Inside XML

Selected Titles from New Riders Publishing

Tim Hill:	*Windows Script Host* ISBN: 1-57870-139-2
Tim Hill:	*Windows NT Shell Scripting* ISBN: 1-57870-047-7
Dave Roth:	*Win32 Perl Programming: The Standard Extensions* ISBN: 1-57870-067-1
Dave Roth:	*Win32 Perl Scripting: The Administrator's Handbook* ISBN: 1-57870-215-1
Thomas Eck:	*Windows NT/2000 ADSI Scripting for System Administration* ISBN: 1-57870-219-4
Duncan Mackenzie and Joel Semeniuk:	*Exchange & Outlook: Constructing Collaborative Solutions* ISBN: 1-57870-252-6
Luke Kenneth Casson Leighton:	*DCE/RPC over SMB: Samba and Windows NT Domain Internals* ISBN: 1-57870-150-3
Gary Nebbett:	*Windows NT/2000 Native API Reference* ISBN: 1-57870-199-6
Eric Harmon:	*Delphi COM Programming* ISBN: 1-57870-221-6
Paul Hinsberg:	*Windows NT Applications: Measuring and Optimizing Performance* ISBN: 1-57870-176-7
Peter G. Viscarola and W. Anthony Mason:	*Windows NT Device Driver Development* ISBN: 1-57870-058-2
William H. Zack:	*Windows 2000 and Mainframe Integration* ISBN: 1-57870-200-3
Sean Deuby:	*Windows 2000 Server: Planning and Migration* ISBN: 1-57870-023-X
Todd Mathers:	*Windows NT/2000 Thin Client Solutions: Implementing Terminal Services and Citrix MetaFrame* ISBN: 1-57870-239-9
Eugene Schultz:	*Windows NT/2000 Network Security* ISBN: 1-57870-253-4
Edgar Brovic, Doug Hauger, and William C. Wade III:	*Windows 2000 Active Directory* ISBN: 0-7357-0870-3
Gary Olsen:	*Windows 2000 Active Directory Design & Deployment* ISBN: 1-57870-242-9

Inside XML

201 West 103rd Street,
Indianapolis, Indiana 46290

Steve Holzner

Inside XML

FIRST EDITION: November

International Standard Book Number: 0-7357-1020-1

Library of Congress Catalog Card Number: 00-102949

05 04 03 02 01   7 6 5 4 3 2 1

Interpretation of the printing code: The rightmost double-digit number is the year of the book's printing; the rightmost single-digit number is the number of the book's printing. For example, the printing code 01-1 shows that the first printing of the book occurred in 2001.

Composed in Bembo and MCPdigital by New Riders Publishing

Printed in the United States of America

Trademarks

All terms mentioned in this book that are known to be trademarks or service marks have been appropriately capitalized. New Riders Publishing cannot attest to the accuracy of this information. Use of a term in this book should not be regarded as affecting the validity of any trademark or service mark.

W3C®—Massachusetts Institute of Technology (MIT), Institut National de Recherche en Informatique et en Automatique (INRIA), Keio University (Keio)

Warning and Disclaimer

This book is designed to provide information about XML. Every effort has been made to make this book as complete and as accurate as possible, but no warranty or fitness is implied.

The information is provided on an as-is basis. The authors and New Riders Publishing shall have neither liability nor responsibility to any person or entity with respect to any loss or damages arising from the information contained in this book or from the use of the discs or programs that may accompany it.

Publisher
David Dwyer

Associate Publisher
Al Valvano

Executive Editor
Stephanie Wall

Managing Editor
Gina Brown

Product Marketing Manager
Stephanie Layton

Publicity Manager
Susan Petro

Development Editor
Robin Drake

Project Editor
Lori Lyons

Copy Editor
Krista Hansing

Indexers
Chris Morris
Lisa Stumpf

Manufacturing Coordinators
Jim Conway
Chris Moos

Book Designer
Louisa Klucznik

Cover Designer
Aren Howell

Composition
Marcia Deboy
Amy Parker

Contents

About the Author

Steven Holzner has been writing about XML about as long as XML has been around. He's written 63 books, all on programming topics, and selling well over a million copies. His books have been translated into 16 languages around the world and include a good number of industry bestsellers. He's a former contributing editor of *PC Magazine*, graduated from MIT, and received his Ph.D. at Cornell. He's been on the faculty of both MIT and Cornell.

About the Technical Reviewers

These reviewers contributed their considerable hands-on expertise to the entire development process for *Inside XML*. As the book was being written, these dedicated professionals reviewed all the material for technical content, organization, and flow. Their feedback was critical to ensuring that *Inside XML* fits our readers' need for the highest quality technical information.

Robert J. Brunner is a Senior Post-Doctoral Scholar in Astronomy at the California Institute of Technology. He has worked for several years on the integration of novel technologies, including XML and Java, into the design of large, highly distributed, collaborative archives. He received a Ph.D. in Astrophysics from the Johns Hopkins University.

Andrew J. Indovina is currently employed in the e-commerce field in Rochester, NY. He is the co-author of the books *Visual Basic 6 Interactive Course*, *Sams Teach Yourself Visual Basic Online in Webtime*, and *Visual C++ 6.0 Unleashed*. He has also done technical edits for books covering Java, Perl, Visual Basic, Visual C++, game development, and project management.

To Nancy, of course!

Acknowledgments

A book like the one you're holding is the work of a great many people, not just the author. The people at New Riders have been great, and I'd like to thank Stephanie Wall, Executive Editor extraordinaire; Chris Zahn and Robin Drake, Development Editors, who did a super job and accepted many chapter updates—and then updates of updates—as we worked to fit in late-breaking news and make this the absolute best XML book anywhere; as well as Lori Lyons and Krista Hansing, Editors, who kept things moving along; and finally the Technical Reviewers, Robert Brunner and Andy Indovina, who did a great job of checking everything. Thanks, everyone, for all your much-appreciated hard work.

Tell Us What You Think

As the reader of this book, you are the most important critic and commentator. We value your opinion and want to know what we're doing right, what we could do better, what areas you'd like to see us publish in, and any other words of wisdom you're willing to pass our way.

As the Executive Editor for the Networking team at New Riders Publishing, I welcome your comments. You can fax, email, or write me directly to let me know what you did or didn't like about this book—as well as what we can do to make our books stronger.

Please note that I cannot help you with technical problems related to the topic of this book, and that due to the high volume of mail I receive, I might not be able to reply to every message.

When you write, please be sure to include this book's title and author as well as your name and phone or fax number. I will carefully review your comments and share them with the author and editors who worked on the book.

Fax: 317-581-4663
Email: `nrfeedback@newriders.com`
Mail: Stephanie Wall
Executive Editor
New Riders Publishing
201 West 103rd Street
Indianapolis, IN 46290 USA

Introduction

Welcome to *Inside XML*. This book is designed to be as comprehensive—and as accessible—as possible for a single book on XML. XML is a standard, not an implementation, and it has become an umbrella for a great number of topics. You'll find XML just about everywhere you look on the Internet today, and even in many places behind the scenes (such as internally in Netscape Navigator). I believe that this book provides the most complete coverage of what's going on in XML than any other XML book today.

You'll find coverage of all the official XML standards here. I'll also take a look at many of the most popular and important implementations of XML that are out there, and I'll put them to work in this book.

That's just part of the story—we'll also put XML to work in depth, pushing the envelope as far as it can go. The best way to learn any topic like XML is by example, and this is an example-oriented book. You'll find hundreds of tested examples here, ready to be used.

Writing XML is not some ordinary and monotonous task: It inspires artistry, devotion, passion, exaltation, and eccentricity—not to mention exasperation and frustration. I'll try to be true to that spirit and capture as much of the excitement and power of XML in this book as I can.

What's Inside?

This book is designed to give you as much of the whole XML story as one book can hold. We'll not only see the full XML syntax—from the most basic to the most advanced—but we'll also dig into many of the ways in which XML is used.

Hundreds of real-world topics are covered in this book, including connecting XML to databases, both locally and on Web servers; styling XML for viewing in today's browsers; reading and using XML documents in browsers; creating your own graphically based browsers; and a great deal more.

Here's a sample of some of the topics in this book—note that each of these topics has many subtopics (too many to list here):

- The complete XML syntax
- Well-formed XML documents
- Valid XML documents
- Document type definitions (DTDs)
- Namespaces

- The XML Document Object Model (DOM)
- Canonical XML
- XML schemas
- Parsing XML with JavaScript
- XML and data binding
- XML and cascading style sheets (CSS)
- XML and Java
- DOM parsers
- SAX parsers
- Extensible Style Language (XSL) transformations
- XSL formatting objects
- XLinks
- XPointers
- XPath
- XBase
- XHTML 1.0 and 1.1
- Resource Description Framework (RDF)
- Channel Definition Format (CDF)
- Vector Markup Language (VML)
- Wireless Markup Language (WML)
- Server-side XML with Java Server Pages (JSP), Active Server Pages (ASP), Java servlets, and Perl

This book starts with the basics. I do assume that you have some knowledge of HTML, but not necessarily much. We'll see how to create XML documents from scratch in this book, starting at the very beginning.

From there, we'll move up to see how to check the syntax of XML documents. The big attraction of XML is that you can define your own tags, such as the `<DOCUMENT>` and `<GREETING>` tags in this document, which we'll see early in Chapter 1, "Essential XML":

```
<?xml version="1.0" encoding="UTF-8"?>
<DOCUMENT>
    <GREETING>
        Hello From XML
    </GREETING>
    <MESSAGE>
        Welcome to the wild and woolly world of XML.
    </MESSAGE>
</DOCUMENT>
```

Because you can create your own tags in XML, it's also important to specify the syntax you want those tags to obey (for example, can a `<MESSAGE>` appear inside a `<GREETING>`?). XML puts a big emphasis on this, too, and there are two main ways to specify the syntax you want your XML to follow—with XML *document type definitions* (DTDs) and XML *schemas*. We'll see how to create both.

And because you can make up your own tags in XML, it's also up to you to specify how they should be used—Netscape Navigator won't know, for example, that a `<KILLER>` tag marks a favorite book in your collection. Because it's up to you to determine what a tag actually means, handling your XML documents in programming is an important part of learning XML, despite what some second-rate XML books try to claim. The two languages I'll use in this book are JavaScript and Java; before using them, I'll introduce them in special sections with plenty of examples, so even if you're not familiar with these languages, you won't have to go anywhere else to get the skills you need.

The major browsers today are becoming more XML-aware, and they use scripting languages to let you work with your XML documents. We'll be using the most popular and powerful of those scripting languages here, JavaScript. Using JavaScript, we'll be able to read XML documents directly in browsers such as Internet Explorer.

It's also important to know how to handle XML outside browsers, because there are plenty of things that JavaScript can't handle. These days, most XML development is taking place in Java, and an endless arsenal of Java resources is available for free on the Internet. In fact, the connection between Java and XML is a natural one, as we'll see. We'll use Java to read XML documents and interpret them, starting in Chapter 11, "Java and the XML DOM." That doesn't mean that you have to be a Java expert—far from it, in fact—because I'll introduce all the Java we'll need right here in this book. And because most XML development is done in Java today, we're going to find a wealth of tools here, ready for use.

You can also design your XML documents to be displayed directly in some modern browsers, and I'll take a look at doing that in two ways—with cascading style sheets (CSS) and the Extensible Style Language (XSL). Using CSS and XSL, you can indicate exactly how a tag that you make up, such as `<PANIC>` or `<BIG_AND_BOLD>` or `<AZURE_UNDERLINED_TEXT>`, should be displayed. I'll take a look at both parts of XSL—XSL transformations and formatting objects—in depth.

In addition, we'll see all the XML specifications in this book, such as XLinks, XBase, and XPointers, which enable you to point to particular items in XML documents in very specific ways. The XML specifications are made by a body called the World Wide Web Consortium (W3C); we'll become very familiar with those specifications here, seeing what they say—and seeing what they lack.

I'll wind up the book by taking a look at a number of the most popular uses of XML on the Internet in several chapters. XML is really a language for *defining* languages, and there are hundreds of such XML-based languages out there now. Some of them are gaining great popularity, and I'll cover them in some depth in this book.

An astonishing wealth of material on XML is available on the Internet today, so I'll also fill this book with the URIs of dozens of those resources (in XML, you use *uniform resource identifiers*, not URLs, although in practice they are the same thing for most purposes today). In nearly every chapter, you'll find lists of free online programs and other resources. (However, there's a hazard here that I should mention: URIs change frequently on the Internet, so don't be surprised if some of these URIs have changed by the time you look for them.)

Who Is This Book For?

This book is designed for just about anyone who wants to learn XML and how it's used today in the real world. The only assumption that I make is that you have some knowledge of how to create documents using Hypertext Markup Language (HTML). You don't have to be any great HTML expert, but a little knowledge of HTML will be helpful. That's really all you need.

However, it's a fact of life that most XML software these days is targeted at Windows. Among other things, that means you should have access to Windows for many of the topics covered in this book. In Chapters 7, "Handling XML Documents with JavaScript," and 8, "XML and Data Binding," we'll be taking a look at the XML support in Internet Explorer. I wish there were more support for the other operating systems that I like, such as UNIX, but right now a lot of it is Windows-only. I'll explore alternatives when I can. One hopeful note for the future is that more Java-based XML tools are appearing daily, and those tools are platform-independent.

At What Level Is This Book Written?

This book is written at several different levels, from basic to advanced, because the XML spectrum is so broad. The general rule is that this book was written to follow HTML books in level. We start at the basic level and gradually get more advanced in a slow, steady way.

I'm not going to assume that you have any programming knowledge (at least until we get to the advanced topics in Chapter 20, "WML, ASP, JSP, Servlets, and Perl," such as Java Server Pages and using Perl with XML) when you start this book. We'll be using both JavaScript and Java in this book, but all you need to know about those languages will be introduced before we use them, and it won't be hard to pick up.

Because there are so many uses of XML available today, this book involves many different software packages; all the ones I'll put to work in the text are free to download from the Internet, and I'll tell you where to get them.

Conventions Used in This Book

I use several conventions in this book that you should be aware of. The most important one is that when I add new sections of code, they'll be highlighted with shading to point out the actual lines I'm discussing so that they stand out. (This sample is written in one of the languages built on XML, the Wireless Markup Language [WML], which is targeted at "microbrowsers" in cellular phones and personal digital assistants [PDAs].)

```
<?xml version="1.0"?>
<!DOCTYPE wml PUBLIC "-//WAPFORUM//DTD WML 1.1//EN"
"http://www.wapforum.org/DTD/wml_1.1.xml">
<wml>
    <card id="Card1" title="First WML Example">
        <!-- This is a comment -->
        <p>
            Greetings from WML.
        </p>
    </card>
</wml>
```

Also, where there's something worth noting or some additional information that adds something to the discussion, I'll add a sidebar. That looks like this:

More on SOAP

With a common name like SOAP, it's hard to search the Internet for more information about the Simple Object Access Protocol unless you're really into pages on personal cleanliness and daytime television. For more information, you might check out this starter list: `http://msdn.microsoft.com/xml/general/soapspec.asp`, `www.oasis-open.org/cover/soap.html`, `www.develop.com/soap/`, and `www.develop.com/soap/soapfaq.xml`.

Finally, many discussions in the text contain syntax examples like this:

```
-config file
```

When using a command or switch shown in a syntax example, substitute the correct value for the characters in *`italic monospace`*. With the switch above, for example, you would substitute the correct configuration filename for *`file`*.

We're ready to go. If you have comments, I encourage you to write to me, care of New Riders. This book is designed to be the new standard in XML coverage, truly more complete and more accessible than ever before. Please do keep in touch with me about ways to improve it and keep it on the forefront. If you think the book lacks anything, let me know—I'll add it because I want to make sure that this book stays on top.

1
Essential XML

Welcome to the world of Extensible Markup Language (XML). This book is your guided tour to that world, so have no worries—you've come to the right place. The world of XML is large and is expanding in unpredictable ways every minute, but we'll become familiar with the lay of the land in detail here. We also have a lot of territory to cover because XML is getting into the most amazing places, and in the most amazing ways, these days.

XML is a language defined by the World Wide Web Consortium (W3C, at `www.w3c.org`), the body that sets the standards for the Web. This first chapter is all about getting a solid overview of that language and how you can use it. For example, you probably already know that you can use XML to create your own elements by designing a customized markup language for your own use. In this way, XML supercedes other markup languages such as Hypertext Markup Language (HTML): In HTML, all the HTML elements you can use are predefined—and there are simply not enough of them. In fact, XML is a meta-markup language because it lets you create your own markup language.

Markup Languages

Markup languages are all about describing the form of the document—that is, the way the content of the document should be interpreted. The markup language that most people are familiar with today, of course, is HTML, which you use to create standard Web pages. Here's a sample HTML page:

```
<HTML>
    <HEAD>
        <TITLE>Hello From HTML</TITLE>
    </HEAD>
    <BODY>
        <CENTER>
            <H1>
                Hello From HTML
            </H1>
        </CENTER>
        Welcome to the wild and woolly world of HTML.
    </BODY>
</HTML>
```

You can see the results of this HTML in Figure 1.1 in Netscape Navigator. Note that the HTML markup in this page—that is, *tags* such as `<HEAD>`, `<CENTER>`, `<H1>`, and so on—is there to give directions to the browser. That's what markup does; it specifies directions on the way the content is to be interpreted.

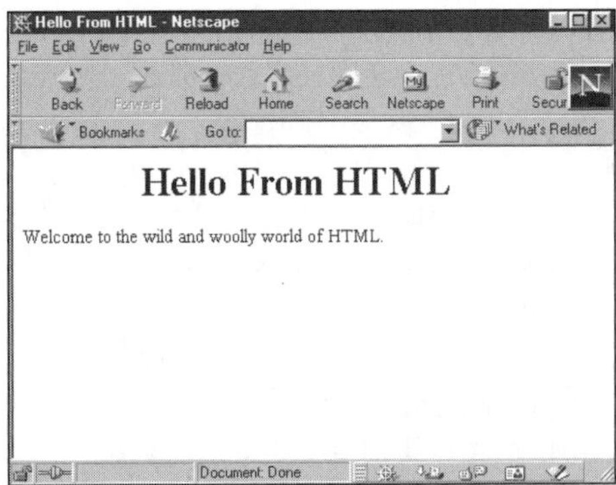

Figure 1.1 An HTML page in a browser.

There is a real relationship between HTML and XML; both are based on *Standard Generalized Markup Language* (*SGML*). As its name implies, SGML is a very general markup language, with enormous capabilities. Because of the large number of things you can do with SGML, however, it can be very difficult to learn, and it hasn't caught on in general use. XML is actually an easier-to-use *subset* of SGML (and technically speaking, HTML is called an *application* of SGML). You can read more about the relationship between SGML and XML at `www.w3.org/TR/NOTE-sgml-xml`.

When you think of markup in terms of specifying how the content of a document is to be handled, it's easy to see that many kinds of markup languages abound already. For example, if you use a word processor to save a document in rich text format (RTF), you'll find all kinds of markup codes embedded in the document. Here's an example; in this case, I've just created an RTF file with the letters "abc" underlined and in bold using Microsoft Word. Try searching for the actual text (hint: it's near the very end):

```
{\rtf1\ansi\ansicpg1252\uc1 \deff0\deflang1033
deflangfe1033{\fonttbl{\f0\froman\fcharset0\fprq2{\*\panose\
02020603050405020304}Times New Roman;}}{\colortbl;\red0
green0\blue0;\red0\green0\blue255;\red0\green255\blue255;\
red0\green255\blue0;\red255\green0\blue255;\red255\green0\
blue0;\red255\green255\blue0;\red255\green255\blue255;\red0\
green0\blue128;\red0\green128\blue128;\red0\green128\blue0;\
red128\green0\blue128;\red128\green0\blue0;\red128\green128\
blue0;\red128\green128\blue128;\red192\green192\blue192;}
{\stylesheet{\widctlpar\adjustright \fs20\cgrid \snext0 Normal;}
{\*\cs10 \additive Default Paragraph Font;}}{\info{\title  }
{\author Steven Holzner}{\operator Steven Holzner}{\creatim
yr2000\mo\dy\hr\min}{\revtim\yr2000\mo4\dy17\hr13\min55}
{\version1}{\edmins1}{\nofpages1}{\nofwords0}{\nofchars1}
{\*\company SteveCo}{\nofcharsws1}{\vern89}}\widowctrl\ftnbj\
aenddoc\formshade\viewkind4\viewscale100\pgbrdrhead\pgbrdrfoot\
fet0\sectd \psz1\linex0\endnhere\sectdefaultcl {\*\pnseclvl1\
pnucrm\pnstart1\pnindent720\pnhang{\pntxta .}}{\*\pnseclvl2\
pnucltr\pnstart1\pnindent720\pnhang{\pntxta .}}{\*\pnseclvl3\
pndec\pnstart1\pnindent720\pnhang{\pntxta .}}{\*\pnseclvl4\
pnlcltr\pnstart1\pnindent720\pnhang{\pntxta )}}{\*\pnseclvl5\
pndec\pnstart1\pnindent720\pnhang{\pntxtb (}{\pntxta )}}
{\*\pnseclvl6\pnlcltr\pnstart1\pnindent720\pnhang{\pntxtb (}
{\pntxta )}}{\*\pnseclvl7\pnlcrm\pnstart1\pnindent720\pnhang
{\pntxtb (}{\pntxta )}}{\*\pnseclvl8\pnlcltr\pnstart1\
pnindent720\pnhang{\pntxtb (}{\pntxta )}}{\*\pnseclvl9\pnlcrm\
pnstart1\pnindent720\pnhang{\pntxtb (}{\pntxta )}}\pard\plain\
sl480\slmult1\widctlpar\adjustright \fs20\cgrid {\b\fs24\ulabc }
{\b\ul \par }}
```

The markup language that most people are familiar with these days is HTML, but it's easy to see how that language doesn't provide enough power for anything beyond creating standard Web pages.

HTML 1.0 consisted of only a dozen or so tags, but the most recent version, HTML 4.01, consists of almost 100—if you include the other tags added by the major browsers, that number is closer to 120. But as handling data on the Web and other nets intensifies, it's clear that 120 tags isn't enough—in fact, you can never have enough.

For example, what if your hobby was building model ships, and you wanted to exchange specifications with others on the topic? HTML doesn't include tags such as `<BEAMWIDTH>`, `<MIZZENHEIGHT>`, `<DRAFT>`, `<SHIPCLASS>`, and others that you might want. What if you worked for a major bank and wanted to exchange financial data with other institutions—would you prefer tags such as `<B>`, `<UL>`, and `<FONT>` or tags such as `<FISCALYEAR>`, `<ACCOUNTNUMBER>`, and `<TRANSFERACCOUNT>`? (In fact, such markup languages, including Extensible Business Reporting Language, exist now and are built on XML.)

Likewise, what if you were a Web browser manufacturer who wanted to create your own markup language to let people configure your browser, adding scrollbars, toolbars, and other elements? You might create your own markup language. In fact, Netscape has done just that with the XML-based User Interface Language, which we'll see in this chapter.

The upshot is that there are as many reasons to create markup languages as there are ways of handling data—and, of course, both are unlimited numbers. That's where XML comes in: It's a meta-markup specification that lets you create your own markup languages.

What Does XML Look Like?

So what does XML look like, and how does it work? Here's an example that mimics the HTML page just introduced:

```
<?xml version="1.0" encoding="UTF-8"?>
<DOCUMENT>
    <GREETING>
        Hello From XML
    </GREETING>
    <MESSAGE>
        Welcome to the wild and woolly world of XML.
    </MESSAGE>
</DOCUMENT>
```

We'll see the parts of an XML document in detail in the next chapter, but in overview, here's how this one works: I start with the XML *processing instruction* `<?xml version="1.0" encoding="UTF-8"?>` (all XML processing instructions start with <? and end with ?>), which indicates that I'm using XML version 1.0 (the only version currently defined) and the UTF-8 *character encoding*, an 8-bit condensed version of Unicode (more on this later in the chapter). Also, when I add new sections of code, they'll be highlighted with shading to point out the actual lines I'm discussing.

```
<?xml version="1.0" encoding="UTF-8"?>


<DOCUMENT>
    <GREETING>
        Hello From XML
    </GREETING>
    <MESSAGE>
        Welcome to the wild and woolly world of XML.
    </MESSAGE>
</DOCUMENT>
```

Next, I create a new tag named `<DOCUMENT>`. As we'll see in the next chapter, you can use any name for a tag, not just DOCUMENT, as long as the name starts with a letter or an underscore (_), and as long as the following characters consist of letters, digits, underscores, dots (.), or hyphens (-), but no spaces. In XML, tags always start with < and end with >.

XML documents are made up of XML *elements*. Much like in HTML, you create XML elements with an opening tag, such as `<DOCUMENT>`, followed by the element content (if any), such as text or other elements, and ending with the matching closing tag that starts with </, such as `</DOCUMENT>`. (There are additional rules we'll see in the next chapter if the element doesn't contain any content.) It's necessary to enclose the entire document, except for processing instructions, in one element, called the *root element*—that's the `<DOCUMENT>` element here:

```
<?xml version="1.0" encoding="UTF-8"?>
<DOCUMENT>
    .
    .
    .
</DOCUMENT>
```

Now I'll add to this XML document a new element that I made up, `<GREETING>`, which encloses text content (in this case, `Hello From XML`), like this:

```
<?xml version="1.0" encoding="UTF-8"?>
<DOCUMENT>
    <GREETING>
        Hello From XML
    </GREETING>
    .
    .
    .
</DOCUMENT>
```

Next, I can add a new element, <MESSAGE>, which also encloses text content, like this:

```
<?xml version="1.0" encoding="UTF-8"?>
<DOCUMENT>
    <GREETING>
        Hello From XML
    </GREETING>
    <MESSAGE>
        Welcome to the wild and woolly world of XML.
    </MESSAGE>
</DOCUMENT>
```

Now the <DOCUMENT> root element contains two elements: <GREETING> and <MESSAGE>. Each of the <GREETING> and <MESSAGE> elements also hold text themselves. In this way, I've created a new XML document.

Note the similarity of this document to the HTML page we saw earlier. Note also, however, that in the HTML document, all the tags were predefined, and a Web browser knew how to handle them. Here, we've just created the tags <DOCUMENT>, <GREETING> and <MESSAGE> from thin air. How can we use an XML document like this one? What would a browser make of these new tags?

What Does XML Look Like in a Browser?

It turns out that a browser such as Microsoft Internet Explorer version 5 or later lets you display raw XML documents directly. For example, if I saved the XML document we just created in a document named greeting.xml and then opened that document in the Internet Explorer, you'd see something like what appears in Figure 1.2.

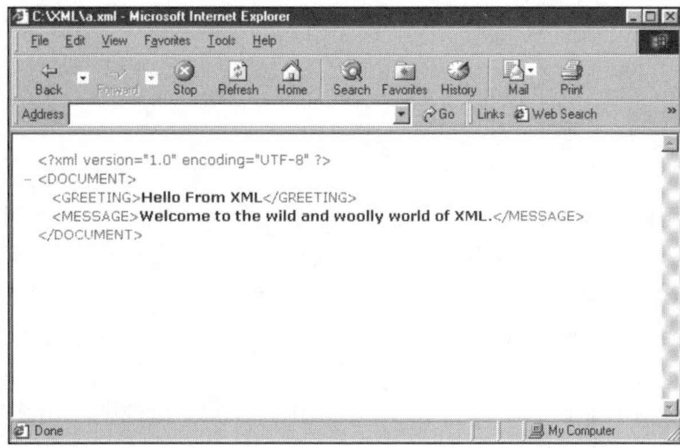

Figure 1.2 An XML document in Internet Explorer.

You can see our complete XML document in Figure 1.2, but it's nothing like the image you see in Figure 1.1; there's no particular formatting at all. So, now that we've created our own markup elements, how do you tell a browser how to display them?

Many people who are new to XML find the claim that you can use XML to create new markup languages very frustrating—after all, what then? It turns out that it's up to you to assign meaning to the new elements you create, and you can do that in two main ways. First, you can use a *style sheet* to indicate to a browser how you want the content of the elements you've created to be formatted. The second way is to use a programming language, such as Java or JavaScript, to handle the XML document in programming code. We'll see both ways throughout this book, and I'll take a quick look at them in this chapter as well. I'll start by adding a style sheet to the XML document we've already created.

There are two main ways of specifying styles when you format XML documents: with cascading style sheets (CSS) and with the Extensible Style Sheets Language (XSL). We'll see both in this book; here, I'll apply a CSS style sheet by using the XML processing instruction `<?xml-stylesheet type="text/css" href="greeting.css"?>`, which tells the browser that the type of the style sheet I'll be using is CSS and that its name is greeting.css:

```
<?xml version="1.0" encoding="UTF-8"?>
<?xml-stylesheet type="text/css" href="greeting.css"?>
<DOCUMENT>
    <GREETING>
        Hello From XML
```

continues ▸

```
    </GREETING>
    <MESSAGE>
        Welcome to the wild and woolly world of XML.
    </MESSAGE>
</DOCUMENT>
```

Here's what the contents of the file greeting.css itself looks like. In this case, I'm customizing the `<GREETING>` element to display its content in red, centered in the browser, and in 36-point font. The `<MESSAGE>` element has been customized to display its text in black 18-point font. The `display: block` part indicates that I want the content of these elements to be displayed in a block, which translates here to being displayed on individual lines:

```
GREETING {display: block; font-size: 36pt; color: #FF0000; text-align: center}
MESSAGE (display: block; font-size: 18pt; color: #000000}
```

You can see the results in two browsers that support XML in Figures 1.3 and 1.4. Figure 1.3 shows greeting.xml in Netscape 6 (available only in a preview version as of this writing), and Figure 1.4 shows the same document in Internet Explorer. As you can see, we've formatted the document as we like it—in fact, this result already represents an advance over HTML because we can format exactly how we want to display the text instead of having to rely on predefined elements such as `<H1>`.

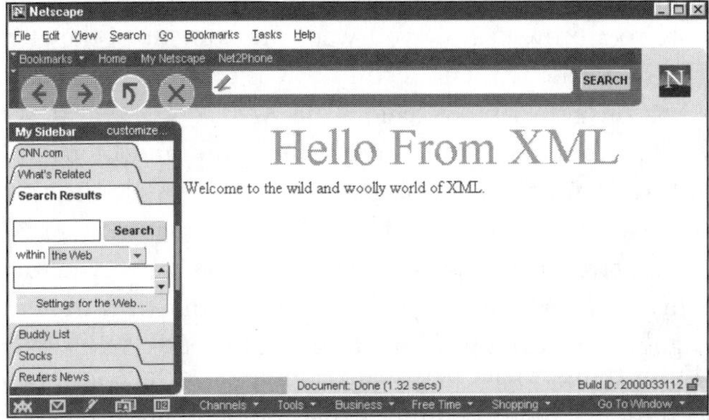

Figure 1.3 An XML document in Netscape 6 (preview version).

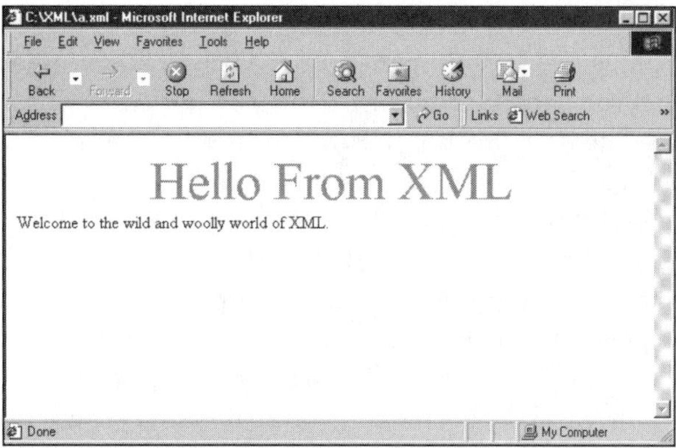

Figure 1.4 An XML document in Internet Explorer.

That gives us a taste of XML. Now we've seen how to create a first XML document and how to use a style sheet to display it in a browser. We've seen what it looks like, so what's so great about XML? Take a look at the overview, coming up next.

What's So Great About XML?

XML is popular for many reasons, and I'll examine some of them here as part of our overview of where XML is today. My own personal favorite is that XML allows easy data handling and exchange.

Easy Data Exchange

I've been involved with computing for a long time, and one of the things I've watched with misgiving is the growth of proprietary data formats. In earlier days, programs could exchange data easily because data was stored as text. Today, however, you need conversion programs or modules to let applications transfer data between themselves. In fact, proprietary data formats have become so complex that frequently one version of a complex application can't even read data from an earlier version of the same application.

In XML, data and markup are stored as text that you can configure. If you like, you can use XML editors to create XML documents, but if something goes wrong, you can examine or modify the document directly because its all just text. The data also is not encoded in some way that has been patented or copyrighted, so it's more accessible.

You might think that binary formats would be more efficient because they can store data more compactly, but that's not the way things have worked out. For example, Microsoft Corporation is notorious for turning out huge applications that store even simple data in huge files (the not-so-affectionate name for this is "bloatware"). If you store only the letters "abc" in a Microsoft Word 97 document, you may be surprised to find that the document is something like 20,000 bytes long. A similar XML file might be 30 or 40 bytes. Even large amounts of data are not necessarily stored efficiently; for instance, Microsoft Excel routinely creates even larger files that are five times as long as the corresponding text. As we'll see, XML provides a very efficient way of storing most data.

In addition, when you standardize markup languages, many different people can use them. I'll take a look at that next.

Customizing Markup Languages

As we've already seen, you can create customized markup languages using XML, and that represents its extraordinary power. When you and a number of other people agree on a markup language, you can create customized browsers or applications to handle that language. Hundreds of such languages already are being standardized now, including these:

- Banking Industry Technology Secretariat (BITS)
- Financial Exchange (IFX)
- Bank Internet Payment System (BIPS)
- Telecommunications Interchange Markup (TIM)
- Schools Interoperability Framework (SIF)
- Common Business Library (CBL)
- Electronic Business XML Initiative (ebXML)
- Product Data Markup Language (PDML)
- Financial Information eXchange protocol (FIX)
- The Text Encoding Initiative (TEI)

Some customized markup languages, such as Chemical Markup Language (CML), let you represent complex molecules graphically, as we'll see later in this chapter. Likewise, you can imagine how useful a language would be that creates graphical building plans for architects when you open a document in a browser.

Not only can you create custom markup languages, but you also can extend them using XML. If someone creates a markup language based on XML, you can add the extensions you want easily. In fact, that's happening now with Extensible Hypertext Markup Language (XHTML), which I'll take a look at briefly in this chapter and in detail later in the book. Using XHTML, you can add your own elements to what a browser displays as normal HTML.

Self-Describing Data

The data in XML documents is self-describing. Take a look at this document:

```
<?xml version="1.0" encoding="UTF-8"?>
<DOCUMENT>
    <GREETING>
        Hello From XML
    </GREETING>
    <MESSAGE>
        Welcome to the wild and woolly world of XML.
    </MESSAGE>
</DOCUMENT>
```

Based solely on the names we've given to each XML element here, you can figure out what's going on: This document has a greeting and a message to impart. Even if you came back to this document years later, you could figure out what's going on. This means that XML documents are, to a large extent, self-documenting. (We'll also see in the next chapter that you can add explicit comments to XML files.)

Structured and Integrated Data

Another powerful aspect of XML is that it lets you specify not only data, but also the structure of that data and how various elements are integrated into other elements. This is important when you're dealing with complex and important data. For example, you could represent a long bank statement in

HTML, but in XML, you actually can build in the semantic rules that specify the structure of the document so that the document can be checked to make sure it's set up correctly.

Take a look at this XML document:

```
<?xml version="1.0"?>
<SCHOOL>
    <CLASS type="seminar">
        <CLASS_TITLE>XML In The Real World</CLASS_TITLE>
        <CLASS_NUMBER>6.031</CLASS_NUMBER>
        <SUBJECT>XML</SUBJECT>
        <START_DATE>6/1/2002</START_DATE>
        <STUDENTS>
            <STUDENT status="attending">
                <FIRST_NAME>Edward</FIRST_NAME>
                <LAST_NAME>Samson</LAST_NAME>
            </STUDENT>
            <STUDENT status="withdrawn">
                <FIRST_NAME>Ernestine</FIRST_NAME>
                <LAST_NAME>Johnson</LAST_NAME>
            </STUDENT>
        </STUDENTS>
    </CLASS>
</SCHOOL>
```

Here I've set up an XML seminar and added two students to it. As we'll see in Chapter 2, "Creating Well-Formed XML Documents," and Chapter 3, "Valid XML Documents: Creating Document Type Definitions," with XML you can specify, for example, that each `<STUDENT>` element needs to enclose a `<FIRST_NAME>` and a `<LAST_NAME>` element, that the `<START_DATE>` element can't go in the `<STUDENTS>` element, and more.

In fact, this emphasis on the correctness of documents is strong in XML. In HTML, a Web author could (and frequently did) write sloppy HTML, knowing that the Web browser would take care of any syntax problems (some Web authors even exploited this intentionally to create special effects in some browsers). In fact, some people estimate that 50% or more of the code in modern browsers is there to take care of sloppy HTML in Web pages. For that kind of reason, the story is different in XML. In XML, browsers are supposed to check your document; if there's a problem, they are not supposed to proceed any further. They should let you know about the problem, but that's as far as they're supposed to go.

So, how does an XML browser check your document? XML browsers can make two main checks: a check to see whether your document is *well-formed*, and a check to see whether it's *valid*. We'll see what these terms mean in more detail in the next chapter, and I'll go over them briefly here.

Well-Formed XML Documents

What does it mean for an XML document to be well-formed? To be well-formed, an XML document must follow the syntax rules set up for XML by W3C in the XML 1.0 specification (which you can find at `www.w3.org/TR/REC-xml`, and which we'll discuss in more detail in the next chapter). Informally, well-formedness often means that the document must contain one or more elements, and one element, the root element, must contain all the other elements. Each element also must nest inside any enclosing elements properly. For example, this document is not well-formed because the `</GREETING>` closing tag comes after the opening `<MESSAGE>` tag for the next element:

```
<?xml version="1.0" encoding="UTF-8"?>
<DOCUMENT>
    <GREETING>
        Hello From XML
    <MESSAGE>
    </GREETING>
        Welcome to the wild and woolly world of XML.
    </MESSAGE>
</DOCUMENT>
```

Valid XML Documents

Most XML browsers will check your document to see whether it is well-formed. Some of them also can check whether it's valid. An XML document is valid if there is a document type definition (DTD) associated with it, and if the document complies with that DTD.

A document's DTD specifies the correct syntax of the document, as we'll see in Chapter 3. DTDs can be stored in a separate file or in the document itself, using a `<!DOCTYPE>` element. Here's an example in which I add a `<!DOCTYPE>` element to the greeting XML document we developed earlier:

```
<?xml version="1.0" encoding="UTF-8"?>
<?xml-stylesheet type="text/css" href="first.css"?>
<!DOCTYPE DOCUMENT [
    <!ELEMENT DOCUMENT (GREETING, MESSAGE)>
    <!ELEMENT GREETING (#PCDATA)>
    <!ELEMENT MESSAGE (#PCDATA)>
]>
<DOCUMENT>
    <GREETING>
        Hello From XML
    </GREETING>
    <MESSAGE>
        Welcome to the wild and woolly world of XML.
    </MESSAGE>
</DOCUMENT>
```

We'll see more about DTDs in Chapter 3, but this DTD indicates that you can have `<GREETING>` and `<MESSAGE>` elements inside a `<DOCUMENT>` element, that the `<DOCUMENT>` element is the root element, and that the `<GREETING>` and `<MESSAGE>` elements can hold text.

Most XML browsers will check XML documents for well-formedness, but only a few will check for validity. I'll talk more about where to find XML validators in the later section "XML Validators."

We've gotten an overview of XML documents now, including how to display them using style sheets, and what constitutes a well-formed and valid document. However, this is only part of the story. Many XML documents are not designed to be displayed in browsers at all, for example, or even if they are, they're are not designed to be used with modern style sheets (such as browsers that convert XML into industry-specific graphics such as molecular structure, physics equations, or even musical scales). The more powerful use of XML involves *parsing* an XML document to break it down into its component parts and then handling the resulting data yourself. Next I'll take a look at a few ways of parsing XML data that are available to us.

Parsing XML Yourself

Let's say that you have this XML document, greeting.xml, which we developed earlier in this chapter:

```
<?xml version="1.0" encoding="UTF-8"?>
<DOCUMENT>
    <GREETING>
        Hello From XML
    </GREETING>
    <MESSAGE>
        Welcome to the wild and woolly world of XML.
    </MESSAGE>
</DOCUMENT>
```

Now say that you want to extract the greeting `Hello From XML` from this XML document. One way of doing that is by using XML data islands in Internet Explorer and then using a scripting language, such as JavaScript, to extract and display the text content of the `<GREETING>` element. Here's how that looks in a Web page:

```
<HTML>
    <HEAD>
        <TITLE>
            Finding Element Values in an XML Document
        </TITLE>

        <XML ID="firstXML" SRC="greeting.xml"></XML>

        <SCRIPT LANGUAGE="JavaScript">
            function getData()
            {
                xmldoc= document.all("firstXML").XMLDocument;

                nodeDoc = xmldoc.documentElement;
                nodeGreeting = nodeDoc.firstChild;

                outputMessage = "Greeting: " +
                     nodeGreeting.firstChild.nodeValue;
                message.innerHTML=outputMessage;
            }
        </SCRIPT>
    </HEAD>

    <BODY>
        <CENTER>
            <H1>
                Finding Element Values in an XML Document
            </H1>
```

continues ▸

```
            <DIV ID="message"></DIV>
            <P>
            <INPUT TYPE="BUTTON" VALUE="Get The Greeting"
                ONCLICK="getData()">
        </CENTER>
    </BODY>
</HTML>
```

This Web page displays a button with the caption "Get The Greeting," as you see in Figure 1.5. When you click the button, the JavaScript code in this page reads in greeting.xml, extracts the text from the <GREETING> element, and displays that text, as you also can see in Figure 1.5. In this way, you can see how you can create applications that handle XML documents in a customized way—even customized XML browsers.

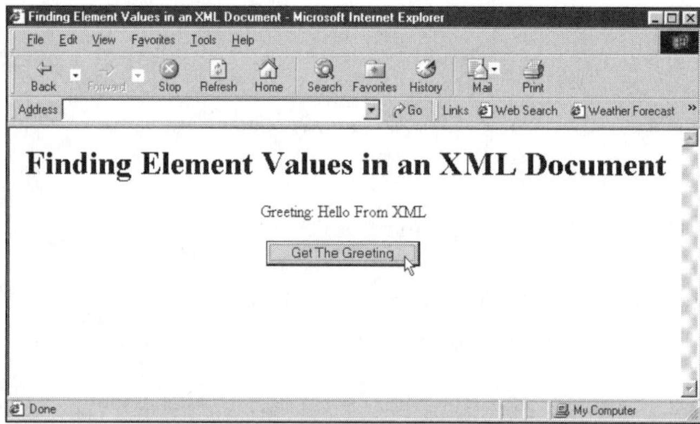

Figure 1.5 Extracting data from an XML document in Internet Explorer.

We'll see more about using JavaScript to work with XML later in this book, and I'll also cover how JavaScript itself works first. If you haven't used JavaScript before, you won't have a problem doing so now.

Although JavaScript is useful for lightweight XML uses, most XML programming is done in Java today, and we'll take advantage of that in this book. Here's an example Java program, readXML.java, using XML4J, probably the most widely used XML parser, which is free from IBM's AlphaWorks. This program also reads greeting.xml and extracts the text content of the <GREETING> element:

```
import org.apache.xerces.parsers.DOMParser;
import org.w3c.dom.Document;
import org.w3c.dom.Element;
import org.w3c.dom.Node;
import org.w3c.dom.Text;

public class readXML
{
    static public void main(String[] argv)
    {
        try {
            DOMParser parser = new DOMParser();
            parser.parse("greeting.xml");
            Document doc = parser.getDocument();

            for (Node node = doc.getDocumentElement().getFirstChild();
                node != null; node = node.getNextSibling()) {

                if (node instanceof Element) {
                    if (node.getNodeName().equals("GREETING")) {

                        StringBuffer buffer = new StringBuffer();

                        for (Node subnode = node.getFirstChild();
                            subnode != null; subnode =
                                subnode.getNextSibling()){
                            if (subnode instanceof Text) {
                                buffer.append(subnode.getNodeValue());
                            }
                        }
                        System.out.println(buffer.toString());
                    }
                }
            }
        } catch (Exception e) {
            e.printStackTrace();
        }
    }
}
```

When you compile and run this program (you'll see how to do so in Chapter 11), the output looks like this. (I'll use "%" to represent the command-line prompt in this book; if you're using UNIX, this prompt may look familiar, or your prompt may look something like /home/steve:. If you're using Windows, you get a command-line prompt by opening an MS-DOS window, and your prompt may look something like C:\XML>.)

```
%java readXML
        Hello From XML
```

(Note that this program returns all the text in the <GREETING> element, including the leading spaces.) We'll see how to use Java to parse XML documents later in this book, mostly using the IBM AlphaWorks XML4J parser, which adheres closely to the W3C Document Object Model. I'll also cover the Java you need to know before getting into the programming, so if you haven't programmed in Java before, that's no problem.

We now have a good overview of how XML works. It's time to take a look at how it's already working in the real world, starting with an overview of the XML resources available to you.

XML Resources

Many XML resources are available to you online. Because it's very important that you know about them to get a solid background in XML, I list them here.

The XML specification is defined by W3C, and that's where you should start looking for XML resources. Here's a good starter list (we'll see all these topics in this book):

- www.w3c.org/xml. W3C's main XML site, the starting point for all things XML.
- www.w3.org/XML/1999/XML-in-10-points. "XML in 10 Points" (actually only seven), an XML overview.
- www.w3.org/TR/REC-xml. The official W3C recommendation for XML 1.0, the current (and only) version. It won't be easy to read, however—that's what this book is all about, translating that kind of document to English.
- www.w3.org/TR/xml-stylesheet/. All about using style sheets and XML.
- www.w3.org/TR/REC-xml-names/. All about XML namespaces.
- www.w3.org/Style/XSL/. All about Extensible Style Language (XSL).
- www.w3.org/TR/xslt. All about XSL transformations (XSLT).
- www.w3.org/XML/Activity.html. An overview of current XML activity at W3C.

- www.w3.org/TR/xmlschema-0/, www.w3.org/TR/xmlschema-1/, and www.w3.org/TR/xmlschema-2/ XML. Information on schemas, the alternative to DTDs.
- www.w3.org/TR/xlink/. The XLinks specification.
- www.w3.org/TR/xptr. The XPointers specification.
- www.w3.org/TR/xhtml1/. The XHTML 1.0 specification.
- www.w3.org/TR/xhtml11/. The XHTML 1.1 specification.
- www.w3.org/DOM/. The W3C Document Object Model, (DOM).

Many non-W3C XML resources are out there, too—a casual search for "XML" on the Web turns up a mere 561,870 pages. Here's a list to get you started:

- www.xml.com; XML.com. A site filled with XML resources, discussions, and notifications of public events.
- www.xml-zone.com. Excellent XML overviews and listings of events.
- www.oasis-open.org. The Organization for the Advancement of Structured Information Standards (OASIS) is dedicated to the adoption of product-independent formats such as XML.
- www.xml.org. XML.ORG is designed to provide information about the use of XML in industrial and commercial settings. It's hosted by OASIS and is a reference for XML vocabularies, DTDs, schemas, and namespaces.
- http://msdn.microsoft.com/xml/default.asp. Microsoft's XML page.

You'll also find quite a few XML tutorials online (searching for "XML Tutorial" brings up more than 500 matches). Here are a few to start with:

- www2.software.ibm.com/developer/education.nsf/xml-onlinecourse-bytitle. IBM's free tutorials.
- **www.ucc.ie/xml/.** A comprehensive frequently asked questions (FAQ) list about XML, kept up by some of the contributors to the W3C's XML Working Group. This is considered by many to be the definitive FAQ on XML.
- msdn.microsoft.com/xml/tutorial/default.asp. Microsoft's XML tutorial.
- www.xml.com/pub/98/10/guide0.html. XML.com's XML overview.
- web2.javasoft.com/xml/docs/tutorial/TOC.html. JavaSoft's XML tutorial.

In addition, you might find some newsgroups on Usenet useful (note that your news server may not carry all these groups):

- `comp.text.xml`. A good, general-purpose, free-floating XML forum.
- `microsoft.public.inetexplorer.ie5beta.programming.xml`. XML discussions and questions concerning Internet Explorer 5.
- `microsoft.public.xml`. The general Microsoft XML forum.

That's a good start on XML resources available on the Internet. What about XML software? Let's take a look at what's out there, starting with XML editors.

XML Editors

To create the XML documents we'll use in this book, all you need is a text editor of some kind, such as vi, emacs, pico, Windows Notepad, or Windows WordPad. By default, XML documents are supposed to be written in Unicode, although in practice you can write them in ASCII, and nearly all of them are written that way so far. Just make sure that when you write an XML document, you save it in your editor's plain-text format.

Using Windows Text Editors

Windows text editors such as WordPad or Notepad have an annoying habit of appending the extension .txt to a filename if they don't understand the extension you've given the file. That's not a problem with .xml files, though, because WordPad understands the extension .xml. For example, if you try to save an XML-based User Interface Language document with the correct extension of .xul, WordPad will give it the extension .xul.txt. To avoid that, place the name of the file in quotation marks when you save it, as in "scrollbars.xul."

However, it can be a lot easier to use an actual XML editor, which is designed explicitly for the job of handling XML. Here's a list of some programs that let you edit your XML:

- **Adobe FrameMaker,** `www.adobe.com`. Great, but expensive, XML support in FrameMaker.
- **XML Pro,** `www.vervet.com/`. A costly but powerful XML editor.
- **XML Writer, on disk, XMLWriter,** `http://xmlwriter.net/`. Color syntax highlighting, with a nice interface.
- **XML Notepad,** `msdn.microsoft.com/xml/notepad/intro.asp`. Microsoft's free XML editor, a little difficult to use.

- **eNotepad,** `www.edisys.com/Products/eNotepad/enotepad.asp`. A WordPad replacement that does well with XML and has a good user interface.
- **XMetal from SoftQuad,** `xmetal.com`. An expensive but very powerful XML editor, and many authors' editor of choice.
- **XML Spy,** `www.xmlspy.com/`. A good and easy-to-use user interface.

You can see XML Spy at work in Figure 1.6, XML Writer in Figure 1.7, XML Notepad in Figure 1.8, and eNotepad in Figure 1.9.

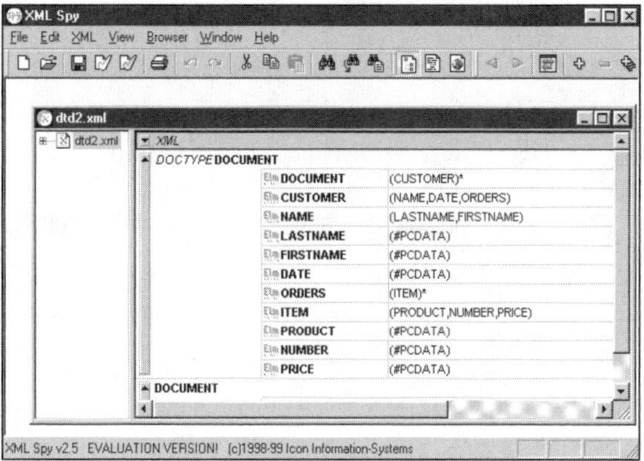

Figure 1.6 XML Spy editing XML.0

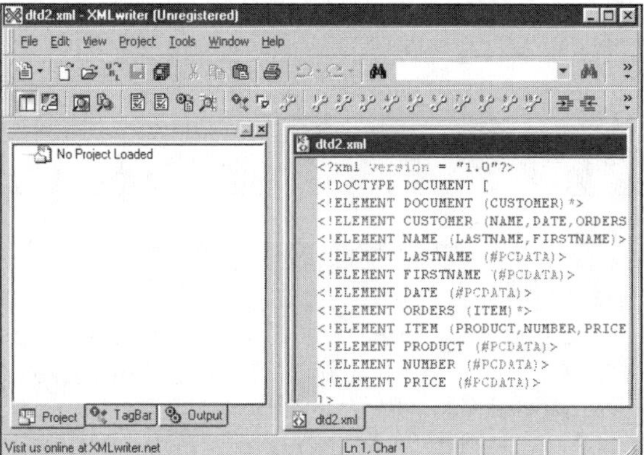

Figure 1.7 XML Writer editing XML.

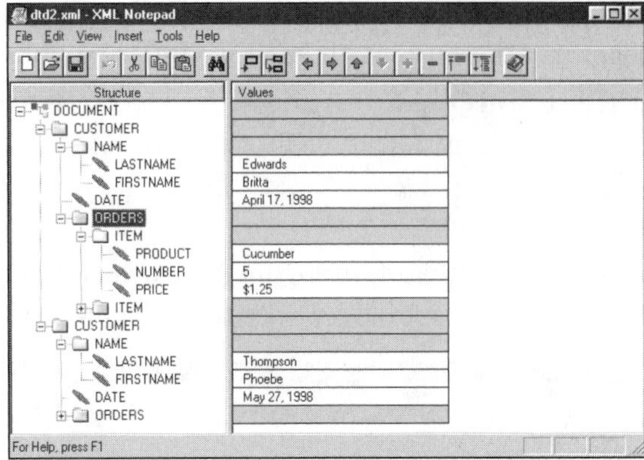

Figure 1.8 XML Notepad editing XML.

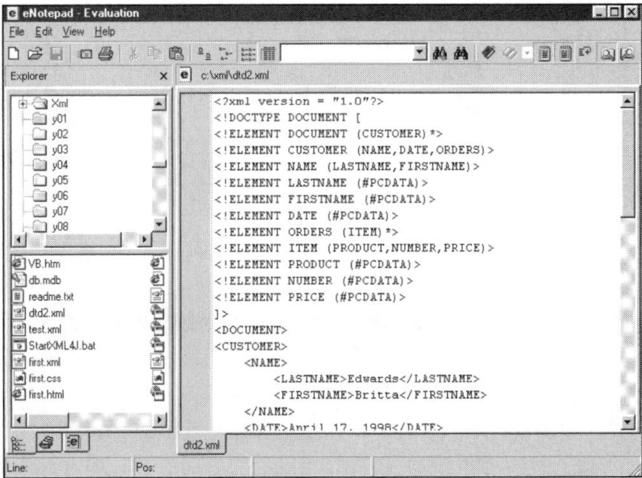

Figure 1.9 eNotepad editing XML.

Now that we've gotten an overview of creating XML documents, what about XML browsers? The list is more limited, but there are a few out there. See the next topic.

XML Browsers

Creating a true XML browser is not easy. Besides supporting XML, the browser would have to support a style language such as CSS or XSL. It also should support a scripting language, such as JavaScript. These are heavy requirements for most third-party vendors, so the true XML browsers out there are few. In fact, no complete, general XML browsers currently exist. None of the browsers listed here validate XML documents—they just check for well-formedness—but a few come close.

Internet Explorer 5

Whether you love or hate Microsoft, the fact remains that Internet Explorer is the most powerful XML browser available now; you currently can get it at `www.microsoft.com/windows/ie/default.htm`.

Internet Explorer can display XML documents directly, as you saw in Figure 1.2, and also can handle them in scripting languages (JScript, Microsoft's version of JavaScript, and Microsoft's VBScript are supported). There is good support for style sheets and other features such as the `<XML>` element, which lets you create XML data islands into which you can load XML documents, and ways of binding XML to ActiveX Data Object (ADO) database recordsets.

Internet Explorer 5.5, in preview at this writing, also supports additional XML features, such as the XPath specification. There's no question that Microsoft's XML commitment is strong—XML has been integrated even into the Office 2000 suite of applications—but Microsoft sometimes swerves significantly from the W3C standards (that is, when Microsoft isn't writing those standards itself).

Netscape Navigator 6

Netscape has just released the preview version of Netscape Navigator 6 (available at `www.netscape.com/download/previewrelease.html`), which has significant XML support. You can see Netscape Navigator 6 at work back in Figure 1.3. This preview version is based on Netscape's open source Mozilla browser, which you can pick up at `www.mozilla.org`. Unfortunately, both Mozilla and the preview version of Netscape Navigator 6 have a reputation for crashing machines frequently.

As with Internet Explorer, support for style sheets is good in Netscape Navigator. The preview version of Netscape Navigator 6 also supports the XML-based User Interface Language (XUL), which lets you configure the controls in the browser. In fact, the preview version's user interface is based on XUL. More XML features will come in Netscape 6, but right now documentation is virtually nonexistent.

Jumbo

One of the more famous true XML browsers that exist is Jumbo, an XML browser designed to work with XML and the CML. You can pick up Jumbo for free at `www.xml-cml.org/jumbo.html`. This browser not only can display XML (although not with style sheets), but it also can use CML to draw molecules, as you see in Figure 1.10.

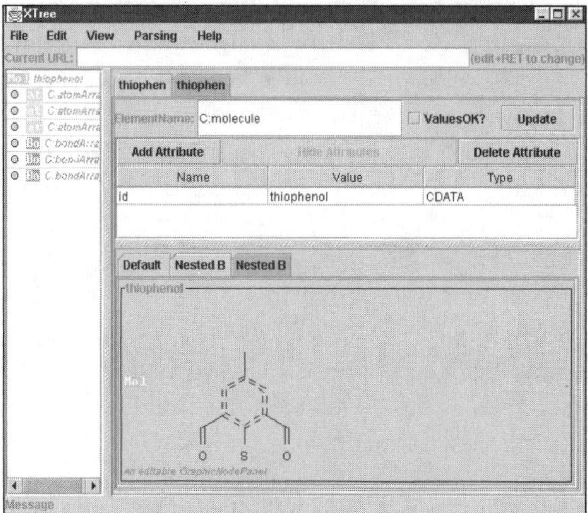

Figure 1.10 Jumbo at work.

Relatively few real XML browsers exist, but there *are* a large number of XML parsers. You can use these parsers to read XML documents and break them up into their component parts.

XML Parsers

XML *parsers* are software packages that you use as part of an application such as Oracle 8i (which includes good XML support) or as part of your own programs. For example, later in this book, I'll use the IBM AlphaWorks XML for Java (XML4J) parser; it is written in Java and connects well to your own Java code. Here's a list of some of the parsers out there:

- **SAX: The Simple API for XML.** Written by David Megginson et al. (`www. megginson.com/SAX/index.html`), SAX is a well-known parser that uses event-based parsing. I'll use SAX in this book.

- **expat.** This famous XML parser was written in the C programming language by James Clark (`www.jclark.com/xml/expat.html`). This parser is used in Netscape Navigator 6 and in the Perl language's XML::Parser module.
- **expat as a Perl Module.** XML::Parser is maintained by Clark Cooper (`ftp://ftp.perl.org/pub/CPAN/modules/by-module/XML/`).
- **TclExpat.** This is expat written for use in the Tcl programming language by Steve Ball. Superceded by TclXML. (`www.zveno.com/zm.cgi/in-tclxml`).
- **LT XML.** This is an XML developers' toolkit from the Language Technology Group at the University of Edinburgh (`www.ltg.ed.ac.uk/software/xml/`).
- **XML for Java –(XML4J).** From IBM AlphaWorks (`www.alphaworks.ibm.com/tech/xml4j`), this is a famous and very widely used XML parser that adheres well to the W3C standards.
- **XML Microsoft's validating XML processor.** This parser requires Internet Explorer 4.01 SP1 and later in order to be fully functional. In addition to various tools, samples, tutorials, and online documentation, this can be found at `msdn.microsoft.com/xml/default.asp`.
- **Lark.** This is a nonvalidating XML processor that was written in Java by Tim Bray (`www.textuality.com/Lark/`), and it's one of the famous ones that have been around a long time.
- **XP.** XP is a nonvalidating XML processor written in Java by James Clark (`www.jclark.com/xml/xp/index.html`).
- **Python and XML Processing Preliminary XML Parser.** This parser offers XML support to the Python programming language (`www.python.org/topics/xml/`).
- **TclXML.** This XML parser was written in Tcl by Steve Ball (`www.zveno.com/zm.cgi/in-tclxml/`).
- **XML Testbed.** This parser was written by Steve Withall (`www.w3.org/XML/1998/08withall/`).
- **SXP.** Silfide XML Parser (SXP) is another famous XML parser and, in fact, a complete XML Application Programming Interface (API) in Java (`www.loria.fr/projets/XSilfide/EN/sxp/`).
- **The Microsoft XML Parser.** The parser used in Internet Explorer is implemented as a COM component at `www.msdn.microsoft.com/downloads/tools/xmlparser/xmlparser.asp`.

- **OmiMark 5 Programming Language.** Includes integrated support for parsing and validation of XML (www.omnimark.com/).
- **Java Standard Extension for XML.** Because XML and Sun Microsystem's Java is such a popular mix, Sun is getting into the act with its own Java package for XML (java.sun.com/products/xml/).

Parsers will break up your document into its component pieces and make them accessible to other parts of a program; some parsers also check for well-formedness and fewer check for document validity. However, if you just want to check whether your XML is both well-formed and valid, all you need is an XML validator.

XML Validators

How do you know whether your XML document is well-formed and valid? One way is to check it with an XML *validator*, and you have plenty to choose from. Validators are packages that will check your XML and give you feedback. For example, if you have the XML for Java parser from IBM's AlphaWorks installed, you can use the DOMWriter example as a complete XML validator. Let's say you wanted to check this document, greeting.xml:

```
<?xml version="1.0" encoding="UTF-8"?>
<DOCUMENT>
    <GREETING>
        Hello From XML
    </GREETING>
    <MESSAGE>
        Welcome to the wild and woolly world of XML.
    </MESSAGE>
</DOCUMENT>
```

To do this, you'd set things up for the XML4J package (we'll see how to do so later in the book) and run the DOMWriter sample on it, like this:

```
%java dom.DOMWriter greeting.xml
greeting.xml:
[Error] greeting.xml:2:11: Element type "DOCUMENT" must be declared
[Error] greeting.xml:3:15: Element type "GREETING" must be declared
[Error] greeting.xml:6:14: Element type "MESSAGE" must be declared.
<?xml version="1.0" encoding="UTF-8"?>
<DOCUMENT>
    <GREETING>
        Hello From XML
```

```
    </GREETING>
    <MESSAGE>
        Welcome to the wild and woolly world of XML.
    </MESSAGE>
</DOCUMENT>
```

If all goes well, DOMWriter simply displays the document you've asked it to validate, but if there are errors, it will display them. Here, DOMWriter is indicating that because we haven't included a DTD in greeting.xml, it can't check for the validity of the document.

That's fine if you have the XML for Java package installed, but more accessible XML validators are available to you as well. Here's a list of some of the XML validators on the Web:

- **W3C XML Validator,** `validator.w3.org/`. This is the official W3C HTML validator. Although it's officially for HTML, it also includes some XML support. Your XML document must be online to be checked with this validator.
- **Tidy,** `www.w3.org/People/Raggett/tidy/`. Tidy is a beloved utility for cleaning up and repairing Web pages, and it includes limited support for XML. Your XML document must be online to be checked with this validator.
- `www.xml.com/xml/pub/tools/ruwf/check.html`. This is XML.com's XML validator based on the Lark processor. Your XML document must be online to be checked with this validator.
- `www.ltg.ed.ac.uk/~richard/xml-check.html`. This is the Language Technology Group at the University of Edinburgh's validator, based on the RXP parser. Your XML document must be online to be checked with this validator.
- `www.stg.brown.edu/service/xmlvalid/`. This is an excellent XML validator from the Scholarly Technology Group at Brown University. This is the only online XML validator I know of that allows you to check XML documents that are not online. You can use the Web page's file upload control to specify the name of the file on your hard disk that you want to have uploaded and checked.

To see a validator at work, take a look at Figure 1.11. There, I'm asking the XML validator from the Scholarly Technology Group to validate this XML document, c:\xml\greeting.xml. I've intentionally exchanged the order of the `<MESSAGE>` and `</GREETING>` tags:

```
<?xml version="1.0" encoding="UTF-8"?>
<!DOCTYPE DOCUMENT [
    <!ELEMENT DOCUMENT (GREETING, MESSAGE)>
    <!ELEMENT GREETING (#PCDATA)>
    <!ELEMENT MESSAGE (#PCDATA)>
]>
<DOCUMENT>
    <GREETING>
        Hello From XML
    <MESSAGE>
    </GREETING>
        Welcome to the wild and woolly world of XML.
    </MESSAGE>
</DOCUMENT>
```

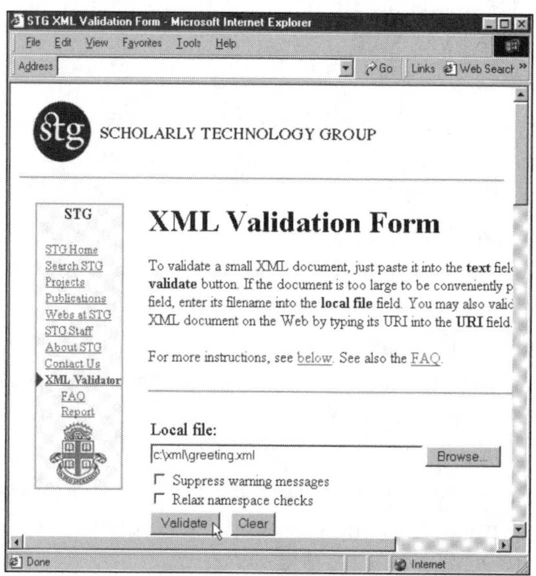

Figure 1.11 Using an XML validator.

You can see the results in Figure 1.12. As you can see, the validator is indicating that there is a problem with these two tags.

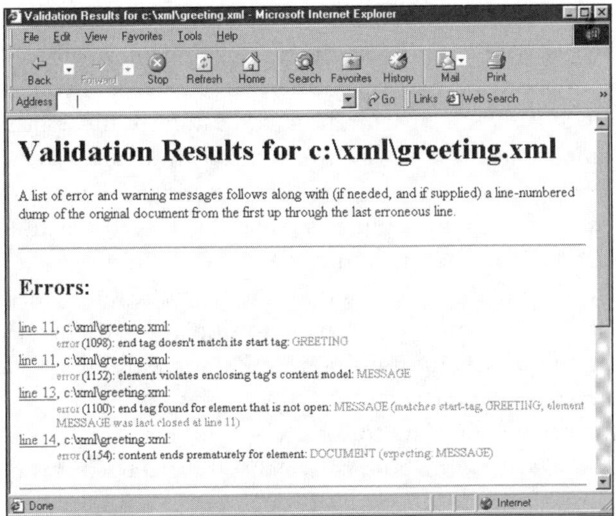

Figure 1.12 The results from an XML validator.

XML validators give you a powerful way of checking your XML documents. That's useful because XML is much stricter than HTML about making sure that a document is correct. (Recall that XML browsers are not supposed to make attempts to fix XML documents if they find a problem; they're just supposed to stop loading the document.)

We've gotten a good overview of XML already in this chapter. In a few pages, I'll start taking a look at a number of XML languages that are already developed. But there are a few more useful topics to cover first, especially if you have programmed in HTML and want to know the differences between XML and HTML.

CSS and XSL

Style sheets are becoming increasingly important in HTML because, in HTML 4, many built-in style features such as the `<CENTER>` element have become deprecated (declared obsolete) in favor of style sheets. However, most HTML programming ignores style sheets entirely.

The story is different in XML because you create your own elements in XML. Thus, if you want a browser to display them, you have to tell it how. This is both good and bad: It's good because it enables you to use the powerful CSS and XSL specifications to customize the appearance of your XML elements far beyond what's possible with standard HTML. It's bad because it can demand a lot of additional work. (One way of getting around the necessity of designing your own style sheets is to use an established XML language that has its own style sheets.)

All this is to say that XML defines the structure and semantics of the document, not its format; if you want to display XML directly, you can either use the default presentation in Internet Explorer, or use a style sheet to set up the presentation yourself.

You have two main ways to specify a style sheet for an XML document: with CSS and with XSL, both of which I'll dig into in this book. CSS is popular with those creating HTML documents and is widely supported. Using CSS, you can specify the formatting of individual elements, create style classes, set up fonts, use colors, and even specify placement of elements in the page.

XSL, on the other hand, is ultimately a better choice to work with XML documents because it's more powerful (in fact, XSL style sheets themselves are well-formed XML documents). XSL documents are made up of rules that are applied to XML documents. When a pattern that you've specified in the XSL document is recognized in the XML document, the rules transform the matched XML into something entirely new. You can even transform XML into HTML in this way.

Although CSS can set only the format and placement of elements, XSL can reorder elements in a document, change them entirely, display some but hide others, select styles based not just on elements but also on element attributes (XML elements can have attributes just as HTML elements can, and I'll introduce them in the next chapter), select styles based on element location, and much more. There are two ways to approach XSL: with XSL transformations and with XSL formatting objects. We'll take a look at both in this book.

Here are some good online resources for style sheets that provide a good reference:

- `www.w3.org/Style/CSS/`. The W3C outline and overview of CSS programming.
- `www.w3.org/TR/REC-CSS1`. The W3C CSS1 specification.

- www.w3.org/TR/REC-CSS2. The W3C CSS2 specification.
- www.w3.org/Style/XSL/. The W3C XSL page.

XLinks and XPointers

It's hard to imagine the World Wide Web without hyperlinks; of course, HTML documents excel at letting you link from one page to another. How about XML? In XML, it turns out, you use XLinks and XPointers.

XLinks let any element become a link, not just a single element such as the HTML <A> element. That's a good thing because XML doesn't have a built-in <A> element. In XML, you define your own elements, and it only makes sense that you can define which of those represent links to other documents.

In fact, XLinks are more powerful than simple hyperlinks. XLinks can be bidirectional, allowing the user to return after following a link. They can even be multidirectional—in fact, they can be sophisticated enough to point to the nearest mirror site from which a resource can be fetched.

XPointers, on the other hand, point not to a whole document, but to a part of a document. In fact, XPointers are smart enough to point to a specific element in a document, or the second instance of such an element, or the 11,904th instance. They can even point to the first child element of another element, and so on. The idea is that XPointers are powerful enough to locate specific parts of another document without forcing you to add additional markup to the target document.

On the other hand, note that the whole idea of XLinks and XPointers is relatively new and is not fully implemented in any browser. We will see what's possible today later in this book.

Here are some XLink and XPointer references online—take a look for more information on these topics:

- www.w3.org/TR/xlink/. The W3C XLink page.
- www.w3.org/TR/xptr. The W3C XPointer page.

URLs versus URIs

Having discussed XLinks and XPointers, I should also mention that the XML specification expands the idea of standard uniform resource locators (URLs) into uniform resource identifiers (URIs).

URLs are well understood and well supported on the Internet today. On the other hand (as you'd expect, given the addition of XLinks and XPointers to XML), the idea of URIs is more general than with simple URLs.

URIs let you represent a way of finding resources on the Internet, and they center more on the resource than the actual location. The idea is that, in theory, URIs can locate the nearest mirror site for a resource or even track a document that has been moved from one location to another.

In practice, the concept of URIs is still being developed, and most software still handles only URLs.

ASCII, Unicode, and the Universal Character System

The actual characters in documents are stored as numeric codes. The most common code set today is the American Standard Code for Information Interchange (ASCII). ASCII codes extend from 0 to 255 (to fit within a single byte); for example, the ASCII code for "A" is 65, the ASCII code for "B" is 66, and so on.

On the other hand, the World Wide Web is just that today: worldwide. Plenty of scripts are not handled by ASCII, such as scripts in Bengali, Armenian, Hebrew, Thai, Tibetan, Japanese Katakana, Arabic, Cyrillic, and other languages.

For that reason, the default character set specified for XML by W3C is Unicode, not ASCII. Unicode codes are made up of 2 bytes, not 1, so they extend from 0 to 65,535, not just 0 to 255. (However, to make things easier, the Unicode codes 0 to 255 do correspond to the ASCII 0 to 255 codes.) Therefore, Unicode can include many of the symbols commonly used in worldwide character and ideograph sets. You can find more on Unicode at `www.unicode.org`.

Only about 40,000 Unicode codes are reserved at this point (of which about 20,000 codes are used for Han ideographs, although more than 80,000 such ideographs are defined; 11,000 are used for Korean Hangul syllables).

In practice, Unicode support, like many parts of the XML technology, is not fully supported on most platforms today. Windows 95/98 does not offer full support for Unicode, although Windows NT and Windows 2000 come much closer (and XML Spy lets you use Unicode to write XML documents in Windows NT). Most often, this means that XML documents are written in simply ASCII, or in UTF-8, which is a compressed version of Unicode that uses 8 bits to represent characters. (In practice, this is well suited to

ASCII documents because multiple bytes are needed for many non-ASCII symbols, and ASCII documents converted to Unicode are two times as long.) Here's how to specify the UTF-8 character encoding in an XML document:

```
<?xml version="1.0" encoding="UTF-8"?>
<DOCUMENT>
    <GREETING>
        Hello From XML
    </GREETING>
    <MESSAGE>
        Welcome to the wild and woolly world of XML.
    </MESSAGE>
</DOCUMENT>
```

The default for XML processors today is to assume that your document is in UTF-8, so if you omit the encoding specification, UTF-8 is assumed. If you're writing XML documents in ASCII, you'll have no trouble.

Actually, not even Unicode has enough space for all symbols in common use. A new specification, the Universal Character System (UCS, also called ISO 10646) uses 4 bytes per symbol, which gives it a range of two billion symbols, far more than needed. You can specify that you want to use pure Unicode encoding in your XML documents by using the UCS-2 encoding (also called ISO-10646-UCS-2), which is compressed 2-byte UCS. You also can use UTF-16, which is a special encoding that represents UCS symbols using 2 bytes so that the result corresponds to UCS-2. Straight UCS encoding is referred to as UCS-4 (also called ISO-10646-UCS-4).

I'll stick to ASCII for most XML documents in this book because support for Unicode and UCS is not yet widespread. For example, I know of no true Unicode editors. On the other hand, you can write documents in a local character set and use a translation utility to convert them to Unicode, or you can insert the actual Unicode codes directly into your documents. For example, the Unicode for π is 03C0 in hexadecimal, so you can insert π into your document with the character entity (more on entities in the next chapter) `π`.

More character sets are available than those mentioned here; for a longer list, take a look at the list posted by the Internet Assigned Numbers Authority (IANA) at `www.isi.edu/in-notes/iana/assignments/character-sets`.

Converting ASCII to Unicode

If you want to convert ASCII files to straight Unicode, you can use the native2ascii program that comes with Sun Microsystem's Java Software Development Kit (the SDK, formerly the JDK). Using this tool, you can convert to Unicode like this: `native2ascii file.txt file.uni`. You also can convert to a number of other encodings besides Unicode, such as compressed Unicode, UTF-8.

XML Applications

We've seen a lot of theory in this chapter, so I'm going to spend the rest of this chapter taking a look at how XML is used in the real world. The world of XML is huge these days; in fact, XML is now used internally even in Netscape and Microsoft products, as well as installations of programming languages such as Perl. You can find a good list of organizations that produce their own XML-based languages at `www.xml.org/xmlorg_catalog.htm`.

It's useful and encouraging to see how XML is being used today in these XML-based languages. It's a new piece of terminology: As you know, XML is a meta-markup language, so it's actually used to create languages. The languages so created are applications of XML, so they're called *XML applications*.

Note that the term *XML application* refers to an application of XML to a specific domain, such as MathML, the mathematics markup language; it does not refer to a program that uses XML (a fact that causes a lot of confusion among people who know nothing about XML).

Thousands of XML applications exist today, and we'll see some of them here. You can see the advantage to various groups (such as physicists or chemists) for defining their own markup languages, allowing them to use the symbols and graphics of their discipline in customized browsers. I'll start with discussing CML.

XML at Work: Chemical Markup Language

Peter Murray-Rust developed CML as a very early XML application, so it has been around quite a while. Many people think of CML as a sort of HTML+Molecules, and that's not a bad characterization. Using CML, you can display the structure of complex molecules.

With CML, chemists can create and publish molecule specifications for easy interchange. Note that the real value of this is not so much in looking at individual chemicals as it is in being able to search CML repositories for molecules matching specific characteristics.

I've already mentioned Jumbo, a famous CML browser that you can download for free from www.xml-cml.org/jumbo.html. Jumbo not only works for handling CML, but you also can use it to display the structure of an XML document in general. However, there's no question that the novelty of Jumbo is that it can use CML to create graphical representations of molecules.

We've already seen an example in Jumbo in Figure 1.10, in which Jumbo is displaying the molecule thiophenol. Here is the file, thiophenol.xml, that it's reading to display that molecule (this document is an example that comes with the Jumbo browser):

```
<?jumbo:namespace ns="http://www.xml-cml.org" prefix="C"
    java="jumbo.cmlxml.*Node" ?>
<C:molecule id="thiophenol">
    <C:atomArray builtin="elsym">
        C C C C C C C S C C O O
    </C:atomArray>
    <C:atomArray builtin="x2" type="float">
        0 0.866 0.866 0 -0.866 -0.866
        0.0 0.0  1.732 -1.732 1.732 -1.732
    </C:atomArray>
    <C:atomArray builtin="y2" type="float">
        1 0.5   -0.5  -1.0 -0.5   0.5
        -2.0  2.0  1.0    1.0    2.0   2.0
    </C:atomArray>
    <C:bondArray builtin="atid1">
        1 2 3 4 5 6 1 4 2 9  6  10
    </C:bondArray>
    <C:bondArray builtin="atid2">
        2 3 4 5 6 1 8 7 9 11 10 12
    </C:bondArray>
    <C:bondArray builtin="order" type="integer">
        4 4 4 4 4 4 1 1 1 2  1  2
    </C:bondArray>
</C:molecule>
```

XML at Work: Mathematical Markup Language

Mathematical Markup Language was designed to fill a significant gap in Web documents: equations. In fact, Tim Berners-Lee first developed the World Wide Web at CERN so that high-energy physicists could exchange papers and documents. Still, there has been no way to display true equations in Web browsers for nearly a decade.

MathML fixes that. MathML is itself a W3C specification, and you can find it at `www.w3.org/Math/`. Using MathML, you can display equations and all kinds of mathematical terms. It's not powerful enough for many specialized areas of the sciences or mathematics yet, but it's growing all the time.

Because of the limited audience for this kind of presentation, no major browser yet supports MathML. However, there is the Amaya browser, which is W3C's own testbed browser for testing new HTML and XHTML elements (unfortunately, it's not an XML browser). You can download Amaya for free from `www.w3.org/Amaya/`.

Here's a MathML document that displays the equation $3Z^2 + 6Z + 12 = 0$ (this document uses an XML namespace, which we'll see more about in the next chapter):

```
<?xml version="1.0"?>
<html xmlns:m="http://www.w3.org/TR/REC-MathML/">
<math>
    <m:mrow>
        <m:mrow>
            <m:mn>3</m:mn>
            <m:mo>&InvisibleTimes;</m:mo>
            <m:msup>
                <m:mi>Z</m:mi>
                <m:mn>2</m:mn>
            </m:msup>
            <m:mo>-</m:mo>
            <m:mrow>
                <m:mn>6</m:mn>
                <m:mo>&InvisibleTimes;</m:mo>
                <m:mi>Z</m:mi>
            </m:mrow>
            <m:mo>+</m:mo>
            <m:mn>12</m:mn>
```

```
        </m:mrow>
        <m:mo>=</m:mo>
        <m:mn>0</m:mn>
    </m:mrow>
</math>
```

You can see the results of this document in the Amaya browser shown in Figure 1.13.

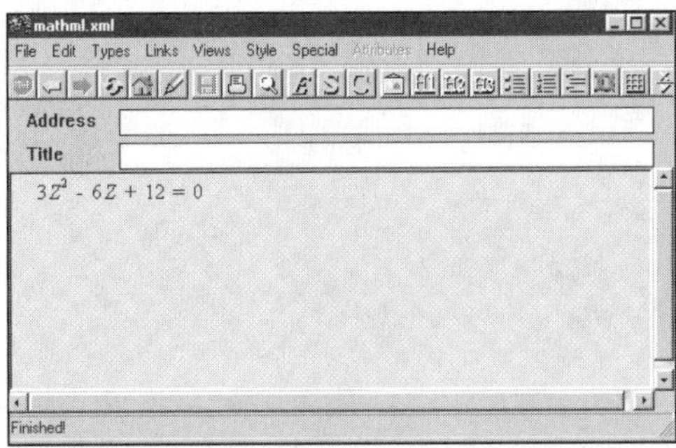

Figure 1.13 Displaying MathML in the Amaya browser.

XML at Work: Channel Definition Format

With the growth of the Web, people are always trying to come up with new ways to use it, and Microsoft is hard at work on this, too. One such innovation from Microsoft is the idea of Web site *channels*, which send documents to the user rather than waiting for the user to come and get them. Channels introduce the idea of Webcasting, or "push" (although it's not true server push in the HTML sense).

CDF documents are actually XML files, and you can learn about them at `msdn.microsoft.com/workshop/delivery/cdf/reference/CDF.asp`. I'll also discuss them later in this book.

Here's the way CDF works: you add a link to a .cdf file to a Web page, and then you give the link text, something like "Subscribe to this channel!" If the user is using Internet Explorer and clicks the hyperlink to navigate to the CDF file, Internet Explorer adds the site to the user's Favorites folder and subscribes to the channel, checking back periodically for updates.

Here's an example: This document, w3c.cdf, lets the user subscribe to the W3C XML and XSL pages:

```
<?xml version="1.0"?>
<CHANNEL HREF="http://www.w3.org/">
  <TITLE>World Wide Web Consortium</TITLE>
  <ABSTRACT>
    Leading the Web to its Full Potential
  </ABSTRACT>

  <ITEM HREF="http://www.w3.org/XML/">
    <TITLE>Extensible Markup Language (XML)
</TITLE>
    <ABSTRACT>
      The Extensible Markup Language (XML) is the universal
      format for structured documents and data on the Web.
    </ABSTRACT>
  </ITEM>

  <ITEM HREF="http://www.w3.org/Style/XSL/">
    <TITLE>Extensible Stylesheet Language (XSL)
</TITLE>
    <ABSTRACT>
      Extensible Stylesheet Language (XSL) is a
      language for expressing style sheets.
      </ABSTRACT>
  </ITEM>
</CHANNEL>
```

You can see the results in Figure 1.14. When the user opens this .cdf file, a W3C channel is added to the Internet Explorer's Favorites folder. (You can see the current channels in Internet Explorer by clicking the Favorites button in the standard toolbar and then double-clicking the Channels folder in the Favorites frame that opens at left.)

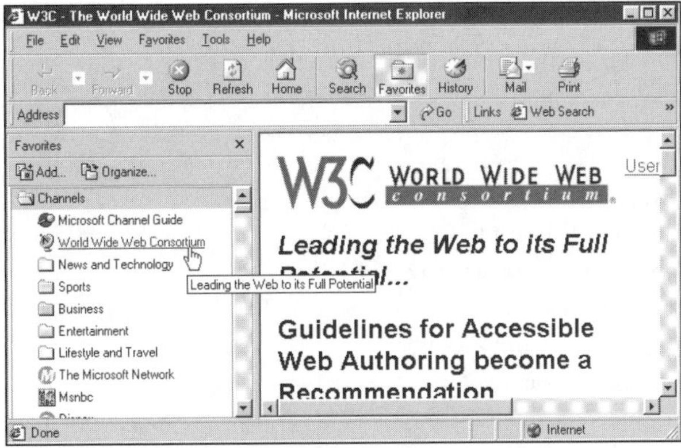

Figure 1.14 Subscribing to a new channel using CDF.

XML at Work: Synchronized Multimedia Integration Language

Synchronized Multimedia Integration Language (SMIL, pronounced "smile") has been around for quite some time. It's a W3C standard that you can find more about at `www.w3.org/AudioVideo/`.

SMIL attempts to fix a problem with modern "multimedia" browsers. Usually, such browsers can handle only one aspect of multimedia—video, or audio, or images—at a time, but never more than that. SMIL lets you create television-like fast cuts and true multimedia presentations.

The idea is that SMIL lets you specify what multimedia files are played when; SMIL itself does not describe or encapsulate any multimedia itself.

Microsoft, Macromedia, and Compaq have a semicompeting specification, HTML+TIME, which I'll take a look at next. As a result, Microsoft hasn't implemented much of SMIL in Internet Explorer yet, although there is limited support for SMIL in the preview version of Internet Explorer 5.5. You can find a SMIL applet written in Java at `www.empirenet.com/~joseram`, as well as some stunning examples of symphonies coordinated with images.

SMIL has become a core part of the RealNetworks streaming software (`http://service.real.com/help/library/guides/production/realpgd.htm`) and Apple Quicktime (`www.apple.com/quicktime/authoring/qtsmil.html`). In addition, the SMIL Boston project (`www.w3.org/TR/smil-boston/`) adds transition effects and event handling to SMIL 1.0. More implementations are also listed at `www.w3.org/AudioVideo`.

Here's an example SMIL document that creates a multimedia sequence, first playing mozart1.wav and amadeus1.mov; then displaying mozart1.htm; next playing mozart2.wav and amadeus2.mov; and finally displaying mozart2.htm:

```
<?xml version="1.0"?>
<!DOCTYPE smil PUBLIC "-//W3C//DTD SMIL 1.0//EN"
  "http://www.w3.org/TR/REC-smil/SMIL10.dtd">
<smil>
    <body>
        <seq id="mozart">
            <audio src="mozart1.wav"/>
            <video src="amadeus1.mov"/>
            <text src="mozart1.htm"/>
            <audio src="mozart2.wav"/>
            <video src="amadeus2.mov"/>
            <text src="mozart2.htm"/>
        </seq>
    </body>
</smil>
```

XML at Work: HTML+TIME

Microsoft, Macromedia, and Compaq have a multimedia alternative to SMIL called Timed Interactive Multimedia Extension (referred to as HTML+TIME), which is an XML application. Although SMIL documents let you manipulate other files, HTML+TIME lets you handle both HTML and multimedia presentations in the same page.

HTML+TIME is not nearly as powerful as SMIL, but Microsoft has shown relatively little interest in SMIL. You can find out about HTML+TIME at `msdn.microsoft.com/workshop/Author/behaviors/time.asp`. HTML+TIME is implemented in Internet Explorer as a *behavior*, which is a new construct in Internet Explorer 5 that lets you separate code from data. You can find more information about Internet Explorer behaviors at `msdn.microsoft.com/workshop/c-frame.htm#/workshop/author/default.asp`.

Here's an example HTML+TIME document that displays the words `Hello`, `there`, `from`, and `HTML+TIME`, spacing the words' appearance apart by two seconds and then repeating:

```
<HTML>
    <HEAD>
        <TITLE>
            Using HTML+TIME
        </TITLE>
        <STYLE>
            .time {behavior: url(#default#time);}
        </STYLE>
    </HEAD>
```

```
    <BODY>
        <DIV CLASS="time" t:REPEAT="5" t:DUR="10" t:TIMELINE="par">
            <DIV CLASS="time" t:BEGIN="0" t:DUR="10">Hello</DIV>
            <DIV CLASS="time" t:BEGIN="2" t:DUR="10">there</DIV>
            <DIV CLASS="time" t:BEGIN="4" t:DUR="10">from</DIV>
            <DIV CLASS="time" t:BEGIN="6" t:DUR="10">HTML+TIME.</DIV>
        </DIV>
    </BODY>
</HTML>
```

You can see the results of this HTML+TIME document in Figure 1.15.

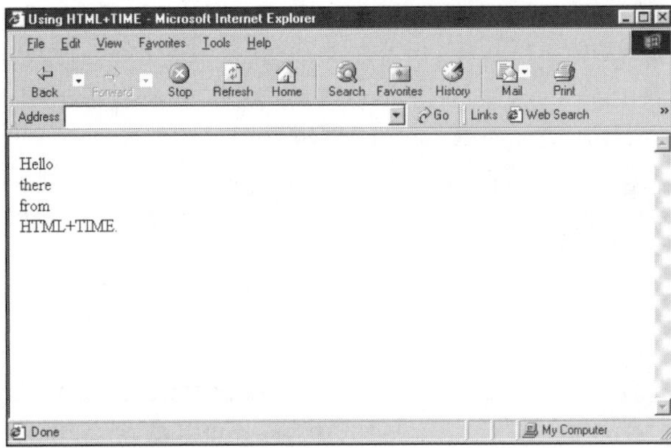

Figure 1.15 An HTML+TIME document at work.

HTML+TIME actually builds on SMIL to a great extent; the example from the previous topic on SMIL would look this way in HTML+TIME:

```
<t:seq id="mozart">
    <t:audio src="mozart1.wav"/>
    <t:video src="amadeus1.mov"/>
    <t:textstream src="mozart1.htm"/>
    <t:audio src="mozart2.wav"/>
    <t:video src="amadeus2.mov"/>
    <t:textstream src="mozart2.htm"/>
</seq>
```

XML at Work: XHTML

One of the biggest XML applications around today is XHTML, the translation of HTML 4.0 into XML by W3C. I'll dig into XHTML in some depth in this book.

W3C introduced XHTML to bridge the gap between HTML and XML, and to introduce more people to XML. XHTML is simply an application that mimics HTML 4.0 in such a way that you can display the results—true XML documents—in current Web browsers. XHTML is an exciting development in the XML world, and we'll be spending some time with it later in this book, in Chapter 16, "Essential XHTML," and Chapter 17, "XHTML at Work."

Here are some XHTML resources online:

- `www.w3.org/MarkUp/Activity.html`. The W3C Hypertext Markup activity page, which has an overview of XHTML.
- `www.w3.org/TR/xhtml1/`. The XHTML 1.0 specification (in more common use than XHTML 1.1 today).
- `www.w3.org/TR/xhtml11/`. The XHTML 1.1 working draft of the XHTML 1.1 module-based specification.

XHTML 1.0 comes in three different versions: transitional, frameset, and strict. The transitional version is the most popular because it supports HTML more or less as it's used today. The frameset version supports XHTML documents that display frames; this version is different from the transitional version because documents in the transitional version are based on the `<body>` element, whereas documents that use frames are based on the `<frameset>` element. The strict version omits all the HTML elements deprecated in HTML 4.0 (of which there were quite a few).

XHTML 1.1 is a form of the XHTML 1.0 strict version made a little more strict by omitting support for some elements and adding support for a few more (such as `<ruby>` for annotated text). You can find a list of the differences between XHTML 1.0 and XHTML 1.1 at `www.w3.org/TR/xhtml11/changes.html#a_changes`. XHTML 1.1 is quite strict, and I think it'll be quite a while before it's in widespread use compared to the XHTML 1.0 transitional version.

Here's an example XHTML document using the XHTML 1.0 transitional DTD. You can display this document in any standard HTML browser, as long as you give the document file the extension .html (note that tag names are all in lowercase text in XHTML):

```
<?xml version="1.0"?>
<!DOCTYPE html PUBLIC "-//W3C//DTD XHTML 1.0 Transitional//EN"
"http://www.w3.org/TR/xhtml1/DTD/xhtml1-transitional.dtd">
<html xmlns="http://www.w3.org/1999/xhtml" xml:lang="en" lang="en">
    <head>
        <title>
            Web page number one!
        </title>
    </head>

    <body>
        <h1>
            Welcome to XHTML!
        </h1>
        <center>
        This is simple text that appears in this page.
            <p>
                Here's a new paragraph!
            </p>
        </center>
    </body>
</html>
```

You can see the results of this XHTML in Figure 1.16. Writing XHTML is a lot like HTML, except that you must adhere to XML syntax (such as making sure that every element has a closing tag).

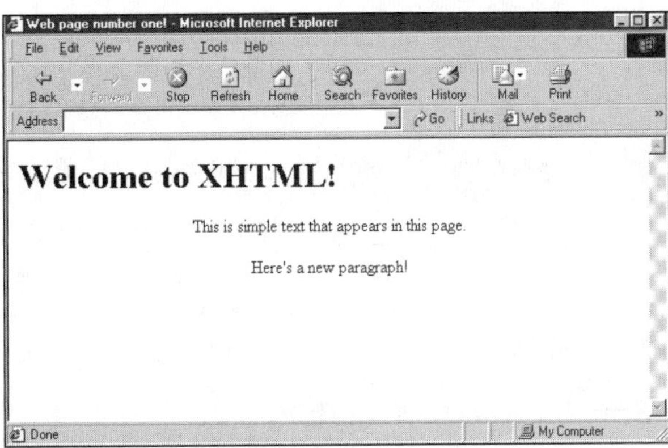

Figure 1.16 Displaying XHTML.

XML at Work: Open Software Description

Open Software Description (OSD) was developed by Marimba and Microsoft; you can find more about this XML application at www.w3.org/TR/NOTE-OSD.html. OSD enables you to specify how and when software is updated via the Internet. In fact, you can use OSD with CDF to make periodic software updates to the user's machine.

Not everyone thinks OSD is a great idea: After all, many users want control over when their software is updated. New versions may have incompatibilities with old versions, for example.

Here's an example .osd file that handles updates for a word processor named SuperDuperTextPro from SuperDuperSoft:

```
<?xml version="1.0"?>
<CHANNEL HREF="http://www.superdupersoft.com/updates.html">
    <TITLE>
        SuperDuperTextPro Updates
    </TITLE>
    <USAGE VALUE="SoftwareUpdate"/>
    <SOFTPKG
        HREF="http://updates.superdupersoft.com/updates.html"
        NAME="{34567A7E-8BE7-99C0-8746-0034829873A3}"
        VERSION="2,4,6">
        <TITLE>
            SuperDuperTextPro
        </TITLE>
        <ABSTRACT>
            SuperDuperTextPro version 206 with sideburns!!!
        </ABSTRACT>
        <IMPLEMENTATION>
             <CODEBASE HREF=
                 "http://www.superdupersoft.com/new.exe"/>
        </IMPLEMENTATION>
    </SOFTPKG>
</CHANNEL>
```

XML at Work: Scalable Vector Graphics

Scalable Vector Graphics (SVG) is another W3C-based XML application that is a good idea but that has found only limited implementation so far (notably, in such programs as CorelDraw and various Adobe products such as Adobe Illustrator). Using SVG, you can draw two-dimensional graphics using markup. You can find the SVG specification at www.w3.org/TR/SVG/ and an overview at www.w3.org/Graphics/SVG/Overview.htm8.

Note that because SVG describes graphics, not text, it's harder for current browsers to implement; no browsers currently have full SVG implementations. Other graphics standards are proposed, such as the Precision Graphics Markup Language (PGML), proposed to W3C (www.w3.org/TR/1998/NOTE-PGML) by IBM, Adobe, Netscape, and Sun.

Here's an example PGML document that draws a blue box:

```
<?xml version="1.0"?>
<!DOCTYPE pgml SYSTEM "/DTDs/pgml.dtd">
<pgml>
  <group fillcolor="blue">
    <path>
      <moveto x="0" y="0"/>
      <lineto x="0" y="1000"/>
      <lineto x="1000" y="1000"/>
      <lineto x="1000" y="0"/>
      <closepath/>
    </path>
  </group>
</pgml>
```

XML at Work: Vector Markup Language

Vector Markup Language (VML) is an alternative to SVG that is implemented in Microsoft Internet Explorer. You can find out more about VML at www.w3.org/TR/NOTE-VML. Using VML, you can draw many vector-based graphics figures. Here's an example, vml.html, that draws a yellow oval, a blue box, and a red squiggle:

```
<HTML xmlns:v="urn:schemas-microsoft-com:vml">

    <HEAD>
        <TITLE>
            Using Vector Markup Language
        </TITLE>

        <STYLE>
        v\:* {behavior: url(#default#VML);}
        </STYLE>
    </HEAD>
```

continues ▸

```
    <BODY>
        <CENTER>
            <H1>
                Using Vector Markup Language
            </H1>
        </CENTER>
        <P>
        <v:oval STYLE='width:100pt; height:75pt'
            fillcolor="yellow"> </v:oval>
        <P>
        <v:rect STYLE='width:100pt; height:75pt' fillcolor="blue"
            strokecolor="red" STROKEWEIGHT="2pt"/>
        <P>
        <v:polyline
            POINTS="20pt,55pt,100pt,-10pt,180pt,65pt,260pt,25pt"
            strokecolor="red" STROKEWEIGHT="2pt"/>
    </BODY>
</HTML>
```

You can see the results of this VML in Figure 1.17.

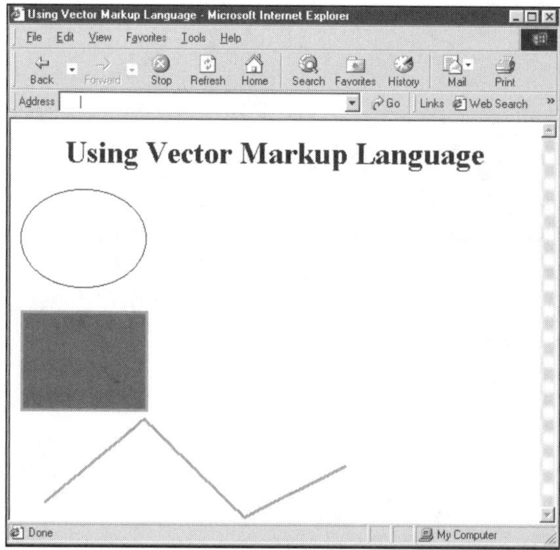

Figure 1.17 Vector Markup Language at work.

XML at Work: XML-Based User Interface Language

XML-based User Interface Language (XUL, pronounced "zuul"), which comes from Netscape and Mozilla, enables you to describe what user-interface elements you want those browsers to display. (The only Netscape Navigator that currently supports XUL is Netscape Navigator 6 preview version,) Here are some online references for XUL:

- `www.mozilla.org/projects/intl/xul-styleguide.html`. A XUL style guide.
- `www.mozilla.org/xpfe/xptoolkit/xulintro.html`. An introduction to XUL.

Here's a sample XUL document, scroll.xul, that adds scrollbars around the browser's document display area. (For formatting reasons, I have to break up the expression `"http://www.mozilla.org/keymaster/gatekeeper/there.is.only.xul"` to two lines in this book; make sure you rejoin that text into a quoted text string on one line before giving this a try).

```
<?xml version="1.0"?>

<window align="horizontal"
    xmlns=
    "http://www.mozilla.org/keymaster/gatekeeper/
        there.is.only.xul">
    <scrollbar align="vertical"/>
    <box align="vertical" flex="100%">
        <scrollbar align="horizontal"/>
        <spring flex="100%" style="background-color: white"/>
        <scrollbar align="horizontal"/>
    </box>
    <scrollbar align="vertical"/>
</window>
```

You can see the results of this XUL document in Figure 1.18.

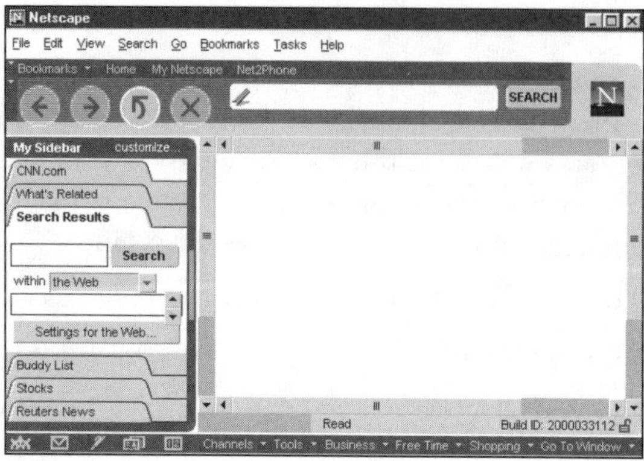

Figure 1.18 Using XUL to create scrollbars.

XML at Work: Extensible Business Reporting Language

Extensible Business Reporting Language (XBRL, formerly named XFRML), is an open specification that uses XML to describe financial statements. You can find more on XBRL at www.xfrml.org/Overview.htm. Using XBRL, you can codify business financial statements in a way that makes it easy to search them en masse and review them quickly, extracting the information you want.

Here's a sample XBRL document that gives you an idea of what this application looks like at work:

```
<?xml version="1.0" encoding="utf-8" ?>
    <group xmlns="http://www.xbrl.org/us/aicpa-us-gaap"
        xmlns:gpsi="http://www.xbrl.org/TaxonomyCustom.xsd"
        id="543-AB" entity="NASDAQ:GPSI" period="1999-05-31"
        schemaLocation="http://www.xbrl.org/TaxonomyCustom.xsd"
        scaleFactor="6" precision="9" type="USGAAP:Financial"
        unit="ISO4217:USD" decimalPattern="" formatName="">
        <item id="IS-025"
            type="operatingExpenses.researchExpense"
            period="P1Y/1999-05-31">20427</item>
        <item id="IS-026"
            type="operatingExpenses.researchExpense"
            period="P1Y/1998-05-31">12586</item>
    </group>
    <group type="gpsi:detail.quarterly" period="1998-05-31">
```

```
    <item period="1997-06-01/1998-07-31">0.12</item>
    <item period="1997-09-01/1997-11-30">0.16</item>
    <item period="1997-12-01/1998-02-28">0.17</item>
    <item period="1998-03-01/1998-05-31">-0.12</item>
    <item period="1998-06-01/1998-05-31">0.33</item>
</group>
<group type="gpsi:detail.quarterly" period="1999-05-31">
    <item period="1998-06-01/1998-08-31">0.15</item>
    <item period="1998-09-01/1998-11-30">0.20</item>
    <item period="1998-12-01/1999-02-28">0.23</item>
    <item period="1999-03-01/1999-05-31">0.28</item>
    <item period="1998-06-01/1999-05-31">0.86</item>
</group>
<group type="gpsi:detail.quarterly" period="1998-05-31">
    <item period="1997-06-01/1998-07-31">0.11</item>
    <item period="1997-09-01/1997-11-30">0.15</item>
    <item period="1997-12-01/1998-02-28">0.17</item>
    <item period="1998-03-01/1998-05-31">-0.12</item>
    <item period="1998-06-01/1998-05-31">0.32</item>
</group>
```

XML at Work: Resource Description Framework

Resource Description Framework (RDF) is an XML application that specializes in meta-data—that is, data about other data.You use RDF to specify information about other resources, such as Web pages, movies, automobiles, or practically anything.You can find more information about RDF at `www.w3.org/RDF/`, and I'll be discussing it later in the book as well, in Chapter 18, "Resource Description Framework and Channel Definition Format."

Using RDF, you create vocabularies that describe resources. For example, the Dublin Core is an RDF vocabulary that handles meta-data for Web pages; you can find more information about it at `http://purl.org/DC/`. Using the Dublin Core, you can specify a great deal of information about Web pages that is designed ultimately to replace the unsystematic use of `<META>` tags in today's pages.When systemized, that information will be much more tractable to Web search engines.

Here's an example RDF page using the Dublin Core that gives information about a Web page:

```
<RDF:RDF xmlns:RDF="http://www.w3.org/1999/02/22-rdf-syntax-ns#"
    xmlns:DC="http://purl.org/DC/">
    <RDF:Description about="http://www.starpowder.com/xml">
        <DC:Format>HTML</DC:Format>
        <DC:Language>en</DC:Language>
        <DC:Date>2002-02-02</DC:date>
        <DC:Type>tutorial</DC:Type>
        <DC:Title>Welcome to XML!</DC:Title>
    </RDF:Description>
</RDF:RDF>
```

Note that many more XML applications exist than can be covered in one chapter—and plenty of them work behind the scenes. For example, Microsoft Office 2000 can handle HTML as well as other types of documents, but because HTML doesn't allow it to store everything it needs in a document, Office 2000 also includes some XML behind the scenes (in fact, Office 2000's vector graphics are done using VML). Even relatively early versions of Netscape Navigator allowed you to look for sites much like the current one you're viewing; to do that, it connected to a CGI program that uses XML internally. As you can see, XML is all around, everywhere you look on the Internet.

That's it for our overview chapter. We've received a solid foundation in XML here. The next step is to start getting all the actual ground rules for creating XML documents under our belts. I'll cover that in Chapter 2.

2 Creating Well-Formed XML Documents

IN THE PREVIOUS CHAPTER, WE GOT OUR start in XML with an overview of how XML lets you structure your own documents, what XML is all about, and what uses you can make of it. It's now time to take a look at XML in more depth and sharpen our XML understanding until it's crystal clear.

In HTML, about 100 elements already are defined. Browsers can check the HTML on a Web page and display that page as they see fit. In XML, you have more freedom—and, thus, more responsibility. In XML, you define your own elements, and it's up to you to decide how they should be used. Despite their apparently free-form nature, however, XML documents are subject to a number of rules that allow them to be handled in a useful and reproducible way.

In fact, the rules to which XML documents are subject are significantly more stringent than the rules to which HTML documents are subject. As mentioned in Chapter 1, "Essential XML," if an XML document cannot be successfully understood by an XML processor, for example, the processor is not supposed to make *any* guesses about the structure of the document at all—it's just supposed to quit, possibly returning an error.

As we also saw in Chapter 1, XML documents are subject to two specific constraints: *well-formedness* and *validity*. As far as the World Wide Web Consortium (W3C) is concerned, well-formedness is the more basic constraint. In the XML 1.0 specification itself, which represents the foundation of this chapter and Chapter 3,"Valid XML Documents: Creating Document Type Definitions," the W3C says that you can't even call a data object an XML document unless it's well-formed:

> *A data object is an XML document if it is well-formed, as defined in this specification. A well-formed XML document may in addition be valid if it meets certain further constraints.*

Why is it so important that XML documents be well-formed? Why does the W3C specify that XML processors should not attempt to fix documents that are not well-formed?

The reason that the W3C makes this stipulation is mainly to stop XML processors from doing the same thing that HTML browsers have done to HTML: By trying to fix things, the major browsers have introduced their own versions of HTML that authors now rely on. The result is that many versions of HTML currently exist.

In this chapter, we'll see what makes an XML document well-formed, which is the minimal requirement that a data object must satisfy to be an XML document. The second constraint that you can require of XML documents is that they be valid, which means that they must obey the document type definition (DTD) or schema that you use to specify the legal syntax of the document. This chapter is all about what makes XML documents well-formed. Chapter 3 is all about what makes them valid.

Now that we're taking a look at how to build XML documents in a formal way, I'll start from the beginning so that we build a complete and solid foundation. That means starting with the W3C itself.

The World Wide Web Consortium

We already know that the W3C is the body responsible for defining exactly what XML is, but who is the W3C? The W3C is not a government body; instead, it's a group made up of member organizations (currently more than 400) that have an interest in the World Wide Web. The W3C is hosted by the Massachusetts Institute of Technology, Laboratory for Computer Science (MIT/LCS), in the United States; the Institut National de Recherche en Informatique et en Automatique (INRIA), in Europe; and the Keio University Shonan Fujisawa Campus, in Japan. Currently, it has about 50 full-time staff members.

How does W3C set up specifications for the Web? It does so by publishing those standards in HTML (and, recently, in XHTML) form at its Web site, www.w3.org. These specifications are given three different levels:

- **Notes.** These are specifications that usually are submitted to the W3C by a member organization, and, that the W3C is making public although not necessarily endorsing. For example, the note submitted by Microsoft to W3C on Vector Markup Language (VML) is at www.w3.org/TR/NOTE-VML.
- **Working drafts.** A working draft is a specification that is under consideration and open to comment. It's inappropriate to refer to such works as standards or as anything other than working drafts. For example, the working draft for XHTML 1.1 is at www.w3.org/TR/xhtml11/.
- **Recommendations.** Working drafts that the W3C has accepted become recommendations. The W3C uses the term *recommendations* when it publishes its standards (because the W3C is not a government body, it does not use the term *standard*). For example, the XML 1.0 recommendation is at www.w3.org/TR/REC-xml.

Besides these official specification levels, W3C also has *candidate recommendations*, which are working drafts that have been proposed but not yet accepted as recommendations, and *companion recommendations*, which augment recommendations. In fact, there are plenty of companion recommendations for XML (such as schemas, XLinks, Xpointers, and so on), and you'll find a good list of them at www.w3c.org/xml.

The recommendation for XML 1.0, which defines XML, is at www.w3.org/TR/REC-xml; you'll also find it in Appendix A, "The XML 1.0 Specification." This specification is the most important one as far as this book is concerned. Together with the associated standards (Unicode and ISO/IEC 10646 for characters, Internet RFC 1766 for language identification tags, ISO 639 for language name codes, and ISO 3166 for country name codes), this recommendation gives you all you need to understand XML Version 1.0 and create XML documents. Now it's time to put this recommendation to work, creating well-formed XML documents.

What Is a Well-Formed XML Document?

The W3C, which is responsible for the term *well-formedness*, defines it this way in the XML 1.0 recommendation (I'll take a look at each of these stipulations later):

> *A textual object is a well-formed XML document if:*
>
> - *Taken as a whole, it matches the production labeled document.*
> - *It meets all the well-formedness constraints given in this specification (that is, www.w3.org/TR/REC-xml).*
> - *Each of the parsed entities which is referenced directly or indirectly within the document is well-formed.*

W3C calls the individual specifications within a working draft or a recommendation *productions*. In this case, to be well-formed, a document must follow the "document" production, which means that the document itself must have three parts: a prolog (which can be empty), a root element, and an optional miscellaneous part.

The prolog, which I'll talk about in a few pages, can and should include an XML declaration (such as `<?xml version = "1.0"?>`) and an optional miscellaneous part that includes comments, processing instructions, and so on.

The root element of the document can itself hold other elements—in fact, it's hard to imagine useful XML documents in which the root element does not contain other elements. Note that each well-formed XML document must have exactly one root element, and all other elements in the document must be enclosed in the root element (this does not apply to the parts of the prolog, of course, because items such as processing instructions and comments are not considered elements).

The optional miscellaneous part can be made up of XML comments, processing instructions, and whitespace (including spaces, tabs, and so on). I'll take a look at the prolog, the root element, and the miscellaneous part later in this chapter.

The next stipulation in the list says that to be well-formed, XML documents must also satisfy the well-formedness constraints listed in the XML 1.0 specification. This means that XML documents must adhere to the syntax rules specified in the XML 1.0 recommendation. I'll talk about those rules in this chapter, including the naming rules that you should follow when naming tags, how to nest elements, and so on.

Well-Formedness Constraint

If you search the XML 1.0 specification, which also appears in Appendix A, you'll see that all constraints that you must satisfy to create a well-formed document are marked with the words "Well-Formedness Constraint."

Finally, the last stipulation in the W3C well-formed document list is that each *parsed entity* must itself be well-formed. What does that mean?

The parts of an XML document are called *entities*. An entity is a part of a document that can hold text or binary data (but not both). An entity may refer to other entities and thus cause them to be included in the document. Entities can be either parsed (character data) or unparsed (character data that can include non-XML text or binary data that the XML processor does not parse). In other words, the term *entity* is just a generic way of referring to a data storage unit in XML. For example, a file with a few XML elements in it is an entity, but it's not a document unless it's also well-formed.

This stipulation about parsed entities means that if you refer to an entity and include that entity's data (which can include data from external sources) in your document, the included data also must be well-formed.

That's the W3C's definition of a well-formed document, but it's far from clear at this point. What are the well-formedness constraints that we need to follow? What exactly can be in a prolog? To answer questions like these, the rest of this chapter examines what these constraints mean in detail.

I'll start by looking at an XML document that we can refer to throughout the chapter as we examine what it means for a document to be well-formed. In this case, I'll store customer data for specific purchases in a document called order.xml. I'll start with the XML declaration itself:

```
<?xml version = "1.0"?>
```

Here, I'm using the `<?xml?>` declaration to indicate that this document is written in XML, and I'm specifying the only version possible at this time, version 1.0. Because all the documents in this chapter are self-contained (that is, they don't refer to or include any external entities), I can also use the `standalone` attribute, setting it to `yes` like this:

```
<?xml version = "1.0" standalone="yes"?>
```

This attribute, which may or may not be used by an XML parser, indicates that the document is completely self-contained. Technically, XML documents do not need to start with the XML declaration, but W3C recommends it.

Next, I add the root element, which I'll call `<DOCUMENT>` in this case (although you can use any name):

```
<?xml version = "1.0" standalone="yes"?>
<DOCUMENT>
    .
    .
    .
</DOCUMENT>
```

The root element can contain other elements, of course. Here, I add elements for three customers to the document:

```
<?xml version = "1.0" standalone="yes"?>
<DOCUMENT>
    <CUSTOMER>
    .
    .
    .
    </CUSTOMER>
    <CUSTOMER>
    .
    .
    .
    </CUSTOMER>
    <CUSTOMER>
    .
    .
    .
    </CUSTOMER>
</DOCUMENT>
```

For each customer, I store a name in a <NAME> element, which itself encloses a <LAST_NAME> and a <FIRST_NAME> element, like this:

```
<?xml version = "1.0" standalone="yes"?>
<DOCUMENT>
    <CUSTOMER>
        <NAME>
            <LAST_NAME>Smith</LAST_NAME>
            <FIRST_NAME>Sam</FIRST_NAME>
        </NAME>
    .
    .
    .
    </CUSTOMER>
    <CUSTOMER>
    .
    .
    .
    </CUSTOMER>
    <CUSTOMER>
    .
    .
    .
    </CUSTOMER>
</DOCUMENT>
```

I can also store the details of customer orders with a new element, <DATE>, and an element named <ORDERS> like this:

```
<?xml version = "1.0" standalone="yes"?>
<DOCUMENT>
    <CUSTOMER>
        <NAME>
            <LAST_NAME>Smith</LAST_NAME>
            <FIRST_NAME>Sam</FIRST_NAME>
        </NAME>
        <DATE>October 15, 2001</DATE>
        <ORDERS>
    .
    .
    .
        </ORDERS>
    .
    .
    .
    </CUSTOMER>
    <CUSTOMER>
    .
    .
    .
    </CUSTOMER>
    <CUSTOMER>
    .
    .
    .
    </CUSTOMER>
</DOCUMENT>
```

I also can record each item that a customer bought with an `<ITEM>` element, which itself is broken up into `<PRODUCT>`, `<NUMBER>`, and `<PRICE>` elements:

```
<?xml version = "1.0" standalone="yes"?>
<DOCUMENT>
    <CUSTOMER>
        <NAME>
            <LAST_NAME>Smith</LAST_NAME>
            <FIRST_NAME>Sam</FIRST_NAME>
        </NAME>
        <DATE>October 15, 2001</DATE>
        <ORDERS>
            <ITEM>
                <PRODUCT>Tomatoes</PRODUCT>
                <NUMBER>8</NUMBER>
                <PRICE>$1.25</PRICE>
            </ITEM>
            <ITEM>
                <PRODUCT>Oranges</PRODUCT>
                <NUMBER>24</NUMBER>
                <PRICE>$4.98</PRICE>
            </ITEM>
```

continues ▸

```
        </ORDERS>
    .
    .
    .
    </CUSTOMER>
    <CUSTOMER>
    .
    .
    .
    </CUSTOMER>
    <CUSTOMER>
    .
    .
    .
    </CUSTOMER>
</DOCUMENT>
```

That's what the data looks like for one customer; here's the full document, including data for all three customers:

```
<?xml version = "1.0" standalone="yes"?>
<DOCUMENT>
    <CUSTOMER>
        <NAME>
            <LAST_NAME>Smith</LAST_NAME>
            <FIRST_NAME>Sam</FIRST_NAME>
        </NAME>
        <DATE>October 15, 2001</DATE>
        <ORDERS>
            <ITEM>
                <PRODUCT>Tomatoes</PRODUCT>
                <NUMBER>8</NUMBER>
                <PRICE>$1.25</PRICE>
            </ITEM>
            <ITEM>
                <PRODUCT>Oranges</PRODUCT>
                <NUMBER>24</NUMBER>
                <PRICE>$4.98</PRICE>
            </ITEM>
        </ORDERS>
    </CUSTOMER>
    <CUSTOMER>
        <NAME>
            <LAST_NAME>Jones</LAST_NAME>
            <FIRST_NAME>Polly</FIRST_NAME>
        </NAME>
        <DATE>October 20, 2001</DATE>
        <ORDERS>
            <ITEM>
                <PRODUCT>Bread</PRODUCT>
                <NUMBER>12</NUMBER>
                <PRICE>$14.95</PRICE>
```

```
            </ITEM>
            <ITEM>
                <PRODUCT>Apples</PRODUCT>
                <NUMBER>6</NUMBER>
                <PRICE>$1.50</PRICE>
            </ITEM>
        </ORDERS>
    </CUSTOMER>
    <CUSTOMER>
        <NAME>
            <LAST_NAME>Weber</LAST_NAME>
            <FIRST_NAME>Bill</FIRST_NAME>
        </NAME>
        <DATE>October 25, 2001</DATE>
        <ORDERS>
            <ITEM>
                <PRODUCT>Asparagus</PRODUCT>
                <NUMBER>12</NUMBER>
                <PRICE>$2.95</PRICE>
            </ITEM>
            <ITEM>
                <PRODUCT>Lettuce</PRODUCT>
                <NUMBER>6</NUMBER>
                <PRICE>$11.50</PRICE>
            </ITEM>
        </ORDERS>
    </CUSTOMER>
</DOCUMENT>
```

Documents like this can grow very long and can consist of markup that is many levels deep. Handling such documents is not a problem for XML parsers, however, as long as the document is well-formed (and, if the parser is a validating parser, valid). In this chapter, I'll refer back to this document, modifying it and taking a look at its parts as we see what makes a document well-formed.

We're ready now to take XML documents apart, piece by piece. I'll start with the basics and work up through the prolog, root element, enclosed elements, and so on. We're going to see it all in this chapter.

At their most basic level, then, XML documents are combinations of *markup* and *character data*. We'll start from that point.

Markup and Character Data

XML documents are made up of markup and character data. Binary data might contribute to XML documents some day, but there is no provision for enclosing binary data in a document made up of markup and character data yet; until there is, you refer to external binary data with entity references, as we'll see.

The markup in a document gives it its structure. Markup includes start tags, end tags, empty element tags, entity references, character references, comments, CDATA section delimiters (we'll see more about CDATA sections in a few pages), document type declarations, and processing instructions. So what's the character data in an XML document? All the text in a document that is not markup is character data.

Here's a quick example using markup and character data that we've already seen:

```
<?xml version="1.0" encoding="UTF-8"?>
<DOCUMENT>
    <GREETING>
        Hello From XML
    </GREETING>
    <MESSAGE>
        Welcome to the wild and woolly world of XML.
    </MESSAGE>
</DOCUMENT>
```

Tags begin with < and end with >, so it's easy to see that the markup here consists of tags, such as <?xml version="1.0" encoding="UTF-8"?>, <DOCUMENT>, and so on. The text Hello From XML and Welcome to the wild and woolly world of XML is the character data.

However, markup does not need to begin and end with < and >. Markup also can start with & and end with ;—in the case of *general entity references* (an entity reference is replaced by the entity it refers to when it's parsed)—or can start with % and end with ;—in the case of *parameter entity references*, which are used in DTDs—as we'll see in Chapter 3. Using entity references, some of the markup in a document can *become* character data when you process that document. For example, the markup > is a general entity reference that is turned into a > when parsed, and the markup < is turned into a < when parsed. Here's an example:

```
<?xml version="1.0" encoding="UTF-8"?>
<DOCUMENT>
    <GREETING>
        This text is inside the &lt;GREETING&gt; element.
    </GREETING>
</DOCUMENT>
```

You can see this XML document in Internet Explorer in Figure 2.1, where you see that the markup > was turned into a >, and that the markup < was turned into a <.

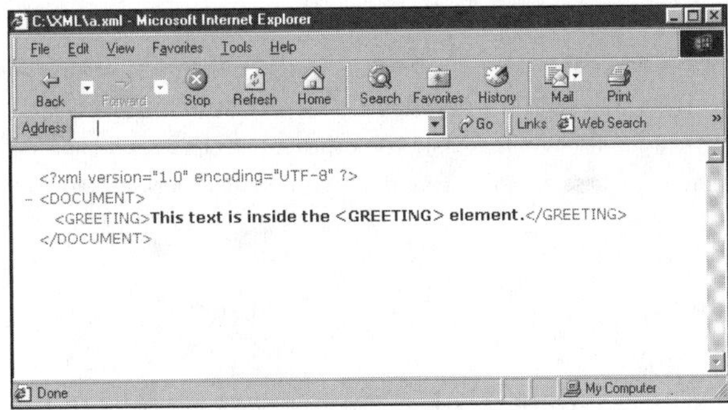

Figure 2.1 Using markup in Internet Explorer.

Because some markup can turn into character data when parsed, the character data that results after everything has been parsed—and markup that should be replaced by character data has been replaced—has a special name: *parsed character data.*

Whitespace

If you're ever concerned about exactly what characters are legal in XML documents, you'll find them listed in the XML 1.0 specification under the production named *Char*. It's worth noting that spaces, carriage returns, line feeds, and tabs are all treated as whitespace in XML. Take a look this document:

```
<?xml version="1.0" encoding="UTF-8"?>
<DOCUMENT>
<GREETING>
Hello From XML
</GREETING>
<MESSAGE>
Welcome to the wild and woolly world of XML.
</MESSAGE>
</DOCUMENT>
```

Practically speaking, that document is equivalent to this one:

```
<?xml version="1.0" encoding="UTF-8"?>
<DOCUMENT><GREETING>Hello From XML</GREETING>
<MESSAGE>Welcome to the wild and woolly world of XML.</MESSAGE></DOCUMENT>
```

It's also worth noting that the XML recommendation specifies that XML documents use the UNIX convention for line endings, which means that lines are ended with a linefeed character only (ASCII code 10). In DOS files, lines are ended with carriage-return linefeed pairs (ASCII codes 13 and 10), but when parsed, that's treated simply as a single linefeed (ASCII code 10).

Handling of Whitespace

You can use the special attribute `xml:space` in an element to indicate that whitespace should be preserved by applications within that element (if you use `xml:space` in documents with a DTD, you also must declare it before using it). You can set this attribute to "default" to indicate that the default handling of whitespace is fine, or you can set this attribute to "preserve" to indicate that you want all applications to preserve whitespace as it is in the document.

That gets us started with what can go into XML documents: markup and character data. It's now time to move to the next step up and begin working on the actual structure of XML documents, starting with the prolog.

The Prolog

Prologs come at the very beginning of XML documents. XML documents actually do not need prologs to be considered well-formed. However, the W3C recommends that you include at least the XML declaration, which indicates the version of XML, in the document's prolog. In general, prologs can contain XML declarations, comments, processing instructions, whitespace, and document type declaration(s).

Here's an example: In this case, I've marked the document's prolog, which contains an XML declaration, a processing instruction, and a DTD (which we'll see more about in Chapter 3):

```
<?xml version = "1.0" standalone="yes"?>
<?xml-stylesheet type="text/css" href="greeting.css"?>
<!DOCTYPE DOCUMENT [
<!ELEMENT DOCUMENT (CUSTOMER)*>
<!ELEMENT CUSTOMER (NAME,DATE,ORDERS)>
<!ELEMENT NAME (LAST_NAME,FIRST_NAME)>
<!ELEMENT LAST_NAME (#PCDATA)>
<!ELEMENT FIRST_NAME (#PCDATA)>
<!ELEMENT DATE (#PCDATA)>
<!ELEMENT ORDERS (ITEM)*>
<!ELEMENT ITEM (PRODUCT,NUMBER,PRICE)>
<!ELEMENT PRODUCT (#PCDATA)>
<!ELEMENT NUMBER (#PCDATA)>
<!ELEMENT PRICE (#PCDATA)>
]>
<DOCUMENT>
    <CUSTOMER>
        <NAME>
            <LAST_NAME>Smith</LAST_NAME>
            <FIRST_NAME>Sam</FIRST_NAME>
        </NAME>
    .
    .
    .
```

Each part of the prolog bears a closer look, and I'll examine them here (except for document type declarations, which we'll explore in Chapter 3).

The XML Declaration

An XML document can (and should, according to W3C) start with an XML declaration, which can indicate that the document is written in XML. If you use an XML declaration, it should be the first line in the document. Nothing should come before the XML declaration. Here's an example:

```
<?xml version = "1.0" standalone="yes" encoding="UTF-8"?>
```

The XML declaration uses the `<?xml?>` element. In earlier drafts of XML, that was `<?XML?>`, but it was made lowercase in the final recommendation; it's an error to use uppercase. (You'll still find applications out there that insist on the original uppercase version, however. Browsers such as Internet Explorer accept either version and are thus not fully compliant with the W3C recommendation.)

You can use three possible attributes in the XML declaration:

- **version.** This is the XML version; currently, only 1.0 is possible here. This attribute is required if you use an XML declaration.
- **encoding.** This is the language encoding for the document. As discussed in Chapter 1, the default here is UTF-8. You also can use Unicode, UCS-2 or UCS-4, and many other character sets, such as ISO character sets. This attribute is optional.
- **standalone.** Set this to "yes" if the document does not refer to any external entities; otherwise, use "no." This attribute is optional.

Comments

XML comments are very much like HTML comments. You can use comments to include explanatory notes in your document that are ignored by XML parsers; comments may appear anywhere in a document outside other markup. As in HTML, you start a comment with `<!--` and end it with `-->`. Here's an example:

```
<?xml version="1.0" encoding="UTF-8"?>
<DOCUMENT>
    <!--Start the document off with a greeting.-->
    <GREETING>
    <!--Here's the greeting's text.-->
```

continues ▸

```
        Hello from XML!
    </GREETING>
</DOCUMENT>
```

You should follow a few rules when adding comments to an XML document. Comments must not come before an XML declaration; for example, this is incorrect:

```
<!--Here's my document.-->
<?xml version="1.0" encoding="UTF-8"?>
<DOCUMENT>
    <GREETING>
        Hello from XML!
    </GREETING>
</DOCUMENT>
```

You also can't put a comment inside markup, like this:

```
<?xml version="1.0" encoding="UTF-8"?>
<DOCUMENT <!--Start the document-->>
    <GREETING>
        Hello from XML!
    </GREETING>
</DOCUMENT>
```

In addition, you cannot use -- inside a comment because XML parsers look for that string inside a comment to indicate the end of the comment. For example, this is incorrect:

```
<?xml version="1.0" encoding="UTF-8"?>
<DOCUMENT>
    <!--Start the document off--politely--with a greeting.-->
    <GREETING>
        Hello from XML!
    </GREETING>
</DOCUMENT>
```

You can use comments to remove parts of documents as long as the enclosed parts do not themselves contain any comments. For example, here I'm commenting out the <MESSAGE> element:

```
<?xml version="1.0" encoding="UTF-8"?>
<DOCUMENT>
    <GREETING>
        Hello From XML
    </GREETING>
<!--
    <MESSAGE>
        Welcome to the wild and woolly world of XML.
    </MESSAGE>
-->
</DOCUMENT>
```

Here's how a parser treats this document:

```
<?xml version="1.0" encoding="UTF-8"?>
<DOCUMENT>
    <GREETING>
        Hello From XML
    </GREETING>
</DOCUMENT>
```

Processing Instructions

As their name implies, processing instructions are instructions to the XML processor. These instructions start with <? and end with ?>. The only restriction here is that you can't use <?xml?> (or <?XML?>, which is also reserved). Processing instructions must be understood by the XML processor, so they're processor-dependant, not built into the XML recommendation.

A very common and well-understood processing instruction (although like other processing instructions, not a part of the XML 1.0 recommendation) is <?xml-stylesheet?>, which connects a style sheet with the document. Here's an example:

```
<?xml version = "1.0" standalone="yes"?>
<?xml-stylesheet type="text/css" href="greeting.css"?>
<DOCUMENT>
    <GREETING>
        Hello From XML
    </GREETING>
    <MESSAGE>
        Welcome to the wild and woolly world of XML.
    </MESSAGE>
</DOCUMENT>
```

XML processors, such as Internet Explorer 5 or Netscape Navigator 6, understand <?xml-stylesheet?> already.

I've now taken a look at everything that a prolog can contain (except DTDs): XML declarations, comments, processing instructions, and whitespace. It's time to take a look at the actual structure of an XML document, as created with tags and elements.

Tags and Elements

You give structure to an XML document using markup, which consists of *elements*. In turn, an XML element consists of a start tag and an end tag, except in the case of elements that are defined to be empty, which consist of only one tag.

A start tag (also called an opening tag) starts with < and ends with >. End tags (also called closing tags) begin with </ and end with >.

Tag Names

The XML specification is very specific about tag names; you can start a tag name with a letter, an underscore, or a colon. The next characters may be letters, digits, underscores, hyphens, periods, and colons (but no whitespace).

Avoid Colons in Tag Names

Although the XML 1.0 recommendation does not say so, you should definitely avoid using colons in tag names because you use a colon when specifying namespaces in XML, as I'll discuss later in this chapter.

Here are some allowable XML tags:

```
<DOCUMENT>

<document>

<_Record>

<customer>

<PRODUCT>
```

Note that because XML processors are case-sensitive, the <DOCUMENT> tag is not the same as a <document> tag. (In fact, you can even have <DOCUMENT> and <document>—and even <DoCuMeNt>—as different tags in the same document, but I really recommend against it.)

Here are the corresponding closing tags:

```
</DOCUMENT>
</document>
</_Record>
</customer>
</PRODUCT>
```

These are some tags that XML considers illegal:

```
<2001DOCUMENT>
<.document>
<Record Number>
<customer*name>
<PRODUCT(ID)>
```

Using start and end tags, you can create elements, as in this example, which has three elements, the <DOCUMENT>, <GREETING>, and <MESSAGE> elements; the <DOCUMENT> element contains the <GREETING> and <MESSAGE> elements:

```
<?xml version = "1.0" standalone="yes"?>
<DOCUMENT>
    <GREETING>
        Hello From XML
    </GREETING>
    <MESSAGE>
        Welcome to the wild and woolly world of XML.
    </MESSAGE>
</DOCUMENT>
```

You also can create elements without using end tags if the elements are explicitly declared to be *empty*.

Empty Elements

Empty elements have only one tag, not a start and end tag. You may be familiar with empty elements from HTML; for example, the HTML `<IMG>`, `<LI>`, `<HR>`, and `<BR>` elements are empty, which is to say that they do not enclose any content (either character data or markup).

Empty elements are represented with only one tag (in HTML, there is no closing `</IMG>`, `</LI>`, `</HR>`, and `</BR>` tags). In XML, you can declare elements to be empty in the document's DTD, as we'll see in Chapter 3.

In XML, you close an empty element with `/>`. For example, if the `<GREETING>` element is empty, it might look like this in an XML document:

```
<?xml version = "1.0" standalone="yes"?>
<DOCUMENT>
    <GREETING TEXT = "Hello From XML" />
</DOCUMENT>
```

This usage might seem a little strange at first, but this is XML's way of making sure that an XML processor isn't left searching for a nonexistent closing tag. In fact, in XHTML, which is a derivation of HTML in XML, the `<IMG>`, `<LI>`, `<HR>`, and `<BR>` tags are actually used as `<IMG />`, `<LI />`, `<HR />`, and `<BR />` (except that XHTML tags use lowercase letters). The additional `/` doesn't seem to give the major browsers any trouble. We'll see how to declare empty tags in Chapter 3.

The Root Element

Each well-formed XML document must contain one element that contains all the other elements. This containing element is called the *root element*. The root element is a very important part of XML documents, especially when you look at them from a programming point of view, because you parse XML documents starting with the root element. In order.xml, developed at the start of this chapter, the root element is the <DOCUMENT> element (although you can give the root element any name):

```
<?xml version = "1.0" standalone="yes"?>
<DOCUMENT>
    <CUSTOMER>
        <NAME>
            <LAST_NAME>Smith</LAST_NAME>
            <FIRST_NAME>Sam</FIRST_NAME>
        </NAME>
        <DATE>October 15, 2001</DATE>
        <ORDERS>
            <ITEM>
                <PRODUCT>Tomatoes</PRODUCT>
                <NUMBER>8</NUMBER>
                <PRICE>$1.25</PRICE>
            </ITEM>
            .
            .
            .
            <ITEM>
                <PRODUCT>Lettuce</PRODUCT>
                <NUMBER>6</NUMBER>
                <PRICE>$11.50</PRICE>
            </ITEM>
        </ORDERS>
    </CUSTOMER>
</DOCUMENT>
```

Attributes

Attributes in XML are much like attributes in HTML—they're name-value pairs that let you specify additional data in start and empty tags. To assign a value to an attribute, you use an equal sign.

For example, I'm assigning values to the STATUS attribute of the <CUSTOMER> elements in this XML to indicate the status of a customer's credit:

```
<?xml version = "1.0" standalone="yes"?>
<DOCUMENT>
    <CUSTOMER STATUS="Good credit">
        <NAME>
            <LAST_NAME>Smith</LAST_NAME>
            <FIRST_NAME>Sam</FIRST_NAME>
        </NAME>
        <DATE>October 15, 2001</DATE>
        <ORDERS>
            <ITEM>
                <PRODUCT>Tomatoes</PRODUCT>
                <NUMBER>8</NUMBER>
                <PRICE>$1.25</PRICE>
```

```
            </ITEM>
            <ITEM>
                <PRODUCT>Oranges</PRODUCT>
                <NUMBER>24</NUMBER>
                <PRICE>$4.98</PRICE>
            </ITEM>
        </ORDERS>
    </CUSTOMER>
    <CUSTOMER STATUS="Lousy credit">
        <NAME>
            <LAST_NAME>Jones</LAST_NAME>
            <FIRST_NAME>Polly</FIRST_NAME>
        </NAME>
        <DATE>October 20, 2001</DATE>
        <ORDERS>
            <ITEM>
                <PRODUCT>Bread</PRODUCT>
                <NUMBER>12</NUMBER>
                <PRICE>$14.95</PRICE>
            </ITEM>
            <ITEM>
                <PRODUCT>Apples</PRODUCT>
                <NUMBER>6</NUMBER>
                <PRICE>$1.50</PRICE>
            </ITEM>
        </ORDERS>
    </CUSTOMER>
    <CUSTOMER STATUS="Good credit">
        <NAME>
            <LAST_NAME>Weber</LAST_NAME>
            <FIRST_NAME>Bill</FIRST_NAME>
        </NAME>
        <DATE>October 25, 2001</DATE>
        <ORDERS>
            <ITEM>
                <PRODUCT>Asparagus</PRODUCT>
                <NUMBER>12</NUMBER>
                <PRICE>$2.95</PRICE>
            </ITEM>
            <ITEM>
                <PRODUCT>Lettuce</PRODUCT>
                <NUMBER>6</NUMBER>
                <PRICE>$11.50</PRICE>
            </ITEM>
        </ORDERS>
    </CUSTOMER>
</DOCUMENT>
```

You can see this XML document in Internet Explorer, including the attributes and their values, in Figure 2.2.

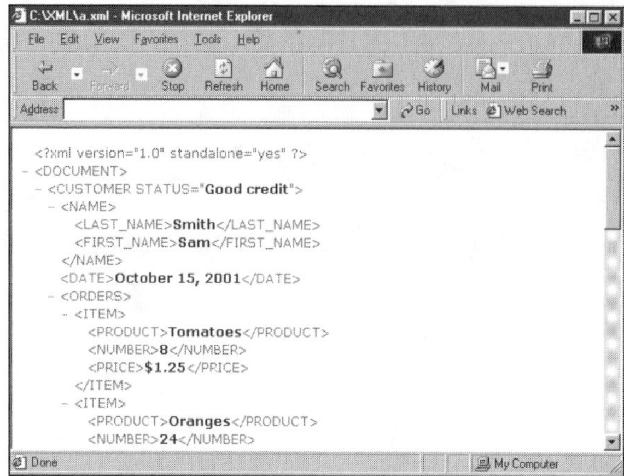

Figure 2.2 Using attributes in Internet Explorer.

An XML processor can read the attributes and their values, and you can put that data to work in your own applications. We'll see how to read attribute values in both JavaScript and Java in this book.

A lot of debate occurs over when you should store data using attributes and when you should store data using elements. There simply is no hard and fast rule, but here are a couple guidelines that I find useful.

First, too many attributes definitely make documents hard to read. For example, take a look at this element:

```
<CUSTOMER>
    <NAME>
        <LAST_NAME>Smith</LAST_NAME>
        <FIRST_NAME>Sam</FIRST_NAME>
    </NAME>
    <DATE>October 15, 2001</DATE>
    <ORDERS>
        <ITEM>
            <PRODUCT>Tomatoes</PRODUCT>
            <NUMBER>8</NUMBER>
            <PRICE>$1.25</PRICE>
        </ITEM>
    </ORDERS>
</CUSTOMER>
```

It's fairly clear what's going on here, even if it is a little involved. However, if you try to convert all this data to attributes, you end up with something like this:

```
<CUSTOMER LAST_NAME="Smith" FIRST_NAME="Sam"
DATE="October 15, 2001" PURCHASE="Tomatoes"
PRICE="$1.25" NUMBER="8" />
```

Clearly, this will be a mess if you have a few such elements.

Another point is that you really can't specify document structure using attributes. For example, the example we've already seen in this chapter stores multiple ordered items per customer. However, attribute names must be unique, so it's much tougher to store data like this using attributes:

```
<CUSTOMER>
    <NAME>
        <LAST_NAME>Smith</LAST_NAME>
        <FIRST_NAME>Sam</FIRST_NAME>
    </NAME>
    <DATE>October 15, 2001</DATE>
    <ORDERS>
        <ITEM>
            <PRODUCT>Tomatoes</PRODUCT>
            <NUMBER>8</NUMBER>
            <PRICE>$1.25</PRICE>
        </ITEM>
        <ITEM>
            <PRODUCT>Oranges</PRODUCT>
            <NUMBER>24</NUMBER>
            <PRICE>$4.98</PRICE>
        </ITEM>
    </ORDERS>
</CUSTOMER>
```

The upshot is that deciding whether to store your data in attributes or to create new elements is really a matter of taste until you get beyond a few attributes per tag. If you find yourself using (not just defining, but using) more than four attributes in a tag, consider breaking up the tag into a number of enclosed tags. Doing so will make the document structure much easier to work with and edit later.

You should follow specific rules when creating attributes, and those include correctly setting attribute names and specifying attribute values.

Attribute Names

According to the XML 1.0 specification, attribute names must follow the same rules as those for tag names, which means that you can start an attribute name with a letter, an underscore, or a colon. The next characters may be letters, digits, underscores, hyphens, periods, and colons (but no whitespace because you separate attribute name-value pairs with whitespace).

Take a look at these examples showing legal attribute names:

```
<circle origin_x="10.0" origin_y="20.0" radius="10.0" />
<image src="image1.jpg">
<pen color="red" width="5">
<book pages="1231" >
```

Here are some illegal attribute names:

```
<circle 1origin_x="10.0" 1origin_y="20.0" 1radius="10.0" />
<image src name="image1.jpg">
<pen color@="red" width@="5">
<book pages(excluding front matter)="1231" >
```

Attribute Values

Because markup is always text, attributes are also text. Even if you're assigning a number to an attribute, you treat that number as a text string and enclose it in quotes, like this:

```
<circle origin_x="10.0" origin_y="20.0" radius="10.0" />
```

Among other things, this means that XML processors will return attribute values as text strings. If you want to treat them as numbers, you'll have to make sure that you translate them to numbers as the programming language you're using allows.

In XML, you must enclose attribute values in quotation marks. Usually, you use double quotes, but consider the case in which the attribute value itself contains double quotes—you can't just surround such a value with double quotes because an XML processor will get confused as to where your text ends. In such a case, you can use single quotes to surround the text, like this:

```
<quotation text='He said, "Not that!"' />
```

What if the attribute value contains both single *and* double quotes? In that case, you can use the XML-defined entity `'` for a single quote and `"` for double quotes, like this (I'll discuss the five XML-defined entity references in a few pages):

```
<person height="5&apos;6&quot;" />
```

> **Assigning Values to Attributes**
>
> If you're going to use an attribute, you must assign it a value. Not doing so is a violation of well-formedness—that is, you cannot have "standalone" attributes in XML, such as the **BORDER** attribute in HTML tables, which need not be assigned a value.

A Useful Attribute *xml:lang*

One general attribute bears mention: `xml:lang`. It's often convenient to specify the language of a document's content and attribute values, especially to help software such as Web search engines. You can specify the language in XML tags with the `xml:lang` attribute. (In valid documents, this attribute, like any other, must be declared if it is used.)

You can set the `xml:lang` attribute to these values:

- A two-letter language code, as defined by [ISO 639].
- A language identifier registered with the Internet Assigned Numbers Authority (IANA). Such identifiers begin with the prefix `i-` (or `I-`).
- A language identifier assigned by you, or for private use. Such identifies must begin with `x-` or `X-`.

As an example, I'm using the `xml:lang` attribute here to indicate that an element's language is English:

```
<p xml:lang="en">The color should be brown.</p>
```

You also can use language *subcodes* if you follow the language code with a hyphen and the subcode. A subcode indicates a dialect or a regional variation. For example, here I'm indicating that one element holds British English content and that one holds American English content:

```
<p xml:lang="en-GB">The colour should be brown.</p>
<p xml:lang="en-US">The color should be brown.</p>
```

Besides defining element content, `xml:lang` also identifies the language used in a tag's attribute values, as in this case, where I'm using German:

```
<p farbe="braun" xml:lang="de">
```

Building Well-Formed Document Structure

We've gotten a lot of the syntax and rules of creating XML documents at the element and character data level down now. It's time to move on to the next level: actually giving your document structure.

The W3C has a lot of rules about how to structure your document in a way to make it well-formed, and I'll take a look at those rules here. In this chapter, I'm going to talk only about standalone documents; in Chapter 3, we'll see that we have to adjust these points somewhat for documents that have a DTD.

Checking Well-Formedness

If you have doubts whether your XML document is well-formed, use an online XML validator, such as the excellent one hosted by the Brown University Scholarly Technology Group at `www.stg.brown.edu/service/xmlvalid/`. You'll get a complete report on your document's well-formedness and validity. To see all the well-formedness constraints as set up by the W3C, look at `www.w3.org/TR/REC-xml` (or Appendix A), and search for the text "Well-Formedness Constraint," which is how W3C marks those constraints.

An XML Declaration Should Begin the Document

The first well-formedness structure constraint is that you should start the document with an XML declaration. Technically, you don't need to include an XML declaration in your document, but if you do, to make the document well-formed, the XML declaration must be the absolute *first* thing in the document, like this (not even whitespace should come before the XML declaration):

```
<?xml version = "1.0" standalone="yes"?>
<DOCUMENT>
    <CUSTOMER STATUS="Good credit">
        <NAME>
            <LAST_NAME>Smith</LAST_NAME>
            <FIRST_NAME>Sam</FIRST_NAME>
        </NAME>
        <DATE>October 15, 2001</DATE>
        <ORDERS>
            <ITEM>
                <PRODUCT>Tomatoes</PRODUCT>
                <NUMBER>8</NUMBER>
                <PRICE>$1.25</PRICE>
            </ITEM>
            <ITEM>
                <PRODUCT>Oranges</PRODUCT>
                <NUMBER>24</NUMBER>
                <PRICE>$4.98</PRICE>
            </ITEM>
        </ORDERS>
    </CUSTOMER>
    .
    .
    .
```

Do You Need an XML Declaration?

The W3C says that XML documents should have an XML declaration, but documents really don't need to have one in all cases. For example, when you're combining XML documents with the same character encoding into one large one, you don't want to include an XML declaration at the head of each section of the document.

Include One or More Elements

To be a well-formed document, a document must include one or more elements. The first element it includes, of course, is the root element, and all other elements are enclosed by that element. The examples we've seen throughout this chapter show how this works, as here, where this XML document contains multiple elements:

```
<?xml version = "1.0" standalone="yes"?>
<DOCUMENT>
    <GREETING>
        Hello From XML
    </GREETING>
    <MESSAGE>
        Welcome to the wild and woolly world of XML.
    </MESSAGE>
</DOCUMENT>
```

Include Both Start and End Tags for Elements That Aren't Empty

In HTML, Web browsers often handle the case where you omit end tags for HTML elements, even if you shouldn't omit those end tags, according to the HTML specification. For example, if you use the `<p>` tag and then follow it with another `<p>` tag—without using a `</p>` tag—the browser will have no problem.

In XML, the story is different. To make sure that a document is well-formed, every element that is not empty must have both a start tag and an end tag, as in the example we just saw:

```
<?xml version = "1.0" standalone="yes"?>
<DOCUMENT>
    <GREETING>
        Hello From XML
    </GREETING>
    <MESSAGE>
        Welcome to the wild and woolly world of XML.
    </MESSAGE>
</DOCUMENT>
```

In fact, there's another well-formedness constraint here: End tags must match start tags to complete an element.

Close Empty Tags with />

Empty elements don't have closing tags. These tags have no content, which means that they do not enclose any character data or markup. Instead, these elements are made up entirely of one tag, like this:

```
<?xml version = "1.0" standalone="yes"?>
<DOCUMENT>
    <GREETING TEXT = "Hello From XML" />
</DOCUMENT>
```

In XML, you must always end empty elements with />, as shown here, if you want your document to be well-formed. In general, the current crop of the major Web browsers deals well with elements such as <BR />; this is a good thing because the alternative was to write such elements as
</BR>, and that can be confusing. In fact, some browsers, such as Netscape, interpret that markup as two <BR> elements.

The Root Element Must Contain All Other Elements

One element in well-formed documents, the root element, contains all other elements. In this case, for example, the root element is the <BOOKS> element:

```
<?xml version = "1.0" standalone="yes"?>
<BOOKS>
    <BOOK>
        <TITLE>
            Inside XML
        </TITLE>
        <REVIEW>
            Excellent
        </REVIEW>
    </BOOK>
    <BOOK>
        <TITLE>
            Other XML Book
        </TITLE>
<REVIEW>
            OK
        </REVIEW>
    </BOOK>
</BOOKS>
```

In this case, the root element must contain all other elements (excluding the XML declaration, comments, and other nonelements). This makes it easy for XML processors to handle XML documents as *trees*, starting at the root element, as we'll see when we start parsing XML documents.

Nest Elements Correctly

A very big part of making sure that documents are well-formed is ensuring that elements nest correctly (in fact, that's one of the reasons for the term *well-formed*). The idea here is that if an element contains a start tag for a tag that's not empty, it must also contain that element's end tag.

For example, this XML is fine:

```
<?xml version = "1.0" standalone="yes"?>
<DOCUMENT>
    <GREETING>
        Hello From XML
    </GREETING>
    <MESSAGE>
        Welcome to the wild and woolly world of XML.
    </MESSAGE>
</DOCUMENT>
```

However, there's a nesting problem in this next document because an XML processor will encounter the <MESSAGE> tag before finding the closing </GREETING> tag:

```
<?xml version = "1.0" standalone="yes"?>
<DOCUMENT>
    <GREETING>
        Hello From XML
    <MESSAGE>
    </GREETING>
        Welcome to the wild and woolly world of XML.
    </MESSAGE>
</DOCUMENT>
```

Because you should nest elements correctly to create a well-formed document, and because XML processors are supposed to refuse documents that are not well-formed, you can always count on every nonroot element to have exactly one (and only one) *parent element* that encloses it. For example, in the example before the previous example that was not well-formed, the <GREETING> and <MESSAGE> elements both have the same parent—the <DOCUMENT> element itself, which is also the root element. Note that a parent element can enclose an indefinite number of *child elements* (which also can mean zero child elements).

Use Unique Attribute Names

One of the well-formedness constraints that the XML 1.0 specification lists is that no attribute name may appear more than once in the same start tag or empty element tag. It's hard to see how you would violate this one other than by mistake, as in this case, where I give a person two last names:

```
<PERSON LAST_NAME="Wooster" LAST_NAME="Jeeves">
```

Note that because XML is case-sensitive, attributes with different capitalizations are treated as being different, as in this case (although it's still hard to see how you'd write this except by mistake):

```
<PERSON LAST_NAME="Wooster" last_name="Jeeves">
```

(In general, using attribute names that differ only in terms of capitalization is a really bad idea.)

Use Only the Five Pre-Existing Entity References

Five predefined *entity references* exist in XML. An entity reference is replaced by the corresponding entity when the XML document is processed. You may already know about entity references from HTML; for example, the HTML entity reference © is replaced by the © symbol when it parses an HTML document.

As in HTML, general entity references in XML start with & and end with ; in XML. Parameter entity references, which we'll use in DTDs in the next chapter, start with % and end with ;. Here are the five predefined entity references in XML and the character they are replaced with when parsed:

&	The & character
<	The < character
>	The > character
'	The ' character
"	The " character

Normally, these characters are tricky to handle in XML documents because XML processors give them special importance—that is, < and > straddle markup tags, you use quotation marks to surround attribute values, and the & character starts entity references. Replacing them with the previous entity references makes them safe because the XML processor will replace them with the appropriate character when processing the document. Using an entity reference for a character is often called *escaping* that character (following the terminology of programming languages that use "escape sequences" to embed special characters in text).

For example, say that you wanted to use the term "The S&O Railway" in a document; you could use the & entity reference for the ampersand this way:

```
<TOUR CAPTION="The S&amp;O Railway" />
```

Although only five predefined entity references exist in XML, you can define new entity references. I'll take a look at how to do that in the next chapter on DTDs.

The Final ; in Entity References

HTML browsers often let you omit the final ; in entity references if the entity reference is followed by whitespace (if the entity reference is embedded in non-whitespace text, you must include the final ; even in HTML). However, you cannot omit the final ; in XML entity references.

Surround Attribute Values with Quotes

In HTML, there's no problem if you omit the quotes around attribute values (as long as those values don't contain any whitespace). For example, this element presents no problem to HTML browsers:

```
<IMG SRC=image.jpg>
```

However, XML processors would refuse such an element because omitting the quotation marks around the attribute value `image.jpg` is a violation of well-formedness. Here's how this element would look when written properly:

```
<IMG SRC="image.jpg" />
```

You can also use single quotation marks, like this:

```
<IMG SRC='image.jpg' />
```

In fact, if the attribute value contains double quotes, you should surround it with single quotes, as we've seen.

```
<quotation text='He said, "Not that!"' />
```

As indicated previously, XML makes provisions for handling single and double quotes inside attribute values. You can always replace single quotes with the entity reference for apostrophes, `'` and double quotes with the entity reference `"`. For example, to assign the attribute `height` the value `5'6"`, you can do it this way:

```
<person height="5&apos;6&quot;" />
```

In XHTML, the derivation of HTML 4.0 in XML, you must surround attribute values in quotation marks, just as in any other XML document. I'm sure that this requirement will be one of the most persistently troublesome for Web authors switching to XHTML, simply because it's so easy to forget.

A few more well-formedness constraints on attribute values bear mention. Attribute values cannot contain direct or indirect references to external entities (more on this in Chapter 3), and you cannot use the `<` character in attribute values. If you must use <, use the entity reference `<` instead, like this, where I'm assigning the text `<--` to the `TEXT` attribute:

```
<ARROW TEXT="&lt;--" />
```

In fact, so strong is the prohibition against using <, except to start markup, that you shouldn't use it anywhere in the document except for that purpose—see the next section, "Use < and & Only to Start Tags and Entities."

Use < and & Only to Start Tags and Entities

XML processors assume that < always starts a tag and that & always starts an entity reference, so you should avoid using those characters for anything else. We've already seen this example where the ampersand in `"The S&O Railway"` is replaced by `&`:

```
<TOUR CAPTION="The S&amp;O Railway" />
```

You should also particularly avoid the < character in nonmarkup text as well. This can be difficult sometimes, as when the < character must be used as the less-than operator in JavaScript, as in this example in XHTML:

```
<?xml version="1.0"?>
<!DOCTYPE html PUBLIC "-//W3C//DTD XHTML 1.0 Transitional//EN"
"http://www.w3.org/tr/xhtml1/DTD/xhtml1-transitional.dtd">
<html xmlns="http://www.w3.org/1999/xhtml" xml:lang="en" lang="en">
    <head>

        <title>
            Using The if Statement In JavaScript
        </title>

    </head>

    <body>

        <script language="javascript">
            var budget
            budget = 234.77
            if (budget < 0) {
                document.writeln("Uh oh.")
            }
        </script>

        <center>
            <h1>
                Using The if Statement In JavaScript
            </h1>
        </center>
    </body>
</html>
```

In cases like this, the W3C suggests that you enclose the JavaScript code in a CDATA section (see the next section) so that the XML processor will ignore it, but unfortunately, no major browser today understands CDATA sections. Another possible solution is to enclose the JavaScript code in a comment, `<!--` and `-->`, but W3C doesn't recommend this because XML processors are allowed to remove comments before passing the XML on to the underlying application and so would remove the JavaScript code entirely from the document.

You can use `<` for the < operator, like this:

```
<?xml version="1.0"?>
<!DOCTYPE html PUBLIC "-//W3C//DTD XHTML 1.0 Transitional//EN"
"http://www.w3.org/tr/xhtml1/DTD/xhtml1-transitional.dtd">
<html xmlns="http://www.w3.org/1999/xhtml" xml:lang="en" lang="en">
    <head>

        <title>
            Using The if Statement In JavaScript
        </title>

    </head>

    <body>

        <script language="javascript">
            var budget
            budget = 234.77
            if (budget &lt; 0) {
                document.writeln("Uh oh.")
            }
        </script>

        <center>
            <h1>
                Using The if Statement In JavaScript
            </h1>
        </center>
    </body>
</html>
```

Practically speaking, however, this still represents a problem for the major browsers, although it's the way you should go in the long run. In the short run, you actually should remove the whole problem from the scope of the browser by placing the script code in an external file, here named script.js:

```
<?xml version="1.0"?>
<!DOCTYPE html PUBLIC "-//W3C//DTD XHTML 1.0 Transitional//EN"
"http://www.w3.org/tr/xhtml1/DTD/xhtml1-transitional.dtd">
```

continues ▸

```
<html xmlns="http://www.w3.org/1999/xhtml" xml:lang="en" lang="en">
    <head>

        <title>
            Using The if Statement In JavaScript
        </title>

    </head>

    <body>

        <script language="javascript" src="script.js">
        </script>

        <center>
            <h1>
                Using The if Statement In JavaScript
            </h1>
        </center>
    </body>
</html>
```

CDATA Sections

As you know, XML processors are very sensitive to characters such as < and &. So what if you had a large section of text that contained a great many < and & characters that you didn't want to interpret as markup? You can escape those characters as `<` and `&`, of course, but with many such characters, that's awkward and hard to read. Instead, you can use a CDATA section.

CDATA sections hold character data that is supposed to remain unparsed by the XML processor. This is a useful asset to XML because otherwise all the text in an XML document is parsed and searched for characters such as < and &. You use CDATA sections simply to tell the XML processor to leave the enclosed text alone and to pass it on unchanged to the underlying application.

You start a CDATA section with the markup `<![CDATA` and end it with `]]>`. Note that this means that CDATA sections *are* actually searched, but only for the ending text `]]>`. Among other things, this means that you cannot include the text `]]>` inside a CDATA section—and it also means that you cannot nest CDATA sections.

Here's an example; in this case, I've added an element named `<MARKUP>` to a document, and this element itself contains markup that I want to preserve as character data (so that it can be printed out, for example). To make sure that the markup inside this element is preserved as text, I enclose it in a CDATA section like this:

```
<?xml version = "1.0" standalone="yes"?>
<DOCUMENT>
    <MARKUP>
    <![CDATA
        <CUSTOMER>
            <NAME>
                <LAST_NAME>Smith</LAST_NAME>
                <FIRST_NAME>Sam</FIRST_NAME>
            </NAME>
            <DATE>October 15, 2001</DATE>
            <ORDERS>
                <ITEM>
                    <PRODUCT>Tomatoes</PRODUCT>
                    <NUMBER>8</NUMBER>
                    <PRICE>$1.25</PRICE>
                </ITEM>
                <ITEM>
                    <PRODUCT>Oranges</PRODUCT>
                    <NUMBER>24</NUMBER>
                    <PRICE>$4.98</PRICE>
                </ITEM>
            </ORDERS>
        </CUSTOMER>
    ]]>
    </MARKUP>
</DOCUMENT>
```

As you can see, CDATA sections are powerful because they enable you to embed character data directly in XML documents without having it parsed. (Normally, character data in XML documents is parsed by the XML processor and becomes parsed character data.)

Here's another example. In this case, I'm adapting the JavaScript example in the previous section to show how the W3C wants to handle script code in XHTML pages—by placing that code in a CDATA section:

```
<?xml version="1.0"?>
<!DOCTYPE html PUBLIC "-//W3C//DTD XHTML 1.0 Transitional//EN"
"http://www.w3.org/tr/xhtml1/DTD/xhtml1-transitional.dtd">
<html xmlns="http://www.w3.org/1999/xhtml" xml:lang="en" lang="en">
    <head>

        <title>
            Using The if Statement In JavaScript
        </title>

    </head>

    <body>
```

continues ▸

```
        <script language="javascript">
            <![CDATA
                var budget
                budget = 234.77
                if (budget < 0) {
                    document.writeln("Uh oh.")
                }
            ]]>
        </script>

        <center>
            <h1>
                Using The if Statement In JavaScript
            </h1>
        </center>
    </body>
</html>
```

Unfortunately, as mentioned in the previous section, the idea of a CDATA section, especially one that starts with the expression `<![CDATA` and ends with the expression `]]>`, confuses the current versions of the major browsers. When those browsers are configured to handle XHTML, this situation will improve.

XML Namespaces

There's considerable freedom in XML because you can define your own tags. However, as more XML applications came to be developed, a problem arose that had been unforeseen by the creators of the original XML specification: tag name conflicts.

As we saw in Chapter 1, two popular XML applications are XHTML—that is, HTML 4.0 as written in XML—and MathML, which lets you display equations. XHTML is useful because it lets you handle all the standard HTML 4.0 tags; if you need to display equations, MathML can be essential. So what if you want to use MathML inside an XHTML Web page? That's a problem because the tags defined in XHTML and MathML overlap (specifically, each application defines a `<var>` and a `<select>` element).

The solution is to use *namespaces*. Namespaces enable you to make sure that one set of tags cannot conflict with another. Namespaces work by letting you prepend a name followed by a colon to tag and attribute names, changing those names so that they don't conflict.

XML namespaces are one of those XML companion recommendations that keep being added to the XML specification; you can find the specification for namespaces at `www.w3.org/TR/REC-xml-names/`. A lot of debate still rages about this one (largely because namespaces can make writing DTDs difficult), but it's now an official W3C recommendation.

Creating a Namespace

Here's an example. In this case, I'll use a fictitious XML application designed for cataloging books whose root element is `<library>`, and I'll add my own reviews to each book. I start off with a book as specified with the fictitious XML application:

```
<library>
   <book>
        <title>
           Earthquakes for Lunch.
        </title>
   </book>
</library>
```

Now I want to add my own comments to this `<book>` item. To do that, I start by confining the book XML application to its own namespace, for which I'll use the prefix `book:`. To define a new namespace, use the `xmlns:`*`prefix`* attribute, where `prefix` is the prefix that you want to use for the namespace:

```
<library
   xmlns:book="http://www.amazingterrificbooks.com/spec">
   <book>
        <title>
           Earthquakes for Lunch.
        </title>
   </book>
</library>
```

To define a namespace, you assign the `xmlns:`*`prefix`* attribute to a unique identifier, which in XML is usually a uniform resource identifier (URI) (a URL, in this case) that may direct the XML processor to a DTD for the namespace (but it doesn't have to). After defining the `book` namespace, you can preface every tag and attribute name in this namespace with `book:`, like this:

```
<book:library
   xmlns:book="http://www.amazingterrificbooks.com/spec">
   <book:book>
        <book:title>
           Earthquakes for Lunch.
        </book:title>
   </book:book>
</book:library>
```

Now the tag and attribute names have actually been changed; for example, `<library>` is now `<book:library>` as far as the XML processor is concerned.

(If you've defined tag and attribute names in a document's DTD, you must redefine the tags and attributes there as well to make the new names legal.)

Because all tag and attribute names from the book namespace are now in their own namespace, I'm free to add my own namespace to the document so that I can add my own comments to each book entry. I start by defining a new namespace named steve:

```
<book:library
   xmlns:book="http://www.amazingterrificbooks.com/spec"
   xmlns:steve="http://www.starpowder.com/steve">
   <book:book>
        <book:title>
           Earthquakes for Lunch.
        </book:title>
   </book:book>
</book:library>
```

Now I can use the new steve namespace to add markup to the document like this, keeping it separate from the other markup:

```
<book:library
   xmlns:book="http://www.amazingterrificbooks.com/spec"
   xmlns:steve="http://www.starpowder.com/steve">
   <book:book>
        <book:title>
           Earthquakes for Lunch.
        </book:title>
        <steve:review>
This book was OK, no great shakes.
        </steve:review>
   </book:book>
</book:library>
```

I also can use attributes in the steve namespace as long as I prefix them with steve:, like this:

```
<book:library
   xmlns:book="http://www.amazingterrificbooks.com/spec"
   xmlns:steve="http://www.starpowder.com/steve">
   <book:book>
        <book:title>
           Earthquakes for Lunch.
        </book:title>
        <steve:review steve:ID="1000034">
           This book was OK, no great shakes.
        </steve:review>
   </book:book>
</book:library>
```

And that's how namespaces work—you can use them to separate tags, even tags with the same name, from each other. As you can see, using multiple namespaces in the same document is no problem at all; just use the `xmlns` attribute in the enclosing element to define the appropriate namespaces.

`xmlns` in Child Elements

In fact, you can use the `xmlns` attribute in child elements to *redefine* an enclosing namespace if you'd like.

Creating Local Namespaces

You don't need to use the `xmlns` attribute in the root element; you can use this attribute in any element. In this case, I've moved the `steve` namespace definition to the element in which it's used:

```
<book:library
   xmlns:book="http://www.amazingterrificbooks.com/spec">
   <book:book>
        <book:title>
           Earthquakes for Lunch.
        </book:title>
        <steve:review
        xmlns:steve="http://www.starpowder.com/steve"
        steve:ID="1000034"/>
           This book was OK, no great shakes.
        </steve:review>
   </book:book>
</book:library>
```

Because namespace prefixes are really just text prepended to tag and attribute names, they follow the same rules for naming tags and attributes—that is, a namespace can start with a letter or an underscore. The following characters can include underscores, letters, digits, hyphens, and periods. Although colons are legal in tag names, you can't use a colon in a namespace name, for obvious reasons. In addition, two namespace names are reserved: `xml` and `xmlns`. Note that because namespace prefixes are merely text prepended to tag and attribute names, followed by a colon (which is legal in names), XML processors that have never heard of namespaces can use them without a problem.

Names of Attributes in Namespaces

You can use two names to refer to the same namespace. Note, however, that because you must use attributes with unique names, you cannot use attributes with those two namespaces that share the same name in the same element.

Default Namespaces

Now I'll return to the example that introduced this topic: the idea of using MathML in an XHTML document. In this case, let's assume that I want to display an equation in an XHTML document. I start off with an XHTML document that looks like this:

```
<?xml version="1.0"?>
<!DOCTYPE html PUBLIC "-//W3C//DTD XHTML 1.0 Transitional//EN"
"http://www.w3.org/tr/xhtml1/DTD/xhtml1-transitional.dtd">
<html xmlns="http://www.w3.org/1999/xhtml" xml:lang="en" lang="en">
    <head>
        <title>
            Embedding MathML In XHTML
        </title>
    </head>

    <body>
        <center>
            <h1>
                Embedding MathML In XHTML
            </h1>
        </center>
        Here's the MathML:
    </body>
</html>
```

This document has a `<!DOCTYPE>` element that you use to connect a DTD to a document, and the `<html>` element defines a namespace with the `xmlns` attribute. Note in particular that this time, the `xmlns` attribute is used by itself, without defining any prefix to specify a namespace (`xmlns="http://www.w3.org/1999/xhtml"`). When you use the `xmlns` attribute alone, without specifying any prefix, you are defining a *default* namespace. All the enclosed elements are assumed to belong to that namespace.

In XHTML documents, it's customary to make the W3C XHTML namespace, `http://www.w3.org/1999/xhtml`, into the default namespace for the document. When you do, you can then use the standard HTML tag names without any prefix, as you see in this example.

However, I want to use MathML markup in this document. To do so, I add a new namespace, which I'll call `m`, to this document, using the namespace that W3C has specified for MathML, `http://www.w3.org/TR/REC-MathML/`:

```
<?xml version="1.0"?>
<!DOCTYPE html PUBLIC "-//W3C//DTD XHTML 1.0 Transitional//EN"
"http://www.w3.org/tr/xhtml1/DTD/xhtml1-transitional.dtd">
<html xmlns="http://www.w3.org/1999/xhtml" xml:lang="en" lang="en"
    xmlns:m="http://www.w3.org/TR/REC-MathML/">
    <head>
```

```
        <title>
            Embedding MathML In XHTML
        </title>
    </head>

    <body>
        <center>
            <h1>
                Embedding MathML In XHTML
            </h1>
        </center>
        Here's the MathML:
    </body>
</html>
```

Now I can add MathML as I like, as long as I restrict that markup to the `m` namespace, like this:

```
<?xml version="1.0"?>
<!DOCTYPE html PUBLIC "-//W3C//DTD XHTML 1.0 Transitional//EN"
"http://www.w3.org/tr/xhtml1/DTD/xhtml1-transitional.dtd">
<html xmlns="http://www.w3.org/1999/xhtml" xml:lang="en" lang="en"
    xmlns:m="http://www.w3.org/TR/REC-MathML/">
    <head>
        <title>
            Embedding MathML In XHTML
        </title>
    </head>

    <body>
        <center>
            <h1>
                Embedding MathML In XHTML
            </h1>
        </center>
        Here's the MathML:
        <m:math>
            <m:mrow>
                <m:mrow>
                <m:mn>3</m:mn>
                    <m:mo>&InvisibleTimes;</m:mo>
                    <m:msup>
                        <m:mi>Z</m:mi>
                        <m:mn>2</m:mn>
                    </m:msup>
                    <m:mo>-</m:mo>
                    <m:mrow>
                        <m:mn>6</m:mn>
                        <m:mo>&InvisibleTimes;</m:mo>
                        <m:mi>Z</m:mi>
```

continues ▸

```
                </m:mrow>
                <m:mo>+</m:mo>
                <m:mn>12</m:mn>
            </m:mrow>
            <m:mo>=</m:mo>
            <m:mn>0</m:mn>
        </m:mrow>
    </m:math>
  </body>
</html>
```

This document works fine, and you can see the result in the W3C Amaya browser in Figure 2.3.

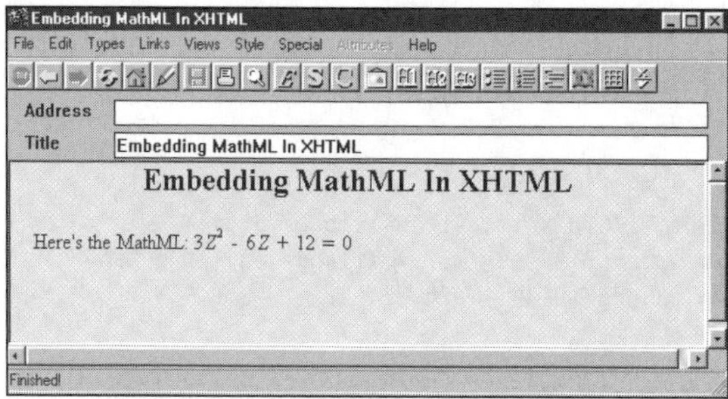

Figure 2.3 A MathML document in the Amaya browser.

We'll have occasions to use namespaces throughout this book, as when we work with the XSL transformation language in Chapter 13 "XSL Transformations."

Infosets

While discussing creating XML documents, it's worth discussing a new XML specification: the XML Information Set specification, which you'll find at `www.w3.org/TR/xml-infoset`.

XML documents excel at storing data, and this has led developers to wonder whether XML will ultimately be able to solve an old problem: being able to directly compare and classify the data in multiple documents. For example, consider the World Wide Web as it stands today. There can be thousands of documents on a particular topic, but how can you possibly compare them? For example, a search for "XML" turns up about 675,000 matches, but it would be extraordinarily difficult to write a program that would compare the data in those documents because all that data isn't stored in any remotely compatible format.

The idea behind XML information sets, also called *infosets*, is to set up an abstract way of looking at an XML document so that it can be compared to others. To have an infoset, XML documents may not use colons in tag and attribute names unless they are used to support namespaces. Documents do not need to be valid to have an infoset, but they need to be well-formed.

An XML document's information set consists of two or more *information items* (the information set for any well-formed XML document contains at least the document information item and one element information item). An information item is an abstract representation of some part of an XML document, and each information item has a set of properties, some of which are considered *core* and some of which are considered *peripheral*.

An XML information set can contain 15 different types of information items, as listed in the W3C Infoset specification:

- *A document information item (core)*
- *Element information items (core)*
- *Attribute information items (core)*
- *Processing instruction information items (core)*
- *Reference to skipped entity information items (core)*
- *Character information items (core)*
- *Comment information items (peripheral)*
- *A document type declaration information item (peripheral)*
- *Entity information items (core for unparsed entities, peripheral for others)*
- *Notation information items (core)*
- *Entity start marker information items (peripheral)*
- *Entity end marker information items (peripheral)*
- *CDATA start marker information items (peripheral)*
- *CDATA end marker information items (peripheral)*
- *Namespace declaration information items (core)*

There is always one document information item in the information set. Here's a list of the core properties of the document information item:

- **[children].** This property holds an ordered list of references to child information items, in the original document order.
- **[notations].** This property holds an unordered set of references to notation information items (which we'll see more about in Chapter 3).
- **[entities].** This property holds an unordered set of references to entity information items, one for each unparsed entity declaration in the DTD.

The document information item can also have these properties:

- **[base URI].** This property holds the absolute URI of the document entity.
- **[children - comments].** This property holds a reference to a comment information item for each comment outside the document element.
- **[children - doctype].** This property holds a reference to one document type declaration information item.
- **[entities - other].** This property holds a reference to an entity information item for each parsed general entity declaration in the DTD.

The other information items, such as element information items and processing instruction information items, have similar properties lists.

Currently, no applications create and work with infosets. However, W3C documentation often refers to the information stored in an XML document as its infoset, so this is an important term to know. The closest you come to working with infosets right now is working with *canonical* XML documents (see the next section, "Canonical XML").

Canonical XML

Although infosets are a good idea, they are only abstract formulations of the information in an XML document. So, without reducing an XML document to its infoset, how can you actually approach the goal of being able to actually compare XML documents byte by byte?

It turns out that there is a way: You can use canonical XML. Canonical XML is a companion standard to XML, and you can read all about it at `www.w3.org/TR/xml-c14n`. Essentially, canonical XML is a strict XML syntax; documents in canonical XML can be compared directly. The information included in the canonical XML version of a document is the same as would appear in its infoset.

As you can imagine, two XML documents that actually contain the same information can be arranged differently. They can differ in terms of their structure, attribute ordering, and even character encoding. That means that it's very hard to compare such documents. However, when you place these documents in canonical XML format, they can be compared on a byte-by-byte level. In the canonical XML syntax, logically equivalent documents are identical byte for byte.

The canonical XML syntax is very strict; for example, canonical XML uses UTF-8 character encoding only, carriage-return linefeed pairs are replaced with linefeeds, tabs in CDATA sections are replaced by spaces, all entity references must be expanded, and much more, as specified in `www.w3.org/TR/xml-c14n`. Because canonical XML is intended to be byte-by-byte correct, the upshot is that if you need a document in canonical form, you should use software to convert your XML documents to that form.

One such package that will convert valid XML documents to canonical form comes with the XML for Java software that you can get from IBM's AlphaWorks (`www.alphaworks.ibm.com/tech/xml4j`); we touched on this in Chapter 1, and we will be using it later in the book, in Chapter 11, "Java and the XML DOM." XML for Java comes with a Java program named DOMWriter that can convert documents to canonical XML form. To use this program, you must make sure that your document is valid, which means giving it a DTD or a schema to be checked against. I'll add a DTD to the example order.xml that we've seen in this chapter (we'll see how to create DTDs in Chapter 3):

```
<?xml version = "1.0" standalone="yes"?>
<!DOCTYPE DOCUMENT [
<!ELEMENT DOCUMENT (CUSTOMER)*>
<!ELEMENT CUSTOMER (NAME,DATE,ORDERS)>
<!ELEMENT NAME (LAST_NAME,FIRST_NAME)>
<!ELEMENT LAST_NAME (#PCDATA)>
<!ELEMENT FIRST_NAME (#PCDATA)>
<!ELEMENT DATE (#PCDATA)>
<!ELEMENT ORDERS (ITEM)*>
<!ELEMENT ITEM (PRODUCT,NUMBER,PRICE)>
<!ELEMENT PRODUCT (#PCDATA)>
<!ELEMENT NUMBER (#PCDATA)>
<!ELEMENT PRICE (#PCDATA)>
]>
<DOCUMENT>
    <CUSTOMER>
        <NAME>
            <LAST_NAME>Smith</LAST_NAME>
            <FIRST_NAME>Sam</FIRST_NAME>
        </NAME>
        <DATE>October 15, 2001</DATE>
        <ORDERS>
            <ITEM>
                <PRODUCT>Tomatoes</PRODUCT>
                <NUMBER>8</NUMBER>
                <PRICE>$1.25</PRICE>
            </ITEM>
            <ITEM>
                <PRODUCT>Oranges</PRODUCT>
                <NUMBER>24</NUMBER>
                <PRICE>$4.98</PRICE>
```

continues ▶

```
            </ITEM>
        </ORDERS>
    </CUSTOMER>
    <CUSTOMER>
        <NAME>
            <LAST_NAME>Jones</LAST_NAME>
            <FIRST_NAME>Polly</FIRST_NAME>
        </NAME>
        <DATE>October 20, 2001</DATE>
        <ORDERS>
            <ITEM>
                <PRODUCT>Bread</PRODUCT>
                <NUMBER>12</NUMBER>
                <PRICE>$14.95</PRICE>
            </ITEM>
            <ITEM>
                <PRODUCT>Apples</PRODUCT>
                <NUMBER>6</NUMBER>
                <PRICE>$1.50</PRICE>
            </ITEM>
        </ORDERS>
    </CUSTOMER>
    <CUSTOMER>
        <NAME>
            <LAST_NAME>Weber</LAST_NAME>
            <FIRST_NAME>Bill</FIRST_NAME>
        </NAME>
        <DATE>October 25, 2001</DATE>
        <ORDERS>
            <ITEM>
                <PRODUCT>Asparagus</PRODUCT>
                <NUMBER>12</NUMBER>
                <PRICE>$2.95</PRICE>
            </ITEM>
            <ITEM>
                <PRODUCT>Lettuce</PRODUCT>
                <NUMBER>6</NUMBER>
                <PRICE>$11.50</PRICE>
            </ITEM>
        </ORDERS>
    </CUSTOMER>
</DOCUMENT>
```

Now you can use the DOMWriter program with the special `-c` switch to convert this document to canonical form; the `> canonical.xml` part at the end sends the output of the program to a file named canonical.xml. (We'll see how to set up the Java `classpath` environment variable as it must be set up to make this work in Chapter 11.).

```
%java dom.DOMWriter -c order.xml > canonical.xml
java -cp xml4j.jar;xerces.jar;xercesSamples.jar dom.DOMWriter -c order.xml >
canonical.xml
```

Here's the result. (Note that DOMWriter has preserved all the whitespace in the document, and the `
` entity references stand for the UTF-8 code for a linefeed.You also can give codes in hexadecimal if you include an "x" before the number like this for a linefeed: `
`.)

```
<DOCUMENT>&#10;    <CUSTOMER>&#10;        <NAME>&#10;
<LAST_NAME>Smith</LAST_NAME>&#10;
<FIRST_NAME>Sam</FIRST_NAME>&#10;        </NAME>&#10;
<DATE>October 15, 2001</DATE>&#10;        <ORDERS>&#10;
<ITEM>&#10;              <PRODUCT>Tomatoes</PRODUCT>&#10;
<NUMBER>8</NUMBER>&#10;
<PRICE>$1.25</PRICE>&#10;             </ITEM>&#10;
<ITEM>&#10;              <PRODUCT>Oranges</PRODUCT>&#10;
<NUMBER>24</NUMBER>&#10;
<PRICE>$4.98</PRICE>&#10;             </ITEM>&#10;
</ORDERS>&#10;    </CUSTOMER>&#10;    <CUSTOMER>&#10;
<NAME>&#10;          <LAST_NAME>Jones</LAST_NAME>&#10;
<FIRST_NAME>Polly</FIRST_NAME>&#10;       </NAME>&#10;
<DATE>October 20, 2001</DATE>&#10;        <ORDERS>&#10;
<ITEM>&#10;              <PRODUCT>Bread</PRODUCT>&#10;
<NUMBER>12</NUMBER>&#10;
<PRICE>$14.95</PRICE>&#10;            </ITEM>&#10;
<ITEM>&#10;              <PRODUCT>Apples</PRODUCT>&#10;
<NUMBER>6</NUMBER>&#10;
<PRICE>$1.50</PRICE>&#10;             </ITEM>&#10;
</ORDERS>&#10;    </CUSTOMER>&#10;    <CUSTOMER>&#10;
<NAME>&#10;          <LAST_NAME>Weber</LAST_NAME>&#10;
<FIRST_NAME>Bill</FIRST_NAME>&#10;        </NAME>&#10;
<DATE>October 25, 2001</DATE>&#10;        <ORDERS>&#10;
<ITEM>&#10;              <PRODUCT>Asparagus</PRODUCT>&#10;
<NUMBER>12</NUMBER>&#10;
<PRICE>$2.95</PRICE>&#10;             </ITEM>&#10;
<ITEM>&#10;              <PRODUCT>Lettuce</PRODUCT>&#10;
<NUMBER>6</NUMBER>&#10;
<PRICE>$11.50</PRICE>&#10;            </ITEM>&#10;
</ORDERS>&#10;    </CUSTOMER>&#10;</DOCUMENT>
```

In their canonical form, documents can be compared directly, and any differences will be readily apparent.

This example is also useful because it shows exactly what a DTD looks like and provides us with the perfect starting point for Chapter 3, which is where we start writing DTDs ourselves and create valid XML documents.

Valid XML Documents: Creating Document Type Definitions

CHAPTER 2, "CREATING WELL-FORMED XML DOCUMENTS," explains all about creating well-formed XML documents. However, there's more to creating good XML documents than the simple (although essential) requirement that they be well-formed. Because you can create your own tags when you create an XML application, it's up to you to set their syntax. For example, can a `<HOUSE>` element contain plain text or only other elements such as `<TENANT>` or `<OWNER>`? Must a `<BOOK>` element contain a `<PAGE_COUNT>` element, or can it get by without one? It's up to you to decide. Using your own custom XML syntax is not only good for making sure that your documents are legible—it can also be essential for programs that deal with documents via code.

XML documents whose syntax has been checked successfully are called *valid* documents; in particular, an XML document is considered valid if there is a *document type definition* (*DTD*) or XML schema associated with it and if the document complies with the DTD or schema. That's all there is to making a document valid. This chapter is all about creating basic DTDs. In the next chapter, I'll elaborate on the DTDs that we create here, showing how to declare entities, attributes, and notations.

You can find the formal rules for DTDs in the XML 1.0 recommendation, `www.w3.org/TR/REC-xml` (which also appears in Appendix A, "The XML 1.0 Specification"). The constraints that documents and DTDs must adhere to create a valid document are marked with the text "Validity Constraint."

Note that DTDs are all about specifying the structure and syntax of XML documents (not their content). Various organizations can share a DTD to put an XML application into practice. We saw quite a few examples of XML applications in Chapter 1, "Essential XML," and those applications can all be enforced with DTDs that the various organizations make public. We'll see how to create public DTDs in this chapter.

Most XML parsers, like the one in Internet Explorer, require XML documents to be well-formed but not necessarily valid. (Most XML parsers do not require a DTD, but if there is one, validating parsers will use it to validate the XML document.)

In fact, we saw a DTD at the end of the previous chapter. In that chapter, I set up an example XML document that stored customer orders named order.xml. At the end of the chapter, I used the DOMWriter program that comes with IBM's XML for Java package to translate the document into canonical XML; to run it through that program, I needed to add a DTD to the document. Here's what it looked like:

```
<?xml version = "1.0" standalone="yes"?>
<!DOCTYPE DOCUMENT [
<!ELEMENT DOCUMENT (CUSTOMER)*>
<!ELEMENT CUSTOMER (NAME,DATE,ORDERS)>
<!ELEMENT NAME (LAST_NAME,FIRST_NAME)>
<!ELEMENT LAST_NAME (#PCDATA)>
<!ELEMENT FIRST_NAME (#PCDATA)>
<!ELEMENT DATE (#PCDATA)>
<!ELEMENT ORDERS (ITEM)*>
<!ELEMENT ITEM (PRODUCT,NUMBER,PRICE)>
<!ELEMENT PRODUCT (#PCDATA)>
<!ELEMENT NUMBER (#PCDATA)>
<!ELEMENT PRICE (#PCDATA)>
]>
<DOCUMENT>
    <CUSTOMER>
        <NAME>
            <LAST_NAME>Smith</LAST_NAME>
            <FIRST_NAME>Sam</FIRST_NAME>
        </NAME>
        <DATE>October 15, 2001</DATE>
        <ORDERS>
            <ITEM>
                <PRODUCT>Tomatoes</PRODUCT>
                <NUMBER>8</NUMBER>
                <PRICE>$1.25</PRICE>
            </ITEM>
            <ITEM>
                <PRODUCT>Oranges</PRODUCT>
                <NUMBER>24</NUMBER>
                <PRICE>$4.98</PRICE>
```

```
            </ITEM>
        </ORDERS>
    </CUSTOMER>
    <CUSTOMER>
        <NAME>
            <LAST_NAME>Jones</LAST_NAME>
            <FIRST_NAME>Polly</FIRST_NAME>
        </NAME>
        <DATE>October 20, 2001</DATE>
        <ORDERS>
            <ITEM>
                <PRODUCT>Bread</PRODUCT>
                <NUMBER>12</NUMBER>
                <PRICE>$14.95</PRICE>
            </ITEM>
            <ITEM>
                <PRODUCT>Apples</PRODUCT>
                <NUMBER>6</NUMBER>
                <PRICE>$1.50</PRICE>
            </ITEM>
        </ORDERS>
    </CUSTOMER>
    <CUSTOMER>
        <NAME>
            <LAST_NAME>Weber</LAST_NAME>
            <FIRST_NAME>Bill</FIRST_NAME>
        </NAME>
        <DATE>October 25, 2001</DATE>
        <ORDERS>
            <ITEM>
                <PRODUCT>Asparagus</PRODUCT>
                <NUMBER>12</NUMBER>
                <PRICE>$2.95</PRICE>
            </ITEM>
            <ITEM>
                <PRODUCT>Lettuce</PRODUCT>
                <NUMBER>6</NUMBER>
                <PRICE>$11.50</PRICE>
            </ITEM>
        </ORDERS>
    </CUSTOMER>
</DOCUMENT>
```

In this chapter, I'm going to take this DTD apart to see what makes it tick. Actually, this DTD is a pretty substantial one, so to get us started and to show how DTDs work in overview, I'll start with a mini-example first:

```
<?xml version="1.0"?>
<!DOCTYPE THESIS [
    <!ELEMENT THESIS (P*)>
    <!ELEMENT P (#PCDATA)>
]>
```

continues ▸

```
<THESIS>
    <P>
        This is my Ph.D. thesis.
    </P>
    <P>
        Pretty good, huh?
    </P>
    <P>
        So, give me a Ph.D. now!
    </P>
</THESIS>
```

Note the `<!DOCTYPE>` element here. Technically, this element is not an element at all, but a document type *declaration* (DTDs are document type *definitions*). You use document type declarations to indicate the DTD used for the document. The basic syntax for the document type declaration is `<!DOCTYPE rootname [DTD]>` (there are other variations we'll see in this chapter) where *`DTD`* is the document type definition that you want to use. DTDs can be internal or external, as we'll see in this chapter—in this case, the DTD is internal:

```
<?xml version="1.0"?>
<!DOCTYPE THESIS [
    <!ELEMENT THESIS (P*)>
    <!ELEMENT P (#PCDATA)>
]>
<THESIS>
    <P>
        This is my Ph.D. thesis.
    </P>
    <P>
        Pretty good, huh?
    </P>
    <P>
        So, give me a Ph.D. now!
    </P>
</THESIS>
```

This DTD follows the W3C syntax conventions, which means that I specify the syntax for each element with `<!ELEMENT>`. Using this declaration, you can specify that the contents of an element can be either parsed character data, `#PCDATA` or other elements that you've created, or both. In this example, I'm indicating that the `<THESIS>` element must contain only `<P>` elements but that it can contain zero or more occurrences of the `<P>` element—which is what the asterisk (`*`) after `P` in `<!ELEMENT THESIS (P*)>` means.

In addition to defining the `<THESIS>` element, I define the `<P>` element so that it can only hold text—that is, parsed character data (which is pure text, without any markup), with the term `#PCDATA`:

```
<?xml version="1.0"?>
<!DOCTYPE THESIS [
    <!ELEMENT THESIS (P*)>
    <!ELEMENT P (#PCDATA)>
]>
<THESIS>
    <P>
        This is my Ph.D. thesis.
    </P>
    <P>
        Pretty good, huh?
    </P>
    <P>
        So, give me a Ph.D. now!
    </P>
</THESIS>
```

In this way, I've specified the syntax of these two elements, `<THESIS>` and `<P>`. A validating XML processor can now validate this document using the DTD that it supplies.

And that's what a DTD looks like in overview; now it's time to dig into the full details. We're going to take a look at all of them here and in the next chapter.

Creating Document Type Declarations

You define the syntax and structure of elements using a document type *definition* (DTD), and you declare that definition in a document using a document type *declaration*. We've seen that you use `<!DOCTYPE>` to create a document type declaration. This element can take many different forms, as you see here (here, *`URL`* is the URL of a DTD, and *`rootname`* is the name of the root element); we'll see all these forms in this chapter:

- `<!DOCTYPE rootname [DTD]>`
- `<!DOCTYPE rootname SYSTEM URL>`
- `<!DOCTYPE rootname SYSTEM URL [DTD]>`
- `<!DOCTYPE rootname PUBLIC identifier URL>`
- `<!DOCTYPE rootname PUBLIC identifier URL [DTD]>`

To use a DTD, you need a document type declaration, which means that you need `<!DOCTYPE>`. The `<!DOCTYPE>` declaration is part of a document's *prolog* (also called *prologue*). Here's how I add a document type declaration to the document order.xml that we developed in Chapter 2:

```
<?xml version = "1.0" standalone="yes"?>
<!DOCTYPE DOCUMENT [
    .
    .
    .
]>
<DOCUMENT>
    <CUSTOMER>
        <NAME>
            <LAST_NAME>Smith</LAST_NAME>
            <FIRST_NAME>Sam</FIRST_NAME>
        </NAME>
        <DATE>October 15, 2001</DATE>
        <ORDERS>
            <ITEM>
                <PRODUCT>Tomatoes</PRODUCT>
                <NUMBER>8</NUMBER>
                <PRICE>$1.25</PRICE>
            </ITEM>
            .
            .
            .
            <ITEM>
                <PRODUCT>Asparagus</PRODUCT>
                <NUMBER>12</NUMBER>
                <PRICE>$2.95</PRICE>
            </ITEM>
            <ITEM>
                <PRODUCT>Lettuce</PRODUCT>
                <NUMBER>6</NUMBER>
                <PRICE>$11.50</PRICE>
            </ITEM>
        </ORDERS>
    </CUSTOMER>
</DOCUMENT>
```

Now it's up to us to supply the actual document type definition, the DTD, that's part of this `<!DOCTYPE>` declaration.

Creating Document Type Definitions

To introduce DTDs, I'll start with a DTD that's internal to the document whose syntax it specifies (we'll see how to create external DTDs later in the chapter). In this case, the DTD itself goes inside the square brackets in `<!DOCTYPE>` (note that I've set the `standalone` attribute to `"yes"` here because this document doesn't rely on any external resources):

```
<?xml version = "1.0" standalone="yes"?>
<!DOCTYPE DOCUMENT [
<!ELEMENT DOCUMENT (CUSTOMER)*>
<!ELEMENT CUSTOMER (NAME,DATE,ORDERS)>
<!ELEMENT NAME (LAST_NAME,FIRST_NAME)>
<!ELEMENT LAST_NAME (#PCDATA)>
<!ELEMENT FIRST_NAME (#PCDATA)>
<!ELEMENT DATE (#PCDATA)>
<!ELEMENT ORDERS (ITEM)*>
<!ELEMENT ITEM (PRODUCT,NUMBER,PRICE)>
<!ELEMENT PRODUCT (#PCDATA)>
<!ELEMENT NUMBER (#PCDATA)>
<!ELEMENT PRICE (#PCDATA)>
]>
<DOCUMENT>
    <CUSTOMER>
        <NAME>
            <LAST_NAME>Smith</LAST_NAME>
            <FIRST_NAME>Sam</FIRST_NAME>
        </NAME>
        <DATE>October 15, 2001</DATE>
        <ORDERS>
            <ITEM>
                <PRODUCT>Tomatoes</PRODUCT>
                <NUMBER>8</NUMBER>
                <PRICE>$1.25</PRICE>
            </ITEM>
            .
            .
            .
            <ITEM>
                <PRODUCT>Asparagus</PRODUCT>
                <NUMBER>12</NUMBER>
                <PRICE>$2.95</PRICE>
            </ITEM>
            <ITEM>
                <PRODUCT>Lettuce</PRODUCT>
                <NUMBER>6</NUMBER>
                <PRICE>$11.50</PRICE>
            </ITEM>
        </ORDERS>
    </CUSTOMER>
</DOCUMENT>
```

When a DTD is in place—and we'll see how to create this DTD in the following sections—you have a valid document.

Having gotten `<!DOCTYPE>` in place, we're ready to start creating the DTD, starting with `<!ELEMENT>`.

Element Declarations

To declare the syntax of an element in a DTD, you use `<!ELEMENT>` like this: `<!ELEMENT NAME CONTENT_MODEL>`. Here, *NAME* is the name of the element that you're declaring; *CONTENT_MODEL* can be set to `EMPTY` or `ANY`, or it can hold mixed content (other elements as well as parsed character data) or child elements.

Here are a few examples. Note the expressions starting with `%` and ending with `;`. Those expressions are *parameter entity references*, much like general entity references except that you use them in DTDs, not the body of the document (we'll see parameter entities in the next chapter):

```
<!ELEMENT direction (left, right, top?)>
<!ELEMENT CHAPTER (INTRODUCTION, (P | QUOTE | NOTE)*, DIV*)>
<!ELEMENT HR EMPTY>
<!ELEMENT p (#PCDATA | I)* >
<!ELEMENT %title; %content; >
<!ELEMENT DOCUMENT ANY>
```

We're going to see how to create `<!ELEMENT>` declarations like these in this and the next chapter. I'll start by declaring the root element of the example document for this chapter, order.xml:

```
<?xml version = "1.0" standalone="yes"?>
<!DOCTYPE DOCUMENT [
<!ELEMENT DOCUMENT ANY>
]>
<DOCUMENT>
</DOCUMENT>
```

Notice that I'm specifying a content model of `ANY` here; see the next section for the details on this keyword.

ANY

When you declare an element with the content model of `ANY`, that means that the declared element can contain any type of content—any element in the document, as well as parsed character data. (Effectively, this means that the contents of elements that you declare with the `ANY` content model are not checked by XML validators. See the later section "Validating Against a DTD" for details on XML validators.)

Here's how you specify a content model of `ANY`:

```
<?xml version = "1.0" standalone="yes"?>
<!DOCTYPE DOCUMENT [
<!ELEMENT DOCUMENT ANY>
]>
<DOCUMENT>
</DOCUMENT>
```

However, giving an element the content model ANY is often not a good idea because it removes syntax checking. It's usually far better to specify an actual content model, and I'll start doing that with a child list of elements.

Child Element Lists

Besides using the content model of ANY, you can specify that the element you're declaring contain another element by giving the name of that element in parentheses, like this:

```
<?xml version = "1.0" standalone="yes"?>
<!DOCTYPE DOCUMENT [
<!ELEMENT DOCUMENT (CUSTOMER)*>
]>
<DOCUMENT>
    .
    .
    .
</DOCUMENT>
```

In this case, I'm indicating that the root element, <DOCUMENT>, can contain any number (including zero) of <CUSTOMER> elements (the way I specify that the <DOCUMENT> element can contain any number of <CUSTOMER> elements is with the asterisk after the parentheses—we'll see how that works in a page or two).

Because the <DOCUMENT> element can contain any number of <CUSTOMER> elements, I can now add a <CUSTOMER> element to the document, like this:

```
<?xml version = "1.0" standalone="yes"?>
<!DOCTYPE DOCUMENT [
<!ELEMENT DOCUMENT (CUSTOMER)*>
]>
<DOCUMENT>
    <CUSTOMER>
    .
    .
    .
    </CUSTOMER>
</DOCUMENT>
```

However, this is not a valid document because I haven't declared the <CUSTOMER> element yet. I'll do that next.

#PCDATA

Say that we want to let the <CUSTOMER> element store some plain text—in particular, say that we want to store the name of a customer. All nonmarkup text is referred to as *parsed character data* in a DTD, and it is abbreviated as

#PCDATA in element declarations. Parsed character data explicitly means text that does not contain markup, just simple character data.

The parsed character data is where you store the actual content of the document as plain text. Note, however, that this is the *only* way to specify the content of the document using DTDs—you can't say anything more about the actual *type* of content.

For example, even though you might be storing numbers, that data is only plain text as far as DTDs are concerned. This lack of precision is one of the reasons that XML schemas, the alternative to DTDs, were developed. With schemas, you can specify much more about the type of data you're storing, such as whether it's in integer, floating point, or even date format, and XML processors can check to make sure the data matches the format that it's supposed to be expressed in. I'll take a look at schemas in Chapter 5, "Creating XML Schemas." (Note, however, that schemas are new enough that there's relatively little software support for them at this point; Internet Explorer has support for schemas, but it implements them according to an old, and unfortunately very out-of-date, W3C note.)

Here's how I declare the <CUSTOMER> element so that it can contain PCDATA (and only PCDATA):

```
<?xml version = "1.0" standalone="yes"?>
<!DOCTYPE DOCUMENT [
<!ELEMENT DOCUMENT (CUSTOMER)*>
<!ELEMENT CUSTOMER (#PCDATA)>
]>
<DOCUMENT>
    <CUSTOMER>
    .
    .
    .
    </CUSTOMER>
</DOCUMENT>
```

Now I can add text to a <CUSTOMER> element in the document like this:

```
<?xml version = "1.0" standalone="yes"?>
<!DOCTYPE DOCUMENT [
<!ELEMENT DOCUMENT (CUSTOMER)*>
<!ELEMENT CUSTOMER (#PCDATA)>
]>
<DOCUMENT>
    <CUSTOMER>
        Sam Smith
    </CUSTOMER>
</DOCUMENT>
```

Note that elements that have been declared to hold PCDATA can hold only PCDATA; you cannot, for example, place another element in the <CUSTOMER> element the way that it has been declared now—this document is not valid:

```
<?xml version = "1.0" standalone="yes"?>
<!DOCTYPE DOCUMENT [
<!ELEMENT DOCUMENT (CUSTOMER)*>
<!ELEMENT CUSTOMER (#PCDATA)>
]>
<DOCUMENT>
    <CUSTOMER>
        Sam Smith
        <CREDIT_RATING>
            Lousy
        </CREDIT_RATING>
    </CUSTOMER>
</DOCUMENT>
```

The content model that supports both PCDATA and other elements inside an element is called the *mixed content model*, and I'll take a look at it in a few pages (you can also support a mixed content model using the ANY content model, of course).

There's another thing to note here now that we're dealing with multiple declarations—the order in which you declare elements doesn't matter, so this DTD, where I've declared the <DOCUMENT> element after the <CUSTOMER> element, works just as well:

```
<?xml version = "1.0" standalone="yes"?>
<!DOCTYPE DOCUMENT [
<!ELEMENT CUSTOMER (#PCDATA)>
<!ELEMENT DOCUMENT (CUSTOMER)*>
]>
<DOCUMENT>
    <CUSTOMER>
    .
    .
    .
    </CUSTOMER>
</DOCUMENT>
```

Note that although the order of element declarations is not supposed to matter—and in practice, that's the way I've always seen it—some XML processors may demand that you declare an element before using it in another declaration.

It's also possible to declare elements in such a way that they can contain multiple children. In fact, you can specify the exact types of child elements that an element can enclose, and in what order those child elements must appear. I'll take a look at that now.

Dealing with Multiple Children

When you want to declare an element that can contain multiple children, you have several options. DTDs use a syntax to deal with multiple children that is much like working with regular expressions in languages such as Perl, in case you're familiar with that. Here's the syntax that you can use (here, `a` and `b` are child elements of the element you're declaring):

- `a+`—One or more occurrences of `a`.
- `a*`—Zero or more occurrences of `a`.
- `a?`—`a` or nothing.
- `a, b`—`a` followed by `b`.
- `a | b`—`a` or `b`, but not both.
- `(expression)`—Surrounding an expression with parentheses means that it's treated as a unit and may have the suffix operator `?`, `*`, or `+`.

If you're not familiar with this kind of syntax, it's not much use asking why things are set up this way; this syntax has been around a long time, and W3C adopted it for DTDs because many people were familiar with it. If this looks totally strange to you, it's just one of the skills you'll have to master when writing DTDs—but, fortunately, it soon becomes second nature.

I'll now take a look at each of these listed possibilities in detail.

One or More Children

If you must specify that the `<DOCUMENT>` element can contain only between 12 and 15 `<CUSTOMER>` elements, you'll have a problem when working with DTDs because the DTD syntax won't allow you to do that without getting very complex. However, you can specify that the `<DOCUMENT>` element must contain one or more `<CUSTOMER>` elements like this, using the `+` operator:

```
<?xml version = "1.0" standalone="yes"?>
<!DOCTYPE DOCUMENT [
<!ELEMENT DOCUMENT (CUSTOMER)+>
<!ELEMENT CUSTOMER (#PCDATA)>
]>
<DOCUMENT>
    <CUSTOMER>
        Sam Smith
    </CUSTOMER>
    <CUSTOMER>
        Fred Smith
    </CUSTOMER>
</DOCUMENT>
```

In this case, the XML processor now knows that you want the <DOCUMENT> element to contain one or more <CUSTOMER> elements, which makes sense if you want a useful document that actually contains some data. In this way, we've been able to specify the syntax of the <DOCUMENT> element in some more detail.

Zero or More Children

Besides specifying one or more child elements, you can also declare elements so that they can enclose zero or more of a particular child element. This is useful if you want to allow an element to have a particular child element, or any number of such elements, but you don't want to force it to have that particular child element.

For example, a <CHAPTER> element might be capable of containing a <FOOTNOTE> element or even several <FOOTNOTE> elements, but you wouldn't necessarily want to force all <CHAPTER> elements to have <FOOTNOTE> elements. Using the * operator, you can do that.

The * operator means that the indicated child element can appear any number of times in the declared element (including zero times). Here's how I indicate that the <DOCUMENT> element can contain any number of <CUSTOMER> elements:

```
<?xml version = "1.0" standalone="yes"?>
<!DOCTYPE DOCUMENT [
<!ELEMENT DOCUMENT (CUSTOMER)*>
<!ELEMENT CUSTOMER (#PCDATA)>
]>
<DOCUMENT>
    <CUSTOMER>
        Sam Smith
    </CUSTOMER>
    <CUSTOMER>
        Fred Smith
    </CUSTOMER>
</DOCUMENT>
```

Zero or One Child

Besides using + to specify one or more occurrences of a particular child element and * to specify zero or more occurrences of a child element, you can also use ? to specify zero or one occurrences of a child element. In other words, using ? indicates that a particular child element *may* be present in the element you're declaring, but it need not be.

For example, a <CHAPTER> element might be capable of containing one <OPENING_QUOTATION> element, but you wouldn't necessarily want to force all

<CHAPTER> elements to have an <OPENING_QUOTATION> element. Using the ? operator, you can do that.

Here's an example; in this case, I'm allowing the <DOCUMENT> element to contain only zero or one <CUSTOMER> element (rather a limited clientele):

```
<?xml version = "1.0" standalone="yes"?>
<!DOCTYPE DOCUMENT [
<!ELEMENT DOCUMENT (CUSTOMER)?>
<!ELEMENT CUSTOMER (#PCDATA)>
]>
<DOCUMENT>
    <CUSTOMER>
        Sam Smith
    </CUSTOMER>
</DOCUMENT>
```

We've advanced a little in DTD power now by allowing multiple child elements, but so far, we've allowed only child elements of the same type in any one declared element—but that's about to change.

DTD Sequences

You can specify exactly what child elements a particular element can contain, and in what order, by using a *sequence*. A sequence is a comma-separated list of element names that tells the XML processor what elements must appear, and in what order.

For example, say that we want to change the <CUSTOMER> element so that instead of containing only PCDATA, it can contain other elements. Here, I'll let the <CUSTOMER> element contain one <NAME> element, one <DATE> element, and one <ORDERS> element, in exactly that order. The resulting declaration looks like this:

```
<!ELEMENT CUSTOMER (NAME,DATE,ORDERS)>
```

I can break this down further, of course; for example, I can specify that the <NAME> element must contain exactly one <LAST_NAME> element and one <FIRST_NAME> element, in that order, like this:

```
<!ELEMENT NAME (LAST_NAME,FIRST_NAME)>
```

White space doesn't matter, of course, so the same declaration could look like this:

```
<!ELEMENT   NAME        (LAST_NAME,       FIRST_NAME)>
```

Being able to specify the exact order that the elements in your document must take can be great when you're working with software that relies on such an order.

Here's how I'll elaborate the order.xml document to include the previous two sequences as well as a third one that makes sure that the <ITEM> element contains exactly one <PRODUCT> element, one <NUMBER> element, and one <PRICE> element, in that order. The resulting DTD enforces the syntax of the order.xml document that we developed in the previous chapter, and you can see the whole document, complete with working DTD, here:

```
<?xml version = "1.0" standalone="yes"?>
<!DOCTYPE DOCUMENT [
<!ELEMENT DOCUMENT (CUSTOMER)*>
<!ELEMENT CUSTOMER (NAME,DATE,ORDERS)>
<!ELEMENT NAME (LAST_NAME,FIRST_NAME)>
<!ELEMENT LAST_NAME (#PCDATA)>
<!ELEMENT FIRST_NAME (#PCDATA)>
<!ELEMENT DATE (#PCDATA)>
<!ELEMENT ORDERS (ITEM)*>
<!ELEMENT ITEM (PRODUCT,NUMBER,PRICE)>
<!ELEMENT PRODUCT (#PCDATA)>
<!ELEMENT NUMBER (#PCDATA)>
<!ELEMENT PRICE (#PCDATA)>
]>
<DOCUMENT>
    <CUSTOMER>
        <NAME>
            <LAST_NAME>Smith</LAST_NAME>
            <FIRST_NAME>Sam</FIRST_NAME>
        </NAME>
        <DATE>October 15, 2001</DATE>
        <ORDERS>
            <ITEM>
                <PRODUCT>Tomatoes</PRODUCT>
                <NUMBER>8</NUMBER>
                <PRICE>$1.25</PRICE>
            </ITEM>
            <ITEM>
                <PRODUCT>Oranges</PRODUCT>
                <NUMBER>24</NUMBER>
                <PRICE>$4.98</PRICE>
            </ITEM>
        </ORDERS>
    </CUSTOMER>
    <CUSTOMER>
        <NAME>
            <LAST_NAME>Jones</LAST_NAME>
            <FIRST_NAME>Polly</FIRST_NAME>
        </NAME>
        <DATE>October 20, 2001</DATE>
        <ORDERS>
            <ITEM>
```

continues ▸

```
                <PRODUCT>Bread</PRODUCT>
                <NUMBER>12</NUMBER>
                <PRICE>$14.95</PRICE>
            </ITEM>
            <ITEM>
                <PRODUCT>Apples</PRODUCT>
                <NUMBER>6</NUMBER>
                <PRICE>$1.50</PRICE>
            </ITEM>
        </ORDERS>
    </CUSTOMER>
    <CUSTOMER>
        <NAME>
            <LAST_NAME>Weber</LAST_NAME>
            <FIRST_NAME>Bill</FIRST_NAME>
        </NAME>
        <DATE>October 25, 2001</DATE>
        <ORDERS>
            <ITEM>
                <PRODUCT>Asparagus</PRODUCT>
                <NUMBER>12</NUMBER>
                <PRICE>$2.95</PRICE>
            </ITEM>
            <ITEM>
                <PRODUCT>Lettuce</PRODUCT>
                <NUMBER>6</NUMBER>
                <PRICE>$11.50</PRICE>
            </ITEM>
        </ORDERS>
    </CUSTOMER>
</DOCUMENT>
```

You can use the same element in a sequence a number of times, if you want. For example, here's how I make sure that the `<CUSTOMER>` element should hold exactly three `<NAME>` elements:

```
<!ELEMENT CUSTOMER (NAME,NAME,NAME)>
```

Here's another important note: You can use `+`, `*`, and `?` operators inside sequences. For example, here's how I specify that there can be one or more `<NAME>` elements for a customer, an optional `<CREDIT_RATING>` element, any number of `<DATE>` elements, and a single orders element:

```
<?xml version = "1.0" standalone="yes"?>
<!DOCTYPE DOCUMENT [
<!ELEMENT DOCUMENT (CUSTOMER)*>
<!ELEMENT CUSTOMER (NAME+,CREDIT_RATING?,DATE*,ORDERS)>
<!ELEMENT NAME (LAST_NAME,FIRST_NAME)>
<!ELEMENT LAST_NAME (#PCDATA)>
<!ELEMENT FIRST_NAME (#PCDATA)>
<!ELEMENT DATE (#PCDATA)>
```

```
<!ELEMENT ORDERS (ITEM)*>
<!ELEMENT ITEM (PRODUCT,NUMBER,PRICE)>
<!ELEMENT PRODUCT (#PCDATA)>
<!ELEMENT NUMBER (#PCDATA)>
<!ELEMENT PRICE (#PCDATA)>
<!ELEMENT CREDIT_RATING (#PCDATA)>
]>
<DOCUMENT>
    <CUSTOMER>
        <NAME>
            <LAST_NAME>Smith</LAST_NAME>
            <FIRST_NAME>Sam</FIRST_NAME>
            .
            .
            .
```

Using +, *, and ? inside sequences provides you with a lot of flexibility because now you can constrain how many times an element can appear in a sequence—and even if it can be absent altogether.

Creating Subsequences with Parentheses

In fact, you can get even more powerful using the +, *, and ? operators inside sequences because, using parentheses, you can create *subsequences*—that is, sequences inside sequences.

For example, say that I wanted the <CUSTOMER> element to be capable of holding one or more <NAME> element; for each <NAME> element, I also want to allow a possible <CREDIT_RATING> element. I can do that like this, creating the subsequence (NAME,CREDIT_RATING?) and allowing that subsequence to appear one or more times in the <CUSTOMER> element:

```
<?xml version = "1.0" standalone="yes"?>
<!DOCTYPE DOCUMENT [
<!ELEMENT DOCUMENT (CUSTOMER)*>
<!ELEMENT CUSTOMER ((NAME,CREDIT_RATING?)+,DATE*,ORDERS)>
<!ELEMENT NAME (LAST_NAME,FIRST_NAME)>
<!ELEMENT LAST_NAME (#PCDATA)>
<!ELEMENT FIRST_NAME (#PCDATA)>
<!ELEMENT DATE (#PCDATA)>
<!ELEMENT ORDERS (ITEM)*>
<!ELEMENT ITEM (PRODUCT,NUMBER,PRICE)>
<!ELEMENT PRODUCT (#PCDATA)>
<!ELEMENT NUMBER (#PCDATA)>
<!ELEMENT PRICE (#PCDATA)>
<!ELEMENT CREDIT_RATING (#PCDATA)>
]>
<DOCUMENT>
    <CUSTOMER>
        <NAME>
```

continues ▸

```
            <LAST_NAME>Smith</LAST_NAME>
            <FIRST_NAME>Sam</FIRST_NAME>
        </NAME>
        <DATE>October 15, 2001</DATE>
        <ORDERS>
            <ITEM>
                <PRODUCT>Tomatoes</PRODUCT>
                <NUMBER>8</NUMBER>
                <PRICE>$1.25</PRICE>
            </ITEM>
            <ITEM>
                <PRODUCT>Oranges</PRODUCT>
                <NUMBER>24</NUMBER>
                <PRICE>$4.98</PRICE>
            </ITEM>
        </ORDERS>
    </CUSTOMER>
    <CUSTOMER>
        <NAME>
            <LAST_NAME>Jones</LAST_NAME>
            <FIRST_NAME>Polly</FIRST_NAME>
        </NAME>
        <DATE>October 20, 2001</DATE>
        <ORDERS>
            <ITEM>
                <PRODUCT>Bread</PRODUCT>
                <NUMBER>12</NUMBER>
                <PRICE>$14.95</PRICE>
            </ITEM>
            <ITEM>
                <PRODUCT>Apples</PRODUCT>
                <NUMBER>6</NUMBER>
                <PRICE>$1.50</PRICE>
            </ITEM>
        </ORDERS>
    </CUSTOMER>
    <CUSTOMER>
        <NAME>
            <LAST_NAME>Weber</LAST_NAME>
            <FIRST_NAME>Bill</FIRST_NAME>
        </NAME>
        <DATE>October 25, 2001</DATE>
        <ORDERS>
            <ITEM>
                <PRODUCT>Asparagus</PRODUCT>
                <NUMBER>12</NUMBER>
                <PRICE>$2.95</PRICE>
            </ITEM>
            <ITEM>
                <PRODUCT>Lettuce</PRODUCT>
                <NUMBER>6</NUMBER>
                <PRICE>$11.50</PRICE>
```

```
            </ITEM>
        </ORDERS>
    </CUSTOMER>
</DOCUMENT>
```

Defining subsequences like this, and using the `+`, `*`, and `?` syntax, allows you to be very flexible when defining elements. Here's another example; in this case, I'm declaring an element named `<COMMENTS>` that must contain a `<DATE>` element and that then can contain one or more sequences of `<TITLE>`, `<AUTHOR>`, and `<TEXT>` elements:

```
<!ELEMENT COMMENTS (DATE,(TITLE,AUTHOR,TEXT)+)>
```

Choices

Besides using sequences, you can also use *choices* in DTDs. A choice lets you specify that one of a number of elements will appear at that particular location. Here's how a choice specifying *one* of the elements `<a>` *or* `<b>` *or* `<c>` looks: `(a | b | c)`. When you use this expression, the XML processor knows that exactly one of the `<a>` *or* `<b>` *or* `<c>` elements can appear.

I'll put choices to work in the order.xml example now; in this case, I'll specify that the `<ITEM>` element must enclose a `<PRODUCT>` element, a `<NUMBER>` element, and exactly one element from the list `<PRICE>`, `<CHARGEACCT>`, and `<SAMPLE>`:

```
<?xml version = "1.0" standalone="yes"?>
<!DOCTYPE DOCUMENT [
<!ELEMENT DOCUMENT (CUSTOMER)*>
<!ELEMENT CUSTOMER (NAME,DATE,ORDERS)>
<!ELEMENT NAME (LAST_NAME,FIRST_NAME)>
<!ELEMENT LAST_NAME (#PCDATA)>
<!ELEMENT FIRST_NAME (#PCDATA)>
<!ELEMENT DATE (#PCDATA)>
<!ELEMENT ORDERS (ITEM)*>
<!ELEMENT ITEM (PRODUCT, NUMBER, (PRICE | CHARGEACCT | SAMPLE))>
<!ELEMENT PRODUCT (#PCDATA)>
<!ELEMENT NUMBER (#PCDATA)>
<!ELEMENT PRICE (#PCDATA)>
<!ELEMENT CHARGEACCT (#PCDATA)>
<!ELEMENT SAMPLE (#PCDATA)>
]>
<DOCUMENT>
    <CUSTOMER>
        <NAME>
            <LAST_NAME>Smith</LAST_NAME>
            <FIRST_NAME>Sam</FIRST_NAME>
        </NAME>
        <DATE>October 15, 2001</DATE>
        <ORDERS>
```

continues ▸

```
            <ITEM>
                <PRODUCT>Tomatoes</PRODUCT>
                <NUMBER>8</NUMBER>
                <PRICE>$1.25</PRICE>
            </ITEM>
            <ITEM>
                <PRODUCT>Oranges</PRODUCT>
                <NUMBER>24</NUMBER>
                <SAMPLE>No Charge</SAMPLE>
            </ITEM>
        </ORDERS>
    </CUSTOMER>
    <CUSTOMER>
        <NAME>
            <LAST_NAME>Jones</LAST_NAME>
            <FIRST_NAME>Polly</FIRST_NAME>
        </NAME>
        <DATE>October 20, 2001</DATE>
        <ORDERS>
            <ITEM>
                <PRODUCT>Bread</PRODUCT>
                <NUMBER>12</NUMBER>
                <CHARGEACCT>299930</CHARGEACCT>
            </ITEM>
            <ITEM>
                <PRODUCT>Apples</PRODUCT>
                <NUMBER>6</NUMBER>
                <CHARGEACCT>299931</CHARGEACCT>
            </ITEM>
        </ORDERS>
    </CUSTOMER>
    <CUSTOMER>
        <NAME>
            <LAST_NAME>Weber</LAST_NAME>
            <FIRST_NAME>Bill</FIRST_NAME>
        </NAME>
        <DATE>October 25, 2001</DATE>
        <ORDERS>
            <ITEM>
                <PRODUCT>Asparagus</PRODUCT>
                <NUMBER>12</NUMBER>
                <PRICE>$2.95</PRICE>
            </ITEM>
            <ITEM>
                <PRODUCT>Lettuce</PRODUCT>
                <NUMBER>6</NUMBER>
                <CHARGEACCT>299932</CHARGEACCT>
            </ITEM>
        </ORDERS>
    </CUSTOMER>
</DOCUMENT>
```

As you might expect, you can use the +, *, and ? with choices as well; here, I'm allowing one or more elements selected from a choice to appear in the <ITEM> element—and allowing the choice to return any number of <CHARGEACCT> elements:

```
<?xml version = "1.0" standalone="yes"?>
<!DOCTYPE DOCUMENT [
<!ELEMENT DOCUMENT (CUSTOMER)*>
<!ELEMENT CUSTOMER (NAME,DATE,ORDERS)>
<!ELEMENT NAME (LAST_NAME,FIRST_NAME)>
<!ELEMENT LAST_NAME (#PCDATA)>
<!ELEMENT FIRST_NAME (#PCDATA)>
<!ELEMENT DATE (#PCDATA)>
<!ELEMENT ORDERS (ITEM)*>
<!ELEMENT ITEM (PRODUCT, NUMBER, (PRICE | CHARGEACCT* | SAMPLE)+)>
<!ELEMENT PRODUCT (#PCDATA)>
<!ELEMENT NUMBER (#PCDATA)>
<!ELEMENT PRICE (#PCDATA)>
<!ELEMENT CHARGEACCT (#PCDATA)>
<!ELEMENT SAMPLE (#PCDATA)>
]>
    .
    .
    .
```

As you can see, DTD syntax enables you to specify syntax fairly exactly (unless you want to specify a range or number of times that an element can appear, or its exact data type, of course). In fact, you can use two more content models as well—mixed content models and empty content models.

Mixed Content

It is actually possible to specify that an element can contain both PCDATA and other elements; such a content model is called *mixed*. To specify a mixed content model, just list #PCDATA along with the child elements that you want to allow:

```
<?xml version = "1.0" standalone="yes"?>
<!DOCTYPE DOCUMENT [
<!ELEMENT DOCUMENT (CUSTOMER)*>
<!ELEMENT CUSTOMER (NAME,DATE,ORDERS)>
<!ELEMENT NAME (LAST_NAME,FIRST_NAME)>
<!ELEMENT LAST_NAME (#PCDATA)>
<!ELEMENT FIRST_NAME (#PCDATA)>
<!ELEMENT DATE (#PCDATA)>
<!ELEMENT ORDERS (ITEM)*>
<!ELEMENT ITEM (PRODUCT, NUMBER, PRICE)>
<!ELEMENT PRODUCT (#PCDATA | PRODUCT_ID)*>
<!ELEMENT NUMBER (#PCDATA)>
```

continues ▸

```
<!ELEMENT PRICE (#PCDATA)>
<!ELEMENT PRODUCT_ID (#PCDATA)>
]>
<DOCUMENT>
    <CUSTOMER>
        <NAME>
            <LAST_NAME>Smith</LAST_NAME>
            <FIRST_NAME>Sam</FIRST_NAME>
        </NAME>
        <DATE>October 15, 2001</DATE>
        <ORDERS>
            <ITEM>
                <PRODUCT>Tomatoes</PRODUCT>
                <NUMBER>8</NUMBER>
                <PRICE>$1.25</PRICE>
            </ITEM>
            <ITEM>
                <PRODUCT>
                    <PRODUCT_ID>
                        124829548702121
                    </PRODUCT_ID>
                </PRODUCT>
                <NUMBER>24</NUMBER>
                <PRICE>$4.98</PRICE>
            </ITEM>
        </ORDERS>
    </CUSTOMER>
    <CUSTOMER>
        <NAME>
            <LAST_NAME>Jones</LAST_NAME>
            <FIRST_NAME>Polly</FIRST_NAME>
        </NAME>
        <DATE>October 20, 2001</DATE>
        <ORDERS>
            <ITEM>
                <PRODUCT>Bread</PRODUCT>
                <NUMBER>12</NUMBER>
                <PRICE>$14.95</PRICE>
            </ITEM>
            <ITEM>
                <PRODUCT>Apples</PRODUCT>
                <NUMBER>6</NUMBER>
                <PRICE>$1.50</PRICE>
            </ITEM>
        </ORDERS>
    </CUSTOMER>
    <CUSTOMER>
        <NAME>
            <LAST_NAME>Weber</LAST_NAME>
            <FIRST_NAME>Bill</FIRST_NAME>
```

```
        </NAME>
        <DATE>October 25, 2001</DATE>
        <ORDERS>
            <ITEM>
                <PRODUCT>Asparagus</PRODUCT>
                <NUMBER>12</NUMBER>
                <PRICE>$2.95</PRICE>
            </ITEM>
            <ITEM>
                <PRODUCT>Lettuce</PRODUCT>
                <NUMBER>6</NUMBER>
                <PRICE>$11.50</PRICE>
            </ITEM>
        </ORDERS>
    </CUSTOMER>
</DOCUMENT>
```

However, there is a big drawback to using the mixed content model—you can specify only the names of the child elements that can occur. You cannot set the child elements' order or number of occurrences. And inside the mixed content model, you cannot use the +, *, or ? operators.

Because of these severe restrictions, I suggest avoiding the mixed content model. You're almost always better off declaring a new element that can hold PCDATA and including that in a standard content model instead.

Why Use the Mixed Content Model?

One possible situation to use the mixed content model is when you're translating simple text documents into XML: Using the mixed content model can handle the case in which part of the document is in XML and part in simple text.

Empty Elements

The last remaining DTD content model is the *empty content model.* In this case, the elements that you declare cannot hold any content (either PCDATA or other elements).

Declaring an element to be empty is easy; you just use the keyword `EMPTY`, like this:

```
<!ELEMENT CREDIT_WARNING EMPTY>
```

Now you can use this new element, `<CREDIT_WARNING>`, like this:

```
<CREDIT_WARNING />
```

Note that although empty elements cannot contain any content, they can have attributes (such as the XHTML `<img>` element)—we'll see how to add attributes to element declarations in the next chapter. Here's how I declare and put the `<CREDIT_WARNING>` element to work:

```
<?xml version = "1.0" standalone="yes"?>
<!DOCTYPE DOCUMENT [
<!ELEMENT DOCUMENT (CUSTOMER)*>
<!ELEMENT CUSTOMER (CREDIT_WARNING?,NAME,DATE,ORDERS)>
<!ELEMENT NAME (LAST_NAME,FIRST_NAME)>
<!ELEMENT LAST_NAME (#PCDATA)>
<!ELEMENT FIRST_NAME (#PCDATA)>
<!ELEMENT DATE (#PCDATA)>
<!ELEMENT ORDERS (ITEM)*>
<!ELEMENT ITEM (PRODUCT, NUMBER, PRICE)>
<!ELEMENT PRODUCT (#PCDATA)>
<!ELEMENT NUMBER (#PCDATA)>
<!ELEMENT PRICE (#PCDATA)>
<!ELEMENT CREDIT_WARNING EMPTY>
]>
<DOCUMENT>
    <CUSTOMER>
        <NAME>
            <LAST_NAME>Smith</LAST_NAME>
            <FIRST_NAME>Sam</FIRST_NAME>
        </NAME>
        <DATE>October 15, 2001</DATE>
        <ORDERS>
            <ITEM>
                <PRODUCT>Tomatoes</PRODUCT>
                <NUMBER>8</NUMBER>
                <PRICE>$1.25</PRICE>
            </ITEM>
            <ITEM>
                <PRODUCT>Oranges</PRODUCT>
                <NUMBER>24</NUMBER>
                <PRICE>$4.98</PRICE>
            </ITEM>
        </ORDERS>
    </CUSTOMER>
    <CUSTOMER>
        <CREDIT_WARNING />
        <NAME>
            <LAST_NAME>Jones</LAST_NAME>
            <FIRST_NAME>Polly</FIRST_NAME>
        </NAME>
        <DATE>October 20, 2001</DATE>
        <ORDERS>
            <ITEM>
                <PRODUCT>Bread</PRODUCT>
                <NUMBER>12</NUMBER>
                <PRICE>$14.95</PRICE>
            </ITEM>
            <ITEM>
                <PRODUCT>Apples</PRODUCT>
                <NUMBER>6</NUMBER>
                <PRICE>$1.50</PRICE>
```

```
            </ITEM>
        </ORDERS>
    </CUSTOMER>
    <CUSTOMER>
        <NAME>
            <LAST_NAME>Weber</LAST_NAME>
            <FIRST_NAME>Bill</FIRST_NAME>
        </NAME>
        <DATE>October 25, 2001</DATE>
        <ORDERS>
            <ITEM>
                <PRODUCT>Asparagus</PRODUCT>
                <NUMBER>12</NUMBER>
                <PRICE>$2.95</PRICE>
            </ITEM>
            <ITEM>
                <PRODUCT>Lettuce</PRODUCT>
                <NUMBER>6</NUMBER>
                <PRICE>$11.50</PRICE>
            </ITEM>
        </ORDERS>
    </CUSTOMER>
</DOCUMENT>
```

DTD Comments

As you can see, DTDs can become fairly complex, especially in longer and more involved documents. To make things easier for the DTD author, the XML specification allows you to place comments inside DTDs.

DTD comments are just like normal XML comments—in fact, they *are* normal XML comments, and they're often stripped out by the XML processor. (W3C allows XML processors to remove comments, but some processors pass comments on to the underlying application.) Here's an example where I have added comments to order.xml:

```
<?xml version = "1.0" standalone="yes"?>
<!DOCTYPE DOCUMENT [
<!-- DOCUMENT is the root element -->
<!ELEMENT DOCUMENT (CUSTOMER)*>
<!-- CUSTOMER stores customer data -->
<!ELEMENT CUSTOMER (NAME,DATE,ORDERS)>
<!-- NAME stores the customer name-->
<!ELEMENT NAME (LAST_NAME,FIRST_NAME)>
<!-- LAST_NAME stores customer's last name -->
<!ELEMENT LAST_NAME (#PCDATA)>
<!-- FIRST_NAME stores customer's last name -->
<!ELEMENT FIRST_NAME (#PCDATA)>
<!-- DATE stores order date -->
<!ELEMENT DATE (#PCDATA)>
```

continues ▸

```
<!-- ORDERS stores customer orders -->
<!ELEMENT ORDERS (ITEM)*>
<!-- ITEM represents a customer purchase -->
<!ELEMENT ITEM (PRODUCT,NUMBER,PRICE)>
<!-- PRODUCT represents a purchased product -->
<!ELEMENT PRODUCT (#PCDATA)>
<!-- NUMBER indicates the number of the item purchased -->
<!ELEMENT NUMBER (#PCDATA)>
<!-- PRICE is the item's price -->
<!ELEMENT PRICE (#PCDATA)>
]>
<DOCUMENT>
    <CUSTOMER>
        <NAME>
            <LAST_NAME>Smith</LAST_NAME>
            <FIRST_NAME>Sam</FIRST_NAME>
        </NAME>
        <DATE>October 15, 2001</DATE>
        <ORDERS>
            <ITEM>
                <PRODUCT>Tomatoes</PRODUCT>
                <NUMBER>8</NUMBER>
                <PRICE>$1.25</PRICE>
            </ITEM>
            <ITEM>
                <PRODUCT>Oranges</PRODUCT>
                <NUMBER>24</NUMBER>
                <PRICE>$4.98</PRICE>
            </ITEM>
        </ORDERS>
    </CUSTOMER>
    <CUSTOMER>
        <NAME>
            <LAST_NAME>Jones</LAST_NAME>
            <FIRST_NAME>Polly</FIRST_NAME>
        </NAME>
        <DATE>October 20, 2001</DATE>
        <ORDERS>
            <ITEM>
                <PRODUCT>Bread</PRODUCT>
                <NUMBER>12</NUMBER>
                <PRICE>$14.95</PRICE>
            </ITEM>
            <ITEM>
                <PRODUCT>Apples</PRODUCT>
                <NUMBER>6</NUMBER>
                <PRICE>$1.50</PRICE>
            </ITEM>
        </ORDERS>
    </CUSTOMER>
    <CUSTOMER>
```

```
        <NAME>
            <LAST_NAME>Weber</LAST_NAME>
            <FIRST_NAME>Bill</FIRST_NAME>
        </NAME>
        <DATE>October 25, 2001</DATE>
        <ORDERS>
            <ITEM>
                <PRODUCT>Asparagus</PRODUCT>
                <NUMBER>12</NUMBER>
                <PRICE>$2.95</PRICE>
            </ITEM>
            <ITEM>
                <PRODUCT>Lettuce</PRODUCT>
                <NUMBER>6</NUMBER>
                <PRICE>$11.50</PRICE>
            </ITEM>
        </ORDERS>
    </CUSTOMER>
</DOCUMENT>
```

A DTD Example

Because being able to create DTDs is an essential XML skill these days (at least, until XML schemas are widely supported), I'll work through another example here.

This new example is a model for a book, complete with `<CHAPTER>`, `<SECTION>`, `<PART>`, and `<SUBTITLE>` elements. Here's what the document will look like:

```
<?xml version="1.0"?>
<!DOCTYPE BOOK [
    <!ELEMENT p (#PCDATA)>
    <!ELEMENT BOOK         (OPENER,SUBTITLE?,INTRODUCTION?,(SECTION | PART)+)>
    <!ELEMENT OPENER       (TITLE_TEXT)*>
    <!ELEMENT TITLE_TEXT   (#PCDATA)>
    <!ELEMENT SUBTITLE     (#PCDATA)>
    <!ELEMENT INTRODUCTION (HEADER, p+)+>
    <!ELEMENT PART         (HEADER, CHAPTER+)>
    <!ELEMENT SECTION      (HEADER, p+)>
    <!ELEMENT HEADER       (#PCDATA)>
    <!ELEMENT CHAPTER      (CHAPTER_NUMBER, CHAPTER_TEXT)>
    <!ELEMENT CHAPTER_NUMBER (#PCDATA)>
    <!ELEMENT CHAPTER_TEXT (p)+>
]>
<BOOK>
    <OPENER>
        <TITLE_TEXT>
            All About Me
        </TITLE_TEXT>
    </OPENER>
```

continues ▸

```
    <PART>
        <HEADER>Welcome To My Book</HEADER>
        <CHAPTER>
            <CHAPTER_NUMBER>CHAPTER 1</CHAPTER_NUMBER>
            <CHAPTER_TEXT>
                <p>Glad you want to hear about me.</p>
                <p>There's so much to say!</p>
                <p>Where should we start?</p>
                <p>How about more about me?</p>
            </CHAPTER_TEXT>
        </CHAPTER>
    </PART>
</BOOK>
```

In this case, I'll start the DTD by declaring the <p> element, which I want to hold text only—that is, PCDATA, which you specify with #PCDATA:

```
<!ELEMENT p             (#PCDATA)>
    .
    .
    .
```

Next, I'll declare the <BOOK> element, which is the root element. In this case, the <BOOK> element contains an <OPENER> element, possibly a <SUBTITLE> element, possibly an <INTRODUCTION> element, and one or more sections or parts declared with the <SECTION> and <PART> elements:

```
<!ELEMENT p             (#PCDATA)>
<!ELEMENT BOOK          (OPENER,SUBTITLE?,INTRODUCTION?,(SECTION | PART)+)>
    .
    .
    .
```

Now I will declare the <OPENER> element. This element will hold the title text for the chapter, which I'll store in <TITLE_TEXT> elements:

```
<!ELEMENT p             (#PCDATA)>
<!ELEMENT BOOK          (OPENER,SUBTITLE?,INTRODUCTION?,(SECTION | PART)+)>
<!ELEMENT OPENER        (TITLE_TEXT)*>
    .
    .
    .
```

I'll declare the <TITLE_TEXT> element so that it contains plain text:

```
<!ELEMENT p             (#PCDATA)>
<!ELEMENT BOOK          (OPENER,SUBTITLE?,INTRODUCTION?,(SECTION | PART)+)>
<!ELEMENT OPENER        (TITLE_TEXT)*>
<!ELEMENT TITLE_TEXT    (#PCDATA)>
    .
    .
    .
```

And I declare the <SUBTITLE> element, which must also contain PCDATA:

```
<!ELEMENT p            (#PCDATA)>
<!ELEMENT BOOK         (OPENER,SUBTITLE?,INTRODUCTION?,(SECTION | PART)+)>
<!ELEMENT OPENER       (TITLE_TEXT)*>
<!ELEMENT TITLE_TEXT   (#PCDATA)>
<!ELEMENT SUBTITLE     (#PCDATA)>
        .
        .
        .
```

I'll set up the <INTRODUCTION> element so that it contains a <HEADER> element and so that it must contain one or more <p> elements. I'll then allow that sequence to repeat, like this:

```
<!ELEMENT p            (#PCDATA)>
<!ELEMENT BOOK         (OPENER,SUBTITLE?,INTRODUCTION?,(SECTION | PART)+)>
<!ELEMENT OPENER       (TITLE_TEXT)*>
<!ELEMENT TITLE_TEXT   (#PCDATA)>
<!ELEMENT SUBTITLE     (#PCDATA)>
<!ELEMENT INTRODUCTION (HEADER, p+)+>
        .
        .
        .
```

Next, the <PART> element contains a <HEADER> and one or more <CHAPTER> elements:

```
<!ELEMENT p            (#PCDATA)>
<!ELEMENT BOOK         (OPENER,SUBTITLE?,INTRODUCTION?,(SECTION | PART)+)>
<!ELEMENT OPENER       (TITLE_TEXT)*>
<!ELEMENT TITLE_TEXT   (#PCDATA)>
<!ELEMENT SUBTITLE     (#PCDATA)>
<!ELEMENT INTRODUCTION (HEADER, p+)+>
<!ELEMENT PART         (HEADER, CHAPTER+)>
        .
        .
        .
```

In addition, I'll specify that the <CHAPTER> element must contain a <CHAPTER_NUMBER> and <CHAPTER_TEXT> element:

```
<!ELEMENT p            (#PCDATA)>
<!ELEMENT BOOK         (OPENER,SUBTITLE?,INTRODUCTION?,(SECTION | PART)+)>
<!ELEMENT OPENER       (TITLE_TEXT)*>
<!ELEMENT TITLE_TEXT   (#PCDATA)>
<!ELEMENT SUBTITLE     (#PCDATA)>
<!ELEMENT INTRODUCTION (HEADER, p+)+>
<!ELEMENT PART         (HEADER, CHAPTER+)>
```

continues ▸

```
<!ELEMENT SECTION      (HEADER, p+)>
<!ELEMENT HEADER       (#PCDATA)>
    <!ELEMENT CHAPTER  (CHAPTER_NUMBER, CHAPTER_TEXT)>
        .
        .
        .
```

The <CHAPTER_NUMBER> element contains parsed character data:

```
<!ELEMENT p            (#PCDATA)>
<!ELEMENT BOOK         (OPENER,SUBTITLE?,INTRODUCTION?,(SECTION | PART)+)>
<!ELEMENT OPENER       (TITLE_TEXT)*>
<!ELEMENT TITLE_TEXT   (#PCDATA)>
<!ELEMENT SUBTITLE     (#PCDATA)>
<!ELEMENT INTRODUCTION (HEADER, p+)+>
<!ELEMENT PART         (HEADER, CHAPTER+)>
<!ELEMENT SECTION      (HEADER, p+)>
<!ELEMENT HEADER       (#PCDATA)>
<!ELEMENT CHAPTER  (CHAPTER_NUMBER, CHAPTER_TEXT)>
<!ELEMENT CHAPTER_NUMBER (#PCDATA)>
        .
        .
        .
```

Finally, the <CHAPTER_TEXT> element can contain <p> paragraph elements:

```
    <!ELEMENT p (#PCDATA)>
    <!ELEMENT BOOK         (OPENER,SUBTITLE?,INTRODUCTION?,(SECTION | PART)+)>
    <!ELEMENT OPENER       (TITLE_TEXT)*>
    <!ELEMENT TITLE_TEXT   (#PCDATA)>
    <!ELEMENT SUBTITLE     (#PCDATA)>
    <!ELEMENT INTRODUCTION (HEADER, p+)+>
    <!ELEMENT PART         (HEADER, CHAPTER+)>
    <!ELEMENT SECTION      (HEADER, p+)>
    <!ELEMENT HEADER       (#PCDATA)>
    <!ELEMENT CHAPTER      (CHAPTER_NUMBER, CHAPTER_TEXT)>
    <!ELEMENT CHAPTER_NUMBER (#PCDATA)>
    <!ELEMENT CHAPTER_TEXT (p)+>
```

And that's it; the DTD is finished. Here's how it looks in the <!DOCTYPE> element in the complete document:

```
<?xml version="1.0"?>
<!DOCTYPE BOOK [
    <!ELEMENT p (#PCDATA)>
    <!ELEMENT BOOK         (OPENER,SUBTITLE?,INTRODUCTION?,(SECTION | PART)+)>
    <!ELEMENT OPENER       (TITLE_TEXT)*>
    <!ELEMENT TITLE_TEXT   (#PCDATA)>
    <!ELEMENT SUBTITLE     (#PCDATA)>
    <!ELEMENT INTRODUCTION (HEADER, p+)+>
    <!ELEMENT PART         (HEADER, CHAPTER+)>
    <!ELEMENT SECTION      (HEADER, p+)>
    <!ELEMENT HEADER       (#PCDATA)>
```

```
    <!ELEMENT CHAPTER       (CHAPTER_NUMBER, CHAPTER_TEXT)>
    <!ELEMENT CHAPTER_NUMBER (#PCDATA)>
    <!ELEMENT CHAPTER_TEXT (p)+>
]>
<BOOK>
    <OPENER>
        <TITLE_TEXT>
            All About Me
        </TITLE_TEXT>
    </OPENER>
    <PART>
        <HEADER>Welcome To My Book</HEADER>
        <CHAPTER>
            <CHAPTER_NUMBER>CHAPTER 1</CHAPTER_NUMBER>
            <CHAPTER_TEXT>
                <p>Glad you want to hear about me.</p>
                <p>There's so much to say!</p>
                <p>Where should we start?</p>
                <p>How about more about me?</p>
            </CHAPTER_TEXT>
        </CHAPTER>
    </PART>
</BOOK>
```

External DTDs

The DTDs I've created in this chapter so far have all been built into the documents that they are targeted for. However, you can also create and use *external* DTDs, where the actual DTD is stored in an external file (usually with the extension .dtd).

Using external DTDs makes it easy to create an XML application that can be shared by many people—in fact, that's the way many XML applications are supported. There are two ways to specify external DTDs—as *private* DTDs or as *public* DTDs. I'll take a look at private DTDs first.

Private DTDs are intended for use by people or groups privately—not for public distribution. You specify an external private DTD with the `SYSTEM` keyword in the `<!DOCTYPE>` element like this (notice also that because this document now depends on an external file, the DTD file order.dtd, I've changed the value of the standalone attribute from `"yes"` to `"no"`):

```
<?xml version = "1.0" standalone="no"?>
<!DOCTYPE DOCUMENT SYSTEM "order.dtd">
<DOCUMENT>
    <CUSTOMER>
        <NAME>
            <LAST_NAME>Smith</LAST_NAME>
            <FIRST_NAME>Sam</FIRST_NAME>
```

continues ▸

```
        </NAME>
        <DATE>October 15, 2001</DATE>
        <ORDERS>
            <ITEM>
                <PRODUCT>Tomatoes</PRODUCT>
                <NUMBER>8</NUMBER>
                <PRICE>$1.25</PRICE>
            </ITEM>
            <ITEM>
                <PRODUCT>Oranges</PRODUCT>
                <NUMBER>24</NUMBER>
                <PRICE>$4.98</PRICE>
            </ITEM>
            .
            .
            .
            <ITEM>
                <PRODUCT>Asparagus</PRODUCT>
                <NUMBER>12</NUMBER>
                <PRICE>$2.95</PRICE>
            </ITEM>
            <ITEM>
                <PRODUCT>Lettuce</PRODUCT>
                <NUMBER>6</NUMBER>
                <PRICE>$11.50</PRICE>
            </ITEM>
        </ORDERS>
    </CUSTOMER>
</DOCUMENT>
```

Here's the file order.dtd that holds the external DTD—note that it simply holds the part of the document that was originally between the [and] in the <!DOCTYPE> element:

```
<!ELEMENT DOCUMENT (CUSTOMER)*>
<!ELEMENT CUSTOMER (NAME,DATE,ORDERS)>
<!ELEMENT NAME (LAST_NAME,FIRST_NAME)>
<!ELEMENT LAST_NAME (#PCDATA)>
<!ELEMENT FIRST_NAME (#PCDATA)>
<!ELEMENT DATE (#PCDATA)>
<!ELEMENT ORDERS (ITEM)*>
<!ELEMENT ITEM (PRODUCT,NUMBER,PRICE)>
<!ELEMENT PRODUCT (#PCDATA)>
<!ELEMENT NUMBER (#PCDATA)>
<!ELEMENT PRICE (#PCDATA)>
```

Using Document Type Definitions with URLs

The previous example just listed the name of an external DTD in the <!DOCTYPE> element, but if the DTD is not in the same directory on the Web site as the document itself, you can specify a URI (which is currently implemented as URLs for today's XML processors) for the DTD like this:

```
<?xml version = "1.0" standalone="no"?>
<!DOCTYPE DOCUMENT SYSTEM
    "http://www.starpowder.com/dtd/order.dtd">
<DOCUMENT>
    <CUSTOMER>
        <NAME>
            <LAST_NAME>Smith</LAST_NAME>
            <FIRST_NAME>Sam</FIRST_NAME>
        </NAME>
        <DATE>October 15, 2001</DATE>
        <ORDERS>
            <ITEM>
                <PRODUCT>Tomatoes</PRODUCT>
                <NUMBER>8</NUMBER>
                <PRICE>$1.25</PRICE>
            </ITEM>
            <ITEM>
                <PRODUCT>Oranges</PRODUCT>
                <NUMBER>24</NUMBER>
                <PRICE>$4.98</PRICE>
            </ITEM>
                .
                .
                .
            <ITEM>
                <PRODUCT>Asparagus</PRODUCT>
                <NUMBER>12</NUMBER>
                <PRICE>$2.95</PRICE>
            </ITEM>
            <ITEM>
                <PRODUCT>Lettuce</PRODUCT>
                <NUMBER>6</NUMBER>
                <PRICE>$11.50</PRICE>
            </ITEM>
        </ORDERS>
    </CUSTOMER>
</DOCUMENT>
```

This is also very useful, of course, if you're using someone else's DTD. In fact, there's a special way of using DTDs intended for public distribution.

Public Document Type Definitions

When you have a DTD that's intended for public use, you use the `PUBLIC` keyword instead of `SYSTEM` in the `<!DOCTYPE>` document type declaration. To use the `PUBLIC` keyword, you must also create a *formal public identifier* (FPI), and there are specific rules for FPIs:

- The first field in an FPI specifies the connection of the DTD to a formal standard. For DTDs that you're defining yourself, this field should be `"-"`. If a nonstandards body has approved the DTD, use `"+"`. For formal standards, this field is a reference to the standard itself (such as `ISO/IEC 13449:2000`).
- The second field must hold the name of the group or person that is going to maintain or be responsible for the DTD. In this case, you should use a name that is unique and that identifies your group easily (for example, W3C simply uses `W3C`).
- The third field must indicate the type of document that is described, preferably followed by a unique identifier of some kind (such as `Version 1.0`). This part should include a version number that you'll update.
- The fourth field specifies the language that your DTD uses (for example, for English you use `EN`). Note that two-letter language specifiers allow only a maximum of $24 \times 24 = 576$ possible languages; expect to see three-letter language specifiers in the near future.
- Fields in an FPI must be separated by double slash (`//`).

Here's how I can modify the previous example to include a public DTD, complete with its own FPI:

```
<?xml version = "1.0" standalone="no"?>
<!DOCTYPE DOCUMENT PUBLIC "-//starpowder//Custom XML Version 1.0//EN"
    "http://www.starpowder.com/steve/order.dtd">
<DOCUMENT>
    <CUSTOMER>
        <NAME>
            <LAST_NAME>Smith</LAST_NAME>
            <FIRST_NAME>Sam</FIRST_NAME>
        </NAME>
        <DATE>October 15, 2001</DATE>
        <ORDERS>
            <ITEM>
                <PRODUCT>Tomatoes</PRODUCT>
                <NUMBER>8</NUMBER>
                <PRICE>$1.25</PRICE>
            </ITEM>
            <ITEM>
```

```
            <PRODUCT>Oranges</PRODUCT>
            <NUMBER>24</NUMBER>
            <PRICE>$4.98</PRICE>
        </ITEM>
        .
        .
        .
        <ITEM>
            <PRODUCT>Asparagus</PRODUCT>
            <NUMBER>12</NUMBER>
            <PRICE>$2.95</PRICE>
        </ITEM>
        <ITEM>
            <PRODUCT>Lettuce</PRODUCT>
            <NUMBER>6</NUMBER>
            <PRICE>$11.50</PRICE>
        </ITEM>
    </ORDERS>
  </CUSTOMER>
</DOCUMENT>
```

Note the syntax of the `<!DOCTYPE>` element in this case: `<!DOCTYPE` *`rootname`* `PUBLIC` *`FPI URL`*`>`. Here's the external DTD, order.dtd, which is the same as in the previous example:

```
<!ELEMENT DOCUMENT (CUSTOMER)*>
<!ELEMENT CUSTOMER (NAME,DATE,ORDERS)>
<!ELEMENT NAME (LAST_NAME,FIRST_NAME)>
<!ELEMENT LAST_NAME (#PCDATA)>
<!ELEMENT FIRST_NAME (#PCDATA)>
<!ELEMENT DATE (#PCDATA)>
<!ELEMENT ORDERS (ITEM)*>
<!ELEMENT ITEM (PRODUCT,NUMBER,PRICE)>
<!ELEMENT PRODUCT (#PCDATA)>
<!ELEMENT NUMBER (#PCDATA)>
<!ELEMENT PRICE (#PCDATA)>
```

Using Both Internal and External DTDs

In fact, you can use *both* internal and external DTDs at the same time, using these forms of the `<!DOCTYPE>` element: `<!DOCTYPE` *`rootname`* `SYSTEM` *`URL`* `[`*`DTD`*`]>` for private external DTDs and `<!DOCTYPE` *`rootname`* `PUBLIC` *`FPI URL`* `[`*`DTD`*`]>` for public external DTDs. In this case, the external DTD is specified by *`URL`* and the internal one by *`DTD`*.

Here's an example where I've removed the `<PRODUCT>` element from the external DTD order.dtd:

```
<!ELEMENT DOCUMENT (CUSTOMER)*>
<!ELEMENT CUSTOMER (NAME,DATE,ORDERS)>
<!ELEMENT NAME (LAST_NAME,FIRST_NAME)>
<!ELEMENT LAST_NAME (#PCDATA)>
<!ELEMENT FIRST_NAME (#PCDATA)>
<!ELEMENT DATE (#PCDATA)>
<!ELEMENT ORDERS (ITEM)*>
<!ELEMENT ITEM (PRODUCT,NUMBER,PRICE)>
<!ELEMENT NUMBER (#PCDATA)>
<!ELEMENT PRICE (#PCDATA)>
```

Now I'll specify that I want to use this external DTD in the document's `<!DOCTYPE>` element—but also add square brackets, `[` and `]`, to enclose an internal DTD as well:

```
<?xml version = "1.0" standalone="no"?>
<!DOCTYPE DOCUMENT SYSTEM "order.dtd" [
    .
    .
    .
]>
<DOCUMENT>
    <CUSTOMER>
        <NAME>
            <LAST_NAME>Smith</LAST_NAME>
            <FIRST_NAME>Sam</FIRST_NAME>
        </NAME>
        <DATE>October 15, 2001</DATE>
        <ORDERS>
            <ITEM>
                <PRODUCT>
                    <PRODUCT_ID>
                        198348209
                    </PRODUCT_ID>
                </PRODUCT>
                <NUMBER>8</NUMBER>
                <PRICE>$1.25</PRICE>
            </ITEM>
            .
            .
            .
            <ITEM>
                <PRODUCT>
                    <PRODUCT_ID>
                        198348206
                    </PRODUCT_ID>
                </PRODUCT>
                <NUMBER>6</NUMBER>
                <PRICE>$11.50</PRICE>
            </ITEM>
        </ORDERS>
    </CUSTOMER>
</DOCUMENT>
```

Next, I add the declaration of the <PRODUCT> element to the internal part of the DTD, like this:

```
<?xml version = "1.0" standalone="no"?>
<!DOCTYPE DOCUMENT SYSTEM "order.dtd" [
<!ELEMENT PRODUCT (PRODUCT_ID)>
<!ELEMENT PRODUCT_ID (#PCDATA)>
]>
<DOCUMENT>
    <CUSTOMER>
        <NAME>
            <LAST_NAME>Smith</LAST_NAME>
            <FIRST_NAME>Sam</FIRST_NAME>
        </NAME>
        <DATE>October 15, 2001</DATE>
        <ORDERS>
            <ITEM>
                <PRODUCT>
                    <PRODUCT_ID>
                        198348209
                    </PRODUCT_ID>
                </PRODUCT>
                <NUMBER>8</NUMBER>
                <PRICE>$1.25</PRICE>
            </ITEM>
            .
            .
            .
            <ITEM>
                <PRODUCT>
                    <PRODUCT_ID>
                        198348206
                    </PRODUCT_ID>
                </PRODUCT>
                <NUMBER>6</NUMBER>
                <PRICE>$11.50</PRICE>
            </ITEM>
        </ORDERS>
    </CUSTOMER>
</DOCUMENT>
```

And that's all it takes; now this DTD uses both internal and external parts.

If It's Both Internal and External, Which Takes Precedence?

Theoretically, if an element or attribute is defined in both an internal and external DTD, the definition in the internal DTD is supposed to take precedence, overwriting the external definition. Things were arranged that way to let you customize external DTDs as you like. However, my experience is that most XML processors simply consider it an error if there is an element or attribute conflict between internal and external DTDs, and they usually just halt.

Namespaces and DTDs

There's one more topic that I want to cover now that we're discussing the basics of creating DTDs—how to use namespaces when you're using DTDs. In fact, this will give us an introduction to the next chapter, where we'll work with declaring attributes as well as elements.

The important thing to recall is that as far as standard XML processors are concerned, namespace prefixes are just text prepended to tag and attribute names with a colon, so they change those tag and attribute names. This means that those names must be declared, with their prefixes, in the DTD.

Here's an example; I'll start with the easy case where I'm using a default namespace like this:

```
<?xml version = "1.0" standalone="yes"?>
<!DOCTYPE DOCUMENT [
<!ELEMENT DOCUMENT (CUSTOMER)*>
<!ELEMENT CUSTOMER (NAME,DATE,ORDERS)>
<!ELEMENT NAME (LAST_NAME,FIRST_NAME)>
<!ELEMENT LAST_NAME (#PCDATA)>
<!ELEMENT FIRST_NAME (#PCDATA)>
<!ELEMENT DATE (#PCDATA)>
<!ELEMENT ORDERS (ITEM)*>
<!ELEMENT ITEM (PRODUCT,NUMBER,PRICE)>
<!ELEMENT PRODUCT (#PCDATA)>
<!ELEMENT NUMBER (#PCDATA)>
<!ELEMENT PRICE (#PCDATA)>
]>
<DOCUMENT xmlns="http://www.starpowder.com/dtd/">
    <CUSTOMER>
        <NAME>
            <LAST_NAME>Smith</LAST_NAME>
            <FIRST_NAME>Sam</FIRST_NAME>
        </NAME>
        <DATE>October 15, 2001</DATE>
        <ORDERS>
            <ITEM>
                <PRODUCT>Tomatoes</PRODUCT>
                <NUMBER>8</NUMBER>
                <PRICE>$1.25</PRICE>
            </ITEM>
    .
    .
    .
            <ITEM>
                <PRODUCT>Asparagus</PRODUCT>
                <NUMBER>12</NUMBER>
                <PRICE>$2.95</PRICE>
            </ITEM>
            <ITEM>
```

```
                <PRODUCT>Lettuce</PRODUCT>
                <NUMBER>6</NUMBER>
                <PRICE>$11.50</PRICE>
            </ITEM>
        </ORDERS>
    </CUSTOMER>
</DOCUMENT>
```

Some validating XML processors aren't going to understand the `xmlns` attribute that you use to declare a namespace. (See the later section "Validating Against a DTD," for details on XML validators.) This means that you must declare that attribute like this; here, I'm using the `<!ATTLIST>` element (as we'll see how to do in the next chapter) to declare this attribute, indicating that the `xmlns` attribute has a fixed value, which I'm setting to the namespace identifier, `"http://www.starpowder.com/dtd/"`:

```
<?xml version = "1.0" standalone="yes"?>
<!DOCTYPE DOCUMENT [
<!ELEMENT DOCUMENT (CUSTOMER)*>
<!ATTLIST DOCUMENT
    xmlns CDATA #FIXED "http://www.starpowder.com/dtd/">
<!ELEMENT CUSTOMER (NAME,DATE,ORDERS)>
<!ELEMENT NAME (LAST_NAME,FIRST_NAME)>
<!ELEMENT LAST_NAME (#PCDATA)>
<!ELEMENT FIRST_NAME (#PCDATA)>
<!ELEMENT DATE (#PCDATA)>
<!ELEMENT ORDERS (ITEM)*>
<!ELEMENT ITEM (PRODUCT,NUMBER,PRICE)>
<!ELEMENT PRODUCT (#PCDATA)>
<!ELEMENT NUMBER (#PCDATA)>
<!ELEMENT PRICE (#PCDATA)>
]>
<DOCUMENT xmlns="http://www.starpowder.com/dtd/">
    <CUSTOMER>
        <NAME>
            <LAST_NAME>Smith</LAST_NAME>
            <FIRST_NAME>Sam</FIRST_NAME>
        </NAME>
        <DATE>October 15, 2001</DATE>
        <ORDERS>
            <ITEM>
                <PRODUCT>Tomatoes</PRODUCT>
                <NUMBER>8</NUMBER>
                <PRICE>$1.25</PRICE>
            </ITEM>
    .
    .
    .
            <ITEM>
```

continues ▸

```
                <PRODUCT>Asparagus</PRODUCT>
                <NUMBER>12</NUMBER>
                <PRICE>$2.95</PRICE>
            </ITEM>
            <ITEM>
                <PRODUCT>Lettuce</PRODUCT>
                <NUMBER>6</NUMBER>
                <PRICE>$11.50</PRICE>
            </ITEM>
        </ORDERS>
    </CUSTOMER>
</DOCUMENT>
```

Now I'm free to use the `xmlns` attribute in the root element. That's all there is to setting up a default namespace when using DTDs.

However, if you want to use a namespace *prefix* throughout a document, the process is a little more involved. In this next example, I use the namespace prefix `doc:` for the namespace `"http://www.starpowder.com/dtd/"`. To do that, I declare a new attribute, `xmlns:doc`, and use that attribute in the root element like this to set up the namespace:

```
<?xml version = "1.0" standalone="yes"?>
<!DOCTYPE DOCUMENT [
<!ELEMENT DOCUMENT (CUSTOMER)*>
<!ATTLIST doc:DOCUMENT
    xmlns:doc CDATA #FIXED "http://www.starpowder.com/dtd/">
<!ELEMENT CUSTOMER (NAME,DATE,ORDERS)>
<!ELEMENT NAME (LAST_NAME,FIRST_NAME)>
<!ELEMENT LAST_NAME (#PCDATA)>
<!ELEMENT FIRST_NAME (#PCDATA)>
<!ELEMENT DATE (#PCDATA)>
<!ELEMENT ORDERS (ITEM)*>
<!ELEMENT ITEM (PRODUCT,NUMBER,PRICE)>
<!ELEMENT PRODUCT (#PCDATA)>
<!ELEMENT NUMBER (#PCDATA)>
<!ELEMENT PRICE (#PCDATA)>
]>
<DOCUMENT xmlns:doc="http://www.starpowder.com/dtd/">
    <CUSTOMER>
        <NAME>
            <LAST_NAME>Smith</LAST_NAME>
            <FIRST_NAME>Sam</FIRST_NAME>
        </NAME>
        <DATE>October 15, 2001</DATE>
        <ORDERS>
            <ITEM>
                <PRODUCT>Tomatoes</PRODUCT>
                <NUMBER>8</NUMBER>
                <PRICE>$1.25</PRICE>
            </ITEM>
    .
    .
    .
```

```
            <ITEM>
                <PRODUCT>Asparagus</PRODUCT>
                <NUMBER>12</NUMBER>
                <PRICE>$2.95</PRICE>
            </ITEM>
            <ITEM>
                <PRODUCT>Lettuce</PRODUCT>
                <NUMBER>6</NUMBER>
                <PRICE>$11.50</PRICE>
            </ITEM>
        </ORDERS>
    </CUSTOMER>
</DOCUMENT>
```

Now I can the doc: prefix throughout the document, where necessary:

```
<?xml version = "1.0" standalone="yes"?>
<!DOCTYPE doc:DOCUMENT [
<!ELEMENT doc:DOCUMENT (doc:CUSTOMER)*>
<!ATTLIST doc:DOCUMENT
    xmlns:doc CDATA #FIXED "http://www.starpowder.com/dtd/">
<!ELEMENT doc:CUSTOMER (doc:NAME,doc:DATE,doc:ORDERS)>
<!ELEMENT doc:NAME (doc:LAST_NAME,doc:FIRST_NAME)>
<!ELEMENT doc:LAST_NAME (#PCDATA)>
<!ELEMENT doc:FIRST_NAME (#PCDATA)>
<!ELEMENT doc:DATE (#PCDATA)>
<!ELEMENT doc:ORDERS (doc:ITEM)*>
<!ELEMENT doc:ITEM (doc:PRODUCT,doc:NUMBER,doc:PRICE)>
<!ELEMENT doc:PRODUCT (#PCDATA)>
<!ELEMENT doc:NUMBER (#PCDATA)>
<!ELEMENT doc:PRICE (#PCDATA)>
]>
<doc:DOCUMENT xmlns:doc="http://www.starpowder.com/dtd/">
    <doc:CUSTOMER>
        <doc:NAME>
            <doc:LAST_NAME>Smith</doc:LAST_NAME>
            <doc:FIRST_NAME>Sam</doc:FIRST_NAME>
        </doc:NAME>
        <doc:DATE>October 15, 2001</doc:DATE>
        <doc:ORDERS>
            <doc:ITEM>
                <doc:PRODUCT>Tomatoes</doc:PRODUCT>
                <doc:NUMBER>8</doc:NUMBER>
                <doc:PRICE>$1.25</doc:PRICE>
            </doc:ITEM>
            <doc:ITEM>
                <doc:PRODUCT>Oranges</doc:PRODUCT>
                <doc:NUMBER>24</doc:NUMBER>
                <doc:PRICE>$4.98</doc:PRICE>
```

continues ▸

```
            </doc:ITEM>
        </doc:ORDERS>
    </doc:CUSTOMER>
    <doc:CUSTOMER>
        <doc:NAME>
            <doc:LAST_NAME>Jones</doc:LAST_NAME>
            <doc:FIRST_NAME>Polly</doc:FIRST_NAME>
        </doc:NAME>
        <doc:DATE>October 20, 2001</doc:DATE>
        <doc:ORDERS>
            <doc:ITEM>
                <doc:PRODUCT>Bread</doc:PRODUCT>
                <doc:NUMBER>12</doc:NUMBER>
                <doc:PRICE>$14.95</doc:PRICE>
            </doc:ITEM>
            <doc:ITEM>
                <doc:PRODUCT>Apples</doc:PRODUCT>
                <doc:NUMBER>6</doc:NUMBER>
                <doc:PRICE>$1.50</doc:PRICE>
            </doc:ITEM>
        </doc:ORDERS>
    </doc:CUSTOMER>
    <doc:CUSTOMER>
        <doc:NAME>
            <doc:LAST_NAME>Weber</doc:LAST_NAME>
            <doc:FIRST_NAME>Bill</doc:FIRST_NAME>
        </doc:NAME>
        <doc:DATE>October 25, 2001</doc:DATE>
        <doc:ORDERS>
            <doc:ITEM>
                <doc:PRODUCT>Asparagus</doc:PRODUCT>
                <doc:NUMBER>12</doc:NUMBER>
                <doc:PRICE>$2.95</doc:PRICE>
            </doc:ITEM>
            <doc:ITEM>
                <doc:PRODUCT>Lettuce</doc:PRODUCT>
                <doc:NUMBER>6</doc:NUMBER>
                <doc:PRICE>$11.50</doc:PRICE>
            </doc:ITEM>
        </doc:ORDERS>
    </doc:CUSTOMER>
</doc:DOCUMENT>
```

And that's all it takes—now this document, complete with namespace, is valid. This example has introduced us to a very important topic—declaring attributes in DTDs. I'll take a look at how that works in the next chapter.

Validating Against a DTD

How do you really know if your XML document is valid? One way is to check it with an XML validator, and there are plenty out there to choose from. As explained in Chapter 1, validators are packages that will check your XML and give you feedback. For example, if you have the XML for Java parser from IBM's AlphaWorks installed, you can use the DOMWriter program as a complete XML validator. In Chapter 1, I created this document, greeting.xml:

```
<?xml version="1.0" encoding="UTF-8"?>
<DOCUMENT>
    <GREETING>
        Hello From XML
    </GREETING>
    <MESSAGE>
        Welcome to the wild and woolly world of XML.
    </MESSAGE>
</DOCUMENT>
```

I tested this document using DOMWriter (we'll see more about the command-line syntax required in Chapter 11, "Java and the XML DOM"):

```
%java dom.DOMWriter greeting.xml
greeting.xml:
[Error] greeting.xml:2:11: Element type "DOCUMENT" must be declared
[Error] greeting.xml:3:15: Element type "GREETING" must be declared
[Error] greeting.xml:6:14: Element type "MESSAGE" must be declared.
<?xml version="1.0" encoding="UTF-8"?>
<DOCUMENT>
    <GREETING>
        Hello From XML
    </GREETING>
    <MESSAGE>
        Welcome to the wild and woolly world of XML.
    </MESSAGE>
</DOCUMENT>
```

In this case, DOMWriter is complaining about the lack of a DTD in greeting.xml, which means that it can't check for the validity of the document.

Here's a list of some of the XML validators on the Web:

- `http://validator.w3.org/`. The official W3C HTML validator. Although it's officially for HTML, it also includes some XML support. Your XML document must be online to be checked with this validator.
- `www.w3.org/People/Raggett/tidy/`. Tidy is a beloved utility for cleaning up and repairing Web pages, and it includes limited support for XML. Your XML document must be online to be checked with this validator.

- `www.xml.com/xml/pub/tools/ruwf/check.html`. This is XML.com's XML validator based on the Lark processor. Your XML document must be online to be checked with this validator.
- `www.ltg.ed.ac.uk/~richard/xml-check.html`. The Language Technology Group at the University of Edinburgh's validator is based on the RXP parser. Your XML document must be online to be checked with this validator.
- `www.stg.brown.edu/service/xmlvalid/`. This is an excellent XML validator from the Scholarly Technology Group at Brown University. This is the only online XML validator that I know of that allows you to check XML documents that are not online—you can use the Web page's file upload control to specify the name of the file on your hard disk that you want to have uploaded and checked.

To see one of these online validators at work, take a look at Figure 3.1. There, I'm asking the XML validator from the Scholarly Technology Group to validate greeting.xml after I've added a DTD and purposely exchanged the order of the `<MESSAGE>` and `</GREETING>` tags:

```
<?xml version="1.0" encoding="UTF-8"?>
<!DOCTYPE DOCUMENT [
    <!ELEMENT DOCUMENT (GREETING, MESSAGE)>
    <!ELEMENT GREETING (#PCDATA)>
    <!ELEMENT MESSAGE (#PCDATA)>
]>
<DOCUMENT>
    <GREETING>
        Hello From XML
    <MESSAGE>
    </GREETING>
        Welcome to the wild and woolly world of XML.
    </MESSAGE>
</DOCUMENT>
```

Figure 3.2 shows the results; the validator indicates that there's a problem with these two tags.

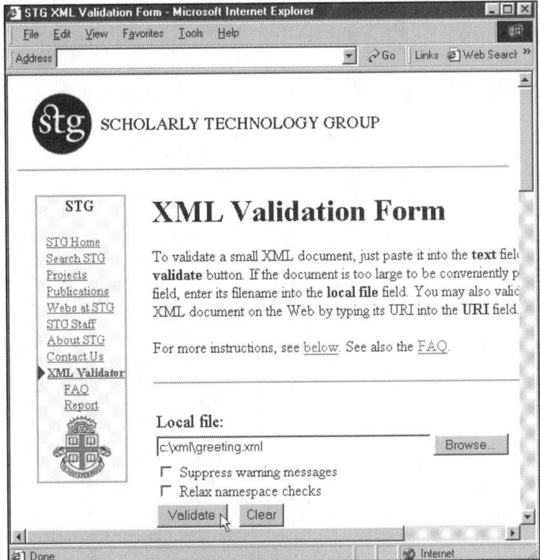

Figure 3.1 Using an XML validator.

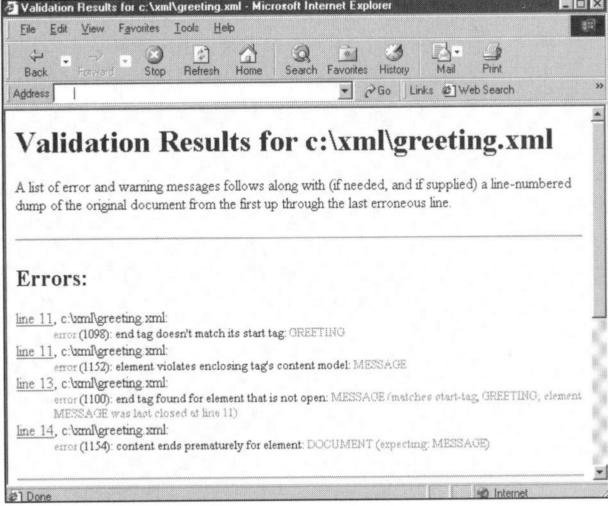

Figure 3.2 The results from an XML validator.

In general, then, you can use a validator to check your document, and there are plenty around. Validators can help a great deal as you're writing long and difficult XML documents because you can often check them at each development stage.

4

DTDs: Entities and Attributes

In Chapter 3, "Valid XML Documents: Creating Document Type Definitions," I discussed creating DTDs and declaring the elements that you use in XML documents. But there's more to DTDs than that—you can also declare *attributes* and *entities*, and we're going to do that in this chapter. We'll also take a look at embedding non-XML data in XML documents.

Entities

In the previous chapter, we received an introduction to the idea of entities in XML documents. Two kinds of entities exist: general entities and parameter entities. General entities are probably used by more XML authors because you use them in the content of your XML document, but parameter entities, which you use in a document's DTD, are also available and are very powerful.

So what exactly is an entity? An *entity* is simply XML's way of referring to a data item; entities are usually text, but they can also be binary data. You declare an entity in a DTD and then refer to it by *reference* in your document. *General entity references* start with `&` and end with `;`, *parameter entity references* start with `%` and end with `;`. For text entities, the entity reference is replaced by the entity itself when parsed by an XML processor.

In other words, you declare an entity in the DTD and refer to it with an entity reference, either in the document's content for general entities, or in the DTD for parameter entities.

Entities can be internal or external. An *internal entity* is defined completely inside the XML document that references it (and, in fact, the document itself is considered an entity in XML). *External entities*, on the other hand, derive their content from an external source, such as a file, and a reference to them usually includes an URI at which they may be found. Entities can also be *parsed* or *unparsed*. The content of parsed entities is well-formed XML text, and unparsed entities hold data that you don't want parsed, such as simple text or binary data. We'll see how to deal with all kinds of entities here.

In fact, we've already seen the five predefined general entity references in XML: `<`, `>`, `&`, `"`, and `'`—they stand for the characters `<`, `>`, `&`, `"`, and `'` respectively. Because these entities are predefined in XML, you don't need to define them in a DTD; for example, here's a document that uses all five predefined entity references:

```
<?xml version = "1.0" standalone="yes"?>
<TEXT>
    This text about the &quot;S&amp;O Railroad&quot;
    is the &lt;TEXT&gt; element&apos;s content.
</TEXT>
```

Each entity reference is replaced by the appropriate character when parsed by an XML processor. For example, Figure 4.1 shows this document open in Internet Explorer. Notice that every entity reference has indeed been replaced.

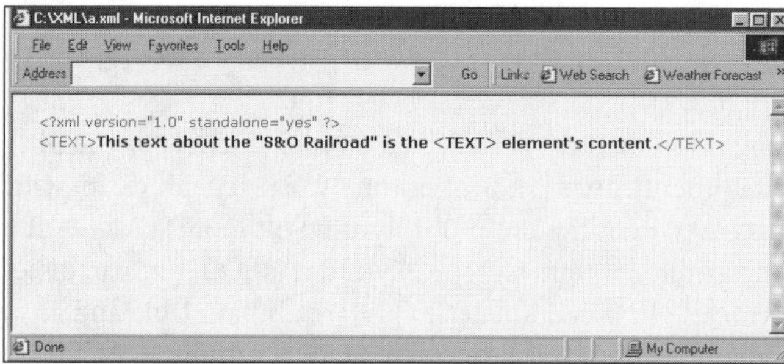

Figure 4.1 Using the predefined entities in Internet Explorer.

The five predefined entity references are very useful when you want to use as text the specific characters that are interpreted as markup.

You can also define your own entities by declaring them in a DTD. To declare an entity, you use the `<!ENTITY>` element (just as you use the `<!ELEMENT>` element to declare an element). Declaring a general entity looks like this:

```
<!ENTITY NAME DEFINITION>
```

Here, *NAME* is the entity's name and *DEFINITION* is its definition. The name of the entity is just the name that you want to use to refer to the entity, and the entity's definition can take several different forms, as we'll see in this chapter.

The simplest possible entity definition is just the text with which you want a reference to that entity to be replaced—here's an example showing how that looks. In this case, I'm defining a general entity named `TODAY` to hold a date, October 15, 2001, in this DTD:

```
<?xml version = "1.0" standalone="yes"?>
<!DOCTYPE DOCUMENT [
<!ELEMENT DOCUMENT (CUSTOMER)*>
<!ELEMENT CUSTOMER (NAME,DATE,ORDERS)>
<!ELEMENT NAME (LAST_NAME,FIRST_NAME)>
<!ELEMENT LAST_NAME (#PCDATA)>
<!ELEMENT FIRST_NAME (#PCDATA)>
<!ELEMENT DATE (#PCDATA)>
<!ELEMENT ORDERS (ITEM)*>
<!ELEMENT ITEM (PRODUCT,NUMBER,PRICE)>
<!ELEMENT PRODUCT (#PCDATA)>
<!ELEMENT NUMBER (#PCDATA)>
<!ELEMENT PRICE (#PCDATA)>
<!ENTITY TODAY "October 15, 2001">
]>
    .
    .
    .
```

And that's all it takes. Now when I put a reference to this entity—`&TODAY;`—into the document, it will be replaced with the text `October 15, 2001` by the XML processor:

```
<?xml version = "1.0" standalone="yes"?>
<!DOCTYPE DOCUMENT [
<!ELEMENT DOCUMENT (CUSTOMER)*>
<!ELEMENT CUSTOMER (NAME,DATE,ORDERS)>
<!ELEMENT NAME (LAST_NAME,FIRST_NAME)>
<!ELEMENT LAST_NAME (#PCDATA)>
<!ELEMENT FIRST_NAME (#PCDATA)>
<!ELEMENT DATE (#PCDATA)>
<!ELEMENT ORDERS (ITEM)*>
<!ELEMENT ITEM (PRODUCT,NUMBER,PRICE)>
<!ELEMENT PRODUCT (#PCDATA)>
<!ELEMENT NUMBER (#PCDATA)>
<!ELEMENT PRICE (#PCDATA)>
<!ENTITY TODAY "October 15, 2001">
]>
<DOCUMENT>
<CUSTOMER>
        <NAME>
            <LAST_NAME>Smith</LAST_NAME>
            <FIRST_NAME>Sam</FIRST_NAME>
```

continues ▸

```
        </NAME>
        <DATE>&TODAY;</DATE>
        <ORDERS>
            <ITEM>
                <PRODUCT>Tomatoes</PRODUCT>
                <NUMBER>8</NUMBER>
                <PRICE>$1.25</PRICE>
            </ITEM>
            <ITEM>
                <PRODUCT>Oranges</PRODUCT>
                <NUMBER>24</NUMBER>
                <PRICE>$4.98</PRICE>
            </ITEM>
        </ORDERS>
    </CUSTOMER>
    <CUSTOMER>
        <NAME>
            <LAST_NAME>Jones</LAST_NAME>
            <FIRST_NAME>Polly</FIRST_NAME>
        </NAME>
        <DATE>&TODAY;</DATE>
        <ORDERS>
            <ITEM>
                <PRODUCT>Bread</PRODUCT>
                <NUMBER>12</NUMBER>
                <PRICE>$14.95</PRICE>
            </ITEM>
            <ITEM>
                <PRODUCT>Apples</PRODUCT>
                <NUMBER>6</NUMBER>
                <PRICE>$1.50</PRICE>
            </ITEM>
        </ORDERS>
    </CUSTOMER>
    <CUSTOMER>
        <NAME>
            <LAST_NAME>Weber</LAST_NAME>
            <FIRST_NAME>Bill</FIRST_NAME>
        </NAME>
        <DATE>&TODAY;</DATE>
        <ORDERS>
            <ITEM>
                <PRODUCT>Asparagus</PRODUCT>
                <NUMBER>12</NUMBER>
                <PRICE>$2.95</PRICE>
            </ITEM>
            <ITEM>
                <PRODUCT>Lettuce</PRODUCT>
                <NUMBER>6</NUMBER>
                <PRICE>$11.50</PRICE>
            </ITEM>
        </ORDERS>
    </CUSTOMER>
</DOCUMENT>
```

Figure 4.2 shows the results of this document in Internet Explorer. Notice that the `&TODAY;` entity references have been replaced with the full text that we've specified.

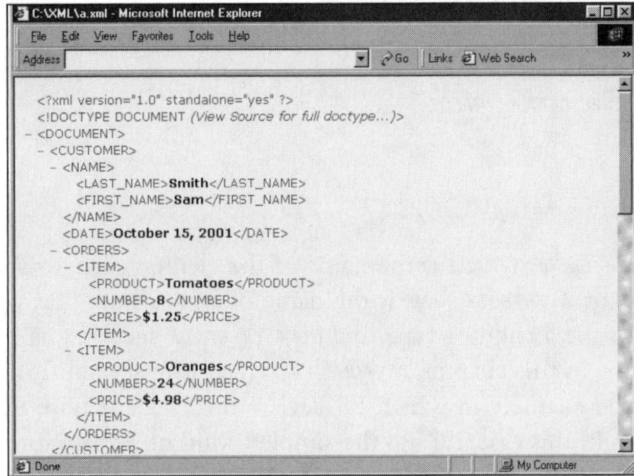

Figure 4.2 Using user-defined entities in Internet Explorer.

Besides general entities as in this example, we'll also see parameter entities in this chapter, which are designed to be used in DTDs themselves. Declaring a parameter entity looks like this (notice the `%`):

```
<!ENTITY % NAME DEFINITION>
```

Besides setting up your own entities in XML, you can customize your document's elements by declaring attributes for those elements.

Attributes

We've already discussed attributes in some detail; they're those name/value pairs that you can use in start tags and empty tags to provide additional information for an element. Here's an example; in this case, I'm adding an attribute named `TYPE` to the `<CUSTOMER>` tag to indicate what type of customer a person is:

```
<CUSTOMER TYPE = "excellent">
        <NAME>
            <LAST_NAME>Smith</LAST_NAME>
            <FIRST_NAME>Sam</FIRST_NAME>
        </NAME>
        <DATE>October 15, 2001</DATE>
    .
    .
    .
```

You can use attributes like this one and assign them values in XML documents, but unless you also declare them, your document won't be valid. You can declare a list of attributes for an element with the `<!ATTLIST>` element in the DTD. Here's the general form of an `<!ATTLIST>` element:

```
<!ATTLIST ELEMENT_NAME
    ATTRIBUTE_NAME TYPE DEFAULT_VALUE
    ATTRIBUTE_NAME TYPE DEFAULT_VALUE
    ATTRIBUTE_NAME TYPE DEFAULT_VALUE
    .
    .
    .
    ATTRIBUTE_NAME TYPE DEFAULT_VALUE>
```

In this case, *ELEMENT_NAME* is the name of the element that you're declaring attributes for, *ATTRIBUTE_NAME* is the name of an attribute that you're declaring, *TYPE* is the attribute's type, and *DEFAULT_VALUE* specifies its default value. As we'll see in this chapter, *DEFAULT_VALUE* can take several forms.

Here's an example in which I'll declare the `TYPE` attribute that we used previously. In this case, I'll use the simplest kind of declaration, making the attribute's type `CDATA`, which is simple character data, and using an `#IMPLIED` default value, which means that you can use this attribute in an element or skip it entirely. This is what the document looks like, including the DTD:

```
<?xml version = "1.0" standalone="yes"?>
<!DOCTYPE DOCUMENT [
<!ELEMENT DOCUMENT (CUSTOMER)*>
<!ELEMENT CUSTOMER (NAME,DATE,ORDERS)>
<!ELEMENT NAME (LAST_NAME,FIRST_NAME)>
<!ELEMENT LAST_NAME (#PCDATA)>
<!ELEMENT FIRST_NAME (#PCDATA)>
<!ELEMENT DATE (#PCDATA)>
<!ELEMENT ORDERS (ITEM)*>
<!ELEMENT ITEM (PRODUCT,NUMBER,PRICE)>
<!ELEMENT PRODUCT (#PCDATA)>
<!ELEMENT NUMBER (#PCDATA)>
<!ELEMENT PRICE (#PCDATA)>
<!ATTLIST CUSTOMER
    TYPE CDATA #IMPLIED>
]>
<DOCUMENT>
<CUSTOMER TYPE = "excellent">
        <NAME>
            <LAST_NAME>Smith</LAST_NAME>
            <FIRST_NAME>Sam</FIRST_NAME>
        </NAME>
        <DATE>October 15, 2001</DATE>
        <ORDERS>
```

```
            <ITEM>
                <PRODUCT>Tomatoes</PRODUCT>
                <NUMBER>8</NUMBER>
                <PRICE>$1.25</PRICE>
            </ITEM>
            <ITEM>
                <PRODUCT>Oranges</PRODUCT>
                <NUMBER>24</NUMBER>
                <PRICE>$4.98</PRICE>
            </ITEM>
            .
            .
            .
            <ITEM>
                <PRODUCT>Asparagus</PRODUCT>
                <NUMBER>12</NUMBER>
                <PRICE>$2.95</PRICE>
            </ITEM>
            <ITEM>
                <PRODUCT>Lettuce</PRODUCT>
                <NUMBER>6</NUMBER>
                <PRICE>$11.50</PRICE>
            </ITEM>
        </ORDERS>
    </CUSTOMER>
</DOCUMENT>
```

That introduces us to the idea of declaring attributes in DTDs. I'll get into the details on entities and attributes now, starting with entities—first general entities and then parameter entities.

Creating Internal General Entities

As discussed at the beginning of the chapter, entities can either be internal or external. We've already seen how to create an internal general reference in this chapter, when we created an internal general entity named `TODAY` and referenced it as `&TODAY;` in the document:

```
<?xml version = "1.0" standalone="yes"?>
<!DOCTYPE DOCUMENT [
<!ELEMENT DOCUMENT (CUSTOMER)*>
<!ELEMENT CUSTOMER (NAME,DATE,ORDERS)>
<!ELEMENT NAME (LAST_NAME,FIRST_NAME)>
<!ELEMENT LAST_NAME (#PCDATA)>
<!ELEMENT FIRST_NAME (#PCDATA)>
<!ELEMENT DATE (#PCDATA)>
<!ELEMENT ORDERS (ITEM)*>
<!ELEMENT ITEM (PRODUCT,NUMBER,PRICE)>
<!ELEMENT PRODUCT (#PCDATA)>
<!ELEMENT NUMBER (#PCDATA)>
```

continues ▶

```
<!ELEMENT PRICE (#PCDATA)>
<!ENTITY TODAY "October 15, 2001">
]>
<DOCUMENT>
<CUSTOMER>
        <NAME>
            <LAST_NAME>Smith</LAST_NAME>
            <FIRST_NAME>Sam</FIRST_NAME>
        </NAME>
        <DATE>&TODAY;</DATE>
        <ORDERS>
            <ITEM>
                <PRODUCT>Tomatoes</PRODUCT>
                <NUMBER>8</NUMBER>
                <PRICE>$1.25</PRICE>
            </ITEM>
            .
            .
            .
            <ITEM>
                <PRODUCT>Lettuce</PRODUCT>
                <NUMBER>6</NUMBER>
                <PRICE>$11.50</PRICE>
            </ITEM>
        </ORDERS>
    </CUSTOMER>
</DOCUMENT>
```

Refer to Figure 4.2 to see the results.

There are a few things to note here; one is that you can *nest* general reference definitions, like this:

```
<!ENTITY NAME "Alfred Hitchcock">
<!ENTITY SIGNATURE "&NAME; 14 Mystery Drive">
```

Another point is that entity references can't be circular, or you'll drive the XML processor crazy. Here's an example:

```
<!ENTITY NAME "Alfred Hitchcock &SIGNATURE;">
<!ENTITY SIGNATURE "&NAME; 14 Mystery Drive">
```

In this case, when the XML processor tries to resolve the `&NAME;` reference, it finds that it needs to substitute the text for the `SIGNATURE` entity in the text for the `NAME` entity, but the `NAME` entity needs the `SIGNATURE` entity's text, and so on, around in a circle that never ends. The result is that circular entity references have been made illegal in valid documents.

Also, it's worth noting that you can't use general entity references to insert text that is supposed to be used only in the DTD, not in the document content itself. Here's an example of something that's considered illegal:

```
<!ENTITY TAGS "(NAME,DATE,ORDERS)">
<!ELEMENT CUSTOMER &TAGS;>
```

The correct way to do this is with parameter entities, not general entities, and I'll cover them in a few pages. You can use general entities in the DTD to insert text that will become part of the document body, however.

Creating External General Entities

Besides internal entities, entities can also be *external*, which means that you should provide a URI directing the XML processor to the entity. You can use references to external entities to embed those entities in your document. As we'll see near the end of this chapter, you can also indicate that an external entity should not be parsed, which means that you can associate binary data with a document (much like associating images with an HTML document).

External entities can be simple strings of text, they can be entire documents, or they can be sections of documents. All that matters is that when they are inserted into the document's content, the XML processor is satisfied that the document is well-formed and valid.

As with DTDs, you can declare external entities using the `SYSTEM` or `PUBLIC` keywords. Entities declared with the `SYSTEM` keyword are for private use by an organization of individuals, and entities declared with `PUBLIC` are public, so they need a formal public identifier (FPI—see Chapter 3 for the rules on creating FPIs). Here's how you use the `SYSTEM` and `PUBLIC` keywords to declare an external entity:

```
<!ENTITY NAME SYSTEM URI>
<!ENTITY NAME PUBLIC FPI URI>
```

For example, say that you've stored a date as the text `October 15, 2001` in a file named date.xml. Here's how you could set up an entity named `TODAY` connected to that file:

```
<!ENTITY TODAY SYSTEM "date.xml">
```

And here's how you could use a reference to that entity to insert the data into a document's content (notice that I changed the value of the `standalone` attribute from `"yes"` to `"no"` here because we're working with an external entity):

```
<?xml version = "1.0" standalone="no"?>
<!DOCTYPE DOCUMENT [
<!ELEMENT DOCUMENT (CUSTOMER)*>
```

continues ▸

```
<!ELEMENT CUSTOMER (NAME,DATE,ORDERS)>
<!ELEMENT NAME (LAST_NAME,FIRST_NAME)>
<!ELEMENT LAST_NAME (#PCDATA)>
<!ELEMENT FIRST_NAME (#PCDATA)>
<!ELEMENT DATE (#PCDATA)>
<!ELEMENT ORDERS (ITEM)*>
<!ELEMENT ITEM (PRODUCT,NUMBER,PRICE)>
<!ELEMENT PRODUCT (#PCDATA)>
<!ELEMENT NUMBER (#PCDATA)>
<!ELEMENT PRICE (#PCDATA)>
<!ENTITY TODAY SYSTEM "date.xml">
]>
<DOCUMENT>
<CUSTOMER>
        <NAME>
            <LAST_NAME>Smith</LAST_NAME>
            <FIRST_NAME>Sam</FIRST_NAME>
        </NAME>
        <DATE>&TODAY;</DATE>
        <ORDERS>
            <ITEM>
                <PRODUCT>Tomatoes</PRODUCT>
                <NUMBER>8</NUMBER>
                <PRICE>$1.25</PRICE>
            </ITEM>
            <ITEM>
                <PRODUCT>Oranges</PRODUCT>
                <NUMBER>24</NUMBER>
                <PRICE>$4.98</PRICE>
            </ITEM>
        </ORDERS>
    </CUSTOMER>
    <CUSTOMER>
        <NAME>
            <LAST_NAME>Jones</LAST_NAME>
            <FIRST_NAME>Polly</FIRST_NAME>
        </NAME>
        <DATE>&TODAY;</DATE>
        <ORDERS>
            <ITEM>
                <PRODUCT>Bread</PRODUCT>
                <NUMBER>12</NUMBER>
                <PRICE>$14.95</PRICE>
            </ITEM>
            <ITEM>
                <PRODUCT>Apples</PRODUCT>
                <NUMBER>6</NUMBER>
                <PRICE>$1.50</PRICE>
            </ITEM>
        </ORDERS>
```

```
    </CUSTOMER>
    <CUSTOMER>
        <NAME>
            <LAST_NAME>Weber</LAST_NAME>
            <FIRST_NAME>Bill</FIRST_NAME>
        </NAME>
        <DATE>&TODAY;</DATE>
        <ORDERS>
            <ITEM>
                <PRODUCT>Asparagus</PRODUCT>
                <NUMBER>12</NUMBER>
                <PRICE>$2.95</PRICE>
            </ITEM>
            <ITEM>
                <PRODUCT>Lettuce</PRODUCT>
                <NUMBER>6</NUMBER>
                <PRICE>$11.50</PRICE>
            </ITEM>
        </ORDERS>
    </CUSTOMER>
</DOCUMENT>
```

Notice how powerful this technique is—now you can create documents that are themselves pieced together from other documents. If you wanted to use a public entity instead of a private one, you could use the SYSTEM keyword with an FPI, like this:

```
<!ENTITY TODAY SYSTEM
"-//starpowder//Custom Entity Version 1.0//EN"
"date.xml">
```

Defining external entities makes them available for multiple documents. This is useful, for example, in case you want to have the same text appear as a signature in all your documents, or you work with text that will change frequently (such as a greeting for the day) that you want to edit in only one place.

Here's another note: Often nonvalidating XML processors (such as Internet Explorer) will read a DTD to pick up any entity declarations that you may have put there, even though they don't use the DTD to validate the document. This means that XML authors sometimes even add partial DTDs to documents that would not be considered valid so that they can use entity references (this is just an expedient programming practice, not a good one). Here's an example (note that this DTD is not complete by any means and that it carries only the declaration for the entity TODAY):

```
<?xml version = "1.0" standalone="no"?>
<!DOCTYPE DOCUMENT [
<!ENTITY TODAY SYSTEM "date.xml">
```

continues ▸

```
]>
<DOCUMENT>
<CUSTOMER>
        <NAME>
            <LAST_NAME>Smith</LAST_NAME>
            <FIRST_NAME>Sam</FIRST_NAME>
        </NAME>
        <DATE>&TODAY;</DATE>
        <ORDERS>
            <ITEM>
                <PRODUCT>Tomatoes</PRODUCT>
                <NUMBER>8</NUMBER>
                <PRICE>$1.25</PRICE>
            </ITEM>
            .
            .
            .
            <ITEM>
                <PRODUCT>Asparagus</PRODUCT>
                <NUMBER>12</NUMBER>
                <PRICE>$2.95</PRICE>
            </ITEM>
            <ITEM>
                <PRODUCT>Lettuce</PRODUCT>
                <NUMBER>6</NUMBER>
                <PRICE>$11.50</PRICE>
            </ITEM>
        </ORDERS>
    </CUSTOMER>
</DOCUMENT>
```

Building a Document from Pieces

One way to use external general entities is to build a document from pieces, in which you treat each piece as a general entity. Here's an example; in this case, I'm including an entity that refers to the file data.xml in my document:

```
<?xml version = "1.0" standalone="no"?>
<!DOCTYPE DOCUMENT [
<!ELEMENT DOCUMENT (CUSTOMER)*>
<!ELEMENT CUSTOMER (NAME,DATE,ORDERS)>
<!ELEMENT NAME (LAST_NAME,FIRST_NAME)>
<!ELEMENT LAST_NAME (#PCDATA)>
<!ELEMENT FIRST_NAME (#PCDATA)>
<!ELEMENT DATE (#PCDATA)>
<!ELEMENT ORDERS (ITEM)*>
<!ELEMENT ITEM (PRODUCT,NUMBER,PRICE)>
<!ELEMENT PRODUCT (#PCDATA)>
<!ELEMENT NUMBER (#PCDATA)>
<!ELEMENT PRICE (#PCDATA)>
```

```
<!ENTITY data SYSTEM "data.xml">
]>
<DOCUMENT>
&data;
</DOCUMENT>
```

The file data.xml itself holds the actual data for the document:

```
<CUSTOMER>
    <NAME>
        <LAST_NAME>Smith</LAST_NAME>
        <FIRST_NAME>Sam</FIRST_NAME>
    </NAME>
    <DATE>October 15, 2001</DATE>
    <ORDERS>
        <ITEM>
            <PRODUCT>Tomatoes</PRODUCT>
            <NUMBER>8</NUMBER>
            <PRICE>$1.25</PRICE>
        </ITEM>
        <ITEM>
            <PRODUCT>Oranges</PRODUCT>
            <NUMBER>24</NUMBER>
            <PRICE>$4.98</PRICE>
        </ITEM>
    </ORDERS>
</CUSTOMER>
<CUSTOMER>
    <NAME>
        <LAST_NAME>Jones</LAST_NAME>
        <FIRST_NAME>Polly</FIRST_NAME>
    </NAME>
    <DATE>October 20, 2001</DATE>
    <ORDERS>
        <ITEM>
            <PRODUCT>Bread</PRODUCT>
            <NUMBER>12</NUMBER>
            <PRICE>$14.95</PRICE>
        </ITEM>
        <ITEM>
            <PRODUCT>Apples</PRODUCT>
            <NUMBER>6</NUMBER>
            <PRICE>$1.50</PRICE>
        </ITEM>
    </ORDERS>
</CUSTOMER>
<CUSTOMER>
    <NAME>
        <LAST_NAME>Weber</LAST_NAME>
        <FIRST_NAME>Bill</FIRST_NAME>
    </NAME>
```

continues ▶

```
        <DATE>October 25, 2001</DATE>
        <ORDERS>
            <ITEM>
                <PRODUCT>Asparagus</PRODUCT>
                <NUMBER>12</NUMBER>
                <PRICE>$2.95</PRICE>
            </ITEM>
            <ITEM>
                <PRODUCT>Lettuce</PRODUCT>
                <NUMBER>6</NUMBER>
                <PRICE>$11.50</PRICE>
            </ITEM>
        </ORDERS>
    </CUSTOMER>
```

In this way, you can put documents together from various pieces, choosing the pieces that you want.

Predefined General Entity References

As we already know, there are five predefined entity references in XML, and they stand for characters that can be interpreted as markup or other control characters:

- & becomes the & character
- ' becomes the ' character
- > becomes the > character
- < becomes the < character
- " becomes the " character

It turns out that you can create entity references for individual characters yourself in XML—all you have to do is to specify the correct character code in the encoding that you're using. For example, in the UTF-8 encoding, the character code for @ is #64 (where the # indicates that this value is in hexadecimal), so you can define an entity named, say, at_new, so that references to at_new will be replaced by @ when parsed. Here's how that entity would look:

```
<!ENTITY at_new "&#64;">
```

In fact, you can even define the predefined entity references yourself, in case you run across an XML processor that doesn't understand them. Here's how I modify the example document at the beginning of this chapter that uses those entity references—this time I define the entities myself:

```
<?xml version = "1.0" standalone="yes"?>
<!DOCTYPE TEXT [
<!ENTITY amp_new "&#38;#38;">
<!ENTITY apos_new "&#39;">
```

```
<!ENTITY gt_new "&#62;">
<!ENTITY lt_new "&#38;#60;">
<!ENTITY quot_new "&#34;">
]>
<TEXT>
    This text about the &quot_new;S&amp_new;O Railroad&quot_new;
    is the &lt_new;TEXT&gt_new; element&apos_new;s content.
</TEXT>
```

Creating Internal Parameter Entities

As we've seen, you use general entity references in documents so that the XML processor will replace them with the entity to which they refer. However, you can use general entities only in a limited way in DTDs—that is, you can use them to insert text that will itself be inserted into the document content, but you can't use them to work with the declarations themselves in the DTD.

To actually work with element and attribute declarations, you use *parameter entities*. Parameter entity references can be used in only the DTD. In fact, there's an additional restriction: Any parameter entity references that you use in any DTD declaration must appear only in the DTD's *external subset* (the external subset is that part of the DTD that is external). You can use parameter entities in the internal subset, but only in a limited way, as we'll see.

Unlike general entity references, parameter entity references start with `%`, not `&`. Creating a parameter entity is just like creating a general entity, except that you include a `%` in the `<!ENTITY>` element, like this:

```
<!ENTITY % NAME DEFINITION>
```

You can also declare external parameter entities using the `SYSTEM` and `PUBLIC` keywords, like this (where *`FPI`* stands for a formal public identifier):

```
<!ENTITY % NAME SYSTEM URI>
<!ENTITY % NAME PUBLIC FPI URI>
```

Here's an example using an internal parameter entity; in this case, I'll declare a parameter entity named `BR` that stands for the text `<!ELEMENT BR EMPTY>` inside this DTD:

```
<?xml version = "1.0" standalone="yes"?>
<!DOCTYPE DOCUMENT [
<!ENTITY % BR "<!ELEMENT BR EMPTY>">
<!ELEMENT DOCUMENT (CUSTOMER)*>
<!ELEMENT CUSTOMER (NAME,DATE,ORDERS)>
<!ELEMENT NAME (LAST_NAME,FIRST_NAME)>
<!ELEMENT LAST_NAME (#PCDATA)>
<!ELEMENT FIRST_NAME (#PCDATA)>
<!ELEMENT DATE (#PCDATA)>
```

continues ▸

```
<!ELEMENT ORDERS (ITEM)*>
<!ELEMENT ITEM (PRODUCT,NUMBER,PRICE)>
<!ELEMENT PRODUCT (#PCDATA)>
<!ELEMENT NUMBER (#PCDATA)>
<!ELEMENT PRICE (#PCDATA)>
]>
    .
    .
    .
```

Now I can reference that parameter entity this way to include the element declaration `<!ELEMENT BR EMPTY>` in the DTD:

```
<?xml version = "1.0" standalone="yes"?>
<!DOCTYPE DOCUMENT [
<!ENTITY % BR "<!ELEMENT BR EMPTY>">
<!ELEMENT DOCUMENT (CUSTOMER)*>
<!ELEMENT CUSTOMER (NAME,DATE,ORDERS)>
<!ELEMENT NAME (LAST_NAME,FIRST_NAME)>
<!ELEMENT LAST_NAME (#PCDATA)>
<!ELEMENT FIRST_NAME (#PCDATA)>
<!ELEMENT DATE (#PCDATA)>
<!ELEMENT ORDERS (ITEM)*>
<!ELEMENT ITEM (PRODUCT,NUMBER,PRICE)>
<!ELEMENT PRODUCT (#PCDATA)>
<!ELEMENT NUMBER (#PCDATA)>
<!ELEMENT PRICE (#PCDATA)>
%BR;
]>
<DOCUMENT>
    <CUSTOMER>
        <NAME>
            <LAST_NAME>Smith</LAST_NAME>
            <FIRST_NAME>Sam</FIRST_NAME>
        </NAME>
        <DATE>October 15, 2001</DATE>
        <ORDERS>
            <ITEM>
                <PRODUCT>Tomatoes</PRODUCT>
                <NUMBER>8</NUMBER>
                <PRICE>$1.25</PRICE>
            </ITEM>
            <ITEM>
                <PRODUCT>Oranges</PRODUCT>
                <NUMBER>24</NUMBER>
                <PRICE>$4.98</PRICE>
            </ITEM>
            .
            .
            .
            <ITEM>
                <PRODUCT>Asparagus</PRODUCT>
```

```
            <NUMBER>12</NUMBER>
            <PRICE>$2.95</PRICE>
        </ITEM>
        <ITEM>
            <PRODUCT>Lettuce</PRODUCT>
            <NUMBER>6</NUMBER>
            <PRICE>$11.50</PRICE>
        </ITEM>
    </ORDERS>
  </CUSTOMER>
</DOCUMENT>
```

Notice that I haven't really saved much time here; I might as well have just put the declaration `<!ELEMENT BR EMPTY>` directly into the DTD. On the other hand, you can't do much more with internal parameter entities (those that are defined in the DTD's internal subset) because you can't use them inside any other declarations. If you want to find out what people really use parameter entities for, we have to take a look at external parameter entities.

External Parameter Entities

When you use a parameter entity in the DTD's external subset, you can reference that entity anywhere in the DTD, including in element declarations. Here's an example; in this case, I'm using an external DTD named order.dtd for this document:

```
<?xml version = "1.0" standalone="no"?>
<!DOCTYPE DOCUMENT SYSTEM "order.dtd">
<DOCUMENT>
    <CUSTOMER>
        <NAME>
            <LAST_NAME>Smith</LAST_NAME>
            <FIRST_NAME>Sam</FIRST_NAME>
        </NAME>
        <DATE>October 15, 2001</DATE>
        <ORDERS>
            <ITEM>
                <PRODUCT>Tomatoes</PRODUCT>
                <NUMBER>8</NUMBER>
                <PRICE>$1.25</PRICE>
            </ITEM>
            <ITEM>
                <PRODUCT>Oranges</PRODUCT>
                <NUMBER>24</NUMBER>
                <PRICE>$4.98</PRICE>
            </ITEM>
            .
            .
            .
```

continues ▸

```
            <ITEM>
                <PRODUCT>Asparagus</PRODUCT>
                <NUMBER>12</NUMBER>
                <PRICE>$2.95</PRICE>
            </ITEM>
            <ITEM>
                <PRODUCT>Lettuce</PRODUCT>
                <NUMBER>6</NUMBER>
                <PRICE>$11.50</PRICE>
            </ITEM>
        </ORDERS>
    </CUSTOMER>
</DOCUMENT>
```

In the external DTD subset, order.dtd, I'm going to set things up so that the <DOCUMENT> element can contain not only <CUSTOMER> elements, but also <BUYER> and <DISCOUNTER> elements. Each of these two new elements, <BUYER> and <DISCOUNTER>, has the same content model as the <CUSTOMER> element (that is, they can contain <NAME>, <DATE>, and <ORDERS> elements), so to save a little time, I'll assign that content model, (NAME,DATE,ORDERS), to a parameter entity named record:

```
<!ENTITY % record "(NAME,DATE,ORDERS)">
<!ELEMENT DOCUMENT (CUSTOMER | BUYER | DISCOUNTER)*>
    .
    .
    .
```

Now I'm free to refer to the record parameter entity where I like; in this case, that means using it to declare the <CUSTOMER>, <BUYER>, and <DISCOUNTER> elements:

```
<!ENTITY % record "(NAME,DATE,ORDERS)">
<!ELEMENT DOCUMENT (CUSTOMER | BUYER | DISCOUNTER)*>
<!ELEMENT CUSTOMER %record;>
<!ELEMENT BUYER %record;>
<!ELEMENT DISCOUNTER %record;>
<!ELEMENT NAME (LAST_NAME,FIRST_NAME)>
<!ELEMENT LAST_NAME (#PCDATA)>
<!ELEMENT FIRST_NAME (#PCDATA)>
<!ELEMENT DATE (#PCDATA)>
<!ELEMENT ORDERS (ITEM)*>
<!ELEMENT ITEM (PRODUCT,NUMBER,PRICE)>
<!ELEMENT PRODUCT (#PCDATA)>
<!ELEMENT NUMBER (#PCDATA)>
<!ELEMENT PRICE (#PCDATA)>
```

Now the document works and parses as expected—I can use <CUSTOMER>, <BUYER>, and <DISCOUNTER> elements inside the <DOCUMENT> element, and all three of those elements have the same content model:

```
<?xml version = "1.0" standalone="no"?>
<!DOCTYPE DOCUMENT SYSTEM "order.dtd">
<DOCUMENT>
    <CUSTOMER>
        <NAME>
            <LAST_NAME>Smith</LAST_NAME>
            <FIRST_NAME>Sam</FIRST_NAME>
        </NAME>
        <DATE>October 15, 2001</DATE>
        <ORDERS>
            <ITEM>
                <PRODUCT>Tomatoes</PRODUCT>
                <NUMBER>8</NUMBER>
                <PRICE>$1.25</PRICE>
            </ITEM>
            <ITEM>
                <PRODUCT>Oranges</PRODUCT>
                <NUMBER>24</NUMBER>
                <PRICE>$4.98</PRICE>
            </ITEM>
        </ORDERS>
    </CUSTOMER>
    <BUYER>
        <NAME>
            <LAST_NAME>Jones</LAST_NAME>
            <FIRST_NAME>Polly</FIRST_NAME>
        </NAME>
        <DATE>October 20, 2001</DATE>
        <ORDERS>
            <ITEM>
                <PRODUCT>Bread</PRODUCT>
                <NUMBER>12</NUMBER>
                <PRICE>$14.95</PRICE>
            </ITEM>
            <ITEM>
                <PRODUCT>Apples</PRODUCT>
                <NUMBER>6</NUMBER>
                <PRICE>$1.50</PRICE>
            </ITEM>
        </ORDERS>
    </BUYER>
    <DISCOUNTER>
        <NAME>
            <LAST_NAME>Weber</LAST_NAME>
            <FIRST_NAME>Bill</FIRST_NAME>
        </NAME>
```

continues ▸

```
        <DATE>October 25, 2001</DATE>
        <ORDERS>
            <ITEM>
                <PRODUCT>Asparagus</PRODUCT>
                <NUMBER>12</NUMBER>
                <PRICE>$2.95</PRICE>
            </ITEM>
            <ITEM>
                <PRODUCT>Lettuce</PRODUCT>
                <NUMBER>6</NUMBER>
                <PRICE>$11.50</PRICE>
            </ITEM>
        </ORDERS>
    </DISCOUNTER>
</DOCUMENT>
```

This example points out probably the biggest reason people use parameter entities: to handle text that's repeated often in element declarations in a DTD. In this case, I specified the content model of three elements using the same parameter entity, but I could just have easily set up a parameter entity to let me specify an attribute list that was the same for as many elements as I like. In this way, you can control the declarations of many elements and attributes, even in a huge DTD. And if you need to modify a declaration, you need to modify only the parameter entity, not each declaration in detail.

For example, you might divide your attributes in a big DTD into various types. When you declare some new element, you might want to give it only the image-handling and URI-handling attributes, which you could do like this (in fact, this is the way the XHTML DTDs are built):

```
<!ATTLIST NEW_ELEMENT %image_attributes; %URI_attributes;>
```

Here's another example showing how to use parameter entities; in this case, I'm going to base my document on the XHTML 1.0 transitional DTD, adding a few elements of my own to XHTML. To do that, I declare the elements that I want to use and then simply include the entire XHTML 1.0 transitional DTD, using a parameter reference like this:

```
<!ENTITY % record "(NAME,DATE,ORDERS)">
<!ELEMENT DOCUMENT (CUSTOMER | BUYER | DISCOUNTER)*>
<!ELEMENT CUSTOMER %record;>
<!ELEMENT BUYER %record;>
<!ELEMENT DISCOUNTER %record;>
<!ELEMENT NAME (LAST_NAME,FIRST_NAME)>
<!ELEMENT LAST_NAME (#PCDATA)>
<!ELEMENT FIRST_NAME (#PCDATA)>
<!ELEMENT DATE (#PCDATA)>
<!ELEMENT ORDERS (ITEM)*>
<!ELEMENT ITEM (PRODUCT,NUMBER,PRICE)>
```

```
<!ELEMENT PRODUCT (#PCDATA)>
<!ELEMENT NUMBER (#PCDATA)>
<!ELEMENT PRICE (#PCDATA)>
<!ENTITY % XHTML1-t.dtd PUBLIC "-//W3C//DTD XHTML 1.0 Transitional//EN"
"http://www.w3.org/TR/xhtml1/DTD/xhtml1-transitional.dtd">
%XHTML1-t.dtd;
```

Using *INCLUDE* and *IGNORE*

Two important DTD directives are often used with parameter entities: `INCLUDE` and `IGNORE`. You use these directives to include or remove sections of a DTD; here's how you use them: `<![ INCLUDE [DTD Section]]>` and `<![ IGNORE [DTD Section]]>`. Using these directives, you can customize your DTD.

Here's an example showing what these two directives look like in practice:

```
<![ INCLUDE [
<!ELEMENT PRODUCT_ID (#PCDATA)>
<!ELEMENT SHIP_DATE (#PCDATA)>
<!ELEMENT SKU (#PCDATA)>
]]>

<![ IGNORE [
<!ELEMENT PRODUCT_ID (#PCDATA)>
<!ELEMENT SHIP_DATE (#PCDATA)>
<!ELEMENT SKU (#PCDATA)>
]]>
```

You might wonder what the big deal is here—after all, you can just use a comment to hide sections of a DTD. The usefulness of `INCLUDE` and `IGNORE` sections becomes more apparent when you use them together with parameter entities to *parameterize* DTDs. When you parameterize a DTD, you can include or ignore multiple sections of a DTD simply by changing the value of a parameter entity from `IGNORE` to `INCLUDE` or back again.

Here's an example; in this case, I'm going to let XML authors include or ignore sections of a DTD just by changing the value of a parameter entity named `includer`. To use a parameter entity in `INCLUDE` and `IGNORE` sections, you must work with the external DTD subset, so I'll set up an external DTD subset named order.dtd:

```
<?xml version = "1.0" standalone="no"?>
<!DOCTYPE DOCUMENT SYSTEM "order.dtd">
<DOCUMENT>
    <CUSTOMER>
        <NAME>
            <LAST_NAME>Smith</LAST_NAME>
            <FIRST_NAME>Sam</FIRST_NAME>
```

continues ▸

```
        </NAME>
        <DATE>October 15, 2001</DATE>
        <ORDERS>
            <ITEM>
                <PRODUCT>Tomatoes</PRODUCT>
                <NUMBER>8</NUMBER>
                <PRICE>$1.25</PRICE>
            </ITEM>
            .
            .
            .
            <ITEM>
                <PRODUCT>Lettuce</PRODUCT>
                <NUMBER>6</NUMBER>
                <PRICE>$11.50</PRICE>
            </ITEM>
        </ORDERS>
    </CUSTOMER>
</DOCUMENT>
```

Here's what order.dtd looks like; first I set up the includer parameter entity, setting it to the text `"INCLUDE"` by default:

```
<!ENTITY % includer "INCLUDE">
<!ELEMENT DOCUMENT (CUSTOMER)*>
<!ELEMENT CUSTOMER (NAME,DATE,ORDERS)>
<!ELEMENT NAME (LAST_NAME,FIRST_NAME)>
<!ELEMENT LAST_NAME (#PCDATA)>
<!ELEMENT FIRST_NAME (#PCDATA)>
<!ELEMENT DATE (#PCDATA)>
<!ELEMENT ORDERS (ITEM)*>
<!ELEMENT ITEM (PRODUCT,NUMBER,PRICE)>
<!ELEMENT PRODUCT (#PCDATA)>
<!ELEMENT NUMBER (#PCDATA)>
<!ELEMENT PRICE (#PCDATA)>
```

Now I can use the value of this entity to set up an `INCLUDE` (or `IGNORE`) section in the DTD like this:

```
<!ENTITY % includer "INCLUDE">
<!ELEMENT DOCUMENT (CUSTOMER)*>
<!ELEMENT CUSTOMER (NAME,DATE,ORDERS)>
<!ELEMENT NAME (LAST_NAME,FIRST_NAME)>
<!ELEMENT LAST_NAME (#PCDATA)>
<!ELEMENT FIRST_NAME (#PCDATA)>
<!ELEMENT DATE (#PCDATA)>
<!ELEMENT ORDERS (ITEM)*>
<!ELEMENT ITEM (PRODUCT,NUMBER,PRICE)>
<!ELEMENT PRODUCT (#PCDATA)>
<!ELEMENT NUMBER (#PCDATA)>
<!ELEMENT PRICE (#PCDATA)>
```

```
<![ %includer; [
<!ELEMENT PRODUCT_ID (#PCDATA)>
<!ELEMENT SHIP_DATE (#PCDATA)>
<!ELEMENT SKU (#PCDATA)>
]]>
```

At this point, you can include or ignore the indicated section of the DTD just by changing the value of the `includer` entity. Using a technique like this makes it easy to centralize the entities that you need to use to customize a whole DTD at one time.

In fact, that's the way the XHTML 1.1 DTD works; XHTML is expressly built to be *modular* to allow devices that can't handle full XHTML to support partial implementations. The main XHTML 1.1 DTD is actually a DTD *driver*, which means that it includes the various XHTML 1.1 modules using parameter entities. For example, here's how the XHTML 1.1 DTD includes the DTD module (that is, a section of a DTD) that supports HTML tables, `xhtml11-table-1.mod`; note that it declares a parameter entity corresponding to that module and then uses an entity reference to include the actual module:

```
<!-- Tables Module ............................................ -->
<!ENTITY % xhtml-table.mod
     PUBLIC "-//W3C//ELEMENTS XHTML 1.1 Tables 1.0//EN"
            "xhtml11-table-1.mod" >
%xhtml-table.mod;
```

However, not all devices that support XHTML might be capable of supporting tables (for example, cell phones or PDAs). So, the XHTML 1.1 DTD also defines a parameter entity named `xhtml-table.module` that's set to `"INCLUDE"` by default and includes the table module with an `INCLUDE` section like this:

```
<!-- Tables Module ............................................ -->
<!ENTITY % xhtml-table.module "INCLUDE" >
<![%xhtml-table.module;[
<!ENTITY % xhtml-table.mod
     PUBLIC "-//W3C//ELEMENTS XHTML 1.1 Tables 1.0//EN"
            "xhtml11-table-1.mod" >
%xhtml-table.mod;]]>
```

Now you can customize the XHTML 1.1 DTD by changing the value of `xhtml-table.module` to `"IGNORE"` to exclude support for tables. Because all the various XHTML 1.1 DTD modules are part of INCLUDE sections based on parameter entities like this, that DTD is considered fully *parameterized*.

All About Attributes

Attributes are name/value pairs that you can use in start and empty tags to add additional information. We've already seen in Chapter 2, "Creating Well-Formed XML Documents," that you can set up attributes as easily in XML as in HTML. Here's an example showing several attributes:

```
<CUSTOMER LAST_NAME="Smith" FIRST_NAME="Sam"
    DATE="October 15, 2001" PURCHASE="Tomatoes"
    PRICE="$1.25" NUMBER="8" />
```

In this case, I'm indicating that the customer's last name is Smith; that his first name is Sam; that the date of the current purchase is October 15, 2001; and that Sam purchased eight tomatoes for a total cost of $1.25.

Because you can declare elements in DTDs, you might expect that you can declare attributes as well, and you'd be right. In fact, there's good support of attribute declarations in DTDs, and we'll take a look at how it works now.

Declaring Attributes in DTDs

Declaring attributes and their types is very useful in XML. If you want your document to be valid, you must declare any attributes you use before using them. You can give attributes default values and even require XML authors who use your DTD to assign values to attributes.

As we saw at the beginning of this chapter, you declare a list of attributes for an element with the `<!ATTLIST>` element:

```
<!ATTLIST ELEMENT_NAME
    ATTRIBUTE_NAME TYPE DEFAULT_VALUE
    ATTRIBUTE_NAME TYPE DEFAULT_VALUE
    ATTRIBUTE_NAME TYPE DEFAULT_VALUE
    .
    .
    .
    ATTRIBUTE_NAME TYPE DEFAULT_VALUE>
```

In this case, *ELEMENT_NAME* is the name of the element that you're declaring attributes for, *ATTRIBUTE_NAME* is the name of an attribute that you're declaring, *TYPE* is the attribute's type, and *DEFAULT_VALUE* represents its default value.

Here are the possible *TYPE* values that you can use:

Type	Description
CDATA	Is simple character data (that is, text that does not include any markup)
ENTITIES	Gives multiple entity names (which must be declared in the DTD), separated by whitespace

`ENTITY`	Names an entity (which must be declared in the DTD)
`Enumerated`	Represents a list of values; any one item from the list is an appropriate attribute value (and you must use one of the items from the list)
`ID`	Is a proper XML name that must be unique (that is, not shared by any other attribute of the `ID` type)
`IDREF`	Will hold the value of an `ID` attribute of some element, usually another element to which the current element is related
`IDREFS`	Shows multiple IDs of elements separated by whitespace
`NMTOKEN`	Shows a proper XML name
`NMTOKENS`	Shows multiple proper XML names in a list, separated by whitespace
`NOTATION`	Shows a notation name (which must be declared in the DTD)

I'll take a look at all these possibilities in this chapter.

Here are the possible *`DEFAULT_VALUE`* settings that you can use:

Method	**Description**
`VALUE`	Shows a simple text value, enclosed in quotes.
`#IMPLIED`	Indicates that there is no default value for this attribute, and this attribute need not be used.
`#REQUIRED`	Indicates that there is no default value, but that a value must be assigned to this attribute.
`#FIXED` *`VALUE`*	In this case, *`VALUE`* is the attribute's value, and the attribute must always have this value.

We saw a simple example at the beginning of this chapter; in this case, I declare a `TYPE` attribute of the `CDATA` type for the `<CUSTOMER>` element and indicate that this attribute can be used as the author prefers:

```
<?xml version = "1.0" standalone="yes"?>
<!DOCTYPE DOCUMENT [
<!ELEMENT DOCUMENT (CUSTOMER)*>
<!ELEMENT CUSTOMER (NAME,DATE,ORDERS)>
<!ELEMENT NAME (LAST_NAME,FIRST_NAME)>
<!ELEMENT LAST_NAME (#PCDATA)>
<!ELEMENT FIRST_NAME (#PCDATA)>
<!ELEMENT DATE (#PCDATA)>
<!ELEMENT ORDERS (ITEM)*>
<!ELEMENT ITEM (PRODUCT,NUMBER,PRICE)>
<!ELEMENT PRODUCT (#PCDATA)>
<!ELEMENT NUMBER (#PCDATA)>
<!ELEMENT PRICE (#PCDATA)>
```

continues ▸

```
<!ATTLIST CUSTOMER
    TYPE CDATA #IMPLIED>
]>
<DOCUMENT>
    <CUSTOMER TYPE = "excellent">
        <NAME>
            <LAST_NAME>Smith</LAST_NAME>
            <FIRST_NAME>Sam</FIRST_NAME>
        </NAME>
        <DATE>October 15, 2001</DATE>
        <ORDERS>
            <ITEM>
                <PRODUCT>Tomatoes</PRODUCT>
                <NUMBER>8</NUMBER>
                <PRICE>$1.25</PRICE>
            </ITEM>
            <ITEM>
                <PRODUCT>Oranges</PRODUCT>
                <NUMBER>24</NUMBER>
                <PRICE>$4.98</PRICE>
            </ITEM>
        </ORDERS>
    </CUSTOMER>
    <CUSTOMER TYPE = "lousy">
        <NAME>
            <LAST_NAME>Jones</LAST_NAME>
            <FIRST_NAME>Polly</FIRST_NAME>
        </NAME>
        <DATE>October 20, 2001</DATE>
        <ORDERS>
            <ITEM>
                <PRODUCT>Bread</PRODUCT>
                <NUMBER>12</NUMBER>
                <PRICE>$14.95</PRICE>
            </ITEM>
            <ITEM>
                <PRODUCT>Apples</PRODUCT>
                <NUMBER>6</NUMBER>
                <PRICE>$1.50</PRICE>
            </ITEM>
        </ORDERS>
    </CUSTOMER>
    <CUSTOMER TYPE="good">
        <NAME>
            <LAST_NAME>Weber</LAST_NAME>
            <FIRST_NAME>Bill</FIRST_NAME>
        </NAME>
        <DATE>October 25, 2001</DATE>
        <ORDERS>
            <ITEM>
```

```
            <PRODUCT>Asparagus</PRODUCT>
            <NUMBER>12</NUMBER>
            <PRICE>$2.95</PRICE>
        </ITEM>
        <ITEM>
            <PRODUCT>Lettuce</PRODUCT>
            <NUMBER>6</NUMBER>
            <PRICE>$11.50</PRICE>
        </ITEM>
    </ORDERS>
  </CUSTOMER>
</DOCUMENT>
```

This example shows how to declare a single attribute, but as its name implies, you can use `<!ATTLIST>` to declare an entire list of attributes for an element; here's an example where I declare the attributes `OWES`, `LAYAWAY`, and `DEFAULTS` for the `<CUSTOMER>` element all at once:

```
<?xml version = "1.0" standalone="yes"?>
<!DOCTYPE DOCUMENT [
<!ELEMENT DOCUMENT (CUSTOMER)*>
<!ELEMENT CUSTOMER (NAME,DATE,ORDERS)>
<!ELEMENT NAME (LAST_NAME,FIRST_NAME)>
<!ELEMENT LAST_NAME (#PCDATA)>
<!ELEMENT FIRST_NAME (#PCDATA)>
<!ELEMENT DATE (#PCDATA)>
<!ELEMENT ORDERS (ITEM)*>
<!ELEMENT ITEM (PRODUCT,NUMBER,PRICE)>
<!ELEMENT PRODUCT (#PCDATA)>
<!ELEMENT NUMBER (#PCDATA)>
<!ELEMENT PRICE (#PCDATA)>
<!ATTLIST CUSTOMER
    OWES CDATA "0"
    LAYAWAY CDATA "0"
    DEFAULTS CDATA "0">
]>
<DOCUMENT>
    <CUSTOMER OWES="$12.13" LAYAWAY="$0" DEFAULTS="0">
        <NAME>
            <LAST_NAME>Smith</LAST_NAME>
            <FIRST_NAME>Sam</FIRST_NAME>
        </NAME>
        <DATE>October 15, 2001</DATE>
        <ORDERS>
            <ITEM>
                <PRODUCT>Tomatoes</PRODUCT>
                <NUMBER>8</NUMBER>
                <PRICE>$1.25</PRICE>
            </ITEM>
            <ITEM>
```

continues ▸

```
                <PRODUCT>Oranges</PRODUCT>
                <NUMBER>24</NUMBER>
                <PRICE>$4.98</PRICE>
            </ITEM>
        </ORDERS>
    </CUSTOMER>
    <CUSTOMER OWES="$132.69" LAYAWAY="$44.99" DEFAULTS="0">
        <NAME>
            <LAST_NAME>Jones</LAST_NAME>
            <FIRST_NAME>Polly</FIRST_NAME>
        </NAME>
        <DATE>October 20, 2001</DATE>
        <ORDERS>
            <ITEM>
                <PRODUCT>Bread</PRODUCT>
                <NUMBER>12</NUMBER>
                <PRICE>$14.95</PRICE>
            </ITEM>
            <ITEM>
                <PRODUCT>Apples</PRODUCT>
                <NUMBER>6</NUMBER>
                <PRICE>$1.50</PRICE>
            </ITEM>
        </ORDERS>
    </CUSTOMER>
    <CUSTOMER OWES="$0" LAYAWAY="$1.99" DEFAULTS="0">
        <NAME>
            <LAST_NAME>Weber</LAST_NAME>
            <FIRST_NAME>Bill</FIRST_NAME>
        </NAME>
        <DATE>October 25, 2001</DATE>
        <ORDERS>
            <ITEM>
                <PRODUCT>Asparagus</PRODUCT>
                <NUMBER>12</NUMBER>
                <PRICE>$2.95</PRICE>
            </ITEM>
            <ITEM>
                <PRODUCT>Lettuce</PRODUCT>
                <NUMBER>6</NUMBER>
                <PRICE>$11.50</PRICE>
            </ITEM>
        </ORDERS>
    </CUSTOMER>
</DOCUMENT>
```

Now that I've declared these attributes, the document is valid.

Setting Default Values for Attributes

I'm going to start the examination of declaring attributes in DTDs by seeing what kind of default values you can specify for attributes.

Immediate Values

You can supply a default value for an attribute simply by giving that value in quotes in the attribute's declaration in the <!ATTLIST> element, as we've seen:

```
<?xml version = "1.0" standalone="yes"?>
<!DOCTYPE DOCUMENT [
<!ELEMENT DOCUMENT (CUSTOMER)*>
<!ELEMENT CUSTOMER (NAME,DATE,ORDERS)>
<!ELEMENT NAME (LAST_NAME,FIRST_NAME)>
<!ELEMENT LAST_NAME (#PCDATA)>
<!ELEMENT FIRST_NAME (#PCDATA)>
<!ELEMENT DATE (#PCDATA)>
<!ELEMENT ORDERS (ITEM)*>
<!ELEMENT ITEM (PRODUCT,NUMBER,PRICE)>
<!ELEMENT PRODUCT (#PCDATA)>
<!ELEMENT NUMBER (#PCDATA)>
<!ELEMENT PRICE (#PCDATA)>
<!ATTLIST CUSTOMER
    OWES CDATA "0"
    LAYAWAY CDATA "0"
    DEFAULTS CDATA "0">
]>
    .
    .
    .
```

However, you can also use other keywords here, such as #REQUIRED.

#REQUIRED

When you use the #REQUIRED keyword as an attribute's default value, it means that you're actually not providing a default value, but that you're requiring anyone using this DTD to do so. Here's an example in which I'm requiring anyone who uses this DTD to supply the <CUSTOMER> element with an OWES attribute:

```
<?xml version = "1.0" standalone="yes"?>
<!DOCTYPE DOCUMENT [
<!ELEMENT DOCUMENT (CUSTOMER)*>
<!ELEMENT CUSTOMER (NAME,DATE,ORDERS)>
<!ELEMENT NAME (LAST_NAME,FIRST_NAME)>
<!ELEMENT LAST_NAME (#PCDATA)>
<!ELEMENT FIRST_NAME (#PCDATA)>
<!ELEMENT DATE (#PCDATA)>
<!ELEMENT ORDERS (ITEM)*>
```

continues ▸

```
<!ELEMENT ITEM (PRODUCT,NUMBER,PRICE)>
<!ELEMENT PRODUCT (#PCDATA)>
<!ELEMENT NUMBER (#PCDATA)>
<!ELEMENT PRICE (#PCDATA)>
<!ATTLIST CUSTOMER
    OWES CDATA #REQUIRED>
]>
<DOCUMENT>
    <CUSTOMER OWES="$0">
        <NAME>
            <LAST_NAME>Smith</LAST_NAME>
            <FIRST_NAME>Sam</FIRST_NAME>
        </NAME>
        <DATE>October 15, 2001</DATE>
        <ORDERS>
            <ITEM>
                <PRODUCT>Tomatoes</PRODUCT>
                <NUMBER>8</NUMBER>
                <PRICE>$1.25</PRICE>
            </ITEM>
            <ITEM>
                <PRODUCT>Oranges</PRODUCT>
                <NUMBER>24</NUMBER>
                <PRICE>$4.98</PRICE>
            </ITEM>
        </ORDERS>
    </CUSTOMER>
    <CUSTOMER OWES="$599.99">
        <NAME>
            <LAST_NAME>Jones</LAST_NAME>
            <FIRST_NAME>Polly</FIRST_NAME>
        </NAME>
        <DATE>October 20, 2001</DATE>
        <ORDERS>
            <ITEM>
                <PRODUCT>Bread</PRODUCT>
                <NUMBER>12</NUMBER>
                <PRICE>$14.95</PRICE>
            </ITEM>
            <ITEM>
                <PRODUCT>Apples</PRODUCT>
                <NUMBER>6</NUMBER>
                <PRICE>$1.50</PRICE>
            </ITEM>
        </ORDERS>
    </CUSTOMER>
    <CUSTOMER OWES="$29.99">
        <NAME>
            <LAST_NAME>Weber</LAST_NAME>
            <FIRST_NAME>Bill</FIRST_NAME>
```

```
        </NAME>
        <DATE>October 25, 2001</DATE>
        <ORDERS>
            <ITEM>
                <PRODUCT>Asparagus</PRODUCT>
                <NUMBER>12</NUMBER>
                <PRICE>$2.95</PRICE>
            </ITEM>
            <ITEM>
                <PRODUCT>Lettuce</PRODUCT>
                <NUMBER>6</NUMBER>
                <PRICE>$11.50</PRICE>
            </ITEM>
        </ORDERS>
    </CUSTOMER>
</DOCUMENT>
```

Requiring a value for an attribute is useful for those cases in which a document should be customized, as when you want to list the document author's name or email. It's also useful, of course, when the element needs more information—such as when you use a `URI` attribute for an element that displays an image or loads an applet.

#IMPLIED

You use the `#IMPLIED` keyword when you don't have a default value for an attribute in mind, and you want to indicate that the document author doesn't even have to use this attribute at all. XML processors will know about this attribute and will not be disturbed if the attribute is not used. (Note that some XML processors will explicitly inform the underlying software application that no value is available for this attribute if no value is given.) The `#IMPLIED` keyword is the one to use when you want to allow the document author to include this attribute but not require it.

Here's an example in which I'm making the `OWES` attribute of the `<CUSTOMER>` element implied, which means that not every element needs to use it:

```
<?xml version = "1.0" standalone="yes"?>
<!DOCTYPE DOCUMENT [
<!ELEMENT DOCUMENT (CUSTOMER)*>
<!ELEMENT CUSTOMER (NAME,DATE,ORDERS)>
<!ELEMENT NAME (LAST_NAME,FIRST_NAME)>
<!ELEMENT LAST_NAME (#PCDATA)>
<!ELEMENT FIRST_NAME (#PCDATA)>
<!ELEMENT DATE (#PCDATA)>
<!ELEMENT ORDERS (ITEM)*>
<!ELEMENT ITEM (PRODUCT,NUMBER,PRICE)>
<!ELEMENT PRODUCT (#PCDATA)>
```

continues ▸

```
<!ELEMENT NUMBER (#PCDATA)>
<!ELEMENT PRICE (#PCDATA)>
<!ATTLIST CUSTOMER
    OWES CDATA #IMPLIED>
]>
<DOCUMENT>
    <CUSTOMER OWES="$23.99">
        <NAME>
            <LAST_NAME>Smith</LAST_NAME>
            <FIRST_NAME>Sam</FIRST_NAME>
        </NAME>
        <DATE>October 15, 2001</DATE>
        <ORDERS>
            <ITEM>
                <PRODUCT>Tomatoes</PRODUCT>
                <NUMBER>8</NUMBER>
                <PRICE>$1.25</PRICE>
            </ITEM>
            <ITEM>
                <PRODUCT>Oranges</PRODUCT>
                <NUMBER>24</NUMBER>
                <PRICE>$4.98</PRICE>
            </ITEM>
        </ORDERS>
    </CUSTOMER>
    <CUSTOMER>
        <NAME>
            <LAST_NAME>Jones</LAST_NAME>
            <FIRST_NAME>Polly</FIRST_NAME>
        </NAME>
        <DATE>October 20, 2001</DATE>
        <ORDERS>
            <ITEM>
                <PRODUCT>Bread</PRODUCT>
                <NUMBER>12</NUMBER>
                <PRICE>$14.95</PRICE>
            </ITEM>
            <ITEM>
                <PRODUCT>Apples</PRODUCT>
                <NUMBER>6</NUMBER>
                <PRICE>$1.50</PRICE>
            </ITEM>
        </ORDERS>
    </CUSTOMER>
    <CUSTOMER>
        <NAME>
            <LAST_NAME>Weber</LAST_NAME>
            <FIRST_NAME>Bill</FIRST_NAME>
        </NAME>
        <DATE>October 25, 2001</DATE>
```

```
        <ORDERS>
            <ITEM>
                <PRODUCT>Asparagus</PRODUCT>
                <NUMBER>12</NUMBER>
                <PRICE>$2.95</PRICE>
            </ITEM>
            <ITEM>
                <PRODUCT>Lettuce</PRODUCT>
                <NUMBER>6</NUMBER>
                <PRICE>$11.50</PRICE>
            </ITEM>
        </ORDERS>
    </CUSTOMER>
</DOCUMENT>
```

It's very common to declare attributes as `#IMPLIED` because that means they either can appear in elements or not, as the document author prefers.

#FIXED

You can even set the value of an attribute so that it must always have that value. To do that, you use the `#FIXED` keyword, which sets a fixed value for the attribute, and then specify the value that you want the attribute to have.

Here's an example in which I'm setting the `LANGUAGE` attribute of the `<CUSTOMER>` elements to English, `EN`, and specifying that this is the only valid value for the attribute. This assumes that the underlying application can handle only English and thus needs data provided in that language:

```
<?xml version = "1.0" standalone="yes"?>
<!DOCTYPE DOCUMENT [
<!ELEMENT DOCUMENT (CUSTOMER)*>
<!ELEMENT CUSTOMER (NAME,DATE,ORDERS)>
<!ELEMENT NAME (LAST_NAME,FIRST_NAME)>
<!ELEMENT LAST_NAME (#PCDATA)>
<!ELEMENT FIRST_NAME (#PCDATA)>
<!ELEMENT DATE (#PCDATA)>
<!ELEMENT ORDERS (ITEM)*>
<!ELEMENT ITEM (PRODUCT,NUMBER,PRICE)>
<!ELEMENT PRODUCT (#PCDATA)>
<!ELEMENT NUMBER (#PCDATA)>
<!ELEMENT PRICE (#PCDATA)>
<!ATTLIST CUSTOMER
    LANGUAGE CDATA #FIXED "EN">
]>
<DOCUMENT>
    <CUSTOMER>
        <NAME>
            <LAST_NAME>Smith</LAST_NAME>
            <FIRST_NAME>Sam</FIRST_NAME>
```

continues ▸

```
        </NAME>
        <DATE>October 15, 2001</DATE>
        <ORDERS>
            <ITEM>
                <PRODUCT>Tomatoes</PRODUCT>
                <NUMBER>8</NUMBER>
                <PRICE>$1.25</PRICE>
            </ITEM>
            <ITEM>
                <PRODUCT>Oranges</PRODUCT>
                <NUMBER>24</NUMBER>
                <PRICE>$4.98</PRICE>
            </ITEM>
        </ORDERS>
    </CUSTOMER>
    <CUSTOMER>
        <NAME>
            <LAST_NAME>Jones</LAST_NAME>
            <FIRST_NAME>Polly</FIRST_NAME>
        </NAME>
        <DATE>October 20, 2001</DATE>
        <ORDERS>
            <ITEM>
                <PRODUCT>Bread</PRODUCT>
                <NUMBER>12</NUMBER>
                <PRICE>$14.95</PRICE>
            </ITEM>
            <ITEM>
                <PRODUCT>Apples</PRODUCT>
                <NUMBER>6</NUMBER>
                <PRICE>$1.50</PRICE>
            </ITEM>
        </ORDERS>
    </CUSTOMER>
    <CUSTOMER>
        <NAME>
            <LAST_NAME>Weber</LAST_NAME>
            <FIRST_NAME>Bill</FIRST_NAME>
        </NAME>
        <DATE>October 25, 2001</DATE>
        <ORDERS>
            <ITEM>
                <PRODUCT>Asparagus</PRODUCT>
                <NUMBER>12</NUMBER>
                <PRICE>$2.95</PRICE>
            </ITEM>
            <ITEM>
                <PRODUCT>Lettuce</PRODUCT>
                <NUMBER>6</NUMBER>
                <PRICE>$11.50</PRICE>
            </ITEM>
```

```
        </ORDERS>
    </CUSTOMER>
</DOCUMENT>
```

Note that I didn't even use the LANGUAGE attribute in the <CUSTOMER> elements here—the XML processor passes that attribute and its value to the underlying application anyway because I've declared them #FIXED. If you do explicitly use this attribute, you must set its value to the value that you've set as the default in the DTD, or the XML processor will generate an error.

That covers the possible default value types that you can specify when declaring attributes; I'll take a look at the possible attribute *types* next.

Attribute Types

So far, I've used just the CDATA attribute type when declaring attributes—and, in fact, that's probably the most common declaration type for attributes because it allows you to use simple text for the attribute's value. However, you can specify a number of different attribute types, and I'll take a look at them here. These types are not (not yet, anyway) detailed enough to indicate specific data types such as float, int, or double, but they can provide you with some ability to check the syntax of a document.

CDATA

The most simple attribute type that you can have is CDATA, which is simple character data. This means that the attribute may be set to a value that is any string of text, as long as the string does not contain markup. The requirement that you can't use markup explicitly excludes any string that includes the characters <, ", or &. If you want to use those characters, use their predefined entity references (<, ", and &) instead because these entity references will be parsed and replaced with the corresponding characters. (Because these attribute values are parsed, you must be careful about including anything that looks like markup—you use the term CDATA for this type, not PCDATA, which is character data that has already been parsed.)

We've already seen a number of examples of attributes declared with the CDATA type, as here:

```
<?xml version = "1.0" standalone="yes"?>
<!DOCTYPE DOCUMENT [
<!ELEMENT DOCUMENT (CUSTOMER)*>
<!ELEMENT CUSTOMER (NAME,DATE,ORDERS)>
<!ELEMENT NAME (LAST_NAME,FIRST_NAME)>
<!ELEMENT LAST_NAME (#PCDATA)>
<!ELEMENT FIRST_NAME (#PCDATA)>
<!ELEMENT DATE (#PCDATA)>
```

continues ▸

```
<!ELEMENT ORDERS (ITEM)*>
<!ELEMENT ITEM (PRODUCT,NUMBER,PRICE)>
<!ELEMENT PRODUCT (#PCDATA)>
<!ELEMENT NUMBER (#PCDATA)>
<!ELEMENT PRICE (#PCDATA)>
<!ATTLIST CUSTOMER
    OWES CDATA "0"
    LAYAWAY CDATA "0"
    DEFAULTS CDATA "0">
]>
    .
    .
    .
```

The CDATA type is the most general type of attribute; from here, we get into more specific types, such as the enumerated type.

Enumerated

The enumerated type does not use a keyword like the other attribute types do; instead, the enumerated type provides a list (or *enumeration*) of possible values. Each possible value must be a valid XML name (following the usual rules that the first character must be a letter or underscore, and so on).

Here's an example: In this case, I'm declaring an attribute named CREDIT_OK that can have only one of two possible values—"TRUE" or "FALSE"—and that has the default value "TRUE":

```
<?xml version = "1.0" standalone="yes"?>
<!DOCTYPE DOCUMENT [
<!ELEMENT DOCUMENT (CUSTOMER)*>
<!ELEMENT CUSTOMER (NAME,DATE,ORDERS)>
<!ELEMENT NAME (LAST_NAME,FIRST_NAME)>
<!ELEMENT LAST_NAME (#PCDATA)>
<!ELEMENT FIRST_NAME (#PCDATA)>
<!ELEMENT DATE (#PCDATA)>
<!ELEMENT ORDERS (ITEM)*>
<!ELEMENT ITEM (PRODUCT,NUMBER,PRICE)>
<!ELEMENT PRODUCT (#PCDATA)>
<!ELEMENT NUMBER (#PCDATA)>
<!ELEMENT PRICE (#PCDATA)>
<!ATTLIST CUSTOMER
    CREDIT_OK (TRUE | FALSE) "TRUE">
]>
<DOCUMENT>
    <CUSTOMER CREDIT_OK = "FALSE">
        <NAME>
            <LAST_NAME>Smith</LAST_NAME>
            <FIRST_NAME>Sam</FIRST_NAME>
        </NAME>
```

```
        <DATE>October 15, 2001</DATE>
        <ORDERS>
            <ITEM>
                <PRODUCT>Tomatoes</PRODUCT>
                <NUMBER>8</NUMBER>
                <PRICE>$1.25</PRICE>
            </ITEM>
            <ITEM>
                <PRODUCT>Oranges</PRODUCT>
                <NUMBER>24</NUMBER>
                <PRICE>$4.98</PRICE>
            </ITEM>
        </ORDERS>
    </CUSTOMER>
    <CUSTOMER>
        <NAME>
            <LAST_NAME>Jones</LAST_NAME>
            <FIRST_NAME>Polly</FIRST_NAME>
        </NAME>
        <DATE>October 20, 2001</DATE>
        <ORDERS>
            <ITEM>
                <PRODUCT>Bread</PRODUCT>
                <NUMBER>12</NUMBER>
                <PRICE>$14.95</PRICE>
            </ITEM>
            <ITEM>
                <PRODUCT>Apples</PRODUCT>
                <NUMBER>6</NUMBER>
                <PRICE>$1.50</PRICE>
            </ITEM>
        </ORDERS>
    </CUSTOMER>
    <CUSTOMER CREDIT_OK="TRUE">
        <NAME>
            <LAST_NAME>Weber</LAST_NAME>
            <FIRST_NAME>Bill</FIRST_NAME>
        </NAME>
        <DATE>October 25, 2001</DATE>
        <ORDERS>
            <ITEM>
                <PRODUCT>Asparagus</PRODUCT>
                <NUMBER>12</NUMBER>
                <PRICE>$2.95</PRICE>
            </ITEM>
            <ITEM>
                <PRODUCT>Lettuce</PRODUCT>
                <NUMBER>6</NUMBER>
                <PRICE>$11.50</PRICE>
            </ITEM>
        </ORDERS>
    </CUSTOMER>
</DOCUMENT>
```

Using enumerations like this is great if you want to set the possible range of values an attribute can take; for example, you might want to restrict an attribute named `WEEKDAY` to these possible values: `"Sunday"`, `"Monday"`, `"Tuesday"`, `"Wednesday"`, `"Thursday"`, `"Friday"`, or `"Saturday"`.

NMTOKEN

Document authors also commonly use another attribute type: `NMTOKEN`. An attribute of this type can take only values that are proper XML names (that is, they must start with a letter or underscore, and the following letters may include digits, letters, and underscores—in particular, note that `NMTOKEN` values cannot include whitespace).

Using `NMTOKEN` attribute values can be useful in some applications; note, for example, that XML names are very close to those that are legal for variables in C++, Java and JavaScript, which means that you could even use those names in underlying applications in fancy ways. `NMTOKEN` values also mean that attribute values must consist of a single word because whitespace of any kind is not allowed; that can be a useful restriction.

Here's an example; in this case, I'm declaring an attribute named `SHIP_STATE` to hold the two-letter state code to which an order was shipped. Declaring that attribute with `NMTOKEM` rules out the possibility of values that are longer than a single term:

```
<?xml version = "1.0" standalone="yes"?>
<!DOCTYPE DOCUMENT [
<!ELEMENT DOCUMENT (CUSTOMER)*>
<!ELEMENT CUSTOMER (NAME,DATE,ORDERS)>
<!ELEMENT NAME (LAST_NAME,FIRST_NAME)>
<!ELEMENT LAST_NAME (#PCDATA)>
<!ELEMENT FIRST_NAME (#PCDATA)>
<!ELEMENT DATE (#PCDATA)>
<!ELEMENT ORDERS (ITEM)*>
<!ELEMENT ITEM (PRODUCT,NUMBER,PRICE)>
<!ELEMENT PRODUCT (#PCDATA)>
<!ELEMENT NUMBER (#PCDATA)>
<!ELEMENT PRICE (#PCDATA)>
<!ATTLIST CUSTOMER
    SHIP_STATE NMTOKEN #REQUIRED>
]>
<DOCUMENT>
    <CUSTOMER SHIP_STATE = "CA">
        <NAME>
            <LAST_NAME>Smith</LAST_NAME>
            <FIRST_NAME>Sam</FIRST_NAME>
        </NAME>
        <DATE>October 15, 2001</DATE>
```

```
        <ORDERS>
            <ITEM>
                <PRODUCT>Tomatoes</PRODUCT>
                <NUMBER>8</NUMBER>
                <PRICE>$1.25</PRICE>
            </ITEM>
            <ITEM>
                <PRODUCT>Oranges</PRODUCT>
                <NUMBER>24</NUMBER>
                <PRICE>$4.98</PRICE>
            </ITEM>
        </ORDERS>
    </CUSTOMER>
    <CUSTOMER SHIP_STATE = "LA">
        <NAME>
            <LAST_NAME>Jones</LAST_NAME>
            <FIRST_NAME>Polly</FIRST_NAME>
        </NAME>
        <DATE>October 20, 2001</DATE>
        <ORDERS>
            <ITEM>
                <PRODUCT>Bread</PRODUCT>
                <NUMBER>12</NUMBER>
                <PRICE>$14.95</PRICE>
            </ITEM>
            <ITEM>
                <PRODUCT>Apples</PRODUCT>
                <NUMBER>6</NUMBER>
                <PRICE>$1.50</PRICE>
            </ITEM>
        </ORDERS>
    </CUSTOMER>
    <CUSTOMER SHIP_STATE = "MA">
        <NAME>
            <LAST_NAME>Weber</LAST_NAME>
            <FIRST_NAME>Bill</FIRST_NAME>
        </NAME>
        <DATE>October 25, 2001</DATE>
        <ORDERS>
            <ITEM>
                <PRODUCT>Asparagus</PRODUCT>
                <NUMBER>12</NUMBER>
                <PRICE>$2.95</PRICE>
            </ITEM>
            <ITEM>
                <PRODUCT>Lettuce</PRODUCT>
                <NUMBER>6</NUMBER>
                <PRICE>$11.50</PRICE>
            </ITEM>
        </ORDERS>
    </CUSTOMER>
</DOCUMENT>
```

NMTOKENS

You can even specify that an attribute value must be made up of `NMTOKEN`s separated by whitespace if you use the `NMTOKENS` attribute type. For example, here I'm giving the attribute `CONTACT_NAME` the type `NMTOKENS` to allow attribute values to hold first and last names, separated by whitespace:

```
<?xml version = "1.0" standalone="yes"?>
<!DOCTYPE DOCUMENT [
<!ELEMENT DOCUMENT (CUSTOMER)*>
<!ELEMENT CUSTOMER (NAME,DATE,ORDERS)>
<!ELEMENT NAME (LAST_NAME,FIRST_NAME)>
<!ELEMENT LAST_NAME (#PCDATA)>
<!ELEMENT FIRST_NAME (#PCDATA)>
<!ELEMENT DATE (#PCDATA)>
<!ELEMENT ORDERS (ITEM)*>
<!ELEMENT ITEM (PRODUCT,NUMBER,PRICE)>
<!ELEMENT PRODUCT (#PCDATA)>
<!ELEMENT NUMBER (#PCDATA)>
<!ELEMENT PRICE (#PCDATA)>
<!ATTLIST CUSTOMER
    CONTACT_NAME NMTOKENS #IMPLIED>
]>
<DOCUMENT>
    <CUSTOMER CONTACT_NAME = "George Starr">
        <NAME>
            <LAST_NAME>Smith</LAST_NAME>
            <FIRST_NAME>Sam</FIRST_NAME>
        </NAME>
        <DATE>October 15, 2001</DATE>
        <ORDERS>
            <ITEM>
                <PRODUCT>Tomatoes</PRODUCT>
                <NUMBER>8</NUMBER>
                <PRICE>$1.25</PRICE>
            </ITEM>
            <ITEM>
                <PRODUCT>Oranges</PRODUCT>
                <NUMBER>24</NUMBER>
                <PRICE>$4.98</PRICE>
            </ITEM>
        </ORDERS>
    </CUSTOMER>
    <CUSTOMER CONTACT_NAME = "Ringo Harrison">
        <NAME>
            <LAST_NAME>Jones</LAST_NAME>
            <FIRST_NAME>Polly</FIRST_NAME>
```

```
        </NAME>
        <DATE>October 20, 2001</DATE>
        <ORDERS>
            <ITEM>
                <PRODUCT>Bread</PRODUCT>
                <NUMBER>12</NUMBER>
                <PRICE>$14.95</PRICE>
            </ITEM>
            <ITEM>
                <PRODUCT>Apples</PRODUCT>
                <NUMBER>6</NUMBER>
                <PRICE>$1.50</PRICE>
            </ITEM>
        </ORDERS>
    </CUSTOMER>
    <CUSTOMER CONTACT_NAME = "Paul Lennon">
        <NAME>
            <LAST_NAME>Weber</LAST_NAME>
            <FIRST_NAME>Bill</FIRST_NAME>
        </NAME>
        <DATE>October 25, 2001</DATE>
        <ORDERS>
            <ITEM>
                <PRODUCT>Asparagus</PRODUCT>
                <NUMBER>12</NUMBER>
                <PRICE>$2.95</PRICE>
            </ITEM>
            <ITEM>
                <PRODUCT>Lettuce</PRODUCT>
                <NUMBER>6</NUMBER>
                <PRICE>$11.50</PRICE>
            </ITEM>
        </ORDERS>
    </CUSTOMER>
</DOCUMENT>
```

ID

You also can declare another very important attribute type: `ID`. XML gives special meaning to an element's `ID` value because that's the value that applications typically use to identify elements. For that reason, XML processors are supposed to make sure that no two elements have the same value for the attribute that is of type `ID` in a document (and you can give elements only one attribute of this type). The actual value that you assign to the attribute of this type must be a proper XML name.

Applications can use the ID value of elements to uniquely identify those elements—but note that you don't have to name the attribute "ID", as you do in HTML because simply specifying an attribute's type to be the ID type makes it into an ID attribute. Here's an example in which I add an ID attribute named CUSTOMER_ID to the <CUSTOMER> elements in this document:

```
<?xml version = "1.0" standalone="yes"?>
<!DOCTYPE DOCUMENT [
<!ELEMENT DOCUMENT (CUSTOMER)*>
<!ELEMENT CUSTOMER (NAME,DATE,ORDERS)>
<!ELEMENT NAME (LAST_NAME,FIRST_NAME)>
<!ELEMENT LAST_NAME (#PCDATA)>
<!ELEMENT FIRST_NAME (#PCDATA)>
<!ELEMENT DATE (#PCDATA)>
<!ELEMENT ORDERS (ITEM)*>
<!ELEMENT ITEM (PRODUCT,NUMBER,PRICE)>
<!ELEMENT PRODUCT (#PCDATA)>
<!ELEMENT NUMBER (#PCDATA)>
<!ELEMENT PRICE (#PCDATA)>
<!ATTLIST CUSTOMER
    CUSTOMER_ID ID #REQUIRED>
]>
<DOCUMENT>
    <CUSTOMER CUSTOMER_ID = "C1232231">
        <NAME>
            <LAST_NAME>Smith</LAST_NAME>
            <FIRST_NAME>Sam</FIRST_NAME>
        </NAME>
        <DATE>October 15, 2001</DATE>
        <ORDERS>
            <ITEM>
                <PRODUCT>Tomatoes</PRODUCT>
                <NUMBER>8</NUMBER>
                <PRICE>$1.25</PRICE>
            </ITEM>
            <ITEM>
                <PRODUCT>Oranges</PRODUCT>
                <NUMBER>24</NUMBER>
                <PRICE>$4.98</PRICE>
            </ITEM>
        </ORDERS>
    </CUSTOMER>
    <CUSTOMER CUSTOMER_ID = "C1232232">
        <NAME>
            <LAST_NAME>Jones</LAST_NAME>
            <FIRST_NAME>Polly</FIRST_NAME>
        </NAME>
        <DATE>October 20, 2001</DATE>
```

```
        <ORDERS>
            <ITEM>
                <PRODUCT>Bread</PRODUCT>
                <NUMBER>12</NUMBER>
                <PRICE>$14.95</PRICE>
            </ITEM>
            <ITEM>
                <PRODUCT>Apples</PRODUCT>
                <NUMBER>6</NUMBER>
                <PRICE>$1.50</PRICE>
            </ITEM>
        </ORDERS>
    </CUSTOMER>
    <CUSTOMER CUSTOMER_ID = "C1232233">
        <NAME>
            <LAST_NAME>Weber</LAST_NAME>
            <FIRST_NAME>Bill</FIRST_NAME>
        </NAME>
        <DATE>October 25, 2001</DATE>
        <ORDERS>
            <ITEM>
                <PRODUCT>Asparagus</PRODUCT>
                <NUMBER>12</NUMBER>
                <PRICE>$2.95</PRICE>
            </ITEM>
            <ITEM>
                <PRODUCT>Lettuce</PRODUCT>
                <NUMBER>6</NUMBER>
                <PRICE>$11.50</PRICE>
            </ITEM>
        </ORDERS>
    </CUSTOMER>
</DOCUMENT>
```

Note that you cannot use the `ID` type with `#FIXED` attributes (because all `#FIXED` attributes have same value). You usually use the `#REQUIRED` keyword instead.

Because `ID` values must be proper XML names, they can't be simple numbers like 12345; these values can't start with a digit.

IDREF

The `IDREF` attribute type represents an attempt to let you use attributes to specify something about a document's structure—in particular, something about the relationship that exists between elements. `IDREF` attributes hold the `ID` value of another element in the document.

For example, say that you wanted to set up a parent-child relationship between elements that was not reflected in the normal nesting structure of the document. In that case, you could set an `IDREF` attribute of an element to the `ID` of its parent. An application could then check the attribute with the `IDREF` type to determine the child's parent.

Here's an example; in this case, I'm declaring two attributes, a `CUSTOMER_ID` attribute of type `ID` and an `EMPLOYER_ID` attribute of type `IDREF` that holds the `ID` value of the customer's employer:

```
<?xml version = "1.0" standalone="yes"?>
<!DOCTYPE DOCUMENT [
<!ELEMENT DOCUMENT (CUSTOMER)*>
<!ELEMENT CUSTOMER (NAME,DATE,ORDERS)>
<!ELEMENT NAME (LAST_NAME,FIRST_NAME)>
<!ELEMENT LAST_NAME (#PCDATA)>
<!ELEMENT FIRST_NAME (#PCDATA)>
<!ELEMENT DATE (#PCDATA)>
<!ELEMENT ORDERS (ITEM)*>
<!ELEMENT ITEM (PRODUCT,NUMBER,PRICE)>
<!ELEMENT PRODUCT (#PCDATA)>
<!ELEMENT NUMBER (#PCDATA)>
<!ELEMENT PRICE (#PCDATA)>
<!ATTLIST CUSTOMER
    CUSTOMER_ID ID #REQUIRED
    EMPLOYER_ID IDREF #IMPLIED>
]>
<DOCUMENT>
    <CUSTOMER CUSTOMER_ID = "C1232231">
        <NAME>
            <LAST_NAME>Smith</LAST_NAME>
            <FIRST_NAME>Sam</FIRST_NAME>
        </NAME>
        <DATE>October 15, 2001</DATE>
        <ORDERS>
            <ITEM>
                <PRODUCT>Tomatoes</PRODUCT>
                <NUMBER>8</NUMBER>
                <PRICE>$1.25</PRICE>
            </ITEM>
            <ITEM>
                <PRODUCT>Oranges</PRODUCT>
                <NUMBER>24</NUMBER>
                <PRICE>$4.98</PRICE>
            </ITEM>
        </ORDERS>
    </CUSTOMER>
    <CUSTOMER CUSTOMER_ID = "C1232232" EMPLOYER_ID="C1232231">
```

```
        <NAME>
            <LAST_NAME>Jones</LAST_NAME>
            <FIRST_NAME>Polly</FIRST_NAME>
        </NAME>
        <DATE>October 20, 2001</DATE>
        <ORDERS>
            <ITEM>
                <PRODUCT>Bread</PRODUCT>
                <NUMBER>12</NUMBER>
                <PRICE>$14.95</PRICE>
            </ITEM>
            <ITEM>
                <PRODUCT>Apples</PRODUCT>
                <NUMBER>6</NUMBER>
                <PRICE>$1.50</PRICE>
            </ITEM>
        </ORDERS>
    </CUSTOMER>
    <CUSTOMER CUSTOMER_ID = "C1232233">
        <NAME>
            <LAST_NAME>Weber</LAST_NAME>
            <FIRST_NAME>Bill</FIRST_NAME>
        </NAME>
        <DATE>October 25, 2001</DATE>
        <ORDERS>
            <ITEM>
                <PRODUCT>Asparagus</PRODUCT>
                <NUMBER>12</NUMBER>
                <PRICE>$2.95</PRICE>
            </ITEM>
            <ITEM>
                <PRODUCT>Lettuce</PRODUCT>
                <NUMBER>6</NUMBER>
                <PRICE>$11.50</PRICE>
            </ITEM>
        </ORDERS>
    </CUSTOMER>
</DOCUMENT>
```

An XML processor can pass on the ID and IDREF structure of a document to an underlying application, which can then use that information to reconstruct the relationships of the elements in the document.

ENTITY

You can also specify that an attribute be of type ENTITY, which means that the attribute can be set to the name of an entity you've declared. For example, say that I declared an entity named SNAPSHOT1 that referred to an external image file. I could then create a new attribute named, say, IMAGE, that I could set to the entity name SNAPSHOT1. Here's how that looks:

```
<?xml version = "1.0" standalone="no"?>
<!DOCTYPE DOCUMENT [
<!ELEMENT DOCUMENT (CUSTOMER)*>
<!ELEMENT CUSTOMER (NAME,DATE,ORDERS)>
<!ELEMENT NAME (LAST_NAME,FIRST_NAME)>
<!ELEMENT LAST_NAME (#PCDATA)>
<!ELEMENT FIRST_NAME (#PCDATA)>
<!ELEMENT DATE (#PCDATA)>
<!ELEMENT ORDERS (ITEM)*>
<!ELEMENT ITEM (PRODUCT,NUMBER,PRICE)>
<!ELEMENT PRODUCT (#PCDATA)>
<!ELEMENT NUMBER (#PCDATA)>
<!ELEMENT PRICE (#PCDATA)>
<!ATTLIST CUSTOMER
    IMAGE ENTITY #IMPLIED>
<!ENTITY SNAPSHOT1 SYSTEM "image.gif">
]>
<DOCUMENT>
    <CUSTOMER IMAGE="SNAPSHOT1">
        <NAME>
            <LAST_NAME>Smith</LAST_NAME>
            <FIRST_NAME>Sam</FIRST_NAME>
        </NAME>
        <DATE>October 15, 2001</DATE>
        <ORDERS>
            <ITEM>
                <PRODUCT>Tomatoes</PRODUCT>
                <NUMBER>8</NUMBER>
                <PRICE>$1.25</PRICE>
            </ITEM>
            .
            .
            .
            <ITEM>
                <PRODUCT>Lettuce</PRODUCT>
                <NUMBER>6</NUMBER>
                <PRICE>$11.50</PRICE>
            </ITEM>
        </ORDERS>
    </CUSTOMER>
</DOCUMENT>
```

This points out how to use the ENTITY attribute type (but actually it's not a complete example because there are specific ways to set up entities to refer to external, non-XML data that we'll see at the end of this chapter). In general, the ENTITY attribute type is a useful one if you declare your own entities; for example, you might want to declare entities named SIGNATURE_HOME,

SIGNATURE_WORK, and so on that hold your name and home address, work address, and so on. If you then declare an attribute named, say, SIGNATURE of the ENTITY type, you can assign the SIGNATURE_HOME or SIGNATURE_WORK entities to the SIGNATURE attribute in the document.

ENTITIES

As with the NMTOKEN attribute type, which has a plural type, NMTOKENS, the ENTITY attribute type also has a plural type, ENTITIES. Attributes of this type can hold lists of entity names, separated by whitespace.

Here's an example; in this case, I'm declaring two entities, SNAPSHOT1 and SNAPSHOT2, and an attribute named IMAGES that you can assign both SNAPSHOT1 and SNAPSHOT2 to at the same time:

```
<?xml version = "1.0" standalone="no"?>
<!DOCTYPE DOCUMENT [
<!ELEMENT DOCUMENT (CUSTOMER)*>
<!ELEMENT CUSTOMER (NAME,DATE,ORDERS)>
<!ELEMENT NAME (LAST_NAME,FIRST_NAME)>
<!ELEMENT LAST_NAME (#PCDATA)>
<!ELEMENT FIRST_NAME (#PCDATA)>
<!ELEMENT DATE (#PCDATA)>
<!ELEMENT ORDERS (ITEM)*>
<!ELEMENT ITEM (PRODUCT,NUMBER,PRICE)>
<!ELEMENT PRODUCT (#PCDATA)>
<!ELEMENT NUMBER (#PCDATA)>
<!ELEMENT PRICE (#PCDATA)>
<!ATTLIST CUSTOMER
    IMAGES ENTITIES #IMPLIED>
<!ENTITY SNAPSHOT1 SYSTEM "image.gif">
<!ENTITY SNAPSHOT2 SYSTEM "image2.gif">
]>
<DOCUMENT>
    <CUSTOMER IMAGES="SNAPSHOT1 SNAPSHOT2">
        <NAME>
            <LAST_NAME>Smith</LAST_NAME>
            <FIRST_NAME>Sam</FIRST_NAME>
        </NAME>
        <DATE>October 15, 2001</DATE>
        <ORDERS>
            <ITEM>
                <PRODUCT>Tomatoes</PRODUCT>
                <NUMBER>8</NUMBER>
                <PRICE>$1.25</PRICE>
            </ITEM>
            .
            .
            .
            <ITEM>
```

continues ▸

```
                <PRODUCT>Lettuce</PRODUCT>
                <NUMBER>6</NUMBER>
                <PRICE>$11.50</PRICE>
            </ITEM>
        </ORDERS>
    </CUSTOMER>
</DOCUMENT>
```

As with the NMTOKENS attribute type, you use the plural ENTITIES type when you want to assign a number of entities to the same attributes. For example, you may have multiple entities defined that represent a customer's usernames and want to assign all of them to an attribute named USERNAMES. Because entities can be quite complex and even can include other entities, this is one way to store detailed data in a document simply using attributes.

NOTATION

The final type of attribute type is NOTATION. When you declare an attribute of this type, you can assign values to it that have been declared *notations*.

A notation specifies the format of non-XML data, and you use it to describe external entities. One popular type of notations are multipurpose Internet mail extensions (MIME) types such as image/gif, application/xml, text/html, and so on. (You can get a list of the registered MIME types at ftp://ftp.isi.edu/in-notes/iana/assignments/media-types/media-types.)

Here's an example; in this case, I'll declare two notations, GIF and JPG, that stand for the MIME types image/gif and image/jpeg. Then I'll set up an attribute that may be assigned either of these values.

To declare a notation, you use the <!NOTATION> element in a DTD like this:

```
<!NOTATION NAME SYSTEM "EXTERNAL_ID">
```

Here, *NAME* is the name of the notation, and *EXTERNAL_ID* is the external ID that you want to use for the notation, often a MIME type.

You can also use the PUBLIC keyword for public notations if you supply a formal public identifier (FPI—see the rules for constructing FPIs in the previous chapter), like this:

```
<!NOTATION NAME PUBLIC FPI "EXTERNAL_ID">
```

Here's how I create the GIF and JPG notations:

```
<?xml version = "1.0" standalone="no"?>
<!DOCTYPE DOCUMENT [
<!ELEMENT DOCUMENT (CUSTOMER)*>
<!ELEMENT CUSTOMER (NAME,DATE,ORDERS)>
<!ELEMENT NAME (LAST_NAME,FIRST_NAME)>
<!ELEMENT LAST_NAME (#PCDATA)>
<!ELEMENT FIRST_NAME (#PCDATA)>
```

```
<!ELEMENT DATE (#PCDATA)>
<!ELEMENT ORDERS (ITEM)*>
<!ELEMENT ITEM (PRODUCT,NUMBER,PRICE)>
<!ELEMENT PRODUCT (#PCDATA)>
<!ELEMENT NUMBER (#PCDATA)>
<!ELEMENT PRICE (#PCDATA)>
<!NOTATION GIF SYSTEM "image/gif">
<!NOTATION JPG SYSTEM "image/jpeg">
    .
    .
    .
```

Now I'm free to create an attribute named, say, `IMAGE_TYPE`, of type `NOTATION` that you can assign either the `GIF` or the `JPG` notations to:

```
<?xml version = "1.0" standalone="no"?>
<!DOCTYPE DOCUMENT [
<!ELEMENT DOCUMENT (CUSTOMER)*>
<!ELEMENT CUSTOMER (NAME,DATE,ORDERS)>
<!ELEMENT NAME (LAST_NAME,FIRST_NAME)>
<!ELEMENT LAST_NAME (#PCDATA)>
<!ELEMENT FIRST_NAME (#PCDATA)>
<!ELEMENT DATE (#PCDATA)>
<!ELEMENT ORDERS (ITEM)*>
<!ELEMENT ITEM (PRODUCT,NUMBER,PRICE)>
<!ELEMENT PRODUCT (#PCDATA)>
<!ELEMENT NUMBER (#PCDATA)>
<!ELEMENT PRICE (#PCDATA)>
<!NOTATION GIF SYSTEM "image/gif">
<!NOTATION JPG SYSTEM "image/jpeg">
<!ATTLIST CUSTOMER
    IMAGE NMTOKEN #IMPLIED
    IMAGE_TYPE NOTATION (GIF | JPG) #IMPLIED>
]>
    .
    .
    .
```

At this point, I'm free to use the `IMAGE_TYPE` attribute:

```
<?xml version = "1.0" standalone="no"?>
<!DOCTYPE DOCUMENT [
<!ELEMENT DOCUMENT (CUSTOMER)*>
<!ELEMENT CUSTOMER (NAME,DATE,ORDERS)>
<!ELEMENT NAME (LAST_NAME,FIRST_NAME)>
<!ELEMENT LAST_NAME (#PCDATA)>
<!ELEMENT FIRST_NAME (#PCDATA)>
<!ELEMENT DATE (#PCDATA)>
<!ELEMENT ORDERS (ITEM)*>
<!ELEMENT ITEM (PRODUCT,NUMBER,PRICE)>
<!ELEMENT PRODUCT (#PCDATA)>
```

continues ▸

```
<!ELEMENT NUMBER (#PCDATA)>
<!ELEMENT PRICE (#PCDATA)>
<!NOTATION GIF SYSTEM "image/gif">
<!NOTATION JPG SYSTEM "image/jpeg">
<!ATTLIST CUSTOMER
    IMAGE NMTOKEN #IMPLIED
    IMAGE_TYPE NOTATION (GIF | JPG) #IMPLIED>
]>
<DOCUMENT>
    <CUSTOMER IMAGE="image.gif" IMAGE_TYPE="GIF">
        <NAME>
            <LAST_NAME>Smith</LAST_NAME>
            <FIRST_NAME>Sam</FIRST_NAME>
        </NAME>
        <DATE>October 15, 2001</DATE>
        <ORDERS>
            <ITEM>
                <PRODUCT>Tomatoes</PRODUCT>
                <NUMBER>8</NUMBER>
                <PRICE>$1.25</PRICE>
            </ITEM>
            <ITEM>
                <PRODUCT>Oranges</PRODUCT>
                <NUMBER>24</NUMBER>
                <PRICE>$4.98</PRICE>
            </ITEM>
            .
            .
            .
            <ITEM>
                <PRODUCT>Asparagus</PRODUCT>
                <NUMBER>12</NUMBER>
                <PRICE>$2.95</PRICE>
            </ITEM>
            <ITEM>
                <PRODUCT>Lettuce</PRODUCT>
                <NUMBER>6</NUMBER>
                <PRICE>$11.50</PRICE>
            </ITEM>
        </ORDERS>
    </CUSTOMER>
</DOCUMENT>
```

This example brings up an interesting point; here, I've just set the value of an attribute, `IMAGE`, to the name of an image file, image.gif—but how do you actually make an unparsed entity like an image part of a document? There's a way of doing that explicitly, and now that we know about notations, we're ready to use it in the next section.

This completes our coverage of creating attributes, but don't forget that there are also two attributes that are in some sense predefined in XML, and we've already covered those: `xml:space`, which you can use to preserve the whitespace in an element, and `xml:lang`, which you can use to specify the language used in an element and its attributes. They're not really predefined because you must declare them if you want to use them, but you shouldn't use these attribute names for anything other than their intended use.

Embedding Non-XML Data in a Document

In the previous example, I associated an image, image.gif, with a document, but only by setting an attribute to the text `"image.gif"`. What if I wanted to make image.gif a real part of the document? I can do that by treating image.gif as an external *unparsed entity*. The creators of XML realized that XML was not ideal for storing data that is not text, so they added the idea of unparsed entities as a way of associating non-XML data, such as non-XML text, or binary data, with XML documents.

To declare an external unparsed entity, use an `<!ENTITY>` element—note the keyword `NDATA`, indicating that I'm referring to an unparsed entity:

```
<!ENTITY NAME SYSTEM VALUE NDATA TYPE>
```

Here, *`NAME`* is the name of the external unparsed entity, *`VALUE`* is the value of the entity, such as the name of an external file (for example, image.gif), and *`TYPE`* is a declared notation. You can also use public external unparsed entities if you use the `PUBLIC` keyword with a formal public identifier:

```
<!ENTITY NAME PUBLIC FPI VALUE NDATA TYPE>
```

Here's an example; in this case, I start by declaring a notation named `GIF` that stands for the image/gif MIME type:

```
<?xml version = "1.0" standalone="no"?>
<!DOCTYPE DOCUMENT [
<!ELEMENT DOCUMENT (CUSTOMER)*>
<!ELEMENT CUSTOMER (NAME,DATE,ORDERS)>
<!ELEMENT NAME (LAST_NAME,FIRST_NAME)>
<!ELEMENT LAST_NAME (#PCDATA)>
<!ELEMENT FIRST_NAME (#PCDATA)>
<!ELEMENT DATE (#PCDATA)>
<!ELEMENT ORDERS (ITEM)*>
<!ELEMENT ITEM (PRODUCT,NUMBER,PRICE)>
<!ELEMENT PRODUCT (#PCDATA)>
<!ELEMENT NUMBER (#PCDATA)>
<!ELEMENT PRICE (#PCDATA)>
<!NOTATION GIF SYSTEM "image/gif">
    .
    .
    .
```

Now I create an external unparsed entity named SNAPSHOT1 to refer to the external image file, image.gif:

```
<?xml version = "1.0" standalone="no"?>
<!DOCTYPE DOCUMENT [
<!ELEMENT DOCUMENT (CUSTOMER)*>
<!ELEMENT CUSTOMER (NAME,DATE,ORDERS)>
<!ELEMENT NAME (LAST_NAME,FIRST_NAME)>
<!ELEMENT LAST_NAME (#PCDATA)>
<!ELEMENT FIRST_NAME (#PCDATA)>
<!ELEMENT DATE (#PCDATA)>
<!ELEMENT ORDERS (ITEM)*>
<!ELEMENT ITEM (PRODUCT,NUMBER,PRICE)>
<!ELEMENT PRODUCT (#PCDATA)>
<!ELEMENT NUMBER (#PCDATA)>
<!ELEMENT PRICE (#PCDATA)>
<!NOTATION GIF SYSTEM "image/gif">
<!ENTITY SNAPSHOT1 SYSTEM "image.gif" NDATA GIF>
    .
    .
    .
```

After you've declared an external unparsed entity like SNAPSHOT1, you can't just embed it in an XML document directly. Instead, you create a new attribute of the ENTITY type that you can assign the entity to. I'll call this new attribute IMAGE:

```
<?xml version = "1.0" standalone="no"?>
<!DOCTYPE DOCUMENT [
<!ELEMENT DOCUMENT (CUSTOMER)*>
<!ELEMENT CUSTOMER (NAME,DATE,ORDERS)>
<!ELEMENT NAME (LAST_NAME,FIRST_NAME)>
<!ELEMENT LAST_NAME (#PCDATA)>
<!ELEMENT FIRST_NAME (#PCDATA)>
<!ELEMENT DATE (#PCDATA)>
<!ELEMENT ORDERS (ITEM)*>
<!ELEMENT ITEM (PRODUCT,NUMBER,PRICE)>
<!ELEMENT PRODUCT (#PCDATA)>
<!ELEMENT NUMBER (#PCDATA)>
<!ELEMENT PRICE (#PCDATA)>
<!NOTATION GIF SYSTEM "image/gif">
<!ENTITY SNAPSHOT1 SYSTEM "image.gif" NDATA GIF>
<!ATTLIST CUSTOMER
    IMAGE ENTITY #IMPLIED>
]>
    .
    .
    .
```

Now, finally, I'm able to assign the IMAGE attribute the value SNAPSHOT1 like this, making image.gif an official part of the document:

```
<?xml version = "1.0" standalone="no"?>
<!DOCTYPE DOCUMENT [
<!ELEMENT DOCUMENT (CUSTOMER)*>
<!ELEMENT CUSTOMER (NAME,DATE,ORDERS)>
<!ELEMENT NAME (LAST_NAME,FIRST_NAME)>
<!ELEMENT LAST_NAME (#PCDATA)>
<!ELEMENT FIRST_NAME (#PCDATA)>
<!ELEMENT DATE (#PCDATA)>
<!ELEMENT ORDERS (ITEM)*>
<!ELEMENT ITEM (PRODUCT,NUMBER,PRICE)>
<!ELEMENT PRODUCT (#PCDATA)>
<!ELEMENT NUMBER (#PCDATA)>
<!ELEMENT PRICE (#PCDATA)>
<!NOTATION GIF SYSTEM "image/gif">
<!ENTITY SNAPSHOT1 SYSTEM "image.gif" NDATA GIF>
<!ATTLIST CUSTOMER
    IMAGE ENTITY #IMPLIED>
]>
<DOCUMENT>
    <CUSTOMER IMAGE="SNAPSHOT1">
        <NAME>
            <LAST_NAME>Smith</LAST_NAME>
            <FIRST_NAME>Sam</FIRST_NAME>
        </NAME>
        <DATE>October 15, 2001</DATE>
        <ORDERS>
            <ITEM>
                <PRODUCT>Tomatoes</PRODUCT>
                <NUMBER>8</NUMBER>
                <PRICE>$1.25</PRICE>
            </ITEM>
            .
            .
            .
            <ITEM>
                <PRODUCT>Lettuce</PRODUCT>
                <NUMBER>6</NUMBER>
                <PRICE>$11.50</PRICE>
            </ITEM>
        </ORDERS>
    </CUSTOMER>
</DOCUMENT>
```

If you use external unparsed entities like this, validating XML processors won't try to read and parse them, but they'll often check to make sure that they're there. So, be sure that the document is complete.

What if I wanted to embed multiple unparsed entities? Take a look at the next topic.

Embedding Multiple Unparsed Entities in a Document

Embedding multiple unparsed entities is no problem; just create an attribute of the `ENTITIES` type and assign multiple entities to it, like this:

```
<?xml version = "1.0" standalone="no"?>
<!DOCTYPE DOCUMENT [
<!ELEMENT DOCUMENT (CUSTOMER)*>
<!ELEMENT CUSTOMER (NAME,DATE,ORDERS)>
<!ELEMENT NAME (LAST_NAME,FIRST_NAME)>
<!ELEMENT LAST_NAME (#PCDATA)>
<!ELEMENT FIRST_NAME (#PCDATA)>
<!ELEMENT DATE (#PCDATA)>
<!ELEMENT ORDERS (ITEM)*>
<!ELEMENT ITEM (PRODUCT,NUMBER,PRICE)>
<!ELEMENT PRODUCT (#PCDATA)>
<!ELEMENT NUMBER (#PCDATA)>
<!ELEMENT PRICE (#PCDATA)>
<!NOTATION GIF SYSTEM "image/gif">
<!ATTLIST CUSTOMER
    IMAGES ENTITIES #IMPLIED>
<!ENTITY SNAPSHOT1 SYSTEM "image.gif" NDATA GIF>
<!ENTITY SNAPSHOT2 SYSTEM "image2.gif" NDATA GIF>
<!ENTITY SNAPSHOT3 SYSTEM "image3.gif" NDATA GIF>
]>
<DOCUMENT>
    <CUSTOMER IMAGES="SNAPSHOT1 SNAPSHOT2 SNAPSHOT3">
        <NAME>
            <LAST_NAME>Smith</LAST_NAME>
            <FIRST_NAME>Sam</FIRST_NAME>
        </NAME>
        <DATE>October 15, 2001</DATE>
        <ORDERS>
            <ITEM>
                <PRODUCT>Tomatoes</PRODUCT>
                <NUMBER>8</NUMBER>
                <PRICE>$1.25</PRICE>
            </ITEM>
            .
            .
            .
            <ITEM>
                <PRODUCT>Lettuce</PRODUCT>
                <NUMBER>6</NUMBER>
                <PRICE>$11.50</PRICE>
            </ITEM>
        </ORDERS>
    </CUSTOMER>
</DOCUMENT>
```

And that's it all it takes.

And that's it for our coverage of constructing and using DTDs as well. In this chapter and the previous chapter, we've seen what goes into a DTD and how to handle elements, attributes, entities, and notations. In the next chapter, we'll take a look at the proposed alternate way of declaring those items in XML documents: XML schemas.

5 Creating XML Schemas

FOR THE PREVIOUS TWO CHAPTERS, WE'VE BEEN WORKING with DTDs. Over time, many people have complained to the W3C about the complexity of DTDs and have asked for something simpler. W3C listened, assigned a committee to work on the problem, and came up with a solution that is much more complex than DTDs ever were: XML schemas.

On the other hand, schemas are also far more powerful and precise than DTDs ever were. With schemas, not only can you specify the syntax of a document as you would with a DTD, but you also can do the following: specify the actual data types of each element's content, inherit syntax from other schemas, annotate schemas, use schemas with multiple namespaces, create simple and complex data types, specify the minimum and maximum number of times that an element can occur, create list types, create attribute groups, restrict the ranges of values that elements can hold, restrict what other schemas can inherit from yours, merge fragments of multiple schemas together, require that attribute or element values be unique, and much more.

Currently, the specification for XML schemas is in the working draft stage, which means that it will probably change before becoming a recommendation. You can find the specification in these three documents:

- `www.w3.org/TR/xmlschema-0/`. XML schema primer, a tutorial introduction to schemas
- `www.w3.org/TR/xmlschema-1/`. XML schema structures, the formal details on creating schemas
- `www.w3.org/TR/xmlschema-2/`. XML schema data types, all about the data types that you can use in schemas

The schema working group expressly set out to tackle a few issues: using namespaces when validating documents, providing for data typing and restrictions, allowing and restricting inheritance between schemas, and creating primitive data types, among others.

Some software is available for modern schema support. W3C had an early schema checker at http://cgi.w3.org/cgi-bin/xmlschema-check, but that page now points to an alpha version of a new schema checker at what looks like a temporary location: www.w3.org/2000/06/webdata/xsv. Apache's Xerces XML parser now contains some support for schemas—see http://xml.apache.org/xerces-j/. Oracle also has some support—see http://technet.oracle.com/tech/xml/schema_java/ index.htm. XML Spy has support at http://new.xmlspy.com/features_schema.html. You can find additional software implementations (including a tool to convert from DTDs to schemas) at www.w3.org/XML/Schema.html.

One of the original proponents of XML schemas was Microsoft. Microsoft's documentation on XML frequently decried DTDs as being too complex and said that schemas would fix the problem. That's not the way it turned out. In fact, the Microsoft implementation of XML schemas in Internet Explorer was promptly outdated not long after it was introduced.

XML Schemas in Internet Explorer

As with many other developers, Microsoft got caught basing its software on a relatively early XML specification, which promptly changed. As implemented in Internet Explorer, Microsoft's schemas are based on the XML-Data Note www.w3.org/TR/1998/NOTE-XML-data-0105/ and the Document Content Description (DCD) note www.w3.org/TR/NOTE-dcd, and are now very outdated.

In this chapter, I'll take a look at schemas as used today in the only implementation that I know of: Internet Explorer. After getting an overview of schemas as used in Internet Explorer, I'll go on to take a look in depth at the most recent XML schema specification and explore how to use it.

You can find the Microsoft XML schema reference at http://msdn.microsoft.com/xml/reference/schema/start.asp. To see how to use schemas in Internet Explorer, I'm going to create an example here. In this case, I'll create a document holding the names of a couple XML programmers in a document whose root is <PROGRAMMING_TEAM>.

```
<?xml version="1.0" ?>
<PROGRAMMING_TEAM>
    <PROGRAMMER>Fred Samson</PROGRAMMER>
    <PROGRAMMER>Edward Fredericks</PROGRAMMER>
    <DESCRIPTION>XML Programming Team</DESCRIPTION>
</PROGRAMMING_TEAM>
```

How do you associate a schema with this document as far as Internet Explorer is concerned? You do so by specifying a default namespace for the document, using the `xmlns` namespace attribute in the root element, and prefacing the name of the schema file with `x-schema:`, like this:

```
<?xml version="1.0" ?>
<PROGRAMMING_TEAM xmlns="x-schema:schema1.xml">
    <PROGRAMMER>Fred Samson</PROGRAMMER>
    <PROGRAMMER>Edward Fredericks</PROGRAMMER>
    <DESCRIPTION>XML Programming Team</DESCRIPTION>
</PROGRAMMING_TEAM>
```

Here, I'm naming the schema file schema1.xml (Internet Explorer does not insist on any special extension for schema files). All that remains is to create the schema file itself. To do that, I start with the `<schema>` element, like this:

```
<schema>
    .
    .
    .
</schema>
```

You can name the schema using the `name` attribute, like this:

```
<schema name="schema1">
    .
    .
    .
</schema>
```

One of the advantages of using schemas is that they allow you to specify the actual data types that you want to use, but those data types weren't fully fleshed out at the time Microsoft decided to implement schemas, so Microsoft implemented its own. To create a schema for Internet Explorer, you set up a default namespace, `urn:schemas-microsoft-com:xml-data`, and a namespace prefix of `dt` for data types: `urn:schemas-microsoft-com:datatypes`:

```
<schema name="schema1"
    xmlns="urn:schemas-microsoft-com:xml-data"
    xmlns:dt="urn:schemas-microsoft-com:datatypes">
    .
    .
    .
</schema>
```

Now Internet Explorer data types are available for use with the `dt` prefix; you'll find those data types in Table 5.1. There's more information at `http://msdn.microsoft.com/xml/reference/schema/datatypes.asp` as well.

Table 5.1 **Microsoft XML Schema Data Types**

Type	Description
`bin.base64`	Base64-encoded binary object.
`bin.hex`	Hexadecimal digits.
`boolean`	`0` or `1` values.
`char`	A one-character string.
`date`	Date (in ISO 8601 format, without the time data, such as `"2001-10-15"`).
`dateTime`	Date and time (in ISO 8601 format, with optional time data, such as `"2001-10-15T09:41:33"`).
`dateTime.tz`	Date, time, and time zone (in ISO 8601 format, with optional time data, and time zone, such as `"2001-10-15T09:41:33-08:00"`).
`fixed.14.4`	Format identical to the `number` format, but with no more than 14 digits to the left of the decimal point, and no more than 4 to the right.
`float`	Floating point number.
`int`	Integer value.
`number`	A simple number, with no limit on digits. This value can have a sign, fractional digits, and an exponent.
`time`	Time in a ISO 8601 format, with no date and no time zone.
`time.tz`	Time in a ISO 8601 format, with no date and with an optional time zone.
`i1`	Integer represented in 1 byte.
`i2`	Integer represented in 1 word.
`i4`	Integer represented in 4 bytes.
`r4`	Real number, with 7-digit precision.
`r8`	Real number, with 15-digit precision.
`ui1`	Unsigned integer, stored in 1 byte.
`ui2`	Unsigned integer, stored in 2 bytes.
`ui4`	Unsigned integer, stored in 4 bytes.
`uri`	Universal resource identifier (URI).
`uuid`	Hexadecimal digits representing octets.

To actually specify the syntax of an element in an Internet Explorer schema currently, you use the `<elementtype>` element, as in this case, where I'm specifying that the `<PROGRAMMER>` and `<DESCRIPTION>` elements can contain only text and that their content model is *closed*—this means that they cannot accept any other content than listed. (In these versions of schemas, if you leave the content model as open, the element can contain content other than what you specify.)

```
<schema name="schema1"
    xmlns="urn:schemas-microsoft-com:xml-data"
    xmlns:dt="urn:schemas-microsoft-com:datatypes">

    <elementtype name="PROGRAMMER" content="textOnly" model="closed"/>
    <elementtype name="DESCRIPTION" content="textOnly" model="closed"/>
    .
    .
    .
</SCHEMA>
```

If I want to specify the type of an element, I can use the `dt:type` attribute like this, specifying a data type from Table 5.1:

```
<schema name="schema1"
    xmlns="urn:schemas-microsoft-com:xml-data"
    xmlns:dt="urn:schemas-microsoft-com:datatypes">

    <elementtype name="PROGRAMMER" content="textOnly" model="closed"/>
    <elementtype name="DESCRIPTION" content="textOnly" model="closed"/>
<elementtype name="counter" dt:type="int"/>
    .
    .
    .
</schema>
```

Unfortunately, Internet Explorer doesn't yet support data type checking using the data types that you specify in schemas. However, you can use data types directly in XML documents like this in Internet Explorer:

```
<document xmlns:dt="urn:schemas-microsoft-com:datatypes"><dt:int>8</dt:int></document>
```

Next, I'll define the `<PROGRAMMING_TEAM>` element in this schema. This element can contain both `<PROGRAMMER>` and `<DESCRIPTION>` elements, but it can contain *only* elements (not text). You specify this by assigning the value `eltOnly` to the `<elementtype>` element's `content` attribute in this version of schemas. Notice that I'm also specifying that the `<PROGRAMMER>` element must occur at least once and that the `<DESCRIPTION>` element must also occur once, but only once, in the `<PROGRAMMING_TEAM>` element, using the `minOccurs` and `maxOccurs` attributes:

```
<schema name="schema1"
    xmlns="urn:schemas-microsoft-com:xml-data"
    xmlns:dt="urn:schemas-microsoft-com:datatypes">

    <elementtype name="PROGRAMMER" content="textOnly" model="closed"/>
    <elementtype name="DESCRIPTION" content="textOnly" model="closed"/>
```

continues ▸

```
    <elementtype name="PROGRAMMING_TEAM" content="eltOnly" model="closed">
        <element type="PROGRAMMER" minOccurs="1" maxOccurs="*"/>
        <element type="DESCRIPTION" minOccurs="1" maxOccurs="1"/>
  </elementtype>
</schema>
```

That's what schemas look like in Internet Explorer. It's not worth fleshing out this example in more detail because it's based on an obsolete schema model; because the XML schema specification has changed a great deal, Microsoft will have to change its implementation.

For that reason, in the rest of this chapter, I'll take a look at the way the W3C says schemas should work. Unfortunately, no software support exists for true XML schemas yet, but it will come in time. Presumably, the Internet Explorer schema model will follow the official schema recommendation when it comes out, at least as a partial implementation. This means that the material in the rest of the chapter is the way things will look in the future, even in Internet Explorer.

W3C XML Schemas

Most of this chapter will center on an example document, book.xml, and its accompanying schema, book.xsd (.xsd is the extension that W3C uses by convention for schema files). This example is all about recording the books loaned by one person, Doug Glass, and borrowed by another, Britta Regensburg. I record the name and address of the borrower and lender, as well as data about the actual books borrowed, including their titles, publication date, replacement value, and maximum number of days that the book may be loaned for. Here's what book.xml looks like:

```
<?xml version="1.0"?>
<transaction borrowDate="2001-10-15">
    <Lender phone="607.555.2222">
        <name>Doug Glass</name>
        <street>416 Disk Drive</street>
        <city>Medfield</city>
        <state>MA</state>
    </Lender>
    <Borrower phone="310.555.1111">
        <name>Britta Regensburg</name>
        <street>219 Union Drive</street>
        <city>Medfield</city>
        <state>CA</state>
    </Borrower>
    <note>Lender wants these back in two weeks!</note>
    <books>
        <book bookID="123-4567-890">
```

```
            <bookTitle>Earthquakes for Breakfast</bookTitle>
            <pubDate>2001-10-20</pubDate>
            <replacementValue>15.95</replacementValue>
            <maxDaysOut>14</maxDaysOut>
        </book>
        <book bookID="123-4567-891">
            <bookTitle>Avalanches for Lunch</bookTitle>
            <pubDate>2001-10-21</pubDate>
            <replacementValue>19.99</replacementValue>
            <maxDaysOut>14</maxDaysOut>
        </book>
        <book bookID="123-4567-892">
            <bookTitle>Meteor Showers for Dinner</bookTitle>
            <pubDate>2001-10-22</pubDate>
            <replacementValue>11.95</replacementValue>
            <maxDaysOut>14</maxDaysOut>
        </book>
        <book bookID="123-4567-893">
            <bookTitle>Snacking on Volcanoes</bookTitle>
            <pubDate>2001-10-23</pubDate>
            <replacementValue>17.99</replacementValue>
            <maxDaysOut>14</maxDaysOut>
        </book>
    </books>
</transaction>
```

Note in particular that this document has a root element named <transaction> and various subelements such as <Lender>, <Borrower>, <books>, and so on. In fact, the subelements themselves have elements, such as the multiple <book> elements inside the <books> element.

In terms of XML schemas, elements that enclose subelements or have attributes are *complex types*. Elements that enclose only simple data such as numbers, strings, or dates—but that do not have any subelements—are *simple types*. In addition, attributes are always simple types because attribute values cannot contain any structure. If you look at a document as a tree, simple types have no subnodes, while complex types can.

The distinction between simple and complex types is an important one because you declare simple and complex types differently. You declare complex types yourself, and the XML schema specification comes with many simple types already declared, as we'll see. You can also declare your own simple types; we'll see how to do that as well.

Here's another thing to note: No part of the document book.xml indicates what schema you should use with it (with DTDs, you use the <!DOCTYPE> element to specify an external DTD). The W3C has not been very clear on what the exact mechanism is for associating schema with documents—in fact, the W3C assumes that an XML processor can find the schema for a document without any information from the document itself.

How this is expected to work in detail is not clear right now, although the W3C seems to want this association between schema and document to be made through the use of namespaces, much like the namespace declaration that we saw in the XML example document used in Internet Explorer:

```
<?xml version="1.0" ?>
<PROGRAMMING_TEAM xmlns="x-schema:schema1.xml">
    <PROGRAMMER>Fred Samson</PROGRAMMER>
    <PROGRAMMER>Edward Fredericks</PROGRAMMER>
    <DESCRIPTION>XML Programming Team</DESCRIPTION>
</PROGRAMMING_TEAM>
```

This relies quite a bit on the XML processor to track down the schema from a namespace declaration; it's less of a problem for this Internet Explorer example because Internet Explorer knows that a namespace that begins with `x-schema:` refers to a schema. In general, however, you'll have to declare a namespace for a document that refers to the schema, something like this:

```
<?xml version="1.0"?>
<transaction borrowDate="2001-10-15"
    xmlns="http://www.starpowder.com/schema">
    <Lender phone="607.555.2222">
        <name>Doug Glass</name>
        <street>416 Disk Drive</street>
        <city>Medfield</city>
        <state>MA</state>
    </Lender>
    .
    .
    .
```

It's then going to be up to the XML processor to find the schema from this description. Inside a schema, you can declare a *target namespace*. When the XML processor finds the schema and verifies that its target namespace is the same as the document's, it can validate the document. More details on this process will become clear as schemas come into more popular use.

Here's the schema for the document book.xml; this schema is named book.xsd, and the prefix `xsd:` is the prefix used by convention to indicate a W3C schema namespace. (I'll take a look at ways of avoiding the `xsd:` prefix later in this chapter, but usually you associate the namespace `xsd` with the W3C schema namespace and prefix W3C schema elements with `xsd:` so that they don't conflict with the elements you're declaring.) Note that, like all schemas, book.xsd is a well-formed XML document:

```
<xsd:schema xmlns:xsd="http://www.w3.org/1999/XMLSchema">

    <xsd:annotation>
        <xsd:documentation>
            Book borrowing transaction schema.
```

```
        </xsd:documentation>
    </xsd:annotation>

    <xsd:element name="transaction" type="transactionType"/>

    <xsd:complexType name="transactionType">
        <xsd:element name="Lender" type="address"/>
        <xsd:element name="Borrower" type="address"/>
        <xsd:element ref="note" minOccurs="0"/>
        <xsd:element name="books" type="books"/>
        <xsd:attribute name="borrowDate" type="xsd:date"/>
    </xsd:complexType>

    <xsd:element name="note" type="xsd:string"/>

    <xsd:complexType name="address">
        <xsd:element name="name" type="xsd:string"/>
        <xsd:element name="street" type="xsd:string"/>
        <xsd:element name="city" type="xsd:string"/>
        <xsd:element name="state" type="xsd:string"/>
        <xsd:attribute name="phone" type="xsd:string"
            use="optional"/>
    </xsd:complexType>

    <xsd:complexType name="books">
        <xsd:element name="book" minOccurs="0" maxOccurs="10">
            <xsd:complexType>
                <xsd:element name="bookTitle" type="xsd:string"/>
                <xsd:element name="pubDate" type="xsd:date" minOccurs='0'/>
                <xsd:element name="replacementValue" type="xsd:decimal"/>
                <xsd:element name="maxDaysOut">
                    <xsd:simpleType base="xsd:integer">
                        <xsd:maxExclusive value="14"/>
                     </xsd:simpleType>
                </xsd:element>
                <xsd:attribute name="bookID" type="catalogID"/>
            </xsd:complexType>
        </xsd:element>
    </xsd:complexType>

    <xsd:simpleType name="catalogID" base="xsd:string">
        <xsd:pattern value="\d{3}-\d{4}-\d{3}"/>
    </xsd:simpleType>

</xsd:schema>
```

We'll go through the various parts of this schema in this chapter, but you can already see some of the structure here. Note, for example, that you use a particular namespace in XML schemas—`"http://www.w3.org/1999/XMLSchema"`—and that the schema elements such as `<xsd:element>` are part of that namespace (you don't have to use the `prefix xsd:`, but it's conventional). As you can see, elements are declared with the `<xsd:element>` element, and attributes are declared with the `<xsd:attribute>` element. Furthermore, you specify the type of elements and attributes when you declare them. To create types, you can use the `<xsd:complexType>` and `<xsd:simpleType>` elements (you can then create elements from the simple or complex types you've created, or use the built-in simple types), schema annotations with the `<xsd:annotation>` element, and so on.

In this case, the root element of the document, `<transaction>`, is defined to be of the type `transactionType`, and this element can contain several other elements, including those of the `address` and `books` types. The `address` type itself is defined to contain elements that hold a person's name and address, and the `books` type holds elements named `<book>` that describe a book, including its title, publication date, and so on. Using this schema, you can describe the syntax of book.xml completely. I'll start taking this schema apart now as we explore it piece by piece.

Declaring Types and Elements

The most basic thing to understand about XML schemas is the concept of using simple and complex types, and how they relate to declaring elements. Unlike with DTDs, you specify the type of the elements that you declare with schemas.

This means that the first step in declaring elements is to make sure that you have the types you want—and that often means defining new complex types. Complex types can enclose elements and have attributes, and simple types cannot do either. You can find the simple types built into XML schemas in Table 5.2. (When you specify these types in schemas, bear in mind that you'll preface them with the W3C schema prefix, usually `xsd:`.)

Table 5.2 Simple Types Built into XML Schema

Type	Description
`binary`	Holds binary values, such as `110001`
`boolean`	Holds values such as `True`, `False`, `1`, `0`
`byte`	Represents a byte value, such as `123`; maximum of `255`
`century`	Holds a century, such as `20`
`date`	Represents a date in YYYY-MM-DD format, such as `2001-10-15`
`decimal`	Holds decimal values, such as `5.4`, `0`, `-219.06`
`double`	Represents a double-precision 64-bit floating point
`ENTITIES`	Represents the XML 1.0 `ENTITIES` attribute type

Type	Description
ENTITY	Represents the XML 1.0 ENTITY attribute type
float	Represents a single-precision 32-bit floating point
ID	Represents the XML 1.0 ID attribute type
IDREF	Represents the XML 1.0 IDREF attribute type
IDREFS	Represents the XML 1.0 IDREFS attribute type
int	Represents an integer, such as 123456789
integer	Represents an integer
language	Holds a language identifier, such as de, fr, or en-US, as defined in XML 1.0
long	Represents a long integer, such as 12345678901234
month	Holds a month, such as 2001-10
Name	Represents the XML 1.0 Name type
NCName	Holds an XML name without a namespace prefix and colon
negativeInteger	Represents a negative integer
NMTOKEN	Represents the XML 1.0 NMTOKEN attribute type
NMTOKENS	Represents the XML 1.0 NMTOKENS attribute type
nonNegativeInteger	Represents a non-negative integer
nonPositiveInteger	Represents a positive integer
NOTATION	Represents the XML 1.0 NOTATION attribute type
positiveInteger	Represents a positive integer
QName	Represents the XML Namespace Qualified Name type
recurringDate	Specifies a recurring date, such as --10-15, which means every October 15th
recurringDay	Specifies a recurring day, such as ----31, which means every 15th day
recurringDuration	Holds a recurring duration, such as --10-15T12:00:00, which means October 15th every year at noon (Co-Ordinated Universal Time)
short	Represents a short integer, such as 12345
string	Represents a string of text.
time	Represents a time, such as 12:00:00.000
timeDuration	Holds a time duration, such as P1Y2M3DT4H5M6.7S, which means 1 year, 2 months, 3 days, 4 hours, 5 minutes, and 6.7 seconds
timeInstant	Holds the time in a format like this: 2001-10-15T12:00:00.000-05:00 (includes time zone adjustment)
timePeriod	Holds a time period, such as 2001-10-15T12:00

continues

Table 5.2 Continued

Type	Description
`unsignedByte`	Represents an unsigned byte value
`unsignedInt`	Represents an unsigned integer
`unsignedLong`	Represents an unsigned long integer
`unsignedShort`	Represents an unsigned short integer
`uriReference`	Holds a URI, such as `http://www.w3c.org`
`year`	Holds a year, such as 2001

To ensure compatibility between XML schemas and XML DTDs, you should use only the simple types `ID`, `IDREF`, `IDREFS`, `ENTITY`, `ENTITIES`, `NOTATION`, `NMTOKEN`, and `NMTOKENS` when declaring attributes.

You create new complex types using the `<xsd:complexType>` element in schemas. A complex type definition itself usually contains element declarations, references to other elements, and attribute declarations. You declare elements with the `<xsd:element>` element, and you declare attributes with the `<xsd:attribute>` element. As in DTDs, element declarations specify the syntax of an element—in schemas, however, element declarations can specify the elements' type as well. In addition, you can also specify the type of attributes.

Here's an example from book.xsd; in this case, I'm declaring a complex type named `address`, which holds the elements that make up a person's address:

```
<xsd:complexType name="address">
    <xsd:element name="name" type="xsd:string"/>
    <xsd:element name="street" type="xsd:string"/>
    <xsd:element name="city" type="xsd:string"/>
    <xsd:element name="state" type="xsd:string"/>
    <xsd:attribute name="phone" type="xsd:string"
        use="optional"/>
</xsd:complexType>
```

I'll use `address` as the type of the `<Lender>` and `<Borrower>` elements so that I can store the addresses of the books' lender and borrower; that declaration looks like this:

```
<xsd:complexType name="transactionType">
    <xsd:element name="Lender" type="address"/>
    <xsd:element name="Borrower" type="address"/>
    <xsd:element ref="note" minOccurs="0"/>
    <xsd:element name="books" type="books"/>
    <xsd:attribute name="borrowDate" type="xsd:date"/>
</xsd:complexType>
```

In the `address` type, I'm indicating that any element of this type must have five elements and one attribute. Those elements are `<name>`, `<street>`, `<city>`, and `<state>`, and the attribute is `phone`. Note how the declarations for these elements set their data types as well: `<name>`, `<street>`, and `<city>` must all be of type `xsd:string`, the `<state>` element must be of type `NMTOKEN`, and the attribute phone must also be of type `xsd:string`.

The definition of the `address` complex type contains only declarations based on the simple types `xsd:string`. On the other hand, complex types can themselves contain elements that are based on complex types. You can see how this works in the `transactionType`, which is the type of book.xml's root element, `<transaction>`; in this case, two of the elements, `<Lender>` and `<Borrower>`, themselves are of the `address` type:

```
<xsd:complexType name="transactionType">
    <xsd:element name="Lender" type="address"/>
    <xsd:element name="Borrower" type="address"/>
    <xsd:element ref="note" minOccurs="0"/>
    <xsd:element name="books" type="books"/>
    <xsd:attribute name="borrowDate" type="xsd:date"/>
</xsd:complexType>
```

Note that the `transactionType` type also includes an attribute, `borrowDate`, which is of the simple type `xsd:date`. Attributes are always of a simple type because attributes can't have internal content.

After you've defined a new type, you can declare new elements of that type. For example, after declaring the `transactionType`, you can declare the `<transaction>` element, which is the root element of the document, to be of that type:

```
<xsd:element name="transaction" type="transactionType"/>
<xsd:complexType name="transactionType">
    <xsd:element name="Lender" type="address"/>
    <xsd:element name="Borrower" type="address"/>
    <xsd:element ref="note" minOccurs="0"/>
    <xsd:element name="books" type="books"/>
    <xsd:attribute name="borrowDate" type="xsd:date"/>
</xsd:complexType>
.
.
.
```

So far, then, we've had a look in overview of how to create new element and attribute declarations—you use `<xsd:element>` and `<xsd:attribute>` elements and set the `type` attribute of those elements to the type that you want. If you want to use a complex type, you'll have to create it; you do that with the `<xsd:complexType>` element (we'll see how to create simple types in a few pages).

Now take a look at the declaration for the `<note>` element in the `transactionType` type:

```
<xsd:complexType name="transactionType">
    <xsd:element name="Lender" type="address"/>
    <xsd:element name="Borrower" type="address"/>
    <xsd:element ref="note" minOccurs="0"/>
    <xsd:element name="books" type="books"/>
    <xsd:attribute name="borrowDate" type="xsd:date"/>
</xsd:complexType>
```

Here, I'm not declaring a new element—instead, I'm including an already existing element by *referring* to it. That is to say, the `<note>` element already exists, like this:

```
<xsd:complexType name="transactionType">
    <xsd:element name="Lender" type="address"/>
    <xsd:element name="Borrower" type="address"/>
    <xsd:element ref="note" minOccurs="0"/>
    <xsd:element name="books" type="books"/>
    <xsd:attribute name="borrowDate" type="xsd:date"/>
</xsd:complexType>

<xsd:element name="note" type="xsd:string"/>
```

Using the `ref` attribute lets you include an element that has already been defined in a complex type definition. However, you can't just include any element by reference. The element that you refer to must have been declared *globally*, which means that it itself is not part of any other complex type. A global element or attribute declaration appears as an immediate child element of the `<xsd:schema>` element; when you declare an element or an attribute globally, it can be used in any complex type. Using the `ref` attribute in this way is a powerful technique because it lets you avoid redefining elements that already exist globally.

Now I'll take a look at how to specify how many times elements can occur in a complex type.

Specifying How Often Elements Can Occur

I've indicated that the `<note>` element can either appear or not appear in elements of the `transactionType` because I've set the `minOccurs` attribute like this, indicating that the minimum number of times this element can occur is 0:

```
<xsd:complexType name="transactionType">
    <xsd:element name="Lender" type="address"/>
    <xsd:element name="Borrower" type="address"/>
    <xsd:element ref="note" minOccurs="0"/>
```

```
    <xsd:element name="books" type="books"/>
    <xsd:attribute name="borrowDate" type="xsd:date"/>
</xsd:complexType>
```

In general, you can specify the minimum number of times that an element appears with the minOccurs attribute and the maximum number of times that it can appear with the maxOccurs attribute. For example, here's how I would say that the <note> element could appear from zero to five times in the transactionType type:

```
<xsd:complexType name="transactionType">
    <xsd:element name="Lender" type="address"/>
    <xsd:element name="Borrower" type="address"/>
    <xsd:element ref="note" minOccurs="0" maxOccurs="5"/>
    <xsd:element name="books" type="books"/>
    <xsd:attribute name="borrowDate" type="xsd:date"/>
</xsd:complexType>
```

The default value for minOccurs is 1; if you don't specify a value for maxOccurs, its default value is the value of minOccurs. To indicate that there is no upper bound to the maxOccurs attribute, set it to the value unbounded.

Specifying Default Values for Elements

Besides the minOccurs and maxOccurs attributes, you can also use the <xsd:element> element's fixed and default attributes to indicate values that an element must have (you use one or the other of these attributes, not both together). For example, setting fixed to 400 means that the element's value must always be 400. Setting the default value to 400, on the other hand, means that the default value for the element is 400, but if the element appears in the document, its actual value is the value it encloses.

For example, here I'm setting the value of an element named <maxTrials> to 100, and specifying that it must always be 100, using the fixed attribute in the <xsd:element> element:

```
<xsd:element name="maxTrials" type="xsd:integer" fixed="100"/>
```

Here I'm giving this element the *default* value of 100 instead of fixing its value at 100, which is useful if you want to provide default values to be used if the user doesn't specify an alternate value:

```
<xsd:element name="maxTrials" type="xsd:integer" default="100"/>
```

Specifying Attribute Constraints and Defaults

As with elements, you can specify the type of attributes. Unlike with elements, however, attributes must be of a simple type. In addition, you don't use `minOccurs` and `maxOccurs` for attributes because attributes can appear only once, at most. Instead, you use a different syntax when constraining attributes.

You declare attributes with the `<xsd:attribute>` element. The `<xsd:attribute>` element itself has a type attribute that gives the attribute's (simple) type. So how do you indicate if an attribute is required or optional, or if there's a default value, or even if the value of the attribute is fixed at a certain value? You use the `<xsd:attribute>` element's `use` and `value` attributes.

The `use` attribute specifies whether the attribute is `required` or `optional`; if the attribute is `optional`, the `use` attribute specifies whether the attribute's value is `fixed` or whether there is a `default`. The second attribute, `value`, holds any value that is needed.

For example, I've added an attribute named `phone` to the `Address` type; this attribute is of type `xsd:string`, and its use is `optional`:

```
<xsd:complexType name="address">
    <xsd:element name="name" type="xsd:string"/>
    <xsd:element name="street" type="xsd:string"/>
    <xsd:element name="city" type="xsd:string"/>
    <xsd:element name="state" type="xsd:string"/>
    <xsd:attribute name="phone" type="xsd:string"
        use="optional"/>
</xsd:complexType>
```

Here are the possible values for the `use` attribute:

- `required`. The attribute is required and may have any value.
- `optional`. The attribute is optional and may have any value.
- `fixed`. The attribute value is fixed, and you set its value with the `value` attribute.
- `default`. If the attribute does not appear, its value is the default value set with the `value` attribute. If it does appear, its value is the value that it is assigned in the document.
- `prohibited`. The attribute must not appear.

For example, consider this attribute declaration:

```
<xsd:attribute name="counter" type="xsd:int
"use="fixed" value="400">
```

This declaration creates an integer attribute named `counter`, whose value is always `400`. Now consider this attribute declaration:

```
<xsd:attribute name="counter" type="xsd:int
"use="default" value="400">
```

This means that the `counter` attribute has a default value of `400` if it is not used, and it has the value assigned to it if it *is* used.

Creating Simple Types

Most of the types that I've used in book.xsd are simple types that come built into the XML schema specification, such as `xsd:string`, `xsd:integer`, `xsd:date`, and so on. However, take a look at the attribute named `bookID`—this attribute is declared to be of the type `catalogID`:

```
<xsd:complexType name="books">
    <xsd:element name="book" minOccurs="0" maxOccurs="10">
        <xsd:complexType>
            <xsd:element name="bookTitle" type="xsd:string"/>
            <xsd:element name="pubDate" type="xsd:date" minOccurs='0'/>
            <xsd:element name="replacementValue" type="xsd:decimal"/>
            <xsd:element name="maxDaysOut">
                <xsd:simpleType base="xsd:integer">
                    <xsd:maxExclusive value="14"/>
                 </xsd:simpleType>
            </xsd:element>
            <xsd:attribute name="bookID" type="catalogID"/>
        </xsd:complexType>
    </xsd:element>
</xsd:complexType>
```

This type, `catalogID`, is itself a simple type that is not built into the XML schema specification; instead, I've defined it with the `<simpleType>` element, like this:

```
<xsd:complexType name="books">
    <xsd:element name="book" minOccurs="0" maxOccurs="10">
        <xsd:complexType>
            <xsd:element name="bookTitle" type="xsd:string"/>
            <xsd:element name="pubDate" type="xsd:date" minOccurs='0'/>
            <xsd:element name="replacementValue" type="xsd:decimal"/>
            <xsd:element name="maxDaysOut">
                <xsd:simpleType base="xsd:integer">
                    <xsd:maxExclusive value="14"/>
                 </xsd:simpleType>
            </xsd:element>
            <xsd:attribute name="bookID" type="catalogID"/>
        </xsd:complexType>
    </xsd:element>
</xsd:complexType>
```

continues ▸

```
<xsd:simpleType name="catalogID" base="xsd:string">
    <xsd:pattern value="\d{3}-\d{4}-\d{3}"/>
</xsd:simpleType>
```

Note in particular that you must base new simple types such as `catalogID` on already existing simple type (either a built-in simple type or one that you've created; here, I'm using the built-in `xsd:string` type). To do that, you use the `base` attribute in the `<xsd:simpleType>` element. In the case of the `catalogID` type, I've based it on the `xsd:string` type with the attribute/value pair `base="xsd:string"`. To describe the properties of new simple types, XML schemas use *facets*, which are discussed in the next section.

Creating Simple Types Using Facets

Using facets lets you restrict the data that a simple type can hold. For example, say that you want to create a simple type named `dayOfMonth` that can hold only values between `1` and `31`, inclusive. In that case, you can define it this way, using the two facets `minInclusive` and `maxInclusive`:

```
<xsd:simpleType name="dayOfMonth" base="xsd:integer">
     <xsd:minInclusive value="1"/>
     <xsd:maxInclusive value="31"/>
 </xsd:simpleType>
```

Now that you've created this new simple type, you can declare elements and attributes of this type.

In book.xsd, the `catalogID` simple type is even more powerful than this `dayOfMonth` simple type. The `catalogID` simple type uses the `pattern` facet to specify a *regular expression* (that is, a pattern set up to match text in the format that you specify) that text strings values for this type must satisfy:

```
<xsd:simpleType name="catalogID" base="xsd:string">
    <xsd:pattern value="\d{3}-\d{4}-\d{3}"/>
</xsd:simpleType>
```

In this case, the text in the `simpleType` type must match the regular expression `"\d{3}-\d{4}-\d{3}"`, which stands for three digits, a hyphen, four digits, another hyphen, and three digits.

About Regular Expressions

The regular expressions used in XML schema facets are the same as those used in the Perl programming language. You can find the complete documentation for Perl regular expressions at the Comprehensive Perl Archive Network (CPAN) Web site: `www.cpan.org/doc/manual/html/pod/perlre.html`. (Regular expressions are not a skill that you'll need in this book.)

The catalogID type is the type of the <book> element's bookID attribute, so I can specify book ID values like this in book.xml, matching the regular expression that I've used for this attribute:

```
<book bookID="123-4567-890">
    <bookTitle>Earthquakes for Breakfast</bookTitle>
    <pubDate>2001-10-20</pubDate>
    <replacementValue>15.95</replacementValue>
    <maxDaysOut>14</maxDaysOut>
</book>
```

What facets are there, and what built-in simple types support them? You'll find the seven general facets, listed by the simple types that support them, in Table 5.3.

Table 5.3 **Simple Types and Applicable Facets**

Type	Length	minLength	maxLength	Pattern	Enumeration
binary	x	x	x	x	x
boolean				x	
byte				x	x
century				x	x
date				x	x
decimal				x	x
double				x	x
ENTITIES	x	x	x		x
ENTITY	x	x	x	x	x
float				x	x
ID	x	x	x	x	x
IDREF	x	x	x	x	x
IDREFS	x	x	x		x
int				x	x
integer				x	x
language	x	x	x	x	x
long				x	x
month				x	x
Name	x	x	x	x	x
NCName	x	x	x	x	x
negativeInteger				x	x

continues

Table 5.3 **Continued**

Type	Length	minLength	maxLength	Pattern	Enumeration
NMTOKEN	x	x	x	x	x
NMTOKENS	x	x	x		x
nonNegativeInteger				x	x
nonPositiveInteger				x	x
NOTATION	x	x	x	x	x
positiveInteger				x	x
QName	x	x	x	x	x
recurringDate			x	x	
recurringDay			x	x	
recurringDuration			x	x	
short				x	x
string	x	x	x	x	x
time				x	x
timeDuration			x	x	
timeInstant			x	x	
timePeriod			x	x	
unsignedByte				x	x
unsignedInt				x	x
unsignedLong				x	x
unsignedShort				x	x
uriReference	x	x	x	x	x
year				x	x

The numeric simple types, and those simple types that can be ordered, also have some additional facets, which you see in Tables 5.4 and 5.5.

Table 5.4 **Ordered Simple Types and Applicable Facets, Part 1**

Type	maxInclusive	maxExclusive	minInclusive
binary			
byte	x	x	x
century	x	x	x
date	x	x	x
decimal	x	x	x

Type	maxInclusive	maxExclusive	minInclusive
double	X	X	X
float	X	X	X
int	X	X	X
integer	X	X	X
long	X	X	X
month	X	X	X
negativeInteger	X	X	X
nonNegativeInteger	X	X	X
nonPositiveInteger	X	X	X
positiveInteger	X	X	X
recurringDate	X	X	X
recurringDay	X	X	X
recurringDuration	X	X	X
short	X	X	X
string	X	X	X
time	X	X	X
timeDuration	X	X	X
timeInstant	X	X	X
timePeriod	X	X	X
unsignedByte	X	X	X
unsignedInt	X	X	X
unsignedLong	X	X	X
unsignedShort	X	X	X
year	X	X	X

Table 5.5 **Ordered Simple Types and Applicable Facets, Part 2**

Type	minExclusive	Precision	Scale	Encoding
binary				X
byte	X	X	X	
century	X			
date	X			
decimal	X	X	X	
double	X			

continues

Table 5.5 **Continued**

Type	minExclusive	Precision	Scale	Encoding
float	x			
int	x	x	x	
integer	x	x	x	
long	x	x	x	
month	x			
negativeInteger	x	x	x	
nonNegativeInteger	x	x	x	
nonPositiveInteger	x	x	x	
positiveInteger	x	x	x	
recurringDate	x			
recurringDay	x			
recurringDuration	x			
short	x	x	x	
string	x			
time	x			
timeDuration	x			
timeInstant	x			
timePeriod	x			
unsignedByte	x	x	x	
unsignedInt	x	x	x	
unsignedLong	x	x	x	
unsignedShort	x	x	x	
year	x			

Some additional facets that have to do with dates and times apply to simple types, and you'll find them in Table 5.6.

Table 5.6 **Time and Date Simple Types and Applicable Facets**

Type	Period	Duration
century	x	x
date	x	x
month	x	x
recurringDate	x	x

Type	Period	Duration
recurringDay	x	x
recurringDuration	x	x
time	x	x
timeDuration	x	x
timeInstant	x	x
timePeriod	x	x
year	x	x

Of all the facets that you see in Tables 5.3, 5.4, and 5.5, my favorites are minInclusive, maxInclusive, pattern, and enumeration. We've seen the first three, but not the enumeration facet yet.

The enumeration facet lets you set up an enumeration of values, exactly as you can do in DTDs (as we saw in the previous chapter). Using an enumeration, you can restrict the possible values of a simple type to a list of values that you specify.

For example, to set up a simple type named weekday whose values can be "Sunday", "Monday", "Tuesday", "Wednesday", "Thursday", "Friday", and "Saturday", you'd define that type like this:

```
<xsd:simpleType name="weekday" base="xsd:string">
    <xsd:enumeration value="Sunday"/>
    <xsd:enumeration value="Monday"/>
    <xsd:enumeration value="Tuesday"/>
    <xsd:enumeration value="Wednesday"/>
    <xsd:enumeration value="Thursday"/>
    <xsd:enumeration value="Friday"/>
    <xsd:enumeration value="Saturday"/>
 </xsd:simpleType>
```

Using Anonymous Type Definitions

So far, all the element declarations that we've used in the book.xsd schema have used the type attribute to indicate the new element's type. But what if you want to use a type only once? Do you have to go to the trouble of declaring it and naming it, all to use it in only one element declaration?

It turns out that there is an easier way. You can use an *anonymous type definition* to avoid having to define a whole new type that you'll reference only once. Using an anonymous type definition simply means that you enclose the <xsd:simpleType> or <xsd:complexType> element inside the <xsd:element> element declaration. In this case, you don't assign an explicit value to the type attribute in the <xsd:element> element because the anonymous type that you're using doesn't have a name. (In fact, you can tell that an anonymous type definition is being used if the `<xsd:complexType>` element doesn't include a `type` attribute.)

Here's an example from book.xsd; in this case, I'll use an anonymous type definition for the `<book>` element. This element holds `<bookTitle>`, `<pubDate>`, `<replacementValue>`, and `<maxDaysOut>` elements. It will also have an attribute named `bookID`, so it looks like a good one to create from a complex type. Instead of declaring a separate complex type, however, I'll just put the `<xsd:complexType>` element *inside* the `<xsd:element>` element that declares `<book>`:

```
<xsd:element name="book" minOccurs="0" maxOccurs="10">
    <xsd:complexType>
    .
    .
    .
    </xsd:complexType>
</xsd:element>
```

Now I'm free to add the elements that I want inside the `<book>` element—without defining a named, separate complex type at all:

```
<xsd:element name="book" minOccurs="0" maxOccurs="10">
    <xsd:complexType>
        <xsd:element name="bookTitle" type="xsd:string"/>
        <xsd:element name="pubDate" type="xsd:date" minOccurs='0'/>
        <xsd:element name="replacementValue" type="xsd:decimal"/>
        .
        .
        .
    </xsd:complexType>
</xsd:element>
```

You can also use simple anonymous types; for example, the `<maxDaysOut>` element holds the maximum number of days that a book is supposed to be out. To set the maximum number of days that a book can be out to `14`, I use a new simple anonymous type so that I can use the `maxExclusive` facet, like this:

```
<xsd:element name="book" minOccurs="0" maxOccurs="10">
    <xsd:complexType>
        <xsd:element name="bookTitle" type="xsd:string"/>
        <xsd:element name="pubDate" type="xsd:date" minOccurs='0'/>
        <xsd:element name="replacementValue" type="xsd:decimal"/>
        <xsd:element name="maxDaysOut">
```

```
            <xsd:simpleType base="xsd:integer">
                <xsd:maxExclusive value="14"/>
             </xsd:simpleType>
        </xsd:element>
        .
        .
        .
    </xsd:complexType>
</xsd:element>
```

You can also include attribute declarations in anonymous type definitions, like this:

```
<xsd:element name="book" minOccurs="0" maxOccurs="10">
    <xsd:complexType>
        <xsd:element name="bookTitle" type="xsd:string"/>
        <xsd:element name="pubDate" type="xsd:date" minOccurs='0'/>
        <xsd:element name="replacementValue" type="xsd:decimal"/>
        <xsd:element name="maxDaysOut">
            <xsd:simpleType base="xsd:integer">
                <xsd:maxExclusive value="14"/>
             </xsd:simpleType>
        </xsd:element>
        <xsd:attribute name="bookID" type="catalogID"/>
    </xsd:complexType>
</xsd:element>
```

Now I'll take a look at declaring empty elements.

Creating Empty Elements

Empty elements have no content, but they can have attributes—so how do you declare them in XML schema? You do that by declaring a complex type and setting the `<xsd:complexType>` element's `content` attribute to `"empty"`.

Here's an example. In this case, I'm going to create a new empty element named `<image>` that can take three attributes: `source`, `width`, and `height`, like this: `<image source="/images/cover.gif" height="256" width=512" />`. I start by declaring this element:

```
<xsd:element name="image">
    .
    .
    .
</xsd:element>
```

I haven't used the type attribute in this element's declaration because I'll use an anonymous type definition to base this element on. To create the anonymous type, I use a <complexType> element; notice that I'm setting the content attribute to "empty":

```
<xsd:element name="image">
    <xsd:complexType content="empty">
    .
    .
    .
    </xsd:complexType>
</xsd:element>
```

Finally, I add the attributes that this element will use:

```
<xsd:element name="image">
    <xsd:complexType content="empty">

        <xsd:attribute name="source" type="xsd:string" />
        <xsd:attribute name="width" type="xsd:decimal" />
        <xsd:attribute name="height" type="xsd:decimal" />

    </xsd:complexType>
</xsd:element>
```

And that's all it takes—now the empty element <image> is ready to be used.

Creating Mixed-Content Elements

So far, the plain text in the documents that we've looked at in this chapter has been confined to the deepest elements in the document—that is, to elements that enclose no child elements, just text. However, as you know, you can also create elements that support *mixed content*, both text and other elements. You can create mixed-content elements with schemas as well as DTDs. In these elements, character data can appear at the same level as child elements.

Here's an example document that shows what mixed-content elements look like using the elements that we've declared in book.xsd; in this case, I'm creating a new element named <reminder> that encloses a reminder letter to a book borrower to return a book:

```
<?xml version="1.0">
<reminder>
    Dear <name>Britta Regensburg</name>:
        The book <bookTitle>Snacking on Volcanoes</bookTitle>
    was supposed to be out for only <maxDaysOut>14</maxDaysOut>
    days. Please return it or pay
    $<replacementValue>17.99</replacementValue>.
    Thank you.
</reminder>
```

This document uses both elements that we've defined before, character data, and the new `<reminder>` element. The `<reminder>` element is the one that has a mixed-content model; to declare it in a schema, I'll start by creating an anonymous new complex type inside the declaration for `<reminder>`:

```
<xsd:element name="reminder">
    <xsd:complexType>
    .
    .
    .
    </xsd:complexType>
</xsd:element>
```

Recall that the `<xsd:complexType>` element has the `content` attribute with which you specify a content model; in this case, the content model is `mixed`:

```
<xsd:element name="reminder">
    <xsd:complexType content="mixed">
    .
    .
    .
    </xsd:complexType>
</xsd:element>
```

Now all I have to do is to add the declarations for the elements that you can use inside the `<reminder>` element, like this:

```
<xsd:element name="reminder">
    <xsd:complexType content="mixed">
        <xsd:element name="name" type="xsd:string"/>
        <xsd:element name="bookTitle" type="xsd:string"/>
        <xsd:element name="maxDaysOut">
            <xsd:simpleType base="xsd:integer">
                <xsd:maxExclusive value="14"/>
            </xsd:simpleType>
        </xsd:element>
        <xsd:element name="replacementValue" type="xsd:decimal"/>
    </xsd:complexType>
</xsd:element>
```

As you might recall from our discussion of DTDs, you can't constrain the order or number of child elements appearing in a mixed-model element. There's more power available when it comes to schemas, however—here, the order and number of child elements does indeed have to correspond to the order and number of child elements that you specify in the schema. In other words, even though DTDs provide only partial syntax specifications for mixed-content models, schemas provide much more complete syntax specifications.

In fact, the demands on XML processors that want to support schemas are great—including, for example, that they must implement the complete syntax for Perl-type regular expressions simply so that they can support the `pattern` facet. The upshot is that it might be a long time until a full implementation of schemas appears (if ever!).

elementOnly and *textOnly* Content Elements

Now that you know that you can use the `content` attribute of `<xsd:complexType>` to specify content models, such as empty and mixed, that raises this question: What model were we using when we used `<xsd:complexType>` without specifying a content model at all? For example, here's how the type `transactionType` is defined in book.xsd:

```
<xsd:element name="transaction" type="transactionType"/>

<xsd:complexType name="transactionType">
    <xsd:element name="Lender" type="address"/>
    <xsd:element name="Borrower" type="address"/>
    <xsd:element ref="note" minOccurs="0"/>
    <xsd:element name="books" type="books"/>
    <xsd:attribute name="borrowDate" type="xsd:date"/>
</xsd:complexType>
```

The default model for complex types is called `elementOnly`, which means that the type can include only elements. In other words, this type definition is the same as this one in which I explicitly make the type `elementOnly`:

```
<xsd:element name="transaction" type="transactionType"/>

<xsd:complexType name="transactionType" content="elementOnly">
    <xsd:element name="Lender" type="address"/>
    <xsd:element name="Borrower" type="address"/>
    <xsd:element ref="note" minOccurs="0"/>
    <xsd:element name="books" type="books"/>
    <xsd:attribute name="borrowDate" type="xsd:date"/>
</xsd:complexType>
```

Actually, I should say that the default complex type content model is `elementOnly`—except in one case. When you derive a complex type from a simple type, the content model is `textOnly`, not `elementOnly`. The `textOnly` content model specifies that the content of elements of this type is text, which means that the XML processor will not apply any syntax rules to that content.

You can also create textOnly content model types explicitly, as in this example, in which I'm creating a new version of the <bookID> element using the textOnly content model to allow it to support different indexing schemes (and, therefore, a different format for book IDs). Because different indexing schemes will have different formats for book ID values, I'm intentionally removing the syntax checking here:

```
<xsd:element name="bookID">
    <xsd:complexType content="textOnly">
        <xsd:attribute name="indexingScheme" type="xsd:string" />
    </xsd:complexType>
</xsd:element>
```

The result is that the <bookID> element may now contain any kind of text (but no elements), and the XML processor won't check it for syntax violations.

As a general rule, W3C suggests that you stay away from removing all syntax checks like this if you can avoid it. In fact, it's not difficult to use regular expressions to specify alternate pattern matches. This means that, in this case, you can still use a simple type based on string and can constrain the syntax of the book ID with the pattern facet.

Annotating Schemas

In DTDs, you can use XML comments to add annotations and provide documentation. In schemas, you might expect that the situation would be a little more complex, and you'd be right. XML schemas define three new elements that you use to add annotations to schemas: <xsd:annotation>, <xsd:documentation>, and <xsd:appInfo>.

Here's how things work: The <xsd:annotation> element is the container element for the <xsd:documentation> and <xsd:appInfo> elements. The <xsd:documentation> element holds text of the kind you'd expect to see in a normal comment—that is, text designed for human readers. As its name implies, the <xsd:appInfo> element, on the other hand, holds annotations suitable for applications that read the document. Such applications can pick up information from <xsd:appInfo> elements if those elements are constructed in a way they recognize.

Here's an example using <xsd:annotation> and <xsd:appInfo> elements. This example is actually from the schema that the W3C publishes for the data types that it uses in the XML schemas, and it's part of what's called the schema of all schemas. This is the declaration of the simple type string, and the <appInfo> element indicates what facets and properties this simple type has in a way that can be read by other applications. (Here it's the <appInfo>, not the <xsd:appInfo> element, because in this schema, the default namespace is the XML schema namespace.)

```
<simpleType name="string" base="urSimpleType">
    <annotation>
        <appinfo>
            <has-facet name="length"/>
            <has-facet name="minLength"/>
            <has-facet name="maxLength"/>
            <has-facet name="pattern"/>
            <has-facet name="enumeration"/>
            <has-facet name="maxInclusive"/>
            <has-facet name="maxExclusive"/>
            <has-facet name="minInclusive"/>
            <has-facet name="minExclusive"/>
            <has-property name="ordered" value="true"/>
            <has-property name="bounded" value="false"/>
            <has-property name="cardinality" value="countably infinite"/>
            <has-property name="numeric" value="false"/>
        </appinfo>
    </annotation>
</simpleType>
```

Here's another example; this one is from book.xsd and uses the <xsd:annotation> and <xsd:documentation> elements, adding an explanatory comment at the beginning of the book.xsd schema:

```
<xsd:schema xmlns:xsd="http://www.w3.org/1999/XMLSchema">

    <xsd:annotation>
        <xsd:documentation>
            Book borrowing transaction schema.
        </xsd:documentation>
    </xsd:annotation>

    <xsd:element name="transaction" type="transactionType"/>

    <xsd:complexType name="transactionType">
        <xsd:element name="Lender" type="address"/>
        <xsd:element name="Borrower" type="address"/>
        <xsd:element ref="note" minOccurs="0"/>
        <xsd:element name="books" type="books"/>
        <xsd:attribute name="borrowDate" type="xsd:date"/>
    </xsd:complexType>
    .
    .
    .
```

In fact, you can use the <xsd:annotation> element at the beginning of most schema constructions, such as the <xsd:schema>, <xsd:complexType>, <xsd:simpleType>, <xsd:element>, and <xsd:attribute> elements, and so on. Here's an example in which I've added an annotation to a complex type in book.xsd:

```
<xsd:schema xmlns:xsd="http://www.w3.org/1999/XMLSchema">

    <xsd:annotation>
        <xsd:documentation>
            Book borrowing transaction schema.
        </xsd:documentation>
    </xsd:annotation>

    <xsd:element name="transaction" type="transactionType"/>

    <xsd:complexType name="transactionType">
    <xsd:annotation>
        <xsd:documentation>
            This type is used by the root element.
        </xsd:documentation>
    </xsd:annotation>
        <xsd:element name="Lender" type="address"/>
        <xsd:element name="Borrower" type="address"/>
        <xsd:element ref="note" minOccurs="0"/>
        <xsd:element name="books" type="books"/>
        <xsd:attribute name="borrowDate" type="xsd:date"/>
    </xsd:complexType>
    .
    .
    .
```

As we've seen with DTDs, you can create choices and sequences of elements—and, as you might expect, you can do the same in schemas.

Creating Choices

A *choice* lets you specify a number of elements, only one of which will be chosen. To create a choice in XML schemas, you use the <xsd:choice> element. Here's an example—in this case, I'll change the transactionType type so that the borrower can borrow either several books or just one book. I do this by creating the <xsd:choice> element that holds both a <books> element and a <book> element (note that in this case, the <book> element needs to be made into a global element so that I can refer to it in this choice, so I remove it from the declaration of the <books> element, as you see here:

```
<xsd:complexType name="transactionType">
    <xsd:element name="Lender" type="address"/>
    <xsd:element name="Borrower" type="address"/>
    <xsd:element ref="note" minOccurs="0"/>
```

continues ▶

```
    <xsd:choice>
        <xsd:element name="books" type="books"/>
        <xsd:element ref="book"/>
    <xsd:choice>
    <xsd:attribute name="borrowDate" type="xsd:date"/>
</xsd:complexType>

<xsd:complexType name="books">
    <xsd:element ref="book" minOccurs="0" maxOccurs="10" />
</xsd:complexType>

<xsd:element name="book">
    <xsd:complexType>
        <xsd:element name="bookTitle" type="xsd:string"/>
        <xsd:element name="pubDate" type="xsd:date" minOccurs='0'/>
        <xsd:element name="replacementValue" type="xsd:decimal"/>
        <xsd:element name="maxDaysOut">
           <xsd:simpleType base="xsd:integer">
                <xsd:maxExclusive value="14"/>
           </xsd:simpleType>
        </xsd:element>
        <xsd:attribute name="bookID" type="catalogID"/>
    </xsd:complexType>
</xsd:element>
```

Next, I'll take a look at creating sequences.

Creating Sequences

By default, complex types in declare sequences of elements must appear in a conforming document. It turns out that you can also create sequences yourself using the `<xsd:sequence>` element.

For example, say that I want to let the borrower borrow not just books, but also a magazine. To do that, I can create a new *group* named `booksAndMagazine`. A group collects elements together. You can name groups, and you can then include a group in other elements using the `<xsd:group>` element and referring to the group by name:

```
<xsd:complexType name="transactionType">
    <xsd:element name="Lender" type="address"/>
    <xsd:element name="Borrower" type="address"/>
    <xsd:element ref="note" minOccurs="0"/>
    <xsd:choice>
        <xsd:element name="books" type="books"/>
        <xsd:element ref="book"/>
        <xsd:group ref="booksAndMagazine"/>
    <xsd:choice>
    <xsd:attribute name="borrowDate" type="xsd:date"/>
</xsd:complexType>
```

To create the group named `booksAndMagazine`, I use the `<xsd:group>` element; to ensure that the elements inside that group appear in a specific sequence, I use the `<xsd:sequence>` element this way:

```
<xsd:complexType name="transactionType">
    <xsd:element name="Lender" type="address"/>
    <xsd:element name="Borrower" type="address"/>
    <xsd:element ref="note" minOccurs="0"/>
    <xsd:choice>
        <xsd:element name="books" type="books"/>
        <xsd:element ref="book"/>
        <xsd:group ref="booksAndMagazine"/>
    <xsd:choice>
    <xsd:attribute name="borrowDate" type="xsd:date"/>
</xsd:complexType>

<xsd:complexType name="books">
    <xsd:element ref="book" minOccurs="0" maxOccurs="10" />
</xsd:complexType>

<xsd:group name="booksAndMagazine">
    <xsd:sequence>
        <xsd:element ref="books"/>
        <xsd:element ref="magazine"/>
    </xsd:sequence>
</xsd:group>

<xsd:element name="book">
    <xsd:complexType>
        <xsd:element name="bookTitle" type="xsd:string"/>
        <xsd:element name="pubDate" type="xsd:date" minOccurs='0'/>
        <xsd:element name="replacementValue" type="xsd:decimal"/>
        <xsd:element name="maxDaysOut">
           <xsd:simpleType base="xsd:integer">
               <xsd:maxExclusive value="14"/>
             </xsd:simpleType>
        </xsd:element>
        <xsd:attribute name="bookID" type="catalogID"/>
    </xsd:complexType>
</xsd:element>

<xsd:element name="magazine">
    <xsd:complexType>
        <xsd:element name="magazineTitle" type="xsd:string"/>
        <xsd:element name="pubDate" type="xsd:date" minOccurs='0'/>
        <xsd:element name="maxDaysOut">
            <xsd:simpleType base="xsd:integer">
                <xsd:maxExclusive value="14"/>
            </xsd:simpleType>
        </xsd:element>
        <xsd:attribute name="magazineID" type="catalogID"/>
    </xsd:complexType>
</xsd:element>
```

Creating Attribute Groups

You can also create groups of attributes using the <xsd:attributeGroup> element. For example, say that I wanted to add a number of attributes to the <book> element that describe the book. To do that, I can create an attribute group named bookDescription and then reference that attribute group in the declaration for <book>:

```
<xsd:element name="book">
    <xsd:complexType>
        <xsd:element name="bookTitle" type="xsd:string"/>
        <xsd:element name="pubDate" type="xsd:date" minOccurs='0'/>
        <xsd:element name="replacementValue" type="xsd:decimal"/>
        <xsd:element name="maxDaysOut">
           <xsd:simpleType base="xsd:integer">
                <xsd:maxExclusive value="14"/>
            </xsd:simpleType>
        </xsd:element>
        <xsd:attributeGroup ref="bookDescription"/>
    </xsd:complexType>
</xsd:element>
```

To create the attribute group bookDescription, I just use the <xsd:attributeGroup> element, enclosing the <xsd:attribute> elements that I use to declare the attributes in the <xsd:attributeGroup> element:

```
<xsd:attributeGroup name="bookDescription">
    <xsd:attribute name="bookID" type="CatalogID"/>
    <xsd:attribute name="numberPages" type="xsd:decimal"/>
    <xsd:attribute name="coverType">
        <xsd:simpleType base="xsd:string">
            <xsd:enumeration value="leather"/>
            <xsd:enumeration value="cloth"/>
            <xsd:enumeration value="vinyl"/>
        </xsd:simpleType>
    </xsd:attribute>
</xsd:attributeGroup><xsd:element name="book">
    <xsd:complexType>
        <xsd:element name="bookTitle" type="xsd:string"/>
        <xsd:element name="pubDate" type="xsd:date" minOccurs='0'/>
        <xsd:element name="replacementValue" type="xsd:decimal"/>
        <xsd:element name="maxDaysOut">
           <xsd:simpleType base="xsd:integer">
                <xsd:maxExclusive value="14"/>
            </xsd:simpleType>
        </xsd:element>
        <xsd:attributeGroup ref="bookDescription"/>
    </xsd:complexType>
</xsd:element>
```

```
<xsd:attributeGroup name="bookDescription">
    <xsd:attribute name="bookID" type="CatalogID"/>
    <xsd:attribute name="numberPages" type="xsd:decimal"/>
    <xsd:attribute name="coverType">
        <xsd:simpleType base="xsd:string">
            <xsd:enumeration value="leather"/>
            <xsd:enumeration value="cloth"/>
            <xsd:enumeration value="vinyl"/>
        </xsd:simpleType>
    </xsd:attribute>
</xsd:attributeGroup>
```

Groups Versus Parameter Entities

The process of creating a group of elements or attributes and then referencing that group in another element mimics the use of parameter entities in DTDs. With DTDs, you do the same thing—include a group, elements, or attributes—in a more or less similar way. There are no such things as parameter entities in schemas, but using groups, you can accomplish most of what parameter entities are used for in DTDs.

As you can see, schemas provide some sophisticated mechanisms for building documents up from pieces.

Creating *all* Groups

Schemas support another type of group: the `all` group. All the elements in an `all` group may appear once or not at all, and they may appear in any order. This group must be used at the top level of the content model, and the group's children must be individual elements—that is, this group must itself contain no groups. In addition, any element in this content model can appear no more than once (which means that the allowed values of `minOccurs` and `maxOccurs` are `0` and `1` only).

Here's an example; in this case, I'm converting the `transactionType` type into an `all` group:

```
<xsd:complexType name="transactionType">
    <xsd:all>
        <xsd:element name="Lender" type="address"/>
        <xsd:element name="Borrower" type="address"/>
        <xsd:element ref="note" minOccurs="0"/>
        <xsd:element name="books" type="books"/>
    </xsd:all>
    <xsd:attribute name="borrowDate" type="xsd:date"/>
</xsd:complexType>
```

This means that the elements in this type may now appear in any order but can appear only once, at most. Another important point is that if you use it, the `<xsd:all>` group must contain all the element declarations in a content model. (That is, you can't declare additional elements that are in the content model but outside the group.)

Schemas and Namespaces

One of the big ideas behind schemas was to allow XML processors to validate documents that use namespaces (which DTDs have a problem with). Toward that end, the `<schema>` element has a new attribute: `targetNamespace`.

The `targetNamespace` attribute specifies the namespace to which the schema is *targeted*—that is, the namespace that it is intended for. This means that if an XML processor is validating a document and is checking elements in a particular namespace, it will know what schema to check, based on the schema's target namespace. That's the idea behind target namespaces: You can indicate what namespace a schema is targeted to so that an XML processor can determine which schema(s) to use to validate a document.

You can also specify whether the elements and attributes that were *locally* declared in a schema need to be qualified when used in a namespace. We've seen globally declared elements and attributes in schemas—they're declared at the top level in the schema, directly under the `<schema>` element. All the other elements and attributes declared in a schema—that is, those not declared as direct children of the `<schema>` element—are locally declared. Schemas allow you to indicate whether locals need to be qualified when used in a document.

Using Unqualified Locals

I'll start looking at how schemas work with target namespaces and locals by beginning with *unqualified locals* (which don't need to be qualified in a document). To indicate whether elements need to be qualified, you use the `elementFormDefault` attribute of the `<schema>` element, and you indicate whether attributes need to be qualified; you use the `attributeFormDefault` attribute of the same element. You can set the `elementFormDefault` and `attributeFormDefault` attributes to either `"qualified"` or `"unqualified"`.

I'll take a look at an example to see how this works. Here, I'm indicating that the target namespace of a schema is `"http://www.starpowder.com/namespace"`. I'm also making the W3C XML schema namespace, `"http://www.w3.org/1999/XMLSchema"`, the default namespace for the document so that I don't have to qualify the XML schema elements such as `<annotation>` and `<complexType>` with a prefix such as `xsd`.

However, I have to be a little careful. When an XML processor dealing with this schema wants to check, say, the `transactionType` complex type, it will need to know what namespace to search—and it won't find the `transactionType` type in the default namespace, which is the W3C XML schema namespace. For that reason, I'll define a new namespace prefix, `t`, and associate that prefix with the same namespace as the target namespace. Now I can use `t:` to prefix types defined in this schema so that an XML processor will know what namespace to search for their definitions.

I'll also indicate that both elements and attributes should be unqualified in this case. Here's what this new schema looks like. (Notice that I qualify types defined in this schema with the `t` prefix, but not types, such as `string`, that are defined in the default `"http://www.w3.org/1999/XMLSchema"` namespace.)

```
<schema xmlns="http://www.w3.org/1999/XMLSchema"
    xmlns:t="http://www.starpowder.com/namespace"
    targetNamespace="http://www.starpowder.com/namespace"
    elementFormDefault="unqualified"
    attributeFormDefault="unqualified">

    <annotation>
        <documentation>
            Book borrowing transaction schema.
        </documentation>
    </annotation>

    <element name="transaction" type="t:transactionType"/>

    <complexType name="transactionType">
        <element name="Lender" type="t:address"/>
        <element name="Borrower" type="t:address"/>
        <element ref="note" minOccurs="0"/>
        <element name="books" type="t:books"/>
        <attribute name="borrowDate" type="date"/>
    </complexType>

    <element name="note" type="string"/>

    <complexType name="address">
        <element name="name" type="string"/>
        <element name="street" type="string"/>
        <element name="city" type="string"/>
        <element name="state" type="string"/>
        <attribute name="phone" type="string"
            use="optional"/>
    </complexType>

    <complexType name="books">
        <element name="book" minOccurs="0" maxOccurs="10">
            <complexType>
```

continues ►

```
                <element name="bookTitle" type="string"/>
                <element name="pubDate" type="date" minOccurs='0'/>
                <element name="replacementValue" type="decimal"/>
                <element name="maxDaysOut">
                    <simpleType base="integer">
                        <maxExclusive value="14"/>
                    </simpleType>
                </element>
                <attribute name="bookID" type="t:catalogID"/>
            </complexType>
        </element>
    </complexType>

    <simpleType name="catalogID" base="string">
        <pattern value="\d{3}-\d{4}-\d{3}"/>
    </simpleType>

</schema>
```

So how does a document that conforms to this schema look? Here's an example—note that locals are unqualified, but I do need to qualify globals such as `<transaction>`, `<note>`, and `<books>`. Note also that the namespace of this document is the same as the target namespace of the schema that specifies its syntax, as it should be.

```
<?xml version="1.0"?>
<at:transaction xmlns:at="http://www.starpowder.com/namespace"
    borrowDate="2001-10-15">
    <Lender phone="607.555.2222">
        <name>Doug Glass</name>
        <street>416 Disk Drive</street>
        <city>Medfield</city>
        <state>MA</state>
    </Lender>
    <Borrower phone="310.555.1111">
        <name>Britta Regensburg</name>
        <street>219 Union Drive</street>
        <city>Medfield</city>
        <state>CA</state>
    </Borrower>
    <at:note>Lender wants these back in two weeks!</at:note>
    <at:books>
        <book bookID="123-4567-890">
            <bookTitle>Earthquakes for Breakfast</bookTitle>
            <pubDate>2001-10-20</pubDate>
            <replacementValue>15.95</replacementValue>
            <maxDaysOut>14</maxDaysOut>
        </book>
        .
        .
        .
    </at:books>
</at:transaction>
```

Using Qualified Locals

You can also require that locals be qualified. Here's an example schema that requires element names to be qualified in conforming documents:

```
<schema xmlns="http://www.w3.org/1999/XMLSchema"
    xmlns:t="http://www.starpowder.com/namespace"
    targetNamespace="http://www.starpowder.com/namespace"
    elementFormDefault="qualified"
    attributeFormDefault="unqualified">

    <annotation>
        <documentation>
            Book borrowing transaction schema.
        </documentation>
    </annotation>
    .
    .
    .
```

What does a document that conforms to this schema look like? Here's an example—note that I qualify all elements explicitly:

```
<?xml version="1.0"?>
<at:transaction xmlns:at="http://www.starpowder.com/namespace"
    borrowDate="2001-10-15">
    <at:Lender phone="607.555.2222">
        <at:name>Doug Glass</at:name>
        <at:street>416 Disk Drive</at:street>
        <at:city>Medfield</at:city>
        <at:state>MA</at:state>
    </at:Lender>
    <at:Borrower phone="310.555.1111">
        <at:name>Britta Regensburg</at:name>
        <at:street>219 Union Drive</at:street>
        <at:city>Medfield</at:city>
        <at:state>CA</at:state>
    </at:Borrower>
    <at:note>Lender wants these back in two weeks!</at:note>
    <at:books>
        <at:book bookID="123-4567-890">
            <at:bookTitle>Earthquakes for Breakfast</at:bookTitle>
            <at:pubDate>2001-10-20</at:pubDate>
            <at:replacementValue>15.95</at:replacementValue>
            <at:maxDaysOut>14</at:maxDaysOut>
        </at:book>
        .
        .
        .
    </at:books>
</at:transaction>
```

Another way of creating a document that conforms to this schema is to replace the explicit qualification of every element with an *implicit* qualification by using a default namespace. Here's what that looks like:

```
<?xml version="1.0"?>
<transaction xmlns="http://www.starpowder.com/namespace"
    borrowDate="2001-10-15">
    <Lender phone="607.555.2222">
        <name>Doug Glass</name>
        <street>416 Disk Drive</street>
        <city>Medfield</city>
        <state>MA</state>
    </Lender>
    <Borrower phone="310.555.1111">
        <name>Britta Regensburg</name>
        <street>219 Union Drive</street>
        <city>Medfield</city>
        <state>CA</state>
    </Borrower>
    <note>Lender wants these back in two weeks!</note>
    <books>
        <book bookID="123-4567-890">
            <bookTitle>Earthquakes for Breakfast</bookTitle>
            <pubDate>2001-10-20</pubDate>
            <replacementValue>15.95</replacementValue>
            <maxDaysOut>14</maxDaysOut>
        </book>
        .
        .
        .
    </books>
</transaction>
```

So far, we've indicated that *all* locals must either be qualified or unqualified. However, there is a way of specifying that individual locals be either qualified or unqualified, and you do that with the `form` attribute.

Here's an example; in this case, I'll leave all locals unqualified, except the `bookID` attribute, which I'll specify must be qualified:

```
<schema xmlns="http://www.w3.org/1999/XMLSchema"
    xmlns:t="http://www.starpowder.com/namespace"
    targetNamespace="http://www.starpowder.com/namespace"
    elementFormDefault="unqualified"
    attributeFormDefault="unqualified">

    <annotation>
        <documentation>
            Book borrowing transaction schema.
        </documentation>
    </annotation>
```

```
    <element name="transaction" type="t:transactionType"/>

    <complexType name="transactionType">
        <element name="Lender" type="t:address"/>
        <element name="Borrower" type="t:address"/>
        <element ref="note" minOccurs="0"/>
        <element name="books" type="t:books"/>
        <attribute name="borrowDate" type="date"/>
    </complexType>

    <element name="note" type="string"/>

    <complexType name="address">
        <element name="name" type="string"/>
        <element name="street" type="string"/>
        <element name="city" type="string"/>
        <element name="state" type="string"/>
        <attribute name="phone" type="string"
            use="optional"/>
    </complexType>

    <complexType name="books">
        <element name="book" minOccurs="0" maxOccurs="10">
            <complexType>
                <element name="bookTitle" type="string"/>
                <element name="pubDate" type="date" minOccurs='0'/>
                <element name="replacementValue" type="decimal"/>
                <element name="maxDaysOut">
                    <simpleType base="integer">
                        <maxExclusive value="14"/>
                    </simpleType>
                </element>
                <attribute name="bookID" type="t:catalogID"
                form="qualified"/>
            </complexType>
        </element>
    </complexType>

    <simpleType name="catalogID" base="string">
        <pattern value="\d{3}-\d{4}-\d{3}"/>
    </simpleType>

</schema>
```

Here's a document that conforms to this schema—note that all locals are unqualified, except the `bookID` attribute, which is qualified:

```
<?xml version="1.0"?>
<at:transaction xmlns:at="http://www.starpowder.com/namespace"
    borrowDate="2001-10-15">
    <Lender phone="607.555.2222">
        <name>Doug Glass</name>
        <street>416 Disk Drive</street>
        <city>Medfield</city>
        <state>MA</state>
    </Lender>
    <Borrower phone="310.555.1111">
        <name>Britta Regensburg</name>
        <street>219 Union Drive</street>
        <city>Medfield</city>
        <state>CA</state>
    </Borrower>
    <at:note>Lender wants these back in two weeks!</at:note>
    <at:books>
        <book at:bookID="123-4567-890">
            <bookTitle>Earthquakes for Breakfast</bookTitle>
            <pubDate>2001-10-20</pubDate>
            <replacementValue>15.95</replacementValue>
            <maxDaysOut>14</maxDaysOut>
        </book>
        .
        .
        .
    </at:books>
</at:transaction>
```

There's plenty more power wrapped up in schemas. For example, you can have one schema inherit functionality from another, much as you would in an object-oriented programming language, and you can restrict the inheritance process, also as you would in an object-oriented programming language. This standard is one that's still evolving—and still expanding. Let's hope that it won't expand past the capabilities of XML processor authors and that we'll see more processors that will support schemas—at least partially—in the near future.

6
Understanding JavaScript

MANY WEB AUTHORS COME TO XML FROM HTML, and they don't have much programming experience beyond writing HTML. Programming experience is not a requirement in HTML, of course, because the HTML is interpreted and displayed by a Web browser. XML is different, however, because it's specifically intended to encapsulate data. And although a browser can make that data accessible to you, it's up to you to go get it—and that means using some programming skills. In this chapter, we'll develop the skills that we need to work with XML in today's browsers. (It's not necessary to write any programming code to simply display XML documents in a browser, of course—you can display it directly, or you can create a style sheet. We'll take a look at that in detail in a few chapters.)

These days, the browser that lets you interact with XML documents in the most powerful and general way is Microsoft's Internet Explorer. Whatever you think of Microsoft, there's no denying that it's making a serious attempt to support XML, and you can write code in Internet Explorer to work with XML documents in either VBScript (Microsoft's proprietary scripting language based on its Visual Basic language) or JavaScript. Other browsers will follow suit—for example, the prototype version of Netscape Navigator 6 already offers some XML support; although this will allow you to access XML documents from code in the future, Netscape hasn't said much publicly on the point yet. To support the largest number of browsers,

I'll use JavaScript to access XML in browsers in this book (and we'll also use Java itself later in the book), and this chapter will provide the foundation for that work. If you're already a JavaScript pro, feel free to skip to Chapter 7, "Handling XML Documents with JavaScript"—you still might want to scan through this chapter first, though.

What Is JavaScript?

JavaScript (which is not actually related to Java) is the most popular scripting language today. Using JavaScript, you can embed programs in Web pages and run those programs. In the next chapter, we'll see how to use those programs to retrieve the contents of XML elements and attributes, and even how to search XML documents for data.

Internet Explorer provides strong XML support with *XML islands* that let you embed XML directly in HTML pages, by letting you read XML documents directly. In this chapter, we'll learn how to use JavaScript; in the next chapter, we'll use it to parse XML documents. In Chapter 8, "XML and Data Binding," we'll use JavaScript to load XML documents into database record sets that have a great deal of support in Internet Explorer, letting you search, order, and display data in many ways.

The programs you write in JavaScript go in the `<SCRIPT>` HTML element, which itself usually goes into the `<HEAD>` section of a Web page. (However, if you use the script to write text directly to the Web page itself, as we'll do often in this chapter, you should place the `<SCRIPT>` element in the page's `<BODY>` element because the `<HEAD>` section may be read before the document's body is available.)

Here's an example to get us started. In this case, this JavaScript is writing the text `Welcome to JavaScript!` directly into a Web page when that Web page is first displayed by the browser:

```
<HTML>
    <HEAD>
        <TITLE>
            Welcome To JavaScript
        </TITLE>
    </HEAD>

    <BODY>
        <SCRIPT LANGUAGE="JavaScript">
        <!--
            document.writeln("Welcome to JavaScript!")
        //-->
        </SCRIPT>
        <CENTER>
            <H1>
```

```
                Welcome To JavaScript!
            </H1>
        </CENTER>
    </BODY>
</HTML>
```

You can see the results of this HTML in Figure 6.1. The JavaScript code wrote the welcoming text you see in the upper-left corner of the page.

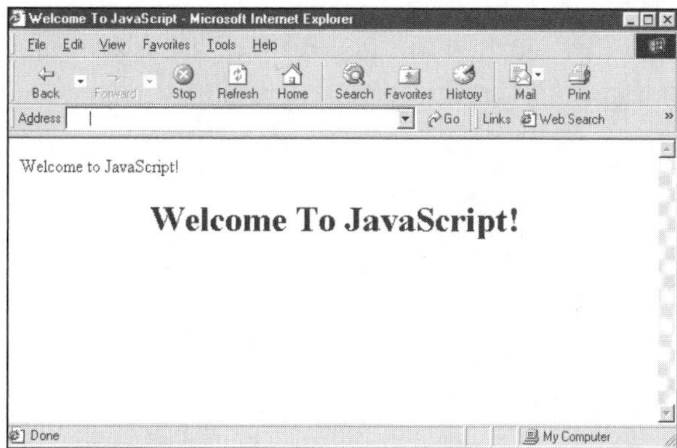

Figure 6.1 Using JavaScript in Internet Explorer.

Internet Explorer may be the premiere general-purpose XML browser today, but others, such as Netscape, will challenge that in the future. Thus, it's worth bearing in mind that there are some differences in the JavaScript implementation between these two browsers. For example, in the same Web page in Netscape, you must first open the document before writing to it, and then you close it like this:

```
<HTML>
    <HEAD>
        <TITLE>
            Welcome To JavaScript
        </TITLE>
    </HEAD>

    <BODY>
        <SCRIPT LANGUAGE="JavaScript">
        <!--
            document.open()
            document.writeln("Welcome to JavaScript!")
            document.close()
        //-->
        </SCRIPT>
```

continues ▸

```
        <CENTER>
            <H1>
                Welcome To JavaScript!
            </H1>
        </CENTER>
    </BODY>
</HTML>
```

Let's take this example apart to get started. Notice that I begin with the <SCRIPT> element and place the JavaScript code into that element. In the <SCRIPT> element, I set the LANGUAGE attribute to "JavaScript" to let the browser know what language the script is in:

```
<HTML>
    <HEAD>
        <TITLE>
            Welcome To JavaScript
        </TITLE>
    </HEAD>

    <BODY>
        <SCRIPT LANGUAGE="JavaScript">
        .
        .
        .
        </SCRIPT>

        <CENTER>
            <H1>
                Welcome To JavaScript!
            </H1>
        </CENTER>

    </BODY>
</HTML>
```

I'll enclose the actual JavaScript code inside an HTML comment. This is just general good practice in JavaScript—unlike an XML browser, if an HTML browser can't understand the contents of an element, it ignores the markup and just displays the text directly. Because some browsers can't understand JavaScript and the <SCRIPT> tag, I place the code in an HTML comment so that it won't be displayed in such browsers. JavaScript-enabled browsers ignore the comment markup—although you should note that, by convention, you must end the HTML comment with //-->, not just -->. This is because // is the JavaScript way of creating a comment (I'll go into more depth about this in a few pages). Otherwise, the browser may try to interpret the --> markup as JavaScript:

```
<HTML>
    <HEAD>
        <TITLE>
            Welcome To JavaScript
        </TITLE>
    </HEAD>

    <BODY>

        <SCRIPT LANGUAGE="JavaScript">
        <!--
        .
        .
        .
        //-->
        </SCRIPT>

        <CENTER>
            <H1>
                Welcome To JavaScript!
            </H1>
        </CENTER>

    </BODY>
</HTML>
```

Handling Browsers That Don't Support JavaScript

There's also a `<NOSCRIPT>` element that you can use to display messages in browsers that don't support JavaScript (such as: `"You're missing some amazing JavaScript action!"`). Browsers that don't handle JavaScript won't understand either the `<SCRIPT>` or `<NOSCRIPT>` elements, but they will display the text in the `<NOSCRIPT>` element directly. (Remember, the JavaScript code in the `<SCRIPT>` element is usually in an HTML comment.) JavaScript-enabled browsers ignore the `<NOSCRIPT>` element.

At this point, we're ready for the JavaScript code. Here, that code is simply the JavaScript expression `document.writeln("Welcome to JavaScript!");` this expression just writes the text `Welcome to JavaScript!` to the Web page:

```
<HTML>
    <HEAD>
        <TITLE>
            Welcome To JavaScript
        </TITLE>
    </HEAD>
```

continues ▸

```
    <BODY>

        <SCRIPT LANGUAGE="JavaScript">
        <!--
            document.writeln("Welcome to JavaScript!")
        //-->
        </SCRIPT>

        <CENTER>
            <H1>
                Welcome To JavaScript!
            </H1>
        </CENTER>

    </BODY>
</HTML>
```

That's our first line of JavaScript: `document.writeln("Welcome to JavaScript!")`. When the Web page is loaded, this JavaScript is read and run by the browser.

The official standard for JavaScript says that each JavaScript statement should end with a semicolon (;). In other words, this first line of JavaScript should technically be `document.writeln("Welcome to JavaScript!");`. However, browsers no longer require the ending semicolon because it's so easy to forget it; most of the JavaScript on the Internet these days omits the semicolon, so I will do the same here.

The two big implementations of JavaScript are Netscape's and Microsoft's. These two browser vendors are not exactly the best of friends, and if you assume that the two implementations of JavaScript have some differences, you're right.

Netscape's JavaScript

You can find documentation for Netscape's JavaScript at `http://developer.netscape.com/tech/javascript/index.html` (bear in mind that such URLs are very subject to change). Netscape has also developed a version of JavaScript designed to be used on the server side, not in browsers at all. You can find Netscape's documentation for server-side JavaScript at `http://docs.iplanet.com/docs/manuals/ssjs.html`.

Microsoft's JScript

Microsoft's implementation of JavaScript is both different and more extensive than the Netscape standards. The implementation of JavaScript in Internet Explorer is actually called JScript, not JavaScript, although JScript is very close to JavaScript. You can find the official documentation for JScript at `http://msdn.microsoft.com/scripting/default.htm?/scripting/jscript/techinfo/jsdocs.htm`. (Note that Microsoft reorganizes its Web sites about every 15 minutes, so by the time you read this, this URL may have changed.)

ECMAScript

There's some animosity between the two main JavaScript implementers, so you might wonder if there isn't some third party that might be capable of sorting things out. In fact, there is—the European Computer Manufacturers Association (ECMA) in Geneva, Switzerland, has standardized JavaScript. You can find the current standard at `www.ecma.ch/ecma1/stand/ecma-262.htm` and `www.ecma.ch/ecma1/stand/ecma-290.htm`. (These URLs seem volatile; they changed while the tech review was being done on this book—if they don't work, go to `www.ecma.ch` and search for "ECMAScript.") In fact, some people even call JavaScript ECMAScript these days. Netscape's version of JavaScript is ECMA-compliant.

There are plenty of free JavaScript resources out there to learn from; here's a starter list:

- `http://home.netscape.com/eng/mozilla/3.0/handbook/javascript/index.html`. Netscape's guide to using and programming JavaScript
- `http://javascript.internet.com`. Ready-to-use, free scripts
- `www.infohiway.com/javascript/`. Ready-to-use, free scripts
- `www.jsworld.com`. Examples and archives of JavaScript
- `www.webteacher.com/javascript/`. Tutorial covering JavaScript in some detail

JavaScript Is Object-Oriented

JavaScript is an *object-oriented* language. The term *object-oriented* should *not* make you nervous because, for us, object-oriented programming will be a lot easier. For our purposes, object-oriented programming just means that JavaScript makes available objects that give us access to some aspect of the browser or document.

For example, we already have used the document object, one of the most powerful JavaScript objects, in this chapter. That object refers to the body of the Web page in the browser, which means that with this object, you have access to the HTML in the page. In the previous example, I used the writeln (which stands for "write line") *method* of the document object to write Welcome to JavaScript! like this:

```
<SCRIPT LANGUAGE="JavaScript">
<!--
    document.writeln("Welcome to JavaScript!")
//-->
</SCRIPT>
```

You can use methods such as writeln to have an object perform some action, such as writing to the Web page. Other methods enable you to force the browser to navigate to a new page, or send data back to scripts on the server, and so on.

The objects that you already have access to in JavaScript give you a great deal of power—for example, we'll use the document object to access XML documents in the next chapter. Here's an overview of some of the most popular JavaScript objects and what they're all about:

Object	Description
document	This object represents the current Web page's body. With this object, you can access all the elements in a Web page, such as links, images, anchors, and so on.
history	This object has a record of what sites the Web browser has been to before opening the current page. Using the methods of this object, you can move backward and forward though the *history list.*
location	This object holds information about the location of the current Web page, including its URL, the domain name, the path, the server port, and so on.
navigator	This object actually refers to the Web browser itself. Using this object, you can determine the type of browser in use.
window	This object refers to the current browser window and provides many powerful methods. In Internet Explorer, you use the event subobject of this object to handle events, as we'll see at the end of the chapter.

There are many more objects in JavaScript, and you can define your own objects—see the JavaScript documentation for details. When you want to create your own objects, you first define a *class*, which you can consider the *type* of the object. Using the JavaScript new operator, you can create objects from classes; we won't create classes here, but we'll use the `new` operator discussed in the later section, "Creating Objects in JavaScript," to create objects in the next chapter.

You need to know about two aspects of objects to be able to get anywhere: *methods*, which we've already seen, and *properties*.

Using Object Properties and Methods in JavaScript

JavaScript programming centers on objects, to a large extent. We've already seen the `document` object and learned that one way to use that object is to use methods such as `writeln` to indicate you want to write to a Web page. To use a method, you use the object's name, followed by a dot (.), followed by the method name, such as `document.writeln`. Here are a few examples of methods:

Method	Description
`document.write`	Writes to the body of the current Web page
`document.writeln`	Writes to the body of the current Web page, and ends the text with a carriage return
`history.go`	Makes the browser navigate to a particular location in the browser's history list
`window.alert`	Makes the browser display an alert dialog box
`window.open`	Makes the browser open a new browser window, possibly displaying a new document

Hundreds of such methods are available in JavaScript, and they enable you to work with a browser as it's running. In addition to using methods to cause the browser to perform some action, you can also read and change the settings in the JavaScript objects using *properties*. For example, the `document.fgcolor` property holds the color of text in the current Web page; by changing the `document.fgcolor` property, you can change the color of that text.

Here are some examples of properties, including the objects they belong to:

Property	Description
`document.bgcolor`	Holds the background color of the current page.
`document.fgcolor`	Holds the foreground (that is, the default text) color of the current page.
`document.lastmodified`	Holds the date that the page was last modified (although many documents do not provide this information).

continues

Property	Description
`document.title`	Holds the title of the current page (which appears in the browser's title bar).
`navigator.appName`	Holds the actual name of the browser, which you can use to determine what browser the user is using. We'll use this property at the end of the chapter to distinguish between Internet Explorer and Netscape.

Using object methods and properties, you have access to what's going on in a Web page, and you have complete programmatic control over the browser in many areas. We'll be putting methods and properties to work in this chapter and the next two chapters.

We've taken a look at the idea of methods and properties, but there's one more concept to cover before getting the actual programming details—using *events* in JavaScript. That topic is discussed next.

Using Events in JavaScript

When you load an XML document in a browser, the browser can keep track of the success or failure of the operation. When the user clicks a button in a Web page or uses the mouse, the browser keeps track of that as well. How does the browser inform your JavaScript code what's going on? It uses *events*.

For example, when the user clicks a Web page, a `mouseDown` event occurs. To handle that event in your code, you can connect code to that event. Most HTML tags now support events using attributes such as `onMouseDown` that you use to connect events to JavaScript code. Here's an example. In this case, when the user clicks the Web page, a `mouseDown` event occurs. Using the `onMouseDown` attribute, I can execute JavaScript code to perform some action, such as turning the background of the Web page green. (This example works only in Internet Explorer—you have to add a little additional code to make it work in Netscape, as we'll see at the end of this chapter.)

```
<HTML>
    <HEAD>
        <TITLE>
            Using JavaScript Events
        </TITLE>
    </HEAD>

    <BODY onMouseDown="document.bgColor='green'">

        <CENTER>
            <H1>
                Click anywhere to turn this page green!
            </H1>
```

```
        </CENTER>

    </BODY>

</HTML>
```

As you can see, when the user clicks the Web page, the code `document.bgColor='green'` is executed, assigning a value of `"green"` to the `document.bgColor` property. You can see this page at work in Figure 6.2.

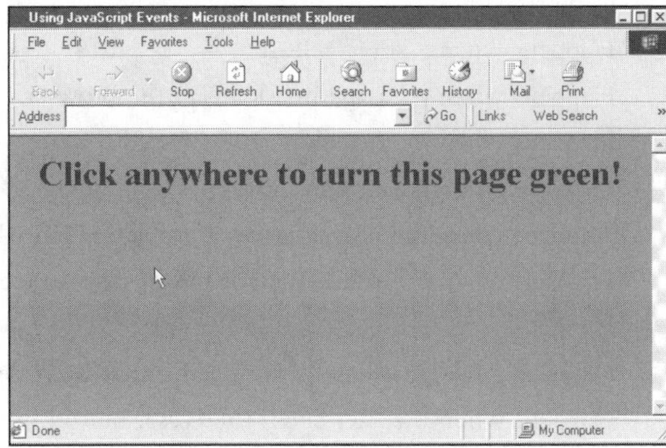

Figure 6.2 Using an event in Internet Explorer.

This example is a very simple one because the JavaScript code is in the `<BODY>` element itself. For longer code, you'll usually store the code in the `<SCRIPT>` element instead and then *call* that code from elements such as `<BODY>`. We'll see how that works in the section "Creating Functions in JavaScript," later in this chapter.

A great number of events are available. Table 6.1 shows the commonly used events. (Note that support for these attributes varies by browser and by HTML tag.)

Table 6.1 **Common Events**

Event	Description
`onBlur`	Happens when an element loses the input *focus*. (The element with the focus is the one to which keystrokes are sent.)
`onChange`	Happens when data in an HTML control changes. (HTML controls include text fields, buttons, lists, and so on.)
`onClick`	Happens when an element is clicked.
`onDblClick`	Happens when an element is double-clicked.

continues

Table 6.1 **Continued**

Event	Description
`onError`	Happens when an error has occurred while executing your code.
`onFocus`	Happens when an element gets the focus. (The element with the focus is the one to which keystrokes are sent.)
`onKeyDown`	Happens when a key is pressed.
`onKeyPress`	Happens when a key is pressed and the struck key's code is available to be read.
`onKeyUp`	Happens when a key is released.
`onLoad`	Happens when the page first loads in the browser.
`onMouseDown`	Happens when a mouse button is pressed.
`onMouseMove`	Happens when the mouse moves.
`onMouseOut`	Happens when the mouse leaves a visible HTML element.
`onMouseOver`	Happens when the mouse cursor moves over an element.
`onMouseUp`	Happens when a mouse button is released.
`onMove`	Happens when an element is moved, either by code or by the user.
`onReset`	Happens when the user clicks the Reset button in an HTML form.
`onResize`	Happens when code or the user resizes an element or page.
`onSelect`	Happens when the user makes a selection.
`onSubmit`	Happens when the user clicks the Submit button in an HTML form.
`onUnload`	Happens when the browser unloads a page.

You use events to handle user and browser actions in real-time in your code, and dozens of events are available. These events are supported by the various HTML tags supported by the browser. You can see which HTML tags support what event attributes in Table 6.3 for Internet Explorer and Table 6.4 for Netscape, later in this chapter.

This overview gives some indication of how powerful JavaScript is. It's now time to turn to the details of writing code in JavaScript so that we can put it to work in the next two chapters.

Programming in JavaScript

In this chapter, we'll build our JavaScript foundation by getting the syntax of the language down. For example, you can make decisions based on your data values with the JavaScript `if` statement. In this code, I'm comparing the value 143 to 719, and if 719 is greater than 143, displaying the message `The first value is greater than the second.`

```
<HTML>
    <HEAD>
        <TITLE>
            Using the JavaScript if Statement
        </TITLE>

    </HEAD>

    <BODY>

        <SCRIPT LANGUAGE="JavaScript">
            if(719 > 143){
                document.writeln(
                    "The first value is greater than the second."
                )
            }
        </SCRIPT>

        <CENTER>
            <H1>
                Using the JavaScript if Statement
            </H1>
        </CENTER>

    </BODY>

</HTML>
```

You can see this Web page at work in Figure 6.3—as indicated in that page, 719 is indeed greater than 143.

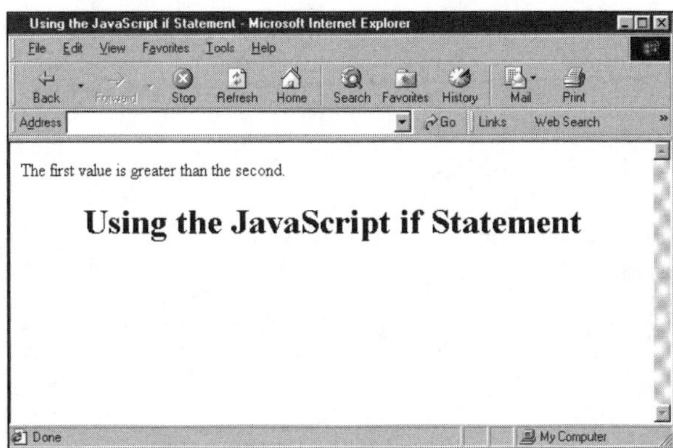

Figure 6.3 Using the JavaScript `if` statement in Internet Explorer.

Testing for Errors in Your Code

While you are developing your JavaScript code, Internet Explorer displays a dialog box indicating what errors are in your code. Netscape, however, simply refuses to run code it considers buggy. To see what the trouble is, just type `"javascript:"` in the Location box, and press Enter. Netscape opens a new window telling you what's wrong with the code.

We're going to see statements such as the `if` statement in the remainder of this chapter—and put them to work in the next two chapters.

Working with Data in JavaScript

Using data is basic to nearly any JavaScript program, and JavaScript supports quite a number of different data types: numbers, Boolean values, text strings, and so on. You store data values in *variables* in JavaScript.

As with other programming languages, variables are simply named locations in memory that you use to store data. You create variables in JavaScript with the `var` statement; when a variable has been created, it's ready for you to store and retrieve data in.

Here's an example; I'm creating a new variable named `temperature` and storing a value of `72` in it using the assignment operator (`=`). When I use this variable in code, JavaScript will replace it with the value `72`, so I can display the temperature like this:

```
<HTML>

    <HEAD>
        <TITLE>
            Using Variables in JavaScript
        </TITLE>

    </HEAD>

    <BODY>

        <SCRIPT LANGUAGE="JavaScript">
            var temperature
            temperature = 72
            document.writeln("The temperature is "
            +  temperature
            + " degrees.")
        </SCRIPT>

        <CENTER>
            <H1>
                Using Variables in JavaScript
            </H1>
```

```
        </CENTER>

    </BODY>

</HTML>
```

Note the text I'm passing to the `document.writeln` method this time: `"The temperature is " + temperature + " degrees."`. In this case, I'm using the JavaScript addition operator, `+`, to join these three expressions into one string. The temperature variable is replaced with the value this variable contains, which is `72`, as shown in Figure 6.4.

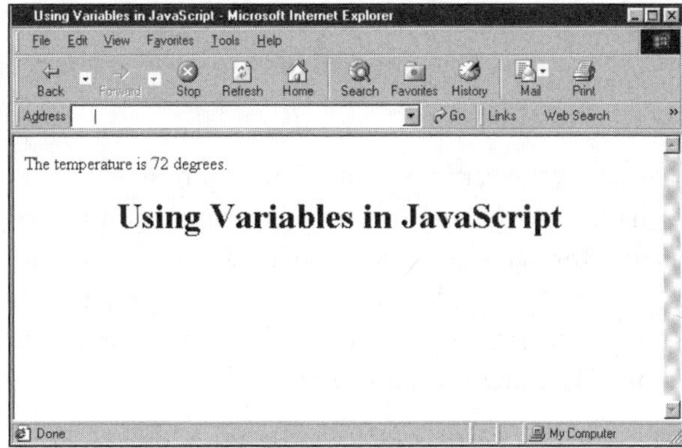

Figure 6.4 Using variables in JavaScript.

You can also create a variable *and* assign a value to it at the same time with the `var` statement. Here's what that looks like:

```
var temperature = 72
document.writeln("The temperature is "
+  temperature
+ " degrees.")
```

Besides storing numbers in JavaScript variables, you can also store text strings. In this next example, I store the entire text `The temperature is 72 degrees.` in the variable named `weatherReport` and then display the text like this:

```
<HTML>
    <HEAD>
        <TITLE>
            Using Variables in JavaScript
        </TITLE>
    </HEAD>

    <BODY>
```

continues ▸

```
        <SCRIPT LANGUAGE="JavaScript">
        <!--
            var weatherReport
            weatherReport = "The temperature is 72 degrees."
            document.writeln(weatherReport)
        //-->
        </SCRIPT>

        <CENTER>
            <H1>
                Using Variables in JavaScript
            </H1>
        </CENTER>

    </BODY>

</HTML>
```

This code produces the same display as in Figure 6.4.

Note the name `weatherReport` here. The convention in JavaScript is to use lowercase names for variables. If you create a name by joining several words, you must capitalize the first letter of the second word, the third word, and so on. Names for JavaScript variables obey the same rules as the names for XML elements. Here are a few examples:

- `counter`
- `numberOfLinks`
- `countLeftUntilFinished`
- `oneOfThoseVeryVeryVeryLongVariableNames`

Commenting Your JavaScript

As with HTML and XML, you can add comments to JavaScript code; in JavaScript, you use a double forward slash (`//`) to start a comment. The JavaScript interpreter in the browser stops reading anything on a line past `//`, so you can comment your code like this:

```
<HTML>
    <HEAD>
        <TITLE>
            Using Variables in JavaScript
        </TITLE>
    </HEAD>

    <BODY>

        <SCRIPT LANGUAGE="JavaScript">
        <!--
```

```
            //Create the weatherReport variable
            var weatherReport
            //Assign a value to weatherReport
            weatherReport = "The temperature is 72 degrees."
            //Display the value in weatherReport
            document.writeln(weatherReport)
        //-->
        </SCRIPT>

        <CENTER>
            <H1>
                Using Variables in JavaScript
            </H1>
        </CENTER>

    </BODY>

</HTML>
```

Working with JavaScript Operators

What if you want to manipulate your data in JavaScript code? Say, for example, that you need to multiply 219 by 45—how would you do it? In JavaScript, you can use the multiplication *operator* (*). Here's an example showing how this works:

```
<HTML>

    <HEAD>
        <TITLE>
            Using Operators In JavaScript
        </TITLE>
    </HEAD>

    <BODY>

        <SCRIPT LANGUAGE="JavaScript">
            var result
            result = 219 * 45
            document.writeln("219 * 45 = " +  result)
        </SCRIPT>

        <CENTER>
            <H1>
                Using Operators In JavaScript
            </H1>
        </CENTER>

    </BODY>

</HTML>
```

Figure 6.5 shows the results of this code.

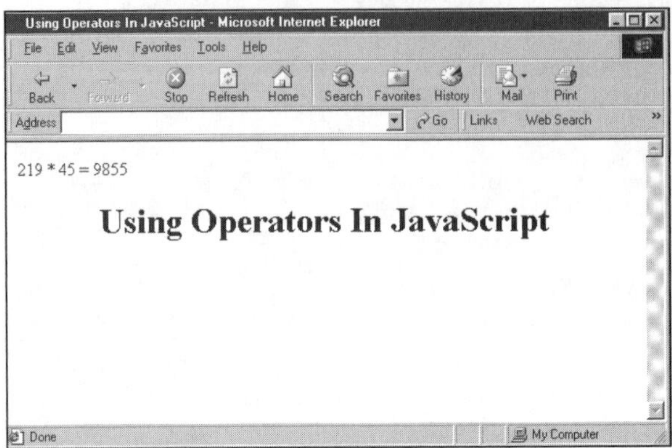

Figure 6.5 Using JavaScript operators in Internet Explorer.

As you might expect, many operators are available in JavaScript. For example, you can use the increment operator, `++`, to add 1 to a numeric value; for example, if `counter` holds `400`, then after you apply the `++` operator—as in `++counter`—`counter` will hold `401`.

Prefix Versus Postfix Operators

As C, C++, Perl, Java, and JavaScript programmers will know, you can apply the ++ increment and -- decrement operators as prefix or postfix operators: `++counter` or `counter++`. Prefix operators are applied before the rest of the statement or expression is evaluated, and postfix operators are applied after the rest of the statement is evaluated.

Table 6.2 lists the JavaScript operators. (As with the rest of the material in this chapter, check the JavaScript documentation for more details.)

Table 6.2 **JavaScript Operators**

Operator	Description
Addition (+)	Adds two numbers or concatenates two strings
Assignment (=)	Assigns a value or an object to a variable
Bitwise `AND` (&)	Performs a bitwise `AND` on two values
Bitwise left shift (<<)	Shifts the bits of an expression to the left a specified number of times
Bitwise `NOT` (~)	Negation; performs a bitwise `NOT` on a value
Bitwise `OR` (|)	Performs a bitwise `OR` operation on two values

Operator	Description
Bitwise right shift (>>)	Shifts the bits of a value to the right (maintaining the sign of the value)
Bitwise XOR (^)	Performs a bitwise exclusive OR on two values
Comma (,)	Causes two expressions to be evaluated sequentially
Conditional (trinary) (?:)	Executes one of two expressions, depending on whether a condition is true or false
Decrement (--)	Decrements a value by 1
Division (/)	Divides two numbers and returns a numeric result
Equality (==)	Compares two expressions to determine if they are equal
Greater than (>)	Compares two expressions to determine if one is greater than the other
Greater than or equal to (>=)	Compares two expressions to determine if one is greater than or equal to the other
Identity (===)	Compares two expressions to determine if they are equal in value and of the same data type
Increment (++)	Increments a value by 1
Inequality (!=)	Compares two expressions to determine if they are unequal
Less than (<)	Compares two values to determine if one is less than the other
Less than or equal to (<=)	Compares two expressions to determine if one is less than or equal to the other
Logical AND (&&)	Performs a logical AND conjunction operation on two expressions
Logical NOT (!)	Performs logical negation on an expression
Logical OR (||)	Performs a logical OR disjunction operation on two expressions
Modulus (%)	Divides two numbers and returns the remainder
Multiplication (*)	Multiplies two numbers
New (new)	Creates a new object
Nonidentity (!==)	Compares two expressions to determine that they are not equal in value or of the same data type
Subtraction (-)	Subtracts one value from another
Typeof (typeof)	Returns a string that identifies the data type of an expression
Unary negation (-)	Returns the negative value of a numeric expression
Unsigned right shift (>>>)	Performs an unsigned right shift of the bits in a value

Besides the operators in this list, you can put together a number of combination operators from two operators. For example, `counterValue += 101` adds 101 to the value in `counterValue`. The combination operators in JavaScript are `+=`, `-=`, `*=`, `/=`, `%=`, `&=`, `|=`, `^=`, `<<=`, `>>=`, and `>>>=`.

It's also worth noting that a number of these operators have to do with comparisons, and you use them to make decisions in code. We've already seen the greater than comparison operator, `>`, like this:

```
if(719 > 143){
    document.writeln(
        "The first value is greater than the second."
    )
}
```

What's really going on here? In this case, I'm using the `if` statement to compare two numbers. The `if` statement is fundamental to JavaScript, and it's the next step up from using simple operators.

Creating JavaScript *if* Statements

You use the `if` statement in JavaScript to test your data and to execute some code if the test is true. Here's the basic form of the `if` statement:

```
if (condition) {
    code
}
```

Here, *`condition`* is the test that you want to make, and *`code`* is the code that you want to execute if the condition is true. One thing to note here is that you must enclose the code to execute in curly braces, `{` and `}`.

So what kind of conditions can you check, and how do you do so? To construct a condition to test, you use the comparison operators, such as `<` (less than), `>` (greater than), `==` (equal to), `<=` (less than or equal to), or `>=` (greater than or equal to).

Here's an example; in this case, I'm making sure that the value in a variable named `temperature` is greater than 32:

```
<HTML>
    <HEAD>
        <TITLE>
            Using the JavaScript if Statement
        </TITLE>
    </HEAD>

    <BODY>

        <SCRIPT LANGUAGE="JavaScript">
            var temperature
            temperature = 45
```

```
            if (temperature > 32) {
                document.writeln("We're above freezing.")
            }
        </SCRIPT>

        <CENTER>
            <H1>
                Using the JavaScript if Statement
            </H1>
        </CENTER>

    </BODY>

</HTML>
```

You can see the results of this code in Figure 6.6.

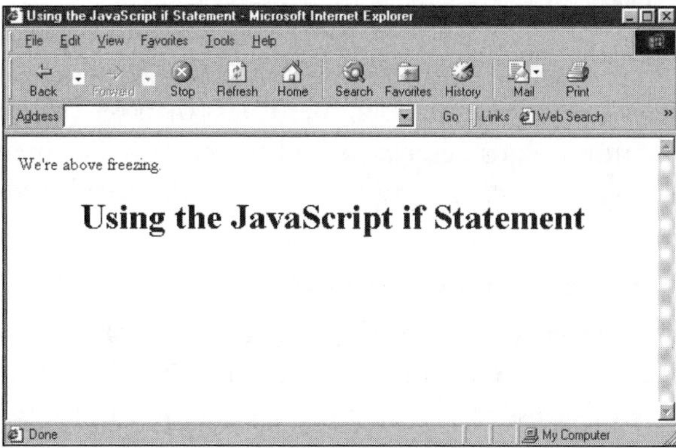

Figure 6.6 Using the `if` statement to check the temperature.

Here are some other `if` statement examples:

```
if (year == 2001) {
    document.writeln("The year is 2001.")
}

if (color == "red") {
    document.writeln("Stop the car.")
}

if (price < 2000.00) {
    document.writeln("Be careful, the price has fallen too low!")
}
```

Besides using the comparison operators, you can also use the *and* operator, `&&`, and the *or* operator, `||`, to combine conditions. Here's how you can use the `&&` operator:

```
if (temperature < 75 && temperature > 65) {
    document.writeln("We're in the comfort zone.")
}
```

Here, the value in the `temperature` variable must be less than 75 *and* greater than 65 for the code to be executed. If the temperature is indeed in that range, the message `We're in the comfort zone.` is displayed.

In this example, both conditions must be true for the overall condition to be considered true. However, you can use the `||` operator as well to connect conditions. Here's an example:

```
if (temperature < 65 || temperature > 75) {
    document.writeln("Outside the comfort zone!")
}
```

In this case, if the value in temperature is less than 65 *or* greater than 75, the overall condition is considered true and the code is executed, which means that the message `Outside the comfort zone!` is displayed in the Web page.

Creating JavaScript *if...else* Statements

In fact, the more general form of the `if` statement also has an `else` clause, which can also hold code. The `else` clause is optional, but if you include it, the code in that clause is executed if the condition in the associated `if` statement is false. Here's how the `if...else` statement looks in general:

```
if (condition) {
    code executed if condition is true
}
else {
    code executed if condition is false
}
```

Here's an example showing how this works; in this case, I'm elaborating on our previous example that made sure the temperature is above freezing. I've added an `else` clause that is executed if the temperature is less than 32°, and the code in that clause displays the message `Time to drain the pool.`

```
<HTML>
    <HEAD>
        <TITLE>
            Using the JavaScript else Clause
        </TITLE>
    </HEAD>
```

```
    <BODY>

        <SCRIPT LANGUAGE="JavaScript">
            var temperature
            temperature = 5
            if (temperature > 32) {
                document.writeln("We're above freezing.")
            }
            else {
                document.writeln("Time to drain the pool.")
            }
        </SCRIPT>

        <CENTER>
            <H1>
                Using the JavaScript else Clause
            </H1>
        </CENTER>

    </BODY>

</HTML>
```

You can see the results of this code in Figure 6.7.

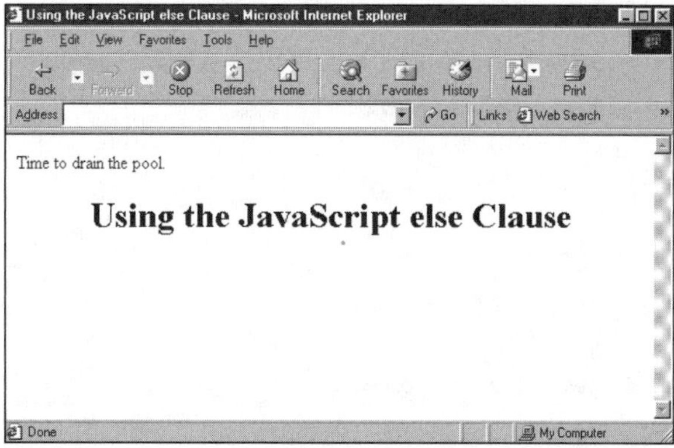

Figure 6.7 Using the `else` clause.

Creating *switch* Statements

The JavaScript `switch` statement is the next step up in decision-making after the `if` statement. You use the `switch` statement if you have a large number of cases that you want to test and don't want to construct a long ladder of `if...else` statements.

Here's how it works—you compare a test expression against a number of values. If one of those values matches, the code associated with the value is executed until the JavaScript interpreter finds a `break` statement. Here's what the `switch` statement looks like in outline:

```
switch(test){
    case value1:
        .
        .
        .
        code executed if test matches value1
        .
        .
        .
        break;
    case value2:
        .
        .
        .
        code executed if test matches value2
        .
        .
        .
        break;
    case value3:
        .
        .
        .
        code executed if test matches value3
        .
        .
        .
        break;
    default:
        .
        .
        .
        code executed if test doesn't matches any case
        .
        .
        .
        break;
}
```

Here, you list the possible values to match against with the `case` statement. When a value given in a `case` statement matches, the corresponding code (that is, the code that follows the `case` statement up to a `break` statement) is executed.

You might also note that I've added a `default` statement to the end of the list of case statements. If no `case` statement's values have matched the text expression, the code in the default statement is executed in case you want to make sure that *some* code is executed. The `default` statement is optional.

Here's an example putting the `switch` statement to work. In this case, I'm checking user input, which I've stored in a variable named `userInput`, against various test strings. Then I'm displaying messages to match the various possibilities:

```
switch(userInput){
    case "EDIT":
        document.writeln("Now entering EDIT mode.")
        break;
    case "HELP":
        //This response should look familiar to users...
        document.writeln("Sorry, no help is available.")
        break;
    case "QUIT":
        document.writeln("Are you sure you want to quit?")
        break;
    default:
        document.writeln("I do not understand that response.")
        break;
}
```

Creating JavaScript *for* Loop Statements

Using loops, you can execute code as many times as you want—which is one of the things computers excel at. The most basic loop is the `for` loop statement, and here's what this statement looks like in general:

```
for (initialization; test; increment) {
    code
}
```

Here's what's happening: You place an expression in the ***`initialization`*** part of the `for` loop (which often initializes a variable, called a *loop index*, to `0`), and then you place a test condition in the ***`test`*** part of the loop to be tested each time the code in the loop has been executed. If the test is false, the loop ends (often the test condition checks whether the value in the loop index exceeds a specified maximum value). On the other hand, if the test condition is true, the body of the loop is executed and the code in the ***`increment`*** part of the loop is executed to get the loop ready for the next iteration (often by incrementing the loop index).

Here's an example to make this clear. In this case, I'll set up a loop to execute 10 times, and each time it will print out the value in a loop index. This example works by setting a loop index variable named `loopIndex` to `0` to start, and then increments it each time when the loop code has executed (using the increment operator, `++`) and checks to make sure that the loop index does not exceed `10`. When the loop index does exceed `10`, the loop terminates. Here's the code (the HTML `<BR>` element, short for *break*, makes the Web browser skip to the next line):

```
<HTML>
    <HEAD>
        <TITLE>
            Using the for Statement
        </TITLE>
    </HEAD>

    <BODY>

        <SCRIPT LANGUAGE = JavaScript>
            for(var loopIndex = 1; loopIndex <= 10; loopIndex++){
                document.writeln("The loop index value is " +
                loopIndex + "<BR>")
            }
        </SCRIPT>

        <CENTER>
            <H1>
                Using the for Statement
            </H1>
        </CENTER>

    </BODY>

</HTML>
```

Here's another thing to note in this example: Because `loopIndex` is a variable that we're using in our code, we must declare it. JavaScript gives you the shortcut of declaring a variable like this right in the `for` loop itself, and you can see the `var` statement inside the initialization part of the `for` loop. This is a common practice, and I'm including it here because you'll see it often.

When you open this page in a browser, you'll see a message displaying the value of the loop index from `1` to `10`, as shown in Figure 6.8.

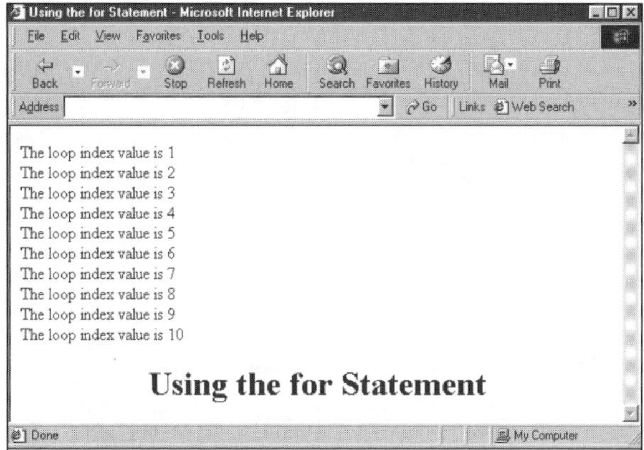

Figure 6.8 Using a JavaScript `for` loop in Internet Explorer.

Creating *while* Loop Statements

There are other loops besides the `for` loop in JavaScript, such as the `while` loop. The `while` loop tests a condition each time the loop is executed. If the condition is true, it executes the code in the loop. Here's what this loop looks like in outline:

```
while (condition){
    code
}
```

For example, here's how you write the example we used for `for` loops as a `while` loop:

```
<HTML>
     <HEAD>
        <TITLE>
            Using the while Statement
        </TITLE>
    </HEAD>

    <BODY>

        <SCRIPT LANGUAGE = JavaScript>
            var loopIndex = 0

            while(loopIndex < 10){
                loopIndex++
                document.writeln("The loop index value is " +
                loopIndex + "<BR>")
            }
```

continues ▸

```
        </SCRIPT>

        <CENTER>
            <H1>
                Using the while Statement
            </H1>
        </CENTER>

    </BODY>

</HTML>
```

You can see the results of this code in Figure 6.9.

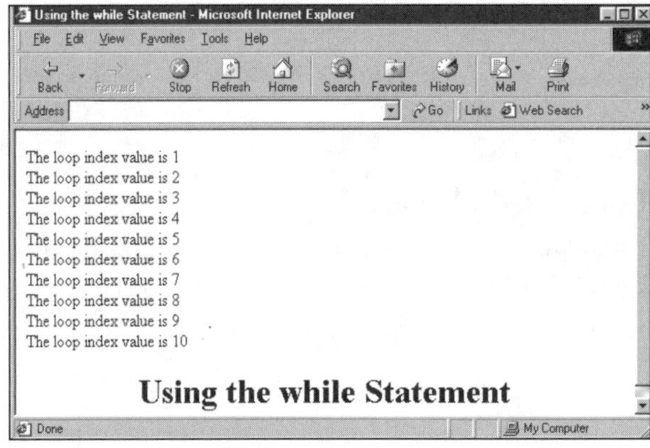

Figure 6.9 Using a JavaScript `while` loop in Internet Explorer.

Creating *do...while* Loops

There's another form of the `while` loop available: the `do...while` loop. This loop is much like the `while` loop, except that it checks the loop condition at the end, after the code in the loop has been executed, not at the beginning. Here's what this loop looks like in outline:

```
do {
    code
} while (condition)
```

Actually, there's a big difference between the `while` and `do...while` loops in programmatic terms—the code in a `do...while` loop is always executed at least once, although that's not true of a `while` loop. Take a look at this example:

```
var number = 25
do {
    document.writeln("The reciprocal of "
    + number + " is "
```

```
    + 1/number + "<BR>")
    --number
} while (number > 0)
```

Here I'm displaying a sequence of reciprocal values, from `1/25` up to `1/1`, using a `do...while` loop. However, this would be a problem if `number` were initialized to `0`, because the first reciprocal the code would attempt to calculate is `1/0`:

```
var number = 0
do {
    document.writeln("The reciprocal of "
    + number + " is "
    + 1/number + "<BR>")
    --number
} while (number > 0)
```

A better choice is to use the `while` loop here, which checks the value in `number` first and won't attempt to calculate a reciprocal if that value equals `0`:

```
var number = 25
while (number > 0) {
    document.writeln("The reciprocal of "
    + number + " is "
    + 1/number + "<BR>")
    --number
}
```

Both forms of the `while` loop have their places, however—for example, if you need to execute the body of the loop before testing to see whether the loop should continue, use the `do...while` loop.

Creating Functions in JavaScript

Functions are a crucial part of JavaScript programming. With a function, you can wrap some code into a programming construct, a *function*, and you call that function to execute that code.

You create functions with the `function` statement. Here's how that statement looks in outline:

```
function functionname([argument1 [, argument2 [, ...argumentn]]])
{
    code
}
```

In this case, I'm *passing* the values `argument1`, `argument2`, and so on to this function. The code in the function has access to these values. A function can also *return* a value; to do that, you use the `return` statement.

Here's an example; in this case, I'm creating a function named `getTime`, which will return the current time. Notice the syntax of the `function` statement here—I'm adding an empty set of parentheses after the name of the function. Those parentheses are always necessary, and when we pass values to a function, they'll be listed in the parentheses. The `getTime` function doesn't accept any passed values, so the parentheses are empty:

```
function getTime()
{
    var now = new Date
    var returnValue = now.getHours() + ":"
    + now.getMinutes()
    return(returnValue)
}
```

In this case, we're using the JavaScript `Date` class and creating a new object of that class named `now` using the `new` operator. I can use the `getHours` and `getMinutes` methods of this new object (these methods are built into the `Date` class) to get the current time.

In fact, methods are just functions built into objects. If you continue on in JavaScript to creating your own classes and objects, the functions that you add to a class will be called methods.

In this example, I place the current time into a string named `returnValue`. That string is what I return from the function, using the `return` statement. After creating this function, you're free to use it in your code. Here's how I place that function in a `<SCRIPT>` element—note that the code in functions is not run automatically when the page loads; it's run only when the function is actually called:

```
<HTML>
    <HEAD>
        <TITLE>
            Using JavaScript Functions
        </TITLE>

    </HEAD>

    <BODY>

        <SCRIPT LANGUAGE = JavaScript>
            document.writeln("The time is " + getTime()
            + " right now.")

            function getTime()
            {
                var now = new Date
                var returnValue = now.getHours() + ":"
                + now.getMinutes()
```

```
                return(returnValue)
            }
        </SCRIPT>

        <CENTER>
            <H1>
                Using JavaScript Functions
            </H1>
        </CENTER>

    </BODY>

</HTML>
```

You can see this page in Internet Explorer in Figure 6.10. As you can see there, things have worked out as we expected—when the page is loaded, the `document.writeln` statement is executed, which means that the call to the `getTime` function is also executed. The `getTime` function returns the current time as a string, which is incorporated into the text that's displayed in the page.

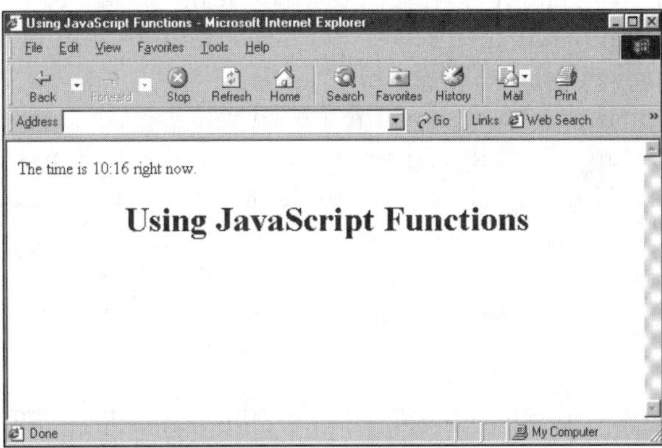

Figure 6.10 Using a JavaScript function in Internet Explorer.

We've seen how to write a function that returns a value now, but what about passing values to functions so that they can work on them? I'll take a look at how that works next.

Passing Values to Functions

The values that you pass to functions are called *arguments*. When you pass data in arguments to a function, the code in the function has access to those values. When you create a function, you specify which arguments are to be passed to the function in an *argument list*.

Here's an example; in this case, I'll create a function named `adder` that will add two values and return their sum. Here's how I start creating `adder`:

```
function adder()
{
    .
    .
    .
}
```

This time, we're going to pass arguments to the function, so we list the arguments that we'll pass by giving them names in the argument list, which is enclosed in the parentheses following the function name. Here, I'll call the two arguments passed to `adder` `value1` and `value2`:

```
function adder(value1, value2)
{
    .
    .
    .
}
```

Note that, by default in JavaScript, what's really passed to functions are not the actual arguments themselves, but *copies* of those arguments. This process is named *calling by value.*

Now you're free to refer to the passed values by the names you've given them in the argument list. To return the sum of `value1` and `value2`, all I have to do is to add those values and use the `return` statement, like this:

```
function adder(value1, value2)
{
    return(value1 + value2)
}
```

To make use of this function, you pass values to it in parentheses, like this, where I'm finding the sum of the values `47` and `99`:

```
<HTML>
    <HEAD>
        <TITLE>
            Passing Arguments to Functions in JavaScript
        </TITLE>
    </HEAD>

    <BODY>

        <SCRIPT LANGUAGE = JavaScript>
```

```
        document.writeln("47 + 99 = " +  adder(47, 99))

        function adder(value1, value2)
        {
            return(value1 + value2)
        }
    </SCRIPT>

    <CENTER>
        <H1>
            Passing Arguments to Functions in JavaScript
        </H1>
    </CENTER>

  </BODY>

</HTML>
```

That's all it takes; now we're passing arguments to the `adder` function. You can see the results in Figure 6.11. As you see there, everything is working perfectly; the sum of `47` and `99` is displayed as it should be. (You might also note that even though the value returned from the `adder` function is a number, JavaScript is smart enough to treat that number as a text string when it's time to print it out with `document.writeln`.)

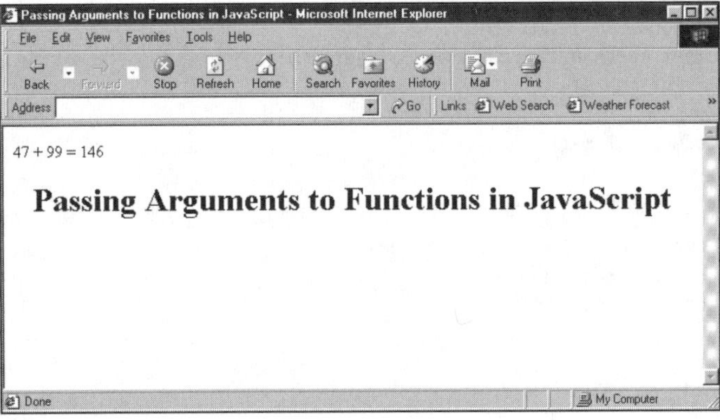

Figure 6.11 Passing arguments to functions in JavaScript.

Using a Variable Number of Arguments

You can actually call a function with fewer arguments than appear in its formal argument list (that is, the number of arguments that you've defined it with). There's no problem unless you try to access by name arguments that had no value passed to them. In addition, you can even pass *more* arguments than a function's formal argument list specifies. If you do that, you can access the additional arguments from the `arguments` *array* (and we'll see more about arrays in a few pages). For example, the first argument passed to `adder` can also be referenced inside the `adder` function as `adder.arguments[0]`, the next as `adder.arguments[1]`, and so on.

Creating Objects in JavaScript

As we already know, JavaScript comes with a number of built-in objects ready for you to use, such as the `document`, `location`, `navigator`, and `history` objects. JavaScript also comes with many classes built in, including classes such as the `Date` class, which handles dates and times, and the `Math` class, which has many built-in methods such as `min` and `max` to compare numbers. You can use built-in classes (and those that you create yourself, although we're not going to do that here) to create objects using the `new` operator.

You can think of a class as an object's *type* because, using the `new` operator, you create objects from classes. Objects can have methods and properties built into them—in fact, most do. We'll be using the `new` operator in the next chapter to create objects that will let us handle XML documents. We've already seen `new` at work in this chapter in this example:

```
<HTML>
    <HEAD>
        <TITLE>
            Using JavaScript Functions
        </TITLE>

    </HEAD>

    <BODY>

        <SCRIPT LANGUAGE = JavaScript>
            document.writeln("The time is " + getTime()
            + " right now.")

            function getTime()
            {
                var now = new Date
                var returnValue = now.getHours() + ":"
                + now.getMinutes()
                return(returnValue)
            }
        </SCRIPT>

        <CENTER>
            <H1>
                Using JavaScript Functions
            </H1>
        </CENTER>

    </BODY>

</HTML>
```

The new operator uses the Date class's *constructor*, which is a special method that classes use to create and return objects. In this case, we didn't pass any arguments to the Date class's constructor, so the object it returns and that we call now will reflect the current date. On the other hand, you could pass a date to the Date class's constructor when you use the new operator, and the Date object returned will reflect that date instead. Here's what that might look like:

```
var then = new Date("10/15/2001")
```

How do you know what kind of values you can pass to a JavaScript class's constructor? Take a look at the JavaScript documentation; what arguments, and what order you pass them in, varies by class.

One important class that's built into JavaScript is the String class, which you use to handle text strings. To get a better idea of how classes, objects, and constructors work, I'll take a look at that class next.

Using String Objects in JavaScript

You handle text strings in JavaScript using the String class. This class enables you to create objects that can hold text strings, and it provides you with plenty of methods to let you work on those strings. Following are the JavaScript methods of this class:

- anchor
- big
- blink
- bold
- charAt
- charCodeAt
- concat
- fixed
- fontcolor
- fontsize
- indexOf
- italics
- lastIndexOf
- link
- match
- replace
- search
- slice
- small
- split
- strike
- sub
- substr
- substring
- sup
- toLowerCase
- toSource
- toUpperCase
- toString
- valueOf

These are the JScript methods of the `String` class:

- `anchor`
- `big`
- `blink`
- `bold`
- `charAt`
- `charCodeAt`
- `concat`
- `fixed`
- `fontcolor`
- `fontsize`
- `fromCharCode`
- `indexOf`
- `italics`
- `lastIndexOf`
- `link`
- `match`
- `replace`
- `search`
- `slice`
- `small`
- `split`
- `strike`
- `sub`
- `substr`
- `substring`
- `sup`
- `toLowerCase`
- `toString`
- `toUpperCase`
- `valueOf`

Here's an example; in this case, I'll create an object of the `String` class. Then I'll use the object's `italics` method to display it in italics, and its `length` property to find its length:

```
<HTML>
    <HEAD>
        <TITLE>
            Using the String Class
        </TITLE>
    </HEAD>

    <BODY>

        <SCRIPT LANGUAGE = JavaScript>
            var string1 = new String("JavaScript and XML are a good mix")

            document.writeln("The text string, " + string1.italics() +
            ", is " + string1.length + " characters long.")
        </SCRIPT>

        <CENTER>
            <H1>
                Using the String Class
            </H1>
        </CENTER>
    </BODY>

</HTML>
```

In this case, I'm passing the text I want in this string, `JavaScript and XML are a good mix`, to the `String` class's constructor. That constructor creates a new `String` object with that text in it and returns it. Now I'm able to use the new object's `italics` method to display the string in italics, and the `length` property to determine the string's length. You can see the results in Figure 6.12.

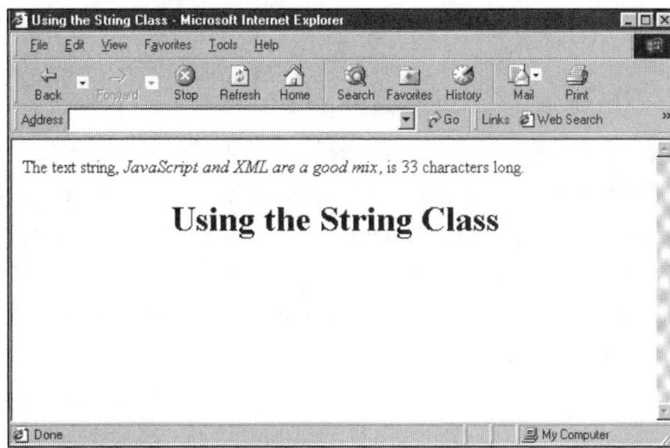

Figure 6.12 Using the `String` class in Internet Explorer.

Here's another important aspect of the `String` class: JavaScript treats this class in a special way, which means that you can actually use it without the `new` operator. You can declare an object of the `String` class as a normal variable (without using the `new` operator or even mentioning the `String` class), and JavaScript will know just what you mean—behind the scenes, it uses the `String` class, but you never need know it, as in this code:

```
<HTML>
    <HEAD>
        <TITLE>
            Using the String Class
        </TITLE>
    </HEAD>

    <BODY>

        <SCRIPT LANGUAGE = JavaScript>
            var string1 = "JavaScript and XML are a good mix"

            document.writeln("The text string, " + string1.italics() +
            ", is " + string1.length + " characters long.")
        </SCRIPT>
```

continues ▸

```
        <CENTER>
            <H1>
                Using the String Class
            </H1>
        </CENTER>
    </BODY>

</HTML>
```

Using the Array Class to Create Arrays

Arrays are programming constructs that can hold a set of data items that you access item by item with a numeric index. Arrays are perfect for programming because, using the array index, you can reach each item in the array so that you can easily iterate over every item in the array using a loop.

To create arrays, you use the JavaScript `Array` class. The following list shows the methods of this class:

- `concat`
- `join`
- `pop`
- `push`
- `reverse`
- `shift`
- `slice`
- `splice`
- `sort`
- `toSource`
- `toString`
- `unshift`
- `valueOf`

These are the methods of the JScript `Array` class:

- `concat`
- `join`
- `reverse`
- `slice`
- `sort`
- `toString`
- `valueOf`

Let's see an example to make this concrete. In this case, I'll create an array that will hold the student scores from an exam. I'll use a `for` loop to add them all, finding the average score by dividing the total by the number of elements in the array.

I start by creating a new array named `scores` to hold the student scores, and a variable named `runningSum` to hold the sum of all the scores:

```
var scores = new Array()
var runningSum = 0
    .
    .
    .
```

You can refer to the first item in the `scores` array as `scores[0]`, the next as `scores[1]`, and so on, so I can store the students' scores in the `scores` array like this. (You can also pass those values to the `Array` class's constructor.)

```
var scores = new Array()
var runningSum = 0


scores[0] = 43
scores[1] = 87
scores[2] = 92
scores[3] = 70
scores[4] = 55
scores[5] = 61
    .
    .
    .
```

Now I can add the scores in a `for` loop this way:

```
var scores = new Array()
var runningSum = 0

scores[0] = 43
scores[1] = 87
scores[2] = 92
scores[3] = 70
scores[4] = 55
scores[5] = 61

for(var loopIndex = 0; loopIndex < scores.length; loopIndex++){
    runningSum += scores[loopIndex]
}
    .
    .
    .
```

All that's left is to divide the total of all the scores by the number of elements in the array, and you can find the length of an array with its `length` property, this way:

```
var scores = new Array()
var runningSum = 0

scores[0] = 43
scores[1] = 87
scores[2] = 92
scores[3] = 70
scores[4] = 55
scores[5] = 61
```

continues ▸

```
for(var loopIndex = 0; loopIndex < scores.length; loopIndex++){
    runningSum += scores[loopIndex]
}

document.write("The average student score is " +
    runningSum / scores.length)
```

Here's the final code in a Web page:

```
<HTML>

    <HEAD>
        <TITLE>
            Using Arrays in JavaScript
        </TITLE>
    </HEAD>

    <BODY>

        <SCRIPT LANGUAGE = JavaScript>
            var scores = new Array()
            var runningSum = 0

            scores[0] = 43
            scores[1] = 87
            scores[2] = 92
            scores[3] = 70
            scores[4] = 55
            scores[5] = 61

            for(var loopIndex = 0; loopIndex < scores.length; loopIndex++){
                runningSum += scores[loopIndex]
            }

            document.write("The average student score is " +
                runningSum / scores.length)
         </SCRIPT>

        <CENTER>
            <H1>
                Using Arrays in JavaScript
            </H1>
        </CENTER>

    </BODY>

</HTML>
```

You can see the results of this JavaScript in Figure 6.13, where you see that the average score is `68`.

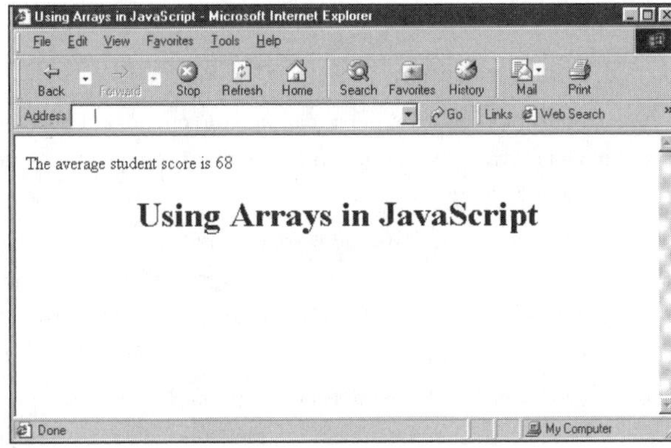

Figure 6.13 Using arrays in JavaScript.

Working with Events

One important aspect of JavaScript is interacting with the user, and you do that through *events*. As discussed earlier, when the user takes some action, such as clicking a button, dragging the mouse, or typing keys, an event happens. In the next chapter, we'll handle not only ordinary events such as button clicks, but also the events that occur as an XML document is loaded into the browser and parsed.

Events are handled tag by tag in browsers, and you use special event attributes to connect code, such as JavaScript code, to an event. For example, when the user presses the mouse button in a Web page, the code connected to the `<BODY>` element with that element's `onMouseDown` attribute is executed. Refer to Table 6.1 in the earlier section, "Using Events in JavaScript," for a list of common events that JavaScript can handle. (Each one is an event attribute that you can use in an HTML tag.)

You can see the complete list of events for various HTML tags in Tables 6.3 for Internet Explorer and 6.4 for Netscape.

Table 6.3 **Events Supported by Internet Explorer**

Element	Event Attributes
`A`	`onbeforecopy, onbeforecut, onbeforeeditfocus, onbeforefocusenter, onbeforefocusleave, onbeforepaste, onblur, onclick, oncontextmenu, oncontrolselect, oncopy, oncut, ondblclick, ondrag, ondragend, ondragenter, ondragleave, ondragover, ondragstart, ondrop, onfocus, onfocusenter, onfocusleave, onhelp, onkeydown, onkeypress, onkeyup, onlosecapture, onmousedown, onmouseenter, onmouseleave, onmousemove,`

continues

Table 6.3 **Continued**

Element	Event Attributes
	onmouseout, onmouseover, onmouseup, onpaste, onpropertychange, onreadystatechange, onresize, onresizeend, onresizestart, onselectstart
BODY	onafterprint, onbeforecut, onbeforefocusenter, onbeforefocusleave, onbeforepaste, onbeforeprint, onbeforeunload, onclick, oncontextmenu, oncontrolselect, oncut, ondblclick, ondrag, ondragend, ondragenter, ondragleave, ondragover, ondragstart, ondrop
BUTTON	onbeforecut, onbeforeeditfocus, onbeforefocusenter, onbeforefocus leave, onbeforepaste, onblur, onclick, oncontextmenu, oncontrolselect, oncut, ondblclick, ondragenter, ondragleave, ondragover, ondrop, onfilterchange, onfocus, onfocusenter, onfocus leave, onhelp, onkeydown, onkeypress, onkeyup, onlosecapture, onmousedown, onmouseenter, onmouseleave, onmousemove, onmouseout, onmouseover, onmouseup, onpaste, onpropertychange, onready statechange, onresize, onresizeend, onresizestart, onselectstart
DIV	onbeforecopy, onbeforecut, onbeforeeditfocus, onbeforefocusenter, onbeforefocusleave, onbeforepaste, onblur, onclick, oncontextmenu, oncontrolselect, oncopy, oncut, ondblclick, ondrag, ondragend, ondragenter, ondragleave, ondragover, ondragstart, ondrop, onfilter-change, onfocus, onfocusenter, onfocusleave, onhelp, onkeydown, onkeypress, onkeyup, onlayoutcomplete, onlosecapture, onmousedown, onmouseenter, onmouseleave, onmousemove, onmouseout, onmouseover, onmouseup, onpaste, onpropertychange, onreadystatechange, onresize, onresizeend, onresizestart, onscroll, onselectstart
FORM	onbeforecopy, onbeforecut, onbeforefocusenter, onbeforefocusleave, onbeforepaste, onblur, onclick, oncontextmenu, oncontrolselect, oncopy, oncut, ondblclick, ondrag, ondragend, ondragenter, ondragleave, ondragover, ondragstart, ondrop, onfocus, onfocusenter, onfocusleave, onhelp, onkeydown, onkeypress, onkeyup, onlosecapture, onmousedown, onmouseenter, onmouseleave, onmousemove, onmouseout, onmouseover, onmouseup, onpaste, onpropertychange, onreadystate-change, onreset, onresize, onresizeend, onresizestart, onselectstart, onsubmit
FRAME	onbeforefocusenter, onbeforefocusleave, onblur, oncontrolselect, onfocus, onfocusenter, onfocusleave, onresize, onresizeend, onresizestart
IFRAME	onbeforefocusenter, onbeforefocusleave, onblur, oncontrolselect, onfocus, onfocusenter, onfocusleave, onresizeend, onresizestart

Element	Event Attributes
IMG	onabort, onbeforecopy, onbeforecut, onbeforefocusenter, onbeforefocusleave, onbeforepaste, onblur, onclick, oncontextmenu, oncontrolselect, oncopy, oncut, ondblclick, ondrag, ondragend, ondragenter, ondragleave, ondragover, ondragstart, ondrop, onerror, onfilterchange, onfocus, onfocusenter, onfocusleave, onhelp, onload, onlosecapture, onmousedown, onmouseenter, onmouseleave, onmousemove, onmouseout, onmouseover, onmouseup, onpaste, onpropertychange, onreadystatechange, onresize, onresizeend, onresizestart, onselectstart
INPUT (button)	onbeforecut, onbeforeeditfocus, onbeforefocusenter, onbeforefocusleave, onbeforepaste, onblur, onclick, oncontextmenu, oncontrolselect, oncut, ondblclick, ondrag, ondragend, ondragenter, ondragleave, ondragover, ondragstart, ondrop, onfilterchange, onfocus, onfocusenter, onfocusleave, onhelp, onkeydown, onkeypress, onkeyup, onlosecapture, onmousedown, onmouseenter, onmouseleave, onmousemove, onmouseout, onmouseover, onmouseup, onpaste, onpropertychange, onreadystatechange, onresize, onresizeend, onresizestart, onselectstart
INPUT (check box)	onbeforecut, onbeforeeditfocus, onbeforefocusenter, onbeforefocusleave, onbeforepaste, onblur, onclick, oncontextmenu, oncontrolselect, oncut, ondblclick, ondrag, ondragend, ondragenter, ondragleave, ondragover, ondragstart, ondrop, onfilterchange, onfocus, onfocusenter, onfocusleave, onhelp, onkeydown, onkeypress, onkeyup, onlosecapture, onmousedown, onmouseenter, onmouseleave, onmousemove, onmouseout, onmouseover, onmouseup, onpaste, onpropertychange, onreadystatechange, onresizeend, onresizestart, onselectstart
INPUT (radio button)	onbeforecut, onbeforeeditfocus, onbeforefocusenter, onbeforefocusleave, onbeforepaste, onblur, onclick, oncontextmenu, oncontrolselect, oncut, ondblclick, ondrag, ondragend, ondragenter, ondragleave, ondragover, ondragstart, ondrop, onfilterchange, onfocus, onfocusenter, onfocusleave, onhelp, onkeydown, onkeypress, onkeyup, onlosecapture, onmousedown, onmouseenter, onmouseleave, onmousemove, onmouseout, onmouseover, onmouseup, onpaste, onpropertychange, onreadystatechange, onresizeend, onresizestart, onselectstart
INPUT (Submit button)	onbeforecut, onbeforeeditfocus, onbeforefocusenter, onbeforefocusleave, onbeforepaste, onblur, onclick, oncontextmenu, oncontrolselect, oncut, ondblclick, ondrag, ondragend, ondragenter, ondragleave, ondragover, ondragstart, ondrop, onfilterchange, onfocus, onfocusenter, onfocusleave, onhelp, onkeydown, onkeypress, onkeyup, onlosecapture, onmousedown, onmouseenter, onmouseleave, onmousemove, onmouseout, onmouseover, onmouseup, onpaste, onpropertychange, onreadystatechange, onresize, onresizeend, onresizestart, onselectstart

continues

Table 6.3 **Continued**

Element	Event Attributes
INPUT (text field)	onafterupdate, onbeforecut, onbeforeeditfocus, onbeforefocusenter, onbeforefocusleave, onbeforepaste, onbeforeupdate, onblur, onchange, onclick, oncontextmenu, oncontrolselect, oncut, ondblclick, ondrag, ondragend, ondragenter, ondragleave, ondragover, ondragstart, ondrop, onerrorupdate, onfilterchange, onfocus, onfocusenter, onfocusleave, onhelp, onkeydown, onkeypress, onkeyup, onlosecapture, onmousedown, onmouseenter, onmouseleave, onmousemove, onmouseout, onmouseover, onmouseup, onpaste, onpropertychange, onreadystatechange, onresize, onresizeend, onresizestart, onselect, onselectstart
LI	onbeforecopy, onbeforecut, onbeforefocusenter, onbeforefocusleave, onbeforepaste, onblur, onclick, oncontextmenu, oncontrolselect, oncopy, oncut, ondblclick, ondrag, ondragend, ondragenter, ondragleave, ondragover, ondragstart, ondrop, onfocus, onfocusenter, onfocusleave, onhelp, onkeydown, onkeypress, onkeyup, onlayout complete, onlosecapture, onmousedown, onmouseenter, object, onmouse-leave, onmousemove, onmouseout, onmouseover, onmouseup, onpaste, onpropertychange, onreadystatechange, onresize, onresizeend, onresizestart, onselectstart
MARQUEE	onbeforecut, onbeforeeditfocus, onbeforefocusenter, onbefore focusleave, onbeforepaste, onblur, onbounce, oncontextmenu, oncontrolselect, oncut, ondblclick, ondrag, ondragend, ondragenter, ondragleave, ondragover, ondragstart, ondrop, onfilterchange, onfin-ish, onfocus, onfocusenter, onfocusleave, onhelp, onkeydown, onkey-press, onkeyup, onlosecapture, onmousedown, onmouseenter, onmouseleave, onmousemove, onmouseout, onmouseover, onmouseup, onpaste, onpropertychange, onreadystatechange, onresize, onresizeend, onresizestart, onscroll, onselectstart, onstart
OBJECT	onbeforeeditfocus, onbeforefocusenter, onbeforefocusleave, onblur, oncellchange, onclick, oncontrolselect, ondataavailable, ondatasetchanged, ondatasetcomplete, ondblclick, ondrag, ondragend, ondragenter, ondragleave, ondragover, ondragstart, ondrop, onerror, onfocus, onfocusenter, onfocusleave, onkeydown, onkeypress, onkeyup, onlosecapture, onpropertychange, onreadystatechange, onresize, onresizeend, onresizestart, onrowenter, onrowexit, onrowsdelete, onrowsinserted, onscroll, onselectstart
P	onbeforecopy, onbeforecut, onbeforefocusenter, onbeforefocusleave, onbeforepaste, onblur, onclick, oncontextmenu, oncontrolselect, oncopy, oncut, ondblclick, ondrag, ondragend, ondragenter, ondragleave, ondragover, ondragstart

Element	Event Attributes
PRE	onbeforecopy, onbeforecut, onbeforefocusenter, onbeforefocusleave, onbeforepaste, onblur, onclick, oncontextmenu, oncontrolselect, oncopy, oncut, ondblclick, ondrag, ondragend, ondragenter, ondragleave, ondragover, ondragstart, ondrop, onfocus, onfocusenter, onfocusleave, onhelp, onkeydown, onkeypress, onkeyup, onlosecapture, onmousedown, onmouseenter, onmouseleave, onmousemove, onmouseout, onmouseover, onmouseup, onpaste, onpropertychange, onreadystatechange, onresize, onresizeend, onresizestart, onselectstart
SELECT	onbeforecut, onbeforeeditfocus, onbeforefocusenter, onbeforefocusleave, onbeforepaste, onblur, onchange, onclick, oncontextmenu, oncontrolselect, oncut, ondblclick, ondragenter, ondragleave, ondragover, ondrop, onfocus, onfocusenter, onfocusleave, onhelp, onkeydown, onkeypress, onkeyup, onlosecapture, onmousedown, onmouseenter, onmouseleave, onmousemove, onmouseout, onmouseover, onmouseup, onpaste, onpropertychange, onreadystatechange, onresize, onresizeend, onresizestart, onscroll, onselectstart
SPAN	onbeforecopy, onbeforecut, onbeforeeditfocus, onbeforefocusenter, onbeforefocusleave, onbeforepaste, onblur, onclick, oncontextmenu, oncontrolselect, oncopy, oncut, ondblclick, ondrag, ondragend, ondragenter, ondragleave, ondragover, ondragstart, ondrop, onfilterchange, onfocus, onfocusenter, onfocusleave, onhelp, onkeydown, onkeypress, onkeyup, onlosecapture, onmousedown, onmouseenter, onmouseleave, onmousemove, onmouseout
TABLE	onbeforecut, onbeforeeditfocus, onbeforefocusenter, onbeforefocusleave, onbeforepaste, onblur, onclick, oncontextmenu, oncontrolselect, oncut, ondblclick, ondrag, ondragend, ondragenter, ondragleave, ondragover, ondragstart, ondrop, onfilterchange, onfocus, onfocusenter, onfocusleave, onhelp, onkeydown, onkeypress, onkeyup, onlosecapture, onmousedown, onmouseenter, onmouseleave, onmousemove, onmouseout, onmouseover, onmouseup, onpaste, onpropertychange, onreadystatechange, onresize, onresizeend, onresizestart, onscroll, onselectstart
TD	onbeforecopy, onbeforecut, onbeforeeditfocus, onbeforefocusenter, onbeforefocusleave, onbeforepaste, onblur, onclick, oncontextmenu, oncontrolselect, oncopy, oncut, ondblclick, ondrag, ondragend, ondragenter, ondragleave, ondragover, ondragstart, ondrop, onfilterchange, onfocus, onfocusenter, onfocusleave, onhelp, onkeydown, onkeypress, onkeyup, onlosecapture, onmousedown, onmouseenter, onmouseleave, onmousemove, onmouseout, onmouseover, onmouseup, onpaste, onpropertychange, onreadystatechange, onresizeend, onresizestart, onselectstart

continues

Table 6.3 **Continued**

Element	Event Attributes
TEXTAREA	onafterupdate, onbeforecopy, onbeforecut, onbeforeeditfocus, onbeforefocusenter, onbeforefocusleave, onbeforepaste, onbeforeupdate, onblur, onchange, onclick, oncontextmenu, oncontrolselect, oncut, ondblclick, ondrag, operation, ondragend, ondragenter, ondragleave, ondragover, ondragstart, ondrop, onerrorupdate, onfilterchange, onfocus, onfocusenter, onfocusleave, onhelp, onkeydown, onkeypress, onkeyup, onlosecapture, onmousedown, onmouseenter, onmouseleave, onmousemove, onmouseout, onmouseover, onmouseup, onpaste, onpropertychange, onreadystatechange, onresize, onresizeend, onresizestart, onscroll, onselect, onselectstart

Table 6.4 **Events Supported by Netscape**

Element	Event Attributes
A	onclick, onmouseout, onmouseover
BODY	onload, onunload, onblur, onfocus
DIV	none
EMBED	none
FORM	onreset, onsubmit
FRAME	None
ILAYER	None
IMG	onabort, onerror, onload
INPUT (button)	onclick
INPUT (check box)	onclick
INPUT (radio button)	onclick
INPUT (Submit button)	onclick
INPUT (text field)	onblur, onchange, onfocus, onselect
LAYER	onmouseover, onmouseout , onfocus, onblur, onload
LI	None
OBJECT	None
P	None
PRE	None
SELECT	onblur, onchange, onclick, onfocus
SPAN	None

Element	Event Attributes
TABLE	None
TD	None
TEXTAREA	onblur, onchange, onfocus, onselect

Let's put this technology to work. In this case, I'll use events with two HTML *controls* (which are what you call the buttons, text fields, lists, and so on in HTML pages)—buttons and text fields. When the user clicks the button, the JavaScript code in the page displays the message `Welcome to event handling.` in the text field.

You create both button and text field controls with the HTML `<INPUT>` element, setting this element's `TYPE` attribute to `"text"` to create a text field and to `"button"` to create a button. You can also give the button a caption with this element's `VALUE` attribute, the text field a length (in characters) with the `LENGTH` attribute, and a name with the `NAME` attribute. When you give a control a name, you can refer to it in code.

You must create controls inside an HTML form to use them, and you create an HTML form with the `<FORM>` element. (A form is just a programming construct and does not appear in the Web page—when you click a Submit button, if there is one, all the data from the controls in a form is sent back to the Web server.) Here's how I add a button and a text field to an HTML page:

```
<HTML>
    <HEAD>
        <TITLE>
            Working With Events in JavaScript
        </TITLE>
    </HEAD>

    <BODY>

        <CENTER>
            <FORM name = "form1">
                <H1>
                    Working With Events in JavaScript
                </H1>
                <BR>
                <H2>
                    Click the button!
                </H2>
                <BR>
                <INPUT TYPE = "text" NAME = "Text" SIZE = "60">
                <BR>
                <BR>
                <INPUT TYPE="button" VALUE="Click Here">
            </FORM>
```

continues ▸

```
        </CENTER>

    </BODY>

</HTML>
```

The next step is to connect the button to some JavaScript code so that when the button is clicked, a JavaScript function named `displayMessage` is called. In that function, I'll add the code that we need to display the message `Welcome to event handling.` in the text field. To connect the `displayMessage` function to the button, I set the button's `onClick` event attribute to the JavaScript I want executed when the button is clicked—`"displayMessage()"`, which will call the `displayMessage` function:

```
<HTML>
    <HEAD>
        <TITLE>
            Working With Events in JavaScript
        </TITLE>
    </HEAD>

    <BODY>

        <CENTER>
            <FORM name = "form1">
                <H1>
                    Working With Events in JavaScript
                </H1>
                <BR>
                <H2>
                    Click the button!
                </H2>
                <BR>
                <INPUT TYPE = "text" NAME = "Text" SIZE = "60">
                <BR>
                <BR>
                <INPUT TYPE="button" VALUE="Click Here"
                    onClick="displayMessage()">
            </FORM>
        </CENTER>

    </BODY>

</HTML>
```

All that we need to do now is to create the JavaScript function named `displayMessage` that places the message `Welcome to event handling.` in the text field. So how do you actually access the text in a text field? All the items in a Web page can be accessed as subobjects of the `document` object. In particular,

I've given the text field the name `Text` by setting the `<INPUT>` element's `NAME` attribute to `"Text"`; it's in the `<FORM>` element, which I've given the name `form1`. This means that you can refer to the text field object as `document.form1.Text`. The actual text in the text field object appears in its `value` property, so you can refer to that text as `document.form1.Text.value` like this:

```
<HTML>
    <HEAD>
        <TITLE>
            Working With Events in JavaScript
        </TITLE>

        <SCRIPT LANGUAGE= "JavaScript">
            function displayMessage(e)
            {
                document.form1.Text.value = "Welcome to event handling."
            }

         </SCRIPT>
    </HEAD>

    <BODY>

        <CENTER>
            <FORM name = "form1">
                <H1>
                    Working With Events in JavaScript
                </H1>
                <BR>
                <H2>
                    Click the button!
                </H2>
                <BR>
                <INPUT TYPE = "text" NAME = "Text" SIZE = "60">
                <BR>
                <BR>
                <INPUT TYPE="button" VALUE="Click Here"
                    onClick="displayMessage()">
            </FORM>
        </CENTER>

    </BODY>

</HTML>
```

That's all it takes—now when the user clicks the button, the message is displayed in the text field, as you can see in Figure 6.14.

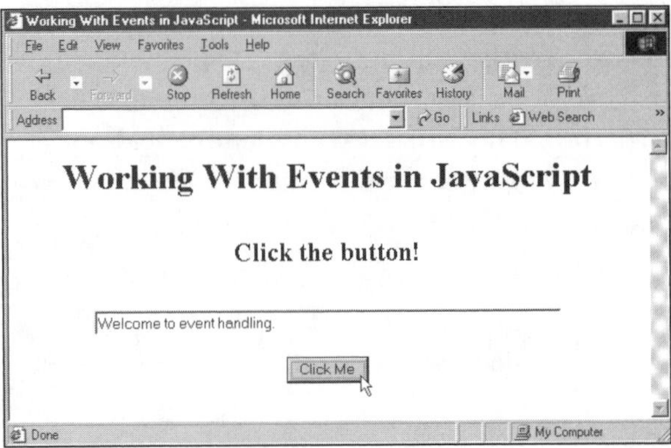

Figure 6.14 Using a button and a text field in Internet Explorer.

Getting Event Information

You might have noticed that I declared the function `displayMessage` as `displayMessage(e)` in the previous example. Why did I indicate that this function would be passed an argument? The answer is that it *is* passed an argument in Netscape. This argument is an object of the `event` class, and you can get information about the event (such as where a mouse click occurred) using this object, which I've named `e`. You'll find the properties of the `event` class in Netscape in Table 6.5.

However, Internet Explorer handles things differently, of course. In Internet Explorer, event-handling functions are not passed an `event` object (JavaScript is flexible enough that even if you declare a function as we have here to handle both browsers as though it does receive an argument—although it really doesn't—there's no problem). Instead of an `event` object that's passed to event-handling functions, you use the `window.event` object (that is, the `event` subobject of the `window` object), which is available globally in code and doesn't have to be passed to a function. You'll find the properties of the `window.event` property in Internet Explorer in Table 6.6.

Table 6.5 **Netscape's Event Object Properties**

Property	Description
`data`	This property holds an array of strings containing the URLs of the dropped objects, used with the `dragdrop` event.
`height`	This property holds a height associated with the event.
`layerX`	This property holds the cursor's horizontal position in pixels, relative to the layer in which the event occurred.

Property	Description
layerY	This property holds the cursor's vertical position in pixels, relative to the layer in which the event occurred.
modifiers	This property holds modifier keys associated with a mouse or key event. Possible values include ALT_MASK, CONTROL_MASK, SHIFT_MASK, and META_MASK.
pageX	This property holds the cursor's horizontal position in pixels, relative to the page.
pageY	This property holds the cursor's vertical position in pixels, relative to the page.
screenX	This property holds the cursor's horizontal position in pixels, relative to the screen.
screenY	This property holds a vertical position in pixels, relative to the screen.
type	This property holds the type of event.
which	This property indicates the mouse button that was pressed or the ASCII value of a pressed key.
width	This property holds a width associated with the event.

Table 6.6 **Internet Explorer's *window.event* Object Properties**

Property	Means
altKey	This property is true if the Alt key is down.
altLeft	This property is true if the left Alt key is down.
button	This property specifies which mouse button, if any, is pressed.
cancelBubble	This property indicates whether this event should move up the event hierarchy.
clientX	This property holds an x coordinate with respect to the client area.
clientY	This property holds a y coordinate with respect to the client area.
ctrlKey	This property is true if the Ctrl key is down.
ctrlLeft	This property is true if the left Ctrl key is down.
fromElement	This property specifies element being moved.
keyCode	This property holds the code of a struck key.
offsetX	This property holds a container-relative x position.
offsetY	This property holds a container-relative y position.

continues

Table 6.6 **Continued**

Property	Means
`reason`	This property holds information about a data transfer.
`returnValue`	This property specifies the return value from the event.
`screenX`	This property holds an x coordinate relative to physical screen size.
`screenY`	This property holds a y coordinate relative to physical screen size.
`shiftKey`	This property is true if the Shift key is down.
`shiftLeft`	This property is true if the left Shift key is down.
`srcElement`	This property holds the element that caused the event.
`srcFilter`	This property holds a filter event if this is a `filterChange` event.
`toElement`	This property specifies the element being moved to, the counterpart of the `fromElement` property.
`type`	This property is the event type, expressed as a string.
`x`	This property holds an x position of the event in context.
`y`	This property holds a y position of the event in context.

For an example that uses the event objects in Tables 6.5 and 6.6, see the next section.

Handling Mouse Events

I'll close this chapter with a reasonably full-scale example that uses the mouse. You can use this in either Netscape or Internet Explorer (even though event handling works differently in those two browsers). The way that I determine which browser the user has is by checking the `appName` property of the `navigator` object; the two possible values of `navigator.appName` are `"Microsoft Internet Explorer"` or `"Netscape"` in these two browsers.

Here are the JavaScript events that this program will use:

- `onMouseDown`. Happens when a mouse button goes down in the page.
- `onMouseUp`. Happens when a mouse button goes up in the page.

When you press or release the mouse button in this page, the code reports the location of the mouse. To find the (x,y) location of the mouse, you use the `window.event.x` and `window.event.y` properties in Internet Explorer, and `e.pageX` and `e.pageY` properties (where `e` is the name I've given the event object passed to the mouse event-handler function) in Netscape.

There's one more point I should mention: In Internet Explorer, you connect the mouseDown and mouseUp events to the <BODY> element this way:

```
<BODY onMouseDown = "mouseDownHandler()" onMouseUp = "mouseUpHandler()">
```

In Netscape, however, the <BODY> element does *not* support the onMouseDown and onMouseUp event attributes. In Netscape, you connect mouse event handlers using the document.onMouseDown and document.onMouseUp properties in the <SCRIPT> element, like this:

```
<SCRIPT LANGUAGE= "JavaScript">

document.onMouseDown = mouseDownHandler
document.onMouseUp = mouseUpHandler
    .
    .
    .
```

Here's what the full code looks like for this example:

```
<HTML>

    <HEAD>

    <TITLE>
        Using JavaScript and the Mouse
    </TITLE>

    <SCRIPT LANGUAGE= "JavaScript">

    document.onMouseDown = mouseDownHandler
    document.onMouseUp = mouseUpHandler

    function mouseDownHandler(e)
    {
        if (navigator.appName == "Microsoft Internet Explorer") {

            document.form1.Text.value = "Mouse button down at: " +
            window.event.x + ", " + window.event.y
        }

        if(navigator.appName == "Netscape") {

            document.form1.Text.value = "Mouse button down at: "
            + e.pageX + ", " + e.pageY
        }
    }

    function mouseUpHandler(e)
    {
        if (navigator.appName == "Microsoft Internet Explorer") {
            document.form1.Text.value = "Mouse button up at: " +
```

continues ▸

```
            window.event.x + ", " + window.event.y
        }

        if(navigator.appName == "Netscape") {
            document.form1.Text.value = "Mouse button up at: "
            + e.pageX + ", " + e.pageY
         }
    }
    </SCRIPT>

    </HEAD>

    <BODY onMouseDown = "mouseDownHandler()" onMouseUp =
        "mouseUpHandler()">

        <CENTER>
            <FORM name = "form1">

            <H1>
                Using JavaScript and the Mouse
            </H1>

            <BR>
            Click the mouse.
            <BR>
            <BR>
            <BR>
            <INPUT TYPE = "text" name = "Text" SIZE = 60>
            </FORM>

        </CENTER>

    </BODY>

</HTML>
```

You can see this example at work in Figure 6.15. If you press or release the mouse button in the page, the JavaScript code will let you know what's going on—and *where* it's going on, as you see in the figure.

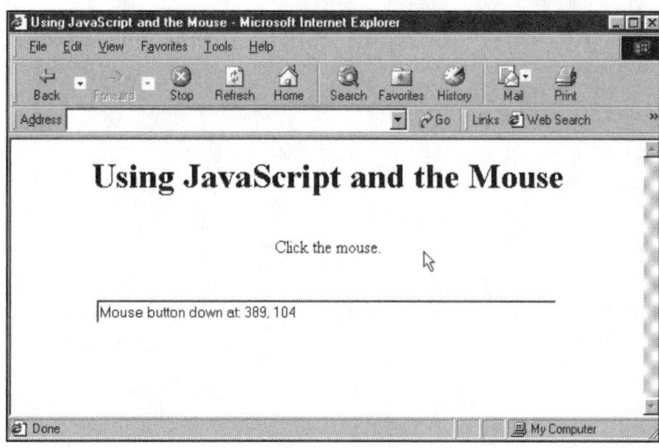

Figure 6.15 Using the mouse in JavaScript.

That brings us up to speed in JavaScript, and we're ready to put it to work in the next chapter. Using a scripting language like JavaScript is how you gain access to XML in a document in the browser. I'll turn to that now.

7
Handling XML Documents with JavaScript

HAVING SUCCESSFULLY MASTERED JAVASCRIPT IN THE PREVIOUS chapter (for our purposes, anyway), we're going to use it in this chapter to work with the *W3C Document Object Model* (*DOM*), the W3C-standardized programming interface for handling XML documents. Before the introduction of the DOM, all XML parsers and processors had different ways of interacting with XML documents—and, worse, they kept changing all the time. With the introduction of the XML DOM, things have settled down (to some extent). Note that this chapter relies on the Microsoft Internet Explorer, which provides the most complete JavaScript-accessible implementation of the DOM.

The W3C DOM

The W3C DOM specifies a way of treating a document as a *tree of nodes*. In this model, every discrete data item is a *node*, and child elements or enclosed text become *subnodes*. Treating a document as a tree of nodes is one good way of handling XML documents (although there are others, as we'll see when we start working with Java) because it makes it relatively easy to explicitly state which elements contain which other elements; the contained elements become subnodes of the container nodes. Everything in a document becomes a node in this model—elements, element attributes, text, and so on. Here are the possible node types in the W3C DOM:

- Element
- Attribute
- Text
- CDATA section
- Entity reference
- Entity
- Processing instruction
- Comment
- Document
- Document type
- Document fragment
- Notation

For example, take a look at this document:

```
<?xml version="1.0" encoding="UTF-8"?>
<DOCUMENT>
    <GREETING>
        Hello From XML
    </GREETING>
    <MESSAGE>
        Welcome to the wild and woolly world of XML.
    </MESSAGE>
</DOCUMENT>
```

This document has a processing instruction node and a root element node corresponding to the `<DOCUMENT>` element. The `<DOCUMENT>` node has two subnodes, the `<GREETING>` and `<MESSAGE>` nodes. These nodes are *child* nodes of the `<DOCUMENT>` node and *sibling* nodes of each other. Both the `<GREETING>` and `<MESSAGE>` elements have one subnode—a text node that holds character data. We'll get used to handling documents like this one as a tree of nodes in this chapter. Figure 7.1 shows what this document looks like.

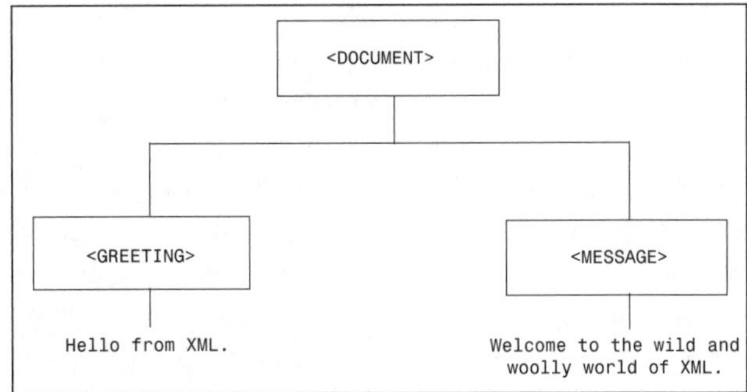

Figure 7.1 Viewing the document as a tree.

Every discrete data item is itself treated as a node. Using the methods defined in the W3C DOM, you can navigate along the various branches of a document's tree using methods such as `nextChild` to move to the `nextChild` node, or `lastSibling` to move to the last sibling node of the current node. Working with a document this way takes a little practice, and that's what this chapter is all about.

There are a number of different levels of DOM:

- **Level 0.** There is no official DOM "level 0," but that's the way W3C refers to the DOM as implemented in relatively early versions of the popular browsers—in particular, Netscape Navigator 3.0 and Microsoft Internet Explorer 3.0.
- **Level 1.** This level of the DOM is the current W3C recommendation, and it concentrates on the HTML and XML document models. You can find the documentation for this level at `www.w3.org/TR/REC-DOM-Level-1/`.
- **Level 2.** Currently at the Candidate Recommendation stage, this level of the DOM is more advanced and includes a style sheet object model. It also adds functionality for manipulating the style information attached to a document. In addition, it enables you to traverse a document, has a built-in event model, and supports XML namespaces. You can find the documentation for this level at `www.w3.org/TR/DOM-Level-2/`.
- **Level 3.** This level is still in the planning stage and will address document loading and saving, as well as content models (such as DTDs and schemas) with document validation support. In addition, it will also address document views and formatting, key events, and event groups. There is no documentation on this level yet.

Practically speaking, the only nearly complete implementation of the XML DOM today is that in Internet Explorer version 5 or later. You can find the documentation for the Microsoft DOM at `http://msdn.microsoft.com/library/psdk/xmlsdk/xmld20ab.htm` as of this writing. However, the Microsoft sites are continually (and annoyingly) being reorganized, so it's quite possible that by the time you read this, that page will be long gone. In that case, your best bet is to go to `http://msdn.microsoft.com` and search for "xml dom." (The general rule is not to trust an URL at a Microsoft site for more than about two months.)

Because Internet Explorer provides substantial support for the W3C DOM level 1, I'm going to use it in this chapter. Let's hope that the translation to other W3C-compliant browsers, as those browsers begin to support the W3C DOM, won't be terribly difficult.

The XML DOM Objects

Here are the official W3C DOM level 1 objects:

Object	Description
`Document`	The document object.
`DocumentFragment`	Reference to a fragment of a document.
`DocumentType`	Reference to the `<!DOCTYPE>` element.
`EntityReference`	Reference to an entity.
`Element`	An element.
`Attr`	An attribute.
`ProcessingInstruction`	A processing instruction.
`Comment`	Content of an XML comment.
`Text`	Text content of an element or attribute.
`CDATAsection`	`CDATA` section
`Entity`	Indication of a parsed or unparsed entity in the XML document.
`Notation`	Holder for a notation.
`Node`	A single node in the document tree.
`NodeList`	A list of node objects. This allows iteration and indexed access operations.
`NamedNodeMap`	Allows iteration and access by name to the collection of attributes.

Microsoft uses different names for these objects and adds its own. In particular, Microsoft defines a set of "base objects" that form the foundation of its XML DOM. The top-level object is the `DOMDocument` object, and it's the only one that you create directly—you reach the other objects through that object. Here's the list of base objects in Internet Explorer. Note the objects designed to treat a document as a tree of nodes—`XMLDOMNode`, `XMLDOMNodeList`, and so on:

Object	Description
`DOMDocument`	The top node of the XML DOM tree.
`XMLDOMNode`	A single node in the document tree. It includes support for data types, namespaces, DTDs, and XML schemas.
`XMLDOMNodeList`	A list of node objects. It allows iteration and indexed access operations.
`XMLDOMNamedNodeMap`	Allows iteration and access by name to the collection of attributes.
`XMLDOMParseError`	Information about the most recent error. It includes error number, line number, character position, and a text description.
`XMLHttpRequest`	Allows communication with HTTP servers.
`XTLRuntime`	Supports methods that you can call from XSL style sheets.

Besides these base objects, the Microsoft XML DOM also provides these XML DOM objects that you use when working with documents in code, including the various types of nodes, which you see supported with objects of types such as `XMLDOMAttribute`, `XMLDOMCharacterData`, and `XMLDOMElement`:

Object	Description
`XMLDOMAttribute`	Stands for an attribute object.
`XMLDOMCDATASection`	Handles CDATA sections so that text is not interpreted as markup language.
`XMLDOMCharacterData`	Provides methods used for text manipulation.
`XMLDOMComment`	Gives the content of an XML comment.
`XMLDOMDocumentFragment`	Is a lightweight object useful for tree insert operations.
`XMLDOMDocumentType`	Holds information connected to the document type declaration.
`XMLDOMElement`	Stands for the element object.

continues

Object	Description
`XMLDOMEntity`	Stands for a parsed or unparsed entity in the XML document.
`XMLDOMEntityReference`	Stands for an entity reference node.
`XMLDOMImplementation`	Supports general DOM methods.
`XMLDOMNotation`	Holds a notation (as declared in the DTD or schema).
`XMLDOMProcessingInstruction`	Is a processing instruction.
`XMLDOMText`	Is text content of an element or attribute.

We'll put many of these objects to work in this chapter, seeing how to parse and access XML documents using the Microsoft XML DOM and handling events as documents are loaded. We'll also see how to alter an XML document at run time.

This previous list of objects is pretty substantial, and each object can contain its own properties, methods, and events. Although most of these properties, methods, and events are specified in the W3C XML DOM, many are added by Microsoft as well (and so are nonstandard). If we're going to work with the XML DOM in practice, it's essential to have a good understanding of these objects, both practically for the purposes of this chapter and also for reference. I'll go through the major objects in some detail to make handling the XML DOM clear, starting with the main object, the `DOMDocument` object.

The *DOMDocument* Object

The `DOMDocument` object is the main object that you work with, and it represents the top node in every document tree. When working with the DOM, this is the only object that you create directly.

As we'll see in this chapter, there are two ways to create document objects in Internet Explorer: using the `Microsoft.XMLDOM` class and using XML *data islands*. Creating a document object with the `Microsoft.XMLDOM` class looks like this, where you explicitly load a document into the object with the `load` method:

```
function readXMLDocument()
{
    var xmldoc
    xmldoc = new ActiveXObject("Microsoft.XMLDOM")
    xmldoc.load("meetings.xml")
    .
    .
    .
```

We'll also see that you can use the `<XML>` HTML element to create a data island in Internet Explorer, and then use the `XMLDocument` property of that element to gain access to the corresponding document object:

```
<XML ID="meetingsXML" SRC="meetings.xml"></XML>

<SCRIPT LANGUAGE="JavaScript">
    function readXMLDocument()
    {
         xmldoc = document.all("meetingsXML").XMLDocument
         .
         .
         .
```

XML DOM and Multithreaded Programs

There's also a "free-threaded" version of the `Microsoft.XMLDOM` class that you can use in multithreaded programs:

```
var xmldoc = new ActiveXObject("Microsoft.FreeThreadedXMLDOM")
```

For more information on this advanced topic, take a look at the Microsoft XML DOM site (at `http://msdn.microsoft.com/library/psdk/xmlsdk/xmld20ab.htm` as of this writing, but very probably moved by the time you read this).

Here are the properties of this object:

Property	Description
`async*`	Indicates whether asynchronous download is allowed. Read/write.
`attributes`	Holds the list of attributes for this node. Read-only.
`baseName*`	Is the base name qualified with the namespace. Read-only.
`childNodes`	Holds a node list containing child nodes for nodes that may have children. Read-only.
`dataType*`	Gives the data type for this node. Read/write.
`definition*`	Gives the definition of the node in the DTD or schema. Read-only.
`doctype`	Specifies the document type node, which is what specifies the DTD for this document. Read-only.
`documentElement`	Gives the root element of the document. Read/write.
`firstChild`	Gives the first child of the current node. Read-only.
`implementation`	Specifies the `XMLDOMImplementation` object for this document. Read-only.

continues

Property	Description
`lastChild`	Gives the last child node of the current node. Read-only.
`namespaceURI`★	Gives the URI for the namespace. Read-only.
`nextSibling`	Specifies the next sibling of the current node. Read-only.
`nodeName`	Specifies the qualified name of the element, attribute, or entity reference. Holds a fixed string for other node types. Read-only.
`nodeType`	Gives the XML DOM node type. Read-only.
`nodeTypedValue`★	Holds this node's value. Read/write.
`nodeTypeString`★	Gives the node type expressed as a string. Read-only.
`nodeValue`	Is the text associated with the node. Read/write.
`ondataavailable`★	Is the event handler for the `ondataavailable` event. Read/write.
`onreadystatechange`★	Is the event handler that handles `readyState` property changes. Read/write.
`ontransformnode`★	Is the event handler for the `ontransformnode` event. Read/write.
`ownerDocument`	Gives the root of the document that contains this node. Read-only.
`parentNode`	Specifies the parent node (for nodes that can have parents). Read-only.
`parsed`★	Is true if this node and all descendants have been parsed; is false otherwise. Read-only.
`parseError`★	Is an `XMLDOMParseError` object with information about the most recent parsing error. Read-only.
`prefix`★	Gives the namespace prefix. Read-only.
`preserveWhiteSpace`★	Is true if processing should preserve whitespace; is false otherwise. Read/write.
`previousSibling`	Specifies the previous sibling of this node. Read-only.
`readyState`★	Gives the current state of the XML document. Read-only.
`resolveExternals`★	Indicates whether external definitions are to be resolved at parse time. Read/write.
`specified`★	Indicates whether the node is explicitly given or derived from a default value. Read-only.
`text`★	Gives the text content of the node and its subtrees. Read/write.
`url`★	Specifies the canonical URL for the most recently loaded XML document. Read-only.

`validateOnParse`*	Indicates whether the parser should validate this document. Read/write.
`xml`*	Gives the XML representation of the node and all its descendants. Read-only.

* *Microsoft extension to the W3C DOM.*

Here are the methods of the `document` object:

Method	Description
`abort`*	Aborts an asynchronous download
`appendChild`	Appends a new child as the last child of the current node
`cloneNode`	Returns a new node that is a copy of this node
`createAttribute`	Returns a new attribute with the given name
`createCDATASection`	Returns a CDATA section node that contains the given data
`createComment`	Returns a comment node
`createDocumentFragment`	Returns an empty `DocumentFragment` object
`createElement`	Returns an element node using the given name
`createEntityReference`	Returns a new `EntityReference` object
`createNode`*	Returns a node using the given type, name, and namespace
`createProcessingInstruction`	Returns a processing instruction node
`createTextNode`	Returns a text node that contains the given data
`getElementsByTagName`	Yields a collection of elements that have the given name
`hasChildNodes`	Is true if this node has children
`insertBefore`	Inserts a child node before the given node
`load`*	Loads an XML document from the given location
`loadXML`*	Loads an XML document using the given string
`nodeFromID`*	Yields the node whose ID attribute matches the given value
`removeChild`	Removes the given child node from the list of children

continues

Method	Description
`replaceChild`	Replaces the given child node with the given new child node
`save`★	Saves an XML document to the given location
`selectNodes`★	Applies the given pattern-matching operation to this node's context, returning a list of matching nodes
`selectSingleNode`★	Applies the given pattern-matching operation to this node's context, returning the first matching node
`transformNode`★	Transforms this node and its children using the given XSL style sheet
`transformNodeToObject`★	Transforms this node and its children to an object, using the given XSL style sheet

★ *Microsoft extension to the W3C DOM.*

Here are the events of the document object:

Event	Description
`ondataavailable`★	Indicates that XML document data is available
`onreadystatechange`★	Indicates when the `readyState` property changes
`ontransformnode`★	Happens before each node in the style sheet is applied in the XML source

★ *Microsoft extension to the W3C DOM.*

The *XMLDOMNode* Object

The Microsoft `XMLDOMNode` object extends the core XML DOM node interface by adding support for data types, namespaces, DTDs, and schemas as implemented in Internet Explorer. We'll use this object a good deal as we traverse document trees. Here are the properties of this object:

Property	Description
`attributes`	The list of attributes for this node. Read-only.
`baseName`★	The base name for the name qualified with the namespace. Read-only.
`childNodes`	A node list containing the child nodes of the current node. Read-only.

`dataType`*	The data type for this node. Read/write.
`definition`*	The definition of the node in the DTD or schema. Read-only.
`firstChild`	The first child of the current node. Read-only.
`lastChild`	The last child of the current node. Read-only.
`namespaceURI`*	The URI for the namespace. Read-only.
`nextSibling`	The next sibling of this node. Read-only.
`nodeName`	Holder for a qualified name for an element, attribute, or entity reference, or a string for other node types. Read-only.
`nodeType`	The XML DOM node type. Read-only.
`nodeTypedValue`*	The node's value. Read/write.
`nodeTypeString`*	The node type in string form. Read-only.
`nodeValue`	The text associated with the node. Read/write.
`ownerDocument`	The root of the document. Read-only.
`parentNode`	The parent node. Read-only.
`parsed`*	True if this node and all descendants have been parsed; false otherwise. Read-only.
`prefix`*	The namespace prefix. Read-only.
`previousSibling`	The previous sibling of this node. Read-only.
`specified`*	Indication of whether a node is explicitly given or derived from a default value. Read-only.
`text`*	The text content of the node and its subtrees. Read/write.
`xml`*	The XML representation of the node and all its descendants. Read-only.

* *Microsoft extension to the W3C DOM.*

Here are the methods of this object:

Method	**Description**
`appendChild`	Appends a new child as the last child of this node
`cloneNode`	Creates a new node that is a copy of this node
`hasChildNodes`	Is true if this node has children
`insertBefore`	Inserts a child node before the given node
`removeChild`	Removes the given child node

continues

Method	Description
`replaceChild`	Replaces the given child node with the given new child node
`selectNodes`*	Applies the given pattern-matching operation to this node's context, returning a list of matching nodes
`selectSingleNode`*	Applies the given pattern-matching operation to this node's context, returning the first matching node
`transformNode`*	Transforms this node and its children using the given XSL style sheet
`transformNodeToObject`*	Transforms this node and its children using the given XSL style sheet, returning the result in an object

* *Microsoft extension to the W3C DOM.*

This object has no events.

The *XMLDOMNodeList* Object

You use the `XMLDOMNodeList` to handle lists of nodes. Node lists are useful because a node itself can have many child nodes. Using a node list, you can handle all the children of a node at once.

For example, here I'm loading a document and getting a list of all `<PERSON>` elements as a node list, using the document object's `getElementsByTagName` method:

```
function readXMLDocument()
{
    var xmldoc, nodeList
    xmldoc = new ActiveXObject("Microsoft.XMLDOM")
    xmldoc.load("meetings.xml")
    nodeList = xmlDoc.getElementsByTagName("PERSON")
    .
    .
    .
```

The `XMLDOMNodeList` object has a single property, `length`, which describes the number of items in the collection and is read-only.

Here are the methods of the `XMLDOMNodeList` object:

Method	Description
`item`	Allows random access to nodes in the collection
`nextNode`*	Indicates the next node in the collection
`reset`*	Resets the list iterator

* *Microsoft extension to the W3C DOM.*

This object has no events.

The *XMLDOMNamedNodeMap* Object

The Microsoft XML DOM also supports an `XMLDOMNamedNodeMap` object, which provides support for namespaces. Here are the properties of this object:

Property	Description
`length`	Gives the number of items in the collection. Read-only.
`item`	Allows random access to nodes in the collection. Read-only.

Here are the methods of this object:

Method	Description
`getNamedItem`	Gets the attribute with the given name
`getQualifiedItem`*	Gets the attribute with the given namespace and attribute name
`nextNode`	Gets the next node
`removeNamedItem`	Removes an attribute
`removeQualifiedItem`	Removes the attribute with the given namespace and attribute name
`reset`	Resets the list iterator
`setNamedItem`	Adds the given node

* *Microsoft extension to the W3C DOM.*

This object has no events.

The *XMLDOMParseError* Object

The Microsoft `XMLDOMParseError` object holds information about the most recent parse error, including the error number, line number, character position, and a text description. Although it's not obvious to anyone who loads an XML document into Internet Explorer, the browser *does* actually validate the document using either a DTD or schema if one is supplied. It's not obvious that this happens because, by default, Internet Explorer does not display any validation error messages. However, if you use the `XMLDOMParseError` object, you can get a full validation report, and I'll do so later in this chapter.

Here are the properties of this object:

Property	Description
`errorCode`	The error code of the most recent parse error. Read-only.
`filepos`	The file position where the error occurred. Read-only.
`line`	The line number that contains the error. Read-only.
`linepos`	The character position in the line where the error happened. Read-only.
`reason`	The reason for the error. Read-only.
`srcText`	The full text of the line containing the error. Read-only.
`url`	The URL of the XML document containing the last error. Read-only.

Note that this object does not have any methods or events, and it does not correspond to any official W3C object in the W3C DOM.

The *XMLDOMAttribute* Object

In both the W3C and Microsoft DOM, attribute objects are node objects (that is, they are based on the `node` object), but they are not actually child nodes of an element and are *not* considered part of the document tree. Instead, attributes are considered *properties* of their associated elements. (This means that properties such as `parentNode`, `previousSibling`, or `nextSibling` are meaningless for attributes.) We'll see how to work with attributes in this chapter.

Here are the properties of the `XMLDOMAttribute` object:

Property	Description
`attributes`	The list of attributes for this node. Read-only.
`baseName`*	The base name for the name qualified with the namespace. Read-only.

`childNodes`	A node list containing child nodes. Read-only.
`dataType`*	The data type of this node. Read/write.
`definition`*	The definition of the node in the DTD or schema. Read-only.
`firstChild`	The first child of the current node. Read-only.
`lastChild`	The last child of the current node. Read-only.
`name`	The attribute name. Read-only.
`namespaceURI`*	The URI for the namespace. Read-only.
`nextSibling`	The next sibling of this node. Read-only.
`nodeName`	The qualified name for an element, attribute, or entity reference, or a string for other node types. Read-only.
`nodeType`	The XML DOM node type. Read-only.
`nodeTypedValue`*	The node's value. Read/write.
`nodeTypeString`*	The node type in string form. Read-only.
`nodeValue`	The text associated with the node. Read/write.
`ownerDocument`	The root of the document. Read-only.
`parentNode`	Holder for the parent node (for nodes that can have parents). Read-only.
`parsed`*	True if this node and all descendants have been parsed; false otherwise. Read-only.
`prefix`*	The namespace prefix. Read-only.
`previousSibling`	The previous sibling of this node. Read-only.
`specified`	Indication of whether the node (usually an attribute) is explicitly specified or derived from a default value. Read-only.
`text`	The text content of the node and its subtrees. Read/write.
`value`	The attribute's value. Read/write.
`xml`	The XML representation of the node and all its descendants. Read-only.

* *Microsoft extension to the W3C DOM.*

Here are the methods of the `XMLDOMAttribute` object:

Method	**Description**
`appendChild`	Appends a new child as the last child of this node
`cloneNode`	Returns a new node that is a copy of this node
`hasChildNodes`	Is true if this node has children
`insertBefore`	Inserts a child node before the given node

continues

Method	Description
`removeChild`	Removes the given child node from the list
`replaceChild`	Replaces the given child node with the given new child node
`selectNodes`	Applies the given pattern-matching operation to this node's context, returning a list of matching nodes
`selectSingleNode`	Applies the given pattern-matching operation to this node's context, returning the first matching node
`transformNode`	Transforms this node and its children using the given XSL style sheet
`transformNodeToObject`	Transforms this node and its children using the given XSL style sheet, and returns the result in an object

This object does not support any events.

The *XMLDOMElement* Object

`XMLDOMElement` objects represent elements and are probably the most common node objects that you'll deal with. Because attributes are not considered child nodes of an element object, you use special methods to get the attributes of an element—for example, you can use the `getAttribute` method, which returns an `XMLDOMNamedNodeMap` object that contains all the element's attributes.

Here are the properties of the `XMLDOMElement` object:

Property	Description
`attributes`	The list of attributes for this node. Read-only.
`baseName`*	The base name for the name qualified with the namespace. Read-only.
`childNodes`	A node list containing the children. Read-only.
`dataType`*	The data type for this node. Read/write.
`definition`*	The definition of the node in the DTD or schema.
`firstChild`	The first child of this node. Read-only.
`lastChild`	The last child node of this node. Read-only.
`namespaceURI`*	The URI for the namespace. Read-only.
`nextSibling`	The next sibling of this node. Read-only.
`nodeName`	Holder for the qualified name of an element, attribute, or entity reference, or a string for other node types. Read-only.
`nodeType`	Indication of the XML DOM node type. Read-only.
`nodeTypeString`*	The node type in string form. Read-only.

`nodeValue`	The text associated with the node. Read/write.
`ownerDocument`	The root of the document. Read-only.
`parentNode`	The parent node of the current node. Read-only.
`parsed`*	True if this node and all descendants have been parsed; false otherwise. Read-only.
`prefix`*	The namespace prefix. Read-only.
`previousSibling`	The previous sibling of this node. Read-only.
`specified`*	Indication of whether the node is explicitly specified or derived from a default value in the DTD or schema. Read-only.
`tagName`	Holder for the element name. Read-only.
`text`*	Holder for the text content of the node and its subtrees. Read/write.
`xml`*	Holder for the XML representation of the node and all its descendants. Read-only.

* *Microsoft extension to the W3C DOM.*

Here are the methods of the `XMLDOMElement` object:

Method	**Description**
`appendChild`	Appends a new child as the last child of the current node
`cloneNode`	Returns a new node that is a copy of this node
`getAttribute`	Gets the value of the named attribute
`getAttributeNode`	Gets the named attribute node
`getElementsByTagName`	Returns a list of all descendant elements that match the given name
`hasChildNodes`	Is true if this node has children
`insertBefore`	Inserts a child node before the given node
`normalize`	Normalizes all descendent elements, combining two or more text nodes next to each other into one text node
`removeAttribute`	Removes or replaces the named attribute
`removeAttributeNode`	Removes the given attribute from this element
`removeChild`	Removes the given child node
`replaceChild`	Replaces the given child node with the given new child node

continues

Method	Description
selectNodes*	Applies the given pattern-matching operation to this node's context, returning the list of matching nodes
selectSingleNode*	Applies the given pattern-matching operation to this node's context, returning the first matching node
setAttribute	Sets the value of a named attribute
setAttributeNode	Adds or changes the given attribute node on this element
transformNode*	Transforms this node and its children using the given XSL style sheet
transformNodeToObject*	Transforms this node and its children using the given XSL style sheet, and returns the resulting transformation as an object

* *Microsoft extension to the W3C DOM.*

This object has no events.

The *XMLDOMText* Object

The XMLDOMText object holds the text content of an element or attribute. If there is no markup inside an element, but there is text, that element will contain only one node—a text node that holds the text. (In mixed-content models, text nodes can have sibling element nodes.)

When a document is first made available to the XML DOM, all text is *normalized*, which means that there is only one text node for each block of text. You can actually create text nodes that are adjacent to each other, although they will not be saved as distinct the next time that the document is opened. (It's worth noting that the normalize method on the XMLDOMElement object merges adjacent text nodes into a single node.)

Here are the properties of the XMLDOMText object:

Property	Description
attributes	Holder for the list of attributes for this node. Read-only.
baseName*	The base name for the name qualified with the namespace. Read-only.
childNodes	A node list containing the child nodes. Read-only.
data	This node's data (what's actually stored depends on the node type). Read/write.
dataType*	The data type for this node. Read/write.

`definition`*	The definition of the node in the DTD or schema. Read-only.
`firstChild`	The first child of the current node. Read-only.
`lastChild`	The last child of the current node. Read-only.
`length`	The length, in characters, of the data. Read-only.
`namespaceURI`*	The URI for the namespace. Read-only.
`nextSibling`	The next sibling of this node. Read-only.
`nodeName`	The qualified name of an element, attribute, or entity reference, or a string for other node types. Read-only.
`nodeType`	Indication of the XML DOM node type. Read-only.
`nodeTypedValue`*	This node's value. Read/write.
`nodeTypeString`*	The node type in string form. Read-only.
`nodeValue`	The text associated with the node. Read/write.
`ownerDocument`	The root of the document. Read-only.
`parentNode`	The parent node. Read-only.
`parsed`*	True if this node and all descendants have been parsed; false otherwise. Read-only.
`prefix`*	The namespace prefix. Read-only.
`previousSibling`	The previous sibling of this node. Read-only.
`specified`	Indication of whether the node is explicitly specified or derived from a default value. Read-only.
`text`*	Holder for the text content of the node and its subtrees. Read/write.
`xml`*	Holder for the XML representation of the node and all its descendants. Read-only.

* *Microsoft extension to the W3C DOM.*

Here are the methods of the `XMLDOMText` object:

Method	**Description**
`appendChild`	Appends a new child as the last child of this node
`appendData`	Appends the given string to the existing string data
`cloneNode`	Returns a new node that is a copy of this node
`deleteData`	Removes the given substring within the string data
`hasChildNodes`	Is true if this node has children
`insertBefore`	Inserts a child node before the specified node

continues

Method	Description
`insertData`	Inserts the supplied string at the specified offset
`removeChild`	Removes the specified child node from the list of children
`replaceChild`	Replaces the specified child node with the given new child node
`selectNodes`★	Replaces the given number of characters with the given string
`selectSingleNode`★	Applies the given pattern-matching operation to this node's context, returning a list of matching nodes
`specified`★	Applies the specified pattern-matching operation to this node's context, returning an object
`splitText`	Breaks this text node into two text nodes
`substringData`	Returns a substring of the full string
`transformNode`★	Transforms this node and its children using the given XSL style sheet
`transformNodeToObject`★	Transforms this node and its children using the given XSL style sheet, and returns the resulting transformation as an object

★ *Microsoft extension to the W3C DOM.*

This object doesn't support any events.

That gives us an overview of the most commonly used objects in the Microsoft XML DOM. Now I'm going to put them to work in the rest of the chapter. I'll start at the beginning—loading an XML document.

Loading XML Documents

Our first step will be to load an XML document into Internet Explorer using code, and to create a document object. Using this object, we'll be able to access all aspects of the document itself.

As mentioned earlier in this chapter, there are two ways to load an XML document into Internet Explorer so that you have access to it using JavaScript. To see how this works, I'll use this XML document, meetings.xml, throughout this chapter—this document records business meetings, including who was present and when the meeting occurred:

```
<?xml version="1.0"?>
<MEETINGS>
   <MEETING TYPE="informal">
       <MEETING_TITLE>XML In The Real World</MEETING_TITLE>
```

```
        <MEETING_NUMBER>2079</MEETING_NUMBER>
        <SUBJECT>XML</SUBJECT>
        <DATE>6/1/2002</DATE>
        <PEOPLE>
            <PERSON ATTENDANCE="present">
                <FIRST_NAME>Edward</FIRST_NAME>
                <LAST_NAME>Samson</LAST_NAME>
            </PERSON>
            <PERSON ATTENDANCE="absent">
                <FIRST_NAME>Ernestine</FIRST_NAME>
                <LAST_NAME>Johnson</LAST_NAME>
            </PERSON>
            <PERSON ATTENDANCE="present">
                <FIRST_NAME>Betty</FIRST_NAME>
                <LAST_NAME>Richardson</LAST_NAME>
            </PERSON>
        </PEOPLE>
    </MEETING>
</MEETINGS>
```

The first way of loading an XML document into Internet Explorer is to create a document object using the `Microsoft.XMLDOM` class.

To see this in action, I'm going to create an example that reads in meetings.xml and retrieves the name of the third person in that document (Betty Richardson). I start by creating a new document object like this (recall that you use the `new` operator to create a new object): `xmldoc = new ActiveXObject("Microsoft.XMLDOM")`. Here's how it looks in code:

```
<HTML>
    <HEAD>
        <TITLE>
            Reading XML element values
        </TITLE>

        <SCRIPT LANGUAGE="JavaScript">
             function readXMLDocument()
             {
                 var xmldoc
                 xmldoc = new ActiveXObject("Microsoft.XMLDOM")
                 .
                 .
                 .
    </HEAD>
</HTML>
```

Now I can load in the XML document meetings.xml:

```
<HTML>
    <HEAD>
        <TITLE>
            Reading XML element values
```

continues ▶

```
        </TITLE>

        <SCRIPT LANGUAGE="JavaScript">
            function readXMLDocument()
            {
                var xmldoc
                xmldoc = new ActiveXObject("Microsoft.XMLDOM")
                xmldoc.load("meetings.xml")
                .
                .
                .
    </HEAD>
</HTML>
```

The next step is to get a node object corresponding to the document's root element, <MEETINGS>. You do that with the documentElement method:

```
<HTML>
    <HEAD>
        <TITLE>
            Reading XML element values
        </TITLE>

        <SCRIPT LANGUAGE="JavaScript">
            function readXMLDocument()
            {
                var xmldoc, meetingsNode
                xmldoc = new ActiveXObject("Microsoft.XMLDOM")
                xmldoc.load("meetings.xml")

                meetingsNode = xmldoc.documentElement
                .
                .
                .
    </HEAD>
</HTML>
```

At this point, I'm free to move around the document as I like, using methods such as firstChild, nextChild, previousChild, and lastChild, which let you access the child elements of an element, and the firstSibling, nextSibling, previousSibling, and lastSibling methods, which let you access elements on the same nesting level. For example, the <MEETING> element is the first child of the document root element, <MEETINGS>, so I can get a node corresponding to the <MEETING> element using the firstChild method:

```
<HTML>
    <HEAD>
        <TITLE>
            Reading XML element values
        </TITLE>
```

```
        <SCRIPT LANGUAGE="JavaScript">
            function readXMLDocument()
            {
                var xmldoc, meetingsNode, meetingNode,
                xmldoc = new ActiveXObject("Microsoft.XMLDOM")
                xmldoc.load("meetings.xml")

                meetingsNode = xmldoc.documentElement
                meetingNode = meetingsNode.firstChild
                .
                .
                .
    </HEAD>
</HTML>
```

I want to track down the third <PERSON> element inside the <PEOPLE> element. The <PEOPLE> element is the last child of the <MEETING> element, so I can get a node corresponding to the <PEOPLE> element this way:

```
<HTML>
    <HEAD>
        <TITLE>
            Reading XML element values
        </TITLE>

        <SCRIPT LANGUAGE="JavaScript">
            function readXMLDocument()
            {
                var xmldoc, meetingsNode, meetingNode, peopleNode
                var first_nameNode, last_nameNode
                xmldoc = new ActiveXObject("Microsoft.XMLDOM")
                xmldoc.load("meetings.xml")

                meetingsNode = xmldoc.documentElement
                meetingNode = meetingsNode.firstChild
                peopleNode = meetingNode.lastChild
                .
                .
                .
    </HEAD>
</HTML>
```

I want the third person in the <PEOPLE> element, which is the last child of this element, so I get access to that person with the `lastChild` method:

```
<HTML>
    <HEAD>
        <TITLE>
            Reading XML element values
        </TITLE>
```

continues ▸

```
        <SCRIPT LANGUAGE="JavaScript">
             function readXMLDocument()
             {
                 var xmldoc, meetingsNode, meetingNode, peopleNode
                 xmldoc = new ActiveXObject("Microsoft.XMLDOM")
                 xmldoc.load("meetings.xml")

                 meetingsNode = xmldoc.documentElement
                 meetingNode = meetingsNode.firstChild
                 peopleNode = meetingNode.lastChild
                 personNode = peopleNode.lastChild
                 .
                 .
                 .
    </HEAD>
</HTML>
```

Finally, I can get a node corresponding to the `<FIRST_NAME>` and `<LAST_NAME>` elements that holds the appropriate person's name using the `firstChild` and `nextSibling` (which gets the current node's next sibling node) methods:

```
<HTML>
    <HEAD>
        <TITLE>
            Reading XML element values
        </TITLE>

        <SCRIPT LANGUAGE="JavaScript">
             function readXMLDocument()
             {
                 var xmldoc, meetingsNode, meetingNode, peopleNode
                 var first_nameNode, last_nameNode
                 xmldoc = new ActiveXObject("Microsoft.XMLDOM")
                 xmldoc.load("meetings.xml")

                 meetingsNode = xmldoc.documentElement
                 meetingNode = meetingsNode.firstChild
                 peopleNode = meetingNode.lastChild
                 personNode = peopleNode.lastChild
                 first_nameNode = personNode.firstChild
                 last_nameNode = first_nameNode.nextSibling
                 .
                 .
                 .
    </HEAD>
</HTML>
```

Now I've walked the tree to get nodes corresponding to the actual elements that I want. Note, however, that the node I want is actually the text nodes *inside* the `<FIRST_NAME>` and `<LAST_NAME>` elements, which hold the person's name. That means that I have to get the first child of those elements (that is, the text node), and then use the `nodeValue` property of that text node to read the person's name.

To actually display the person's first and last names, I'll use a little dynamic HTML—here, I'm going to use an HTML `<DIV>` element and the `innerHTML` property of that element (which holds the text content of the `<DIV>` element) to display the person's name, like this:

```
<HTML>
    <HEAD>
         <TITLE>
             Reading XML element values
         </TITLE>

         <SCRIPT LANGUAGE="JavaScript">
              function readXMLDocument()
              {
                  var xmldoc, meetingsNode, meetingNode, peopleNode
                  var first_nameNode, last_nameNode, outputText
                  xmldoc = new ActiveXObject("Microsoft.XMLDOM")
                  xmldoc.load("meetings.xml")

                  meetingsNode = xmldoc.documentElement
                  meetingNode = meetingsNode.firstChild
                  peopleNode = meetingNode.lastChild
                  personNode = peopleNode.lastChild
                  first_nameNode = personNode.firstChild
                  last_nameNode = first_nameNode.nextSibling

                  outputText = "Third name: " +
                        first_nameNode.firstChild.nodeValue + ' '
                      + last_nameNode.firstChild.nodeValue
                  messageDIV.innerHTML=outputText
              }
         </SCRIPT>
    </HEAD>

    <BODY>
        <CENTER>
            <H1>
                Reading XML element values
            </H1>

            <INPUT TYPE="BUTTON" VALUE="Get the name of the third person"
                ONCLICK="readXMLDocument()">
            <P>
```

continues ▸

```
            <DIV ID="messageDIV"></DIV>
        </CENTER>
    </BODY>
</HTML>
```

I've also added a button with the caption `Get the name of the third person` that will call the JavaScript function we've defined, `readXMLDocument`, and that function reads and displays the document.

You can see this page at work in Internet Explorer in Figure 7.2. When the user clicks the button, the XML document meetings.xml is read and parsed, and we retrieve and display the third person's name. We've made substantial progress.

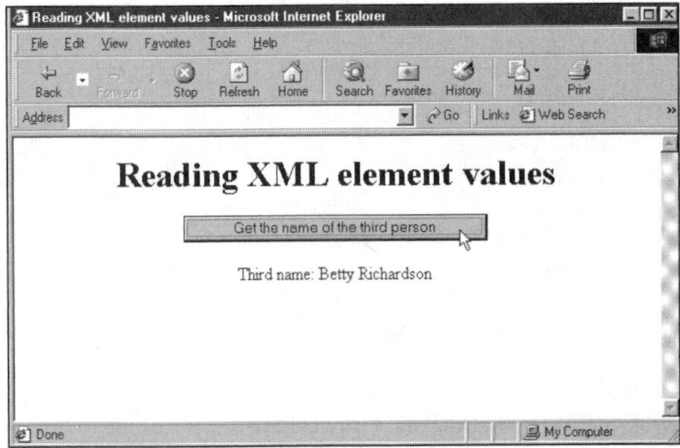

Figure 7.2 Reading an XML element in Internet Explorer.

Using XML Data Islands

As of Internet Explorer version 5, you can also use *XML data islands* to actually embed XML inside HTML pages. Internet Explorer supports an HTML `<XML>` element (which is not part of the HTML standard) that you can simply enclose an XML document inside, like this:

```
<XML ID="greeting">
    <DOCUMENT>
        <GREETING>Hi there XML!</GREETING>
    </DOCUMENT>
</XML>
```

The Internet Explorer <XML> element has some attributes worth noting:

Attribute	Description
ID	The ID with which you can refer to the <XML> element in code. Set to an alphanumeric string.
NS	The URI of the XML namespace used by the XML content. Set to a URI.
PREFIX	Namespace prefix of the XML contents. Set to an alphanumeric string.
SRC	Source for the XML document, if the document is external. Set to a URI.

When you use this element, you access it using its ID value in code. To reach the element, you can use the `all` collection, passing it the ID that you gave the element, like this, for the above example: `document.all("greeting")`. To get the document object corresponding to the XML document, you can then use the `XMLDocument` property. Here's how I convert the previous example to use a data island instead of the `Microsoft.XMLDOM` object:

```
<HTML>
    <HEAD>
        <TITLE>
            Reading element values with XML data islands
        </TITLE>

        <XML ID="meetingsXML" SRC="meetings.xml"></XML>

        <SCRIPT LANGUAGE="JavaScript">
            function readXMLDocument()
            {
                var xmldoc, meetingsNode, meetingNode, peopleNode
                var first_nameNode, last_nameNode, outputText

                xmldoc= document.all("meetingsXML").XMLDocument

                meetingsNode = xmldoc.documentElement
                meetingNode = meetingsNode.firstChild
                peopleNode = meetingNode.lastChild
                personNode = peopleNode.lastChild
                first_nameNode = personNode.firstChild
                last_nameNode = first_nameNode.nextSibling

                outputText = "Third name: " +
                      first_nameNode.firstChild.nodeValue + ' '
                    + last_nameNode.firstChild.nodeValue
                messageDIV.innerHTML=outputText
            }
        </SCRIPT>
```

continues ▸

```
    </HEAD>

    <BODY>
        <CENTER>
            <H1>
                Reading element values with XML data islands
            </H1>

            <INPUT TYPE="BUTTON" VALUE="Get the name of the third person"
                ONCLICK="readXMLDocument()">
            <P>
            <DIV ID="messageDIV"></DIV>
        </CENTER>
    </BODY>
</HTML>
```

This example works as the previous example did, as shown in Figure 7.3.

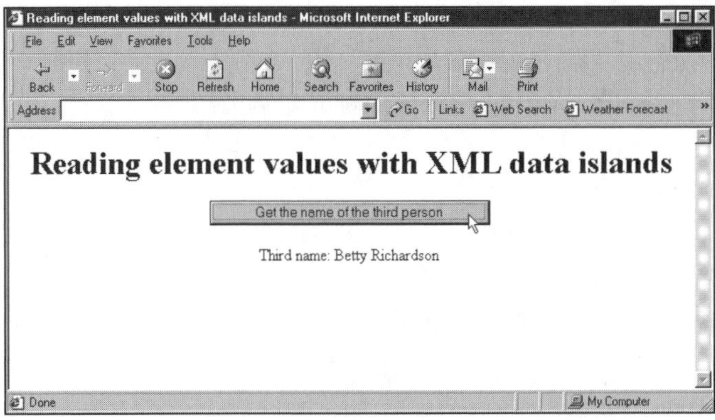

Figure 7.3 Using XML data islands in Internet Explorer.

In the previous example, I used an external XML document, meetings.xml, which I referenced with the `<XML>` element's `SRC` attribute. However, you can also enclose the entire XML document in the `<XML>` element, like this:

```
<HTML>
    <HEAD>
        <TITLE>
            Creating An XML Data Island
        </TITLE>

        <XML ID="meetingsXML">
            <?xml version="1.0"?>
            <MEETINGS>
                <MEETING TYPE="informal">
                    <MEETING_TITLE>XML In The Real World</MEETING_TITLE>
                    <MEETING_NUMBER>2079</MEETING_NUMBER>
```

```
                <SUBJECT>XML</SUBJECT>
                <DATE>6/1/2002</DATE>
                <PEOPLE>
                    <PERSON ATTENDANCE="present">
                        <FIRST_NAME>Edward</FIRST_NAME>
                        <LAST_NAME>Samson</LAST_NAME>
                    </PERSON>
                    <PERSON ATTENDANCE="absent">
                        <FIRST_NAME>Ernestine</FIRST_NAME>
                        <LAST_NAME>Johnson</LAST_NAME>
                    </PERSON>
                    <PERSON ATTENDANCE="present">
                        <FIRST_NAME>Betty</FIRST_NAME>
                        <LAST_NAME>Richardson</LAST_NAME>
                    </PERSON>
                </PEOPLE>
            </MEETING>
        </MEETINGS>
    </XML>

    <SCRIPT LANGUAGE="JavaScript">
        function readXMLDocument()
        {
            var xmldoc, meetingsNode, meetingNode, peopleNode
            var first_nameNode, last_nameNode, outputText

            xmldoc= document.all("meetingsXML").XMLDocument

            meetingsNode = xmldoc.documentElement
            meetingNode = meetingsNode.firstChild
            peopleNode = meetingNode.lastChild
            personNode = peopleNode.lastChild
            first_nameNode = personNode.firstChild
            last_nameNode = first_nameNode.nextSibling

            outputText = "Third name: " +
                  first_nameNode.firstChild.nodeValue + ' '
                + last_nameNode.firstChild.nodeValue
            messageDIV.innerHTML=outputText
        }
    </SCRIPT>
</HEAD>

<BODY>
    <CENTER>
        <H1>
            Reading element values with XML data islands
        </H1>

        <INPUT TYPE="BUTTON" VALUE="Get the name of the third person"
            ONCLICK="readXMLDocument()">
        <P>
```

continues ▸

```
            <DIV ID="messageDIV"></DIV>
        </CENTER>
    </BODY>
</HTML>
```

So far, I've used the `XMLDocument` property of the object corresponding to the XML data island to get the document object, but you can also use the `documentElement` property of the data island directly to get the root element of the XML document, like this:

```
<HTML>
    <HEAD>
         <TITLE>
             Reading XML element values
         </TITLE>

         <XML ID="meetingsXML" SRC="meetings.xml"></XML>

         <SCRIPT LANGUAGE="JavaScript">
              function readXMLDocument()
              {
                  var xmldoc, meetingsNode, meetingNode, peopleNode
                  var first_nameNode, last_nameNode, outputText

                  meetingsNode = meetingsXML.documentElement
                  meetingNode = meetingsNode.firstChild
                  peopleNode = meetingNode.lastChild
                  personNode = peopleNode.lastChild
                  first_nameNode = personNode.firstChild
                  last_nameNode = first_nameNode.nextSibling
                  .
                  .
                  .
</HTML>
```

Getting Elements by Name

So far in this chapter, I've used the navigation methods such as `nextSibling` and `nextChild` to navigate through XML documents. However, you can also get individual elements by searching for them by name. Here's an example; in this case, I'll use the document object's `getElementsByTagName` method to return a node list object holding all elements of a given name. In particular, I'm searching for `<FIRST_NAME>` and `<LAST_NAME>` elements, so I get lists of those elements like this:

```
<HTML>
    <HEAD>
         <TITLE>
```

```
            Reading XML element values
        </TITLE>

        <SCRIPT LANGUAGE="JavaScript">
             function loadDocument()
             {
                 var xmldoc, listNodesFirstName, listNodesLastName

                 xmldoc = new ActiveXObject("Microsoft.XMLDOM")
                 xmldoc.load("meetings.xml")

                 listNodesFirstName = xmldoc.getElementsByTagName("FIRST_NAME")
                 listNodesLastName = xmldoc.getElementsByTagName("LAST_NAME")<HTML>
    .
    .
    .
```

Like all node lists, the `listNodesFirstName` and `listNodesLastName` node lists are indexed by number starting at 0, so the third element in these lists is element number 2, which you refer to as `listNodesLastName.item(2)`. This means that I can find the first and last name of the third person. (Recall that I actually need the first child of the `<FIRST_NAME>` and `<LAST_NAME>` nodes, which is the text node inside those elements that holds the person's name, so I use the `firstChild` method here.)

```
<HTML>
    <HEAD>
        <TITLE>
            Reading XML element values
        </TITLE>

        <SCRIPT LANGUAGE="JavaScript">
             function loadDocument()
             {
                 var xmldoc, listNodesFirstName, listNodesLastName

                 xmldoc = new ActiveXObject("Microsoft.XMLDOM")
                 xmldoc.load("meetings.xml")

                 listNodesFirstName = xmldoc.getElementsByTagName("FIRST_NAME")
                 listNodesLastName = xmldoc.getElementsByTagName("LAST_NAME")

                 outputText = "Third name: " +
                        listNodesFirstName.item(2).firstChild.nodeValue + ' '
                      + listNodesLastName.item(2).firstChild.nodeValue
                 messageDIV.innerHTML=outputText
             }
        </SCRIPT>
    </HEAD>
```

continues ▸

```
    <BODY>
        <CENTER>
            <H1>
                Reading XML element values
            </H1>

            <INPUT TYPE="BUTTON" VALUE="Get the name of the third person"
                ONCLICK="loadDocument()">
            <P>
            <DIV ID="messageDIV"></DIV>
        </CENTER>
    </BODY>
</HTML>
```

We've made some progress here and have been able to read in an XML document in various ways to access specific elements in the document. I'll move on to the next step now—accessing not just an element's text content, but also the element's *attributes*.

Getting Attribute Values from XML Elements

To see how to read attribute values from an XML document, I'll read the value of the ATTENDANCE attribute of the third person in the XML document meetings.xml:

```
<?xml version="1.0"?>
<MEETINGS>
   <MEETING TYPE="informal">
       <MEETING_TITLE>XML In The Real World</MEETING_TITLE>
       <MEETING_NUMBER>2079</MEETING_NUMBER>
       <SUBJECT>XML</SUBJECT>
       <DATE>6/1/2002</DATE>
       <PEOPLE>
           <PERSON ATTENDANCE="present">
               <FIRST_NAME>Edward</FIRST_NAME>
               <LAST_NAME>Samson</LAST_NAME>
           </PERSON>
           <PERSON ATTENDANCE="absent">
               <FIRST_NAME>Ernestine</FIRST_NAME>
               <LAST_NAME>Johnson</LAST_NAME>
           </PERSON>
           <PERSON ATTENDANCE="present">
               <FIRST_NAME>Betty</FIRST_NAME>
               <LAST_NAME>Richardson</LAST_NAME>
           </PERSON>
       </PEOPLE>
   </MEETING>
</MEETINGS>
```

How do you read attribute values? You start by getting a named node map object of the attributes of the current element using that element's attribute's property. In this case, we want the attributes of the third `<PERSON>` element, and we get a named node map of those attributes, like this:

```
<HTML>
    <HEAD>
        <TITLE>
            Reading attribute values from XML documents
        </TITLE>

        <XML ID="meetingsXML" SRC="meetings.xml"></XML>

        <SCRIPT LANGUAGE="JavaScript">
            function readXMLDocument()
            {
                var xmldoc, meetingsNode, meetingNode, peopleNode
                var first_nameNode, last_nameNode, outputText
                var attributes

                xmldoc= document.all("meetingsXML").XMLDocument

                meetingsNode = xmldoc.documentElement
                meetingNode = meetingsNode.firstChild
                peopleNode = meetingNode.lastChild
                personNode = peopleNode.lastChild
                first_nameNode = personNode.firstChild
                last_nameNode = first_nameNode.nextSibling
                attributes = personNode.attributes
                .
                .
                .
</HTML>
```

Now I can recover the actual node for the `ATTENDANCE` node with the named node map object's `getNamedItem` method:

```
<HTML>
    <HEAD>
        <TITLE>
            Reading attribute values from XML documents
        </TITLE>

        <XML ID="meetingsXML" SRC="meetings.xml"></XML>

        <SCRIPT LANGUAGE="JavaScript">
            function readXMLDocument()
            {
                var xmldoc, meetingsNode, meetingNode, peopleNode
                var first_nameNode, last_nameNode, outputText
```

continues ▸

```
                xmldoc= document.all("meetingsXML").XMLDocument

                meetingsNode = xmldoc.documentElement
                meetingNode = meetingsNode.firstChild
                peopleNode = meetingNode.lastChild
                personNode = peopleNode.lastChild
                first_nameNode = personNode.firstChild
                last_nameNode = first_nameNode.nextSibling
                attributes = personNode.attributes
                attendancePerson = attributes.getNamedItem("ATTENDANCE")
                .
                .
                .
</HTML>
```

Now I have a node corresponding to the `ATTENDANCE` attribute, and I can get the value of that attribute using the `value` property (attribute nodes don't have internal text nodes):

```
<HTML>
    <HEAD>
        <TITLE>
            Reading attribute values from XML documents
        </TITLE>

        <XML ID="meetingsXML" SRC="meetings.xml"></XML>

        <SCRIPT LANGUAGE="JavaScript">
            function readXMLDocument()
            {
                var xmldoc, meetingsNode, meetingNode, peopleNode
                var first_nameNode, last_nameNode, outputText
                var attributes, attendancePerson

                xmldoc= document.all("meetingsXML").XMLDocument

                meetingsNode = xmldoc.documentElement
                meetingNode = meetingsNode.firstChild
                peopleNode = meetingNode.lastChild
                personNode = peopleNode.lastChild
                first_nameNode = personNode.firstChild
                last_nameNode = first_nameNode.nextSibling
                attributes = personNode.attributes
                attendancePerson = attributes.getNamedItem("ATTENDANCE")
                outputText = first_nameNode.firstChild.nodeValue
                    + ' ' + last_nameNode.firstChild.nodeValue
                    + " is " + attendancePerson.value
                messageDIV.innerHTML=outputText
                .
                .
                .
</HTML>
```

And that's all it takes. Here's what the whole page looks like:

```
<HTML>
    <HEAD>
         <TITLE>
             Reading attribute values from XML documents
         </TITLE>

         <XML ID="meetingsXML" SRC="meetings.xml"></XML>

         <SCRIPT LANGUAGE="JavaScript">
             function readXMLDocument()
             {
                  var xmldoc, meetingsNode, meetingNode, peopleNode
                  var first_nameNode, last_nameNode, outputText
                  var attributes, attendancePerson

                  xmldoc= document.all("meetingsXML").XMLDocument

                  meetingsNode = xmldoc.documentElement
                  meetingNode = meetingsNode.firstChild
                  peopleNode = meetingNode.lastChild
                  personNode = peopleNode.lastChild
                  first_nameNode = personNode.firstChild
                  last_nameNode = first_nameNode.nextSibling
                  attributes = personNode.attributes
                  attendancePerson = attributes.getNamedItem("ATTENDANCE")
                  outputText = first_nameNode.firstChild.nodeValue
                      + ' ' + last_nameNode.firstChild.nodeValue
                      + " is " + attendancePerson.value
                  messageDIV.innerHTML=outputText
             }
         </SCRIPT>
    </HEAD>

    <BODY>
        <CENTER>
            <H1>
                Reading attribute values from XML documents
            </H1>

            <INPUT TYPE="BUTTON" VALUE="Get attendance of the third person"
                ONCLICK="readXMLDocument()">
            <P>
            <DIV ID="messageDIV"></DIV>
        </CENTER>
    </BODY>
</HTML>
```

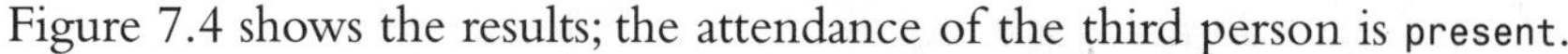

Figure 7.4 shows the results; the attendance of the third person is `present`.

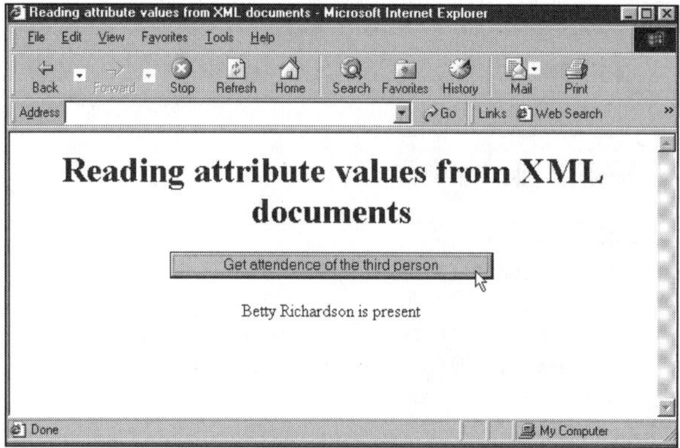

Figure 7.4 Reading attributes in Internet Explorer.

Parsing XML Documents in Code

Up to this point, I've gone after a specific element in a Web page, but there are other ways of handling documents, too. For example, you can parse—that is, read and interpret—the entire document at once. Here's an example; in this case, I'll work through this entire XML document, meetings.xml, displaying all its nodes in an HTML Web page.

To handle this document, I'll create a function, `iterateChildren`, that will read and display all the children of a node. As with most parsers, this function is a recursive function, which means that it can call itself to get the children of the current node. To get the name of a node, I will use the `nodeName` property. To parse an entire document, then, you just have to pass the root node of the entire document to the `iterateChildren` function, and it will work through the entire document, displaying all the nodes in that document:

```
<HTML>
    <HEAD>
        <TITLE>
            Parsing an XML Document
        </TITLE>

        <XML ID="meetingsXML" SRC="meetings.xml"></XML>

        <SCRIPT LANGUAGE="JavaScript">
            function parseDocument()
            {
```

```
                documentXML = document.all("meetingsXML").XMLDocument
                resultsDIV.innerHTML = iterateChildren(documentXML, "")
            }
    .
    .
    .
```

Note that I've also passed an empty string ("") to the `iterateChildren` function. I'll use this string to indent the various levels of the display, to indicate what nodes are nested inside what other nodes. In the `iterateChildren` function, I start by creating a new text string with the current indentation string (which is either an empty string or a string of spaces), as well as the name of the current node and a `<BR>` element so that the browser will skip to the next line:

```
<HTML>
    <HEAD>
        <TITLE>
            Parsing an XML Document
        </TITLE>

        <XML ID="meetingsXML" SRC="meetings.xml"></XML>

        <SCRIPT LANGUAGE="JavaScript">
            function parseDocument()
            {
                documentXML = document.all("meetingsXML").XMLDocument
                resultsDIV.innerHTML = iterateChildren(documentXML, "")
            }

            function iterateChildren(theNode, indentSpacing)
            {
                var text = indentSpacing + theNode.nodeName + "<BR>"
                .
                .
                .
                return text
            }
        </SCRIPT>
    </HEAD>
    .
    .
    .
```

I can determine whether the current node has children by checking the `childNodes` property, which holds a node list of the children of the current node. I can determine whether the current node has any children by checking the length of this list with its `length` property; if it does have children, I call `iterateChildren` on all child nodes. (Note also that I indent this next level of the display by adding four nonbreaking spaces—which you specify with the ` ` entity reference in HTML—to the current indentation string.)

```
<HTML>
    <HEAD>
        <TITLE>
            Parsing an XML Document
        </TITLE>

        <XML ID="meetingsXML" SRC="meetings.xml"></XML>

        <SCRIPT LANGUAGE="JavaScript">
            function parseDocument()
            {
                documentXML = document.all("meetingsXML").XMLDocument
                resultsDIV.innerHTML = iterateChildren(documentXML, "")
            }

            function iterateChildren(theNode, indentSpacing)
            {
                var text = indentSpacing + theNode.nodeName + "<BR>"

                if (theNode.childNodes.length > 0) {
                    for (var loopIndex = 0; loopIndex <
                        theNode.childNodes.length; loopIndex++) {
                        text += iterateChildren(theNode.childNodes(loopIndex),
                        indentSpacing + "    ")
                    }
                }
                return text
            }
        </SCRIPT>
    </HEAD>
    .
    .
    .
```

And that's all it takes; here's the whole Web page:

```
<HTML>
    <HEAD>
        <TITLE>
            Parsing an XML Document
        </TITLE>

        <XML ID="meetingsXML" SRC="meetings.xml"></XML>
```

```
        <SCRIPT LANGUAGE="JavaScript">
            function parseDocument()
            {
                documentXML = document.all("meetingsXML").XMLDocument
                resultsDIV.innerHTML = iterateChildren(documentXML, "")
            }

            function iterateChildren(theNode, indentSpacing)
            {
                var text = indentSpacing + theNode.nodeName + "<BR>"

                if (theNode.childNodes.length > 0) {
                    for (var loopIndex = 0; loopIndex <
                        theNode.childNodes.length; loopIndex++) {
                        text += iterateChildren(theNode.childNodes(loopIndex),
                        indentSpacing + "    ")
                    }
                }
                return text
            }
        </SCRIPT>
    </HEAD>

    <BODY>
        <CENTER>
            <H1>
                Parsing an XML Document
            </H1>
        </CENTER>

        <CENTER>
            <INPUT TYPE="BUTTON" VALUE="Parse and display the document"
                ONCLICK="parseDocument()">
        </CENTER>
        <DIV ID="resultsDIV"></DIV>
    </BODY>
</HTML>
```

When you click the button in this page, it will read meetings.xml and display its structure as shown in Figure 7.5. You can see all the nodes listed there, indented as they should be. Note also the "meta-names" that Internet Explorer gives to document and text nodes—`#document` and `#text`.

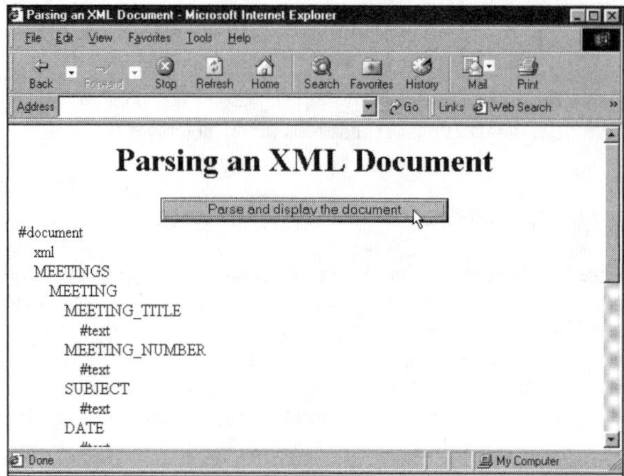

Figure 7.5 Parsing a document in Internet Explorer.

Parsing an XML Document to Display Node Type and Content

In the previous example, the code listed the names of each node in the meetings.xml document. However, you can do more than that—you can also use the `nodeValue` property to list the value of each node, and I'll do that in this section. In addition, you can indicate the type of each node that you come across by checking the `nodeType` property. Here are the possible values for this property:

Value	Description
1	Element
2	Attribute
3	Text
4	CDATA section
5	Entity reference
6	Entity
7	Processing instruction
8	Comment
9	Document
10	Document type
11	Document fragment
12	Notation

Here's how I determine the type of a particular node, using a JavaScript `switch` statement of the kind that we saw in the previous chapter:

```
<HTML>
    <HEAD>
        <TITLE>
            Parsing an XML document and displaying node type and content
        </TITLE>

        <XML ID="meetingsXML" SRC="meetings.xml"></XML>

        <SCRIPT LANGUAGE="JavaScript">
            function parseDocument()
            {
                documentXML = document.all("meetingsXML").XMLDocument
                resultsDIV.innerHTML = iterateChildren(documentXML, "")
            }

            function iterateChildren(theNode, indentSpacing)
            {
                var typeData
                switch (theNode.nodeType) {
                    case 1:
                        typeData = "element"
                        break
                    case 2:
                        typeData = "attribute"
                        break
                    case 3:
                        typeData = "text"
                        break
                    case 4:
                        typeData = "CDATA section"
                        break
                    case 5:
                        typeData = "entity reference"
                        break
                    case 6:
                        typeData = "entity"
                        break
                    case 7:
                        typeData = "processing instruction"
                        break
                    case 8:
                        typeData = "comment"
                        break
                    case 9:
                        typeData = "document"
                        break
                    case 10:
                        typeData = "document type"
                        break
```

continues ▸

```
                case 11:
                    typeData = "document fragment"
                    break
                case 12:
                    typeData = "notation"
            }
            .
            .
            .
```

If the node has a value (which I check by comparing `nodeValue` to `null`, which is the value that it will have if there is no actual node value), I can display that value like this:

```
<HTML>
    <HEAD>
        <TITLE>
            Parsing an XML document and displaying node type and content
        </TITLE>

        <XML ID="meetingsXML" SRC="meetings.xml"></XML>

        <SCRIPT LANGUAGE="JavaScript">
            function parseDocument()
            {
                documentXML = document.all("meetingsXML").XMLDocument
                resultsDIV.innerHTML = iterateChildren(documentXML, "")
            }

            function iterateChildren(theNode, indentSpacing)
            {
                var typeData

                switch (theNode.nodeType) {
                    case 1:
                        typeData = "element"
                        break
                    case 2:
                        typeData = "attribute"
                        break
                    case 3:
                        typeData = "text"
                        break
                    case 4:
                        typeData = "CDATA section"
                        break
                    case 5:
                        typeData = "entity reference"
                        break
                    case 6:
                        typeData = "entity"
                        break
```

```
                case 7:
                    typeData = "processing instruction"
                    break
                case 8:
                    typeData = "comment"
                    break
                case 9:
                    typeData = "document"
                    break
                case 10:
                    typeData = "document type"
                    break
                case 11:
                    typeData = "document fragment"
                    break
                case 12:
                    typeData = "notation"
            }
              var text

              if (theNode.nodeValue != null) {
                  text = indentSpacing + theNode.nodeName
                  + "  = " + theNode.nodeValue
                  + "  (Node type: " + typeData
                  + ")<BR>"
              } else {
                  text = indentSpacing + theNode.nodeName
                  + "  (Node type: " + typeData
                  + ")<BR>"
              }

             if (theNode.childNodes.length > 0) {
                for (var loopIndex = 0; loopIndex <
                    theNode.childNodes.length; loopIndex++) {
                    text += iterateChildren(theNode.childNodes(loopIndex),
                    indentSpacing + "    ")
                }
            }
            return text
        }
    </SCRIPT>
</HEAD>

<BODY>
    <CENTER>
        <H1>
            Parsing an XML document and displaying node type and content
        </H1>
    </CENTER>

    <CENTER>
        <INPUT TYPE="BUTTON" VALUE="Parse and display the document"
            ONCLICK="parseDocument()">
```

continues ▸

```
        </CENTER>

        <DIV ID="resultsDIV"></DIV>
    </BODY>
</HTML>
```

And that's all it takes; the results are shown in Figure 7.6. As you see there, the entire document is listed, as is the type of each node. In addition, if the node has a value, that value is displayed.

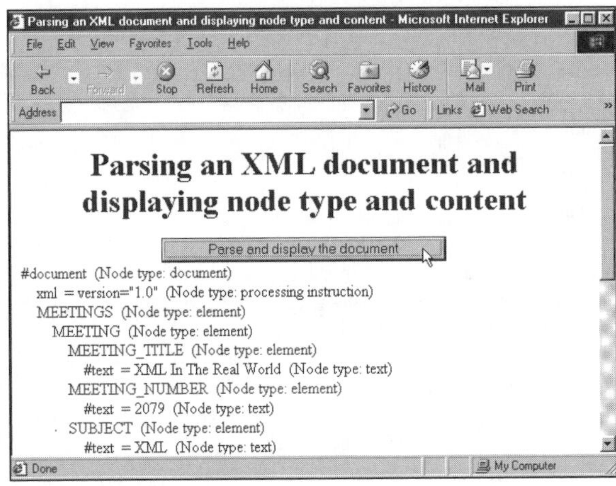

Figure 7.6 Using JavaScript to display element content and type.

This example listed the nodes of a document—on the other hand, some of the elements in meetings.xml have attributes as well. So how do you handle attributes?

Parsing an XML Document to Display Attribute Values

You can get access to an element's attributes with the element's `attributes` property. You can get attribute names and values with the `name` and `value` properties of attribute objects—I used the `value` property earlier in this chapter. It's also worth noting that because attributes are themselves nodes, you can use the `nodeName` and `nodeValue` properties to do the same thing; I'll do that in this example to show how it works.

Here's how I augment the previous example, looping over all the attributes that an element has and listing them. (Note that you could use the `name` and `value` properties here instead of `nodeName` and `nodeValue`.)

```
<HTML>
    <HEAD>
        <TITLE>
            Parsing XML to read attributes
        </TITLE>

        <XML ID="meetingsXML" SRC="meetings.xml"></XML>

        <SCRIPT LANGUAGE="JavaScript">

            function parseDocument()
            {
                documentXML = document.all("meetingsXML").XMLDocument
                resultsDIV.innerHTML = iterateChildren(documentXML, "")
            }

            function iterateChildren(theNode, indentSpacing)
            {
                var typeData

                switch (theNode.nodeType) {
                    case 1:
                        typeData = "element"
                        break
                    case 2:
                        typeData = "attribute"
                        break
                    case 3:
                        typeData = "text"
                        break
                    case 4:
                        typeData = "CDATA section"
                        break
                    case 5:
                        typeData = "entity reference"
                        break
                    case 6:
                        typeData = "entity"
                        break
                    case 7:
                        typeData = "processing instruction"
                        break
                    case 8:
                        typeData = "comment"
                        break
                    case 9:
                        typeData = "document"
                        break
```

continues ▸

```
                case 10:
                    typeData = "document type"
                    break
                case 11:
                    typeData = "document fragment"
                    break
                case 12:
                    typeData = "notation"
            }
              var text

              if (theNode.nodeValue != null) {
                  text = indentSpacing + theNode.nodeName
                  + "  = " + theNode.nodeValue
                  + "  (Node type: " + typeData
                  + ")"
              } else {
                  text = indentSpacing + theNode.nodeName
                  + "  (Node type: " + typeData
                  + ")"
              }

            if (theNode.attributes != null) {
                 if (theNode.attributes.length > 0) {
                     for (var loopIndex = 0; loopIndex <
                         theNode.attributes.length; loopIndex++) {
                         text += " (Attribute: " +
                             theNode.attributes(loopIndex).nodeName +
                             " = \"" +
                             theNode.attributes(loopIndex).nodeValue
                             + "\")"
                     }
                 }
             }

             text += "<BR>"

             if (theNode.childNodes.length > 0) {
                for (var loopIndex = 0; loopIndex <
                    theNode.childNodes.length; loopIndex++) {
                    text += iterateChildren(theNode.childNodes(loopIndex),
                    indentSpacing + "    ")
                }
            }
            return text
        }

    </SCRIPT>
</HEAD>

<BODY>
    <CENTER>
```

```
            <H1>
                Parsing XML to read attributes
            </H1>
        </CENTER>

        <CENTER>
            <INPUT TYPE="BUTTON" VALUE="Parse and display the document"
                ONCLICK="parseDocument()">
        </CENTER>
        <DIV ID="resultsDIV"></DIV>
    </BODY>
</HTML>
```

You can see the results of this page in Figure 7.7; both elements and attributes are listed in that figure.

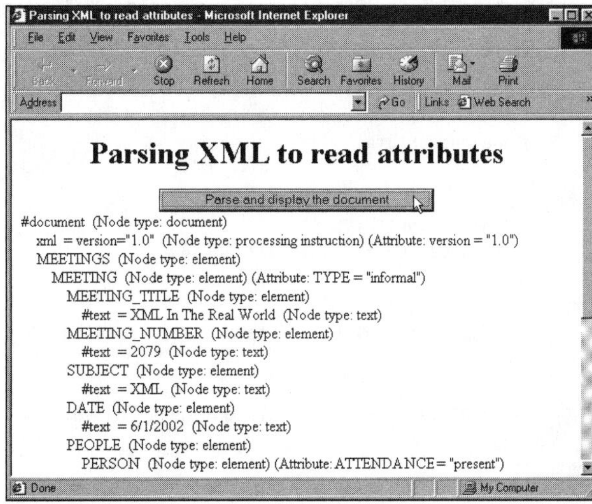

Figure 7.7 Listing elements and attributes in Internet Explorer.

Handling Events While Loading XML Documents

Internet Explorer also lets you track the progress of an XML document as it's being loaded. In particular, you can use the `onreadystatechange` and `ondataavailable` events to watch what's happening. The `readyState` property in the `onreadystatechange` event informs you about the current status of a document. Here's an example showing how this works:

```
<HTML>
    <HEAD>
        <TITLE>
            Handling document loading events
        </TITLE>
```

continues ▸

```
    <SCRIPT LANGUAGE="JavaScript">
        var xmldoc

        function loadDocument()
        {
            xmldoc = new ActiveXObject("microsoft.XMLDOM")

            xmldoc.ondataavailable = dataAvailableHandler
            xmldoc.onreadystatechange = stateChangeHandler

            xmldoc.load('meetings.xml')
        }

        function dataAvailableHandler()
        {
            messageDIV.innerHTML += "Status: data available.<BR>"
        }

        function stateChangeHandler()
        {
            switch (xmldoc.readyState)
            {
                case 1:
                    messageDIV.innerHTML +=
                        "Status: data uninitialized.<BR>"
                    break
                case 2:
                    messageDIV.innerHTML += "Status: data loading.<BR>"
                    break
                case 3:
                    messageDIV.innerHTML += "Status: data loaded.<BR>"
                    break
                case 4:
                    messageDIV.innerHTML +=
                        "Status: data loading complete.<BR>"
                    if (xmldoc.parseError.errorCode != 0) {
                        messageDIV.innerHTML += "Status: error.<BR>"
                    }
                    else {
                        messageDIV.innerHTML +=
                            "Status: data loaded alright.<BR>"
                    }
                    break
            }
        }
    </SCRIPT>
</HEAD>

<BODY>
    <CENTER>
        <H1>
            Handling document loading events
```

```
            </H1>
        </CENTER>

        <CENTER>
            <INPUT TYPE="BUTTON" VALUE="Load the document"
                ONCLICK="loadDocument()">
        </CENTER>
        <DIV ID="messageDIV"></DIV>
    </BODY>
</HTML>
```

The results of this Web page appear in Figure 7.8, and you can see the progress that Internet Explorer made in loading a document in that page.

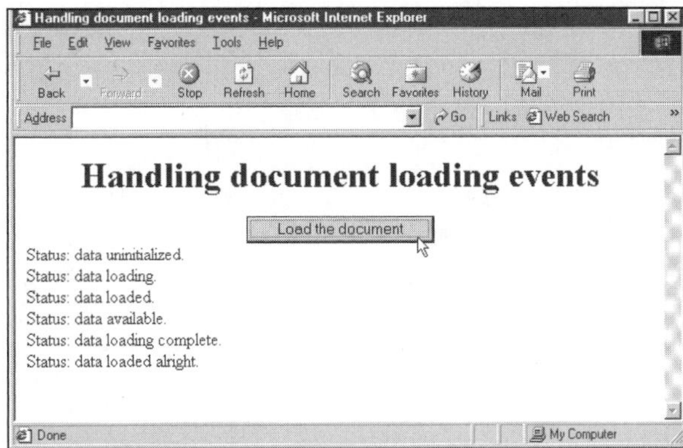

Figure 7.8 Monitoring XML loading events in Internet Explorer.

Validating XML Documents with Internet Explorer

By default, Internet Explorer actually does validate XML documents as it loads them, but you won't see any validation errors unless you check the `parseError` object.

> **Turning Validation On and Off**
> You can turn document validation on or off with the document object's `validateOnParse` property, which is set to true by default.

Here's an example; in this case, I'll load this XML document, error.xml. This document has a validation problem because the `<NAME>` element is declared to contain only a `<FIRST_NAME>` element, not a `<LAST_NAME>` element:

```
<?xml version = "1.0" standalone="yes"?>
<!DOCTYPE DOCUMENT [
<!ELEMENT DOCUMENT (CUSTOMER)*>
<!ELEMENT CUSTOMER (NAME,DATE,ORDERS)>
<!ELEMENT NAME (FIRST_NAME)>
<!ELEMENT LAST_NAME (#PCDATA)>
<!ELEMENT FIRST_NAME (#PCDATA)>
<!ELEMENT DATE (#PCDATA)>
<!ELEMENT ORDERS (ITEM)*>
<!ELEMENT ITEM (PRODUCT,NUMBER,PRICE)>
<!ELEMENT PRODUCT (#PCDATA)>
<!ELEMENT NUMBER (#PCDATA)>
<!ELEMENT PRICE (#PCDATA)>
]>
<DOCUMENT>
    <CUSTOMER>
        <NAME>
            <LAST_NAME>Smith</LAST_NAME>
            <FIRST_NAME>Sam</FIRST_NAME>
        </NAME>
        <DATE>October 15, 2001</DATE>
        <ORDERS>
            <ITEM>
                <PRODUCT>Tomatoes</PRODUCT>
                <NUMBER>8</NUMBER>
                <PRICE>$1.25</PRICE>
            </ITEM>
            <ITEM>
                <PRODUCT>Asparagus</PRODUCT>
                <NUMBER>12</NUMBER>
                <PRICE>$2.95</PRICE>
            </ITEM>
            <ITEM>
                <PRODUCT>Lettuce</PRODUCT>
                <NUMBER>6</NUMBER>
                <PRICE>$11.50</PRICE>
            </ITEM>
        </ORDERS>
    </CUSTOMER>
</DOCUMENT>
```

Here's what the Web page that reads in and checks this document looks like—here I'm using the `parseError` object's `errorCode`, `url`, `line`, `linepos`, `errorString`, and `reason` properties to track down the error:

```
<HTML>
    <HEAD>
        <TITLE>
            Validating documents
        </TITLE>

        <SCRIPT LANGUAGE="JavaScript">
            var xmldoc
```

```
        function loadDocument()
        {
            xmldoc = new ActiveXObject("microsoft.XMLDOM")

            xmldoc.onreadystatechange = stateChangeHandler
            xmldoc.ondataavailable = dataAvailableHandler

            xmldoc.load('error.xml')
        }

        function dataAvailableHandler()
        {
            messageDIV.innerHTML += "Status: data available.<BR>"
        }

        function stateChangeHandler()
        {
            if(xmldoc.readyState == 4){
                var errorString = xmldoc.parseError.srcText
                errorString =
                xmldoc.parseError.srcText.replace(/\</g, "&lt;")
                errorString = errorString.replace(/\>/g, "&gt;")
                if (xmldoc.parseError.errorCode != 0) {
                    messageDIV.innerHTML = "Problem in " +
                    xmldoc.parseError.url +
                    " line " + xmldoc.parseError.line +
                    " position " + xmldoc.parseError.linepos +
                    ":<BR>Error source: " + errorString +
                    "<BR>" + xmldoc.parseError.reason +
                    "<BR>" +  "Error: " +
                    xmldoc.parseError.errorCode
                }
                else {
                    messageDIV.innerHTML =
                    "Status: document loaded alright.<BR>"
                }
            }
        }
    </SCRIPT>
</HEAD>

<BODY>
    <CENTER>
        <H1>
            Validating documents
        </H1>
    </CENTER>

    <DIV ID="messageDIV"></DIV>

    <CENTER>
        <INPUT TYPE="BUTTON" VALUE="Load the document"
```

continues ▸

```
            ONCLICK="loadDocument()">
        </CENTER>
    </BODY>
</HTML>
```

Figure 7.9 shows the results of this Web page, where the validation error is reported.

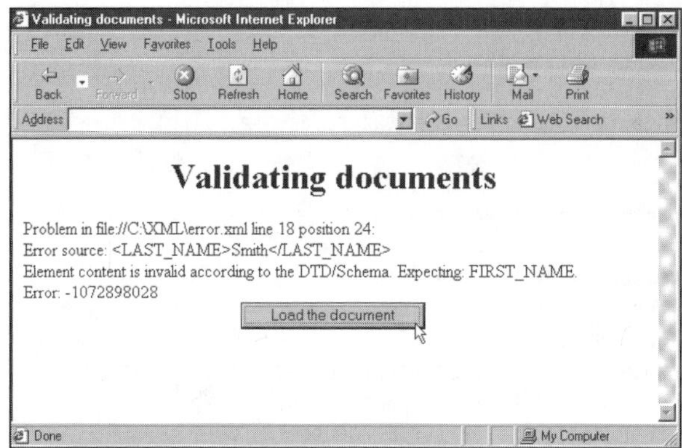

Figure 7.9 Validating XML documents in Internet Explorer.

You might note that the `errorString` property holds the error-causing text from the XML document. Because that text is `<LAST_NAME>Smith</LAST_NAME>`, there's a problem—the browser will try to interpret this as markup. To avoid that, I use the JavaScript `String` object's `replace` method to replace < with `<` and > with `>`. (You pass a regular expression to the replace method; to change all < characters to `<`, the regular expression that you use is `/\</g`. To change all > characters to `>`, you match to the regular expression `/\>/g`.)

Scripting XML Elements

Internet Explorer provides limited support for scripting XML elements. For example, I can add an `onclick` event attribute to an XML element named `<xlink>` in an XHTML document. (We'll take a look at Xlinks and XHTML later in this book; see Chapters 15, 16, and 17.)

```
<?xml version="1.0" encoding="UTF-8"?>
<?xml-stylesheet TYPE="text/css" href="xlink.css"?>

<!DOCTYPE html SYSTEM "t3.dtd">
```

```
<html>
    <head>
    </head>

    <body>
    Want to check out <xlink xml:link = "simple" inline="false"
    href = "http://www.w3c.org"
    onclick="location.href='http://www.w3c.org'">W3C</xlink>?
    </body>
</html>
```

I can specify in a style sheet, xlink.css, that `<xlink>` elements should be displayed in blue and underlined, as a hyperlink might appear, and I can also specify that the mouse cursor should change to a hand when over this element, just as it would for an HTML hyperlink:

```
xlink {color: #0000FF; text-decoration: underline; cursor: hand}
```

The results appear in Figure 7.10—when the user clicks the `<xlink>` element, Internet Explorer executes the code in the `onclick` event attribute. In this case, that navigates the browser to `http://www.w3c.org`. As you can see, you can script XML elements in Internet Explorer, adding event attributes such as `onclick`.

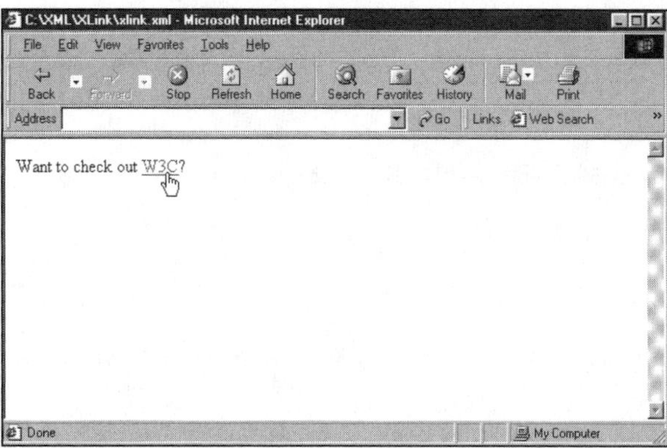

Figure 7.10 Creating a "hyperlink" in an XML document in Internet Explorer.

Editing XML Documents with Internet Explorer

You can alter the contents of an XML document in Internet Explorer. To do this, you use methods such s `createElement`, `insertBefore`, `createTextNode`, and `appendChild`.

As an example, I'll alter the document meetings.xml by inserting a new element, `<MEETING_CHAIR>`, like this:

```
<?xml version="1.0"?>
<MEETINGS>
   <MEETING TYPE="informal">
       <MEETING_CHAIR>Ted Bond</MEETING_CHAIR>
       <MEETING_TITLE>XML In The Real World</MEETING_TITLE>
       <MEETING_NUMBER>2079</MEETING_NUMBER>
       <SUBJECT>XML</SUBJECT>
       <DATE>6/1/2002</DATE>
       <PEOPLE>
           <PERSON ATTENDANCE="present">
               <FIRST_NAME>Edward</FIRST_NAME>
               <LAST_NAME>Samson</LAST_NAME>
           </PERSON>
               .
               .
               .
```

I begin by creating the new node, corresponding to the `<MEETING_CHAIR>` element, and inserting it into the document with the `insertBefore` method:

```
<HTML>
    <HEAD>
        <XML ID="meetingsXML" SRC="meetings.xml"></XML>

        <SCRIPT LANGUAGE="JavaScript">
        <!—
            function alterDocument()
            {
                var xmldoc, rootNode, meetingsNode, meetingNode, createdNode,
createdTextNode

                xmldoc = document.all.meetingsXML
                rootNode = xmldoc.documentElement
                meetingsNode = rootNode.firstChild
                meetingNode = meetingsNode.firstChild

                createdNode = xmldoc.createElement("MEETING_CHAIR")
                createdNode = meetingsNode.insertBefore(createdNode, meetingNode)
                .
                .
                .
```

Now I will create the text node inside this new element. The text node will hold the text `"Ted Bond"`, and I'll create it with the `createTextNode` method and append it to the `<MEETING_CHAIR>` element with the `appendChild` method:

```
<HTML>
    <HEAD>
        <XML ID="meetingsXML" SRC="meetings.xml"></XML>

        <SCRIPT LANGUAGE="JavaScript">
        <!--
            function alterDocument()
            {
                var xmldoc, rootNode, meetingsNode, meetingNode, createdNode,
createdTextNode

                xmldoc = document.all.meetingsXML
                rootNode = xmldoc.documentElement
                meetingsNode = rootNode.firstChild
                meetingNode = meetingsNode.firstChild

                createdNode = xmldoc.createElement("MEETING_CHAIR")
                createdNode = meetingsNode.insertBefore(createdNode, meetingNode)

                createdTextNode = xmldoc.createTextNode("Ted Bond")
                createdNode.appendChild(createdTextNode)
                .
                .
                .
```

Now I've altered the document—but at this point, it exists only inside the `xmldoc` object. How do I display it in the browser? The `DOMDocument` object actually has a `save` method that enables you to save the document to a new file like this: `xmldoc.save("new.xml")`. However, you can't use that method without changing the security settings in Internet Explorer—by default, browsers aren't supposed to be capable of writing files on the host machine.

I'll take a different approach. In this case, I'll store the XML document's text in a hidden control in an HTML form (a hidden control simply holds text invisible to the user), and send the data in that form to a server-side Active Server Pages (ASP) script. That script will just echo the document back to the browser, which, in turn, will display it. Here's the ASP script, echo.asp, where I set the MIME type of this document to `"text/xml"`, add an `<?xml?>` processing instruction, and echo the XML data back to Internet Explorer. (ASP scripts such as this one are beyond the scope of this book, but we'll take a brief look at them in Chapter 20, "WML, ASP, JSP, Servlets, and Perl.")

```
<%@ LANGUAGE="VBSCRIPT" %>
<%
Response.ContentType = "text/xml"
Response.Write "<?xml version=" & Chr(34) &
"1.0" & Chr(34) & "?>" & Chr(13) & Chr(10)
Response.Write Request("data")
%>
```

I have an ASP server on my host machine, so the URI that I'll send the XML document to is `http://default/db/echo.asp`. I do that by using the HTML form's `submit` method (which works exactly as if the user had clicked a Submit button in the form) after loading the XML document into the page's hidden control:

```
<HTML>
    <HEAD>
        <XML ID="meetingsXML" SRC="meetings.xml"></XML>

        <SCRIPT LANGUAGE="JavaScript">
        <!--
            function alterDocument()
            {
                var xmldoc, rootNode, meetingsNode, meetingNode, createdNode,
createdTextNode

                xmldoc = document.all.meetingsXML
                rootNode = xmldoc.documentElement
                meetingsNode = rootNode.firstChild
                meetingNode = meetingsNode.firstChild

                createdNode = xmldoc.createElement("MEETING_CHAIR")
                createdNode = meetingsNode.insertBefore(createdNode, meetingNode)

                createdTextNode = xmldoc.createTextNode("Ted Bond")
                createdNode.appendChild(createdTextNode)

                document.all.data.value = meetingsXML.documentElement.xml
                document.form1.submit()
            }
        //-->
        </SCRIPT>
    </HEAD>

    <BODY>
        <CENTER>
            <FORM NAME="form1" ACTION="http://default/db/echo.asp" METHOD="POST">
            <INPUT TYPE="HIDDEN" NAME="data">
            <INPUT TYPE="BUTTON" VALUE="Alter the document" onclick="alterDocument()">
            </FORM>
        </CENTER>
    </BODY>
</HTML>
```

Now when the user clicks the button with the caption `Alter the document`, the code in this page alters the XML document and sends it to the server. The ASP script on the server echoes the XML document back to the browser, which displays it, as you see in Figure 7.11. You can see the new `<MEETING_CHAIR>` element in that figure.

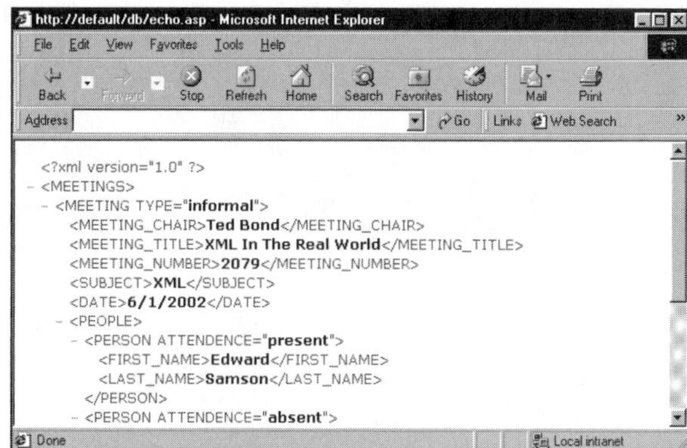

Figure 7.11 Altering an XML document in Internet Explorer.

We've put JavaScript to work in this chapter, parsing and accessing XML documents. In the next chapter, I'm going to put JavaScript to work treating XML data as database objects.

8

XML and Data Binding

IN THE PREVIOUS CHAPTER, WE TOOK A LOOK AT WORKING WITH XML documents in Internet Explorer using the DOM. In that chapter, we used methods such as `firstChild`, `lastChild`, `lastSibling`, and so on to work through a document. Using methods such as those give you complete access to the data in an XML document, but regarding an XML document as a node tree can be confusing, especially if you forget that the character data in an element is stored in its own node.

There's another way of handling XML documents in Internet Explorer, however, and it also bears exploration, which we'll do in this chapter. Internet Explorer enables you to read both HTML and XML documents and to store them in a database. Using the database methods that we'll see in this chapter, you can move from record to record through your data in a way that many programmers find easier to use than the DOM methods.

Data Binding in Internet Explorer

Internet Explorer specializes in *data binding*. With data binding, you can connect the data in documents to an *ActiveX Data Object* (*ADO*) database and then work with that data in an easy way. This technique is useful because data from a database can be sent as an XML document over the Internet and can be immediately converted back to a database in the browser, which means that programmers familiar with database programming can concentrate on using database methods, not DOM methods.

I'll take a look at data binding in Internet Explorer in general first, and then I'll work specifically with XML documents in this chapter. There are two parts to working with bound data in Internet Explorer—using *data source objects* (*DSOs*) and binding data to the HTML elements in a Web page.

More Details on Data Binding

You can find information about data binding in Internet Explorer at http://msdn.microsoft.com/workshop/c-frame.htm#/workshop/author/default.asp.

Using Data Source Objects

There are four data source objects in Internet Explorer: the *Microsoft HTML* (*MSHTML*) control, the *tabular data control* (*TDC*), the XML DSO, and XML data islands. (In fact, Internet Explorer also supports the relatively sophisticated *Remote Data Service* [*RDS*] DSO, which you use to connect to database applications, such as those that run in SQL-enabled application on a Web server.) Two of these DSOs, the XML DSO and XML data islands, support XML documents.

A DSO doesn't appear in a Web page (although, as we'll see at the end of the chapter, the XML DSO can display status messages in a page). You use a DSO to read a document and make its data available to the rest of the page. For a DSO to read data from a document, that data must be formatted correctly.

Here's an example HTML document, customer.htm, that holds data on sales made to customers. Here, I'm recording the customers' names and IDs, the date of the purchase, the department of the item purchased, and the name of the item. Note how I'm structuring an HTML page to hold data for Internet Explorer—by using the `<SPAN>` element. (You can also use other elements such as `<DIV>`) and can assign a type to each data item with the enclosing element's ID tag. As you can see, this technique cries out for XML formatting.)

```
<HTML>
    <HEAD>
        <TITLE>
            Customer Data
        </TITLE>
    </HEAD>

    <BODY>
        Name: <SPAN ID="NAME">Charles</SPAN><BR>
        ID: <SPAN ID="CUSTOMER_ID">58704</SPAN><BR>
```

```
    Purchase date: Date: <SPAN ID="PURCHASE_DATE">
        10/15/2001</SPAN><BR>
    Department: <SPAN ID="DEPARTMENT">
        Meat</SPAN><BR>
    Product: <SPAN ID="PRODUCT_NAME">Ham</SPAN><BR>

    Name: <SPAN ID="NAME">Franklin</SPAN><BR>
    ID: <SPAN ID="CUSTOMER_ID">58705</SPAN><BR>
    Purchase date: <SPAN ID="PURCHASE_DATE">
        10/15/2001</SPAN><BR>
    Department: <SPAN ID="DEPARTMENT">
        Produce</SPAN><BR>
    Product: <SPAN ID="PRODUCT_NAME">Tomatoes</SPAN><BR>

    Name: <SPAN ID="NAME">Phoebe</SPAN><BR>
    ID: <SPAN ID="CUSTOMER_ID">58706</SPAN><BR>
    Purchase date: <SPAN ID="PURCHASE_DATE">
        10/15/2001</SPAN><BR>
    Department: <SPAN ID="DEPARTMENT">
        Meat</SPAN><BR>
    Product: <SPAN ID="PRODUCT_NAME">Turkey</SPAN><BR>

    Name: <SPAN ID="NAME">Mark</SPAN><BR>
    ID: <SPAN ID="CUSTOMER_ID">58707</SPAN><BR>
    Purchase date: <SPAN ID="PURCHASE_DATE">
        10/15/2001</SPAN><BR>
    Department: <SPAN ID="DEPARTMENT">
        Meat</SPAN><BR>
    Product: <SPAN ID="PRODUCT_NAME">Beef</SPAN><BR>

    Name: <SPAN ID="NAME">Nancy</SPAN><BR>
    ID: <SPAN ID="CUSTOMER_ID">58708</SPAN><BR>
    Purchase date: <SPAN ID="PURCHASE_DATE">
        10/15/2001</SPAN><BR>
    Department: <SPAN ID="DEPARTMENT">
        Frozen</SPAN><BR>
    Product: <SPAN ID="PRODUCT_NAME">Broccoli</SPAN><BR>

    </BODY>
</HTML>
```

The most common way of handling data formatted as HTML documents is with the MSHTML DSO, and I'm going to use it here. A DSO reads a document like this one and converts it into a *recordset*. Each record in the recordset comes from the HTML or XML elements that you've used to store the data. For example, here's what the HTML for one record looks like:

```
Name: <SPAN ID="NAME">Charles</SPAN><BR>
ID: <SPAN ID="CUSTOMER_ID">58704</SPAN><BR>
Purchase date: Date: <SPAN ID="PURCHASE_DATE">
    10/15/2001</SPAN><BR>
```

continues ▸

```
Department: <SPAN ID="DEPARTMENT">
    Meat</SPAN><BR>
Product: <SPAN ID="PRODUCT_NAME">Ham</SPAN><BR>
```

This record has five *fields*: NAME, CUSTOMER_ID, PURCHASE_DATE, DEPARTMENT, and PRODUCT_NAME. A recordset is much like an array holding records; when you work with a particular record, you can access the data in the fields in each record individually. For example, to determine what item Charles has purchased, you just need to find his record and then check the PRODUCT_NAME field in that record.

Using the Internet Explorer <OBJECT> element, you can create an MSHTML DSO and bind it to customer.htm. Here, I'm naming this DSO dsoCustomer:

```
<OBJECT ID="dsoCustomer" DATA="customer.htm" HEIGHT="0" WIDTH="0">
</OBJECT>
```

The DSO will read and interpret customer.htm and convert that document into an ADO recordset (the type of recordset actually used in Internet Explorer is read-only, called an *ADOR* recordset). The DSO holds data from only one record at a time, and that record is called the *current record*. You can use the built-in methods of a recordset to navigate through your data by making other records the current record; some common methods are moveFirst, moveLast, moveNext, and movePrevious, which let you navigate from record to record. To actually display the data from this DSO, you can bind it to HTML elements.

Binding Data to HTML Elements

Quite a few elements in Internet Explorer support data properties that you can use to bind them to DSO. To connect to those properties, you use the DATASRC and DATAFLD attributes in those elements. You set the DATASRC attribute to the name of a DSO, and you set the DATAFLD attribute to the name of the data field to which you want to bind the element. The element will then display the data in the current record in the DSO. You can use the moveFirst, moveLast, moveNext, and movePrevious methods to make other records the current record, and the data in the bound elements will be updated automatically.

For example, if you've bound a text field control to the dsoCustomer DSO and to the NAME field in the DSO's records, that control will display the name "Charles" when the page first loads. Executing the moveNext method will make the next record in the recordset the current record, and the text field will display the name Franklin.

Here's a list of HTML elements in Internet Explorer detailing what property is actually bound when you use the `DATASRC` and `DATAFLD` attributes:

Element	Bound Properties
`A`	Binds to the `href` property; does not update data.
`APPLET`	Binds to the `param` property; updates data.
`BUTTON`	Binds to the `value` property; does not update data.
`DIV`	Binds to the `innerText` and `innerHTML` properties; does not update data.
`FRAME`	Binds to the `src` property; does not update data.
`IFRAME`	Binds to the `src` property; does not update data.
`IMG`	Binds to the `src` property; does not update data.
`INPUT TYPE=BUTTON`	Binds to the `value` property; does not update data.
`INPUT TYPE=CHECKBOX`	Binds to the `checked` property; updates data.
`INPUT TYPE=HIDDEN`	Binds to the `value` property; updates data.
`INPUT TYPE=PASSWORD`	Binds to the `value` property; updates data.
`INPUT TYPE=RADIO`	Binds to the `checked` property; updates data.
`INPUT TYPE=TEXT`	Binds to the `value` property; updates data.
`LABEL`	Binds to the `value` property; does not update data.
`MARQUEE`	Binds to the `innerText` and `innerHTML` properties; does not update data.
`OBJECT`	Binds to the `objects` property; updates data.
`PARAM`	Binds to the `param` property; updates data.
`SELECT`	Binds to the `text` property of an option; updates data.
`SPAN`	Binds to the `innerText` and `innerHTML` properties; does not update data.
`TABLE`	Constructs an entire table; does not update data.
`TEXTAREA`	Binds to the `value` property; updates data.

In addition, HTML tags have certain events that you use with data bindings:

Event	Description
`onafterupdate`	Happens after the data in the element is updated to the DSO
`onbeforeunload`	Happens before the page is unloaded
`onbeforeupdate`	Happens just before the data in the element is updated in the DSO
`onerrorupdate`	Happens if there an error stopped data from being updated in the DSO

It's time to put this to work. I'll start by adding an MSHTML control named `dsoCustomer` to a Web page, and connecting that DSO to customer.htm:

```
<HTML>
    <HEAD>
        <TITLE>
            Data Binding With the MSHTML DSO
        </TITLE>
    </HEAD>

    <BODY>

        <CENTER>
            <H1>
                Data Binding With the MSHTML DSO
            </H1>

            <OBJECT ID="dsoCustomer" DATA="customer.htm" HEIGHT="0" WIDTH="0">
            </OBJECT>
            .
            .
            .
```

Now I'll bind this DSO to a text field by setting that text field's `DATASRC` attribute to `#dsoCustomer` (Internet Explorer requires the # symbol before a DSO's name). Because a text field can display only one field of data at a time, I'll bind the `NAME` field to this control by setting its `DATAFLD` attribute to `NAME`:

```
<HTML>
    <HEAD>
        <TITLE>
            Data Binding With the MSHTML DSO
        </TITLE>
    </HEAD>

    <BODY>

        <CENTER>
            <H1>
                Data Binding With the MSHTML DSO
            </H1>

            <OBJECT ID="dsoCustomer" DATA="customer.htm" HEIGHT="0" WIDTH="0">
            </OBJECT>

            Name: <INPUT TYPE="TEXT" DATASRC="#dsoCustomer"
                DATAFLD="NAME" SIZE="10">
            .
            .
            .
```

I'll bind the `CUSTOMER_ID` field to another text field as well. I can also display text data from the DSO directly in a Web page—without using a text field control—by binding that DSO to a `<SPAN>` element in this way:

```
<HTML>
    <HEAD>
        <TITLE>
            Data Binding With the MSHTML DSO
        </TITLE>
    </HEAD>

    <BODY>

        <CENTER>
            <H1>
                Data Binding With the MSHTML DSO
            </H1>

            <OBJECT ID="dsoCustomer" DATA="customer.htm" HEIGHT="0" WIDTH="0">
            </OBJECT>

            Name: <INPUT TYPE="TEXT" DATASRC="#dsoCustomer"
                DATAFLD="NAME" SIZE="10">

            <P>
            ID: <INPUT TYPE="TEXT" DATASRC="#dsoCustomer"
                DATAFLD="CUSTOMER_ID" SIZE="5">

            <P>
            Purchase date: <SPAN DATASRC="#dsoCustomer"
                DATAFLD="PURCHASE_DATE"></SPAN>
    .
    .
    .
```

To show how to bind to other controls, I'll bind the `DEPARTMENT` field, which can take the values `Produce`, `Meat`, or `Frozen`, to a `<SELECT>` control, which displays a drop-down list. You bind this control to the `dsoCustomer` DSO as you do other controls, but you must also specify all possible values that the field you're binding, `DEPARTMENT`, can take as `<OPTION>` elements in the `<SELECT>` control, like this:

```
<HTML>
    <HEAD>
        <TITLE>
            Data Binding With the MSHTML DSO
        </TITLE>
    </HEAD>

    <BODY>
```

continues ▸

```
<CENTER>
    <H1>
        Data Binding With the MSHTML DSO
    </H1>

    <OBJECT ID="dsoCustomer" DATA="customer.htm" HEIGHT="0" WIDTH="0">
    </OBJECT>

    Name: <INPUT TYPE="TEXT" DATASRC="#dsoCustomer"
        DATAFLD="NAME" SIZE="10">

    <P>
    ID: <INPUT TYPE="TEXT" DATASRC="#dsoCustomer"
        DATAFLD="CUSTOMER_ID" SIZE="5">

    <P>
    Purchase date: <SPAN DATASRC="#dsoCustomer"
        DATAFLD="PURCHASE_DATE"></SPAN>

    <P>
    Department: <SELECT DATASRC="#dsoCustomer"
        DATAFLD="DEPARTMENT" SIZE="1">
        <OPTION VALUE="Produce">Produce
        <OPTION VALUE="Meat">Meat
        <OPTION VALUE="Frozen">Frozen
    </SELECT>

    <P>
    Product: <SPAN DATASRC="#dsoCustomer" DATAFLD="PRODUCT_NAME">
    </SPAN>
        .
        .
        .
```

Note that I'm also binding the `PRODUCT_NAME` field to another `<SPAN>` element. When the page first loads, you'll see the customer name, customer ID, purchase date, department, and product ID of the first record displayed in the elements that we've put in the page. But there's a problem—as you may recall, DSOs don't appear in the page, so how can the user move from record to record?

To let the user navigate through the recordset, you use the recordset's `moveFirst`, `moveLast`, `moveNext`, and `movePrevious` methods, and connect those methods to buttons. You can reach the recordset object inside the DSO as `dsoCustomer.recordset`, so using the `moveFirst` method to move to the first record in the recordset looks like this: `dsoCustomer.recordset.moveFirst()`. Following common usage, I'll give the buttons these captions:

Caption	Action
<<	Moves to the first record
<	Moves to the previous record
>	Moves to the next record
>>	Moves to the last record

Here's what the HTML for these buttons looks like:

```
<BUTTON ONCLICK=
    "dsoCustomer.recordset.moveFirst()" >&lt;&lt;
</BUTTON>
<BUTTON ONCLICK
    "dsoCustomer.recordset.movePrevious()" >&lt;
</BUTTON>
<BUTTON ONCLICK
    "dsoCustomer.recordset.moveNext()" >&gt;
</BUTTON>
<BUTTON ONCLICK=
    "dsoCustomer.recordset.moveLast()">&gt;&gt;
</BUTTON>
```

Before using the `moveNext` and `movePrevious` methods, however, it's worth checking to make sure that there actually is a next or previous record to move to. (If you move past the end of the recordset, the bound elements in your page will appear blank.) You can use the `recordset` object's `BOF` (beginning of file) property to see if you're at the beginning of the recordset, and the `EOF` (end of file) property to see if you're at the end of the recordset. To make sure that we're not trying to move outside the recordset, I'll use this code:

```
<HTML>
    <HEAD>
        <TITLE>
            Data Binding With the MSHTML DSO
        </TITLE>
    </HEAD>

    <BODY>

        <CENTER>
            <H1>
                Data Binding With the MSHTML DSO
            </H1>

            <OBJECT ID="dsoCustomer" DATA="customer.htm" HEIGHT="0" WIDTH="0">
            </OBJECT>

            Name: <INPUT TYPE="TEXT" DATASRC="#dsoCustomer"
```

continues ►

```
            DATAFLD="NAME" SIZE="10">

        <P>
        ID: <INPUT TYPE="TEXT" DATASRC="#dsoCustomer"
            DATAFLD="CUSTOMER_ID" SIZE="5">

        <P>
        Purchase date: <SPAN DATASRC="#dsoCustomer"
            DATAFLD="PURCHASE_DATE"></SPAN>

        <P>
        Department: <SELECT DATASRC="#dsoCustomer"
            DATAFLD="DEPARTMENT" SIZE="1">
            <OPTION VALUE="Produce">Produce
            <OPTION VALUE="Meat">Meat
            <OPTION VALUE="Frozen">Frozen
        </SELECT>

        <P>
        Product: <SPAN DATASRC="#dsoCustomer" DATAFLD="PRODUCT_NAME">
        </SPAN>

        <P>
        <BUTTON ONCLICK=
            "dsoCustomer.recordset.moveFirst()" >&lt;&lt;
        </BUTTON>
        <BUTTON ONCLICK="if (!dsoCustomer.recordset.BOF)
            dsoCustomer.recordset.movePrevious()" >&lt;
        </BUTTON>
        <BUTTON ONCLICK="if (!dsoCustomer.recordset.EOF)
            dsoCustomer.recordset.moveNext()" >&gt;
        </BUTTON>
        <BUTTON ONCLICK=
            "dsoCustomer.recordset.moveLast()">&gt;&gt;
        </BUTTON>
    </CENTER>
  </BODY>
</HTML>
```

You can see this page in operation in Figure 8.1. As you see in that page, the data from customer.htm is displayed. The user can move from record to record using the buttons at the bottom of the page.

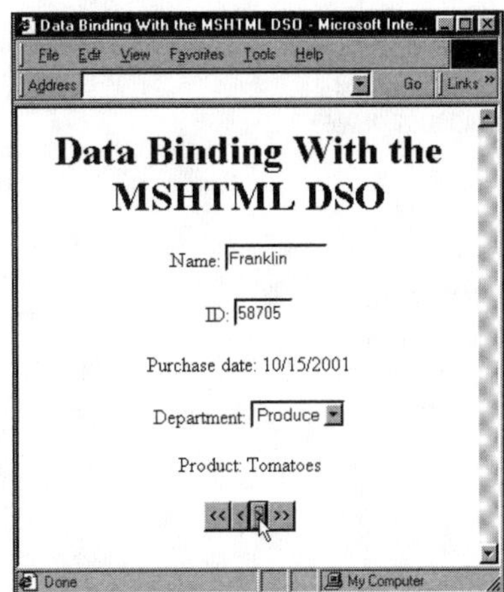

Figure 8.1 Using data binding in Internet >Explorer.

So much for data binding and HTML; it's time to start working with XML.

Data Binding with XML

I'll start by converting customer.htm into XML. In customer.htm, I had to use the `ID` attribute of `<SPAN>` elements to name the fields in a record; in XML, I can simply create a new element. Here's what customer.htm looks like in XML format:

```
<?xml version="1.0"?>
<CUSTOMERS>

    <CUSTOMER>
        <NAME>Charles</NAME>
        <CUSTOMER_ID>58704</CUSTOMER_ID>
        <PURCHASE_DATE>10/15/2001</PURCHASE_DATE>
        <DEPARTMENT>Meat</DEPARTMENT>
        <PRODUCT_NAME>Ham</PRODUCT_NAME>
    </CUSTOMER>

    <CUSTOMER>
        <NAME>Franklin</NAME>
        <CUSTOMER_ID>58705</CUSTOMER_ID>
        <PURCHASE_DATE>10/15/2001</PURCHASE_DATE>
        <DEPARTMENT>Produce</DEPARTMENT>
        <PRODUCT_NAME>Tomatoes</PRODUCT_NAME>
    </CUSTOMER>

    <CUSTOMER>
        <NAME>Phoebe</NAME>
```

continues ▸

```
        <CUSTOMER_ID>58706</CUSTOMER_ID>
        <PURCHASE_DATE>10/15/2001</PURCHASE_DATE>
        <DEPARTMENT>Meat</DEPARTMENT>
        <PRODUCT_NAME>Turkey</PRODUCT_NAME>
    </CUSTOMER>

    <CUSTOMER>
        <NAME>Mark</NAME>
        <CUSTOMER_ID>58707</CUSTOMER_ID>
        <PURCHASE_DATE>10/15/2001</PURCHASE_DATE>
        <DEPARTMENT>Meat</DEPARTMENT>
    <PRODUCT_NAME>Beef</PRODUCT_NAME>
    </CUSTOMER>

    <CUSTOMER>
        <NAME>Nancy</NAME>
        <CUSTOMER_ID>58708</CUSTOMER_ID>
        <PURCHASE_DATE>10/15/2001</PURCHASE_DATE>
        <DEPARTMENT>Frozen</DEPARTMENT>
        <PRODUCT_NAME>Broccoli</PRODUCT_NAME>
    </CUSTOMER>

</CUSTOMERS>
```

As you can see, each record has become a `<CUSTOMER>` element. You can use whatever name you want for elements, and Internet Explorer will understand what you mean. In the previous HTML example, I used the MSHTML control as a DSO, but that's not going to work here. Instead, you can use either an XML data island or a special applet-based XML DSO that comes with Internet Explorer. I'm going to start with XML data islands.

XML Single-Record Binding Using XML Data Islands

To see how to bind HTML elements to an XML data island, I'll write an example. In this case, I'll add a data island for customer.xml with the ID `customers` to a new Web page, like this:

```
<HTML>
    <HEAD>
        <TITLE>
            Single Record Binding Using XML Data Islands
        </TITLE>
    </HEAD>

    <XML SRC="customer.xml" ID="customers"></XML>
    .
    .
    .
```

Now customers can act like a DSO, just like any other DSO (which is why data islands are called data islands). I can bind this DSO to assorted HTML elements as we've already seen in this chapter:

```
<HTML>
    <HEAD>
        <TITLE>
            Single Record Binding Using XML Data Islands
        </TITLE>
    </HEAD>

    <XML SRC="customer.xml" ID="customers"></XML>

    <BODY>
        <CENTER>
            <H1>
                Single Record Binding Using XML Data Islands
            </H1>

            Name: <INPUT TYPE="TEXT" DATASRC="#customers"
                DATAFLD="NAME" SIZE=10>

            <P>
            CUSTOMER_ID: <INPUT TYPE="TEXT" DATASRC="#customers"
                DATAFLD="CUSTOMER_ID" SIZE=5>

            <P>
            Department: <SELECT DATASRC="#customers"
                DATAFLD="DEPARTMENT" SIZE=1>

                <OPTION VALUE="Meat">Meat
                <OPTION VALUE="Produce">Produce
                <OPTION VALUE="Frozen">Frozen
            </SELECT>

            <P>
            Purchase date: <SPAN DATASRC="#customers"
                DATAFLD="PURCHASE_DATE"></SPAN>

            <P>
            Product: <SPAN DATASRC="#customers" DATAFLD="PRODUCT_NAME"></SPAN><P>
            .
            .
            .
        </CENTER>
    </BODY>
</HTML>
```

Properties, Methods, and Events of XML DSOs

In the example at the beginning of this chapter, we saw that you could use recordset methods such as `moveFirst`, `moveLast`, `moveNext`, and `movePrevious` to move around in a recordset. I'll make that more systematic now. In particular, the recordset object in an XML DSO has these properties:

Property	Description
`absolutePage`	The page where the current record is
`absolutePosition`	The position in a recordset of the current record
`BOF`	True if the current record position is before the first record
`cacheSize`	The number of records from a recordset object that are cached locally
`cursorLocation`	The location of the cursor for the recordset
`cursorType`	The type of database cursor used
`editMode`	Specification for whether editing is in progress
`EOF`	True if the current position is after the last record
`lockType`	The type of database locking in force
`maxRecords`	The maximum number of records to return to a recordset from a query
`pageCount`	The number of pages of data that the recordset contains
`pageSize`	The number of records that make up one page
`recordCount`	The number of records in the recordset
`state`	The state of the recordset (open or closed)
`status`	The status of the current record
`stayInSync`	Specification for whether a hierarchical recordset should remain in contact with the data source

Here are the methods of the recordset objects inside XML DSOs:

Method	Description
`addNew`	Adds a new record to the recordset.
`cancel`	Cancels execution of a pending `Execute` or `Open` request.
`cancelUpdate`	Cancels a pending update operation.
`clone`	Creates a copy of the recordset.
`close`	Closes a recordset.
`delete`	Deletes the current record (or group of records).

`find`	Searches the record set (although the Structured Query Language syntax required here is not supported in Internet Explorer yet).
`getRows`	Reads records and stores them in an array.
`getString`	Gets the recordset as a string.
`move`	Moves the position of the current record.
`moveFirst`, `moveLast`, `moveNext`, `movePrevious`	Enable you to navigate to various positions in the recordset.
`nextRecordSet`	Clears the current recordset object and returns the next recordset. This is used with hierarchical recordsets.
`open`	Opens a database.
`requery`	Re-executes the query that created the recordset.
`save`	Saves the recordset in a file.
`supports`	Indicates the features that the recordset supports. You must pass long integer values that correspond to the various ADO methods, as defined in the Microsoft ADO documentation. For example, passing this method a value of `0x1000400` (`0x` specifies a hexadecimal value) returns a value of `true`, indicating that the recordset supports the `addNew` method; passing a value of `0x10000` returns a value of `false`, indicating that the recordset does not support the `updateBatch` method.

XML DSOs also have a number of events that you can handle. (Recall that we saw how to handle XML document events in Internet Explorer at the end of the previous chapter.)

Event	Description
`onDataAvailable`	Happens each time a batch of data is downloaded
`onDatasetChanged`	Happens when the data set was changed
`onDatasetComplete`	Happens when the data is downloaded and ready for use
`onReadyStateChange`	Happens when the `ReadyState` property changes
`onRowEnter`	Happens when a new record becomes the current one
`onRowExit`	Happens just before exiting the current record
`onRowsDelete`	Happens when a row is deleted
`onRowsInserted`	Happens when a row is inserted
`onCellChange`	Happens when the data in a bound control changes and the focus leaves that cell

To let the user navigate around in the recordset created from customer.xml, I'll add the same buttons that we saw in the earlier HTML example, using methods such as `customers.recordset.moveNext()` to navigate, like this:

```
<HTML>
    <HEAD>
        <TITLE>Single Record Binding Using XML Data Islands</TITLE>
    </HEAD>

    <XML SRC="customer.xml" ID="customers"></XML>

    <BODY>
        <CENTER>
            <H1>
                Single Record Binding Using XML Data Islands
            </H1>

            Name: <INPUT TYPE="TEXT" DATASRC="#customers"
                DATAFLD="NAME" SIZE=10>
            <P>

            Customer ID: <INPUT TYPE="TEXT" DATASRC="#customers"
                DATAFLD="CUSTOMER_ID" SIZE=5>

            <P>
            Purchase date: <SPAN DATASRC="#customers"
                DATAFLD="PURCHASE_DATE"></SPAN><P>
            Product: <SPAN DATASRC="#customers" DATAFLD="PRODUCT_NAME"></SPAN>

            <P>
            Department: <SELECT DATASRC="#customers"
                DATAFLD="DEPARTMENT" SIZE=1>

            <OPTION VALUE="Meat">Meat
            <OPTION VALUE="Produce">Produce
            <OPTION VALUE="Frozen">Frozen
            </SELECT>

            <P>
            <BUTTON ONCLICK="customers.recordset.moveFirst()" >
                 &lt;&lt;
            </BUTTON>
            <BUTTON ONCLICK="if (!customers.recordset.BOF)
                customers.recordset.movePrevious()" >
                &lt;
            </BUTTON>
            <BUTTON ONCLICK="if (!customers.recordset.EOF)
                customers.recordset.moveNext()" >
                &gt;
            </BUTTON>
            <BUTTON ONCLICK="customers.recordset.moveLast()">
                &gt;&gt;
            </BUTTON>
```

```
</CENTER>
    </BODY>
</HTML>
```

You can see this page in Figure 8.2, where you see the fields of the current record displayed in bound HTML elements. The user can click the buttons in the page to navigate through the recordset.

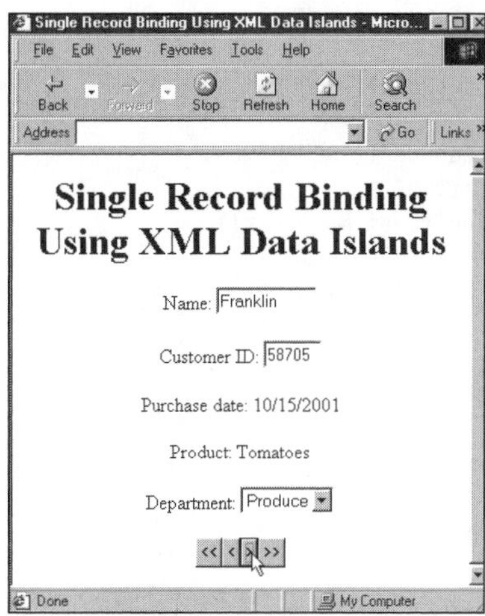

Figure 8.2 Using data binding to display an XML document in Internet Explorer.

As you can see in the previous table, there's a lot more you can do with a recordset than just navigate through it. For example, it's often useful to access the individual fields in a record. Say that you wanted to get the value in the `CUSTOMER_ID` field of the current record in the DSO. You could use the expression `customers.recordset("CUSTOMER_ID")` to do that.

You might note how much easier accessing data in recordset fields is than using DOM methods such as `nextChild` and `lastSibling` to navigate a node tree. If you consider an XML document as a database, it can make life a good deal easier.

I'll access individual fields in records now in an example to make this concrete. In this case, I'll loop over all the records in the database (which I can do with a `while` loop, looping until the recordset's `EOF` property is true) and display the customer name, the item purchased, and what department the purchase was made in. Here's what the code looks like:

```
<HTML>
    <HEAD>
        <TITLE>
            Accessing individual data fields
```

continues ▸

```
        </TITLE>

        <XML ID="customer" SRC="customer.xml"></XML>

        <SCRIPT LANGUAGE="JavaScript">
            function viewData()
            {
                while (!customer.recordset.EOF) {
                    div1.innerHTML +=
                    customer.recordset("NAME") +
                    " bought " +
                    customer.recordset("PRODUCT_NAME") +
                    " from the " +
                    customer.recordset("DEPARTMENT") +
                    " department.<BR>"
                    customer.recordset.moveNext()
                }
            }
        </SCRIPT>
    </HEAD>

    <BODY>
        <CENTER>
            <H1>
                Accessing individual data fields
            </H1>
        </CENTER>

        <FORM>
            <CENTER>
                <INPUT TYPE="BUTTON" VALUE="View data"
                    ONCLICK="viewData()">
            </CENTER>
        </FORM>
        <DIV ID="div1">
        </DIV>
    </BODY>
</HTML>
```

You can see this page in operation in Figure 8.3. As you can see there, the data from the individual fields in the various records has been assembled and displayed.

Besides working with single records as we have up to this point, you can also work with all the data in an XML document at once when you bind it to a table.

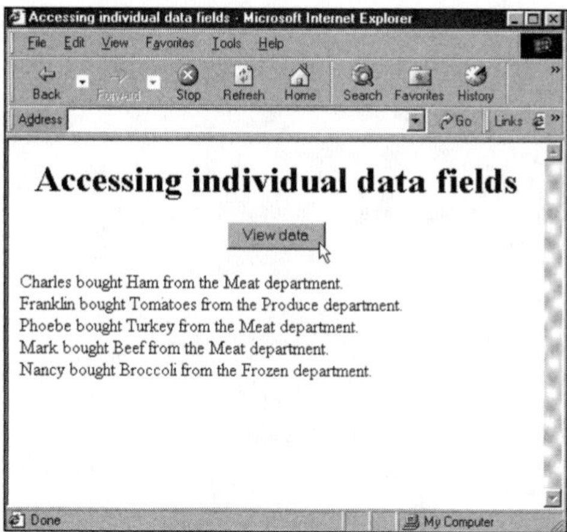

Figure 8.3 Accessing individual data fields.

Tabular Data Binding and XML

When you bind a recordset to an HTML table, the table can display the entire recordset. Here's an example; in this case, I'll bind the data in customer.xml to a table. I start by creating an XML data island, giving the data island the ID `customers`:

```
<HTML>
    <HEAD>
        <TITLE>
            Tabular Binding with XML Data Islands
        </TITLE>
    </HEAD>

    <BODY>
        <CENTER>
            <H1>
                Tabular Binding with XML Data Islands
            </H1>

            <XML SRC="customer.xml" ID="customers"></XML>
            .
            .
            .
```

To bind the data in customer.xml to a table, all I have to do is set a table's DATASRC attribute to customers:

```
<HTML>
    <HEAD>
        <TITLE>
            Tabular Binding with XML Data Islands
        </TITLE>
    </HEAD>

    <BODY>
        <CENTER>
            <H1>
                Tabular Binding with XML Data Islands
            </H1>

            <XML SRC="customer.xml" ID="customers"></XML>

             <TABLE DATASRC="#customers" CELLSPACING="10">
                .
                .
                .
```

The fields in the records of customer.xml are NAME, CUSTOMER_ID, PURCHASE_DATE, DEPARTMENT, and DATE. I will bind those fields to the individual cells in a table. Here's how that works:

```
<HTML>
    <HEAD>
        <TITLE>
            Tabular Binding with XML Data Islands
        </TITLE>
    </HEAD>

    <BODY>
        <CENTER>
            <H1>
                Tabular Binding with XML Data Islands
            </H1>

            <XML SRC="customer.xml" ID="customers"></XML>

             <TABLE DATASRC="#customers" CELLSPACING="10">
                 <THEAD>
                     <TR>
                         <TH>Name</TH>
                         <TH>Customer ID</TH>
                         <TH>Purchase Date</TH>
                         <TH>Department</TH>
                         <TH>Product</TH>
                     </TR>
                  </THEAD>
```

```
                <TBODY>
                    <TR>
                        <TD>
                            <SPAN DATAFLD="NAME">
                            </SPAN>
                        </TD>
                        <TD>
                            <SPAN DATAFLD="CUSTOMER_ID">
                            </SPAN>
                        </TD>
                        <TD>
                            <SPAN DATAFLD="PURCHASE_DATE">
                            </SPAN>
                        </TD>
                        <TD>
                            <SPAN DATAFLD="DEPARTMENT">
                            </SPAN>
                        </TD>
                        <TD>
                            <SPAN DATAFLD="PRODUCT_NAME">
                            </SPAN>
                        </TD>
                    </TR>
                </TBODY>
            </TABLE>
        </CENTER>
    </BODY>
</HTML>
```

You can see the results in Figure 8.4, where the data from customer.xml is displayed in a table.

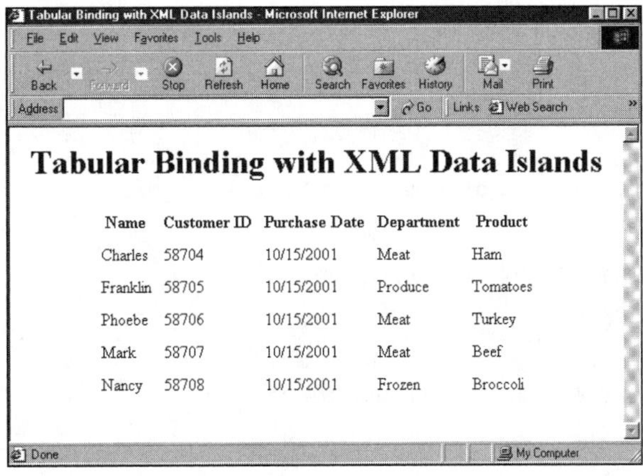

Figure 8.4 Binding data to a table in Internet Explorer.

There's another DSO that you can use with XML documents in Internet Explorer—the XML DSO.

Single-Record Data Binding with the XML DSO

Starting in Internet Explorer 4, Microsoft has included an XML DSO expressly designed to be used with XML. This DSO is a little odd because it's not internal to Internet Explorer; instead, it's implemented as a Java applet. You can embed this applet in a page and create an XML DSO like this with the HTML <APPLET> element:

```
<APPLET
    CODE="com.ms.xml.dso.XMLDSO.class"
    ID="IDNAME"
    WIDTH="0"
    HEIGHT="0"
    MAYSCRIPT="true">
    <PARAM NAME="URL" VALUE="XMLPageURL">
</APPLET>
```

Here, you pass the URL of the XML document as a parameter to the XML DSO applet, using the <PARAM> element, and then give this DSO a name with the <APPLET> ID attribute.

In the next example, I'll put the XML DSO to work, connecting it to customer.xml. To bind customer.xml to HTML elements, I start by adding the XML applet to a Web page, calling this DSO `dsoCustomer`, and then passing it the URL of the document to read as a parameter:

```
<HTML>
    <HEAD>
        <TITLE>
            Single Record Binding Using the XML DSO
        </TITLE>
    </HEAD>

    <BODY>
        <CENTER>
            <H1>
                Single Record Binding Using the XML DSO
            </H1>

            <APPLET CODE="com.ms.xml.dso.XMLDSO.class"
                ID="dsoCustomer"
                WIDTH="0" HEIGHT="0"
                MAYSCRIPT="true">
                <PARAM NAME="URL" VALUE="customer.xml">
            </APPLET>

            .
            .
            .
```

That's all it takes. This DSO exposes a recordset object as XML data islands do, so I can bind HTML elements to it as we've done before:

```
<HTML>
    <HEAD>
        <TITLE>
            Single Record Binding Using the XML DSO
        </TITLE>
    </HEAD>

    <BODY>
        <CENTER>
            <H1>
                Single Record Binding Using the XML DSO
            </H1>

            <APPLET CODE="com.ms.xml.dso.XMLDSO.class"
                ID="dsoCustomer"
                WIDTH="0" HEIGHT="0"
                MAYSCRIPT="true">
               <PARAM NAME="URL" VALUE="customer.xml">
            </APPLET>

            Name:
            <INPUT TYPE="TEXT" DATASRC="#dsoCustomer"
                DATAFLD="NAME" SIZE=10>

            <P>
            Customer ID:
            <INPUT TYPE="TEXT" DATASRC="#dsoCustomer"
                DATAFLD="CUSTOMER_ID" SIZE=5>

            <P>
            Purchase date:
            <SPAN DATASRC="#dsoCustomer"
                DATAFLD="PURCHASE_DATE"></SPAN>

            <P>
            Department:
            <SELECT DATASRC="#dsoCustomer"
                DATAFLD="DEPARTMENT" SIZE=1>

                <OPTION VALUE="Meat">Meat
                <OPTION VALUE="Produce">Produce
                <OPTION VALUE="Frozen">Frozen
            </SELECT>

            <P>
            Product:
            <SPAN DATASRC="#dsoCustomer" DATAFLD="PRODUCT_NAME">
            </SPAN>
            .
            .
            .
```

I can use the recordset object's methods, such as `moveNext` to move to the next record, or `movePrevious` to move to the previous one, with buttons like this:

```
<HTML>
    <HEAD>
        <TITLE>
            Single Record Binding Using the XML DSO
        </TITLE>
    </HEAD>

    <BODY>
        <CENTER>
            <H1>
                Single Record Binding Using the XML DSO
            </H1>

            <APPLET CODE="com.ms.xml.dso.XMLDSO.class"
                ID="dsoCustomer"
                WIDTH="0" HEIGHT="0"
                MAYSCRIPT="true">
                <PARAM NAME="URL" VALUE="customer.xml">
            </APPLET>

            Name:
            <INPUT TYPE="TEXT" DATASRC="#dsoCustomer"
                DATAFLD="NAME" SIZE=10>

            <P>
            Customer ID:
            <INPUT TYPE="TEXT" DATASRC="#dsoCustomer"
                DATAFLD="CUSTOMER_ID" SIZE=5>

            <P>
            Purchase date:
            <SPAN DATASRC="#dsoCustomer"
                DATAFLD="PURCHASE_DATE"></SPAN>

            <P>
            Department:
            <SELECT DATASRC="#dsoCustomer"
                DATAFLD="DEPARTMENT" SIZE=1>

                <OPTION VALUE="Meat">Meat
                <OPTION VALUE="Produce">Produce
                <OPTION VALUE="Frozen">Frozen
            </SELECT>

            <P>
            Product:
            <SPAN DATASRC="#dsoCustomer" DATAFLD="PRODUCT_NAME">
            </SPAN>

            <P>
```

```
<BUTTON ONCLICK="dsoCustomer.recordset.moveFirst()" >
    &lt;&lt;
</BUTTON>
<BUTTON ONCLICK="if (!dsoCustomer.recordset.BOF)
    dsoCustomer.recordset.movePrevious()" >
    &lt;
</BUTTON>
<BUTTON ONCLICK="if (!dsoCustomer.recordset.EOF)
    dsoCustomer.recordset.moveNext()" >
    &gt;
</BUTTON>
<BUTTON ONCLICK="dsoCustomer.recordset.moveLast()">
    &gt;&gt;
</BUTTON>

        </CENTER>

    </BODY>
</HTML>
```

You can see this page at work in Figure 8.5. The XML DOS applet works as expected, but the fact that it has remained an applet external to Internet Explorer suggests that Microsoft may discard it sooner or later in favor of XML islands.

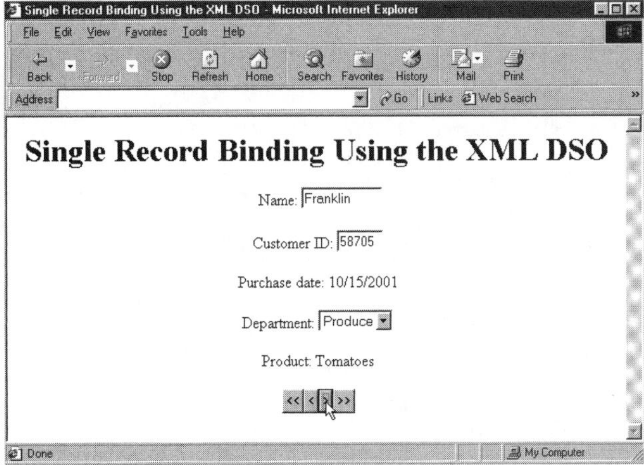

Figure 8.5 Single-record binding using the XML DSO in Internet Explorer.

As with XML data islands, you can also bind the XML DSO to tables, as described in the next section.

Tabular Data Binding with the XML DSO

It's as easy to bind the XML DSO to tables as it was to bind XML data islands to tables. Here's an example to show how this works. In this case, I'm just binding customer.xml to a table using the XML DSO, and I'm displaying all the fields in the various records of customer.xml at once:

```
<HTML>
    <HEAD>
        <TITLE>
            Binding the XML DSO to Tables
        </TITLE>
    </HEAD>

    <BODY>
        <CENTER>
            <H1>
                Binding the XML DSO to Tables
            </H1>

            <APPLET CODE="com.ms.xml.dso.XMLDSO.class"
                ID="customers"
                WIDTH="0" HEIGHT="0"
                MAYSCRIPT="true">
                <PARAM NAME="URL" VALUE="customer.xml">
            </APPLET>

             <TABLE DATASRC="#customers" CELLSPACING="10">
                 <THEAD>
                     <TR>
                         <TH>Name</TH>
                         <TH>Customer ID</TH>
                         <TH>Purchase Date</TH>
                         <TH>Department</TH>
                         <TH>Product</TH>
                     </TR>
                 </THEAD>

                 <TBODY>
                     <TR>
                         <TD>
                             <SPAN DATAFLD="NAME">
                             </SPAN>
                         </TD>
                         <TD>
                             <SPAN DATAFLD="CUSTOMER_ID">
                             </SPAN>
                         </TD>
                         <TD>
                             <SPAN DATAFLD="PURCHASE_DATE">
                             </SPAN>
                         </TD>
```

```
                    <TD>
                        <SPAN DATAFLD="DEPARTMENT">
                        </SPAN>
                    </TD>
                    <TD>
                        <SPAN DATAFLD="PRODUCT_NAME">
                        </SPAN>
                    </TD>
                </TR>
            </TBODY>
        </TABLE>
    </CENTER>
  </BODY>
</HTML>
```

That's all it takes; you can see this page in action in Figure 8.6.

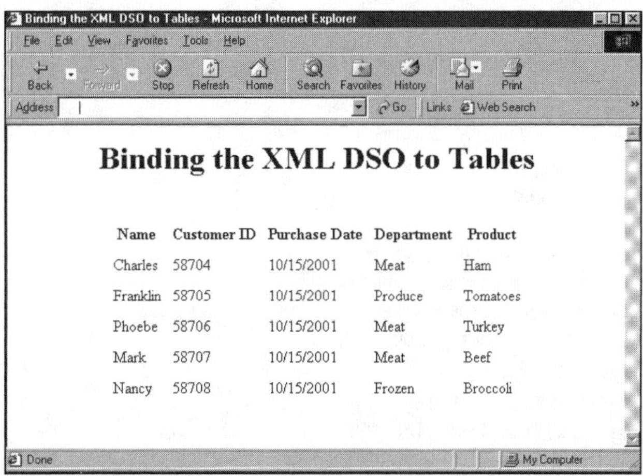

Figure 8.6 Tabular data binding with the XML DSO in Internet Explorer.

XML and Hierarchical Data

One of the most interesting developments in database handling is the capability to create hierarchical recordsets, where a record can actually contain an entire new recordset. XML documents represent a perfect way of storing hierarchical recordsets because you can enclose one set of elements inside another easily.

Here's an example; in this case, I'm adding records about deliveries made to the customers in customer.xml in a new XML document, deliveries.xml:

```
<?xml version="1.0"?>
<CUSTOMERS>
    <CUSTOMER>
        <NAME>Charles</NAME>
        <RECORD>
            <CUSTOMER_ID>58704</CUSTOMER_ID>
            <PURCHASE_DATE>10/15/2001</PURCHASE_DATE>
            <DEPARTMENT>Meat</DEPARTMENT>
            <PRODUCT_NAME>Ham</PRODUCT_NAME>
            <DELIVERY>
                <DATE>10/20/2001</DATE>
                <TOTAL_COST>$1.99</TOTAL_COST>
            </DELIVERY>
            <DELIVERY>
                <DATE>10/25/2001</DATE>
                <TOTAL_COST>$1.49</TOTAL_COST>
            </DELIVERY>
        </RECORD>
    </CUSTOMER>
    <CUSTOMER>
        <NAME>Franklin</NAME>
        <RECORD>
            <CUSTOMER_ID>58705</CUSTOMER_ID>
            <PURCHASE_DATE>10/15/2001</PURCHASE_DATE>
            <DEPARTMENT>Produce</DEPARTMENT>
            <PRODUCT_NAME>Tomatoes</PRODUCT_NAME>
            <DELIVERY>
                <DATE>10/20/2001</DATE>
                <TOTAL_COST>$3.00</TOTAL_COST>
            </DELIVERY>
            <DELIVERY>
                <DATE>10/25/2001</DATE>
                <TOTAL_COST>$2.95</TOTAL_COST>
            </DELIVERY>
        </RECORD>
    </CUSTOMER>
    <CUSTOMER>
        <NAME>Phoebe</NAME>
        <RECORD>
            <CUSTOMER_ID>58706</CUSTOMER_ID>
            <PURCHASE_DATE>10/15/2001</PURCHASE_DATE>
            <DEPARTMENT>Meat</DEPARTMENT>
            <PRODUCT_NAME>Turkey</PRODUCT_NAME>
            <DELIVERY>
                <DATE>10/20/2001</DATE>
                <TOTAL_COST>$4.99</TOTAL_COST>
            </DELIVERY>
```

```
            <DELIVERY>
                <DATE>10/25/2001</DATE>
                <TOTAL_COST>$8.99</TOTAL_COST>
            </DELIVERY>
        </RECORD>
    </CUSTOMER>
    <CUSTOMER>
        <NAME>Mark</NAME>
        <RECORD>
            <CUSTOMER_ID>58707</CUSTOMER_ID>
            <PURCHASE_DATE>10/15/2001</PURCHASE_DATE>
            <DEPARTMENT>Meat</DEPARTMENT>
            <PRODUCT_NAME>Beef</PRODUCT_NAME>
            <DELIVERY>
                <DATE>10/20/2001</DATE>
                <TOTAL_COST>$3.95</TOTAL_COST>
            </DELIVERY>
            <DELIVERY>
                <DATE>10/25/2001</DATE>
                <TOTAL_COST>$6.95</TOTAL_COST>
            </DELIVERY>
        </RECORD>
    </CUSTOMER>
    <CUSTOMER>
        <NAME>Nancy</NAME>
        <RECORD>
            <CUSTOMER_ID>58708</CUSTOMER_ID>
            <PURCHASE_DATE>10/15/2001</PURCHASE_DATE>
            <DEPARTMENT>Frozen</DEPARTMENT>
            <PRODUCT_NAME>Broccoli</PRODUCT_NAME>
            <DELIVERY>
                <DATE>10/20/2001</DATE>
                <TOTAL_COST>$1.99</TOTAL_COST>
            </DELIVERY>
            <DELIVERY>
                <DATE>10/25/2001</DATE>
                <TOTAL_COST>$2.99</TOTAL_COST>
            </DELIVERY>
        </RECORD>
    </CUSTOMER>
</CUSTOMERS>
```

In this case, each `<RECORD>` element itself contains two `<DELIVERY>` elements (which contain `<DATE>` and `<TOTAL_COST>` elements). A DSO can't simply treat multiple enclosed records like this as a single record because that would give two or more fields in the record the same name. Instead, Internet Explorer makes the recordset into a hierarchical recordset and gives each `<DELIVERY>` element its own subrecordset.

How do you refer to a subrecordset in a hierarchical database? For example, how can you refer to the `<DELIVERY>` elements in each `<RECORD>` element? You do that by referring to a new recordset, `RECORD.DELIVERY`. This expression refers to the child recordset made up of the `<DELIVERY>` elements in the current record.

As usual, this is made easier to understand with an example, so take a look at this code. Here, I'm binding deliveries.xml to a table and displaying the `<DELIVERY>` records for each customer using tables. I start by binding a table to an XML data island and displaying the name of each customer, like this:

```
<HTML>
    <HEAD>
        <TITLE>
            Using XML With Hierarchical Records
        </TITLE>
    </HEAD>

    <BODY>

        <CENTER>
            <H1>
                Using XML With Hierarchical Records
            </H1>

            <XML SRC="deliveries.xml" ID=dsoCustomer></XML>

            <TABLE DATASRC="#dsoCustomer" BORDER="1">
                <TR>
                    <TH><DIV DATAFLD="NAME"></DIV></TH>
                    <TD>
            .
            .
            .
```

Next, I bind a table to the `RECORD` field in the current record:

```
<HTML>
    <HEAD>
        <TITLE>
            Using XML With Hierarchical Records
        </TITLE>
    </HEAD>

    <BODY>

        <CENTER>
            <H1>
                Using XML With Hierarchical Records
            </H1>
```

```
        <XML SRC="deliveries.xml" ID=dsoCustomer></XML>

        <TABLE DATASRC="#dsoCustomer" BORDER="1">
            <TR>
                <TH><DIV DATAFLD="NAME"></DIV></TH>
                <TD>
                    <TABLE DATASRC="#dsoCustomer"
                    DATAFLD="RECORD">
        .
        .
        .
```

To display the data from the <DATE> and <TOTAL_COST> elements in each <DELIVERY> record, I bind one final internal table to the RECORD.DELIVERY recordset:

```
<HTML>
    <HEAD>
        <TITLE>
            Using XML With Hierarchical Records
        </TITLE>
    </HEAD>

    <BODY>

        <CENTER>
            <H1>
                Using XML With Hierarchical Records
            </H1>

            <XML SRC="deliveries.xml" ID=dsoCustomer></XML>

            <TABLE DATASRC="#dsoCustomer" BORDER="1">
                <TR>
                    <TH><DIV DATAFLD="NAME"></DIV></TH>
                    <TD>
                        <TABLE DATASRC="#dsoCustomer"
                        DATAFLD="RECORD">
                            <TR>
                                <TD>
                                <TABLE DATASRC="#dsoCustomer"
                                    CELLPADDING = "5"
                                    DATAFLD="RECORD.DELIVERY">
                                    <TR ALIGN = "LEFT">
                                        <TH>Date</TH>
                                        <TH>Total Cost</TH>
                                    </TR>
                                    <TR ALIGN = "LEFT">
                                        <TD><DIV DATAFLD="DATE">
                                        </DIV></TD>
                                        <TD><DIV
                                        DATAFLD="TOTAL_COST">
```

continues ▸

```
                                        </DIV></TD>
                                    </TR>
                                </TABLE>
                                </TD>
                            </TR>
                        </TABLE>
                    </TD>
                </TR>
            </TABLE>
        </CENTER>
    </BODY>
</HTML>
```

This page appears in Internet Explorer in Figure 8.7. As you can see there, each customer's name is displayed next to the dates and costs of their deliveries. Now you're handling hierarchical recordsets and XML.

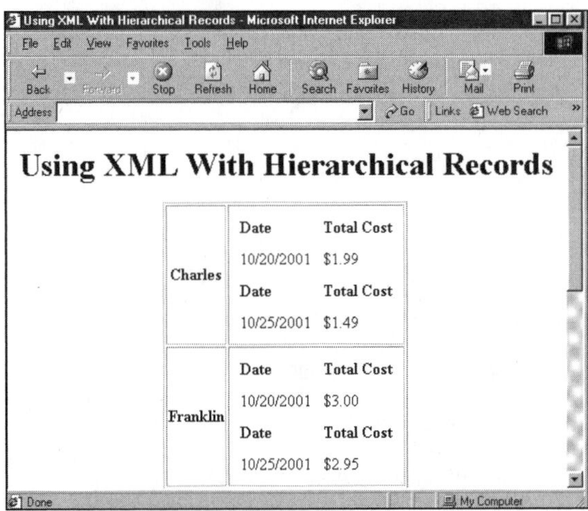

Figure 8.7 Displaying hierarchical recordsets in Internet Explorer.

Handling Variable-Size Hierarchical Data in XML Documents

We've seen that Internet Explorer DSOs can handle hierarchical recordsets when each record itself has an internal recordset. The internal recordsets that I used each contained two records, but that's hardly a realistic example; in real-world documents, recordsets can be of any length. How do the DSOs in Internet Explorer stack up here? Take a look at this new document, variable.xml, in which each internal recordset has between one and three `<DELIVERY>` records:

```
<?xml version="1.0"?>
<CUSTOMERS>

    <CUSTOMER>
        <NAME>Charles</NAME>
        <RECORD>
            <CUSTOMER_ID>58704</CUSTOMER_ID>
            <PURCHASE_DATE>10/15/2001</PURCHASE_DATE>
            <DEPARTMENT>Meat</DEPARTMENT>
            <PRODUCT_NAME>Ham</PRODUCT_NAME>
            <DELIVERY>
                <DATE>10/20/2001</DATE>
                <TOTAL_COST>$1.99</TOTAL_COST>
            </DELIVERY>
            <DELIVERY>
                <DATE>10/25/2001</DATE>
                <TOTAL_COST>$1.49</TOTAL_COST>
            </DELIVERY>
            <DELIVERY>
                <DATE>10/25/2001</DATE>
                <TOTAL_COST>$1.49</TOTAL_COST>
            </DELIVERY>
        </RECORD>
    </CUSTOMER>

    <CUSTOMER>
        <NAME>Franklin</NAME>
        <RECORD>
            <CUSTOMER_ID>58705</CUSTOMER_ID>
            <PURCHASE_DATE>10/15/2001</PURCHASE_DATE>
            <DEPARTMENT>Produce</DEPARTMENT>
            <PRODUCT_NAME>Tomatoes</PRODUCT_NAME>
            <DELIVERY>
                <DATE>10/20/2001</DATE>
                <TOTAL_COST>$3.00</TOTAL_COST>
            </DELIVERY>
        </RECORD>
    </CUSTOMER>

    <CUSTOMER>
        <NAME>Phoebe</NAME>
        <RECORD>
            <CUSTOMER_ID>58706</CUSTOMER_ID>
            <PURCHASE_DATE>10/15/2001</PURCHASE_DATE>
            <DEPARTMENT>Meat</DEPARTMENT>
            <PRODUCT_NAME>Turkey</PRODUCT_NAME>
            <DELIVERY>
                <DATE>10/20/2001</DATE>
                <TOTAL_COST>$4.99</TOTAL_COST>
            </DELIVERY>
            <DELIVERY>
                <DATE>10/25/2001</DATE>
```


continues ▸

```
                <TOTAL_COST>$8.99</TOTAL_COST>
            </DELIVERY>
        </RECORD>
    </CUSTOMER>

    <CUSTOMER>
        <NAME>Mark</NAME>
        <RECORD>
            <CUSTOMER_ID>58707</CUSTOMER_ID>
            <PURCHASE_DATE>10/15/2001</PURCHASE_DATE>
            <DEPARTMENT>Meat</DEPARTMENT>
            <PRODUCT_NAME>Beef</PRODUCT_NAME>
            <DELIVERY>
                <DATE>10/20/2001</DATE>
                <TOTAL_COST>$3.95</TOTAL_COST>
            </DELIVERY>
            <DELIVERY>
                <DATE>10/25/2001</DATE>
                <TOTAL_COST>$6.95</TOTAL_COST>
            </DELIVERY>
        </RECORD>
    </CUSTOMER>

    <CUSTOMER>
        <NAME>Nancy</NAME>
        <RECORD>
            <CUSTOMER_ID>58708</CUSTOMER_ID>
            <PURCHASE_DATE>10/15/2001</PURCHASE_DATE>
            <DEPARTMENT>Frozen</DEPARTMENT>
            <PRODUCT_NAME>Broccoli</PRODUCT_NAME>
            <DELIVERY>
                <DATE>10/20/2001</DATE>
                <TOTAL_COST>$1.99</TOTAL_COST>
            </DELIVERY>
            <DELIVERY>
                <DATE>10/25/2001</DATE>
                <TOTAL_COST>$2.99</TOTAL_COST>
            </DELIVERY>
            <DELIVERY>
                <DATE>5-3-2002</DATE>
                <TOTAL_COST>$7200.00</TOTAL_COST>
            </DELIVERY>
        </RECORD>
    </CUSTOMER>

</CUSTOMERS>
```

In fact, this is not a problem; here's the page I'll use to display this data:

```
<HTML>
    <HEAD>
        <TITLE>
            Variable Size Hierarchical Records
        </TITLE>
    </HEAD>

    <BODY>

        <CENTER>
            <H1>
                Variable Size Hierarchical Records
            </H1>

            <XML SRC="variable.xml" ID="customers"></XML>

            <TABLE DATASRC="#customers" BORDER="1">
                <TR>
                    <TH><DIV DATAFLD="NAME"></DIV></TH>
                    <TD>
                        <TABLE DATASRC="#customers"
                        DATAFLD="RECORD">
                            <TR>
                                <TD>
                                <TABLE DATASRC="#customers"
                                    CELLPADDING = "3"
                                    DATAFLD="RECORD.DELIVERY">
                                    <TR ALIGN = "LEFT">
                                        <TH>Date</TH>
                                        <TH>Amount</TH>
                                    </TR>
                                    <TR ALIGN = "LEFT">
                                        <TD><DIV DATAFLD="DATE">
                                        </DIV></TD>
                                        <TD><DIV
                                        DATAFLD="TOTAL_COST">
                                        </DIV></TD>
                                    </TR>
                                </TABLE>
                                </TD>
                            </TR>
                        </TABLE>
                    </TD>
                </TR>
            </TABLE>
        </CENTER>
    </BODY>
</HTML>
```

You can see the results in Figure 8.8, where each <DELIVERY> recordset is correctly displayed, even though they have different number of records.

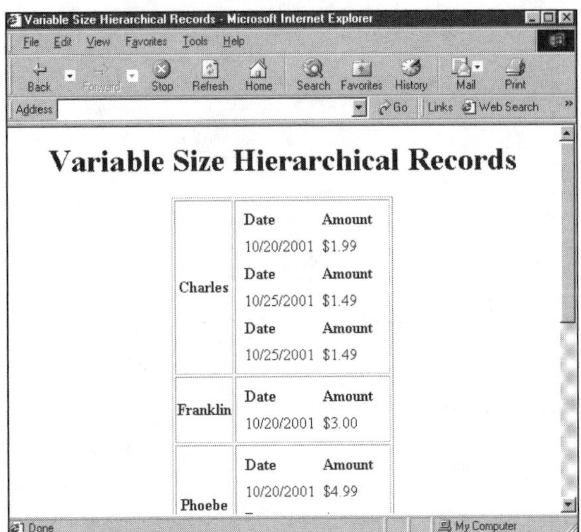

Figure 8.8 Variable-size hierarchical records in Internet Explorer.

You can also create the same page using the XML DSO applet instead of data islands:

```
<HTML>
    <HEAD>
        <TITLE>
            Variable Size Hierarchical Records
        </TITLE>
    </HEAD>

    <BODY>
        <CENTER>
            <H1>
                Variable Size Hierarchical Records
            </H1>

            <APPLET CODE="com.ms.xml.dso.XMLDSO.class"
                ID="customers"
                WIDTH="0" HEIGHT="0"
                MAYSCRIPT="true">
                <PARAM NAME="URL" VALUE="variable.xml">
            </APPLET>

            <TABLE DATASRC="#customers" BORDER="1">
                <TR>
                    <TH><DIV DATAFLD="NAME"></DIV></TH>
                    <TD>
                        <TABLE DATASRC="#customers"
                        DATAFLD="RECORD">
```

```
                    <TR ALIGN = CENTER>
                        <TD>Sales</TD>
                    </TR>
                    <TR>
                    .
                    .
                    .
                    </TR>
                </TABLE>
            </TD>
        </TR>
      </TABLE>
    </CENTER>
  </BODY>
</HTML>
```

Searching XML Data

You can do a great many things with recordsets, as we've seen in this chapter. In this chapter's final example, I'll take a look at how to search a database for a specific item. In particular, I'll let the user search for a match to a customer's name that this user specifies.

For this example, I'll modify customer.xml by adding a second customer with the name Nancy to make sure that we catch all instances of a match, naming this new document multiple.xml:

```
<?xml version="1.0"?>
<CUSTOMER>

    <CUSTOMER>
        <NAME>Charles</NAME>
        <CUSTOMER_ID>58704</CUSTOMER_ID>
        <PURCHASE_DATE>10/15/2001</PURCHASE_DATE>
        <DEPARTMENT>Meat</DEPARTMENT>
        <PRODUCT_NAME>Ham</PRODUCT_NAME>
    </CUSTOMER>

    <CUSTOMER>
        <NAME>Franklin</NAME>
        <CUSTOMER_ID>58705</CUSTOMER_ID>
        <PURCHASE_DATE>10/15/2001</PURCHASE_DATE>
        <DEPARTMENT>Produce</DEPARTMENT>
        <PRODUCT_NAME>Tomatoes</PRODUCT_NAME>
    </CUSTOMER>

    <CUSTOMER>
        <NAME>Phoebe</NAME>
        <CUSTOMER_ID>58706</CUSTOMER_ID>
        <PURCHASE_DATE>10/15/2001</PURCHASE_DATE>
```

continues ▸

```
        <DEPARTMENT>Meat</DEPARTMENT>
        <PRODUCT_NAME>Turkey</PRODUCT_NAME>
    </CUSTOMER>

    <CUSTOMER>
        <NAME>Mark</NAME>
        <CUSTOMER_ID>58707</CUSTOMER_ID>
        <PURCHASE_DATE>10/15/2001</PURCHASE_DATE>
        <DEPARTMENT>Meat</DEPARTMENT>
    <PRODUCT_NAME>Beef</PRODUCT_NAME>
    </CUSTOMER>

    <CUSTOMER>
        <NAME>Nancy</NAME>
        <CUSTOMER_ID>58708</CUSTOMER_ID>
        <PURCHASE_DATE>10/15/2001</PURCHASE_DATE>
        <DEPARTMENT>Frozen</DEPARTMENT>
        <PRODUCT_NAME>Broccoli</PRODUCT_NAME>
    </CUSTOMER>

    <CUSTOMER>
        <NAME>Nancy</NAME>
        <CUSTOMER_ID>58709</CUSTOMER_ID>
        <PURCHASE_DATE>10/15/2001</PURCHASE_DATE>
        <DEPARTMENT>Produce</DEPARTMENT>
        <PRODUCT_NAME>Tomatoes</PRODUCT_NAME>
    </CUSTOMER>

</CUSTOMER>
```

After setting up an XML data island and connecting it to multiple.xml, I'll define a new function named `findMatches` that will search for matches to the customer name the user wants to search for. Although ADOR recordset objects do have a method called `find` for searching databases, you set the search criterion in that method using a Structured Query Language (SQL, the language many database applications use) expression, and Internet Explorer doesn't appear to support such expressions. Instead, I'll set up a JavaScript loop that will find matches to the name the user is searching for.

The user can enter the name to search for in a text field that I'll call `text1`. When that user clicks a button, the `findMatches` function is called. I'll convert the name the user wants to search for into lowercase (using the JavaScript `String` object's `toLowerCase` method) to make the search case-insensitive, and I'll store it in a variable named `searchFor`:

```
<HTML>
    <HEAD>
        <TITLE>
            Searching XML-Based Databases
        </TITLE>
```

```
        <XML ID="customers" SRC="multiple.xml"></XML>

        <SCRIPT LANGUAGE="JavaScript">
            function findMatches()
            {
                var searchFor = form1.text1.value.toLowerCase()
    .
    .
    .
```

Now I'll loop over all the records in the recordset, storing the name in the current record in a variable named `currentName`, which I also convert to lowercase:

```
<HTML>
    <HEAD>
        <TITLE>
            Searching XML-Based Databases
        </TITLE>

        <XML ID="customers" SRC="multiple.xml"></XML>

        <SCRIPT LANGUAGE="JavaScript">
            function findMatches()
            {
                var searchFor = form1.text1.value.toLowerCase()

                while (!customers.recordset.EOF) {
                    var currentName = new String(customers.recordset("NAME"))
                    currentName = currentName.toLowerCase()
                    .
                    .
                    .
                    customers.recordset.moveNext()
                }
            }
        </SCRIPT>
    </HEAD>
```

I'll use the JavaScript `String` object's `indexOf` method to see whether the current name matches the name that the user is searching for. The `indexOf` method returns a value of `0` or greater if a match was found, so I use that method like this:

```
<HTML>
    <HEAD>
        <TITLE>
            Searching XML-Based Databases
        </TITLE>
```

continues ▸

```
        <XML ID="customers" SRC="multiple.xml"></XML>

        <SCRIPT LANGUAGE="JavaScript">
            function findMatches()
            {
                var searchFor = form1.text1.value.toLowerCase()

                while (!customers.recordset.EOF) {
                    var currentName = new String(customers.recordset("NAME"))
                    currentName = currentName.toLowerCase()
                    if (currentName.indexOf(searchFor) >= 0) {
                    .
                    .
                    .
                    }
                    customers.recordset.moveNext()
                }
            }
        </SCRIPT>
    </HEAD>
    .
    .
    .
```

All that remains is to display the matching records in a `<DIV>` element, as we have before in this chapter, and add the button and text field that we'll use to let the user interact with our code:

```
<HTML>
    <HEAD>
        <TITLE>
            Searching XML-Based Databases
        </TITLE>

        <XML ID="customers" SRC="multiple.xml"></XML>

        <SCRIPT LANGUAGE="JavaScript">
            function findMatches()
            {
                var searchFor = form1.text1.value.toLowerCase()

                while (!customers.recordset.EOF) {
                    var currentName = new String(customers.recordset("NAME"))
                    currentName = currentName.toLowerCase()
                    if (currentName.indexOf(searchFor) >= 0) {
                        divMessage.innerHTML +=
                        customers.recordset("NAME") +
                        " (ID " +
                        customers.recordset("CUSTOMER_ID") +
                        ") bought " +
                        customers.recordset("PRODUCT_NAME") +
```

```
                    " from the " +
                    customers.recordset("DEPARTMENT") +
                    " department on " +
                    customers.recordset("PURCHASE_DATE") +
                    ".<BR>"
                }
                customers.recordset.moveNext()
            }
        }
    </SCRIPT>
</HEAD>

<BODY>
    <CENTER>
        <H1>
            Searching XML-Based Databases
        </H1>

        <FORM ID="form1">
            Search for this name: <INPUT TYPE="TEXT" NAME="text1">
            <BR>
            <BR>
            <INPUT TYPE="BUTTON" VALUE="Search for matches"
                ONCLICK="findMatches()">
        </FORM>
    </CENTER>
    <DIV ID="divMessage">
    </DIV>
</BODY>
</HTML>
```

You can see the results in Figure 8.9, where we've matched both customers named Nancy.

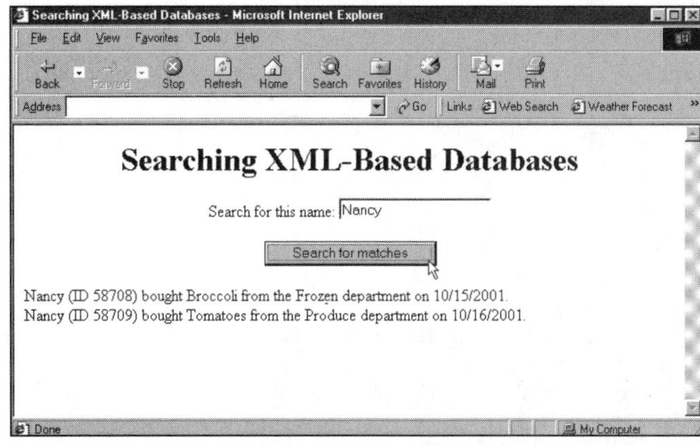

Figure 8.9 Searching for matches in XML-based databases.

In this example, I've used XML data islands, but of course you can also use the XML DSO applet to load the file multiple.xml. I'll do that here to demonstrate another aspect of the XML DSO applet: Up until now, I've given the applet a zero width and height, but in fact, this applet does display the status of its operations if you give it some space in the Web page. I'll do that like this:

```
<HTML>
    <HEAD>
        <TITLE>
            Searching XML-Based Databases
        </TITLE>

        <SCRIPT LANGUAGE="JavaScript">
            function findMatches()
            {
                var searchFor = form1.text1.value.toLowerCase()

                while (!customers.recordset.EOF) {
                    var currentName = new String(customers.recordset("NAME"))
                    currentName = currentName.toLowerCase()
                    if (currentName.indexOf(searchFor) >= 0) {
                        divMessage.innerHTML +=
                        customers.recordset("NAME") +
                        " (ID " +
                        customers.recordset("CUSTOMER_ID") +
                        ") bought " +
                        customers.recordset("PRODUCT_NAME") +
                        " from the " +
                        customers.recordset("DEPARTMENT") +
                        " department on " +
                        customers.recordset("PURCHASE_DATE") +
                        ".<BR>"
                    }
                    customers.recordset.moveNext()
                }
            }
        </SCRIPT>
    </HEAD>

    <BODY>
        <CENTER>
            <H1>
                Searching XML-Based Databases
            </H1>

            <APPLET CODE="com.ms.xml.dso.XMLDSO.class"
                ID="customers"
                WIDTH="400" HEIGHT="50"
                MAYSCRIPT="true">
                <PARAM NAME="URL" VALUE="multiple.xml">
            </APPLET>
```

```
<FORM ID="form1">
            Search for this name: <INPUT TYPE="TEXT" NAME="text1">
            <BR>
            <BR>
            <INPUT TYPE="BUTTON" VALUE="Search for matches"
                ONCLICK="findMatches()">
        </FORM>
    </CENTER>
    <DIV ID="divMessage">
    </DIV>
  </BODY>
</HTML>
```

You can see the results in Figure 8.10, where the XML DSO is displaying the message `Successfully loaded XML from "file:/C:/xml/multiple.xml"`. The background of this applet is green because there was no error; if an error occurred, the background would be red and the applet would display error messages.

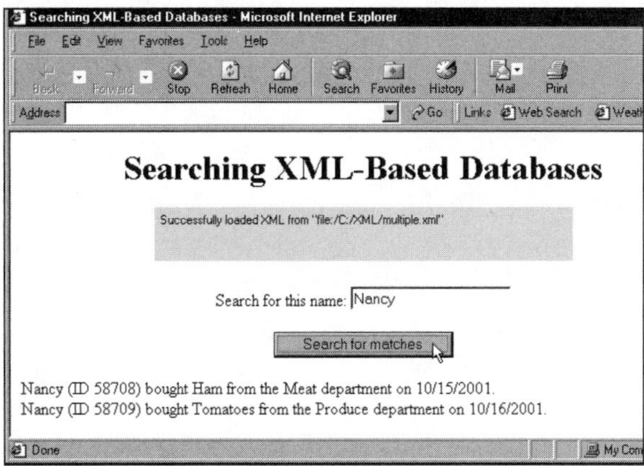

Figure 8.10 Searching for matches in XML-based databases using the XML DSO.

That completes our data-binding work with the Internet Explorer. In the next chapter, I'll take a look at XML and cascading style sheets.

9

Cascading Style Sheets

IF YOU WANT TO DISPLAY XML PAGES IN A BROWSER, you have a problem. Unless the browser you're using can handle your XML markup (such as the Jumbo browser, which handles Chemical Markup Language), the best that it can do is to display your document in some default way. For example, take a look at this document, which holds the beginning text of the stoic philosopher (and Roman emperor) Marcus Aurelius's *The Meditations* (`http://classics.mit.edu/Antoninus/meditations.html`):

```
<?xml version="1.0" standalone="yes"?>
<DOCUMENT>
    <TITLE>The Meditations</TITLE>
    <AUTHOR>By Marcus Aurelius</AUTHOR>
    <SECTION>Book One</SECTION>
    <P>
        From my grandfather, Verus, I learned good morals
        and the government of my temper.
    </P>
    <P>
        From the reputation and remembrance of my father,
        modesty and a manly character.
    </P>
    <P>
        From my mother, piety and beneficence, and abstinence,
        not only from evil deeds, but even from evil
        thoughts; and further, simplicity in my way of living,
        far removed from the habits of the rich.
    </P>
    <P>
```

continues ▸

```
        From my great-grandfather, not to have frequented
        public schools, and to have had good teachers at home,
        and to know that on such things a man should spend
        freely.
    </P>
</DOCUMENT>
```

Internet Explorer can display this document, but because it has no idea what you want to do with the various tags as far as presentation goes, it leaves them in, as you see in Figure 9.1.

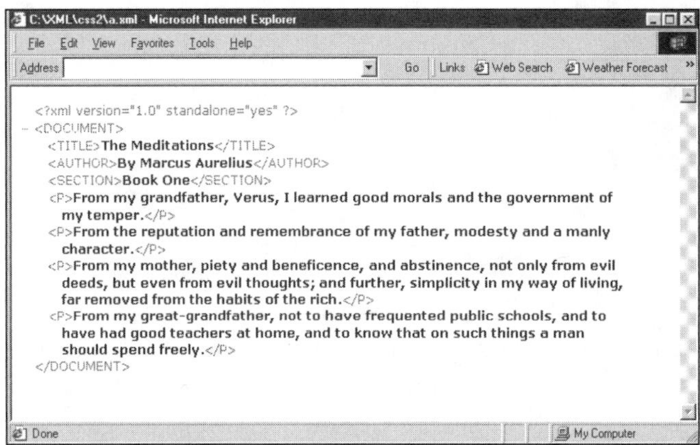

Figure 9.1 Displaying an XML document in Internet Explorer.

This chapter is all about fixing this situation by telling browsers exactly how to display the elements that you've created in a document. To do this, I'll use *cascading style sheets* (*CSS*), which were first introduced in December 1996. CSS is now widely supported in the major browsers; using CSS, you can specify exactly how you want your documents to appear in browsers. Although CSS was developed for use with HTML, it works with XML—in fact, it works even better with XML because there are some conflicts between CSS and HTML (such as the CSS `nowrap` specification and the HTML `NOWRAP` attribute) that XML doesn't have. What's more, in HTML, you're restricted to working with the predefined HTML elements, while in XML, you can style sophisticated nestings of elements and more.

Two levels of CSS exist today, and they're both W3C specifications—*CSS1* and *CSS2*. You'll find these specifications at `www.w3.org/TR/REC-CSS1` and `www.w3.org/TR/REC-CSS2`. CSS2 includes all of CSS1 and adds some additional features such as aural style sheets, support for various media types, and other advanced features. In fact, CSS3 is under development; you can read all about it at `www.w3.org/Style/CSS/current-work`.

The actual support that you'll find in browsers for CSS varies widely, as you might expect. The support in both Netscape and Internet Explorer is good—although somewhat different—so some experimentation in both browsers is usually a good idea. In fact, until fairly recently, no browser even supported CSS1 completely (Internet Explorer 5.0 for the Macintosh, shipped March 27, 2000, is apparently the first complete CSS1 browser). I can't stress this enough: Test your style sheets in as many browsers as you can because style sheet implementation varies a great deal from browser to browser.

More on Style Sheets

There are many more styles in CSS2—such as aural style sheets—than I can include in this chapter. See `www.w3.org/TR/REC-CSS2/` for details.

Here are a few online CSS resources:

- The W3C CSS validator, located at `http://jigsaw.w3.org/css-validator/`, will check the CSS in your pages for you.
- The W3C TIDY program can convert styles in HTML document to CSS for you. You can find TIDY at `www.w3.org/People/Raggett/tidy`.
- Many CSS resources are available at the W3C CSS page, `www.w3.org/Style/CSS/`, including CSS tutorials and links to free tools. If you will be using a lot of CSS, take a look at this page first.

So what are style sheets? A style sheet is a list of style *rules*, and it's attached to a document to indicate how you want the elements in the document displayed. For example, the document that we've just seen uses `<TITLE>`, `<AUTHOR>`, `<SECTION>`, and `<P>` elements. In a style sheet, I can supply a rule for all these elements. A rule consists of a *selector*, which specifies what element or elements you want the rule to apply to, and the rule specification itself, which is enclosed in curly braces, `{` and `}`. Here's a sample style sheet, style.css, for the XML document that we've already seen:

```
TITLE {display: block; font-size: 24pt; font-weight: bold;
    text-align: center; text-decoration: underline}
AUTHOR {display: block; font-size: 18pt; font-weight: bold;
    text-align: center}
SECTION {display: block; font-size: 16pt; font-weight: bold;
    text-align: center; font-style: italic}
P {display: block; margin-top: 10}
```

How do you attach this style sheet to the XML document that we saw at the beginning of this chapter? Take a look at the next section to find out.

Attaching Style Sheets to XML Documents

In HTML, there are three ways to connect style sheets to documents: You can use the `<STYLE>` HTML element to attach an internal style sheet or an external one, or you can use the `STYLE` attribute in HTML elements to style an individual element. In XML, there's really only one way to connect a style sheet to an XML document, and that's by using the `<?xml-stylesheet?>` processing instruction. (In fact, `<?xml-stylesheet?>` is only an agreed-upon convention and does *not* appear in the XML 1.0 W3C recommendation.) To use `<?xml-stylesheet?>` with CSS style sheets, you set the `type` attribute to `"text/css"` and the `href` attribute to the URI of the style sheet. For example, to attach style.css to the XML document, I can use a `<?xml-stylesheet?>` processing instruction like this:

```
<?xml version="1.0" standalone="yes"?>
<?xml-stylesheet type="text/css" href="style.css"?>
<DOCUMENT>
    <TITLE>The Meditations</TITLE>
    <AUTHOR>By Marcus Aurelius</AUTHOR>
    <SECTION>Book One</SECTION>
    <P>
        From my grandfather, Verus, I learned good morals
        and the government of my temper.
    </P>
    <P>
        From the reputation and remembrance of my father,
        modesty and a manly character.
    </P>
    <P>
        From my mother, piety and beneficence, and abstinence,
        not only from evil deeds, but even from evil
        thoughts; and further, simplicity in my way of living,
        far removed from the habits of the rich.
    </P>
    <P>
        From my great-grandfather, not to have frequented
        public schools, and to have had good teachers at home,
        and to know that on such things a man should spend
        freely.
    </P>
</DOCUMENT>
```

That's all it takes; now you can open this document in a browser as you see in Figure 9.2, and the browser will know how to handle the document.

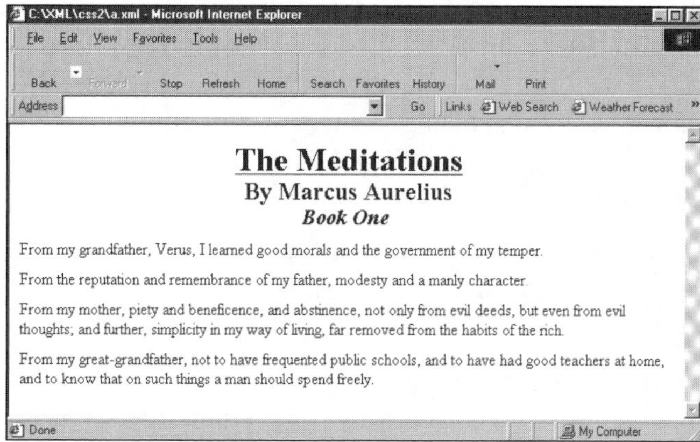

Figure 9.2 A style XML document.

Although I've said that using the `<?xml-stylesheet?>` processing instruction is the only way to attach a style sheet to an XML document, some browsers, such as Internet Explorer, also support a `STYLE` attribute in XML elements. You can specify styles using this attribute, like this:

```
From my grandfather, <UL STYLE="text-decoration: underline">Verus</UL>,
I learned good morals and the government of my temper.
```

I'll take a look at this way of styling individual elements—called *inline styling*—as well, but it's worth noting that it's even less standard than the `<?xml-stylesheet?>` processing instruction; its use is discouraged by style purists (mainly because it decentralizes your style specification for a document).

Selecting Elements in Style Sheet Rules

This chapter is dedicated to understanding how to create style sheets. After going through the mechanics, we'll see a lot of examples at work and then spend some time with the actual CSS specification.

I'll start by taking a look at how to create *selectors*, which indicate the element or elements to which you want to attach a style rule. In the style sheet we've already seen, style.css, the selectors are of the simplest kind and select just one element by giving the name of that element:

```
TITLE {display: block; font-size: 24pt; font-weight: bold;
text-align: center; text-decoration: underline}
AUTHOR {display: block; font-size: 18pt; font-weight: bold;
text-align: center}
SECTION {display: block; font-size: 16pt; font-weight: bold;
text-align: center; font-style: italic}
P {display: block; margin-top: 10}
```

For example, here I'm applying this style specification to the `<TITLE>` element:

```
{display: block; font-size: 24pt; font-weight: bold;
text-align: center; text-decoration: underline}
```

I'm applying this one to the `<AUTHOR>` element:

```
{display: block; font-size: 18pt; font-weight: bold;
text-align: center}
```

As you can see, one type of selector just lists the element that you want to style. However, you can create many other types of selectors, such as *grouping* elements, as described in the next section.

Grouping Elements in Selectors

Another way of creating an element selector in a style rule is to list a number of elements, separated by commas. The same rule applies to the whole group of elements, as in this case, where I'm styling the `<TITLE>` and `<AUTHOR>` elements the same way in style.css:

```
TITLE, AUTHOR {display: block; font-size: 24pt; font-weight: bold;
text-align: center; text-decoration: underline}
SECTION {display: block; font-size: 16pt; font-weight: bold;
text-align: center; font-style: italic}
P {display: block; margin-top: 10}
```

You can see this style sheet applied to the XML document that we've been using in Figure 9.3. As you see in that figure, the `<TITLE>` and `<AUTHOR>` elements are indeed styled the same way in that figure.

Creating Pseudo-Elements

Besides using elements as selectors for rules, you can also use *pseudo-elements*. There are two pseudo-elements in CSS1: `first-letter`, which refers to the first letter of a block of text, and `first-line`, which refers to the block's first line. Two more pseudo-elements were introduced in CSS2—`before` and `after`, which let you specify what should go immediately before and after elements. You use these pseudo-elements like this: `P:first-letter` to refer to the first letter of a `<P>` element.

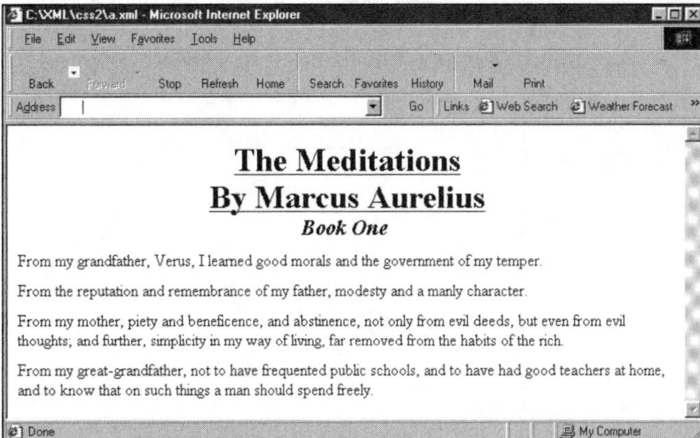

Figure 9.3 Using a group selector in a style sheet.

Here's an example. In this case, I'm styling the first letter of <P> elements to be larger than the rest of the text and to be a "drop cap," which means that it will appear lower than the rest of the text on the first line. (I'll specify that the top of the first letter should align with the top of the rest of the text on the first line with `vertical-align: text-top`, and we'll see how this works later in the chapter.)

```
TITLE {display: block; font-size: 24pt; font-weight: bold;
text-align: center; text-decoration: underline}
AUTHOR {display: block; font-size: 18pt; font-weight: bold;
text-align: center}
SECTION {display: block; font-size: 16pt; font-weight: bold;
text-align: center; font-style: italic}
P {display: block; margin-top: 10}
P:first-letter {font-size: 18pt; float: left; vertical-align: text-top}
```

These pseudo-elements are not implemented in Internet Explorer, but they are implemented in the preview version of Netscape Navigator 6.You can see this style sheet applied to the XML document in Figure 9.4.

You can also use the `before` and `after` pseudo-elements to specify what comes before or after another element. In this case, I'm adding a line of hyphens and asterisks after the <P> element. (The `\A` refers to line breaks—A is the hexadecimal digit for 10 decimal, and that's the UTF-8 code for a line feed character.)

```
P:after {content: "\A-*-*-*-*-*-*-*-*-*-*-*-*-*-*-*-*-*-*-*-*-*-*-*\A"}
```

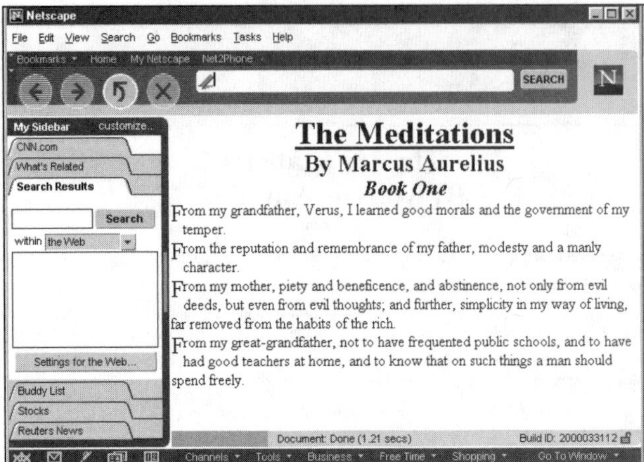

Figure 9.4 Using pseudo-elements in Netscape Navigator 6.

Classes

Besides elements, you can also create selectors using *classes*. Here's an example. In this case, I'll create a class named `RED` to specify that elements to which it's applied must use a foreground (text) color of red and a background color of pink. To define a general class such as `RED`, you must preface it with a dot (.), as `.RED`:

```
TITLE {display: block; font-size: 24pt; font-weight: bold;
text-align: center; text-decoration: underline}
AUTHOR {display: block; font-size: 18pt; font-weight: bold;
text-align: center}
SECTION {display: block; font-size: 16pt; font-weight: bold;
text-align: center; font-style: italic}
P {display: block; margin-top: 10}
.RED {color:red; background-color: pink}
```

To apply this class to an individual element, such as the `<TITLE>` element in our XML document, I can add a `CLASS` attribute to that element—assuming that the browser I'm using can understand that attribute:

```
<?xml version="1.0" standalone="yes"?>
<?xml-stylesheet type="text/css" href="style.css"?>
<DOCUMENT>
    <TITLE CLASS="RED">The Meditations</TITLE>
    <AUTHOR>By Marcus Aurelius</AUTHOR>
    <SECTION>Book One</SECTION>
    <P>
```

```
        From my grandfather, Verus, I learned good morals
        and the government of my temper.
    </P>
    <P>
        From the reputation and remembrance of my father,
        modesty and a manly character.
    </P>
    <P>
        From my mother, piety and beneficence, and abstinence,
        not only from evil deeds, but even from evil
        thoughts; and further, simplicity in my way of living,
        far removed from the habits of the rich.
    </P>
    <P>
        From my great-grandfather, not to have frequented
        public schools, and to have had good teachers at home,
        and to know that on such things a man should spend
        freely.
    </P>
</DOCUMENT>
```

Browsers such as Internet Explorer understand the CLASS attribute, so you can see what this document looks like in Figure 9.5.

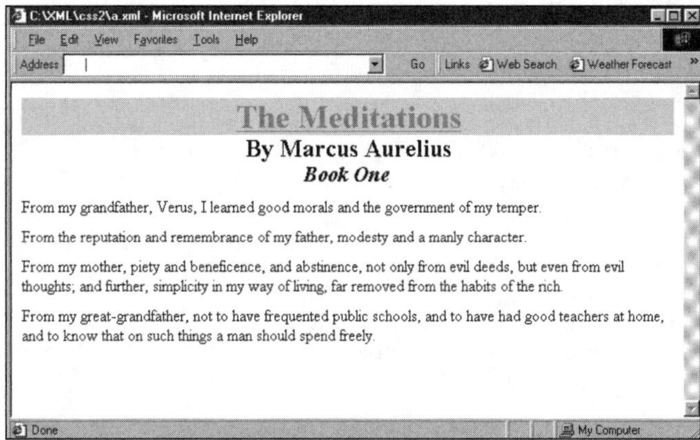

Figure 9.5 Using style classes.

Note that if you want to make this a valid document, you must declare the CLASS attribute. That might look like this in a DTD:

```
<!ELEMENT TITLE (CDATA)*>
<!ATTLIST TITLE CLASS CDATA #IMPLIED>
```

You can also create classes that apply only to specific elements. For example, here's how I style the first paragraph in a document to add some space before that paragraph, creating a class named TOP that applies to only <P> elements, which I specify by calling this class P.TOP. (Note that general classes such as RED apply to all elements, which is why you declare them as .RED.)

```
TITLE {display: block; font-size: 24pt; font-weight: bold;
text-align: center; text-decoration: underline}
AUTHOR {display: block; font-size: 18pt; font-weight: bold;
text-align: center}
SECTION {display: block; font-size: 16pt; font-weight: bold;
text-align: center; font-style: italic}
P {display: block; margin-top: 10}
P.TOP {display: block; margin-top: 30}
```

Now I can use this new class with the first paragraph in the document:

```
<?xml version="1.0" standalone="yes"?>
<?xml-stylesheet type="text/css" href="style.css"?>
<DOCUMENT>
    <TITLE>The Meditations</TITLE>
    <AUTHOR>By Marcus Aurelius</AUTHOR>
    <SECTION>Book One</SECTION>
    <P CLASS="TOP">
        From my grandfather, Verus, I learned good morals
        and the government of my temper.
    </P>
    <P>
        From the reputation and remembrance of my father,
        modesty and a manly character.
    </P>
    <P>
        From my mother, piety and beneficence, and abstinence,
        not only from evil deeds, but even from evil
        thoughts; and further, simplicity in my way of living,
        far removed from the habits of the rich.
    </P>
    <P>
        From my great-grandfather, not to have frequented
        public schools, and to have had good teachers at home,
        and to know that on such things a man should spend
        freely.
    </P>
</DOCUMENT>
```

You can see the results in Figure 9.6.

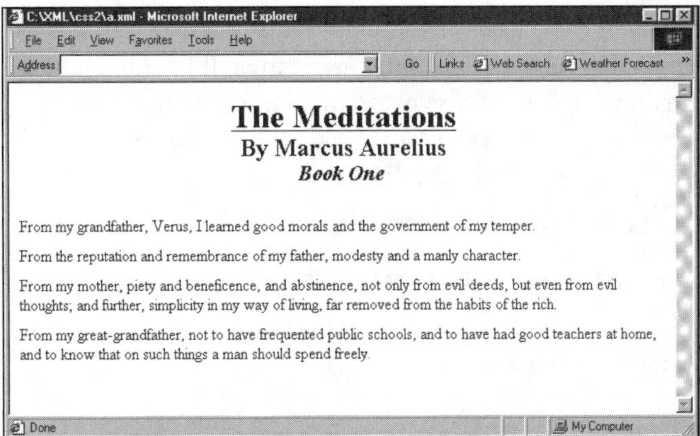

Figure 9.6 Styling just one paragraph.

Creating Pseudo-Classes

CSS also defines a number of *pseudo-classes*. Here's a sampling of pseudo-classes, which can act as selectors:

Pseudo-class	Description
`:focus`	Refers to the element with the focus (the item that is the target of keystrokes). For example, `P:focus` selects the `<P>` element with the focus.
`:first-child`	Refers to the first child of the indicated element. For example, `P:first-child` selects the first child of the `<P>` element.
`:link`, `:visited`, `:active`, `:hover`	Refers to hyperlink-like elements. The `:link` pseudo-class refers to elements that have been designated as links, `:visited` specifies the style of visited links, `:active` specifies the style of links as they're being activated, and `:hover` specifies the style as the mouse hovers over them.
`:lang()`	Refers to elements that use a specified language. The language is usually set in elements with the `xml:lang` attribute.

Selecting by ID

Another way of selecting elements is by their ID values, which you set with an `ID` attribute. To create a selector that targets elements with a certain ID, you use the syntax *`ELEMENT_NAME#ID_VALUE`*. For example, here's how I create a rule for `<P>` elements with the ID value `"TOP"`:

```
TITLE {display: block; font-size: 24pt; font-weight: bold;
text-align: center; text-decoration: underline}
AUTHOR {display: block; font-size: 18pt; font-weight: bold;
text-align: center}
SECTION {display: block; font-size: 16pt; font-weight: bold;
text-align: center; font-style: italic}
P {display: block; margin-top: 10}
P#TOP {display: block; margin-top: 30}
```

To give an element the ID `"TOP"`, I can add an `ID` attribute like this, assuming that the browser can understand this attribute:

```
<?xml version="1.0" standalone="yes"?>
<?xml-stylesheet type="text/css" href="style.css"?>
<DOCUMENT>
    <TITLE>The Meditations</TITLE>
    <AUTHOR>By Marcus Aurelius</AUTHOR>
    <SECTION>Book One</SECTION>
    <P ID="TOP">
        From my grandfather, Verus, I learned good morals
        and the government of my temper.
    </P>
    <P>
        From the reputation and remembrance of my father,
        modesty and a manly character.
    </P>
    <P>
        From my mother, piety and beneficence, and abstinence,
        not only from evil deeds, but even from evil
        thoughts; and further, simplicity in my way of living,
        far removed from the habits of the rich.
    </P>
    <P>
        From my great-grandfather, not to have frequented
        public schools, and to have had good teachers at home,
        and to know that on such things a man should spend
        freely.
    </P>
</DOCUMENT>
```

Internet Explorer lets you use `ID` attributes with XML elements, so selecting by `ID` like this gives you the same results that you see in Figure 9.6. Note that, as with the `CLASS` attribute, you must declare the `ID` attribute if you want to use it; such a declaration might look like this in a DTD (note that I'm declaring this attribute of type ID):

```
<!ELEMENT P (#PCDATA)>
<!ATTLIST P ID ID #REQUIRED>
```

Using Contextual Selectors

You can use *contextual* selectors to specify the style of elements that appear within other elements. For example, you might want an element to appear one way when it's by itself, but another way when enclosed in another element. Here's how that might look—in this case, I'm specifying that when used inside <P> elements, the <UL> element must underline its enclosed text:

```
TITLE {display: block; font-size: 24pt; font-weight: bold;
text-align: center; text-decoration: underline}
AUTHOR {display: block; font-size: 18pt; font-weight: bold;
text-align: center}
SECTION {display: block; font-size: 16pt; font-weight: bold;
text-align: center; font-style: italic}
P {display: block; margin-top: 10}
P UL {text-decoration: underline}
```

Now I can use the <UL> element inside a <P> element:

```
<?xml version="1.0" standalone="yes"?>
<?xml-stylesheet type="text/css" href="style.css"?>
<DOCUMENT>
    <TITLE>The Meditations</TITLE>
    <AUTHOR>By Marcus Aurelius</AUTHOR>
    <SECTION>Book One</SECTION>
    <P>
        From my grandfather, <UL>Verus</UL>, I learned good morals
        and the government of my temper.
    </P>
    <P>
        From the reputation and remembrance of my father,
        modesty and a manly character.
    </P>
    <P>
        From my mother, piety and beneficence, and abstinence,
        not only from evil deeds, but even from evil
        thoughts; and further, simplicity in my way of living,
        far removed from the habits of the rich.
    </P>
    <P>
        From my great-grandfather, not to have frequented
        public schools, and to have had good teachers at home,
        and to know that on such things a man should spend
        freely.
    </P>
</DOCUMENT>
```

And you can see the results in Figure 9.7, where you can see the <UL> tag doing its job on the name Verus in the first sentence.

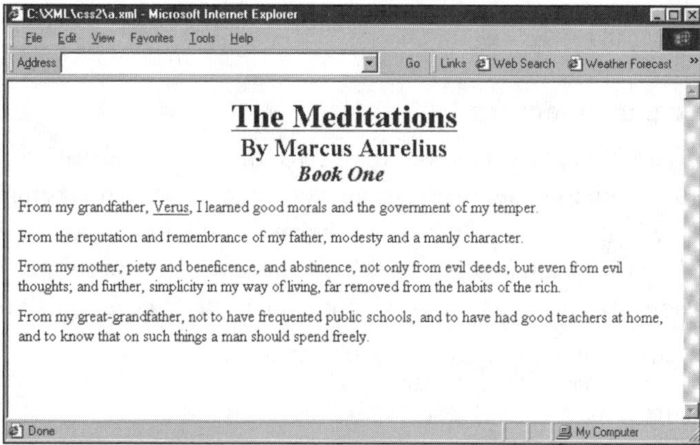

Figure 9.7 Using contextual selectors.

Using Inline Styles

As mentioned earlier, you can also create inline styles using the STYLE attribute, if the browser that you're using understands that attribute in XML documents. Using the STYLE attribute, you can specify a rule directly. For example, here's how I style the <UL> element used in the previous example using the STYLE attribute:

```
<?xml version="1.0" standalone="yes"?>
<?xml-stylesheet type="text/css" href="style.css"?>
<DOCUMENT>
    <TITLE>The Meditations</TITLE>
    <AUTHOR>By Marcus Aurelius</AUTHOR>
    <SECTION>Book One</SECTION>
    <P>
        From my grandfather,
        <UL STYLE="text-decoration: underline">Verus</UL>,
        I learned good morals and the government of my temper.
    </P>
    <P>
        From the reputation and remembrance of my father,
        modesty and a manly character.
    </P>
    <P>
        From my mother, piety and beneficence, and abstinence,
        not only from evil deeds, but even from evil
        thoughts; and further, simplicity in my way of living,
        far removed from the habits of the rich.
```

```
    </P>
    <P>
        From my great-grandfather, not to have frequented
        public schools, and to have had good teachers at home,
        and to know that on such things a man should spend
        freely.
    </P>
</DOCUMENT>
```

This document gives the same results that you see in Figure 9.7. Note that if you want to make this document valid, you'll have to declare the `STYLE` attribute, which might look like this in a DTD:

```
<!ELEMENT UL (CDATA)*>
<!ATTLIST UL STYLE CDATA #IMPLIED>
```

Style purists recommend that you stay away from the `STYLE` attribute because using this attribute means that your style declarations will be all over the document, not just in a centralized style sheet. However, this attribute is certainly recognized by browsers, so the choice is up to you.

Using Inheritance

You might have noticed that although the `<UL>` element in the previous examples specified only one aspect of the element's style—that is, that text should be underlined (by using this rule: `UL {text-decoration: underline}`)—the underlined text appeared in the same font as the surrounding text, as you see in Figure 9.7. The reason is that styled elements *inherit* the styles of their parent elements; in this case, the `<UL>` element's parent element is `<P>`:

```
<?xml-stylesheet type="text/css" href="style.css"?>
<DOCUMENT>
    <TITLE>The Meditations</TITLE>
    <AUTHOR>By Marcus Aurelius</AUTHOR>
    <SECTION>Book One</SECTION>
    <P>
        From my grandfather, <UL>Verus</UL>, I learned good morals
        and the government of my temper.
    </P>
    <P>
        From the reputation and remembrance of my father,
        modesty and a manly character.
    </P>
    <P>
        From my mother, piety and beneficence, and abstinence,
        not only from evil deeds, but even from evil
        thoughts; and further, simplicity in my way of living,
        far removed from the habits of the rich.
    </P>
```

continues ▸

```
    <P>
        From my great-grandfather, not to have frequented
        public schools, and to have had good teachers at home,
        and to know that on such things a man should spend
        freely.
    </P>
</DOCUMENT>
```

Inheritance is very useful: As you see, you don't have to specify all aspects of a child element's style if you want it to retain those aspects from the parent element. When you want to override some aspects of a style from the parent's style, you just need to define them in a rule for the child element.

Because style rules can inherit other rules, the order in which rules are applied becomes important; this ordering process is called a style *cascade*, from which cascading style sheets take their name.

Understanding Cascades

You can use multiple style sheets for one XML document in several ways because there are multiple ways of attaching style sheets. For example, you can use the `<?xml-stylesheet?>` processing instruction, and you can use the `@import` directive. This directive will import a style sheet:

```
@import url(http://www.starpowder.com/style.css);
```

In a style sheet to *import* another style sheet, the reader of a document may use browser-specific techniques to use style sheets; in fact, the reader's software can even supply default style sheets.

In addition, the author or reader of a document can use another declaration, the `!important` declaration, to specify that some aspect of a style should not be overridden by inheritance. For example, this declaration specifies that it's important for `<UL>` elements color their text red:

```
UL {color: red !important text-decoration: underline}).
```

When multiple style rules are involved, what order are they applied in? Generally speaking, the most *specific* rules are the ones that are applied if a conflict arises. For example, rules that you apply by ID are preferred to those applied by class. However, rules applied by class are preferred to those applied to all elements of the same type. If no selector fits the situation, the element will inherit styles from its parent; if there is no parent, a default style is used.

If there's a conflict, here's the order in which the rules are applied: rules that the document author specified as important are preferred, followed by rules that the reader specified as important, followed by general author rules (that is, those not marked as important), followed by general reader rules, and followed by the most recent rule in the style sheet(s) that applies.

Creating Style Rules

We've seen how to create selectors in rules; it's time to take a look at creating rules themselves. A rule is composed of a selector followed by a semicolon-separated list of *property-value* pairs enclosed in curly braces, like this:

```
TITLE {display: block; font-size: 24pt; font-weight: bold;
text-align: center; text-decoration: underline}
```

In this case, I'm setting values for the `display`, `font-size`, `font-weight`, `text-align`, and `text-decoration` properties. You assign a value to a property by following the name of the property with a colon, whitespace, and the value that you want to assign.

Quite a number of properties are defined in CSS, and the best way to get a grip on what's going on is to actually *use* them, so we're about to see a lot of examples.

Creating Block Elements

You might have noticed the property-value pair `display: block` in the rules in style.css:

```
TITLE {display: block; font-size: 24pt; font-weight: bold;
text-align: center; text-decoration: underline}
AUTHOR {display: block; font-size: 18pt; font-weight: bold;
text-align: center}
SECTION {display: block; font-size: 16pt; font-weight: bold;
text-align: center; font-style: italic}
P {display: block; margin-top: 10}
```

In particular, `display: block` specifies that the element in question get its own *block*, which means that these elements start on a new line, and the element following them starts on a new line as well—that is, you use `display: block` to create *block-level* elements.

The `display` property is more important in XML style sheets than it is in HTML style sheets because HTML styles such as `<H1>` already inherit the `display: block` style. To create elements that you want set off from other elements, such as paragraphs and headers, use `display: block`. (For example, using this style specification is the reason that elements such as `<TITLE>`, `<AUTHOR>`, `<SECTION>`, and so on appear on their own lines, as shown earlier in Figure 9.2.

Specifying Height and Width

You can specify the width and height of a block using the `width` and `height` properties; see the section "Displaying Images," later in this chapter, for more details.

Styling Text

Setting text styles is one of the more important aspects of cascading style sheets, but the process is not straightforward. Here are some properties that you can use with text:

Property	Description
`float`	Indicates how text should flow around this element. Set this to `left` to move the element to the left of the display area and have text flow around it to the right; set this to `right` to move the element to the right and have text flow around the element to the left; or set this to `none`.
`font-family`	Sets the font face. Note that you can specify a number of options here, separated by commas, and the first face supported by the browser will be used.
`font-size`	Sets the size of the text font.
`font-stretch`	Indicates the desired amount of condensing or expansion in the letters used to draw the text.
`font-style`	Specifies whether the text is to be rendered using a normal, italic, or oblique face.
`font-variant`	Indicates whether the text is to be rendered using the normal letters or small-cap letters for lowercase characters.
`font-weight`	Refers to the boldness or lightness of the glyphs used to render the text, relative to other fonts in the same font family.
`line-height`	Indicates the height given to each line. Set this to an absolute measurement or a percentage value such as `200%` to create double-spacing.
`text-align`	Sets the alignment of text; set this to `left`, `right`, `center`, or `justify`.
`text-decoration`	To underline the text, set to `underline`, `overline`, `line-through`, or `blink`; to remove inherited decorations, set to `none`.
`text-indent`	Sets the indentation of the first line of block-level elements. Set this to an absolute value such as 10 pixels, `10px`, or 4 points, `4pt`.
`text-transform`	Indicates whether you want to display text in all uppercase, all lowercase, or with initial letters capitalized. Set this to `capitalize`, `uppercase`, `lowercase`, or `none`.
`vertical-align`	Sets the vertical alignment of text; set this to `baseline`, `sub`, `super`, `top`, `text-top`, `middle`, `bottom`, or `text-bottom`.

Here's an example of putting some of these properties to use. In this case, I'll specify 18-point (a point is 1/72 of an inch) centered text in italic Arial (or Helvetica, if the browser can't find the Arial font face):

```
TITLE {display: block; font-size: 24pt; font-weight: bold;
text-align: center; text-decoration: underline}
AUTHOR {display: block; font-size: 18pt; font-weight: bold;
text-align: center}
SECTION {display: block; font-size: 16pt; font-weight: bold;
text-align: center; font-style: italic}
P {display: block; font-size: 18pt; font-style: italic; font-family:
Arial, Helvetica; text-align: center; margin-top: 10}
```

You can see the results of using this style sheet with the previous XML document in Figure 9.8.

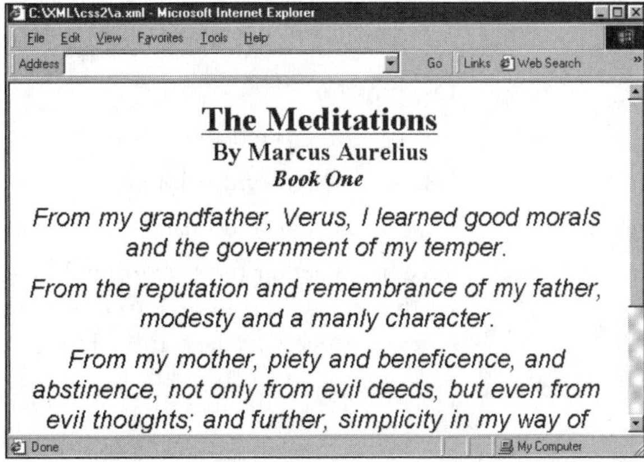

Figure 9.8 Using font properties.

As with many groups of properties, you can use a *shortcut* property to set the `font-style`, `font-variant`, `font-weight`, `font-size`, `line-height`, and `font-family` properties all at once—the `font` property. To use this shortcut property, you just specify values for all these properties (in the order that I've given here), separating the `font-size` and `line-height` values with a forward slash (`/`) and listing all values without commas (except between font family names, if you list more than one). Here's an example using the `font` shorthand property:

```
TITLE {display: block; font-size: 24pt; font-weight: bold;
text-align: center; text-decoration: underline}
AUTHOR {display: block; font-size: 18pt; font-weight: bold;
text-align: center}
SECTION {display: block; font-size: 16pt; font-weight: bold;
text-align: center; font-style: italic}
```

continues ▸

```
P {display: block; font: italic normal bold 12pt/10pt arial,
        helvetica; text-align: center}
```

Most groups of properties—such as the font properties, or those you use to set borders—have a shortcut property that lets you set multiple property values at once. I'll list some of these shortcut properties and how to use them at the end of this chapter.

Generic Font Selections

As a last resort, you can assign a generic font family to `font-family` to use in case the user's computer doesn't have the one you specified. The browser will select a font family that's similar. Generic font families include `serif`, `sans serif`, `cursive`, `fantasy`, and `monospace`.

Setting Colors and Backgrounds

Here are the properties that you use to set color and backgrounds:

Property	Description
`color`	Sets the foreground (text) color
`background-color`	Sets the background color
`background-image`	Sets the background image
`background-repeat`	Specifies whether the background image should be tiled; set this to `repeat`, `repeat-x` (repeat in the x direction), `repeat-y` (repeat in the y direction) or `no-repeat`
`background-attachment`	Specifies whether the background scrolls with the rest of the document
`background-position`	Sets the initial position of the background

There's also a `background` shorthand property that you can set to the background `color`, `image`, `repeat`, `attachment`, and `position` all at once (list those values in order). I'll cover more on how to use this shorthand property at the end of the chapter.

In this next example, I'm styling both the background and the foreground (that is, the text color) of a document. In this case, I'm setting the background color of the `<DOCUMENT>` element to coral. Note that because all the other elements in the document are children of this element, they'll all inherit this background color—except for the `<P>` element, in which I'm specifically setting the background to white and coloring the text blue:

```
DOCUMENT {background-color: coral}
TITLE {display: block; font-size: 24pt; font-weight: bold;
text-align: center; text-decoration: underline}
```

```
AUTHOR {display: block; font-size: 18pt; font-weight: bold;
text-align: center}
SECTION {display: block; font-size: 16pt; font-weight: bold;
text-align: center; font-style: italic}
P {display: block; background-color: white; color: blue}
```

You can see the results in Figure 9.9 (of course, the coral background appears gray here).

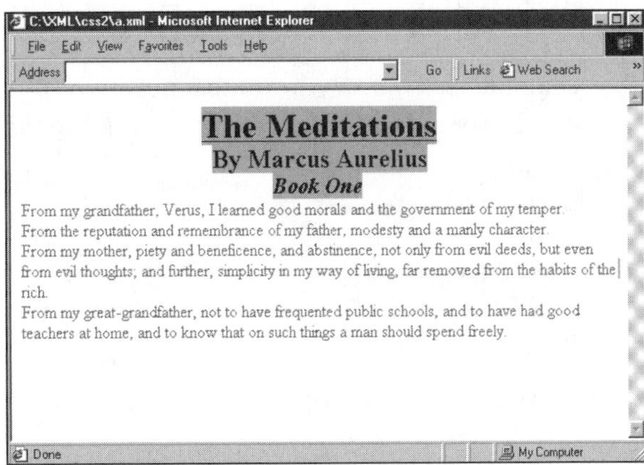

Figure 9.9 Using font properties to style foreground and background.

Although dozens of colors are predefined in most browsers, the CSS standards define only 16 colors:

- Aqua
- Black
- Blue
- Fuchsia
- Gray
- Green
- Lime
- Maroon
- Navy
- Olive
- Purple
- Red
- Silver
- Teal
- White
- Yellow

In this example, I used the predefined colors coral, blue, and white, but you can also define your own colors as color triplets: `#rrggbb`. Here, *rr*, *gg*, and *bb* are two-digit hexadecimal values that you use to specify the red, green, and blue components of a color, just as you do in HTML. For example, white is `#ffffff`, black is `#000000`, pure blue is `#0000ff`, pure red is `#ff0000`, pink is

`#ffcccc`, orange is `#ffcc00`, and coral is `#ff7f50`. Using color triplets, here's what the previous style sheet looks like:

```
DOCUMENT {background-color: #ff7f50}
TITLE {display: block; font-size: 24pt; font-weight: bold;
text-align: center; text-decoration: underline}
AUTHOR {display: block; font-size: 18pt; font-weight: bold;
text-align: center}
SECTION {display: block; font-size: 16pt; font-weight: bold;
text-align: center; font-style: italic}
P {display: block; background-color: #ffffff; color: #0000ff}
```

Here's another example that we saw in the beginning of this chapter, where I gave the `<TITLE>` element a pink background and red foreground:

```
<?xml version="1.0" standalone="yes"?>
<?xml-stylesheet type="text/css" href="style.css"?>
<DOCUMENT>
    <TITLE CLASS="RED">The Meditations</TITLE>
    <AUTHOR>By Marcus Aurelius</AUTHOR>
    <SECTION>Book One</SECTION>
    <P>
        From my grandfather, Verus, I learned good morals
        and the government of my temper.
    </P>
    <P>
        From the reputation and remembrance of my father,
        modesty and a manly character.
    </P>
    <P>
        From my mother, piety and beneficence, and abstinence,
        not only from evil deeds, but even from evil
        thoughts; and further, simplicity in my way of living,
        far removed from the habits of the rich.
    </P>
    <P>
        From my great-grandfather, not to have frequented
        public schools, and to have had good teachers at home,
        and to know that on such things a man should spend
        freely.
    </P>
</DOCUMENT>
```

The `RED` class was defined this way:

```
TITLE {display: block; font-size: 24pt; font-weight: bold;
text-align: center; text-decoration: underline}
AUTHOR {display: block; font-size: 18pt; font-weight: bold;
text-align: center}
SECTION {display: block; font-size: 16pt; font-weight: bold;
text-align: center; font-style: italic}
P {display: block; margin-top: 10}
.RED {color:red; background-color: pink}
```

Margins, Indentations, and Alignments

Here are the properties that you use to work with margins, indentations, and alignments:

Property	Description
`line-height`	Indicates the height given to each line. Set this to an absolute measurement or a percentage value such as `200%` to create double-spacing.
`margin-left`	Sets the left margin of a block element.
`margin-right`	Sets the right margin of a block element.
`margin-top`	Sets the top margin of a block element.
`text-align`	Sets the alignment of text; set this to `left`, `right`, `center`, or `justify`.
`text-indent`	Sets the indentation of the first line of block-level elements. Set this to an absolute value such as 10 pixels, `10px`, or 4 points, `4pt`.
`vertical-align`	Sets the vertical alignment of text; set this to `baseline`, `sub`, `super`, `top`, `text-top`, `middle`, `bottom`, or `text-bottom`.

Here's an example showing how to put some of these properties to work. In this style sheet, I'm indenting the first line of each paragraph by 40 pixels. (For more on the kinds of units that you use to specify lengths, see Table 9.1, later in this chapter.) I'm also indenting all the text in paragraphs by 20 pixels:

```
TITLE {display: block; font-size: 24pt; font-weight: bold;
text-align: center; text-decoration: underline}
AUTHOR {display: block; font-size: 18pt; font-weight: bold;
text-align: center}
SECTION {display: block; font-size: 16pt; font-weight: bold;
text-align: center; font-style: italic}
P {display: block; text-indent: 40px; margin-left: 20px}
```

You can see the results in Figure 9.10. As you see there, the first line of each paragraph is indeed indented, and the paragraph text is also moved to the left.

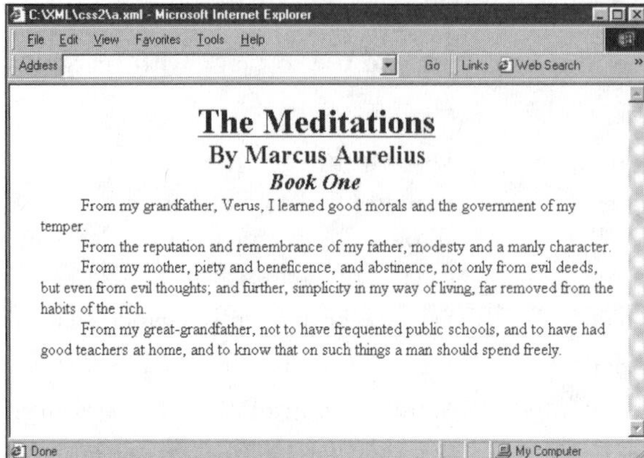

Figure 9.10 Indenting text using a style sheet.

Applying Styles to Lists

This table describes the properties you typically use with lists:

Property	Description
`list-item`	Set the `display` property to this value to create a list.
`list-style-image`	Sets the image that will be used as the list item marker. This is used in Internet Explorer 5 and later only.
`list-style-type`	Sets the appearance of the list item marker, such as `disc`, `circle`, `square`, `decimal`, `lowercase Roman`, `uppercase Roman`, and others.

Here's an example; in this case, I'm setting the marker in front of each list item in an unordered list to a square using `list-style-type`—note that you have to set the `display` property to `list-item`:

```
TITLE {display: block; font-size: 24pt; font-weight: bold;
text-align: center; text-decoration: underline}
AUTHOR {display: block; font-size: 18pt; font-weight: bold;
text-align: center}
SECTION {display: block; font-size: 16pt; font-weight: bold;
text-align: center; font-style: italic}
P {display:list-item; list-style-type: square}
```

Creating Borders

You can also create borders for elements using CSS, setting the border style, border width, border color, and so on. These border properties are available:

Property	Description
`border-bottom-width`	Width of the bottom of the border; set this to an absolute measurement such as `10px` for 10 pixels, or `4pt` for 4 points, or a keyword: `thin`, `medium`, or `thick`.
`border-color`	The color in which you want the border to be displayed (use a predefined color or a color triplet). Setting this property to one value sets the color of the whole border; two values set the top and bottom borders to the first value, and the right and left borders to the second; four values set the color of all border parts in order: top, right, bottom, and left.
`border-left-width`	Width of the left edge of the border; set this to an absolute measurement such as `10px` for 10 pixels, or `4pt` for four points, or a keyword: `thin`, `medium`, or `thick`.
`border-right-width`	Width of the right edge of the border; set this to an absolute measurement such as `10px` for 10 pixels, or `4pt` for 4 points, or a keyword: `thin`, `medium`, or `thick`.
`border-style`	Sets the border style. Possible values include `dotted`, `dashed`, `solid`, `double`, `groove`, `ridge`, `inset`, and `outset`.
`border-top-width`	Width of the top of the border; set this to an absolute measurement such as `10px` for 10 pixels, or `4pt` for 4 points, or a keyword: `thin`, `medium`, or `thick`.

There are also five shorthand border properties:

Property	Description
`border-top`	Sets the style of the top border
`border-right`	Sets the style of the right border
`border-bottom`	Sets the style of the bottom border
`border-left`	Sets the style of the left border
`border`	Sets the border style all at once

You set the shorthand properties to a width, style, and color all at once like this:

```
P {border 10pt solid cyan}
```

Here's an example; in this case, I'm adding a border to the <SECTION> element in our XML document:

```
TITLE {display: block; font-size: 24pt; font-weight: bold;
text-align: center; text-decoration: underline}
AUTHOR {display: block; font-size: 18pt; font-weight: bold;
text-align: center}
SECTION {display: block; font-size: 16pt; font-weight: bold;
text-align: center; font-style: italic; border-style: solid}
P {display:block}
```

You can see the results in Figure 9.11, where you can see the solid border around the <SECTION> element. (I might note in passing that it's a good thing that we selected a solid border for this element: Internet Explorer currently cannot draw anything but solid borders around elements.)

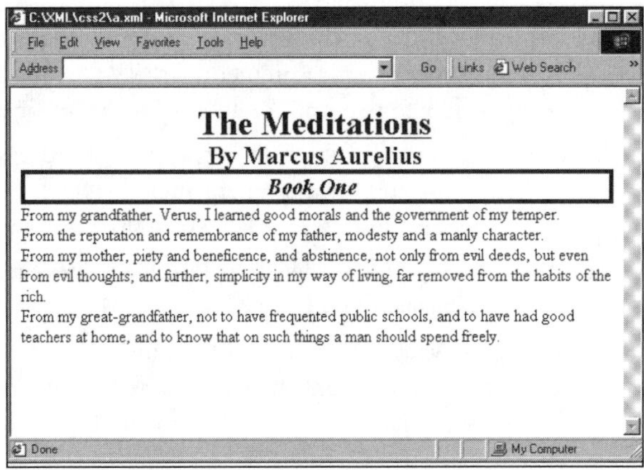

Figure 9.11 Enclosing an element in a block.

Displaying Images

You can use several properties with images:

Property	Description
`background-image`	Sets a background image; set this to an URL.
`background-repeat`	Specifies whether the background image should be tiled; set this to `repeat`, `repeat-x` (repeat in the x direction), `repeat-y` (repeat in the y direction), or `no-repeat`.
`background-attachment`	Specifies whether the background scrolls with the rest of the document.

`background-position`	Sets the initial position of the background. Specify an x and y coordinate here (where the origin is at upper-left), such as `background-position: 0% 100%` to add a background image to the lower-left.

There's also a `background` shorthand property that you can set to the background `color`, `image`, `repeat`, `attachment`, and `position` all at once (list those values in order).

Here's an example showing how to use a background image. In this case, I'll add a background image to appear behind text in `<P>` elements, making that image repeat until it fills all the space behind the `<P>` element—note that you specify an URL with the `url` keyword:

```
TITLE {display: block; font-size: 24pt; font-weight: bold;
text-align: center; text-decoration: underline}
AUTHOR {display: block; font-size: 18pt; font-weight: bold;
text-align: center}
SECTION {display: block; font-size: 16pt; font-weight: bold;
text-align: center; font-style: italic}
P {background-image: url(image.jpg);
    background-repeat: repeat}
```

For this example, I'll condense all the `<P>` elements in our XML document into one `<P>` element so that the result, showing the background image, will be clearer:

```
<?xml version="1.0" standalone="yes"?>
<?xml-stylesheet type="text/css" href="style.css"?>
<DOCUMENT>
    <TITLE CLASS="RED">The Meditations</TITLE>
    <AUTHOR>By Marcus Aurelius</AUTHOR>
    <SECTION>Book One</SECTION>
    <P>
        From my grandfather, Verus, I learned good morals
        and the government of my temper.
        From the reputation and remembrance of my father,
        modesty and a manly character.
        From my mother, piety and beneficence, and abstinence,
        not only from evil deeds, but even from evil
        thoughts; and further, simplicity in my way of living,
        far removed from the habits of the rich.
        From my great-grandfather, not to have frequented
        public schools, and to have had good teachers at home,
        and to know that on such things a man should spend
        freely.
    </P>
</DOCUMENT>
```

You can see the results in Figure 9.12, where the background image does indeed appear behind the text.

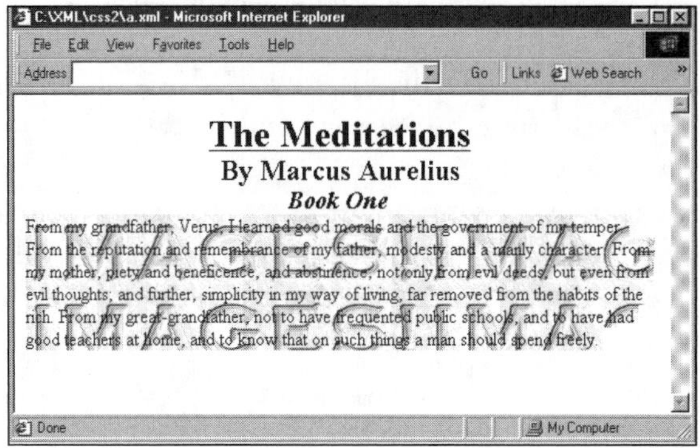

Figure 9.12 Displaying a background image.

What if you just want to display an image by itself? In that case, you can create a dedicated element that uses the image as its background image. Here's an example—note that I'm setting the `height` and `width` properties to the size of the image. Note also that I'm using the `float` property to indicate that text should flow around the left of this element:

```
TITLE {display: block; font-size: 24pt; font-weight: bold;
text-align: center; text-decoration: underline}
AUTHOR {display: block; font-size: 18pt; font-weight: bold;
text-align: center}
SECTION {display: block; font-size: 16pt; font-weight: bold;
text-align: center; font-style: italic}
P {display:block}
IMG {background: url(image.jpg) no-repeat center center;
    height: 66px;
    width: 349px;
    float: right}
```

Here's how I add the `<IMG>` element to the document:

```
<?xml version="1.0" standalone="yes"?>
<?xml-stylesheet type="text/css" href="style.css"?>
<DOCUMENT>
    <TITLE CLASS="RED">The Meditations</TITLE>
    <AUTHOR>By Marcus Aurelius</AUTHOR>
    <SECTION>Book One</SECTION>
    <IMG></IMG>
    <P>
```

```
        From my grandfather, Verus, I learned good morals
        and the government of my temper.
        From the reputation and remembrance of my father,
        modesty and a manly character.
        From my mother, piety and beneficence, and abstinence,
        not only from evil deeds, but even from evil
        thoughts; and further, simplicity in my way of living,
        far removed from the habits of the rich.
        From my great-grandfather, not to have frequented
        public schools, and to have had good teachers at home,
        and to know that on such things a man should spend
        freely.
    </P>
</DOCUMENT>
```

You can see the results in Figure 9.13.

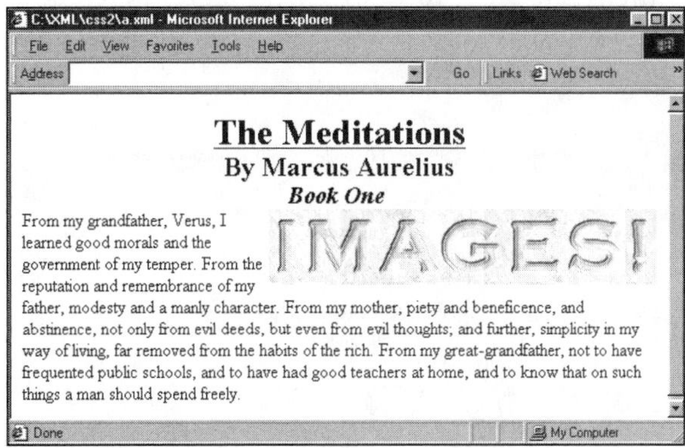

Figure 9.13 Displaying an image.

Absolute Positioning

You can use the `position` property to set the position of elements in a Web page. I'll take a look at positioning items in absolute terms in this section and in relative terms in the next section. Here are the properties that you commonly use when working with positioning:

Property	Description
`position`	Holds values such as `absolute` and `relative`
`top`	Offsets the top of the element
`bottom`	Offsets the bottom of the element
`left`	Offsets the left edge of the element
`right`	Offsets the right edge of the element

In this example, I'll set the absolute position of the image that we used in the previous example so that it's directly on top of the text:

```
TITLE {display: block; font-size: 24pt; font-weight: bold;
text-align: center; text-decoration: underline}
AUTHOR {display: block; font-size: 18pt; font-weight: bold;
text-align: center}
SECTION {display: block; font-size: 16pt; font-weight: bold;
text-align: center; font-style: italic}
P {display: block; }

IMG {background: url(image.jpg) no-repeat center center;
    height: 66px;
    width: 349px;
    position:absolute; left:50; top:160;
    border-width: thick}
```

You can see the results in Figure 9.14; as you see there, the image has indeed moved so that it's now on top of the text. Using this technique, you can place elements as you like.

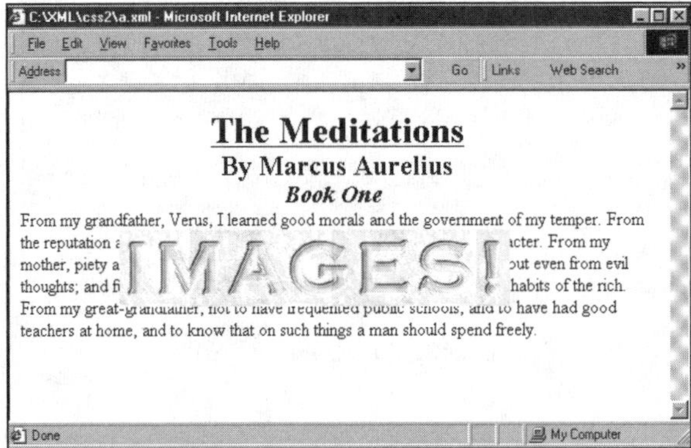

Figure 9.14 Using absolute positioning.

Relative Positioning

In addition to absolute positioning, you can use *relative* positioning. When you use relative positioning, elements are positioned relative to the location that they would have had in the normal flow of elements in the Web browser.

To position items in a relative way, you set the `position` property to `relative`. You can also set the other properties to indicate the new relative position. In this example, I'm moving some text—the name `Verus`—up 5 pixels from the normal position at which the browser would place this text with a new element, `<SUP>`, where I'm using a `STYLE` attribute to set the relative position:

```
<?xml version="1.0" standalone="yes"?>
<?xml-stylesheet type="text/css" href="style.css"?>
<DOCUMENT>
    <TITLE>The Meditations</TITLE>
    <AUTHOR>By Marcus Aurelius</AUTHOR>
    <SECTION>Book One</SECTION>
    <P>
        From my grandfather,
        <SUP STYLE="position: relative; top: -5">Verus</SUP>,
        I learned good morals and the government of my temper.
    </P>
    <P>
        From the reputation and remembrance of my father,
        modesty and a manly character.
    </P>
    <P>
        From my mother, piety and beneficence, and abstinence,
        not only from evil deeds, but even from evil
        thoughts; and further, simplicity in my way of living,
        far removed from the habits of the rich.
    </P>
    <P>
        From my great-grandfather, not to have frequented
        public schools, and to have had good teachers at home,
        and to know that on such things a man should spend
        freely.
    </P>
</DOCUMENT>
```

You can see the results in Figure 9.15, where, as you can see, the text inside the `<SUP>` element is positioned higher than the rest.

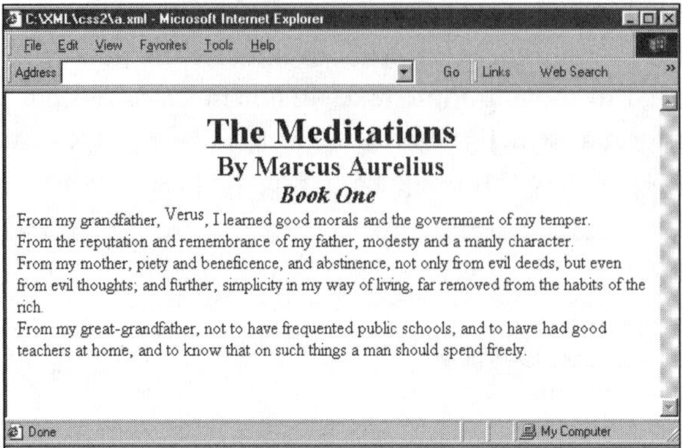

Figure 9.15 Using relative positioning.

Formal Style Property Specifications

We've seen quite a few CSS examples in this chapter. When you get more serious about CSS, you're going to need very in-depth information. For that reason, the rest of this chapter covers the most commonly used CSS styles and their formal specifications.

The W3C CSS style specifications give the possible values that CSS properties can take, the default value of those properties, and so on. The syntax that the W3C specifications use is a little complex. Here's an example—the style specification for the background-color property.

background-color

- CSS1 values: <color> | transparent
- CSS2 values: inherit
- Default value: transparent
- Element support: All elements
- Browser support: [IE4, IE5, NS4]
- Style inherited: No

Here you can see the way a style is specified, listing the possible values that the property can take for the CSS1 level specification, as well as the possible values CSS2 adds, the property's default value, which types of elements are supported (such as block-level elements), and whether the style is inherited by child elements. I'm also adding which of the two major browsers support the property, and what versions of those browsers do.

Note the expression `<color>|transparent`, which indicates the possible values you can assign this property. This expression means that you can set the `background-color` property to *either* a valid color value *or* the word `transparent`. The W3C syntax for style properties such as this is worth getting to know so that you can refer to the W3C documentation when you need it. Here's the syntax rules the W3C uses:

- Terms in angle brackets, `<` and `>`, specify valid units for values—see Table 9.1 for the details.
- Values separated with `|` specify alternatives. Only one alternative may be used.
- Values separated with `||` specify options. You can use one or more of them in any order.
- Brackets, `[` and `]`, specify group statements. These are evaluated like mathematical statements.
- `*` means that the preceding term can occur zero or more times (as in DTD syntax).
- `+` means that the preceding term occurs one or more times (as in DTD syntax).
- `?` means that the preceding term is optional (as in DTD syntax).
- Curly braces, `{` and `}`, enclose a comma-separated pair of numbers giving the minimum and maximum number of times that a term may occur, such as `{0, 10}`.

The expressions that you see in angle brackets, such as `<color>`, use a specific format, and I list those formats in Table 9.1. For example, there you'll see that `<color>` can be set to a red, green, blue triplet color value, or a predefined color. This means that you could assign a color value to the `background-color` property like this in a style rule: `{background-color: #0000ff}`. Or, you could do so like this: `{background-color: azure}`.

Table 9.1 **Units in the W3C Property Style Specifications**

Unit Measurement	**Description**
`<absolute-size>`	Absolute font sizes—may be `xx-small`, `x-small`, `small`, `medium`, `large`, `x-large`, or `xx-large`.
`<angle>`	Angle—may be `deg`, `grad`, or `rad (degrees, gradients, or radians)`.
`<border-style>`	Border style—may be `none`, `dotted`, `dashed`, `solid`, `double`, `groove`, `ridge`, `inset`, or `outset`.

continues

Table 9.1 **Continued**

Unit Measurement	Description
`<border-width>`	Width of a border—may be `thin`, `medium`, `thick`, or an explicit length.
`<color>`	Color—may be specified with a predefined color value (theoretically one of the 16 predefined CSS colors, but in practice, any color name that the browser recognizes) or RGB triplet color value.
`<family-name>`	Name of a font family, such as `Times New Roman`, `Courier New`, or `Arial`.
`<frequency>`	Frequency values—units may be `Hz` or `kHz`.
`<generic-family>`	Generic names for fonts specified as a last resort if the browser can't find a specific font face. For example, you can set this type to `serif` (for a serif font), `sans-serif` (for a sans-serif font), or `monospace` (for a monospace font).
`<generic-voice>`	Aural voices—may be set to `male`, `female`, or `child`.
`<integer>`	Standard integer values.
`<length>`	Length—can start with a `+` or `-` followed by a number. The number can include a decimal point and can be followed by a unit identifier, which may be `em` (font size of the relevant font), `ex` (the x-height of the font), `px` (pixels), `pt` (points, 1/72 of an inch), `in` (inches), `cm` (centimeters), `mm` (millimeters), or `pc` (picas, 1/6 of an inch).
`<number>`	Number—can include a sign and a decimal point.
`<percentage>`	Percentage—can include a value followed by a percent sign (`%`).
`<relative-size>`	Font size relative to the parent element—can be either `larger` or `smaller`.
`<shape>`	Shape—can be only a rectangle currently, like this: `rect (<top> <right> <bottom> <left>)`.
`<time>`	Time units—given as a number followed by `ms` (milliseconds) or `s` (seconds).
`<uri>`	Uniform resource indicator.

You also should know about two special property values: `auto` and a new CSS2 value, `inherit`. You set a property to `auto` when you want the browser to assign an automatic value to the property. Usually, the value set will depend on the context, such as the style or color of surrounding text. The `inherit` value is new in CSS2 and means that the value of this property should be *inherited* from its parent (instead of using the default initial value), if the element has a parent.

There's one more term to understand as well: *box*. A box is the area in which an element is drawn in the browser—that is, the box is the invisible rectangle surrounding the display area of the element. Because boxes are constructed with borders, padding, and margins, many style properties refer to them.

Keep in mind that I'm listing the style properties as the W3C defines them here. The way your browser uses these style properties may differ.

That's all the introduction we need to the actual style property specifications. I'll take a look at the most common style properties now, as well as the values they can take and what kind of elements you can use them with. Bear in mind that you can find the complete CSS property specifications at `www.w3.org/TR/REC-CSS1` and `www.w3.org/TR/REC-CSS2`.

Text Properties

Probably the most common reason people think of style sheets is to format text, so I'll start with the CSS text properties.

letter-spacing

- CSS1 values: normal | <length>
- CSS2 values: inherit
- Default value: normal
- Element support: All elements
- Browser support: [IE4, IE5]
- Style inherited: Yes

This property sets the spacing between text characters and is implemented in Internet Explorer, but the implementation appears to be a little spotty.

line-height

- CSS1 values: normal | <number> | <length> | <percentage>
- CSS2 values: inherit
- Default value: normal
- Element support: All elements
- Browser support: [IE3, IE4, IE5, NS4]
- Style inherited: Yes

This property gives the minimum height of the element's box. It is usually used to specify single- or double-spacing.

text-align

- CSS1 values: left | right | center | justify
- CSS2 values: <string> | inherit
- Default value: Varies
- Element support: Block-level elements
- Browser support: [IE3, IE4, IE5, NS4]
- Style inherited: Yes

This property indicates the alignment of the content of a block: left, right, center, or justified. Note that in CSS2, you can specify a string to align with respect to.

text-decoration

- CSS1 values: None | [underline | | overline | | line-through | | blink]
- CSS2 values: inherit
- Default value: None
- Element support: All elements
- Browser support: [IE3, IE4, IE5, NS4]
- Style inherited: No

This property indicates the "decorations" for text display, including underlining, overlining, and line-through (strikethrough). The blink value is not implemented anywhere yet, as far as I know.

text-indent

- CSS1 values: <length> | <percentage>
- CSS2 values: inherit
- Default value: 0
- Element support: Block-level elements
- Browser support: [IE3, IE4, IE5, NS4]
- Style inherited: Yes

This property indicates the indentation of the first line of text. Note that this property applies only to block-level elements (which you set with `display: block`).

text-shadow

- CSS2 values:
  None | [<color> | | <length><length><length>?,]*[<color> | | <length>
  <length><length>?] | inherit
- Default value: None
- Element support: All elements
- Browser support: [IE5]
- Style inherited: No

This property gives a comma-separated list of shadow effects that should be used for text.

vertical-align

- CSS1 values: baseline | sub | super | top | text-top | middle | bottom |
  text-
  bottom | <percentage> | <length>
- CSS2 values: inherit
- Default value: baseline
- Element support: Inline-level and table cell elements
- Browser support: [IE4, IE5]
- Style inherited: No

This property indicates the vertical alignment of text in the element. For example, setting this value to `text-top` and using a larger initial character in a block of text is how you create "drop caps."

white-space

- CSS1 values: normal | pre | nowrap
- CSS2 values: inherit
- Default value: normal
- Element support: Block-level elements
- Browser support: [NS4]
- Style inherited: Yes

This property indicates how whitespace should be handled. Theoretically, setting this property to `pre` should be like setting `xml:space` to `preserve`.

word-spacing

- CSS1 values: normal | <length>
- CSS2 values: inherit
- Default value: normal
- Element support: All elements
- Browser support: [None]
- Style inherited: Yes

This property sets the spacing between words.

Font Properties

Besides the text properties, probably the next most common set of style properties used is the font properties. I'll take a look at them here, starting with the `font` shorthand property.

font

- CSS1 values: [[<font-style> | | <font-variant> | | <font-weight>]? <font-size>[/<line-height>]?<font-family>
- CSS2 values: caption | icon | menu | message-box | small-caption | status-bar | inherit
- Default value: Varies
- Element support: All elements
- Browser support: [IE3, IE4, IE5]
- Style inherited: Yes

This shorthand property indicates `font-style`, `font-variant`, `font-weight`, `font-size`, `line-height`, and `font-family` properties. You list those properties in that order—and without commas between them, except between items in a list of alternate font families. You can also set all these properties individually.

font-family

- CSS1 values: [[<family-name> | <generic-family>],]*[<family-name> | <generic-family>]
- CSS2 values: inherit

- Default value: Depends on the browser
- Element support: All elements
- Browser support: [IE3, IE4, IE5, NS4]
- Style inherited: Yes

You set this property to a list of font family names or generic family names. Your document may be viewed in a browser that doesn't support the font face that you want, so you can list alternates, as we have in this chapter. You can also list generic font families, such as `serif` or `sans-serif`.

font-size

- CSS1 values: <absolute-size> | <relative-size> | <length> | <percentage>
- CSS2 values: inherit
- Default value: medium
- Element support: All elements
- Browser support: [IE3, IE4, IE5, NS4]
- Style inherited: Yes

This property sets the size of a font face. It is usually set in terms of points, but you can use any valid measurement.

font-stretch

- CSS2 values: normal | wider | narrower | ultra-condensed | extra-condensed | condensed | semi-condensed | semi-expanded | expanded | extra-expanded | ultra-expanded | inherit
- Default value: normal
- Element support: All elements
- Browser support: [None]
- Style inherited: Yes

You use this property to set a normal, condensed, or extended font face.

font-style

- CSS1 values: normal | italic | oblique
- CSS2 values: inherit
- Default value: normal

- Element support: All elements
- Browser support: [IE3, IE4, IE5, NS4]
- Style inherited: Yes

This property specifies font styles, such as `normal` (also called upright or standard), `italic`, and `oblique` fonts.

font-variant

- CSS1 values: normal | small-caps
- CSS2 values: inherit
- Default value: normal
- Element support: All elements
- Browser support: [IE4, IE5]
- Style inherited: Yes

This property indicates whether a font is a normal or special "small-caps" font.

font-weight

- CSS1 values: normal | bold | bolder | lighter | 100 | 200 | 300 | 400 | 500 | 600 | 700 | 800 | 900
- CSS2 values: inherit
- Default value: normal
- Element support: All elements
- Browser support: [IE3, IE4, IE5, NS4]
- Style inherited: Yes

This property gives the *weight* of a font, such as `normal`, `bold`, or a numeric value.

Background and Color Properties

You can also use CSS to specify backgrounds, images, and colors. What follows is a synopsis of these properties.

background

- CSS1 values: [<background-color> | | <background-image> | | <background-repeat> | | <background-attachment> | | <background-position>]
- CSS2 values: inherit
- Default value: Not defined
- Element support: All elements
- Browser support: [IE3, IE4, IE5, NS4]
- Style inherited: No

This shorthand property lets you list the background properties (such as `background-color`, `background-image`, `background-repeat`, `background-attachment`, and `background-position`) all at the same time. Of course, you can set these properties individually as well.

background-attachment

- CSS1 values: scroll | fixed
- CSS2 values: inherit
- Default value: scroll
- Element support: All elements
- Browser support: [IE4, IE5]
- Style inherited: No

This property indicates whether a background image is fixed or moves when a user scrolls the rest of the document. You can create some interesting effects by letting text "float" over a background this way.

background-color

- CSS1 values: <color> | transparent
- CSS2 values: inherit
- Default value: transparent
- Element support: All elements
- Browser support: [IE4, IE5, NS4]
- Style inherited: No

This property indicates the background color of an element. You set it to either a `<color>` value or the keyword `transparent`. The `transparent` setting makes the underlying color visible.

background-image

- CSS1 values: <uri> | none
- CSS2 values: inherit
- Default value: None
- Element support: All elements
- Browser support: [IE4, IE5, NS4]
- Style inherited: No

This property sets an element's background image. One thing to keep in mind is that, when setting a background image, you might also want to set a background color in case the image is unavailable.

background-position

- CSS1 values: [[<percentage> | <length>]{1,2} | [[top | center | bottom] | | [left | center | right]]]
- CSS2 values: inherit
- Default value: 0% 0%
- Element support: Block-level and replaced elements
- Browser support: [IE4, IE5]
- Style inherited: No

Set this property to indicate a background image's starting position. For example, setting this property to **`50% 50%`** starts it at the middle of the page.

background-repeat

- CSS1 values: repeat | repeat-x | repeat-y | no-repeat
- CSS2 values: inherit
- Default value: repeat
- Element support: All elements
- Browser support: [IE4, IE5]
- Style inherited: No

You use this property to specify whether a background image is repeated, "tiling" the background, and if so, how it is to be repeated.

color

- CSS1 values: <color>
- CSS2 values: inherit
- Default value: Browser dependent
- Element support: All elements
- Browser support: [IE3, IE4, IE5, NS4]
- Style inherited: Yes

This property sets a foreground (text) color. Set it to a color value.

Table Properties

CSS also supports a number of properties targeted especially to tables. There are quite a few table properties, but as yet the support for them is slight.

border-collapse

- CSS2 values: collapse | separate | inherit
- Default value: collapse
- Element support: Table and inline table elements
- Browser support: [IE5]
- Style inherited: Yes

This property gives a table's border model. For more information on table models, see the W3C CSS documentation.

border-spacing

- CSS2 values: <length><length>? | inherit
- Default value: 0
- Element support: Table and inline table elements
- Browser support: [None]
- Style inherited: Yes

Although it's not supported anywhere yet, this property is supposed to give the distance between cell borders.

column-span, row-span

- CSS2 values: <integer> | inherit
- Default value: 1
- Element support: Table cells, table columns, and table-column-group elements
- Browser support: [None]
- Style inherited: No

This property indicates how many columns or rows are spanned by a cell.

empty-cells

- CSS2 values: show | hide | inherit
- Default value: show
- Element support: Table cell elements
- Browser support: [None]
- Style inherited: Yes

You use this property to control how borders are drawn around cells that are empty.

table-layout

- CSS2 values: auto | fixed | inherit
- Default value: auto
- Element support: Table and inline table elements
- Browser support: [IE5]
- Style inherited: No

This property specifies how to lay out table cells, rows, and columns. For more information on table layouts, see the W3C CSS documentation.

Positioning and Block Properties

As you may recall, we took a look at absolute and relative positioning in this chapter, moving text and images around. Because the positioning style properties refer to position, they also refer to an element's box quite a bit. As mentioned earlier, an element's box is just the invisible rectangle that it's drawn in.

bottom, top, left, right

- CSS2 values: <length> | <percentage> | auto | inherit
- Default value: auto
- Element support: All elements
- Browser support: [IE3, IE4, IE5, NS4]
- Style inherited: No

This property specifies how far a box's bottom, top, left, or right content edge should be from the box's containing area. You use these properties to position the box.

direction

- CSS1 values: ltr | rtl
- CSS2 values: inherit
- Default value: ltr
- Element support: All elements
- Browser support: [IE5]
- Style inherited: Yes

This property gives the base writing direction of text (left to right or right to left).

display

- CSS1 values: inline | block | list-item
- CSS2 values: run-in | compact | marker | table | inline-table | table-row-group | table-header-group | table-footer-group | table-row | table-column-group | table-column | table-cell | table-caption | none | inherit
- Default value: inline
- Element support: All elements
- Browser support: [IE4, IE5]
- Style inherited: No

This property indicates how an element should be displayed. If you set this property to `block`, creating a block-level element, the element will be displayed starting on a new line, and the following element will also start on a new line. The `inline` value, which is the default, specifies that elements should be displayed in the normal flow of elements.

float

- CSS1 values: left | right | none
- CSS2 values: inherit
- Default value: None
- Element support: All but positioned elements
- Browser support: [IE4, IE5, NS4]
- Style inherited: No

You use this property to indicate whether a box should be positioned to the left, right, or not at all; text will flow around the element.

position

- CSS2 values: static | relative | absolute | fixed | inherit
- Default value: static
- Element support: All elements, but not generated content
- Browser support: [IE4, IE5, NS4]
- Style inherited: No

This property indicates which positioning algorithm to use. This setting is important when you set properties such as `left` or `right`.

unicode-bidi

- CSS2 values: normal | embed | bidi-override | inherit
- Default value: normal
- Element support: All elements
- Browser support: [IE5]
- Style inherited: No

You use this property to work with elements with reversed Unicode order.

z-index

- CSS2 values: auto | <integer> | inherit
- Default value: auto
- Element support: Positioned elements
- Browser support: [IE4, IE5, NS4]
- Style inherited: No

This property indicates the *stacking* level of a box, and you use it when you position elements to indicate which element goes on top of which other element.

Box Properties

An element's box is an important part of its display, and quite a few style properties work with the box.

border

- CSS1 values: [<border-width> | | <border-style> | | <color>]
- CSS2 values: inherit
- Default value: Varies
- Element support: All elements
- Browser support: [IE4, IE5, NS4]
- Style inherited: No

This shorthand property lets you set the `border-width`, `border-style`, and `color` for all four borders of a box at once. List values for those properties in that order. Of course, you can also set these properties individually.

border-top, border-right, border-bottom, border-left

- CSS1 values: [<border-top/right/bottom/left-width> | | <border-style> | | <color>]
- CSS2 values: inherit
- Default value: Varies
- Element support: All elements
- Browser support: [IE4, IE5]
- Style inherited: No

These properties give the width, style, and color of the top, right, bottom, and left border of a box. Refer to Table 9.1 for possible settings.

border-color

- CSS1 values: <color>{1,4} | transparent
- CSS2 values: inherit
- Default value: Varies

- Element support: All elements
- Browser support: [IE4, IE5, NS4]
- Style inherited: No

This property gives the color of all four borders of a box.

border-top-color, border-right-color, border-bottom-color, border-left-color

- CSS1 values: <color>
- CSS2 values: inherit
- Default value: Varies
- Element support: All elements
- Browser support: [IE4, IE5]
- Style inherited: No

These properties give the color of one border of a box, such as the border's bottom.

border-style

- CSS1 values: <border-style>{1,4}
- CSS2 values: inherit
- Default value: Varies
- Element support: All elements
- Browser support: [IE4, IE5, NS4]
- Style inherited: No

This property indicates the style of the four borders of a box. It can have from one to four values (the values will be set on the different sides of the box).

border-top-style, border-right-style, border-bottom-style, border-left-style

- CSS1 values: <border-style>
- CSS2 values: inherit
- Default value: None
- Element support: All elements
- Browser support: [IE4, IE5]
- Style inherited: No

This property lets you specify the style of one border edge of a box. Refer to Table 9.1 for possible values.

border-width

- CSS1 values: <border-width>{1,4}
- CSS2 values: inherit
- Default value: Not defined
- Element support: All elements
- Browser support: [IE4, IE5, NS4]
- Style inherited: No

This property lets you set specify the border width, setting the `border-top-width`, `border-right-width`, `border-bottom-width`, and `border-left-width` properties all at the same time.

border-top-width, border-right-width, border-bottom-width, border-left-width

- CSS1 values: <border-width>
- CSS2 values: inherit
- Default value: medium
- Element support: All elements
- Browser support: [IE4, IE5, NS4]
- Style inherited: No

These properties let you set the border widths of a box's sides, one by one.

clear

- CSS1 values: None | left | right | both
- CSS2 values: inherit
- Default value: None
- Element support: Block-level elements
- Browser support: [IE4, IE5, NS4]
- Style inherited: No

This property lets you specify how another box should "clear" the current one, much like the `CLEAR` attribute in HTML. In particular, it specifies which borders of an element's boxes may not be next to an earlier floating element.

height, width

- CSS1 values: <length> | <percentage> | auto
- CSS2 values: inherit
- Default value: auto
- Element support: All elements except inline elements, table columns, and column groups
- Browser support: [IE4, IE5, NS4]
- Style inherited: No

These properties set the height or width of boxes.

margin

- CSS1 values: <margin-width>{1,4}
- CSS2 values: inherit
- Default value: Not defined
- Element support: All elements
- Browser support: [IE3, IE4, IE5, NS4]
- Style inherited: No

This shorthand property sets the `margin-top`, `margin-right`, `margin-bottom`, and `margin-left` properties all at the same time.

margin-top, margin-right, margin-bottom, margin-left

- CSS1 values: <margin-width>
- CSS2 values: inherit
- Default value: 0
- Element support: All elements
- Browser support: [IE3, IE4, IE5, NS4]
- Style inherited: No

These properties let you set the width of the top, right, bottom, or left margins of a box.

max-height, max-width

- CSS2 values: <length> | <percentage> | none | inherit
- Default value: None
- Element support: All elements except nonreplaced inline elements and table elements
- Browser support: [IE4, IE5]
- Style inherited: No

These properties let you restrict box heights and widths to a range that you specify.

min-height

- CSS2 values: <length> | <percentage>inherit
- Default value: 0
- Element support: All elements except nonreplaced inline elements and table elements
- Browser support: [None]
- Style inherited: No

This property lets you set the minimum height of a box.

min-width

- CSS2 values: <length> | <percentage>inherit
- Default value: 0
- Element support: All elements except nonreplaced inline elements and table elements
- Browser support: [None]
- Style inherited: No

This property lets you set the minimum width of a box.

padding

- CSS1 values: <length> | <percentage>
- CSS2 values: inherit
- Default value: Not defined
- Element support: All elements

- Browser support: [IE4, IE5, NS4]
- Style inherited: No

This property lets you set the `padding-top`, `padding-right`, `padding-bottom`, and `padding-left` properties all at the same time and to the same value.

padding-top, padding-right, padding-bottom, padding-left

- CSS1 values: <length> | <percentage>
- CSS2 values: inherit
- Default value: 0
- Element support: All elements
- Browser support: [IE4, IE5, NS4]
- Style inherited: No

These properties let you set the top, right, bottom, and left padding of a box, which surrounds the content of the box.

Visual Effects Properties

New in CSS2, visual effect properties let you describe how elements are drawn. I'm including a sampling of these properties here.

clip

- CSS2 values: <shape> | auto | inherit
- Default value: auto
- Element support: Block-level and replaced elements
- Browser support: [IE5]
- Style inherited: No

The clipping region of an element indicates what part of the element is drawn and therefore, what part is visible. This property lets you set an element's clipping region.

overflow

- CSS2 values: visible | hidden | scroll | auto | inherit
- Default value: visible
- Element support: Block-level and replaced elements

- Browser support: [IE5]
- Style inherited: No

This property specifies whether the content of a block-level element should be clipped if it extends past the edges of the element's box.

visibility

- CSS2 values: visible | hidden | collapse | inherit
- Default value: inherit
- Element support: All elements
- Browser support: [IE5]
- Style inherited: No

This property indicates whether the element should be displayed.

List Properties

CSS also includes a number of styles that you use with lists. Although Internet Explorer indicates that it supports many of them, I've found the support to be spotty. To use these styles, you should set the display property to `list-item`.

list-style

- CSS1 values: [<list-style-type> | | <list-style-position> | | <list-style-image>]
- CSS2 values: inherit
- Default value: Not defined
- Element support: List items
- Browser support: [IE4, IE5]
- Style inherited: Yes

This shorthand property sets the values of the `list-style-type`, `list-style-position`, and `list-style-image` properties all at the same time and in that order.

list-style-image

- CSS1 values: <uri> | none
- CSS2 values: inherit
- Default value: None

- Element support: List items
- Browser support: [IE4, IE5]
- Style inherited: Yes

You can use this property to indicate an image that should be used next to every list item.

list-style-position

- CSS1 values: inside | outside
- CSS2 values: inherit
- Default value: outside
- Element support: List items
- Browser support: [IE4, IE5]
- Style inherited: Yes

This property sets the position of the list item marker; `outside` means that the marker should appear to the left of the text, and `inside` indicates that the marker should appear where the text's first character would normally appear.

list-style-type

- CSS1 values: disc | circle | square | decimal | decimal-leading-zero | lower-roman | upper-roman | lower-alpha | upper-alpha | none
- CSS2 values: lower-greek | lower-latin | upper-latin | hebrew | armenian | georgian | cjk-ideographic | hiragana | katakana | hiragana-iroha | katakana-iroha | inherit
- Default value: Disc
- Element support: List items
- Browser support: [IE4, IE5, NS4]
- Style inherited: Yes

This property lets you set the type of list item marker if you don't use the `list-style-image` property. The default value is `none`, which is also this property's value if the image specified cannot be displayed.

That finishes our work on cascading style sheets for the moment; in the next chapter, we'll start working with XML and Java.

10
Understanding Java

CHAPTER 7, "HANDLING XML DOCUMENTS WITH JAVASCRIPT," and Chapter 8, "XML and Data Binding," describe how to work with XML and JavaScript in Internet Explorer. However, JavaScript is a relatively lightweight language, and most serious XML programming doesn't take place in browsers such as Internet Explorer. Today, the most common way of handling XML in code is to use Java. Working with XML by using Java has become a central XML topic, and no XML book can ignore this connection.

Java should not be confused with JavaScript; despite their names and similar syntax, they are not truly related. Java is a creation of Sun Microsystems and JavaScript of Netscape. Java is far deeper and far more extensive than JavaScript.

On the other hand, now that we have used JavaScript, we've got a good leg up on Java because much of the basic syntax is similar (because both are based on the C++ model, not because JavaScript and Java are directly related). In the next two chapters, we'll see how to work with the most popular XML package written for Java—the XML for Java package from IBM's AlphaWorks.

In this chapter, we'll come up to speed with Java, building on what we already know of JavaScript. We'll get the skills that we need for the next two chapters in this chapter, including creating Java classes and windowed applications.

In general, creating serious applications with Java is more involved than working with JavaScript because Java is so much more extensive. As you can imagine, there's way more Java than we can cover in one chapter, so if you want to learn more, pick up a good book on the subject. Try *Special Edition Java 2 Platform* by Joseph Weber, published by Que, or *Sams Teach Yourself Java 2 in 24 Hours, 2nd Edition* by Roger Candenhead, published by Sams. On the other hand, this chapter introduces all the Java coding skills we'll use in the next two chapters. If you're already comfortable with Java, feel free to skip to the next chapter, where I work with the XML DOM in Java (not JavaScript, as in Chapter 7).

Java Resources

Java is a product of Sun Microsystems. These are some Web sites that contain Java resources online, most of them at Sun:

- `http://developer.netscape.com/tech/java/`. Netscape's "Java Developer Central" site, which contains a good amount of useful information
- `http://java.sun.com`. The main Java site; it's filled with information
- `http://java.sun.com/docs/`. Java documentation available online; this is *the* reference Web site.
- `http://java.sun.com/js2e/`. The site for the current Java software development kit (this URL is very subject to change).
- `http://java.sun.com/j2se/1.3/`. The home of Java Version 1.3, which is the current version as of this writing (actually called Java 2 Platform, Standard Edition, version 1.3), of the Java software development kit
- `www.javaworld.com`. A great number of Java resources and discussions

Here's another list that you might want to look into; these are free online tutorials that you can use to develop your Java skills:

- `http://java.sun.com/docs/books/tutorial/index.html`. Sun's own, very extensive Java tutorial
- `http://gamelan.earthweb.com/javaprogramming/javanotes/`. Gamelan's Java tutorial
- `www.javacoffeebreak.com`. A good online Java tutorial
- `www-4.ibm.com/software/developer/education/buildapplet/`. IBM's Java tutorial with some outstanding features

Here's an important note—Java programming is not for everyone. Java is a complex language, and to cover it fully would take thousands of pages. We can't ignore it because it has come to play such a big part in the XML world, but if you're not into programming, you can skip the Java chapters (this and the next two chapters) and continue on with the rest of the book. Many people prefer to get their Java XML applications written by someone else, and that's fine. However, these days, to really work with XML, it usually comes down sooner or later to working with Java.

Writing Java Programs

You're probably already familiar with Java, if only because of Java *applets*. Applets—windowed Java applications designed to work in browsers—took the world by storm when first introduced, and all major browsers support some version of Java these days. You can find millions of applets on the Internet, and you can pick up whole banks of them for free. There are even applets out there that work with XML.

A Java applet takes up a predefined area in a browser and can display graphics, *controls* (such as buttons and text fields), text, and more. It's interactive because it runs in your browser. As mentioned, applets took the Internet by storm when first introduced. However, they're on the wane now, largely because of other solutions that can be easier to program, such as Dynamic HTML, or more powerful, such as Shockwave.

Don't worry about Java though—as applets have become less popular (although still very popular), Java *applications* have gathered strength. The main reason that Java applications have become so powerful is that they're nearly as powerful as C++, but they're also cross-platform—you can use the same application in Windows or UNIX, for example. Many large corporations have switched from using C++ internally to using Java for most programming.

A Java application does not run in a browser like an applet—it's a free-standing program. Java applications can themselves create windows, such as applets, and we'll see how to do that here. In fact, Java applications can act as browsers, and we'll see an example of that in the next chapter with a Java application that reads an XML document from the Internet and uses it to display graphics. In that case, the XML document will specify circles to draw, and we'll be creating a graphical, not text-based, browser, which is typical of the kinds of things you can do when you create your own XML applications.

Our XML Java work will center on writing Java applications, not applets. (For security reasons, applets are very restricted in terms of what they can do, and they can't handle most types of file access—we don't want to restrict our XML programs to work only in browsers.) So how do you create a Java application? You write applications as Java code and then *compile* them with the Java Software Development Kit (SDK). (Before Java 2, the SDK was called the Java Development Kit [JDK], and some people, including some Web pages at Sun, still call it that.) The compiled application is ready to run, and we'll see how to do that here.

I'll make this more concrete with an immediate example. Here's how to create an application named app, which I'll store in a file named app.java (I'll go through the details of this application in this chapter):

```
public class app
{
    public static void main(String[] args)
    {
        System.out.println("Welcome to Java");
    }
}
```

I can use the Java compiler, which is named javac, to compile this file into a bytecode file named app.class, and app.class is what you actually run. The bytecodes in app.class are what Java reads and executes. (Java bytecodes are very compact compared to text, which makes applets fast to download. You can run the same bytecode file on many different operating systems, which makes it cross-platform.) Here's how you use javac to compile app.java (I'm using `%` as a generic command-line prompt, following the UNIX usage, where the prompt often is `%`; on an operating platform such as Windows, this prompt will be something like `C:\XML>`):

```
%javac app.java
```

This creates app.class, and it's that file you use when running that application. To run the application, you use the tool named java (which comes with the Java SDK), like this:

```
%javac app.java
%java app
Welcome to Java
```

As you can see, the `java` tool executes the bytecode file app.class, and the result—the text `Welcome to Java`—appears. As mentioned, I'm using `%` as a generic command-line prompt because Java is available on many platforms. In Windows, you use these tools in an MS DOS window like this:

```
C:\>java app
Welcome to Java
```

That's what running a Java application looks like. As we'll see, there are many similarities between Java and JavaScript—but there are also significant differences. For example, we'll need to indicate the *type* of variables in Java, which you don't have to do in JavaScript, and Java is also a lot more object-oriented than JavaScript.

Java Is Object-Oriented from the Ground Up

We first got a look at object-oriented programming when working with JavaScript, but that was only a quick glance. Object-oriented programming is integral to every aspect of Java. For example, take a look at the application we just saw:

```
public class app
{
    public static void main(String[] args)
    {
        System.out.println("Welcome to Java");
    }
}
```

The very first line—`public class app`—defines a *class* named `app`. Our whole program is based on that class because, unlike JavaScript, every line of code that you write in Java must be part of a class (or an *interface*, which is a more generalized form of class). When Java runs this application, it creates an object of this class and gives that object control. So, although you can optionally use objects in JavaScript, there's no avoiding them in Java.

I'll take a closer look at the idea behind classes now because we'll have to understand more about them than we did when discussing JavaScript. Object-oriented programming is really just another technique to let you implement that famous programming dictum: Divide and conquer.

Here's the idea: You *encapsulate* data and functions into *objects*, which makes objects into self-contained units. The data inside an object can be purely internal to the object, in which case it's called *private data*, or it can be accessible externally, in which case it's called *public data*.

The functions built into an object can also be purely private, or they can be public. In fact, ideally, the object should interact with the rest of the program only through a well-defined interface as created by its public functions. As we saw in Chapter 6, "Understanding JavaScript," functions that are part of classes or objects are called *methods*.

Object-oriented programming was first developed to let programmers handle larger programs by breaking them up into functional units that can be easily conceptualized. As you know, you can already break your code up into functions; object-oriented programming goes a step further than that, letting you create objects that can contain not just one function, but many, as well as internal data items. When you encapsulate part of your code into an object, it lets you think of that part of the program in an easily conceptualized way, and that's the motivation behind object-oriented programming.

For example, consider a car—but consider it not as a sleek new automobile, but as an assemblage of pipes, wires, valves, switches, gasoline, and all the various parts that make it work. Now imagine that you are responsible yourself for handling everything that the car usually does itself, such as pumping the fuel, igniting the fuel, transmitting power to the wheels, regulating electrical power, and more. A device requiring such attention would be impossible to drive. Now imagine all those functions back where they should be, internal to the car, and interacting with each other automatically as needed when you step on the gas. You think of the result simply as a car—an easily imagined single concept. All you have to do is to turn it on and step on the gas.

That's the idea behind encapsulation—you can take a complex system that requires a lot of attention and turn it into an object that handles the details internally when you pass control to it. If the first dictum of object-oriented programming is, "Divide and conquer," then the second is surely "Out of sight, out of mind."

In Java, object-oriented programming revolves around a few key concepts: classes, data members, inheritance, methods, and objects. This list summarizes these terms:

- **Class.** A class can be thought of as a template from which you can create objects. The definition of the class includes the formal specifications for the class and any data and methods in it.
- **Data members.** The data members of a class are the variables that are part of an object. You store the data that the object uses in its data members.

- **Inheritance.** This is the process of deriving one class, called the *derived class*, from another, the *base class*, and being able to make use of the base class's methods in the derived class, while adding new functionality to the derived class.
- **Method.** A method is a function built into an object. Methods can be part of classes (*class methods*) or objects (*object methods*), as we'll see in this chapter.
- **Object.** This is an *instance* of a class—what you create with classes. You can think of a class as the *type* of an object. When you've created an object, you can customize it by storing data in it (which you can't do with a class).

All these constructs are important to object-oriented programming, and we'll get more details on each of them in this chapter as we see how to create our own classes.

Getting the Java SDK

To create your own Java applications, you'll need to get and install the Java SDK, at `http://java.sun.com/js2e`. After downloading the Java SDK, usually as one executable package that installs itself, follow the installation instructions on the `http://java.sun.com` site.

At this point, I'd love to be able to give detailed instructions on how to install the Java SDK, but that's a trap too many books have fallen into. The actual installation procedure has changed so often and so many times that any book that covers Java (and I've written many on Java) and tries to give those instructions is sure to make itself obsolete immediately. On the other hand, in recent versions, all you have to do is run an executable program that you download, and it'll do all the work for you.

As indicated in the Sun installation instructions, you must make sure that your machine can find the Java tools, including the Java compiler, javac. To do this, make sure that the Java bin subdirectory is in your computer's path. For example, in Windows, the bin subdirectory is `c:\jdk1.2.2\bin` for the Java 2 SDK by default, version 1.2.2. You add a line like the following to autoexec.bat:

```
SET PATH=%PATH%;C:\JDK1.2.2\BIN
```

Depending on your operating system, you must reboot your computer to make these changes take effect. Now that the bin directory is in the path, you'll be able to use the Java tools from the command line; otherwise, you'll have to preface them with a pathname each time you want to use them.

Creating Java Files

The actual Java code that we'll write is stored in plain text files holding Java statements and declarations. To store Java code in a file, you can use a simple text editor or as fancy a word processor as you like, as long as the result is a plain text file without any fancy formatting that the Java compiler can't handle. You can use whatever text editor you prefer, such as vi in UNIX, or WordPad in Windows.

You should give such files the extension .java because the Java compiler expects that extension. As you saw, I saved the application named app in a file named app.java. This Java file is the one that you'll pass to the Java compiler to create a bytecode file. A very important point to remember is that the file into which you save a java class must have the same name as the java class itself.

The tools we'll use are ready; it's time to start writing code.

Writing Code: Creating an Application

Here's the sample Java application that I'll develop through to the compiling and running stages over the next few sections. Place this code in a file named app.java:

```
public class app
{
    public static void main(String[] args)
    {
        System.out.println("Welcome to Java");
    }
}
```

As we've seen, this application will print out the text `Welcome to Java` when you run it. For example, here's how things would look in a DOS window under Windows:

```
C:\>java app
Welcome to Java
```

As you can see, this is not the most powerful of programs, but it's simple enough to get us started. We'll work up from this point to windowed Java applications at the end of the chapter. To see what's going on in app.java, the following sections take it apart, line by line.

public class app

Note the first line in app.java:

```
public class app
{
    .
    .
    .
}
```

This line of code says that we're creating a new Java class named `app`. When we translate this file into a bytecode file, Java itself will create an object of this class and give it control.

Note also the keyword `public` in this line of code. This keyword is an *access specifier*. When you use the `public` access specifier for a class, that class is accessible anywhere in your program. The main class for a Java application must always be `public`. In fact, Java insists that you name the file after the `public` class in it, which is why this file is named app.java (note that capitalization counts—app.java must hold a public class named `app`, not `APP` or `App`). Because the name of a public class sets the name of the file in which that class is defined, you should have only one public class in a file.

Following the `public class app` line is the actual implementation of the class, which goes in curly braces:

```
public class app
{
    .
    .
    .
}
```

As with the code that you write for methods, the code that you write for objects must go inside curly braces.

public static void main(String[] args)

The next line of code in the application is as follows:

```
public class app
{
    public static void main(String[] args)
    {
        .
        .
        .
    }
}
```

What's going on here? In this case, I'm defining a function that's part of an object (because it's defined inside the object's definition), which makes it a method. I'm also declaring this method public, which means that it's accessible (may be called) outside the object. Methods that I declare private cannot be called from outside the object (and are usually utility methods that other methods inside the object call). As with functions in JavaScript, you can pass arguments to Java methods, and you can have methods return values. I'll go into more detail on this process later in the section "Creating Methods in Java," but here I'm indicating that this method is named `main` and does not return any value, which I indicate with the `void` keyword. The `main` method is a special one in Java because it's the one that will be called automatically when Java starts this application. When Java finds the `main` method, it passes control to it. (Applets don't need a `main` method—in fact, that's a major programming difference between programming applets and applications.) You place the code that you want run as soon as the application starts in the `main` method.

In addition, I'm indicating that this method is passed an array of Java `String` objects by enclosing the code `String[] args` in parentheses after the method name. You must declare the type of every argument that you pass to a method, and I'm listing that type as `String[]` here, which is an array of strings. I'm also naming that array `args`, which is how I can refer to it in the method's code. This array is passed to every application's `main` method; as we'll see later in the section "Creating Methods in Java," you can use it to read the command-line arguments passed to the application. (For example, if you were to start the application like this: `%java app Welcome to Java`, the command-line arguments are `Welcome`, `to`, and `Java`.)

There's one more point here—note the `static` keyword. Technically speaking, the `main` method is a method of the application's main class, `app`. You don't create an object of the `app` class yourself in code; it remains as a class. For that reason, the methods and data items in the `app` class are class methods and data items (as opposed to object methods and data items). There is a rule for class methods and data items: They must be declared `static`, which gives Java a special way of storing them. When you've declared them `static`, you have access to the methods and data items in a class without having to create an object of that class.

This line of code starts the `main` method, and the rest of this method's code is inside curly braces, as usual:

```
public class app
{
    public static void main(String[] args)
    {
        .
        .
        .
    }
}
```

The purpose of this method is to print out the text `Welcome to Java`, and I'll do that in the next line of code.

System.out.println("Welcome to Java");

The `main` method has just one line of code in it, and here it is:

```
public class app
{
    public static void main(String[] args)
    {
        System.out.println("Welcome to Java");
    }
}
```

This line of code is the only one that actually produces anything as far as the user sees; it prints out `Welcome to Java`. So what's going on here?

In this case, I'm using some of the built-in functionality that comes with Java. Like JavaScript, Java has plenty of classes and objects ready for you to use. In Java, that functionality is available in Java *packages* (which are class libraries). One of the Java packages that is available in any Java program is `java.lang`, the Java language package itself, and this package includes a class named `System`, which contains a static object named `out` that enables you to communicate with the user. In particular, I'm using the `out` object's `println` method here to display text on the user's console.

Here's another thing to notice: This line of code ends with a semicolon (;). Ending each simple statement with a semicolon has become standard in languages such as C, C++, Java, and even JavaScript. In JavaScript, we were able to omit the semicolon because browsers don't require it—in fact, most people do omit it. In Java, it's another story. The semicolons are required. If you're coming to Java from JavaScript, you may get the feeling that Java is a very prickly language by comparison to JavaScript: Not only do you have to put in the semicolons, but you also have to specify a data type for each data item. When you try to assign a value of one type to a variable of another (which may be legal in JavaScript), Java will give you warning and error reports.

At this point, you've created your new application and stored it in a file named app.java. What's the next step? How do you get it to actually *run*? Take a look at the next section.

Compiling Code

We have the complete file, app.java, and we're ready to run it. The first step is compiling it into a bytecode file, app.class. To compile app.java, you use the Java tool javac, the Java compiler (on Windows machines, this program is called javac.exe and is located in the bin subdirectory of the JDK installation). Here's how you use javac in general. (All the arguments here are optional, and I'll place them in square brackets to indicate that, which is the convention Sun itself uses in the Java documentation.)

```
javac [options] [sourcefiles] [files]
```

Here are the arguments to `javac`:

Argument	Description
options	Command-line options; see the Java documentation for the details; we won't need any command-line options here.
sourcefiles	One or more code files to be compiled (here, that'll be just app.java).
files	One or more files that list command-line options code files to compile.

In this case, I'll compile app.java with this command:

```
%javac app.java
```

The Java compiler, javac, compiles the file app.java (assuming that there are no errors), translating it and creating a new file named app.class. If errors occur, the Java compiler will tell you what they are, including what line of code is wrong, as in this case, where I've forgotten the name of the `println` method and tried to use one called `printText`:

```
%javac app.java
app.java:5: Method printText(java.lang.String) not found in class
java.io.Print
Stream.
        System.out.printText("Welcome to Java");
                             ^
1 error
```

At this point, we've created the file app.class, the bytecode file that Java will need to run the application. This bytecode file will run unchanged on any system that supports Java.

So, how do you actually run app.class? I'll take a look at that in the next section.

Running Java Applications

The way you actually run Java applications is with the Java tool named, appropriately enough, java. This tool is a program that comes with the Java SDK (java.exe in Windows, in the Java bin directory).

> **Running Java Apps Without the SDK**
>
> You don't need the full Java SDK to simply run Java applications. You can get the java tool in the Java Runtime Environment, or JRE, which you can get from the Sun Java site, at `http://java.sun.com/js2e`.

To run the app application, I use the java tool like this on the command line:

```
%java app
```

The result appears at once:

```
%java app
Welcome to Java
```

You can see what this looks like in Figure 10.1, where I'm running this application in a DOS window in Windows.

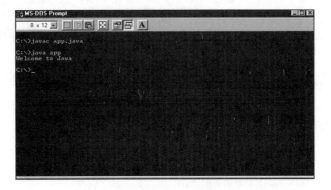

Figure 10.1 Running a Java application.

That's all it takes—you've created, compiled, and run your first Java application. (Note that if your application isn't responding or you want to stop it for some reason, you can type Ctrl+C. If that doesn't work, try the Escape key.)

While we're on the topic of compiling and running code, we should cover another detail—commenting your Java code.

Commenting Your Code

As with JavaScript, you can comment your Java code. Comments serve the same purpose here as they do in XML or JavaScript—they hold descriptive text that explains what's going on in your code. There are two ways to insert comments in a Java program. The first way is to surround comments, especially multiline comments, with the characters `/*` and `*/`, like this:

```
/* This application is designed to display
   the message "Welcome to Java" on the console
*/
public class app
{
    public static void main(String[] args)
    {
        System.out.println("Welcome to Java");
    }
}
```

As with any type of comment, the Java compiler will ignore the text in the comment—that is, any text between the `/*` and `*/` markers.

As with JavaScript, Java also supports a one-line comment, using a double slash (`//`). The Java compiler will ignore everything on a line after the `//` marker, so you can create whole lines that are comments, or just add a comment to an individual line, like this:

```
/* This application is designed to display
   the message "Welcome to Java" on the console
*/

public class app          //Define the class app
{
    //Define main(), the first method to be called.
    public static void main(String[] args)
    {
        //Display the message "Welcome to Java"
        System.out.println("Welcome to Java");
    }
}
```

In fact, there's even another type of comments, JavaDoc comments, that start with `/**` and end with `*/`, and are used by the javadoc tool to provide documentation for a program.)

Importing Java Packages and Classes

As mentioned, the classes that Sun has put together already for you to use are stored in class libraries called packages. The classes that we'll use to interact with XML documents in the next two chapters are also stored in packages. Although the `java.lang` package is already available to your code by default, the classes in other packages are not, and you must *import* those packages to use them. You can also import individual classes, as well as whole packages. Knowing how to do this is very important in Java programming because a great deal of the resources that most programs use are in packages that you must import.

To import a package, you use the Java `import` statement, which looks like this:

```
import [package1[.package2...].](classname|*);
```

Following the Sun conventions, items in square brackets (`[]`) are optional, and the upright bar (`|`) means *or*, much as it does when you write DTDs.

Note that you put a dot (.) between package and class names to keep them separate. The standard Java packages themselves are stored in a large package called `java`, so the `util` package is really called the `java.util` package. (Other large packages like the `java` package are available—for example, the extensive `Swing` package is stored in the `javax` package.)

Here's an example; in this case, I want to use the `Date` class in the `java.util` package. To do that, I can import that class this way in code:

```
import java.util.Date;

public class app
{
    public static void main(String[] args)
    {
    .
    .
    .
    }
}
```

Now I'm able to use the `Date` class in code. To do that, I create a new `Date` object with the `new` operator—which is how you create objects from classes in JavaScript as well. (In fact, we used the JavaScript `Date` class and created a new object of that class in Chapter 6.) The new `Date` object represents today's date, which I can display like this—note that I'm also adding a pair of empty parentheses after the `Date` class to indicate that I'm not passing any value to that class's constructor. (As we saw in Chapter 6, a class's constructor is a method that runs when an object is created from the class, allowing you to initialize the object.)

```
import java.util.Date;

public class app
{
    public static void main(String[] args)
    {
        System.out.println("Today's date is " + new Date());
    }
}
```

When you compile and run this application, this is the kind of result you'll see:

```
%java app
Today's date is Mon May 22 16:28:53 EDT 2001
```

In this case, I imported a specific class, the `Date` class, from the `java.util` package. However, you can import all classes from a package at once with the `*` wildcard, like this, where I'm importing all `java.util` classes. (Note that this does not make the `app.class` file any larger—only those classes that are actually referenced in the code are used when building the final bytecode file—the bytecode file `app.class` will be the same size if you use either the statement `import java.util.Date;` or the statement `import java.util.*;`.)

```
import java.util.*;

public class app
{
    public static void main(String[] args)
    {
        System.out.println("Today's date is " + new Date());
    }
}
```

You can also import classes that you've created. For example, say that you've created a class named `Display` that uses a method named `showImage` to display an image on the user's screen. You might create a new object of the `Display` class and use the `showImage` method something like this:

```
public class app
{
    public static void main(String[] args)
    {
        (new Display()).showImage("flowers.gif");
    }
}
```

When you've created the file `Display.class`, you can import the `Display` class into your program like this:

```
import Display;

public class app
{
    public static void main(String[] args)
    {
        (new Display()).showImage("flowers.gif");
    }
}
```

This technique relies on having `Display.class` in the same directory as the application you're compiling so that the `import` statement can find it. On the other hand, you might want to store `Display.class` in another directory, such as C:\display. In that case, you have to add `c:\display` to the Java environment variable `CLASSPATH`. We'll see more about this in the next chapter, or you can see the Java documentation for all the details.

Creating Variables in Java

We've seen that Java applications are class-based, and we've gotten enough Java down now to create basic programs. The next step in Java programming is to start storing your data so that you can work on that data. As with JavaScript, variables serve as locations in memory in which you can store your data. However, unlike JavaScript, Java variables are strongly *typed*, which means that you must declare a type for each variable and be careful about mixing those types. (This is actually one of the strengths of Java because the basic data types are always the same, and the programmer does not need to worry about arcane floating point standards or word orders.)

For example, one of the most common variable types is int, which stands for *integer.* This type sets aside 4 bytes of memory, which means that you can store values between –2,147,483,648 and 2,147,483,647 in int variables. Quite a few different variable types are built into Java, such as integers, floating point numbers, and individual characters.

When you want to use a variable in Java, you must declare it, specifying the variable's type:

```
type name [= value][, name [= value]...];
```

Here's an example showing how to declare a variable of the int type. This variable is named counter:

```
public class app
{
    public static void main(String[] args)
    {
        int counter;
        .
        .
        .
    }
}
```

What I've done is set aside 4 bytes of memory for the variable named counter. I can store a value of 2001 in that counter like this, using the Java assignment operator:

```
public class app
{
    public static void main(String[] args)
    {
        int counter;

        counter = 2001;
    .
    .
    .
    }
}
```

And I can display the value in the counter variable with a println statement, like this:

```
public class app
{
    public static void main(String[] args)
    {
        int counter;

        counter = 2001;
```

```
        System.out.println("The current counter value is " + counter);
    }
}
```

Here's the result of this code:

```
%java app
The current counter value is 2001
```

As in JavaScript, you can use a shortcut to both declare a variable and assign a value to it at the same time:

```
public class app
{
    public static void main(String[] args)
    {
        int counter = 2001;

        System.out.println("The current counter value is " + counter);
    }
}
```

Plenty of variable types are built into Java besides `int`:

- **Boolean.** The `boolean` type holds only two types of values: `true` and `false`.
- **Characters.** The `char` type holds representations of characters such as letters and numbers.
- **Floating point numbers.** There are two types here—`float` and `double` (for double precision), which hold signed floating point numbers.
- **Integers.** There are a number of integer types, such as `byte` (1 byte of storage), `short` (usually 2 bytes), `int` (usually 4 bytes), and `long` (usually 8 bytes), which hold signed (that is, plus or minus), whole-value numbers.

Because Java is a very strongly typed language, it's very particular about mixing data types. For example, look at this code, where I'm declaring a floating point number and an integer, and then assigning the floating point number to the integer:

```
public class app
{
    public static void main(String[] args)
    {
        float counter = 2001;
        int counter2;

        counter2 = counter;

        System.out.println("The current counter2 value is " + counter2);
    }
}
```

Java regards this as a problem because the floating point type can hold numbers with greater precision than the `int` type. It returns an error when you try to compile this code, saying that an "explicit cast" is required to convert a floating point number to an integer:

```
%javac app.java
app.java:8: Incompatible type for =. Explicit cast
needed to convert float to int.
        counter2 = counter;
                 ^
1 error
```

To solve a problem like this, you can explicitly request Java to convert the floating point number to an integer with the *cast* `(int)`:

```
public class app
{
    public static void main(String[] args)
    {
        float counter = 2001;
        int counter2;

        counter2 = (int) counter;

        System.out.println("The current counter2 value is " + counter2);
    }
}
```

You can convert between types like this if required, but bear in mind that you could lose some numerical precision this way.

Creating Arrays in Java

Simple data types of the kind we saw in the previous section are fine for storing single data items, but data is often more complex. Like JavaScript, Java supports arrays as well. Here's an example; in this case, I'll store the balances in customers' charge accounts in an array named `chargesDue`. I start by declaring that array, making it of type `double`:

```
public class app
{
    public static void main(String[] args)
    {
        double chargesDue[];
    .
    .
    .
```

Before using the array, you also have to allocate the number of elements that you want the array to hold. You do that like this, using the new operator:

```
public class app
{
    public static void main(String[] args)
    {
        double chargesDue[];

        chargesDue = new double[100];
    .
    .
    .
```

You can combine the array declaration and definition into one statement, like this:

```
public class app
{
    public static void main(String[] args)
    {
        double chargesDue[] = new double[100];
    .
    .
    .
```

After the array has been created, you can address individual elements using square brackets and an array index, like this:

```
public class app
{
    public static void main(String[] args)
    {
        double chargesDue[] = new double[100];

        chargesDue[4] = 99.06;

        System.out.println("Customer 4 owes $" + chargesDue[4]);
    }
}
```

Here's the result of this code:

```
%java app
Customer 4 owes $99.06
```

In Java, the lower bound of an array that you declare this way is `0`, so the statement `chargesDue = new double[100]` creates an array with a first item of `chargesDue[0]` and a last item of `chargesDue[99]`.

You can also initialize arrays with values at the same time you create them. You do that by specifying a comma-separated list of values in curly braces, like this (note that the number of elements in the created array will be the number of elements in the list):

```
public class app
{
    public static void main(String[] args)
    {
        double chargesDue[] = {1093.66, 667.19, 45.99, 890.30, 99.06};

        System.out.println("Customer 4 owes $" + chargesDue[4]);
    }
}
```

I'll elaborate this example now. Say that the store we're handling customer balances for opens a new branch, so now there are both eastern and western branches. If customers can open accounts in both branches, we'll need to keep track of two balances for each customer. You can do that by using a two-dimensional array, like this:

```
public class app
{
    public static void main(String[] args)
    {
        double chargesDue[][] = new double[2][100];
    .
    .
    .
```

Now you refer to every element in the array with two array indices, not just one, as in the previous, one-dimensional version of this array:

```
public class app
{
    public static void main(String[] args)
    {
        double chargesDue[][] = new double[2][100];

        chargesDue[0][4] = 99.06;
        chargesDue[1][4] = 23.17;
    .
    .
    .
```

I can display the balance in both a customer's eastern and western branch accounts, like this:

```
public class app
{
    public static void main(String[] args)
    {
        double chargesDue[][] = new double[2][100];

        chargesDue[0][4] = 99.06;
        chargesDue[1][4] = 23.17;

        System.out.println("Customer 4 owes $" +
        chargesDue[0][4] + " in the eastern branch.");
        System.out.println("Customer 4 owes $" +
        chargesDue[1][4] + " in the western branch.");
    }
}
```

Here's the result:

```
%java app
Customer 4 owes $99.06 in the eastern branch.
Customer 4 owes $23.17 in the western branch.
```

You can also initialize a two-dimensional array by assigning values when declaring such an array:

```
public class app
{
    public static void main(String[] args)
    {
        double chargesDue[][] = {{1093.66, 667.19, 45.99, 890.30, 99.06},
                                 {2019.00, 129.99, 19.01, 630.90, 23.17}};

        System.out.println("Customer 4 owes $" +
            chargesDue[0][4] + " in the eastern branch.");
        System.out.println("Customer 4 owes $" +
            chargesDue[1][4] + " in the western branch.");
}
}
```

Determining the Length of an Array

Need to find the length of an array? Just use the array's `length` property, like this: `scores.length`.

Creating Strings in Java

You may have noticed that you can combine strings with the + operator in Java, just as you can in JavaScript:

```
public class app
{
    public static void main(String[] args)
    {
        double chargesDue[][] = {{1093.66, 667.19, 45.99, 890.30, 99.06},
                                 {2019.00, 129.99, 19.01, 630.90, 23.17}};

        System.out.println("Customer 4 owes $" +
            chargesDue[0][4] + " in the eastern branch.");
        System.out.println("Customer 4 owes $" +
            chargesDue[1][4] + " in the western branch.");
    }
}
```

The reason this works is that strings are supported by the built-in class `String` in Java. In fact, the `String` class is treated in a special way in Java, and you can use it just as you would any built-in data type, as in the following case. (Note that I don't have to use the `new` operator or call the `String` class's constructor here.)

```
public class app
{
    public static void main(String[] args)
    {
        String welcome = "Welcome to Java";
        .
        .
        .
```

You can treat this new `String` variable as you would other simple variables, including printing it out like this:

```
public class app
{
    public static void main(String[] args)
    {
        String welcome = "Welcome to Java";

        System.out.println(welcome);
    }
}
```

In fact, there are really two string classes that are available in Java—the `String` and `StringBuffer` classes. `String` objects are read-only because they don't allow you to change their internal data. However, you can change the internal text in the `StringBuffer` class. Both these classes have many methods built into them, which you can find in the Java documentation.

Java Operators

As in JavaScript, operators are an important part of programming in Java. Here's an example adding two values using the Java + operator:

```
public class app
{
    public static void main(String[] args)
    {
        int int1 = 130, int2 = 250, sum;

        sum = int1 + int2;

        System.out.println(int1 + " + " + int2 +
            " = " + sum);
    }
}
```

Here are the results of this code:

```
%java app
130 + 250 = 380
```

So what operators are available in Java? Table 10.1 contains all of them—note that JavaScript shares nearly all of them as well.

Table 10.1 **Java Operators**

Operator	Operation Performed
++	Increment
--	Decrement
=	Assignment
==	Equal to
+	Addition
+=	Addition assignment
-	Subtraction
-=	Subtraction assignment
*	Multiplication
*=	Multiplication assignment

continues

Table 10.1 **Continued**

<table>
<tr><th>Operator</th><th>Operation Performed</th></tr>
<tr><td>/</td><td>Division</td></tr>
<tr><td>/=</td><td>Division assignment</td></tr>
<tr><td><</td><td>Less than</td></tr>
<tr><td><=</td><td>Less than or equal to</td></tr>
<tr><td><<</td><td>Shift left</td></tr>
<tr><td><<=</td><td>Shift left assignment</td></tr>
<tr><td>></td><td>Greater than</td></tr>
<tr><td>>=</td><td>Greater than or equal to</td></tr>
<tr><td>>></td><td>Shift right</td></tr>
<tr><td>>>=</td><td>Shift right assignment</td></tr>
<tr><td>>>></td><td>Shift right with zero fill</td></tr>
<tr><td>>>>=</td><td>Shift right zero fill assignment</td></tr>
<tr><td>^</td><td>Logical Xor</td></tr>
<tr><td>^=</td><td>Bitwise Xor assignment</td></tr>
<tr><td>|</td><td>Logical Or</td></tr>
<tr><td>||</td><td>Short-circuit Or</td></tr>
<tr><td>|=</td><td>Bitwise Or assignment</td></tr>
<tr><td>~</td><td>Bitwise unary Not</td></tr>
<tr><td>!</td><td>Logical unary Not</td></tr>
<tr><td>!=</td><td>Not equal to</td></tr>
<tr><td>&</td><td>Logical And</td></tr>
<tr><td>&&</td><td>Short-circuit And</td></tr>
<tr><td>&=</td><td>Bitwise And assignment</td></tr>
<tr><td>?:</td><td>Ternary <code>if...else</code></td></tr>
<tr><td>%</td><td>Modulus</td></tr>
<tr><td>%=</td><td>Modulus assignment</td></tr>
</table>

Java Conditional Statements: *if, if...else, switch*

After operators, the next level up is to use conditional statements, and Java supports the same conditional statements as JavaScript: `if`, `if...else`, and `switch`.

The `if` statement enables you to check a condition, which you create using the Java conditional operators such as <, >, and ==:

```
if (condition) {
    code executed if condition is true
}
else {
    code executed if condition is false
}
```

For example, say that you had two `double` variables, `assets` and `debts`, and you wanted to compare the two to make sure that you're solvent. You might want the code to display a message, such as `You're solvent.` You can do that like this (note the \ before the `'` in this code; you must add the \ to let Java know that the `'` is not a quotation mark):

```
public class app
{
    public static void main(String[] args)
    {
        double assets = 175.99;
        double debts = 115.99;

        if (assets > debts) {
            System.out.println("You\'re solvent.");
}
    }
}
```

As we've seen when discussing JavaScript, the `if` statement checks its condition and, if that condition evaluates to true, executes the code in the `if` statement's body. In this case, the code will display the message; here are the results:

```
%java app
You're solvent.
```

You can also explicitly handle the case in which the condition in an `if` statement turns out to be false by including an `else` clause. If the condition in the `if` statement evaluates to false, the code in the `else` clause is executed if the `if` statement has such a clause. Here's an example; in this case, the second message will be displayed if the amount in `assets` is less than or equal to the amount in `debts`:

```
public class app
{
    public static void main(String[] args)
    {
        double assets = 175.99;
        double debts = 115.99;
```

continues ▸

```
        if (assets > debts) {
            System.out.println("You\'re solvent.");
}
        else {
            System.out.println("Uh oh.");
        }
    }
}
```

You can also create "ladders" of `if..else` statements, like this, where I'm handling the cases in which the amount in `assets` is either the same as or greater than that in `debts`:

```
public class app
{
    public static void main(String[] args)
    {
        double assets = 175.99;
        double debts = 115.99;

        if (assets > debts) {
            System.out.println("You\'re solvent.");
}
        else {
            if(assets == debts) {
                System.out.println("You\'re broke.");
            }
            else {
                System.out.println("Uh oh.");
            }
        }
    }
}
```

As with JavaScript, Java also supports a `switch` statement:

```
switch(test){
    case value1:
            .
            .
            .
        code executed if test matches value1
            .
            .
            .
        break;
    case value2:
            .
            .
            .
```

```
        code executed if test matches value2
          .
          .
          .
        break;
    default:
          .
          .
          .
        code executed if test doesn't matches any case
          .
          .
          .
        break;
}
```

But there's a catch: You can't use it with most of the many variable types Java defines. The only values that you can check in `switch` statements are `byte`, `char`, `short`, or `int` values. Here's an example where I'm working with integers:

```
public class app
{
    public static void main(String[] args)
    {
        int day = 5;

        switch(day) {
            case 0:
                System.out.println("Today is Sunday.");
                break;
            case 1:
                System.out.println("Today is Monday.");
                break;
            case 2:
                System.out.println("Today is Tuesday.");
                break;
            case 3:
                System.out.println("Today is Wednesday.");
                break;
            case 4:
                System.out.println("Today is Thursday.");
                break;
            case 5:
                System.out.println("Today is Friday.");
                break;
            default:
                System.out.println("It must be Saturday.");
        }
    }
}
```

There's another useful way of handling `if...else` situations—you can use the Java `?:` operator. This operator returns one of two values depending on whether an expression evaluates to true or false. You put the condition in front of the `?`, the value that this operator should return if the condition is true immediately after the `?`, and the value that the operator should return if the condition is false after the colon (:). Here's an example, where I've converted the earlier `if...else` example to use the `?:` operator:

```
public class app
{
    public static void main(String[] args)
    {
        double assets = 175.99;
        double debts = 115.99;
        String output;

        output = assets > debts ? "You\'re solvent." : "Uh oh.";

        System.out.println(output);
    }
}
```

Java Loops: *for, while, do...while*

The next step after working with conditional statements is to handle loops. Like JavaScript, Java supports a `for` loop, a `while` loop, and a `do...while` loop.

Here's how you use a Java `for` loop in general; note that the statement that makes up the body of the `for` loop can be a compound statement—it can be made up of several single statements enclosed in curly braces:

```
for (initialization_expression; test_condition; iteration_expression) {
    statement
}
```

You place an expression in the *`initialization`* part of the `for` loop (which often initializes a variable—that is, a loop index—to `0`), and then you place a test condition in the *`test`* part of the loop to be tested each time the code in the loop has been executed. If the test is false, the loop ends (often the test condition checks whether the value in the loop index exceeds a specified maximum value). On the other hand, if the test condition is true, the body of the loop is executed and the code in the *`iteration`* part of the loop is executed to get the loop ready for the next iteration (often by incrementing the loop index).

Here's an example; in this case, I'm summing the values in five bank accounts, as stored in an array named accounts, using a for loop:

```
public class app
{
    public static void main(String[] args)
    {
        double accounts[] =
            {365.55, 789.19, 532.11, 1079.96, 185.19};
        double sum = 0;

        for (int loopIndex = 0; loopIndex < accounts.length;
            loopIndex++) {
            sum += accounts[loopIndex];
        }

        System.out.println("The total in all accounts is $" + sum);
    }
}
```

Here are the results of this code:

```
%java app
The total in all accounts is $2952
```

Java also supports a while loop. I'll create an example showing how to use this loop and how you can read input from the keyboard. In this case, I'll keep reading from the keyboard until the user types the word quit.

You can use the System.in.read method to read character by character from the keyboard. This method waits until the user presses Enter at the end of the line, at which point Java stores all those typed characters. When you call this method, it reads the next character from those that were typed and returns it.

To read what the user has typed using this method, I'll start by creating a string named input, and I'll add all the waiting characters to this string in succession by repeatedly calling the System.in.read method. I'll then search the string for the word quit. I can use the String class's indexOf method to search this string for that word and keep looping until that word is found. The indexOf method returns the starting location of the string that you're searching for, or -1 if that string is not found. Here's how I can keep waiting for quit until it's found:

```
public class app
{
    public static void main(String[] args)
    {
        String input = "";
```

continues ▸

```
        while (input.indexOf("quit") < 0){
            .
            .
            .
        }
    }
}
```

Each time the user enters a new line, I can use `System.in.read` to read the characters the user has typed, and add them one by one to the `input` string. The `System.in.read` method actually returns ASCII codes as integers, so we'll need an explicit cast, `(char)`, to convert those values to characters we can add to the `input` string.

The creators of Java knew that I/O operations are prone to errors, so they allowed the `System.in.read` to generate errors that your program can handle, called *trappable* errors or *exceptions* in Java. Generating such an error is called *throwing an exception.* You must enclose the code that can cause errors in a special construct called a `try` block:

```
public class app
{
    public static void main(String[] args)
    {
        String input = "";

        while (input.indexOf("quit") < 0){
            try {
                input += (char) System.in.read();
            }
            .
            .
            .
        }
    }
}
```

You follow the `try` block with a `catch` block to catch any errors that occurred. The `catch` block is passed an object of class `Exception`, and I'll name that object `e` here. I can use that object's `printStackTrace` method to display the error that occurred, sending the text from that method to the `System.err` output channel (which corresponds to the console by default), like this:

```
public class app
{
    public static void main(String[] args)
    {
        String input = "";
```

```
        while (input.indexOf("quit") < 0){
            try {
                input += (char) System.in.read();
            } catch (Exception e) {
                e.printStackTrace(System.err);
            }
        }
    }
}
```

That's all we need; now the user can enter text, which the application will read—and when the user types the word `quit` anywhere in that text, the application will terminate:

```
%java app
Hi there!
This is great.
Anything happening?
Well, looks like it's time to quit.
```

Not bad; now we've seen one way to read from the keyboard as well as use the `while` loop.

Declaring and Creating Objects

In Java, you must declare new objects, then you create them with the `new` operator. For example, here's how I create an object of the Java `String` class, passing the text `Welcome to Java` to that class's constructor:

```
public class app
{
    public static void main(String[] args)
    {
        String greeting1;

        greeting1 = new String("Welcome to Java");
    .
    .
    .
```

Note that I first declared the `greeting1` object, giving the object's class, `String`, as its type. Then I create the object with the `new` operator.

Overloading Constructors

Classes can have different constructors that handle different types of data. For example, I passed a string to the `String` class's constructor in the previous example, but I can also pass an array of characters this way, which is useful if my data is stored as such an array:

```
public class app
{
    public static void main(String[] args)
    {
        String greeting1, greeting2, greeting3;

        greeting1 = new String("Welcome to Java");

        char characters[] = {'W', 'e', 'l', 'c', 'o', 'm', 'e',
                    ' ', 't', 'o', ' ', 'J', 'a', 'v', 'a'};

        greeting2 = new String(characters);
        .
        .
        .
    }
}
```

Constructors and methods that can take different argument lists are called *overloaded.*

To overload a constructor or method, you just define it a number of times, each with a different argument list.

Assigning Objects

You can also assign one object to another, using the = assignment operator:

```
public class app
{
    public static void main(String[] args)
    {
        String greeting1, greeting2, greeting3;

        greeting1 = new String("Welcome to Java");

        char characters[] = {'W', 'e', 'l', 'c', 'o', 'm', 'e',
                    ' ', 't', 'o', ' ', 'J', 'a', 'v', 'a'};

        greeting2 = new String(characters);

        greeting3 = greeting2;
        .
        .
        .
    }
}
```

To end this example, I'll print out all the strings that we've created:

```
public class app
{
    public static void main(String[] args)
    {
        String greeting1, greeting2, greeting3;

        greeting1 = new String("Welcome to Java");

        char characters[] = {'W', 'e', 'l', 'c', 'o', 'm', 'e',
                   ' ', 't', 'o', ' ', 'J', 'a', 'v', 'a'};

        greeting2 = new String(characters);

        greeting3 = greeting2;

        System.out.println(greeting1);
        System.out.println(greeting2);
        System.out.println(greeting3);
    }
}
```

Here's what this application looks like when run:

```
%java app
Welcome to Java
Welcome to Java
Welcome to Java
```

That's how to declare and create objects in Java. It's similar to the way you declare and create simple variables, with the added power of configuring objects by passing data to a class's constructor.

Creating Methods in Java

In JavaScript, we created functions; in Java, everything is object-oriented, so we'll be creating methods. A method is just a function that's part of a class or object. As an example, I'll create a method now named `adder` that will add two integers and return their sum.

To start, I'll need two numbers to add, and I'll let the user enter them as command-line arguments. I can read those arguments from the array passed to the `main` method, which I name `args`, and then store them in integers `value1` and `value2`, like this:

```
public class app
{
    public static void main(String[] args)
    {
        int value1 = Integer.parseInt(args[0]);
```

continues ▸

```
        int value2 = Integer.parseInt(args[1]);
    .
    .
    .
}
```

Now I display those values, pass them to the `adder` method, and display the value that `adder` returned, like this:

```
public class app
{
    public static void main(String[] args)
    {
        int value1 = Integer.parseInt(args[0]);
        int value2 = Integer.parseInt(args[1]);

        System.out.println(value1 + " + " + value2 +
        " = " + adder(value1, value2));
    }
    .
    .
    .
}
```

All that remains is to create the `adder` method.You can give methods access specifiers such as `public` or `private`. If you give it the access specifier `public`, the method is accessible outside the object or class. If you give it the access specifier `private` (which is the default if you don't use an access specifier), it's accessible only inside the object or class. I'll use `public` here.

In addition, you must specify the return type of the value the method returns (you can use the keyword `void` if the method doesn't return a value). And you must give a comma-separated argument list for the method, giving the type of each argument in parentheses following the method's name (if the method takes no arguments, leave the parentheses empty). All this gives us the following skeleton for the definition of `adder`:

```
public class app
{
    public static void main(String[] args)
    {
        int value1 = Integer.parseInt(args[0]);
        int value2 = Integer.parseInt(args[1]);

        System.out.println(value1 + " + " + value2 +
        " = " + adder(value1, value2));
    }
```

```
    public static int adder(int int1, int int2)
    {
    .
    .
    .
    }
}
```

In the body of the method, I can refer to the two values passed using the names I've given them in the argument list, `int1` and `int2`. I add those values and return the result using the `return` statement:

```
public class app
{
    public static void main(String[] args)
    {
        int value1 = Integer.parseInt(args[0]);
        int value2 = Integer.parseInt(args[1]);

        System.out.println(value1 + " + " + value2 +
        " = " + adder(value1, value2));
    }

    public static int adder(int int1, int int2)
    {
        return int1 + int2;
    }
}
```

Now the user can enter values to add on the command line, and the application will handle them without problem:

```
%java app 180 120
180 + 180 = 300
```

Using return

You can use the `return` statement even in methods that you don't return any value from if you want to terminate execution and return from the method—just use the `return` statement alone, without specifying any values to return.

Creating Java Classes

We've already seen how to create classes in a rudimentary way: You need to create a class to do anything at all, as when we created the main class for the applications that we've built:

```
public class app
{
    public static void main(String[] args)
    {
        System.out.println("Welcome to Java");
    }
}
```

In preparation for the next chapter, let's take a look at a more advanced example. In this case, I'll create a new class named `AppFrame` based on the Java `Frame` class, which is what you use to create *frame windows* (a frame window has a frame, including a border and title bar) in Java. There are two ways to work with graphics in Java: the Abstract Windowing Toolkit (AWT) and the Swing Java packages. In the interests of space, I'm going to stick with the AWT in this book because just starting to understand how Swing works would be a whole chapter itself. However, if you find yourself doing a lot of Java development, I encourage you to examine what Swing has to offer.

Here's what it will look like in the `main` method; I'll create a new object named `f` of the `AppFrame` class, passing the text that we want to appear in that window to that class's constructor:

```
public class window
{
   public static void main(String argv[]) {

       AppFrame f = new AppFrame("Creating windowed Java applications...");
           .
           .
           .
   }
}
```

Because the `AppFrame` class is built on the Java `Frame` class, I can use the `Frame` class's `setSize` method to give this new window a size of 400 × 200 pixels, and I can use the `show` method to display it on the screen:

```
public class window
{
   public static void main(String argv[]) {

       AppFrame f = new AppFrame("Creating windowed Java applications...");
```

```
        f.setSize(400, 200);

        f.show();
    }
}
```

Creating New Classes

The `AppFrame` class is based on the Java `Frame` class, which means that `AppFrame` will have all the built-in `Frame` class's methods. You can find those methods in Table 10.2.

Table 10.2 **Methods of the Frame Class**

Method	Description
`void addNotify()`	Allows this frame to be displayed by connecting it to a native screen resource
`protected void finalize()`	Called when the frame is about to be disposed of
`int getCursorType()`	Replaced by `Component.getCursor()`
`static Frame[] getFrames()`	Returns an array containing all frames created by the application
`Image getIconImage()`	Returns the image to be displayed in the minimized icon
`MenuBar getMenuBar()`	Returns the menu bar
`int getState()`	Returns the current state of the frame
`String getTitle()`	Returns the frame's title
`boolean isResizable()`	Specifies whether this frame is resizable by the user
`protected String paramString()`	Returns the parameter string of this frame
`void remove(MenuComponent m)`	Removes the given menu bar from this frame
`void removeNotify()`	Makes this frame undisplayable
`void setCursor(int cursorType)`	Replaced by `Component.setCursor(Cursor)`
`void setIconImage(Image image)`	Sets the image to be displayed in the minimized icon for this frame
`void setMenuBar(MenuBar mb)`	Sets the menu bar for this frame to the specified menu bar
`void setResizable(boolean resizable)`	Specifies whether this frame is resizable by the user
`void setState(int state)`	Sets the state of this frame
`void setTitle(String title)`	Sets the title for this frame to the given string

You can create your own classes with the `class` statement in Java, as we've seen. The `AppFrame` class is built on the `Frame` class, which in object-oriented terms means that `AppFrame` *inherits* the `Frame` class. To indicate that you want one class to be based on another, you use the `extends` keyword, like this. (Note that I'm not using an access specifier when defining `AppFrame`, which means that this class will use the default access specifier, which is `private`.)

```
import java.awt.*;

public class window
{
   public static void main(String argv[]) {

       AppFrame f = new AppFrame("Creating windowed Java applications...");

       f.setSize(400, 200);

       f.addWindowListener(new WindowAdapter() {public void
          windowClosing(WindowEvent e) {System.exit(0);}});

       f.show();
   }
}

class AppFrame extends Frame
{
    .
    .
    .
}
```

Note also that the Java `Frame` class is part of the Java Abstract Windowing Toolkit (AWT) package. This means that I must import that package with the statement `import java.awt.*;`.

Creating a Constructor

This new class needs a constructor because I want to pass the text the window should display to that constructor. You create a constructor simply by creating a method in a class that has the same name as the class. In this case, that's `AppFrame` (constructors do not specify any return value):

```
import java.awt.*;
import java.awt.event.*;

public class window
{
   public static void main(String argv[]) {
```

```
        AppFrame f = new AppFrame("Creating windowed Java applications...");

        f.setSize(400, 200);

        f.addWindowListener(new WindowAdapter() {public void
            windowClosing(WindowEvent e) {System.exit(0);}});

        f.show();
    }
}

class AppFrame extends Frame
{
    String displayText;

    public AppFrame(String text)
    {
    .
    .
    .
    }
}
```

You might notice that the methods I'm adding to the `AppFrame` class are not declared `static`. That's because these methods will be used only as part of an object, not as class methods. In particular, I create an object of the `AppFrame` class named `f` in the `main` method, and I use the methods of that object.

I'll store the text passed to the constructor in a string named `displayText` this way:

```
import java.awt.*;
import java.awt.event.*;

public class window
{
    public static void main(String argv[]) {

        AppFrame f = new AppFrame("Creating windowed Java applications...");

        f.setSize(400, 200);

        f.addWindowListener(new WindowAdapter() {public void
            windowClosing(WindowEvent e) {System.exit(0);}});

        f.show();
    }
}

class AppFrame extends Frame
{
```

continues ▸

```
    String displayText;

    public AppFrame(String text)
    {
        displayText = text;
    }
}
```

Using Graphics Objects

The next step is to display the text in the window itself. The `Frame` class has a method named `paint` that is automatically called whenever the window needs to be drawn on the screen. This method is passed an object of the Java `Graphics` class, which I will call `g`:

```
import java.awt.*;
import java.awt.event.*;

public class window
{
   public static void main(String argv[]) {

       AppFrame f = new AppFrame("Creating windowed Java applications...");

       f.setSize(400, 200);

       f.addWindowListener(new WindowAdapter() {public void
           windowClosing(WindowEvent e) {System.exit(0);}});

       f.show();
   }
}

class AppFrame extends Frame
{
    String displayText;

    public AppFrame(String text)
    {
        displayText = text;
    }

    public void paint(Graphics g)
    {
    .
    .
    .
    }
}
```

You can use the `Graphics` object's methods to draw in a window, and you'll find those methods in Table 10.3.

Table 10.3 **Methods of the Graphics Class**

Method	Description
`abstract void clearRect(int x, int y, int width, int height)`	Clears a rectangle (fills it with the background color)
`abstract void clipRect(int x, int y, int width, int height)`	Clips a rectangle
`abstract void copyArea(int x, int y, int width, int height, int dx, int dy)`	Copies an area of size `dx` and `dy`
`abstract Graphics create()`	Creates a new graphics object and makes it a copy of the current one
`Graphics create(int x, int y, int width, int height)`	Creates a new graphics object, with a new translation and clip area
`abstract void dispose()`	Disposes of a graphics context
`void draw3DRect(int x, int y, int width, int height, boolean raised)`	Displays a 3D rectangle
`abstract void drawArc(int x, int y, int width, int height, int startAngle, int arcAngle)`	Draws a circular or elliptical arc
`void drawBytes(byte[] data, int offset, int length, int x, int y)`	Draws the text stored in the byte array
`void drawChars(char[] data, int offset, int length, int x, int y)`	Draws the text stored in the character array
`abstract boolean drawImage(Image img, int x, int y, Color bgcolor, ImageObserver observer)`	Draws as much of the specified image as is possible, letting you specify a background color
`abstract boolean drawImage(Image img, int x, int y, ImageObserver observer)`	Draws as much of the specified image as possible
`abstract boolean drawImage(Image img, int x, int y, int width, int height, Color bgcolor, ImageObserver observer)`	Draws as much of the image as can fit inside the rectangle
`abstract boolean drawImage(Image img, int x, int y, int width, int height, ImageObserver observer)`	Draws as much of the given image as has been scaled to fit inside the rectangle

continues

Table 10.3 **Continued**

Method	Description
abstract boolean drawImage (Image *img*, int *dx1*, int *dy1*, int *dx2*, int *dy2*, int *sx1*, int *sy1*, int *sx2*, int *sy2*, Color *bgcolor*, ImageObserver *observer*)	Draws as much of the image as possible, scaling it to fit inside the given area
abstract boolean drawImage(Image *img*, int *dx1*, int *dy1*, int *dx2*, int *dy2*, int *sx1*, int *sy1*, int *sx2*, int *sy2*, ImageObserver *observer*)	Draws as much of the area of the image as possible, scaling it to fit inside the given area of the destination surface
abstract void drawLine(int *x1*, int *y1*, int *x2*, int *y2*)	Draws a line, in the current default color between the points (*x1*, *y1*) and (*x2*, *y2*)
abstract void drawOval(int *x*, int *y*, int *width*, int *height*)	Draws the outline of an oval
abstract void drawPolygon(int[] *xPoints*, int[] *yPoints*, int *nPoints*)	Draws a closed polygon as defined by the x and y coordinate arrays
void drawPolygon(Polygon *p*)	Draws a polygon defined by the given `Polygon` object
abstract void drawPolyline (int[] *xPoints*, int[] *yPoints*, int *nPoints*)	Draws a sequence of connected lines
void drawRect(int *x*, int *y*, int *width*, int *height*)	Draws the specified rectangle
abstract void drawRoundRect(int *x*, int *y*, int *width*, int *height*, int *arcWidth*, int *arcHeight*)	Draws a round-cornered rectangle
abstract void drawString (AttributedCharacterIterator *iterator*, int *x*, int *y*)	Draws the text given by the iterator
abstract void drawString (String *str*, int *x*, int *y*)	Draws the text given by the string
void fill3DRect(int *x*, int *y*, int *width*, int *height*, boolean raised)	Paints a filled 3D rectangle
abstract void fillArc(int *x*, int *y*, int *width*, int *height*, int *startAngle*, int *arcAngle*)	Fills a circular or elliptical arc
abstract void fillOval(int *x*, int *y*, int *width*, int *height*)	Fills an oval bounded by the given rectangle

Method	Description
`abstract void fillPolygon(int[] xPoints, int[] yPoints, int nPoints)`	Fills a closed polygon defined by arrays of x and y coordinates
`void fillPolygon(Polygon p)`	Fills the polygon defined by the `Polygon` object with the current color
`abstract void fillRect(int x, int y, int width, int height)`	Fills the specified rectangle
`abstract void fillRoundRect(int x, int y, int width, int height, int arcWidth, int arcHeight)`	Fills a rounded corner rectangle
`void finalize()`	Called when the object is about to be disposed of
`abstract Shape getClip()`	Returns the clipping area
`abstract Rectangle getClipBounds()`	Returns the bounding rectangle of the clipping area
`Rectangle getClipBounds(Rectangle r)`	Returns the bounding rectangle of the clipping area for a specific rectangle
`Rectangle getClipRect()`	Replaced by `getClipBounds()`
`abstract Color getColor()`	Returns this graphics context's current foreground color
`abstract Font getFont()`	Returns the current font
`FontMetrics getFontMetrics()`	Returns the font metrics of the default font
`abstract FontMetrics getFontMetrics(Font f)`	Returns the font metrics for the given font
`boolean hitClip(int x, int y, int width, int height)`	Is true if the given area intersects the rectangle of the clipping area
`abstract void setClip(int x, int y, int width, int height)`	Sets the current clip to the given rectangle
`abstract void setClip(Shape clip)`	Sets the clipping area to a shape
`abstract void setColor(Color c)`	Sets the graphics context's foreground color
`abstract void setFont(Font font)`	Sets the graphics context's font
`abstract void setPaintMode()`	Sets the paint mode
`abstract void setXORMode(Color c1)`	Sets the paint mode to use XOR painting
`String toString()`	Returns a `String` object that represents the `Graphics` object
`abstract void translate (int x, int y)`	Translates the origin of the graphics context to a new origin

In this case, I'll use the `drawString` method to display the text in the window, like this:

```
import java.awt.*;
import java.awt.event.*;

public class window
{
   public static void main(String argv[]) {

       AppFrame f = new AppFrame("Creating windowed Java applications...");

       f.setSize(400, 200);

       f.addWindowListener(new WindowAdapter() {public void
           windowClosing(WindowEvent e) {System.exit(0);}});

       f.show();
   }
}

class AppFrame extends Frame
{
    String displayText;

    public AppFrame(String text)
    {
        displayText = text;
    }

    public void paint(Graphics g)
    {
        g.drawString(displayText, 60, 100);
    }
}
```

Closing Application Windows

There's one more refinement to make; when the user clicks the Close button at the upper right in the window we're creating, we'll need to handle the window closing event that occurs. To handle events in Java, you use an *event listener*. In this case, I'll use an event listener to catch the window closing event and, when that event occurs, end the program using the call `System.exit(0);`. This call ends the program and passes a value of `0` (which indicates normal termination) as an exit code to the operating system.

Handling Java events in detail is beyond the scope of this book, but here's how it works—in this case, I'll add a window listener to the `AppFrame` object that will "listen" for window closing events and, when one occurs, end the program. Note that to handle events with AWT objects, you must import the classes in the `java.awt.event` package:

```
import java.awt.*;
import java.awt.event.*;

public class window
{
   public static void main(String argv[]) {

        AppFrame f = new AppFrame("Creating windowed Java applications...");

        f.setSize(400, 200);

        f.addWindowListener(new WindowAdapter() {public void
            windowClosing(WindowEvent e) {System.exit(0);}});

        f.show();
   }
}

class AppFrame extends Frame
{
    String displayText;

    public AppFrame(String text)
    {
        displayText = text;
    }

    public void paint(Graphics g)
    {
        g.drawString(displayText, 60, 100);
    }
}
```

You can see the results of this code in Figure 10.2. When you start this application, the window appears, displaying the text as shown.

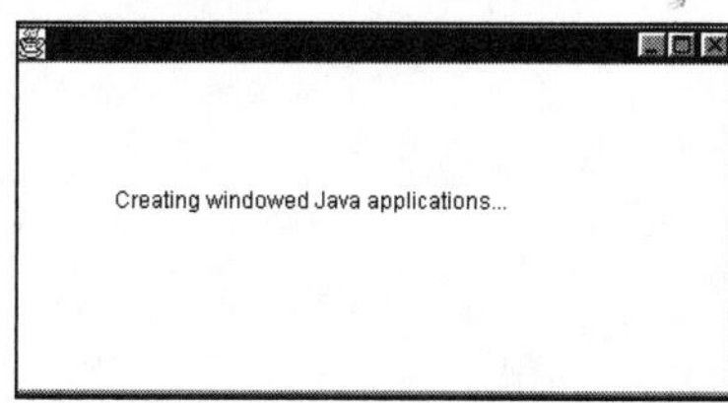

Figure 10.2 Running a windowed Java application.

Now that we're in the Java business, it's time to put all this technology to work with XML. I'll do that in the next chapter.

11
Java and the XML DOM

THIS CHAPTER IS ALL ABOUT USING XML WITH JAVA to create standalone programs. In fact, I'll even create a few browsers in this chapter. Here, the programs we write will be based on the XML DOM, and I'll use the XML for Java (XML4J) packages from IBM alphaWorks (`www.alphaworks.ibm.com/tech/xml4j`). This is the famous XML parser that adheres to the W3C standards and has implemented the W3C DOM level 1 (and part of level 2). It's the most widely used standalone XML Java parser available. As of this writing, the current version is 3.0.1, and it's based on the Apache Xerces XML Parser Version 1.0.3.

The alphaWorks site proudly announces:

> *XML Parser for Java is a validating XML parser written in 100% pure Java. The package (`com.ibm.xml.parser`) contains classes and methods for parsing, generating, manipulating, and validating XML documents. XML Parser for Java is believed to be the most robust XML processor currently available and conforms most closely to the XML 1.0 Recommendation.*

In fact, this points out one of the problems with working with modern XML Java parsers—they're always in a state of flux. It turns out that the `com.ibm.xml.parser` package mentioned here is now *deprecated*, which in Java terms means that it's obsolete (although still supported) and scheduled to be removed in a future release. Instead, we'll use the `org.apache.xerces.parsers` package, which is the successor to `com.ibm.xml.parser`.

This is an occupational hazard when working with third-party parsers, which historically have been extremely volatile. For example, when XML was still very young, I wrote a book based largely on the Microsoft XML Java parser, which was the only commercial-grade Java XML parser available at that time. And just before the book appeared on shelves, Microsoft changed its parser utterly so that virtually none of the code in the book worked. (The Microsoft XML Java parser is not even available as a standalone package anymore.) That's not an uncommon experience.

On the other hand, the alphaWorks parser has been changed so that it's now based on the W3C DOM (the package we'll be using to support nodes and elements in code will be alphaWork's `org.w3c.dom` package), which means that things have finally become standardized. However, the package names and the actual parsers we'll use, such as `org.apache.xerces.parsers.DOMParser` in this chapter, are still subject to change. By the time you read this, the alphaWorks packages may well have changed, something that's beyond our control here. In that case, you should refer to the XML for Java documentation to see what changes you need to make to your code—now that the W3C DOM is available, those changes should be minimized compared to what happened in the past.

This chapter and the next one provide you with a good introduction to the XML for Java parser. However, there's enough material here to take up a whole book—in fact, such books have been published, as recently as last year. (Those books are now obsolete because of changes in the parser—surprise!) The XML for Java packages are extensive and come with hundreds of pages of documentation, so if you want to pursue XML for Java programming beyond the techniques that you see in these chapters, dig into that documentation.

We saw XML for Java in this book as early as Chapter 1, "Essential XML," where I used an example that comes with XML for Java named DOMWriter that lets you validate XML documents based on DTDs. In Chapter 1, we saw this document, `greeting.xml`:

```
<?xml version="1.0" encoding="UTF-8"?>
<DOCUMENT>
    <GREETING>
        Hello From XML
    </GREETING>
    <MESSAGE>
        Welcome to the wild and woolly world of XML.
    </MESSAGE>
</DOCUMENT>
```

I tested this document using DOMWriter like this, where you can see that it reports validation errors:

```
%java dom.DOMWriter greeting.xml
greeting.xml:
[Error] greeting.xml:2:11: Element type "DOCUMENT" must be declared
[Error] greeting.xml:3:15: Element type "GREETING" must be declared
[Error] greeting.xml:6:14: Element type "MESSAGE" must be declared.
<?xml version="1.0" encoding="UTF-8"?>
<DOCUMENT>
    <GREETING>
        Hello From XML
    </GREETING>
    <MESSAGE>
        Welcome to the wild and woolly world of XML.
    </MESSAGE>
</DOCUMENT>
```

In this chapter, we'll build our own Java programs using XML for Java directly, including parsing and filtering XML documents, as well as creating standalone browsers and even a specialized graphical browser that uses XML documents not to display text, but to display circles. That's one advantage of being able to create your own programs using parsers like the ones in XML for Java: You can create your own specialized browsers.

Getting XML for Java

The first step is to download XML for Java at `www.alphaworks.ibm.com/tech/xml4j`. Currently, you only need to navigate to that site, click the Download button, then select a file to download, and click the Download Selected File button. For example, if you're on a UNIX system, you can select the file labeled `Binary distribution packaged as a UNIX Tar.gz file`, which is `XML4J-bin.3.0.1.tar.gz` as of this writing. If you're on Windows, you can select the file labeled `Binary distribution packaged as a Windows ZIP file`, which is `XML4J-bin.3.0.1.zip` as of this writing. You can also download the XML for Java source code, which means that you can build everything for yourself.

After you've downloaded the compressed XML for Java file, you must uncompress it yourself (in Windows, make sure that you use an unzip utility that can handle long filenames). That's all for actually installing XML for Java—now you must make sure that Java can find it.

Setting *CLASSPATH*

As far as we're concerned, XML for Java is a huge set of classes ready for us to use. Those classes are stored in Java JAR (Java Archive) files, and we must make sure that Java can search those JAR files for the classes that it needs.

I discussed this process a little in the last chapter when I mentioned using the Java `CLASSPATH` environment variable. This is the variable that you set to tell Java where to look for additional classes your code may require. In our case, the JAR files we'll need to search for classes are called `xerces.jar` and `xercesSamples.jar` (these names may have changed by the time you read this).

Unfortunately, the way you set the `CLASSPATH` variable can vary by system. For example, to permanently set the class path in Windows NT, you use the Control Panel. In the System Properties dialog box, you click the Environment tab, then click the `CLASSPATH` variable, and enter the new value there. In Windows 95 or 98, you can use the MS-DOS `SET` command in autoexec.bat, which sets the value of environment variables. Note, however, that you can also use the MS-DOS `SET` command to set the class path in Windows 95, 98, and NT to set the class path until the MS-DOS window is closed, which is perhaps the easiest way. For example, if `xerces.jar` and `xercesSamples.jar` are in the directory C:\xmlparser\XML4J_3_0_1 on your system, you could use a SET command like this (and put it all on one line):

```
C:\>SET CLASSPATH=%CLASSPATH%;C:\xmlparser\XML4J_3_0_1\xerces.jar;
C:\xmlparser\XML4J_3_0_1\xercesSamples.jar
```

Take a look at the Java documentation to see how to set `CLASSPATH` on your system. There's a shortcut if you can't get the `CLASSPATH` variable working; you can use the `-classpath` switch when working with the javac and java tools. For example, here's how I compile and run a program named browser.java using that switch to specify the class path I want to use (both commands should be on one line):

```
%javac -classpath C:\xmlparser\XML4J_3_0_1\xerces.jar;
C:\xmlparser\XML4J_3_0_1\xercesSamples.jar browser.java
%java -classpath C:\xmlparser\XML4J_3_0_1\xerces.jar;
C:\xmlparser\XML4J_3_0_1\xercesSamples.jar browser
```

We're ready to start working with code. I'll start by writing an example that parses an XML document.

Creating a Parser

This first XML for Java example will get us started by parsing an XML document and displaying the number of a certain element in it. In this chapter, I'm taking a look at using the XML DOM with Java, and I'll use the XML for Java `DOMParser` class, which creates a W3C DOM tree as its output.

The document we'll parse is one we've seen before—`customer.xml`:

```
<?xml version = "1.0" standalone="yes"?>
<DOCUMENT>
    <CUSTOMER>
        <NAME>
            <LAST_NAME>Smith</LAST_NAME>
            <FIRST_NAME>Sam</FIRST_NAME>
        </NAME>
        <DATE>October 15, 2001</DATE>
        <ORDERS>
            <ITEM>
                <PRODUCT>Tomatoes</PRODUCT>
                <NUMBER>8</NUMBER>
                <PRICE>$1.25</PRICE>
            </ITEM>
            <ITEM>
                <PRODUCT>Oranges</PRODUCT>
                <NUMBER>24</NUMBER>
                <PRICE>$4.98</PRICE>
            </ITEM>
        </ORDERS>
    </CUSTOMER>
    <CUSTOMER>
        <NAME>
            <LAST_NAME>Jones</LAST_NAME>
            <FIRST_NAME>Polly</FIRST_NAME>
        </NAME>
        <DATE>October 20, 2001</DATE>
        <ORDERS>
            <ITEM>
                <PRODUCT>Bread</PRODUCT>
                <NUMBER>12</NUMBER>
                <PRICE>$14.95</PRICE>
            </ITEM>
            <ITEM>
                <PRODUCT>Apples</PRODUCT>
                <NUMBER>6</NUMBER>
                <PRICE>$1.50</PRICE>
            </ITEM>
        </ORDERS>
    </CUSTOMER>
    <CUSTOMER>
        <NAME>
            <LAST_NAME>Weber</LAST_NAME>
            <FIRST_NAME>Bill</FIRST_NAME>
        </NAME>
        <DATE>October 25, 2001</DATE>
        <ORDERS>
            <ITEM>
                <PRODUCT>Asparagus</PRODUCT>
```

continues ▸

```
            <NUMBER>12</NUMBER>
            <PRICE>$2.95</PRICE>
        </ITEM>
        <ITEM>
            <PRODUCT>Lettuce</PRODUCT>
            <NUMBER>6</NUMBER>
            <PRICE>$11.50</PRICE>
        </ITEM>
    </ORDERS>
  </CUSTOMER>
</DOCUMENT>
```

In this example, the code will scan `customer.xml` and report how many `<CUSTOMER>` elements the document has.

To start this program, I'll import the XML for Java classes that we'll need—the `org.w3c.dom` classes, which support the W3C DOM interfaces, such as `Node` and `Element`, and the XML for Java DOM parser we'll use is `org.apache.xerces.parsers.DOMParser`:

```
import org.w3c.dom.*;
import org.apache.xerces.parsers.DOMParser;
    .
    .
    .
```

I'll call this first program `FirstParser.java`, so the public class in that file is `FirstParser`:

```
import org.w3c.dom.*;
import org.apache.xerces.parsers.DOMParser;

public class FirstParser
{
    public static void main(String[] args)
    {
    .
    .
    .
}
```

To parse the XML document, you need a `DOMParser` object, which I'll call `parser`:

```
import org.w3c.dom.*;
import org.apache.xerces.parsers.DOMParser;

public class FirstParser
{
    public static void main(String[] args)
    {
```

```
            DOMParser parser = new DOMParser();
            .
            .
            .
    }
}
```

The `DOMParser` class is derived from the `XMLParser` class, which in turn is based on the `java.lang.Object` class:

```
java.lang.Object
|
+--org.apache.xerces.framework.XMLParser
   |
   +--org.apache.xerces.parsers.DOMParser
```

The default constructor for the `DOMParser` class is `DOMParser()`. The methods of the `DOMParser` class are listed in Table 11.1.

The keyword `protected` is an access specifier, just like `private` and `public`. The `protected` access specifier is the same as `private`, except that derived classes also have access to members that were declared `protected` in the base class. In addition, the *callback* methods listed in Table 11.1 are called by `DOMParser` objects. We'll see how to work with callback methods in the next chapter.

Table 11.1 **DOMParser Methods**

Method	Description
`void attlistDecl(int elementTypeIndex, int attrNameIndex, int attType, java.lang.String enumString, int attDefaultType, int attDefaultValue)`	Serves as a callback for attribute declarations
`void characters(int dataIndex)`	Serves as a callback for characters
`void comment(int dataIndex)`	Serves as a callback for comments
`void elementDecl(int elementTypeIndex, XMLValidator.ContentSpec contentSpec)`	Serves as a callback for element declarations
`void endCDATA()`	Serves as a callback for the end of `CDATA` section
`void endDocument()`	Serves as a callback for the end of the document
`void endDTD()`	Is called at the end of the DTD
`void endElement(int elementTypeIndex)`	Serves as a callback for the end of elements

continues

Table 11.1 **Continued**

Method	Description
`void endEntityReference(int entityName, int entityType, int entityContext)`	Serves as a callback for the end of entity references
`void endNamespaceDeclScope(int prefix)`	Serves as a callback for the end of the scope of a namespace declaration
`void externalEntityDecl(int entityNameIndex, int publicIdIndex, int systemIdIndex)`	Serves as a callback for external entity references
`void externalPEDecl(int entityName, int publicId, int systemId)`	Serves as a callback for external parameter entities declarations
`boolean getCreateEntityReferenceNodes()`	Is true if entity references in the document are included in the document as `EntityReference` nodes
`protected Element getCurrentElementNode()`	Returns the current element node
`protected boolean getDeferNodeExpansion()`	Is true if the expansion of nodes is deferred
`Document getDocument()`	Returns the document itself
`protected java.lang.String getDocumentClassName()`	Returns the qualified class name of the document factory
`boolean getFeature(java.lang.String featureId)`	Gets the current state of any feature in a SAX2 parser
`java.lang.String[] getFeaturesRecognized()`	Gets a list of features that this parser recognizes
`boolean getIncludeIgnorableWhitespace()`	Is true if there are ignorable whitespace text nodes in the DOM tree
`java.lang.String[] getPropertiesRecognized()`	Gets a list of properties that the parser recognizes
`java.lang.Object getProperty(java.lang.String propertyId)`	Gets the value of a property in a SAX2 parser
`void ignorableWhitespace(int dataIndex)`	Serves as a callback for ignorable whitespace
`protected void init()`	Initializes or reinitializes the parser to a pre-parse state
`void internalEntityDecl(int entityNameIndex, int entityValueIndex)`	Serves as a callback for an internal entity declaration
`void internalPEDecl(int entityName, int entityValue)`	Serves as a callback for an internal parameter entity declaration
`void internalSubset(int internalSubset)`	Supports DOM Level 2 `internalSubsets`
`void notationDecl(int notationNameIndex, int publicIdIndex, int systemIdIndex)`	Serves as a callback for notation declarations

void processingInstruction(int *targetIndex*, int *dataIndex*)	Serves as a callback for processing instructions
void reset()	Resets the parser
void resetOrCopy()	Resets or copies the parser
protected void setCreateEntityReferenceNodes(boolean create)	Indicates whether entity references in the document are part of the document as EntityReference nodes
protected void setDeferNodeExpansion(boolean deferNodeExpansion)	Indicates whether the expansion of the nodes is deferred
protected void setDocumentClassName(java.lang.String *documentClassName*)	Lets you decide which document factory to use
void setFeature(java.lang.String *featureId*, boolean state)	Sets the state of any feature in a SAX2 parser
void setIncludeIgnorableWhitespace(boolean include)	Specifies whether ignorable whitespace text nodes are included in the DOM tree
void setProperty(java.lang.String *propertyId*, java.lang.Object *value*)	Sets the value of any property in a SAX2 parser
void startCDATA()	Serves as a callback for the start of a CDATA section
void startDocument(int *versionIndex*, int *encodingIndex*, int *standAloneIndex*)	Serves as a callback for the start of a document
void startDTD(int *rootElementType*, int *publicId*, int *systemId*)	Serves as a callback for the start of a DTD
void startElement(int *elementTypeIndex*, XMLAttrList *xmlAttrList*, int *attrListIndex*)	Serves as a callback for the start of an element
void startEntityReference(int *entityName*, int *entityType*, int *entityContext*)	Serves as a callback for the start of an entity reference
void startNamespaceDeclScope(int *prefix*, int *uri*)	Serves as a callback for the start of the scope of a namespace declaration
void unparsedEntityDecl(int *entityNameIndex*, int *publicIdIndex*, int *systemIdIndex*, int *notationNameIndex*)	Serves as a callback for an unparsed entity declaration

The DOMParser class is based on the XMLParser class, and the XMLParser class has a great deal of functionality that you frequently use in XML for Java programming. The XMLParser constructor is protectedXMLParser(). The methods of the XMLParser class are listed in Table 11.2.

Table 11.2 ***XMLParser* Methods**

Method	Description
`void addRecognizer(org.apache.xerces.readers. XMLDeclRecognizer` *`recognizer`*`)`	Adds a recognizer
`abstract void attlistDecl(int` *`elementType`*`, int` *`attrName`*`, int` *`attType`*`, java.lang. String` *`enumString`*`, int` *`attDefaultType`*`, int` *`attDefaultValue`*`)`	Serves as a callback for an attribute list declaration
`void callCharacters(int` *`ch`*`)`	Calls the characters callback
`void callComment(int` *`comment`*`)`	Calls the comment callback
`void callEndDocument()`	Calls the end document callback
`boolean callEndElement(int` *`readerId`*`)`	Calls the end element callback
`void callProcessingInstruction (int` *`target`*`, int` *`data`*`)`	Calls the processing instruction callback
`void callStartDocument(int` *`version`*`, int` *`encoding`*`, int` *`standalone`*`)`	Calls the start document callback
`void callStartElement(int` *`elementType`*`)`	Calls the start element callback
`org.apache.xerces.readers.XMLEntityHandler. EntityReader changeReaders()`	Is called by the reader subclasses at the end of input
`abstract void characters(char[]` *`ch`*`, int` *`start`*`, int` *`length`*`)`	Serves as a callback for characters
`abstract void characters(int` *`data`*`)`	Serves as a callback for characters using string pools
`abstract void comment(int` *`comment`*`)`	Serves as a callback for comment
`void commentInDTD(int` *`comment`*`)`	Serves as a callback for comment in DTD
`abstract void elementDecl(int` *`elementType`*`, XMLValidator.ContentSpec` *`contentSpec`*`)`	Serves as a callback for an element declaration
`abstract void endCDATA()`	Serves as a callback for end of the `CDATA` section
`abstract void endDocument()`	Serves as a callback for the end of the document
`abstract void endDTD()`	Serves as a callback for the end of the DTD
`abstract void endElement(int` *`elementType`*`)`	Serves as a callback for end of the element
`void endEntityDecl()`	Serves as a callback for the end of an entity declaration

Method	Description
abstract void endEntityReference (int *entityName*, int *entityType*, int *entityContext*)	Serves as a callback for the end of an entity reference
abstract void endNamespaceDeclScope (int *prefix*)	Serves as a callback for the end of a namespace declaration scope
java.lang.String expandSystemId (java.lang.String *systemId*)	Expands a system ID and returns the system ID as an URL
abstract void externalEntityDecl (int *entityName*, int *publicId*, int *systemId*)	Serves as a callback for an external general entity declaration
abstract void externalPEDecl(int *entityName*, int *publicId*, int *systemId*)	Serves as a callback for an external parameter entity declaration
protected boolean getAllowJavaEncodings()	Is true if Java encoding names are allowed in the XML document
int getColumnNumber()	Gives the column number of the current position in the document
protected boolean getContinueAfterFatalError()	Is true if the parser will continue after a fatal error
org.apache.xerces.readers.XMLEntityHandler. EntityReader *getEntityReader()*	Gets the `Entity` reader
EntityResolver getEntityResolver()	Gets the current entity resolver
ErrorHandler getErrorHandler()	Gets the current error handler
boolean getFeature(java.lang.String *featureId*)	Gets the state of a feature
java.lang.String[] getFeaturesRecognized()	Gets a list of features recognized by this parser
int getLineNumber()	Gets the current line number in the document
Locator getLocator()	Gets the locator used by the parser
protected boolean getNamespaces()	Is true if the parser preprocesses name-spaces
java.lang.String[] getPropertiesRecognized()	Gets the list of recognized properties for the parser
java.lang.Object getProperty(java.lang. String *propertyId*)	Gets the value of a property
java.lang.String getPublicId()	Gets the public ID of the `InputSource`
protected org.apache.xerces.validators. schema.XSchemaValidator *getSchemaValidator()*	Gets the current XML schema validator

continues

Table 11.2 **Continued**

Method	Description
`java.lang.String getSystemId()`	Gets the system ID of the `InputSource`
`protected boolean getValidation()`	Is true if validation is turned on
`protected boolean getValidationDynamic()`	Is true if validation is determined based on whether a document contains a grammar
`protected boolean getValidation WarnOnDuplicateAttdef()`	Is true if an error is created when an attribute is redefined in the grammar
`protected boolean getValidation WarnOnUndeclaredElemdef()`	Is true if the parser creates an error when an undeclared element is referenced
`abstract void ignorableWhitespace (char[]` *ch*`, int` *start*`, int` *length*`)`	Serves as a callback for ignorable whitespace
`abstract void ignorableWhitespace(int` *data*`)`	Serves as a callback for ignorable whitespace based on string pools
`abstract void internalEntityDecl (int` *entityName*`, int` *entityValue*`)`	Serves as a callback for internal general entity declaration
`abstract void internalPEDecl (int` *entityName*`, int` *entityValue*`)`	Serves as a callback for an internal parameter entity declaration
`abstract void internalSubset (int` *internalSubset*`)`	Supports DOM Level 2 `internalSubsets`
`boolean isFeatureRecognized (java.lang.String` *featureId*`)`	Is true if the given feature is recognized
`boolean isPropertyRecognized (java.lang.String` *propertyId*`)`	Is true if the given property is recognized
`abstract void notationDecl(int` *notationName*`, int` *publicId*`, int` *systemId*`)`	Serves as a callback for a notation declaration
`void parse(InputSource` *source*`)`	Parses the given input source
`void parse(java.lang.String` *systemId*`)`	Parses the input source given by a system identifier
`boolean parseSome()`	Supports application-driven parsing
`boolean parseSomeSetup(InputSource` *source*`)`	Sets up application-driven parsing
`void processCharacters(char[]` *chars*`, int` *offset*`, int` *length*`)`	Processes character data given a character array
`void processCharacters(int` *data*`)`	Processes character data
`abstract void processingInstruction (int` *target*`, int` *data*`)`	Serves as a callback for processing instructions

Method	Description
`void processingInstructionInDTD (int target, int data)`	Serves as a callback for processing instructions in a DTD
`void processWhitespace(char[] chars, int offset, int length)`	Processes whitespace
`void processWhitespace(int data)`	Processes whitespace based on string pools
`void reportError(Locator locator, java.lang.String errorDomain, int majorCode, int minorCode, java.lang.Object[] args, int errorType)`	Reports errors
`void reset()`	Resets the parser so that it can be reused
`protected void resetOrCopy()`	Resets or copies the parser
`int scanAttributeName(org.apache.xerces. readers.XMLEntityHandler.EntityReader entityReader, int elementType)`	Scans an attribute name
`int scanAttValue(int elementType, int attrName)`	Scans an attribute value
`void scanDoctypeDecl(boolean standalone)`	Scans a `doctype` declaration
`int scanElementType(org.apache.xerces. readers.XMLEntityHandler.EntityReader entityReader, char fastchar)`	Scans an element type
`boolean scanExpectedElementType (org.apache.xerces.readers.XMLEntityHandler. EntityReader entityReader, char fastchar)`	Scans an expected element type
`protected void setAllowJavaEncodings (boolean allow)`	Supports the use of Java encoding names
`protected void setContinueAfterFatalError (boolean continueAfterFatalError)`	Lets the parser continue after fatal errors
`void setEntityResolver(EntityResolver resolver)`	Specifies the resolver (resolves external entities)
`void setErrorHandler(ErrorHandler handler)`	Sets the error handler
`void setFeature(java.lang.String featureId, boolean state)`	Sets the state of a feature
`void setLocale(java.util.Locale locale)`	Sets the locale
`void setLocator(Locator locator)`	Sets the locator
`protected void setNamespaces(boolean process)`	Specifies whether the parser preprocesses namespaces

continues

Table 11.2 **Continued**

Method	Description
`void setProperty(java.lang.String` *`propertyId`*`, java.lang.Object` *`value`*`)`	Sets the value of a property
`void setReaderFactory(org.apache.xerces. readers.XMLEntityReaderFactory` *`readerFactory`*`)`	Sets the reader factory
`protected void setSendCharDataAsCharArray) (boolean flag)`	Sets character data processing preferences
`void setValidating(boolean flag)`	Indicates to the parser that we are validating
`protected void setValidation(boolean validate)`	Specifies whether the parser validates
`protected void setValidationDynamic (boolean dynamic)`	Lets the parser validate a document only if it contains a grammar
`protected void setValidationWarnOn) DuplicateAttdef(boolean warn)`	Specifies whether an error is created when attributes are redefined in the grammar
`protected void setValidationWarnOn UndeclaredElemdef(boolean warn)`	Specifies whether the parser causes an error when an element's content model references an element by name that is not declared
`abstract void startCDATA()`	Serves as a callback for start of the `CDATA` section
`abstract void startDocument(int` *`version`*`, int` *`encoding`*`, int` *`standAlone`*`)`	Serves as a callback for the start of the document
`abstract void startDTD(int` *`rootElementType`*`, int` *`publicId`*`, int` *`systemId`*`)`	Serves as a callback for the start of the DTD
`abstract void startElement(int` *`elementType`*`, XMLAttrList` *`attrList`*`, int` *`attrListHandle`*`)`	Serves as a callback for the start of the element
`boolean startEntityDecl(boolean isPE, int` *`entityName`*`)`	Serves as a callback for the start of an entity declaration
`abstract void startEntityReference (int` *`entityName`*`, int` *`entityType`*`, int` *`entityContext`*`)`	Serves as a callback for start of an entity reference
`abstract void startNamespaceDeclScope (int` *`prefix`*`, int` *`uri`*`)`	Serves as a callback for the start of a namespace declaration scope
`boolean startReadingFromDocument (InputSource` *`source`*`)`	Starts reading from a document

Method	Description
`boolean startReadingFromEntity(int entityName, int readerDepth, int context)`	Starts reading from an external entity
`void startReadingFromExternalSubset (java.lang.String publicId, java.lang.String systemId, int readerDepth)`	Starts reading from an external DTD subset
`void stopReadingFromExternalSubset()`	Stops reading from an external DTD subset
`abstract void unparsedEntityDecl (int entityName, int publicId, int systemId, int notationName)`	Serves as a callback for unparsed entity declarations
`boolean validEncName(java.lang.String encoding)`	Is true if the given encoding is valid
`boolean validVersionNum(java.lang.String version)`	Is true if the given version is valid

To actually parse the XML document, you use the `parse` method of the `parser` object. I'll let the user specify the name of the document to parse on the command by parsing `args[0]`. Note that you don't need to pass the name of a local file to the `parse` method—you can pass the URL of a document on the Internet, and the `parse` method will retrieve that document.

When you use the `parse` method, you need to enclose your code in a `try` block to catch possible errors, like this:

```
import org.w3c.dom.*;
import org.apache.xerces.parsers.DOMParser;

public class FirstParser
{
    public static void main(String[] args)
    {

        try {
            DOMParser parser = new DOMParser();
            parser.parse(args[0]);
            .
            .
            .
        } catch (Exception e) {
            e.printStackTrace(System.err);
        }
    }
}
```

If the document is successfully parsed, you can get a `Document` object based on the W3C DOM, corresponding to the parsed document, using the parser's `getDocument` method:

```
import org.w3c.dom.*;
import org.apache.xerces.parsers.DOMParser;

public class FirstParser
{
    public static void main(String[] args)
    {

        try {
            DOMParser parser = new DOMParser();
            parser.parse(args[0]);
            Document doc = parser.getDocument();
            .
            .
            .
        } catch (Exception e) {
            e.printStackTrace(System.err);
        }
    }
}
```

The `Document` interface is part of the W3C DOM, and you can find the methods of this interface in Table 11.3.

Table 11.3 **Document Interface Methods**

Method	Description
`Attr createAttribute(java.lang.String` *`name`*`)`	Creates an attribute of the given name
`Attr createAttributeNS(java.lang.String` *`namespaceURI`*`, java.lang.String` *`qualifiedName`*`)`	Creates an attribute of the given qualified name and namespace
`CDATASection createCDATASection (java.lang.String` *`data`*`)`	Creates a `CDATASection` node
`Comment createComment(java.lang.String` *`data`*`)`	Creates a `Comment` node
`DocumentFragment createDocumentFragment()`	Creates an empty `DocumentFragment` object
`Element createElement(java.lang.String` *`tagName`*`)`	Creates an element of the type given
`Element createElementNS(java.lang.String` *`namespaceURI`*`, java.lang.String` *`qualifiedName`*`)`	Creates an element of the given qualified name and namespace
`EntityReference createEntityReference (java.lang.String` *`name`*`)`	Creates an `EntityReference` object

Method	Description
`ProcessingInstruction createProcessingInstruction(java.lang.String target, java.lang.String data)`	Creates a `ProcessingInstruction` node with the given name and data
`Text createTextNode(java.lang.String data)`	Creates a `Text` node
`DocumentType getDoctype()`	Gets the document type declaration for this document
`Element getDocumentElement()`	Gets the root element of the document
`Element getElementById(java.lang.String elementId)`	Gets the element with the given ID
`NodeList getElementsByTagName(java.lang.String tagname)`	Returns a `NodeList` of all the elements with a given tag name
`NodeList getElementsByTagNameNS(java.lang.String namespaceURI, java.lang.String localName)`	Returns a `NodeList` of all the elements with a given local name and namespace URI
`DOMImplementation getImplementation()`	Gets the `DOMImplementation` object
`Node importNode(Node importedNode, boolean deep)`	Imports a node from another document

The `Document` interface is based on the `Node` interface, which supports the W3C `Node` object. Nodes represent a single node in the document tree (as you recall, everything in the document tree, including text and comments, is treated as a node). The `Node` interface has many methods that you can use to work with nodes; for example, you can use methods such as `getNodeName` and `getNodeValue` to get information about the node, and we'll use this kind of information a great deal in this chapter. This interface also has data members, called *fields*, which hold constant values corresponding to various node types, and we'll see them in this chapter as well. You'll find the `Node` interface fields in the following bulleted list and the methods of this interface in Table 11.4. As you see in Table 11.4, the `Node` interface contains all the standard W3C DOM methods for navigating in a document that we already used with JavaScript in Chapter 7, "Handling XML Documents with JavaScript," including `getNextSibling`, `getPreviousSibling`, `getFirstChild`, `getLastChild`, and `getParent`. We'll put those methods to work here as well.

- `static short ATTRIBUTE_NODE`
- `static short CDATA_SECTION_NODE`
- `static short COMMENT_NODE`
- `static short DOCUMENT_FRAGMENT_NODE`

- static short DOCUMENT_NODE
- static short DOCUMENT_TYPE_NODE
- static short ELEMENT_NODE
- static short ENTITY_NODE
- static short ENTITY_REFERENCE_NODE
- static short NOTATION_NODE
- static short PROCESSING_INSTRUCTION_NODE
- static short TEXT_NODE

Table 11.4 **Node Interface Methods**

Method	Description
`Node appendChild(Node newChild)`	Adds the *newChild* node as the last child node of this node
`Node cloneNode(boolean deep)`	Creates a duplicate of this node
`NamedNodeMap getAttributes()`	Gets a `NamedNodeMap` containing the attributes of this node
`NodeList getChildNodes()`	Gets a `NodeList` that contains all children of this node
`Node getFirstChild()`	Gets the first child of this node
`Node getLastChild()`	Gets the last child of this node
`java.lang.String getLocalName()`	Gets the local name of the node
`java.lang.String getNamespaceURI()`	Gets the namespace URI of this node
`Node getNextSibling()`	Gets the node immediately following this one
`java.lang.String getNodeName()`	Gets the name of this node
`short getNodeType()`	Gets a code representing the type of the node
`java.lang.String getNodeValue()`	Gets the value of this node
`Document getOwnerDocument()`	Gets the `Document` object that owns this node
`Node getParentNode()`	Gets the parent of this node
`java.lang.String getPrefix()`	Gets the namespace prefix of this node
`Node getPreviousSibling()`	Gets the node immediately before this one
`boolean hasChildNodes()`	Is true if this node has any children
`Node insertBefore(Node newChild, Node refChild)`	Inserts the node *newChild* before the child node *refChild*

Method	Description
`void normalize()`	Normalizes text nodes by making sure that there are no immediately adjacent or empty text nodes
`Node removeChild(Node oldChild)`	Removes the child node `oldChild`
`Node replaceChild(Node newChild, Node oldChild)`	Replaces the child node `oldChild` with `newChild`
`void setNodeValue (java.lang.String nodeValue)`	Sets a node's value
`void setPrefix(java.lang.String prefix)`	Sets a prefix
`boolean supports(java.lang.String feature, java.lang.String version)`	Is true if the DOM implementation implements a specific feature supported by this node

At this point, we have access to the root node of the document. Our goal here is to check how many `<CUSTOMER>` elements the document has, so I'll use the `getElementsByTagName` method to get a `NodeList` object containing a list of all `<CUSTOMER>` elements:

```
import org.w3c.dom.*;
import org.apache.xerces.parsers.DOMParser;

public class FirstParser
{
    public static void main(String[] args)
    {

        try {
            DOMParser parser = new DOMParser();
            parser.parse(args[0]);
            Document doc = parser.getDocument();

            NodeList nodelist = doc.getElementsByTagName("CUSTOMER");
            .
            .
            .
        } catch (Exception e) {
            e.printStackTrace(System.err);
        }
    }
}
```

The `NodeList` interface supports an ordered collection of nodes. You can access nodes in such a collection by index, and we'll do that in this chapter. You can find the methods of the `NodeList` interface in Table 11.5.

Table 11.5 **NodeList Interface Methods**

Method	Description
`int getLength()`	Gets the number of nodes in this list
`Node item(int index)`	Gets the item at the specified index value in the collection

In Table 11.5, you'll see that the `NodeList` interface supports a `getLength` method that returns the number of nodes in the list. This means that we can find how many `<CUSTOMER>` elements there are in the document like this:

```
import org.w3c.dom.*;
import org.apache.xerces.parsers.DOMParser;

public class FirstParser
{
    public static void main(String[] args)
    {

        try {
            DOMParser parser = new DOMParser();
            parser.parse(args[0]);
            Document doc = parser.getDocument();

            NodeList nodelist = doc.getElementsByTagName("CUSTOMER");
            System.out.println(args[0] + " has " +
            nodelist.getLength() + " <CUSTOMER> elements.");

        } catch (Exception e) {
            e.printStackTrace(System.err);
        }
    }
}
```

You can see the results of this code here, indicating that `customer.xml` has three `<CUSTOMER>` elements, which is correct:

```
%java FirstParser customer.xml
customer.xml has 3 <CUSTOMER> elements.
```

If you prefer to use the `-classpath` switch instead of explicitly setting the class path, you could use `javac` like this, assuming the needed `.jar` files are in the current directory:

```
javac -classpath xerces.jar;xercesSamples.jar FirstParser.java
```

And then execute the code like this:

```
javac -classpath xerces.jar;xercesSamples.jar FirstParser customer.xml
```

That's all it takes to get started with the XML for Java parsers.

Displaying an Entire Document

In this next example, I'm going to write a program that will parse and display an entire document, indenting each element, processing instruction, and so on, as well as displaying attributes and their values. For example, if you pass `customer.xml` to this program, which I'll call `IndentingParser.java`, that program will display the whole document properly indented.

I start by letting the user specify what document to parse and then parsing that document as before. To actually parse the document, I'll call a new method, `displayDocument`, from the `main` method:

```
public static void main(String args[])
{
    displayDocument(args[0]);
    .
    .
    .
}
```

In the `displayDocument` method, I'll parse the document and get an object corresponding to that document:

```
import org.w3c.dom.*;
import org.apache.xerces.parsers.DOMParser;

public class IndentingParser
{
    public static void displayDocument(String uri)
    {
        try {
            DOMParser parser = new DOMParser();
            parser.parse(uri);
            Document document = parser.getDocument();
            .
            .
            .
        } catch (Exception e) {
            e.printStackTrace(System.err);
        }
    .
    .
    .
```

The actual method that will parse the document, `display`, will be recursive, as we saw when working with JavaScript. I'll pass the document to parse to that method, as well as the current indentation string (which will grow by four spaces for every successive level of recursion):

```
import org.w3c.dom.*;
import org.apache.xerces.parsers.DOMParser;

public class IndentingParser
{
    public static void displayDocument(String uri)
    {
        try {
            DOMParser parser = new DOMParser();
            parser.parse(uri);
            Document document = parser.getDocument();

            display(document, "");

        } catch (Exception e) {
            e.printStackTrace(System.err);
        }
    }
    .
    .
    .
```

In the `display` method, I'll check to see whether the node passed to us is really a node—if not, return from the method. The next job is to display the node, and how we do that depends on the type of node we're working with. To get the type of node, you can use the node's `getNodeType` method; I'll set up a long `switch` statement to handle the different types:

```
import org.w3c.dom.*;
import org.apache.xerces.parsers.DOMParser;

public class IndentingParser
{
    public static void displayDocument(String uri)
    {
    .
    .
    .
    }

    public static void display(Node node, String indent)
    {
        if (node == null) {
            return;
        }

        int type = node.getNodeType();

        switch (type) {
    .
    .
    .
```

To handle output from this program, I'll create an array of strings, `displayStrings`, placing each line of the output into one of those strings. I'll also store our current location in that array in an integer named `numberDisplayLines`:

```
public class IndentingParser
{
    static String displayStrings[] = new String[1000];
    static int numberDisplayLines = 0;
    .
    .
    .
```

I'll start handling various types of nodes in this `switch` statement now.

Handling Document Nodes

At the beginning of the document is the XML declaration, and the type of this node matches the constant `Node.DOCUMENT_NODE` defined in the `Node` interface (see Table 11.4). This declaration takes up one line of output, so I'll start the first line of output with the current indent string, followed by a default XML declaration.

The next step is to get the document element of the document we're parsing (the *root element*), and you do that with the `getDocumentElement` method. The root element contains all other elements, so I pass that element to the `display` method, which will display all those elements:

```
public static void display(Node node, String indent)
{
    if (node == null) {
        return;
    }

    int type = node.getNodeType();

    switch (type) {
        case Node.DOCUMENT_NODE: {
            displayStrings[numberDisplayLines] = indent;
            displayStrings[numberDisplayLines] +=
              "<?xml version=\"1.0\" encoding=\""+
              "UTF-8" + "\"?>";
            numberDisplayLines++;
            display(((Document)node).getDocumentElement(), "");
            break;
        }
.
.
.
```

Handling Element Nodes

To handle an element node, we should display the name of the element, as well as any attributes the element has. I start by checking whether the current node type is `Node.ELEMENT_NODE`; if so, I place the current indent string into a display string, followed by a < and the element's name, which I can get with the `getNodeName` method:

```
switch (type) {
    .
    .
    .
    case Node.ELEMENT_NODE: {
        displayStrings[numberDisplayLines] = indent;
        displayStrings[numberDisplayLines] += "<";
        displayStrings[numberDisplayLines] += node.getNodeName();
        .
        .
        .
```

Handling Attributes

Now we've got to handle the attributes of this element, if it has any. Because the current node is an element node, you can use the method `getAttributes` to get a `NodeList` object holding all its attributes, which are stored as `Attr` objects. I'll convert the node list to an array of `Attr` objects, `attributes`, like this—note that I first create the `attributes` array after finding the number of items in the `NodeList` object with the `getLength` method:

```
switch (type) {
    .
    .
    .
    case Node.ELEMENT_NODE: {
        displayStrings[numberDisplayLines] = indent;
        displayStrings[numberDisplayLines] += "<";
        displayStrings[numberDisplayLines] += node.getNodeName();

        int length = (node.getAttributes() != null) ?
            node.getAttributes().getLength() : 0;
        Attr attributes[] = new Attr[length];
        for (int loopIndex = 0; loopIndex < length; loopIndex++) {
            attributes[loopIndex] =
            (Attr)node.getAttributes().item(loopIndex);
        }
        .
        .
        .
```

You can find the methods of the `Attr` interface in Table 11.6.

Table 11.6 ***Attr* Interface Methods**

Method	Description
`java.lang.String getName()`	Gets the name of this attribute
`Element getOwnerElement()`	Gets the `Element` node to which this attribute is attached
`boolean getSpecified()`	Is true if this attribute was explicitly given a value in the original document.
`java.lang.String getValue()`	Gets the value of the attribute as a string

Because the `Attr` interface is built on the `Node` interface, you can use either the `getNodeName` and `getNodeValue` methods to get the attribute's name and value, or the `Attr` methods `getName` and `getValue` methods. I'll use `getNodeName` and `getNodeValue` here. In this case, I'm going to loop over all the attributes in the `attributes` array, adding them to the current display line: *`AttrName`* `= "`*`AttrValue`*`"`. (Note that I escape the quotation marks around the attribute values as `\"` so that Java doesn't interpret them as the end of the string.)

```
switch (type) {
    .
    .
    .
    case Node.ELEMENT_NODE: {
        displayStrings[numberDisplayLines] = indent;
        displayStrings[numberDisplayLines] += "<";
        displayStrings[numberDisplayLines] += node.getNodeName();

        int length = (node.getAttributes() != null) ?
            node.getAttributes().getLength() : 0;
        Attr attributes[] = new Attr[length];
        for (int loopIndex = 0; loopIndex < length; loopIndex++) {
            attributes[loopIndex] =
            (Attr)node.getAttributes().item(loopIndex);
        }

        for (int loopIndex = 0; loopIndex < attributes.length; loopIndex++) {
            Attr attribute = attributes[loopIndex];
            displayStrings[numberDisplayLines] += " ";
            displayStrings[numberDisplayLines] += attribute.getNodeName();
            displayStrings[numberDisplayLines] += "=\"";
            displayStrings[numberDisplayLines] += attribute.getNodeValue();
            displayStrings[numberDisplayLines] += "\"";
        }
        displayStrings[numberDisplayLines] += ">";

        numberDisplayLines++;
        .
        .
        .
```

This element may have child elements, of course, and we have to handle them as well. I do that by storing all the child nodes in a `NodeList` object with the `getChildNodes` method. If there are any child nodes, I add four spaces to the indent string and loop over those child nodes, calling `display` to display each of them:

```
switch (type) {
    .
    .
    .
    case Node.ELEMENT_NODE: {
        displayStrings[numberDisplayLines] = indent;
        displayStrings[numberDisplayLines] += "<";
        displayStrings[numberDisplayLines] += node.getNodeName();

        int length = (node.getAttributes() != null) ?
            node.getAttributes().getLength() : 0;
        Attr attributes[] = new Attr[length];
        for (int loopIndex = 0; loopIndex < length; loopIndex++) {
            attributes[loopIndex] =
            (Attr)node.getAttributes().item(loopIndex);
        }

        for (int loopIndex = 0; loopIndex < attributes.length; loopIndex++) {
            Attr attribute = attributes[loopIndex];
            displayStrings[numberDisplayLines] += " ";
            displayStrings[numberDisplayLines] += attribute.getNodeName();
            displayStrings[numberDisplayLines] += "=\"";
            displayStrings[numberDisplayLines] += attribute.getNodeValue();
            displayStrings[numberDisplayLines] += "\"";
        }
        displayStrings[numberDisplayLines] += ">";

        numberDisplayLines++;

        NodeList childNodes = node.getChildNodes();
        if (childNodes != null) {
            length = childNodes.getLength();
            indent += "    ";
            for (int loopIndex = 0; loopIndex < length; loopIndex++ ) {
               display(childNodes.item(loopIndex), indent);
            }
        }
        break;
    }
    .
    .
    .
```

That's it for handling elements; I'll handle `CDATA` sections next.

Handling *CDATA* Section Nodes

Handling CDATA sections is particularly easy. All I have to do here is to enclose the value of the CDATA section's node inside "<![CDATA[" and "[[>":

```
case Node.CDATA_SECTION_NODE: {
    displayStrings[numberDisplayLines] = indent;
    displayStrings[numberDisplayLines] += "<![CDATA[";
    displayStrings[numberDisplayLines] += node.getNodeValue();
    displayStrings[numberDisplayLines] += "]]>";
    numberDisplayLines++;
    break;
}
.
.
.
```

Handling Text Nodes

The W3C DOM specifies that the text in elements must be stored in text nodes, and those nodes have the type Node.TEXT_NODE. For these nodes, I'll add the current indent string to the display string, and then I'll trim off leading and trailing whitespace from the node's value with the Java String object's trim method:

```
case Node.TEXT_NODE: {
    displayStrings[numberDisplayLines] = indent;
    String newText = node.getNodeValue().trim();
.
.
.
```

The XML for Java parser treats all text as text nodes, including the spaces used for indenting elements in customer.xml. I'll filter out the text nodes corresponding to indentation spacing; if a text node contains only displayable text, however, I'll add that text to the strings in the displayStrings array:

```
case Node.TEXT_NODE: {
    displayStrings[numberDisplayLines] = indent;
    String newText = node.getNodeValue().trim();
    if(newText.indexOf("\n") < 0 && newText.length() > 0) {
        displayStrings[numberDisplayLines] += newText;
        numberDisplayLines++;
    }
    break;
}
.
.
.
```

Handling Processing Instruction Nodes

The W3C DOM also lets you handle processing instructions. Here, the node type is `Node.PROCESSING_INSTRUCTION_NODE`, and the node value is simply the processing instruction itself. For example, let's say that this is the processing instruction:

```
<?xml-stylesheet type="text/css" href="style.css"?>
```

Then this is the value of the associated processing instruction node:

```
xml-stylesheet type="text/css" href="style.css"
```

That means all we have to do is to straddle the value of a processing instruction node with `<?` and `?>`. Here's what the code looks like:

```
    case Node.PROCESSING_INSTRUCTION_NODE: {
        displayStrings[numberDisplayLines] = indent;
        displayStrings[numberDisplayLines] += "<?";
        String text = node.getNodeValue();
        if (text != null && text.length() > 0) {
            displayStrings[numberDisplayLines] += text;
        }
        displayStrings[numberDisplayLines] += "?>";
        numberDisplayLines++;
        break;
    }
}
.
.
.
```

And that finishes the `switch` statement that handles the various types of nodes. There's only one more point to cover.

Closing Element Tags

Displaying element nodes takes a little more thought than displaying other types of nodes. In addition to displaying `<`, the name of the element, and `>`, you also must display a closing tag, `</`, the name of the element, and `>`, at the end of the element.

For that reason, I'll place some code after the `switch` statement to add closing tags to elements after all their children have been displayed. (Note that I'm also subtracting four spaces from the indent string, using the Java String `substr` method so that the closing tag lines up vertically with the opening tag.)

```
    if (type == Node.ELEMENT_NODE) {
        displayStrings[numberDisplayLines] = indent.substring(0,
            indent.length() - 4);
        displayStrings[numberDisplayLines] += "</";
        displayStrings[numberDisplayLines] += node.getNodeName();
        displayStrings[numberDisplayLines] += ">";
        numberDisplayLines++;
        indent += "    ";
    }
}
```

And that's it. I parse and display `customer.xml` like this after compiling `IndentingParser.java`—in this case, I'll pipe the output through the `more` filter to stop it scrolling off the screen. (The `more` filter is available in MS-DOS and certain UNIX ports; it displays one screenful of information, and waits for you to type a key to display the next screenful.)

```
%java IndentingParser customer.xml | more
```

You can see the results in Figure 11.1. As you see in that figure, the program works as it should—the document appears with all elements and text intact, indented properly. Congratulations—now you're able to handle most of what you'll find in XML documents using the XML for Java packages. The complete listing for `IndentingParser.java` is in Listing 11.1. Note that you can use this program as a text-based browser: You can give it the name of any XML document on the Internet—not just local documents—to parse, and it'll fetch that document and parse it.

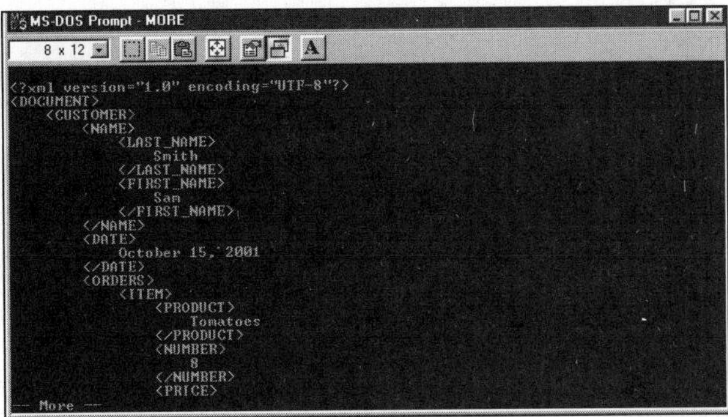

Figure 11.1 Parsing an XML document.

Listing 11.1 ***IndentingParser.java***

```
import org.w3c.dom.*;
import org.apache.xerces.parsers.DOMParser;

public class IndentingParser
{
    static String displayStrings[] = new String[1000];
    static int numberDisplayLines = 0;

    public static void displayDocument(String uri)
    {
        try {
            DOMParser parser = new DOMParser();
            parser.parse(uri);
            Document document = parser.getDocument();

            display(document, "");

        } catch (Exception e) {
            e.printStackTrace(System.err);
        }
    }

    public static void display(Node node, String indent)
    {
        if (node == null) {
            return;
        }

        int type = node.getNodeType();

        switch (type) {
            case Node.DOCUMENT_NODE: {
                displayStrings[numberDisplayLines] = indent;
                displayStrings[numberDisplayLines] +=
                  "<?xml version=\"1.0\" encoding=\""+
                  "UTF-8" + "\"?>";
                numberDisplayLines++;
                display(((Document)node).getDocumentElement(), "");
                break;
             }

             case Node.ELEMENT_NODE: {
                 displayStrings[numberDisplayLines] = indent;
                 displayStrings[numberDisplayLines] += "<";
                 displayStrings[numberDisplayLines] += node.getNodeName();

                 int length = (node.getAttributes() != null) ?
                     node.getAttributes().getLength() : 0;
                 Attr attributes[] = new Attr[length];
                 for (int loopIndex = 0; loopIndex < length; loopIndex++) {
```

```
            attributes[loopIndex] =
            (Attr)node.getAttributes().item(loopIndex);
        }

        for (int loopIndex = 0; loopIndex < attributes.length;
            loopIndex++) {
            Attr attribute = attributes[loopIndex];
            displayStrings[numberDisplayLines] += " ";
            displayStrings[numberDisplayLines] +=
                attribute.getNodeName();
            displayStrings[numberDisplayLines] += "=\"";
            displayStrings[numberDisplayLines] +=
                attribute.getNodeValue();
            displayStrings[numberDisplayLines] += "\"";
        }
        displayStrings[numberDisplayLines] += ">";

        numberDisplayLines++;

        NodeList childNodes = node.getChildNodes();
        if (childNodes != null) {
            length = childNodes.getLength();
            indent += "    ";
            for (int loopIndex = 0; loopIndex < length; loopIndex++ ) {
               display(childNodes.item(loopIndex), indent);
            }
        }
        break;
    }

    case Node.CDATA_SECTION_NODE: {
        displayStrings[numberDisplayLines] = indent;
        displayStrings[numberDisplayLines] += "<![CDATA[";
        displayStrings[numberDisplayLines] += node.getNodeValue();
        displayStrings[numberDisplayLines] += "]]>";
        numberDisplayLines++;
        break;
    }

    case Node.TEXT_NODE: {
        displayStrings[numberDisplayLines] = indent;
        String newText = node.getNodeValue().trim();
        if(newText.indexOf("\n") < 0 && newText.length() > 0) {
            displayStrings[numberDisplayLines] += newText;
            numberDisplayLines++;
        }
        break;
    }

    case Node.PROCESSING_INSTRUCTION_NODE: {
        displayStrings[numberDisplayLines] = indent;
        displayStrings[numberDisplayLines] += "<?";
```

continues

Listing 11.1 **Continued**

```
                displayStrings[numberDisplayLines] += node.getNodeName();
                String text = node.getNodeValue();
                if (text != null && text.length() > 0) {
                    displayStrings[numberDisplayLines] += text;
                }
                displayStrings[numberDisplayLines] += "?>";
                numberDisplayLines++;
                break;
            }
        }

        if (type == Node.ELEMENT_NODE) {
            displayStrings[numberDisplayLines] = indent.substring(0,
                indent.length() - 4);
            displayStrings[numberDisplayLines] += "</";
            displayStrings[numberDisplayLines] += node.getNodeName();
            displayStrings[numberDisplayLines] += ">";
            numberDisplayLines++;
            indent += "    ";
        }
    }

    public static void main(String args[])
    {
        displayDocument(args[0]);

        for(int loopIndex = 0; loopIndex < numberDisplayLines; loopIndex++){
            System.out.println(displayStrings[loopIndex]);
        }
    }
}
```

Filtering XML Documents

The previous example displayed the entire document, but you can be more selective than that through a process called *filtering*. When you filter a document, you extract only those elements that you're interested in.

Here's an example named `searcher.java`. In this case, I'll let the user specify what document to search and what element name to search for like this, which will display all `<ITEM>` elements in `customer.xml`:

```
%java searcher customer.xml ITEM
```

I'll start this program by creating a new class, `FindElements`, to make the programming a little easier. All I have to do is to pass the document to search and the element name to search for to the constructor of this new class:

```
import org.w3c.dom.*;
import org.apache.xerces.parsers.DOMParser;

public class searcher
{
    public static void main(String args[])
    {
        FindElements findElements = new FindElements(args[0], args[1]);
    }
}
```

In the `FindElements` class constructor, I'll save the name of the element to search for in a string named `searchFor` and then call the `displayDocument` method as in the previous example to display the document. That method will fill the `displayStrings` array with the output strings, which we print:

```
class FindElements
{
    static String displayStrings[] = new String[1000];
    static int numberDisplayLines = 0;
    static String searchFor;

    public FindElements (String uri, String searchString)
    {

        searchFor = searchString;
        displayDocument(uri);

        for(int loopIndex = 0; loopIndex < numberDisplayLines; loopIndex++){
            System.out.println(displayStrings[loopIndex]);
        }
    }s
```

In the `displayDocument` method, we want to display only the elements with the name that's in the `searchFor` string. To find those elements, I use the `getElementsByTagName` method, which returns a node list of matching elements. I loop over all elements in that list, calling the `display` method to display each element and its children:

```
public static void displayDocument(String uri)
{
    try {
        DOMParser parser = new DOMParser();
        parser.parse(uri);
        Document document = parser.getDocument();

        NodeList nodeList = document.getElementsByTagName(searchFor);

        if (nodeList != null) {
            for (int loopIndex = 0; loopIndex < nodeList.getLength();
                loopIndex++ ) {
                display(nodeList.item(loopIndex), "");
            }
        }
```

continues ▸

```
    } catch (Exception e) {
        e.printStackTrace(System.err);
    }
}
```

The display method is the same as in the previous example.

That's all it takes; here I search customer.xml for all <ITEM> elements:

```
%java searcher customer.xml ITEM | more
```

You can see the results in Figure 11.2. The complete code for searcher.java is in Listing 11.2.

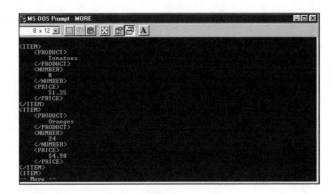

Figure 11.2 Filtering an XML document.

Listing 11.2 *searcher.java*

```
import org.w3c.dom.*;
import org.apache.xerces.parsers.DOMParser;

public class searcher
{
    public static void main(String args[])
    {
        FindElements findElements = new FindElements(args[0], args[1]);
    }
}

class FindElements
{
    static String displayStrings[] = new String[1000];
    static int numberDisplayLines = 0;
    static String searchFor;

    public FindElements (String uri, String searchString)
    {
```

```
    searchFor = searchString;
    displayDocument(uri);

    for(int loopIndex = 0; loopIndex < numberDisplayLines; loopIndex++){
        System.out.println(displayStrings[loopIndex]);
    }
}

public static void displayDocument(String uri)
{
    try {
        DOMParser parser = new DOMParser();
        parser.parse(uri);
        Document document = parser.getDocument();

        NodeList nodeList = document.getElementsByTagName(searchFor);

        if (nodeList != null) {
            for (int loopIndex = 0; loopIndex < nodeList.getLength();
                loopIndex++ ) {
                display(nodeList.item(loopIndex), "");
            }
        }
    } catch (Exception e) {
        e.printStackTrace(System.err);
    }
}

public static void display(Node node, String indent)
{
    if (node == null) {
        return;
    }

    int type = node.getNodeType();

    switch (type) {
        case Node.DOCUMENT_NODE: {
            displayStrings[numberDisplayLines] = indent;
            displayStrings[numberDisplayLines] +=
                "<?xml version=\"1.0\" encoding=\""+
                "UTF-8" + "\"?>";
            numberDisplayLines++;
            display(((Document)node).getDocumentElement(), "");
            break;
         }

         case Node.ELEMENT_NODE: {
             displayStrings[numberDisplayLines] = indent;
             displayStrings[numberDisplayLines] += "<";
             displayStrings[numberDisplayLines] += node.getNodeName();
```

continues

Listing 11.2 **Continued**

```
            int length = (node.getAttributes() != null) ?
                node.getAttributes().getLength() : 0;
            Attr attrs[] = new Attr[length];
            for (int loopIndex = 0; loopIndex < length; loopIndex++) {
                attrs[loopIndex] =
                (Attr)node.getAttributes().item(loopIndex);
            }

            for (int loopIndex = 0; loopIndex < attrs.length;
                loopIndex++) {
                Attr attr = attrs[loopIndex];
                displayStrings[numberDisplayLines] += " ";
                displayStrings[numberDisplayLines] += attr.getNodeName();
                displayStrings[numberDisplayLines] += "=\"";
                displayStrings[numberDisplayLines] +=
                    attr.getNodeValue();
                displayStrings[numberDisplayLines] += "\"";
            }
            displayStrings[numberDisplayLines] += ">";

            numberDisplayLines++;

            NodeList childNodes = node.getChildNodes();
            if (childNodes != null) {
                length = childNodes.getLength();
                indent += "    ";
                for (int loopIndex = 0; loopIndex < length; loopIndex++ ) {
                   display(childNodes.item(loopIndex), indent);
                }
            }
            break;
        }

        case Node.CDATA_SECTION_NODE: {
            displayStrings[numberDisplayLines] = indent;
            displayStrings[numberDisplayLines] += "<![CDATA[";
            displayStrings[numberDisplayLines] += node.getNodeValue();
            displayStrings[numberDisplayLines] += "]]>";
            numberDisplayLines++;
            break;
        }

        case Node.TEXT_NODE: {
            displayStrings[numberDisplayLines] = indent;
            String newText = node.getNodeValue().trim();
            if(newText.indexOf("\n") < 0 && newText.length() > 0) {
                displayStrings[numberDisplayLines] += newText;
                numberDisplayLines++;
            }
            break;
```

```
            }

            case Node.PROCESSING_INSTRUCTION_NODE: {
                displayStrings[numberDisplayLines] = indent;
                displayStrings[numberDisplayLines] += "<?";
                displayStrings[numberDisplayLines] += node.getNodeName();
                String text = node.getNodeValue();
                if (text != null && text.length() > 0) {
                    displayStrings[numberDisplayLines] += text;
                }
                displayStrings[numberDisplayLines] += "?>";
                numberDisplayLines++;
                break;
            }
        }

        if (type == Node.ELEMENT_NODE) {
            displayStrings[numberDisplayLines] = indent.substring(0,
                indent.length() - 4);
            displayStrings[numberDisplayLines] += "</";
            displayStrings[numberDisplayLines] += node.getNodeName();
            displayStrings[numberDisplayLines] += ">";
            numberDisplayLines++;
            indent+= "    ";
        }
    }
}
```

The examples we've created so far have all created text-based output using the `System.out.println` method. However, few browsers these days work that way. In the next section, I'll take a look at creating a windowed browser.

Creating a Windowed Browser

Converting the code we've written to display a document in a window isn't difficult because that code was purposely written to store the output in an array of strings; I can display those strings in a Java window. In this example, I'll upgrade that code to a new program, `browser.java`, which will use XML for Java to display XML documents in a window.

Here's how it works; I start by parsing the document that the user wants to parse in the `main` method:

```
public static void main(String args[]) {

    displayDocument(args[0]);
    .
    .
    .
```

Then I'll create a new window using the techniques we've seen in the previous chapter. Specifically, I'll create a new class named `AppFrame`, create an object of that class, and display it:

```
public static void main(String args[]) {

    displayDocument(args[0]);

    AppFrame f = new AppFrame(displayStrings, numberDisplayLines);

    f.setSize(300, 500);

    f.addWindowListener(new WindowAdapter() {public void
        windowClosing(WindowEvent e) {System.exit(0);}});

    f.show();
}
```

The `AppFrame` class is specially designed to display the output strings in the `displayStrings` array in a Java window. To do that, I pass that array and the number of lines to display to the `AppFrame` constructor, and store them in this new class:

```
class AppFrame extends Frame
{
    String displayStrings[];
    int numberDisplayLines;

    public AppFrame(String[] strings, int number)
    {
        displayStrings = strings;
        numberDisplayLines = number;
    }
        .
        .
        .
```

All that's left is to display the strings in the `displayStrings` array. When you display text in a Java window, you're responsible for positioning that text as you want it. To display multiline text, we'll need to know the height of a line of text in the window, and you can find that with the Java `FontMetrics` class's `getHeight` method.

Here's how I display the output text in the `AppFrame` window. I create a new Java `Font` object using Courier font, and install it in the `Graphics` object passed to the `paint` method. Then I find the height of each line of plain text:

```
public void paint(Graphics g)
{
    Font font = new Font("Courier", Font.PLAIN, 12);
    g.setFont(font);

    FontMetrics fontmetrics = getFontMetrics(getFont());
    int y = fontmetrics.getHeight();
    .
    .
    .
```

Finally, I loop over all lines of text, using the Java `Graphics` object's `drawString` method:

```
public void paint(Graphics g)
{
    Font font = new Font("Courier", Font.PLAIN, 12);
    g.setFont(font);

    FontMetrics fontmetrics = getFontMetrics(getFont());
    int y = fontmetrics.getHeight();

    for(int index = 0; index < numberDisplayLines; index++){
        y += fontmetrics.getHeight();
        g.drawString(displayStrings[index], 5, y);
    }
}
```

You can see the result in Figure 11.3. As you see in that figure, `customer.xml` is displayed in our windowed browser. The code for this example, `browser.java`, appears in Listing 11.3.

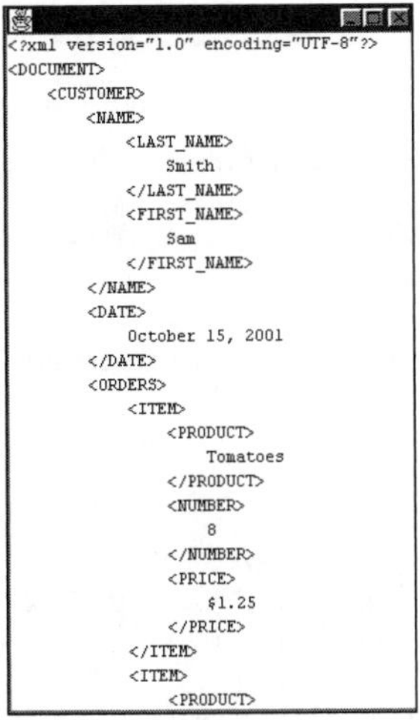

Figure 11.3 A graphical browser.

Listing 11.3 ***browser.java***

```
import java.awt.*;
import java.awt.event.*;

import org.w3c.dom.*;
import org.apache.xerces.parsers.DOMParser;

public class browser
{
    static String displayStrings[] = new String[1000];
    static int numberDisplayLines = 0;

    public static void displayDocument(String uri)
    {
        try {
            DOMParser parser = new DOMParser();
            parser.parse(uri);
            Document document = parser.getDocument();

            display(document, "");

        } catch (Exception e) {
            e.printStackTrace(System.err);
        }
    }

    public static void display(Node node, String indent)
    {
        if (node == null) {
            return;
        }

        int type = node.getNodeType();

        switch (type) {
            case Node.DOCUMENT_NODE: {
                displayStrings[numberDisplayLines] = indent;
                displayStrings[numberDisplayLines] +=
                    "<?xml version=\"1.0\" encoding=\""+
                    "UTF-8" + "\"?>";
                numberDisplayLines++;
                display(((Document)node).getDocumentElement(), "");
                break;
             }

             case Node.ELEMENT_NODE: {
                 displayStrings[numberDisplayLines] = indent;
                 displayStrings[numberDisplayLines] += "<";
                 displayStrings[numberDisplayLines] += node.getNodeName();

                 int length = (node.getAttributes() != null) ?
```

```
            node.getAttributes().getLength() : 0;
        Attr attrs[] = new Attr[length];
        for (int loopIndex = 0; loopIndex < length; loopIndex++) {
            attrs[loopIndex] =
            (Attr)node.getAttributes().item(loopIndex);
        }

        for (int loopIndex = 0; loopIndex < attrs.length;
            loopIndex++) {
            Attr attr = attrs[loopIndex];
            displayStrings[numberDisplayLines] += " ";
            displayStrings[numberDisplayLines] += attr.getNodeName();
            displayStrings[numberDisplayLines] += "=\"";
            displayStrings[numberDisplayLines] +=
                attr.getNodeValue();
            displayStrings[numberDisplayLines] += "\"";
        }
        displayStrings[numberDisplayLines] += ">";

        numberDisplayLines++;

        NodeList childNodes = node.getChildNodes();
        if (childNodes != null) {
            length = childNodes.getLength();
            indent += "    ";
            for (int loopIndex = 0; loopIndex < length; loopIndex++ ) {
               display(childNodes.item(loopIndex), indent);
            }
        }
        break;
    }

    case Node.CDATA_SECTION_NODE: {
        displayStrings[numberDisplayLines] = indent;
        displayStrings[numberDisplayLines] += "<![CDATA[";
        displayStrings[numberDisplayLines] += node.getNodeValue();
        displayStrings[numberDisplayLines] += "]]>";
        numberDisplayLines++;
        break;
    }

    case Node.TEXT_NODE: {
        displayStrings[numberDisplayLines] = indent;
        String newText = node.getNodeValue().trim();
        if(newText.indexOf("\n") < 0 && newText.length() > 0) {
            displayStrings[numberDisplayLines] += newText;
            numberDisplayLines++;
        }
        break;
    }

    case Node.PROCESSING_INSTRUCTION_NODE: {
```

continues

Listing 11.3 **Continued**

```
                displayStrings[numberDisplayLines] = indent;

                displayStrings[numberDisplayLines] += "<?";
                displayStrings[numberDisplayLines] += node.getNodeName();
                String text = node.getNodeValue();
                if (text != null && text.length() > 0) {
                    displayStrings[numberDisplayLines] += text;
                }
                displayStrings[numberDisplayLines] += "?>";
                numberDisplayLines++;
                break;
            }
        }

        if (type == Node.ELEMENT_NODE) {
            displayStrings[numberDisplayLines] = indent.substring(0,
                indent.length() - 4);
            displayStrings[numberDisplayLines] += "</";
            displayStrings[numberDisplayLines] += node.getNodeName();
            displayStrings[numberDisplayLines] += ">";
            numberDisplayLines++;
            indent+= "    ";
        }
    }

    public static void main(String args[]) {

        displayDocument(args[0]);

        AppFrame f = new AppFrame(displayStrings, numberDisplayLines);

        f.setSize(300, 500);

        f.addWindowListener(new WindowAdapter() {public void
            windowClosing(WindowEvent e) {System.exit(0);}});

        f.show();
    }
}

class AppFrame extends Frame
{
    String displayStrings[];
    int numberDisplayLines;

    public AppFrame(String[] strings, int number)
    {
        displayStrings = strings;
        numberDisplayLines = number;
    }
```

```
    public void paint(Graphics g)
    {
        Font font = new Font("Courier", Font.PLAIN, 12);
        g.setFont(font);

        FontMetrics fontmetrics = getFontMetrics(getFont());
        int y = fontmetrics.getHeight();

        for(int index = 0; index < numberDisplayLines; index++){
            y += fontmetrics.getHeight();
            g.drawString(displayStrings[index], 5, y);
        }
    }
}
```

Now that we're parsing and displaying XML documents in windows, there's no reason to restrict ourselves to displaying the text form of an XML document. Take a look at the next topic.

Creating a Graphical Browser

In Java, text is just a form of graphics, so we've already been working with graphics. In this next example, I'll create a nontext browser that reads an XML document and uses it to draw graphics figures—circles. Here's what a document this browser might read, `circles.xml`, looks like—I'm specifying the (x, y) origin of the circle and the radius of the circle as attributes of the `<CIRCLE>` element:

```
<?xml version = "1.0" ?>
<!DOCTYPE DOCUMENT [
<!ELEMENT DOCUMENT (CIRCLE|ELLIPSE)*>
<!ELEMENT CIRCLE EMPTY>
<!ELEMENT ELLIPSE EMPTY>
<!ATTLIST CIRCLE
    X CDATA #IMPLIED
    Y CDATA #IMPLIED
    RADIUS CDATA #IMPLIED>
<!ATTLIST ELLIPSE
    X CDATA #IMPLIED
    Y CDATA #IMPLIED
    WIDTH CDATA #IMPLIED
    HEIGHT CDATA #IMPLIED>
]>
<DOCUMENT>
    <CIRCLE X='200' Y='160' RADIUS='50' />
    <CIRCLE X='170' Y='100' RADIUS='15' />
    <CIRCLE X='80' Y='200' RADIUS='45' />
    <CIRCLE X='200' Y='140' RADIUS='35' />
```

continues ▸

```
    <CIRCLE X='130' Y='240' RADIUS='25' />
    <CIRCLE X='270' Y='300' RADIUS='45' />
    <CIRCLE X='210' Y='240' RADIUS='25' />
    <CIRCLE X='60' Y='160' RADIUS='35' />
    <CIRCLE X='160' Y='260' RADIUS='55' />
</DOCUMENT>
```

I'll call this example `circles.java`. We'll need to decode the XML document and store the specification of each circle. To store that data, I'll create an array named `x` to hold the x coordinates of the circles, `y` to hold the y coordinates, and `radius` to hold the radii of the circles. I'll also store our current location in these arrays in an integer named `numberFigures`:

```
public class circles
{
    static int numberFigures = 0;
    static  int x[] = new int[100];
    static int y[] = new int[100];
    static int radius[] = new int[100];
    .
    .
    .
```

As we parse the document, I'll filter out elements and search for `<CIRCLE>` elements. When I find a `<CIRCLE>` element, I'll store its x, y, and radius values in the appropriate array. To check whether the current node is a `<CIRCLE>` element, I'll compare the node's name, which I get with the `getNodeName` method, to `"CIRCLE"` using the Java `String` method `equals`, which you must use with `String` objects instead of the `==` operator:

```
if (node.getNodeType() == Node.ELEMENT_NODE) {

        if (node.getNodeName().equals("CIRCLE")) {
        .
        .
        .
        }
.
.
.
```

To find the value of the `X`, `Y`, and `RADIUS` attributes, I'll use the `getAttributes` method to get a `NamedNodeMap` object representing all the attributes of this element. To get the value of specific attributes, I get the node corresponding to that attribute with the `getNamedItem` method. I get the attribute's actual value with `getNodeValue` like this, where I'm converting the attribute data from strings to integers using the Java `Integer` class's `parseInt` method:

```
if (node.getNodeType() == Node.ELEMENT_NODE) {

    if (node.getNodeName().equals("CIRCLE")) {

        NamedNodeMap attrs = node.getAttributes();

        x[numberFigures] =
        Integer.parseInt((String)attrs.getNamedItem("X").getNodeValue());

        y[numberFigures] =
        Integer.parseInt((String)attrs.getNamedItem("Y").getNodeValue());

        radius[numberFigures] =
        Integer.parseInt((String)attrs.getNamedItem("RADIUS").getNodeValue());

        numberFigures++;
    }
    .
    .
    .
```

You can find the methods of the `NamedNodeMap` interface in Table 11.7.

Table 11.7 ***NamedNodeMap* Interface Methods**

Method	Description
`int getLength()`	Returns the number of nodes in this map
`Node getNamedItem(java.lang.String` *`name`*`)`	Gets a node indicated by name
`Node getNamedItemNS(java.lang.String` *`namespaceURI`*`, java.lang.String` *`localName`*`)`	Gets a node indicated by a local name and namespace URI
`Node item(int` *`index`*`)`	Gets an item in the map by index
`Node removeNamedItem (java.lang.String` *`name`*`)`	Removes a node given by name
`Node removeNamedItemNS(java.lang. String` *`namespaceURI`*`, java.lang.S tring` *`localName`*`)`	Removes a node given by a local name and namespace URI
`Node setNamedItem(Node` *`arg`*`)`	Adds a node specified by its `nodeName` attribute
`Node setNamedItemNS(Node` *`arg`*`)`	Adds a node specified by its `namespaceURI` and `localName`

After parsing the document, the required data is in the x, y, and radius arrays. All that's left is to display the corresponding circles, and I'll use the Java `Graphics` object's `drawOval` method to do that. This method draws ellipses and takes the (x, y) location of the figure's origin, as well as the minor and major axes' length. To draw circles, I'll set both those lengths to the radius value for the circle. It all looks like this in the `AppFrame` class, which is where we draw the browser's window:

```
class AppFrame extends Frame
{
    int numberFigures;
    int[] xValues;
    int[] yValues;
    int[] radiusValues;

    public AppFrame(int number, int[] x, int[] y, int[] radius)
    {
        numberFigures = number;
        xValues = x;
        yValues = y;
        radiusValues = radius;
    }

    public void paint(Graphics g)
    {
        for(int loopIndex = 0; loopIndex < numberFigures; loopIndex++){
            g.drawOval(xValues[loopIndex], yValues[loopIndex],
            radiusValues[loopIndex], radiusValues[loopIndex]);
        }
    }
```

And that's all it takes; you can see the results in Figure 11.4, where the browser is displaying `circles.xml`. The complete listing appears in Listing 11.4.

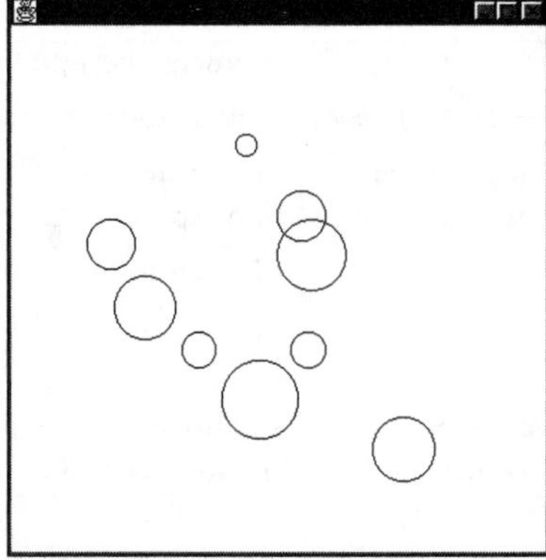

Figure 11.4 Creating a graphical XML browser.

Listing 11.4 ***circles.java***

```
import java.awt.*;
import java.awt.event.*;

import org.w3c.dom.*;
import org.apache.xerces.parsers.DOMParser;

public class circles
{
```

```
static int numberFigures = 0;
static  int x[] = new int[100];
static int y[] = new int[100];
static int radius[] = new int[100];

public static void displayDocument(String uri)
{
    try {
        DOMParser parser = new DOMParser();
        parser.parse(uri);
        Document document = parser.getDocument();

        display(document);

    } catch (Exception e) {
        e.printStackTrace(System.err);
    }
}

public static void display(Node node)
{
    if (node == null) {
        return;
    }

    int type = node.getNodeType();

    if (node.getNodeType() == Node.DOCUMENT_NODE) {
        display(((Document)node).getDocumentElement());
    }

    if (node.getNodeType() == Node.ELEMENT_NODE) {

        if (node.getNodeName().equals("CIRCLE")) {

            NamedNodeMap attrs = node.getAttributes();

            x[numberFigures] =
        Integer.parseInt((String)attrs.getNamedItem("X").getNodeValue());

            y[numberFigures] =
        Integer.parseInt((String)attrs.getNamedItem("Y").getNodeValue());

            radius[numberFigures] =
    Integer.parseInt((String)attrs.getNamedItem("RADIUS").getNodeValue());

            numberFigures++;
        }

        NodeList childNodes = node.getChildNodes();

        if (childNodes != null) {
```

continues

Listing 11.4 **Continued**

```
                int length = childNodes.getLength();
                for (int loopIndex = 0; loopIndex < length; loopIndex++) {
                    display(childNodes.item(loopIndex));
                }
            }
        }
    }

    public static void main(String args[])
    {
        displayDocument(args[0]);

        AppFrame f = new AppFrame(numberFigures, x, y, radius);

        f.setSize(400, 400);

        f.addWindowListener(new WindowAdapter() {public void
            windowClosing(WindowEvent e) {System.exit(0);}});

        f.show();
    }
}

class AppFrame extends Frame
{
    int numberFigures;
    int[] xValues;
    int[] yValues;
    int[] radiusValues;

    public AppFrame(int number, int[] x, int[] y, int[] radius)
    {
        numberFigures = number;
        xValues = x;
        yValues = y;
        radiusValues = radius;
    }

    public void paint(Graphics g)
    {
        for(int loopIndex = 0; loopIndex < numberFigures; loopIndex++){
            g.drawOval(xValues[loopIndex], yValues[loopIndex],
                radiusValues[loopIndex], radiusValues[loopIndex]);
        }
    }
}
```

Navigating in XML Documents

As you saw earlier in Table 11.4, the `Node` interface contains all the standard W3C DOM methods for navigating in a document that we've already used with JavaScript in Chapter 7, including `getNextSibling`, `getPreviousSibling`, `getFirstChild`, `getLastChild`, and `getParent`. You can put those methods to work here as easily as in Chapter 7; for example, here's the XML document that we navigated through in Chapter 7, `meetings.xml`:

```
<?xml version="1.0"?>
<MEETINGS>
   <MEETING TYPE="informal">
       <MEETING_TITLE>XML In The Real World</MEETING_TITLE>
       <MEETING_NUMBER>2079</MEETING_NUMBER>
       <SUBJECT>XML</SUBJECT>
       <DATE>6/1/2002</DATE>
       <PEOPLE>
           <PERSON ATTENDANCE="present">
               <FIRST_NAME>Edward</FIRST_NAME>
               <LAST_NAME>Samson</LAST_NAME>
           </PERSON>
           <PERSON ATTENDANCE="absent">
               <FIRST_NAME>Ernestine</FIRST_NAME>
               <LAST_NAME>Johnson</LAST_NAME>
           </PERSON>
           <PERSON ATTENDANCE="present">
               <FIRST_NAME>Betty</FIRST_NAME>
               <LAST_NAME>Richardson</LAST_NAME>
           </PERSON>
       </PEOPLE>
   </MEETING>
</MEETINGS>
```

In Chapter 7, we navigated through this document to display the third person's name, and I'll do the same here. The main difference between the XML for Java and the JavaScript implementations in this case is that the XML for Java implementation treats all text as text nodes—including the spacing used to indent `meetings.xml`. This means that I can use essentially the same code to navigate through the document here that we used in Chapter 7, bearing in mind that we must step over the text nodes which only contain indentation text. Here's what that looks like in a program named `nav.java`:

```
import org.w3c.dom.*;
import org.apache.xerces.parsers.DOMParser;

public class nav
{
    public static void displayDocument(String uri)
    {
```

continues ▸

```
        try {
            DOMParser parser = new DOMParser();
            parser.parse(uri);
            Document document = parser.getDocument();

            display(document);

        } catch (Exception e) {
            e.printStackTrace(System.err);
        }
    }

    public static void display(Node node)
    {
        Node textNode;
        Node meetingsNode = ((Document)node).getDocumentElement();
        textNode = meetingsNode.getFirstChild();
        Node meetingNode = textNode.getNextSibling();
        textNode = meetingNode.getLastChild();
        Node peopleNode = textNode.getPreviousSibling();
        textNode = peopleNode.getLastChild();
        Node personNode = textNode.getPreviousSibling();
        textNode = personNode.getFirstChild();
        Node first_nameNode = textNode.getNextSibling();
        textNode = first_nameNode.getNextSibling();
        Node last_nameNode = textNode.getNextSibling();

        System.out.println("Third name: " +
            first_nameNode.getFirstChild().getNodeValue() + ' '
            + last_nameNode.getFirstChild().getNodeValue());
    }

    public static void main(String args[])
    {
        displayDocument("meetings.xml");
    }
}
```

And here are the results of this program:

```
%java nav
Third name: Betty Richardson
```

Ignoring Whitespace

You can eliminate the indentation spaces, called "ignorable" whitespace, if you want. In that case, you must provide the XML for Java parser some way of checking the grammar of your XML document so that it knows what kind of whitespace it may ignore, and you can do that by giving the document a DTD:

```
<?xml version="1.0"?>
<!DOCTYPE MEETINGS [
<!ELEMENT MEETINGS (MEETING*)>
<!ELEMENT MEETING (MEETING_TITLE,MEETING_NUMBER,SUBJECT,DATE,PEOPLE*)>
<!ELEMENT MEETING_TITLE (#PCDATA)>
<!ELEMENT MEETING_NUMBER (#PCDATA)>
<!ELEMENT SUBJECT (#PCDATA)>
<!ELEMENT DATE (#PCDATA)>
<!ELEMENT FIRST_NAME (#PCDATA)>
<!ELEMENT LAST_NAME (#PCDATA)>
<!ELEMENT PEOPLE (PERSON*)>
<!ELEMENT PERSON (FIRST_NAME,LAST_NAME)>
<!ATTLIST MEETING
    TYPE CDATA #IMPLIED>
<!ATTLIST PERSON
    ATTENDANCE CDATA #IMPLIED>
]>
<MEETINGS>
    <MEETING TYPE="informal">
       <MEETING_TITLE>XML In The Real World</MEETING_TITLE>
       <MEETING_NUMBER>2079</MEETING_NUMBER>
       <SUBJECT>XML</SUBJECT>
       <DATE>6/1/2002</DATE>
       <PEOPLE>
           <PERSON ATTENDANCE="present">
               <FIRST_NAME>Edward</FIRST_NAME>
               <LAST_NAME>Samson</LAST_NAME>
           </PERSON>
           <PERSON ATTENDANCE="absent">
               <FIRST_NAME>Ernestine</FIRST_NAME>
               <LAST_NAME>Johnson</LAST_NAME>
           </PERSON>
           <PERSON ATTENDANCE="present">
               <FIRST_NAME>Betty</FIRST_NAME>
               <LAST_NAME>Richardson</LAST_NAME>
           </PERSON>
       </PEOPLE>
   </MEETING>
</MEETINGS>
```

Now I call the parser method `setIncludeIgnorableWhitespace` with a value of `false` to turn off ignorable whitespace, and I don't have to worry about the indentation spaces showing up as text nodes, which makes the code considerably shorter:

```
import org.w3c.dom.*;
import org.apache.xerces.parsers.DOMParser;

public class nav
{
    public static void displayDocument(String uri)
    {
        try {
            DOMParser parser = new DOMParser();
```

continues ▸

```
            parser.setIncludeIgnorableWhitespace(false);
            parser.parse(uri);
            Document document = parser.getDocument();

            display(document);

        } catch (Exception e) {
            e.printStackTrace(System.err);
        }
    }

    public static void display(Node node)
    {
        Node meetingsNode = ((Document)node).getDocumentElement();
        Node meetingNode = meetingsNode.getFirstChild();
        Node peopleNode = meetingNode.getLastChild();
        Node personNode = peopleNode.getLastChild();
        Node first_nameNode = personNode.getFirstChild();
        Node last_nameNode = first_nameNode.getNextSibling();

        System.out.println("Third name: " +
            first_nameNode.getFirstChild().getNodeValue() + ' '
            + last_nameNode.getFirstChild().getNodeValue());
    }

    public static void main(String args[])
    {
        displayDocument("meetings.xml");
    }
}
```

Modifying XML Documents

As you saw earlier in Table 11.4, the `Node` interface contains a number of methods for modifying documents by adding or removing nodes. These methods include `appendChild`, `insertBefore`, `removeChild`, `replaceChild`, and so on. You can use these methods to modify XML documents on the fly.

If you do modify a document, however, you still have to write it out. (In Chapter 7, we couldn't do that using JavaScript in a browser, so I sent the whole document to an ASP script that echoed it back to be displayed in the browser.) The XML for Java packages do support an interface named `Serializer` that you can use to serialize (store) documents. However, that interface is not included in the standard JAR files that we've already downloaded—in fact, it's easy enough to simply store the modified XML document ourselves because we print out that document anyway. Instead of using `System.out.println` to display the modified document on the console, I'll use a Java `FileWriter` object to write that document to disk.

In this example, I'll assume that all the people listed in `customer.xml` (you can see this document at the beginning of this chapter) are experienced XML programmers. In addition to the `<FIRST_NAME>` and `<LAST_NAME>` elements, I'll give each of them `XML` as a middle name by adding a `<MIDDLE_NAME>` element. Like `<FIRST_NAME>` and `<LAST_NAME>`, `<MIDDLE_NAME>` will be a child element of the `<NAME>` element:

```
<NAME>
    <LAST_NAME>
        Jones
    </LAST_NAME>
    <FIRST_NAME>
        Polly
    </FIRST_NAME>
    <MIDDLE_NAME>
        XML
    </MIDDLE_NAME>
</NAME>
```

Adding a `<MIDDLE_NAME>` element to every `<NAME>` element is easy enough to do—all I have to do is make sure that we're parsing the `<NAME>` element, and then use the `createElement` method to create a new element named `<MIDDLE_NAME>`:

```
case Node.ELEMENT_NODE: {

    if(node.getNodeName().equals("NAME")) {
        Element middleNameElement = document.createElement("MIDDLE_NAME");
    .
    .
    .
```

Because all text is stored in text nodes, I also create a new text node with the `createTextNode` method to hold the text `XML`:

```
case Node.ELEMENT_NODE: {

    if(node.getNodeName().equals("NAME")) {
        Element middleNameElement = document.createElement("MIDDLE_NAME");
        Text textNode = document.createTextNode("XML");
    .
    .
    .
```

Now I can append the text node to the new element with `appendChild`:

```
case Node.ELEMENT_NODE: {

    if(node.getNodeName().equals("NAME")) {
        Element middleNameElement = document.createElement("MIDDLE_NAME");
        Text textNode = document.createTextNode("XML");
```

continues ▸

```
        middleNameElement.appendChild(textNode);
    .
    .
    .
```

Finally, I append the new element to the <NAME> node, like this:

```
case Node.ELEMENT_NODE: {

    if(node.getNodeName().equals("NAME")) {
        Element middleNameElement = document.createElement("MIDDLE_NAME");
        Text textNode = document.createTextNode("XML");
        middleNameElement.appendChild(textNode);
        node.appendChild(middleNameElement);
    }
    .
    .
    .
```

Using this code, I'm able to modify the document in memory. As before, the lines of this document are stored in the array `displayStrings`, and I can write that array out to a file called `customer2.xml`. To do that, I use the Java `FileWriter` class, which writes text stored as character arrays in files. To create those character arrays, I can use the Java `String` object's handy `toCharArray` method, like this:

```
public static void main(String args[])
{
    displayDocument(args[0]);

    try {
        FileWriter filewriter = new FileWriter("customer2.xml");

        for(int loopIndex = 0; loopIndex < numberDisplayLines; loopIndex++){
            filewriter.write(displayStrings[loopIndex].toCharArray());
            filewriter.write('\n');
        }

        filewriter.close();
        }
    catch (Exception e) {
        e.printStackTrace(System.err);
    }
}
```

That's all there is to it; after running this code, this is the result, `customer2.xml`, complete with the new <MIDDLE_NAME> elements:

```
<?xml version="1.0" encoding="UTF-8"?>
<DOCUMENT>
    <CUSTOMER>
        <NAME>
            <LAST_NAME>
                Smith
```

```
            </LAST_NAME>
            <FIRST_NAME>
                Sam
            </FIRST_NAME>
            <MIDDLE_NAME>
                XML
            </MIDDLE_NAME>
        </NAME>
        <DATE>
            October 15, 2001
        </DATE>
        <ORDERS>
            <ITEM>
                <PRODUCT>
                    Tomatoes
                </PRODUCT>
                <NUMBER>
                    8
                </NUMBER>
                <PRICE>
                    $1.25
                </PRICE>
            </ITEM>
            <ITEM>
                <PRODUCT>
                    Oranges
                </PRODUCT>
                <NUMBER>
                    24
                </NUMBER>
                <PRICE>
                    $4.98
                </PRICE>
            </ITEM>
        </ORDERS>
    </CUSTOMER>
    <CUSTOMER>
        <NAME>
            <LAST_NAME>
                Jones
            </LAST_NAME>
            <FIRST_NAME>
                Polly
            </FIRST_NAME>
            <MIDDLE_NAME>
                XML
            </MIDDLE_NAME>
        </NAME>
        <DATE>
            October 20, 2001
        </DATE>
```

continues ▸

```
        <ORDERS>
            <ITEM>
                <PRODUCT>
                    Bread
                </PRODUCT>
                <NUMBER>
                    12
                </NUMBER>
                <PRICE>
                    $14.95
                </PRICE>
            </ITEM>
            <ITEM>
                <PRODUCT>
                    Apples
                </PRODUCT>
                <NUMBER>
                    6
                </NUMBER>
                <PRICE>
                    $1.50
                </PRICE>
            </ITEM>
        </ORDERS>
    </CUSTOMER>
    <CUSTOMER>
        <NAME>
            <LAST_NAME>
                Weber
            </LAST_NAME>
            <FIRST_NAME>
                Bill
            </FIRST_NAME>
            <MIDDLE_NAME>
                XML
            </MIDDLE_NAME>
        </NAME>
        <DATE>
            October 25, 2001
        </DATE>
        <ORDERS>
            <ITEM>
                <PRODUCT>
                    Asparagus
                </PRODUCT>
                <NUMBER>
                    12
                </NUMBER>
                <PRICE>
                    $2.95
                </PRICE>
```

```
            </ITEM>
            <ITEM>
                <PRODUCT ID="5231" TYPE="3133">
                    Lettuce
                </PRODUCT>
                <NUMBER>
                    6
                </NUMBER>
                <PRICE>
                    $11.50
                </PRICE>
            </ITEM>
        </ORDERS>
    </CUSTOMER>
</DOCUMENT>
```

You can find the code for this example, `XMLWriter.java`, in Listing 11.5.

Listing 11.5 ***XMLWriter.java***

```
import java.awt.*;
import java.io.*;
import java.awt.event.*;

import org.w3c.dom.*;
import org.apache.xerces.parsers.DOMParser;
import org.apache.xerces.*;

public class XMLWriter
{
    static String displayStrings[] = new String[1000];
    static int numberDisplayLines = 0;
    static Document document;
    static Node c;

    public static void displayDocument(String uri)
    {
        try {
            DOMParser parser = new DOMParser();
            parser.parse(uri);
            document = parser.getDocument();

            display(document, "");

        } catch (Exception e) {
            e.printStackTrace(System.err);
        }
    }

    public static void display(Node node, String indent)
    {
        if (node == null) {
```

continues

Listing 11.5 **Continued**

```
        return;
    }

    int type = node.getNodeType();

    switch (type) {
        case Node.DOCUMENT_NODE: {
            displayStrings[numberDisplayLines] = indent;
            displayStrings[numberDisplayLines] +=
                "<?xml version=\"1.0\" encoding=\""+
                "UTF-8" + "\"?>";
            numberDisplayLines++;
            display(((Document)node).getDocumentElement(), "");
            break;
        }

         case Node.ELEMENT_NODE: {

             if(node.getNodeName().equals("NAME")) {
                 Element middleNameElement = document.createElement("MIDDLE_NAME");
                 Text textNode = document.createTextNode("XML");
                 middleNameElement.appendChild(textNode);
                 node.appendChild(middleNameElement);
             }

             displayStrings[numberDisplayLines] = indent;
             displayStrings[numberDisplayLines] += "<";
             displayStrings[numberDisplayLines] += node.getNodeName();

             int length = (node.getAttributes() != null) ?
                 node.getAttributes().getLength() : 0;
             Attr attributes[] = new Attr[length];
             for (int loopIndex = 0; loopIndex < length; loopIndex++) {
                 attributes[loopIndex] = (Attr)node.getAttributes().item(loopIndex);
             }

             for (int loopIndex = 0; loopIndex < attributes.length; loopIndex++) {
                 Attr attribute = attributes[loopIndex];
                 displayStrings[numberDisplayLines] += " ";
                 displayStrings[numberDisplayLines] += attribute.getNodeName();
                 displayStrings[numberDisplayLines] += "=\"";
                 displayStrings[numberDisplayLines] += attribute.getNodeValue();
                 displayStrings[numberDisplayLines] += "\"";
             }
             displayStrings[numberDisplayLines]+=">";

             numberDisplayLines++;

             NodeList childNodes = node.getChildNodes();
             if (childNodes != null) {
```

```
                    length = childNodes.getLength();
                    indent += "    ";
                    for (int loopIndex = 0; loopIndex < length; loopIndex++ ) {
                       display(childNodes.item(loopIndex), indent);
                    }
                }
                break;
            }

            case Node.CDATA_SECTION_NODE: {
                displayStrings[numberDisplayLines] = indent;
                displayStrings[numberDisplayLines] += "<![CDATA[";
                displayStrings[numberDisplayLines] += node.getNodeValue();
                displayStrings[numberDisplayLines] += "]]>";
                numberDisplayLines++;
                break;
            }

            case Node.TEXT_NODE: {
                displayStrings[numberDisplayLines] = indent;
                String newText = node.getNodeValue().trim();
                if(newText.indexOf("\n") < 0 && newText.length() > 0) {
                    displayStrings[numberDisplayLines] += newText;
                    numberDisplayLines++;
                }
                break;
            }

            case Node.PROCESSING_INSTRUCTION_NODE: {
                displayStrings[numberDisplayLines] = indent;
                displayStrings[numberDisplayLines] += "<?";
                displayStrings[numberDisplayLines] += node.getNodeName();
                String text = node.getNodeValue();
                if (text != null && text.length() > 0) {
                    displayStrings[numberDisplayLines] += text;
                }
                displayStrings[numberDisplayLines] += "?>";
                numberDisplayLines++;
                break;
            }
        }

        if (type == Node.ELEMENT_NODE) {
            displayStrings[numberDisplayLines] = indent.substring(0,
                indent.length() - 4);
            displayStrings[numberDisplayLines] += "</";
            displayStrings[numberDisplayLines] += node.getNodeName();
            displayStrings[numberDisplayLines] += ">";
            numberDisplayLines++;
            indent += "    ";
        }
    }
```

continues

Listing 11.4 **Continued**

```
    public static void main(String args[])
    {
        displayDocument(args[0]);

        try {
            FileWriter filewriter = new FileWriter("customer2.xml");

            for(int loopIndex = 0; loopIndex < numberDisplayLines; loopIndex++){
                filewriter.write(displayStrings[loopIndex].toCharArray());
                filewriter.write('\n');
            }

            filewriter.close();
        }
        catch (Exception e) {
            e.printStackTrace(System.err);
        }
    }
}
```

As you see, there's a lot of power in XML for Java. In fact, there's another way to do all this besides using the DOM. It's called SAX, and I'll take a look at it in the next chapter.

12
Java and SAX

THE PREVIOUS CHAPTER WAS ALL ABOUT USING JAVA and the XML DOM. Some people, however, find using the DOM difficult and see the whole concept of treating an XML document as a tree unnecessarily complex. Rather than having to navigate through the whole document, they say, wouldn't it be great if the whole document came to you? That's the idea behind the Simple API for XML (SAX), and this chapter is dedicated to it. SAX really is a lot easier to use for many—possibly even most—XML parsing that you have to do.

You may be surprised to learn that we've already been putting the idea behind SAX to work throughout the entire previous chapter. You may recall that in that chapter, I set up a recursive method named `display` that was called for every node in the DOM tree. In `display`, I used a `switch` statement to make things easier. That `switch` statement had `case` statements to handle different types of nodes:

```
public static void display(Node node, String indent)
{
    if (node == null) {
        return;
    }

    int type = node.getNodeType();

    switch (type) {
        case Node.DOCUMENT_NODE: {
            displayStrings[numberDisplayLines] = indent;
```

continues ▸

```
        displayStrings[numberDisplayLines] +=
            "<?xml version=\"1.0\" encoding=\""+
            "UTF-8" + "\"?>";
        numberDisplayLines++;
        display(((Document)node).getDocumentElement(), "");
        break;
    }

    case Node.ELEMENT_NODE: {
        displayStrings[numberDisplayLines] = indent;
        displayStrings[numberDisplayLines] += "<";
        displayStrings[numberDisplayLines] += node.getNodeName();

        int length = (node.getAttributes() != null) ?
            node.getAttributes().getLength() : 0;
        Attr attributes[] = new Attr[length];
        for (int loopIndex = 0; loopIndex < length; loopIndex++) {
            attributes[loopIndex] = (Attr)node.getAttributes().item(loopIndex);
        }
        .
        .
        .
```

I was able to add the code that handled elements to one `case` statement, the code to handle processing instructions to another `case` statement, and so on.

In essence, we were handling XML documents the same way that SAX does. Instead of navigating through the document ourselves, we let the document come to us, having the code call various `case` statements for the various nodes in the document. That's what SAX does. It's *event-based*, which means that when the SAX parser encounters an element, it treats that as an event and calls the code that you specify should be called for elements; when it encounters a processing instruction, it treats that as an event and calls the code that you specify should be called for processing instructions, and so on. In this way, you don't have to navigate through the document yourself—it comes to you. The fact that we've already based a significant amount of programming on this technique indicates how useful it is.

The XML for Java package from alphaWorks that we used in the previous chapter (`www.alphaworks.ibm.com/tech/xml4j`) also supports SAX. That means you can use the same JAR files in this chapter that we used in the previous chapter; just make sure that they're added to your `CLASSPATH` like this in Windows (and make the command all one line):

```
C:\>SET
CLASSPATH=%CLASSPATH%;C:\xmlparser\XML4J_3_0_1\xerces.jar;
C:\xmlparser\XML4J_3_0_1\xercesSamples.jar
```

Or, use the `-classpath` switch, as discussed in the previous chapter:

```
%javac -classpath C:\xmlparser\XML4J_3_0_1\xerces.jar;
C:\xmlparser\XML4J_3_0_1\xercesSamples.jar browser.java
%java -classpath C:\xmlparser\XML4J_3_0_1\xerces.jar;
C:\xmlparser\XML4J_3_0_1\xercesSamples.jar browser
```

Working with SAX

This first example will show how to work with SAX. In this case, I'll use SAX to count the number of `<CUSTOMER>` elements in `customer.xml`, just as the first example in the previous chapter did. Here's `customer.xml`:

```
<?xml version = "1.0" standalone="yes"?>
<DOCUMENT>
    <CUSTOMER>
        <NAME>
            <LAST_NAME>Smith</LAST_NAME>
            <FIRST_NAME>Sam</FIRST_NAME>
        </NAME>
        <DATE>October 15, 2001</DATE>
        <ORDERS>
            <ITEM>
                <PRODUCT>Tomatoes</PRODUCT>
                <NUMBER>8</NUMBER>
                <PRICE>$1.25</PRICE>
            </ITEM>
            <ITEM>
                <PRODUCT>Oranges</PRODUCT>
                <NUMBER>24</NUMBER>
                <PRICE>$4.98</PRICE>
            </ITEM>
        </ORDERS>
    </CUSTOMER>
    <CUSTOMER>
        <NAME>
            <LAST_NAME>Jones</LAST_NAME>
            <FIRST_NAME>Polly</FIRST_NAME>
        </NAME>
        <DATE>October 20, 2001</DATE>
        <ORDERS>
            <ITEM>
                <PRODUCT>Bread</PRODUCT>
                <NUMBER>12</NUMBER>
                <PRICE>$14.95</PRICE>
            </ITEM>
            <ITEM>
                <PRODUCT>Apples</PRODUCT>
                <NUMBER>6</NUMBER>
                <PRICE>$1.50</PRICE>
            </ITEM>
```

continues ►

```
        </ORDERS>
    </CUSTOMER>
    <CUSTOMER>
        <NAME>
            <LAST_NAME>Weber</LAST_NAME>
            <FIRST_NAME>Bill</FIRST_NAME>
        </NAME>
        <DATE>October 25, 2001</DATE>
        <ORDERS>
            <ITEM>
                <PRODUCT>Asparagus</PRODUCT>
                <NUMBER>12</NUMBER>
                <PRICE>$2.95</PRICE>
            </ITEM>
            <ITEM>
                <PRODUCT>Lettuce</PRODUCT>
                <NUMBER>6</NUMBER>
                <PRICE>$11.50</PRICE>
            </ITEM>
        </ORDERS>
    </CUSTOMER>
</DOCUMENT>
```

Here, I'll base the new program on a new class named `FirstParserSAX`. We'll need an object of that class to pass to the SAX parser so that it can call the methods in that object when it encounters elements, the start of the document, the end of the document, and so on. I begin by creating an object of the `FirstParserSAX` class named `SAXHandler`:

```
import org.xml.sax.*;
import org.apache.xerces.parsers.SAXParser;

public class FirstParserSAX
{
    public static void main(String[] args)
    {
        FirstParserSAX SAXHandler = new FirstParserSAX();
            .
            .
            .
    }
}
```

Next, I create the actual SAX parser that we'll work with. This parser is an object of the `org.apache.xerces.parsers.SAXParser` class (just like the DOM parser objects we worked with in the previous chapter were objects of the `org.apache.xerces.parsers.DOMParser` class). To use the `SAXParser` class, I import that class and the supporting classes in the `org.xml.sax` package, and I'm free to create a new SAX parser named `parser`:

```
import org.xml.sax.*;
import org.apache.xerces.parsers.SAXParser;

public class FirstParserSAX
{
    public static void main(String[] args)
    {
        FirstParserSAX SAXHandler = new FirstParserSAX();

        SAXParser parser = new SAXParser();
            .
            .
            .
    }
}
```

The `SAXParser` class is derived from the `XMLParser` class, which in turn is based on the `java.lang.Object` class:

```
java.lang.Object
  |
  +--org.apache.xerces.framework.XMLParser
        |
        +--org.apache.xerces.parsers.SAXParser
```

The constructor of the `SAXParser` class is `SAXParser()`; the methods of the `SAXParser` class are listed in Table 12.1. The constructor of the `XMLParser` class is `protectedXMLParser()`; the methods of the `XMLParser` class are listed in Table 12.2.

Table 12.1 ***SAXParser*** **Methods**

Method	Description
`void attlistDecl(int elementTypeIndex, int attrNameIndex, int attType, java.lang. String enumString, int attDefaultType, int attDefaultValue)`	Callback for attribute type declarations
`void characters(char[] ch, int start, int length)`	Callback for characters that specifies the characters in an array
`void comment(int dataIndex)`	Callback for comments
`void commentInDTD(int dataIndex)`	Callback for comments in a DTD
`void elementDecl(int elementType, XMLValidator.ContentSpec contentSpec)`	Callback for an element type declaration

continues

Table 12.1 **Continued**

Method	Description
`void endCDATA()`	Callback for the end of `CDATA` sections
`void endDocument()`	Callback for the end of a document
`void endDTD()`	Callback for the end of the DTD
`void endElement(int` *`elementType`*`)`	Callback for the end of an `Element` element
`void endEntityReference(int` *`entityName`*`, int` *`entityType`*`, int` *`entityContext`*`)`	Callback for the end of an entity reference
`void endNamespaceDeclScope(int` *`prefix`*`)`	Callback for the end of the scope of a namespace declaration
`void externalEntityDecl(int` *`entityName`*`, int` *`publicId`*`, int` *`systemId`*`)`	Callback for a parsed external general entity declaration
`void externalPEDecl(int` *`entityName`*`, int` *`publicId`*`, int` *`systemId`*`)`	Callback for a parsed external parameter entity declaration
`ContentHandler getContentHandler()`	Instruction to get the content handler
`protected DeclHandler getDeclHandler()`	Instruction to get the DTD declaration event handler
`DTDHandler getDTDHandler()`	Instruction to get the current DTD handler
`boolean getFeature(java.lang.String` *`featureId`*`)`	Instruction to get the state of a parser feature
`java.lang.String[] getFeaturesRecognized()`	Instruction to get a list of features that the parser recognizes
`protected LexicalHandler getLexicalHandler()`	Instruction to get the lexical handler for this parsers
`protected boolean getNamespacePrefixes()`	Instruction to get the value of namespace prefixes
`java.lang.String[] getPropertiesRecognized()`	Instruction to get a list of properties that the parser recognizes
`java.lang.Object getProperty (java.lang.String` *`propertyId`*`)`	Instruction to get the value of a property
`void ignorableWhitespace(char[]` *`ch`*`, int` *`start`*`, int` *`length`*`)`	Callback for ignorable whitespace
`void internalEntityDecl(int` *`entityName`*`, int` *`entityValue`*`)`	Callback for an internal general entity declaration

Method	Description
`void internalPEDecl(int entityName, int entityValue)`	Callback for an internal parameter entity declaration
`void internalSubset(int internalSubset)`	Callback from DOM Level 2
`void notationDecl(int notationName, int publicId, int systemId)`	Callback for notification of a notation declaration event
`void processingInstruction (int piTarget, int piData)`	Callback for processing instructions
`void processingInstructionInDTD (int piTarget, int piData)`	Callback for processing instructions in DTD
`void setContentHandler(ContentHandler handler)`	Instruction to set a content handler to let an application handle SAX events
`protected void setDeclHandler (DeclHandler handler)`	Instruction to set the DTD declaration event handler
`void setDocumentHandler(DocumentHandler handler)`	Instruction to set the document handler
`void setDTDHandler(DTDHandler handler)`	Instruction to set the DTD handler
`void setFeature(java.lang.String featureId, boolean state)`	Instruction to set the state of any feature
`protected void setLexicalHandler (LexicalHandler handler)`	Instruction to set the lexical event handler
`protected void setNamespacePrefixes (boolean process)`	Specifier for how the parser reports raw prefixed names, as well as if xmlns attributes are reported
`void setProperty(java.lang.String propertyId, java.lang.Object value)`	Instruction to set the value of any property
`void startCDATA()`	Callback for the start of a `CDATA` section
`void startDocument(int versionIndex, int encodingIndex, int standaloneIndex)`	Callback for the start of the document
`void startDTD(int rootElementType, int publicId, int systemId)`	Callback for a `<!DOCTYPE...>` declaration
`void startElement(int elementType, XMLAttrList attrList, int attrListIndex)`	Callback for the start of an element
`void startEntityReference(int entityName, int entityType, int entityContext)`	Callback for the start of an entity reference
`void startNamespaceDeclScope(int prefix, int uri)`	Callback for the start of the scope of a namespace declaration
`void unparsedEntityDecl(int entityName, int publicId, int systemId, int notationName)`	Callback for an unparsed entity declaration event

Table 12.2 ***XMLParser* Methods**

Method	Description
`void addRecognizer(org.apache.xerces.readers.XMLDeclRecognizer recognizer)`	Adds a recognizer
`abstract void attlistDecl(int elementType, int attrName, int attType, java.lang.String enumString, int attDefaultType, int attDefaultValue)`	Serves as a callback for an attribute list declaration
`void callCharacters(int ch)`	Calls the characters callback
`void callComment(int comment)`	Calls the comment callback
`void callEndDocument()`	Calls the end document callback
`boolean callEndElement(int readerId)`	Calls the end element callback
`void callProcessingInstruction (int target, int data)`	Calls the processing instruction callback
`void callStartDocument(int version, int encoding, int standalone)`	Calls the start document callback
`void callStartElement(int elementType)`	Calls the start element callback
`org.apache.xerces.readers.XMLEntityHandler.EntityReader changeReaders()`	Is called by the reader subclasses at the end of input
`abstract void characters(char[] ch, int start, int length)`	Serves as a callback for characters
`abstract void characters(int data)`	Serves as a callback for characters using string pools
`abstract void comment(int comment)`	Serves as a callback for comment
`void commentInDTD(int comment)`	Serves as a callback for comment in DTD
`abstract void elementDecl(int elementType, XMLValidator.ContentSpec contentSpec)`	Serves as a callback for an element declaration
`abstract void endCDATA()`	Serves as a callback for the end of the CDATA section
`abstract void endDocument()`	Serves as a callback for the end of a document
`abstract void endDTD()`	Serves as a callback for the end of the DTD
`abstract void endElement(int elementType)`	Serves as a callback for the end of an element
`void endEntityDecl()`	Serves as a callback for the end of an entity declaration

Method	Description
`abstract void endEntityReference (int entityName, int entityType, int entityContext)`	Serves as a callback for an end of entity reference
`abstract void endNamespaceDeclScope(int prefix)`	Serves as a callback for the end of a namespace declaration scope
`java.lang.String expandSystemId(java.lang. String systemId)`	Expands a system ID and method returns the system ID as an URL
`abstract void externalEntityDecl (int entityName, int publicId, int systemId)`	Serve as a callback for a external general entity declaration
`abstract void externalPEDecl(int entityName, int publicId, int systemId)`	Serves as a callback for an external parameter entity declaration
`protected boolean getAllowJavaEncodings()`	Is True if Java encoding names are allowed in the XML document
`int getColumnNumber()`	Gives the column number of the current position in the document
`protected boolean getContinueAfterFatalError()`	Is True if the parser will continue after a fatal error
`org.apache.xerces.readers.XMLEntityHandler. EntityReader getEntityReader()`	Gets the entity reader
`EntityResolver getEntityResolver()`	Gets the current entity resolver
`ErrorHandler getErrorHandler()`	Gets the current error handler
`boolean getFeature(java.lang.String featureId)`	Gets the state of a feature
`java.lang.String[] getFeaturesRecognized()`	Gets a list of features recognized by this parser
`int getLineNumber()`	Gets the current line number in the document
`Locator getLocator()`	Gets the locator used by the parser
`protected boolean getNamespaces()`	Is True if the parser preprocesses namespaces
`java.lang.String[] getPropertiesRecognized()`	Gets the list of recognized properties for the parser
`java.lang.Object getProperty(java.lang. String propertyId)`	Gets the value of a property
`java.lang.String getPublicId()`	Gets the public ID of the `InputSource`
`protected org.apache.xerces.validators.schema. XSchemaValidator getSchemaValidator()`	Gets the current XML schema validator

continues

Table 12.2 **Continued**

Method	Description
`java.lang.String getSystemId()`	Gets the system ID of the `InputSource`
`protected boolean getValidation()`	Is True if validation is turned on.
`protected boolean getValidationDynamic()`	Is True if validation is determined based on whether a document contains a grammar
`protected boolean getValidationWarnOn DuplicateAttdef()`	Is True if an error is created when an attribute is redefined in the grammar
`protected boolean getValidationWarnOn UndeclaredElemdef()`	Is True if the parser creates an error when an undeclared element is referenced
`abstract void ignorableWhitespace(char[] ch, int start, int length)`	Serves as a callback for ignorable whitespace
`abstract void ignorableWhitespace(int data)`	Serves as a callback for ignorable whitespace based on string pools
`abstract void internalEntityDecl (int entityName, int entityValue)`	Serves as a callback for an internal general entity declaration
`abstract void internalPEDecl(int entityName, int entityValue)`	Serves as a callback for an internal parameter entity declaration
`abstract void internalSubset (int internalSubset)`	Supports DOM Level 2 `internalSubsets`
`boolean isFeatureRecognized(java.lang. String featureId)`	Is True if the given feature is recognized
`boolean isPropertyRecognized(java.lang. String propertyId)`	Is True if the given property is recognized
`abstract void notationDecl(int notationName, int publicId, int systemId)`	Serves as a callback for a notation declaration
`void parse(InputSource source)`	Parses the given input source
`void parse(java.lang.String systemId)`	Parses the input source given by a system identifier
`boolean parseSome()`	Supports application-driven parsing
`boolean parseSomeSetup(InputSource source)`	Sets up application-driven parsing
`void processCharacters(char[] chars, int offset, int length)`	Processes character data given a character array
`void processCharacters(int data)`	Processes character data
`abstract void processingInstruction (int target, int data)`	Serves as a callback for processing instructions

Method	Description
`void processingInstructionInDTD (int target, int data)`	Serves as a callback for processing instructions in a DTD
`void processWhitespace(char[] chars, int offset, int length)`	Processes whitespace
`void processWhitespace(int data)`	Processes whitespace based on string pools
`void reportError(Locator locator, java.lang. String errorDomain, int majorCode, int minorCode, java.lang.Object[] args, int errorType)`	Reports errors
`void reset()`	Resets the parser so that it can be reused
`protected void resetOrCopy()`	Resets or copies the parser
`int scanAttributeName(org.apache.xerces. readers.XMLEntityHandler.EntityReader entityReader, int elementType)`	Scans an attribute name
`int scanAttValue(int elementType, int attrName)`	Scans an attribute value
`void scanDoctypeDecl(boolean standalone)`	Scans a doctype declaration
`int scanElementType(org.apache.xerces. readers.XMLEntityHandler.EntityReader entityReader, char fastchar)`	Scans an element type
`boolean scanExpectedElementType(org.apache. xerces.readers.XMLEntityHandler.EntityReader entityReader, char fastchar)`	Scans an expected element type
`protected void setAllowJavaEncodings (boolean allow)`	Supports the use of Java encoding names
`protected void setContinueAfterFatalError (boolean continueAfterFatalError)`	Lets the parser continue after fatal errors
`void setEntityResolver(EntityResolver resolver)`	Specifies the resolver (resolves external entities)
`void setErrorHandler(ErrorHandler handler)`	Sets the error handler
`void setFeature(java.lang.String featureId, boolean state)`	Sets the state of a feature
`void setLocale(java.util.Locale locale)`	Sets the locale
`void setLocator(Locator locator)`	Sets the locator
`protected void setNamespaces(boolean process)`	Specifies whether the parser preprocesses namespaces

continues

Table 12.2 **Continued**

Method	Description
`void setProperty(java.lang.String` *`propertyId`*`, java.lang.Object` *`value`*`)`	Sets the value of a property
`void setReaderFactory(org.apache.xerces.readers.XMLEntityReaderFactory` *`readerFactory`*`)`	Sets the reader factory
`protected void setSendCharDataAsCharArray(boolean flag)`	Sets character data processing preferences
`void setValidating(boolean flag)`	Indicates to the parser that you are validating
`protected void setValidation(boolean validate)`	Specifies whether the parser validates
`protected void setValidationDynamic(boolean dynamic)`	Lets the parser validate a document only if it contains a grammar
`protected void setValidationWarnOnDuplicateAttdef(boolean warn)`	Specifies whether an error is created when attributes are redefined in the grammar
`protected void setValidationWarnOnUndeclaredElemdef(boolean warn)`	Specifies whether the parser causes an error when an element's content model references an element by name that is not declared
`abstract void startCDATA()`	Serves as a callback for the start of the CDATA section
`abstract void startDocument(int` *`version`*`, int` *`encoding`*`, int` *`standAlone`*`)`	Serves as a callback for the start of the document
`abstract void startDTD(int` *`rootElementType`*`, int` *`publicId`*`, int` *`systemId`*`)`	Serves as a callback for the start of the DTD
`abstract void startElement(int` *`elementType`*`, XMLAttrList` *`attrList`*`, int` *`attrListHandle`*`)`	Serves as a callback for the start of an element
`boolean startEntityDecl(boolean isPE, int` *`entityName`*`)`	Serves as a callback for the start of an entity declaration
`abstract void startEntityReference(int` *`entityName`*`, int` *`entityType`*`, int` *`entityContext`*`)`	Serves as a callback for the start of an entity reference
`abstract void startNamespaceDeclScope(int` *`prefix`*`, int` *`uri`*`)`	Serves as a callback for the start of a namespace declaration scope
`boolean startReadingFromDocument(InputSource` *`source`*`)`	Starts reading from a document

Method	Description
`boolean startReadingFromEntity (int entityName, int readerDepth, int context)`	Starts reading from an external entity
`void startReadingFromExternalSubset (java.lang.String publicId, java.lang. String systemId, int readerDepth)`	Starts reading from an external DTD subset
`void stopReadingFromExternalSubset()`	Stops reading from an external DTD subset
`abstract void unparsedEntityDecl (int entityName, int publicId, int systemId, int notationName)`	Serves as a callback for unparsed entity declarations
`boolean validEncName(java.lang. String encoding)`	Is True if the given encoding is valid
`boolean validVersionNum(java.lang. String version)`	Is True if the given version is valid

We have a `SAXParser` object now, and we need to register the `SAXHandler` object we created with the `SAXParser` object so the methods of the `SAXHandler` object are called when the parser starts the document, finds a new element, and so forth. SAX parsers call quite a number of methods, such as those for elements, processing instructions, declarations in DTDs, and so on. The methods a SAX parser calls to inform you that a new item has been found in the document are called *callback* methods, and you must register those methods with the SAX parser.

Four core SAX interfaces support the various callback methods:

- `EntityResolver` implements customized handling for external entities.
- `DTDHandler` handles DTD events.
- `ContentHandler` handles the content of a document, such as elements and processing instructions.
- `ErrorHandler` handles errors that occur while parsing.

There are many callback methods in these interfaces; if you want to use an interface, you have to implement all those methods. The XML for Java package makes it easier for you by creating a class called `DefaultHandler`, which has default implementations for all the required callback methods. The constructor of the `DefaultHandler` class is `DefaultHandler()`; its methods are listed in Table 12.3.

Table 12.3 ***DefaultHandler* Methods**

Method	Description
`void characters(char[] ch, int start, int length)`	Callback for character data inside an element
`void endDocument()`	Callback for the end of the document
`void endElement(java.lang.String uri, java.lang.String localName, java.lang.String rawName)`	Callback for the end of an element
`void endPrefixMapping(java.lang.String prefix)`	Callback for the end of a namespace mapping
`void error(SAXParseException e)`	Callback for a recoverable parser error
`void fatalError(SAXParseException e)`	Callback for a fatal XML parsing error
`void ignorableWhitespace(char[] ch, int start, int length)`	Callback for ignorable whitespace in element content
`void notationDecl(java.lang.String name, java.lang.String publicId, java.lang.String systemId)`	Callback for a notation declaration
`void processingInstruction(java.lang.String target, java.lang.String data)`	Callback for a processing instruction
`InputSource resolveEntity(java.lang.String publicId, java.lang.String systemId)`	Callback for an external entity
`void setDocumentLocator(Locator locator)`	Sets a `Locator` object for document events
`void skippedEntity(java.lang.String name)`	Callback for a skipped entity
`void startDocument()`	Callback for the beginning of the document
`void startElement(java.lang.String uri, java.lang.String localName, java.lang.String rawName, Attributes attributes)`	Callback for the start of an element
`void startPrefixMapping(java.lang.String prefix, java.lang.String uri)`	Callback for the start of a namespace mapping
`void unparsedEntityDecl(java.lang.String name, java.lang.String publicId, java.lang.String systemId, java.lang.String notationName)`	Callback for an unparsed entity declaration
`void warning(SAXParseException e)`	Callback for parser warnings

If you base your program on the `DefaultHandler` interface, you need to implement only the callback methods you're interested in, so I'll derive the main class of this program, `FirstParserSAX`, on the `DefaultHandler` interface, which you do with the `extends` keyword:

```
import org.xml.sax.*;
import org.xml.sax.helpers.DefaultHandler;
import org.apache.xerces.parsers.SAXParser;

public class FirstParserSAX extends DefaultHandler
{
    public static void main(String[] args)
    {
        FirstParserSAX SAXHandler = new FirstParserSAX();

        SAXParser parser = new SAXParser();
            .
            .
            .
    }
}
```

Now we're ready to register the `FirstParserSAX` class with the SAX parser. In this case, I'm not going to worry about handling DTD events or resolving external entities; I'll just handle the document's content and any errors with the `setContentHandler` and `setErrorHandler` methods:

```
import org.xml.sax.*;
import org.xml.sax.helpers.DefaultHandler;
import org.apache.xerces.parsers.SAXParser;

public class FirstParserSAX extends DefaultHandler
{
    public static void main(String[] args)
    {
        FirstParserSAX SAXHandler = new FirstParserSAX();

        SAXParser parser = new SAXParser();
        parser.setContentHandler(SAXHandler);
        parser.setErrorHandler(SAXHandler);
            .
            .
            .
    }
}
```

This registers the `SAXHandler` object so that it will receive SAX content and error events. I'll add the methods that will be called after finishing the `main` method.

To actually parse the XML document, you use the `parse` method of the `parser` object. I'll let the user specify the name of the document to parse on the command by parsing `args[0]`. (Note that you don't need to pass the name of a local file to the `parse` method—you can pass the URL of a document on the Internet, and the `parse` method will retrieve that document.) The `parse` method can throw Java exceptions, which means that you have to enclose it in a `try` block, which has a subsequent `catch` block:

```
import org.xml.sax.*;
import org.xml.sax.helpers.DefaultHandler;
import org.apache.xerces.parsers.SAXParser;

public class FirstParserSAX extends DefaultHandler
{
    public static void main(String[] args)
    {
        try {
            FirstParserSAX SAXHandler = new FirstParserSAX();

            SAXParser parser = new SAXParser();
            parser.setContentHandler(SAXHandler);
            parser.setErrorHandler(SAXHandler);
            parser.parse(args[0]);
        }
        catch (Exception e) {
            e.printStackTrace(System.err);
        }
    }
}
```

That completes the `main` method, so I'll implement the methods that are called when the SAX parser parses the XML document. In this case, the goal is to determine how many `<CUSTOMER>` elements the document has, so I implement the `startElement` method like this:

```
import org.xml.sax.*;
import org.xml.sax.helpers.DefaultHandler;
import org.apache.xerces.parsers.SAXParser;

public class FirstParserSAX extends DefaultHandler
{
    public void startElement(String uri, String localName, String rawName,
        Attributes attributes)
    {
    .
    .
    .
    }
```

```
    public static void main(String[] args)
    {
        try {
            FirstParserSAX SAXHandler = new FirstParserSAX();

            SAXParser parser = new SAXParser();
            parser.setContentHandler(SAXHandler);
            parser.setErrorHandler(SAXHandler);
            parser.parse(args[0]);
        }
        catch (Exception e) {
            e.printStackTrace(System.err);
        }
    }
}
```

The `startElement` method is called each time the SAX parser sees the start of an element, and the `endElement` method is called when the SAX parser sees the end of an element.

Note that two element names are passed to the `startElement` method: `localName` and `rawName`. You use the `localName` argument with namespace processing; this argument holds the name of the element without any namespace prefix. The `rawName` argument holds the full, qualified name of the element, including any namespace prefix.

We're just going to count the number of `<CUSTOMER>` elements, so I'll take a look at the element's `rawName` argument. If that argument equals `"CUSTOMER"`, I'll increment a variable named `customerCount`:

```
import org.xml.sax.*;
import org.xml.sax.helpers.DefaultHandler;
import org.apache.xerces.parsers.SAXParser;

public class FirstParserSAX extends DefaultHandler
{
    int customerCount = 0;

    public void startElement(String uri, String localName, String rawName,
        Attributes attributes)
    {
        if (rawName.equals("CUSTOMER")) {
            customerCount++;
        }
    }

    public static void main(String[] args)
    {
        try {
```

continues ▸

```
            FirstParserSAX SAXHandler = new FirstParserSAX();

            SAXParser parser = new SAXParser();
            parser.setContentHandler(SAXHandler);
            parser.setErrorHandler(SAXHandler);
            parser.parse(args[0]);
        }
        catch (Exception e) {
            e.printStackTrace(System.err);
        }
    }
}
```

How do you know when you've reached the end of the document and there are no more `<CUSTOMER>` elements to count? You use the `endDocument` method, which is called when the end of the document is reached. I'll display the number of tallied `<CUSTOMER>` elements in that method:

```
import org.xml.sax.*;
import org.xml.sax.helpers.DefaultHandler;
import org.apache.xerces.parsers.SAXParser;

public class FirstParserSAX extends DefaultHandler
{
    int customerCount = 0;

    public void startElement(String uri, String localName, String rawName,
        Attributes attributes)
    {
        if (rawName.equals("CUSTOMER")) {
            customerCount++;
        }
    }

    public void endDocument()
    {
        System.out.println("The document has "
        + customerCount + " <CUSTOMER> elements.");
    }

    public static void main(String[] args)
    {
        try {
            FirstParserSAX SAXHandler = new FirstParserSAX();

            SAXParser parser = new SAXParser();
            parser.setContentHandler(SAXHandler);
            parser.setErrorHandler(SAXHandler);
            parser.parse(args[0]);
        }
        catch (Exception e) {
            e.printStackTrace(System.err);
```

```
        }
    }
}
```

You can compile and run this program like this:

```
%java FirstParserSAX customer.xml
The document has 3 <CUSTOMER> elements.
```

And that's all it takes to get started with SAX.

Displaying an Entire Document

In this next example, as in the previous chapter, I'm going to write a program that parses and displays an entire document, indenting each element, processing instruction, and so on, as well as displaying attributes and their values. Here, however, I'll use SAX methods, not DOM methods. If you pass `customer.xml` to this program, which I'll call `IndentingParserSAX.java`, the program will display the whole document properly indented.

I start by letting the user specify what document to parse and then parsing that document as before. To actually parse the document, I'll call a new method, `displayDocument`, from the `main` method. The `displayDocument` method will fill the array `displayStrings` with the formatted document, and the `main` method will print it out:

```
import org.xml.sax.*;
import org.xml.sax.helpers.DefaultHandler;
import org.apache.xerces.parsers.SAXParser;

public class IndentingParserSAX extends DefaultHandler
{
    public static void displayDocument(String uri)
    {
    .
    .
    .
    }

    public static void main(String args[])
    {
        displayDocument(args[0]);

        for(int index = 0; index < numberDisplayLines; index++){
            System.out.println(displayStrings[index]);
        }
    }
}
```

In the `displayDocument` method, I'll create a SAX parser and register an object of the program's main class with that parser so that the methods of the object will be called for SAX events:

```
import org.xml.sax.*;
import org.xml.sax.helpers.DefaultHandler;
import org.apache.xerces.parsers.SAXParser;

public class IndentingParserSAX extends DefaultHandler
{

    public static void displayDocument(String uri)
    {
        try {
            IndentingParserSAX SAXHandler = new IndentingParserSAX();

            SAXParser parser = new SAXParser();
            parser.setContentHandler(SAXHandler);
            parser.setErrorHandler(SAXHandler);
            parser.parse(uri);
        }
        catch (Exception e) {
            e.printStackTrace(System.err);
        }
    }

    public static void main(String args[])
    {
        displayDocument(args[0]);

        for(int index = 0; index < numberDisplayLines; index++){
            System.out.println(displayStrings[index]);
        }
    }
}
```

All that's left is to create the various methods that will be called for SAX events, and I'll start with the beginning of the document.

Handling the Beginning of Documents

When the SAX parser encounters the beginning of the document to parse, it calls the `startDocument` method. This method is not passed any arguments, so I'll just have the program display the XML declaration. As in the previous chapter, I'll store the text to display in the array of `String` objects named `displayStrings`, our location in that array in the integer variable `numberDisplayLines`, and the current indentation level in a `String` object named `indent`. Using an array of strings like this will facilitate the conversion process when we adapt this program to display in a Java window.

Here's how I add the XML declaration to the display strings in `startDocument`:

```
import org.xml.sax.*;
import org.xml.sax.helpers.DefaultHandler;
import org.apache.xerces.parsers.SAXParser;

public class IndentingParserSAX extends DefaultHandler
{
    static String displayStrings[] = new String[1000];
    static int numberDisplayLines = 0;
    static String indent = "";

    public static void displayDocument(String uri)
    {
        try {
            IndentingParserSAX SAXHandler = new IndentingParserSAX();

            SAXParser parser = new SAXParser();
            parser.setContentHandler(SAXHandler);
            parser.setErrorHandler(SAXHandler);
            parser.parse(uri);
        }
        catch (Exception e) {
            e.printStackTrace(System.err);
        }
    }

    public void startDocument()
    {
        displayStrings[numberDisplayLines] = indent;
        displayStrings[numberDisplayLines] += "<?xml version=\"1.0\" encoding=\""+
            "UTF-8" + "\"?>";
        numberDisplayLines++;
    }
    .
    .
    .
    public static void main(String args[])
    {
        displayDocument(args[0]);

        for(int index = 0; index < numberDisplayLines; index++){
            System.out.println(displayStrings[index]);
        }
    }
}
```

I'll take a look at handling processing instructions next.

Handling Processing Instructions

You can handle processing instructions with the `processingInstruction` callback. This method is called with two arguments: the processing instruction's target, and its data. For example, in the `<?xml-stylesheet type="text/css" href="style.css"?>`, its target is `xml-stylesheet` and its data is `type="text/css" href="style.css"`.

Here's how I handle processing instructions, adding them to the display strings—note that I check first to make sure there is some data before adding it to the processing instruction's display:

```
import org.xml.sax.*;
import org.xml.sax.helpers.DefaultHandler;
import org.apache.xerces.parsers.SAXParser;

public class IndentingParserSAX extends DefaultHandler
{
    static String displayStrings[] = new String[1000];
    static int numberDisplayLines = 0;
    static String indent = "";

    public void processingInstruction(String target, String data)
    {
        displayStrings[numberDisplayLines] = indent;
        displayStrings[numberDisplayLines] += "<?";
        displayStrings[numberDisplayLines] += target;
        if (data != null && data.length() > 0) {
            displayStrings[numberDisplayLines] += ' ';
            displayStrings[numberDisplayLines] += data;
        }
        displayStrings[numberDisplayLines] += "?>";
        numberDisplayLines++;
    }

    public static void main(String args[])
    {
    .
    .
    .
    }
}
```

Handling the Beginning of Elements

You can handle the start of elements with the `startElement` method. Because we've found a new element, I'll add four spaces to the current indentation to handle any children the element has, and I'll display its name using the `rawName` argument:

```
import org.xml.sax.*;
import org.xml.sax.helpers.DefaultHandler;
import org.apache.xerces.parsers.SAXParser;

public class IndentingParserSAX extends DefaultHandler
{
    static String displayStrings[] = new String[1000];
    static int numberDisplayLines = 0;
    static String indent = "";

    public void startElement(String uri, String localName, String rawName,
        Attributes attributes)
    {
        displayStrings[numberDisplayLines] = indent;

        indent += "    ";

        displayStrings[numberDisplayLines] += '<';
        displayStrings[numberDisplayLines] += rawName;
        displayStrings[numberDisplayLines] += '>';
        numberDisplayLines++;
    }

    public static void main(String args[])
    {
    .
    .
    .
    }
}
```

That's enough to display the opening tag of an element, but what if the element has attributes?

Handling Attributes

One of the arguments passed to the `startElement` method is an object that implements the `Attributes` interface:

```
public void startElement(String uri, String localName, String rawName,
    Attributes attributes)
{
.
.
.
}
```

This object gives you access to the attributes of the element; you can find the methods of the `Attributes` interface in Table 12.4. You can reach the attributes in an object that implements this interface based on index, name, or namespace-qualified name.

Table 12.4 ***Attributes* Interface Methods**

Method	Description
`int getIndex(java.lang.String` *`rawName`*`)`	Gets the index of an attribute given its raw name
`int getIndex(java.lang.String` *`uri`*`, java.lang.String` *`localPart`*`)`	Gets the index of an attribute by namespace and local name
`int getLength()`	Gets the number of attributes in the list
`java.lang.String getLocalName(int` *`index`*`)`	Gets an attribute's local name by index
`java.lang.String getRawName(int` *`index`*`)`	Gets an attribute's raw name by index
`java.lang.String getType(int` *`index`*`)`	Gets an attribute's type by index
`java.lang.String getType(java.lang.String` *`rawName`*`)`	Gets an attribute's type by raw name
`java.lang.String getType(java.lang.String` *`uri`*`, java.lang.String` *`localName`*`)`	Gets an attribute's type by namespace and local name
`java.lang.String getURI(int` *`index`*`)`	Gets an attribute's namespace URI by index
`java.lang.String getValue(int` *`index`*`)`	Gets an attribute's value by index
`java.lang.String getValue(java.lang.String` *`rawName`*`)`	Gets an attribute's value by raw name
`java.lang.String getValue(java.lang.String` *`uri`*`, java.lang.String` *`localName`*`)`	Gets an attribute's value by namespace name and local name

So how do we find and display all the attributes an element has? I'll find the number of attributes using the `Attributes` interface's `getLength` method, and then I'll get the names and values of the attributes with the `getRawName` and `getValue` methods, referring to attributes by index—note that I first make sure that this element actually has attributes by checking to make sure that the `attributes` argument is not null:

```
import org.xml.sax.*;
import org.xml.sax.helpers.DefaultHandler;
import org.apache.xerces.parsers.SAXParser;

public class IndentingParserSAX extends DefaultHandler
{
    static String displayStrings[] = new String[1000];
```

```
    static int numberDisplayLines = 0;
    static String indent = "";

    public void startElement(String uri, String localName, String rawName,
        Attributes attributes)
    {
        displayStrings[numberDisplayLines] = indent;

        indent += "    ";

        displayStrings[numberDisplayLines] += '<';
        displayStrings[numberDisplayLines] += rawName;

        if (attributes != null) {
            int numberAttributes = attributes.getLength();
            for (int loopIndex = 0; loopIndex < numberAttributes; loopIndex++) {
                displayStrings[numberDisplayLines] += ' ';
                displayStrings[numberDisplayLines] += attributes.getRawName(loopIndex);
                displayStrings[numberDisplayLines] += "=\"";
                displayStrings[numberDisplayLines] += attributes.getValue(loopIndex);
                displayStrings[numberDisplayLines] += '"';
            }
        }

        displayStrings[numberDisplayLines] += '>';
        numberDisplayLines++;
    }

    public static void main(String args[])
    {
    .
    .
    .
    }
}
```

That's all it takes; now we're handling the element's attributes as well.

Handling Text

Many of the elements in `customer.xml` contain text, such as the `<FIRST_NAME>` and `<LAST_NAME>` elements, and we want to display that text. To handle element text, you use the `characters` callback.

This method is called with three arguments—an array of type `char` that holds the actual character text, the starting location in the array, and the length of the text. For elements that contain only one text node, the starting location is always `0` in the character array.

To add the text inside an element to the display strings, I implement the `characters` method, converting the character array to a Java `String` object named `characterData` like this—note that I use the `String` class's `trim` method to trim the text of leading and trailing spaces:

```
import org.xml.sax.*;
import org.xml.sax.helpers.DefaultHandler;
import org.apache.xerces.parsers.SAXParser;

public class IndentingParserSAX extends DefaultHandler
{
    static String displayStrings[] = new String[1000];
    static int numberDisplayLines = 0;
    static String indent = "";

    public void characters(char characters[], int start, int length)
    {
        String characterData = (new String(characters, start, length)).trim();
        .
        .
        .
    }

    public static void main(String args[])
    {
    .
    .
    .
    }
}
```

To eliminate indentation text—the spaces used to indent the elements in the file `customer.xml`—I add an `if` statement and then add the text itself to the display strings this way:

```
import org.xml.sax.*;
import org.xml.sax.helpers.DefaultHandler;
import org.apache.xerces.parsers.SAXParser;

public class IndentingParserSAX extends DefaultHandler
{
    static String displayStrings[] = new String[1000];
    static int numberDisplayLines = 0;
    static String indent = "";

    public void characters(char characters[], int start, int length)
    {
        String characterData = (new String(characters, start, length)).trim();
```

```
        if(characterData.indexOf("\n") < 0 && characterData.length() > 0) {
            displayStrings[numberDisplayLines] = indent;
            displayStrings[numberDisplayLines] += characterData;
            numberDisplayLines++;
        }
    }

    public static void main(String args[])
    {
    .
    .
    .
    }
}
```

That's all there is to it. By default, the XML for Java SAX parser reports the whitespace a document uses for indentation, which is called "ignorable" whitespace.

Handling Ignorable Whitespace

So how do you actually ignore "ignorable" whitespace? It's actually easier to ignore ignorable whitespace with the SAX parser than with the DOM parser. The SAX parser needs to know only what text it can ignore, so you must indicate what the proper grammar of the document is, which you could do with a DTD in `customer.xml`:

```
<?xml version = "1.0" standalone="yes"?>
<!DOCTYPE DOCUMENT [
<!ELEMENT DOCUMENT (CUSTOMER)*>
<!ELEMENT CUSTOMER (NAME,DATE,ORDERS)>
<!ELEMENT NAME (LAST_NAME,FIRST_NAME)>
<!ELEMENT LAST_NAME (#PCDATA)>
<!ELEMENT FIRST_NAME (#PCDATA)>
<!ELEMENT DATE (#PCDATA)>
<!ELEMENT ORDERS (ITEM)*>
<!ELEMENT ITEM (PRODUCT,NUMBER,PRICE)>
<!ELEMENT PRODUCT (#PCDATA)>
<!ELEMENT NUMBER (#PCDATA)>
<!ELEMENT PRICE (#PCDATA)>
]>
<DOCUMENT>
    <CUSTOMER>
        <NAME>
            <LAST_NAME>Smith</LAST_NAME>
            <FIRST_NAME>Sam</FIRST_NAME>
        </NAME>
        <DATE>October 15, 2001</DATE>
        <ORDERS>
```

continues ▸

```
            <ITEM>
                <PRODUCT>Tomatoes</PRODUCT>
                <NUMBER>8</NUMBER>
                <PRICE>$1.25</PRICE>
            </ITEM>
            <ITEM>
                <PRODUCT>Oranges</PRODUCT>
                <NUMBER>24</NUMBER>
                <PRICE>$4.98</PRICE>
            </ITEM>
        </ORDERS>
    </CUSTOMER>
    <CUSTOMER>
        <NAME>
            <LAST_NAME>Jones</LAST_NAME>
            <FIRST_NAME>Polly</FIRST_NAME>
        </NAME>
        <DATE>October 20, 2001</DATE>
        <ORDERS>
            <ITEM>
                <PRODUCT>Bread</PRODUCT>
                <NUMBER>12</NUMBER>
                <PRICE>$14.95</PRICE>
            </ITEM>
            <ITEM>
                <PRODUCT>Apples</PRODUCT>
                <NUMBER>6</NUMBER>
                <PRICE>$1.50</PRICE>
            </ITEM>
        </ORDERS>
    </CUSTOMER>
    <CUSTOMER>
        <NAME>
            <LAST_NAME>Weber</LAST_NAME>
            <FIRST_NAME>Bill</FIRST_NAME>
        </NAME>
        <DATE>October 25, 2001</DATE>
        <ORDERS>
            <ITEM>
                <PRODUCT>Asparagus</PRODUCT>
                <NUMBER>12</NUMBER>
                <PRICE>$2.95</PRICE>
            </ITEM>
            <ITEM>
                <PRODUCT ID = "5231" TYPE = "3133">Lettuce</PRODUCT>
                <NUMBER>6</NUMBER>
                <PRICE>$11.50</PRICE>
            </ITEM>
        </ORDERS>
    </CUSTOMER>
</DOCUMENT>
```

Now, the SAX parser will not call the `characters` callback when it sees ignorable whitespace (such as indentation spaces); it will call a method named `ignorableWhitespace`. That means you can comment out the `if` statement I used to filter out ignorable whitespace before:

```
public void characters(char characters[], int start, int length)
{
    String characterData = (new String(characters, start, length)).trim();
    //if(characterData.indexOf("\n") < 0 && characterData.length() > 0) {
        displayStrings[numberDisplayLines] = indent;
        displayStrings[numberDisplayLines] += characterData;
        numberDisplayLines++;
    //}
}
```

That's all it takes—to filter out ignorable whitespace, just give the SAX parser some way of figuring out what is ignorable, such as adding a DTD to your document.

Note that you can add code to the `ignorableWhitespace` to handle that whitespace if you like—in fact, you can even pass it on to the `characters` callback, as I'm doing here:

```
public void ignorableWhitespace(char characters[], int start, int length)
{
    characters(characters, start, length);
}
```

Handling the End of Elements

So far, we've handled the start of each element and incremented the indentation level each time to handle any possible children. We also must display the end tag for each element and decrement the indentation level; I'll do that in the `endElement` callback, which is called each time the SAX parser reaches the end of an element. Here's what that looks like in code:

```
import org.xml.sax.*;
import org.xml.sax.helpers.DefaultHandler;
import org.apache.xerces.parsers.SAXParser;

public class IndentingParserSAX extends DefaultHandler
{
    static String displayStrings[] = new String[1000];
    static int numberDisplayLines = 0;
    static String indent = "";
```

continues ▸

```
    public void endElement(String uri, String localName, String rawName)
    {
        indent = indent.substring(0, indent.length() - 4);
        displayStrings[numberDisplayLines] = indent;
        displayStrings[numberDisplayLines] += "</";
        displayStrings[numberDisplayLines] += rawName;
        displayStrings[numberDisplayLines] += '>';
        numberDisplayLines++;
    }

    public static void main(String args[])
    {
    .
    .
    .
    }
}
```

There's one last topic to cover: handling errors and warnings.

Handling Errors and Warnings

The `DefaultHandler` interface defines several callbacks to handle warnings and errors from the parser. These methods are `warning`, which handles parser warnings; `error`, which handles parser errors; and `fatalError`, which handles errors so severe that the parser can't continue.

Each of these methods is passed an object of the class `SAXParseException`, and that object supports a method, `getMessage`, that will return the warning or error message. I display those messages using `System.err.println` message, which prints to the Java `err` output channel, which corresponds to the console by default:

```
import org.xml.sax.*;
import org.xml.sax.helpers.DefaultHandler;
import org.apache.xerces.parsers.SAXParser;

public class IndentingParserSAX extends DefaultHandler
{
    static String displayStrings[] = new String[1000];
    static int numberDisplayLines = 0;
    static String indent = "";
    .
    .
    .
    public void warning(SAXParseException exception)
    {
        System.err.println("WARNING! " +
            exception.getMessage());
    }
```

```
    public void error(SAXParseException exception)
    {
        System.err.println("ERROR! " +
            exception.getMessage());
    }

    public void fatalError(SAXParseException exception)
    {
        System.err.println("FATAL ERROR! " +
            exception.getMessage());
    }

    public static void main(String args[])
    {
    .
    .
    .
    }
}
```

That's all we need; you can see the results of parsing `customer.xml` in Figure 12.1, where I'm using the MS-DOS `more` filter to stop the display from scrolling off the top of the window. This program is a success, and you can find the complete code in Listing 12.1.

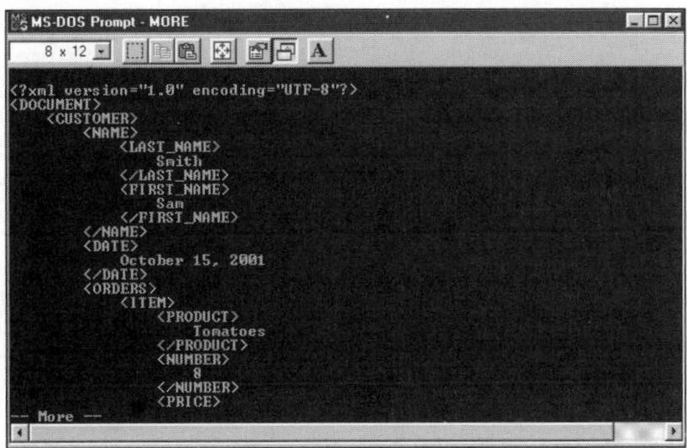

Figure 12.1 Parsing an XML document with a SAX parser.

Listing 12.1 ***IndentingParserSAX.java***

```
import org.xml.sax.*;
import org.xml.sax.helpers.DefaultHandler;
import org.apache.xerces.parsers.SAXParser;

public class IndentingParserSAX extends DefaultHandler
{
    static String displayStrings[] = new String[1000];
    static int numberDisplayLines = 0;
    static String indent = "";

    public static void displayDocument(String uri)
    {
        try {
            IndentingParserSAX SAXHandler = new IndentingParserSAX();

            SAXParser parser = new SAXParser();
            parser.setContentHandler(SAXHandler);
            parser.setErrorHandler(SAXHandler);
            parser.parse(uri);
        }
        catch (Exception e) {
            e.printStackTrace(System.err);
        }
    }

    public void startDocument()
    {
        displayStrings[numberDisplayLines] = indent;
        displayStrings[numberDisplayLines] += "<?xml version=\"1.0\" encoding=\""+
            "UTF-8" + "\"?>";
        numberDisplayLines++;
    }

    public void processingInstruction(String target, String data)
    {
        displayStrings[numberDisplayLines] = indent;
        displayStrings[numberDisplayLines] += "<?";
        displayStrings[numberDisplayLines] += target;
        if (data != null && data.length() > 0) {
            displayStrings[numberDisplayLines] += ' ';
            displayStrings[numberDisplayLines] += data;
        }
        displayStrings[numberDisplayLines] += "?>";
        numberDisplayLines++;
    }

    public void startElement(String uri, String localName, String rawName,
        Attributes attributes)
    {
        displayStrings[numberDisplayLines] = indent;
```

```
        indent += "    ";

        displayStrings[numberDisplayLines] += '<';
        displayStrings[numberDisplayLines] += rawName;
        if (attributes != null) {
            int numberAttributes = attributes.getLength();
            for (int loopIndex = 0; loopIndex < numberAttributes; loopIndex++) {
                displayStrings[numberDisplayLines] += ' ';
                displayStrings[numberDisplayLines] += attributes.getRawName(loopIndex);
                displayStrings[numberDisplayLines] += "=\"";
                displayStrings[numberDisplayLines] += attributes.getValue(loopIndex);
                displayStrings[numberDisplayLines] += '"';
            }
        }
        displayStrings[numberDisplayLines] += '>';
        numberDisplayLines++;
    }

    public void characters(char characters[], int start, int length)
    {
        String characterData = (new String(characters, start, length)).trim();
        if(characterData.indexOf("\n") < 0 && characterData.length() > 0) {
            displayStrings[numberDisplayLines] = indent;
            displayStrings[numberDisplayLines] += characterData;
            numberDisplayLines++;
        }
    }

    public void ignorableWhitespace(char characters[], int start, int length)
    {
        //characters(characters, start, length);
    }

    public void endElement(String uri, String localName, String rawName)
    {
        indent = indent.substring(0, indent.length() - 4);
        displayStrings[numberDisplayLines] = indent;
        displayStrings[numberDisplayLines] += "</";
        displayStrings[numberDisplayLines] += rawName;
        displayStrings[numberDisplayLines] += '>';
        numberDisplayLines++;
    }

    public void warning(SAXParseException exception)
    {
        System.err.println("WARNING! " +
            exception.getMessage());
    }

    public void error(SAXParseException exception)
    {
```

continues ▸

Listing 12.1 **Continued**

```
        System.err.println("ERROR! " +
            exception.getMessage());
    }

    public void fatalError(SAXParseException exception)
    {
        System.err.println("FATAL ERROR! " +
            exception.getMessage());
    }

    public static void main(String args[])
    {
        displayDocument(args[0]);

        for(int index = 0; index < numberDisplayLines; index++){
            System.out.println(displayStrings[index]);
        }
    }
}
```

Filtering XML Documents

The previous example displayed the entire document, but you can be more selective than that through a process called *filtering*. When you filter a document, you extract only those elements you're interested in.

Here's a new example named `searcherSAX.java`. In this case, I'll let the user specify what document to search and what element name to search for, like this, which will display all `<ITEM>` elements in `customer.xml`:

```
%java searcherSAX customer.xml ITEM
```

This program is not difficult to write, now that we've written the indenting parser example. Note, however, that we must handle not just the specific element the user is searching for, but also the element's children that are contained inside the element. I'll adapt the `IndentingParserSAX.java` program to create `searcherSAX.java`; all we'll have to control is when we display elements and when we don't. If the current element matches the element the user is searching for, I'll set a Boolean variable named `printFlag` to true:

```
public void startElement(String uri, String localName,

    String rawName, Attributes attributes)
{
    if(rawName.equals(searchFor)){
        printFlag=true;
    }
.
.
.
}
```

Now I can check whether `printFlag` is true; if so, I'll add the current element and its attributes to the display strings:

```
public void startElement(String uri, String localName, String rawName, Attributes
attributes)
{
    if(rawName.equals(searchFor)){
        printFlag=true;
    }

    if (printFlag){
        displayStrings[numberDisplayLines] = indent;

        indent += "    ";

        displayStrings[numberDisplayLines] += '<';
        displayStrings[numberDisplayLines] += rawName;
        if (attributes != null) {
            int numberAttributes = attributes.getLength();
            for (int loopIndex = 0; loopIndex < numberAttributes; loopIndex++) {
                displayStrings[numberDisplayLines] += ' ';
                displayStrings[numberDisplayLines] +=
                    attributes.getRawName(loopIndex);
                displayStrings[numberDisplayLines] += "=\"";
                displayStrings[numberDisplayLines] +=
                    attributes.getValue(loopIndex);
                displayStrings[numberDisplayLines] += '"';
            }
        }
        displayStrings[numberDisplayLines] += '>';
        numberDisplayLines++;
    }
}
```

And I can do the same in other callback methods that add text to the `displayStrings` array, such as the `character` callback:

```
public void characters(char characters[], int start, int length) {
    if(printFlag){
        String characterData = (new String(characters, start, length)).trim();
        if(characterData.indexOf("\n") < 0 && characterData.length() > 0) {
            displayStrings[numberDisplayLines] = indent;
            displayStrings[numberDisplayLines] += characterData;
            numberDisplayLines++;
        }
    }
}
```

Note that we don't want to set `printFlag` to false until after the element that the user is searching for ends, at which point we've displayed the whole element and all its children. When the element ends, I set `printFlag` to false this way:

```
public void endElement(String uri, String localName, String rawName)
{
    if(printFlag){
        indent = indent.substring(0, indent.length() - 4);
        displayStrings[numberDisplayLines] = indent;
        displayStrings[numberDisplayLines] += "</";
        displayStrings[numberDisplayLines] += rawName;
        displayStrings[numberDisplayLines] += '>';
        numberDisplayLines++;
    }
    if(rawName.equals(searchFor)){
        printFlag=false;
    }
}
```

That's all it takes. I'll filter `customer.xml` for `<ITEM>` elements like this:

```
%java searcherSAX customer.xml ITEM | more
```

You can see the results in Figure 12.2, where I'm filtering `customer.xml` to find all `<ITEM>` elements. The complete code appears in Listing 12.2.

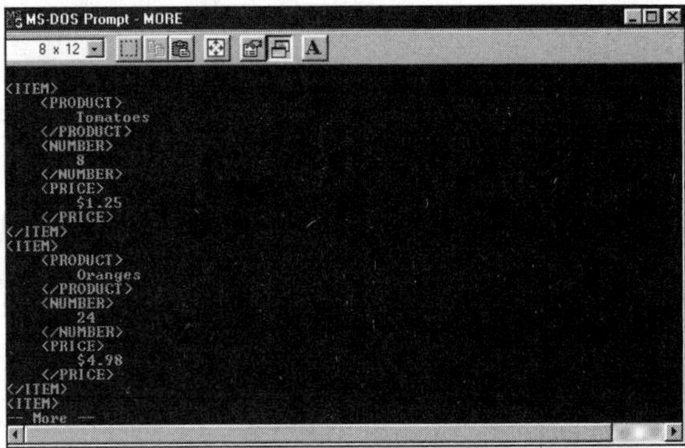

Figure 12.2 Filtering an XML document using a SAX parser.

Listing 12.2 ***searcherSAX.java***

```
import org.xml.sax.*;
import org.xml.sax.helpers.DefaultHandler;
import org.apache.xerces.parsers.SAXParser;
```

```
public class searcherSAX extends DefaultHandler
{
    static String displayStrings[] = new String[1000];
    static int numberDisplayLines = 0;
    static String indent = "";
    static boolean printFlag;
    static String searchFor;

    public static void displayDocument(String uri)
    {
        try {
            searcherSAX SAXHandler = new searcherSAX();

            SAXParser parser = new SAXParser();
            parser.setContentHandler(SAXHandler);
            parser.setErrorHandler(SAXHandler);
            parser.parse(uri);
        }
        catch (Exception e) {
            e.printStackTrace(System.err);
        }
    }

    public void processingInstruction(String target, String data)
    {
        if(printFlag){
            displayStrings[numberDisplayLines] = indent;
            displayStrings[numberDisplayLines] += "<?";
            displayStrings[numberDisplayLines] += target;
            if (data != null && data.length() > 0) {
                displayStrings[numberDisplayLines] += ' ';
                displayStrings[numberDisplayLines] += data;
            }
            displayStrings[numberDisplayLines] += "?>";
            numberDisplayLines++;
        }
    }

    public void startDocument()
    {
        if(printFlag){
            displayStrings[numberDisplayLines] = indent;
            displayStrings[numberDisplayLines] += "<?xml version=\"1.0\" encoding=\""+
                "UTF-8" + "\"?>";
            numberDisplayLines++;
        }
    }

    public void startElement(String uri, String localName,
        String rawName, Attributes attributes)
    {
```

continues ▸

Listing 12.2 **Continued**

```
        if(rawName.equals(searchFor)){
            printFlag=true;
        }

        if (printFlag){
            displayStrings[numberDisplayLines] = indent;

            indent += "    ";

            displayStrings[numberDisplayLines] += '<';
            displayStrings[numberDisplayLines] += rawName;
            if (attributes != null) {
                int numberAttributes = attributes.getLength();
                for (int loopIndex = 0; loopIndex < numberAttributes; loopIndex++) {
                    displayStrings[numberDisplayLines] += ' ';
                    displayStrings[numberDisplayLines] +=
                        attributes.getRawName(loopIndex);
                    displayStrings[numberDisplayLines] += "=\"";
                    displayStrings[numberDisplayLines] +=
                        attributes.getValue(loopIndex);
                    displayStrings[numberDisplayLines] += '"';
                }
            }
            displayStrings[numberDisplayLines] += '>';
            numberDisplayLines++;
        }
    }

    public void characters(char characters[], int start, int length) {
        if(printFlag){
            String characterData = (new String(characters, start,
                length)).trim();
            if(characterData.indexOf("\n") < 0 && characterData.length() > 0) {
                displayStrings[numberDisplayLines] = indent;
                displayStrings[numberDisplayLines] += characterData;
                numberDisplayLines++;
            }
        }
    }

    public void ignorableWhitespace(char characters[], int start, int length)
    {
        if(printFlag){
            //characters(ch, start, length);
        }
    }

    public void endElement(String uri, String localName, String rawName)
    {
```

```
        if(printFlag){
            indent = indent.substring(0, indent.length() - 4);
            displayStrings[numberDisplayLines] = indent;
            displayStrings[numberDisplayLines] += "</";
            displayStrings[numberDisplayLines] += rawName;
            displayStrings[numberDisplayLines] += '>';
            numberDisplayLines++;
        }
        if(rawName.equals(searchFor)){
            printFlag=false;
        }
    }

    public void warning(SAXParseException exception)
    {
        System.err.println("WARNING! " +
            exception.getMessage());
    }

    public void error(SAXParseException exception)
    {
        System.err.println("ERROR! " +
            exception.getMessage());
    }

    public void fatalError(SAXParseException exception)
    {
        System.err.println("FATAL ERROR! " +
            exception.getMessage());
    }

    public static void main(String args[])
    {
        String arg = args[0];
        searchFor = args[1];

        displayDocument(arg);

        for(int index = 0; index < numberDisplayLines; index++){
            System.out.println(displayStrings[index]);
        }
    }
}
```

The examples we've created so far have all created text-based output using the `System.out.println` method. As noted in the previous chapter, however, few browsers these days work that way. In the next section, I'll take a look at creating a windowed browser.

Creating a Windowed Browser

We wrote the indenting parser example to store the display text in an array named `displayStrings`, so it's easy to display that text in a Java window as we did in the previous chapter. To do that, I'll create a new example named `browserSAX.java`; in this program, I create a new object of a class I'll call `AppFrame`. Then I pass `displayStrings` and the number of lines to display to the `AppFrame` class's constructor, and then call the `AppFrame` object's `show` method to show the window:

```
import java.awt.*;
import java.awt.event.*;

import org.apache.xerces.parsers.SAXParser;
import org.xml.sax.*;
import org.xml.sax.helpers.DefaultHandler;

public class browserSAX extends DefaultHandler
{
    .
    .
    .
    public static void main(String args[])
    {
       displayDocument(args[0]);

       AppFrame f = new AppFrame(displayStrings, numberDisplayLines);

       f.setSize(300, 500);

       f.addWindowListener(new WindowAdapter() {public void
           windowClosing(WindowEvent e) {System.exit(0);}});

       f.show();
    }
}
```

The `AppFrame` class is based on the Java `Frame` class, and displays the text we've passed to it:

```
class AppFrame extends Frame
{
    String displayStrings[];
    int numberDisplayLines;

    public AppFrame(String[] d, int n)
    {
       displayStrings = d;
       numberDisplayLines = n;
    }
```

```
    public void paint(Graphics g)
    {
        Font font;

        font = new Font("Courier", Font.PLAIN, 12);
        g.setFont(font);

        FontMetrics fontmetrics = g.getFontMetrics(getFont());
        int y = fontmetrics.getHeight();

        for(int index = 0; index < numberDisplayLines; index++){
            y += fontmetrics.getHeight();
            g.drawString(displayStrings[index], 5, y);
        }
    }
}
```

You can see the `browerSAX` program at work in Figure 12.3, where `customer.xml` is displayed in a Java window. The complete code appears in Listing 12.3.

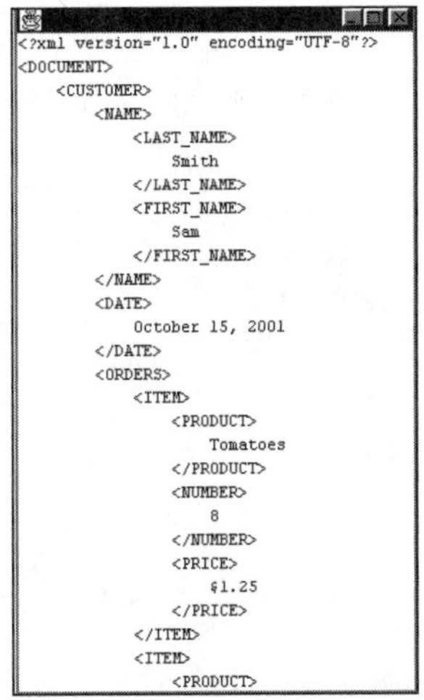

Figure 12.3 A window-based browser using a SAX parser.

Listing 12.3 ***browserSAX.java***

```
import java.awt.*;
import java.awt.event.*;

import org.apache.xerces.parsers.SAXParser;
import org.xml.sax.*;
```

continues ▸

Listing 12.3 **Continued**

```
import org.xml.sax.helpers.DefaultHandler;

public class browserSAX extends DefaultHandler
{
    static String displayStrings[] = new String[1000];
    static int numberDisplayLines = 0;
    static String indent = "";

    public static void displayDocument(String uri)
    {
        try {
            browserSAX SAXHandler = new browserSAX();

            SAXParser parser = new SAXParser();
            parser.setContentHandler(SAXHandler);
            parser.setErrorHandler(SAXHandler);
            parser.parse(uri);
        }
        catch (Exception e) {
            e.printStackTrace(System.err);
        }
    }

    public void processingInstruction(String target, String data)
    {
        displayStrings[numberDisplayLines] = indent;
        displayStrings[numberDisplayLines] += "<?";
        displayStrings[numberDisplayLines] += target;
        if (data != null && data.length() > 0) {
            displayStrings[numberDisplayLines] += ' ';
            displayStrings[numberDisplayLines] += data;
        }
        displayStrings[numberDisplayLines] += "?>";
        numberDisplayLines++;
    }

    public void startDocument()
    {
        displayStrings[numberDisplayLines] = indent;
        displayStrings[numberDisplayLines] += "<?xml version=\"1.0\" encoding=\""+
            "UTF-8" + "\"?>";
        numberDisplayLines++;
    }

    public void startElement(String uri, String localName, String rawName,
        Attributes attributes)
    {
        displayStrings[numberDisplayLines] = indent;

        indent += "    ";
```

```
        displayStrings[numberDisplayLines] += '<';
        displayStrings[numberDisplayLines] += rawName;
        if (attributes != null) {
            int numberAttributes = attributes.getLength();
            for (int loopIndex = 0; loopIndex < numberAttributes; loopIndex++) {
                displayStrings[numberDisplayLines] += ' ';
                displayStrings[numberDisplayLines] += attributes.getRawName(loopIndex);
                displayStrings[numberDisplayLines] += "=\"";
                displayStrings[numberDisplayLines] += attributes.getValue(loopIndex);
                displayStrings[numberDisplayLines] += '"';
            }
        }
        displayStrings[numberDisplayLines] += '>';
        numberDisplayLines++;
    }

    public void characters(char characters[], int start, int length)
    {
        String characterData = (new String(characters, start, length)).trim();
        if(characterData.indexOf("\n") < 0 && characterData.length() > 0) {
            displayStrings[numberDisplayLines] = indent;
            displayStrings[numberDisplayLines] += characterData;
            numberDisplayLines++;
        }
    }

    public void ignorableWhitespace(char characters[], int start, int length)
    {
        //characters(characters, start, length);
    }

    public void endElement(String uri, String localName, String rawName)
    {
        indent = indent.substring(0, indent.length() - 4);
        displayStrings[numberDisplayLines] = indent;
        displayStrings[numberDisplayLines] += "</";
        displayStrings[numberDisplayLines] += rawName;
        displayStrings[numberDisplayLines] += '>';
        numberDisplayLines++;
    }

    public void warning(SAXParseException exception)
    {
        System.err.println("WARNING! " +
            exception.getMessage());
    }

    public void error(SAXParseException exception)
    {
        System.err.println("ERROR! " +
            exception.getMessage());
    }
```

continues ▸

Listing 12.3 **Continued**

```
    public void fatalError(SAXParseException exception)
    {
        System.err.println("FATAL ERROR! " +
            exception.getMessage());
    }

    public static void main(String args[])
    {
       displayDocument(args[0]);

       AppFrame f = new AppFrame(displayStrings, numberDisplayLines);

       f.setSize(300, 500);

       f.addWindowListener(new WindowAdapter() {public void
           windowClosing(WindowEvent e) {System.exit(0);}});

       f.show();
    }
}

class AppFrame extends Frame
{
    String displayStrings[];
    int numberDisplayLines;

    public AppFrame(String[] d, int n)
    {
        displayStrings = d;
        numberDisplayLines = n;
    }

    public void paint(Graphics g)
    {
        Font font;

        font = new Font("Courier", Font.PLAIN, 12);
        g.setFont(font);

        FontMetrics fontmetrics = g.getFontMetrics(getFont());
        int y = fontmetrics.getHeight();

        for(int index = 0; index < numberDisplayLines; index++){
            y += fontmetrics.getHeight();
            g.drawString(displayStrings[index], 5, y);
        }
    }
}
```

Now that we're parsing and displaying XML documents in windows, there's no reason to restrict ourselves to displaying the text form of an XML document. Take a look at the next topic.

Creating a Graphical Browser

In the previous chapter, I adapted the DOM parser browser we wrote to display circles. It will be instructive to do the same here for the SAX parser browser because it will show how to retrieve specific attribute values. Here's what the document this browser, `circlesSAX.java`, might read—this document is called `circles.xml`, and as in the previous chapter, I'm specifying the (x, y) origin of each circle and the radius of the circle as attributes of the `<CIRCLE>` element:

```
<?xml version = "1.0" ?>
<!DOCTYPE DOCUMENT [
<!ELEMENT DOCUMENT (CIRCLE|ELLIPSE)*>
<!ELEMENT CIRCLE EMPTY>
<!ELEMENT ELLIPSE EMPTY>
<!ATTLIST CIRCLE
    X CDATA #IMPLIED
    Y CDATA #IMPLIED
    RADIUS CDATA #IMPLIED>
<!ATTLIST ELLIPSE
    X CDATA #IMPLIED
    Y CDATA #IMPLIED
    WIDTH CDATA #IMPLIED
    HEIGHT CDATA #IMPLIED>
]>
<DOCUMENT>
    <CIRCLE X='200' Y='160' RADIUS='50' />
    <CIRCLE X='170' Y='100' RADIUS='15' />
    <CIRCLE X='80' Y='200' RADIUS='45' />
    <CIRCLE X='200' Y='140' RADIUS='35' />
    <CIRCLE X='130' Y='240' RADIUS='25' />
    <CIRCLE X='270' Y='300' RADIUS='45' />
    <CIRCLE X='210' Y='240' RADIUS='25' />
    <CIRCLE X='60' Y='160' RADIUS='35' />
    <CIRCLE X='160' Y='260' RADIUS='55' />
</DOCUMENT>
```

Here the trick will be to recover the values of the attributes `X`, `Y`, and `RADIUS`. I'll store those values in arrays named `x`, `y`, and `radius`. Getting an element's attribute values is easier using the XML for Java's SAX parser than it is with the DOM parser. The `startElement` method is passed an object of `Attributes` interface, and all you have to do is use that object's `getValue` method, passing it the name of the attribute you're interested in:

```
import java.awt.*;
import java.awt.event.*;

import org.xml.sax.*;
import org.xml.sax.helpers.DefaultHandler;
import org.apache.xerces.parsers.SAXParser;

public class circlesSAX extends DefaultHandler
{
    static int numberFigures = 0;
    static int x[] = new int[100];
    static int y[] = new int[100];
    static int radius[] = new int[100];
    .
    .
    .
    public void startElement(String uri, String localName,
        String rawName, Attributes attrs)
    {
        if (rawName.equals("CIRCLE")) {
            x[numberFigures] = Integer.parseInt(attrs.getValue("X"));
            y[numberFigures] = Integer.parseInt(attrs.getValue("Y"));
            radius[numberFigures] =
                Integer.parseInt(attrs.getValue("RADIUS"));
            numberFigures++;
        }
    }
    .
    .
    .
    public static void main(String args[])
    {
        displayDocument(args[0]);

        AppFrame f = new AppFrame(numberFigures, x, y, radius);

        f.setSize(400, 400);

        f.addWindowListener(new WindowAdapter() {public void
            windowClosing(WindowEvent e) {System.exit(0);}});

        f.show();
    }
}
```

Having stored all the circles' data, I display them in the `AppFrame` class as we did in the previous chapter:

```
class AppFrame extends Frame
{
    int numberFigures;
    int[] xValues;
    int[] yValues;
    int[] radiusValues;

    public AppFrame(int number, int[] x, int[] y, int[] radius)
    {
        numberFigures = number;
        xValues = x;
        yValues = y;
        radiusValues = radius;
    }

    public void paint(Graphics g)
    {
        for(int loopIndex = 0; loopIndex < numberFigures; loopIndex++){
            g.drawOval(xValues[loopIndex], yValues[loopIndex],
            radiusValues[loopIndex], radiusValues[loopIndex]);
        }
    }
}
```

And that's all it takes; you can see the results in Figure 12.4, where the browser is displaying `circles.xml`. The complete listing appears in Listing 12.4.

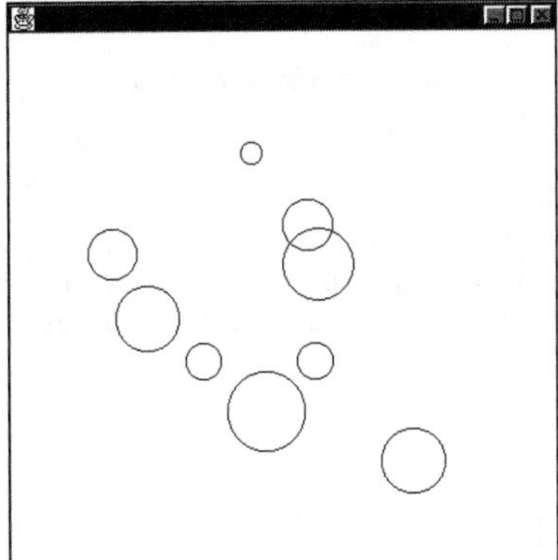

Figure 12.4 Creating a graphical XML browser using a SAX parser.

Listing 12.4 *circlesSAX.java*

```
import java.awt.*;
import java.awt.event.*;

import org.xml.sax.*;
import org.w3c.dom.*;
import org.xml.sax.helpers.DefaultHandler;
import org.apache.xerces.parsers.SAXParser;

public class circlesSAX extends DefaultHandler
{
    static int numberFigures = 0;
    static int x[] = new int[100];
    static int y[] = new int[100];
    static int radius[] = new int[100];

    public static void displayDocument(String uri)
    {
        try {
            circlesSAX SAXHandler = new circlesSAX();

            SAXParser parser = new SAXParser();
            parser.setContentHandler(SAXHandler);
            parser.setErrorHandler(SAXHandler);
            parser.parse(uri);
        }
        catch (Exception e) {
            e.printStackTrace(System.err);
        }
    }

    public void startElement(String uri, String localName,
        String rawName, Attributes attrs)
    {
        if (rawName.equals("CIRCLE")) {
            x[numberFigures] = Integer.parseInt(attrs.getValue("X"));
            y[numberFigures] = Integer.parseInt(attrs.getValue("Y"));
            radius[numberFigures] = Integer.parseInt(attrs.getValue("RADIUS"));
            numberFigures++;
        }
    }

    public void warning(SAXParseException exception)
    {
        System.err.println("WARNING! " +
            exception.getMessage());
    }

    public void error(SAXParseException exception)
    {
        System.err.println("ERROR! " +
```

```
            exception.getMessage());
    }

    public void fatalError(SAXParseException exception)
    {
        System.err.println("FATAL ERROR! " +
            exception.getMessage());
    }

    public static void main(String args[])
    {
        displayDocument(args[0]);

        AppFrame f = new AppFrame(numberFigures, x, y, radius);

        f.setSize(400, 400);

        f.addWindowListener(new WindowAdapter() {public void
            windowClosing(WindowEvent e) {System.exit(0);}});

        f.show();
    }
}

class AppFrame extends Frame
{
    int numberFigures;
    int[] xValues;
    int[] yValues;
    int[] radiusValues;

    public AppFrame(int number, int[] x, int[] y, int[] radius)
    {
        numberFigures = number;
        xValues = x;
        yValues = y;
        radiusValues = radius;
    }

    public void paint(Graphics g)
    {
        for(int loopIndex = 0; loopIndex < numberFigures; loopIndex++){
            g.drawOval(xValues[loopIndex], yValues[loopIndex],
            radiusValues[loopIndex], radiusValues[loopIndex]);
        }
    }
}
```

Navigating in XML Documents

The Node interface available that is when you use the DOM parser contains all the standard W3C DOM methods for navigating in a document, including getNextSibling, getPreviousSibling, getFirstChild, getLastChild, and getParent. It's different when you use a SAX parser, however, because this parser does not create a tree of nodes, so those methods don't apply.

Instead, if you want to find a particular element, you have to find it yourself. In the previous chapter, I found the third person's name in meetings.xml:

```
<?xml version="1.0"?>
<MEETINGS>
   <MEETING TYPE="informal">
       <MEETING_TITLE>XML In The Real World</MEETING_TITLE>
       <MEETING_NUMBER>2079</MEETING_NUMBER>
       <SUBJECT>XML</SUBJECT>
       <DATE>6/1/2002</DATE>
       <PEOPLE>
           <PERSON ATTENDANCE="present">
               <FIRST_NAME>Edward</FIRST_NAME>
               <LAST_NAME>Samson</LAST_NAME>
           </PERSON>
           <PERSON ATTENDANCE="absent">
               <FIRST_NAME>Ernestine</FIRST_NAME>
               <LAST_NAME>Johnson</LAST_NAME>
           </PERSON>
           <PERSON ATTENDANCE="present">
               <FIRST_NAME>Betty</FIRST_NAME>
               <LAST_NAME>Richardson</LAST_NAME>
           </PERSON>
       </PEOPLE>
   </MEETING>
</MEETINGS>
```

It's not difficult to do the same thing here, but in SAX programming, finding a specific element takes a little code. I start by finding the third <PERSON> element and setting a variable named thirdPersonFlag true when I find it:

```
public void startElement(String uri, String localName,
String rawName, Attributes attributes)
{
    if(rawName.equals("PERSON")) {
        personCount++;
    }

    if(personCount == 3) {
        thirdPersonFlag = true;
    }
    .
    .
    .
}
```

When the SAX parser is parsing the third person's <FIRST_NAME> element, I'll set a variable named firstNameFlag to true; when it's parsing the third person's <LAST_NAME> element, I'll set a variable named lastNameFlag to true.

```
public void startElement(String uri, String localName,
String rawName, Attributes attributes)
{
    if(rawName.equals("PERSON")) {
        personCount++;
    }

    if(personCount == 3) {
        thirdPersonFlag = true;
    }

    if(rawName.equals("FIRST_NAME") && thirdPersonFlag) {
        firstNameFlag = true;
    }

    if(rawName.equals("LAST_NAME")  && thirdPersonFlag) {
        firstNameFlag = false;
        lastNameFlag = true;
    }
}
```

Watching the variables firstNameFlag and lastNameFlag, I can store the person's first and last names in the character callback:

```
public void characters(char characters[], int start, int length)
{
    String characterData = (new String(characters, start, length)).trim();
    if(characterData.indexOf("\n") < 0 && characterData.length() > 0) {
        if(firstNameFlag) {
            firstName = characterData;
        }
        if(lastNameFlag) {
            lastName = characterData;
        }
    }
}
```

When the SAX parser is done parsing the third <PERSON> element, I'll display that person's name:

```
public void endElement(String uri, String localName, String rawName)
{
    if(thirdPersonFlag && lastNameFlag){
        System.out.println("Third name: " + firstName + " " + lastName);
        thirdPersonFlag = false;
        firstNameFlag = false;
        lastNameFlag = false;
    }
}
```

And that's the technique you use when you're hunting a specific element using a SAX parser—you just wait until the parser hands it to you. Here are the results:

```
%java navSAX meetings.xml
Third name: Betty Richardson
```

You can see the full code for this program, `navSAX.java`, in Listing 12.5.

Listing 12.5 ***navSAX.java***

```
import org.xml.sax.*;
import org.xml.sax.helpers.DefaultHandler;
import org.apache.xerces.parsers.SAXParser;

public class navSAX extends DefaultHandler
{
    int personCount;
    boolean thirdPersonFlag = false, firstNameFlag = false, lastNameFlag = false;
    String firstName, lastName;

    public static void displayDocument(String uri)
    {
        try {
            navSAX SAXHandler = new navSAX();

            SAXParser parser = new SAXParser();
            parser.setContentHandler(SAXHandler);
            parser.setErrorHandler(SAXHandler);
            parser.parse(uri);
        }
        catch (Exception e) {
            e.printStackTrace(System.err);
        }
    }

    public void startElement(String uri, String localName, String rawName,
        Attributes attributes)
    {
        if(rawName.equals("PERSON")) {
            personCount++;
        }

        if(personCount == 3) {
            thirdPersonFlag = true;
        }

        if(rawName.equals("FIRST_NAME") && thirdPersonFlag) {
            firstNameFlag = true;
        }
```

```
        if(rawName.equals("LAST_NAME")  && thirdPersonFlag) {
            firstNameFlag = false;
            lastNameFlag = true;
        }

    }

    public void characters(char characters[], int start, int length)
    {
        String characterData = (new String(characters, start, length)).trim();
        if(characterData.indexOf("\n") < 0 && characterData.length() > 0) {
            if(firstNameFlag) {
                firstName = characterData;
            }
            if(lastNameFlag) {
                lastName = characterData;
            }
        }
    }

    public void endElement(String uri, String localName, String rawName)
    {
        if(thirdPersonFlag && lastNameFlag){
            System.out.println("Third name: " + firstName + " " + lastName);
            thirdPersonFlag = false;
            firstNameFlag = false;
            lastNameFlag = false;
        }
    }

    public void warning(SAXParseException exception)
    {
        System.err.println("WARNING! " +
            exception.getMessage());
    }

    public void error(SAXParseException exception)
    {
        System.err.println("ERROR! " +
            exception.getMessage());
    }

    public void fatalError(SAXParseException exception)
    {
        System.err.println("FATAL ERROR! " +
            exception.getMessage());
    }

    public static void main(String args[])
    {
        displayDocument(args[0]);
    }
}
```

Modifying XML Documents

In the previous chapter, we saw that the XML for Java DOM parser has several methods that let you modify a document in memory, such as `insertBefore` and `addChild`, and so on. SAX parsers don't give you access to the whole document tree at once, so no similar methods exist here.

However, if you want, you can "modify" the structure of a document when using a SAX parser simply by calling various callback methods yourself. In the previous chapter, I modified `customer.xml` to create `customer2.xml`, adding a `<MIDDLE_NAME>` element with the text `XML` to each `<PERSON>` element in addition to the `<FIRST_NAME>` and `<LAST_NAME>` elements. It's easy enough to do the same here using SAX methods. All I have to do is to wait for a `<FIRST_NAME>` element and then "create" a new element by calling the `startElement`, `characters`, and `endElement` callbacks myself:

```
public void endElement(String uri, String localName, String rawName)
{
    indent = indent.substring(0, indent.length() - 4);
    displayStrings[numberDisplayLines] = indent;
    displayStrings[numberDisplayLines] += "</";
    displayStrings[numberDisplayLines] += rawName;
    displayStrings[numberDisplayLines] += '>';
    numberDisplayLines++;

    if (rawName.equals("FIRST_NAME")) {
        startElement("", "MIDDLE_NAME", "MIDDLE_NAME", null);
        characters("XML".toCharArray(), 0, "XML".length());
        endElement("", "MIDDLE_NAME", "MIDDLE_NAME");
    }
}
```

In the `main` method, I'll write this new document out to customer2.xml:

```
public static void main(String args[])
{
    displayDocument(args[0]);

    try {
        FileWriter filewriter = new FileWriter("customer2.xml");

        for(int loopIndex = 0; loopIndex < numberDisplayLines; loopIndex++){
            filewriter.write(displayStrings[loopIndex].toCharArray());
            filewriter.write('\n');
        }

        filewriter.close();
    }
    catch (Exception e) {
        e.printStackTrace(System.err);
    }
}
```

And that's it; here's what the resulting file, `customer2.xml`, looks like, with the new `<MIDDLE_NAME>` elements:

```
<?xml version="1.0" encoding="UTF-8"?>
<DOCUMENT>
    <CUSTOMER>
        <NAME>
            <LAST_NAME>
                Smith
            </LAST_NAME>
            <FIRST_NAME>
                Sam
            </FIRST_NAME>
            <MIDDLE_NAME>
                XML
            </MIDDLE_NAME>
        </NAME>
        <DATE>
            October 15, 2001
        </DATE>
        <ORDERS>
            <ITEM>
                <PRODUCT>
                    Tomatoes
                </PRODUCT>
                <NUMBER>
                    8
                </NUMBER>
                <PRICE>
                    $1.25
                </PRICE>
            </ITEM>
            <ITEM>
                <PRODUCT>
                    Oranges
                </PRODUCT>
                <NUMBER>
                    24
                </NUMBER>
                <PRICE>
                    $4.98
                </PRICE>
            </ITEM>
        </ORDERS>
    </CUSTOMER>
    <CUSTOMER>
        <NAME>
            <LAST_NAME>
                Jones
            </LAST_NAME>
            <FIRST_NAME>
```

continues ▸

```
            Polly
        </FIRST_NAME>
        <MIDDLE_NAME>
            XML
        </MIDDLE_NAME>
    </NAME>
    <DATE>
        October 20, 2001
    </DATE>
    <ORDERS>
        <ITEM>
            <PRODUCT>
                Bread
            </PRODUCT>
            <NUMBER>
                12
            </NUMBER>
            <PRICE>
                $14.95
            </PRICE>
        </ITEM>
        <ITEM>
            <PRODUCT>
                Apples
            </PRODUCT>
            <NUMBER>
                6
            </NUMBER>
            <PRICE>
                $1.50
            </PRICE>
        </ITEM>
    </ORDERS>
</CUSTOMER>
<CUSTOMER>
    <NAME>
        <LAST_NAME>
            Weber
        </LAST_NAME>
        <FIRST_NAME>
            Bill
        </FIRST_NAME>
        <MIDDLE_NAME>
            XML
        </MIDDLE_NAME>
    </NAME>
    <DATE>
        October 25, 2001
    </DATE>
    <ORDERS>
        <ITEM>
```

```
                <PRODUCT>
                    Asparagus
                </PRODUCT>
                <NUMBER>
                    12
                </NUMBER>
                <PRICE>
                    $2.95
                </PRICE>
            </ITEM>
            <ITEM>
                <PRODUCT>
                    Lettuce
                </PRODUCT>
                <NUMBER>
                    6
                </NUMBER>
                <PRICE>
                    $11.50
                </PRICE>
            </ITEM>
        </ORDERS>
    </CUSTOMER>
</DOCUMENT>
```

That finishes our work with the XML for Java package and with Java for the moment. In the next chapter, I'm going to start taking a look at working with XSL transformations.

13 XSL Transformations

IN THIS CHAPTER, I'M GOING TO START WORKING WITH THE Extensible Styles Language (XSL). XSL has two parts—a transformation language and a formatting language.

The *transformation language* lets you transform documents into different forms, while the *formatting language* actually formats and styles documents in various ways. These two parts of XSL can function quite independently, and you can think of XSL as two languages, not one. In practice, you often transform a document before formatting it because the transformation process lets you add the tags the formatting process requires. In fact, that is one of the main reasons that W3C supports XSLT as the first stage in the formatting process, as we'll see in the next chapter.

This chapter covers the transformation language, and the next details the formatting language. The XSL transformation language is often called XSLT, and it has been a W3C recommendation since November 11, 1999. You can find the W3C recommendation for XSLT at `www.w3.org/TR/xslt`.

XSLT is a relatively new specification, and it's still developing in many ways. There are some XSLT processors of the kind we'll use in this chapter, but bear in mind that the support offered by publicly available software is not very strong as yet. A few packages support XSLT fully, and we'll see them here. However, no browser supports XSLT fully yet.

I'll start this chapter with an example to show how XSLT works.

Using XSLT Style Sheets in XML Documents

You use XSLT to manipulate documents, changing and working with their markup as you want. One of the most common transformations is from XML documents to HTML documents, and that's the kind of transformation we'll see in the examples in this chapter.

To create an XSLT transformation, you need two documents—the document to transform, and the style sheet that specifies the transformation. Both documents are well-formed XML documents.

Here's an example; this document, planets.xml, is a well-formed XML document that holds data about three planets—Mercury, Venus, and Earth. Throughout this chapter, I'll transform this document to HTML in various ways. For programs that can understand it, you can use the `<?xml-stylesheet?>` processing instruction to indicate what XSLT style sheet to use, where you set the `type` attribute to `"text/xml"` and the `href` attribute to the URI of the XSLT style sheet, such as `planets.xsl` in this example (XSLT style sheets usually have the extension `.xsl`).

```
<?xml version="1.0"?>
<?xml-stylesheet type="text/xml" href="planets.xsl"?>
<PLANETS>

    <PLANET>
        <NAME>Mercury</NAME>
        <MASS UNITS="(Earth = 1)">.0553</MASS>
        <DAY UNITS="days">58.65</DAY>
        <RADIUS UNITS="miles">1516</RADIUS>
        <DENSITY UNITS="(Earth = 1)">.983</DENSITY>
        <DISTANCE UNITS="million miles">43.4</DISTANCE><!--At perihelion-->
    </PLANET>

    <PLANET>
        <NAME>Venus</NAME>
        <MASS UNITS="(Earth = 1)">.815</MASS>
        <DAY UNITS="days">116.75</DAY>
        <RADIUS UNITS="miles">3716</RADIUS>
        <DENSITY UNITS="(Earth = 1)">.943</DENSITY>
        <DISTANCE UNITS="million miles">66.8</DISTANCE><!--At perihelion-->
    </PLANET>

    <PLANET>
        <NAME>Earth</NAME>
        <MASS UNITS="(Earth = 1)">1</MASS>
        <DAY UNITS="days">1</DAY>
        <RADIUS UNITS="miles">2107</RADIUS>
        <DENSITY UNITS="(Earth = 1)">1</DENSITY>
        <DISTANCE UNITS="million miles">128.4</DISTANCE><!--At perihelion-->
    </PLANET>

</PLANETS>
```

XSL Style Sheets

Here's what the style sheet planets.xsl might look like. In this case, I'm converting planets.xml into HTML, stripping out the names of the planets, and surrounding those names with HTML `<P>` elements:

```
<?xml version="1.0"?>
<xsl:stylesheet version="1.0" xmlns:xsl="http://www.w3.org/1999/XSL/Transform">

    <xsl:template match="PLANETS">
        <HTML>
            <xsl:apply-templates/>
        </HTML>
    </xsl:template>

    <xsl:template match="PLANET">
        <P>
            <xsl:value-of select="NAME"/>
        </P>
    </xsl:template>

</xsl:stylesheet>
```

All right, we have an XML document and the style sheet we'll use to transform it. So, how exactly do you transform the document?

Making a Transformation Happen

You can transform documents in three ways:

- **In the server.** A server program, such as a Java servlet, can use a style sheet to transform a document automatically and serve it to the client. One such example is the XML Enabler, which is a servlet that you'll find at the XML for Java Web site, `www.alphaworks.ibm.com/tech/xml4j`.
- **In the client.** A client program, such as a browser, can perform the transformation, reading in the style sheet that you specify with the `<?xml-stylesheet?>` processing instruction. Internet Explorer can handle transformations this way to some extent.
- **With a separate program.** Several standalone programs, usually based on Java, will perform XSLT transformations. I'll use these programs primarily in this chapter.

In this chapter, I'll use standalone programs to perform transformations because those programs offer by far the most complete implementations of XSLT. I'll also take a look at using XSLT in Internet Explorer.

Two popular programs will perform XSLT transformations: XT and XML for Java.

James Clark's XT

You can get James Clark's XT at `www.jclark.com/xml/xt.html`. Besides XT itself, you'll also need a SAX-compliant XML parser, such as the one we used in the previous chapter that comes with the XML for Java packages, or James Clark's own XP parser, which you can get at `www.jclark.com/xml/xp/ index.html`.

XT is a Java application. Included in the XT download is the JAR file you'll need, xt.jar. The XT download also comes with sax.jar, which holds James Clark's SAX parser. You can also use the XML for Java parser with XT; to do that, you must include both `xt.jar` and `xerces.jar` in your `CLASSPATH`, something like this:

```
%set CLASSPATH=%CLASSPATH%;C:\XML4J_3_0_1\xerces.jar;C:\xt\xt.jar;
```

Then you can use the XT transformation class, `com.jclark.xsl.sax.Driver`. You supply the name of the SAX parser you want to use, such as the XML for Java class `org.apache.xerces.parsers.SAXParser`, by setting the `com.jclark.xsl.sax.parser` variable with the `java -D` switch. Here's how I use XT to transform planets.xml, using `planets.xsl`, into planets.html:

```
%java -Dcom.jclark.xsl.sax.parser=
org.apache.xerces.parsers.SAXParser
com.jclark.xsl.sax.Driver planets.xml planets.xsl planets.html
```

XT is also packaged as a Win32 exe. To use `xt.exe`, however, you will need the Microsoft Java Virtual Machine (VM) installed (included with Internet Explorer). Here's an example in Windows that performs the same transformation as the previous command:

```
C:\>xt planets.xml planets.xsl planets.html
```

XML for Java

You can also use the IBM alphaWorks XML for Java XSLT package, called LotusXSL. LotusXSL implements an XSLT processor in Java that can be used from the command line, in an applet or a servlet, or as a module in another program. By default, it uses the XML4J XML parser, but it can interface to any XML parser that conforms to the either the DOM or the SAX specification.

Here's what the XML for Java site says about LotusXSL: "LotusXSL 1.0.1 is a complete and a robust reference implementation of the W3C Recommendations for XSL Transformations (XSLT) and the XML Path Language (XPath)."

You can get LotusXSL at `www.alphaworks.ibm.com/tech/xml4j`; just click the XML item in the frame at left, click LotusXSL, and then click the Download button (or you can go directly to `www.alphaworks.ibm.com/tech/lotusxsl`, although that URL may change). The download includes xerces.jar, which includes the parsers that the rest of the LotusXSL package uses (although you can use other parsers), and xalan.jar, which is the LotusXSL JAR file. To use LotusXSL, make sure that you have `xalan.jar` in your `CLASSPATH`; to use the XML for Java SAX parser, make sure that you also have `xerces.jar` in your `CLASSPATH`, something like this:

```
%set CLASSPATH=
%CLASSPATH%;C:\lotusxsl_1_0_1\xalan.jar;C:\xsl\lotusxsl_1_0_1\xerces.jar;
```

Unfortunately, the LotusXSL package does not have a built-in class that will take a document name, a style sheet name, and an output file name like XT. However, I'll create one named xslt, and you can use this class quite generally for transformations. Here's what xslt.java looks like:

```
import org.apache.xalan.xslt.*;

public class xslt
{
    public static void main(String[] args)
    {
        try {
            XSLTProcessor processor = XSLTProcessorFactory.getProcessor();
            processor.process(new XSLTInputSource(args[0]),
                new XSLTInputSource(args[1]),
                new XSLTResultTarget(args[2]));
        }
        catch (Exception e)
        {
            System.err.println(e.getMessage());
        }
    }
}
```

After you've set the `CLASSPATH` as indicated, you can create `xslt.class` with javac like this:

```
%javac xslt.java
```

The file xslt.class is all you need. After you've set the `CLASSPATH` as indicated, you can use xslt.class like this to transform planets.xml, using the style sheet `planets.xsl`, into planets.html:

```
%java xslt planets.xml planets.xsl planets.html
```

What does planets.html look like? In this case, I've set up `planets.xsl` to simply place the names of the planets in `<P>` HTML elements. Here are the results, in planets.html:

```
<HTML>

    <P>Mercury</P>

    <P>Venus</P>

    <P>Earth</P>

</HTML>
```

That's the kind of transformation we'll see in this chapter.

There's another way to transform XML documents without a standalone program—you can use a client program such as a browser to transform documents.

Using Browsers to Transform XML Documents

Internet Explorer includes a partial implementation of XSLT; you can read about Internet Explorer support at `http://msdn.microsoft.com/xml/XSLGuide/`. That support is based on the W3C XSL working draft of December 16, 1998 (which you can find at `www.w3.org/TR/1998/WD-xsl-19981216.html`); as you can imagine, things have changed considerably since then.

To use planets.xml with Internet Explorer, I have to make a few modifications. For example, I have to convert the type attribute in the `<?xml-stylesheet?>` processing instruction from `"text/xml"` to `"text/xsl"`:

```
<?xml version="1.0"?>
<?xml-stylesheet type="text/xsl" href="planets.xsl"?>
<PLANETS>

    <PLANET>
        <NAME>Mercury</NAME>
        <MASS UNITS="(Earth = 1)">.0553</MASS>
        <DAY UNITS="days">58.65</DAY>
        <RADIUS UNITS="miles">1516</RADIUS>
        <DENSITY UNITS="(Earth = 1)">.983</DENSITY>
        <DISTANCE UNITS="million miles">43.4</DISTANCE><!--At perihelion-->
    </PLANET>

    <PLANET>
        <NAME>Venus</NAME>
        <MASS UNITS="(Earth = 1)">.815</MASS>
        <DAY UNITS="days">116.75</DAY>
```

```
        <RADIUS UNITS="miles">3716</RADIUS>
        <DENSITY UNITS="(Earth = 1)">.943</DENSITY>
        <DISTANCE UNITS="million miles">66.8</DISTANCE><!--At perihelion-->
    </PLANET>

    <PLANET>
        <NAME>Earth</NAME>
        <MASS UNITS="(Earth = 1)">1</MASS>
        <DAY UNITS="days">1</DAY>
        <RADIUS UNITS="miles">2107</RADIUS>
        <DENSITY UNITS="(Earth = 1)">1</DENSITY>
        <DISTANCE UNITS="million miles">128.4</DISTANCE><!--At perihelion-->
    </PLANET>

</PLANETS>
```

I can also convert the style sheet `planets.xsl` for use in Internet Explorer. A major difference between the W3C XSL recommendation and the XSL implementation in Internet Explorer is that Internet Explorer doesn't implement any default XSL rules (which I'll discuss in this chapter). This means that I have to explicitly include an XSL rule for the root of the document, which you specify with `/`. I also have to use a different namespace in the style sheet, `http://www.w3.org/TR/WD-xsl`, and omit the `version` attribute in the `<xsl:stylesheet>` element:

```
<?xml version="1.0"?>
<xsl:stylesheet xmlns:xsl="http://www.w3.org/TR/WD-xsl">

    <xsl:template match="/">
        <HTML>
            <xsl:apply-templates/>
        </HTML>
    </xsl:template>

    <xsl:template match="PLANETS">
        <xsl:apply-templates/>
    </xsl:template>

    <xsl:template match="PLANET">
        <P>
            <xsl:value-of select="NAME"/>
        </P>
    </xsl:template>

</xsl:stylesheet>
```

You can see the results of this transformation in Figure 13.1.

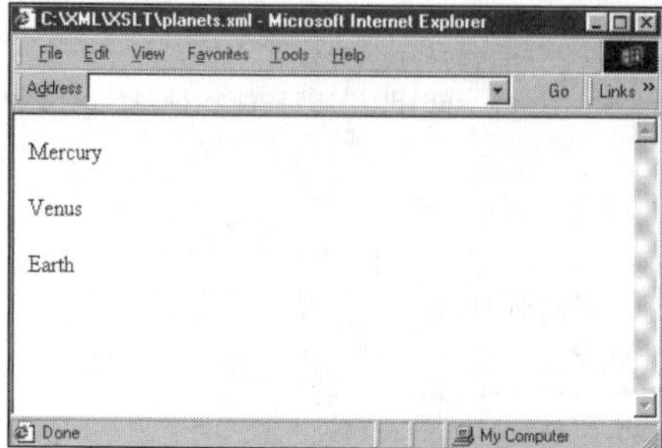

Figure 13.1 Performing an XSL transformation in Internet Explorer.

We now have an overview of XSL transformations and have seen them at work. It's time to see how to create XSLT style sheets in detail.

Creating XSLT Style Sheets

XSLT transformations accept a document tree as input and produce a tree as output. From the XSLT point of view, documents are trees built of nodes, and there are seven types of nodes XSLT recognizes; here are those nodes, and how XSLT processors treat them:

Node	Description
Document root	Is the very start of the document
Attribute	Holds the value of an attribute after entity references have been expanded and surrounding whitespace has been trimmed
Comment	Holds the text of a comment, not including `<!--` and `-->`
Element	Consists of all character data in the element, which includes character data in any of the children of the element
Namespace	Holds the namespace's URI
Processing instruction	Holds the text of the processing instruction, which does not include `<?` and `?>`
Text	Holds the text of the node

To indicate what node or nodes you want to work on, XSLT supports various ways of matching or selecting nodes. For example, the character `/` stands for the root node. To get us started, I'll create a short example here that will replace the root node—and, therefore, the whole document—with an HTML page.

As you might expect, XSLT style sheets must be well-formed XML documents, so you start a style sheet with the XML declaration. Next, you use a `<stylesheet>` element; XSLT style sheets use the namespace `xsl`, which, now that XSLT has been standardized, corresponds to `http://www.w3.org/1999/XSL/Transform`. You must also include the `version` attribute in the `<stylesheet>` element, setting that attribute to the only current version, 1.0:

```
<?xml version="1.0"?>
<xsl:stylesheet version="1.0" xmlns:xsl="http://www.w3.org/1999/XSL/Transform">
    .
    .
    .
```

That's how you start an XSLT style sheet (in fact, if you're using a standalone program that requires you to give the name of the style sheet you're using, you can usually omit the `<xsl:stylesheet>` element). To work with specific nodes in an XML document, XSLT uses *templates*. When you match or select nodes, a template tells the XSLT processor how to transform the node for output. In this example, I want to replace the root node with a whole new HTML document, so I start by creating a template with the `<xsl:template>` element, setting the match attribute to the node to match, `"/"`:

```
<?xml version="1.0"?>
<xsl:stylesheet version="1.0" xmlns:xsl="http://www.w3.org/1999/XSL/Transform">

    <xsl:template match="/">
        .
        .
        .
    </xsl:template>

</xsl:stylesheet>
```

When the root node is matched, the template is applied to that node. In this case, I want to replace the root node with an HTML document, so I just include that HTML document directly as the content of the `<xsl:template>` element:

```
<?xml version="1.0"?>
<xsl:stylesheet version="1.0" xmlns:xsl="http://www.w3.org/1999/XSL/Transform">

    <xsl:template match="/">
        <HTML>
            <HEAD>
                <TITLE>
                    A trivial transformation
                </TITLE>
            </HEAD>
```

continues ▶

```
            <BODY>
                This transformation has replaced
                the entire document.
            </BODY>
        </HTML>
    </xsl:template>

</xsl:stylesheet>
```

And that's all it takes; by using the `<xsl:template>` element, I've set up a *rule* in the style sheet. When the XSL processor reads the document, the first node that it sees is the root node. This rule matches that root node, so the XSL processor replaces it with the HTML document, producing this result:

```
<HTML>
    <HEAD>
        <TITLE>
            A trivial transformation
        </TITLE>
    </HEAD>
    <BODY>
        This transformation has replaced
        the entire document.
    </BODY>
</HTML>
```

That's our first, rudimentary transformation. All we've done is replace the entire document with another one. But, of course, that's just the beginning.

The *xsl:apply-templates* Element

The template I used in the previous section applied to only one node—the root node—and performed a trivial action, replacing the entire XML document with an HTML document. However, you can also apply templates to the *children* of a node that you've matched, and you do that with the `<xsl:apply-templates>` element.

For example, say that I want to convert planets.xml to HTML. The document node in that document is `<PLANETS>`, so I can match that element with a template, setting the `match` attribute to the name of the element I want to match. Then I replace the `<PLANETS>` element with an `<HTML>` element, like this:

```
<?xml version="1.0"?>
<xsl:stylesheet version="1.0" xmlns:xsl="http://www.w3.org/1999/XSL/Transform">

    <xsl:template match="PLANETS">
        <HTML>
    .
    .
    .
```

```
        </HTML>
    </xsl:template>
    .
    .
    .
</xsl:stylesheet>
```

But what about the children of the <PLANETS> element? To make sure that they are transformed correctly, you use the <xsl:apply-templates> element this way:

```
<?xml version="1.0"?>
<xsl:stylesheet version="1.0" xmlns:xsl="http://www.w3.org/1999/XSL/Transform">

    <xsl:template match="PLANETS">
        <HTML>
            <xsl:apply-templates/>
        </HTML>
    </xsl:template>
    .
    .
    .
</xsl:stylesheet>
```

Now you can provide templates for the child nodes. In this case, I'll just replace each of the three <PLANET> elements with some text, which I place directly into the template for the <PLANET> element:

```
<?xml version="1.0"?>
<xsl:stylesheet version="1.0" xmlns:xsl="http://www.w3.org/1999/XSL/Transform">

    <xsl:template match="PLANETS">
        <HTML>
            <xsl:apply-templates/>
        </HTML>
  </xsl:template>

    <xsl:template match="PLANET">
        <P>
            Planet data will go here....
        </P>
    </xsl:template>

</xsl:stylesheet>
```

And that's it; now the <PLANETS> element is replaced by an <HTML> element, and the <PLANET> elements are also replaced:

```
<HTML>

    <P>
        Planet data will go here....
    </P>

    <P>
        Planet data will go here....
    </P>

    <P>
        Planet data will go here....
    </P>

</HTML>
```

You can see that this transformation works, but it's still less than useful; all we've done is replace the <PLANET> elements with some text. What if we wanted to access some of the data in the <PLANET> element? For example, say that we wanted to place the text from the <NAME> element in each <PLANET> element in the output document:

```
    <PLANET>
        <NAME>Mercury</NAME>
        <MASS UNITS="(Earth = 1)">.0553</MASS>
        <DAY UNITS="days">58.65</DAY>
        <RADIUS UNITS="miles">1516</RADIUS>
        <DENSITY UNITS="(Earth = 1)">.983</DENSITY>
        <DISTANCE UNITS="million miles">43.4</DISTANCE><!--At perihelion-->
    </PLANET>
```

To gain access to this kind of data, you can use the select attribute of the <xsl:value-of> element.

Getting the Value of Nodes with *xsl:value-of*

In this example, I'll extract the name of each planet and insert that name into the output document. To get the name of each planet, I'll use the <xsl:value-of> element in a template targeted at the <PLANET> element, and I'll select the <NAME> element with the select attribute like this:

```
<?xml version="1.0"?>
<xsl:stylesheet version="1.0" xmlns:xsl="http://www.w3.org/1999/XSL/Transform">

    <xsl:template match="PLANETS">
        <HTML>
```

```
            <xsl:apply-templates/>
        </HTML>
    </xsl:template>

    <xsl:template match="PLANET">
        <xsl:value-of select="NAME"/>
    </xsl:template>

</xsl:stylesheet>
```

Using `select` like this, you can select nodes. The `select` attribute is much like the `match` attribute of the `<xsl:template>` element, except that the `select` attribute is more powerful. With it, you can specify the node or nodes to select using the full XPath XML specification, as we'll see later in this chapter. The `select` attribute is an attribute of the `<xsl:apply-templates>`, `<xsl:value-of>`, `<xsl:for-each>`, and `<xsl:sort>` elements, all of which we'll also see in this chapter.

Applying the previous style sheet, the `<xsl:value-of select="NAME"/>` element directs the XSLT processor to insert the name of each planet into the output document, so that document looks like this:

```
<HTML>

  Mercury

  Venus

  Earth

</HTML>
```

Handling Multiple Selections with *xsl:for-each*

The `select` attribute selects only the first node that matches its selection criterion. What if you have multiple nodes that could match? For example, say that you can have multiple `<NAME>` elements for each planet:

```
<PLANET>
    <NAME>Mercury</NAME>
    <NAME>Closest planet to the sun</NAME>
    <MASS UNITS="(Earth = 1)">.0553</MASS>
    <DAY UNITS="days">58.65</DAY>
    <RADIUS UNITS="miles">1516</RADIUS>
    <DENSITY UNITS="(Earth = 1)">.983</DENSITY>
    <DISTANCE UNITS="million miles">43.4</DISTANCE><!--At perihelion-->
</PLANET>
```

The <xsl:value-of> element's `select` attribute by itself will select only the first <NAME> element; to loop over all possible matches, you can use the <xsl:for-each> element like this:

```
<?xml version="1.0"?>
<xsl:stylesheet version="1.0" xmlns:xsl="http://www.w3.org/1999/XSL/Transform">

    <xsl:template match="PLANETS">
        <HTML>
            <xsl:apply-templates/>
        </HTML>
    </xsl:template>

<xsl:template match="PLANET">
    <xsl:for-each select="NAME">
        <P>
            <xsl:value-of select="."/>
        </P>
    </xsl:for-each>
</xsl:template>

</xsl:stylesheet>
```

This style sheet will catch all <NAME> elements, place their values in a <P> element, and add them to the output document, like this:

```
<HTML>

    <P>Mercury</P>
    <P>Closest planet to the sun</P>

    <P>Venus</P>

    <P>Earth</P>

</HTML>
```

We've seen now that you can use the `match` and `select` attributes to indicate what nodes you want to work with. The actual syntax that you can use with these attributes is fairly complex but worth knowing. I'll take a look at the `match` attribute in more detail first, and I'll examine the `select` attribute later in this chapter.

Specifying Patterns for the *match* Attribute

You can use an involved syntax with the <xsl:template> element's `match` attribute, and an even more involved syntax with the `select` attribute of the <xsl:apply-templates>, <xsl:value-of>, <xsl:for-each>, <xsl:copy-of>, and <xsl:sort> elements. We'll see them both in this chapter, starting with the syntax you can use with the `match` attribute.

Matching the Root Node

As we've already seen, you can match the root node with /, like this:

```
<xsl:template match="/">
    <HTML>
        <xsl:apply-templates/>
    </HTML>
</xsl:template>
```

Matching Elements

You can match specific XML elements simply by giving their name, as we've also seen:

```
<xsl:template match="PLANETS">
    <HTML>
        <xsl:apply-templates/>
    </HTML>
</xsl:template>
```

Matching Children

You can use the / operator to separate element names when you want to refer to a child of a particular node. For example, say that you wanted to create a rule that applies only to <NAME> elements that are children of <PLANET> elements. In that case, you can match to the expression "PLANET/NAME". Here's a rule that will surround the text of such elements in an <H3> element:

```
<xsl:template match="PLANET/NAME">
  <H3><xsl:value-of select="."/></H3>
</xsl:template>
```

Notice the expression "." here. You use "." with the select attribute to specify the current node, as we'll see when discussing the select attribute.

You can also use the * character as a wildcard, standing for any element (* can match only elements). For example, this rule applies to all <NAME> elements that are *grandchildren* of <PLANET> elements:

```
<xsl:template match="PLANET/*/NAME">
  <H3><xsl:value-of select="."/></H3>
</xsl:template>
```

Matching Element Descendants

In the previous section, I used the expression "PLANET/NAME" to match all <NAME> elements that are direct children of <PLANET> elements, and I used the expression "PLANET/*/NAME" to match all <NAME> elements that are grandchildren of <PLANET> elements. However, there's an easier way to perform both matches: Just use the expression "PLANET//NAME", which matches all

<NAME> elements that are inside <PLANET> elements, no matter how many levels deep. (The matched elements are called *descendants* of the <PLANET> element). In other words, "PLANET//NAME" matches "PLANET/NAME", "PLANET/*/NAME", "PLANET/*/*/NAME", and so on:

```
<xsl:template match="PLANETS//NAME">
  <H3><xsl:value-of select="."/></H3>
</xsl:template>
```

Matching Attributes

You can match attributes if you preface their name with @. Here's an example; in this case, I'll display the data in planets.xml in an HTML table. You might note, however, that the units for the various measurements are stored in attributes, like this:

```
<PLANET>
    <NAME>Earth</NAME>
    <MASS UNITS="(Earth = 1)">1</MASS>
    <DAY UNITS="days">1</DAY>
    <RADIUS UNITS="miles">2107</RADIUS>
    <DENSITY UNITS="(Earth = 1)">1</DENSITY>
    <DISTANCE UNITS="million miles">128.4</DISTANCE><!--At perihelion-->
</PLANET>
```

To recover the units and display them as well as the values for the mass and so on, I'll match the UNITS attribute with @UNITS. Here's how that looks—note that I'm using the element <xsl:text> element to insert a space into the output document (more on <xsl:text> later):

```
<?xml version="1.0"?>
<xsl:stylesheet version="1.0"
xmlns:xsl="http://www.w3.org/1999/XSL/Transform">

    <xsl:template match="/PLANETS">
        <HTML>
            <HEAD>
                <TITLE>
                    The Planets Table
                </TITLE>
            </HEAD>
            <BODY>
                <H1>
                    The Planets Table
                </H1>
                <TABLE>
                    <TD>Name</TD>
                    <TD>Mass</TD>
                    <TD>Radius</TD>
```

```
                    <TD>Day</TD>
                    <xsl:apply-templates/>
                </TABLE>
            </BODY>
        </HTML>
    </xsl:template>

    <xsl:template match="PLANET">
       <TR>
          <TD><xsl:value-of select="NAME"/></TD>
          <TD><xsl:apply-templates select="MASS"/></TD>
          <TD><xsl:apply-templates select="RADIUS"/></TD>
       </TR>
   </xsl:template>

    <xsl:template match="MASS">
        <xsl:value-of select="."/>
        <xsl:text> </xsl:text>
        <xsl:value-of select="@UNITS"/>
    </xsl:template>

    <xsl:template match="RADIUS">
        <xsl:value-of select="."/>
        <xsl:text> </xsl:text>
        <xsl:value-of select="@UNITS"/>
    </xsl:template>

    <xsl:template match="DAY">
        <xsl:value-of select="."/>
        <xsl:text> </xsl:text>
        <xsl:value-of select="@UNITS"/>
    </xsl:template>

</xsl:stylesheet>
```

Now the resulting HTML table includes not only values, but also their units of measurement. (The spacing leaves a little to be desired, but HTML browsers will have no problem with it; we'll take a look at ways of handling whitespace later in this chapter.)

```
<HTML>
<HEAD>
<TITLE>
                        The Planets Table
                    </TITLE>
</HEAD>
<BODY>
<H1>
                        The Planets Table
                    </H1>
```

continues ▸

```
<TABLE>
<TD>Name</TD><TD>Mass</TD><TD>Radius</TD><TD>Day</TD>

    <TR>
<TD>Mercury</TD><TD>.0553 (Earth = 1)</TD><TD>1516 miles</TD>
</TR>

    <TR>
<TD>Venus</TD><TD>.815 (Earth = 1)</TD><TD>3716 miles</TD>
</TR>

    <TR>
<TD>Earth</TD><TD>1 (Earth = 1)</TD><TD>2107 miles</TD>
</TR>

</TABLE>
</BODY>
</HTML>
```

You can also use the `@*` wildcard to select all attributes of an element. For example, `"PLANET/@*"` selects all attributes of `<PLANET>` elements.

Matching by ID

You can also match elements that have a specific ID value using the pattern `id()`. To use this selector, you must give elements an `ID` attribute, and you must declare that attribute of type `ID`, as you can do in a DTD. Here's an example rule that adds the text of all elements that have the ID `Christine`:

```
<xsl:template match = "id('Christine')">
    <H3><xsl:value-of select="."/></H3>
</xsl:template>
```

Matching Comments

You can match the text of comments with the pattern `comment()`. You should not store data that should go into the output document in comments in the input document, of course. However, you might want to convert comments from the `<!--`*`comment`*`-->` form into something another markup language might use, such as a `<COMMENT>` element.

Here's an example; planet.xml was designed to include comments so that we could see how to extract them:

```
<PLANET>
    <NAME>Venus</NAME>
    <MASS UNITS="(Earth = 1)">.815</MASS>
    <DAY UNITS="days">116.75</DAY>
    <RADIUS UNITS="miles">3716</RADIUS>
    <DENSITY UNITS="(Earth = 1)">.943</DENSITY>
```

```
    <DISTANCE UNITS="million miles">66.8</DISTANCE><!--At perihelion-->
</PLANET>
```

To extract comments and put them into <COMMENT> elements, I'll include a rule just for comments:

```
<?xml version="1.0"?>
<xsl:stylesheet version="1.0" xmlns:xsl="http://www.w3.org/1999/XSL/Transform">

    <xsl:template match="PLANETS">
        <HTML>
            <xsl:apply-templates/>
        </HTML>
    </xsl:template>

<xsl:template match="comment()">
    <COMMENT>
        <xsl:value-of select="."/>
    </COMMENT>
</xsl:template>

</xsl:stylesheet>
```

Here's what the result is for Venus, where I've transformed the comment into a <COMMENT> element:

```
Venus
.815
116.75
3716
.943
66.8<COMMENT>At perihelion</COMMENT>
```

Note that the text for the other elements in the <PLANET> element is also inserted into the output document. The reason for that is that the *default rule* for each element is to include its text in the output document. Because I haven't provided a rule for elements, their text is simply included in the output document. I'll take a closer look at default rules later in the chapter.

Matching Text Nodes with *text()*

You can match the text in a node with the pattern `text()`. There's really not much reason to ever use `text()`, however, because XSLT includes a default rule: If there are no other rules for a text node, the text in that node is inserted into the output document. If you were to make that default rule explicit, it might look like this:

```
<xsl:template match="text()">
    <xsl:value-of select="."/>
</xsl:template>
```

You can override this rule by *not* sending the text in text nodes to the output document, like this:

```
<xsl:template match="text()">
</xsl:template>
```

In the previous example, you can see that a great deal of text made it from the input document to the output document because there was no explicit rule besides the default one for text nodes—the only output rule that I used was for comments. If you turn off the default rule for text nodes by adding the previous two lines to the version of `planets.xsl` used in the previous example, the text of those text nodes does not go into the output document. This is the result:

```
<HTML>
<COMMENT>At perihelion</COMMENT>
<COMMENT>At perihelion</COMMENT>
<COMMENT>At perihelion</COMMENT>
</HTML>
```

Matching Processing Instructions

You can use the pattern `processing-instruction()` to match processing instructions.

```
<xsl:template match="/processing-instruction()">
    <I>
        Found a processing instruction.
    </I>
</xsl:template>
```

You can also specify what processing instruction you want to match by giving the name of the processing instruction (excluding `<?` and `?>`), as in this case, where I'm matching the processing instruction `<?xml-include?>`:

```
<xsl:template match="/processing-instruction(xml-include)">
    <I>
        Found an xml-include processing instruction.
    </I>
</xsl:template>
```

One of the major reasons that XML makes a distinction between the root node (at the very beginning of the document) and the document node is so that you have access to the processing instructions and other nodes in the document's prolog.

Using the Or Operator

You can match to a number of possible patterns, which is very useful when your documents get a little more involved than the ones we've been using so far in this chapter. Here's an example; in this case, I want to display <NAME> and <MASS> elements in bold, which I'll do with the HTML <B> tag. To match either <NAME> *or* <MASS> elements, I'll use the Or operator, which is a vertical bar (|), in a new rule, like this:

```
<?xml version="1.0"?>
<xsl:stylesheet version="1.0" xmlns:xsl="http://www.w3.org/1999/XSL/Transform">

    <xsl:template match="PLANETS">
        <HTML>
            <xsl:apply-templates/>
        </HTML>
    </xsl:template>

    <xsl:template match="PLANET">
        <P>
            <xsl:apply-templates/>
        </P>
    </xsl:template>

    <xsl:template match="NAME | MASS">
        <B>
            <xsl:apply-templates/>
        </B>
    </xsl:template>

</xsl:stylesheet>
```

Here are the results; note that the name and mass values are both enclosed in <B> elements. (Also note that, because of the XSL default rules, the text from the other child elements of the <PLANET> element is also displayed.)

```
<HTML>

  <P>
    <B>Mercury</B>
    <B>.0553</B>
    58.65
    1516
    .983
    43.4
  </P>

  <P>
    <B>Venus</B>
    <B>.815</B>
    116.75
    3716
```

continues ▸

```
    .943
    66.8
  </P>

  <P>
    <B>Earth</B>
    <B>1</B>
    1
    2107
    1
    128.4
  </P>

</HTML>
```

You can use any valid pattern with the | operator, such as expressions like PLANET | PLANET//NAME, and you can use multiple | operators, such as NAME | MASS | DAY, and so on.

Testing with *[]*

You can use the [] operator to test whether a certain condition is true. For example, you can test the following:

- The value of an attribute in a given string
- The value of an element
- Whether an element encloses a particular child, attribute, or other element
- The position of a node in the node tree

Here are some examples:

- This expression matches <PLANET> elements that have child <NAME> elements:

  ```
  <xsl:template match = "PLANET[NAME]">
  ```

- This expression matches any element that has a <NAME> child element:

  ```
  <xsl:template match = "*[NAME]">
  ```

- This expression matches any <PLANET> element that has either a <NAME> or a <MASS> child element:

  ```
  <xsl:template match="PLANET[NAME | MASS]">
  ```

Say that we gave the <PLANET> elements in planets.xml a new attribute—COLOR—which holds the planet's color:

```
<?xml version="1.0"?>
<?xml-stylesheet type="text/xml" href="planets.xsl"?>
<PLANETS>
```

```
  <PLANET COLOR="RED">
    <NAME>Mercury</NAME>
    <MASS UNITS="(Earth = 1)">.0553</MASS>
    <DAY UNITS="days">58.65</DAY>
    <RADIUS UNITS="miles">1516</RADIUS>
    <DENSITY UNITS="(Earth = 1)">.983</DENSITY>
    <DISTANCE UNITS="million miles">43.4</DISTANCE><!--At perihelion-->
  </PLANET>

  <PLANET COLOR="WHITE">
    <NAME>Venus</NAME>
    <MASS UNITS="(Earth = 1)">.815</MASS>
    <DAY UNITS="days">116.75</DAY>
    <RADIUS UNITS="miles">3716</RADIUS>
    <DENSITY UNITS="(Earth = 1)">.943</DENSITY>
    <DISTANCE UNITS="million miles">66.8</DISTANCE><!--At perihelion-->
  </PLANET>

  <PLANET COLOR="BLUE">
    <NAME>Earth</NAME>
    <MASS UNITS="(Earth = 1)">1</MASS>
    <DAY UNITS="days">1</DAY>
    <RADIUS UNITS="miles">2107</RADIUS>
    <DENSITY UNITS="(Earth = 1)">1</DENSITY>
    <DISTANCE UNITS="million miles">128.4</DISTANCE><!--At perihelion-->
  </PLANET>

</PLANETS>
```

This expression matches `<PLANET>` elements that have `COLOR` attributes:

```
<xsl:template match="PLANET[@COLOR]">
```

What if you wanted to match planets whose `COLOR` attribute was `BLUE`? You can do that with the `=` operator, like this:

```
<?xml version="1.0"?>
<xsl:stylesheet version="1.0" xmlns:xsl="http://www.w3.org/1999/XSL/Transform">

    <xsl:template match="PLANETS">
        <HTML>
            <xsl:apply-templates/>
        </HTML>
    </xsl:template>

    <xsl:template match="PLANET[@COLOR = 'BLUE']">
            The <xsl:value-of select="NAME"/> is blue.
    </xsl:template>

    <xsl:template match="text()">
    </xsl:template>

</xsl:stylesheet>
```

This style sheet filters out all planets whose color is blue and omits the others by turning off the default rule for text nodes. Here's the result:

```
<HTML>
        The Earth is blue.
</HTML>
```

In fact, the expressions you can use in the `[]` operators are W3C XPath expressions. XPath expressions give you ways of specifying nodes in an XML document using a fairly involved syntax. And because the `select` attribute, which we're about to cover, uses XPath, I'll take a look at XPath as well.

Specifying Patterns for the *select* Attribute

I've taken a look at the kinds of expressions that you can use with the `<xsl:template>` element's `match` attribute. You can use an even more involved syntax with the `select` attribute of the `<xsl:apply-templates>`, `<xsl:value-of>`, `<xsl:for-each>`, `<xsl:copy-of>`, and `<xsl:sort>` elements.

The `select` attribute uses XPath expressions, which is a W3C recommendation as of November 16, 1999. You can find the XPath specification at www.w3.org/TR/xpath.

We've seen that you can use the `match` attribute to find nodes by name, child element(s), attributes, or even descendant. We've also seen that you can make some tests to see whether elements or attributes have certain values. You can do all that and more with the XPath specification supported by the `select` attribute, including finding nodes by parent or sibling elements, as well as much more involved tests. XPath is much more of a true language than the expressions you can use with the `match` attribute; for example, XPath expressions can return not only lists of nodes, but also Boolean, string, and numeric values.

The XML for Java package has a handy example program, `ApplyXPath.java`, that enables you to apply an XPath expression to a document and see what the results would be. This is great for testing. For example, if I applied the XPath expression `"PLANET/NAME"` to planets.xml, here is what the result would look like, displaying the values of all `<NAME>` elements that are children of `<PLANET>` elements (the `<output>` tags are added by `ApplyXPath`):

```
%java ApplyXPath planets.xml PLANET/NAME
<output>
<NAME>Mercury</NAME><NAME>Venus</NAME><NAME>Earth</NAME></output>
```

XPath expressions are more powerful than the `match` expressions we've seen; for one thing, they're not restricted to working with the current node or child nodes because you can work with parent nodes, ancestor nodes, and more. Specifying what node you want to work in relation to is called *specifying an axis* in XPath. I'll take a look at XPath syntax in detail next.

Understanding XPath

To specify a node or set of nodes in XPath, you use a *location path*. A location path, in turn, consists of one or more *location steps*, separated by `/` or `//`. If you start the location path with `/`, the location path is called an *absolute location path* because you're specifying the path from the root node; otherwise, the location path is *relative*, starting with the current node, which is called the *context node*. Got all that? Good, because there's more.

A location step is made up of an *axis*, a *node test*, and zero or more *predicates*. For example, in the expression `child::PLANET[position() = 5]`, `child` is the name of the axis, `PLANET` is the node test, and `[position() = 5]` is a predicate. You can create location paths with one or more location steps, such as `/descendant::PLANET/child::NAME`, which selects all the `<NAME>` elements that have a `<PLANET>` parent. The best way to understand all this is by example, and we'll see plenty of them in a few pages. In the meantime, I'll take a look at what kind of axes, node tests, and predicates XPath supports.

XPath Axes

In the location path `child::NAME`, which refers to a `<NAME>` element that is a child of the current node, the child is called the *axis*. XPath supports many different axes, and it's important to know what they are. Here's the list:

Axis	Description
`ancestor`	Holds the ancestors of the context node. The ancestors of the context node are the parent of context node and the parent's parent and so forth, back to and including the root node.
`ancestor-or-self`	Holds the context node and the ancestors of the context node.
`attribute`	Holds the attributes of the context node.
`child`	Holds the children of the context node.
`descendant`	Holds the descendants of the context node. A descendant is a child or a child of a child, and so on.

continues

Axis	Description
`descendant-or-self`	Contains the context node and the descendants of the context node.
`following`	Holds all nodes in the same document as the context node that come after the context node.
`following-sibling`	Holds all the following siblings of the context node. A sibling is a node on the same level as the context node.
`namespace`	Holds the namespace nodes of the context node.
`parent`	Holds the parent of the context node.
`preceding`	Contains all nodes that come before the context node.
`preceding-sibling`	Contains all the preceding siblings of the context node. A sibling is a node on the same level as the context node.
`self`	Contains the context node.

You can use axes to specify a location step or path, as in this example, where I'm using the `child` axis to indicate that I want to match to child nodes of the context node, which is a `<PLANET>` element. (We'll see later that an abbreviated version lets you omit the `child::` part.)

```
<xsl:template match="PLANET">
    <HTML>
        <CENTER>
            <xsl:value-of select="child::NAME"/>
        </CENTER>
        <CENTER>
            <xsl:value-of select="child::MASS"/>
        </CENTER>
        <CENTER>
            <xsl:value-of select="child::DAY"/>
        </CENTER>
    </HTML>
</xsl:template>
```

In these expressions, `child` is the axis, and the element names `NAME`, `MASS`, and `DAY` are *node tests*.

XPath Node Tests

You can use names of nodes as node tests, or you can use the wild card `*` to select element nodes. For example, the expression `child::*/child::NAME` selects all `<NAME>` elements that are grandchildren of the context node. Besides nodes and the wild card character, you can also use these node tests:

Node Test	Description
`comment()`	Selects comment nodes.
`node()`	Selects any type of node.
`processing-instruction()`	Selects a processing instruction node. You can specify the name of the processing instruction to select in the parentheses.
`text()`	Selects a text node.

XPath Predicates

The predicate part of an XPath step is perhaps its most intriguing part because it gives you the most power. You can work with all kinds of expressions in predicates; here are the possible types:

- Node sets
- Booleans
- Numbers
- Strings
- Result tree fragments

I'll take a look at these various types in turn.

XPath Node Sets

As its name implies, a *node set* is simply a set of nodes. An expression such as `child::PLANET` returns a node set of all `<PLANET>` elements. The expression `child::PLANET/child::NAME` returns a node list of all `<NAME>` elements that are children of `<PLANET>` elements. To select a node or nodes from a node set, you can use various functions that work on node sets in predicates.

Function	Description
`last()`	Returns the number of nodes in a node set.
`position()`	Returns the position of the context node in the context node set (starting with 1).

continues

Function	Description
`count(`*`node-set`*`)`	Returns the number of nodes in *node-set*. Omitting *node-set* makes this function use the context node.
`id(string `*`ID`*`)`	Returns a node set containing the element whose ID matches the string passed to the function, or returns an empty node set if no element has the specified ID.You can list multiple IDs separated by whitespace, and this function will return a node set of the elements with those IDs.
`local-name(`*`node-set`*`)`	Returns the local name of the first node in the node set. Omitting *node-set* makes this function use the context node.
`namespace-uri(`*`node-set`*`)`	Returns the URI of the namespace of the first node in the node set. Omitting *node-set* makes this function use the context node.
`name(`*`node-set`*`)`	Returns the full, qualified name of the first node in the node set. Omitting *node-set* makes this function use the context node.

Here's an example; in this case, I'll number the elements in the output document using the `position()` function:

```
<?xml version="1.0"?>
<xsl:stylesheet version="1.0" xmlns:xsl="http://www.w3.org/1999/XSL/Transform">

    <xsl:template match="PLANETS">
        <HTML>
            <HEAD>
                <TITLE>
                    The Planets
                </TITLE>
            </HEAD>
            <BODY>
                <xsl:apply-templates select="PLANET"/>
            </BODY>
        </HTML>
    </xsl:template>

    <xsl:template match="PLANET">
        <P>
            <xsl:value-of select="position()"/>.
            <xsl:value-of select="NAME"/>
        </P>
    </xsl:template>

</xsl:stylesheet>
```

Here's the result, where you can see that the planets are numbered:

```
<HTML>
<HEAD>
<TITLE>
                The Planets
            </TITLE>
</HEAD>
<BODY>
<P>1.
          Mercury</P>
<P>2.
          Venus</P>
<P>3.
          Earth</P>
</BODY>
</HTML>
```

You can use functions that operate on node sets in predicates, as in `child::PLANET[position() = last()]`, which selects the last `<PLANET>` child of the context node.

XPath Booleans

You can also use Boolean values in XPath expressions. Numbers are considered false if they're zero and are considered true otherwise. An empty string (`""`) is also considered false, and all other strings are considered true.

You can use XPath logical operators to produce Boolean true/false results; here are the logical operators:

Operator	Description
`!=`	Is not equal to.
`<`	Is less than. (Use `<` in XML documents.)
`<=`	Is less than or equal to. (Use `<=` in XML documents.)
`=`	Is equal to. (C, C++, Java, JavaScript programmers take note—this operator is one `=` sign, not two.)
`>`	Is greater than.
`>=`	Is greater than or equal to.

You shouldn't use `<` directly in XML documents; use the entity reference `<` instead.

You can also use the keywords `and` and `or` to connect Boolean clauses with a logical And or Or operation, as we've seen when working with JavaScript and Java.

Here's an example using the logical operator >. This rule applies to all <PLANET> elements after position 5:

```
<xsl:template match="PLANET[position() > 5]">
    <xsl:value-of select="."/>

</xsl:template>
```

There is also a `true()` functions that always returns a value of true, and a `false()` function that always returns a value of false.

You can also use the `not()` function to reverse the logical sense of an expression, as in this case, where I'm selecting all but the last <PLANET> element:

```
<xsl:template match="PLANET[not(position() = last())]">
    <xsl:value-of select="."/>
</xsl:template>
```

Finally, the `lang()` function returns true or false, depending on whether the language of the context node (which is given by `xml:lang` attributes) is the same as the language you pass to this function.

XPath Numbers

In XPath, numbers are actually stored as in double-precision floating-point format. (See Chapter 10, "Understanding Java," for more details on doubles; technically speaking, all XPath numbers are stored in 64-bit IEEE 754 floating-point double-precision format.) All numbers are stored as doubles, even integers such as `5`, as in the example we just saw:

```
<xsl:template match="PLANET[position() > 5]">
    <xsl:value-of select="."/>
</xsl:template>
```

You can use several operators on numbers:

Operator	Action
+	Adds.
-	Subtracts.
*	Multiplies.
div	Divides. (The / character, which stands for division in other languages, is already heavily used in XML and XPath.)
mod	Returns the modulus of two numbers (the remainder after dividing the first by the second).

For example, the element `<xsl:value-of select="180 + 420"/>` inserts the string `"600"` into the output document. This example selects all planets whose day (measured in earth days) divided by its mass (where the mass of Earth = 1) is greater than 100:

```
<xsl:template match="PLANETS">
    <HTML>
        <BODY>
            <xsl:apply-templates select="PLANET[DAY div MASS > 100]"/>
        </BODY>
    </HTML>
</xsl:template>
```

XPath also supports these functions that operate on numbers:

Function	Description
`ceiling()`	Returns the smallest integer larger than the number that you pass it
`floor()`	Returns the largest integer smaller than the number that you pass it
`round()`	Rounds the number that you pass it to the nearest integer
`sum()`	Returns the sum of the numbers that you pass it

For example, here's how you can find the average mass of the planets in planets.xml:

```
<xsl:template match="PLANETS">
    <HTML>
        <BODY>
            The average planetary mass is:
            <xsl:value-of select="sum(child::MASS)
            div count(descendant::MASS)"/>
        </BODY>
    </HTML>
</xsl:template>
```

XPath Strings

In XPath, strings are made up of Unicode characters. A number of functions are specially designed to work on strings, as shown in this table.

Function	Description
`starts-with(string` *`string1`*`, string` *`string2`*`)`	Returns true if the first string starts with the second string
`contains(string` *`string1`*`, string` *`string2`*`)`	Returns true if the first string contains the second one

continues

Function	Description
`substring(string string1, number offset, number length)`	Returns *length* characters from the string, starting at *offset*
`substring-before(string string1, string string2)`	Returns the part of *string1* up to the first occurrence of *string2*
`substring-after(string string1, string string2)`	Returns the part of *string1* after the first occurrence of *string2*
`string-length(string string1)`	Returns the number of characters in *string1*
`normalize-space(string string1)`	Returns *string1* after leading and trailing whitespace is stripped and multiple consecutive whitespace is replaced with a single space
`translate(string string1, string string2, string string3)`	Returns *string1* with all occurrences of the characters in *string2* replaced by the matching characters in *string3*
`concat(string string1, string string2, ...)`	Returns all strings concatenated (that is, joined) together
`format-number(number number1, string string2, string string3)`	Returns a string holding the formatted string version of *number1*, using *string2* as a format ting string (create formatting strings as you would for Java's `java.text.DecimalFormat` method), and *string3* as the optional locale string

XPath Result Tree Fragments

A *result tree fragment* is a part of an XML document that is not a complete node or complete set of nodes. You can create result tree fragments in various ways, such as with the `document()` function when you point to somewhere inside another document.

You really can't do much with result tree fragments in XPath. Actually, you can do only two things: use the `string()` or `boolean()` functions to turn them into strings or Booleans.

XPath Examples

We've seen a lot of XPath in theory; how about some examples? Here's a number of location path examples—note that XPath enables you to use `and` or `or` in predicates to apply logical tests using multiple patterns.

Example	Action
`child::PLANET`	Returns the `<PLANET>` element children of the context node.
`child::*`	Returns all element children (`*` only matches elements) of the context node.
`child::text()`	Returns all text node children of the context node.
`child::node()`	Returns all the children of the context node, no matter what their node type is.
`attribute::UNIT`	Returns the `UNIT` attribute of the context node.
`descendant::PLANET`	Returns the `<PLANET>` element descendants of the context node.
`ancestor::PLANET`	Returns all `<PLANET>` ancestors of the context node.
`ancestor-or-self::PLANET`	Returns the `<PLANET>` ancestors of the context node. If the context node is a `<PLANET>` as well, also returns the context node.
`descendant-or-self::PLANET`	Returns the `<PLANET>` element descendants of the context node. If the context node is a `<PLANET>` as well, also returns the context node.
`self::PLANET`	Returns the context node if it is a `<PLANET>` element.
`child::NAME/descendant::PLANET`	Returns the `<PLANET>` element descendants of the child `<NAME>` elements of the context node.
`child::*/child::PLANET`	Returns all `<PLANET>` grandchildren of the context node.
`/`	Returns the document root (that is, the parent of the document element).
`/descendant::PLANET`	Returns all the `<PLANET>` elements in the document.
`/descendant::PLANET/child::NAME`	Returns all the `<NAME>` elements that have a `<PLANET>` parent.
`child::PLANET[position() = 3]`	Returns the third `<PLANET>` child of the context node.
`child::PLANET[position() = last()]`	Returns the last `<PLANET>` child of the context node.
`/descendant::PLANET[position() = 3]`	Returns the third `<PLANET>` element in the document.

`child::PLANETS/child::PLANET [position() = 4 ]/child::NAME [position() = 3]`	Returns the third <NAME> element of the fourth <PLANET> element of the <PLANETS> element.
`child::PLANET[position() > 3]`	Returns all the <PLANET> children of the context node after the first three.
`preceding-sibling::NAME [position() = 2]`	Returns the second previous <NAME> sibling element of the context node.
`child::PLANET[attribute:: COLOR = "RED"]`	Returns all <PLANET> children of the context node that have a COLOR attribute with value of RED.
`child::PLANET[attribute::] COLOR = "RED"][position() = 3`	Returns the third <PLANET> child of the context node that has a COLOR attribute with value of RED.
`child::PLANET[position() = 3][attribute::COLOR="RED"]`	Returns the third <PLANET> child of the context node, only if that child has a COLOR attribute with value of RED.
`child::MASS[child::NAME = "VENUS" ]`	Returns the <MASS> children of the context node that have <NAME> children whose text is VENUS.
`child::PLANET[child::NAME]`	Returns the <PLANET> children of the context node that have <NAME> children.
`child::*[self::NAME or self::MASS ]`	Returns both the <NAME> and <MASS> children of the context node.
`child::*[self::NAME or self::MASS][position() = first()]`	Returns the first <NAME> or <MASS> child of the context node.

As you can see, some of this syntax is pretty involved and a little lengthy to type. However, there is an abbreviated form of XPath syntax.

XPath Abbreviated Syntax

You can take advantage of a number of abbreviations in XPath syntax. Here are the rules:

Expression	Abbreviation
`self::node()`	`.`
`parent::node()`	`..`
`child::`*`childname`*	*`childname`*
`attribute::`*`childname`*	`@`*`childname`*
`/descendant-or-self::node()/`	`//`

You can also abbreviate predicate expressions such as `[position() = 3]` as `[3]`, `[position() = last()]` as `[last()]`, and so on. Using the abbreviated syntax makes XPath expressions a lot easier to use. Here are some examples of location paths using abbreviated syntax—note how well these fit the syntax we saw with the `match` attribute earlier in the chapter:

Path	Description
`PLANET`	Returns the <PLANET> element children of the context node.
`*`	Returns all element children of the context node.
`text()`	Returns all text node children of the context node.
`@UNITS`	Returns the UNITS attribute of the context node.
`@*`	Returns all the attributes of the context node.
`PLANET[3]`	Returns the third <PLANET> child of the context node.
`PLANET[first()]`	Returns the first <PLANET> child of the context node
`*/PLANET`	Returns all <PLANET> grandchildren of the context node.
`/PLANETS/PLANET[3]/NAME[2]`	Returns the second <NAME> element of the third <PLANET> element of the <PLANETS> element.
`//PLANET`	Returns all the <PLANET> descendants of the document root.
`PLANETS//PLANET`	Returns the <PLANET> element descendants of the <PLANETS> element children of the context node.
`//PLANET/NAME`	Returns all the <NAME> elements that have an <PLANET> parent.
`.`	Returns the context node itself.
`.//PLANET`	Returns the <PLANET> element descendants of the context node.
`..`	Returns the parent of the context node.
`../@UNITS`	Returns the UNITS attribute of the parent of the context node.

continues

Path	Description
PLANET[NAME]	Returns the <PLANET> children of the context node that have <NAME> children.
PLANET[NAME="Venus"]	Returns the <PLANET> children of the context node that have <NAME> children with text equal to Venus.
PLANET[@UNITS = "days"]	Returns all <PLANET> children of the context node that have a UNITS attribute with value days.
PLANET[6][@UNITS = "days"]	Returns the sixth <PLANET> child of the context node, only if that child has a UNITS attribute with value days. Can also be written as PLANET[@UNITS = "days"][6].
PLANET[@COLOR and @UNITS]	Returns all the <PLANET> children of the context node that have both a COLOR attribute and a UNITS attribute.

Here's an example in which I put the abbreviated syntax to work, moving up and down inside a <PLANET> element:

```
<?xml version="1.0"?>
<xsl:stylesheet version="1.0"
xmlns:xsl="http://www.w3.org/1999/XSL/Transform">

    <xsl:template match="PLANETS">
        <HTML>
            <xsl:apply-templates select="PLANET"/>
        </HTML>
    </xsl:template>

    <xsl:template match="PLANET">
        <xsl:apply-templates select="MASS"/>
    </xsl:template>

    <xsl:template match="MASS">
        <xsl:value-of select="../NAME"/>
        <xsl:value-of select="../DAY"/>
        <xsl:value-of select="."/>
   </xsl:template>

</xsl:stylesheet>
```

Default XSLT Rules

XSLT has some built-in, default rules that we've already seen in action. For example, the default rule for text nodes is to add the text in that node to the output document.

The most important default rule applies to elements and can be expressed like this:

```
<xsl:template match="/ | *">
    <xsl:apply-templates/>
</xsl:template>
```

This rule is simply there to make sure that every element, from the root on down, is processed with `<xsl:apply-templates/>` if you don't supply some other rule. If you do supply another rule, it overrides the corresponding default rule.

The default rule for text can be expressed like this, where, by default, the text of a text node is added to the output document:

```
<xsl:template match="text()">
    <xsl:value-of select="."/>
</xsl:template>
```

The same kind of default rule applies to attributes, which are added to the output document with a default rule like this:

```
<xsl:template match="@*">
    <xsl:value-of select="."/>
</xsl:template>
```

By default, processing instructions are not inserted in the output document, so their default rule can be expressed simply like this:

```
<xsl:template match="processing-instruction()"/>
```

The same goes for comments, whose default rule can be expressed this way:

```
<xsl:template match="comment()"/>
```

The upshot of the default rules is that if you don't supply any rules at all, all the parsed character data in the input document is inserted in the output document. Here's what an XSLT style sheet with no explicit rules looks like:

```
<?xml version="1.0"?>
<xsl:stylesheet version="1.0" xmlns:xsl="http://www.w3.org/1999/XSL/Transform">
</xsl:stylesheet>
```

Here's the results of applying this style sheet to planet.xml:

```
<?xml version="1.0" encoding="UTF-8"?>



    Mercury
    .0553
    58.65
    1516
    .983
    43.4



    Venus
    .815
    116.75
    3716
    .943
    66.8



    Earth
    1
    1
    2107
    1
    128.4
```

XSLT Rules and Internet Explorer

One of the problems of working with XSLT in Internet Explorer is that that browser doesn't supply any default rules. You have to supply all the rules yourself.

Altering Document Structure Based on Input

So far, the templates in this chapter have been fairly rigid skeletons, specifying exactly what should go into the output document in what order. But you can use XSLT elements such as `<xsl:element>`, `<xsl:attribute>`, `<xsl:text>`, and so on to create new nodes on the fly, based on what you find in the input document. I'll take a look at how this works now.

Creating Attribute Templates

Say that you wanted to convert the text in some elements to attributes in other elements—how could you do it? Attribute values must be quoted in XML, but you can't just use expressions like these, where I'm taking the values of <NAME>, <MASS>, and <DAY> elements and trying to make them into attribute values:

```
<xsl:template match="PLANET">
    <PLANET NAME="<xsl:value-of select='NAME'/>"
        MASS="<xsl:value-of select='MASS'/>"
        DAY="<xsl:value-of select='DAY'/>"
    />
```

This won't work because you can't use < inside attribute values, as I have here. Instead, you must use an expression like {NAME}; here's the proper XSLT:

```
<?xml version="1.0"?>
<xsl:stylesheet version="1.0" xmlns:xsl="http://www.w3.org/1999/XSL/Transform">

<xsl:template match="PLANETS">
    <HTML>
        <HEAD>
            <TITLE>
                Planets
            </TITLE>
        </HEAD>
        <BODY>
            <xsl:apply-templates select="PLANET"/>
        </BODY>
    </HTML>
</xsl:template>

<xsl:template match="PLANET">
    <PLANET NAME="{NAME}"
        MASS="{MASS}"
        DAY="{DAY}"
    />
</xsl:template>

</xsl:stylesheet>
```

Here's the resulting document—note that I've been able to convert the values in various elements to attributes:

```
<HTML>
<HEAD>
<TITLE>
                Planets
            </TITLE>
</HEAD>
```

continues ▸

```
<BODY>
<PLANET DAY="58.65" MASS=".0553" NAME="Mercury">
</PLANET>
<PLANET DAY="116.75" MASS=".815" NAME="Venus">
</PLANET>
<PLANET DAY="1" MASS="1" NAME="Earth">
</PLANET>
</BODY>
</HTML>
```

You can even include multiple expressions in curly braces, like this, where I'm adding the units for mass and day measurements from the `UNITS` attribute in the original elements:

```
<?xml version="1.0"?>
<xsl:stylesheet version="1.0" xmlns:xsl="http://www.w3.org/1999/XSL/Transform">

<xsl:template match="PLANETS">
    <HTML>
        <HEAD>
            <TITLE>
                Planets
            </TITLE>
        </HEAD>
        <BODY>
            <xsl:apply-templates select="PLANET"/>
        </BODY>
    </HTML>
</xsl:template>

<xsl:template match="PLANET">
    <PLANET NAME="{NAME}"
        MASS="{MASS} {MASS/@UNITS}"
        DAY="{DAY} {DAY/@UNITS}"
    />
</xsl:template>

</xsl:stylesheet>
```

Creating New Elements

You can create new elements with the `<xsl:element>` element. For example, say that I store the name of planets in a `NAME` attribute instead of a `<NAME>` element in planets.xml, like this:

```
<?xml version="1.0"?>
<?xml-stylesheet type="text/xml" href="planets.xsl"?>
<PLANETS>
```

```
<PLANET NAME="Mercury">
    <MASS UNITS="(Earth = 1)">.0553</MASS>
    <DAY UNITS="days">58.65</DAY>
    <RADIUS UNITS="miles">1516</RADIUS>
    <DENSITY UNITS="(Earth = 1)">.983</DENSITY>
    <DISTANCE UNITS="million miles">43.4</DISTANCE><!—At perihelion—>
</PLANET>
  .
  .
  .
```

I could create a new element using the name of the planet with `<xsl:element>`, supplying the name of the new planet with the `name` attribute, and enclosing a `<MASS>` element this way:

```
<?xml version="1.0"?>
<xsl:stylesheet version="1.0" xmlns:xsl="http://www.w3.org/1999/XSL/Transform">

<xsl:template match="PLANETS">
    <HTML>
        <HEAD>
            <TITLE>
                Planets
            </TITLE>
        </HEAD>
        <BODY>
            <xsl:apply-templates select="PLANET"/>
        </BODY>
    </HTML>
</xsl:template>

<xsl:template match="PLANET">
    <xsl:element name="{@NAME}">
        <MASS><xsl:value-of select="MASS"/></MASS>
    </xsl:element>
</xsl:template>

</xsl:stylesheet>
```

Here is the result, where I've created a new `<mercury>` element:

```
<HTML>
<HEAD>
<TITLE>
                Planets
            </TITLE>
</HEAD>
<BODY>
<Mercury>
<MASS>.0553</MASS>
</Mercury>
    .
    .
    .
```

In this way, you can create new elements and name them when the XSLT transformation takes place.

Creating New Attributes

Just as you can create new elements with `<xsl:element>` and set the element name and content under programmatic control, you can do the same for attributes using the `<xsl:attribute>` element.

Here's an example; in this case, I'm creating new `<PLANET>` elements with attributes corresponding to the various planet names, and values taken from the `COLOR` attribute in the original `<PLANET>` elements:

```
<?xml version="1.0"?>
<xsl:stylesheet version="1.0" xmlns:xsl="http://www.w3.org/1999/XSL/Transform">

<xsl:template match="PLANETS">
    <HTML>
        <HEAD>
            <TITLE>
                Planets
            </TITLE>
        </HEAD>
        <BODY>
            <xsl:apply-templates select="PLANET"/>
        </BODY>
    </HTML>
</xsl:template>

<xsl:template match="PLANET">
    <PLANET>
        <xsl:attribute name="{NAME}">
            <xsl:value-of select="@COLOR"/>
        </xsl:attribute>
    </PLANET>
</xsl:template>

</xsl:stylesheet>
```

Here are the results; as you can see, I've created new attributes on the fly, using the names of the planets:

```
<HTML>
<HEAD>
<TITLE>
                Planets
            </TITLE>
</HEAD>
<BODY>
<PLANET Mercury="RED">
</PLANET>
```

```
<PLANET Venus="WHITE">
</PLANET>
<PLANET Earth="BLUE">
</PLANET>
</BODY>
</HTML>
```

Generating Comments with *xsl:comment*

You can also create comments on the fly with the `<xsl:comment>` element. Here's an example; in this case, I'm creating comments that will replace `<PLANET>` elements, and I'll include the name of the planet in the text of the comment:

```
<?xml version="1.0"?>
<xsl:stylesheet version="1.0" xmlns:xsl="http://www.w3.org/1999/XSL/Transform">

<xsl:template match="PLANETS">
    <HTML>
        <HEAD>
            <TITLE>
                Planets
            </TITLE>
        </HEAD>
        <BODY>
            <xsl:apply-templates select="PLANET"/>
        </BODY>
    </HTML>
</xsl:template>

<xsl:template match="PLANET">
    <xsl:comment>This was the <xsl:value-of select="NAME"/> element</xsl:comment>
</xsl:template>

</xsl:stylesheet>
```

Here's the result:

```
<HTML>
<HEAD>
<TITLE>
                Planets
            </TITLE>
</HEAD>
<BODY>
<!--This was the Mercury element-->
<!--This was the Venus element-->
<!--This was the Earth element-->
</BODY>
</HTML>
```

Generating Text with *xsl:text*

You can create text nodes with the <xsl:text> element, allowing you to do things such as replace whole elements with text on the fly. One reason you can use <xsl:text> is to preserve whitespace, as in this example from earlier in the chapter, where I used <xsl:text> to insert spaces:

```
<?xml version="1.0"?>
<xsl:stylesheet version="1.0"
xmlns:xsl="http://www.w3.org/1999/XSL/Transform">

    <xsl:template match="/PLANETS">
        <HTML>
            <HEAD>
                <TITLE>
                    The Planets Table
                </TITLE>
            </HEAD>
            <BODY>
                <H1>
                    The Planets Table
                </H1>
                <TABLE>
                    <TD>Name</TD>
                    <TD>Mass</TD>
                    <TD>Radius</TD>
                    <TD>Day</TD>
                    <xsl:apply-templates/>
                </TABLE>
            </BODY>
        </HTML>
    </xsl:template>

    <xsl:template match="PLANET">
       <TR>
        <TD><xsl:value-of select="NAME"/></TD>
        <TD><xsl:apply-templates select="MASS"/></TD>
        <TD><xsl:apply-templates select="RADIUS"/></TD>
      </TR>
   </xsl:template>

   <xsl:template match="MASS">
     <xsl:value-of select="."/>
     <xsl:text> </xsl:text>
     <xsl:value-of select="@UNITS"/>
   </xsl:template>

   <xsl:template match="RADIUS">
     <xsl:value-of select="."/>
     <xsl:text> </xsl:text>
     <xsl:value-of select="@UNITS"/>
   </xsl:template>
```

```
    <xsl:template match="DAY">
      <xsl:value-of select="."/>
      <xsl:text> </xsl:text>
      <xsl:value-of select="@UNITS"/>
    </xsl:template>

</xsl:stylesheet>
```

Another reason to use `<xsl:text>` is when you want characters such as `<` and `&` to appear in your output document, not `<` and `&`. To do that, you set the `<xsl:text>` element's `disable-output-escaping` attribute to `"yes"`:

```
<?xml version="1.0"?>
<xsl:stylesheet version="1.0" xmlns:xsl="http://www.w3.org/1999/XSL/Transform">

<xsl:template match="PLANETS">
    <HTML>
        <HEAD>
            <TITLE>
                Planets
            </TITLE>
        </HEAD>
        <BODY>
            <xsl:apply-templates select="PLANET"/>
        </BODY>
    </HTML>
</xsl:template>

<xsl:template match="PLANET">
    <xsl:text disable-output-escaping = "yes">
        &lt;PLANET&gt;
    </xsl:text>
</xsl:template>

</xsl:stylesheet>
```

Here is the result:

```
<HTML>
<HEAD>
<TITLE>
                Planets
            </TITLE>
</HEAD>
<BODY>
      <PLANET>

      <PLANET>

      <PLANET>
  </BODY>
</HTML>
```

Copying Nodes

You can use the <xsl:copy> element to copy nodes, specifying just what parts you want to copy. The default rule for elements is that only the text in the element is copied. However, you can change that with <xsl:copy>, which can copy whole elements, text nodes, attributes, processing instructions and more, as you direct.

Here's an example; in this case, I'll strip all comments, processing instructions, and attributes out of planets.xml, simply by copying only text and elements:

```
<?xml version="1.0"?>
<xsl:stylesheet version="1.0" xmlns:xsl="http://www.w3.org/1999/XSL/Transform">

<xsl:template match="* | text()">
    <xsl:copy>
        <xsl:apply-templates select="* | text()"/>
    </xsl:copy>
</xsl:template>

</xsl:stylesheet>
```

Here's the output of this transformation:

```
<?xml version="1.0" encoding="UTF-8"?>
<PLANETS>

  <PLANET>
    <NAME>Mercury</NAME>
    <MASS>.0553</MASS>
    <DAY>58.65</DAY>
    <RADIUS>1516</RADIUS>
    <DENSITY>.983</DENSITY>
    <DISTANCE>43.4</DISTANCE>
  </PLANET>
     .
     .
     .
```

Sorting Elements

You can use the <xsl:sort> element to sort node sets. You use this element inside <xsl:apply-templates> and then use its select attribute to specify what to sort on. For example, here's how I sort the planets based on density:

```
<?xml version="1.0"?>
<xsl:stylesheet version="1.0" xmlns:xsl="http://www.w3.org/1999/XSL/Transform">

    <xsl:template match="PLANETS">
        <HTML>
            <HEAD>
                <TITLE>
                    Planets
                </TITLE>
            </HEAD>
            <BODY>
                <H1>Planets sorted by density</H1>
                <TABLE>
                    <TD>Planet</TD>
                    <TD>Mass</TD>
                    <TD>Day</TD>
                    <TD>Density</TD>
                    <xsl:apply-templates>
                        <xsl:sort select="DENSITY"/>
                    </xsl:apply-templates>
                </TABLE>
            </BODY>
        </HTML>
    </xsl:template>

    <xsl:template match="PLANET">
        <TR>
            <TD><xsl:apply-templates select="NAME"/></TD>
            <TD><xsl:apply-templates select="MASS"/></TD>
            <TD><xsl:apply-templates select="DAY"/></TD>
            <TD><xsl:apply-templates select="DENSITY"/></TD>
        </TR>
    </xsl:template>

</xsl:stylesheet>
```

Here are the results of this transformation:

```
<HTML>
<HEAD>
<TITLE>
                    Planets
                </TITLE>
</HEAD>
<BODY>
<H1>Planets sorted by density</H1>
```

```
<TABLE>
<TD>Planet</TD><TD>Mass</TD><TD>Day</TD><TD>Density</TD>

<TR>
<TD>Venus</TD><TD>.815</TD><TD>116.75</TD><TD>.943</TD>
</TR>
<TR>
<TD>Mercury</TD><TD>.0553</TD><TD>58.65</TD><TD>.983</TD>
</TR>
<TR>
<TD>Earth</TD><TD>1</TD><TD>1</TD><TD>1</TD>
</TR>
</TABLE>
</BODY>
</HTML>
```

You can see this HTML page in Figure 13.2.

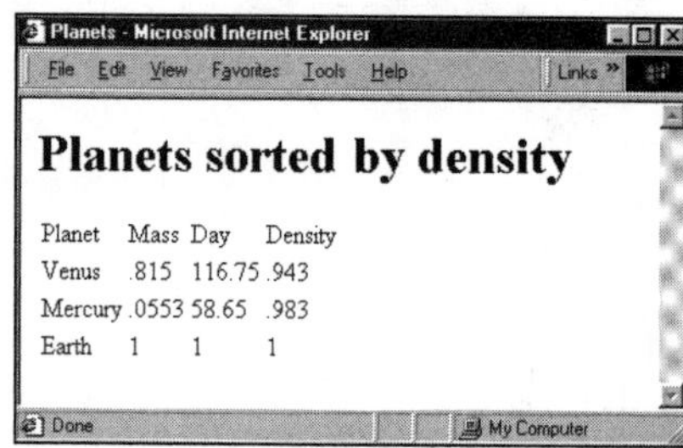

Figure 13.2 Sorting elements.

Note that, by default, `<xsl:sort>` performs an alphabetic sort, which means that `10` will come before `2`. You can perform a true numeric sort by setting the `data-type` attribute to `"number"`, like this:

```
<xsl:sort data-type="number" select="DENSITY"/>
```

You can also create descending sorts by setting the `<xsl:sort>` element's `order` attribute to `"descending"`.

Using *xsl:if*

You can make choices based on the input document using the `<xsl:if>` element. To use this element, you simply set its `test` attribute to an expression that evaluates to a Boolean value.

Here's an example. In this case, I'll list the planets one after the other and add a HTML horizontal rule, <HR>, element after the last element—but only after the last element. I can do that with <xsl:if>, like this:

```
<?xml version="1.0"?>
<xsl:stylesheet version="1.0" xmlns:xsl="http://www.w3.org/1999/XSL/Transform">

<xsl:template match="PLANETS">
    <HTML>
        <HEAD>
            <TITLE>
                Planets
            </TITLE>
        </HEAD>
        <BODY>
            <xsl:apply-templates select="PLANET"/>
        </BODY>
    </HTML>
</xsl:template>

<xsl:template match="PLANET">
    <P>
    <xsl:value-of select="NAME"/>
    is planet number <xsl:value-of select="position()"/> from the sun.
    </P>
    <xsl:if test="position() = last()"><xsl:element name="HR"/></xsl:if>
</xsl:template>

</xsl:stylesheet>
```

Here is the result; as you can see, the <HR> element appears after only the last planet has been listed:

```
<HTML>
<HEAD>
<TITLE>
                Planets
            </TITLE>
</HEAD>
<BODY>
<P>Mercury
    is planet number 1 from the sun.
    </P>
<P>Venus
    is planet number 2 from the sun.
    </P>
<P>Earth
    is planet number 3 from the sun.
    </P>
<HR>
</BODY>
</HTML>
```

Using *xsl:choose*

The <xsl:choose> element is much like the Java switch statement, which enables you to compare a test value against several possible matches. Suppose that we add COLOR attributes to each <PLANET> element in planets.xml:

```
<?xml version="1.0"?>
<?xml-stylesheet type="text/xml" href="planets.xsl"?>
<PLANETS>

  <PLANET COLOR="RED">
    <NAME>Mercury</NAME>
    <MASS UNITS="(Earth = 1)">.0553</MASS>
    <DAY UNITS="days">58.65</DAY>
    <RADIUS UNITS="miles">1516</RADIUS>
    <DENSITY UNITS="(Earth = 1)">.983</DENSITY>
    <DISTANCE UNITS="million miles">43.4</DISTANCE><!--At perihelion-->
  </PLANET>

  <PLANET COLOR="WHITE">
    <NAME>Venus</NAME>
    <MASS UNITS="(Earth = 1)">.815</MASS>
    <DAY UNITS="days">116.75</DAY>
    <RADIUS UNITS="miles">3716</RADIUS>
    <DENSITY UNITS="(Earth = 1)">.943</DENSITY>
    <DISTANCE UNITS="million miles">66.8</DISTANCE><!--At perihelion-->
  </PLANET>

  <PLANET COLOR="BLUE">
    <NAME>Earth</NAME>
    <MASS UNITS="(Earth = 1)">1</MASS>
    <DAY UNITS="days">1</DAY>
    <RADIUS UNITS="miles">2107</RADIUS>
    <DENSITY UNITS="(Earth = 1)">1</DENSITY>
    <DISTANCE UNITS="million miles">128.4</DISTANCE><!--At perihelion-->
  </PLANET>

</PLANETS>
```

Now say that we want to display the names of the various planets, formatted in different ways using HTML <B>, <I>, and <U> tags, depending on the value of the COLOR attribute. I can do this with an <xsl:choose> element. Each case in the <xsl:choose> element is specified with an <xsl:when> element, and you specify the actual test for the case with the test attribute. Here's what it looks like:

```
<?xml version="1.0"?>
<xsl:stylesheet version="1.0" xmlns:xsl="http://www.w3.org/1999/XSL/Transform">
```

```
<xsl:template match="PLANETS">
    <HTML>
        <HEAD>
            <TITLE>
                Planets
            </TITLE>
        </HEAD>
        <BODY>
            <xsl:apply-templates select="PLANET"/>
        </BODY>
    </HTML>
</xsl:template>

<xsl:template match="PLANET">
    <xsl:choose>
        <xsl:when test="@COLOR = 'RED'">
            <B>
                <xsl:value-of select="NAME"/>
            </B>
        </xsl:when>
        <xsl:when test="@COLOR = 'WHITE'">
            <I>
                <xsl:value-of select="NAME"/>
            </I>
        </xsl:when>
        <xsl:when test="@COLOR = 'BLUE'">
            <U>
                <xsl:value-of select="NAME"/>
            </U>
        </xsl:when>
        <xsl:otherwise>
             <PRE>
                 <xsl:value-of select="."/>
             </PRE>
        </xsl:otherwise>
    </xsl:choose>
</xsl:template>

</xsl:stylesheet>
```

Note also the `<xsl:otherwise>` element in this example, which acts the same way as the `default:` case in a `switch` statement—that is, if no other case matches, the `<xsl:otherwise>` element is applied. Here is the result of this XSLT:

```
<HTML>
<HEAD>
<TITLE>
                Planets
            </TITLE>
</HEAD>
```

continues ▸

```
<BODY>
<B>Mercury</B>
<I>Venus</I>
<U>Earth</U>
</BODY>
</HTML>
```

Controlling Output Type

A lot of the examples in this chapter have converted XML into HTML, and you might have wondered how an XSLT processor knows to omit the `<?xml?>` declaration from the beginning of such output documents. It turns out that there's a special rule here: If the document node of the output document is `<HTML>`, the XSLT processor knows that the output document type is HTML and writes the document accordingly.

In fact, you can specify three types of output documents:

- **XML.** This is the default, and such documents start with an `<?xml?>` declaration. In addition, entity references will not be replaced with characters such as `<` or `&` in the output document; the actual entity reference will appear in the output.
- **HTML.** This is standard HTML 4.0, without a XML declaration or any need to close elements that don't normally have a closing tag in HTML 4.0. Empty elements can end with `>`, not `/>`, and `<` and `&` characters in text are not escaped with the corresponding character entity references.
- **Text.** This type of output represents pure text. In this case, the output document is simply the plain text of the document tree.

You can set the output method by setting the `<xsl:output>` element's `method` attribute to `"xml"`, `"html"`, or `"text"`. For example, if you want to create an HTML document, even though the root element is not `<HTML>`, you can use this `<xsl:output>` element:

```
<xsl:output method = "html"/>
```

Another useful attribute of `<xsl:output>` is the `indent` attribute, which enables the XSLT processor (but does not force it) to insert whitespace to indent the output. Here's how you can use this attribute:

```
<xsl:output indent = "yes"/>
```

This next table shows some `<xsl:output>` attributes that you can use to create or modify XML declarations:

Attribute	Description
encoding	Specifies the value for the XML declaration's encoding attribute.
omit-xml-declaration	Specifies whether the processor should omit the XML declaration. Set this to yes or no.
standalone	Specifies the value for the XML declaration's standalone attribute. Set this to yes or no.
version	Specifies the value for the XML declaration's version attribute.

Another useful attribute of `<xsl:output>` is `media-type`, which enables you to specify the MIME type of the output document. Here's an example:

```
<xsl:output media-type="text/xml"/>
```

You can also use the `<xsl:output>` `doctype-system` and `doctype-public` attributes to specify an external DTD. For example, take a look at the following `<xsl:output>` element:

```
<xsl:output doctype-system = "planets.dtd"/>
```

It produces a `<!DOCTYPE>` element in the output document, like this:

```
<!DOCTYPE PLANETS SYSTEM "planets.dtd">
```

As you can see, there's a tremendous amount going on in XSL transformations. In fact, there's more than we can cover here—for plenty of additional details, take a look at the W3C XSLT specification at www.w3.org/TR/xslt, and the XPath specification at www.w3.org/TR/xpath.

There's more to XSL—besides XSL transformations, XSL also includes a whole formatting language, and I'm going to take a look at that in the next chapter.

14
XSL Formatting Objects

IN THE PREVIOUS CHAPTER, WE TOOK A LOOK AT THE XSL transformation language. In this chapter, we'll take a look at the second half of XSL: formatting objects.

The W3C has defined such formatting objects as `root`, `block`, and `character` that support different properties such as `font-weight`, `line-height`, and `border`. Using these predefined objects, you can specify the exact formatting for a document. At this writing, there are 56 formatting objects and 177 properties that apply to these objects. Each of these objects has its own XML tag, and the properties that it supports are attributes of that tag. (Many of these properties come from CSS2, which you can read more about in Chapter 9, "Cascading Style Sheets.")

Like other XML applications, XSL formatting objects have their own namespace, `"http://www.w3.org/1999/XSL/Format"`, and the namespace prefix that people use for that namespace is almost invariably `fo`, for "formatting objects." For example, here's how I can create a block (recall from CSS that blocks are rectangular areas in the output document) that displays the text `Welcome to XSL formatting.` in 36 point sans-serif font using the `<fo:block>` formatting object:

```
<fo:block font-family="sans-serif" line-height="48pt" font-size="36pt">
    Welcome to XSL formatting.
</fo:block>
```

The formatting object that I'm using here is fo:block, and the properties that I'm assigning values to are font-family, line-height, and font-size. After you've created a document using the XSL formatting objects, you can let an XSL processor format that document. We'll see one such program in this chapter that creates files in PDF format (*portable document format*, the common format that you see on the Web for document exchange) from documents written with the XSL formatting objects.

That's the idea—if you write your documents using the formatting objects, you can actually specify how that document will be displayed, down to the last comma and figure. Unfortunately, very little software actually interprets and uses the XSL formatting objects yet. In this chapter, we'll use the only such package that I know of: the Apache XML Project's FOP processor.

The <fo:block> and all the other formatting objects are defined by the W3C, and you can find the W3C recommendation for the XSL formatting objects at www.w3.org/TR/xsl. The specification for all the formatting objects is at www.w3.org/TR/xsl/slice6.html, and the specification of the properties that you can use with these objects is at www.w3.org/TR/xsl/slice7.html.

We can't cover the entire field of formatting objects here because that would take a book by itself. For all the details, refer to www.w3.org/TR/xsl.

Formatting an XML Document

Writing an entire document using the XSL formatting objects is not an easy task except for short documents. I have a hard time imagining anyone using the formatting objects to write a book, for example. W3C foresaw that difficulty, and that's one of the main reasons that it also introduced the transformation language we took a look at in the previous chapter. You can write a document using your own tags, and you can use XSLT to transform the document so that it uses the XSL formatting objects. In practice, that's almost invariably the way it's done, which means that all you have to supply is an XSLT style sheet that can be used to convert your document to use formatting objects. In this way, an XSLT processor can do all the work for you, transforming a document from a form you're comfortable working with to formatting an object form, which you can then feed to a program that can handle formatting objects and display the formatted result.

To make all this self-evident, I'll write an example here using the planets.xml document we saw in the previous chapter:

```
<?xml version="1.0"?>
<?xml-stylesheet type="text/xml" href="planets.xsl"?>
<PLANETS>
```

```
  <PLANET COLOR="RED">
    <NAME>Mercury</NAME>
    <MASS UNITS="(Earth = 1)">.0553</MASS>
    <DAY UNITS="days">58.65</DAY>
    <RADIUS UNITS="miles">1516</RADIUS>
    <DENSITY UNITS="(Earth = 1)">.983</DENSITY>
    <DISTANCE UNITS="million miles">43.4</DISTANCE><!--At perihelion-->
  </PLANET>

  <PLANET COLOR="WHITE">
    <NAME>Venus</NAME>
    <MASS UNITS="(Earth = 1)">.815</MASS>
    <DAY UNITS="days">116.75</DAY>
    <RADIUS UNITS="miles">3716</RADIUS>
    <DENSITY UNITS="(Earth = 1)">.943</DENSITY>
    <DISTANCE UNITS="million miles">66.8</DISTANCE><!--At perihelion-->
  </PLANET>

  <PLANET COLOR="BLUE">
    <NAME>Earth</NAME>
    <MASS UNITS="(Earth = 1)">1</MASS>
    <DAY UNITS="days">1</DAY>
    <RADIUS UNITS="miles">2107</RADIUS>
    <DENSITY UNITS="(Earth = 1)">1</DENSITY>
    <DISTANCE UNITS="million miles">128.4</DISTANCE><!--At perihelion-->
  </PLANET>

</PLANETS>
```

In this chapter, I'll write an XSLT style sheet for this document, transforming it so that it uses formatting objects. Then I'll use the FOP processor to turn the new document into a PDF file. I'll also take a look at the formatted document with Adobe Acrobat.

Creating the XSLT Style Sheet

I could translate planets.xsl into a document using the formatting objects by hand. As mentioned, however, that doesn't really work for anything but short documents in general. The usual technique is to create an XSLT style sheet that you can use to transform a document so that it uses the XSL formatting objects, and I'll do that in this chapter. Here's what that style sheet, planets.xsl, will look like; in this case, I'm using a large font for 36-point text:

```
<?xml version='1.0'?>
<xsl:stylesheet xmlns:xsl="http://www.w3.org/1999/XSL/Transform"
    xmlns:fo="http://www.w3.org/1999/XSL/Format"
    version='1.0'>

    <xsl:template match="PLANETS">
        <fo:root>
```

continues ▶

```
            <fo:layout-master-set>
                <fo:simple-page-master master-name="page"
                    page-height="400mm" page-width="300mm"
                    margin-top="10mm" margin-bottom="10mm"
                    margin-left="20mm" margin-right="20mm">

                    <fo:region-body
                      margin-top="0mm" margin-bottom="10mm"
                      margin-left="0mm" margin-right="0mm"/>

                    <fo:region-after extent="10mm"/>
                </fo:simple-page-master>
            </fo:layout-master-set>

            <fo:page-sequence master-name="page">

                <!-- Added for fop -->
                <fo:sequence-specification>
                    <fo:sequence-specifier-single master-name="page"/>
                </fo:sequence-specification>
                <!-- Added for fop -->

                <fo:flow>
                    <xsl:apply-templates/>
                </fo:flow>
            </fo:page-sequence>

        </fo:root>
    </xsl:template>

    <xsl:template match="PLANET/NAME">
        <fo:block font-weight="bold" font-size="36pt"
            line-height="48pt" font-family="sans-serif">
            Name:
            <xsl:apply-templates/>
        </fo:block>
    </xsl:template>

    <xsl:template match="PLANET/MASS">
        <fo:block font-size="36pt" line-height="48pt"
            font-family="sans-serif">
            Mass (Earth = 1):
            <xsl:apply-templates/>
        </fo:block>
    </xsl:template>

    <xsl:template match="PLANET/DAY">
        <fo:block font-size="36pt" line-height="48pt" font-family="sans-serif">
            Day (Earth = 1):
            <xsl:apply-templates/>
        </fo:block>
    </xsl:template>
```

```
    <xsl:template match="PLANET/RADIUS">
        <fo:block font-size="36pt" line-height="48pt" font-family="sans-serif">
            Radius (in miles):
            <xsl:apply-templates/>
        </fo:block>
    </xsl:template>

    <xsl:template match="PLANET/DENSITY">
        <fo:block font-size="36pt" line-height="48pt" font-family="sans-serif">
            Density (Earth = 1):
            <xsl:apply-templates/>
        </fo:block>
    </xsl:template>

    <xsl:template match="PLANET/DISTANCE">
        <fo:block font-size="36pt" line-height="48pt" font-family="sans-serif">
            Distance (million miles):
            <xsl:apply-templates/>
        </fo:block>
    </xsl:template>

</xsl:stylesheet>
```

Transforming a Document into a Formatting Object Form

To transform planets.xml into a document that uses formatting objects, which I'll call planets.fo, all I have to do is to apply the style sheet planets.xsl. You can do that using the XSLT techniques we saw in the previous chapter. For example, to use the `xslt` Java class I created in that chapter, you first set the class path to include the alphaWorks' xalan.jar and xerces.jar files, something like this:

```
%set classpath=%classpath%;C:\lotusxsl_1_0_1\xalan.jar;C:\xsl\lotusxsl_1_0_1\xerces.jar;
```

Then you apply planets.xsl to planets.xml to produce planets.fo:

```
%java xslt planets.xml planets.xsl planets.fo
```

The document planets.fo uses the XSL formatting objects to specify how the document should be formatted. Here's what planets.fo looks like:

```
<?xml version="1.0" encoding="UTF-8"?>
<fo:root xmlns:fo="http://www.w3.org/1999/XSL/Format">

    <fo:layout-master-set>
        <fo:simple-page-master margin-right="20mm"
            margin-left="20mm" margin-bottom="10mm"
            margin-top="10mm" page-width="300mm"
```

continues ▸

```
            page-height="400mm" master-name="page">

            <fo:region-body margin-right="0mm"
                margin-left="0mm" margin-bottom="10mm"
                margin-top="0mm"/>

         <fo:region-after extent="10mm"/>

        </fo:simple-page-master>
    </fo:layout-master-set>

    <fo:page-sequence master-name="page">

        <!-- Added for fop -->
        <fo:sequence-specification>
            <fo:sequence-specifier-single master-name="page"/>
        </fo:sequence-specification>
        <!-- Added for fop -->

        <fo:flow>

            <fo:block font-family="sans-serif" line-height="48pt"
                font-size="36pt" font-weight="bold">
                Name:
                Mercury
            </fo:block>
            <fo:block font-family="sans-serif" line-height="48pt"
                font-size="36pt">
                Mass (Earth = 1):
                .0553</fo:block>
            <fo:block font-family="sans-serif" line-height="48pt"
                font-size="36pt">
                Day (Earth = 1):
                58.65</fo:block>
            <fo:block font-family="sans-serif" line-height="48pt"
                font-size="36pt">
                Radius (in miles):
                1516</fo:block>
            <fo:block font-family="sans-serif" line-height="48pt"
                font-size="36pt">
                Density (Earth = 1):
                .983</fo:block>
            <fo:block font-family="sans-serif" line-height="48pt"
                font-size="36pt">
                Distance (million miles):
                43.4</fo:block>

            <fo:block font-family="sans-serif" line-height="48pt"
                font-size="36pt" font-weight="bold">
                Name:
                Venus
            </fo:block>
```

```
<fo:block font-family="sans-serif" line-height="48pt"
    font-size="36pt">
    Mass (Earth = 1):
    .815
</fo:block>
<fo:block font-family="sans-serif" line-height="48pt"
    font-size="36pt">
    Day (Earth = 1):
    116.75
</fo:block>
<fo:block font-family="sans-serif" line-height="48pt"
    font-size="36pt">
    Radius (in miles):
    3716
</fo:block>
<fo:block font-family="sans-serif" line-height="48pt"
    font-size="36pt">
    Density (Earth = 1):
    .943
</fo:block>
<fo:block font-family="sans-serif" line-height="48pt"
    font-size="36pt">
     Distance (million miles):
     66.8
</fo:block>

<fo:block font-family="sans-serif" line-height="48pt"
    font-size="36pt" font-weight="bold">
    Name:
    Earth
</fo:block>
<fo:block font-family="sans-serif" line-height="48pt"
    font-size="36pt">
    Mass (Earth = 1):
    1
</fo:block>
<fo:block font-family="sans-serif" line-height="48pt"
    font-size="36pt">
    Day (Earth = 1):
    1
</fo:block>
<fo:block font-family="sans-serif" line-height="48pt"
    font-size="36pt">
    Radius (in miles):
    2107
</fo:block>
<fo:block font-family="sans-serif" line-height="48pt"
    font-size="36pt">
    Density (Earth = 1):
    1
</fo:block>
<fo:block font-family="sans-serif" line-height="48pt"
```

continues ▸

```
            font-size="36pt">
            Distance (million miles):
            128.4
        </fo:block>

    </fo:flow>
  </fo:page-sequence>
</fo:root>
```

Okay, now we have planets.fo. How can we use it to create a formatted PDF file?

Creating a Formatted Document

To process planets.fo and create a formatted document, I'll use the only XSL formatting object processor currently available as far as I know: James Tauber's FOP (formatting objects processor), which has now been donated to the Apache XML Project. (The alphaWorks XML for Java parsers I've been using for several chapters is based on the Apache XML Project's Xerces XML parser.)

Here's how the Apache XML Project describes FOP:

> *FOP is the world's first print formatter driven by XSL formatting objects. It is a Java application that reads a formatting object tree and then turns it into a PDF document. The formatting object tree can be in the form of an XML document (output by an XSLT engine like XT or Xalan) or can be passed in memory as a DOM document or (in the case of XT) SAX events.*

Here's how the Apache XML Project describes the objectives of FOP:

> *The goals of the Apache XML FOP Project are to deliver an XSL FO->PDF formatter that is compliant to at least the Basic conformance level described in the 27 March 2000 XSL WD [W3C Working Draft], and that complies with the 11 March 1999 Portable Document Format Specification (Version 1.3) from Adobe Systems.*

You can get FOP at `http://xml.apache.org/fop`; just click the Download button to download it. The FOP package, including documentation, comes zipped, and you must unzip it. It's implemented as a Java JAR file, `fop_bin_0_12_1`.jar (this jar file is updated frequently; during tech review of this book, a new version, `fop_bin_0_13_0.jar`, appeared). You can use FOP from the command line with a class that at this writing is `org.apache.fop.apps.CommandLine`. You must provide the parser you want to use; I'll use the XML for Java parsers in xerces.jar.

Here's how I use FOP to convert planets.fo to planets.pdf with the java tool; note that I'm specifying the class path with the `-cp` switch to include `fop_bin_0_12_1.jar` and `xerces.jar`:

```
%java -cp fop_bin_0_12_1.jar;xerces.jar

org.apache.fop.apps.CommandLine planets.fo planets.pdf
```

And that's it; you can see the final results, planets.pdf, in the Adobe Acrobat PDF reader (which you can get for free at `www.adobe.com/products/acrobat/readermain.html`) in Figure 14.1. The planets.xml document appears in that figure formatted exactly as it should be.

The PDF format is a good one for formatting object output, although it has some limitations—for example, it can't handle dynamic tables that can expand or collapse at the click of a mouse, or interactive multiple-target links, both of which are part of the formatting objects specification. Although FOP is, as far as I know, the only software package that handles formatting objects (even partially), formatting objects most likely will be supported in the major browsers one day.

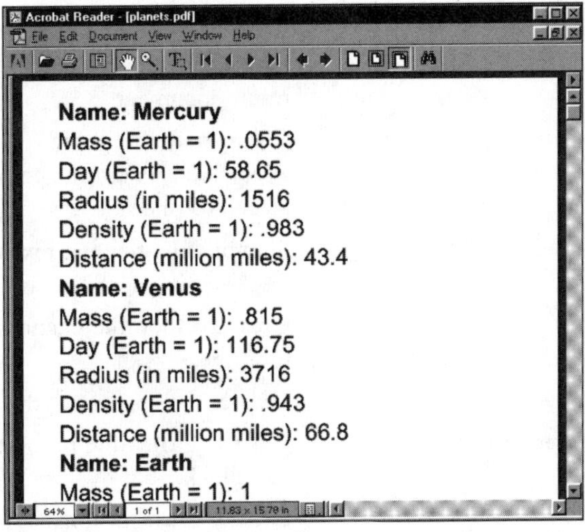

Figure 14.1 A PDF document created with formatting objects.

Now you've seen how the process works; it's time to get to the details, starting with an overview of the available formatting objects.

XSL Formatting Objects

Here's an overview of the 56 formatting objects that exist as of this writing—we'll see a good number of them in action in this chapter.

Object	Description
`bidi-override`	Overrides the default Unicode-bidirectionality algorithm direction in mixed-language documents.
`block`	Creates a display block, often used for formatting paragraphs, titles, headlines, figure and table captions, and so on.
`block-container`	Generates a block-level reference area.
`character`	Represents a character that is associated with a glyph for display.
`color-profile`	Declares a color profile for a style sheet.
`conditional-page-master-reference`	Specifies a page master to be used when the given conditions are met.
`declarations`	Groups global declarations for a style sheet.
`external-graphic`	Adds an inline graphic to the document, where the graphics data is outside the XML result document.
`float`	Can specify that some content is formatted in a separate area at the beginning of the page or placed to one side.
`flow`	Supports the flowing text content that is displayed in pages.
`footnote`	Creates a footnote citation and the associated footnote.
`footnote-body`	Creates the content of the footnote.
`initial-property-set`	Sets the formatting properties for the first line of a block.
`inline`	Usually is used to format part of the text with a background or to give it a border.
`inline-container`	Creates an inline reference area.
`instream-foreign-object`	Is used to insert an inline graphic or other object where the object data is a descendant of the `fo:instream-foreign-object`.
`layout-master-set`	Is a wrapper for all the masters used in the document.

Object	Description
`leader`	Creates a rule or row of repeating characters or a repeating pattern of characters that is used between two text-formatting objects.
`list-block`	Is used to format a list.
`list-item`	Holds the label and the body of an item in a list.
`list-item-body`	Holds the content of the body of a list item.
`list-item-label`	Holds the content of the label of a list item.
`marker`	Is used with `fo:retrieve-marker` to create on-the-fly headers or footers.
`multi-case`	Adds flow objects that the parent object, `fo:multi-switch`, can be used to show or hide.
`multi-properties`	Switches between two or more property sets that are connected to a given part of the content.
`multi-property-set`	Indicates an alternative set of formatting properties that can be applied to the content.
`multi-switch`	Switches between two or more subtrees of formatting objects.
`multi-toggle`	Is used inside an `fo:multi-case` object to switch to another `fo:multi-case`.
`page-number`	Holds the current page number.
`page-number-citation`	References the page number for the page containing the cited formatting object.
`page-sequence`	Specifies how to create a sequence of pages within a document.
`page-sequence-master`	Contains sequences of page masters that are used to generate sequences of pages.
`region-after`	Refers to the region located after a `fo:region-body` region.
`region-before`	Refers to the region before a `fo:region-body` region.
`region-body`	Refers to the region in the center of the `fo:simple-page-master`.
`region-end`	Refers to the region at the end of a `fo:region-body` region.

continues ▸

Object	Description
`region-start`	Refers to the region starting a `fo:region-body` region.
`repeatable-page-master-alternatives`	Indicates a subsequence made up of repeated instances of a set of alternative page masters.
`repeatable-page-master-reference`	Indicates a subsequence of repeated instances of a single page master.
`retrieve-marker`	Is used with `fo:marker` to create on-the-fly headers or footers.
`root`	Is the top node of an XSL formatted document.
`simple-link`	Represents the start location in a simple link.
`simple-page-master`	Gives the geometry of a page, which may be divided into up to five regions.
`single-page-master-reference`	Indicates a subsequence made up of a single instance of a single page master.
`static-content`	Contains a sequence of formatting objects that should be presented in a single region or repeated in like-named regions on one or more pages in the page-sequence. This most often is used for repeating headers and footers.
`table`	Formats the data in a table.
`table-and-caption`	Formats the data and caption of a table.
`table-body`	Holds the content of the table body.
`table-caption`	Holds block-level formatting objects that, in turn, hold the caption for a table.
`table-cell`	Groups content to be placed in a table cell.
`table-column`	Sets characteristics for table cells that have the same column.
`table-footer`	Holds the content of the table footer.
`table-header`	Holds the content of the table header.
`table-row`	Groups table cells into rows.
`title`	Gives a document a title. The content of the `fo:title` object can be formatted and displayed in the document.
`wrapper`	Indicates inherited properties for a group of formatting objects.

XSL Formatting Properties

The formatting objects in the previous section have properties that you can use to customize what they do. As we'll see in this chapter, a typical formatting object can support quite a few properties. Here are the current formatting properties that the W3C formatting objects specification supports—many of these properties are taken from and behave the same as in CSS, and you set lengths and other units exactly as you do in CSS (using units such as `px` for pixels, `pt` for points, `mm` for millimeters, `%` for percentages, and so on)—you can find more details at `www.w3.org/TR/xsl/sliceC.html#prtab1` and `www.w3.org/TR/xsl/sliceC.html#prtab2`:

- `absolute-position`
- `active-state`
- `alignment-adjust`
- `auto-restore`
- `azimuth`
- `background`
- `background-attachment`
- `background-color`
- `background-image`
- `background-position`
- `background-position-horizontal`
- `background-position-vertical`
- `background-repeat`
- `baseline-identifier`
- `baseline-shift`
- `blank-or-not-blank`
- `block-progression-dimension`
- `border`
- `border-after-color`
- `border-after-style`
- `border-after-width`
- `border-before-color`
- `border-before-style`
- `border-before-width`
- `border-bottom`
- `border-bottom-color`
- `border-bottom-style`
- `border-bottom-width`
- `border-collapse`
- `border-color`
- `border-end-color`
- `border-end-style`
- `border-end-width`
- `border-left`
- `border-left-color`
- `border-left-style`
- `border-left-width`
- `border-right`
- `border-right-color`
- `border-right-style`
- `border-right-width`
- `border-separation`
- `border-spacing`
- `border-start-color`

- border-start-style
- border-start-width
- border-style
- border-top
- border-top-color
- border-top-style
- border-top-width
- border-width
- bottom
- break-after
- break-before
- caption-side
- case-name
- case-title
- character
- clear
- clip
- color
- color-profile-name
- column-count
- column-gap
- column-number
- column-width
- content-height
- content-type
- content-width
- country
- cue
- cue-after
- cue-before
- destination-placement-offset
- direction
- display-align
- dominant-baseline
- elevation
- empty-cells
- end-indent
- ends-row
- extent
- external-destination
- float
- flow-name
- font
- font-family
- font-height-override-after
- font-height-override-before
- font-size
- font-size-adjust
- font-stretch
- font-style
- font-variant
- font-weight
- force-page-count
- format
- glyph-orientation-horizontal
- glyph-orientation-vertical
- grouping-separator
- grouping-size
- height
- hyphenate
- hyphenation-character
- hyphenation-keep
- hyphenation-ladder-count
- hyphenation-push-character-count

- hyphenation-remain-character-count
- id
- indicate-destination
- initial-page-number
- inline-progression-dimension
- internal-destination
- keep-together
- keep-with-next
- keep-with-previous
- language
- last-line-end-indent
- leader-alignment
- leader-length
- leader-pattern
- leader-pattern-width
- left
- letter-spacing
- letter-value
- linefeed-treatment
- line-height
- line-height-shift-adjustment
- line-stacking-strategy
- margin
- margin-bottom
- margin-left
- margin-right
- margin-top
- marker-class-name
- master-name
- max-height
- maximum-repeats
- max-width
- min-height
- min-width
- number-columns-repeated
- number-columns-spanned
- number-rows-spanned
- odd-or-even
- orphans
- overflow
- padding
- padding-after
- padding-before
- padding-bottom
- padding-end
- padding-left
- padding-right
- padding-start
- padding-top
- page-break-after
- page-break-before
- page-break-inside
- page-height
- page-position
- page-width
- pause
- pause-after
- pause-before
- pitch
- pitch-range
- play-during
- position
- precedence
- provisional-distance-between-starts

- provisional-label-separation
- reference-orientation
- ref-id
- region-name
- relative-align
- relative-position
- rendering-intent
- retrieve-boundary
- retrieve-class-name
- retrieve-position
- richness
- right
- role
- rule-style
- rule-thickness
- scaling
- scaling-method
- score-spaces
- script
- show-destination
- size
- source-document
- space-after
- space-before
- space-end
- space-start
- space-treatment
- span
- speak
- speak-header
- speak-numeral
- speak-punctuation
- speech-rate
- src
- start-indent
- starting-state
- starts-row
- stress
- suppress-at-line-break
- switch-to
- table-layout
- table-omit-footer-at-break
- table-omit-header-at-break
- text-align
- text-align-last
- text-decoration
- text-indent
- text-shadow
- text-transform
- top
- treat-as-word-space
- unicode-bidi
- vertical-align
- visibility
- voice-family
- volume
- white-space
- white-space-collapse
- widows
- width
- word-spacing
- wrap-option
- writing-mode
- xml:lang
- z-index

Working with Formatting Objects

This chapter is all about working with the XSL formatting objects, and I'll cover those objects in depth. Knowing how to use these objects is crucial to the whole formatting process because, even if you use a transformation style sheet to transform XML documents to formatting-object form, you still have to know how to create the style sheet to do so. By the end of this chapter, you'll have a solid idea of exactly how that works.

The first formatting object I'll cover is `fo:root`, the root object of any formatting object document.

The Document Root: *fo:root*

The `fo:root` object is the top node of the formatting object tree that makes up a formatting object document—that is, the document node of the formatting object document *must* be `fo:root`.

The children of the `fo:root` formatting object are a single `fo:layout-master-set` and a sequence of one or more `fo:page-sequences`. The `fo:layout-master-set` formatting object holds all "masters" used in the document, which you use to specify how each page will actually be built. Each `fo:page-sequence` represents a sequence of pages formatted the way you want them. For example, each chapter of a book could be made up of its own page sequence, and you can give each sequence the same header and footer, such as `Chapter 2: The Plot Thickens`.

In planets.xml, the document node is `<PLANETS>`; however, the document node of a formatting object document is `<fo:root>`, which means that we must replace `<PLANETS>` with `<fo:root>`. That looks like this in planets.xsl, the transformation style sheet:

```
<?xml version='1.0'?>
<xsl:stylesheet xmlns:xsl="http://www.w3.org/1999/XSL/Transform"
    xmlns:fo="http://www.w3.org/1999/XSL/Format"
    version='1.0'>

    <xsl:template match="PLANETS">
        <fo:root>
            .
            .
            .
```

The `fo:root` object can contain both master set layouts and page sequences. I'll take a look at the `fo:layout-master-set` object first.

The Master Set Layout: *fo:layout-master-set*

You use *masters* to create templates for pages, page sequences, and regions. The `fo:layout-master-set` object contain all the masters used in the document, including page sequence master objects, page master objects, and region master objects, which you apply to create page sequences, pages, and regions.

The name of each master ends in `-master` in XSL. For example, the page master that we'll use is the `simple-page-master` object. *Page masters* specify the subdivisions of a page and the geometry of these subdivisions. *Page sequence masters* specify the sequence of page masters that will be used to generate pages during the formatting.

You list the masters you want to use in the document in the `<fo:layout-master-set>` element, so I'll add that element to `planets.xsl` now:

```
<?xml version='1.0'?>
<xsl:stylesheet xmlns:xsl="http://www.w3.org/1999/XSL/Transform"
    xmlns:fo="http://www.w3.org/1999/XSL/Format"
    version='1.0'>

    <xsl:template match="PLANETS">
        <fo:root>

            <fo:layout-master-set>
    .
    .
    .
```

To configure each page, you use a page master; the one I'll use here is the `fo:simple-page-master` object.

Using a Page Master: *fo:simple-page-master*

A page master is a master template that is used to generate a page, and it specifies the actual layout of the page. You can use a page master whenever you want to in a document, and each page master has a unique name.

In the current XSL specification, there is only one kind of page-master, the `fo:simple-page-master` object (in the future, the XSL specification may support additional page masters). You use the `fo:simple-page-master` object to generate pages and define the geometry of the page.

To set the overall geometry of the page, you can use these properties of the `fo:simple-page-master` object:

- Common margin properties for blocks: `margin-top`, `margin-bottom`, `margin-left`, `margin-right`, `space-before`, `space-after`, `start-indent`, `end-indent`
- `master-name`
- `page-height`

- `page-width`
- `reference-orientation`
- `writing-mode`

In planets.xsl, I'll name the simple page master `"page"` using the `master-name` property; when I want to create pages using this master, I'll be able to refer to it by name. I'll also specify the page dimensions and margins like this:

```
<?xml version='1.0'?>
<xsl:stylesheet xmlns:xsl="http://www.w3.org/1999/XSL/Transform"
    xmlns:fo="http://www.w3.org/1999/XSL/Format"
    version='1.0'>

    <xsl:template match="PLANETS">
        <fo:root>

            <fo:layout-master-set>
                <fo:simple-page-master master-name="page"
                    page-height="400mm" page-width="300mm"
                    margin-top="10mm" margin-bottom="10mm"
                    margin-left="20mm" margin-right="20mm">
    .
    .
    .
```

Besides laying out the margins of a page, an `fo:simple-page-master` has children that specify one or more *regions* in the page, enabling you to customize the layout in detail.

Creating Regions

In version 1.0 of the XSL recommendation, page masters have up to five regions. The central region, which corresponds to the body of the page, is called the *body region*. The top part of the page, the header, is called the *before region*, the bottom part of the page, the footer, is called the *after region*. In languages that read left to right, such as English, the left side of the page is called the *start region*, and the right side is called the *end region*. In languages that read right to left, the start and end regions are reversed. You can think of start and end regions as sidebars that flank the body region.

Five XSL formatting objects correspond to these regions:

- `fo:region-before`
- `fo:region-after`
- `fo:region-body`
- `fo:region-start`
- `fo:region-end`

You can use these properties with these formatting objects:

- Common border, padding, and background properties: `background-attachment`, `background-color`, `background-image`, `background-repeat`, `background-position-horizontal`, `background-position-vertical`, `border-before-color`, `border-before-style`, `border-before-width`, `border-after-color`, `border-after-style`, `border-after-width`, `border-start-color`, `border-start-style`, `border-start-width`, `border-end-color`, `border-end-style`, `border-end-width`, `border-top-color`, `border-top-style`, `border-top-width`, `border-bottom-color`, `border-bottom-style`, `border-bottom-width`, `border-left-color`, `border-left-style`, `border-left-width`, `border-right-color`, `border-right-style`, `border-right-width`, `padding-before`, `padding-after`, `padding-start`, `padding-end`, `padding-top`, `padding-bottom`, `padding-left`, `padding-right`
- Common margin properties for blocks: `margin-top`, `margin-bottom`, `margin-left`, `margin-right`, `space-before`, `space-after`, `start-indent`, `end-indent`
- `clip`
- `column-count`
- `column-gap`
- `display-align`
- `extent`
- `overflow`
- `region-name`
- `reference-orientation`
- `writing-mode`

You can customize the regions of a page as you like, as in planets.xsl, where I'm setting margins for the body region. The four outer regions (but not the body region) have an `extent` property that sets the size of those regions, and I'll use that here:

```
<?xml version='1.0'?>
<xsl:stylesheet xmlns:xsl="http://www.w3.org/1999/XSL/Transform"
    xmlns:fo="http://www.w3.org/1999/XSL/Format"
    version='1.0'>

    <xsl:template match="PLANETS">
        <fo:root>

            <fo:layout-master-set>
                 <fo:simple-page-master master-name="page"
                     page-height="400mm" page-width="300mm"
                     margin-top="10mm" margin-bottom="10mm"
                     margin-left="20mm" margin-right="20mm">
```

```
            <fo:region-body
              margin-top="0mm" margin-bottom="10mm"
              margin-left="0mm" margin-right="0mm"/>

            <fo:region-after extent="10mm"/>
        </fo:simple-page-master>
    </fo:layout-master-set>
.
.
.
```

That ends the only master I'll have in this document, the simple page master named `"page"`, so that completes the `fo:layout-master-set` object.

As mentioned, besides the `fo:layout-master-set`, a formatting object document usually also contains one or more `fo:page-sequence` objects that define page sequences using the masters you define in the `fo:layout-master-set`.

Creating Page Sequences: *fo:page-sequence*

The pages in the output document are actually created when the XSL processor processes `fo:page-sequence` objects. A page sequence consists of a run of pages that share the same characteristics, such as a chapter in a book.

Each `fo:page-sequence` object references either an `fo:page-sequence-master` or a page master, and the actual layout of the pages is specified by those masters. You can get fairly involved here, creating sequences in which the page numbering alternates from side to side on the page, as when you're creating pages for a book.

These properties apply to the `fo:page-sequence` object:

- `country`
- `format`
- `language`
- `letter-value`
- `grouping-separator`
- `grouping-size`
- `id`
- `initial-page-number`
- `force-page-count`
- `master-name`

In the current W3C XSL recommendation, you specify what page master you want to use for a page sequence with the `<fo:page-sequence>` element's `master-name` attribute. I named the simple page master we created `"page"`, so I'll set that attribute to that name here. However, FOP is based on an earlier version of XSL and requires an `<fo:sequence-specification>` element—which is no longer supported in the XSL recommendation—to let you specify the page master. So, in addition to using the `master-name` attribute, I'll add an `<fo:sequence-specification>` element for FOP, enclosing an `<fo:sequence-specifier-single>` element, which also is no longer supported, and setting that element's `master-name` attribute to `"page"`. (For future XSL formatting processors that conform to the current XSL recommendation, remove the `<fo:sequence-specification>` and `<fo:sequence-specifier-single>` elements.)

```
<?xml version='1.0'?>
<xsl:stylesheet xmlns:xsl="http://www.w3.org/1999/XSL/Transform"
    xmlns:fo="http://www.w3.org/1999/XSL/Format"
    version='1.0'>

    <xsl:template match="PLANETS">
        <fo:root>

            <fo:layout-master-set>
                <fo:simple-page-master master-name="page"
                    page-height="400mm" page-width="300mm"
                    margin-top="10mm" margin-bottom="10mm"
                    margin-left="20mm" margin-right="20mm">

                    <fo:region-body
                      margin-top="0mm" margin-bottom="10mm"
                      margin-left="0mm" margin-right="0mm"/>

                    <fo:region-after extent="10mm"/>
                </fo:simple-page-master>
            </fo:layout-master-set>

            <fo:page-sequence master-name="page">

                <!-- Added for fop -->
                <fo:sequence-specification>
                    <fo:sequence-specifier-single master-name="page"/>
                </fo:sequence-specification>
                <!-- Added for fop -->
                .
                .
                .
```

That specifies what page master we want to use for a page sequence. Next, you must specify the *content* of the page sequence. The content of these pages comes from *flow* children of the `fo:page-sequence`.

Creating Flows: *fo:flow*

Flow objects are so called because the text in them "flows" and is arranged to fit the page by the displaying software. The content of a page is handled with flow objects.

Two kinds of flow objects exist: `fo:static-content` and `fo:flow`. An `fo:static-content` flow object holds content, such as the text that goes into headers and footers, that is repeated on the pages of the page sequence. The `fo:flow` flow object, on the other hand, holds the text itself that makes up the content of the document. The `fo:flow` object has a single property, `flow-name`.

I'll add a `fo:flow` object to `planets.xsl` to handle the text content of `planets.xml`. To make sure that the text content of `planets.xml` is transformed into that flow, I'll use an `<xsl:apply-templates>` element, which we first saw in the previous chapter. The `<xsl:apply-templates>` element will make the XSL processor process the various elements in planets.xml (note that I also add the declaration of the `xsl` namespace) and will insert them into the flow:

```
<?xml version='1.0'?>
<xsl:stylesheet xmlns:xsl="http://www.w3.org/1999/XSL/Transform"
    xmlns:fo="http://www.w3.org/1999/XSL/Format"
    version='1.0'>

    <xsl:template match="PLANETS">
        <fo:root>

            <fo:layout-master-set>
                 <fo:simple-page-master master-name="page"
                     page-height="400mm" page-width="300mm"
                     margin-top="10mm" margin-bottom="10mm"
                     margin-left="20mm" margin-right="20mm">

                     <fo:region-body
                       margin-top="0mm" margin-bottom="10mm"
                       margin-left="0mm" margin-right="0mm"/>

                     <fo:region-after extent="10mm"/>
                 </fo:simple-page-master>
             </fo:layout-master-set>

             <fo:page-sequence master-name="page">
                 <!-- Added for fop -->
                 <fo:sequence-specification>
                     <fo:sequence-specifier-single master-name="page"/>
```

continues ▸

```
            </fo:sequence-specification>
            <!-- Added for fop -->

            <fo:flow>
                <xsl:apply-templates/>
            </fo:flow>
        </fo:page-sequence>

    </fo:root>
</xsl:template>
.
.
.
```

That completes the `fo:page-sequence` object; we've specified a master to use for this sequence and provided the XSL processor a way to get the content that will go into the pages in the formatted document. Besides `fo:flow`, there's another flow object: `fo:static-content`.

Creating Static Content: *fo:static-content*

The `fo:static-content` formatting object holds formatting objects that are to be presented in a single region or repeated in regions on one or more pages in the page sequence. It is most often used to create repeating headers and footers because its content is repeated on every page to which it is assigned.

Like the `fo:flow` flow object, the `fo:static-content` formatting object has a single property, `flow-name`.

Creating Block-level Content: *fo:block*

You use blocks in XSL just as we did in CSS: to create a rectangular display area set off from other display areas in a document. You use the `fo:block` formatting object for formatting such items as paragraphs, titles, headlines, figure and table captions, and so on. Here's an example from the beginning of the chapter:

```
<fo:block font-family="sans-serif" line-height="48pt" font-size="36pt">
    Welcome to XSL formatting.
</fo:block>
```

You can use these properties with `fo:block`:

- Common accessibility properties: `source-document`, `role`
- Common aural properties: `azimuth`, `cue-after`, `cue-before`, `elevation`, `pause-after`, `pause-before`, `pitch`, `pitch-range`, `play-during`, `richness`, `speak`, `speak-header`, `speak-numeral`, `speak-punctuation`, `speech-rate`, `stress`, `voice-family`, `volume`

- Common border, padding, and background properties: `background-attachment`, `background-color`, `background-image`, `background-repeat`, `background-position-horizontal`, `background-position-vertical`, `border-before-color`, `border-before-style`, `border-before-width`, `border-after-color`, `border-after-style`, `border-after-width`, `border-start-color`, `border-start-style`, `border-start-width`, `border-end-color`, `border-end-style`, `border-end-width`, `border-top-color`, `border-top-style`, `border-top-width`, `border-bottom-color`, `border-bottom-style`, `border-bottom-width`, `border-left-color`, `border-left-style`, `border-left-width`, `border-right-color`, `border-right-style`, `border-right-width`, `padding-before`, `padding-after`, `padding-start`, `padding-end`, `padding-top`, `padding-bottom`, `padding-left`, `padding-right`
- Common font properties: `font-family`, `font-size`, `font-stretch`, `font-size-adjust`, `font-style`, `font-variant`, `font-weight`
- Common hyphenation properties: `country`, `language`, `script`, `hyphenate`, `hyphenation-character`, `hyphenation-push-character-count`, `hyphenation-remain-character-count`
- Common margin properties for blocks: `margin-top`, `margin-bottom`, `margin-left`, `margin-right`, `space-before`, `space-after`, `start-indent`, `end-indent`
- `break-after`
- `break-before`
- `color`
- `font-height-override-after`
- `font-height-override-before`
- `hyphenation-keep`
- `hyphenation-ladder-count`
- `id`
- `keep-together`
- `keep-with-next`
- `keep-with-previous`
- `last-line-end-indent`
- `linefeed-treatment`
- `line-height`
- `line-height-shift-adjustment`
- `line-stacking-strategy`

- orphans
- relative-position
- space-treatment
- span
- text-align
- text-align-last
- text-indent
- visibility
- white-space-collapse
- widows
- wrap-option
- z-index

Note that the data in planets.xml is broken up into various child elements of a <PLANET> element, such as <NAME>, <MASS>, and so on like this:

```
<PLANET COLOR="RED">
  <NAME>Mercury</NAME>
  <MASS UNITS="(Earth = 1)">.0553</MASS>
  <DAY UNITS="days">58.65</DAY>
  <RADIUS UNITS="miles">1516</RADIUS>
  <DENSITY UNITS="(Earth = 1)">.983</DENSITY>
  <DISTANCE UNITS="million miles">43.4</DISTANCE><!--At perihelion-->
</PLANET>
```

In this example, I'll give the data in each of the children of a <PLANET> element its own block in the formatted document. To do that, I add a rule to planets.xsl for each of those children, specifying the font to use for each block:

```
<?xml version='1.0'?>
<xsl:stylesheet xmlns:xsl="http://www.w3.org/1999/XSL/Transform"
    xmlns:fo="http://www.w3.org/1999/XSL/Format"
    version='1.0'>

    <xsl:template match="PLANETS">
        <fo:root>

            <fo:layout-master-set>
                <fo:simple-page-master master-name="page"
                    page-height="400mm" page-width="300mm"
                    margin-top="10mm" margin-bottom="10mm"
                    margin-left="20mm" margin-right="20mm">

                    <fo:region-body
                      margin-top="0mm" margin-bottom="10mm"
```

```
                    margin-left="0mm" margin-right="0mm"/>

                <fo:region-after extent="10mm"/>
            </fo:simple-page-master>
        </fo:layout-master-set>

        <fo:page-sequence master-name="page">

            <!-- Added for fop -->
            <fo:sequence-specification>
                <fo:sequence-specifier-single master-name="page"/>
            </fo:sequence-specification>
            <!-- Added for fop -->

            <fo:flow>
                <xsl:apply-templates/>
            </fo:flow>
        </fo:page-sequence>

    </fo:root>
</xsl:template>

<xsl:template match="PLANET/NAME">
    <fo:block font-weight="bold" font-size="36pt"
        line-height="48pt" font-family="sans-serif">
        Name:
        <xsl:apply-templates/>
    </fo:block>
</xsl:template>

<xsl:template match="PLANET/MASS">
    <fo:block font-size="36pt" line-height="48pt"
        font-family="sans-serif">
        Mass (Earth = 1):
        <xsl:apply-templates/>
    </fo:block>
</xsl:template>

<xsl:template match="PLANET/DAY">
    <fo:block font-size="36pt" line-height="48pt"
        font-family="sans-serif">
        Day (Earth = 1):
        <xsl:apply-templates/>
    </fo:block>
</xsl:template>

<xsl:template match="PLANET/RADIUS">
    <fo:block font-size="36pt" line-height="48pt"
        font-family="sans-serif">
        Radius (in miles):
        <xsl:apply-templates/>
    </fo:block>
```

continues ▸

```
    </xsl:template>

    <xsl:template match="PLANET/DENSITY">
        <fo:block font-size="36pt" line-height="48pt"
            font-family="sans-serif">
            Density (Earth = 1):
            <xsl:apply-templates/>
        </fo:block>
    </xsl:template>

    <xsl:template match="PLANET/DISTANCE">
        <fo:block font-size="36pt" line-height="48pt"
            font-family="sans-serif">
            Distance (million miles):
            <xsl:apply-templates/>
        </fo:block>
    </xsl:template>

</xsl:stylesheet>
```

And now we've handled all the elements in planets.xml, so that completes planets.xsl. You can see the results in Figure 14.2—congratulations, you've completed your first transformation to XSL formatting objects.

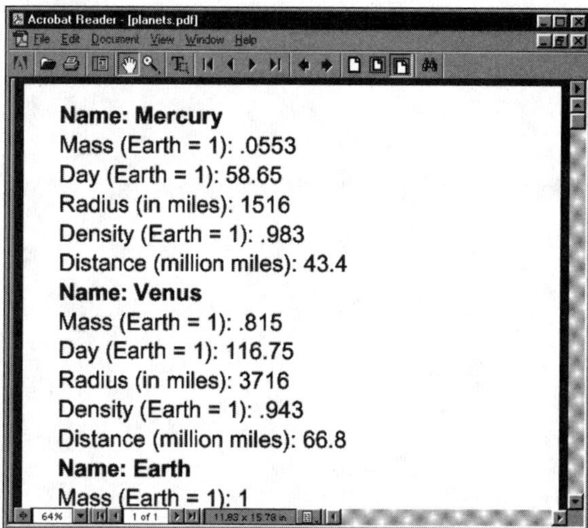

Figure 14.2 Using planets.xsl for formatting.

Inline-Level Formatting Objects

Besides block objects, you can also create *inline* objects. Inline objects are usually used to format part of the text as that text follows the normal flow in the page. For example, you can make the first character in a paragraph larger, make the whole first line smaller, insert page numbers into text, and so on.

Here are the inline formatting objects:

- `fo:bidi-override`
- `fo:character`
- `fo:initial-property-set`
- `fo:external-graphic`
- `fo:instream-foreign-object`
- `fo:inline`
- `fo:inline-container`
- `fo:leader`
- `fo:page-number`
- `fo:page-number-citation`

I'll take a look at a few of the more common of these objects next.

Using fo:character

The `fo:character` object enables you to handle the characters in a document individually, which is very useful if you want to write an XSL processor, but not necessarily that useful otherwise. You can use `fo:character` to replace characters with other characters. Here's an example; in this case, I'm matching an element named `<MASKED>` and replacing the characters in it with a hyphen (-):

```
<xsl:template match="MASKED">
    <fo:character character="-">
        <xsl:value-of select="."/>
    </fo:character>
</xsl:template>
```

You can use these properties with `fo:character`:

- Common aural properties: `azimuth`, `cue-after`, `cue-before`, `elevation`, `pause-after`, `pause-before`, `pitch`, `pitch-range`, `play-during`, `richness`, `speak`, `speak-header`, `speak-numeral`, `speak-punctuation`, `speech-rate`, `stress`, `voice-family`, `volume`
- Common border, padding, and background properties: `background-attachment`, `background-color`, `background-image`, `background-repeat`, `background-position-horizontal`, `background-position-vertical`, `border-before-color`, `border-before-style`, `border-before-width`, `border-after-color`, `border-after-style`, `border-after-width`, `border-start-color`, `border-start-style`, `border-start-width`, `border-end-color`, `border-end-style`, `border-end-width`, `border-top-color`, `border-top-style`, `border-top-width`, `border-bottom-color`,

border-bottom-style, border-bottom-width, border-left-color, border-left-style, border-left-width, border-right-color, border-right-style, border-right-width, padding-before, padding-after, padding-start, padding-end, padding-top, padding-bottom, padding-left, padding-right

- Common font properties: font-family, font-size, font-stretch, font-size-adjust, font-style, font-variant, font-weight
- Common hyphenation properties: country, language, script, hyphenate, hyphenation-character, hyphenation-push-character-count, hyphenation-remain-character-count
- Common margin properties–inline: space-end, space-start
- alignment-adjust
- treat-as-word-space
- baseline-identifier
- baseline-shift
- character
- color
- dominant-baseline
- font-height-override-after
- font-height-override-before
- glyph-orientation-horizontal
- glyph-orientation-vertical
- id
- keep-with-next
- keep-with-previous
- letter-spacing
- line-height
- line-height-shift-adjustment
- relative-position
- score-spaces
- suppress-at-line-break
- text-decoration
- text-shadow
- text-transform
- word-spacing

fo:initial-property-set

You can format the first line of an `fo:block` object with `fo:initial-property-set` (it's much like the CSS `first-line` pseudoelement). Here's an example where I'm setting the first line of a block in small caps:

```
<fo:block>
    <fo:initial-property-set font-variant="small-caps" />
    Here is the actual text of the paragraph; the first line,
    and only the first line, will be displayed in small caps.
</fo:block>
```

You can use these properties with `fo:initial-property-set`:

- Common accessibility properties: `source-document`, `role`
- Common aural properties: `azimuth`, `cue-after`, `cue-before`, `elevation`, `pause-after`, `pause-before`, `pitch`, `pitch-range`, `play-during`, `richness`, `speak`, `speak-header`, `speak-numeral`, `speak-punctuation`, `speech-rate`, `stress`, `voice-family`, `volume`
- Common border, padding, and background properties: `background-attachment`, `background-color`, `background-image`, `background-repeat`, `background-position-horizontal`, `background-position-vertical`, `border-before-color`, `border-before-style`, `border-before-width`, `border-after-color`, `border-after-style`, `border-after-width`, `border-start-color`, `border-start-style`, `border-start-width`, `border-end-color`, `border-end-style`, `border-end-width`, `border-top-color`, `border-top-style`, `border-top-width`, `border-bottom-color`, `border-bottom-style`, `border-bottom-width`, `border-left-color`, `border-left-style`, `border-left-width`, `border-right-color`, `border-right-style`, `border-right-width`, `padding-before`, `padding-after`, `padding-start`, `padding-end`, `padding-top`, `padding-bottom`, `padding-left`, `padding-right`
- Common font properties: `font-family`, `font-size`, `font-stretch`, `font-size-adjust`, `font-style`, `font-variant`, `font-weight`
- `color`
- `id`
- `letter-spacing`
- `line-height`
- `line-height-shift-adjustment`
- `relative-position`
- `score-spaces`
- `text-decoration`
- `text-shadow`
- `text-transform`
- `word-spacing`

Adding Graphics: fo:external-graphic

Another inline formatting object that is available is `fo:external-graphic`, which you use to embed an image in a document. (Unfortunately, `fo:external-graphic` is not supported by FOP yet.)

You can set the size of the image in the document with the `content-height`, `content-width`, and `scaling` properties; if you don't set these properties, the image is displayed in its original size. Here's an example displaying an image and a caption:

```
<?xml version="1.0" encoding="UTF-8"?>
<fo:root xmlns:fo="http://www.w3.org/1999/XSL/Format">

    <fo:layout-master-set>
        <fo:simple-page-master margin-right="20mm"
            margin-left="20mm" margin-bottom="10mm"
            margin-top="10mm" page-width="300mm"
            page-height="400mm" master-name="page">

            <fo:region-body margin-right="0mm"
                margin-left="0mm" margin-bottom="10mm"
                margin-top="0mm"/>

         <fo:region-after extent="10mm"/>

        </fo:simple-page-master>
    </fo:layout-master-set>

    <fo:page-sequence master-name="page">

        <!-- Added for fop -->
        <fo:sequence-specification>
            <fo:sequence-specifier-single master-name="page"/>
        </fo:sequence-specification>
        <!-- Added for fop -->

        <fo:flow>

            <fo:block>
                <fo:external-graphic src="alps15.jpg"/>
            </fo:block>

            <fo:block space-before="10pt" start-indent="10mm"
                end-indent="0mm">
                A view of the Austrian Alps near Wolfgang See
            </fo:block>

        </fo:flow>
    </fo:page-sequence>
</fo:root>
```

You can use these properties with `fo:external-graphic`:

- Common accessibility properties: `source-document`, `role`
- Common aural properties: `azimuth`, `cue-after`, `cue-before`, `elevation`, `pause-after`, `pause-before`, `pitch`, `pitch-range`, `play-during`, `richness`, `speak`, `speak-header`, `speak-numeral`, `speak-punctuation`, `speech-rate`, `stress`, `voice-family`, `volume`
- Common border, padding, and background properties: `background-attachment`, `background-color`, `background-image`, `background-repeat`, `background-position-horizontal`, `background-position-vertical`, `border-before-color`, `border-before-style`, `border-before-width`, `border-after-color`, `border-after-style`, `border-after-width`, `border-start-color`, `border-start-style`, `border-start-width`, `border-end-color`, `border-end-style`, `border-end-width`, `border-top-color`, `border-top-style`, `border-top-width`, `border-bottom-color`, `border-bottom-style`, `border-bottom-width`, `border-left-color`, `border-left-style`, `border-left-width`, `border-right-color`, `border-right-style`, `border-right-width`, `padding-before`, `padding-after`, `padding-start`, `padding-end`, `padding-top`, `padding-bottom`, `padding-left`, `padding-right`
- Common margin properties–inline: `space-end`, `space-start`
- `alignment-adjust`
- `baseline-identifier`
- `baseline-shift`
- `block-progression-dimension`
- `content-height`
- `content-type`
- `content-width`
- `dominant-baseline`
- `height`
- `id`
- `inline-progression-dimension`
- `keep-with-next`
- `keep-with-previous`
- `line-height`
- `line-height-shift-adjustment`
- `relative-position`

- overflow
- scaling
- scaling-method
- src
- width

The Inline Formatting Object: fo:inline

You can use the fo:inline formatting object to format a part of your text with a background or surround it with a border. This object is fairly general and lets you format an inline area almost as though it were a block.

You can use these properties with fo:inline:

- Common accessibility properties: source-document, role
- Common aural properties: azimuth, cue-after, cue-before, elevation, pause-after, pause-before, pitch, pitch-range, play-during, richness, speak, speak-header, speak-numeral, speak-punctuation, speech-rate, stress, voice-family, volume
- Common border, padding, and background properties: background-attachment, background-color, background-image, background-repeat, background-position-horizontal, background-position-vertical, border-before-color, border-before-style, border-before-width, border-after-color, border-after-style, border-after-width, border-start-color, border-start-style, border-start-width, border-end-color, border-end-style, border-end-width, border-top-color, border-top-style, border-top-width, border-bottom-color, border-bottom-style, border-bottom-width, border-left-color, border-left-style, border-left-width, border-right-color, border-right-style, border-right-width, padding-before, padding-after, padding-start, padding-end, padding-top, padding-bottom, padding-left, padding-right
- Common font properties: font-family, font-size, font-stretch, font-size-adjust, font-style, font-variant, font-weight
- Common margin properties–inline: space-end, space-start
- alignment-adjust
- baseline-identifier
- baseline-shift
- color
- dominant-baseline
- id

- keep-together
- keep-with-next
- keep-with-previous
- line-height
- line-height-shift-adjustment
- relative-position
- text-decoration
- visibility
- z-index

Creating Page Numbers: fo:page-number

Another useful inline formatting object is fo:page-number, which creates an inline area displaying the current page number. Here's an example:

```
<fo:block>
    <xsl:text>This is page </xsl:text><fo:page-number/>.
</fo:block>
```

You can use these properties with fo:page-number:

- Common accessibility properties: source-document, role
- Common aural properties: azimuth, cue-after, cue-before, elevation, pause-after, pause-before, pitch, pitch-range, play-during, richness, speak, speak-header, speak-numeral, speak-punctuation, speech-rate, stress, voice-family, volume
- Common border, padding, and background properties: background-attachment, background-color, background-image, background-repeat, background-position-horizontal, background-position-vertical, border-before-color, border-before-style, border-before-width, border-after-color, border-after-style, border-after-width, border-start-color, border-start-style, border-start-width, border-end-color, border-end-style, border-end-width, border-top-color, border-top-style, border-top-width, border-bottom-color, border-bottom-style, border-bottom-width, border-left-color, border-left-style, border-left-width, border-right-color, border-right-style, border-right-width, padding-before, padding-after, padding-start, padding-end, padding-top, padding-bottom, padding-left, padding-right
- Common font properties: font-family, font-size, font-stretch, font-size-adjust, font-style, font-variant, font-weight
- Common margin properties–inline: space-end, space-start

- `alignment-adjust`
- `baseline-identifier`
- `baseline-shift`
- `dominant-baseline`
- `id`
- `keep-with-next`
- `keep-with-previous`
- `letter-spacing`
- `line-height`
- `line-height-shift-adjustment`
- `relative-position`
- `score-spaces`
- `text-decoration`
- `text-shadow`
- `text-transform`
- `word-spacing`

Creating Tables

Some of the most useful constructs you can format with XSL are tables. A table in XSL is much like one in HTML—a rectangular grid of rows and columns of cells. You can use nine formatting objects to create tables:

- `fo:table-and-caption`
- `fo:table`
- `fo:table-column`
- `fo:table-caption`
- `fo:table-header`
- `fo:table-footer`
- `fo:table-body`
- `fo:table-row`
- `fo:table-cell`

Creating tables is a little involved in XSL. You create a `fo:table object`, format each column with an `fo:table-column` object, and then create a `table-body object`, as well as `table-row` objects for each row and `table-cell` objects for each cell in each row. Here's an example creating a 3 × 3 table with the words `Tic`, `Tac`, and `Toe` repeated on each line:

```
<?xml version="1.0" encoding="UTF-8"?>
<fo:root xmlns:fo="http://www.w3.org/1999/XSL/Format">
    <fo:layout-master-set>
        <fo:simple-page-master margin-right="20mm"
            margin-left="20mm" margin-bottom="20mm"
            margin-top="20mm" page-width="300mm"
            page-height="400mm" master-name="page">

            <fo:region-body margin-right="0mm" margin-left="0mm"
                margin-bottom="20mm" margin-top="0mm"/>

            <fo:region-after extent="20mm"/>

        </fo:simple-page-master>
    </fo:layout-master-set>

    <fo:page-sequence master-name="page">

        <!-- Added for fop -->
        <fo:sequence-specification>
            <fo:sequence-specifier-single master-name="page"/>
        </fo:sequence-specification>
        <!-- Added for fop -->

        <fo:flow>
            <fo:table width="12cm" table-layout="fixed">
                <fo:table-column column-number="1" column-width="25mm">
                </fo:table-column>
                <fo:table-column column-number="2" column-width="25mm">
                </fo:table-column>
                <fo:table-column column-number="3" column-width="25mm">
                </fo:table-column>
                <fo:table-body>
                     <fo:table-row line-height="20mm">
                         <fo:table-cell column-number="1">
                             <fo:block font-family="sans-serif"
                                 font-size="36pt">
                                 Tic
                             </fo:block>
                         </fo:table-cell>
                         <fo:table-cell column-number="2">
                             <fo:block font-family="sans-serif"
                                 font-size="36pt">
                                 Tac
                             </fo:block>
```

continues ▸

```
                    </fo:table-cell>
                    <fo:table-cell column-number="3">
                        <fo:block font-family="sans-serif"
                            font-size="36pt">
                            Toe
                        </fo:block>
                    </fo:table-cell>
                </fo:table-row>
                <fo:table-row line-height="20mm">
                    <fo:table-cell column-number="1">
                        <fo:block font-family="sans-serif"
                            font-size="36pt">
                            Tic
                        </fo:block>
                    </fo:table-cell>
                    <fo:table-cell column-number="2">
                        <fo:block font-family="sans-serif"
                            font-size="36pt">
                            Tac
                        </fo:block>
                    </fo:table-cell>
                    <fo:table-cell column-number="3">
                        <fo:block font-family="sans-serif"
                            font-size="36pt">
                            Toe
                        </fo:block>
                    </fo:table-cell>
                </fo:table-row>
                <fo:table-row line-height="20mm">
                    <fo:table-cell column-number="1">
                        <fo:block font-family="sans-serif"
                            font-size="36pt">
                            Tic
                        </fo:block>
                    </fo:table-cell>
                    <fo:table-cell column-number="2">
                        <fo:block font-family="sans-serif"
                            font-size="36pt">
                            Tac
                        </fo:block>
                    </fo:table-cell>
                    <fo:table-cell column-number="3">
                        <fo:block font-family="sans-serif"
                            font-size="36pt">
                            Toe
                        </fo:block>
                    </fo:table-cell>
                </fo:table-row>
            </fo:table-body>
        </fo:table>
    </fo:flow>
  </fo:page-sequence>
</fo:root>
```

After running this file, `table.fo`, through FOP and creating `table.pdf`, you can see the result in Figure 14.3.

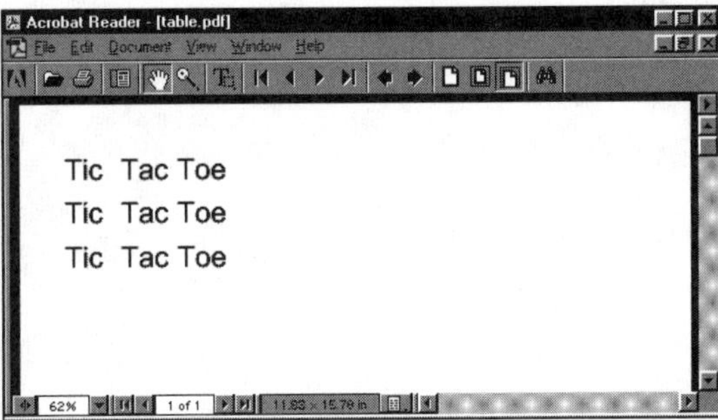

Figure 14.3 An XSL formatted table in Adobe Acrobat.

I'll now take a look at the various objects you use to create tables.

fo:table

You use the `fo:table` object to create a new table. The table itself consists of an optional header, an optional footer, and one or more table bodies. The actual grid of cells, arranged into rows and columns, appears in a table body.

You can use these properties with the `fo:table` object:

- Common accessibility properties: `source-document`, `role`
- Common aural properties: `azimuth`, `cue-after`, `cue-before`, `elevation`, `pause-after`, `pause-before`, `pitch`, `pitch-range`, `play-during`, `richness`, `speak`, `speak-header`, `speak-numeral`, `speak-punctuation`, `speech-rate`, `stress`, `voice-family`, `volume`
- Common border, padding, and background properties: `background-attachment`, `background-color`, `background-image`, `background-repeat`, `background-position-horizontal`, `background-position-vertical`, `border-before-color`, `border-before-style`, `border-before-width`, `border-after-color`, `border-after-style`, `border-after-width`, `border-start-color`, `border-start-style`, `border-start-width`, `border-end-color`, `border-end-style`, `border-end-width`, `border-top-color`, `border-top-style`, `border-top-width`, `border-bottom-color`, `border-bottom-style`, `border-bottom-width`, `border-left-color`, `border-left-style`, `border-left-width`, `border-right-color`, `border-right-style`, `border-right-width`, `padding-before`, `padding-after`, `padding-start`, `padding-end`, `padding-top`, `padding-bottom`, `padding-left`, `padding-right`
- Common margin properties–block: `margin-top`, `margin-bottom`, `margin-left`, `margin-right`, `space-before`, `space-after`, `start-indent`, `end-indent`

- block-progression-dimension
- border-collapse
- border-separation
- break-after
- break-before
- id
- inline-progression-dimension
- height
- keep-together
- keep-with-next
- keep-with-previous
- relative-position
- table-layout
- table-omit-footer-at-break
- table-omit-header-at-break
- width
- writing-mode

fo:table-column

You can use the `fo:table-column` formatting object to indicate characteristics that apply to table cells that have the same column. Probably the most important property here is the `column-width` property, which you use to set the width of each column.

You can use these properties with the `fo:table-column` object:

- Common border, padding, and background properties: background-attachment, background-color, background-image, background-repeat, background-position-horizontal, background-position-vertical, border-before-color, border-before-style, border-before-width, border-after-color, border-after-style, border-after-width, border-start-color, border-start-style, border-start-width, border-end-color, border-end-style, border-end-width, border-top-color, border-top-style, border-top-width, border-bottom-color, border-bottom-style, border-bottom-width, border-left-color, border-left-style, border-left-width, border-right-color, border-right-style, border-right-width, padding-before, padding-after, padding-start, padding-end, padding-top, padding-bottom, padding-left, padding-right

- column-number
- column-width
- number-columns-repeated
- number-columns-spanned
- visibility

fo:table-body

The actual content of tables appears in fo:table-body objects. The object is the one that contains the actual fo:table-row objects, which, in turn, contain the fo:table-cell objects that hold the data for the table.

You can use these properties with the fo:table-body object:

- Common border, padding, and background properties: background-attachment, background-color, background-image, background-repeat, background-position-horizontal, background-position-vertical, border-before-color, border-before-style, border-before-width, border-after-color, border-after-style, border-after-width, border-start-color, border-start-style, border-start-width, border-end-color, border-end-style, border-end-width, border-top-color, border-top-style, border-top-width, border-bottom-color, border-bottom-style, border-bottom-width, border-left-color, border-left-style, border-left-width, border-right-color, border-right-style, border-right-width, padding-before, padding-after, padding-start, padding-end, padding-top, padding-bottom, padding-left, padding-right
- id
- relative-position

fo:table-row

You use the fo:table-row object is used to group table cells into rows. The XSL processor determines the dimensions of the table by how many rows you've added to the table.

You can use these properties with the fo:table-row object:

- Common accessibility properties: source-document, role
- Common aural properties: azimuth, cue-after, cue-before, elevation, pause-after, pause-before, pitch, pitch-range, play-during, richness, speak, speak-header, speak-numeral, speak-punctuation, speech-rate, stress, voice-family, volume

- Common border, padding, and background properties: background-attachment, background-color, background-image, background-repeat, background-position-horizontal, background-position-vertical, border-before-color, border-before-style, border-before-width, border-after-color, border-after-style, border-after-width, border-start-color, border-start-style, border-start-width, border-end-color, border-end-style, border-end-width, border-top-color, border-top-style, border-top-width, border-bottom-color, border-bottom-style, border-bottom-width, border-left-color, border-left-style, border-left-width, border-right-color, border-right-style, border-right-width, padding-before, padding-after, padding-start, padding-end, padding-top, padding-bottom, padding-left, padding-right
- block-progression-dimension
- break-after
- break-before
- id
- height
- keep-together
- keep-with-next
- keep-with-previous
- relative-position

fo:table-cell

You place the content for each cell in an `fo:table-cell` object. To specify the font and other characteristics of that content, you can enclose an `fo:block` object inside each `fo:table-cell` object. You can connect a table cell with a table column using the `column-number` property.

You can use these properties with the `fo:table-cell` object:

- Common accessibility properties: source-document, role
- Common aural properties: azimuth, cue-after, cue-before, elevation, pause-after, pause-before, pitch, pitch-range, play-during, richness, speak, speak-header, speak-numeral, speak-punctuation, speech-rate, stress, voice-family, volume
- Common border, padding, and background properties: background-attachment, background-color, background-image, background-repeat, background-position-horizontal, background-position-vertical, border-before-color, border-before-style,

border-before-width, border-after-color, border-after-style, border-after-width, border-start-color, border-start-style, border-start-width, border-end-color, border-end-style, border-end-width, border-top-color, border-top-style, border-top-width, border-bottom-color, border-bottom-style, border-bottom-width, border-left-color, border-left-style, border-left-width, border-right-color, border-right-style, border-right-width, padding-before, padding-after, padding-start, padding-end, padding-top, padding-bottom, padding-left, padding-right

- block-progression-dimension
- column-number
- display-align
- empty-cells
- ends-row
- height
- id
- number-columns-spanned
- number-rows-spanned
- relative-align
- relative-position
- starts-row
- width

Creating Lists

Besides tables, another XSL construct that is very close to the corresponding construct in HTML are lists. An XSL list presents a vertical arrangement of items, just as in HTML. You use four formatting objects to construct lists:

- fo:list-block
- fo:list-item
- fo:list-item-label
- fo:list-item-body

You enclose the whole list in an `fo:list-block` object, and you enclose each item in the list in an `fo:list-item` object. To create a label for the list item, you use an `fo:list-item-label` object; to insert the actual data for each list item, you use an `fo:list-item-body` object.

Here's an example creating a numbered list with three list items: `Tic`, `Tac`, and `Toe`:

```
<?xml version="1.0" encoding="UTF-8"?>
<fo:root xmlns:fo="http://www.w3.org/1999/XSL/Format">
    <fo:layout-master-set>
        <fo:simple-page-master margin-right="20mm" margin-left="20mm"
            margin-bottom="10mm" margin-top="10mm" page-width="300mm"
            page-height="400mm" master-name="page">

            <fo:region-body margin-right="0mm" margin-left="0mm"
            margin-bottom="10mm" margin-top="0mm"/>

            <fo:region-after extent="10mm"/>
        </fo:simple-page-master>
    </fo:layout-master-set>

    <fo:page-sequence master-name="page">
        <!-- Added for fop -->
        <fo:sequence-specification>
            <fo:sequence-specifier-single master-name="page"/>
        </fo:sequence-specification>
        <!-- Added for fop -->

        <fo:flow>
            <fo:list-block
                provisional-distance-between-starts="15mm"
                provisional-label-separation="5mm">

                 <fo:list-item line-height="20mm">
                    <fo:list-item-label>
                        <fo:block font-family="sans-serif"
                            font-size="36pt">
                            1.
                        </fo:block>
                    </fo:list-item-label>
                    <fo:list-item-body>
                        <fo:block font-family="sans-serif"
                            font-size="36pt">
                            Tic.
                        </fo:block>
                    </fo:list-item-body>
                </fo:list-item>
                <fo:list-item line-height="20mm">
                    <fo:list-item-label>
                        <fo:block font-family="sans-serif"
                            font-size="36pt">
                            2.
                        </fo:block>
                    </fo:list-item-label>
                    <fo:list-item-body>
                        <fo:block font-family="sans-serif"
```

```
                        font-size="36pt">
                        Tac.
                    </fo:block>
                </fo:list-item-body>
            </fo:list-item>
             <fo:list-item line-height="20mm">
                <fo:list-item-label>
                    <fo:block font-family="sans-serif"
                        font-size="36pt">
                        3.
                    </fo:block>
                </fo:list-item-label>
                <fo:list-item-body>
                    <fo:block font-family="sans-serif"
                        font-size="36pt">
                        Toe.
                    </fo:block>
                </fo:list-item-body>
            </fo:list-item>
        </fo:list-block>
    </fo:flow>
</fo:page-sequence>
</fo:root>
```

You can see the resulting PDF file displayed in the Adobe Acrobat in Figure 14.4, showing the list.

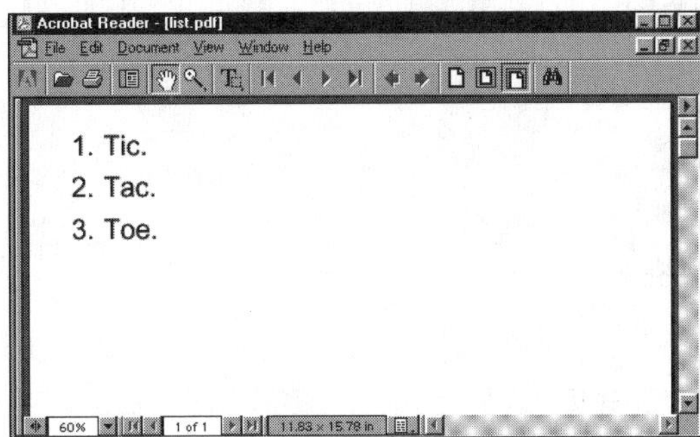

Figure 14.4 An XSL formatted list in Adobe Acrobat.

I'll take a look at the list formatting objects in more detail now.

fo:list-block

You use `fo:list-block` to format a list; this object encloses `fo:list-item` objects.

You can use these properties with the `fo:list-block` object:

- Common accessibility properties: `source-document`, `role`
- Common aural properties: `azimuth`, `cue-after`, `cue-before`, `elevation`, `pause-after`, `pause-before`, `pitch`, `pitch-range`, `play-during`, `richness`, `speak`, `speak-header`, `speak-numeral`, `speak-punctuation`, `speech-rate`, `stress`, `voice-family`, `volume`
- Common border, padding, and background properties: `background-attachment`, `background-color`, `background-image`, `background-repeat`, `background-position-horizontal`, `background-position-vertical`, `border-before-color`, `border-before-style`, `border-before-width`, `border-after-color`, `border-after-style`, `border-after-width`, `border-start-color`, `border-start-style`, `border-start-width`, `border-end-color`, `border-end-style`, `border-end-width`, `border-top-color`, `border-top-style`, `border-top-width`, `border-bottom-color`, `border-bottom-style`, `border-bottom-width`, `border-left-color`, `border-left-style`, `border-left-width`, `border-right-color`, `border-right-style`, `border-right-width`, `padding-before`, `padding-after`, `padding-start`, `padding-end`, `padding-top`, `padding-bottom`, `padding-left`, `padding-right`
- Common margin properties-block: `margin-top`, `margin-bottom`, `margin-left`, `margin-right`, `space-before`, `space-after`, `start-indent`, `end-indent`
- `break-after`
- `break-before`
- `id`
- `keep-together`
- `keep-with-next`
- `keep-with-previous`
- `provisional-distance-between-starts`
- `provisional-label-separation`
- `relative-position`

fo:list-item

You use a `fo:list-item` object to contain the label and the body of an item in a list.

You can use these properties with the `fo:list-item` object:

- Common accessibility properties: `source-document`, `role`
- Common aural properties: `azimuth`, `cue-after`, `cue-before`, `elevation`, `pause-after`, `pause-before`, `pitch`, `pitch-range`, `play-during`, `richness`, `speak`, `speak-header`, `speak-numeral`, `speak-punctuation`, `speech-rate`, `stress`, `voice-family`, `volume`
- Common border, padding, and background properties: `background-attachment`, `background-color`, `background-image`, `background-repeat`, `background-position-horizontal`, `background-position-vertical`, `border-before-color`, `border-before-style`, `border-before-width`, `border-after-color`, `border-after-style`, `border-after-width`, `border-start-color`, `border-start-style`, `border-start-width`, `border-end-color`, `border-end-style`, `border-end-width`, `border-top-color`, `border-top-style`, `border-top-width`, `border-bottom-color`, `border-bottom-style`, `border-bottom-width`, `border-left-color`, `border-left-style`, `border-left-width`, `border-right-color`, `border-right-style`, `border-right-width`, `padding-before`, `padding-after`, `padding-start`, `padding-end`, `padding-top`, `padding-bottom`, `padding-left`, `padding-right`
- Common margin properties–block: `margin-top`, `margin-bottom`, `margin-left`, `margin-right`, `space-before`, `space-after`, `start-indent`, `end-indent`
- `break-after`
- `break-before`
- `id`
- `keep-together`
- `keep-with-next`
- `keep-with-previous`
- `relative-align`
- `relative-position`

fo:list-item-label

You use the `fo:list-item-label` object to hold the label of a list item, usually to enumerate or decorate (as with a bullet) the body of the list item.

You can use these properties with the `fo:list-item-label` object:

- Common accessibility properties: `source-document`, `role`
- `id`
- `keep-together`

fo:list-item-body

You use the `fo:list-item-body` object to hold the actual body of a list item. To format the item's body the way you want it, you can enclose an `fo:block` object in an `fo:list-item-body` object.

You can use these properties with the `fo:list-item-body` object:

- Common accessibility properties: `source-document`, `role`
- `id`
- `keep-together`

As you can see, there's a lot to XSL formatting objects; in fact, there's a lot more that we don't have the space to cover here. For more details, take a look at the W3C site. Not a lot of software packages can put formatting objects to work yet, but that should change in the future.

In the next chapter, I'm going to start taking an in-depth look at another important part of the XML specification—XLinks and XPointers.

15
XLinks and XPointers

THIS CHAPTER IS ALL ABOUT CREATING CONNECTIONS BETWEEN documents and parts of documents—the XLink and XPointer specifications. In HTML, you have hyperlinks, but XML has gone far beyond that, using the XLink, XPointer, XPath, and XBase specifications.

Unfortunately, this is another area of XML where the W3C is far ahead of the rest of the world. There are no concrete implementations of any of these specifications yet. Microsoft, which has been burned many times by implementing XML standards that have then changed, is just beginning to add support for XLinks and XPointers to Internet Explorer. Certainly, we'll see all these specifications implemented in future software, but for now, most of the material in this chapter is waiting for actual implementations.

Overview: Linking with XLinks and XPointers

XLinks specify how one document links to another document. XPointers specify locations inside a document, building on the XPath recommendation that we covered in Chapter 13, "XSL Transformations." I'll take a look at an overview now.

As of this writing, the XLink specification is a W3C working draft, released on February 21, 2000. You can find the most current version of this specification at `www.w3.org/TR/xlink`. You use XLinks to link one document to another. Here's what W3C says in the W3C working draft:

> *This specification defines the XML Linking Language (XLink), which allows elements to be inserted into XML documents in order to create and describe links between resources. It uses XML syntax to create structures that can describe the simple unidirectional hyperlinks of today's HTML, as well as more sophisticated links.*

Here's an example to give you an idea what an XLink looks like. Unlike HTML hyperlinks, any element can be a link in XML. You specify that an element is a link with the attribute `xlink:type` like this, where I'm creating a simple XLink:

```
<MOVIE_REVIEW xmlns:xlink = "http://www.w3.org/1999/xlink"
    xlink:type = "simple"
    xlink:show = "new"
    xlink:href = "http://www.starpowdermovies.com/reviews.xml">
    Mr. Blandings Builds His Dream House
</MOVIE_REVIEW>
```

In this case, I'm creating a simple XLink, which is much like an HTML hyperlink, by setting the `xlink:type` attribute to `"simple"`. I'm also setting the `xlink:show` attribute to `"new"`, which means that XLink-aware software should open the linked-to document in a new window or other display context. I'm also setting the `xlink:href` attribute to the URI of the new document (which can be quite general and need not be in the URL form I've used here).

For the sake of familiarity, I'm starting with a simple XLink because it's much like an HTML link (although XLinks can become quite involved, as we'll see in this chapter). Besides basic unidirectional links, such as the simple link I've created here, you can also create bidirectional links as well as links between many documents and even document sets. In addition, you can do much more, including storing your links in link databases called *linkbases*.

XLinks let you link to a particular document, but you often need to be more precise than that. XPointers let you point to specific locations inside a document—without having to modify that document by embedding special tags or markers.

To point to a specific location in a document, the XPointer specification builds on the XPath specification. As you recall, we covered the XPath specification in Chapter 13; it let you identify specific nodes in a document with expressions like this:

```
/child::*[position()=126]/child::*[position()=first()]
```

XPointers are now in the W3C candidate recommendation stage. As of this writing, the current document is as of June 7, 2000; you can find the most current version of this specification at www.w3.org/TR/xptr. Here's what W3C says about XPointers:

> *This specification defines the XML Pointer Language (XPointer), the language to be used as a fragment identifier for any URI-reference that locates a resource of Internet media type text/xml or application/xml. XPointer, which is based on the XML Path Language (XPath), supports addressing into the internal structures of XML documents. It allows for traversals of a document tree and choice of its internal parts based on various properties, such as element types, attribute values, character content, and relative position.*

Although XPointers are built on the XPath specification (which you'll find covered in Chapter 13 and at www.w3.org/TR/xpath), the XPointer specification extends XPaths in ways that we'll see in this chapter.

How do you add an XPointer to a document's URI to identify a specific location in a document? You just append # (following the HTML usage for URLs that specify link targets) and then xpointer(), placing the XPath expression you want to use in the parentheses. Here's an example:

```
<MOVIE_REVIEW xmlns:xlink = "http://www.w3.org/1999/xlink"
    xlink:type = "simple"
    xlink:show = "new"
    xlink:href = "http://www.starpowdermovies.com/reviews.xml#
        xpointer(/child::*[position()=126]/child::*[position()=first()])">
    Mr. Blandings Builds His Dream House
</MOVIE_REVIEW>
```

That gives us an overview of XLinks and XPointers. I'm going to cover both these specifications in this chapter, as well as the XBase specification, starting now with XLinks.

XML Volatility

As in most areas of XML not bound by W3C recommendations, it's important to realize that the XLink, XPointer, and XBase specifications are subject to change. They've been around for a while and are close to becoming candidate recommendations, so things shouldn't change much from what you see in this chapter. However, bear in mind that things can change—when software implementations of these specifications appear, those implementations may also vary from the specifications in significant ways. It's the same old story once again—watch out for standards that change under your feet.

All About XLinks

Hyperlinks have long been an important part of HTML, and you create them with the HTML `<A>` element, like this:

```
<A HREF = "http://www.starpowdermovies.com/reviews.html#blandings">
    Mr. Blandings Builds His Dream House
<A>
```

The hyperlink appears in an HTML document either as text—typically underlined and colored—or as a clickable image. When clicked, the hyperlink can perform a variety of actions: navigating to a new document, as well as a specific location in that document; opening the new document in an existing frame or even a new window if you use the `TARGET` attribute; or executing JavaScript if you use the `javascript:` URL. Table 15.1 lists the official HTML attributes for the `<A>` element:

Table 15.1 **Official HTML Attributes for the <*A*> Element**

Attribute	Description
ACCESSKEY	Assigns a keyboard shortcut to the hyperlink.
CHARSET	Specifies the character encoding of the target of the hyperlink. You set this to a RFC 2045 language character set string (the default value is `ISO-8859-1`).
CLASS	Gives the style class of the element.
COORDS	Sets the coordinate values (in pixels) appropriate to the accompanying `SHAPE` attribute to define a region of an image for image maps.
DIR	Gives the direction of directionally neutral text. Set it to `LTR` for left-to-right text, or `RTL` for right-to-left text.
HREF	Holds the target URL of the hyperlink. Either this attribute or the `NAME` attribute must be used.
HREFLANG	Specifies the base language of the target indicated in the `HREF` attribute. Set this to RFC 1766 values.
ID	Gives a unique identifier for the tag.
LANG	Serves as the base language used for the tag.
NAME	Set this to an anchor name, the name you want to use to refer to the enclosed items (such as text, images, and so on). Either this attribute or the `HREF` attribute must be used.
REL	Specifies the relationship described by the hyperlink.
REV	Essentially is the same as the `REL` attribute, but the syntax works in the reverse direction.

Attribute	Description
SHAPE	Defines the type of region to be defined for mapping in an HTML AREA tag.
STYLE	Is the inline style indicating how to render the element.
TABINDEX	Sets the tab sequence of hyperlinks in the page.
TARGET	Indicates the named frame for the HREF hyperlink to jump to. Set this to the name of a frame.
TITLE	Holds title information for the element.
TYPE	Specifies the MIME type of the target given in the HREF attribute.

There's a lot of functionality here, but it all relies on the <A> element and the simplest type of hyperlink—one that waits to be clicked and then navigates to a new document or document location.

Relationships between documents can be far more complex than that. For example, you might want to do one or more of the following:

- Set up a link to point to 10 mirror sites of a main site, and let the browser select the one that's closest.
- Link to an entire set of documents, complete with subsets, that the browser should search for the resource you want.
- Set up a series of paths that lets the user navigate between a set of documents in various directions, but not in others.

And so on. XLinks let you perform all these kinds of linking.

XLinks are not restricted to any one element like the <A> element, which is to say that XLinks may not always appear in your documents in the traditional blue, underlined text (although, of course, they could, if you wanted them that way). Being able to make any element into an XLink is great because you can create elements that are always links to other resources. Users might even come to expect that, for example, if they come across anything formatted with, the <CITATION> element, that element will be linked to the cited material.

You create an XLink with attributes, not with specific elements. Specifically, you use the `xlink:type` attribute to create an XLink, setting it to one of the allowable types of XLinks: `"simple"`, `"extended"`, `"locator"`, `"arc"`, `"resource"`, `"title"`, or `"none"`.

Table 15.2 lists the current XLink attributes.

Table 15.2 **The Current XLink Attributes**

Attribute	Description
`xlink:actuate`	This attribute determines when traversal operations occur. You can set this attribute to the official values of `"onLoad"`, `"onRequest"`, or `"undefined"`, or other values as required by the software you're using.
`xlink:from`	This attribute defines starting resources.
`xlink:href`	This is the *locator* attribute, which supplies the data that allows an XLink application to find a remote resource.
`xlink:role`	You use the `role` attribute to describe the function of a link's remote resource in a machine-readable fashion and, in the case of extended-type elements, to serve as a resource category label for traversal rules in arc-type elements. For example, search engines will be capable of reading this attribute.
`xlink:show`	You use this attribute to indicate how you want to display the linked-to resource. XLink applications must recognize the following values: `"new"` (open a new display space), `"replace"` (replace the currently displayed data), `"embed"` (embed the new resource in the current one), and `"undefined"` (leaving the `show` function up to the displaying software).
`xlink:title`	You use the `title` attribute to describe the function of a link's remote resource for people to understand.
`xlink:to`	This attribute defines target or ending resources.
`xlink:type`	This attribute sets the type of the XLink; it can be one of `"simple"`, `"extended"`, `"locator"`, `"arc"`, `"resource"`, `"title"`, or `"none"`. We'll see what these types mean in this chapter.

Using the XLink attributes, you can make an XLink mockup in browsers such as Internet Explorer. As an example, I'll create a mockup of a simple XLink here. Internet Explorer supports the `onClick` attribute, if you use it with an XML element. I'll add some JavaScript to that attribute to make the browser navigate to a new URI, using Internet Explorer's `location` object:

```
<?xml version="1.0" encoding="UTF-8"?>
<?xml-stylesheet type="text/css" href="xlink_example.css"?>

<!DOCTYPE html SYSTEM "xlink_example.dtd">

<DOCUMENT>
```

```
    <P>
        Want to check out
        <LINK xml:type = "simple" href = "http://www.w3c.org"
        onClick="location.href='http://www.w3c.org'">W3C</LINK>?
    </P>
</DOCUMENT>
```

I'm even supplying a style sheet, xlink_example.css, to make this XLink appear in the standard blue, underlined font; in fact, you can even make Internet Explorer's cursor change to a hand as it does for HTML hyperlinks with the `cursor` CSS property:

```
LINK {color: #0000FF; text-decoration: underline; cursor: hand}
```

The result appears in Figure 15.1, where the simple XLink functions much like an HTML hyperlink (which, of course, limits the whole concept of XLinks badly). You can click this link to make Internet Explorer navigate to a new document.

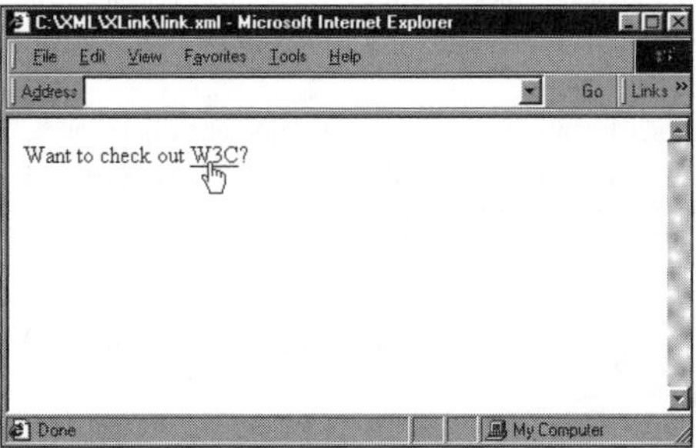

Figure 15.1 A mockup of a simple XLink in Internet Explorer.

So when do you use which XLink attributes? It all depends on the type of link you're creating, as given by the `xlink:type` attribute. Depending on link type, some of these attributes are required, and some are optional. You can find the complete rules in Table 15.3, where the rows correspond to the various XLink attributes, and the columns correspond to the various XLink types.

Table 15.3 **Required and optional attributes by *xlink:type***

	simple	extended	locator	arc	resource	title
`type`	Required	Required	Required	Required	Required	Required
`href`	Optional	Omitted	Required	Omitted	Omitted	Omitted
`role`	Optional	Optional	Optional	Optional	Optional	Omitted
`title`	Optional	Optional	Optional	Optional	Optional	Omitted
`show`	Optional	Omitted	Omitted	Optional	Omitted	Omitted
`actuate`	Optional	Omitted	Omitted	Optional	Omitted	Omitted
`from`	Omitted	Omitted	Omitted	Optional	Omitted	Omitted
`to`	Omitted	Omitted	Omitted	Optional	Omitted	Omitted

Note that each of these attributes uses the `xlink` namespace; this namespace always has the value `"http://www.w3.org/1999/xlink"`, as we saw in the earlier simple link example:

```
<MOVIE_REVIEW xmlns:xlink = "http://www.w3.org/1999/xlink"
    xlink:type = "simple"
    xlink:show = "new"
    xlink:href = "http://www.starpowdermovies.com/reviews.xml#
        xpointer(/child::*[position()=126]/child::*[position()=first()])">
    Mr. Blandings Builds His Dream House
</MOVIE_REVIEW>
```

XML Base (XBase)

Another W3C specification bears discussion while talking about linking and the relationship between documents: the XBase specification.

As of this writing, the XBase specification is in working draft stage, released on June 7, 2000. You can find the current version of this document at `www.w3.org/TR/xmlbase`. This specification lets you provide a base URI for XML documents, just like the HTML `<BASE>` element. In fact, the HTML `<BASE>` element is exactly the reason XBase exists—W3C is committed to giving XLink all the power that HTML 4.0 linking has and then building on that. One of the aspects of linking in HTML 4.0 is the `<BASE>` element.

Here's how it works. You can use the `xml:base` element in an XML document to set the document's base URI. The other URIs in the document are then resolved using that value as a base. Note that `xml:base` uses the `xml` namespace, not the `xlink` namespace; the `xml` namespace is predefined in

XML (that is, you don't have to define it to be able to use it in most XML parsers) as `"http://www.w3.org/XML/1998/namespace"`. Here's an example:

```
<MOVIE_REVIEW xmlns:xlink = "http://www.w3.org/1999/xlink"
    xml:base="http://www.starpowder.com"
    xlink:type = "simple"
    xlink:show = "new"
    xlink:href = "reviews.xml">
    Mr. Blandings Builds His Dream House
</MOVIE_REVIEW>
```

Using the value assigned to the `xml:base` attribute, the URI in this example's `xlink:href` attribute, `"reviews.xml"`, is resolved to the full URI `"http://www.starpowder.com/reviews.xml"`. In this way, you can use `xml:base` to provide a base URI for a document (or even a specific element).

Declaring the XLink Attributes

Note that if you're creating valid XML documents, you must declare XLink attributes, just like any other attributes. For example, you might use a declaration in a DTD like this for the previous example:

```
<?xml version = "1.0" standalone="yes"?>
<!DOCTYPE MOVIE_REVIEW [
<!ELEMENT MOVIE_REVIEW (#PCDATA)>
<!ATTLIST MOVIE_REVIEW
    xmlns:xlink CDATA #IMPLIED
    xml:base CDATA #IMPLIED
    xlink:type CDATA #REQUIRED
    xlink:href CDATA #IMPLIED
    xlink:show CDATA #IMPLIED
    xlink:actuate CDATA #IMPLIED
    xlink:title CDATA #IMPLIED>
]>
<MOVIE_REVIEW xmlns:xlink = "http://www.w3.org/1999/xlink"
    xml:base="http://www.starpowder.com"
    xlink:type = "simple"
    xlink:show = "new"
    xlink:href = "reviews.xml">
    Mr. Blandings Builds His Dream House
</MOVIE_REVIEW>
```

You can also hard-code the values for most of the values in the XLink attributes, if you prefer, in which case, you have to supply a value for only the `xlink:href` attribute:

```
<?xml version = "1.0" standalone="yes"?>
<!DOCTYPE MOVIE_REVIEW [
<!ELEMENT MOVIE_REVIEW (#PCDATA)>
<!ATTLIST MOVIE_REVIEW
```

continues ▸

```
    xmlns:xlink CDATA #FIXED "http://www.w3.org/1999/xlink"
    xml:base CDATA #FIXED "http://www.starpowder.com"
    xlink:type CDATA #FIXED "simple"
    xlink:href CDATA #REQUIRED
    xlink:show CDATA #FIXED "new"
    xlink:actuate CDATA #FIXED "onRequest"
    xlink:title CDATA #IMPLIED>
]>
<MOVIE_REVIEW xlink:href = "reviews.xml">
    Mr. Blandings Builds His Dream House
</MOVIE_REVIEW>
```

Because XLink is so general, declaring your XLink elements can get fairly involved—XLink elements may even have child XLink elements, which have their own XLink children, and so on. But keep in mind that if you want to create a valid document, you have to declare them all in a DTD or schema.

We've seen the attributes you can use with XLinks in overview now. Because these attributes define XLinks, I'll take a look at each of them more detail now, starting with the most important one of all, the `xlink:type` attribute.

The *xlink:type* Attribute

The `xlink:type` attribute defines the type of XLink you're creating. You can set this attribute to these values:

Value	Description
`simple`	Creates a simple link.
`extended`	Creates an extended link.
`locator`	Creates a locator link that points to a resource.
`arc`	Creates an arc with multiple resources and various traversal paths.
`resource`	Creates a resource link, which indicates a specific resource.
`title`	Creates a title link. Such elements are useful, for example, for cases in which human-readable label information needs further element markup, or in which multiple titles are necessary for internationalization purposes.

We've already seen how to create simple links:

```
<MOVIE_REVIEW xmlns:xlink = "http://www.w3.org/1999/xlink"
    xlink:type = "simple"
    xlink:show = "new"
    xlink:href =
"http://www.starpowdermovies.com/reviews.xml#
        xpointer(/child::*[position()=126]/child::*[position()=first()])">
    Mr. Blandings Builds His Dream House
</MOVIE_REVIEW>
```

I'll take a look at the various other kinds of links in this chapter.

Locating Resources with *xlink:href*

The `xlink:href` attribute is also called the *locator* attribute. This is the attribute that supplies the data that allows an XLink application to find a remote resource.

URI Definition

Although XLinks can be quite general, they commonly use URIs to locate resources, and you usually use a URI in `xlink:href`. Now that we're examining the way linking works in XML, you might want to look up the formal definition of URIs, which you can find in its entirety at `www.ics.uci.edu/pub/ietf/uri/rfc2396.txt`.

We've seen that you can set the `xlink:href` attribute to specify a document and an XPointer:

```
<MOVIE_REVIEW xmlns:xlink = "http://www.w3.org/1999/xlink"
    xlink:type = "simple"
    xlink:show = "new"
    xlink:href = "http://www.starpowdermovies.com/reviews.xml#
        xpointer(/child::*[position()=126]/child::*[position()=first()])">
    Mr. Blandings Builds His Dream House
</MOVIE_REVIEW>
```

We'll see how the values you assign to this attribute can become fairly involved when we work with XPointers.

Describing Resources: *xlink:role* and *xlink:title*

Two important XLink attributes are `xlink:role` and `xlink:title`, which let you describe a remote resource. Both these attributes are optional. Here's an example putting both attributes to work:

```
<MOVIE_REVIEW xmlns:xlink = "http://www.w3.org/1999/xlink"
    xlink:type = "simple"
    xlink:show = "new"
    xlink:role = "MOVIE_REVIEW[EN]"
    xlink:title = "Review of 'Mr. Blandings Builds His Dream House'"
    xlink:href = "http://www.starpowdermovies.com/reviews.xml#
        xpointer(/child::*[position()=126]/child::*[position()=first()])">
    Mr. Blandings Builds His Dream House
</MOVIE_REVIEW>
```

The `xlink:title` attribute here has the value `"Review of 'Mr. Blandings Builds His Dream House'"`. This is a human-readable description of the resource to which the link links; the idea here is that a person can read this text to get more information about the remote resource the link points to. An application might display this text on demand.

The text of the `xlink:role` attribute, on the other hand, is designed to be read by software. A link's role indicates the category of a link. In this case, the text of the link's role is `"MOVIE_REVIEW[EN]"`.

There has been no attempt to standardize roles as there has been in the Remote Description Framework language that we first saw in Chapter 1, "Essential XML," because there are simply too many possibilities. Although search engines can use the link's role to classify the link, you usually use roles to define directional links when creating extended links, and I'll take a look at that soon.

If you want to create valid documents, you must declare the `xlink:role` and `xlink:title` attributes, as in this case, where I'm using a DTD and giving `xlink:role` the fixed value `"MOVIE_REVIEW[EN]"` in `<MOVIE_REVIEW>` elements:

```
<!ELEMENT MOVIE_REVIEW (#PCDATA)>
<!ATTLIST MOVIE_REVIEW
    xmlns:xlink CDATA  #FIXED "http://www.w3.org/1999/xlink"
    xlink:type  CDATA  #FIXED "simple"
    xlink:href  CDATA  #REQUIRED
    xlink:title CDATA  #IMPLIED
    xlink:role  CDATA  #FIXED "MOVIE_REVIEW[EN]"
>
```

The *xlink:show* Attribute

You use the XLink `xlink:show` attribute to indicate how you want the linked-to resource displayed when the link is activated. The `xlink:show` attribute has four values that are predefined:

Value	Description
`replace`	Replaces the current resource in the same window, if there is one
`new`	Opens a new display area, such as a new window, to display the new resource
`embed`	Embeds the linked-to resource in the current resource
`undefined`	Indicates that you are requesting no specific `xlink:show` setting

Even though `xlink:show` has these predefined values, you can set your own values as well.

The default behavior of HTML links is to navigate to a linked-to document, replacing the current document with the new one. You can mimic that operation by assigning `xlink:show` a value of `"replace"`:

```
<MOVIE_REVIEW xmlns:xlink = "http://www.w3.org/1999/xlink"
    xlink:type = "simple"
    xlink:show = "replace"
    xlink:href = "http://www.starpowdermovies.com/reviews.xml">
    Mr. Blandings Builds His Dream House
</MOVIE_REVIEW>
```

What this actually means in practice is application-specific. Although you'd expect the current document to be replaced with a new one, there are plenty of other possibilities. For example, a spreadsheet application may replace the displayed data, but not the overall display, with data from the linked-to resource. Or, the `xlink:show` attribute can make the application use a different style sheet when the link is activated. Again, the actual implementation is up to the software designer.

If the value of `xlink:show` is `"new"`, activating the link typically opens a new window that displays the linked-to resource:

```
<MOVIE_REVIEW xmlns:xlink = "http://www.w3.org/1999/xlink"
    xlink:type = "simple"
    xlink:show = "new"
    xlink:href = "http://www.starpowdermovies.com/reviews.xml">
    Mr. Blandings Builds His Dream House
</MOVIE_REVIEW>
```

However, as before, there are plenty of possibilities; a value of `"new"` might simply mean that a new column is added to a table or that a new line is displayed in a graph. It's a good idea to be considerate here—bear in mind that users coming from HTML will not be used to having links that automatically open new windows, if that's what your link is going to do. You might make sure you add some explanatory text—otherwise, such behavior might be annoying.

Similarly, the attribute value `"embed"` is subject to interpretation. The idea here is that when a link is activated, the linked-to resource is embedded in the current display or document, although what is actually embedded and how is up to the application. For example, say that we linked to `planets.xml`, which we saw in the previous few chapters:

```
<?xml version="1.0"?>
<?xml-stylesheet type="text/xml" href="planets.xsl"?>
<PLANETS>

    <PLANET>
        <NAME>Mercury</NAME>
```

continues ▸

```
        <MASS UNITS="(Earth = 1)">.0553</MASS>
        <DAY UNITS="days">58.65</DAY>
        <RADIUS UNITS="miles">1516</RADIUS>
        <DENSITY UNITS="(Earth = 1)">.983</DENSITY>
        <DISTANCE UNITS="million miles">43.4</DISTANCE><!--At perihelion-->
    </PLANET>

    <PLANET>
        <NAME>Venus</NAME>
        <MASS UNITS="(Earth = 1)">.815</MASS>
        <DAY UNITS="days">116.75</DAY>
        <RADIUS UNITS="miles">3716</RADIUS>
        <DENSITY UNITS="(Earth = 1)">.943</DENSITY>
        <DISTANCE UNITS="million miles">66.8</DISTANCE><!--At perihelion-->
    </PLANET>

    <PLANET>
        <NAME>Earth</NAME>
        <MASS UNITS="(Earth = 1)">1</MASS>
        <DAY UNITS="days">1</DAY>
        <RADIUS UNITS="miles">2107</RADIUS>
        <DENSITY UNITS="(Earth = 1)">1</DENSITY>
        <DISTANCE UNITS="million miles">128.4</DISTANCE><!--At perihelion-->
    </PLANET>

</PLANETS>
```

Here's how the links to the various planets might look. I'm anticipating the use of XPointers here to pick out the specific planets in `planets.xml`; note that the `xlink:show` values are all `"embed"` here:

```
<?xml version = "1.0">
<ASTRO_NEWS>
    <PLANET_DATA xmlns:xlink = "http://www.w3.org/1999/xlink"
        xlink:type = "simple"
        xlink:show = "embed"
        xlink:href = "http://www.starpowdermovies.com/planets.xml#
            xpointer(/descendant::PLANET[position() = 1]">
        Mercury
    </PLANET_DATA>
    <PLANET_DATA xmlns:xlink = "http://www.w3.org/1999/xlink"
        xlink:type = "simple"
        xlink:show = "embed"
        xlink:href = "http://www.starpowdermovies.com/planets.xml#
            xpointer(/descendant::PLANET[position() = 2]">
        Venus
    </PLANET_DATA>
    <PLANET_DATA xmlns:xlink = "http://www.w3.org/1999/xlink"
        xlink:type = "simple"
        xlink:show = "embed"
        xlink:href = "http://www.starpowdermovies.com/planets.xml#
            xpointer(/descendant::PLANET[position() = 3]">
```

```
        Earth
    </PLANET_DATA>
<ASTRO_NEWS>
```

After all these links are activated, the data from the various <PLANET> elements might be inserted into the current display, something like this (again, the details are up to the host application):

```
<?xml version = "1.0">
<ASTRO_NEWS>
    <PLANET_DATA xmlns:xlink = "http://www.w3.org/1999/xlink"
        <NAME>Mercury</NAME>
        <MASS UNITS="(Earth = 1)">.0553</MASS>
        <DAY UNITS="days">58.65</DAY>
        <RADIUS UNITS="miles">1516</RADIUS>
        <DENSITY UNITS="(Earth = 1)">.983</DENSITY>
        <DISTANCE UNITS="million miles">43.4</DISTANCE><!--At perihelion-->
    </PLANET_DATA>
    <PLANET_DATA xmlns:xlink = "http://www.w3.org/1999/xlink"
        <NAME>Venus</NAME>
        <MASS UNITS="(Earth = 1)">.815</MASS>
        <DAY UNITS="days">116.75</DAY>
        <RADIUS UNITS="miles">3716</RADIUS>
        <DENSITY UNITS="(Earth = 1)">.943</DENSITY>
        <DISTANCE UNITS="million miles">66.8</DISTANCE><!--At perihelion-->
    </PLANET_DATA>
    <PLANET_DATA xmlns:xlink = "http://www.w3.org/1999/xlink"
        <NAME>Earth</NAME>
        <MASS UNITS="(Earth = 1)">1</MASS>
        <DAY UNITS="days">1</DAY>
        <RADIUS UNITS="miles">2107</RADIUS>
        <DENSITY UNITS="(Earth = 1)">1</DENSITY>
        <DISTANCE UNITS="million miles">128.4</DISTANCE><!--At perihelion-->
    </PLANET_DATA>
<ASTRO_NEWS>
```

You can also set `xlink:show` to a value of `"undefined"`, in which case you're indicating to the application that you don't have a display preference, which usually means that it's up to the application. In fact, it's up to the application what happens in any case, because the application may ignore any of the values you carefully assign to `xlink:show`, especially if it's not capable of handling what you want (as when you set `xlink:show` to `"new"` but the browser can't handle multiple windows).

You're also free to set `xlink:show` to your own values. For example, setting it to `"new_row"` might add a new row to a table for displaying data. You might also use this attribute to indicate something about the *format* in which documents are displayed, rather than *how* they are displayed, as when you set `xlink:show` to the name of a style sheet. Or, you might set JavaScript code to execute in this attribute's value when the link is activated.

Don't forget that you need to declare `xlink:show` if you want to create valid documents. That might look something like this in a DTD:

```
<!ELEMENT ASTRO_NEWS>
<!ATTLIST ASTRO_NEWS
    xmlns:xlink CDATA #FIXED "http://www.w3.org/1999/xlink"
    xlink:type CDATA #FIXED "simple"
    xlink:href CDATA #REQUIRED
    xlink:show (new | replace | embed | undefined) #IMPLIED "replace">
```

The *xlink:actuate* Attribute

You can use the `xlink:actuate` attribute to indicate when a link should be traversed. The `xlink:actuate` attribute has these predefined values:

Value	Description
`onRequest`	Indicates that the link should be traversed only on the user's request
`onLoad`	Indicates that the link should be traversed when the document or resource is loaded
`undefined`	Indicates that you have no preference for the xlink:actuate action

You can also set your own values for `xlink:actuate`.

The first of the predefined values, `"onRequest"`, indicates that the user should request the link to be traversed before any action takes place. Typically, the user request takes the form of a mouse click, as in our earlier mockup of a simple link in Internet Explorer, where we can use the `"onRequest"` value:

```
<?xml version="1.0" encoding="UTF-8"?>
<?xml-stylesheet type="text/css" href="xlink_example.css"?>

<!DOCTYPE html SYSTEM "xlink_example.dtd">

<DOCUMENT>
    <P>
        Want to check out
        <LINK xml:type = "simple" href = "http://www.w3c.org"
        xlink:actuate = "onRequest" onClick=
        "location.href='http://www.w3c.org'">W3C</LINK>?
    </P>
</DOCUMENT>
```

If you set the value of `xlink:actuate` to `"onLoad"`, the link is traversed when the resource containing it is loaded. For example, you might have a link to an image map's image and want to load it as soon as the containing document is loaded. That might look something like this:

```
<IMAGE_MAP xmlns:xlink="http://www.w3.org/1999/xlink"
    xlink:type="simple"
    xlink:href="http://www.starpowder.com/gifs/image_map.gif"
    xlink:actuate="onLoad">
</IMAGE_MAP>
```

You can also set `xlink:actuate` to `"undefined"`, which means that when the link is traversed is up to the application. (Of course, it's up to the application in any case, even when you specify any other value for `xlink:actuate`.)

You can also set your own values for `xlink:actuate`. For example, you might define your own application-specific values, such as `"onLoadData"`, `"onShowImage"`, or `"onUnload"`.

If you want to create valid XML documents, of course, you'll have to declare `xlink:actuate`, and that might look something like this in a DTD:

```
<!ELEMENT ASTRO_NEWS>
<!ATTLIST ASTRO_NEWS
    xmlns:xlink CDATA #FIXED "http://www.w3.org/1999/xlink"
    xlink:type CDATA #FIXED "simple"
    xlink:href CDATA #REQUIRED
    xlink:show (new | replace | embed | undefined) #IMPLIED "replace"
    xlink:actuate (onRequest | onLoad | undefined) #IMPLIED "onRequest">
```

Extended Links

You may be accustomed to the idea of simple links much as they work in HTML, and as I've discussed them previously, but here's where we broaden things by getting into *extended links*. Extended links are very general and really indicate relationships between resources. An extended link can involve multiple resources, multiple paths between those resources, bidirectional paths, and "out-of-line" links. It helps to think very generally here, in terms of all the possible relationships you might have between data resources.

Extended Link Terminology

The upcoming concepts may seem very vague when compared to the concrete functionality of simple links, but keep in mind that W3C is trying to let you describe, in XML terms, all the possible relationships that there might be among multiple resources and how those relationships work. It's a big job. In technical terms, an extended link is called a *directed labeled graph*. The resources that it connects are called the *vertices*, and the actual links between resources are the *edges* of the graph.

In general terms, then, an extended link is made up of the connections between a set of resources. Such resources may be *local*, which means that they're actually part of the extended link element, or *remote*, which means that they're not part of the extended link element (but does not mean that they have to be in another document). If a link does not contain any local resources at all, it's called an *out-of-line* link.

So how does an application use an extended link? That's completely up to the application. I'll provide some ideas here, but so far, things are really up in the air. To my knowledge, no generally available software packages implement true extended links.

A hypothetical example might be an *expert system* (for example, artificial intelligence or intelligent agents), in which the links between multiple resources are traversed depending on yes or no answers to questions. The idea here is that by answering a series of questions, an expert system can progressively narrow a search and direct you to a resource that will provide the answer to quite complex queries.

As mentioned, resources that participate in an extended link can be either local or remote. A local resource is part of the extended link itself and is contained in an element that has its `xlink:type` attribute set to `"resource"`.

On the other hand, remote resources are outside the extended link element, but not necessarily in another document. You use *locator elements* to point to remote resources; those elements have their `xlink:type` attributes set to `"locator"`. When you create a locator element, you must also give its `xlink:href` attribute a value that points to the remote resource.

Here's an example of an extended link. This link contains four resources—two inline links and two out-of-line links:

```
<ASTRO_DATA xmlns:xlink="http://www.w3.org/1999/xlink"
        xlink:type="extended" xlink:title="Planetary Data">
    <NAME xlink:type="resource" xlink:role="NAME">
        Planetary Data
    </NAME>
    <DATE xlink:type="resource" xlink:role="LAST_UPDATED">
        September 1, 2001
    </DATE>
    <PLANET_DATA xmlns:xlink = "http://www.w3.org/1999/xlink"
        xlink:type = "locator"
        xlink:show = "embed"
        xlink:href = "http://www.starpowdermovies.com/planets.xml#
            xpointer(/descendant::PLANET[position() = 1]">
        xlink:title="Mercury"
        xlink:role="PLANETARY_DATA"
    </PLANET_DATA>
    <PLANET_DATA xmlns:xlink = "http://www.w3.org/1999/xlink"
        xlink:type = "locator"
```

```
        xlink:show = "embed"
        xlink:href = "http://www.starpowdermovies.com/planets.xml#
            xpointer(/descendant::PLANET[position() = 2]">
        xlink:title="Venus"
        xlink:role="PLANETARY_DATA"
    </PLANET_DATA>
    <PLANET_DATA xmlns:xlink = "http://www.w3.org/1999/xlink"
        xlink:type = "locator"
        xlink:show = "embed"
        xlink:href = "http://www.starpowdermovies.com/planets.xml#
            xpointer(/descendant::PLANET[position() = 3]">
        xlink:title="Earth"
        xlink:role="PLANETARY_DATA"
    </PLANET_DATA>
</ASTRO_DATA>
```

The inline links here are those links that have the `xlink:type` value `"resource"` and whose resources are actually contained in the linking element. In this case, that's the `<NAME>` and `<DATE>` links, both of which contain a local resource (which is simply text here, although it could consist of multiple nested XML elements, if you prefer).

The out-of-line links here have the `xlink:type` attribute value `"locator"`. These links serve to locate remote resources, which may be in the same document or in another document. In this example, the remote resources are all in another document, `planets.xml`.

As before, if you want to create valid documents, you must declare the attributes and elements you're using. In this example, that might look like this, where I'm adding a DTD:

```
<?xml version = "1.0"?>
<!DOCTYPE ASTRO_DATA  [
<!ELEMENT ASTRO_DATA (NAME, DATE, PLANET_DATA*) >
<!ATTLIST ASTRO_DATA
    xmlns:xlink CDATA #FIXED "http://www.w3.org/1999/xlink"
    xlink:type (extended) #FIXED "extended"
    xlink:title CDATA #IMPLIED
    xlink:role CDATA #IMPLIED>

<!ELEMENT NAME (#PCDATA)>
<!ATTLIST NAME
    xmlns:xlink CDATA #FIXED "http://www.w3.org/1999/xlink"
    xlink:type CDATA #FIXED "resource"
    xlink:role CDATA #IMPLIED
    xlink:title CDATA #IMPLIED
>

<!ELEMENT DATE (#PCDATA)>
<!ATTLIST DATE
    xmlns:xlink CDATA #FIXED "http://www.w3.org/1999/xlink"
```

continues ▶

```
    xlink:type CDATA #FIXED "resource"
    xlink:role CDATA #IMPLIED
    xlink:title CDATA #IMPLIED
>

<!ELEMENT PLANET_DATA (#PCDATA)>
<!ATTLIST PLANET_DATA
    xmlns:xlink CDATA #FIXED "http://www.w3.org/1999/xlink"
    xlink:type CDATA #FIXED "locator"
    xlink:href CDATA #REQUIRED
    xlink:role CDATA #IMPLIED
    xlink:title CDATA #IMPLIED
    xlink:show CDATA #IMPLIED
>
]>

<ASTRO_DATA xmlns:xlink="http://www.w3.org/1999/xlink"
         xlink:type="extended" xlink:title="Planetary Data">
    <NAME xlink:type="resource" xlink:role="NAME">
        Planetary Data
    </NAME>
    <DATE xlink:type="resource" xlink:role="LAST_UPDATED">
        September 1, 2001
    </DATE>
    <PLANET_DATA xmlns:xlink = "http://www.w3.org/1999/xlink"
        xlink:type = "locator"
        xlink:show = "embed"
        xlink:href = "http://www.starpowdermovies.com/planets.xml#
            xpointer(/descendant::PLANET[position() = 1]">
        xlink:title="Mercury"
        xlink:role="PLANETARY_DATA">
    </PLANET_DATA>
    <PLANET_DATA xmlns:xlink = "http://www.w3.org/1999/xlink"
        xlink:type = "locator"
        xlink:show = "embed"
        xlink:href = "http://www.starpowdermovies.com/planets.xml#
            xpointer(/descendant::PLANET[position() = 2]">
        xlink:title="Venus"
        xlink:role="PLANETARY_DATA">
    </PLANET_DATA>
    <PLANET_DATA xmlns:xlink = "http://www.w3.org/1999/xlink"
        xlink:type = "locator"
        xlink:show = "embed"
        xlink:href = "http://www.starpowdermovies.com/planets.xml#
            xpointer(/descendant::PLANET[position() = 3]">
        xlink:title="Earth"
        xlink:role="PLANETARY_DATA">
    </PLANET_DATA>
</ASTRO_DATA>
```

So far, all we've done is indicate what elements that participate in an extended link represent local or remote resources. You can do more if you use the `xlink:from` and `xlink:to` attributes, which enable you to create directed links, or *arcs*.

Creating Arcs with the *xlink:from* and *xlink:to* Attributes

In simple links, there's little question where to go when the link is activated: The `xlink:href` attribute tells you all you need to know. However, extended links are more complex—when you want to traverse the link we created in the last section, what should happen? There are all kinds of paths among the various resources.

Each of the possible paths between resources is called an *arc*. You represent arcs in XML elements by setting the `xlink:type` attribute to `"arc"`.

To specify how an arc works, you can use attributes like `xlink:show` and `xlink:actuate`. Here's the important part: Arc elements also have `xlink:from` and `xlink:to` elements to specify traversal paths. The `xlink:from` attribute indicates what resource an arc comes from, and the `xlink:to` attribute indicates what resource it goes to. You set the values of `xlink:from` and `xlink:to` to match the `xlink:role` attribute of the source and target resources.

Here's an example. In this case, I'll modify the previous example by renaming the `<NAME>` element `<START>`, and I'll include three arcs: one from the `<START>` element to each of the three `<PLANET_DATA>` elements (individual arcs always go from one source resource to one target resource). I'll support the arcs with elements named `<LOOKUP>`. Here's what it looks like:

```
<?xml version = "1.0"?>
<ASTRO_DATA xmlns:xlink="http://www.w3.org/1999/xlink"
        xlink:type="extended" xlink:title="Planetary Data">

    <START xlink:type="resource" xlink:role="START">
        Planetary Data
    </START>

    <DATE xlink:type="resource" xlink:role="LAST_UPDATED">
        September 1, 2001
    </DATE>

    <PLANET_DATA xmlns:xlink = "http://www.w3.org/1999/xlink"
        xlink:type = "locator"
        xlink:show = "embed"
        xlink:href = "http://www.starpowdermovies.com/planets.xml#
            xpointer(/descendant::PLANET[position() = 1]">
        xlink:title="Mercury"
        xlink:role="Mercury">
    </PLANET_DATA>
```

continues ▸

```
    <PLANET_DATA xmlns:xlink = "http://www.w3.org/1999/xlink"
        xlink:type = "locator"
        xlink:show = "embed"
        xlink:href = "http://www.starpowdermovies.com/planets.xml#
            xpointer(/descendant::PLANET[position() = 2]">
        xlink:title="Venus"
        xlink:role="Venus">
    </PLANET_DATA>

    <PLANET_DATA xmlns:xlink = "http://www.w3.org/1999/xlink"
        xlink:type = "locator"
        xlink:show = "embed"
        xlink:href = "http://www.starpowdermovies.com/planets.xml#
            xpointer(/descendant::PLANET[position() = 3]">
        xlink:title="Earth"
        xlink:role="Earth">
    </PLANET_DATA>

    <LOOKUP xlink:type = "arc" xlink:from = "START"
        xlink:to = "Mercury" xlink:show="new"
        xlink:actuate="onRequest">
    </LOOKUP>

    <LOOKUP xlink:type = "arc" xlink:from = "START"
        xlink:to = "Venus" xlink:show="new"
        xlink:actuate="onRequest">
    </LOOKUP>

    <LOOKUP xlink:type = "arc" xlink:from = "START"
        xlink:to = "Earth" xlink:show="new"
        xlink:actuate="onRequest">
    </LOOKUP>
</ASTRO_DATA>
```

As usual, you must declare the elements and attributes you're using if you want a valid document; that might look something like this with a DTD:

```
<?xml version = "1.0"?>
<!DOCTYPE ASTRO_DATA [
<!ELEMENT ASTRO_DATA (START, DATE, PLANET_DATA*, LOOKUP*) >
<!ATTLIST ASTRO_DATA
    xmlns:xlink CDATA #FIXED "http://www.w3.org/1999/xlink"
    xlink:type (extended) #FIXED "extended"
    xlink:title CDATA #IMPLIED
    xlink:role CDATA #IMPLIED>

<!ELEMENT START (#PCDATA)>
<!ATTLIST START
    xmlns:xlink CDATA #FIXED "http://www.w3.org/1999/xlink"
    xlink:type CDATA #FIXED "resource"
    xlink:role CDATA #IMPLIED
    xlink:title CDATA #IMPLIED>
```

```
<!ELEMENT DATE (#PCDATA)>
<!ATTLIST DATE
    xmlns:xlink CDATA #FIXED "http://www.w3.org/1999/xlink"
    xlink:type CDATA #FIXED "resource"
    xlink:role CDATA #IMPLIED
    xlink:title CDATA #IMPLIED>

<!ELEMENT PLANET_DATA (#PCDATA)>
<!ATTLIST PLANET_DATA
    xmlns:xlink CDATA #FIXED "http://www.w3.org/1999/xlink"
    xlink:type CDATA #FIXED "locator"
    xlink:href CDATA #REQUIRED
    xlink:role CDATA #IMPLIED
    xlink:title CDATA #IMPLIED
    xlink:show CDATA #IMPLIED>

<!ELEMENT LOOKUP (#PCDATA)>
<!ATTLIST LOOKUP
    xlink:type CDATA #FIXED "arc"
    xlink:from CDATA #IMPLIED
    xlink:to CDATA #IMPLIED
    xlink:show CDATA #IMPLIED
    xlink:actuate (onRequest | onLoad | undefined) #IMPLIED>
]>

<ASTRO_DATA xmlns:xlink="http://www.w3.org/1999/xlink"
         xlink:type="extended" xlink:title="Planetary Data">

    <START xlink:type="resource" xlink:role="START">
        Planetary Data
    </START>

    <DATE xlink:type="resource" xlink:role="LAST_UPDATED">
        September 1, 2001
    </DATE>

    <PLANET_DATA xmlns:xlink = "http://www.w3.org/1999/xlink"
        xlink:type = "locator"
        xlink:show = "embed"
        xlink:href = "http://www.starpowdermovies.com/planets.xml#
            xpointer(/descendant::PLANET[position() = 1]">
        xlink:title="Mercury"
        xlink:role="Mercury">
    </PLANET_DATA>

    <PLANET_DATA xmlns:xlink = "http://www.w3.org/1999/xlink"
        xlink:type = "locator"
        xlink:show = "embed"
        xlink:href = "http://www.starpowdermovies.com/planets.xml#
            xpointer(/descendant::PLANET[position() = 2]">
        xlink:title="Venus"
        xlink:role="Venus">
    </PLANET_DATA>
```

continues ▸

```
    <PLANET_DATA xmlns:xlink = "http://www.w3.org/1999/xlink"
        xlink:type = "locator"
        xlink:show = "embed"
        xlink:href = "http://www.starpowdermovies.com/planets.xml#
            xpointer(/descendant::PLANET[position() = 3]">
        xlink:title="Earth"
        xlink:role="Earth">
    </PLANET_DATA>

    <LOOKUP xlink:type = "arc" xlink:from = "START"
        xlink:to = "Mercury" xlink:show="new"
        xlink:actuate="onRequest">
    </LOOKUP>

    <LOOKUP xlink:type = "arc" xlink:from = "START"
        xlink:to = "Venus" xlink:show="new"
        xlink:actuate="onRequest">
    </LOOKUP>

    <LOOKUP xlink:type = "arc" xlink:from = "START"
        xlink:to = "Earth" xlink:show="new"
        xlink:actuate="onRequest">
    </LOOKUP>
</ASTRO_DATA>
```

You don't need to have an arc refer to one specific resource, as I've done here. For example, here all three <PLANET_DATA> elements have the same role, PLANETARY_DATA, so this single <LOOKUP> element defines three arcs, one to each <PLANET_DATA> resource:

```
<?xml version = "1.0"?>
<ASTRO_DATA xmlns:xlink="http://www.w3.org/1999/xlink"
         xlink:type="extended" xlink:title="Planetary Data">

    <START xlink:type="resource" xlink:role="START">
        Planetary Data
    </START>

    <DATE xlink:type="resource" xlink:role="LAST_UPDATED">
        September 1, 2001
    </DATE>

    <PLANET_DATA xmlns:xlink = "http://www.w3.org/1999/xlink"
        xlink:type = "locator"
        xlink:show = "embed"
        xlink:href = "http://www.starpowdermovies.com/planets.xml#
            xpointer(/descendant::PLANET[position() = 1]">
        xlink:title="Mercury"
        xlink:role="PLANETARY_DATA">
    </PLANET_DATA>
```

```
    <PLANET_DATA xmlns:xlink = "http://www.w3.org/1999/xlink"
        xlink:type = "locator"
        xlink:show = "embed"
        xlink:href = "http://www.starpowdermovies.com/planets.xml#
            xpointer(/descendant::PLANET[position() = 2]">
        xlink:title="Venus"
        xlink:role="PLANETARY_DATA">
    </PLANET_DATA>

    <PLANET_DATA xmlns:xlink = "http://www.w3.org/1999/xlink"
        xlink:type = "locator"
        xlink:show = "embed"
        xlink:href = "http://www.starpowdermovies.com/planets.xml#
            xpointer(/descendant::PLANET[position() = 3]">
        xlink:title="Earth"
        xlink:role="PLANETARY_DATA">
    </PLANET_DATA>

    <LOOKUP xlink:type = "arc" xlink:from = "START"
        xlink:to = "PLANETARY_DATA" xlink:show="new"
        xlink:actuate="onRequest">
    </LOOKUP>
</ASTRO_DATA>
```

In fact, you can omit an `xlink:from` or `xlink:to` attribute altogether, in which case arcs are created between the particular element and all the locator elements in the extended link (which can include the element that omits the `xlink:from` or `xlink:to` attribute itself).

The way the `xlink:from` and `xlink:to` attributes are actually used is up to the application that's reading the containing document.

Inline Versus Out-of-Line Links

When a link does not contain any of the resources it's linking to, it's called an *out-of-line link*. Inline links are part of the resources they're part of, but out-of-line links are not part of the same resource. There's a big movement to try to separate markup from content as much as possible. (This is the motivation behind the big switch in HTML 4.0 to working with style sheets instead of dedicated elements such as `<CENTER>` and the external code modules called *behaviors* in Internet Explorer.) Using out-of-line links is very attractive, if that's the way you want to go.

You can place out-of-line links in their own documents, called *linkbases*. The actual set of out-of-line links in a linkbase is called a *linkset*.

Here's an example. In this case, all the links in this document are to resources that are not part of the document, so this is a linkbase:

```
<?xml version = "1.0"?>
<ASTRO_DATA xmlns:xlink="http://www.w3.org/1999/xlink"
        xlink:type="extended" xlink:title="Planetary Data">

    <PLANET_DATA xmlns:xlink = "http://www.w3.org/1999/xlink"
        xlink:type = "locator"
        xlink:show = "embed"
        xlink:href = "http://www.starpowdermovies.com/planets.xml">
        xlink:title="START"
        xlink:role="START">
    </PLANET_DATA>

    <PLANET_DATA xmlns:xlink = "http://www.w3.org/1999/xlink"
        xlink:type = "locator"
        xlink:show = "embed"
        xlink:href = "http://www.starpowdermovies.com/planets.xml#
            xpointer(/descendant::PLANET[position() = 1]">
        xlink:title="Mercury"
        xlink:role="Mercury">
    </PLANET_DATA>

    <PLANET_DATA xmlns:xlink = "http://www.w3.org/1999/xlink"
        xlink:type = "locator"
        xlink:show = "embed"
        xlink:href = "http://www.starpowdermovies.com/planets.xml#
            xpointer(/descendant::PLANET[position() = 2]">
        xlink:title="Venus"
        xlink:role="Venus">
    </PLANET_DATA>

    <PLANET_DATA xmlns:xlink = "http://www.w3.org/1999/xlink"
        xlink:type = "locator"
        xlink:show = "embed"
        xlink:href = "http://www.starpowdermovies.com/planets.xml#
            xpointer(/descendant::PLANET[position() = 3]">
        xlink:title="Earth"
        xlink:role="Earth">
    </PLANET_DATA>

    <LOOKUP xlink:type = "arc" xlink:from = "START"
        xlink:to = "Mercury" xlink:show="new"
        xlink:actuate="onRequest">
    </LOOKUP>

    <LOOKUP xlink:type = "arc" xlink:from = "START"
        xlink:to = "Venus" xlink:show="new"
        xlink:actuate="onRequest">
    </LOOKUP>
```

```
    <LOOKUP xlink:type = "arc" xlink:from = "START"
        xlink:to = "Earth" xlink:show="new"
        xlink:actuate="onRequest">
    </LOOKUP>
</ASTRO_DATA>
```

In this case, all the resources linked to are outside the document. I've added locator links to all the planets in `planets.xml`, and arcs from the starting position in that document to the planets as well. You typically have three types of links in a linkbase: extended links, locator links, and arcs. You cannot have any links that are of type `resource`.

Linkbases are subject to the same rules as other XML documents, so you can provide them with DTD if you want to validate them, something like this:

```
<?xml version = "1.0"?>
<!DOCTYPE ASTRO_DATA  [
<!ELEMENT ASTRO_DATA (PLANET_DATA*, LOOKUP*) >
<!ATTLIST ASTRO_DATA
    xmlns:xlink CDATA #FIXED "http://www.w3.org/1999/xlink"
    xlink:type (extended) #FIXED "extended"
    xlink:title CDATA #IMPLIED
    xlink:role CDATA #IMPLIED>

<!ELEMENT PLANET_DATA (#PCDATA)>
<!ATTLIST PLANET_DATA
    xmlns:xlink CDATA #FIXED "http://www.w3.org/1999/xlink"
    xlink:type CDATA #FIXED "locator"
    xlink:href CDATA #REQUIRED
    xlink:role CDATA #IMPLIED
    xlink:title CDATA #IMPLIED
    xlink:show CDATA #IMPLIED>

<!ELEMENT LOOKUP (#PCDATA)>
<!ATTLIST LOOKUP
    xlink:type CDATA #FIXED "arc"
    xlink:from CDATA #IMPLIED
    xlink:to CDATA #IMPLIED
    xlink:show CDATA #IMPLIED
    xlink:actuate (onRequest | onLoad | undefined) #IMPLIED>
]>
<ASTRO_DATA xmlns:xlink="http://www.w3.org/1999/xlink"
        xlink:type="extended" xlink:title="Planetary Data">

    <PLANET_DATA xmlns:xlink = "http://www.w3.org/1999/xlink"
        xlink:type = "locator"
        xlink:show = "embed"
        xlink:href = "http://www.starpowdermovies.com/planets.xml">
        xlink:title="START"
        xlink:role="START">
    </PLANET_DATA>
```

continues ▸

```
    <PLANET_DATA xmlns:xlink = "http://www.w3.org/1999/xlink"
        xlink:type = "locator"
        xlink:show = "embed"
        xlink:href = "http://www.starpowdermovies.com/planets.xml#
            xpointer(/descendant::PLANET[position() = 1]">
        xlink:title="Mercury"
        xlink:role="Mercury">
    </PLANET_DATA>

    <PLANET_DATA xmlns:xlink = "http://www.w3.org/1999/xlink"
        xlink:type = "locator"
        xlink:show = "embed"
        xlink:href = "http://www.starpowdermovies.com/planets.xml#
            xpointer(/descendant::PLANET[position() = 2]">
        xlink:title="Venus"
        xlink:role="Venus">
    </PLANET_DATA>

    <PLANET_DATA xmlns:xlink = "http://www.w3.org/1999/xlink"
        xlink:type = "locator"
        xlink:show = "embed"
        xlink:href = "http://www.starpowdermovies.com/planets.xml#
            xpointer(/descendant::PLANET[position() = 3]">
        xlink:title="Earth"
        xlink:role="Earth">
    </PLANET_DATA>

    <LOOKUP xlink:type = "arc" xlink:from = "START"
        xlink:to = "Mercury" xlink:show="new"
        xlink:actuate="onRequest">
    </LOOKUP>

    <LOOKUP xlink:type = "arc" xlink:from = "START"
        xlink:to = "Venus" xlink:show="new"
        xlink:actuate="onRequest">
    </LOOKUP>

    <LOOKUP xlink:type = "arc" xlink:from = "START"
        xlink:to = "Earth" xlink:show="new"
        xlink:actuate="onRequest">
    </LOOKUP>
</ASTRO_DATA>
```

You can elaborate out-of-line linksets as much as you like; here, I'm adding arcs that will add a `"next"` and `"previous"` link to each planet:

```
<?xml version = "1.0"?>
<ASTRO_DATA xmlns:xlink="http://www.w3.org/1999/xlink"
         xlink:type="extended" xlink:title="Planetary Data">

    <PLANET_DATA xmlns:xlink = "http://www.w3.org/1999/xlink"
        xlink:type = "locator"
        xlink:show = "embed"
```

```
    xlink:href = "http://www.starpowdermovies.com/planets.xml">
    xlink:title="START"
    xlink:role="START">
</PLANET_DATA>

<PLANET_DATA xmlns:xlink = "http://www.w3.org/1999/xlink"
    xlink:type = "locator"
    xlink:show = "embed"
    xlink:href = "http://www.starpowdermovies.com/planets.xml#
        xpointer(/descendant::PLANET[position() = 1]">
    xlink:title="Mercury"
    xlink:role="Mercury">
</PLANET_DATA>

<PLANET_DATA xmlns:xlink = "http://www.w3.org/1999/xlink"
    xlink:type = "locator"
    xlink:show = "embed"
    xlink:href = "http://www.starpowdermovies.com/planets.xml#
        xpointer(/descendant::PLANET[position() = 2]">
    xlink:title="Venus"
    xlink:role="Venus">
</PLANET_DATA>

<PLANET_DATA xmlns:xlink = "http://www.w3.org/1999/xlink"
    xlink:type = "locator"
    xlink:show = "embed"
    xlink:href = "http://www.starpowdermovies.com/planets.xml#
        xpointer(/descendant::PLANET[position() = 3]">
    xlink:title="Earth"
    xlink:role="Earth">
</PLANET_DATA>

<LOOKUP xlink:type = "arc" xlink:from = "START"
    xlink:to = "Mercury" xlink:show="new"
    xlink:actuate="onRequest">
</LOOKUP>

<LOOKUP xlink:type = "arc" xlink:from = "START"
    xlink:to = "Venus" xlink:show="new"
    xlink:actuate="onRequest">
</LOOKUP>

<LOOKUP xlink:type = "arc" xlink:from = "START"
    xlink:to = "Earth" xlink:show="new"
    xlink:actuate="onRequest">
</LOOKUP>

<NEXT xlink:type = "arc" xlink:from = "Mercury"
    xlink:to = "Venus" xlink:show="new"
    xlink:actuate="onRequest">
</NEXT>
```

continues ▸

```
    <NEXT xlink:type = "arc" xlink:from = "Venus"
        xlink:to = "Earth" xlink:show="new"
        xlink:actuate="onRequest">
    </NEXT>

    <NEXT xlink:type = "arc" xlink:from = "Earth"
        xlink:to = "Mercury" xlink:show="new"
        xlink:actuate="onRequest">
    </NEXT>

    <PREVIOUS xlink:type = "arc" xlink:from = "Earth"
        xlink:to = "Venus" xlink:show="new"
        xlink:actuate="onRequest">
    </PREVIOUS>

    <PREVIOUS xlink:type = "arc" xlink:from = "Venus"
        xlink:to = "Mercury" xlink:show="new"
        xlink:actuate="onRequest">
    </PREVIOUS>

    <PREVIOUS xlink:type = "arc" xlink:from = "Mercury"
        xlink:to = "Earth" xlink:show="new"
        xlink:actuate="onRequest">
    </PREVIOUS>
</ASTRO_DATA>
```

The next question is this: Because out-of-line links are outside all resources they reference, how does application software that deals with those resources know how to find those links? The W3C specification is unclear on this point, much as it is on connecting external style sheets to XML documents. The idea here is that the application itself is responsible for finding such linkbases.

Admittedly, it is hard to specify how applications should find linkbases if you want to keep markup and content separate, which means that you can't embed a link to a linkbase in a resource (as when you're annotating someone else's work but don't have access to the source documents).

However, if you can add a link to a linkbase in a resource, W3C suggests a way to do so: You can use the predefined role `xlink:external-linkbase` to create links to a linkbase, something like this:

```
<EXTERNAL_LINKS xlink:type="simple"
    xmlns:xlink="http://www.w3.org/1999/xlink"
    xlink:role="xlink:external-linkset"
    xlink:href="linkbase.xml"/>
</EXTERNAL_LINKS>
```

So far in this chapter, I've said that you use the `xlink:href` attribute to locate resources, and I've left it at that. However, there is more to it than that: You can do more than just place a URI in this attribute—you can also use XPointers to locate specific locations or sections of a document.

All About XPointers

In the beginning of this chapter, I took a look at a link that used an XPointer to locate a specific element in a document; that example looked like this:

```
<MOVIE_REVIEW xmlns:xlink = "http://www.w3.org/1999/xlink"
    xlink:type = "simple"
    xlink:show = "new"
    xlink:href = "http://www.starpowdermovies.com/reviews.xml#
        xpointer(/child::*[position()=126]/child::*[position()=first()])">
    Mr. Blandings Builds His Dream House
</MOVIE_REVIEW>
```

You can see the XPointer part here:

```
xpointer(/child::*[position()=126]/child::*[position()=first()])
```

This XPointer is appended to the URI I'm using here, following a `#` character.

You might notice that this XPointer expression looks a lot like the XPath expressions we used in Chapter 13, and with good reason—XPointers are built on XPaths, with certain additions that I'll note here.

Because XPointers are built on XPaths, they have all the power of XPaths. Among other things, this means that you can use an XPointer made up of location steps that target an individual location in a document without having to add any markup to that document. You can also use the `id()` function to target specific elements if you do want to add ID attributes to those elements.

However, because XPointers extend XPaths, there are some differences. The biggest difference is that because users can select parts of documents using the mouse, if they prefer, XPointers enable you to select *points* and *ranges* in addition to the normal XPath nodes. A point is just what it sounds like: a specific location in a document. A range is made up of all the XML between two points, which can include part of elements and text strings.

To support points and ranges, XPointer extends the idea of nodes into *locations*. Every location is an XPath node, a point, or a range. Therefore, node sets become *location sets* in the XPointer specification.

How do you create an XPointer? Like XPaths, XPointers are made of location paths that are divided into location steps, separated by the / character. A location step is made up of an axis, a node test, and zero or more predicates, like this:

```
axis::node_test[predicate]
```

For example, in the expression

```
child::PLANET[position() = 5]
```

child is the name of the axis, PLANET is the node test, and [position() = 5] is a predicate.

You can create location paths with one or more location steps, such as /descendant::PLANET/child::NAME, which selects all the <NAME> elements that have a <PLANET> parent.

XPointers augment what's available with XPaths, so I'm going to take a look at these three parts—axes, node tests, and predicates—for XPointers now.

XPointer Axes

The XPointer axes are the same as the XPath axes, and we're already familiar with them. Axes tell you which direction you should search and give you a starting position to search from. Here's the list of possible axes:

Axis	Description
ancestor	Holds the ancestors of the context node. The ancestors of the context node are the parent of the context node and the parent's parent and so forth, back to and including the root node.
ancestor-or-self	Holds the context node and the ancestors of the context node.
attribute	Holds the attributes of the context node.
child	Holds the children of the context node.
descendant	Holds the descendants of the context node. A descendant is a child, or a child of a child, and so on.
descendant-or-self	Contains the context node and the descendants of the context node.
following	Holds all nodes in the same document as the context node that come after the context node.
following-sibling	Holds all the following siblings of the context node. A sibling is a node on the same level as the context node.

Axis	Description
`namespace`	Holds the namespace nodes of the context node.
`parent`	Holds the parent of the context node.
`preceding`	Contains all nodes that come before the context node.
`preceding-sibling`	Contains all the preceding siblings of the context node. A sibling is a node on the same level as the context node.
`self`	Contains the context node.

Although XPointers use the same axes as XPaths, there are some new node tests. We'll take a look at these next.

XPointer Node Tests

Here are the node tests you can use with XPointers, and what they match:

Node Test	Matches
`*`	Any element
`node()`	Any node
`text()`	A text node
`comment()`	A comment node
`processing-instruction()`	A processing instruction node
`point()`	A point in a resource
`range()`	A range in a resource

Note in particular the last two—`point()` and `range()`. These correspond to the two new constructs added in XPointers, points and ranges, and I'll talk more about them at the end of this chapter.

To extend XPath to include points and ranges, the XPointer specification created the concept of a location, which can be an XPath node, a point, or a range. However, node tests are still called node tests, not location tests; when discussing node tests, the XPointer specification specifically extends the definition of node types to include points and ranges so that node tests can work with those types. For the moment, then, we're stuck with the idea that locations can be XPath nodes, points, or ranges—and that the node types in node tests can also be XPath nodes, points, or ranges. Presumably, this contradiction will be cleared up in the final XPointer recommendation.

XPointer Predicates

XPointers support the same types of expressions as XPaths. As in Chapter 13, these are the possible types of expressions you can use in predicates (refer to Chapter 13 for more information):

- Node sets
- Booleans
- Numbers
- Strings
- Result tree fragments

As we saw in Chapter 13, there are functions to deal with all these types in XPath. The XPointer specification supports all those functions and also adds functions to cast subexpressions to the particular types defined in XPath, such as `boolean()`, `string()`, `text()`, and `number()`. It also adds the function `unique()`, to enable you to test whether an XPointer locates a single location rather than multiple locations or no locations.

XPointer also makes some additions to the functions that return location sets, and I'll take a look at those functions now.

XPointer Location Set Functions

Four XPointer functions return location sets:

Function	Description
`id()`	Returns all the elements with a specific ID
`root()`	Returns a location set with one location, the root node
`here()`	Returns a location set with one location, the current location
`origin()`	Same as `here()`, except that this function is used with out-of-line links

The `id()` function is the one we saw in Chapter 13 when discussing XPath. You can use this function to return all locations with a given ID.

The `root()` function works just like the `/` character—it refers to the root node (which is not the same as the document node—the root node corresponds to the very beginning of the prolog, while the document node corresponds to the top-level element in the document). The `root()` function is not actually part of the XPath specification, but the XPointer specification refers to it as if it were. Whether or not it will be included in the final XPointer recommendation is unclear.

The `here()` function refers to the current element. This is useful because XPointers are usually stored in text nodes or attribute values, and you might want to refer to the current element (not just the current node). For example, you might want to refer to the second previous `<NAME>` sibling element of the element that contains an XPointer, and you can use an expression like this to do so:

```
here()/preceding-sibling::NAME[position() = 2]
```

The `origin()` function is much like the `here()` function, but you use it with out-of-line links. It refers to the original element, which may be in another document, from which the current link was activated. This can be very helpful if the link itself is in a linkbase and needs to refer not to the element that the link is in, but the original element from which the link is activated.

You can use the abbreviated XPath syntax in XPointers as well. I'll take a look at a few examples, using `planets.xml` as the document we'll be navigating:

```
<?xml version="1.0"?>
<?xml-stylesheet type="text/xml" href="planets.xsl"?>
<PLANETS>

    <PLANET>
        <NAME>Mercury</NAME>
        <MASS UNITS="(Earth = 1)">.0553</MASS>
        <DAY UNITS="days">58.65</DAY>
        <RADIUS UNITS="miles">1516</RADIUS>
        <DENSITY UNITS="(Earth = 1)">.983</DENSITY>
        <DISTANCE UNITS="million miles">43.4</DISTANCE><!—At perihelion—>
    </PLANET>

    <PLANET>
        <NAME>Venus</NAME>
        <MASS UNITS="(Earth = 1)">.815</MASS>
        <DAY UNITS="days">116.75</DAY>
        <RADIUS UNITS="miles">3716</RADIUS>
        <DENSITY UNITS="(Earth = 1)">.943</DENSITY>
        <DISTANCE UNITS="million miles">66.8</DISTANCE><!—At perihelion—>
    </PLANET>

    <PLANET>
        <NAME>Earth</NAME>
        <MASS UNITS="(Earth = 1)">1</MASS>
        <DAY UNITS="days">1</DAY>
        <RADIUS UNITS="miles">2107</RADIUS>
        <DENSITY UNITS="(Earth = 1)">1</DENSITY>
        <DISTANCE UNITS="million miles">128.4</DISTANCE><!—At perihelion—>
    </PLANET>

</PLANETS>
```

Here are a few XPointer examples—note that, as with XPath, you can use the [] operator; here, it extracts a particular location from a location set.

Example	Description
PLANET	Returns the <PLANET> element children of the context node.
*	Returns all element children of the context node.
text()	Returns all text node children of the context node.
@UNITS	Returns the UNITS attribute of the context node.
@*	Returns all the attributes of the context node.
PLANET[3]	Returns the third <PLANET> child of the context node.
PLANET[first()]	Returns the first <PLANET> child of the context node.
*/PLANET	Returns all <PLANET> grandchildren of the context node.
/PLANETS/PLANET[3]/NAME[2]	Returns the second <NAME> element of the third <PLANET> element of the <PLANETS> element.
//PLANET	Returns all the <PLANET> descendants of the document root.
PLANETS//PLANET	Returns the <PLANET> element descendants of the <PLANETS> element children of the context node.
//PLANET/NAME	Returns all the <NAME> elements that have a <PLANET> parent.
.	Returns the context node itself.
.//PLANET	Returns the <PLANET> element descendants of the context node.
..	Returns the parent of the context node.
../@UNITS	Returns the UNITS attribute of the parent of the context node.
PLANET[NAME]	Returns the <PLANET> children of the context node that have <NAME> children.
PLANET[NAME="Venus"]	Returns the <PLANET> children of the context node that have <NAME> children with text equal to "Venus".
PLANET[@UNITS = "days"]	Returns all <PLANET> children of the context node that have a UNITS attribute with value "days".
PLANET[6][@UNITS = "days"]	Returns the sixth <PLANET> child of the context node, only if that child has a UNITS attribute with value "days". Can also be written as PLANET[@UNITS = "days"][6].
PLANET[@COLOR and @UNITS]	Returns all the <PLANET> children of the context node that have both a COLOR attribute and a UNITS attribute.

In XPath, you can locate data only at the node level. That's fine when you're working with software that handles XML data in terms of nodes, such as XSL transformations, but it's not good enough for all purposes. For example, a user working with a displayed XML document might be able to click the mouse at a particular point, or even select a range of XML content. (Note that such ranges might not start and end on node boundaries at all—they might contain parts of various trees and subtrees.) To give you finer control over XML data, you can work with *points* and *ranges* in XPointer.

Using XPointer Points

How do you define a point in the XPointer specification? To do so, you must use two items—a node, and an index that can hold a positive integer or zero. The node specifies an origin for the point, and the index indicates how far the point you want is from that origin.

But what should the index be measured in terms of—characters in the document, or number of nodes? In fact, there are two different types of points, and the index value you use is measured differently for those types.

Node-points

When the origin node, also called the *container* node, of a point can have child nodes (which means that it's an element node or the root node), then the point is called a *node-point*.

The index of a node-point is measured in child nodes. Here, the index of a node-point must be equal to or less than the number of child nodes in the origin node. If you use an index of zero, the point is immediately before any child nodes. An index of 5 locates a point immediately after the fifth child node.

You can use axes with node-points: A node-point's siblings are the children of the container node before or after the node-point. Points don't have any children, however.

Character-points

If the origin node can't contain any child nodes, only text, then the index is measured in characters. Points like these are called *character-points*.

The index of a character-point must be a positive integer or zero, and less than or equal to the length of the text string in the node. If the index is zero, the point is immediately before the first character; an index of `5` locates the point immediately after the fifth character. Character-points do not have preceding or following siblings, or children.

For example, you can treat <DOCUMENT> as a container node in this document:

```
<DOCUMENT>
Hi there!
</DOCUMENT>
```

In this case, there are nine character-points here, one before every character. The character-point at index 0 is right before the first character, H; the character-point at index 1 is right before the i; and so on.

In addition, you should note that the XPointer specification collapses all consecutive whitespace into a single space, so four spaces is the same as one space when calculating an index for a character-point. Also, you cannot place points inside a start tag, end tag, processing instruction, or comment, or inside any markup.

Creating Points

To create a point, you use the start-point() function with a predicate, like this:

```
start-point()[position()=10]
```

Here's an example; say that I wanted to position a point just before the e in the text in Mercury's <NAME> element:

```
<?xml version="1.0"?>
<?xml-stylesheet type="text/xml" href="planets.xsl"?>
<PLANETS>

    <PLANET>
        <NAME>Mercury</NAME>
        <MASS UNITS="(Earth = 1)">.0553</MASS>
        <DAY UNITS="days">58.65</DAY>
        <RADIUS UNITS="miles">1516</RADIUS>
        <DENSITY UNITS="(Earth = 1)">.983</DENSITY>
        <DISTANCE UNITS="million miles">43.4</DISTANCE><!--At perihelion-->
    </PLANET>
    .
    .
    .
```

In this case, I could use an expression like this to refer to the point right before the character e:

```
xpointer(/PLANETS/PLANET[1]/NAME/text()/start-point()[position() = 1])
```

Similarly, I can access the point right before the 6 in the text in Mercury's <DAY> element, 58.65 (which, of course, is text, not a number), this way:

```
xpointer(/PLANETS/PLANET[1]/DAY/text()/start-point()[position() = 3])
```

Using XPointer Ranges

You can create ranges with two points, a start point and an end point, as long as they are in the same document and the start point is not after the end point. (If the start point and the end point are the same, the range is *collapsed.*) A range is all of the XML structure between those two points.

A range doesn't have to be a neat subsection of a document; it can extend from one subtree to another in the document, for example. All you need are a valid start point and a valid end point in the same document.

Creating Ranges

To create a range, you use two location paths, separated with the keyword `to` in the `xpointer()` function. For example, here's how to create a range that includes the whole word `Mercury` in `planets.xml`:

```
xpointer(/PLANETS/PLANET[1]/NAME/text()/start-point()[position() = 0] to
/PLANETS/PLANET[1]/NAME/text()/start-point()[position() = 7])
```

Here's how to create a range that includes the entire text value in Mercury's `<RADIUS>` element, `1516`:

```
xpointer(/PLANETS/PLANET[1]/RADIUS/text()/start-point()[position() = 0] to
/PLANETS/PLANET[1]/RADIUS/text()/start-point()[position() = 4])
```

Range Functions

The XPointer specification adds a number of functions to those available in XPath to handle ranges:

Function	Description
`range-to(`*`location-set`*`)`	This function takes the locations you pass to it and returns a range that completely covers the location. For example, an element location is converted to a range by returning the element's parent as the origin node, the start point as the number of previous siblings the element has, and the end point as one greater than the start point. In other words, this function is intended to cover locations with ranges.
`range-inside(`*`location-set`*`)`	This function returns a range or ranges covering each location in the argument location set. For example, if you pass an element location, the result is a range that encloses all that is inside the element.

continues

`start-point(location-set)` This function returns a location set with start points in it. Those points are the start points of ranges that would cover the passed locations. For example, `start-point(//PLANET[2])` would return the point immediately before the second `<PLANET>` element in the document, and `start-point (//PLANET)` would return a location set of the points just before each `<PLANET>` element.

`end-point(location-set)` This is the same as `start-point()`, except that it returns the corresponding endpoints of the ranges that cover the locations passed to it.

Using String Ranges

The XPointer specification also includes a function for basic string matching, `string-range()`. This function returns a location set with one range for every nonoverlapping match to the search string. The match operation is case-sensitive.

You can also specify optional index and length arguments to specify how many characters after the match the range should start and how many characters should be in the range. Here's how you use `string-range()` in general:

```
string-range(location_set, string, [index, [length]])
```

Matching an Empty String

An empty string, `""`, matches to the location immediately before any character, so you can use an empty string to match to the very beginning of any string.

For example, this expression returns a location set containing ranges covering all matches to the word `"Saturn"`:

```
string-range(/, "Saturn")
```

To extract a specific match from the location set returned, you use the `[]` operator. For example, this expression returns a range covering the second occurrence of `"Saturn"` in the document:

```
string-range(/, "Saturn")[2]
```

This expression returns a range covering the third occurrence of the word `"Jupiter"` in the `<NAME>` element of the sixth `<PLANET>` element in a document:

```
string-range(//PLANET[6]/NAME, "Jupiter")[3]
```

You can also specify the range you want to return using the `index` (which starts with a value of 1) and `length` arguments. For example, this expression returns a range covering the letters `er` in the third occurrence of the word `"Jupiter"` in the <NAME> element of the sixth <PLANET> element:

```
string-range(//PLANET[6]/NAME, "Jupiter", 6, 2)[3]
```

If you want to locate a specific point, you can create a collapsed (zero-length) range, like this:

```
string-range(//PLANET[6]/NAME, "Jupiter", 6, 0)[3]
```

Another way to get a specific point is to use the `start-point()` function, which returns the start point of a range:

```
start-point(string-range(//PLANET[6]/NAME, "Jupiter", 6, 2)[3])
```

Here's an expression that locates the second `@` character in any text node in the document and the five characters following it:

```
string-range(/, "@", 1, 6)[2]
```

XPointer Abbreviations

Because it's so common to refer to elements by location or ID, XPointer adds a few abbreviated forms of reference. Here's an example; suppose that you wanted to locate Venus's <DAY> element in `planets.xml`:

```
<?xml version="1.0"?>
<?xml-stylesheet type="text/xml" href="planets.xsl"?>
<PLANETS>

    <PLANET>
        <NAME>Mercury</NAME>
        <MASS UNITS="(Earth = 1)">.0553</MASS>
        <DAY UNITS="days">58.65</DAY>
        <RADIUS UNITS="miles">1516</RADIUS>
        <DENSITY UNITS="(Earth = 1)">.983</DENSITY>
        <DISTANCE UNITS="million miles">43.4</DISTANCE><!--At perihelion-->
    </PLANET>

    <PLANET>
        <NAME>Venus</NAME>
        <MASS UNITS="(Earth = 1)">.815</MASS>
        <DAY UNITS="days">116.75</DAY>
        <RADIUS UNITS="miles">3716</RADIUS>
        <DENSITY UNITS="(Earth = 1)">.943</DENSITY>
        <DISTANCE UNITS="million miles">66.8</DISTANCE><!--At perihelion-->
    </PLANET>
    .
    .
    .
```

You could do so with this rather formidable expression:

```
http://www.starpowdermovies.com/planets.xml#
xpointer(/child::*[position()=1]/
child::*[position()=2]/child::*[position()=3])
```

As you know from Chapter 13, the `child::` part is optional in XPath expressions, and the predicate `[position() = x]` can be abbreviated as `[x]`. In XPointer, you can abbreviate this still more, omitting the `[` and `]`. Here's the result, which is fairly compact:

```
http://www.starpowdermovies.com/planets.xml#1/2/3
```

When you see location steps made up of single numbers in this way, those location steps correspond to the location of elements.

In a similar way, you can use words as location steps, not just numbers, if those words correspond to ID values of elements in the document. For example, say that I give Venus's `<PLANET>` element the ID `"Planet_Of_Love"`. (Here I'm assuming that this element's ID attribute is declared with the type `ID` in a DTD.)

```
<?xml version="1.0"?>
<?xml-stylesheet type="text/xml" href="planets.xsl"?>
<PLANETS>

    <PLANET>
        <NAME>Mercury</NAME>
        <MASS UNITS="(Earth = 1)">.0553</MASS>
        <DAY UNITS="days">58.65</DAY>
        <RADIUS UNITS="miles">1516</RADIUS>
        <DENSITY UNITS="(Earth = 1)">.983</DENSITY>
        <DISTANCE UNITS="million miles">43.4</DISTANCE><!--At perihelion-->
    </PLANET>

    <PLANET ID = "Planet_Of_Love">
        <NAME>Venus</NAME>
        <MASS UNITS="(Earth = 1)">.815</MASS>
        <DAY UNITS="days">116.75</DAY>
        <RADIUS UNITS="miles">3716</RADIUS>
        <DENSITY UNITS="(Earth = 1)">.943</DENSITY>
        <DISTANCE UNITS="million miles">66.8</DISTANCE><!--At perihelion-->
    </PLANET>
    .
    .
    .
```

Now you could reach the `<DAY>` element in Venus's `<PLANET>` element like this:

```
http://www.starpowdermovies.com/planets.xml#
xpointer(//child::*[id("Planet_Of_Love")]/child::*[position()=3]
```

However, there's also an abbreviated version that's much shorter. In this case, I use the fact that you can use an element's ID value as a location step, and the result looks like this:

```
http://www.starpowdermovies.com/planets.xml#Planet_Of_Love/3
```

As you can see, this form is considerably shorter.

In this example, I used the `id()` function; to use that function, you should declare ID attributes so that they have the type ID. However, not all documents have a DTD or schema, so XPointer enables you to specify *alternative* patterns using multiple XPointers. Here's how that might look in this case, where I specify two XPointers in one location step:

```
http://www.starpowdermovies.com/planets.xml#
xpointer(id("Planet_Of_Love"))xpointer(//*[@id="Planet_Of_Love"])/3
```

If the first XPointer, which relies on the `id()` function, fails, the second XPointer is supposed to be used instead, and that one locates any element that has an attribute named `ID` with the required value. It remains to be seen how much of this syntax applications will actually implement.

That's it for XLinks and XPointers. As you can see, there's a lot of power here—far more than with simple HTML hyperlinks. However, the XLink and XPointer standards have been proposed for quite a few years now, and there have been practically no implementations of them. Hopefully the future will bring more concrete results.

In the next chapter, I'm going to start looking at some popular XML applications in depth, starting with the most popular one of all: XHTML.

16 Essential XHTML

PROBABLY THE BIGGEST XML APPLICATION TODAY IS XHTML, which is W3C's implementation of HTML 4.0 in XML. XHTML is a true XML application, which means that XHTML documents are XML documents that can be checked for well-formedness and validity.

There are two big advantages to using XHTML. First, HTML predefines all its elements and attributes, and that's not something you can change—unless you use XHTML. Because XHTML is really XML, you can extend it with your own elements, and we'll see how to do that in the next chapter. Need `<INVOICE>`, `<DELIVERY_DATE>`, and `<PRODUCT_ID>` elements in your Web page? Now you can add them. (This aspect of XHTML isn't supported by the major browsers yet, but it's coming.) The other big advantage, as far as HTML authors are concerned, is that you can display XHTML documents in today's browsers without modification. That's the whole idea behind XHTML—it's supposed to provide a bridge between XML and HTML. XHTML is true XML, but you can use it today in browsers. And that has made it very popular.

Here's an example; this page is written in standard HTML:

```
<HTML>
    <HEAD>
        <TITLE>
            Welcome to my page
        </TITLE>
    </HEAD>
```

continues ▸

```
    <BODY>
        <H1>
            Welcome to HTML!
        </H1>
    </BODY>
</HTML>
```

Here's the same page, written in XHTML, with the message changed from `Welcome to HTML!` to `Welcome to XHTML!`:

```
<?xml version="1.0"?>
<!DOCTYPE html PUBLIC "-//W3C//DTD XHTML 1.0 Transitional//EN"
"http://www.w3.org/TR/xhtml1/DTD/xhtml1-transitional.dtd">
<html xmlns="http://www.w3.org/1999/xhtml" xml:lang="en" lang="en">
    <head>
        <title>
            Welcome to my page
        </title>
    </head>

    <body>
        <h1>
            Welcome to XHTML!
        </h1>
    </body>
</html>
```

I'll go through exactly what's happening here in this chapter.

You save XHTML documents with the extension .html to make sure that browsers treat those documents as HTML. This document produces the same result as the previous HTML document, except that this document says `Welcome to XHTML!` instead, as you can see in Figure 16.1.

Figure 16.1 An XHTML document in Netscape.

Take a look at this XHTML document; as you can see, it's true XML, starting with the XML declaration:

```
<?xml version="1.0"?>
    .
    .
    .
```

Next comes a `<!DOCTYPE>` element:

```
<?xml version="1.0"?>
<!DOCTYPE html PUBLIC "-//W3C//DTD XHTML 1.0 Transitional//EN"
"http://www.w3.org/TR/xhtml1/DTD/xhtml1-transitional.dtd">
    .
    .
    .
```

This is just a standard `<!DOCTYPE>` element; in this case, it indicates that the document element is `<html>`. Note the lowercase here—`<html>`, not `<HTML>`. All elements in XHTML (except the `<!DOCTYPE>` element) are lowercase. That's the XHTML standard—if you're accustomed to using uppercase tag names, it'll take a little getting used to.

The DTDs that XHTML use are public DTDs, created by W3C. Here, the formal public identifier (FPI) for the DTD that I'm using is `"-//W3C//DTD XHTML 1.0 Transitional//EN"`, which is one of several DTDs available, as we'll see. I'm also giving the URL for the DTD, which for this DTD is `"http://www.w3.org/TR/xhtml1/DTD/xhtml1-transitional.dtd"`.

Using an XHTML DTD, browsers can validate XHTML documents, at least theoretically (and, in fact, browsers such as Internet Explorer will read in the DTD and check the document against it, although as we've seen, you must explicitly check whether errors occurred because the browser won't announce them).

Note also that the URI for the DTD is at W3C itself: `"http://www.w3.org/TR/xhtml1/DTD/xhtml1-transitional.dtd"`. Now imagine 40 million browsers trying to validate XHTML documents all at the same time by downloading XHTML DTDs like this one from the W3C site—quite a problem. To avoid bottlenecks like this, you can copy the XHTML DTDs and store them locally (I'll give their URIs and discuss this in a few pages), or do without a DTD in your documents. However, my guess is that when we get fully enabled validating XHTML browsers, they'll have the various XHTML DTDs stored internally for immediate access, without having to download the XHTML DTDs from the Internet. (As it stands now, it takes Internet Explorer 10 to 20 seconds to download a typical XHTML DTD on a typical modem line.)

After the <!DOCTYPE> element comes the <html> element, which is the document element. It starts the actual document content:

```
<?xml version="1.0"?>
<!DOCTYPE html PUBLIC "-//W3C//DTD XHTML 1.0 Transitional//EN"
"http://www.w3.org/TR/xhtml1/DTD/xhtml1-transitional.dtd">
<html xmlns="http://www.w3.org/1999/xhtml" xml:lang="en" lang="en">
    .
    .
    .
```

I'm using three attributes of this XHTML element here, as is usual:

- `xmlns` defines an XML namespace for the document.
- `xml:lang` sets the language for the document when it's interpreted as XML.
- The standard HTML attribute `lang` sets the language when the document is treated as HTML.

Note in particular the namespace used for XHTML: `"http://www.w3.org/1999/xhtml"`, which is the official XHTML namespace. All the XHTML elements must be in this namespace.

The remainder of the page is very like the HTML document we saw earlier—the only real difference is that the tag names are now lowercase:

```
<?xml version="1.0"?>
<!DOCTYPE html PUBLIC "-//W3C//DTD XHTML 1.0 Transitional//EN"
"http://www.w3.org/TR/xhtml1/DTD/xhtml1-transitional.dtd">
<html xmlns="http://www.w3.org/1999/xhtml" xml:lang="en" lang="en">
    <head>
        <title>
            Welcome to my page
        </title>
    </head>

    <body>
        <h1>
            Welcome to XHTML!
        </h1>
    </body>
</html>
```

XHTML Versions

As you see in the <!DOCTYPE> element, I'm using the XHTML DTD that's called "XHTML 1.0 Transitional". That's only one of the XHTML DTDs available, although it's currently the most popular one. So, what XHTML DTDs are available, and what do they mean? That all depends on what version of XHTML that you are using.

XHTML Version 1.0

The standard version of XHTML, version 1.0, is just a rewrite of HTML 4.0 in XML. You can find the W3C recommendation for XHTML 1.0 at www.w3.org/TR/xhtml1. Essentially, it's just a set of DTDs that provide validity checks for documents that are supposed to mimic HTML 4.0 (actually, HTML 4.01). The W3C has created several DTDs for HTML 4.0, and the XHTML DTDs are based on those, translated into straight XML. As with HTML 4.0, XHTML 1.0 has three versions, which correspond to three DTDs here:

- **The strict XHTML 1.0 DTD.** The strict DTD is based on straight HTML 4.0 and does not include support for elements and attributes that the W3C considers deprecated. This is the version of XHTML 1.0 that the W3C hopes people will migrate to in time.
- **The transitional XHTML 1.0 DTD.** The transitional DTD is based on the *transitional* HTML 4.0 DTD. This DTD has support for the many elements and attributes that were deprecated in HTML 4.0 but that are still popular, such as the <CENTER> and <FONT> elements. This DTD is also named the "loose" DTD. It is the most popular version of XHTML at the moment.
- **The frameset XHTML 1.0 DTD.** The frameset DTD is based on the frameset HTML 4.0 DTD. This is the DTD you should work with when you're creating pages based on frames: In that case, you replace the <BODY> element with a <FRAMESET> element. The DTD must reflect that, so you use the frameset DTD when working with frames. That's the difference between the XHTML 1.0 transitional and frameset DTDs—the frameset DTD replaces the <BODY> element with the <FRAMESET> element.

Here are the actual <!DOCTYPE> elements you should use in XHTML for these various DTDs—strict, transitional, and frameset—including the URIs for these DTDs:

```
<!DOCTYPE html
     PUBLIC "-//W3C//DTD XHTML 1.0 Strict//EN"
     "http://www.w3.org/TR/xhtml1/DTD/xhtml1-strict.dtd">

<!DOCTYPE html
     PUBLIC "-//W3C//DTD XHTML 1.0 Transitional//EN"
     "http://www.w3.org/TR/xhtml1/DTD/xhtml1-transitional.dtd">

<!DOCTYPE html
     PUBLIC "-//W3C//DTD XHTML 1.0 Frameset//EN"
     "http://www.w3.org/TR/xhtml1/DTD/xhtml1-frameset.dtd">
```

Because I'm giving the DTDs' URIs here, you can copy them and cache a local copy if you want for faster access. For example, if you place the DTD files in a directory named DTD in your Web site, your <!DOCTYPE> elements might look more like this:

```
<!DOCTYPE html
     PUBLIC "-//W3C//DTD XHTML 1.0 Strict//EN"
     "DTD/xhtml1-strict.dtd">

<!DOCTYPE html
     PUBLIC "-//W3C//DTD XHTML 1.0 Transitional//EN"
     "DTD/xhtml1-transitional.dtd">

<!DOCTYPE html
     PUBLIC "-//W3C//DTD XHTML 1.0 Frameset//EN"
     "DTD/xhtml1-frameset.dtd">
```

If you cache these DTDs locally, there should be less of a bottleneck when XHTML becomes very popular and users try to download your documents.

XHTML Version 1.1

There's also a new version of XHTML available, version 1.1. This version is not yet in W3C recommendation form; it's a working draft. You can find the current working draft of XHTML 1.1 at www.w3.org/TR/xhtml11.

XHTML 1.1 is a strict version of XHTML, and it's clear that the W3C wants to wean HTML authors away from their loose ways into writing very tight XML. How far those HTML authors will follow is yet to be determined. XHTML 1.1 removes all the elements and attributes deprecated in HTML 4.0, and a few more as well.

<APPLET> Versus <OBJECT>

There's another interesting thing going on in XHTML 1.1: The W3C has long said that it wants to replace the `<APPLET>` and other elements with the Microsoft-supported `<OBJECT>` element. However, and surprisingly, `<OBJECT>` is missing from XHTML 1.1. And—surprise—the `<APPLET>` element is back.

XHTML 1.1 is so far ahead of the pack that many of the features that today's HTML authors and browsers use aren't supported there at all. Therefore, I'm going to stick to XHTML 1.0 transitional in the examples in this chapter and the next chapter. However, I'll also indicate which elements and attributes are supported by what versions of XHTML, including XHTML 1.1, throughout these chapters.

XHTML 1.0 Versus XHTML 1.1

You can find the differences between XHTML 1.0 and XHTML 1.1 at `www.w3.org/TR/xhtml11/changes.html#a_changes`.

When you want to use XHTML 1.1, here's the `<!DOCTYPE>` element you should use (there's only one XHTML 1.1 DTD, not three, as in XHTML 1.0):

```
<!DOCTYPE html PUBLIC "-//W3C//DTD XHTML 1.1//EN"
    "http://www.w3.org/TR/xhtml11/DTD/xhtml11.dtd">
```

Another big difference between XHTML 1.1 and XHTML 1.0 goes beyond the support offered to various elements and attributes. XHTML is designed to be modular. In practice, this means that the XHTML 1.1 DTD is actually relatively short—it's a *driver* DTD, which inserts various other DTDs as modules. The benefit of modular DTDs is that you can omit the modules that your application doesn't support.

For example, if you're supporting XHTML 1.1 on a nonstandard device such as a PDA or even a cell phone or pager (the W3C has all kinds of big ideas for the future), you might not be able to support everything, such as tables or hyperlinks. With XHTML 1.1, all you need to do is to omit the DTD modules corresponding to tables and hyperlinks. (Several modules are marked as required in the XHTML 1.1 DTD, and those cannot be omitted.)

XHTML Basic

In fact, there's another version of XHTML that is also in the working draft stage: XHTML Basic. XHTML Basic is a very small subset of XHTML, reduced to a very minimum so that it can be supported by devices considerably simpler than standard PCs. You can find the current working draft for XHTML Basic at `www.w3.org/TR/xhtml-basic`.

If you want to use XML Basic, here's the <!DOCTYPE> element you should use:

```
<!DOCTYPE html PUBLIC "-//W3C//DTD XHTML Basic 1.0//EN"
     "http://www.w3.org/TR/xhtml-basic/xhtml-basic10.dtd">
```

XHTML Checklist

The W3C has a number of requirements for documents before they can be called true XHTML documents. Here's the list of requirements that documents must meet:

- The document must successfully validate against one of the W3C XHTML DTDs.
- The document element must be <html>.
- The document element, <html>, must set an XML namespace for the document, using the xmlns attribute. This namespace must be "http://www.w3.org/1999/xhtml".
- There must be a <!DOCTYPE> element, and it must appear before the document element.

XHTML is designed to be displayed in today's browsers, and it works well (largely because those browsers ignore elements that they don't understand, such as <?xml?> and <!DOCTYPE>). However, because XHTML is also XML, a number of differences exist between legal HTML and legal XHTML.

XHTML Versus HTML

As you know, XML is more particular about many aspects of writing documents than HTML is. For example, you need to place all attribute values in quotes in XML, although HTML documents can use unquoted values because HTML browsers will accept that. One of the problems the W3C is trying to solve with XHTML, in fact, is the thicket of nonstandard HTML that's out there on the Web, mostly because browsers support it. Some observers estimate that half of the code in browsers is there to handle nonstandard use of HTML, and that discourages any but the largest companies from creating HTML browsers. XHTML is supposed to be different—if a document isn't in perfect XHTML, the browser is supposed to quit loading it and display an error, *not* guess what the document author was trying to do. Hopefully, that will make it easier to write XHTML browsers.

Here are some of the major differences between HTML and XHTML:

- XHTML documents must be well-formed XML documents.
- Element and attribute names must be in lowercase.
- Elements that aren't empty need end tags; end tags can't be omitted as they can sometimes in HTML.
- Attribute values must always be quoted.
- You cannot use "standalone" attributes that are not assigned values. If need be, assign a dummy value to an attribute, as in `action = "action"`.
- Empty elements must end with the `/>` characters. In practice, this does not seem to be a problem for the major browsers, which is a lucky thing for XHTML because it's definitely not standard HTML.
- The `<a>` element cannot contain other `<a>` elements.
- The `<pre>` element cannot contain the `<img>`, `<object>`, `<big>`, `<small>`, `<sub>`, or `<sup>` elements.
- The `<button>` element cannot contain the `<input>`, `<select>`, `<textarea>`, `<label>`, `<button>`, `<form>`, `<fieldset>`, `<iframe>`, or `<isindex>` elements.
- The `<label>` element cannot contain other `<label>` elements.
- The `<form>` element cannot contain other `<form>` elements.
- You must use the `id` attribute, not the `name` attribute, even on elements that have also had a `name` attribute. In XHTML 1.0, the `name` attribute of the `<a>`, `<applet>`, `<form>`, `<frame>`, `<iframe>`, `<img>`, and `<map>` elements is formally deprecated. In practice, this is a little difficult in browsers such as Netscape that support `name` and not `id`; in that case, you should use both attributes in the same element, even though it's not legal XHTML.
- You must escape sensitive characters. For example, when an attribute value contains an ampersand (`&`), the ampersand must be expressed as a character entity reference, as `&`.

As we'll see in the next chapter, there are some additional requirements—for example, if you use < characters in your scripts, you should either escape such characters as `<`, or, if the browser can't handle that, place the script in an external file. (The W3C's suggestion—to place scripts in `CDATA` sections—is definitely not understood by any major browser today.)

Automatic Conversion from HTML to XHTML

You may already have a huge Web site full of HTML pages, and you might be reading all this with some trepidation—how are you going to convert all those pages to the far more strict XHTML? In fact, a utility out there can do it for you—the Tidy utility, created by Dave Raggett. This utility is available for a wide variety of platforms, and you can download it for free from www.w3.org/People/Raggett/tidy. There's also a complete set of instructions on that page.

Here's an example: I'll use Tidy in Windows to convert a file from HTML to XHTML. In this case, I'll use the example HTML file we developed earlier, as saved in a file named index.html:

```
<HTML>
    <HEAD>
        <TITLE>
            Welcome to my page
        </TITLE>
    </HEAD>

    <BODY>
        <H1>
            Welcome to XHTML!
        </H1>
    </BODY>
</HTML>
```

After downloading Tidy, you run it at the command prompt. Here are the command-line switches, or options, that you can use with Tidy:

Switch	Description
-config *file*	Use the configuration file named *file*
-indent or -i	Indent element content
-omit or -o	Omit optional end tags
-wrap 72	Wrap text at column 72 (default is 68)
-upper or -u	Force tags to uppercase (default is lowercase)
-clean or -c	Replace font, nobr, &, and center tags, by CSS
-raw	Don't substitute entities for characters 128 to 255
-ascii	Use ASCII for output, and Latin-1 for input
-latin1	Use Latin-1 for both input and output
-utf8	Use UTF-8 for both input and output
-iso2022	Use ISO2022 for both input and output
-numeric or -n	Output numeric rather than named entities
-modify or -m	Modify original files
-errors or -e	Show only error messages
-quiet or -q	Suppress nonessential output
-f *file*	Write errors to *file*

`-xml`	Use this when input is in XML
`-asxml`	Convert HTML to XML
`-slides`	Burst into slides on h2 elements
`-help`	List command-line options
`-version`	Show release date

In this example, I'll use three switches:

- `-m` indicates that I want Tidy to modify the file I pass to it, which will be `index.html`
- `-i` indicates that I want it to indent the resulting XHTML elements
- `-config` indicates that I want to use a configuration file named `config.txt`.

Here's how I use Tidy from the command line:

```
%tidy -m -i -config configuration.txt index.html
```

Tidy is actually a utility that cleans up HTML, as you might gather from its name. To make it create XHTML, you must use a configuration file, which I've named `configuration.txt` here. You can see all the configuration file options on the Tidy Web site. Here are the contents of `configuration.txt`, which I'll use to convert `index.html` to XHTML:

```
output-xhtml: yes
add-xml-pi: yes
doctype: loose
```

Here, `output-xhtml` indicates that I want Tidy to create XHTML output. Using `add-xml-pi` indicates that the output should also include an XML declaration, and `doctype: loose` means that I want to use the transitional XHTML DTD. If you don't specify what DTD to use, Tidy will guess, based on your HTML.

Here's the resulting XHTML document:

```
<?xml version="1.0"?>
<!DOCTYPE html PUBLIC "-//W3C//DTD XHTML 1.0 Transitional//EN"
    "http://www.w3.org/TR/xhtml1/DTD/xhtml1-transitional.dtd">

<html xmlns="http://www.w3.org/1999/xhtml">
  <head>
    <meta name="generator" content="HTML Tidy, see www.w3.org" />

    <title>Welcome to my page</title>
  </head>

  <body>
    <h1> Welcome to XHTML!</h1>
  </body>
</html>
```

You can even teach Tidy about new XHTML tags that you've added. If you're ever stuck and want a quick way of translating HTML into XHTML, check out Tidy; it's fast, it's effective, and it's free.

Validating Your XHTML Document

The W3C has a validator you can use to check the validity of your XHTML document, and you can find this validator at `http://validator.w3.org`. To use the XHTML validator, you just enter the URI of your document and click the Validate This Page button. The W3C validator checks the document and gives you a full report. Here's an example response:

```
Congratulations, this document validates as XHTML1.0 Transitional!
To show your readers that you have taken the care to create an
interoperable Web page, you may display this icon on any page that
validates. Here is the HTML you could use to add this icon to your
Web page:
  <p>
    <a href="http://validator.w3.org/check/referer"><img
        src="http://validator.w3.org/images/vxhtml10"
        alt="Valid XHTML 1.0!" height="31" width="88" /></a>
  </p>
```

In this case, the document I tested validated properly, and the W3C validator says that I can add the official W3C XHTML 1.0 Transitional logo to the document. That logo appears in Figure 16.2.

Figure 16.2 The W3C transitional XHTML logo.

Actually, the W3C XHTML validator does not do a complete job—it doesn't check to see if values are supplied for required attributes, for example, or make sure that child elements are allowed to be nested inside the particular type of their parents. However, it does a reasonably good job.

XHTML Programming

In the remainder of this chapter, I'm going to get to the actual XHTML programming, starting with the document element, `<html>`.

Document Element (<*html*>)

This element is supported in XHTML 1.0 Strict, XHTML 1.0 Transitional, XHTML 1.0 Frameset, and XHTML 1.1. Here are its attributes:

Attribute	Description
`dir`	Sets the direction of text that doesn't have an inherent direction in which you should read it, called *directionally neutral text*. You can set this attribute to `LTR`, for left-to-right text, or `RTL`, for right-to-left text.
`lang`	Specifies the base language used in the element. Applies only when the document is interpreted as HTML.
`xml:lang`	Specifies the base language for the element when the document is interpreted as XML.
`xmlns`	Is required. Set this attribute to `"http://www.w3.org/1999/xhtml"`.

The document element for all XHTML elements is `<html>`, which is how XHTML matches the `<HTML>` element in HTML documents. This element must contain all the content of the document, as in this example:

```
<?xml version="1.0"?>
<!DOCTYPE html PUBLIC "-//W3C//DTD XHTML 1.0 Transitional//EN"
"http://www.w3.org/TR/xhtml1/DTD/xhtml1-transitional.dtd">
<html xmlns="http://www.w3.org/1999/xhtml" xml:lang="en" lang="en">
    <head>
        <title>
            Welcome to my page
        </title>
    </head>

    <body>
        <h1>
            Welcome to XHTML!
        </h1>
    </body>
</html>
```

The document element is very important in XML documents, of course. Note that this is one of the big differences between XHTML and HTML—in HTML, the `<HTML>` tag is optional because it's the default. To be valid XHTML, a document must have an `<html>` element.

Of all the attributes of this element, only one is required—`xmlns`, which sets the XML namespace. Most XML applications set up their own namespace to avoid overlap, and XHTML is no exception; you must set the `xmlns` attribute to `"http://www.w3.org/1999/xhtml"` in XHTML documents.

This tag also supports the `lang` and `xml:lang` attributes to let you specify the language of the document. If you specify values for both these attributes, the `xml:lang` attribute takes precedence in XHTML.

In XHTML, the <html> element can contain a <head> and a <body> element (or a <head> and a <frameset> element, in the XHTML 1.0 frameset document).

Creating a Web Page Heading (*<head>*)

The <head> element contains the head of an XHTML document, which should contain at least a <title> element. The <head> element is supported in XHTML 1.0 Strict, XHTML 1.0 Transitional, XHTML 1.0 Frameset, and XHTML 1.1. Here are the attributes of this element:

Attribute	Description
dir	Sets the direction of directionally neutral text. You can set this attribute to LTR, for left-to-right text, or RTL, for right-to-left text.
lang	Specifies the base language used in the element. Applies only when the document is interpreted as HTML.
profile	Specifies the location of one or more whitespace-separated metadata profile URIs.
xml:lang	Specifies the base language for the element when the document is interpreted as an XML document.

Each XHTML document should have a <head> element, like the one in this example:

```
<?xml version="1.0"?>
<!DOCTYPE html PUBLIC "-//W3C//DTD XHTML 1.0 Transitional//EN"
"http://www.w3.org/TR/xhtml1/DTD/xhtml1-transitional.dtd">
<html xmlns="http://www.w3.org/1999/xhtml" xml:lang="en" lang="en">
    <head>
        <title>
            Welcome to my page
        </title>
    </head>

    <body>
        <h1>
            Welcome to XHTML!
        </h1>
    </body>
</html>
```

The head of an XHTML document holds information that isn't directly displayed in the document itself, such as a title for the document (which usually appears in the browser's title bar), keywords that search engines can pick up, the base address for URIs, and so on. The head of every XHTML document is supposed to contain a <title> element, which holds the title of the document.

This element also supports the usual attributes, such as `lang` and `xml:lang`, as well as one attribute that is specific to `<head>` elements: `profile`. The profile attribute can hold a whitespace-separated list of URIs that hold information about the document, such as a description of the document, the author's name, copyright information, and so forth. (None of the major browsers implement this attribute yet.)

Here are the elements that can appear in the head:

Element	Description
`<base>`	Specifies the base URI for the document
`<isindex>`	Supports rudimentary input control
`<link>`	Specifies the relationship between the document and an external object
`<meta>`	Contains information about the document
`<noscript>`	Contains text that appears only if the browser does not support the `<script>` tag
`<object>`	Embeds an object
`<script>`	Contains programming scripts, such as JavaScript code
`<style>`	Contains style information used for rendering elements
`<title>`	Gives the document's title, which appears in the browser

As mentioned, each `<head>` element should contain exactly one `<title>` element.

Document Title (*<title>*)

As in HTML, the `<title>` element contains a title for the document, stored as simple text. Most browsers will read the document's title and display it in its title bar. The title of a document is also used by search engines. This element is supported in XHTML 1.0 Strict, XHTML 1.0 Transitional, XHTML 1.0 Frameset, and XHTML 1.1. Here are the attributes for this element:

Attribute	Description
`dir`	Sets the direction of directionally neutral text. You can set this attribute to `LTR`, for left-to-right text or `RTL`, for right-to-left text.
`lang`	Specifies the base language used in the element. Applies only when the document is interpreted as HTML.
`xml:lang`	Specifies the base language for the element when the document is interpreted as an XML document.

You use the <title> element to specify the document's title to browsers and search engines; browsers usually display the title in the title bar. The W3C XHTML DTDs say, "Exactly one title is required per document." However, the W3C XHTML validator doesn't complain if you omit a title. Nonetheless, you should put a <title> element in every document.

We saw an example <title> element at the beginning of this chapter:

```
<?xml version="1.0"?>
<!DOCTYPE html PUBLIC "-//W3C//DTD XHTML 1.0 Transitional//EN"
"http://www.w3.org/TR/xhtml1/DTD/xhtml1-transitional.dtd">
<html xmlns="http://www.w3.org/1999/xhtml" xml:lang="en" lang="en">
    <head>
        <title>
            Welcome to my page
        </title>
    </head>

    <body>
        <h1>
            Welcome to XHTML!
        </h1>
    </body>
</html>
```

No major browser will react badly if you don't give a document a title. However, XHTML documents should have one, according to the W3C.

We've completed the head section of XHTML documents; next comes the body.

Document Body (*<body>*)

The document's body is where the action is—the content that the document is designed to contain, that is. The <body> element is supported in XHTML 1.0 Strict, XHTML 1.0 Transitional, and XHTML 1.1. Here are this element's attributes, all of which are supported in XHTML 1.0 Strict, XHTML 1.0 Transitional, and XHTML 1.1, unless otherwise noted:

Attribute	Description
alink	Is deprecated in HTML 4.0. Sets the color of hyperlinks when they're being activated. (XHTML 1.0 Transitional, XHTML 1.0 Frameset.)
background	Is deprecated in HTML 4.0. Holds the URI of an image to be used in tiling the browser's background. (XHTML 1.0 Transitional, XHTML 1.0 Frameset.)

`bgcolor`	Is deprecated in HTML 4.0. Sets the color of the browser's background. (XHTML 1.0 Transitional, XHTML 1.0 Frameset.)
`class`	Gives the style class of the element.
`dir`	Sets the direction of directionally neutral text. You can set this attribute to `LTR`, for left-to-right text or `RTL`, for right-to-left text.
`id`	Use the ID to refer to the element; set this attribute to a unique identifier.
`lang`	Specifies the base language used in the element. Applies only when the document is interpreted as HTML.
`link`	Is deprecated in HTML 4.0. Sets the color of hyperlinks that have not yet been visited. (XHTML 1.0 Transitional, XHTML 1.0 Frameset.)
`style`	Set to an inline style to specify how the browser should display the element.
`text`	Is deprecated in HTML 4.0. Sets the color of the text in the document. (XHTML 1.0 Transitional, XHTML 1.0 Frameset.)
`title`	Contains the title of the body (which might be displayed in ToolTips).
`vlink`	Is deprecated in HTML 4.0. Sets the color of hyperlinks that have been visited already. (XHTML 1.0 Transitional, XHTML 1.0 Frameset.)
`xml:lang`	Specifies the base language for the element when the document is interpreted as an XML document.

This element also supports these events in XHTML: `onclick`, `ondblclick`, `onload`, `onmousedown`, `onmouseup`, `onmouseover`, `onmousemove`, `onmouseout`, `onkeypress`, `onkeydown`, `onkeyup`, and `onunload`. You can use scripts like JavaScript with events like these, and I'll take a look at how in the next chapter.

If you place descriptions of your document in the `<head>` element, you place the actual content of the document in the `<body>` element—unless you're sectioning your page into frames, in which case you should use the `<frameset>` element instead of the `<body>` element.

We've already seen a simple example in which the content of a page is just an `<h1>` heading, like this:

```
<?xml version="1.0"?>
<!DOCTYPE html PUBLIC "-//W3C//DTD XHTML 1.0 Transitional//EN"
"http://www.w3.org/TR/xhtml1/DTD/xhtml1-transitional.dtd">
<html xmlns="http://www.w3.org/1999/xhtml" xml:lang="en" lang="en">
```

continues ▸

```
    <head>
        <title>
            Welcome to my page
        </title>
    </head>

    <body>
        <h1>
            Welcome to XHTML!
        </h1>
    </body>
</html>
```

If you've written HTML before, you may be startled to discover that many cherished attributes are now considered deprecated in XHTML, which means that they're omitted from XHTML 1.0 Strict and XHTML 1.1. Deprecated attributes of the `<body>` element include these:

- `alink`
- `background`
- `bgcolor`
- `link`
- `text`
- `vlink`

Instead of using these attributes, you're now supposed to use style sheets. Here's an example showing how to replace deprecated attributes. In this case, I'll set the browser's background to white, the color of displayed text to black, the color of hyperlinks (created with the `<a>` element, which I'll take a look at in the next chapter) to red, the color of activated links to blue, and the color of visited links to green, all using deprecated attributes of the `<body>` element:

```
<?xml version="1.0"?>
<!DOCTYPE html PUBLIC "-//W3C//DTD XHTML 1.0 Transitional//EN"
"http://www.w3.org/TR/xhtml1/DTD/xhtml1-transitional.dtd">
<html xmlns="http://www.w3.org/1999/xhtml" xml:lang="en" lang="en">
    <head>
        <title>
            Welcome to my page
        </title>
    </head>

    <body bgcolor="white" text="black" link="red" alink="blue"
        vlink="green">
        Welcome to my XHTML document.
        Want to check out more about XHTML?
```

```
        Go to
        <a href="http://www.w3c.org">W3C</a>.
    </body>
</html>
```

You can see this document displayed in Netscape in Figure 16.3. It works as it should, but the fact is that it's not strict XHTML.

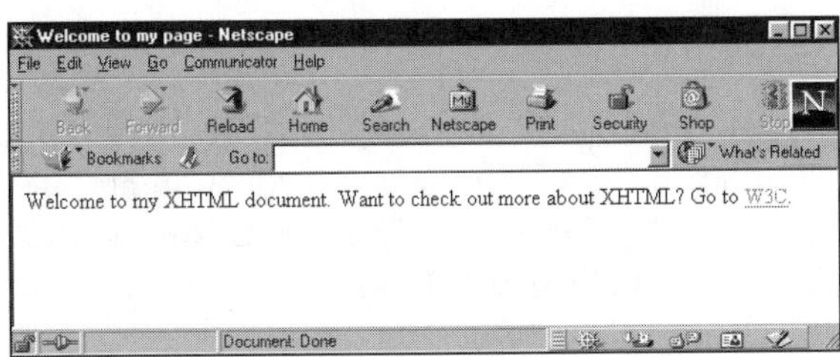

Figure 16.3 Displaying a hyperlink in Netscape.

To make the same page adhere to the XHTML strict standard, you use style sheets. Here's how this page looks using a `<style>` element to set up the same colors (I'll take a look at the `<style>` element more closely in the next chapter):

```
<?xml version="1.0"?>
<!DOCTYPE html PUBLIC "-//W3C//DTD XHTML 1.0 Transitional//EN"
"http://www.w3.org/TR/xhtml1/DTD/xhtml1-transitional.dtd">
<html xmlns="http://www.w3.org/1999/xhtml" xml:lang="en" lang="en">
    <head>
        <title>
            Welcome to my page
        </title>
        <style type="text/css">
            body {background: white; color: black}
            a:link {color: red}
            a:visited {color: green}
            a:active {color: blue}
        </style>
    </head>

    <body>
        Welcome to my XHTML document.
        Want to check out more about XHTML?
        Go to
        <a href="http://www.w3c.org">W3C</a>.
    </body>
</html>
```

In this case, I'm using CSS to style this document. To separate content from markup, the W3C is relying on style sheets a great deal these days. Note, however, that the contents of a `<style>` element are still part of the XHTML document. This means that if you use sensitive characters such as `&` or `<` in it, you should either escape those characters or use an external style sheet, which I'll take a look at in the next chapter.

Comments (<!-->)

Because XHTML documents are actually XML, they support XML comments, which you can use to annotate your document. These annotations will not be displayed by the browser. XHTML comments are supported in XHTML 1.0 Strict, XHTML 1.0 Transitional, XHTML 1.0 Frameset, and XHTML 1.1. Comments have no attributes.

We're familiar with comments from XML; you enclose the text in a comment like this: `<!--This page was last updated July 3.-->`. Using comments, you can describe to readers what's going on in your document.

Here's how I might add comments to an XHTML document:

```
<?xml version="1.0"?>
<!DOCTYPE html PUBLIC "-//W3C//DTD XHTML 1.0 Transitional//EN"
"http://www.w3.org/TR/xhtml1/DTD/xhtml1-transitional.dtd">
<html xmlns="http://www.w3.org/1999/xhtml" xml:lang="en" lang="en">
    <!-- This is the document head -->
    <head>
        <!-- This is the document title -->
        <title>
            Welcome to my page
        </title>
    </head>

    <!-- This is the document body element -->
    <body>
        <h1>
            <!-- This is an h1 heading element -->
            Welcome to XHTML!
        </h1>
    </body>
</html>
```

As with any XML documents, the comments are supposed to be stripped out by the XML processor that reads the document. On the other hand, keep in mind that comments are text—if you have a lot of them in a lengthy document, you can increase the download time of your document significantly.

Headings (*<h1>* Through *<h6>*)

You use the `<h1>` through `<h6>` elements to creating headings in your documents. These are the familiar headings from HTML: `<h1>` creates the largest text, and `<h6>` creates the smallest. These elements are supported in 1.0 Strict, 1.0 Transitional, 1.0 Frameset, and XHTML 1.1. This table lists the possible attributes of these elements. Unless otherwise noted, versions 1.0 Strict, 1.0 Transitional, 1.0 Frameset, and XHTML 1.1 support them:

Attribute	Description
`align`	Gives the alignment of text in the heading. The possible values are `left` (the default), `center`, `right`, and `justify`. (XHTML 1.0 Transitional, XHTML 1.0 Frameset.)
`class`	Gives the style class of the element.
`dir`	Sets the direction of directionally neutral text. You can set this attribute to `LTR`, for left-to-right text, or `RTL`, for right-to-left text.
`id`	Use the ID to refer to the element; set this attribute to a unique identifier.
`lang`	Specifies the base language used in the element. Applies only when the document is interpreted as HTML.
`style`	Set this to an inline style to specify how the browser should display the element.
`title`	Contains the title of the element (which might be displayed in ToolTips).
`xml:lang`	Specifies the base language for the element when the document is interpreted as an XML document.

These elements also support these events in XHTML: `onclick`, `ondblclick`, `onmousedown`, `onmouseup`, `onmouseover`, `onmousemove`, `onmouseout`, `onkeypress`, `onkeydown`, and `onkeyup`.

Headings act much like headlines in newspapers. They are block elements that present text in bold and that often are larger than other text. Six heading tags exist: `<h1>`, `<h2>`, `<h3>`, `<h4>`, `<h5>`, and `<h6>`. Because headings are block elements, they get their own line in a displayed XHTML document.

Here's an example that shows these headings in action:

```
<?xml version="1.0"?>
<!DOCTYPE html PUBLIC "-//W3C//DTD XHTML 1.0 Transitional//EN"
"http://www.w3.org/TR/xhtml1/DTD/xhtml1-transitional.dtd">
<html xmlns="http://www.w3.org/1999/xhtml" xml:lang="en" lang="en">
    <head>
        <title>
```

continues ▸

```
            The &lt;h1&gt; - &lt;h6&gt; Elements
        </title>
    </head>

    <body>
        <center>
            <h1>This is an &lt;h1&gt; heading</h1>
            <h2>This is an &lt;h2&gt; heading</h2>
            <h3>This is an &lt;h3&gt; heading</h3>
            <h4>This is an &lt;h4&gt; heading</h4>
            <h5>This is an &lt;h5&gt; heading</h5>
            <h6>This is an &lt;h6&gt; heading</h6>
        </center>
    </body>

</html>
```

You can see this XHTML displayed in Netscape in Figure 16.4. Headings such as these help break up the text in a page, just as they do in newspapers, and they let the structure of your document stand out.

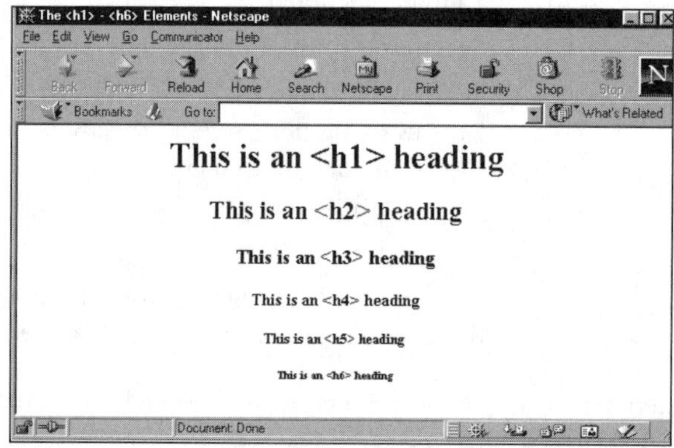

Figure 16.4 Displaying the six levels of headings in Netscape.

Handling Text

Displaying simple text works the same way in XHTML as it does in HTML: You just place the text directly in a document. XHTML elements that display text have mixed content models, so they can contain both text and other elements, as in the example we saw earlier:

```
<?xml version="1.0"?>
<!DOCTYPE html PUBLIC "-//W3C//DTD XHTML 1.0 Transitional//EN"
"http://www.w3.org/TR/xhtml1/DTD/xhtml1-transitional.dtd">
```

```
<html xmlns="http://www.w3.org/1999/xhtml" xml:lang="en" lang="en">
    <head>
        <title>
            Welcome to my page
        </title>
    </head>
    <body bgcolor="white" text="black" link="red" alink="blue"
        vlink="green">
        Welcome to my XHTML document.
        Want to check out more about XHTML?
        Go to
        <a href="http://www.w3c.org">W3C</a>.
    </body>
</html>
```

The text in this document is displayed directly in the browser, as you see in Figure 16.3. It's up to you to format the text the way you want it. In early versions of HTML, you used elements such as <b> (bold), <i> (italic), and <u> (underline) to format text, but as formatting has become more sophisticated, the emphasis has switched to using style sheets.

As you know, there are five predefined entity references in XML, and they stand for characters that can be interpreted as markup or other control characters:

This	Displays This Character
&	&
'	'
>	>
<	<
"	"

There are a great many more character entities in HTML 4.0, and they're supported in XHTML as well. You can find them in Table 16.1.

Table 16.1 **Character Entities in XHTML (Support Varies by Browser)**

Entity	Number	Displays This
Aacute	Á	Latin capital letter A with acute accent
aacute	á	Latin small letter a with acute accent
Acirc	Â	Latin capital letter A with circumflex
acirc	â	Latin small letter a with circumflex
acute	´	Acute accent
AElig	Æ	Latin capital letter AE

continues

Table 16.1 **Continued**

Entity	Number	Displays This
aelig	æ	Latin small letter ae
Agrave	À	Latin capital letter A with grave accent
agrave	à	Latin small letter a with grave accent
alefsym	ℵ	Alef symbol = first transfinite cardinal
Alpha	Α	Greek capital letter alpha
alpha	α	Greek small letter alpha
amp	&	Ampersand
and	∧	Logical and
ang	∠	Angle
Aring	Å	Latin capital letter A with ring above
aring	å	Latin small letter a with ring above
asymp	≈	Almost equal to = asymptotic to
Atilde	Ã	Latin capital letter A with tilde
atilde	ã	Latin small letter a with tilde
Auml	Ä	Latin capital letter A with diaeresis (umlaut)
auml	ä	Latin small letter a with diaeresis (umlaut)
bdquo	„	Double low-9 quotation mark
Beta	Β	Greek capital letter beta
beta	β	Greek small letter beta
brvbar	¦	Broken bar = broken vertical bar
bull	•	Bullet = black small circle
cap	∩	Intersection = cap
Ccedil	Ç	Latin capital letter C with cedilla
ccedil	ç	Latin small letter c with cedilla
cedil	¸	Cedilla
cent	¢	Cent sign
Chi	Χ	Greek capital letter chi
chi	χ	Greek small letter chi
circ	ˆ	Modifier letter circumflex accent
clubs	♣	Black club suit = shamrock
cong	≅	Approximately equal to
copy	©	Copyright sign
crarr	↵	Downward arrow with corner leftward

Entity	Number	Displays This
cup	∪	Union = cup
curren	¤	Currency sign
dagger	†	Dagger
Dagger	‡	Double dagger
darr	↓	Downward arrow
dArr	⇓	Downward double arrow
deg	°	Degree sign
Delta	Δ	Greek capital letter delta
delta	δ	Greek small letter delta
diams	♦	Black diamond suit
divide	÷	Division sign
Eacute	É	Latin capital letter E with acute
eacute	é	Latin small letter e with acute
Ecirc	Ê	Latin capital letter E with circumflex
ecirc	ê	Latin small letter e with circumflex
Egrave	È	Latin capital letter E with grave accent
egrave	è	Latin small letter e with grave accent
empty	∅	Empty set = null set = diameter
emsp		Em space
ensp		En space
Epsilon	Ε	Greek capital letter epsilon
epsilon	ε	Greek small letter epsilon
equiv	≡	Identical to
Eta	Η	Greek capital letter eta
eta	η	Greek small letter eta
ETH	Ð	Latin capital letter ETH
eth	ð	Latin small letter eth
Euml	Ë	Latin capital letter E with diaeresis (umlaut)
euml	ë	Latin small letter e with diaeresis
euro	€	Euro sign
exist	∃	There exists
fnof	ƒ	Latin small f with hook = function
forall	∀	For all
frac12	½	Vulgar fraction one-half

continues

Table 16.1 **Continued**

Entity	Number	Displays This
frac14	¼	Vulgar fraction one-quarter
frac34	¾	Vulgar fraction three-quarters
frasl	⁄	Fraction slash
Gamma	Γ	Greek capital letter gamma
gamma	γ	Greek small letter gamma
ge	≥	Greater than or equal to
gt	>	Greater than sign
harr	↔	Left right arrow
hArr	⇔	Left right double arrow
hearts	♥	Black heart suit = valentine
hellip	…	Horizontal ellipsis = three-dot leader
Iacute	Í	Latin capital letter I with acute accent
iacute	í	Latin small letter i with acute accent
Icirc	Î	Latin capital letter I with circumflex
icirc	î	Latin small letter i with circumflex
iexcl	¡	Inverted exclamation mark
Igrave	Ì	Latin capital letter I with grave accent
igrave	ì	Latin small letter i with grave accent
image	ℑ	Blackletter capital I = imaginary part
infin	∞	Infinity
int	∫	Integral
Iota	Ι	Greek capital letter iota
iota	ι	Greek small letter iota
iquest	¿	Inverted question mark
isin	∈	Element of
Iuml	Ï	Latin capital letter I with diaeresis (umlaut)
iuml	ï	Latin small letter i with diaeresis
Kappa	Κ	Greek capital letter kappa
kappa	κ	Greek small letter kappa
Lambda	Λ	Greek capital letter lambda
lambda	λ	Greek small letter lambda
lang	〈	Left-pointing angle bracket = bra
laquo	«	Left-pointing double angle quotation mark

Entity	Number	Displays This
larr	←	Leftward arrow
lArr	⇐	Leftward double arrow
lceil	⌈	Left ceiling = apl upstile
ldquo	“	Left double quotation mark
le	≤	Less than or equal to
lfloor	⌊	Left floor = apl downstile
lowast	∗	Asterisk operator
loz	◊	Lozenge
lrm	‎	Left-to-right mark
lsaquo	‹	Single left-pointing angle quotation mark
lsquo	‘	Left single quotation mark
lt	<	Less than
macr	¯	Macron = spacing macron
mdash	—	Em dash
micro	µ	Micro sign
middot	·	Middle dot
minus	−	Minus sign
Mu	Μ	Greek capital letter mu
mu	μ	Greek small letter mu
nabla	∇	Nabla = backward difference
nbsp		No-break space = nonbreaking space
ndash	–	En dash
ne	≠	Not equal to
ni	∋	Contains as member
not	¬	Not sign
notin	∉	Not an element of
nsub	⊄	Not a subset of
Ntilde	Ñ	Latin capital letter N with tilde
ntilde	ñ	Latin small letter n with tilde
Nu	Ν	Greek capital letter nu
nu	ν	Greek small letter nu
Oacute	Ó	Latin capital letter O with acute accent
oacute	ó	Latin small letter o with acute accent
Ocirc	Ô	Latin capital letter O with circumflex

continues

Table 16.1 **Continued**

Entity	Number	Displays This
ocirc	ô	Latin small letter o with circumflex
OElig	Œ	Latin capital ligature OE
oelig	œ	Latin small ligature oe
Ograve	Ò	Latin capital letter O with grave accent
ograve	ò	Latin small letter o with grave accent
oline	‾	Overline = spacing overscore
Omega	Ω	Greek capital letter omega
omega	ω	Greek small letter omega
Omicron	Ο	Greek capital letter omicron
omicron	ο	Greek small letter omicron
oplus	⊕	Circled plus = direct sum
or	∨	Logical or = vee
ordf	ª	Feminine ordinal indicator
ordm	º	Masculine ordinal indicator
Oslash	Ø	Latin capital letter O with stroke
oslash	ø	Latin small letter o with stroke
Otilde	Õ	Latin capital letter O with tilde
otilde	õ	Latin small letter o with tilde
otimes	⊗	Circled times = vector product
Ouml	Ö	Latin capital letter O with diaeresis (umlaut)
ouml	ö	Latin small letter o with diaeresis (umlaut)
para	¶	Pilcrow sign
part	∂	Partial differential
permil	‰	Per mille sign
perp	⊥	Up tack = orthogonal to = perpendicular
Phi	Φ	Greek capital letter phi
phi	φ	Greek small letter phi
Pi	Π	Greek capital letter pi
pi	π	Greek small letter pi
piv	ϖ	Greek pi symbol
plusmn	±	Plus-minus sign
pound	£	Pound sign

Entity	Number	Displays This
prime	′	Prime = minutes = feet
Prime	″	Double prime = seconds = inches
prod	∏	N-ary product = product sign
prop	∝	Proportional to
Psi	Ψ	Greek capital letter psi
psi	ψ	Greek small letter psi
quot	"	Quotation mark = APL quote
radic	√	Square root = radical sign
rang	〉	Right-pointing angle bracket = ket
raquo	»	Right-pointing double angle quotation mark
rarr	→	Rightward arrow
rArr	⇒	Rightward double arrow
rceil	⌉	Right ceiling
rdquo	”	Right double quotation mark
real	ℜ	Blackletter capital R = real part symbol
reg	®	Registered sign
rfloor	⌋	Right floor
Rho	Ρ	Greek capital letter rho
rho	ρ	Greek small letter rho
rlm	‏	Right-to-left mark
rsaquo	›	Single right-pointing angle quotation mark
rsquo	’	Right single quotation mark
sbquo	‚	Single low-9 quotation mark
Scaron	Š	Latin capital letter S with caron
scaron	š	Latin small letter s with caron
sdot	⋅	Dot operator
sect	§	Section sign
shy		Soft hyphen
Sigma	Σ	Greek capital letter sigma
sigma	σ	Greek small letter sigma
sigmaf	ς	Greek small letter final sigma
sim	∼	Tilde operator
spades	♠	Black spade suit

continues

Table 16.1 **Continued**

Entity	Number	Displays This
sub	⊂	Subset of
sube	⊆	Subset of or equal to
sum	∑	N-ary summation
sup	⊃	Superset of
sup1	¹	Superscript 1
sup2	²	Superscript 2
sup3	³	Superscript 3
supe	⊇	Superset of or equal to
szlig	ß	Latin small letter sharp s
Tau	Τ	Greek capital letter tau
tau	τ	Greek small letter tau
there4	∴	Therefore
Theta	Θ	Greek capital letter theta
theta	θ	Greek small letter theta
thetasym	ϑ	Greek small letter theta symbol
thinsp		Thin space
THORN	Þ	Latin capital letter THORN
thorn	þ	Latin small letter thorn
tilde	˜	Small tilde
times	×	Multiplication sign
trade	™	Trademark sign
Uacute	Ú	Latin capital letter U with acute accent
uacute	ú	Latin small letter u with acute accent
uarr	↑	Upward arrow
uArr	⇑	Upward double arrow
Ucirc	Û	Latin capital letter U with circumflex
ucirc	û	Latin small letter u with circumflex
Ugrave	Ù	Latin capital letter U with grave accent
ugrave	ù	Latin small letter u with grave accent
uml	¨	Diaeresis (umlaut)
upsih	ϒ	Greek upsilon with hook symbol
Upsilon	Υ	Greek capital letter upsilon
upsilon	υ	Greek small letter upsilon

Entity	Number	Displays This
Uuml	Ü	Latin capital letter U with diaeresis (umlaut)
uuml	ü	Latin small letter u with diaeresis
weierp	℘	Script capital P = power set
Xi	Ξ	Greek capital letter xi
xi	ξ	Greek small letter xi
Yacute	Ý	Latin capital letter Y with acute accent
yacute	ý	Latin small letter y with acute accent
yen	¥	Yen sign = yuan sign
Yuml	Ÿ	Latin capital letter Y with diaeresis
yuml	ÿ	Latin small letter y with diaeresis
Zeta	Ζ	Greek capital letter zeta
zeta	ζ	Greek small letter zeta
zwj	‍	Zero-width joiner
zwnj	‌	Zero-width nonjoiner

As I mentioned before, as with HTML, XHTML supports the various text-formatting tags, such as `<b>` for bold text, `<i>` for italic text, and `<u>` for underlined text. I'll take a look at them briefly because they're still very popular.

Making Text Bold (<*b*>) or Italic (<*i*>)

The `<b>` element gives you a simple inline way of bolding text. Although plenty of experts would prefer that you use style sheets to display text in bold, you can still use the `<b>` element. Like the `<b>` element, the `<i>` element offers some rudimentary text formatting—in this case, creating italic text. Both elements are supported in XHTML 1.0 Strict, XHTML 1.0 Transitional, XHTML 1.0 Frameset, and XHTML 1.1. Here are their attributes:

Attribute	Description
class	Gives the style class of the element.
dir	Sets the direction of directionally neutral text. You can set this attribute to LTR, for left-to-right text, or RTL, for right-to-left text.
id	Use the ID to refer to the element; set this attribute to a unique identifier.
lang	Specifies the base language used in the element. Applies only when the document is interpreted as HTML.

continues

Attribute	Description
`style`	Set this to an inline style to specify how the browser should display the element.
`title`	Contains the title of the element (which might be displayed in ToolTips).
`xml:lang`	Specifies the base language for the element when the document is interpreted as an XML document.

Here are the official XHTML events that these elements support: `onclick`, `ondblclick`, `onmousedown`, `onmouseup`, `onmouseover`, `onmousemove`, `onmouseout`, `onkeypress`, `onkeydown`, and `onkeyup`.

Here's an example that displays text in both italic and bold (I'm using the line break, `<br>` element, which we'll see later, to separate the lines of text):

```
<?xml version="1.0"?>
<!DOCTYPE html PUBLIC "-//W3C//DTD XHTML 1.0 Transitional//EN"
"http://www.w3.org/TR/xhtml1/DTD/xhtml1-transitional.dtd">
<html xmlns="http://www.w3.org/1999/xhtml" xml:lang="en" lang="en">
    <head>
        <title>
            Bold and Italic Text
        </title>
    </head>

    <body>
        <i>This text is italic.</i>
        <br />
        <b>This text is bold.</b>
        <br />
        <b><i>This text is both.</i></b>
    </body>
</html>
```

The results of this XHTML appear in Figure 16.5, where you can see text that's bold, italic, and both bold and italic. The `<b>` and `<i>` tags are favorites among Web page authors because they're so easy to use.

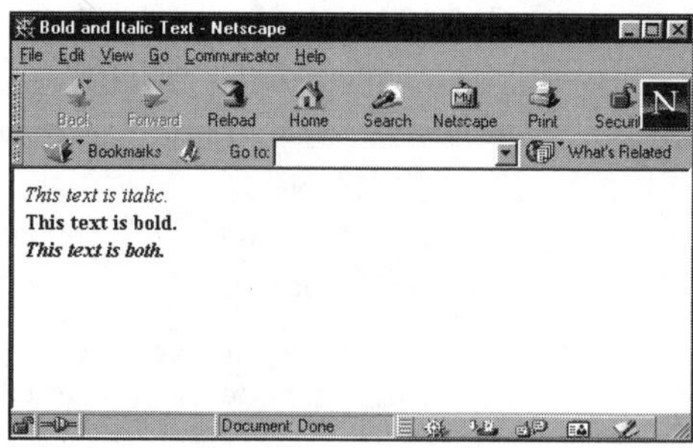

Figure 16.5 Displaying bold and italic text in Netscape.

Underlining Text (<*u*>)

The <u> element displays underlined text. This element was deprecated in HTML 4.0, so it is not supported in XHTML 1.0 Strict or XHTML 1.1. It is supported in XHTML 1.0 Transitional and XHTML 1.0 Frameset, however. Note, of course, that if your readers are very traditional, they might mistake underlined text for a hyperlink. Here are the attributes of this element:

Attribute	Description
`class`	Gives the style class of the element.
`dir`	Sets the direction of directionally neutral text. You can set this attribute to `LTR`, for left-to-right text, or `RTL`, for right-to-left text.
`id`	Use the ID to refer to the element; set this attribute to a unique identifier.
`lang`	Specifies the base language used in the element. Applies only when the document is interpreted as HTML.
`style`	Set this to an inline style to specify how the browser should display the element.
`title`	Contains the title of the element (which might be displayed in ToolTips).
`xml:lang`	Specifies the base language for the element when the document is interpreted as an XML document.

Here are the official XHTML events this element supports: `onclick`, `ondblclick`, `onmousedown`, `onmouseup`, `onmouseover`, `onmousemove`, `onmouseout`, `onkeypress`, `onkeydown`, and `onkeyup`.

The <u> element offers another easy formatting option, underlining its enclosed text. This element is deprecated in HTML 4.0, so you can't use it in strict XHTML 1.0 or XHTML 1.1. Here's an example putting <u> to work:

```
<?xml version="1.0"?>
<!DOCTYPE html PUBLIC "-//W3C//DTD XHTML 1.0 Transitional//EN"
"http://www.w3.org/TR/xhtml1/DTD/xhtml1-transitional.dtd">
<html xmlns="http://www.w3.org/1999/xhtml" xml:lang="en" lang="en">
    <head>
        <title>
            Using the &lt;u&gt; Element
        </title>
    </head>

    <body>
        You can <u>underline</u> text for a little more emphasis.
    </body>

</html>
```

The results of this XHTML appear in Figure 16.6.

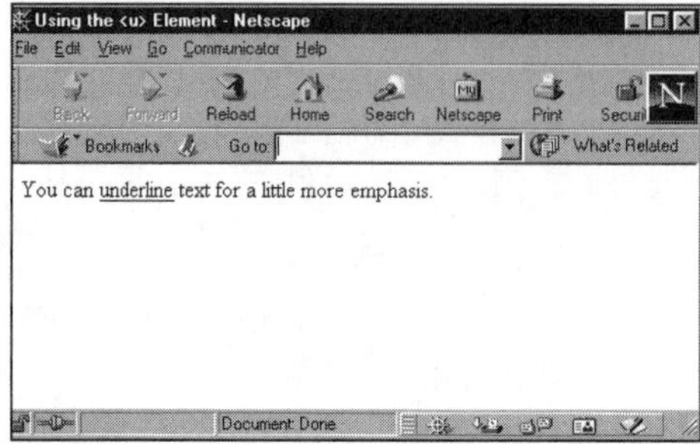

Figure 16.6 Displaying underlined text in Netscape.

Specifying a Text Font (*<font>*)

Using the `<font>` element, you can select text size, color, and face. The `<font>` element has always been very popular among HTML authors, but with the new emphasis on handling styles in style sheets, you can imagine that it was headed for extinction. And it has indeed been deprecated in HTML 4.0, so it's not available in XHTML 1.1 or XHTML 1.0 Strict. It's supported in XHTML 1.0 Transitional and XHTML 1.0 Frameset. Because it's so popular still, I'll cover it here briefly.

Here are this element's attributes:

Attribute	Description
`class`	Gives the style class of the element.
`color`	Is deprecated. Sets the color of the text.
`dir`	Sets the direction of directionally neutral text. You can set this attribute to `LTR`, for left-to-right text, or `RTL`, for right-to-left text.
`face`	Is deprecated. You can set this attribute to a single font name or a list of names separated by commas. The browser will select the first font face from the list that it can find.
`id`	Use the ID to refer to the element; set this attribute to a unique identifier.
`lang`	Specifies the base language used in the element. Applies only when the document is interpreted as HTML.
`size`	Is deprecated. Gives the size of the text. Possible values range from 1 through 7.

`style`	Set this to an inline style to specify how the browser should display the element.
`title`	Contains the title of the element (which might be displayed in ToolTips).
`xml:lang`	Specifies the base language for the element when the document is interpreted as an XML document.

This element does not support any XHTML events.

You can use the `<font>` element to set a font face, size, and color for text. Here's an example; in this case, I'm displaying text in a large red Arial font:

```
<?xml version="1.0"?>
<!DOCTYPE html PUBLIC "-//W3C//DTD XHTML 1.0 Transitional//EN"
"http://www.w3.org/TR/xhtml1/DTD/xhtml1-transitional.dtd">
<html xmlns="http://www.w3.org/1999/xhtml" xml:lang="en" lang="en">
    <head>
        <title>
            Using the &lt;font&gt; Element
        </title>
    </head>

    <body>
        <font size="6" color="#ff0000" face="Arial">
        Putting the &lt;font&gt; element to work.
        </font>
    </body>

</html>
```

The results of this XHTML appear in Figure 16.7.

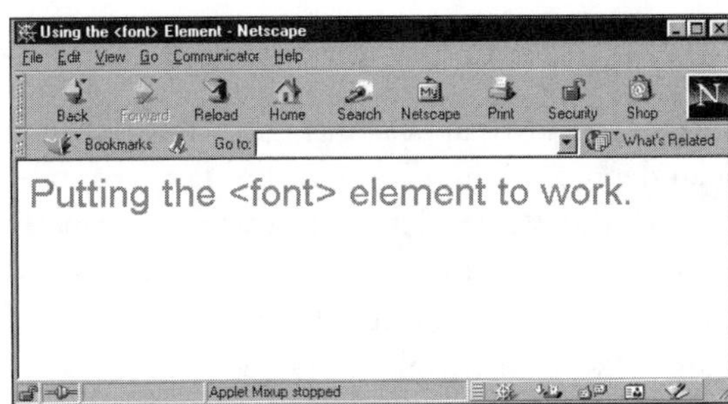

Figure 16.7 Using the `<font>` element in Netscape.

You specify font sizes by using the values 1 through 7. In practice, font size 1 is about 6 points, font size 2 is about 12 points, and so on, but actual sizes vary by system. Here's an example showing the range of possible sizes:

```
<?xml version="1.0"?>
<!DOCTYPE html PUBLIC "-//W3C//DTD XHTML 1.0 Transitional//EN"
"http://www.w3.org/TR/xhtml1/DTD/xhtml1-transitional.dtd">
<html xmlns="http://www.w3.org/1999/xhtml" xml:lang="en" lang="en">
    <head>
        <title>
            Using the &lt;font&gt; Element
        </title>
    </head>

    <body>
        <center>
            <h1>
                Using the &lt;font&gt; Element
            </h1>
            <font size="1">This is font size 1.</font>
            <br />
            <font size="2">This is font size 2.</font>
            <br />
            <font size="3">This is font size 3.</font>
            <br />
            <font size="4">This is font size 4.</font>
            <br />
            <font size="5">This is font size 5.</font>
            <br />
            <font size="6">This is font size 6.</font>
            <br />
            <font size="7">This is font size 7.</font>
        </center>
    </body>
</html>
```

The results of this XHTML appear in Figure 16.8. As mentioned earlier, `<font>` has been deprecated in HTML 4.0 in favor of style sheets. So how should you replace the `<font>` element? See the section "Formatting Text Inline (`<span>`)," at the end of this chapter, for a good substitute.

Besides the simple text formatting elements, HTML also contains elements to arrange text in the display; XHTML supports those elements as well.

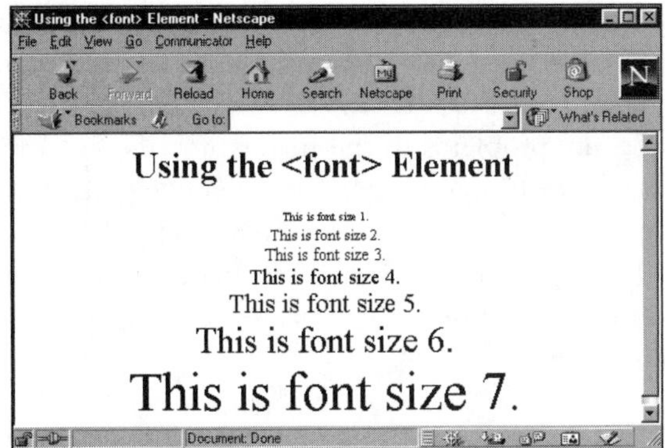

Figure 16.8 Displaying various font sizes in Netscape.

Line Breaks (<*br*>) and Text Paragraphs (<*p*>)

The `<br>` element is an empty element that inserts a line break into text. Because this element is empty, you use it like this in XHTML: `<br />`. This element is supported in XHTML 1.0 Strict, XHTML 1.0 Transitional, XHTML 1.0 Frameset, and XHTML 1.1. Here are the attributes of this element:

Attribute	Description
`class`	Gives the style class of the element.
`clear`	Is used to move past-aligned images or other elements. Set this to `none` (the default—just a normal break), `left` (breaks line and moves down until there is a clear left margin past the aligned element), `right` (breaks line and moves down until there is a clear right margin past the aligned element), or `all` (breaks line and moves down until both margins are clear of the aligned element). (XHTML 1.0 Transitional, XHTML 1.0 Frameset.)
`id`	Use the ID to refer to the element; set this attribute to a unique identifier.
`style`	Set this to an inline style to specify how the browser should display the element.
`title`	Contains the title of the element (which might be displayed in ToolTips).

This element does not support any XHTML events.

You use the <br> element to arrange the text in a document by adding a line break, making the browser skip to the next text line. This usage actually does not cause any problems in the major browsers, and the fact that those browsers are capable of handling empty elements with the usual XML /> closing characters is one of the reasons that XHTML actually works as it should in HTML browsers. In fact, you can also insert line breaks as
</br>, but that usage does turn out to be confusing to some browsers and XML validators.

Letting the Browser Handle the Formatting

Ideally, you should let the browser handle text formatting as much as possible. The text flow is supposed to be handled by the browser to display that text as best as possible to fit the display area. This means that if you add a lot of line breaks, you may interfere with the best possible display (unless you're adding line breaks to specifically separate discrete elements, such as images). It's usually best to format your text into paragraphs that the browser can handle as appropriate, rather than expressly adding line breaks to text yourself.

The <p> element enables you to break text up into paragraphs. Paragraphs are block elements that you can format as you like in style sheets or with style attributes, including indenting the first line and so forth. If you're coming to XHTML from HTML, one thing to recall is that every <p> tag needs a corresponding </p> tag, which is easy to forget because HTML doesn't require that. In addition, note that paragraphs are block elements, which in XHTML means that you cannot display other block elements, such as headings, in them. The <p> element is supported in XHTML 1.0 Strict, XHTML 1.0 Transitional, XHTML 1.0 Frameset, and XHTML 1.1. Here are this element's attributes:

Attribute	Description
`align`	Is deprecated in HTML 4. Sets the alignment of the text. Possible values include `left` (the default), `right`, `center`, and `justify`. (XHTML 1.0 Transitional, XHTML 1.0 Frameset.)
`class`	Gives the style class of the element.
`dir`	Sets the direction of directionally neutral text. You can set this attribute to `LTR`, for left-to-right text, or `RTL`, for right-to-left text.
`id`	Use the ID to refer to the element; set this attribute to a unique identifier.

`lang`	Specifies the base language used in the element. Applies only when the document is interpreted as HTML.
`style`	Set this to an inline style to specify how the browser should display the element.
`title`	Contains the title of the element (which might be displayed in ToolTips).
`xml:lang`	Specifies the base language for the element when the document is interpreted as an XML document.

This element supports these XHTML events: `onclick`, `ondblclick`, `onmousedown`, `onmouseup`, `onmouseover`, `onmousemove`, `onmouseout`, `onkeypress`, `onkeydown`, and `onkeyup`.

You use the `<p>` element to organize your text. The browser adds a little vertical space on top of paragraphs to separate them from other elements. The browser formats the text in a paragraph to fit the current page width.

Here's an example; in this case, I'm using `<br>` elements to introduce line breaks, and a `<p>` element to create a new paragraph:

```
<?xml version="1.0"?>
<!DOCTYPE html PUBLIC "-//W3C//DTD XHTML 1.0 Transitional//EN"
"http://www.w3.org/TR/xhtml1/DTD/xhtml1-transitional.dtd">
<html xmlns="http://www.w3.org/1999/xhtml" xml:lang="en" lang="en">
    <head>
        <title>
            Using the &lt;br&gt; and &lt;p&gt; Elements
        </title>
    </head>

    <body>
        <center>
            <h1>
                Using the &lt;br&gt; and &lt;p&gt; Elements
            </h1>
        </center>
        This is a line of text.
        <br />
        Using a line break skips to the next line.
        <p style="font-weight: bold">
            This is a line of bold text in a paragraph.
            <br />
            Here's a new line of text in the same paragraph.
        </p>
    </body>
</html>
```

The results of this code appear in Figure 16.9. As you can see, inserting a `<br>` element makes the browser move to the next line of text.

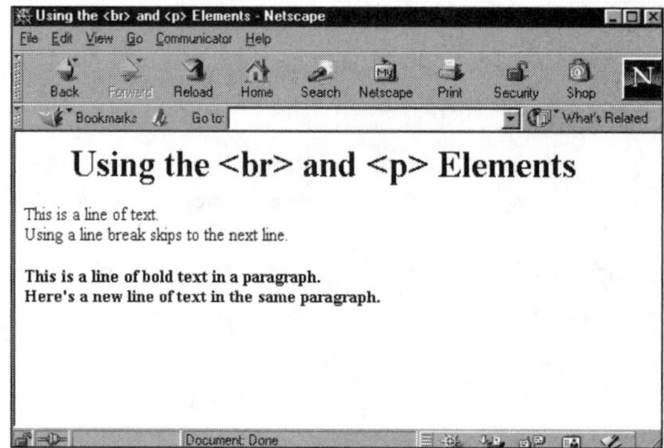

Figure 16.9 Using line breaks and paragraphs in Netscape.

This example points out the difference between `<br>` and `<p>`. The `<br>` element is empty and just makes the flow of text skip to the next line. The `<p>` element, on the other hand, is a block element that encloses content. You can apply styles to the content in a `<p>` element, and those styles are applied to all text in the paragraph, even if they're broken up with line breaks—as you see in Figure 16.9, where the bold style of text applies to both lines in the paragraph.

Creating Horizontal Rules (*<hr>*)

Another handy element to arrange text is the `<hr>` horizontal rule element. This element just causes the browser to draw a horizontal line to separate or group elements vertically. It's supported in XHTML 1.0 Strict, XHTML 1.0 Transitional, XHTML 1.0 Frameset, and XHTML 1.1. Here are the attributes of this element—note that it includes a few attributes that have been deprecated:

Attribute	**Description**
`align`	Is deprecated. Sets the alignment of the rule; set this to `left`, `center` (the default), or `right`. To set this attribute, you must also set the `width` attribute. (XHTML 1.0 Transitional, XHTML 1.0 Frameset.)
`class`	Gives the style class of the element.
`id`	Use the ID to refer to the element; set this attribute to a unique identifier.

`noshade`	Is deprecated. Displays the rule with a two-dimensional, not three-dimensional (the default), appearance. (XHTML 1.0 Transitional, XHTML 1.0 Frameset.)
`size`	Is deprecated. Sets the vertical size of the horizontal rule in pixels. (XHTML 1.0 Transitional, XHTML 1.0 Frameset.)
`style`	Set this to an inline style to specify how the browser should display the element.
`title`	Contains the title of the element (which might be displayed in ToolTips).
`width`	Is deprecated. Sets the horizontal width of the rule. You can set this attribute to a pixel measurement or a percentage of the display area. (XHTML 1.0 Transitional, XHTML 1.0 Frameset.)
`xml:lang`	Specifies the base language for the element when the document is interpreted as an XML document.

These are the XHTML events supported by this element: `onclick`, `ondblclick`, `onmousedown`, `onmouseup`, `onmouseover`, `onmousemove`, `onmouseout`, `onkeypress`, `onkeydown`, and `onkeyup`.

It's easy to break your text up with horizontal rules, using the `<hr>` element. This can be very useful in longer documents, and it serves to organize your document visually into sections. This element is empty and just instructs the browser to insert a horizontal rule.

As with many style attributes in HTML 4.0, the `<hr>` element's `align`, `width`, `noshade`, and `size` attributes are all deprecated. However, they're still in the XHTML 1.0 Transitional or Frameset DTDs. Here's an example that displays a few horizontal rules of varying width and alignment:

```
<?xml version="1.0"?>
<!DOCTYPE html PUBLIC "-//W3C//DTD XHTML 1.0 Transitional//EN"
"http://www.w3.org/TR/xhtml1/DTD/xhtml1-transitional.dtd">
<html xmlns="http://www.w3.org/1999/xhtml" xml:lang="en" lang="en">
    <head>
        <title>
            Using the &lt;hr&gt; Element
        </title>
    </head>

    <body>
        <center>
            <h1>
                Using the &lt;hr&gt; Element
            </h1>
        </center>
```

```
        This is &lt;hr /&gt;:
        <hr />
        <br />
        This is &lt;hr align="left" width="60%" /&gt;:
        <hr align="left" width="60%" />
        <br />
        This is &lt;hr align="center" width="60%" /&gt;:
        <hr align="center" width="60%" />
        <br />
        This is &lt;hr align="right" width="60%" /&gt;:
        <hr align="right" width="60%" />
        <br />
    </body>
</html>
```

You can see the results of this XHTML in Figure 16.10, which shows a number of ways to configure horizontal rules. Here's another note: When you set the `align` attribute, you must also set the `width` attribute.

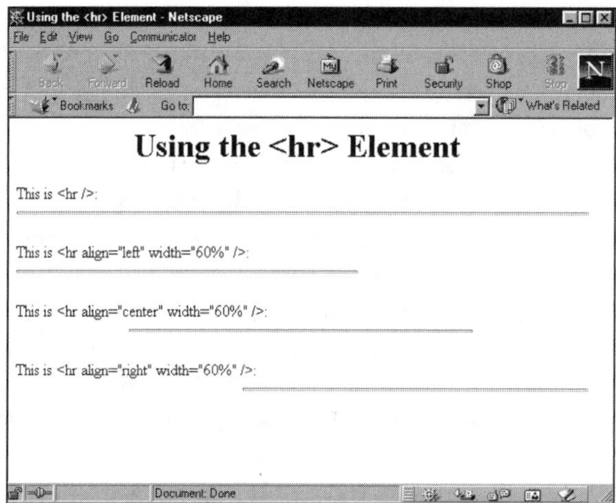

Figure 16.10 Displaying horizontal rules in Netscape.

Centering Displayed Text (*<center>*)

The `<center>` element does just what its name implies: It centers text and elements in the browser's display area. The W3C deprecated `<center>` in HTML 4, so you won't find it in the XHTML 1.0 strict or XHTML 1.1 DTDs. Nonetheless, `<center>` remains a favorite element and will be in use for a long time to come.

Here are the attributes of this element:

Attribute	Description
`class`	Gives the style class of the element.
`dir`	Sets the direction of directionally neutral text. You can set this attribute to `LTR`, for left-to-right text, or `RTL`, for right-to-left text.
`id`	You use the ID to refer to the element; set this attribute to a unique identifier.
`lang`	Specifies the base language used in the element. Applies only when the document is interpreted as HTML.
`style`	Set this to an inline style to specify how the browser should display the element.
`title`	Contains the title of the element (which might be displayed in ToolTips).
`xml:lang`	Specifies the base language for the element when the document is interpreted as an XML document.

This element supports the following XHTML events: `onclick`, `ondblclick`, `onmousedown`, `onmouseup`, `onmouseover`, `onmousemove`, `onmouseout`, `onkeypress`, `onkeydown`, and `onkeyup`.

Here's an example of `<center>` at work centering multiline text:

```
<?xml version="1.0"?>
<!DOCTYPE html PUBLIC "-//W3C//DTD XHTML 1.0 Transitional//EN"
"http://www.w3.org/TR/xhtml1/DTD/xhtml1-transitional.dtd">
<html xmlns="http://www.w3.org/1999/xhtml" xml:lang="en" lang="en">
    <head>
        <title>
            Using the &lt;center&gt; Element
        </title>
    </head>

    <body>
        <center>
            <h1>
                Using the &lt;center&gt; Element
            </h1>
        </center>
        <center>
            The &lt;center&gt; element is a
            <br />
            useful one for centering
            <br />
            text made up of
            <br />
```

continues ▸

```
            multiple lines.
        </center>
    </body>
</html>
```

You can see the results of this XHTML in Figure 16.11.

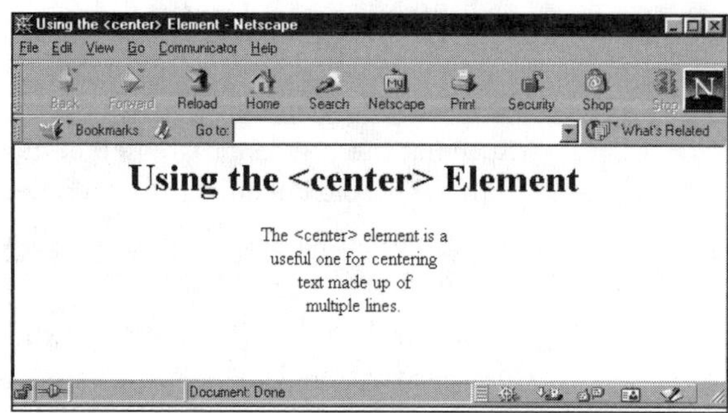

Figure 16.11 Using the `<center>` element.

The `<center>` element is still in widespread use, which is why I'm taking a look at it here; however, it has been deprecated, which means that it will disappear from XHTML one day. So, what are you supposed to use instead? Take a look at the next topic, the `<div>` element.

Formatting Text Blocks (*<div>*)

You can use the `<div>` element to select or enclose a block of text, usually so that you can apply styles to it. This element is supported in XHTML 1.0 Strict, XHTML 1.0 Transitional, XHTML 1.0 Frameset, and XHTML 1.1. Here are its attributes:

Attribute	Description
`align`	Is deprecated. Sets the horizontal alignment of the element. Set this to `left` (the default), `right`, `center`, or `justify`. (XHTML 1.0 Transitional, XHTML 1.0 Frameset.)
`class`	Gives the style class of the element.
`dir`	Sets the direction of directionally neutral text. You can set this attribute to `LTR`, for left-to-right text, or `RTL`, for right-to-left text.
`id`	Use the ID to refer to the element; set this attribute to a unique identifier.
`lang`	Specifies the base language used in the element. Applies only when the document is interpreted as HTML.

`style`	Set this to an inline style to specify how the browser should display the element.
`title`	Contains the title of the element (which might be displayed in ToolTips).
`xml:lang`	Specifies the base language for the element when the document is interpreted as an XML document.

This element supports these XHTML events: `onclick`, `ondblclick`, `onmousedown`, `onmouseup`, `onmouseover`, `onmousemove`, `onmouseout`, `onkeypress`, `onkeydown`, and `onkeyup`.

The `<div>` element enables you to refer to an entire section of your document by name. You can replace the text in it from JavaScript code, as we did in Chapter 7, "Handling XML Documents with JavaScript," where we read in XML documents and worked with them, displaying results using the `<div>` element's `innerHTML` property in Internet Explorer as in this HTML document:

```
<HTML>
    <HEAD>
         <TITLE>
             Reading XML element values
         </TITLE>

         <SCRIPT LANGUAGE="JavaScript">
              function readXMLDocument()
              {
                  var xmldoc, meetingsNode, meetingNode, peopleNode
                  var first_nameNode, last_nameNode, outputText
                  xmldoc = new ActiveXObject("Microsoft.XMLDOM")
                  xmldoc.load("meetings.xml")

                  meetingsNode = xmldoc.documentElement
                  meetingNode = meetingsNode.firstChild
                  peopleNode = meetingNode.lastChild
                  personNode = peopleNode.lastChild
                  first_nameNode = personNode.firstChild
                  last_nameNode = first_nameNode.nextSibling

                  outputText = "Third name: " +
                        first_nameNode.firstChild.nodeValue + ' '
                     + last_nameNode.firstChild.nodeValue

                  messageDIV.innerHTML=outputText
              }
         </SCRIPT>
    </HEAD>
```

```
    <BODY>
        <CENTER>
            <H1>
                Reading XML element values
            </H1>

            <INPUT TYPE="BUTTON" VALUE="Get the name of the third person"
                ONCLICK="readXMLDocument()">
            <P>
            <DIV ID="messageDIV"></DIV>
        </CENTER>
    </BODY>
</HTML>
```

Here's an XHTML example; in this case, I'm enclosing some text in a `<div>` element and styling the text in bold red italics with an XHTML `<style>` element. (More on the `<style>` element comes in the next chapter.)

```
<?xml version="1.0"?>
<!DOCTYPE html PUBLIC "-//W3C//DTD XHTML 1.0 Transitional//EN"
"http://www.w3.org/TR/xhtml1/DTD/xhtml1-transitional.dtd">
<html xmlns="http://www.w3.org/1999/xhtml" xml:lang="en" lang="en">
    <head>
        <title>
            Using the &lt;div&gt; tag
        </title>
        <style>
            div {color: red; font-weight: bold; font-style: italic}
        </style>
    </head>

    <body>
        <center>
            <h1>
                Using the &lt;div&gt; Element
            </h1>
        </center>

        <p>
            <div>
                This text, which
                <br />
                takes up multiple lines,
                <br />
                was formatted all at once
                <br />
                in a single &lt;div&gt; element.
            </div>
        </p>
    </body>
</html>
```

You can see the results of this XHTML in Figure 16.12 where, as you see, all the lines in the <div> element were styled in the same way.

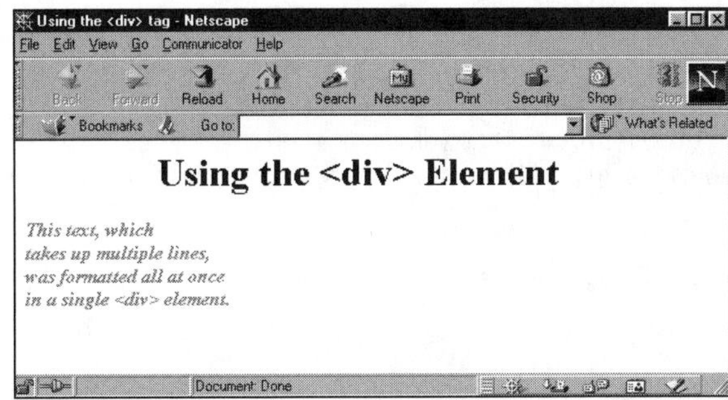

Figure 16.12 Styling text with the <div> element.

The W3C suggests that you use the <div> element's align attribute to replace the now deprecated <center> element by setting align to "center". That would look like this, where I'm modifying the example from the previous section:

```
<?xml version="1.0"?>
<!DOCTYPE html PUBLIC "-//W3C//DTD XHTML 1.0 Transitional//EN"
"http://www.w3.org/TR/xhtml1/DTD/xhtml1-transitional.dtd">
<html xmlns="http://www.w3.org/1999/xhtml" xml:lang="en" lang="en">
    <head>
        <title>
            Using the &lt;div&gt; Element
        </title>
    </head>

    <body>
        <div align="center">
            <h1>
                Using the &lt;div&gt; Element
            </h1>
        </div>
        <div align="center">
            The &lt;div&gt; element is a
            <br />
            useful one for centering
            <br />
            text made up of
            <br />
            multiple lines.
        </div>
    </body>
</html>
```

In fact, although W3C documentation suggests that you use the `align` attribute, the W3C seems to have forgotten that it deprecated that attribute in HTML 4.0. The way to center text now is setting a `<div>` element's `text-align` style property to `"center"`. That might look like this:

```
<?xml version="1.0"?>
<!DOCTYPE html PUBLIC "-//W3C//DTD XHTML 1.0 Transitional//EN"
"http://www.w3.org/TR/xhtml1/DTD/xhtml1-transitional.dtd">
<html xmlns="http://www.w3.org/1999/xhtml" xml:lang="en" lang="en">
    <head>
        <title>
            Using the &lt;div&gt; Element
        </title>
        <style>
            div {text-align: center}
        </style>
    </head>

    <body>
        <div>
            <h1>
                Using the &lt;div&gt; Element
            </h1>
        </div>
        <div>
            The &lt;div&gt; element is a
            <br />
            useful one for centering
            <br />
            text made up of
            <br />
            multiple lines.
        </div>
    </body>
</html>
```

This works as planned—the text is indeed centered in the browser.

Using the positioning style properties, you can also position text with the `<div>` tag, even overlapping displayed text blocks. There's another handy element that you can use to select text and apply styles: `<span>`.

Formatting Text Inline (*<span>*)

The `<span>` element lets you select inline text to apply styles. It's supported in XHTML 1.0 Strict, XHTML 1.0 Transitional, XHTML 1.0 Frameset, and XHTML 1.1. Here are the attributes of this element:

Attribute	Description
`class`	Gives the style class of the element.
`dir`	Sets the direction of directionally neutral text. You can set this attribute to `LTR`, for left-to-right text, or `RTL`, for right-to-left text.
`id`	Use the ID to refer to the element; set this attribute to a unique identifier.
`lang`	Specifies the base language used in the element. Applies only when the document is interpreted as HTML.
`style`	Set this to an inline style to specify how the browser should display the element.
`title`	Contains the title of the element (which might be displayed in ToolTips).
`xml:lang`	Specifies the base language for the element when the document is interpreted as an XML document.

This element supports these XHTML events: `onclick`, `ondblclick`, `onmousedown`, `onmouseup`, `onmouseover`, `onmousemove`, `onmouseout`, `onkeypress`, `onkeydown`, and `onkeyup`.

You usually use `<span>` to apply styles inline, for example, in the middle of a sentence, to a few words or even characters. When styling blocks of text, you can use `<div>`; for individual characters, words, or sentences, use `<span>`.

As we saw, you can use `<div>` to replace the deprecated `<center>` element; there's also a deprecated element that you can replace with `<span>`: the `<font>` element. Using `<span>`, you can apply styles inline to a few characters or words, which is what Web authors previously used `<font>` for. For example, here I'm applying a style to a section of text using `<span>`, displaying that text in bold red italic:

```
<?xml version="1.0"?>
<!DOCTYPE html PUBLIC "-//W3C//DTD XHTML 1.0 Transitional//EN"
"http://www.w3.org/TR/xhtml1/DTD/xhtml1-transitional.dtd">
<html xmlns="http://www.w3.org/1999/xhtml" xml:lang="en" lang="en">
    <head>
        <title>
            Using the &lt;span&gt; Element
        </title>

        <style>
            span {color: red; font-weight: bold; font-style: italic}
        </style>
```

continues ▸

```
    </head>

    <body>
        <center>
            <h1>
                Using the &lt;span&gt; Element
            </h1>
        </center>
        <h2>
            Sometimes, for <span>emphasis</span>, you might want to
            target <span>specific words</span> in your text.
        </h2>
    </body>
</html>
```

You can see the results of this XHTML in Figure 16.13, where the words we want styled in a specific way are indeed styled as we want them.

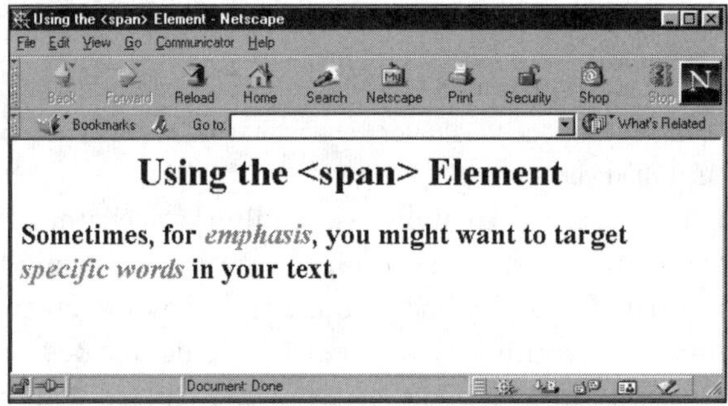

Figure 16.13 Using `<span>` to style text.

There's more XHTML to come—take a look at the next chapter.

17 XHTML at Work

WE GOT STARTED WITH XHTML IN THE PREVIOUS chapter, and I'll continue exploring it here. In this chapter, I'll take a look at how XHTML implements images, hyperlinks, style sheets, tables, and forms, and I'll also cover how to extend XHTML by creating custom tags. I'll start with handling images.

Displaying an Image (*<img>*)

As in HTML, the `<img>` element is an empty element that you use to insert images into Web pages. This element is supported in XHTML 1.0 Strict, XHTML 1.0 Transitional, XHTML 1.0 Frameset, and XHTML 1.1. Here are its attributes (which apply to XHTML 1.0 Strict, XHTML 1.0 Transitional, XHTML 1.0 Frameset, and XHTML 1.1, unless otherwise noted):

Attribute	Description
`align`	Sets the alignment of text relative to the image on the screen. Possible settings are `left`, `right`, `top`, `texttop`, `middle`, `absmiddle`, `baseline`, `bottom`, and `absbottom`. (XHTML 1.0 Transitional, XHTML 1.0 Frameset.)
`alt`	Is required. This attribute holds the text that should be displayed instead of an image for browsers that cannot handle graphics or have graphics disabled.

continues

Attribute	Description
`border`	Specifies whether the image has a border and, if so, how thick the border is. Set this to 0 for no border, or a positive integer pixel value. (XHTML 1.0 Transitional, XHTML 1.0 Frameset.)
`class`	Gives the style class of the element.
`height`	Specifies the height of the image, in pixels.
`hspace`	Sets the horizontal spacing (both left and right sides) around the image. Set this to pixel measurements. (XHTML 1.0 Transitional, XHTML 1.0 Frameset.)
`id`	Use the ID to refer to the element; set this attribute to a unique identifier.
`ismap`	Specifies that this image is to be used as an image map along with a map file.
`lang`	Specifies the base language used in the element. Applies only when the document is interpreted as HTML.
`longdesc`	Contains a longer description of the image. Allows descriptions that can contain markup. Set this to a URI.
`src`	Is required. Specifies the URI of the image to display.
`style`	Gives the inline style indicating how to render the element.
`title`	Contains the title of the body (which might be displayed in ToolTips).
`usemap`	Specifies the URI—usually inside the current document—of a client-side image map.
`vspace`	Sets the vertical spacing around the image. Set this to pixel measurements. (XHTML 1.0 Transitional, XHTML 1.0 Frameset.)
`width`	Indicates the width of the image. Set this to pixel measurements.
`xml:lang`	Specifies the base language for the element when the document is interpreted as an XML document.

This element supports these XHTML events: `onclick`, `ondblclick`, `onmousedown`, `onmouseup`, `onmouseover`, `onmousemove`, `onmouseout`, `onkeypress`, `onkeydown`, and `onkeyup`.

You use the XHTML `<img>` element to insert images into a Web page as well as image maps. When you use this element, you supply the URI of the image in the `src` attribute. Besides `src`, the `alt` attribute, which specifies alternate text to display in case the image can't be displayed, is required.

Interestingly, the `align` attribute is not deprecated in the `<img>` element as it is for virtually every other XHTML element that supports it.

Here's a simple example using the `<img>` element:

```
<?xml version="1.0"?>
<!DOCTYPE html PUBLIC "-//W3C//DTD XHTML 1.0 Transitional//EN"
"http://www.w3.org/TR/xhtml1/DTD/xhtml1-transitional.dtd">
<html xmlns="http://www.w3.org/1999/xhtml" xml:lang="en" lang="en">
    <head>
        <title>
            Using the &lt;img&gt; Element
        </title>
    </head>

    <body>
        <center>
            <h1>
                Using the &lt;img&gt; Element
            </h1>
            <img src="image.jpg"
                width="428" height="86" alt="an image" />
        </center>
    </body>
</html>
```

You can see the result in Figure 17.1.

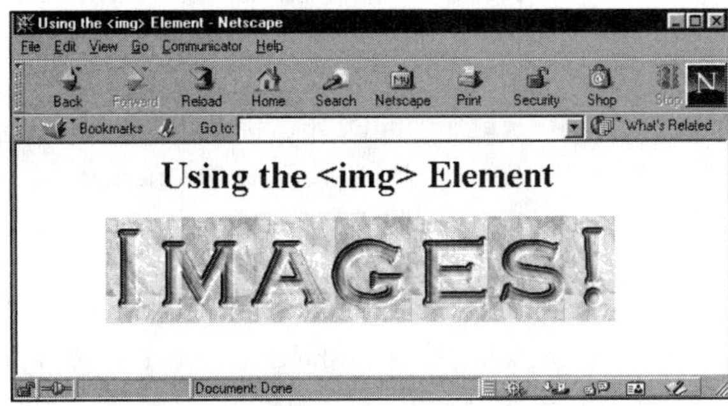

Figure 17.1 Displaying an image in XHTML.

Creating a Hyperlink or Anchor (<*a*>)

The `<a>` element creates a hyperlink (use the `href` attribute) or anchor (use the `id` or the deprecated `name` attribute for browsers that need to use `name`, such as Netscape). This element is supported in XHTML 1.0 Strict, XHTML 1.0 Transitional, XHTML 1.0 Frameset, and XHTML 1.1. Here are this element's attributes:

Attribute	Description
`accesskey`	Assigns a keyboard access key to the hyperlink. (XHTML 1.0 Strict, XHTML 1.0 Transitional.)
`charset`	Indicates the character encoding of the hyperlink's target. Set this to an RFC (Request for Comments) 2045 language character set string. The default value is ISO-8859-1.
`class`	Gives the style class of the element.
`coords`	Sets the coordinate values (in pixels) appropriate to the corresponding `shape` attribute to define a region of an image for image maps.
`dir`	Sets the direction of text that doesn't have an inherent direction in which you should read it, called directionally neutral text. You can set this attribute to `ltr`, for left-to-right text, or `rtl`, for right-to-left text.
`href`	Holds the target URI of the hyperlink. You must assign a value to either this attribute or the `id` attribute.
`hreflang`	Gives the base language of the target indicated in the `href` attribute. Set this to RFC 1766 values.
`id`	Use the ID to refer to the element; set this attribute to a unique identifier.
`lang`	Specifies the base language used in the element. Applies only when the document is interpreted as HTML.
`name`	Is available in the three XHTML 1.0 DTDs, but is deprecated and not available in the XHTML 1.1 DTD (use `id` instead). Gives the anchor a name, which may be used as the target of a hyperlink. (XHTML 1.0 Strict, XHTML 1.0 Transitional, XHTML 1.0 Frameset.)
`rel`	Specifies the relationship described by the hyperlink.
`rev`	Is the same as the `rel` attribute, but the syntax works in the reverse direction. For example, a link from A to B with `rel="X"` signifies the same relationship as a link from B to A with `rev="X"`.

`shape`	Specifies the type of region for mapping in an `<area>` element. Used with the `coords` attribute. Possible values are `rect` (the default), `circ`, `circle`, `POLY`, and `polygon`.
`style`	Is an inline style indicating how to render the element.
`tabindex`	Specifies the tab sequence of hyperlinks in the page for keyboard navigation. (XHTML 1.0 Strict, XHTML 1.0 Transitional, XHTML 1.0 Frameset.)
`target`	Indicates the named frame that serves as the target of the hyperlink. (XHTML 1.0 Transitional, XHTML 1.0 Frameset.)
`title`	Contains the title of the element (which might be displayed in ToolTips).
`type`	Specifies the Multipurpose Internet Mail Extensions (MIME) type of the target given in the `href` attribute.
`xml:lang`	Specifies the base language for the element when the document is interpreted as an XML document.

This element supports these XHTML events: `onclick`, `ondblclick`, `onfocus`, `onblur`, `onmousedown`, `onmouseup`, `onmouseover`, `onmousemove`, `onmouseout`, `onkeypress`, `onkeydown`, and `onkeyup`.

The `<a>` element is a big part of what makes the Web work. You use this element to create hyperlinks and anchors (an anchor can serve as the target of a hyperlink). In this element, you must set either the `href` attribute to set the target URI of a hyperlink, or the `id` attribute to create an anchor. Here's an example using `href`, specifying the W3C site as the target of a hyperlink:

```
<?xml version="1.0"?>
<!DOCTYPE html PUBLIC "-//W3C//DTD XHTML 1.0 Transitional//EN"
"http://www.w3.org/TR/xhtml1/DTD/xhtml1-transitional.dtd">
<html xmlns="http://www.w3.org/1999/xhtml" xml:lang="en" lang="en">
    <head>
        <title>
            Using the &lt;a&gt; Element
        </title>
    </head>

    <body>

       <center>

           <h1>
            Using the &lt;a&gt; Element
           </h1>

           Want to learn more about XHTML? Go to:
```

continues ▸

```
        <a href="http://w3c.org">W3C</a>.
    </center>

  </body>
</html>
```

You can see the results of this XHTML in Figure 17.2; as is standard in HTML browsers, the hyperlink appears as underlined text (largely because the browser thinks that this *is* standard HTML). You can also use graphical hyperlinks if you enclose an `<img>` element in the `<a>` element.

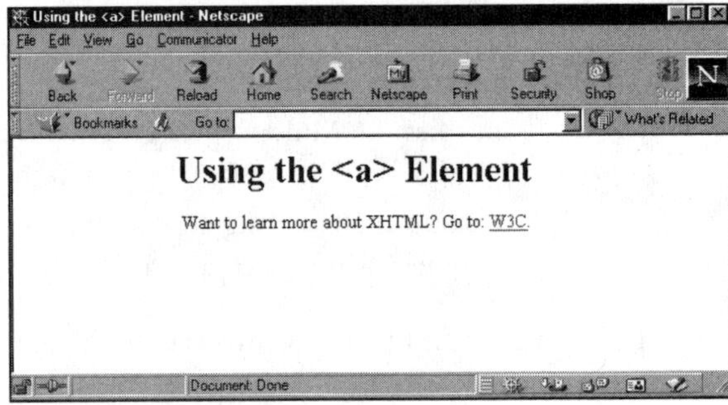

Figure 17.2 Displaying a hyperlink.

Setting Link Information (*<link>*)

You use the XHTML `<link>` element to indicate the relationship of other documents to the current one, such as specifying an external style sheet. This element is empty and goes in the `<head>` section of a document. This element is supported in XHTML 1.0 Strict, XHTML 1.0 Transitional, XHTML 1.0 Frameset, and XHTML 1.1. Here are the attributes of `<link>`:

Attribute	Description
`charset`	Specifies the character encoding of the linked document. Set this to an RFC 2045 language character set string; the default value is ISO-8859-1.
`class`	Gives the style class of the element.
`dir`	Sets the direction of directionally neutral text. You can set this attribute to `ltr`, for left-to-right text, or `rtl`, for right-to-left text.
`href`	Contains the target URI of the resource. You must assign a value to either this attribute or the `id` attribute.

`hreflang`	Indicates the base language of the target indicated in the `href` attribute. Set this to RFC 1766 values.
`id`	Use the ID to refer to the element; set this attribute to a unique identifier.
`lang`	Specifies the base language used in the element. Applies only when the document is interpreted as HTML.
`media`	Specifies the device that the document will be displayed on; possible values are `screen` (the default), `print`, `projection`, `braille`, `speech`, and `all` (style information should be used for all devices).
`rel`	Gives the relationship described by the hyperlink.
`rev`	Is the same as the `rel` attribute, but the syntax works in the reverse direction. For example, a link from A to B with `rel="X"` signifies the same relationship as a link from B to A with `rev="X"`.
`style`	Is an inline style indicating how to render the element.
`target`	Indicates the named frame that serves as the target of the link. (XHTML 1.0 Transitional, XHTML 1.0 Frameset.)
`title`	Contains the title of the element.
`type`	Indicates the MIME type of the target given in the `href` attribute.
`xml:lang`	Specifies the base language for the element when the document is interpreted as an XML document.

This element supports these event attributes: `onclick`, `ondblclick`, `onmousedown`, `onmouseup`, `onmouseover`, `onmousemove`, `onmouseout`, `onkeypress`, `onkeydown`, and `onkeyup`.

The `<link>` element specifies the relationship of the current document to other documents. I'll use this element to handle external style sheets. You indicate the relationship with the `rel` attribute, which can take these values:

Value	**Links to**
`rel=alternate`	An alternate resource
`rel=appendix`	An appendix
`rel=bookmark`	Bookmarks, which provide entry points into a document
`rel=chapter`	A chapter
`rel=contents`	The contents section
`rel=copyright`	A copyright document for the current document
`rel=glossary`	A document providing a glossary of terms

continues

Value	Links to
rel=help	A document providing help
rel=home	A home page
rel=index	A document providing an index
rel=next	The next document
rel=previous	The previous document
rel=section	A section
rel=start	The start of a resource
rel=stylesheet	An external style sheet
rel=subsection	A subsection
rel=toc	A document that holds a table of contents
rel=up	The parent of the current document

Here's an example showing how to use an external style sheet, where I'm setting `rel` to `"stylesheet"` to indicate that the linked-to item is a style sheet, and `href` to the URI of the style sheet:

```
<!DOCTYPE html PUBLIC "-//W3C//DTD XHTML 1.0 Transitional//EN"
"http://www.w3.org/tr/xhtml1/DTD/xhtml1-transitional.dtd">
<html xmlns="http://www.w3.org/1999/xhtml" xml:lang="en" lang="en">
    <head>
        <title>
            Working With External Style Sheets
        </title>

        <link rel="stylesheet" href="style.css">

    </head>

    <body>

       <center>

           <h1>
               Working With External Style Sheets
           </h1>

           <p>
           This document is displayed using an external style sheet.
           </p>

       </center>

    </body>
</html>
```

Here's the style sheet I'm using, `style.css`:

```
body {background-color: #FFFFCC; font-family: Arial}
a:link {color: #0000FF}
a:visited {color: #FFFF00}
a:hover {color: #00FF00}
a:active {color: #FF0000}
p {font-style: italic}
```

That's all it takes—you can see the results in Figure 17.3. I'll take a closer look at working with style sheets later in this chapter (see the section "Using Style Sheets in XHTML").

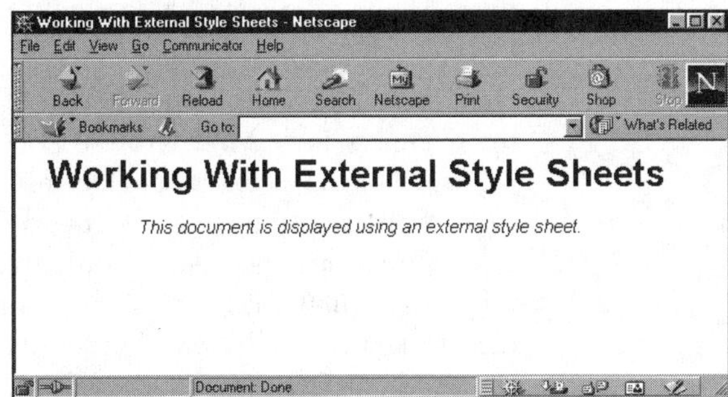

Figure 17.3 Using an external style sheet in Netscape.

Creating Tables (*<table>*)

The `<table>` element is always a popular one, and you use it to create tables. To build a table, you enclose other elements in `<table>`, such as `<caption>`, `<tr>`, `<th>`, `<td>`, `<colspan>`, `<col>`, `<thead>`, `<tbody>`, and `<tfoot>`. This element is supported in XHTML 1.0 Strict, XHTML 1.0 Transitional, XHTML 1.0 Frameset, and XHTML 1.1. Here are its attributes:

Attribute	Description
`align`	Is deprecated in HTML 4.0. Sets the horizontal alignment of the table in the browser window. Set this to `left`, `center`, or `right`. (XHTML 1.0 Transitional, XHTML 1.0 Frameset.)
`bgcolor`	Is deprecated in HTML 4.0. Sets the background color of table cells. Even though this attribute is deprecated, style sheet support for tables is still limited and inconsistent among browsers today. (XHTML 1.0 Transitional, XHTML 1.0 Frameset.)

continues

Attribute	Description
`border`	Sets the border width as measured in pixels. If you set this attribute to `0`, the border is invisible. (XHTML 1.0 Transitional, XHTML 1.0 Frameset.)
`cellpadding`	Specifies the spacing between cell walls and cell contents in pixels.
`cellspacing`	Specifies the distance between cells. Set this to a value in pixels.
`class`	Gives the style class of the element.
`dir`	Sets the direction of directionally neutral text. You can set this attribute to `ltr`, for left-to-right text, or `rtl`, for right-to-left text.
`frame`	Determines the outer border display of the table using the Complex Table Model. You use this attribute with the `rules` attribute. Possible values are `void` (no borders), `above` (border on top side only), `below` (border on bottom side only), `hsides` (horizontal borders only), `vsides` (vertical borders only), `lhs` (border on left side only), `rhs` (border on right side only), `box` (border on all four sides), and `border` (the default, the same as `box`).
`id`	You use the ID to refer to the element; set this attribute to a unique identifier.
`lang`	Specifies the base language used in the element. Applies only when the document is interpreted as HTML.
`rules`	Specifies the interior struts in a table using the Complex Table Model. Set this to `none` (no interior struts), `groups` (horizontal struts displayed between table groups created with the `thead`, `tbody`, `tfoot`, and `colgroup` tags), `rows` (horizontal struts displayed between all table rows), `cols` (vertical struts displayed between all table columns), and `all` (struts displayed between all table cells).
`style`	Is an inline style indicating how to render the element.
`summary`	Gives summary information for nonvisual browsers.
`title`	Contains the title of the element.
`width`	Sets the width of the table; set this to a pixel value or a percentage of the display area (add a percent sign [`%`] to such values).
`xml:lang`	Specifies the base language for the element when the document is interpreted as an XML document.

Here are the XHTML events that this element supports: onclick, ondblclick, onfocus, onblur, onmousedown, onmouseup, onmouseover, onmousemove, onmouseout, onkeypress, onkeydown, and onkeyup.

The <table> element is what you use to create tables in XHTML. To create a table, you enclose everything in a <table> element:

```
<table>
    .
    .
    .
</table>
```

That creates a table, but nothing happens on the screen with this markup—you need to give the table some rows. See the next section to start fleshing things out.

Creating Table Rows (<*tr*>)

You use <tr> to create rows in a table. This element can contain <th> (table header) and <td> (table data) elements, and it is supported in XHTML 1.0 Strict, XHTML 1.0 Transitional, XHTML 1.0 Frameset, XHTML 1.1. Here are this element's attributes:

Attribute	Description
align	Specifies the horizontal alignment of the text in this table row. Set this to left, center, right, justify, or char. Unlike other align attributes, this one is not deprecated.
bgcolor	Is deprecated in HTML 4.0. Specifies the background color of the table cells. (XHTML 1.0 Transitional, XHTML 1.0 Frameset.)
char	Specifies a character to align text on.
charoff	Sets the alignment offset to the first character to align on (which you set with char).
class	Gives the style class of the element.
dir	Sets the direction of directionally neutral text. You can set this attribute to ltr, for left-to-right text, or rtl, for right-to-left text.
id	Use the ID to refer to the element; set this attribute to a unique identifier.
lang	Specifies the base language used in the element. Applies only when the document is interpreted as HTML.
style	Is an inline style indicating how to render the element.

continues

Attribute	Description
title	Contains the title of the element.
valign	Sets the vertical alignment of the data in this row. Possible values are top, middle, bottom, and baseline.
xml:lang	Specifies the base language for the element when the document is interpreted as an XML document.

Here are the events supported by this element: onclick, ondblclick, onfocus, onblur, onmousedown, onmouseup, onmouseover, onmousemove, onmouseout, onkeypress, onkeydown, and onkeyup.

You use <tr> inside <table> to create a row in a table. Here's how that looks:

```
<table>
    <tr>
      .
      .
      .
    </tr>
    .
    .
    .
</table>
```

There's a <tr> element for every row in an XHTML table, and the browser knows how many rows there will be in the table by counting the number of <tr> elements. This element contains <tr> elements, which you use to create table headers, and <td> elements, which hold the actual data in the cells in a table.

Creating Table Headings (<*th*>)

You use the <th> element to create table headings, which are usually displayed in bold text and label the columns in a table. This element is supported in XHTML 1.0 Strict, XHTML 1.0 Transitional, XHTML 1.0 Frameset, and XHTML 1.1. Here are its attributes:

Attribute	Description
abbr	Holds an abbreviated name for a header.
align	Sets the horizontal alignment of content in table cells. Possible values are left, center, right, justify, and char.
axis	Contains a name for a cell (usually used only with table heading cells). Allows the table to be mapped to a tree hierarchy for access in code.

`bgcolor`	Is deprecated in HTML 4.0. Sets the background color of table cells. (XHTML 1.0 Transitional, XHTML 1.0 Frameset.)
`char`	Specifies a character to align text on.
`charoff`	Sets the alignment offset to the first character to align on (which you set with `char`).
`class`	Gives the style class of the element.
`colspan`	Specifies how many columns of the table this header should span. (The default is one).
`dir`	Sets the direction of directionally neutral text. You can set this attribute to `ltr`, for left-to-right text, or `rtl`, for right-to-left text.
`headers`	Species a list of header cells that supply header information.
`height`	Is deprecated in HTML 4.0. Sets the height of the header in pixels. (XHTML 1.0 Transitional, XHTML 1.0 Frameset.)
`id`	Use the ID to refer to the element; set this attribute to a unique identifier.
`lang`	Specifies the base language used in the element. Applies only when the document is interpreted as HTML.
`nowrap`	Is deprecated in HTML 4.0. Indicates that content should not be wrapped by the browser by adding line breaks. (XHTML 1.0 Transitional, XHTML 1.0 Frameset.)
`rowspan`	Specifies how many rows of the table this header should span.
`scope`	Specifies a set of data cells for which the header cell provides header information. Set this to `row`, `col`, `rowgroup`, or `colgroup`.
`style`	Is an inline style indicating how to render the element.
`title`	Contains the title of the element.
`valign`	Sets the vertical alignment of the data in this cell. Set this to `top`, `middle`, `bottom`, or `baseline`.
`width`	Is deprecated in HTML 4.0. Gives the width of the header. (XHTML 1.0 Transitional, XHTML 1.0 Frameset.)
`xml:lang`	Specifies the base language for the element when the document is interpreted as an XML document.

Here are the XHTML events supported by this element: onclick, ondblclick, onfocus, onblur, onmousedown, onmouseup, onmouseover, onmousemove, onmouseout, onkeypress, onkeydown, and onkeyup.

You use the <th> element to put a header on top of columns in a table. Headers such as these can span several columns if you use the colspan attribute. Here's an example:

```
<table>
    <tr>
        <th>TIC</th>
        <th>TAC</th>
        <th>TOE</th>
    </tr>
    .
    .
    .
</table>
```

This adds three table headers on top of three columns: TIC, TAC, and TOE. The next step is adding cells to the table that can contain some data, and you do that with the <td> element.

Creating Table Data (<td>)

The <td> element is where you place the data that you want in a cell in a table. You use this element inside the <tr> element. It's supported in XHTML 1.0 Strict, XHTML 1.0 Transitional, XHTML 1.0 Frameset, and XHTML 1.1. Here are this element's attributes:

Attribute	Description
abbr	Gives an abbreviated name for a cell (XHTML 1.0 Strict, XHTML 1.0 Transitional, XHTML 1.0 Frameset, XHTML 1.1.)
align	Sets the horizontal alignment of content in the table cell. Set this to left, center, right, justify, or char.
axis	Contains a name for a cell (usually used only with table heading cells). Allows the table to be mapped to a tree hierarchy.
bgcolor	Is deprecated in HTML 4.0. Sets the background color of table cells. (XHTML 1.0 Transitional, XHTML 1.0 Frameset.)
char	Specifies a character to align text on.
charoff	Sets the alignment offset to the first character to align on (which you set with char).

`class`	Gives the style class of the element.
`colspan`	Specifies how many columns this cell should span.
`dir`	Sets the direction of directionally neutral text. You can set this attribute to `ltr`, for left-to-right text, or `rtl`, for right-to-left text.
`headers`	Species a list of header cells that supply header information.
`height`	Is deprecated in HTML 4.0. Sets the height of the cell in pixels. (XHTML 1.0 Transitional, XHTML 1.0 Frameset.)
`id`	Use the ID to refer to the element; set this attribute to a unique identifier.
`lang`	Specifies the base language used in the element. Applies only when the document is interpreted as HTML.
`nowrap`	Is deprecated in HTML 4.0. Indicates that content should not be wrapped by the browser by adding line breaks. (XHTML 1.0 Transitional, XHTML 1.0 Frameset.)
`rowspan`	Specifies how many rows of the table this cell should span.
`scope`	Specifies a set of data cells for which the header cell provides header information. Set this to `row`, `col`, `rowgroup`, or `colgroup`.
`style`	Is an inline style indicating how to render the element.
`title`	Contains the title of the element.
`valign`	Sets the vertical alignment of the data in this cell. Set this to `top`, `middle`, `bottom`, or `baseline`.
`width`	Is deprecated in HTML 4.0. Gives the width of the header. (XHTML 1.0 Transitional, XHTML 1.0 Frameset.)
`xml:lang`	Specifies the base language for the element when the document is interpreted as an XML document.

Here are the events that this element supports: `onclick`, `ondblclick`, `onfocus`, `onblur`, `onmousedown`, `onmouseup`, `onmouseover`, `onmousemove`, `onmouseout`, `onkeypress`, `onkeydown`, and `onkeyup`.

You use `<td>` elements to hold the data in a table's cells. The browser knows how many columns to create in the table, depending on how many `<td>` or `<th>` elements you put into a row. For example, here's how I add data to the rows of a table using `<td>` elements:

```
<!DOCTYPE html PUBLIC "-//W3C//DTD XHTML 1.0 Transitional//EN"
"http://www.w3.org/tr/xhtml1/DTD/xhtml1-transitional.dtd">
<html xmlns="http://www.w3.org/1999/xhtml" xml:lang="en" lang="en">
```

continues ▸

```
    <head>
        <title>
            Working With XHTML Tables
        </title>
    </head>

    <body>
       <center>
           <h1>
               Working With XHTML Tables
           </h1>
            <table>
                <tr>
                   <th>TIC</th>
                   <th>TAC</th>
                   <th>TOE</th>
                </tr>
                <tr>
                     <td>0</td>
                     <td>X</td>
                     <td>0</td>
                 </tr>
                 <tr>
                     <td>X</td>
                     <td>0</td>
                     <td>X</td>
                 </tr>
                 <tr>
                     <td>0</td>
                     <td>X</td>
                     <td>0</td>
                </tr>
            </table>
        </center>
    </body>
</html>
```

You can see the results in Figure 17.4. That's all it takes to create simple tables in XHTML. The process is just like HTML—you enclose everything in a `<table>` element, use `<tr>` to create the rows of a table, and enter the data in each cell using `<td>` (or `<th>` for header text).

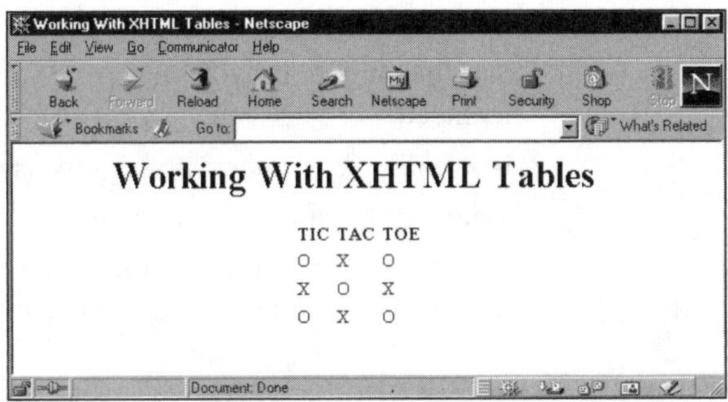

Figure 17.4 A table written in XHTML.

Creating Documents with Frames (*<frameset>*)

You use the `<frameset>` element when you want to display frames in a document. The `<frameset>` element replaces the `<body>` element in such documents; in XHTML 1.0, that means you use the XHTML 1.0 Frameset DTD. This element is supported in XHTML 1.0 Frameset only. The `<frame>` and `<frameset>` elements are *not* supported in XHTML 1.1; the XHTML 1.1 DTD does not makes any mention of these elements or of frames at all, and these elements are specifically listed as unsupported in XHTML 1.1. Why aren't frames supported in XHTML 1.1? They're not supported because the W3C expects style sheets to handle the presentation techniques that you use frames for today; whether the Web community will ultimately accept that is anyone's guess.

Here are the attributes of this element:

Attribute	**Description**
`class`	Gives the style class of the element.
`cols`	Sets the number of columns (vertical framed bands) in the frameset.
`dir`	Sets the direction of directionally neutral text . You can set this attribute to `ltr`, for left-to-right text, or `rtl`, for right-to-left text.
`id`	Use the ID to refer to the element; set this attribute to a unique identifier.
`lang`	Specifies the base language used in the element. Applies only when the document is interpreted as HTML.

continues

Attribute	Description
rows	Sets the number of rows (horizontal framed bands) in the frameset.
style	Is an inline style indicating how to render the element.
title	Contains the title of the element.
xml:lang	Specifies the base language for the element when the document is interpreted as an XML document.

This element supports no XHTML events.

You use the <frameset> element and the XHTML frameset DTD to format a page into frames. This element takes the place of the <body> element in documents that display frames. To create the frames themselves, you use the <frame> element.

To format the display into frames, you use the rows or cols attribute of the <frameset> element. You indicate the number or rows or columns that you want to use by giving their heights or widths in a comma-separated list. To specify those heights or widths, you can give pixel measurements or a percentage measurement (such as "40%") to request a percentage of the available display area. If you use an asterisk, the browser will try to give you the remaining display area; for example, cols="200, *" creates one vertical frame of 200 pixels and a second vertical frame filling the remainder of the display area. I recommend using percentage measurements rather than pixel measurements because the user may resize the browser window.

For example, here's how I create two columns—that is, two vertical frames—each of which takes up half the available width (note that I'm using the XHTML 1.0 frameset DTD):

```
<?xml version="1.0"?>
<!DOCTYPE html PUBLIC "-//W3C//DTD XHTML 1.0 Frameset//EN"
"http://www.w3.org/TR/xhtml1/DTD/xhtml1-frameset.dtd">
<html xmlns="http://www.w3.org/1999/xhtml" xml:lang="en" lang="en">
    <head>
        <title>
            Using XHTML Frames
        </title>
    </head>

    <frameset cols = "50%, 50%">
        .
        .
        .
    </frameset>
</html>
```

So how do you actually create the frames that should be displayed? Take a look at the next topic.

Creating Individual Frames (<*frame*>)

You use the `<frame>` element to create an individual frame. This element is an empty element, and you use it inside the `<frameset>` element. It's supported in XHTML 1.0 Frameset only. This table lists its attributes:

Attribute	Description
`class`	Gives the style class of the element.
`dir`	Sets the direction of directionally neutral text. You can set this attribute to `ltr`, for left-to-right text, or `rtl`, for right-to-left text.
`frameborder`	Sets whether borders enclose the frame. In Netscape, you set this attribute to `yes` (the default) or `no`; in Internet Explorer, you set it to `1` (the default) or `0` (no border).
`id`	Use the ID to refer to the element; set this attribute to a unique identifier.
`lang`	Specifies the base language used in the element. Applies only when the document is interpreted as HTML.
`longdesc`	Specifies the URI for a long description of the frame contents, which may include markup.
`marginheight`	Sets the height of the top and bottom margins used in the frame.
`marginwidth`	Sets the width of the right and left margins used in the frame.
`name`	Sets the name of the frame, which you can use as target destinations for `<a>`, `<area>`, `<base>`, and `<form>` elements.
`noresize`	Indicates that the frame may not be resized. The default is that frames may be resized by dragging the border.
`scrolling`	Sets scrollbar action; possible values are `auto`, `yes`, and `no`.
`src`	Is required. Holds the URI of the frame document.
`style`	Is an inline style indicating how to display the element.
`title`	Contains the title of the element.
`xml:lang`	Specifies the base language for the element when the document is interpreted as an XML document.

This element does not support any XHTML events.

You can use the <frame> element inside a <frameset> element to create a frame. This element exists so that you can specify the document that is displayed in a URI. That's the one required attribute in this element—src, which holds the URI of the document that the frame is to display.

For example, here's how I might display two frames, placing the contents of the document frame1.html in one, and the contents of frame2.html in the other:

```
<?xml version="1.0"?>
<!DOCTYPE html PUBLIC "-//W3C//DTD XHTML 1.0 Frameset//EN"
"http://www.w3.org/TR/xhtml1/DTD/xhtml1-frameset.dtd">
<html xmlns="http://www.w3.org/1999/xhtml" xml:lang="en" lang="en">
    <head>
        <title>
            Using XHTML Frames
        </title>
    </head>

    <frameset cols = "50%, 50%">
        <frame src="frame1.html" />
        <frame src="frame2.html" />
    </frameset>

</html>
```

Here's frame1.html:

```
<?xml version="1.0"?>
<!DOCTYPE html PUBLIC "-//W3C//DTD XHTML 1.0 Frameset//EN"
"http://www.w3.org/TR/xhtml1/DTD/xhtml1-frameset.dtd">
<html xmlns="http://www.w3.org/1999/xhtml" xml:lang="en" lang="en">
    <head>
        <title>
            Using XHTML Frames
        </title>
    </head>

    <body bgcolor=red>
    <h1>
        <center>
        This is frame 1.
        </center>
    </h1>
    </body>
</html>
```

And here's frame2.html:

```
<?xml version="1.0"?>
<!DOCTYPE html PUBLIC "-//W3C//DTD XHTML 1.0 Frameset//EN"
"http://www.w3.org/TR/xhtml1/DTD/xhtml1-frameset.dtd">
```

```
<html xmlns="http://www.w3.org/1999/xhtml" xml:lang="en" lang="en">
    <head>
        <title>
            Using XHTML Frames
        </title>
    </head>

    <body bgcolor=cyan>
    <h1>
        <center>
        This is frame 2.
        </center>
    </h1>
    </body>
</html>
```

The result of this XHTML appears in Figure 17.5.

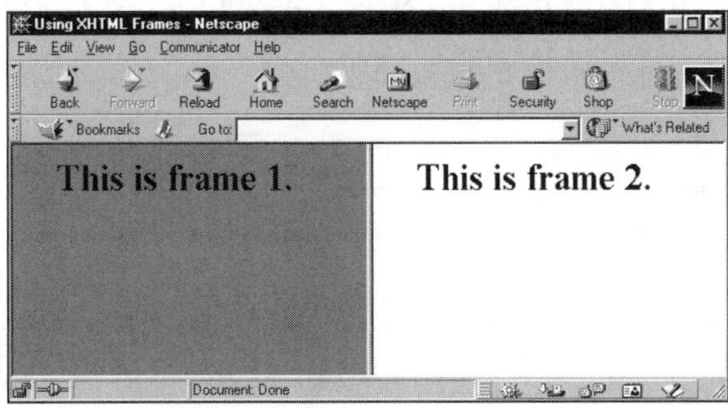

Figure 17.5 Displaying XHTML frames.

That's all it takes to create and display frames in XHTML, but bear in mind that the W3C has apparently targeted frames for extinction. Will style sheets be capable of taking over what frames do today? That remains to be seen. I'll take a look at handling style sheets now.

Using Style Sheets in XHTML

There are several ways to use style sheets in XHTML. As we already saw in this chapter, you can use the `<link>` element to connect an external style sheet to a document, like this:

```
<!DOCTYPE html PUBLIC "-//W3C//DTD XHTML 1.0 Transitional//EN"
"http://www.w3.org/tr/xhtml1/DTD/xhtml1-transitional.dtd">
<html xmlns="http://www.w3.org/1999/xhtml" xml:lang="en" lang="en">
    <head>
        <title>
            Working With External Style Sheets
        </title>
```

continues ▸

```
        <link rel="stylesheet" href="style.css">
    </head>

    <body>
       <center>
          <h1>
             Working With External Style Sheets
          </h1>
          <p>
          This document is displayed using an external style sheet.
          </p>
       </center>
    </body>
</html>
```

This XHTML links the Web page to an external style sheet named `style.css`, written in CSS (refer to Chapter 9, "Cascading Style Sheets," for more on CSS). Here's how that style sheet looks:

```
body {background-color: #FFFFCC; font-family: Arial}
a:link {color: #0000FF}
a:visited {color: #FFFF00}
a:hover {color: #00FF00}
a:active {color: #FF0000}
p {font-style: italic}
```

XHTML documents can be interpreted in two ways by browsers today—as HTML or as XML (and in the future, presumably, as XHTML). If you treat an XHTML document as XML (that is, by giving it the extension `.xml`), you use an XML processing instruction, `<?xml-stylesheet?>`, to indicate what style sheet you want to use, as we did in Chapter 9:

```
<?xml version="1.0"?>
<!DOCTYPE html PUBLIC "-//W3C//DTD XHTML 1.0 Transitional//EN"
"http://www.w3.org/tr/xhtml1/DTD/xhtml1-transitional.dtd">
<?xml-stylesheet type="text/css" href="style.css"?>
<html xmlns="http://www.w3.org/1999/xhtml" xml:lang="en" lang="en">
    <head>
        <title>
            Working With External Style Sheets
        </title>
        <link rel="stylesheet" href="style.css">
    </head>

    <body>
       <center>
          <h1>
             Working With External Style Sheets
          </h1>
```

```
            <p>
            This document is displayed using an external style sheet.
            </p>
        </center>
    </body>
</html>
```

Besides linking to external style sheets, XHTML documents that are interpreted as HTML can also use *embedded* style sheets if you use the <style> element.

Creating Embedded Style Sheets in XHTML (<*style*>)

The <style> element lets you embed full style sheets in XHTML documents. It is supported in XHTML 1.0 Strict, XHTML 1.0 Transitional, XHTML 1.0 Frameset, and XHTML 1.1. Here are the attributes of this element:

Attribute	Description
dir	Sets the direction of directionally neutral text. You can set this attribute to ltr, for left-to-right text, or rtl, for right-to-left text.
lang	Specifies the base language used in the element. Applies only when the document is interpreted as HTML.
media	Specifies the target media for the style sheet. Possible values are screen (the default), print, projection, braille, speech, and all.
title	Names the style sheet so that the browser can build a menu of alternative style sheets.
type	Is required. Indicates the MIME type of the <style> element content.
xml:lang	Specifies the base language for the element when the document is interpreted as an XML document.
xml:space	Set this to preserve to preserve spacing.

This element does not support any XHTML events.

The <style> element usually goes in a Web page's head, and you can use it to set styles, just as you can with an external style sheet. Here's an example that creates the same display as the example in the previous topic—note that the type attribute is required in XHTML:

```
<?xml version="1.0"?>
<!DOCTYPE html PUBLIC "-//W3C//DTD XHTML 1.0 Transitional//EN"
"http://www.w3.org/tr/xhtml1/DTD/xhtml1-transitional.dtd">
<html xmlns="http://www.w3.org/1999/xhtml" xml:lang="en" lang="en">
    <head>
        <title>
```

continues ▸

```
            Working With External Style Sheets
        </title>
        <style type="text/css">
            body {background-color: #FFFFCC; font-family: Arial}
            a:link {color: #0000FF}
            a:visited {color: #FFFF00}
            a:hover {color: #00FF00}
            a:active {color: #FF0000}
            p {font-style: italic}
        </style>
    </head>

    <body>
        <center>
            <h1>
                Working With External Style Sheets
            </h1>

            <p>
            This document is displayed using an external style sheet.
            </p>
        </center>
    </body>
</html>
```

Here's an important note: XHTML browsers are allowed to read and interpret every part of your document, so if your style sheet includes the characters `<`, `&`, `]]>`, or `--`, you should make your style sheet *external* so that those characters are not parsed and mistaken for markup. Also, XML parsers, like the ones inside XHTML browsers, are permitted to remove comments, so the practice of "hiding" style sheets inside comments as Web authors sometimes did to make documents backward-compatible might not work as expected in XHTML.

Using Inline Styles in XHTML

In XHTML, you can also *create* inline styles, where you apply styles to one XHTML element only. You create inline styles with the `style` attribute that most XHTML elements have. Here's an example. This example creates the same result as the previous two examples, but this time I'm using the `style` attribute, not the `<link>` element to link to an external style sheet, or the `<style>` element to create an embedded style sheet:

```
<?xml version="1.0"?>
<!DOCTYPE html PUBLIC "-//W3C//DTD XHTML 1.0 Transitional//EN"
"http://www.w3.org/tr/xhtml1/DTD/xhtml1-transitional.dtd">
<html xmlns="http://www.w3.org/1999/xhtml" xml:lang="en" lang="en">
    <head>
```

```
        <title>
            Working With External Style Sheets
        </title>
    </head>

    <body style="background-color: #FFFFCC; font-family: Arial">
        <center>
            <h1>
                Working With External Style Sheets
            </h1>

            <p style="font-style: italic">
            This document is displayed using an external style sheet.
            </p>
        </center>
    </body>
</html>
```

You usually use inline styles for short amounts of text; in fact, style purists insist that you should stay away from inline styles because it decentralizes the definition of styles, mixing markup with content more than they like. Note that as with embedded style sheets, if your style sheet includes the characters `<`, `&`, `]]>`, or `--`, you should make your style sheet external.

Using Script Programming (*<script>*)

You use the `<script>` element to embed a script, such as those written in JavaScript in an XHTML document. You usually place this element in a document's `<head>` section, except when the code writes directly to the document's body, in which case you should place it in the document's body. This element is supported in XHTML 1.0 Strict, XHTML 1.0 Transitional, XHTML 1.0 Frameset, and XHTML 1.1. Here are the attributes of this element:

Attribute	Description
`charset`	Gives the character encoding of the script contents.
`defer`	Tells the browser that the script is not going to generate any document content.
`language`	Specifies the scripting language. This attribute is required if the `src` attribute is not set and is optional otherwise. (XHTML 1.0 Strict, XHTML 1.0 Transitional, XHTML 1.0 Frameset.)
`src`	Holds a URI for the script code. (XHTML 1.0 Strict, XHTML 1.0 Transitional, XHTML 1.0 Frameset.)

continues

Attribute	Description
type	Is required. Holds the Multipurpose Internet Mail Extension (MIME) type of the scripting code. (XHTML 1.0 Strict, XHTML 1.0 Transitional, XHTML 1.0 Frameset.)
xml:space	Set this to preserve to preserve spacing.

This element does not support any XHTML events.

You use the `<script>` element to embed a script in a document. In XHTML, the `type` attribute, which you set to `"text/javascript"` in JavaScript, is required. Here's an example; note that normally, `<script>` goes in a document's `<head>` element, but because this script writes a message, `Welcome to XHTML scripting!`, to the document's body, it's supposed to be in the `<body>` element. (Note also that the `document.open()` and `document.close()` calls are not needed in Internet Explorer.)

```
<?xml version="1.0"?>
<!DOCTYPE html PUBLIC "-//W3C//DTD XHTML 1.0 Transitional//EN"
"http://www.w3.org/tr/xhtml1/DTD/xhtml1-transitional.dtd">
<html xmlns="http://www.w3.org/1999/xhtml" xml:lang="en" lang="en">
    <head>
        <title>
            Welcome to XHTML scripting
        </title>
    </head>

    <body>
        <script type = "text/javascript" language="javascript">
            document.open()
            document.writeln("Welcome to XHTML scripting!")
            document.close()
        </script>
    </body>
</html>
```

You can see the results of this XHTML in Figure 17.6.

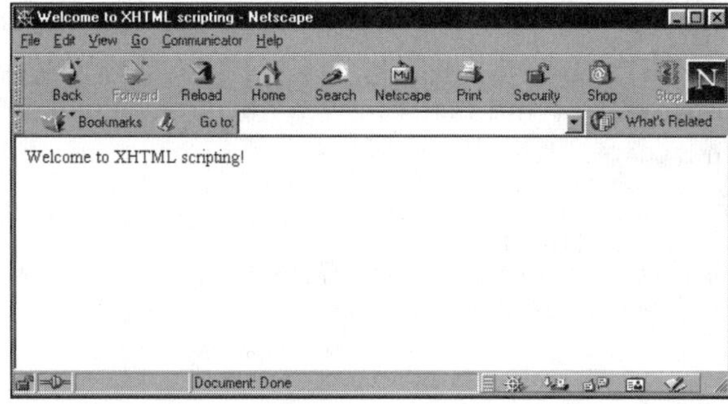

Figure 17.6 Running JavaScript in XHTML.

In HTML programming, you enclosed the actual JavaScript in an HTML comment like this. (Note that I ended the comment with a JavaScript comment marker, `//`; if I didn't, some HTML browsers would assume that the script code was actually commented out.)

```
<?xml version="1.0"?>
<!DOCTYPE html PUBLIC "-//W3C//DTD XHTML 1.0 Transitional//EN"
"http://www.w3.org/tr/xhtml1/DTD/xhtml1-transitional.dtd">
<html xmlns="http://www.w3.org/1999/xhtml" xml:lang="en" lang="en">
    <head>
        <title>
            Welcome To JavaScript
        </title>
    </head>

    <body>
        <script type = "text/javascript" language="javascript">
            <!--
            document.open()
            document.writeln("Welcome to XHTML scripting!")
            document.close()
            //-->
        </script>
    </body>
</html>
```

The reason that you had to do that is because if a browser doesn't understand the `<script>` tag, it displays what's inside the `<script>` element—the JavaScript code—as text. If you enclose that text in what looks like an HTML comment to the browser, it won't display the code. However, that's no good in XML because XML parsers are allowed to remove what they consider to be comments from the document entirely, and not pass them on to the browser.

While we're on the topic, it's worth noting that if your script contains sensitive characters such as < or &, they may be treated as markup by an XHTML browser. To avoid that, the W3C helpfully suggests that you enclose the script in a CDATA section:

```
<?xml version="1.0"?>
<!DOCTYPE html PUBLIC "-//W3C//DTD XHTML 1.0 Transitional//EN"
"http://www.w3.org/tr/xhtml1/DTD/xhtml1-transitional.dtd">
<html xmlns="http://www.w3.org/1999/xhtml" xml:lang="en" lang="en">
    <head>
        <title>
            Welcome to XHTML scripting
        </title>
    </head>

    <body>
        <script type = "text/javascript" language="javascript">
            <![CDATA[
            document.open()
            document.writeln("Welcome to XHTML scripting!")
            document.close()
            ]]>
        </script>
    </body>
</html>
```

Unfortunately, no major HTML browser today has any idea what to do with CDATA sections in documents that they consider HTML. Your only real alternative here is to store the script in an external file so that it won't be parsed, and assign the src attribute the URI of that file. Here's how that looks—in this case, I'm storing the JavaScript code in a file named script.js:

```
<?xml version="1.0"?>
<!DOCTYPE html PUBLIC "-//W3C//DTD XHTML 1.0 Transitional//EN"
"http://www.w3.org/tr/xhtml1/DTD/xhtml1-transitional.dtd">
<html xmlns="http://www.w3.org/1999/xhtml" xml:lang="en" lang="en">
    <head>
        <title>
            Welcome to XHTML scripting
        </title>
    </head>

    <body>
        <script type = "text/javascript" language="javascript"
        src="script.js">
        </script>
    </body>
</html>
```

Here, `script.js`, stored in the same directory as the Web page itself, contains this code:

```
document.open()
document.writeln("Welcome to XHTML scripting!")
document.close()
```

This XHTML gives the same results as the earlier examples. What's important to remember here is that you should use external scripts if your script uses the characters `<`, `&`, `]]>`, or `--` because an XHTML browser may interpret those characters as markup.

Creating XHTML Forms (*<form>*)

You use the `<form>` element to create an XHTML form, which you use to contain XHTML controls such as buttons and text fields. This element is supported in XHTML 1.0 Strict, XHTML 1.0 Transitional, XHTML 1.0 Frameset, and XHTML 1.1. Here are its attributes:

Attribute	Description
`accept`	Holds a comma-separated list of content types that a server processing this form will handle correctly. (XHTML 1.0 Strict, XHTML 1.0 Transitional, XHTML 1.0 Frameset, XHTML 1.1.)
`accept-charset`	Holds a list of possible language character sets for the form data. (XHTML 1.0 Strict, XHTML 1.0 Transitional, XHTML 1.0 Frameset, XHTML 1.1.)
`action`	Is required. Gives the URI that will handle the form data.
`class`	Gives the style class of the element.
`dir`	Sets the direction of directionally neutral text. You can set this attribute to `ltr`, for left-to-right text, or `rtl`, for right-to-left text.
`enctype`	Sets the MIME type used to encode the name/value pairs when sent to the action URI. The default is `"application/x-www-form-urlencoded"`.
`id`	Use the ID to refer to the element; set this attribute to a unique identifier.
`lang`	Specifies the base language used in the element. Applies only when the document is interpreted as HTML.

continues

Attribute	Description
`method`	Indicates a method or protocol for sending data to the target action URI. The `GET` method is the default; the other alternative is `POST`.
`name`	Is deprecated. Gives a name to the form so that you can reference it in code; use the `id` attribute instead in browsers that understand it. (XHTML 1.0 Transitional, XHTML 1.0 Frameset.)
`style`	Is an inline style indicating how to render the element.
`target`	Indicates a named frame for the browser to display the form results in. (XHTML 1.0 Transitional, XHTML 1.0 Frameset.)
`title`	Contains the title of the element.
`xml:lang`	Specifies the base language for the element when the document is interpreted as an XML document.

This element supports these XHTML events: `onclick`, `ondblclick`, `onmousedown`, `onmouseup`, `onmouseover`, `onmousemove`, `onmouseout`, `onkeypress`, `onkeydown`, `onkeyup`, `onsubmit`, and `onreset`.

When you want to use controls in a Web page, such as buttons and text fields, you should enclose the control elements in a `<form>` element. (Controls won't even appear in Netscape unless you enclose them in a `<form>` element.)

Forms originally were intended to be used to send data (such as the contents of text fields) back to the server. The target URI to send that data to is placed in the `action` attribute, and the W3C has made that attribute required for forms. We'll see how to send data to a server in Chapter 20, "WML, ASP, JSP, Servlets, and Perl," and we'll use the `action` attribute there; until then, I'll just set the `action` attribute to `"action"`. In addition, note that in XHTML, you're supposed to give XHTML forms an ID with the ID attribute—some browsers, such as Netscape, however, don't understand that attribute and use `name` instead. The only alternative in this case is to use both the `ID` and the `name` attributes here.

Let's see an example; here, the document will display a message that, when clicked, will display the message `Hello from JavaScript.` in a text field. Here's the code:

```
<?xml version="1.0"?>
<!DOCTYPE html PUBLIC "-//W3C//DTD XHTML 1.0 Transitional//EN"
"http://www.w3.org/tr/xhtml1/DTD/xhtml1-transitional.dtd">
<html xmlns="http://www.w3.org/1999/xhtml" xml:lang="en" lang="en">
    <head>
        <title>
```

```
            Using Forms in XHTML
        </title>

        <script language = "javascript">
            function displayMessage()
            {
                document.form1.textfield.value = "Hello from JavaScript."
            }
        </script>
    </head>

    <body>
        <center>
            <h1>
                Using Forms in XHTML
            </h1>
            <form name = "form1" id = "form1" action = "action">
                <input type = "text" name = "textfield" size = "25" />
                <br />
                <br />
                <input type = "button" value = "Click Me"
                    onclick = "displayMessage()" />
            </form>
        </center>
    </body>
</html>
```

You can see the results of this XHTML in Figure 17.7.

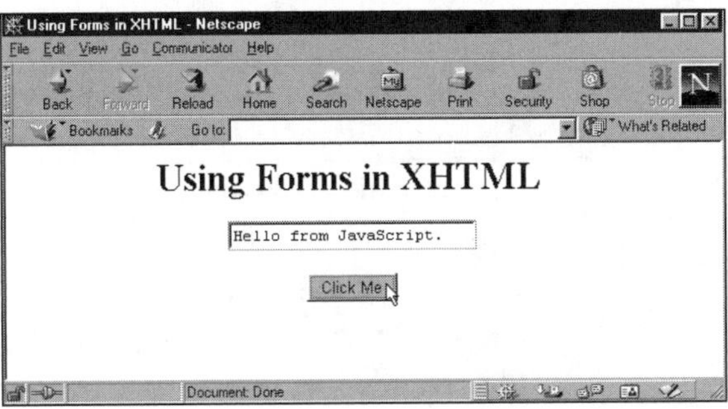

Figure 17.7 Using an XHTML form in Netscape.

This document used both a button and a text field, and I'll take a look at how to create those two controls in XHTML next.

Creating Controls (*<input type = "button">*)

You use the `<input>` element to create controls such as buttons and text fields. Setting the `type` attribute indicates what kind of control you want to create, and this element supports different attributes based on control type. This element is empty and is supported in XHTML 1.0 Strict, XHTML 1.0 Transitional, XHTML 1.0 Frameset, and XHTML 1.1. Here are the attributes for `<input type="button">`:

Attribute	Description
`accesskey`	Assigns a keyboard access key to the button. (XHTML 1.0 Strict, XHTML 1.0 Transitional.)
`class`	Gives the style class of the element.
`dir`	Sets the direction of directionally neutral text. You can set this attribute to `ltr`, for left-to-right text, or `rtl`, for right-to-left text.
`disabled`	Indicates that the element should be disabled when first displayed.
`id`	Use the ID to refer to the element; set this attribute to a unique identifier.
`lang`	Specifies the base language used in the element. Applies only when the document is interpreted as HTML.
`name`	Gives the element a name.
`size`	Sets the size of the control.
`style`	Is an inline style indicating how to render the element.
`tabindex`	Specifies the tab sequence of hyperlinks in the page for keyboard navigation.
`title`	Contains the title of the element.
`type`	Specifies the type of the element.
`value`	Specifies the caption of the element.
`xml:lang`	Specifies the base language for the element when the document is interpreted as an XML document.

This element supports these XHTML events: `onclick`, `ondblclick`, `onmousedown`, `onmouseup`, `onmouseover`, `onmousemove`, `onmouseout`, `onkeypress`, `onkeydown`, `onkeyup`, `onfocus`, `onblur`, `onselect`, and `onchange`.

You can create buttons in XHTML with the `<input type="button">` element (and also with the `<button>` element). We saw an example in the previous section:

```
<?xml version="1.0"?>
<!DOCTYPE html PUBLIC "-//W3C//DTD XHTML 1.0 Transitional//EN"
"http://www.w3.org/tr/xhtml1/DTD/xhtml1-transitional.dtd">
<html xmlns="http://www.w3.org/1999/xhtml" xml:lang="en" lang="en">
    <head>
        <title>
            Using Forms in XHTML
        </title>

        <script language = "javascript">
            function displayMessage()
            {
                document.form1.textfield.value = "Hello from JavaScript."
            }
        </script>
    </head>

    <body>
        <center>
            <h1>
                Using Forms in XHTML
            </h1>
            <form name = "form1" id = "form1" action = "action">
                <input type = "text" name = "textfield" size = "25" />
                <br />
                <br />
                <input type = "button" value = "Click Me"
                    onclick = "displayMessage()" />
            </form>
        </center>
    </body>
</html>
```

Of course, you can create plenty of other controls. I'll take a brief look at creating text fields next.

Creating Text Fields (*<input type="text">*)

You use the `<input type = "text">` element to create text fields. This element is an empty element and is supported in XHTML 1.0 Strict, XHTML 1.0 Transitional, XHTML 1.0 Frameset, and XHTML 1.1. Here are its attributes:

Attribute	Description
`accesskey`	Assigns a keyboard access key to the button. (XHTML 1.0 Strict, XHTML 1.0 Transitional.)
`class`	Gives the style class of the element.
`dir`	Sets the direction of directionally neutral text. You can set this attribute to `ltr`, for left-to-right text, or `rtl`, for right-to-left text.
`disabled`	Indicates that the element should be disabled when first displayed.
`id`	Use the ID to refer to the element; set this attribute to a unique identifier.
`lang`	Specifies the base language used in the element. Applies only when the document is interpreted as HTML. (XHTML 1.0 Strict, XHTML 1.0 Transitional, XHTML 1.0 Frameset, XHTML 1.1, IE4, IE5.)
`maxlength`	Sets the maximum number of characters that can be entered into the text field. The text field will scroll as needed if `maxlength` is greater than value of the `size` attribute.
`name`	Gives the element a name.
`readonly`	Specifies that the content of the text field is read-only, which means that it cannot be modified.
`size`	Sets the size of the text field, as measured in characters.
`style`	Is an inline style indicating how to render the element.
`tabindex`	Specifies the tab sequence of hyperlinks in the page for keyboard navigation.
`title`	Contains the title of the element.
`type`	Specifies the type of the element.
`value`	Holds the initial text in the text field. Set this to alphanumeric characters.
`xml:lang`	Specifies the base language for the element when the document is interpreted as an XML document.

This element supports these XHTML events: onclick, ondblclick, onmousedown, onmouseup, onmouseover, onmousemove, onmouseout, onkeypress, onkeydown, onkeyup, onfocus, onblur, onselect, and onchange.

You can create a text field with the <input type="text"> element. You can set the size of the text field in characters with the size attribute, and the maximum length of text (text fields will scroll if the maximum length is greater than its size) with the maxlength attribute.

Here's an example. In this case, I'm connecting JavaScript code to display the message Hello from JavaScript. in the text field to the onkeyup event, so every time you type something in this text field, the text is immediately replaced with that message.

```
<?xml version="1.0"?>
<!DOCTYPE html PUBLIC "-//W3C//DTD XHTML 1.0 Transitional//EN"
"http://www.w3.org/tr/xhtml1/DTD/xhtml1-transitional.dtd">
<html xmlns="http://www.w3.org/1999/xhtml" xml:lang="en" lang="en">
    <head>
        <title>
            Using Forms in XHTML
        </title>

        <script language = "javascript">
            function displayMessage()
            {
                document.form1.textfield.value = "Hello from JavaScript."
            }
        </script>
    </head>

    <body>
        <center>
            <h1>
                Using Forms in XHTML
            </h1>
            <form name = "form1" id = "form1" action = "action">
                <input type = "text" name = "textfield" size = "25"
                onkeyup = "displayMessage()" />
            </form>
        </center>
    </body>
</html>
```

You can see results in Figure 17.8.

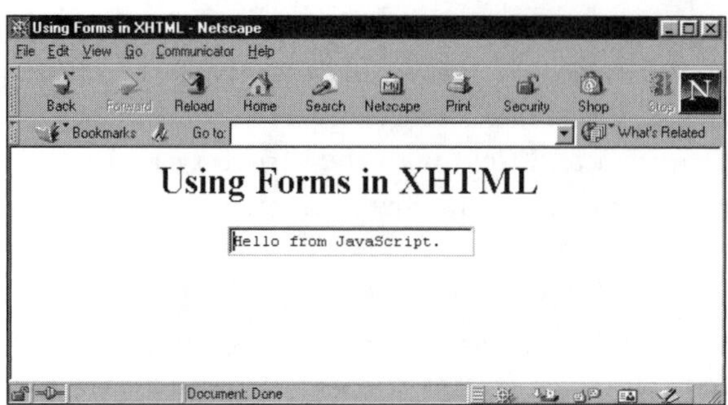

Figure 17.8 Using a text field in XHTML.

Extending XHTML 1.0

One of the attractions of XHTML is that you can extend it with your own elements because it's based on XML. The way you actually do this is has changed in the various XHTML working drafts over time; the current working draft on this topic is at `www.w3.org/TR/xhtml-building/`.

Here's an example. As you know, XHTML documents have `<head>` and `<body>` elements. Here, I'll add a `<foot>` element to XHTML 1.0. The W3C says that all custom XHTML elements should have their own namespace, so I'll give that element the namespace `doc`. I'll also create an attribute for this element, `footattribute`, like this in a new DTD, `extend.dtd`:

```
<!ELEMENT doc:foot (#PCDATA) >
<!ATTLIST doc:foot
    footattribute    CDATA   #IMPLIED
>
    .
    .
    .
```

You also must indicate where the new element fits into the XHTML element hierarchy. In the XHTML 1.0 Transitional DTD, here's how the `<html>` element is defined:

```
<!ELEMENT html (head, body)>
```

I can add `<doc:foot>` to this content model this way:

```
<!ELEMENT doc:foot (#PCDATA) >
<!ATTLIST doc:foot
    footattribute    CDATA   #IMPLIED
>
```

```
<!ELEMENT html (head, body, doc:foot)>
    .
    .
    .
```

Redefining the <html> element's content model in extend.dtd means that this new content model will be used instead of the old version. To complete extend.dtd, I include the entire XHTML 1.0 Transitional DTD using a parameter entity this way:

```
<!ELEMENT doc:foot (#PCDATA) >
<!ATTLIST doc:foot
     footattribute    CDATA   #IMPLIED
>

<!ELEMENT html (head, body, doc:foot)>

<!ENTITY % xhtml10T.dtd PUBLIC "-//W3C//DTD XHTML 1.0 Transitional//EN"
       "http://www.w3.org/TR/xhtml1/DTD/xhtml1-transitional.dtd">
%xhtml10T.dtd;
```

You can specify how you want the new element displayed with a style sheet. For example, I'll call this style sheet extend.css and use it with this new element:

```
doc:foot {font-size: 8pt; color: #0000FF}
p (color: #000000}
```

Here's an XHTML document that uses this new element. In this case, I'm creating a formal public identifier (FPI) for the new DTD ("-//Extender//DTD XHTML-Extensions 1.0//EN"). I'm also setting the default namespace to the XHTML namespace, and defining the doc namespace for the <doc:foot> element:

```
<!DOCTYPE html PUBLIC "-//Extender//DTD XHTML-Extensions 1.0//EN"
"http://www.starpowder.com/steve/extend.dtd" >
<html xmlns="http://www.w3.org/1999/xhtml"
xmlns:doc="http://www.starpowder.com/steve/extend.dtd">
    <head>
        <title>
            Extending XHTML
        </title>

        <link rel="stylesheet" href="extend.css" />
    </head>

    <body>
        <p>
            Here is some text.
        </p>
```

continues ▸

```
    </body>

    <doc:foot>
            This is the page's foot.
    </doc:foot>
</html>
```

And that's all there is to it. Here are the general rules for creating FPIs:

- The first field in an FPI specifies the connection of the DTD to a formal standard. For DTDs that you're defining yourself, this field should be –. If a non-standards body has approved the DTD, use `+`. For formal standards, this field is a reference to the standard itself (such as `ISO/IEC 13449:2000`).
- The second field must hold the name of the group or person that will maintain or be responsible for the DTD. In this case, you should use a name that is unique and that identifies your group easily (for example, the W3C simply uses `W3C`).
- The third field must indicate the type of document that is described, preferably followed by a unique identifier of some kind (such as `Version 1.0`). This part should include a version number that you'll update.
- The fourth field specifies the language that your DTD uses (for example, for English, you use `EN`. Note that two-letter language specifiers allow only a maximum of 24 × 24 = 576 possible languages; expect to see three-letter language specifiers in the near future).
- Fields in an FPI must be separated by double slash (`//`).

So far, I've only extended XHTML 1.0. The process is similar in XHTML 1.1, but you have to know how to integrate new elements into the XHTML 1.1 content models; to do that, you have to know how XHTML 1.1 modules work.

All About XHTML 1.1 Modules

The XHTML 1.1 DTD is a driver DTD that includes DTD *modules*. A DTD module is a section of a DTD that has two parts—an abstract part, which specifies what the DTD does in human-readable language, and the module itself, which is a DTD fragment that contains element types, a set of attribute list declarations, and a set of content model declarations.

You can find the XHTML 1.1 driver DTD at `www.w3.org/TR/xhtml11/xhtml11_dtd.html#a_xhtml11_driver`, and the actual implementation of the XHTML 1.1 modules (there's one for forms, one for text, one for images, and so on) at www.w3.org/TR/xhtmlmodularization/dtd_module_defs.html#a_xhtml11_modules. You'll find the XHTML 1.1 modules listed in Table 17.1.

Table 17.1 **The XHTML 1.1 Modules**

Module	Contents
xhtml-applet.module	Java Applet Element Module
xhtml-base.module	Base Element Module
xhtml-bdo.module	BIDI Override Module
xhtml-csismap.module	Client-side Image Map Module
xhtml-edit.module	Edit Module (<del> and <ins>)
xhtml-events.module	Events Module
xhtml-form.module	Forms Module
xhtml-framework.module	Modular Framework Module
xhtml-hypertext.module	Hypertext Module
xhtml-image.module	Image Module
xhtml-link.module	Link Element Module
xhtml-list.module	Lists Module
xhtml-meta.module	Document Metainformation Module
xhtml-param.module	Param Element Module
xhtml-postfw-redecl.module	Post-Framework Redeclaration Module
xhtml-prefw-redecl.module	Pre-Framework Redeclaration Module
xhtml-pres.module	Presentation Module
xhtml-ruby.module	Ruby Module
xhtml-script.module	Scripting Module
xhtml-ssismap.module	Server-side Image Map Module
xhtml-struct.module	Document Structure Module
xhtml-style.module	Stylesheets Module
xhtml-table.module	Tables Module
xhtml-text.module	Basic Text Module

Each module has two parts, and I'll take a look at them here in overview.

XHTML 1.1 Abstract Modules

Each XHTML 1.1 module has an description called an *abstract module* that specifies what elements and attributes are in the module, and gives a minimal content model for each element. You can find these abstract versions of the

XHTML 1.1 modules at www.w3.org/TR/xhtml-modularization/xhtml_modules.html#s_xhtmlmodules. An abstract module is really just a table listing the elements, attributes, and minimal content models in the module. For example, the Basic Text abstract module appears in Table 17.2.

Table 17.2 **The Basic Text Abstract Module**

Element	Attributes	Minimal Content Model
abbr	Common	(PCDATA | Inline)*
acronym	Common	(PCDATA | Inline)*
address	Common	(PCDATA | Inline)*
blockquote	Common, cite	(PCDATA | Heading | Block)*
br	Core	EMPTY
cite	Common	(PCDATA | Inline)*
code	Common	(PCDATA | Inline)*
dfn	Common	(PCDATA | Inline)*
div	Common	(Heading | Block | List)*
em	Common	(PCDATA | Inline)*
h1	Common	(PCDATA | Inline)*
h2	Common	(PCDATA | Inline)*
h3	Common	(PCDATA | Inline)*
h4	Common	(PCDATA | Inline)*
h5	Common	(PCDATA | Inline)*
h6	Common	(PCDATA | Inline)*
kbd	Common	(PCDATA | Inline)*
p	Common	(PCDATA | Inline)*
pre	Common	(PCDATA | Inline)*
q	Common, cite	(PCDATA | Inline)*
samp	Common	(PCDATA | Inline)*
span	Common	(PCDATA | Inline)*
strong	Common	(PCDATA | Inline)*
var	Common	(PCDATA | Inline)*

The Basic Text abstract module in Table 17.2 lists two attribute groups—`Common` and `Core`. Here's what they contain:

- The `Common` attribute groups contains the `class`, `id`, `title`, `dir`, `xml:lang`, `style`, `onclick`, `ondblclick`, `onmousedown`, `onmouseup`, `onmouseover`, `onmousemove`, `onmouseout`, `onkeypress`, `onkeydown`, and `onkeyup` attributes.
- The `Core` attribute group contains the `class`, `id`, and `title` attributes.

The content models in Table 17.2 also use the `Heading`, `Block`, and `Inline` content models; here's what elements they contain:

- The `Heading` content model contains <h1>, <h2>, <h3>, <h4>, <h5>, and <h6>.
- The `Block` content model contains <address>, <blockquote>, <div>, <p>, and <pre>.
- The `Inline` content model contains <abbr>, <acronym>, <br>, <cite>, <code>, <dfn>, <em>, <kbd>, <q>, <samp>, <span>, <strong>, and <var>.

An abstract module like the Basic Text module is only so that you can find out what's in a module—it isn't actually used by any software, nor does it appear in any actual module implementation. What actually makes these modules work is their *implementations*.

XHTML 1.1 Module Implementations

As far as an XML processor is concerned, a module is really just a DTD fragment that is included in a driver DTD. This DTD fragment can contain *element declarations*, *attribute declarations*, and *content model declarations*. You can find the XHTML 1.1 module implementations at `www.w3.org/TR/xhtml-modularization/dtd_module_defs.html`. For example, here's the XHTML 1.1 images module, `xhtml11-image-1.mod`:

```
<!--
.......................................................................
-->
<!-- XHTML 1.1 Images Module
.................................................. -->
<!-- file: xhtml11-image-1.mod

     This is XHTML XHTML 1.1, a modular variant of XHTML 1.0.
     Copyright 1998-2000 W3C (MIT, INRIA, Keio), All Rights Reserved.
     Rovision: $Id: dtd_module_defs.html,v 1.2 2000/01/05 20:58:33
shane Exp $ SMI

     This DTD module is identified by the PUBLIC and SYSTEM
identifiers:
```

continues ▸

```
     PUBLIC "-//W3C//ELEMENTS XHTML 1.1 Images 1.0//EN"
     SYSTEM "xhtml11-image-1.mod"

     Revisions:
     (none)
     .....................................................................
-->

<!-- Images

        img

     This module provides markup to support basic image embedding.
-->

<!-- To avoid problems with text-only UAs as well as to make
     image content understandable and navigable to users of
     non-visual UAs, you need to provide a description with
     the 'alt' attribute, and avoid server-side image maps.
-->

<!ENTITY % Img.element  "INCLUDE" >
<![%Img.element;[
<!ENTITY % Img.content  "EMPTY" >
<!ELEMENT img  %Img.content; >
<!-- end of Img.element -->]]>

<!ENTITY % Img.attlist  "INCLUDE" >
<![%Img.attlist;[
<!ATTLIST img
      %Common.attrib;
      src          %URI.datatype;           #REQUIRED
      alt          %Text.datatype;          #REQUIRED
      longdesc     %URI.datatype;           #IMPLIED
      height       %Length.datatype;        #IMPLIED
      width        %Length.datatype;        #IMPLIED
>
<!-- end of Img.attlist -->]]>

<!-- end of xhtml11-image-1.mod -->
```

Here's how that module is included in the XHTML 1.1 driver DTD:

```
<!-- Image Module ............................................... -->
<!ENTITY % xhtml-image.module "INCLUDE" >
<![%xhtml-image.module;[
<!ENTITY % xhtml-image.mod
PUBLIC "-//W3C//ELEMENTS XHTML 1.1 Images 1.0//EN" "xhtml11-image-1.mod" >
%xhtml-image.mod;]]>
```

Note the parameter entity `xhtml-image.module` here. This entity is set to `"INCLUDE"` by default, as you see here, but you can set it to `"IGNORE"` if you want to exclude the image module in a customized version of XHTML 1.1. That W3C calls the XHTML 1.1 DTD *fully parameterized*, and that's what it means—you can include or exclude modules just by changing parameter entities.

You'll find various suffixes used in the XHTML 1.1 driver DTD; for example, the name of the actual image module file is `xhtml-image.mod`. Here are the suffixes, such as `.mod`, that you'll find in the XHTML 1.1 driver DTD, along with what they mean. Using these suffixes, you can decipher what the various parameter entities in the DTD do:

Suffix	Description
`.attrib`	Indicates a group of tokens that indicate attribute specifications. Used in `ATTLIST` declarations.
`.class`	Groups elements of the same class together.
`.content`	Specifies the content model of a particular element. You specify what elements go inside what other elements with the content model. For example, here's how that looks for the `<head>` element: `<!ENTITY % Head.content "( %Head-opts.mix;, title, %Head-opts.mix; )" >`.
`.mix`	Specifies a collection of elements from different classes.
`.mod`	Is used for DTD modules, such as the term `xhtml-image.mod` that we've already seen.
`.module`	Is used for parameter entities that are used to control inclusion or exclusion of DTD modules. You can set them to `INCLUDE` (the default) to include a module, or `IGNORE` to exclude the module.

Extending XHTML 1.1

As mentioned, extending XHTML 1.1 works much like extending XHTML 1.0, except that integrating the new element into the element hierarchy is a little different. For example, instead of modifying the declaration of the `<html>` element directly, you modify the `Html.content` parameter entity, which looks like this in XHTML 1.1:

```
<!ENTITY % Html.content "( head, body )" >
```

This means that I can modify the DTD that I developed earlier, `extend.dtd`, to work with XHTML 1.1 by modifying this content model, adding `<doc:foot>` and including the entire XHTML 1.1 DTD this way:

```
<!ELEMENT doc:foot (#PCDATA) >
<!ATTLIST doc:foot
    footattribute    CDATA    #IMPLIED
>
```

```
<!ENTITY % Html.content "( head, body, doc:foot )" >

<!ENTITY % xhtml11.dtd PUBLIC "-//W3C//DTD XHTML 1.1//EN"
"http://www.w3.org/TR/xhtml11/DTD/xhtml11.dtd"> %xhtml11.dtd;
```

Now I can use this new DTD as we've used the XHTML 1.0 version of `extend.dtd`:

```
<!DOCTYPE html PUBLIC "-//Extender//DTD XHTML-Extensions
1.0//EN" "http://www.starpowder.com/steve/extend.dtd" >
<html xmlns="http://www.w3.org/1999/xhtml"
xmlns:doc="http://www.starpowder.com/steve/extend.dtd">
    <head>
        <title>
            Extending XHTML
        </title>

        <link rel="stylesheet" href="extend.css" />
    </head>

    <body>
        <p>
            Here is some text.
        </p>
    </body>

    <doc:foot>
            This is the page's foot.
    </doc:foot>
</html>
```

And that's it for our look at XHTML. These two chapters have provided an introduction to the subject, and we've hit the major differences between HTML and XHTML. You're now ready to create XHTML documents of substantial complexity. However, there are more details in XHTML than we can cover in two chapters—for example, what attributes are required in each of the more than 100 XHTML elements. For more information, see the W3C XHTML sites using the various URIs that I've listed—everything you need is there.

In the next chapter, I'm going to take a look at two more popular XML applications: Resource Description Framework (RDF) and Channel Definition Format (CDF).

18

Resource Description Framework and Channel Definition Format

THIS CHAPTER IS ABOUT TWO XML APPLICATIONS THAT WORK with metadata. Metadata is data that describes data, and the applications I'm going to take a look at are Resource Description Framework (RDF) and Channel Definition Format (CDF).

As you can gather from its name, RDF is a language that lets you describe resources. Although it's typically used to describe Web documents and sites, you can also use it to describe CD collections, books in a library, a collection of antique pen knives, and more. It's a general-purpose XML application that is helping to standardize the way people handle data on the Internet. Some consistent way of working with vast amounts of data on the Internet is sorely needed, and RDF is one possible solution. You may recall our discussion of canonical XML, which puts XML documents into a format that may easily be compared—RDF is actually stored in documents separate from the resources it describes, and it provides a standard description language.

CDF is similar, but more targeted. It's a language supported by only Internet Explorer, and it's designed to let you create *channels* in that browser to provide easy access to Web documents and sites to users. Creating a channel means letting Internet Explorer know all about what documents you want the user to be able to access and when—even providing for scheduled automatic download of entire Web sites or software updates. Using channels, the user needs only to click an icon to download the documents referenced by the CDF that created the channel.

I'll start with RDF, taking a look at that XML application in overview.

RDF Overview

As mentioned, RDF is a language for describing resources. Although you can use it to describe any kind of resource, it's usually used to describe Web documents and sites. RDF is a W3C recommendation, and its main page is at www.w3.org/RDF. You can find the RDF model and syntax specification at www.w3.org/TR/REC-rdf-syntax, and the RDF schema specification at www.w3.org/TR/rdf-schema. Here's what the W3C says about RDF:

> *The Resource Description Framework (RDF) is a foundation for processing metadata; it provides interoperability between applications that exchange machine-understandable information on the Web. RDF uses XML to exchange descriptions of Web resources, but the resources being described can be of any type, including XML and non-XML resources.*

What does RDF look like? Here's an example:

```
<?xml version="1.0" ?>
<rdf:RDF
    xmlns:rdf="http://www.w3.org/1999/02/22-rdf-syntax-ns#">
    <rdf:Description about="http://www.starpowder.com/planets.html">
        <Creator>Nicolas Copernicus</Creator>
    </rdf:Description>
</rdf:RDF>
```

This RDF document describes the document at "www.starpowder.com/planets.html" and lists that document's creator, Nicolas Copernicus. RDF is general enough to support all kinds of resource descriptions, but complete generality may not be what you need—to be useful, descriptions should use agreed-upon terms. Several sublanguages or grammars use RDF and define specific XML elements for describing resources. In this chapter, I'll take a look at the most popular such sublanguage, the *Dublin Core*. For example, RDF itself does not define an element named <Creator> to indicate the resource's creator; however, <Creator> is an element in the Dublin Core, which means that Web search engines that support the Dublin Core will know enough to search for <Creator> elements when they want to find a particular Web resource's author.

Support for RDF is growing. Here's a partial list of what's available in RDF today:

- www710.univ-lyon1.fr/~champin/rdf-tutorial. An RDF tutorial online. (It's in English, even though the Web page is in France.)

- `www.pro-solutions.com/rdfdemo`. A terrific online RDF parser. All you have to do is paste the RDF you want parsed into a box and then click the Send the RTF button. This program will tell you how an RDF parser will unpack the information in the RDF you tested.
- `www.w3.org/1999/02/26-modules`. The PerlXmlParser, which is a set of Comprehensive Perl Archive Network (CPAN) modules by Eric Prud'Hommeaux (a W3C member), supports an RDF SAX parser and a simple database interface for Perl.
- `www.ics.forth.gr/proj/isst/RDF`. This validating RDF parser by ICS-FORTH is a Java parser with some support for RDF schemas.
- `www.megginson.com/DATAX`. David Megginson's DATAX (Data Exchange in XML) and www.megginson.com/Software is his RDF Filter. Both of these are Java tools for parsing and filtering RDF.
- `http://nestroy.wi-inf.uni-essen.de/xwmf`. The Extensible Web Modeling Framework (XWMF) offers a number of tools, including an RDF parser.
- `www.w3.org/Library/src/HTRDF`. This is John Punin's RDF parser in C.
- `www.mozilla.org/rdf/doc`. This site explains about Mozilla's RDF implementation. I'll say more about this later in the chapter.
- `www.w3.org/RDF/Implementations/SiRPAC`. SiRPAC, a Simple RDF Parser and Compiler, was written by Janne Saarela, of W3C.
- `www.pro-solutions.com/download`. This is the Perl `RDF::Parser` module, written by Pro Solutions, Ltd. There's also an online demo available.
- `http://lists.w3.org/Archives/Public/www-rdf-interest/2000May/0009.html`. This is an RDF parser in XSLT, by Dan Connolly.

One of the most useful of these resources is the Pro Solutions online RDF parser, which you can see in Figure 18.1. All you have to do to is paste the RDF that you want to parse into the parser and click the Send the RTF button. You can see one of the built-in examples supported by this parser, which uses the Dublin Core, in Figure 18.1.

The results of parsing the RDF document appear in Figure 18.2, where the document has been broken up into subjects, predicates, and objects. I'll cover what those terms mean when we get to the RDF syntax.

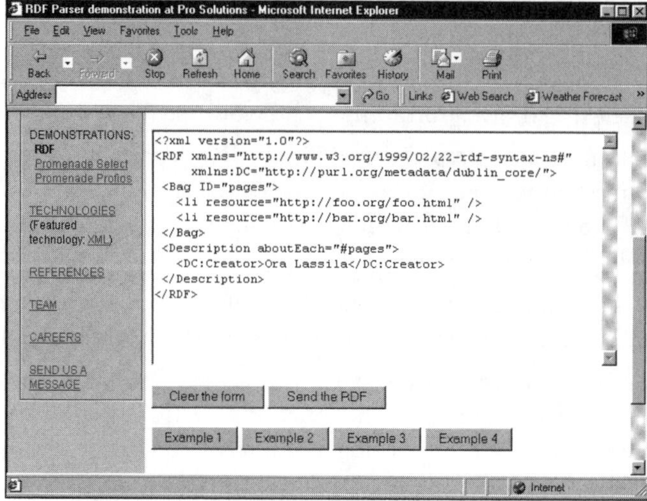

Figure 18.1 The online Pro Solutions RDF parser.

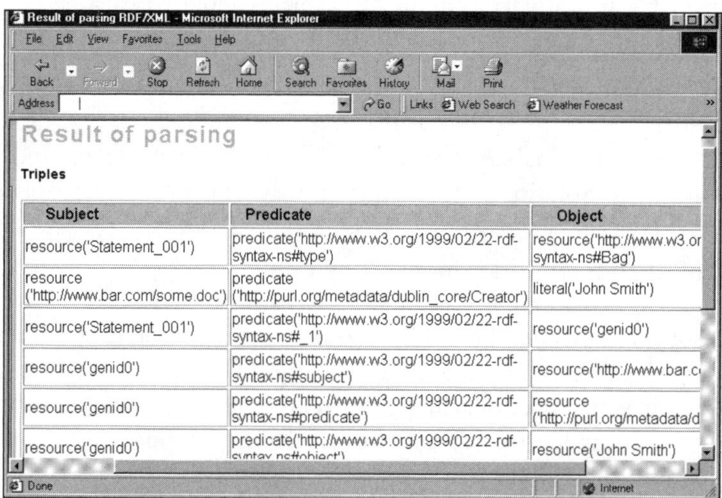

Figure 18.2 The results of parsing an RDF document.

Although no major browser has yet supported RDF in a big way, Mozilla, Netscape's open source version, has a lot of RDF support built into it. Here are some of the documents covering RDF in Mozilla:

- `www.mozilla.org/rdf/50-words.html`. One of Mozilla's "In Fifty Words Or Less" articles. This is an overview of RDF and how it fits with Mozilla. It also includes examples.

- `www.mozilla.org/rdf/back-end-architecture.html`. A very detailed document that describes how the RDF "back end" works in Mozilla. Although it doesn't have sample code now, it will one day, showing how to use the back end directly as a client and showing how to write your own RDF data source.
- `www.mozilla.org/rdf/doc/faq.html`. The RDF-in-Mozilla FAQ. It also has some sample code.
- `www.mozilla.org/rdf/doc/datasource-howto.html`. A cookbook approach to creating an RDF datasource.
- `www.mozilla.org/rdf/rdf-nglayout.html`. Description of how RDF is handled in Mozilla to create a content model consistent with W3C Level 1 DOM.
- `www.mozilla.org/rdf/doc/api.html`. The RDF Technical Overview; it provides an overview of the Mozilla RDF implementation.
- `www.mozilla.org/rdf/doc/vocabs.html`. The Mozilla RDF metadata vocabularies.

You can also get more information about software support for RDF in Mozilla at these locations:

- `www.mozilla.org/rdf/doc/SmartBrowsing.html`. Mozilla's SmartBrowsing system, which allows third-party metadata servers to provide XML/RDF "related link" annotations.
- `www.mozilla.org/rdf/doc/aurora.html`. Mozilla's Aurora project, which is the code name for the user interface in Mozilla that handles RDF data sources.
- `www.mozilla.org/rdf/doc/flash-spec.html`. The Mozilla Flash Specification. The Flash system offers an XML/RDF system for offering up-to-the-minute information about events that are of interest to the user.
- `www.mozilla.org/rdf/doc/z3950.html`. The Mozilla RDF/Z39.50 Integration Project, which lets you connect to digital library systems. This project is all about using the ANSI/NISO Z39.50 search protocol from inside Mozilla.

What about RDF support in Internet Explorer? There really isn't any—at least, not yet. However, Microsoft does offer an RDF viewer at `http://msdn.microsoft.com/downloads/samples/Internet/xml/xml_rdf_viewer/sample.asp`. (Keep in mind that Microsoft URIs seem to change every 15 minutes, so this link may be obsolete by the time you read this.)

Here's Microsoft's description of the RDF viewer:

> *The sample is written in Visual Basic 6.0 and consists of a single form. Users can enter the URL of a known RDF file or they can choose buttons that represent RDF files from three different sources. The form then retrieves the RDF file, which is then parsed using the MSXML parser. The contents of the RDF file are presented in a list box and any URL links attached to each item are stored in an array. When an item in the list box is selected, the page represented by the associated URL is displayed in the browser control.*

To run the viewer, however, you need Internet Explorer 5.0, Visual Basic 6.0, and Windows 98, Windows NT 4.0, or Windows 2000.

As you can see, there's a lot of material out there on RDF. It's time to get to the RDF details now, starting with RDF syntax.

RDF Syntax

RDF documents are made of RDF statements that describe resources. Each statement has three parts, so it's called a *triple*. Here are the three parts of an RDF statement:

- **Resource.** Resources are typically Web documents that you point to with a URI.
- **Named property.** Such a property is a specific characteristic or attribute of the resource, such as the resource's creator.
- **Property value.** The value of the property is the property's content. For example, the value of the `<Creator>` property is usually the name of the resource's creator.

An RDF statement, then, is made up of a resource, a named property, and a property value. In RDF, you name these three parts like this:

- The resource is called the *subject* of the statement.
- The named property is called the *predicate* of the statement.
- The property value is called the *object* of the statement.

Here's a simple example RDF document:

```
<?xml version="1.0" ?>
<rdf:RDF
    xmlns:rdf="http://www.w3.org/1999/02/22-rdf-syntax-ns#">
    <rdf:Description about="http://www.starpowder.com/planets.html">
        <Creator>Nicolas Copernicus</Creator>
    </rdf:Description>
</rdf:RDF>
```

In this case, the subject is the document "http://www.starpowder.com/planets.html", the predicate is the named property Creator, and the object is the name of the document's creator, Nicolas Copernicus. To understand RDF, I'm going to take this document apart piece by piece now.

The RDF Root Element

Because RDF documents are also XML documents, they start with the <?xml?> declaration. These documents also must have a specific root element, <RDF>, which encloses the rest of the document. Because the namespace you use with RDF is usually given the prefix rdf, you often specify the <RDF> element as <rdf:RDF>, like this:

```
<?xml version="1.0" ?>
<rdf:RDF
        .
        .
        .
</rdf:RDF>
```

Also, note that RDF documents must use the RDF namespace.

The RDF Namespace

The official, W3C-defined, RDF namespace is "http://www.w3.org/1999/02/22-rdf-syntax-ns#" (the # on the end, which may look pretty funny, is not an error; it's there to help applications create valid XPointers). All RDF documents must use this namespace. The conventional prefix for this namespace is rdf, so I'll declare that prefix like this:

```
<?xml version="1.0" ?>
<rdf:RDF
    xmlns:rdf="http://www.w3.org/1999/02/22-rdf-syntax-ns#">
        .
        .
        .
</rdf:RDF>
```

The RDF Description Element

Each resource that you want to describe in RDF gets its own `<rdf:Description>` element. This element has several attributes:

Attribute	Description
`about`	Lets you specify what resource the element describes
`aboutEach`	Lets you make statements about each of the element's children
`aboutEachPrefix`	Lets you select RDF container items by prefix
`bagID`	Specifies the ID of an associated bag container
`ID`	Lets you give the element an ID value
`type`	Specifies the description's type

In fact, you can also convert the properties you list in the `<rdf:Description>` element into attributes, as we'll see when we take a look at the RDF abbreviated syntax.

In our example, the resource being described is the document `"http://www.starpowder.com/planets.html"`, so I assign that URI to the `about` attribute of the `<rdf:Description>` element:

```
<?xml version="1.0" ?>
<rdf:RDF
    xmlns:rdf="http://www.w3.org/1999/02/22-rdf-syntax-ns#">
    <rdf:Description about="http://www.starpowder.com/planets.html">
    .
    .
    .
    </rdf:Description>
</rdf:RDF>
```

In other words, you use the `about` attribute to specify the statement's subject.

To actually say something about the resource, you use property elements.

RDF Property Elements

Inside the `<rdf:Description>` element, you store the actual elements that describe the subject. In the current example, the predicate is the `Creator` property, which specifies the document's author, and the object is the name of the author, `Nicolas Copernicus`:

```
<?xml version="1.0" ?>
<rdf:RDF
    xmlns:rdf="http://www.w3.org/1999/02/22-rdf-syntax-ns#">
    <rdf:Description about="http://www.starpowder.com/planets.html">
        <Creator>Nicolas Copernicus</Creator>
    </rdf:Description>
</rdf:RDF>
```

The `Creator` property is not built into the RDF specification—in fact, no properties are. It's up to you to create the named properties you want to use to describe a resource. In fact, a number of property sets, called *RDF content description models*, already are available. That's useful because they provide some agreement on property names—which means that applications such as Web search engines can make some sense out of the properties you use. The most popular and well-supported of these RDF content description models is the Dublin Core.

The Dublin Core

The Dublin Core calls itself a "metadata initiative," and it provides an RDF content model that is in wide use to describe Web resources. The Dublin Core has attracted the attention of museums, libraries, government agencies, and commercial groups as a way of standardizing RDF for Web resources. You can find out all about the Dublin Core at its home page, `www.purl.org/dc`.

In the previous example, I used a `<Creator>` property, without specifying a namespace for that property. However, when you create your own properties, you should use a namespace to avoid conflicts. The Dublin Core's namespace is `"http://purl.org/DC/"`. In fact, the `<Creator>` property I've been using is modeled after the Dublin Core's `<Creator>` property. I can declare the Dublin Core's namespace—which is usually given the prefix `dc`—in the example document, and indicate that `<Creator>` is part of that namespace, like this:

```
<?xml version="1.0" ?>
<rdf:RDF
    xmlns:rdf="http://www.w3.org/1999/02/22-rdf-syntax-ns#"
    xmlns:dc="http://purl.org/DC/">
    <rdf:Description about="http://www.starpowder.com/planets.html">
        <dc:Creator>Nicolas Copernicus</dc:Creator>
    </rdf:Description>
</rdf:RDF>
```

The `<Creator>` property is just one Dublin Core property; you can find all the defined Dublin Core properties in Table 18.1.

Table 18.1 **Dublin Core Properties**

Element	Description
`Contributor`	Names the person or organization that has contributed in some way to this resource.
`Coverage`	Gives the extent or scope of the content of the resource. For example, this might include location, time, or jurisdiction.
`Creator`	Names the person, organization, or service responsible for creating the resource. Typically it refers to the resource's author.
`Date`	Gives a date connected to the resource, such as its last update or its creation date. The recommended practice for encoding the date value is defined in ISO 8601, which follows the YYYY-MM-DD format.
`Description`	Gives the description of the resource. For example, this could be an abstract, table of contents, or text description of the resource.
`Format`	Gives the format used for the resource. Usually, the format includes the media type or dimensions of the resource. Readers may use `Format` to determine the software, hardware, or other equipment needed. You usually use a MIME type here.
`Identifier`	Gives an ID value for the resource in its context. Recommended practice is to identify the resource by means of a string or number as part of a formal identification system. For example, you might use a URI or an International Standard Book Number (ISBN).
`Language`	Specifies the language of the resource. Recommended practice is to use values defined by RFC 1766, which includes a two-letter Language Code (from the ISO 639 standard), with an optional two-letter Country Code (from the ISO 3166 standard).
`Publisher`	Names the agent responsible for making the resource available. Usually, this is a person, an organization, or a service.
`Relation`	Is a reference to a related resource or relationship type.
`Rights`	Gives information about rights about the resource. For example, a `Rights` element can contain intellectual property rights, copyright, or various other property rights.
`Source`	Refers to a resource from which the current resource is derived.
`Subject`	Gives the topic of the content of the resource. Recommended practice is to select a value from a formal classification scheme. For example, subjects might be keywords, key phrases, or classification codes.
`Title`	Is a name given to the resource.
`Type`	Gives the type of the content of the resource, usually a term describing general categories or functions. Recommended practice is to select a value from a formally defined and publicly available vocabulary.

Each Dublin Core element also 10 ten attributes, which are taken from the ISO/IEC 11179 standard:

Attribute	Description
`Comment`	Is a comment about the use of the data in the element
`Datatype`	Specifies the type of data in the element
`Definition`	Defines the concept behind the data in the element
`Identifier`	Is a unique identifier assigned to the element that identifies it
`Language`	Specifies the language of the data in the element
`Maximum Occurrence`	Puts a limit on how many times the element may occur
`Name`	is the name you've assigned to the data element
`Obligation`	Specifies whether the element is required
`Registration Authority`	Refers to the agency or group authorized to register the element
`Version`	Gives the version of the element

In fact, 6 of these 10 attributes are common to all the Dublin Core elements, and they have fixed values. Here they are, along with their values:

Attribute	Value
Version	`1.1`
Registration Authority	`Dublin Core Metadata Initiative`
Language	`en` (that is, English)
Obligation	`Optional`
Datatype	`Character String`
Maximum Occurrence	`Unlimited`

The Dublin Core also lists a set of default resource *types* that you can use with the `<Type>` element:

- `collection`
- `dataset`
- `event`
- `image`
- `interactive resource`
- `model`
- `party`
- `physical object`
- `place`
- `service`
- `software`
- `sound`
- `text`

You can find these types defined in detail at `http://purl.org/DC/documents/wd-typelist.htm`.

Describing Multiple Properties

The example RDF document that we've seen so far has defined only one property for the `"http://www.starpowder.com/planets.html"` resource—the `<Creator>` property. In fact, you can assign multiple properties to resources, and now that we've seen all the available Dublin Core elements, I'll put more of them to work. For example, here's how I describe that resource's creator, title, and type:

```
<?xml version="1.0" ?>
<rdf:RDF
    xmlns:rdf="http://www.w3.org/1999/02/22-rdf-syntax-ns#"
    xmlns:dc="http://purl.org/DC/">

    <rdf:Description about="http://www.starpowder.com/planets.html">
        <dc:Creator>Nicolas Copernicus</dc:Creator>
        <dc:Title>Mercury</dc:Title>
        <dc:Type>text</dc:Type>
    </rdf:Description>

</rdf:RDF>
```

Describing Multiple Resources

An RDF document can also describe multiple resources—all you have to do is use multiple `<rdf:Description>` elements. For example, here's an RDF document that describes three resources, `mercury.html`, `venus.html`, and `earth.html`:

```
<?xml version="1.0" ?>
<rdf:RDF
    xmlns:rdf="http://www.w3.org/1999/02/22-rdf-syntax-ns#"
    xmlns:dc="http://purl.org/DC/">

    <rdf:Description about="http://www.starpowder.com/mercury.html">
        <dc:Creator>Nicolas Copernicus</dc:Creator>
        <dc:Title>Mercury</dc:Title>
        <dc:Type>text</dc:Type>
    </rdf:Description>

    <rdf:Description about="http://www.starpowder.com/venus.html">
        <dc:Creator>Nicolas Copernicus</dc:Creator>
        <dc:Title>Venus</dc:Title>
        <dc:Type>text</dc:Type>
    </rdf:Description>
```

```
    <rdf:Description about="http://www.starpowder.com/earth.html">
        <dc:Creator>Nicolas Copernicus</dc:Creator>
        <dc:Title>Earth</dc:Title>
        <dc:Type>text</dc:Type>
    </rdf:Description>

</rdf:RDF>
```

Nesting Resources

What if a property itself needs more description? For example, what if the creator of the resource is described by a Web page, and you want to refer the reader to that page? In that case, you can nest `<rdf:Resource>` elements. For example, if you want to describe Nicolas Copernicus, the creator of `planets.html`, with another Web page, `NickC.html`, that might look like this:

```
<?xml version="1.0" ?>
<rdf:RDF xmlns="http://www.w3.org/1999/02/22-rdf-syntax-ns#"
    xmlns:dc="http://www.purl.org/DC/">

    <rdf:Description about="http://www.starpowder.com/planets.html">
        <dc:Title>Mercury</dc:Title>
        <dc:Creator>
            <rdf:Description about="http://www.starpowder.com/NickC.html">
                <dc:Title>Nicolas Copernicus</dc:Title>
                <dc:Language>en</dc:Language>
            </rdf:Description>
        </dc:Creator>
    </rdf:Description>
</rdf:RDF>
```

Referring to Resources by Reference

There's another way to refer to a resource that describes a property—you can give the resource's URI using the `rdf:resource` attribute. You use this attribute in the property element. Here's an example; in this case, I'm referring to the resource `NickC.html` to describe the creator of various documents:

```
<?xml version="1.0" ?>
<rdf:RDF
    xmlns:rdf="http://www.w3.org/1999/02/22-rdf-syntax-ns#"
    xmlns:dc="http://www.purl.org/DC/">

    <rdf:Description about="http://www.starpowder.com/mercury.html">
        <dc:Title>Mercury</dc:Title>
```

continues ▸

```
        <dc:Creator rdf:resource="http://www.starpowder.com/NickC.html"/>
    </rdf:Description>

    <rdf:Description about="http://www.starpowder.com/venus.html">
        <dc:Title>Venus</dc:Title>
        <dc:Creator rdf:resource="http://www.starpowder.com/NickC.html"/>
    </rdf:Description>

    <rdf:Description about="http://www.starpowder.com/earth.html">
        <dc:Title>Earth</dc:Title>
        <dc:Creator rdf:resource="http://www.starpowder.com/NickC.html"/>
    </rdf:Description>

</rdf:RDF>
```

As you can see, using the `rdf:resource` attribute makes it easy to connect the same property to a number of resources; in this case, I'm giving the `mercury.html`, `venus.html`, and `earth.html` all the same creator properties.

Using XML in Property Elements

Although property values are mostly text or resources that you reference, they can also be straight XML. In that case, you just set the `parseType` attribute of the property to `"Literal"`.

For example, I'm using my own XML elements, such as `<BirthCity>` and `<BirthCountry>` in the `<Creator>` property here, and giving them their own namespace, `ns`:

```
<?xml version="1.0" ?>
<rdf:RDF
    xmlns:rdf="http://www.w3.org/1999/02/22-rdf-syntax-ns#"
    xmlns:dc="http://www.purl.org/DC/"
    xmlns:ns="http://www.starpowder.com/namespace/">

    <rdf:Description about="http://www.starpowder.com/planets.html">
        <dc:Creator parseType="Literal">
            <ns:FirstName>Nicolas</nm:FirstName>
            <ns:LastName>Copernicus</nm:LastName>
            <ns:Birth>1473</nm:Birth>
            <ns:Death>1543</nm:Death>
            <ns:BirthCity>Torun</nm:BirthCity>
            <ns:BirthCountry>Poland</nm:BirthCountry>
        </dc:Creator>
    </rdf:Description>

</rdf:RDF>
```

Using Abbreviated RDF Syntax

The W3C also defines an abbreviated RDF syntax to make things a little easier. To use the abbreviated syntax, you just convert property elements to attributes of the `<rdf:Description>` element. For example, here's what an unabbreviated document might look like:

```
<?xml version="1.0" ?>
<rdf:RDF
    xmlns:rdf="http://www.w3.org/1999/02/22-rdf-syntax-ns#"
    xmlns:dc="http://purl.org/DC/">

    <rdf:Description about="http://www.starpowder.com/mercury.html">
        <dc:Creator>Nicolas Copernicus</dc:Creator>
        <dc:Title>Mercury</dc:Title>
        <dc:Type>text</dc:Type>
    </rdf:Description>

    <rdf:Description about="http://www.starpowder.com/venus.html">
        <dc:Creator>Nicolas Copernicus</dc:Creator>
        <dc:Title>Venus</dc:Title>
        <dc:Type>text</dc:Type>
    </rdf:Description>
    .
    .
    .
```

Here's the abbreviated form:

```
<?xml version="1.0" ?>
<rdf:RDF
    xmlns:rdf="http://www.w3.org/1999/02/22-rdf-syntax-ns#"
    xmlns:dc="http://purl.org/DC/">

    <rdf:Description about="http://www.starpowder.com/mercury.html"
        dc:Creator = "Nicolas Copernicus"
        dc:Title = "Mercury"
        dc:Type = "text">
    </rdf:Description>

    <rdf:Description about="http://www.starpowder.com/venus.html"
        dc:Creator = "Nicolas Copernicus">
        dc:Title = "Venus"
        dc:Type = "text">
    </rdf:Description>
    .
    .
    .
```

Why is this useful? One big reason is that it makes RDF easier to handle in HTML browsers in case that RDF is embedded in an HTML document. Recall that HTML browsers will ignore any tags they don't understand and simply treat the element's content as plain text. If you convert the property elements to attributes, there are no property elements to be mishandled in that way.

The situation is a little more complex if your properties themselves contain resources. In that case, it's best to refer to those resources by reference using the `rdf:resource` attribute:

```
<?xml version="1.0" ?>
<rdf:RDF
    xmlns:rdf="http://www.w3.org/1999/02/22-rdf-syntax-ns#"
    xmlns:dc="http://www.purl.org/DC/">

    <rdf:Description about="http://www.starpowder.com/mercury.html"
        dc:Title = "Mercury">
        <dc:Creator rdf:resource="http://www.starpowder.com/NickC.html"/>
    </rdf:Description>

    <rdf:Description about="http://www.starpowder.com/venus.html"
        dc:Title = "Venus">
        <dc:Creator rdf:resource="http://www.starpowder.com/NickC.html"/>
    </rdf:Description>
    .
    .
    .
```

Even though this still uses `<dc:Creator>` property elements, there is still no element content to be treated as plain text by an HTML browser.

RDF Containers

RDF also enables you to group properties together by defining property *containers*. Three containers exist:

Container	Description
`Bag`	A group of properties without any particular order.
`Seq`	A sequence of properties in a specific order.
`Alt`	A list of properties giving alternate choices. Only one of all these choices is actually chosen.

These containers are supported with the `<rdf:Bag>`, `<rdf:Seq>`, and `<rdf:Alt>` elements, which have `ID` and `aboutEach` attributes. (The W3C RDF syntax specification mistakenly defines these elements with only an `ID` attribute, but then uses both attributes in the text). I'll use both those attributes in this chapter.

Using the *Bag* Container

You use a `Bag` container to indicate that a property has multiple, although unordered, values. How do you specify the multiple items in a container? You use the `<rdf:li>` element (modeled after the HTML `<LI>`, list item, element).

Here's an example; in this case, I'm indicating that the `planets.html` resource has multiple subjects—`Mercury`, `Venus`, `Mars`, and `Earth`:

```
<?xml version="1.0" ?>
<rdf:RDF
    xmlns:rdf="http://www.w3.org/1999/02/22-rdf-syntax-ns#"
    xmlns:dc="http://www.purl.org/DC#">

    <rdf:Description about="http://www.starpowder.com/planets.html">
        <dc:Title>Planets</dc:Title>
        <dc:Creator>Nicolas Copernicus</dc:Creator>
        <dc:Type>text</dc:Type>
        <dc:Subject>
            <rdf:Bag>
                <rdf:li>Mercury</rdf:li>
                <rdf:li>Venus</rdf:li>
                <rdf:li>Earth</rdf:li>
                <rdf:li>Mars</rdf:li>
            </rdf:Bag>
        </dc:Subject>
    </rdf:Description>

</rdf:RDF>
```

The items in a bag can also be resource references, of course, like this:

```
<?xml version="1.0" ?>
<rdf:RDF
    xmlns:rdf="http://www.w3.org/1999/02/22-rdf-syntax-ns#"
    xmlns:dc="http://www.purl.org/DC#">

    <rdf:Description about="http://www.starpowder.com/planets.html">
        <dc:Title>Planets</dc:Title>
        <dc:Creator>Nicolas Copernicus</dc:Creator>
        <dc:Subject>
            <rdf:Bag>
                <rdf:li
                    rdf:resource="http://www.starpowder.com/mercury.html"/>
                <rdf:li
                    rdf:resource="http://www.starpowder.com/venus.html"/>
                <rdf:li
                    rdf:resource="http://www.starpowder.com/earth.html"/>
                <rdf:li
                    rdf:resource="http://www.starpowder.com/mars.html"/>
            </rdf:Bag>
```

continues ▸

```
        </dc:Subject>
    </rdf:Description>
</rdf:RDF>
```

Using the *Seq* Container

You use a `Seq` to indicate that a property has multiple ordered values. In this case, you are indicating that the multiple property values have some order. For example, this document indicates that `planet.html` covers the topics `Mercury`, `Venus`, `Earth`, and `Mars`, in that order:

```
<?xml version="1.0" ?>
<rdf:RDF
    xmlns:rdf="http://www.w3.org/1999/02/22-rdf-syntax-ns#"
    xmlns:dc="http://www.purl.org/DC#">

    <rdf:Description about="http://www.starpowder.com/planets.html">
        <dc:Title>Planets</dc:Title>
        <dc:Creator>Nicolas Copernicus</dc:Creator>
        <dc:Subject>
            <rdf:Seq>
                <rdf:li>Mercury</rdf:li>
                <rdf:li>Venus</rdf:li>
                <rdf:li>Earth</rdf:li>
                <rdf:li>Mars</rdf:li>
            </rdf:Seq>
        </dc:Subject>
    </rdf:Description>

</rdf:RDF>
```

Using the *Alt* Container

The `Alt` container provides alternatives, such as different language versions of a resource, or mirror sites. In general, you use it to associate alternative resources with a document. Here's an example; in this case, I'm listing various versions of a document in different formats, plain text, HTML, Rich Text Format (RTF), and XML:

```
<?xml version="1.0" ?>
<rdf:RDF
    xmlns:rdf="http://www.w3.org/1999/02/22-rdf-syntax-ns#"
    xmlns:dc="http://www.purl.org/DC#">

    <rdf:Description about="http://www.starpowder.com/planets">
        <dc:Title>Planets</dc:Title>
        <dc:Creator>Nicolas Copernicus</dc:Creator>
```

```
        <dc:Format>
            <rdf:Alt>
                <rdf:li resource =
                 "http://www.starpowder.com/planets.html">
                     text/html
                </rdf:li>
                <rdf:li resource =
                 "http://www.starpowder.com/planets.txt">
                    text/plain
                </rdf:li>
                <rdf:li resource =
                 "http://www.starpowder.com/planets.rtf">
                    text/rtf
                </rdf:li>
                <rdf:li resource =
                 "http://www.starpowder.com/planets.xml">
                    text/xml
                </rdf:li>
            </rdf:Alt>
        </dc:Format>
    </rdf:Description>

</rdf:RDF>
```

Making Statements About Containers

You can use a container's ID attribute to make a statement about the container as a whole, separate from the items in the container. Here's an example. In this case, I'm giving a creation date for a bag container; to do that, I give the bag container the ID `"planets"` and then create a new `<rdf:Description>` element about `"#planets"` to describe the bag container and give its date:

```
<?xml version="1.0" ?>
<rdf:RDF
    xmlns:rdf="http://www.w3.org/1999/02/22-rdf-syntax-ns#"
    xmlns:dc="http://www.purl.org/DC#">

    <rdf:Description
        about="http://www.starpowder.com/planets.html">
        <dc:Title>XML Links</dc:Title>
        <dc:Creator>Nicolas Copernicus</dc:Creator>
        <dc:Subject>
            <rdf:Bag ID="planets">
                <rdf:li
                    rdf:resource="http://www.starpowder.com/mercury.html"/>
                <rdf:li
                    rdf:resource="http://www.starpowder.com/venus.html"/>
                <rdf:li
```

continues ▸

```
                rdf:resource="http://www.starpowder.com/earth.html"/>
            <rdf:li
                rdf:resource="http://www.starpowder.com/mars.html"/>
        </rdf:Bag>
    </dc:Subject>
</rdf:Description>

<rdf:Description about="#planets">
    <dc:Date>
        1501-10-15
    </dc:Date>
</rdf:Description>

</rdf:RDF>
```

Making Statements About the Items in a Container

You can also make statements about each item in a container by using the container's `aboutEach` attribute. For example, suppose that I want to indicate that each item in a bag has the same creation date; in that case, I could assign the value `"creationDate"` to the bag's `aboutEach` attribute, and add a new `<rdf:Description>` element about `"#creationDate"`, like this:

```
<?xml version="1.0" ?>
<rdf:RDF
    xmlns:rdf="http://www.w3.org/1999/02/22-rdf-syntax-ns#"
    xmlns:dc="http://www.purl.org/DC#">

    <rdf:Description about="http://www.starpowder.com/planets.html">
        <dc:Title>Mercury</dc:Title>
        <dc:Creator>Nicolas Copernicus</dc:Creator>
        <dc:Subject>
            <rdf:Bag aboutEach="creationDate">
                <rdf:li
                    resource="http://www.starpowder.com/mercury.html"/>
                <rdf:li
            resource="http://www.starpowder.com/venus.html"/>
                <rdf:li
                    resource="http://www.starpowder.com/earth.html"/>
                <rdf:li
                resource="http://www.starpowder.com/mars.html"/>
            </rdf:Bag>
        </dc:Subject>
    </rdf:Description>

    <rdf:Description aboutEach="#creationDate">
        <dc:Date>
            1501-10-15
        </dc:Date>
    </rdf:Description>
</rdf:RDF>
```

Selecting Container Items by Prefix

In fact, you can make statements about groups of resources that have the same prefixes (which may or may not be members of one container). For example, say that I want to connect a date with all resources that start with `"http://www.starpowder.com/"`. I can do that with the `aboutEachPrefix` attribute of `<rdf:Description>`, like this:

```
<?xml version="1.0" ?>
<rdf:RDF
    xmlns:rdf="http://www.w3.org/1999/02/22-rdf-syntax-ns#"
    xmlns:dc="http://www.purl.org/DC#">

    <rdf:Description about="http://www.starpowder.com/planets.html">
        <dc:Title>Mercury</dc:Title>
        <dc:Creator>Nicolas Copernicus</dc:Creator>
        <dc:Subject>
            <rdf:Bag>
                <rdf:li
                    resource="http://www.starpowder.com/mercury.html"/>
                <rdf:li
            resource="http://www.starpowder.com/venus.html"/>
                <rdf:li
                    resource="http://www.starpowder.com/earth.html"/>
                <rdf:li
                resource="http://www.starpowder.com/mars.html"/>
            </rdf:Bag>
        </dc:Subject>
    </rdf:Description>

    <rdf:Description aboutEachPrefix="#http://www.starpowder.com/">
        <dc:Date>
            1501-10-15
        </dc:Date>
    </rdf:Description>
</rdf:RDF>
```

Creating RDF Schemas

So far, the property elements you use in RDF are up to you to define, unless you use someone else's RDF content model, such as the Dublin Core. Until recently, there was no real way to make sure that RDF software would be capable of checking the syntax of your RDF extensions.

However, the W3C has been working hard on creating an RDF schema language, and you can find the details at `www.w3.org/TR/rdf-schema`. It's not finalized yet (the specification is a candidate recommendation at this writing) and is not supported by any software, but when available, it will let RDF parsers check the full syntax of the extensions you make to RDF.

The Dublin Core Metatdata Initiative is solidly behind the idea of creating schemas to let RDF software check the syntax of RDF documents; you can read the group's thoughts on the matter at `http://purl.org/DC/schemas/index.htm`. Here's a partial extract from that page:

> *The diversity of metadata needs on the Web requires an infrastructure that supports the coexistence of complementary, independently maintained metadata packages. The World Wide Web Consortium (W3C) has begun implementing an architecture for metadata for the Web. The Resource Description Framework, or RDF, is designed to support the many different metadata needs of vendors and information providers. The Dublin Core Metadata Initiative expects to support the infrastructure for registries provided by RDF Schemas. Developments in this area will be reflected on these pages as they develop.*

CDF Overview

Channel Definition Format (CDF) is a Microsoft XML application for use with Internet Explorer. As mentioned in the introduction to this chapter, CDF enables automatic user notification when a Web site changes.

XML and Microsoft

XML has been steadily gaining support at Microsoft over the years. As of this writing, Microsoft has just indicated that the next version of Visual Studio, which is the host for such products as Visual Basic and Visual C++, is going to rely heavily on XML, as will MS Office applications.

How does CDF look in practice? Take a look at Figure 18.3. There, I've added a channel named Planets, complete with a simple icon, to Internet Explorer. To see the available channels, you click the Favorites button in Internet Explorer's button bar, which opens the Favorites bar as you see in Figure 18.3. (You can close the Favorites bar by clicking the X button at upper right in the bar.) The top folder in the Favorites bar is the Channels folder, which you click to open. The Channels bar shows the current channels, and the user has only to click a channel to download the channel's main page (channels can represent not only single pages, but whole Web sites).

Figure 18.3 Internet Explorer showing a new channel.

That's how channels work—when activated, the page or pages they represent are downloaded so that they may be viewed by the user without additional fetches from the Internet, even offline. Channel content may be downloaded on demand or on a set schedule. Besides a main page, most channels include a collection of other pages; we'll see how to create channel children, and how the user can access them, later in this chapter (see the later section "Adding `<ITEM>` Children").

How do channels actually work? The complete specification for a channel is stored in a CDF document, which is separate from other Web pages but usually linked to one of those Web pages. The user has only to open the CDF file—which usually means clicking a hyperlink with the text `Subscribe to this page` or something similar—to establish the channel in Internet Explorer. They can delete the channel later by removing it from the Favorites bar (for example, by right-clicking the channel and selecting the Delete item).

A fair number of CDF resources are available, nearly all of them at Microsoft. Microsoft did submit the specification for CDF to the W3C, and the W3C seems to have politely accepted it, posted it on its Web site, and done nothing else with it. Here's a starter list of CDF resources—keep in mind that Microsoft URIs change very frequently:

- `http://msdn.microsoft.com/workshop/delivery/cdf/reference/CDF.asp.` The CDF reference at Microsoft.
- `www.w3.org/TR/NOTE-CDFsubmit.html.` The Microsoft-submitted CDF note giving the CDF specification, now at the W3C.

- `http://support.microsoft.com/support/kb/articles/Q174/6/87.ASP`. An article on creating personalized channels using Active Server Pages (ASP) with Microsoft Internet Information Server (IIS). All about how content providers can dynamically generate custom CDF files to send personalized information to users, taking into account user preferences.
- `http://msdn.microsoft.com/downloads/tools/cdfgen/cdfgenerator.asp`. An automatic CDF generator.
- `http://support.microsoft.com/support/kb/articles/Q241/8/39.ASP`. A discussion on how to create a CDF file that works with Microsoft FrontPage 2000.
- `http://msdn.microsoft.com/workshop/delivery/channel/tutorial/tutorial.asp`. Microsoft's CDF tutorial.

We might also note that Microsoft has a CDF generator; you can use this generator, which is free to download, to create CDF files. Here's how Microsoft describes it:

- It has a simple and intuitive graphical interface that you will get used to in a few minutes.
- It doesn't require previous knowledge of channels.
- It supports all CDF tags.
- It supports UTF-8 encoding.
- It can also be used for testing purposes because it parses the CDF files and detects the errors.
- It supports drag and drop, so there's less to type.

Microsoft also has another tool, which is even easier to use—the Channel Wizard. As of this writing, it is at `http://msdn.microsoft.com/workshop/delivery/channel/cdfwiz/intro.asp`. This tool lets you construct channels without knowing the first thing about CDF. This wizard asks you questions about the channel you want and generates the `.cdf` file and the link to it that you can embed in a Web page. This tool runs entirely online, and you can see it at work in Figure 18.4.

The Channel Wizard also provides dynamic HTML samples that will allow you to add special effects to your channel pages.

Microsoft supports the CDF File Verification Tool, which checks CDF files for validity, as well. As of this writing, this tool is at `http://msdn.microsoft.com/downloads/tools/cdftest/cdftest.asp`. You can use this tool to discover problems with CDF files, such as missing end tags and incorrect or misspelled tags. However, it doesn't run online; you must download this tool to use it.

That gives us an overview of CDF—it's time to start creating CDF files and channels.

Figure 18.4 The Microsoft Channel Wizard.

CDF Syntax

CDF files are true XML documents. They must be well-formed, but they can't be valid because there is no current publicly available CDF DTD or schema. There is an early CDF DTD in the CDF note at the W3C, at `www.w3.org/TR/NOTE-CDFsubmit.html`, but it's out of date. However, you can see how simple it is—it's almost trivial, which suggests that you can create your own CDF DTD easily enough. (Note that several of these elements no longer exist and that others have been added.)

```
<!ELEMENT LastMod EMPTY>
<!ATTLIST LastMod VALUE CDATA #REQUIRED>
<!ELEMENT Title EMPTY>
<!ATTLIST Title VALUE CDATA #REQUIRED>
<!ELEMENT Abstract EMPTY>
<!ATTLIST Abstract VALUE CDATA #REQUIRED>
<!ELEMENT Author EMPTY>
<!ATTLIST Author VALUE CDATA #REQUIRED>
<!ELEMENT Publisher EMPTY>
<!ATTLIST Publisher VALUE CDATA #REQUIRED>
<!ELEMENT Copyright EMPTY>
<!ATTLIST Copyright VALUE CDATA #REQUIRED>
```

continues ▸

```
<!ELEMENT PublicationDate EMPTY>
<!ATTLIST PublicationDate VALUE CDATA #REQUIRED>
<!ELEMENT Keywords EMPTY>
<!ATTLIST Keywords VALUE CDATA #REQUIRED>
<!ELEMENT Category EMPTY>
<!ATTLIST Category VALUE CDATA #REQUIRED>
<!ELEMENT Rating EMPTY>
<!ATTLIST Rating PICS-Label CDATA #REQUIRED>
```

Note that because CDF files are XML documents, you must escape the characters <, >, ', ", and & as <, >, ', ", and &, respectively, in CDF files.

Here are all the CDF elements:

Element	Description
<?XML?>	Is the XML declaration.
<A>	Creates a hyperlink.
<ABSTRACT>	Gives abstract text for the channel; appears in ToolTips.
<CHANNEL>	Creates a channel.
<EARLIESTTIME>	Gives the earliest time for updates.
<HTTP-EQUIV>	Supplies information that can also be provided through HTTP response headers.
<INTERVALTIME>	Specifies the time between updates.
<ITEM>	Is a Web document that is part of the channel.
<LATESTTIME>	Gives the latest time for updates.
<LOG>	Indicates that the URL of the parent ITEM should be recorded in a page-hit log file.
<LOGIN>	Indicates that the channel requires authentication for updates.
<LOGO>	Are images to be used for the channel in Internet Explorer
<LOGTARGET>	Indicates where to send a CDF client page-hit log file.
<PURGETIME>	Indicates the maximum age of valid page hits when the log file is being uploaded.
<SCHEDULE>	Sets the schedule used for channel updating.
<TITLE>	Gives the title of the channel, for the Favorites bar.
<USAGE>	Indicates how the parent element should be used. Can be set to "Channel", "DesktopComponent", "Email", "NONE", "ScreenSaver", or "SoftwareUpdate".

When you create a channel, you must decide what page or pages to include in the channel. As we'll see, you can include as many pages as you'd like in a channel, all of which may be downloaded to the user's computer. In this chapter, I'll use a simple HTML document, `planets.html` (refer to Figure 18.3):

```
<HTML>
    <HEAD>
        <TITLE>
            The Planets
        </TITLE>
    </HEAD>

    <BODY>
        <CENTER>
            <H1>
                Welcome to the Planets!
            </H1>
            <BR>
            This is where you'll find all things planetary.
        </CENTER>
    </BODY>
</HTML>
```

After you've decided what will be in your channel, you must create the CDF file that will define that channel.

Creating a CDF File

Here's just about the simplest possible CDF file for `planets.html`, which I'll call `planets.cdf`:

```
<?xml version="1.0"?>
<CHANNEL HREF="http://www.starpowder.com/planets.html">
</CHANNEL>
```

This example just creates the most basic possible channel, based on a single Web page. The user has to click the channel to be able to download any content because we haven't set up a schedule for automatic updating yet.

As you can see, this document is a very simple one—all you need is the XML declaration and a `<CHANNEL>` element. The `<CHANNEL>` element uses a single attribute, `HREF`, to specify the URI of a page that will become the channel's main page, displayed in Internet Explorer when the user clicks the channel (refer to Figure 18.3).

On the other hand, most channels aren't made up of a single page, but rather several pages. You add those pages with the `<ITEM>` element.

Adding *<ITEM>* Children

To add child pages to a channel, you use the `<ITEM>` element. For example, say that I want to keep `planets.html` as the main page for the channel, but I want to add child pages for various planets: `mercury.html`, `venus.html`, `earth.html`, and `venus.html`. I can do that with the `<ITEM>` element, setting that element's `HREF` attribute to the URI of each child page in turn:

```
<?xml version="1.0"?>
<CHANNEL HREF="http://www.starpowder.com/planets.html">
    <ITEM HREF="http://www.starpowder.com/mercury.html">
    </ITEM>
    <ITEM HREF="http://www.starpowder.com/venus.html">
    </ITEM>
    <ITEM HREF="http://www.starpowder.com/earth.html">
    </ITEM>
    <ITEM HREF="http://www.starpowder.com/venus.html">
    </ITEM>
</CHANNEL>
```

Now we have five pages in this channel. So how do you install this channel in Internet Explorer?

Connecting a CDF File to a Web Page

To subscribe to a channel, the user only needs to open the channel's CDF file. You usually link to a CDF file and let the user subscribe to your channel simply by clicking the link. For example, here's how I might add such a hyperlink to `planets.html`—note that the target of the hyperlink is simply the CDF file, `planets.cdf`:

```
<HTML>
    <HEAD>
        <TITLE>
            The Planets
        </TITLE>
    </HEAD>

    <BODY>
        <CENTER>
            <H1>
                Welcome to the Planets!
            </H1>
            <BR>
            This is where you'll find all things planetary.
            <BR>
            <A HREF="planets.cdf">Subscribe to this page!</A>
        </CENTER>
    </BODY>
</HTML>
```

Now when the user clicks the link, Internet Explorer informs the user that a new page, corresponding to this channel, will be added to the Favorites list, as you see in Figure 18.5.

Figure 18.5 Subscribing to a channel.

So far, so good—we've created a channel with a main page and four children. Note that the name of the channel in Figure 18.5 is simply the name of the page because we haven't given the channel a title. I'll do that next.

Describing a Channel

You can describe a channel to a user in three ways—with titles, abstracts, and logos. I'll take a look at those possibilities in order.

Channel Titles

If you give a channel a title, that title will appear in the Favorites bar. You can also give a title to each child page in the channel. All this happens with the `<TITLE>` element. For example, here's how I add a title to the channel and all the child pages in `planets.cdf`:

```
<?xml version="1.0"?>
<CHANNEL HREF="http://www.starpowder.com/planets.html">
    <TITLE>Planets</TITLE>
    <ITEM HREF="http://www.starpowder.com/mercury.html">
        <TITLE>All about Mercury</TITLE>
    </ITEM>
    <ITEM HREF="http://www.starpowder.com/venus.html">
        <TITLE>All about Venus</TITLE>
    </ITEM>
```

continues ▸

```
    <ITEM HREF="http://www.starpowder.com/earth.html">
        <TITLE>All about Earth</TITLE>
    </ITEM>
    <ITEM HREF="http://www.starpowder.com/mars.html">
        <TITLE>All about Mars</TITLE>
    </ITEM>
</CHANNEL>
```

You can see the results in Figure 18.6—as you can see, all the pages in the channel now have easily readable titles. If the user is interested in updating any of these pages, he or she must only click them.

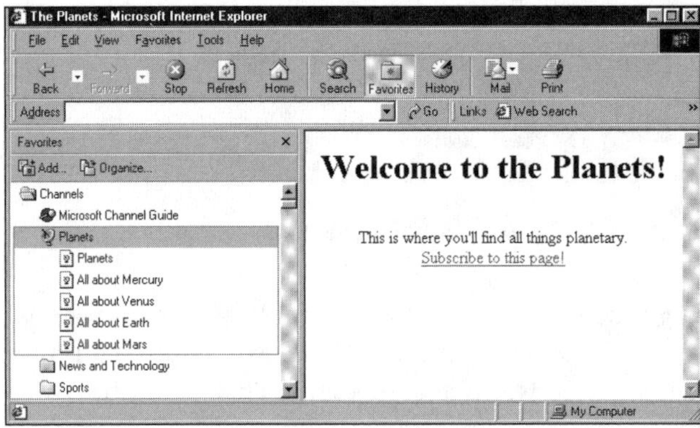

Figure 18.6 Channels with titles.

Besides using titles, you can also add *abstracts* to the pages in a channel.

Channel Abstracts

Channel titles are fine, but necessarily brief. A channel abstract can hold more information about the channel, but its text must also be fairly brief because that text appears in a ToolTip (one of those small yellow boxes with explanatory text that appear near the mouse pointer) for the associated channel page.

You can create an abstract for a page in a channel with the <ABSTRACT> element. For example, I can add abstracts to the various pages in the Planets channel like this:

```
<?xml version="1.0"?>
<CHANNEL HREF="http://www.starpowder.com/planets.html">
    <TITLE>Planets</TITLE>
    <ITEM HREF="http://www.starpowder.com/mercury.html">
        <TITLE>All about Mercury</TITLE>
```

```
        <ABSTRACT>
            All planetary information for
            Mercury, including orbital specifications.
        </ABSTRACT>
    </ITEM>
    <ITEM HREF="http://www.starpowder.com/venus.html">
        <TITLE>All about Venus</TITLE>
        <ABSTRACT>
            All planetary information for
            Venus, including orbital specifications.
        </ABSTRACT>
    </ITEM>
    <ITEM HREF="http://www.starpowder.com/earth.html">
        <TITLE>All about Earth</TITLE>
        <ABSTRACT>
            All planetary information for
            Earth, including orbital specifications.
        </ABSTRACT>
    </ITEM>
    <ITEM HREF="http://www.starpowder.com/mars.html">
        <TITLE>All about Mars</TITLE>
        <ABSTRACT>
            All planetary information for
            Mars, including orbital specifications.
        </ABSTRACT>
    </ITEM>
</CHANNEL>
```

You can see the results in Figure 18.7, where you see an abstract displayed as a ToolTip.

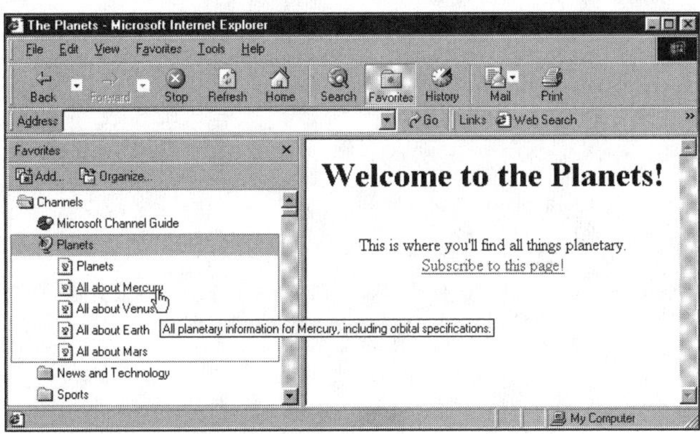

Figure 18.7 Channels with abstracts.

Another way to describe a channel is with *logos*. We'll look at these next.

Channel Logos

You can add logos—icons and images—to channels, using the <LOGO> element to the <CHANNEL> or <ITEM> elements. You specify what type of logo you're creating with the STYLE attribute, which takes these values:

Value	Description
ICON	16 × 16 pixel icon. This image appears in the Favorites bar hierarchy.
IMAGE	80 × 32 pixel image. In Active Desktop installations, this logo is placed in the desktop Channel bar, which provides quick access to the channel's main page.
IMAGE-WIDE	194 × 32 pixel image. Wide logos appear in the browser's Favorites bar to provide a link to the main channel page. When clicked, this image expands or contracts the channel's child list if the channel has children.

Here's an example where I'm adding logos to the Planets channel:

```
<?xml version="1.0"?>
<CHANNEL HREF="http://www.starpowder.com/planets.html">
    <TITLE>Planets</TITLE>

    <LOGO HREF="http://www.starpowder.com/icon.gif" STYLE="ICON"/>
    <LOGO HREF="http://www.starpowder.com/image.gif" STYLE="IMAGE"/>
    <LOGO HREF="http://www.starpowder.com/image-wide.gif" STYLE="IMAGE-WIDE"/>

    <ITEM HREF="http://www.starpowder.com/mercury.html">
        <TITLE>All about Mercury</TITLE>
        <ABSTRACT>
            All planetary information for
            Mercury, including orbital specifications.
        </ABSTRACT>
    </ITEM>

    <ITEM HREF="http://www.starpowder.com/venus.html">
        <TITLE>All about Venus</TITLE>
        <ABSTRACT>
            All planetary information for
            Venus, including orbital specifications.
        </ABSTRACT>
    </ITEM>

    <ITEM HREF="http://www.starpowder.com/earth.html">
        <TITLE>All about Earth</TITLE>
        <ABSTRACT>
            All planetary information for
            Earth, including orbital specifications.
```

```
        </ABSTRACT>
    </ITEM>

    <ITEM HREF="http://www.starpowder.com/mars.html">
        <TITLE>All about Mars</TITLE>
        <ABSTRACT>
            All planetary information for
            Mars, including orbital specifications.
        </ABSTRACT>
    </ITEM>
</CHANNEL>
```

The icon image for the planets channel—a red circle—has replaced the default icon for the channel (see Figure 18.8).

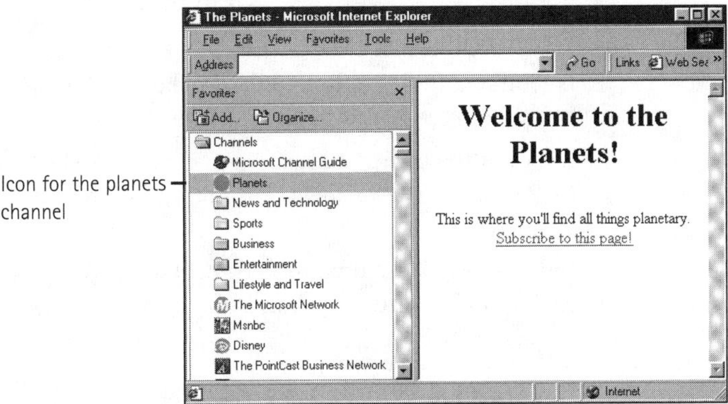

Figure 18.8 Replacing the Channel icon.

Scheduling Automatic Updates

You can set up a channel so that the browser downloads channel content automatically if it has been updated. (The browser relies on the `Last-Modified` item in the HTTP header of a Web page to check when the page was last modified.) I advise you to use this feature with caution—few things annoy users more than when software such as Internet Explorer seems to take over by itself and do mysterious things.

You use a <SCHEDULE> element to create a channel schedule. This element has three attributes:

Attribute	Description
STARTDATE	Indicates when the schedule is to start.
STOPDATE	Indicates when schedule is to end (if you don't use this attribute, the schedule never expires).
TIMEZONE	Gives the difference in hours between the server's time zone and Greenwich Mean Time. For example, EST is -0500, CST is -0600, MST is -0700, PST -0800, and Alaska and Hawaii are -1000.

The <SCHEDULE> element can itself have three child elements:

Element	Description
<INTERVALTIME>	Is required. Indicates how often to check for updates. Has DAY (1–7), HOUR (0–23), and MIN (0–59) attributes.
<EARLIESTTIME>	Indicates the earliest time to update. Has DAY (1–7), HOUR (0–23), and TIMEZONE (default is the user's timezone) attributes.
<LATESTTIME>	Indicates the latest time to update. Has DAY (1–7), HOUR (0–23), and TIMEZONE (default is the user's timezone) attributes.

For example, say that I wanted to have Internet Explorer check once every five days if a channel's content has changed and so needs to be downloaded automatically, and I wanted to download new content only between 3 and 5 a.m. That looks like this:

```
<?xml version="1.0"?>
<CHANNEL HREF="http://www.starpowder.com/planets.html">
    <TITLE>Planets</TITLE>

    <LOGO HREF="http://www.starpowder.com/icon.gif" STYLE="ICON"/>
    <LOGO HREF="http://www.starpowder.com/image.gif" STYLE="IMAGE"/>
    <LOGO HREF="http://www.starpowder.com/image-wide.gif" STYLE="IMAGE-WIDE"/>

    <SCHEDULE TIMEZONE="-0800">
        <INTERVALTIME DAY="5"/>
        <EARLIESTTIME HOUR="3" TIMEZONE="-0800"/>
        <LATESTTIME HOUR="5" TIMEZONE="-0800"/>
    </SCHEDULE>

    <ITEM HREF="http://www.starpowder.com/mercury.html">
        <TITLE>All about Mercury</TITLE>
        <ABSTRACT>
```

```
            All planetary information for
            Mercury, including orbital specifications.
        </ABSTRACT>
    </ITEM>

    <ITEM HREF="http://www.starpowder.com/venus.html">
        <TITLE>All about Venus</TITLE>
        <ABSTRACT>
            All planetary information for
            Venus, including orbital specifications.
        </ABSTRACT>
    </ITEM>

    <ITEM HREF="http://www.starpowder.com/earth.html">
        <TITLE>All about Earth</TITLE>
        <ABSTRACT>
            All planetary information for
            Earth, including orbital specifications.
        </ABSTRACT>
    </ITEM>

    <ITEM HREF="http://www.starpowder.com/mars.html">
        <TITLE>All about Mars</TITLE>
        <ABSTRACT>
            All planetary information for
            Mars, including orbital specifications.
        </ABSTRACT>
    </ITEM>

</CHANNEL>
```

Again, you should be very cautious when setting up automatic updates—they can be confusing to the user, who may get very annoyed and have no idea how to cancel such updating.

Turning Off Precaching

When channel content is downloaded, it is cached automatically so that the user may view it later. However, if you want to turn off precaching, you can set the `<CHANNEL>` element's `PRECACHE` attribute to `"NO"`:

```
<CHANNEL PRECACHE="NO" HREF=...
        .
        .
        .
</CHANNEL>
```

If you do turn off precaching, nothing will be downloaded automatically from the channel.

Downloading Pages in a Hierarchy

You can also make Internet Explorer download a whole Web site, not just those pages listed in <ITEM> elements, although this can be very wasteful of bandwidth. To do this, you use the <CHANNEL> element's LEVEL attribute, which indicates how many levels deep in a page hierarchy you want the browser to fetch pages from (the hierarchy is constructed by linking pages with hyperlinks).

You can set LEVEL to values from 0 to 3, as here, where I set it to 2:

```
<?xml version="1.0"?>
<CHANNEL LEVEL="2"
    HREF="http://www.starpowder.com/planets.html">
    <TITLE>Planets</TITLE>

    <LOGO HREF="http://www.starpowder.com/icon.gif" STYLE="ICON"/>
    <LOGO HREF="http://www.starpowder.com/image.gif" STYLE="IMAGE"/>
    <LOGO HREF="http://www.starpowder.com/image-wide.gif" STYLE="IMAGE-WIDE"/>

    <SCHEDULE TIMEZONE="-0800">
        <INTERVALTIME DAY="5"/>
        <EARLIESTTIME HOUR="3" TIMEZONE="-0800"/>
        <LATESTTIME HOUR="5" TIMEZONE="-0800"/>
    </SCHEDULE>

    <ITEM HREF="http://www.starpowder.com/mercury.html">
        <TITLE>All about Mercury</TITLE>
        <ABSTRACT>
            All planetary information for
            Mercury, including orbital specifications.
        </ABSTRACT>
    </ITEM>
    .
    .
    .
</CHANNEL>
```

In this case, Internet Explorer will "Web crawl" two levels deep and retrieve all the documents when the main channel page changes. Note, however, that this is almost always wasteful, unless you really change your whole Web site when the main channel page changes.

Logging User Access

Using the <LOG> and <LOGTARGET> elements, which are children of the <CHANNEL> element, you can track which downloaded channel pages a user looks at offline. This can be useful if you have advertisements on those pages and need to know which pages were actually viewed. From the user's point of view, of course, it can also feel like another invasion of privacy.

To set up logging, you use the `<LOG>` element like this; you need the `VALUE` attribute (it's required), and the only valid value currently is `"document:view"`:

```
<LOG VALUE="document:view"/>
```

The `<LOGTARGET>` element specifies where to send logging information. This information is sent in a way that can be handled by CGI scripts. This element has these attributes:

Attribute	Description
`HREF`	Specifies the URI to send logging information to.
`METHOD`	Specifies the method used to send logging information; can be `POST` or `PUT`.
`SCOPE`	Specifies what types of page viewing to count. It can be `ALL`, `ONLINE`, or `OFFLINE`.

The `<LOGTARGET>` element also has two possible child elements:

Attribute	Description
`<PURGETIME>`	Specifies the number of hours for which logging information is valid. Set the `HOUR` attribute to a number of hours.
`<HTTP-EQUIV>`	Allows you to set key value pairs in the HTTP MIME header to send to the logging target.

For example, here's how I could enable offline logging in `planets.cdf`, sending updates to a CGI script named `log.cgi`:

```
<?xml version="1.0"?>
<CHANNEL HREF="http://www.starpowder.com/planets.html">
    <TITLE>Planets</TITLE>

    <LOGO HREF="http://www.starpowder.com/icon.gif" STYLE="ICON"/>
    <LOGO HREF="http://www.starpowder.com/image.gif" STYLE="IMAGE"/>
    <LOGO HREF="http://www.starpowder.com/image-wide.gif" STYLE="IMAGE-WIDE"/>

    <SCHEDULE TIMEZONE="-0800">
        <INTERVALTIME DAY="5"/>
        <EARLIESTTIME HOUR="3" TIMEZONE="-0800"/>
        <LATESTTIME HOUR="5" TIMEZONE="-0800"/>
    </SCHEDULE>

    <LOG VALUE="document:view"/>

    <LOGTARGET METHOD="POST" SCOPE="OFFLINE"
        HREF="http://www.starpowder.com/cgi-bin/log.cgi">
        <PURGETIME HOUR="24"/>
        <HTTP-EQUIV NAME="ENCODING-TYPE" VALUE="text"/>
    </LOGTARGET>
```

continues ▸

```
    <ITEM HREF="http://www.starpowder.com/mercury.html">
        <TITLE>All about Mercury</TITLE>
        <ABSTRACT>
            All planetary information for
            Mercury, including orbital specifications.
        </ABSTRACT>
    </ITEM>
    .
    .
    .
</CHANNEL>
```

Setting a Channel Base URI

You can use the `BASE` attribute of the `<CHANNEL>` element to set a base URI for the channel, much as you can with the `<BASE>` element in HTML. The value that you assign to `BASE` must end with `/`. Here's an example; in this case, I'm setting a base URI for the channel, which then makes all other URIs relative to that base:

```
<?xml version="1.0"?>
<CHANNEL BASE="http://www.starpowder.com/">
    <TITLE>Planets</TITLE>

    <LOGO HREF="icon.gif" STYLE="ICON"/>
    <LOGO HREF="image.gif" STYLE="IMAGE"/>
    <LOGO HREF="image-wide.gif" STYLE="IMAGE-WIDE"/>

    <SCHEDULE TIMEZONE="-0800">
        <INTERVALTIME DAY="5"/>
        <EARLIESTTIME HOUR="3" TIMEZONE="-0800"/>
        <LATESTTIME HOUR="5" TIMEZONE="-0800"/>
    </SCHEDULE>

    <ITEM HREF="mercury.html">
        <TITLE>All about Mercury</TITLE>
        <ABSTRACT>
            All planetary information for
            Mercury, including orbital specifications.
        </ABSTRACT>
    </ITEM>
    .
    .
    .
</CHANNEL>
```

Setting Last Modified Dates

The browser can check whether channel pages have been modified by reading the MIME header that comes with those pages and by checking the `Last-Modified` item in the header. In fact, the browser can request only the page's header, which means that it can check the last modified date without having to download the whole page.

On the other hand, this creates a lot of header requests. One way of changing that is the `LASTMOD` attribute of the `<CHANNEL>` and `<ITEM>` elements, which you set to a date and Greenwich Mean Time (GMT) like this: `"2001-10-15T01:00:00"`. The browser can get the last modified time of a page from an element that uses the `LASTMOD` attribute in the CDF file, and download the document only if the cached version is dated earlier than the `LASTMOD` time. In this way, the browser can check `LASTMOD` times instead of having to query the server for MIME headers. Here's an example where I'm assigning a value to `LASTMOD`:

```
<?xml version="1.0"?>
<CHANNEL HREF="http://www.starpowder.com/planets.html"
   LASTMOD="2001-10-15T01:00:00">
   <TITLE>Planets</TITLE>

   <LOGO HREF="http://www.starpowder.com/icon.gif" STYLE="ICON"/>
   <LOGO HREF="http://www.starpowder.com/image.gif" STYLE="IMAGE"/>
   <LOGO HREF="http://www.starpowder.com/image-wide.gif" STYLE="IMAGE-WIDE"/>

   <SCHEDULE TIMEZONE="-0800">
       <INTERVALTIME DAY="5"/>
       <EARLIESTTIME HOUR="3" TIMEZONE="-0800"/>
       <LATESTTIME HOUR="5" TIMEZONE="-0800"/>
   </SCHEDULE>

   <ITEM HREF="mercury.html">
       <TITLE>All about Mercury</TITLE>
       <ABSTRACT>
           All planetary information for
           Mercury, including orbital specifications.
       </ABSTRACT>
   </ITEM>
   .
   .
   .
</CHANNEL>
```

Setting Channel Usage

With the `<USAGE>` element, you can set various ways of using channels beyond active channels. To determine the usage of a channel, you assign a value to the `VALUE` attribute from this list:

Value	Description
`Channel`	The default. The items in a channel appear in the browser's Favorites bar.
`DesktopComponent`	Items displayed directly on the desktop in Active Desktop installations.
`Email`	The parent element that will be emailed to the user when updated.
`None`	Item will not appear in the Favorites bar.
`Screensaver`	Item that is a screen saver.
`SoftwareUpdate`	Item that is a software update.

We've already seen the default value, `"Channel"` at work. Using the `"None"` value just turns the item off as far as channels go. I'll take a look at the other possibilities here.

Updating Desktop Components

In Microsoft Active Desktop installations, desktop components are displayed directly on the Windows desktop and can be updated automatically. For example, say that some users want to keep tabs on all the major planets and want images continually updated on their desktops of those planets.

Here's how you might implement that, updating the image of Mercury every 20 minutes; note the child elements of `<USAGE>` in this case—`<WIDTH>`, `<HEIGHT>`, `<OPENAS>`, and `<CANRESIZE>`:

```
<?xml version="1.0"?>
<CHANNEL HREF="http://www.starpowder.com/planets.html">
    <TITLE>
        Planetary Images
    </TITLE>
    <ABSTRACT>
        These are updated planetary images.
    </ABSTRACT>

    <ITEM
        HREF="http://www.starpowder.com/mercury.gif">
        <TITLE>Image of Mercury</TITLE>
```

```
        <SCHEDULE TIMEZONE="-0800">
            <INTERVALTIME MIN="20"/>
            <EARLIESTTIME HOUR="0"/>
            <LATESTTIME HOUR="23"/>
        </SCHEDULE>

        <USAGE VALUE="DesktopComponent">
            <WIDTH VALUE="400"/>
            <HEIGHT VALUE="400"/>
            <OPENAS VALUE="Image"/>
            <CANRESIZE VALUE="No"/>
        </USAGE>
    </ITEM>
</CHANNEL>
```

Updating Through Email

You can also indicate how to handle email updates; in this case, you can set the usage to `"Email"`, which means that the parent item will be sent to the user in email. For example, here's how I indicate that I want `update.html` sent to the user when updates occur:

```
<?xml version="1.0"?>
<CHANNEL HREF="http://www.starpowder.com/planets.html">
    <TITLE>Planets</TITLE>

    <LOGO HREF="http://www.starpowder.com/icon.gif" STYLE="ICON"/>
    <LOGO HREF="http://www.starpowder.com/image.gif" STYLE="IMAGE"/>
    <LOGO HREF="http://www.starpowder.com/image-wide.gif" STYLE="IMAGE-WIDE"/>

    <SCHEDULE TIMEZONE="-0800">
        <INTERVALTIME DAY="5"/>
        <EARLIESTTIME HOUR="3" TIMEZONE="-0800"/>
        <LATESTTIME HOUR="5" TIMEZONE="-0800"/>
    </SCHEDULE>

    <ITEM HREF="update.html">
        <USAGE VALUE="Email"/>
    </ITEM>

    <ITEM HREF="mercury.html">
        <TITLE>All about Mercury</TITLE>
        <ABSTRACT>
            All planetary information for
            Mercury, including orbital specifications.
        </ABSTRACT>
    </ITEM>
    .
    .
    .
</CHANNEL>
```

Updating Screen Savers

If you set the usage of an item to `"Screensaver"`, that HTML page will be downloaded and used as the new screen saver. To use this option, the user must have selected the `"Channel Screen Saver"` as the current screen saver, as shown in Figure 18.9; if the user has not, Windows will ask whether to do so when the screen saver's CDF file is opened.

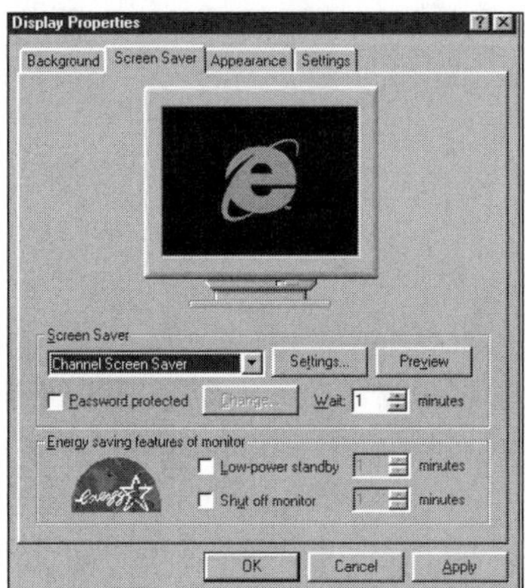

Figure 18.9 Selecting a channel screen saver.

Here's an example where I'm adding a screen saver (you can set only one per CDF file) to `planets.cdf`:

```
<?xml version="1.0"?>
<CHANNEL HREF="http://www.starpowder.com/planets.html">
    <TITLE>Planets</TITLE>

    <LOGO HREF="http://www.starpowder.com/icon.gif" STYLE="ICON"/>
    <LOGO HREF="http://www.starpowder.com/image.gif" STYLE="IMAGE"/>
    <LOGO HREF="http://www.starpowder.com/image-wide.gif" STYLE="IMAGE-WIDE"/>

    <SCHEDULE TIMEZONE="-0800">
        <INTERVALTIME DAY="5"/>
        <EARLIESTTIME HOUR="3" TIMEZONE="-0800"/>
        <LATESTTIME HOUR="5" TIMEZONE="-0800"/>
    </SCHEDULE>

    <ITEM HREF="http://www.starpowder.com/planets.gif">
        <USAGE VALUE="ScreenSaver"/>
    </ITEM>
```

```
    <ITEM HREF="mercury.html">
        <TITLE>All about Mercury</TITLE>
        <ABSTRACT>
            All planetary information for
            Mercury, including orbital specifications.
        </ABSTRACT>
    </ITEM>
    .
    .
    .
</CHANNEL>
```

Updating Software

You can also update software packages automatically using the <USAGE> element in CDF files and setting its VALUE attribute to "SoftwareUpdate". You also must indicate what you want to have happen, using Open Software Description (OSD) in a special element, <SOFTPKG>. You can learn more about OSD here:

- http://msdn.microsoft.com/workshop/management/osd/osdfaq.asp. Microsoft's OSD FAQ
- http://msdn.microsoft.com/workshop/delivery/osd/overview/osd.asp. An overview of OSD

Here's an example; in this case, I'll set up updating for a software package named StarGazerKing. The actual installation uses Cabinet (CAB) files of the type that the Microsoft Visual Studio products such as Visual Basic create. I'm listing three alternate CABs, one for each of three operating systems—you can add a <SCHEDULE> element if you want the browser to check for updates regularly:

```
<?xml version="1.0"?>
<CHANNEL HREF="http://www.starpowder.com/planets.html">
    <TITLE>StarGazerKing Update</TITLE>
    <ABSTRACT>
        StarGazerKing now comes with a spellchecker!
    </ABSTRACT>

    <USAGE VALUE="SoftwareUpdate"/>

    <SOFTPKG NAME="StarGazerKing"
        AUTOINSTALL="No"
```

```
        VERSION="2, 1, 0, 0"
        STYLE="ActiveSetup">

        <TITLE>StarGazerKing</TITLE>

        <ABSTRACT>
            StarGazerKing now comes with spellchecking,
            and it'll increase your productivity greatly!
        </ABSTRACT>

        <IMPLEMENTATION>
            <OS VALUE="win95" />
            <CODEBASE HREF="http://www.starpowder.com/cabs/sgk95.cab">
        </IMPLEMENTATION>

        <IMPLEMENTATION>
            <OS VALUE="winnt" />
            <CODEBASE HREF="http://www.starpowder.com/cabs/sgknt.cab">
        </IMPLEMENTATION>

        <IMPLEMENTATION>
            <OS VALUE="mac" />
            <CODEBASE HREF="http://www.starpowder.com/cabs/sgkmac.cab">
        </IMPLEMENTATION>

    </SOFTPKG>

</CHANNEL>
```

Windows will ask users whether they want the update to take place because I set `AUTOINSTALL` to `"No"`; you can set it to `"Yes"` to make the installation automatic, but that also has the potential of making users angry because they'll be installing new versions of software without their consent. I suggest that you avoid automatic installation. There are a great many more options here—if you are interested, take a look at the software update material on the Microsoft CDF sites.

That completes our look at RDF and CDF, two popular XML applications. In the next chapter, I'll take a look at another XML application: VML.

19
Vector Markup Language

THE WAY YOU PRESENT XML IN BROWSERS SHOULD not be limited to simple text—in fact, there are various initiatives to create graphics-based XML applications. We created graphical browsers in Chapter 11, "Java and the XML DOM," and Chapter 12, "Java and SAX," to use XML to display circles. I also discussed the W3C language, Scalable Vector Graphics (SVG), in Chapter 1, "Essential XML." SVG has been around for a long time but has not been very widely implemented. Today, the most widespread graphics-based XML application is the Vector Markup Language (VML) from Microsoft.

Here's how Microsoft describes VML: "VML is an application of Extensible Markup Language (XML) 1.0 which defines a format for the encoding of vector information together with additional markup to describe how that information may be displayed and edited."

VML supports the markup of vector graphic information in the same way that HTML supports the markup of textual information. Besides its own XML elements, VML also supports CSS, so you can style and position shapes as you like. It's supported in Microsoft Office 2000—Microsoft Word, PowerPoint, and Excel. When you create graphics in those programs, the graphics are stored in VML. Internet Explorer also supports VML. You can use the tools that come with Microsoft Office to draw VML figures, or you can create VML yourself. We'll do it ourselves in this chapter.

There are two primary online resources for VML: the VML reference at Microsoft, and the note that Microsoft wrote and sent to the W3C, which the W3C has posted (not much has come of that note; no one besides Microsoft seems very inclined to implement VML). Here are these resources (bear in mind that URIs on Microsoft's sites change very frequently):

- `http://msdn.microsoft.com/standards/vml/ref/`. The Microsoft VML reference, with examples.
- `www.w3.org/TR/NOTE-VML`. The VML note at W3C, dated May 13, 1998.

VML was added to Internet Explorer before that browser added its built-in XML support, so the way you implement VML does not involve Internet Explorer XML islands or any such mechanism. Instead, you use a namespace for VML and then use the VML engine in Internet Explorer, which is actually implemented as an Internet Explorer *behavior* (an external code module). We saw this example in Chapter 1, and I'll take a closer look at it in this chapter:

```
<HTML xmlns:v="urn:schemas-microsoft-com:vml">

    <HEAD>
        <TITLE>
            Using Vector Markup Language
        </TITLE>

        <STYLE>
        v\:* {behavior: url(#default#VML);}
        </STYLE>
    </HEAD>

    <BODY>
        <CENTER>
            <H1>
                Using Vector Markup Language
            </H1>
        </CENTER>
        <P>
        <v:oval STYLE='width:100pt; height:75pt'
            fillcolor="yellow" />
        <P>
        <v:rect STYLE='width:100pt; height:75pt' fillcolor="blue"
            strokecolor="red" STROKEWEIGHT="2pt"/>
        <P>
        <v:polyline
            POINTS="20pt,55pt,100pt,-10pt,180pt,65pt,260pt,25pt"
            strokecolor="red" STROKEWEIGHT="2pt"/>
    </BODY>
</HTML>
```

Internet Explorer Behaviors

You can find out more about Internet Explorer behaviors, which represent one of Microsoft's techniques for separating markup from document content, at `http://msdn.microsoft.com/workshop/c-frame.htm#/workshop/author/default.asp`.

This example just drew a few VML shapes, and you can see the results of this page in Figure 19.1.

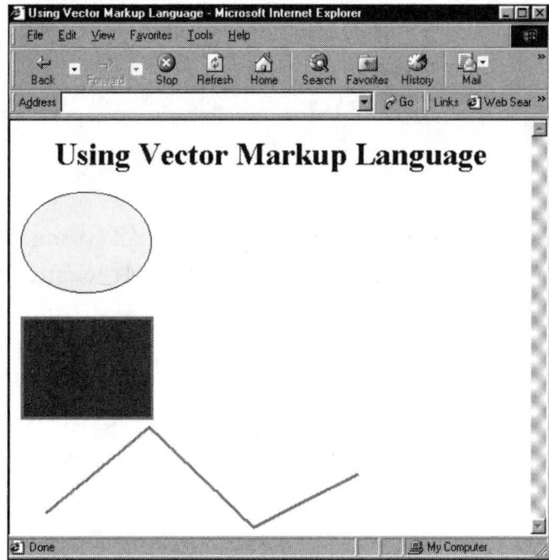

Figure 19.1 A VML page sample page.

Now that we're discussing VML in depth, the syntax of this document bears a little examination.

Creating VML Documents

In Internet Explorer, VML is embedded in HTML documents. You start by declaring this namespace, v:

```
<HTML xmlns:v="urn:schemas-microsoft-com:vml">
    .
    .
    .
```

You must also instantiate the VML engine, which is implemented as an Internet Explorer behavior. To implement this behavior, you use a <STYLE> element, connecting the v namespace to the VML default behavior:

```
<HTML xmlns:v="urn:schemas-microsoft-com:vml">

    <HEAD>
        <TITLE>
            Using Vector Markup Language
        </TITLE>

        <STYLE>
            v\:* {behavior: url(#default#VML);}
        </STYLE>
    </HEAD>
    .
    .
    .
```

This indicates to Internet Explorer that the VML in the page should be handled by the VML engine. Now you can add VML elements such as <oval> if you use the proper namespace, v:

```
<HTML xmlns:v="urn:schemas-microsoft-com:vml">

    <HEAD>
        <TITLE>
            Using Vector Markup Language
        </TITLE>

        <STYLE>
            v\:* {behavior: url(#default#VML);}
        </STYLE>
    </HEAD>

    <BODY>
        <CENTER>
            <H1>
                Using Vector Markup Language
            </H1>
        </CENTER>
        <P>
        <v:oval STYLE='width:100pt; height:75pt'
            fillcolor="yellow" />
        <P>
        <v:rect STYLE='width:100pt; height:75pt' fillcolor="blue"
            strokecolor="red" STROKEWEIGHT="2pt"/>
        <P>
        <v:polyline
            POINTS="20pt,55pt,100pt,-10pt,180pt,65pt,260pt,25pt"
            strokecolor="red" STROKEWEIGHT="2pt"/>
    </BODY>
</HTML>
```

I'll take a look at what VML elements are available now.

The VML Elements

Twenty elements are defined in VML, as shown in Table 19.1.

Table 19.1 **The VML Elements**

Element	Description
`<arc>`	Draws an arc
`<background>`	Adds a background
`<curve>`	Draws a curve
`<fill>`	Fills a shape
`<formulas>`	Specifies a formula that lets you scale shapes
`<group>`	Groups shapes
`<handles>`	Draws handles on shapes
`<image>`	Supports images
`<imagedata>`	Specifies an image to be rendered on top of a shape
`<line>`	Draws a line
`<oval>`	Draws an oval
`<path>`	Specifies a path for rendering
`<polyline>`	Draws a shape from line segments
`<roundrect>`	Draws a rounded rectangle
`<shadow>`	Adds a shadow to a shape
`<shape>`	Creates a basic shape
`<shapetype>`	Defines a reusable shape
`<stroke>`	Specifies how to draw a path
`<textbox>`	Creates a text box
`<textpath>`	Specifies a path for text to be drawn along.

The overall structure of VML is based on the two primary elements: `<shape>` and `<group>`. The `<shape>` element is the most basic VML element, and you use it to define general graphic shapes in VML. You can use the `<group>` element to group shapes together so that they can be handled as a single unit.

Besides the `<shape>` and `<group>` elements, VML also defines additional top-level elements to help make the editing and representation of complex graphical information more compact and convenient. For example, you can use the <shapetype> element to define a definition of a shape. A <shape> element may then reference a <shapetype> element to instantiate several copies of the same shape.

You also can use a number of predefined shapes, based on the <shape> element. Using the predefined shapes means that you don't have to explicitly declare the shape you want to use. These predefined shapes are <line>, <polyline>, <curve>, <rect>, <roundrect>, <oval>, <arc>, and <image>.

Common Attributes

You can find parts (but only parts) of the VML DTD in the VML note at www.w3.org/TR/NOTE-VML. Two important parts are the entity parameters coreattrs and shapeattrs, which define attribute lists, because many of the elements we'll see in this chapter use those attributes. Here's how coreattrs is defined:

```
<!entity %coreattrs
id id #implied -- document-wide unique id --
class cdata #implied -- space separated list of classes --
style cdata #implied -- associated style info --
title cdata #implied -- advisory title/amplification --
href cdata #implied -- URL link if the element is clicked on --
target cdata #implied -- target frame for href ---
alt cdata #implied -- alternate text if element cannot be displayed --
coordsize cdata #implied -- size of coordinate space inside the element --
coordorigin cdata #implied -- coordinate at top-left corner of element --
wrapcoords cdata #implied -- outline to use for tight text wrapping --
>
```

Here is the shapeattrs parameter entity:

```
<!entity %shapeattrs
opacity cdata #implied -- opacity of the shape --
chromakey cdata #implied -- color to be made transparent --
stroke cdata #implied -- Boolean whether to stroke the outline or not --
strokecolor cdata #implied -- RGB color to use for the stroke --
strokeweight cdata #implied -- weight of the line to use for stroking --
fill cdata #implied -- Boolean whether to fill the shape or not --
fillcolor cdata #implied -- RGB color to use for the fill --
print cdata #implied -- Boolean whether the element is to be printed --
>
```

VML Uses CSS

VML uses CSS to position and orient shapes. In addition to standard CSS layout, the VML elements may also be rotated or flipped. Each element also establishes a coordinate space for its content, which allows scaling of the content with respect to the containing elements.

VML used a number ofVML styles to augment CSS2, and I'll take a look at them here.

The *rotation* Property

You can use the `rotation` property to specify a rotation for a shape or group. The rotation is measured in clockwise degrees about its center.

The *flip* Property

You use the `flip` property to specify that a shape or group should be flipped about its center on either the x or the y axis. Here are the two values that you can assign to the `flip` property:

Value	Description
x	Flip the rotated shape about the y axis
y	Flip the rotated shape about the x axis

The *center-x* and *center-y* Properties

You use the `center-x` and `center-y` properties to specify the center of the block that contains the shape. These properties can be used as an alternative to the customary CSS positioning properties, `left` and `top`.

Local Coordinate Space

The <shape> and `<group>` elements are CSS block-level elements. Inside their blocks, a local coordinate system is defined for any subelements using the `coordsize` and `coordorigin` attributes, and all CSS2 positioning information is expressed in terms of this local coordinate space. We'll run into these attributes in this chapter when we group shapes.

The VML `coordsize` attribute defines how many units there are along the width of the containing block. The `coordorigin` attribute defines the coordinate at the top left corner of the containing block. For example, take a look at a group defined as follows:

```
<v:shape style='width: 500px; height: 200px'
coordsize="100,100" coordorigin="-50,-50" />
```

Here, the containing block would be 500 pixels wide by 200 pixels high. The coordinate system inside the block ranges from -50.0 to 50.0 along the x axis and -50.0 to 50.0 along the y-axis. The point (0, 0) is right in the center of the block. Shapes inside the group are positioned and sized according to this local coordinate system. That's useful because, no matter how the width and height of the group is changed, the local coordinate system inside will remain the same.

The *<shape>* Element

The `<shape>` element is the primary one in VML, although I rarely find myself using it in practice (I mostly use the predefined shapes based on `<shape>`). This element may appear by itself or within a `<group>` element. The `<shape>` element includes all the attributes in `coreattrs` and `shapeattrs`, and adds three more:

```
<!attlist shape %coreattrs; %shapeattrs;
type cdata #implied -- reference to shapetype --
adj cdata #implied -- list of adjust values for parameterized paths --
path cdata #implied -- string with command set describing a path --
>
```

For the sake of reference, all the attributes of this element and their descriptions appear in Table 19.2; note that VML attributes can be part of either the VML or the CSS namespaces.

Table 19.2 **Attributes of the *<shape>* Element**

Namespace	Attribute	Type	Default Value	Description
CSS	flip	String	null	Specifies that the shape image inside the reference rectangle should be flipped along the given axes in the order specified. Takes the values "x", "y", or both.
CSS	height	Number	100	Specifies the height of the containing block of the shape.
CSS	left, margin-left, center-x, etc	Number	0	Sets the position of the left of the containing block of the shape.
CSS	position	string	"static"	Sets the CSS type of positioning. When inside a group, this value must always be "absolute".
CSS	rotation	number	0	Specifies the angle by which to rotate.
CSS	top, margin-top, center-y, etc	number	0	Sets the position of the top of the containing block of the shape.
CSS	visibility	string	visible	Sets the visibility of shapes.
CSS	width	number	100	Specifies the width of the container rectangle of the shape.

Namespace	Attribute	Type	Default Value	Description
CSS	z-index	number	0	Specifies the z-index of the shape. Positive numbers come out of the screen, and negative ones go into it.
VML	adj	string	null	Is a comma-separated list of numbers that are "adjusting" parameters for the formulas that define the path of the shape.
VML	alt	string	null	Text associated with the shape that may appear instead of the shape.
VML	chromakey	color	null	Sets a color value that will be transparent so that anything behind the shape will show through.
VML	class	string	null	Gives the CSS class of this shape.
VML	coordorigin	Vector2D	"0 0"	Gives the coordinates at the top-left corner of the containing block.
VML	coordsize	Vector2D	"1000 1000"	Gives the width and height of the coordinate space inside the containing block of this shape.
VML	fill	boolean	true	If "true", the path defining the shape will be filled.
VML	fillcolor	color	"white"	Specifies the color of the brush to use to fill the path of this shape.
VML	href	string	null	Specifies the URI to jump to when this shape is clicked.
VML	id	string	null	A unique identifier for the shape.
VML	opacity	number	1.0	Sets the opacity of the entire shape. Set this to values between 0 (transparent) and 1 (opaque.)
VML	path	string	null	Specifies the path that defines the shape—a string containing the commands that define the path.
VML	print	boolean	true	If true, this shape should be printed.
VML	stroke	boolean	true	If true, the path defining the shape will be stroked (rendered) using a solid line, unless there is a stroke subelement.

continues

Table 19.2 **Attributes of the <*shape*> Element**

Namespace	Attribute	Type	Default Value	Description
VML	strokecolor	color	"black"	Sets the color of the brush to use to draw the path of this shape.
VML	stroke weight	number	"0.75pt"	Sets the width of the brush to use to stroke the path.
VML	target	string	null	The target frame URI.
VML	title	string	null	Gives the title of the shape.
VML	type	string	null	Holds a shapetype ID that describes the shape.
VML	v	string	null	A string containing the commands that define the path.
VML	Wrapcoords	string	null	Used for the wrapping text around an object.

Microsoft gives all VML elements an "XML template" that specifies default values for each of its attributes; here's the XML template for the `<shape>` element:

```
<shape
type=null
adj=null
path=null
opacity="100%"
chromakey="none"
stroke="true"
strokecolor="black"
strokeweight="0.75pt"
fill="true"
fillcolor="white"
print="true"
id=null
class=null
style='visibility: visible'
title=null
href=null
target=null
alt=null
coordsize="1000, 1000"
coordorigin="0, 0"
wrapcoords=null
/>
```

Using the `<shape>` element to draw shapes can be a little complex because you need to define the whole shape yourself, which you do by specifying a VML *path*. Doing that means giving the actual locations to use to draw the shape. To show how that works, I'll use a shape that Microsoft supports in its reference material; it draws a heart:

```
<HTML xmlns:v="urn:schemas-microsoft-com:vml">

    <HEAD>
        <TITLE>
            Using Vector Markup Language
        </TITLE>

        <STYLE>
        v\:* {behavior: url(#default#VML);}
        </STYLE>
    </HEAD>

    <BODY>
        <CENTER>
            <H1>
                VML Shapes
            </H1>
            <v:shape fillcolor="red"
                strokecolor="red" coordsize="21600,21600"
                path="m10860,2187c10451,1746,9529,1018,9015,730,
                7865,152,6685,,5415,,4175, 152,2995,575,1967,
                1305,1150,2187,575,3222,242,4220,,5410,242,6560,
                575,7597l10860, 21600,20995,7597c21480,6560,
                21600,5410,21480,4220,21115,3222,20420,2187,19632,
                1305,18575,575,17425,152,16275,,15005,,13735,152,
                12705,730,12176,1018,11254,1746, 10860,2187xe"
                style='width:200;height:160;'/>
        </CENTER>
    </BODY>
</HTML>
```

You can see the results in Figure 19.2.

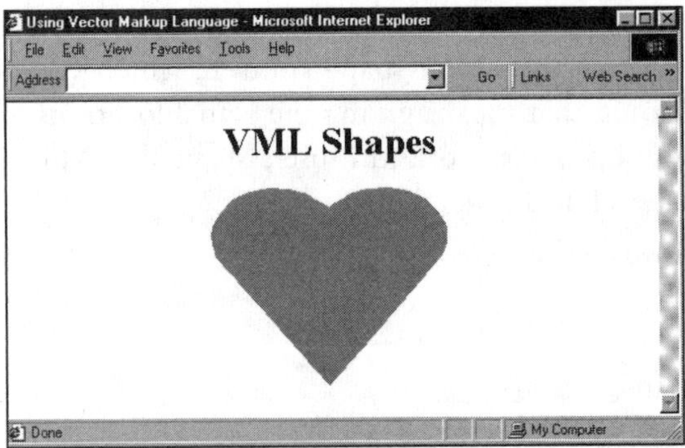

Figure 19.2 Using the <shape> element.

Another way of drawing this shape is to specify the shape's path in a <shapetype> element and then reference the <shapetype> element's ID with the <shape> element's type attribute:

```
<HTML xmlns:v="urn:schemas-microsoft-com:vml">

    <HEAD>
        <TITLE>
            Using Vector Markup Language
        </TITLE>

        <STYLE>
        v\:* {behavior: url(#default#VML);}
        </STYLE>
    </HEAD>

    <BODY>
        <CENTER>
            <H1>
                VML Shapes
            </H1>
            <v:shapetype id="Valentine" fillcolor="red"
                strokecolor="red" coordsize="21600,21600"
                path="m10860,2187c10451,1746,9529,1018,9015,730,
                7865,152,6685,,5415,,4175, 152,2995,575,1967,
                1305,1150,2187,575,3222,242,4220,,5410,242,6560,
                575,7597l10860, 21600,20995,7597c21480,6560,
                21600,5410,21480,4220,21115,3222,20420,2187,19632,
                1305,18575,575,17425,152,16275,,15005,,13735,152,
                12705,730,12176,1018,11254,1746, 10860,2187xe">
            </v:shapetype>
            <v:shape type="#Valentine" style='width:200;height:160;'/>
        </CENTER>
    </BODY>
</HTML>
```

However, unless you have a drawing tool of some kind, it's pretty tedious to calculate all the points in a path; it's usually far easier to use the predefined shapes.

Using Predefined Shapes

There are quite a few predefined shapes in VML, and using them can save you a lot of effort. In this section, I'll take a look at how to draw graphics using these elements.

The *<rect>* Element

The `<rect>` element just draws rectangles. This element supports both the `coreattrs` and `shapeattrs` attributes; here is its XML template, showing the default values for those attributes:

```
<rect
id=null
href=null
target=null
class=null
title=null
alt=null
style='visibility: visible'
opacity="1.0"
chromakey="null"
stroke="true"
strokecolor="black"
strokeweight="1"
fill="true"
fillcolor="white"
print="true"
coordsize="1000,1000"
coordorigin="0 0"
/>
```

Here's an example; in this case, I'll draw a rectangle that's red with a green border of 4 points wide:

```
<HTML xmlns:v="urn:schemas-microsoft-com:vml">

    <HEAD>
        <TITLE>
            Using Vector Markup Language
        </TITLE>

        <STYLE>
            v\:* {behavior: url(#default#VML);}
        </STYLE>
```

continues ►

```
    </HEAD>

    <BODY>
        <CENTER>
            <H1>
                VML Rectangles
            </H1>
            <v:rect style='width:200pt;height:100pt'
                fillcolor="red" strokecolor="green"
                strokeweight="4pt"/>
        </CENTER>
    </BODY>
</HTML>
```

You can see the results in Figure 19.3.

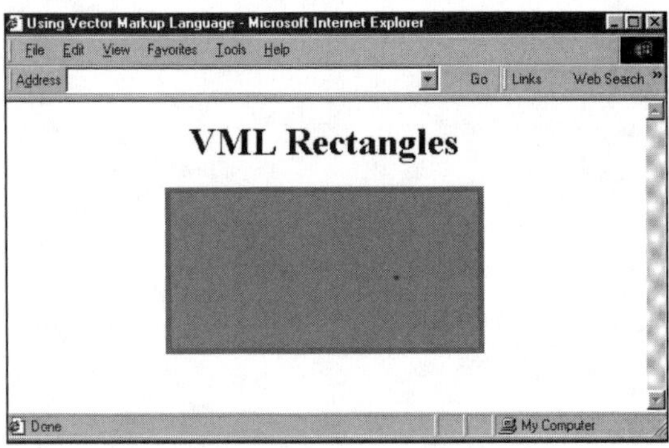

Figure 19.3 Using the <rect> element.

The *<roundrect>* Element

You can use the `<roundrect>` element to draw a rectangle with rounded corners. This element supports the `coreattrs` and `shapeattrs` attributes, along with one additional attribute, `arcsize`:

```
<!attlist roundrect %coreattrs; %shapeattrs;
arcsize cdata #implied -- size of arc on corners of rectangle --
>
```

The `arcsize` attribute defines the rounded corners as a percentage of half the smaller dimension of the rectangle. Here's the XML template for this element:

```
<roundrect
arcsize="0.2"
id=null
href=null
target=null
class=null
```

```
title=null
alt=null
style='visibility: visible'
opacity="1.0"
chromakey="null"
stroke="true"
strokecolor="black"
strokeweight="0.75pt"
fill="true"
fillcolor="white"
print="true"
coordsize="1000,1000"
coordorigin="0 0"
/>
```

As an example, I'll convert the rectangle in the previous example to a rounded rectangle with rounded corners 20% of half the smaller dimension of the rectangle. To do that, you specify an `arcsize` of `"0.2"`:

```
<HTML xmlns:v="urn:schemas-microsoft-com:vml">

    <HEAD>
        <TITLE>
            Using Vector Markup Language
        </TITLE>

        <STYLE>
        v\:* {behavior: url(#default#VML);}
        </STYLE>
    </HEAD>

    <BODY>
        <CENTER>
            <H1>
                VML Rounded Rectangles
            </H1>
            <v:roundrect style="width:200pt;height:100pt"
                arcsize="0.2" fillcolor="red"
                strokecolor="green" strokeweight="4pt"/>
        </CENTER>
    </BODY>
</HTML>
```

You can see the results of this VML in Figure 19.4.

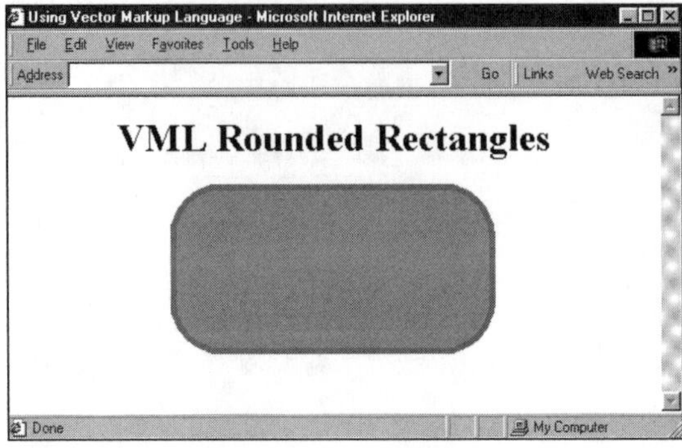

Figure 19.4 Using the <roundrect> element.

The *<line>* Element

You use the `<line>` element to create a straight line. Here are the attributes of this element:

```
<!attlist line %coreattrs; %shapeattrs;
from cdata #implied
to cdata #implied
>
```

These are the two attributes specific to the `<line>` element:

Attribute	**Description**
`from`	The starting point of the line. Specified using Vector2D format, like this: `"100 100"`.
`to`	The ending point of the line. Specified using Vector2D format, like this: `"100 100"`.

And here's the XML template for this element:

```
<line
from="0 0"
to="10 10"
id=null
href=null
target=null
class=null
title=null
alt=null
style='visibility: visible'
opacity="1.0"
chromakey="null"
stroke="true"
```

```
strokecolor="black"
strokeweight="1"
fill="true"
fillcolor="white"
print="true"
coordsize="1000,1000"
coordorigin="0 0"
/>
```

Here's an example; in this case, I'm drawing a thick blue line from the pixel coordinates (20, 20) to (400, 100):

```
<HTML xmlns:v="urn:schemas-microsoft-com:vml">

    <HEAD>
        <TITLE>
            Using Vector Markup Language
        </TITLE>

        <STYLE>
            v\:* {behavior: url(#default#VML);}
        </STYLE>
    </HEAD>

    <BODY>
        <CENTER>
            <H1>
                VML Lines
            </H1>
            <v:line from="20px,20px" to="400px,100px"
                strokecolor="blue" strokeweight="4pt">
        </CENTER>
    </BODY>
</HTML>
```

You can see the results of this VML in Figure 19.5.

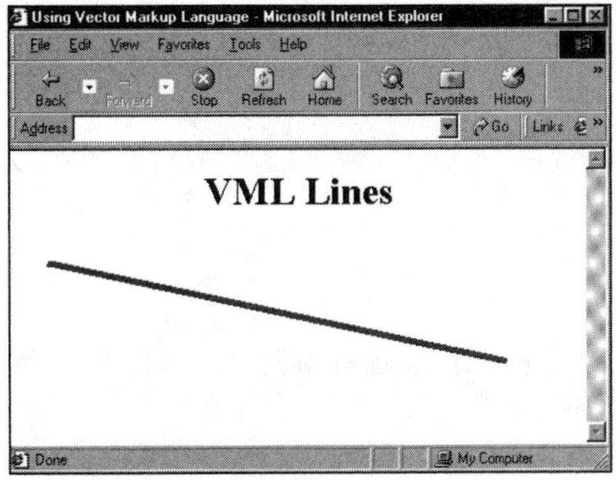

Figure 19.5 Using the <line> element.

The *<oval>* Element

You use the `<oval>` element to draw ovals and circles. This element supports the `coreattrs` and `shapeattrs` attributes. Here is the `<oval>` element's XML template:

```
<oval
position="0 0"
size="100 100"
id=null
href=null
target=null
class=null
title=null
alt=null
style='visibility: visible'
opacity="1.0"
chromakey="null"
stroke="true"
strokecolor="black"
strokeweight="0.75pt"
fill="true"
fillcolor="white"
print="true"
coordsize="1000,1000"
coordorigin="0 0"
/>
```

Here's an example where I'm drawing a blue oval; as with other elements, you can specify the size of the oval using the CSS `style` attribute:

```
<HTML xmlns:v="urn:schemas-microsoft-com:vml">

    <HEAD>
        <TITLE>
            Using Vector Markup Language
        </TITLE>

        <STYLE>
            v\:* {behavior: url(#default#VML);}
        </STYLE>
    </HEAD>

    <BODY>
        <CENTER>
            <H1>
                VML Ovals
            </H1>

            <v:oval style='width:200pt;height:100pt'
                fillcolor="blue" />

        </CENTER>
    </BODY>
</HTML>
```

You can see the results of this VML in Figure 19.6.

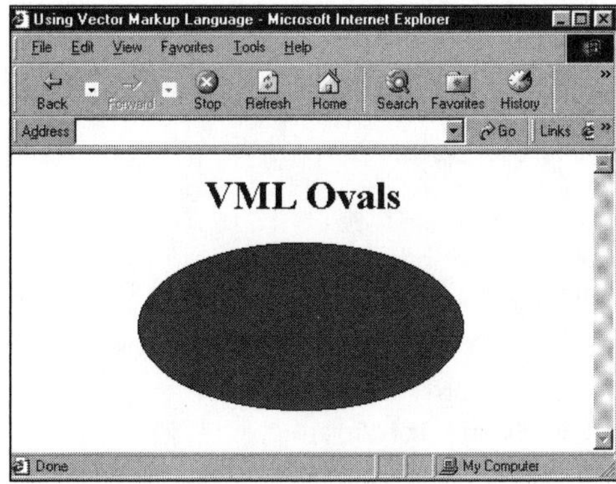

Figure 19.6 Using the `<oval>` element.

The *<polyline>* Element

You can use the `<polyline>` element to define shapes that are created from connected line segments. You use this element to draw your own shapes. Here's the attribute list for this element:

```
<!attlist polyline %coreattrs; %shapeattrs;
points cdata #implied
>
```

The `points` attribute is a string that defines the polyline shape to draw using pairs of values that specify points, such as `"0 0 10 10 40 40"`. Here is the XML template for this element:

```
<polyline
points="0 0 10 10 20 0"
id=null
href=null
target=null
class=null
title=null
alt=null
style='visibility: visible'
opacity="1.0"
chromakey="null"
stroke="true"
strokecolor="black"
strokeweight="1"
fill="true"
fillcolor="white"
```

continues ▸

```
print="true"
coordsize="1000,1000"
coordorigin="0 0"
/>
```

For example, to draw a polyline shape, here's some VML:

```
<HTML xmlns:v="urn:schemas-microsoft-com:vml">

    <HEAD>
        <TITLE>
            Using Vector Markup Language
        </TITLE>

        <STYLE>
            v\:* {behavior: url(#default#VML);}
        </STYLE>
    </HEAD>

    <BODY>
        <CENTER>
            <H1>
                VML Polylines
            </H1>
            <v:polyline points="0pt,0pt,90pt,-9pt,180pt,60pt,0pt,20pt
                -180pt,60pt,-90pt,-9pt,0pt,0pt"
                strokecolor="red" strokeweight="2pt"/>
        </CENTER>
    </BODY>
</HTML>
```

You can see the results of this VML in Figure 19.7.

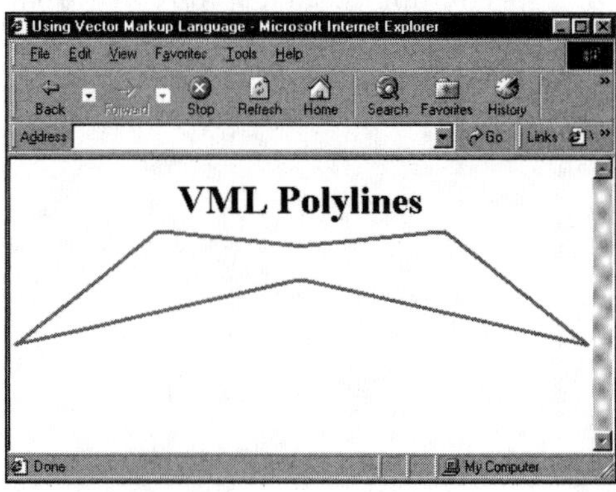

Figure 19.7 Using the <polyline> element.

The *<curve>* Element

You can use the <curve> element to draw a cubic bèzier curve. Here is the attribute list of this element:

```
<!attlist curve %coreattrs; %shapeattrs;
from cdata #implied
control1 cdata #implied
control2 cdata #implied
to cdata #implied
>
```

These are the custom attributes for this element:

Attribute	Description
from	The starting point of the line in the coordinate space of the parent element. Specified using Vector2D format, like this: "100 100".
control1	The first control point for the curve. Specified using Vector2D format, like this: "100 100".
control2	The second control point for the curve. Specified using Vector2D format, like this: "100 100".
to	The ending point of the line in the coordinate space of the parent element. Specified using Vector2D format, like this: "100 100".

The control points let you specify the bounding rectangle for the curve and so specify its shape. Here is this element's XML template:

```
<curve
from="0 0"
control1="10 10"
control2="20 0"
to="10 10"
id=null
href=null
target=null
class=null
title=null
alt=null
style='visibility: visible'
opacity="1.0"
chromakey="null"
stroke="true"
strokecolor="black"
strokeweight="1"
fill="true"
fillcolor="white"
print="true"
```

continues ▸

```
coordsize="1000,1000"
coordorigin="0 0"
/>
```

For example, I'll draw a curve using this VML:

```
<HTML xmlns:v="urn:schemas-microsoft-com:vml">

    <HEAD>
        <TITLE>
            Using Vector Markup Language
        </TITLE>

        <STYLE>
            v\:* {behavior: url(#default#VML);}
        </STYLE>
    </HEAD>

    <BODY>
        <CENTER>
            <H1>
                VML Curves
            </H1>
            <v:curve style='position:absolute'
            from="-100pt,0" control1="100pt,100pt"
            control2="200pt,100pt" to="100pt,0"
            strokecolor="blue" strokeweight="4pt"/>
        </CENTER>
    </BODY>
</HTML>
```

You can see the results of this VML in Figure 19.8.

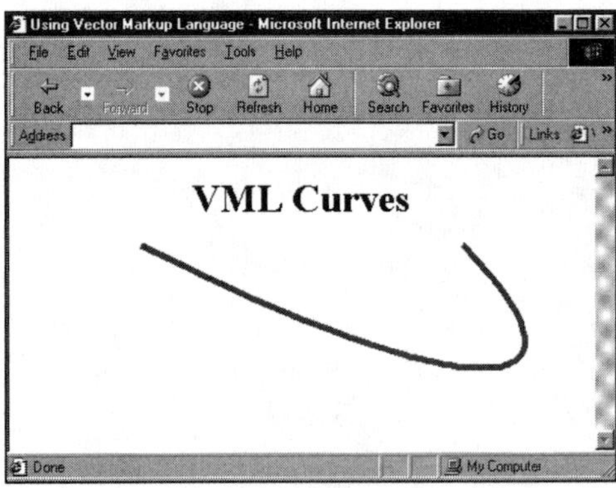

Figure 19.8 Using the <curve> element.

The <*arc*> Element

You can use the <arc> element to draw an arc. The arc is defined by the intersection of the oval with the start and end radius vectors given by angles. Here is the attribute list of this element:

```
<!attlist arc %coreattrs; %shapeattrs;
startangle cdata #implied
endangle cdata #implied
>
```

These are the custom attributes for this element:

Attribute	Description
startangle	Specifies the angle where the arc starts
endangle	Specifies the angle where the arc ends

Here is the XML template for this element:

```
<arc
startangle="0"
endangle="90"
id=null
href=null
target=null
class=null
title=null
alt=null
style='visibility: visible'
opacity="1.0"
chromakey="null"
stroke="true"
strokecolor="black"
strokeweight="0.75pt"
fill="true"
fillcolor="white"
print="true"
coordsize="1000,1000"
coordorigin="0 0"
/>
```

For example, here's how to take an arc from an oval, extending from 0° to 160°:

```
<HTML xmlns:v="urn:schemas-microsoft-com:vml">

    <HEAD>
        <TITLE>
            Using Vector Markup Language
        </TITLE>

        <STYLE>
```

continues ▸

```
        v\:* {behavior: url(#default#VML);}
    </STYLE>
</HEAD>

<BODY>
    <CENTER>
        <H1>
            VML Arcs
        </H1>
        <v:arc style='width:200pt;height:100pt'
            startangle="0" endangle="160"
            strokecolor="blue" strokeweight="4pt"/>
    </CENTER>
</BODY>
</HTML>
```

You can see the results of this VML in Figure 19.9.

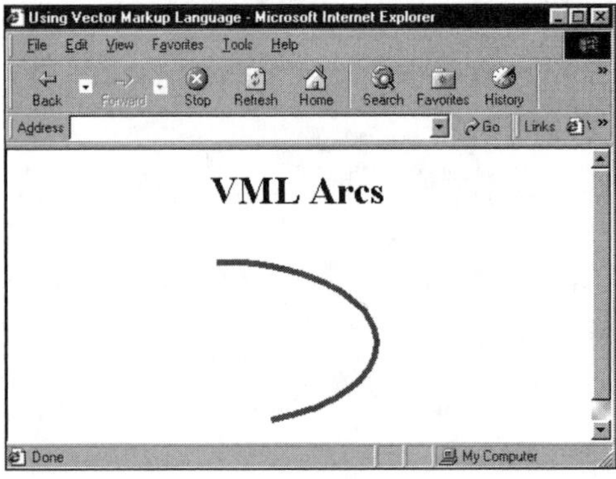

Figure 19.9 Using the <arc> element.

Coloring Shapes

You may have noticed that I've specified colors so far using words such as `"red"`, `"blue"`, `"green"`, and so on. In fact, there are three ways to specify colors in VML:

- Using a predefined color name: `fillcolor="red"`
- Using the `rgb` function: `fillcolor="rgb(255,0,0)"`
- Specifying a direct value: `fillcolor="#FF0000"`

You can use the HTML 4.0 predefined color names in VML:

- aqua
- black
- blue
- fuchsia
- gray
- green
- lime
- maroon
- navy
- olive
- purple
- red
- silver
- teal
- white
- yellow

You can also specify colors by giving the red, green, and blue color values in the rgb function, like this: rgb(*rrr*, *ggg*, *bbb*). Here, *rrr* is the red color value, *ggg* is the green color value, and *bbb* is the blue color value, all of which range from 0 to 255. Or, you can give those color values directly using hexadecimal digits, as you would in HTML, like this: "#*rrrgggbbb*". For example, "000000" is black, "#0000FF" is bright blue, "#FFFFFF" is white, and so on.

Scaling Shapes

You may also have noticed that you can set the size for shapes with the style attribute, as in this case, where I'm setting the size of the bounding rectangle of an oval:

```
<HTML xmlns:v="urn:schemas-microsoft-com:vml">

    <HEAD>
        <TITLE>
            Using Vector Markup Language
        </TITLE>

        <STYLE>
            v\:* {behavior: url(#default#VML);}
        </STYLE>
    </HEAD>

    <BODY>
        <CENTER>
            <H1>
                VML Ovals
            </H1>
```

continues ▸

```
            <v:oval style='width:200pt;height:100pt'
                fillcolor="blue" />
        </CENTER>
    </BODY>
</HTML>
```

To scale a shape, all you have to do is change the width and height, as specified with the style attribute. For example, to double the oval's size in both dimensions, I could assign style a value of `"width:400pt;height:200pt"`.

Positioning Shapes

VML uses the same syntax defined in CSS2 to position shapes on a Web page. You can use static, relative, or absolute positioning to determine where the base point is located on a Web page. You can also use the `top` and `left`, or `center-x` and `center-y`, style attributes to specify the offset from the base point at which the containing box for the shape will be positioned.

You can also use `z-index` to specify the z-order of shapes on a Web page. In addition, VML provides `rotation` and `flip` to rotate or flip shapes. I'll take a look at a few of the position styles here.

The *static* Position Style

The default position style is *static*, which makes the browser insert a shape at the current point in the browser's text flow. Here's an example putting static positioning to work, where I'm drawing a rectangle following some text:

```
<HTML xmlns:v="urn:schemas-microsoft-com:vml">

    <HEAD>
        <TITLE>
            Using Vector Markup Language
        </TITLE>

        <STYLE>
            v\:* {behavior: url(#default#VML);}
        </STYLE>
    </HEAD>

    <BODY>
        <CENTER>
            <H1>
                VML Positioning
            </H1>
            Here is the rectangle:
```

```
            <v:rect style='width:200pt;height:100pt'
                fillcolor="red" strokecolor="green"
                strokeweight="4pt"/>
        </CENTER>
    </BODY>
</HTML>
```

The results appear in Figure 19.10. As you see there, the shape's base line is aligned with the baseline of the text.

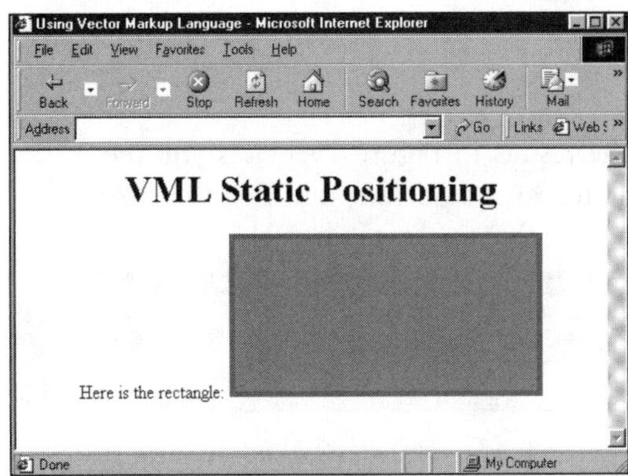

Figure 19.10 Using static positioning.

The *relative* Position Style

When you use static positioning, a shape is positioned with respect to the current location in the text flow. You can also position shapes *relative* to the current location in the text flow. To do so, you use the `position:relative` style and use the `top` and `left` style properties.

Here's an example where I position a shape 30 points to the left of the current text location and 15 points higher:

```
<HTML xmlns:v="urn:schemas-microsoft-com:vml">

    <HEAD>
        <TITLE>
            Using Vector Markup Language
        </TITLE>

        <STYLE>
            v\:* {behavior: url(#default#VML);}
        </STYLE>
    </HEAD>
```

continues ▸

```
    <BODY>
        <CENTER>
            <H1>
                VML Relative Positioning
            </H1>
            Here is the rectangle:
            <v:rect style='position:relative;left:30pt;
                top:-15pt;width:200pt;height:100pt'
                fillcolor="red" strokecolor="green"
                strokeweight="4pt"/>
        </CENTER>
    </BODY>
</HTML>
```

You can see the results in Figure 19.11. As you see in the figure, the shape is positioned relative to the current text flow location.

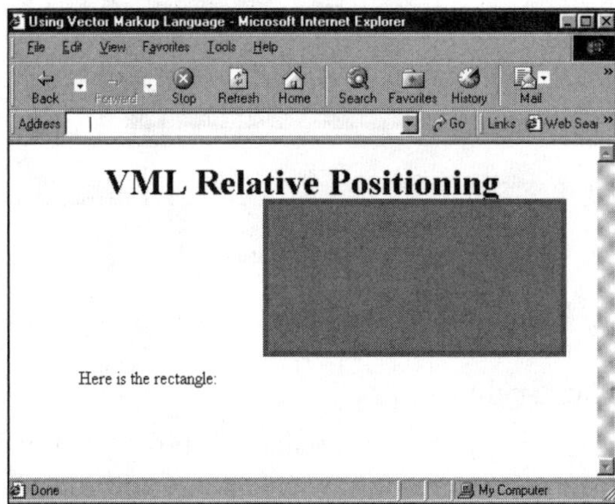

Figure 19.11 Using relative positioning.

The *absolute* Position Style

You can also position shapes in *absolute* terms. When you set the `position` style property to `absolute`, the shape is positioned with respect to the upper-left corner of its container. You can use the `top` and `left` style properties to position the top left of the shape with regard to the container's origin.

Here's an example. In this case, I'll position a VML shape 100 points from the top and left of the shape's container, which is the browser's display area in this case:

```
<HTML xmlns:v="urn:schemas-microsoft-com:vml">

    <HEAD>
        <TITLE>
            Using Vector Markup Language
        </TITLE>

        <STYLE>
            v\:* {behavior: url(#default#VML);}
        </STYLE>
    </HEAD>

    <BODY>
        <CENTER>
            <H1>
                VML Absolute Positioning
            </H1>
            Here is the rectangle:
            <v:rect style='position:absolute;left:100pt;
                top:100pt;width:200pt;height:100pt'
                fillcolor="red" strokecolor="green"
                strokeweight="4pt"/>
        </CENTER>
    </BODY>
</HTML>
```

You can see the results in Figure 19.12. The rectangle is positioned in absolute terms in the browser's display area; note that when you position shapes absolutely, they are not considered part of the text flow.

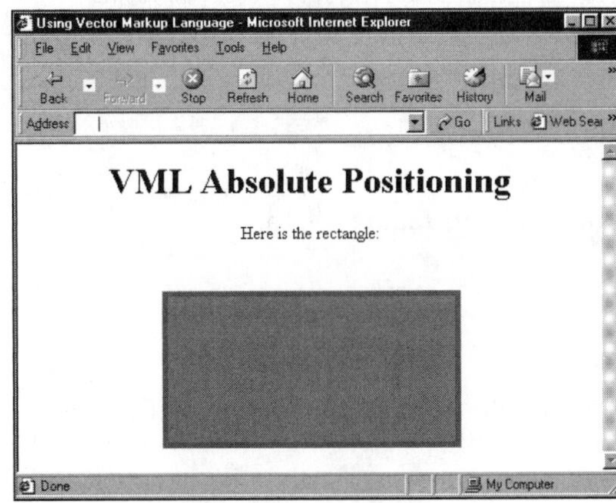

Figure 19.12 Using absolute positioning.

The *z-index* Position Style

It is possible to position a shape that overlaps another shape. In VML, you can control the z-order by using the `z-index` style attribute. You can set this attribute to zero, a positive integer, or a negative integer. The shape that has a larger `z-index` value appears on top of the shape that has a smaller `z-index` value. When both shapes have the same `z-index` value, the shape that was displayed last appears on top.

For example, in the following VML, the blue oval is displayed on top of the red rectangle. This is because the `z-index` value of the blue oval is greater than the `z-index` value of the red rectangle:

```
<HTML xmlns:v="urn:schemas-microsoft-com:vml">

    <HEAD>
        <TITLE>
            Using Vector Markup Language
        </TITLE>

        <STYLE>
            v\:* {behavior: url(#default#VML);}
        </STYLE>
    </HEAD>

    <BODY>
        <CENTER>
            <H1>
                VML Z-Index Positioning
            </H1>
            <v:rect style='position:absolute;left:100pt;top:100pt;
             width:200pt;height:100pt;z-index:0'
                fillcolor="red" strokecolor="green"
                strokeweight="4pt"/>
            <v:oval style='position:absolute;left:150pt;top:60pt;
                width:100pt;height:100pt;z-index:1'
                fillcolor="blue" />
        </CENTER>
    </BODY>
</HTML>
```

You can see the results in Figure 19.13.

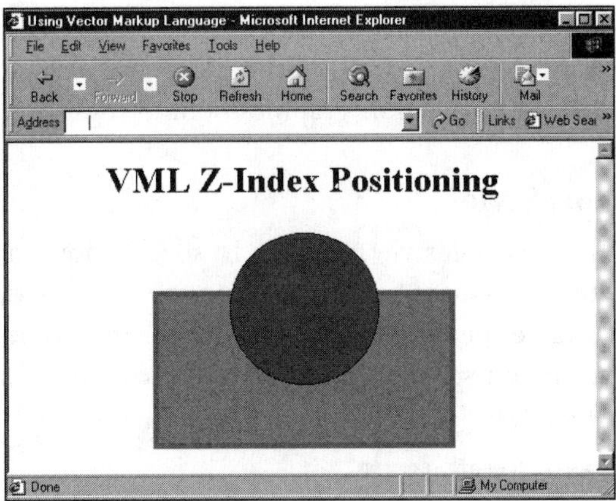

Figure 19.13 Using `z-index` positioning.

If you reverse the `z-index` of the shapes, the blue oval would move behind the red rectangle:

```
<v:rect style='position:absolute;left:100pt;top:100pt;
 width:200pt;height:100pt;z-index:1'
    fillcolor="red" strokecolor="green"
    strokeweight="4pt"/>
<v:oval style='position:absolute;left:150pt;top:60pt;
    width:100pt;height:100pt;z-index:0'
     fillcolor="blue" />
```

You can see the new result in Figure 19.14.

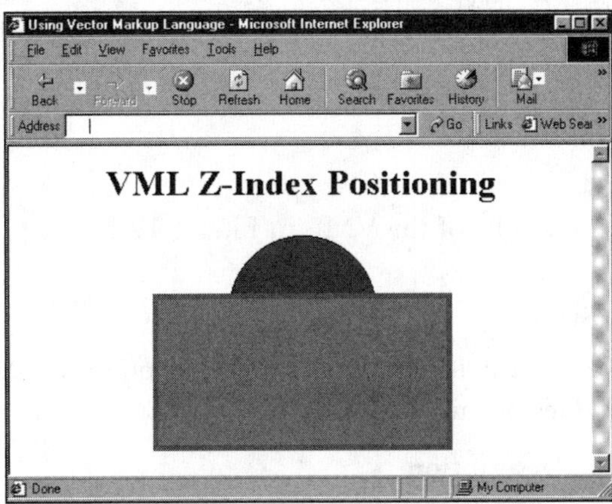

Figure 19.14 Reversing `z-index` positioning.

Positive `z-index` values are considered out of the screen, and negative values are considered into the screen. Note that if you provide a negative integer, you can use `z-index` to position graphics behind the normal flow of text.

The *rotation* Position Style

You can use the `rotation` style property to specify how many degrees you want a shape to be rotated. A positive value specifies a clockwise rotation, and a negative value specifies a counterclockwise rotation.

For example, if you specify `style='rotation:45'`, you can rotate this rectangle 45° clockwise:

```
<HTML xmlns:v="urn:schemas-microsoft-com:vml">

    <HEAD>
        <TITLE>
            Using Vector Markup Language
        </TITLE>

        <STYLE>
            v\:* {behavior: url(#default#VML);}
        </STYLE>
    </HEAD>

    <BODY>
        <CENTER>
            <H1>
                VML Rotation Positioning
            </H1>
            <v:rect style='position:absolute;left:100pt;top:100pt;
                width:200pt;height:100pt;rotation:45'
                fillcolor="red" strokecolor="green"
                strokeweight="4pt"/>
        </CENTER>
    </BODY>
</HTML>
```

You can see the results of this VML in Figure 19.15.

The *flip* Position Style

You can use the `flip` style attribute to flip a shape on its x or y axis. Here are the possible values of this property:

Value	Description
`x`	Flip the rotated shape about the y axis
`y`	Flip the rotated shape about the x axis

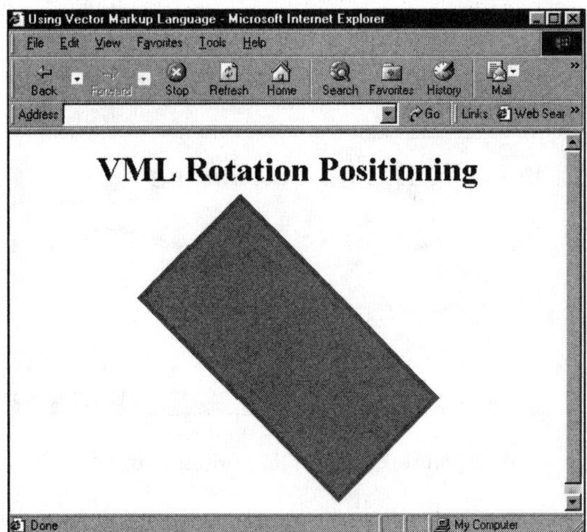

Figure 19.15 Rotation positioning.

You can use either `x` or `y` or both. If you use `style='flip:x y'`, the shape will flip on both its x and y axis. As an example, here's how to flip the shape in Figure 19.7, with respect to the y axis:

```
<HTML xmlns:v="urn:schemas-microsoft-com:vml">

    <HEAD>
        <TITLE>
            Using Vector Markup Language
        </TITLE>

        <STYLE>
            v\:* {behavior: url(#default#VML);}
        </STYLE>
    </HEAD>

    <BODY>
        <CENTER>
            <H1>
                VML Flip Positioning
            </H1>
            <v:polyline points="0pt,0pt,90pt,-9pt,180pt,60pt,0pt,
                20pt -180pt,60pt,-90pt,-9pt,0pt,0pt"
                style="flip: y"
                strokecolor="red" strokeweight="2pt"/>
        </CENTER>
    </BODY>
</HTML>
```

The flipped shape appears in Figure 19.16.

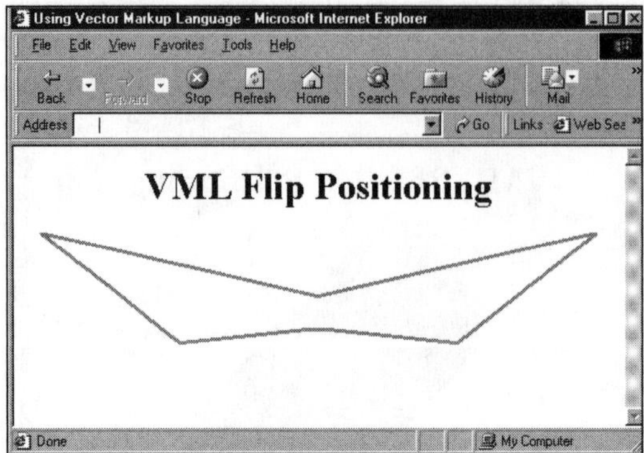

Figure 19.16 Flip positioning.

The *<group>* Element

You can group shapes with the `<group>` element, which enables you to treat a number of shapes as one unit. To create a group, you use the `<group>` element, which supports the `coreattrs` attributes. Here is this element's XML template:

```
<group
id=null
class=null
style='visibility: visible'
title=null
href=null
target=null
alt=null
coordsize="1000, 1000"
coordorigin="0, 0"
wrapcoords=null
/>
```

Here's an example. In this case, I'll group a rectangle and an oval together. I do that by creating a `<group>` element this way:

```
<HTML xmlns:v="urn:schemas-microsoft-com:vml">

    <HEAD>
        <TITLE>
            Using Vector Markup Language
        </TITLE>

        <STYLE>
            v\:* {behavior: url(#default#VML);}
        </STYLE>
```

```
    </HEAD>

    <BODY>
        <CENTER>
            <H1>
                VML Grouping Elements
            </H1>
            <v:group id="Group1" style='position:absolute;
                left:150pt;top:60pt;width:200pt;height:100pt'
                coordsize="100,100">
                .
                .
                .
            </v:group>
        </CENTER>
    </BODY>
</HTML>
```

You position grouped shapes together, so I'm specifying the absolute position and dimensions of the group with the `<group>` element's `style` property.

Here's an important point—the shapes in a group use the group's coordinate system because the group is their container. To specify the group's coordinates, you can use the `coordsize` and `coordorigin` attributes. By default, the coordinate size is set to 1000 × 1000, and the origin is set to (0, 0) in a group (there are no units for these values—they're relative measurements expressed simply as numbers).

In this example, I've set the coordinate size to 100 × 100, so I draw the contained shapes using that coordinate system:

```
<HTML xmlns:v="urn:schemas-microsoft-com:vml">

    <HEAD>
        <TITLE>
            Using Vector Markup Language
        </TITLE>

        <STYLE>
            v\:* {behavior: url(#default#VML);}
        </STYLE>
    </HEAD>

    <BODY>
        <CENTER>
            <H1>
                VML Grouping Elements
            </H1>
            <v:group id="Group1" style='position:absolute;
                left:150pt;top:60pt;width:200pt;height:100pt'
                coordsize="100,100">
```

continues ▶

```
            <v:rect
                fillcolor="red" strokecolor="green"
                style='width:50;height:50'
                strokeweight="4pt" />
            <v:oval
                fillcolor="blue"
                style='width:50;height:50' />
        </v:group>
    </CENTER>
  </BODY>
</HTML>
```

You can see the results of this VML in Figure 19.17. The group of shapes is treated as one unit, which is useful because it enables you to position and scale all the shapes in the group at once.

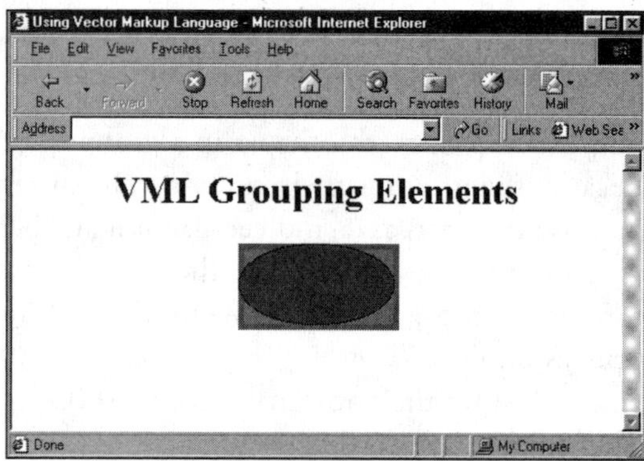

Figure 19.17 Grouping elements.

The *<shadow>* Element

You can use the `<shadow>` element to add shadows to VML shapes, as well as create embossing effects and even double shadows. Here's the attribute list for this element:

```
<!attlist shadow
id id #implied -- document-wide unique id --
on cdata #implied
type cdata #implied
obscured cdata #implied
color cdata #implied
opacity cdata #implied
offset cdata #implied
color2 cdata #implied
```

```
offset2 cdata #implied
origin cdata #implied
matrix cdata #implied
>
```

You can find the attributes of this element in Table 19.3.

Table 19.3 **Attributes of the *<shadow>* Element**

Namespace	Attribute	Type	Default Value	Description
VML	`color`	Boolean	`gray RGB (128,128,128)`	Sets the color of the primary shadow.
VML	`color2`	Boolean	`gray RGB (203,203,203)`	Sets the color of the second shadow, or the highlight in an embossed shadow.
VML	`id`	string	`null`	Gives a unique identifier for the shadow.
VML	`matrix`	string	`null`	Is a perspective transform matrix using the form `"scalexx,scalexy,scaleyx, scaleyy,perspectivex, perspectivey"`. The perspective units are measured in inverse fractions of the shape size.
VML	`obscured`	Boolean	`false`	Determines whether you can see the shadow if the shape is not filled.
VML	`offset`	vector2D	`2pt,2pt`	Amount of x,y offset for the shadow from the shape's location.
VML	`offset2`	vector2D	`0pt,0pt`	Amount of x,y offset for the second shadow from the shape's location.
VML	`on`	Boolean	`true`	Turns the display of the shadow on and off.
VML	`opacity`	number	`1.0`	Sets the opacity of the shadow.
VML	`origin`	vector2D	`0,0`	Sets the origin. Set this to fractional values.
VML	`type`	string	`single`	Sets the shadow type. This can be single, double, emboss, or perspective.

This is the XML template for this element:

```
<shadow
id=null
on="false"
type="single"
obscured="false"
color="rgb(128,128,128)"
opacity="1.0"
offset="2pt,2pt"
color2="rgb(203,203,203)"
opacity2="1.0"
offset2="0pt,0pt"
origin="0,0"
matrix=null
</shadow>
```

You place the `<shadow>` element inside the `<shape>`, `<shapetype>`, or any predefined shape element to draw a shape with a shadow. When creating a shadow, the tricky part is getting the perspective transform matrix to indicate how to create the shadow as you want it. In this example, I've created a matrix that will add a shadow to any VML shape—that shape is a rectangle here, but you can use an oval or whatever you like—pointing to the right and up at 45°:

```
<HTML xmlns:v="urn:schemas-microsoft-com:vml">

    <HEAD>
        <TITLE>
            Using Vector Markup Language
        </TITLE>

        <STYLE>
        v\:* {behavior: url(#default#VML);}
        </STYLE>
    </HEAD>

    <BODY>
        <CENTER>
            <H1>
                VML Shadows
            </H1>
            <v:rect style='width:120pt;height:100pt;'
                fillcolor="blue">
                <v:shadow on="true" type="perspective"
                origin=".5,.5"
                matrix="1,-1,0,1,0,-5e-7"/>
            </v:rect>
        </CENTER>
    </BODY>
</HTML>
```

The result appears in Figure 19.18, where you can see the shadow apparently coming from a light source at the lower left.

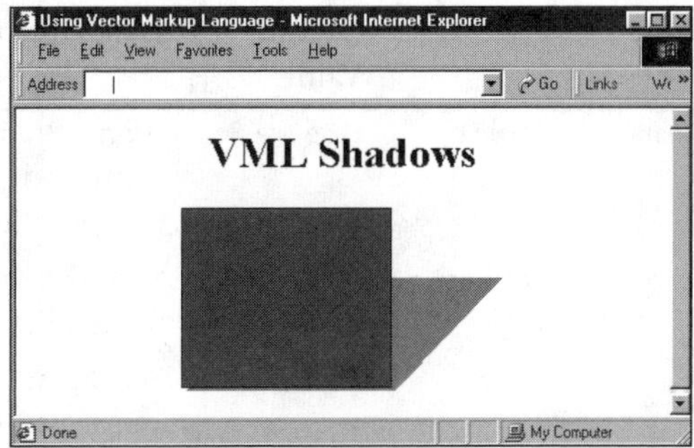

Figure 19.18 Creating VML shadows.

The *<fill>* Element

As we've seen, you can use the `fill` attribute to set fill colors. The `<fill>` element works like the `fill` attribute, except that it's an element you enclose in VML shape elements. I'll take a look at this element here, including some of its more advanced capabilities. Here is the attribute list for the `<fill>` element:

```
<!attlist fill
id id #implied -- document-wide unique id --
type cdata #implied
on cdata #implied
color cdata #implied
color2 cdata #implied
opacity cdata #implied
src cdata #implied
size cdata #implied
origin cdata #implied
position cdata #implied
alignshape cdata #implied
colors cdata #implied
angle cdata #implied
focus cdata #implied
focussize cdata #implied
focusposition cdata #implied
method cdata #implied
>
```

You can find these attributes explained in Table 19.4.

Table 19.4 **Attributes of the <*fill*> Element**

Namespace	Attribute	Type	Default Value	Description
VML	`alignshape`	Boolean	`true`	Aligns the image with the shape if true; otherwise, aligns the image with the window.
VML	`angle`	number	`"0"`	Specifies the angle along which the gradient is directed.
VML	`aspect`	string	`"ignore"`	Set this to `"ignore"` to ignore aspect issues, to `"atleast"` to specify that the image is at least as big as imageSize, or to `"atmost"` to specify that the image is no bigger than imageSize.
VML	`color`	color	`"white"`	Sets the fill color.
VML	`color2`	color	`"white"`	Sets the secondary fill color for patterns.
VML	`colors`	string	`null`	Sets intermediate colors in the gradient and their relative positions along the gradient—for example: `"20% red, 60% blue, 80% green"`.
VML	`focus`	number	`"0"`	Sets the focus point for linear gradient fill; possible values range from –100 to 100.
VML	`focusposition`	Vector2D	`0,0`	For radial gradients, sets the position of the innermost rectangle.
VML	`focussize`	Vector2D	`0,0`	For radial gradients, sets the size of the innermost rectangle.
VML	`id`	string	`null`	Gives a unique identifier for the shape.
VML	`method`	string	`"sigma"`	Sets the fill method; set this to `"none"`, `"linear"`, `"sigma"` or `"any"`.
VML	`on`	Boolean	`true`	Turns fill display on or off.
VML	`opacity`	number	`1.0`	Sets the opacity of the fill.

Namespace	Attribute	Type	Default Value	Description
VML	`origin`	Vector2D	`"auto"`	Sets the origin, relative to the upper left of the image. By default, sets to the center of the image.
VML	`position`	Vector2D	`"auto"`	Is a point in the reference rectangle of the shape used to position the origin of the image. Specified as a fraction of the image size.
VML	`size`	Vector2D	`"auto"`	Gives the size of the image.
VML	`src`	string	`null`	Gives the URI of an image to load for image and pattern fills.
VML	`type`	string	`"solid"`	Sets the fill type. May be `"solid"`, `"gradient"`, `"gradientradial"`, `"tile"`, `"pattern"`, or `"frame"`.

This is the XML template for this element, showing the default values for its attributes:

```
<fill
id=null
type="solid"
on="true"
color="white"
opacity="1.0"
color2="white"
opacity2="1.0"
src=null
size="auto"
origin="center"
position="center"
aspect="ignore"
alignshape="true"
colors=null
angle="0"
focus="0"
focussize="0,0"
focusposition="0,0"
method="sigma"
/>
```

You can create all kinds of fills, such as gradient fills, pattern fills, and picture fills.

Creating Gradient Fills

To draw a gradient-filled shape, you can set the `type` property attribute of the `<fill>` subelement to `"gradient"` or `"gradientradial"`, and then specify other property attributes of the `<fill>` subelement, such as `method`, `color2`, `focus`, and `angle`. Here's an example; in this case, I'm creating a shaded egg shape with a standard gradient fill:

```
<HTML xmlns:v="urn:schemas-microsoft-com:vml">

    <HEAD>
        <TITLE>
            Using Vector Markup Language
        </TITLE>

        <STYLE>
        v\:* {behavior: url(#default#VML);}
        </STYLE>
    </HEAD>

    <BODY>
        <CENTER>
            <H1>
                VML Gradient Fills
            </H1>
            <v:oval style='width:200pt;height:100pt'
                fillcolor="blue" strokecolor="white">
                <v:fill method="linear sigma" angle="45"
                 type="gradient" />
            </v:oval>
        </CENTER>
    </BODY>
</HTML>
```

You can see the results of this VML in Figure 19.19.

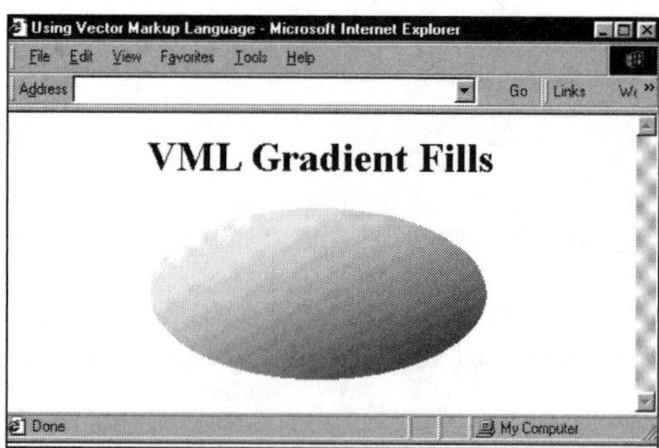

Figure 19.19 A gradient fill.

Another option is the `gradientradial` fill type, where the fill gradient is directed radially. Here's an example, this time with a rectangle:

```
<HTML xmlns:v="urn:schemas-microsoft-com:vml">

    <HEAD>
        <TITLE>
            Using Vector Markup Language
        </TITLE>

        <STYLE>
        v\:* {behavior: url(#default#VML);}
        </STYLE>
    </HEAD>

    <BODY>
        <CENTER>
            <H1>
                VML Gradient Radial Fills
            </H1>
            <v:rect style='width:200pt;height:100pt'
                fillcolor="blue" strokecolor="white">
                <v:fill method="linear sigma" angle="45"
                    type="gradientradial" />
            </v:rect>
        </CENTER>
    </BODY>
</HTML>
```

You can see the results of this VML in Figure 19.20.

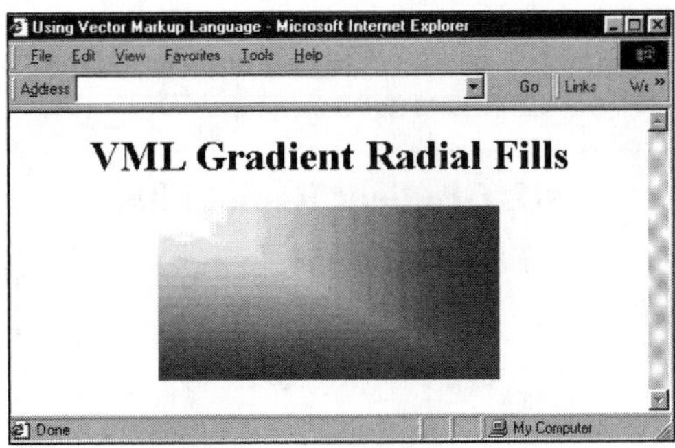

Figure 19.20 A gradient radial fill.

You can also set the origin of gradient radial fills, as in this case, where I'm setting the gradient origin to the center of the rectangle for an intriguing effect:

```
<HTML xmlns:v="urn:schemas-microsoft-com:vml">

    <HEAD>
        <TITLE>
            Using Vector Markup Language
        </TITLE>

        <STYLE>
        v\:* {behavior: url(#default#VML);}
        </STYLE>
    </HEAD>

    <BODY>
        <CENTER>
            <H1>
                VML Gradient Radial Fills
            </H1>
            <v:rect style='width:200pt;height:100pt' fillcolor="blue" strokecolor="white">
                <v:fill method="linear sigma" angle="45"
                    focus="100%" focusposition=".5,.5" focussize="0,0"
                    type="gradientradial" />
            </v:rect>
        </CENTER>
    </BODY>
</HTML>
```

You can see the results of this VML in Figure 19.21.

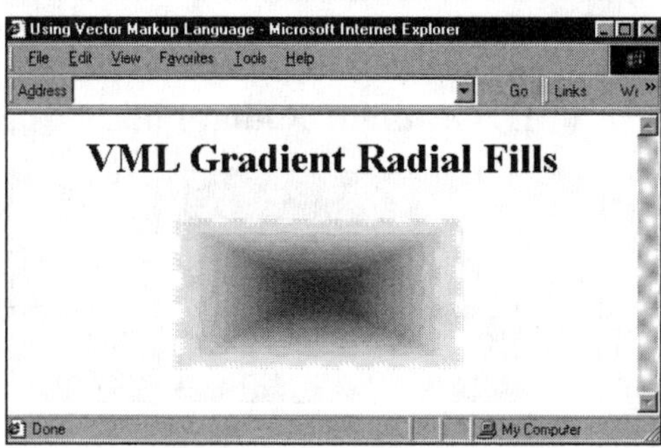

Figure 19.21 A gradient radial fill with origin at the center.

Creating Pattern Fills

To draw a pattern-filled shape, you can set the `type` property attribute of the `<fill>` element to `"pattern"`, and then set the `src` property to the URI of an image file. For example, here's how I use the image `bubbles.bmp`, which comes with Windows, as a fill pattern (after converting `bubbles.bmp` to a GIF file so that Internet Explorer can handle it):

```
<HTML xmlns:v="urn:schemas-microsoft-com:vml">

    <HEAD>
        <TITLE>
            Using Vector Markup Language
        </TITLE>

        <STYLE>
        v\:* {behavior: url(#default#VML);}
        </STYLE>
    </HEAD>

    <BODY>
        <CENTER>
            <H1>
                VML Fill Patterns
            </H1>
            <v:rect style='width:200pt;height:100pt'
                fillcolor="blue">
                <v:fill type="pattern" src="bubbles.gif"/>
            </v:rect>
        </CENTER>
    </BODY>
</HTML>
```

Note that you can also specify the color of the fill you want, as in this case, where I'm making it blue (the original image is black and white). You can see the results of this VML in Figure 19.22, where the bubbles pattern is repeatedly tiled inside a rectangle.

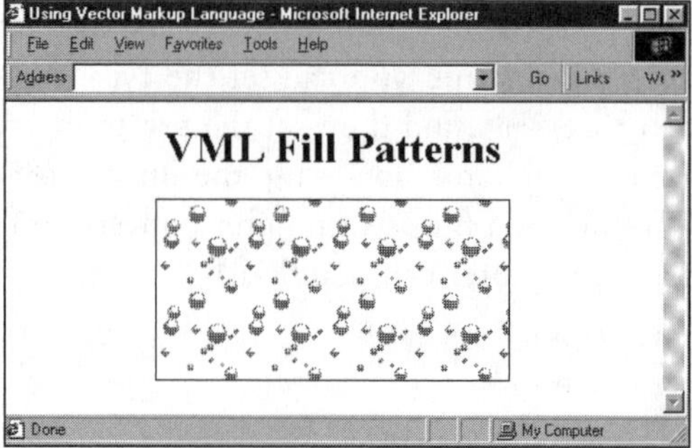

Figure 19.22 A pattern fill.

Creating Picture Fills

To draw a picture-filled shape, you can set the type property attribute of the <fill> element to "frame", and then set the src property to the URI of the image you want to use. Here's an example; in this case, I'll display the image fill.jpg:

```
<HTML xmlns:v="urn:schemas-microsoft-com:vml">

    <HEAD>
        <TITLE>
            Using Vector Markup Language
        </TITLE>

        <STYLE>
        v\:* {behavior: url(#default#VML);}
        </STYLE>
    </HEAD>

    <BODY>
        <CENTER>
            <H1>
                VML Picture Fills
            </H1>
            <v:rect style='width:673px;height:89px'>
                <v:fill type="frame" src="fill.jpg"/>
            </v:rect>
        </CENTER>
    </BODY>
</HTML>
```

You can see the results of this VML in Figure 19.23.

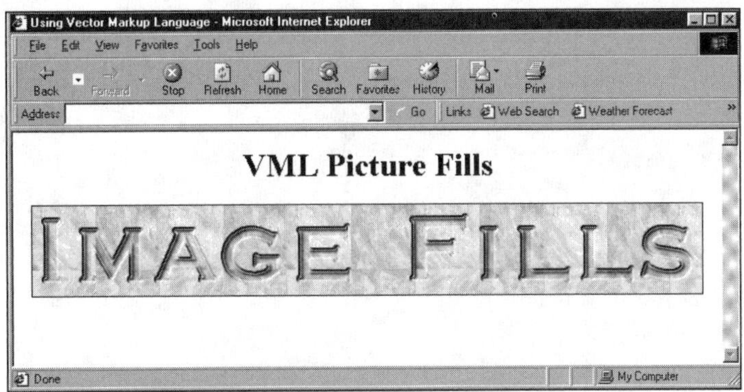

Figure 19.23 A picture fill.

Using the *<shapetype>* Element

You can parameterize the creation of shapes with the `<shapetype>` element. The `<shapetype>` element defines a shape type, and you can instantiate shapes of that type. You create a shape type and give it a name with the ID attribute of `<shapetype>`, and you use that shape type with the `<shape>` element's `type` attribute.

Here's the attribute list of the `<shapetype>` element:

```
<!attlist shapetype %coreattrs; %shapeattrs;
adj cdata #implied -- list of adjust values for parameterized paths --
path cdata #implied -- string with command set describing a path --
>
```

These are the custom attributes of this element:

Attribute	Description
`adj`	A comma-separated list of numbers that are "adjusting" parameters for the formulas that define the path of the shape
`path`	The path that defines the shape; a string containing the commands that define the path

Here is the `<shapetype>` element's XML template:

```
<shapetype
adj=null
path=null
opacity="100%"
chromakey="none"
stroke="true"
strokecolor="black"
strokeweight="0.75pt"
```

continues ►

```
fill="true"
fillcolor="white"
print="true"
id=null
class=null
style='visibility: visible'
title=null
href=null
target=null
alt=null
coordsize="1000, 1000"
coordorigin="0, 0"
wrapcoords=null
/>
```

We saw an example using the <shapetype> element earlier in this chapter. In that example, the shape was defined with the path attribute, like this:

```
<v:shapetype id="Valentine" fillcolor="red"
    strokecolor="red" coordsize="21600,21600"
    path="m10860,2187c10451,1746,9529,1018,9015,730,
    7865,152,6685,,5415,,4175, 152,2995,575,1967,
    1305,1150,2187,575,3222,242,4220,,5410,242,6560,
    575,7597l10860, 21600,20995,7597c21480,6560,
    21600,5410,21480,4220,21115,3222,20420,2187,19632,
    1305,18575,575,17425,152,16275,,15005,,13735,152,
    12705,730,12176,1018,11254,1746, 10860,2187xe">
</v:shapetype>
```

The path defined here defines the shape. Specifying a path in the <shapetype> element is a little involved; you specify pairs of points along the path and use commands such as m (start a path), x (close the path), e (end the path), and so on. You can find the available commands in Table 19.5. This table also indicates how many parameters each command takes, using DTD notation; for example, 2* indicates that the command takes pairs of parameters. You can also skip any values that are zero when specifying points, so the point specification 16275,,15005,,13735,152 is the same as 16275,0,15005,0,13735,152.

Table 19.5 **Commands for the *path* Attribute**

Command	Name	Parameters	Description
ae	angleellipseto	6*	center (*x*,*y*), size (*w*,*h*), start-angle, end-angle. Draws a segment of an ellipse.
al	angleellipse	6*	Same as angleellipseto, except that there is an implied move to the starting point of the segment.

Command	Name	Parameters	Description
ar	arc	8*	left, top, right, bottom, start (x,y), end (x,y). Same as arcto, except that a new subpath is started by an implied move to the start point.
at	arcto	8*	left, top, right, bottom, start (x,y), end (x,y). The first four values define the bounding box of an ellipse, and the second four define two radial vectors. This command draws a segment of the ellipse, starting at the angle defined by the start radius vector and ending at the angle defined by the end vector.
c	curveto	6*	Draws a cubic bèzier curve from the current point to the coordinate given by the final two parameters. The control points are given by the first four parameters.
e	end	0	End of the current set of subpaths.
l	lineto	2*	Draws a line from the current point to the given point.
m	moveto	2	Begins a new subpath at the given coordinate.
nf	nofill	0	Ensures that the current set of subpaths will not be filled.
ns	nostroke	0	Ensures that the current set of subpaths will not be drawn (stroked).
qb	quadraticbezier	2+2*	(controlpoint(x,y))*, end(x,y) Defines one or more quadratic be`zier curves with a set of control points and an endpoint.

continues

Table 19.5 **Coontinued**

Command	Name	Parameters	Description
qx	ellipticalqaudrantx	2*	end(*x*,*y*). Draws a quarter ellipse from the current point to the endpoint.
qy	ellipticalquadranty	2*	end(*x*,*y*). Same as ellipticalquadrantx, except that the segment starts out vertical.
r	rlineto	2*	Draws a line from the current point to the given point.
t	rmoveto	2*	Starts a new subpath at the indicated coordinate.
v	rcurveto	6*	Creates a cubic bèzier curve using the given coordinate relative to the current point.
wa	clockwisearcto	8*	left, top, right, bottom, start (*x*,*y*), end (*x*,*y*). Same as arcto, except that here the arc is drawn in a clockwise direction.
wr	clockwisearc	8*	left, top, right, bottom start (*x*,*y*), end (*x*,*y*). Same as arc, except here the arc is drawn in a clockwise direction.
x	close	0	Closes the current subpath. Draws a straight line from the current point to the original moveto point.

Here's how you can use this <shapetype> element to create a shape as we've done earlier in the chapter:

```
<HTML xmlns:v="urn:schemas-microsoft-com:vml">

    <HEAD>
        <TITLE>
            Using Vector Markup Language
        </TITLE>

        <STYLE>
        v\:* {behavior: url(#default#VML);}
        </STYLE>
    </HEAD>
```

```
    <BODY>
        <CENTER>
            <H1>
                VML Shapes
            </H1>
            <v:shapetype id="Valentine" fillcolor="red"
                strokecolor="red" coordsize="21600,21600"
                path="m10860,2187c10451,1746,9529,1018,9015,730,
                7865,152,6685,,5415,,4175, 152,2995,575,1967,
                1305,1150,2187,575,3222,242,4220,,5410,242,6560,
                575,7597l10860, 21600,20995,7597c21480,6560,
                21600,5410,21480,4220,21115,3222,20420,2187,19632,
                1305,18575,575,17425,152,16275,,15005,,13735,152,
                12705,730,12176,1018,11254,1746, 10860,2187xe">
            </v:shapetype>
            <v:shape type="#Valentine" style='width:200;height:160;'/>
        </CENTER>
    </BODY>
</HTML>
```

The results of this VML appear earlier in Figure 19.2.

You can list properties for the shape in the `<shapetype>` element, as in this example, which assigns a value to the `fillcolor` property. However, if you want to override those properties, you can do so; just specify new values in the `<shape>` element when you instantiate the shape. For example, here's how I turn the heart this VML draws blue:

```
<HTML xmlns:v="urn:schemas-microsoft-com:vml">

    <HEAD>
        <TITLE>
            Using Vector Markup Language
        </TITLE>

        <STYLE>
        v\:* {behavior: url(#default#VML);}
        </STYLE>
    </HEAD>

    <BODY>
        <CENTER>
            <H1>
                VML Shapes
            </H1>
            <v:shapetype id="Valentine" fillcolor="red"
                strokecolor="red" coordsize="21600,21600"
                path="m10860,2187c10451,1746,9529,1018,9015,730,
                7865,152,6685,,5415,,4175, 152,2995,575,1967,
                1305,1150,2187,575,3222,242,4220,,5410,242,6560,
```

continues ▶

```
            575,7597l10860, 21600,20995,7597c21480,6560,
            21600,5410,21480,4220,21115,3222,20420,2187,19632,
            1305,18575,575,17425,152,16275,,15005,,13735,152,
            12705,730,12176,1018,11254,1746, 10860,2187xe">
        </v:shapetype>
        <v:shape type="#Valentine" fillcolor="blue"
            style='width:200;height:160;'/>
    </CENTER>
  </BODY>
</HTML>
```

More Advanced VML

Besides the material we've seen in this chapter, there's plenty more in VML. Like many graphics languages, VML has a lot of depth. Here's a last example, adapted from the examples in the Microsoft VML reference, which displays text along a VML *text path*, specified using VML *formulae*:

```
<HTML xmlns:v="urn:schemas-microsoft-com:vml">

    <HEAD>
        <TITLE>
            Using Vector Markup Language
        </TITLE>

        <STYLE>
        v\:* {behavior: url(#default#VML);}
        </STYLE>
    </HEAD>

    <BODY>
        <CENTER>
            <H1>
                VML Text Paths
            </H1>
            <v:shapetype id="MyShape"
                coordsize="21600,21600" adj="9931"
                path="m0@0c7200@2,14400@1,21600,
                0m0@5c7200@6,14400@6,21600@5e">
                <v:formulas>
                    <v:f eqn="val #0"/>
                    <v:f eqn="prod #0 3 4"/>
                    <v:f eqn="prod #0 5 4"/>
                    <v:f eqn="prod #0 3 8"/>
                    <v:f eqn="prod #0 1 8"/>
                    <v:f eqn="sum 21600 0 @3"/>
                    <v:f eqn="sum @4 21600 0"/>
                    <v:f eqn="prod #0 1 2"/>
                    <v:f eqn="prod @5 1 2"/>
                    <v:f eqn="sum @7 @8 0"/>
                    <v:f eqn="prod #0 7 8"/>
```

```
                <v:f eqn="prod @5 1 3"/>
                <v:f eqn="sum @1 @2 0"/>
                <v:f eqn="sum @12 @0 0"/>
                <v:f eqn="prod @13 1 4"/>
                <v:f eqn="sum @11 14400 @14"/>
            </v:formulas>
            <v:path textpathok="t" />
            <v:textpath on="t" fitshape="t" xscale="t"/>
        </v:shapetype>

        <v:shape type="#MyShape"
            style='position:absolute; top:60pt; left:60pt;
            width:207pt;height:63pt;' adj="8717"
            fillcolor="blue" strokeweight="1pt">
            <v:fill method="linear sigma" focus="100%"
            type="gradient"/>
            <v:shadow on="t" offset="3pt"/>
            <v:textpath style='font-family:"Times New Roman";
                v-text-kern:t'trim="t" fitpath="t" xscale="f"
                string="VML"/>
        </v:shape>
    </CENTER>
  </BODY>
</HTML>
```

You can see the results of this VML in Figure 19.24. You may have seen text graphics like this in Microsoft Office products such as Word and PowerPoint, and now you know how it's done.

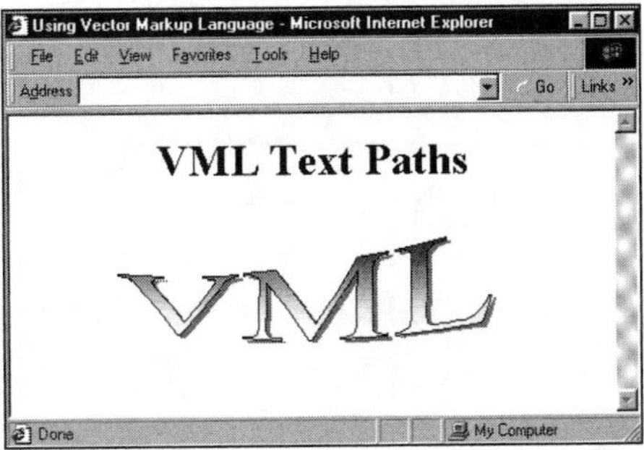

Figure 19.24 Using a VML text path.

For more information on VML, take a look at the Microsoft VML site. VML is a powerful language, but it's limited to Internet Explorer. One day, browsers will implement a W3C language such as SVG, and I'll be able to rewrite this chapter.

It's time to take a look at using Perl and XML on the server side, and I'm going to do that in the next chapter.

20

WML, ASP, JSP, Servlets, and Perl

THIS CHAPTER COVERS A NUMBER OF TOPICS, including Wireless Markup Language (WML), a popular XML application targeted at cordless phones, PDAs, and other relatively simple devices that support the Wireless Application Protocol (WAP). WML is easy to use; you can find it in many places these days, and WAP servers are popping up all over. This chapter takes a look at creating WML documents and viewing them in WML browsers (often called microbrowsers).

This chapter is also about using XML with existing server technologies such as Active Server Pages (ASP), Java Server Pages (JSP), Java servlets, and Perl. A lot of companies are jumping on the XML-on-the-Internet bandwagon, with a resulting explosion of XML Internet software—take a look at Microsoft's page at `http://msdn.microsoft.com/xml/demos/default.asp` for a survey. One popular server-side technology is the Simple Object Access Protocol (SOAP). SOAP is a simple protocol for message exchange in a distributed environment—and those messages are written in XML. SOAP is often used to send commands in HTTP headers because remote method invocation protocols such as Microsoft's DCOM haven't really proven simple enough or adaptable enough to be extended to the Internet. In fact, Microsoft is one of the heavy hitters in SOAP, which may make you wonder what its future plans are for DCOM. IBM and Lotus are also involved.

More on SOAP

With a common name like SOAP, it's hard to search the Internet for more information unless you're really into pages on personal cleanliness and daytime television. For more information, check out this starter list:

- http://msdn.microsoft.com/xml/general/soapspec.asp
- www.oasis-open.org/cover/soap.html, www.develop.com/soap/
- www.develop.com/soap/soapfaq.xml

This chapter takes a look at how to create XML documents from the server side. To do that, I'll extract data from a database file, db.mdb, written in common Microsoft Access format, on various servers. Then I'll format that data using XML and send the resulting XML back to the client. This database file was written to be a simple example, holding just the names of eight students and a letter grade for each student, as shown in Table 20.1.

Table 20.1 **Students in db.mdb**

Student	Grade
Ann	C
Mark	B
Ed	A
Frank	A
Ted	A
Mabel	B
Ralph	B
Tom	B

I'll start by using ActiveX Data Objects (ADO) on a server to search db.mdb and create an XML document displaying the results with Active Server Pages.

Server-Side Programming

The first half of this chapter, which describes server-side programming, moves through many technologies fairly quickly. Unfortunately, there's no way to provide all the background you need to program in Active Server Pages, Java Server Pages, Java servlets, and Perl here; you can find that background elsewhere if you need it. When discussing WML (an XML application) in the second half of the chapter, I don't make any such assumptions. There, I'll start from the ground up.

XML and Active Server Pages

Active Server Pages (*ASP*) is a Microsoft Internet server-side technology that lets you create Web documents on the fly; it runs on servers such as the Microsoft Internet Information Server (IIS). In this case, I'll search db.mdb for the names of the students and return them in an XML document like this, using `<document>` as the document element and `<student>` for each student:

```
<?xml version="1.0"?>
<document>
    <student>
        Ann
    </student>
    <student>
        Mark
    </student>
    <student>
        Ed
    </student>
    <student>
        Frank
    </student>
    <student>
        Ted
    </student>
    <student>
        Mabel
    </student>
    <student>
        Ralph
    </student>
    <student>
        Tom
    </student>
</document>
```

The main trick in the .asp file is to make sure that your code creates an XML document because the default document type is HTML. If the content type item in the HTTP header doesn't indicate that a document is XML, the browser won't treat it as an XML document (and probably will treat it as HTML). You do this in the ASP script with `<% Response.ContentType %>`, setting the content type header item to `"application/xml"` this way:

```
<% Response.ContentType = "application/xml" %>
     .
     .
     .
```

I also need to add the XML declaration for the resulting document as well as the document element, <document>:

```
<% Response.ContentType = "application/xml" %>

<?xml version="1.0"?>
<document>
    .
    .
    .
```

Now I need to fetch the names of the students from db.mdb. I'll do this using the Microsoft ADO protocol because ASP is targeted to run on Microsoft platforms such as IIS. I'll create an ADO connection to db.mdb and use an SQL statement to return a record set of all records:

```
<% Response.ContentType = "application/xml" %>

<?xml version="1.0"?>
<document>
<%

DIM adoConnect
DIM adoRecordset

Set adoConnect = Server.CreateObject("ADODB.Connection")

adoConnect.open "Provider=Microsoft.Jet.OLEDB.4.0;" _
    & "Data Source=C:\xml\db.mdb"

Set adoRecordset = adoConnect.Execute("SELECT * FROM Students")
    .
    .
    .
```

All that's left is to loop over each record and create the corresponding XML <student> element:

```
<% Response.ContentType = "application/xml" %>

<?xml version="1.0"?>
<document>

<%

DIM adoConnect
DIM adoRecordset

Set adoConnect = Server.CreateObject("ADODB.Connection")

adoConnect.open "Provider=Microsoft.Jet.OLEDB.4.0;" _
    & "Data Source=C:\xml\db.mdb"
```

```
Set adoRecordset = adoConnect.Execute("SELECT * FROM Students")

Do While Not adoRecordset.EOF
    Response.Write "<student>" + adoRecordset("Name") + "</student>"
    adoRecordset.MoveNext
Loop

adoRecordset.Close

set adoRecordset = Nothing

%>
</document>
```

That creates the XML we want. Figure 20.1 shows the results created by this ASP file.

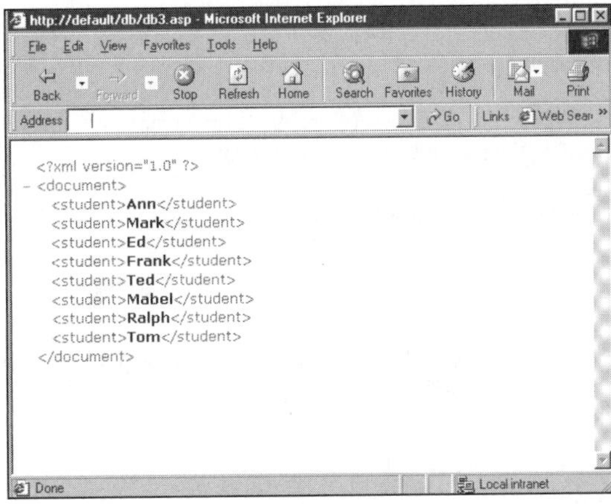

Figure 20.1 Creating XML documents with ASP.

Note that the next few figures look a lot like this one; be sure to watch the title bars for differences.

XML and Java Servlets

Java servlets are supposed to be to Web servers what Java applets are to Web clients. You can use servlets to create Web documents on suitably enabled servers. To create servlets, you can download the Java Servlet Development Kit (JSDK) from `java.sun.com` (as of this writing, the main page for servlets is `http://java.sun.com/products/servlet/index.html`) and create servlets using the classes in servlet.jar and server.jar.

To read the names of the students from db.mdb, I'll use the Java Database Connectivity package (JBDC), interfacing to db.mdb after registering that database as an open database connectivity (ODBC) data source. After searching for all the students, I'll return their names in an XML document and send that document back to the client.

Again, the key here is to create an XML document, not the default HTML document. In servlets, you create an XML document with the `ServletResponse` class's `setContentType` method, setting the content type to `"application/xml"` like this:

```
import java.net.*;
import java.sql.*;
import java.awt.*;
import java.awt.event.*;
import java.io.*;
import javax.servlet.*;

public class xml extends GenericServlet
{
    public void service(ServletRequest request, ServletResponse
        response) throws ServletException, IOException
    {
        response.setContentType("application/xml");
    .
    .
    .
```

Next, I send the XML declaration and document element back to the client:

```
import java.net.*;
import java.sql.*;
import java.awt.*;
import java.awt.event.*;
import java.io.*;
import javax.servlet.*;

public class xml extends GenericServlet
{
    Connection connection;
    Statement statement;

    public void service(ServletRequest request, ServletResponse
        response) throws ServletException, IOException
    {
        response.setContentType("application/xml");
        PrintWriter printwriter = response.getWriter();

        printwriter.println("<?xml version=\"1.0\"?>");
        printwriter.println("<document>");
    .
    .
    .
```

At this point, I can use JDBC to create a result set with all records from db.mdb, using an SQL statement:

```
import java.net.*;
import java.sql.*;
import java.awt.*;
import java.awt.event.*;
import java.io.*;
import javax.servlet.*;

public class xml extends GenericServlet
{
    Connection connection;
    Statement statement;

    public void service(ServletRequest request, ServletResponse
        response) throws ServletException, IOException
    {
        response.setContentType("application/xml");
        PrintWriter printwriter = response.getWriter();

        printwriter.println("<?xml version=\"1.0\"?>");
        printwriter.println("<document>");

        try
        {
            Class.forName("sun.jdbc.odbc.JdbcOdbcDriver");

            connection = DriverManager.getConnection(
                "jdbc:odbc:students", "Steve", "password");

            statement = connection.createStatement();

            String SQL = "SELECT Name FROM Students";
            ResultSet resultset = statement.executeQuery(SQL);
    .
    .
    .
```

All that's left is to loop over the result set with the next method, getting the student names and sending them back to the client in `<student>` elements like this:

```
import java.net.*;
import java.sql.*;
import java.awt.*;
import java.awt.event.*;
import java.io.*;
import javax.servlet.*;
```

```
public class xml extends GenericServlet
{
    Connection connection;
    Statement statement;

    public void service(ServletRequest request, ServletResponse
        response) throws ServletException, IOException
    {
        response.setContentType("application/xml");
        PrintWriter printwriter = response.getWriter();

        printwriter.println("<?xml version=\"1.0\"?>");
        printwriter.println("<document>");

        try
        {
             Class.forName("sun.jdbc.odbc.JdbcOdbcDriver");

             connection = DriverManager.getConnection(
                 "jdbc:odbc:students", "Steve", "password");

             statement = connection.createStatement();

             String SQL = "SELECT Name FROM Students";
             ResultSet resultset = statement.executeQuery(SQL);

             while (resultset.next()) {
                 printwriter.println("<student>" +
                 resultset.getString(1) + "</student>");
             }
        }
        catch(Exception e) {}

        printwriter.println("</document>");
        printwriter.close();
    }
}
```

And that's all it takes. This servlet is running in Figure 20.2, where the same XML document discussed in the preceding section is delivered to the client.

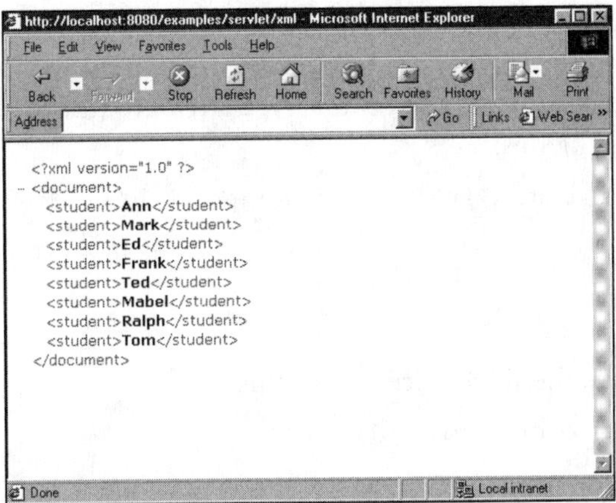

Figure 20.2 Creating XML documents with Java servlets.

Another Java technology that's becoming popular for serving XML documents is Java Server Pages, as discussed in the next section.

Java Server Pages

Java Server Pages (*JSP*) are Java's answer to Active Server Pages, and they enable you to create dynamic Web content in much the same way—by running scripts on the server. You can read all about them at the main JSP page (as of this writing, `http://java.sun.com/products/jsp/index.html`). Using JSP is fairly close to using ASP.

In this example, I'll use the Apache Tomcat server, which is the official reference implementation for JSP (and Java servlets, for that matter). You can download Tomcat at the Tomcat main page, currently at `http://jakarta.apache.org/tomcat/`.

I'll create the same XML document as in the previous two examples by searching db.mdb for all students and returning them in an XML document. Because we're working in Java again here, I'll use JDBC to connect to db.mdb.

Again, a major point is to make sure that the content type of the document we send to the client is `"application/xml"`, not the default HTML type. In JSP, you do that with the `contentType` attribute (this one took me a while to find out), like this:

```
<%@ page language="java" contentType="application/xml"
    import="java.sql.*" %>
    .
    .
    .
```

I also initialize the JDBC driver like this:

```
<%@ page language="java" contentType="application/xml"
    import="java.sql.*" %>

<% Class.forName("sun.jdbc.odbc.JdbcOdbcDriver") ; %>
    .
    .
    .
```

Then I send the XML declaration and the document element back to the client like this:

```
<%@ page language="java" contentType="application/xml"
    import="java.sql.*" %>

<% Class.forName("sun.jdbc.odbc.JdbcOdbcDriver") ; %>

<?xml version="1.0"?>
<document>
    .
    .
    .
```

Now I get a JDBC result set with all the students' records by using an SQL statement:

```
<%@ page language="java" contentType="application/xml"
    import="java.sql.*" %>

<% Class.forName("sun.jdbc.odbc.JdbcOdbcDriver") ; %>

<?xml version="1.0"?>
<document>
```

```
<%
Connection connection = DriverManager.getConnection(
    "jdbc:odbc:students", "Steve", "password");

Statement statement = connection.createStatement() ;
ResultSet resultset =
    statement.executeQuery("select * from Students") ; %>
    .
    .
    .
```

All that's left is to loop over the students' records and send the matching `<student>` elements back to the client:

```
<%@ page language="java" contentType="application/xml"
    import="java.sql.*" %>

<% Class.forName("sun.jdbc.odbc.JdbcOdbcDriver") ; %>

<?xml version="1.0"?>
<document>

<%
Connection connection = DriverManager.getConnection(
    "jdbc:odbc:students", "Steve", "password");

Statement statement = connection.createStatement() ;
ResultSet resultset =
    statement.executeQuery("select * from Students") ; %>

<% while(resultset.next()){ %>
  <student> <%= resultset.getString(1)  %>  </student>
<% } %>

</document>
```

Figure 20.3 shows the results of this JSP script. As the figure shows, JSP works as well as ASP when serving XML documents. In fact, I know plenty of XML developers who prefer JSP over ASP for this purpose because working with XML using Java is so natural, as I've shown in Chapters 11, "Java and the XML DOM," and 12, "Java and SAX."

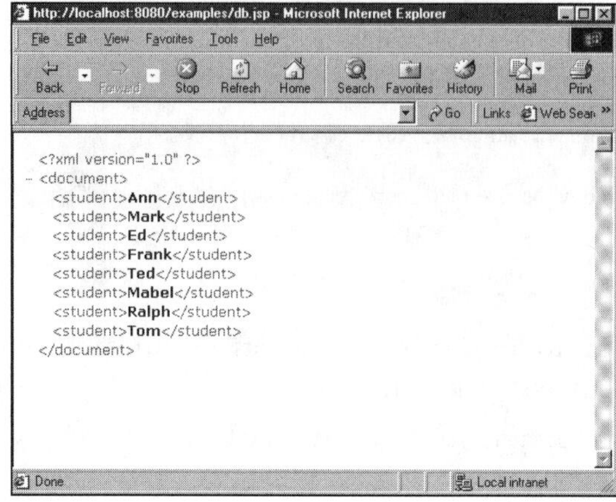

Figure 20.3 Creating XML documents with Java Server Pages.

XML and Perl

The *Practical Extraction and Reporting Language* (*PERL*) has long been a mainstay of server-side programming and a foundation of Common Gateway Interface (CGI) programming. Perl has been getting into XML in a big way, and one could easily write a book on the subject.

Perl modules are distributed at the Comprehensive Perl Archive Network (CPAN) site, at `www.cpan.org`, and plenty of them deal with XML (I counted 156). Table 20.2 provides a selection of Perl XML modules, along with their descriptions as given on the CPAN site.

Table 20.2 **XML Modules in Perl with CPAN Descriptions**

Module	Description
`Apache::AxKit::XMLFinder`	Detects XML files
`Apache::MimeXML`	mod_perl mime encoding sniffer for XML files
`Boulder::XML`	XML format input/output for Boulder streams
`Bundle::XML`	Bundle to install all XML-related modules
`CGI::XMLForm`	Extension of CGI.pm that reads/generates formatted XML
`Data::DumpXML`	Dumps arbitrary data structures as XML
`DBIx::XML_RDB`	Perl extension for creating XML from existing DBI data sources

Module	Description
GoXML::XQI	Perl extension for the XML Query Interface at xqi.goxml.com.
Mail::XML	Adds toXML() method to Mail::Internet.
MARC::XML	Subclass of MARC.pm to provide XML support
PApp::XML	pxml sections and more
XML::Catalog	Resolves public identifiers and remaps system identifiers
XML::CGI	Perl extension for converting CGI.pm variables to/from XML
XML::Checker	Perl module for validating XML
XML::Checker::Parser	XML::Parser that validates at parse time
XML::DOM	Perl module for building DOM Level 1 compliant document structures
XML::DOM::NamedNodeMap	Hash table interface for XML::DOM
XML::DOM::NodeList	Node list as used by XML::DOM
XML::DOM::PerlSAX	Old name of XML::Handler::BuildDOM
XML::DOM::ValParser	XML::DOM::Parser that validates at parse time
XML::Driver::HTML	SAX driver for non–well-formed HTML
XML::DT	Package for down translation of XML to strings
XML::Edifact	Perl module to handle XML::Edifact messages
XML::Encoding	Perl module for parsing XML encoding maps
XML::ESISParser	PerlSAX parser using nsgmls
XML::Filter::DetectWS	PerlSAX filter that detects ignorable whitespace
XML::Filter::Hekeln	SAX stream editor
XML::Filter::Reindent	Reformats whitespace for prettyprinting XML
XML::Filter::SAXT	Replicates SAX events to several SAX event handlers
XML::Generator	Perl extension for generating XML
XML::Grove	Perl-style XML objects
XML::Grove::AsCanonXML	Outputs XML objects in canonical XML
XML::Grove::AsString	Outputs content of XML objects as a string
XML::Grove::Builder	PerlSAX handler for building an XML::Grove
XML::Grove::Factory	Simplifies creation of XML::Grove objects
XML::Grove::Path	Returns the object at a path
XML::Grove::PerlSAX	PerlSAX event interface for XML objects

continues

Table 20.2 **Continued**

Module	Description
`XML::Grove::Sub`	Runs a filter sub over a grove
`XML::Grove::Subst`	Substitutes values into a template
`XML::Handler::BuildDOM`	PerlSAX handler that creates `XML::DOM` document structures
`XML::Handler::CanonXMLWriter`	Outputs XML in canonical XML format
`XML::Handler::Composer`	XML printer/writer/generator
`XML::Handler::PrintEvents`	Prints PerlSAX events (for debugging)
`XML::Handler::PyxWriter`	Converts PerlSAX events to ESIS of nsgmls
`XML::Handler::Sample`	Trivial PerlSAX handler
`XML::Handler::Subs`	PerlSAX handler base class for calling user-defined subs
`XML::Handler::XMLWriter`	PerlSAX handler for writing readable XML
`XML::Handler::YAWriter`	Yet another PerlSAX XML Writer 0.15
`XML::Node`	Node-based XML parsing: a simplified interface to XML
`XML::Parser`	Perl module for parsing XML documents
`XML::Parser::Expat`	Low-level access to James Clark's expat XML parser
`XML::Parser::PerlSAX`	PerlSAX parser using `XML::Parser`
`XML::Parser::PyxParser`	Convert ESIS of nsgmls or Pyxie to PerlSAX
`XML::PatAct::Amsterdam`	Action module for simplistic style sheets
`XML::PatAct::MatchName`	Pattern module for matching element names
`XML::PatAct::ToObjects`	Action module for creating Perl objects
`XML::PYX`	XML to PYX generator
`XML::QL`	XML query language
`XML::RegExp`	Regular expressions for XML tokens
`XML::Registry`	Perl module for loading and saving an XML registry
`XML::RSS`	Creates and updates RSS files
`XML::SAX2Perl`	Translates PerlSAX methods to Java/CORBA-style methods
`XML::Simple`	Trivial API for reading and writing XML (esp. config files)
`XML::Stream`	Creates an XML Stream connection and parses return data
`XML::Stream::Namespace`	Object to make defining namespaces easier
`XML::Template`	Perl XML template instantiation

Module	Description
XML::Twig	Perl module for processing huge XML documents in tree mode
XML::UM	Converts UTF-8 strings to any encoding supported by XML::Encoding
XML::Writer	Perl extension for writing XML documents
XML::XPath	Set of modules for parsing and evaluating XPath
XML::XPath::Boolean	Boolean true/false values
XML::XPath::Builder	SAX handler for building an XPath tree
XML::XPath::Literal	Simple string values
XML::XPath::Node	Internal representation of a node
XML::XPath::NodeSet	List of XML document nodes
XML::XPath::Number	Simple numeric values
XML::XPath::PerlSAX	PerlSAX event generator
XML::XPath::XMLParser	Default XML parsing class that produces a node tree
XML::XQL	Perl module for querying XML tree structures with XQL
XML::XQL::Date	Adds an XQL::Node type for representing and comparing dates and times
XML::XQL::DOM	Adds XQL support to XML::DOM nodes
XML::XSLT	Perl module for processing XSLT
XMLNews::HTMLTemplate	Module for converting NITF to HTML
XMLNews::Meta	Module for reading and writing XMLNews metadata files

Most of the Perl XML modules that appear in Table 20.2 must be downloaded and installed before you can use them. (The process is lengthy, if straightforward; download manager tools exist for Windows and UNIX that can manage the download and installation process and make things easier.) The Perl distribution comes with some XML support built in, such as the `XML::Parser` module.

Here's an example putting `XML::Parser` to work. In this case, I'll parse an XML document and print it out using Perl. The `XML::Parser` module can handle callbacks—calling subroutines when the beginning of an element is encountered—as well as the text content in an element and the end of an element. Here's how I set up such calls to the handler subroutines `start_handler`, `char_handler`, and `end_handler`, respectively, creating a new parser object named `$parser` in Perl:

```
use XML::Parser;

$parser = new XML::Parser(Handlers => {Start => \&start_handler,
        End   => \&end_handler,
        Char  => \&char_handler});
    .
    .
    .
```

Now I need an XML document to parse. I'll use a document we've seen before, meetings.xml (in Chapter 7, "Handling XML Documents with JavaScript"):

```
<?xml version="1.0"?>
<MEETINGS>
   <MEETING TYPE="informal">
       <MEETING_TITLE>XML</MEETING_TITLE>
       <MEETING_NUMBER>2079</MEETING_NUMBER>
       <SUBJECT>XML</SUBJECT>
       <DATE>6/1/2002</DATE>
       <PEOPLE>
           <PERSON ATTENDANCE="present">
               <FIRST_NAME>Edward</FIRST_NAME>
               <LAST_NAME>Samson</LAST_NAME>
           </PERSON>
           <PERSON ATTENDANCE="absent">
               <FIRST_NAME>Ernestine</FIRST_NAME>
               <LAST_NAME>Johnson</LAST_NAME>
           </PERSON>
           <PERSON ATTENDANCE="present">
               <FIRST_NAME>Betty</FIRST_NAME>
               <LAST_NAME>Richardson</LAST_NAME>
           </PERSON>
       </PEOPLE>
   </MEETING>
</MEETINGS>
```

I can parse that document using the `$parser` object's `parsefile` method:

```
use XML::Parser;

$parser = new XML::Parser(Handlers => {Start => \&start_handler,
        End   => \&end_handler,
        Char  => \&char_handler});

$parser->parsefile('meetings.xml');
    .
    .
    .
```

All that remains is to create the subroutines `start_handler`, `char_handler`, and `end_handler`. I'll begin with `start_handler`, which is called when the start of an XML element is encountered. The name of the element is stored in item 1 of the standard Perl array `@_`, which holds the arguments passed to subroutines. I can display that element's opening tag like this:

```
use XML::Parser;

$parser = new XML::Parser(Handlers => {Start => \&start_handler,
        End   => \&end_handler,
        Char  => \&char_handler});

$parser->parsefile('meetings.xml');

sub start_handler
{
    print "<$_[1]>\n";
}
    .
    .
    .
```

I'll also print out the closing tag in the `end_handler` subroutine:

```
use XML::Parser;

$parser = new XML::Parser(Handlers => {Start => \&start_handler,
        End   => \&end_handler,
        Char  => \&char_handler});

$parser->parsefile('meetings.xml');

sub start_handler
{
    print "<$_[1]>\n";
}

sub end_handler
{
    print "</$_[1]>\n";
}
    .
    .
    .
```

I can print out the text content of the element in the `char_handler` subroutine, after removing discardable whitespace:

```
use XML::Parser;

$parser = new XML::Parser(Handlers => {Start => \&start_handler,
        End   => \&end_handler,
        Char  => \&char_handler});

$parser->parsefile('meetings.xml');

sub start_handler
{
    print "<$_[1]>\n";
}

sub end_handler
{
    print "</$_[1]>\n";
}

sub char_handler
{
    if(index($_[1], " ") < 0 && index($_[1], "\n") < 0){
        print "$_[1]\n";
    }
}
```

That completes the code. Running this Perl script gives you the following result, showing that meetings.xml was indeed parsed successfully:

```
<MEETINGS>
<MEETING>
<MEETING_TITLE>
XML
</MEETING_TITLE>
<MEETING_NUMBER>
2079
</MEETING_NUMBER>
<SUBJECT>
XML
</SUBJECT>
<DATE>
6/1/2002
</DATE>
<PEOPLE>
<PERSON>
<FIRST_NAME>
Edward
</FIRST_NAME>
<LAST_NAME>
```

```
Samson
</LAST_NAME>
</PERSON>
<PERSON>
<FIRST_NAME>
Ernestine
</FIRST_NAME>
<LAST_NAME>
Johnson
</LAST_NAME>
</PERSON>
<PERSON>
<FIRST_NAME>
Betty
</FIRST_NAME>
<LAST_NAME>
Richardson
</LAST_NAME>
</PERSON>
</PEOPLE>
</MEETING>
</MEETINGS>
```

Writing this script, parsing the document, and implementing callbacks like this in Perl may remind you quite closely of the Java SAX work in Chapter 12.

I'll take a look at serving XML documents from Perl scripts next. Unfortunately, Perl doesn't come with a built-in database protocol as powerful as JDBC and its ODBC handler, or ASP and its ADO support. The database support that comes built into Perl is based on DBM files, which are hash-based databases. (Now, of course, you can install many Perl modules to interface to other database protocols, from ODBC to Oracle.)

In this case, I'll write a Perl script that will let you enter a key (such as `vegetable`) and a value (such as `broccoli`) to store in a database built in the NDBM database format, which is a default format that Perl supports. This database will be stored on the server. When you enter a key into the page created by this script, the code checks the database for a match to that key; if found, it returns the key and its value. For example, when I enter the key `vegetable` and the value `broccoli`, that key/value pair is stored in the database. When I subsequently search for a match to the key `vegetable`, the script returns both that key and the matching value, `broccoli`, in an XML document using the tags `<key>` and `<value>`:

```
<?xml version="1.0" ?>
<document>
    <key>vegetable</key>
    <value>broccoli</value>
</document>
```

Figure 20.4 shows the results of the CGI script. To add an entry to the database, you enter a key into the text field marked Key To Add to the Database and a corresponding value in the text field marked Value to Add to the Database, and then click the Add to Database button. In Figure 20.4, I'm storing the value `broccoli` under the key `vegetable`.

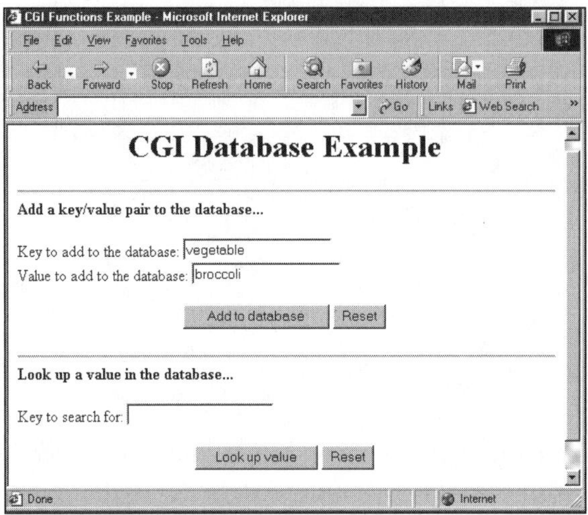

Figure 20.4 A Perl CGI script database manager.

To retrieve a value from the database, you enter the value's key in the box marked Key to Search For, and click the Look Up Value button. The database is searched and an XML document with the results is sent to the client, as shown in Figure 20.5. In this case, I've searched for the key `vegetable`. Although this XML document is displayed in a browser, it's relatively easy to use Internet sockets in Perl code to let you read and handle such XML without a browser.

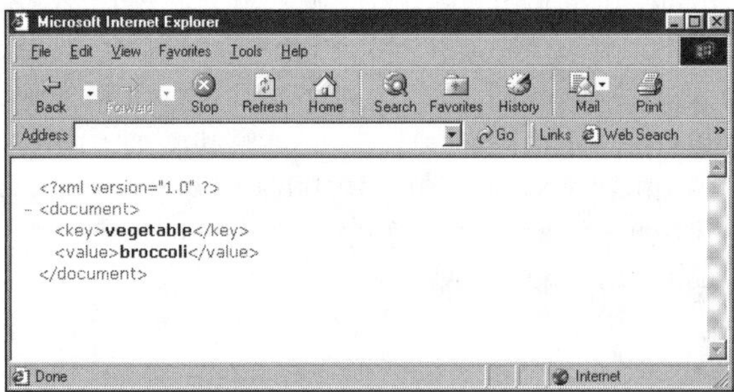

Figure 20.5 An XML document generated by a Perl script.

In this Perl script, I'll use CGI.pm, the official Perl CGI module that comes with the standard Perl distribution. I begin by creating the Web page shown earlier in Figure 20.4, including all the HTML controls we'll need:

```
#!/usr/local/bin/perl
use Fcntl;
use NDBM_File;
use CGI;
$co = new CGI;

if(!$co->param()) {
print $co->header,
$co->start_html('CGI Functions Example'),
$co->center($co->h1('CGI Database Example')),
$co->hr,
$co->b("Add a key/value pair to the database..."),
$co->start_form,
"Key to add to the database: ",
$co->textfield(-name=>'key',-default=>'', -override=>1),
$co->br,
"Value to add to the database: ",
$co->textfield(-name=>'value',-default=>'', -override=>1),
$co->br,
$co->hidden(-name=>'type',-value=>'write', -override=>1),
$co->br,
$co->center(
    $co->submit('Add to database'),
    $co->reset
),
$co->end_form,
$co->hr,
$co->b("Look up a value in the database..."),
$co->start_form,
"Key to search for: ",$co->textfield(-name=>'key',-default=>'', -override=>1),
$co->br,
$co->hidden(-name=>'type',-value=>'read', -override=>1),
$co->br,
$co->center(
    $co->submit('Look up value'),
    $co->reset
),
$co->end_form,
$co->hr;
print $co->end_html;
}
    .
    .
    .
```

This CGI creates two HTML forms—one for use when you want to store key/value pairs, and one when you want to enter a key to search for. I didn't specify a target for these two HTML forms in this page to send their data, so the data will simply be sent back to the same script. I can check whether the script has been called with data to be processed by checking the return value of the CGI.pm `param` method; if it's true, data is waiting for us to work on.

The document this script returns is an XML document, not the default HTML—so how do you set the content type in the HTTP header to indicate that? You do so by using the `header` method, setting the `type` named parameter to `"application/xml"`. This code follows the previous code in the script:

```
if($co->param()) {
    print $co->header(-type=>"application/xml");
    print "<?xml version = \"1.0\"?>";
    print "<document>";
    .
    .
    .
```

I keep the two HTML forms separate with a hidden data variable named `type`. If that variable is set to `"write"`, I enter the data that the user supplied into the database:

```
if($co->param()) {
    print $co->header(-type=>"application/xml");
    print "<?xml version = \"1.0\"?>";
    print "<document>";
    if($co->param('type') eq 'write') {
        tie %dbhash, "NDBM_File", "dbdata", O_RDWR|O_CREAT, 0644;
        $key = $co->param('key');
        $value = $co->param('value');
        $dbhash{$key} = $value;
        untie %dbhash;
        if ($!) {
            print "There was an error: $!";
        } else {
            print "$key=>$value stored in the database";
        }
    }
    .
    .
    .
}
```

Otherwise, I search the database for the key the user has specified, and return both the key and the corresponding value in an XML document:

```
if($co->param()) {
    print $co->header(-type=>"application/xml");
    print "<?xml version = \"1.0\"?>";
    print "<document>";
    if($co->param('type') eq 'write') {
        tie %dbhash, "NDBM_File", "dbdata", O_RDWR | O_CREAT, 0644;
        $key = $co->param('key');
        $value = $co->param('value');
```

```
        $dbhash{$key} = $value;
        untie %dbhash;
        if ($!) {
            print "There was an error: $!";
        } else {
            print "$key=>$value stored in the database";
        }
    } else {
        tie %dbhash, "NDBM_File", "dbdata", O_RDWR | O_CREAT, 0644;
        $key = $co->param('key');
        $value = $dbhash{$key};
        print "<key>";
        print $key;
        print "</key>";
        print "<value>";
        print $value;
        print "</value>";
        if ($value) {
           if ($!) {
                print "There was an error: $!";
            }
        } else {
            print "No match found for that key";
        }
        untie %dbhash;
    }
    print "</document>";
}
```

In this way, we've been able to store data in a database using Perl, and retrieve that data formatted as XML. Listing 20.1 provides the complete listing for this CGI script, dbxml.cgi. Of course, doing everything yourself like this is the hard way—if you get into Perl XML development, you should take a close look at the dozens of Perl XML modules available at CPAN.

Listing 20.1 **dbxml.cgi**

```
#!/usr/local/bin/perl
use Fcntl;
use NDBM_File;
use CGI;
$co = new CGI;

if(!$co->param()) {
print $co->header,
$co->start_html('CGI Functions Example'),
$co->center($co->h1('CGI Database Example')),
$co->hr,
```

continues ▸

Listing 20.1 **Continued**

```
$co->b("Add a key/value pair to the database..."),
$co->start_form,
"Key to add to the database: ",
$co->textfield(-name=>'key',-default=>'', -override=>1),
$co->br,
"Value to add to the database: ",
$co->textfield(-name=>'value',-default=>'', -override=>1),
$co->br,
$co->hidden(-name=>'type',-value=>'write', -override=>1),
$co->br,
$co->center(
    $co->submit('Add to database'),
    $co->reset
),
$co->end_form,
$co->hr,
$co->b("Look up a value in the database..."),
$co->start_form,
"Key to search for: ",$co->textfield(-name=>'key',-default=>'', -override=>1),
$co->br,
$co->hidden(-name=>'type',-value=>'read', -override=>1),
$co->br,
$co->center(
    $co->submit('Look up value'),
    $co->reset
),
$co->end_form,
$co->hr;
print $co->end_html;
}

if($co->param()) {
    print $co->header(-type=>"application/xml");
    print "<?xml version = \"1.0\"?>";
    print "<document>";
    if($co->param('type') eq 'write') {
        tie %dbhash, "NDBM_File", "dbdata", O_RDWR | O_CREAT, 0644;
        $key = $co->param('key');
        $value = $co->param('value');
        $dbhash{$key} = $value;
        untie %dbhash;
        if ($!) {
            print "There was an error: $!";
        } else {
            print "$key=>$value stored in the database";
        }
```

```
    } else {
        tie %dbhash, "NDBM_File", "dbdata", O_RDWR | O_CREAT, 0644;
        $key = $co->param('key');
        $value = $dbhash{$key};
        print "<key>";
        print $key;
        print "</key>";
        print "<value>";
        print $value;
        print "</value>";
        if ($value) {
           if ($!) {
               print "There was an error: $!";
           }
        } else {
            print "No match found for that key";
        }
        untie %dbhash;
    }
    print "</document>";
}
```

Wireless Markup Language

One of the XML applications getting a lot of attention these days is *Wireless Markup Language* (*WML*). WML and its associated protocol, the *Wireless Application Protocol* (*WAP*), are targeted at handheld devices such as cellular phones, PDAs, and other devices with restricted hardware capabilities. WML represents a limited-syntax language that's relatively easy to implement for such devices, and the programs that use WML in those devices are often called *microbrowsers*.

The following list describes some WML resources:

- `www.wapforum.org`. A great resource for all things WML. Acts as a clearinghouse for information.
- `http://wap.colorline.no/wap-faq/`. An independent WAP FAQ, with lots of information, including a list of WAP service providers.
- `www.apachesoftware.com`. All about Klondike, a popular WML browser.
- `http://hotfiles.zdnet.com/cgi-bin/texis/swlib/hotfiles/info.html?fcode=0018AV`. Download site for Klondike.
- `www.apachesoftware.com/wml/wmldemo.wml`. Klondike WML examples.
- `www.wap-uk.com/Developers/Tutorial.htm`. A WML tutorial.

- www.wapdesign.org.uk/tutorial.html. Another WML tutorial.
- www.wapdesign.org.uk/server.html. Tutorial about serving WAP documents.
- www.wapforum.org/DTD/wml_1.1.xml. The WML 1.1 (the current version) DTD. A great place to check to resolve syntax questions.

Table 20.3 lists all the WML elements and their attributes.

Table 20.3 **WML Elements**

Element	Does This	Attributes
a	Hyperlink	class, href, id, title, xml:lang
access	Access element	class, domain, id, path
anchor	Creates an anchor	class, id, title, xml:lang
b	Bold	class, id, xml:lang
big	Big text	class, id, xml:lang
br	Line break	class, id, xml:lang
card	Creates a card	class, do, id, label, name, newcontext, onenterbackward, onenterforward, ontimer, optional, ordered, title, type, xml:lang, xml:lang
em	Emphasized	class, id, xml:lang
fieldset	Field set	class, id, title, xml:lang
go	Navigates	accept-charset, class, href, id, method, sendreferer
head	Head section	class, id
i	Italic	class, id, xml:lang
img	Handles images	align, alt, class, height, hspace, id, localsrc, src, vspace, width, xml:lang
input	Text field	class, emptyok, format, id, maxlength, name, size, tabindex, title, type, value, xml:lang
meta	Holds metadata	class, content, forua, http-equiv, id, name, scheme
noop	No operation (placeholder)	class, id
onevent	Handles an event	class, id, type
optgroup	Creates an option group	class, id, title, xml:lang

Element	Does This	Attributes
option	Creates an option	class, id, onpick, title, value, xml:lang
p	Paragraph	align, mode, xml:lang, class, id
postfield	Posts field data	class, id, name, value
prev	Moves to previous card	(none)
refresh	Handles refreshes	class, id
select	Selects control	class, id, iname, ivalue, multiple, name, tabindex, title, value xml:lang
setvar	Sets a variable	class, id, name, value
small	Small text	class, id, xml:lang
strong	Strong	class, id, xml:lang
table	Creates a table	align, class, columns, id, title, xml:lang
td	Table cell data	class, id, xml:lang
template	Template	class, id, onenterbackward, onenterforward, ontimer
timer	Creates a timer	class, id, name, value
tr	Table row	class, id
u	Underlines	class, id, xml:lang

In addition, WML supports these character entities:

- & is an ampersand (&)
- ' is an apostrophe (')
- > is the greater than symbol (>)
- < is the less than symbol (<)
-   is a nonbreaking space (' ')
- " is a quotation mark (")
- is a soft hyphen (-).

In the following sections, I use the popular Apache Klondike WML browser, which you can download for free from links at www.apachesoftware.com. It's a well-designed browser; if you want to follow along, I encourage you to install it.

Getting Starting with WML

Microbrowsers don't have a lot of display area to spare, so WML documents are divided into *cards*, which are displayed one at a time. A WML document is called a *deck* of such cards. A deck begins and ends with the <wml> tag, and each card in a deck begins and ends with the <card> tag. When a microbrowser reads a WML document, it reads the whole deck, although you see only one card at a time.

You start WML documents with the XML declaration:

```
<?xml version="1.0"?>
    .
    .
    .
```

Like XHTML, WML uses a <!DOCTYPE> element with a formal public identifier, except that the authorization body is the WAP Forum, not W3C:

```
<?xml version="1.0"?>
<!DOCTYPE wml PUBLIC "-//WAPFORUM//DTD WML 1.1//EN"
    "http://www.wapforum.org/DTD/wml_1.1.xml">
    .
    .
    .
```

The document, or deck, element is <wml>:

```
<?xml version="1.0"?>
<!DOCTYPE wml PUBLIC "-//WAPFORUM//DTD WML 1.1//EN"
    "http://www.wapforum.org/DTD/wml_1.1.xml">
<wml>
    .
    .
    .
</wml>
```

You create a card in this deck with the <card> element. In this case, I'll give this card the ID `Card1` and the title `First WML Example` (which will appear in Klondike's title bar):

```
<?xml version="1.0"?>
<!DOCTYPE wml PUBLIC "-//WAPFORUM//DTD WML 1.1//EN"
    "http://www.wapforum.org/DTD/wml_1.1.xml">
<wml>
    <card id="Card1" title="First WML Example">
    .
    .
    .
    </card>
</wml>
```

You can use comments in WML just as you can in XML:

```
<?xml version="1.0"?>
<!DOCTYPE wml PUBLIC "-//WAPFORUM//DTD WML 1.1//EN"
    "http://www.wapforum.org/DTD/wml_1.1.xml">
<wml>
```

```
    <card id="Card1" title="First WML Example">
        <!-- This is a comment -->
        .
        .
        .
    </card>
</wml>
```

Every card must have a <p> (paragraph) element, and I'll place some greeting text in that element:

```
<?xml version="1.0"?>
<!DOCTYPE wml PUBLIC "-//WAPFORUM//DTD WML 1.1//EN"
    "http://www.wapforum.org/DTD/wml_1.1.xml">
<wml>
    <card id="Card1" title="First WML Example">
        <!-- This is a comment -->
        <p>
            Greetings from WML.
        </p>
    </card>
</wml>
```

That's all it takes. Figure 20.6 shows this WML document displayed in Klondike.

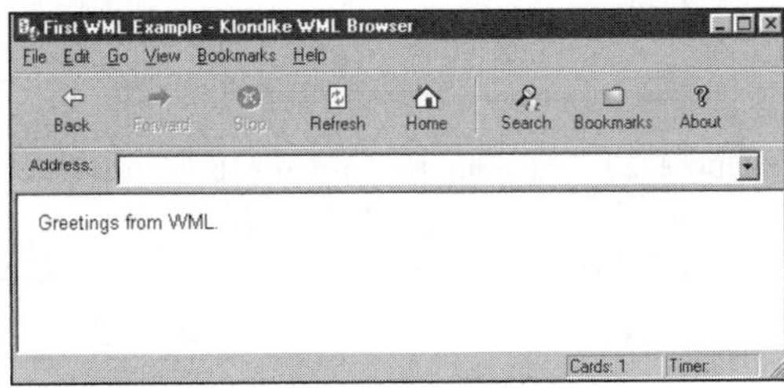

Figure 20.6 A first WML document.

Setting Text Alignment

The <p> element has an `align` attribute, which is supported by Klondike and which is useful for aligning text. You can assign this attribute the value `"left"`, `"center"`, or `"right"`. There's also a `mode` attribute that you can use to specify whether you want text wrapped by assigning values of `"wrap"` or `"nowrap"`.

The following example demonstrates text alignment, using these attributes of the <p> element:

```
<?xml version="1.0"?>
<!DOCTYPE wml PUBLIC "-//WAPFORUM//DTD WML 1.1//EN"
    "http://www.wapforum.org/DTD/wml_1.1.xml">
<wml>
    <card id="Card1" title="Text Alignment">
        <p align="center"><b>Text Alignment</b></p>
        <p align="left">Left-aligned text</p>
        <p align="center">Center-aligned text</p>
        <p align="right">Right-aligned text</p>
        <p mode="nowrap">Non-wrapped text in a long line of text....</p>
    </card>
</wml>
```

Figure 20.7 shows this WML document in Klondike.

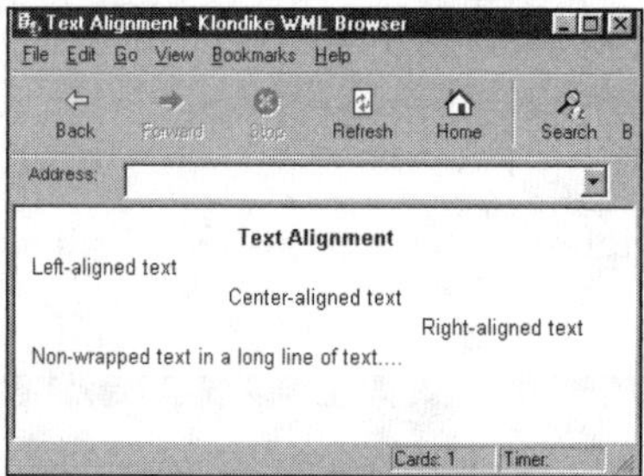

Figure 20.7 Aligning text in a WML document.

Basic Text Styling

WML also supports several basic text-styling elements modeled after HTML, such as <b> for bold text, <i> for italic text, <u> for underlined text, and so on. Here's an example putting these basic text-styling elements to work (note that not all microbrowsers will support all these styling elements):

```
<?xml version="1.0"?>
<!DOCTYPE wml PUBLIC "-//WAPFORUM//DTD WML 1.1//EN"
    "http://www.wapforum.org/DTD/wml_1.1.xml">
<wml>
    <card id="Card1" title="Text Formatting">
        <p align="center"><b>Text Formatting</b></p>
        <p>
```

```
            WML supports these text styles:
            <b>bold</b>,
            <big>big</big>,
            <em>emphasis</em>,
            <i>italic</i>,
            <small>small</small>,
            <strong>strong</strong>,
            and <u>underline</u>.
        </p>
    </card>
</wml>
```

Figure 20.8 shows the results displayed in the Klondike browser.

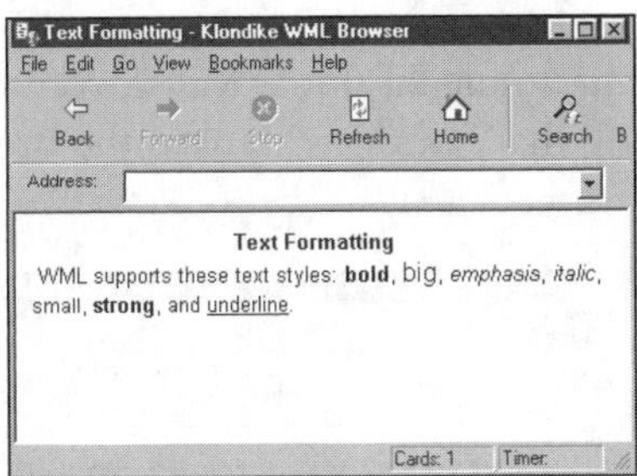

Figure 20.8 Text formatting in WML.

Buttons

You can create buttons in WML with the `<do>` element. For example, suppose that I want to let the user navigate to the WML document page at `www.starpowder.com/planets.wml`. In that case, I'd start with the `<do>` element, setting the `type` attribute to `"accept"` and adding a label with the `label` attribute to create the new button:

```
<?xml version="1.0"?>
<!DOCTYPE wml PUBLIC "-//WAPFORUM//DTD WML 1.1//EN"
    "http://www.wapforum.org/DTD/wml_1.1.xml">
<wml>
    <card id="Card1" title="Buttons">
        <p align="center"><b>Buttons</b></p>
        <do type="accept" label="Go to a new page...">
        .
        .
        .
        </do>
    </card>
</wml>
```

You can navigate to the new document with the <go> element, specifying the target URI with the href element:

```
<?xml version="1.0"?>
<!DOCTYPE wml PUBLIC "-//WAPFORUM//DTD WML 1.1//EN"
    "http://www.wapforum.org/DTD/wml_1.1.xml">
<wml>
    <card id="Card1" title="Buttons">
        <p align="center"><b>Buttons</b></p>
        <do type="accept" label="Go to a new page...">
            <go href="http://www.starpowder.com/planets.wml"/>
        </do>
    </card>
</wml>
```

Figure 20.9 shows the results of this WML document; the button appears in the browser. Clicking that button will make the browser navigate to www.starpowder.com/planets.wml.

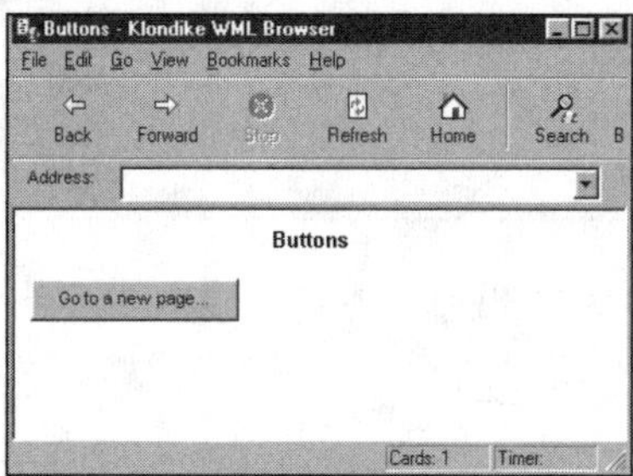

Figure 20.9 Displaying a button in a WML document.

As mentioned earlier, you can have multiple cards in a deck, but you see only one at a time. So how do you get to the others? You do so with buttons. In this case, you assign the ID of the target card to the href attribute in the <go> element.

Here's an example with two cards and a button that lets the user navigate from the first card to the second one—note that the href attribute of the button's <go> element points to the ID value of the target card:

```
<?xml version="1.0"?>
<!DOCTYPE wml PUBLIC "-//WAPFORUM//DTD WML 1.1//EN"
    "http://www.wapforum.org/DTD/wml_1.1.xml">
 <wml>
    <card id="Card1" title="Multiple Cards">
        <p align="center"><b>Multiple Cards</b></p>
        <do type="accept" label="Go to Card 2">
```

```
            <go href="#Card2"/>
        </do>
    </card>
    <card id="Card2" title="Card 2">
        <p>
            This is card 2.
        </p>
    </card>
</wml>
```

For the results of this WML, see Figure 20.10. When the user clicks the button, the browser navigates to card 2 in the deck. That's how you get from card to card in WML—with browser navigation techniques.

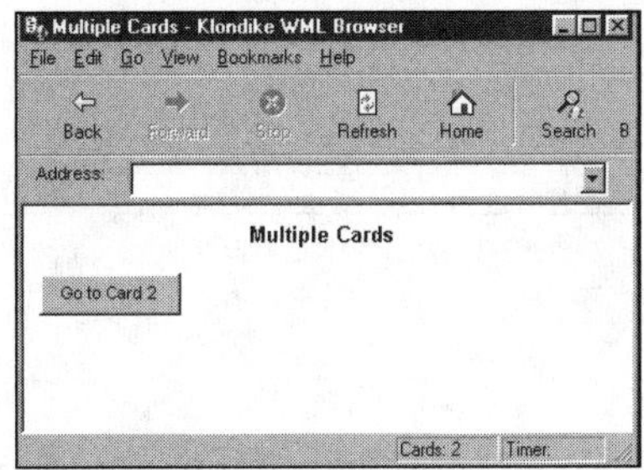

Figure 20.10 Displaying a navigation button in a WML document.

So, having navigated to card 2, how does the user get back to card 1? Take a look at the next topic.

The Back Button

WML supports a special button that you'll often see displayed—the Back button. To add a Back button to card 2, I use the WML <prev> element like this:

```
<?xml version="1.0"?>
<!DOCTYPE wml PUBLIC "-//WAPFORUM//DTD WML 1.1//EN"
    "http://www.wapforum.org/DTD/wml_1.1.xml">
 <wml>
    <card id="Card1" title="Multiple Cards">
        <p align="center"><b>Multiple Cards</b></p>
        <do type="accept" label="Go to Card 2">
            <go href="#Card2"/>
        </do>
    </card>
    <card id="Card2" title="Card 2">
        <p>
            This is card 2.
        </p>
```

continues ▸

```
        <do type="prev" label="Back">
            <prev/>
        </do>
    </card>
</wml>
```

That's all it takes. As Figure 20.11 shows, a Back button appears in card 2. When the user clicks this button, the browser navigates back to the previous card. Bear in mind that the user uses buttons to navigate from card to card in a deck, so it's a good idea to include a Back button on every card (microbrowsers typically won't have a built-in Back button, although Klondike does).

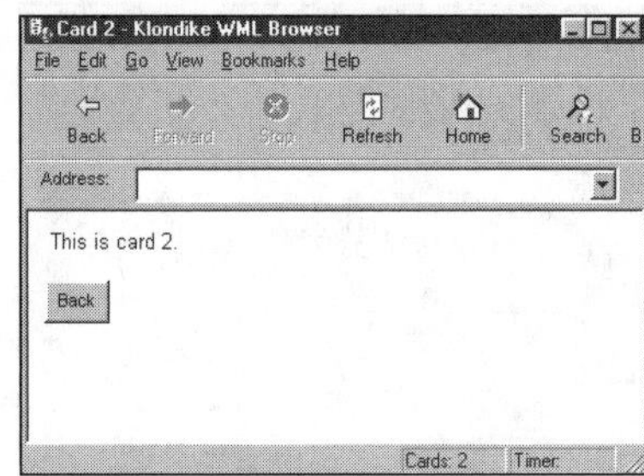

Figure 20.11 Displaying a Back button.

Hyperlinks

WML also supports an `<a>` element for hyperlinks. Like the HTML version of this element, you use the `href` attribute to specify the target URI to which you want to navigate. Here's an example that takes the user to the Apache WML example:

```
<?xml version="1.0"?>
<!DOCTYPE wml PUBLIC "-//WAPFORUM//DTD WML 1.1//EN"
    "http://www.wapforum.org/DTD/wml_1.1.xml">
 <wml>
    <card id="Card1" title="Hyperlinks">
        <p align="center"><b>Hyperlinks</b></p>
        <p>
            Want to see some WML examples?
            Take a look at the
            <a href="http://www.apachesoftware.com/wml/wmldemo.wml">
                Apache examples
            </a>.
```

```
        </p>
    </card>
    </card>
</wml>
```

Figure 20.12 shows the results. When the user clicks the hyperlink, Klondike navigates to the target URI.

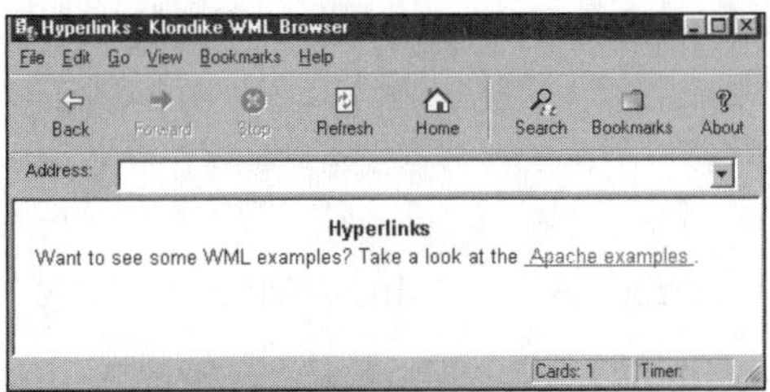

Figure 20.12 A WML hyperlink.

Tables

You can create tables in WML using markup that matches the HTML `<table>`, `<tr>` , and `<td>` elements (there are no `<th>`, `<tbody>`, `<thead>`, or `<tfoot>` elements). Notice how closely the following example resembles an HTML table:

```
<?xml version="1.0"?>
<!DOCTYPE wml PUBLIC "-//WAPFORUM//DTD WML 1.1//EN"
    "http://www.wapforum.org/DTD/wml_1.1.xml">
<wml>
    <card id="Card1" title="Tables">
        <p align="center"><b>Tables</b></p>
        <p align="center">
            <table columns="3">
                <tr>
                    <td>TIC</td>
                    <td>TAC</td>
                    <td>TOE</td>
                </tr>
                <tr>
                    <td>x</td>
                    <td>o</td>
                    <td>x</td>
                </tr>
                <tr>
```

continues ▸

```
                <td>o</td>
                <td>x</td>
                <td>o</td>
            </tr>
            <tr>
                <td>x</td>
                <td>o</td>
                <td>x</td>
            </tr>
        </table>
    </p>
  </card>
</wml>
```

Figure 20.13 shows the results of this WML.

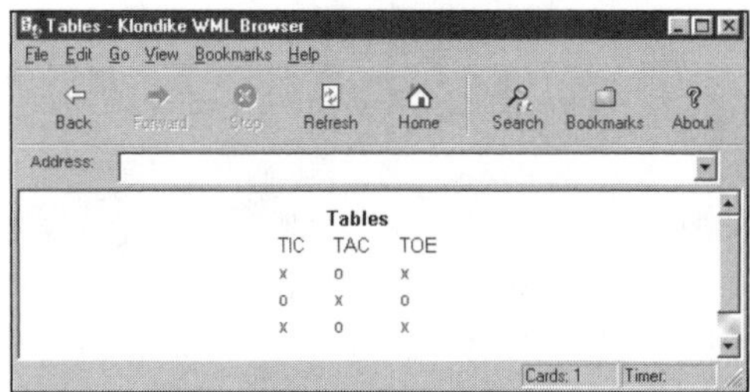

Figure 20.13 WML tables.

Text Input

WML also supports an `<input>` element. If you set this element's `type` attribute to `"text"`, you can display a text field, much like HTML text fields (not all microbrowsers support this element, however).

In this example, I'll let the user enter the URI of a local file in a text field. When the user clicks a button labeled Go, the browser navigates to that URI. I begin by creating the text field:

```
<?xml version="1.0"?>
<!DOCTYPE wml PUBLIC "-//WAPFORUM//DTD WML 1.1//EN"
    "http://www.wapforum.org/DTD/wml_1.1.xml">
<wml>
    <card id="Card1" title="Text Input">
        <p align="center"><b>Text Input</b></p>
        <p>
            Navigate to:
            <input type="text" name="uri"/>
    .
    .
    .
```

When the user clicks the Go button, I need some way to read what was entered in the text field. Here, I've given the text field the name `uri`. I can refer to the text in the text field as `$(uri)` this way in the Go button's `<go>` element:

```
<?xml version="1.0"?>
<!DOCTYPE wml PUBLIC "-//WAPFORUM//DTD WML 1.1//EN"
    "http://www.wapforum.org/DTD/wml_1.1.xml">
<wml>
    <card id="Card1" title="Text Input">
        <p align="center"><b>Text Input</b></p>
        <p>
            Navigate to:
            <input type="text" name="uri"/>
            <do type="accept" label="Go">
                <go href="$(uri)"/>
            </do>
        </p>
    </card>
</wml>
```

Figure 20.14 shows the results. When the user enters the URI of a local document in the text field—I'm using `b.wml` in this figure—and clicks the Go button, the browser reads the name of the document from the text field and opens that document.

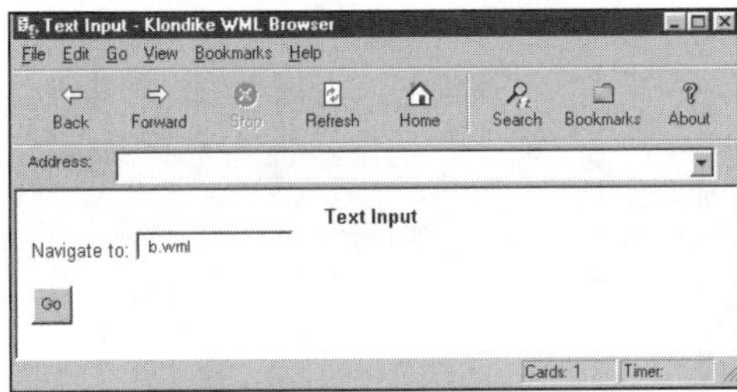

Figure 20.14 Handling text input.

This topic has also introduced us to the concept of WML variables, such as `$(uri)`. Being capable of handling variables directly like this gives WML an interesting mix of markup and scripting capabilities. There's also a `<setvar>` element that lets you set the value of variables like this:

```
<setvar name="uri" value="b.wml" />
```

I'll put variables to work in the next topic.

Select Elements

Like HTML, WML supports a <select> element to display a *select control* (which is like a drop-down list). As an example, I'll create a select control. After making a selection, the user can click a Read Selection button, which navigates to a new card that displays the selection.

I start by creating the select control and giving it the name "selection":

```
<?xml version="1.0"?>
<!DOCTYPE wml PUBLIC "-//WAPFORUM//DTD WML 1.1//EN"
    "http://www.wapforum.org/DTD/wml_1.1.xml">
<wml>
    <card id="Card1" title="Select">
        <p align="center"><b>Select</b></p>
        <select name="selection">
        .
        .
        .
        </select>
```

As in HTML, you specify the items in the select control with <option> elements:

```
<?xml version="1.0"?>
<!DOCTYPE wml PUBLIC "-//WAPFORUM//DTD WML 1.1//EN"
    "http://www.wapforum.org/DTD/wml_1.1.xml">
<wml>
    <card id="Card1" title="Select">
        <p align="center"><b>Select</b></p>
        <select name="selection">
            <option value="broccoli">Broccoli</option>
            <option value="green beans">Green Beans</option>
            <option value="spinach">Spinach</option>
        </select>
        .
        .
        .
```

Now I add the Read Selection button that will navigate to a new card, card 2:

```
<?xml version="1.0"?>
<!DOCTYPE wml PUBLIC "-//WAPFORUM//DTD WML 1.1//EN"
    "http://www.wapforum.org/DTD/wml_1.1.xml">
<wml>
    <card id="Card1" title="Select">
        <p align="center"><b>Select</b></p>
        <select name="selection">
            <option value="broccoli">Broccoli</option>
            <option value="green beans">Green Beans</option>
            <option value="spinach">Spinach</option>
```

```
        </select>
        <do type="accept" label="Read selection">
            <go href="#card2"/>
        </do>
    .
    .
    .
```

In card 2, I'll display the value in the select control, which I can refer to as `$(selection)`. The value of a select control is the string in the `value` attribute of the currently selected item's `<option>` element. In card 2, here's the WML to display the current selection:

```
<?xml version="1.0"?>
<!DOCTYPE wml PUBLIC "-//WAPFORUM//DTD WML 1.1//EN"
    "http://www.wapforum.org/DTD/wml_1.1.xml">
<wml>
    <card id="Card1" title="Select">
        <p align="center"><b>Select</b></p>
        <select name="selection">
            <option value="broccoli">Broccoli</option>
            <option value="green beans">Green Beans</option>
            <option value="spinach">Spinach</option>
        </select>
        <do type="accept" label="Read selection">
            <go href="#card2"/>
        </do>
    </card>
    <card id="card2" title="Card 2">
        <p>
            You selected $(selection).
        </p>
    </card>
</wml>
```

Figure 20.15 shows how this works; I've selected the item `Broccoli`.

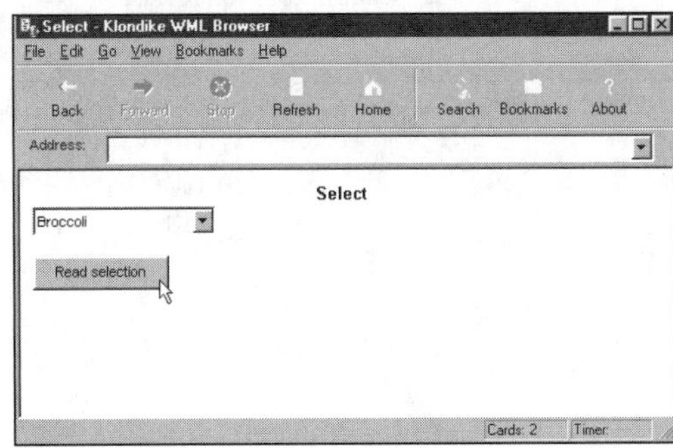

Figure 20.15 Making selections.

Clicking the Read Selection button goes to card 2, which reports the selection, as shown in Figure 20.16.

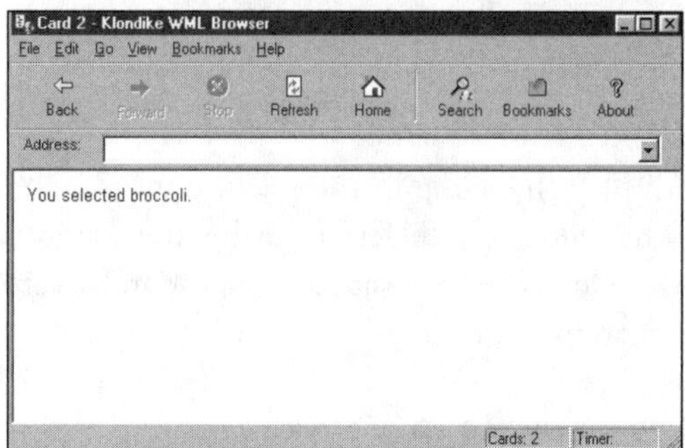

Figure 20.16 Reporting selections.

Another useful aspect of select controls is the `onpick` attribute of `<option>` elements, which enables you to navigate to new URIs as soon as the user chooses an item in a select control. Here's an example. All I have to do is to set the `onpick` attribute of a number of `<option>` elements to URIs; when the user chooses one, the browser navigates to the corresponding URI:

```
<?xml version="1.0"?>
<!DOCTYPE wml PUBLIC "-//WAPFORUM//DTD WML 1.1//EN"
   "http://www.wapforum.org/DTD/wml_1.1.xml">
<wml>
    <card id="Card1" title="Select">
        <p align="center"><b>Select</b></p>
        <select name="selection">
           <option onpick="http://www.starpowder.com/mercury.wml">
               Mercury
           </option>
           <option onpick="http://www.starpowder.com/venus.wml">
               Venus
           </option>
           <option onpick="http://www.starpowder.com/earth.wml">
               Earth
           </option>
        </select>
    </card>
</wml>
```

Timers

In WML, you can use a *timer* to measure a time period, and the browser will undertake some action when that period has expired. For example, if I assign a card's `ontimer` attribute to the ID of another card, the browser navigates to that card when the timer finishes:

```
<?xml version="1.0"?>
<!DOCTYPE wml PUBLIC "-//WAPFORUM//DTD WML 1.1//EN"
    "http://www.wapforum.org/DTD/wml_1.1.xml">
<wml>
    <card id="Card1" ontimer="#card2" title="Timers">
    .
    .
    .
    </card>
    .
    .
    .
```

You create a timer with the `<timer>` element and give it a time period (measured in tenths of a second) with the `value` attribute. Here I'm giving this card's timer a period of 10 seconds:

```
<?xml version="1.0"?>
<!DOCTYPE wml PUBLIC "-//WAPFORUM//DTD WML 1.1//EN"
    "http://www.wapforum.org/DTD/wml_1.1.xml">
<wml>
    <card id="Card1" ontimer="#card2" title="Timers">
        <p align="center"><b>Timers</b></p>
        <timer value="100"/>
        <p>
            In ten seconds, you'll be redirected
            to the second card.
        </p>
    </card>
    .
    .
    .
```

All that remains is to add the targeted card, card2:

```
<?xml version="1.0"?>
<!DOCTYPE wml PUBLIC "-//WAPFORUM//DTD WML 1.1//EN"
    "http://www.wapforum.org/DTD/wml_1.1.xml">
<wml>
    <card id="Card1" ontimer="#card2" title="Timers">
        <p align="center"><b>Timers</b></p>
        <timer value="100"/>
        <p>
```

continues ▸

```
            In ten seconds, you'll be redirected
            to the second card.
        </p>
    </card>
    <card id="card2" title="Welcome">
        <p>
            Welcome to card 2.
        </p>
    </card>
</wml>
```

When you open this deck, card 1 is displayed, as shown in Figure 20.17. After 10 seconds, the browser navigates to card 2. Klondike features a timer counter at lower right; in the figure, the timer indicates that 7 seconds are left in the timer.

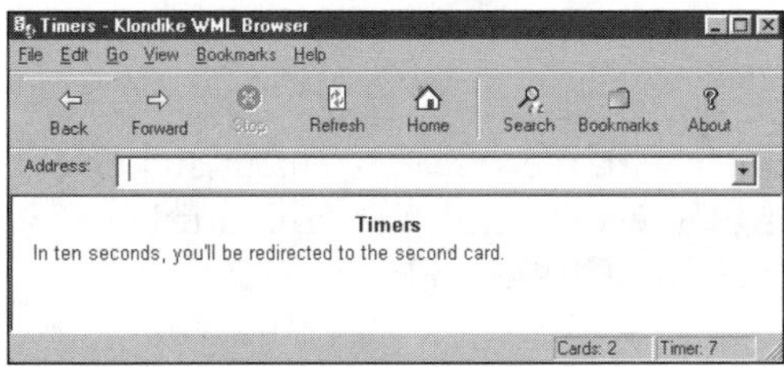

Figure 20.17 Using a timer.

Connecting to the Server

You can also create forms in WML, which are much like HTML forms. The data in a WML form is encoded just as in HTML, so it can be uploaded to CGI scripts (not all microbrowsers support forms, however).

In the following example, I ask for user comments and send them back to a CGI script named comments.cgi. To start, I create a button with the label Upload Data, setting its `method` attribute to `"post"` and its `href` attribute to the URI to post to, `"http://www.starpowder.com/comments.cgi"`, just as you might in an HTML form:

```
<?xml version="1.0"?>
<!DOCTYPE wml PUBLIC "-//WAPFORUM//DTD WML 1.1//EN"
    "http://www.wapforum.org/DTD/wml_1.1.xml">
<wml>
    <card id="Card1" title="Uploading">
        <p align="center"><b>Uploading</b></p>
        <do type="accept" label="Upload data">
```

```
            <go method="post"
                href="http://www.starpowder.com/comments.cgi">
                .
                .
                .
            </go>
            .
            .
            .
```

All that's left is to indicate the value of the data to upload and how to name that data. You do that with the `<postfield>` element's `name` and `value` attributes. In this case, I'll upload the text from a text field named `"comments"`:

```
<?xml version="1.0"?>
<!DOCTYPE wml PUBLIC "-//WAPFORUM//DTD WML 1.1//EN"
    "http://www.wapforum.org/DTD/wml_1.1.xml">
<wml>
    <card id="Card1" title="Uploading">
        <p align="center"><b>Uploading</b></p>
        <do type="accept" label="Upload data">
            <go method="post"
                href="www.starpowder.com/comments.cgi">
                <postfield name="comments" value="$(comments)"/>
            </go>
        </do>
        <p>
        Please give us your comments:
            <input type="text" name="comments"/>
        </p>
    </card>
</wml>
```

That's all it takes. The CGI script can now read the uploaded data as it would from any HTML document. Note that when you send back a response, you should format that response in WML, which means setting the Content Type HTTP header item to the WML MIME type, `"text/vnd.wap.wml"`.

Images

You can also display images in WMF, but there's a catch. Images must be in a special WBMP format, and that format doesn't exactly permit the rich depth of colors to which you may be accustomed. In fact, WBMP format is black and white with no grayscale—just 1 bit per pixel.

The following list describes some WBMP resources available online:

- www.creationflux.com/laurent/wbmp.html. A shareware Adobe Photoshop plug-in for creating WBMP files.
- www.gingco.de/wap/content/download.html. A downloadable image converter that converts images to WBMP format.
- www.phnet.fi/public/jiikoo/ WAPDraw. A useful WBMP drawing program.
- www.teraflops.com/wbmp Teraflops. An online converter that converts image files to WBMP files with a few simple clicks. Any HTML browser can download the resulting images—unless the browser understands WBMP format, in which case the image will be displayed.

To display images, you probably won't be surprised to learn that WML has an `<img>` element. You set the `alt`, `src`, `width`, and `height` attributes of this element to display images, as in this example:

```
<?xml version="1.0"?>
<!DOCTYPE wml PUBLIC "-//WAPFORUM//DTD WML 1.1//EN"
    "http://www.wapforum.org/DTD/wml_1.1.xml">
<wml>
    <card id="Card1" title="Images">
        <p align="center"><b>Images</b></p>
        <p align="center">
            <img alt="WML Image"
                src="image.wbmp" width="217" height="164"/>
        </p>
    </card>
</wml>
```

Figure 20.18 shows this WML document, along with a WBMP image that I created for it to display.

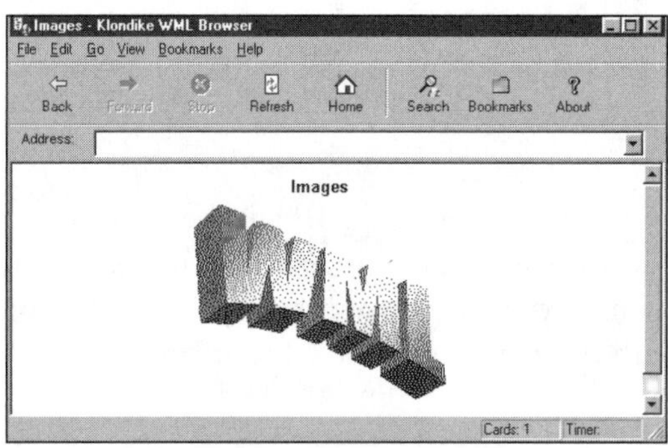

Figure 20.18 Displaying an image.

And that's it for our exploration of WML—and XML. We've come far in this book, from the very beginning up through valid and well-formed documents, DTDs, schemas, parsing XML with JavaScript, data binding, CSS, XML and Java, DOM and SAX parsers, XSL transformations, XSL formatting objects, XLinks, Xpointers, XHTML, RDF, CDF, and VML, and now WML and XML with JSP, ASP, Java servlets, and Perl. All that remains now is for you is to put all this incredible technology to work for yourself.

A

The XML 1.0 Specification

THIS APPENDIX LISTS THE W3C XML 1.0 recommendation from `www.w3.org/TR/REC-xml` and was written by the authors listed at the end of the appendix. Note that formal syntax of XML is given using a simple *Extended Backus-Naur Form notation* (*EBNF*). This notation is explained in Section 6 of the appendix.

REC-xml-19980210

Extensible Markup Language (XML) 1.0

W3C Recommendation 10-February-1998

This version:

http://www.w3.org/TR/1998/REC-xml-19980210
http://www.w3.org/TR/1998/REC-xml-19980210.xml
http://www.w3.org/TR/1998/REC-xml-19980210.html
http://www.w3.org/TR/1998/REC-xml-19980210.pdf
http://www.w3.org/TR/1998/REC-xml-19980210.ps

Latest version:

http://www.w3.org/TR/REC-xml

Previous version:

http://www.w3.org/TR/PR-xml-971208

Editors:
Tim Bray (Textuality and Netscape) <tbray@textuality.com>
Jean Paoli (Microsoft) <jeanpa@microsoft.com>
C. M. Sperberg-McQueen (University of Illinois at Chicago) <cmsmcq@uic.edu>

Abstract

The Extensible Markup Language (XML) is a subset of SGML that is completely described in this document. Its goal is to enable generic SGML to be served, received, and processed on the Web in the way that is now possible with HTML. XML has been designed for ease of implementation and for interoperability with both SGML and HTML.

Status of this document

This document has been reviewed by W3C Members and other interested parties and has been endorsed by the Director as a W3C Recommendation. It is a stable document and may be used as reference material or cited as a normative reference from another document. W3C's role in making the Recommendation is to draw attention to the specification and to promote its widespread deployment. This enhances the functionality and interoperability of the Web.

This document specifies a syntax created by subsetting an existing, widely used international text processing standard (Standard Generalized Markup Language, ISO 8879:1986(E) as amended and corrected) for use on the World Wide Web. It is a product of the W3C XML Activity, details of which can be found at `http://www.w3.org/XML`. A list of current W3C Recommendations and other technical documents can be found at `http://www.w3.org/TR`.

This specification uses the term URI, which is defined by [Berners-Lee et al.], a work in progress expected to update [IETF RFC1738] and [IETF RFC1808].

The list of known errors in this specification is available at `http://www.w3.org/XML/xml-19980210-errata`.

Please report errors in this document to `xml-editor@w3.org`.

Extensible Markup Language (XML) 1.0

Table of Contents

Appendices

1. Introduction

Extensible Markup Language, abbreviated XML, describes a class of data objects called XML documents and partially describes the behavior of computer programs which process them. XML is an application profile or restricted form of SGML, the Standard Generalized Markup Language [ISO 8879]. By construction, XML documents are conforming SGML documents.

XML documents are made up of storage units called entities, which contain either parsed or unparsed data. Parsed data is made up of characters, some of which form character data, and some of which form markup. Markup encodes a description of the document's storage layout and logical structure. XML provides a mechanism to impose constraints on the storage layout and logical structure.

A software module called an **XML processor** is used to read XML documents and provide access to their content and structure. It is assumed that an XML processor is doing its work on behalf of another module, called the **application**. This specification describes the required behavior of an XML processor in terms of how it must read XML data and the information it must provide to the application.

1.1 Origin and Goals

XML was developed by an XML Working Group (originally known as the SGML Editorial Review Board) formed under the auspices of the World Wide Web Consortium (W3C) in 1996. It was chaired by Jon Bosak of Sun Microsystems with the active participation of an XML Special Interest Group (previously known as the SGML Working Group) also organized by the W3C. The membership of the XML Working Group is given in an appendix. Dan Connolly served as the WG's contact with the W3C.

The design goals for XML are:

1. XML shall be straightforwardly usable over the Internet.
2. XML shall support a wide variety of applications.
3. XML shall be compatible with SGML.
4. It shall be easy to write programs which process XML documents.
5. The number of optional features in XML is to be kept to the absolute minimum, ideally zero.
6. XML documents should be human-legible and reasonably clear.
7. The XML design should be prepared quickly.
8. The design of XML shall be formal and concise.
9. XML documents shall be easy to create.
10. Terseness in XML markup is of minimal importance.

This specification, together with associated standards (Unicode and ISO/IEC 10646 for characters, Internet RFC 1766 for language identification tags, ISO 639 for language name codes, and ISO 3166 for country name codes), provides all the information necessary to understand XML Version 1.0 and construct computer programs to process it.

This version of the XML specification may be distributed freely, as long as all text and legal notices remain intact.

1.2 Terminology

The terminology used to describe XML documents is defined in the body of this specification. The terms defined in the following list are used in building those definitions and in describing the actions of an XML processor:

may

Conforming documents and XML processors are permitted to but need not behave as described.

must

Conforming documents and XML processors are required to behave as described; otherwise they are in error.

error

A violation of the rules of this specification; results are undefined. Conforming software may detect and report an error and may recover from it.

fatal error

An error which a conforming XML processor must detect and report to the application. After encountering a fatal error, the processor may continue processing the data to search for further errors and may report such errors to the application. In order to support correction of errors, the processor may make unprocessed data from the document (with intermingled character data and markup) available to the application. Once a fatal error is detected, however, the processor must not continue normal processing (i.e., it must not continue to pass character data and information about the document's logical structure to the application in the normal way).

at user option

Conforming software may or must (depending on the modal verb in the sentence) behave as described; if it does, it must provide users a means to enable or disable the behavior described.

validity constraint

A rule which applies to all valid XML documents. Violations of validity constraints are errors; they must, at user option, be reported by validating XML processors.

well-formedness constraint

A rule which applies to all well-formed XML documents. Violations of well-formedness constraints are fatal errors.

match

(Of strings or names:) Two strings or names being compared must be identical. Characters with multiple possible representations in ISO/IEC 10646 (e.g. characters with both precomposed and base+diacritic forms) match only if they have the same representation in both strings. At user option, processors may normalize such characters to some canonical form. No case folding is performed. (Of strings and rules in the grammar:) A string matches a grammatical production if it belongs to the language generated by that production. (Of content and content models:) An element matches its declaration when it conforms in the fashion described in the constraint "Element Valid".

for compatibility

A feature of XML included solely to ensure that XML remains compatible with SGML.

for interoperability

A non-binding recommendation included to increase the chances that XML documents can be processed by the existing installed base of SGML processors which predate the WebSGML Adaptations Annex to ISO 8879.

2. Documents

A data object is an **XML document** if it is well-formed, as defined in this specification. A well-formed XML document may in addition be valid if it meets certain further constraints.

Each XML document has both a logical and a physical structure. Physically, the document is composed of units called entities. An entity may refer to other entities to cause their inclusion in the document. A document begins in a "root" or document entity. Logically, the document is composed of declarations, elements, comments, character references, and processing instructions, all of which are indicated in the document by explicit markup. The logical and physical structures must nest properly, as described in "4.3.2 Well-Formed Parsed Entities".

2.1 Well-Formed XML Documents

A textual object is a well-formed XML document if:

1. Taken as a whole, it matches the production labeled document.
2. It meets all the well-formedness constraints given in this specification.
3. Each of the parsed entities which is referenced directly or indirectly within the document is well-formed.

Document

```
[1]  document ::= prolog element Misc*
```

Matching the document production implies that:

1. It contains one or more elements.
2. There is exactly one element, called the **root**, or document element, no part of which appears in the content of any other element. For all other elements, if the start-tag is in the content of another element, the

end-tag is in the content of the same element. More simply stated, the elements, delimited by start- and end-tags, nest properly within each other.

As a consequence of this, for each non-root element `C` in the document, there is one other element `P` in the document such that `C` is in the content of `P`, but is not in the content of any other element that is in the content of `P`. `P` is referred to as the **parent** of `C`, and `C` as a **child** of `P`.

2.2 Characters

A parsed entity contains **text**, a sequence of characters, which may represent markup or character data. A **character** is an atomic unit of text as specified by ISO/IEC 10646 [ISO/IEC 10646]. Legal characters are tab, carriage return, line feed, and the legal graphic characters of Unicode and ISO/IEC 10646. The use of "compatibility characters", as defined in section 6.8 of [Unicode], is discouraged.

Character Range

```
[2]  Char ::= #x9 | #xA | #xD | [#x20-#xD7FF]         /* any Unicode
                                                         character,
              | [#xE000-#xFFFD] | [#x10000-#x10FFFF]     excluding the
                                                         surrogate blocks,
                                                         FFFE, and FFFF. */
```

The mechanism for encoding character code points into bit patterns may vary from entity to entity. All XML processors must accept the UTF-8 and UTF-16 encodings of 10646; the mechanisms for signaling which of the two is in use, or for bringing other encodings into play, are discussed later, in "4.3.3 Character Encoding in Entities".

2.3 Common Syntactic Constructs

This section defines some symbols used widely in the grammar.

`S` (white space) consists of one or more space (#x20) characters, carriage returns, line feeds, or tabs.

White Space

```
[3]  S ::=  (#x20 | #x9 | #xD | #xA)+
```

Characters are classified for convenience as letters, digits, or other characters. Letters consist of an alphabetic or syllabic base character possibly followed by one or more combining characters, or of an ideographic character. Full definitions of the specific characters in each class are given in "B. Character Classes".

A **Name** is a token beginning with a letter or one of a few punctuation characters, and continuing with letters, digits, hyphens, underscores, colons, or full stops, together known as name characters. Names beginning with the string "`xml`", or any string which would match `(('X'|'x') ('M'|'m') ('L'|'l'))`, are reserved for standardization in this or future versions of this specification.

Note: The colon character within XML names is reserved for experimentation with name spaces. Its meaning is expected to be standardized at some future point, at which point those documents using the colon for experimental purposes may need to be updated. (There is no guarantee that any name-space mechanism adopted for XML will in fact use the colon as a name-space delimiter.) In practice, this means that authors should not use the colon in XML names except as part of name-space experiments, but that XML processors should accept the colon as a name character.

An `Nmtoken` (name token) is any mixture of name characters.

Names and Tokens

```
[4]  NameChar ::=  Letter | Digit | '.' | '-' | '_' | ':'
                   | CombiningChar | Extender
[5]      Name ::=  (Letter | '_' | ':') (NameChar)*
[6]     Names ::=  Name (S Name)*
[7]   Nmtoken ::=  (NameChar)+
[8]  Nmtokens ::=  Nmtoken (S Nmtoken)*
```

Literal data is any quoted string not containing the quotation mark used as a delimiter for that string. Literals are used for specifying the content of internal entities (`EntityValue`), the values of attributes (`AttValue`), and external identifiers (`SystemLiteral`). Note that a `SystemLiteral` can be parsed without scanning for markup.

Literals

```
[9]     EntityValue ::=  '"' ([^%&"] | PEReference | Reference)* '"'
                         | "'" ([^%&'] | PEReference | Reference)* "'"
[10]       AttValue ::=  '"' ([^<&"] | Reference)* '"'
                         | "'" ([^<&'] | Reference)* "'"
[11]  SystemLiteral ::=  ('"' [^"]* '"') | ("'" [^']* "'")
[12]  PubidLiteral ::=   '"' PubidChar* '"' | "'" (PubidChar - "'")* "'"
[13]     PubidChar ::=   #x20 | #xD | #xA | [a-zA-Z0-9]
                         | [-'()+,./:=?;!*#@$_%]
```

2.4 Character Data and Markup

Text consists of intermingled character data and markup. **Markup** takes the form of start-tags, end-tags, empty-element tags, entity references, character references, comments, CDATA section delimiters, document type declarations, and processing instructions.

All text that is not markup constitutes the **character data** of the document.

The ampersand character (`&`) and the left angle bracket (`<`) may appear in their literal form *only* when used as markup delimiters, or within a comment, a processing instruction, or a CDATA section. They are also legal within the literal entity value of an internal entity declaration; see "4.3.2 Well-Formed Parsed Entities". If they are needed elsewhere, they must be escaped using either numeric character references or the strings "`&`" and "`<`" respectively. The right angle bracket (`>`) may be represented using the string "`>`", and must, for compatibility, be escaped using "`>`" or a character reference when it appears in the string "`]]>`" in content, when that string is not marking the end of a CDATA section.

In the content of elements, character data is any string of characters which does not contain the start-delimiter of any markup. In a CDATA section, character data is any string of characters not including the CDATA-section-close delimiter, "`]]>`".

To allow attribute values to contain both single and double quotes, the apostrophe or single-quote character (`'`) may be represented as "`'`", and the double-quote character (`"`) as "`"`".

Character Data

```
[14]  CharData ::=  [^<&]* - ([^<&]* ']]>' [^<&]*)
```

2.5 Comments

Comments may appear anywhere in a document outside other markup; in addition, they may appear within the document type declaration at places allowed by the grammar. They are not part of the document's character data; an XML processor may, but need not, make it possible for an application to retrieve the text of comments. For compatibility, the string "`--`" (double-hyphen) must not occur within comments.

Comments

```
[15] Comment ::= '<!--' ((Char - '-') | ('-' (Char - '-')))* '-->'
```

An example of a comment:

```
<!-- declarations for <head> & <body> -->
```

2.6 Processing Instructions

Processing instructions (PIs) allow documents to contain instructions for applications.

Processing Instructions

```
[16]       PI ::=  '<?' PITarget (S (Char* - (Char* '?>' Char*)))? '?>'
[17] PITarget ::=  Name - (('X' | 'x') ('M' | 'm') ('L' | 'l'))
```

PIs are not part of the document's character data, but must be passed through to the application. The PI begins with a target (`PITarget`) used to identify the application to which the instruction is directed. The target names "`XML`", "`xml`", and so on are reserved for standardization in this or future versions of this specification. The XML Notation mechanism may be used for formal declaration of PI targets.

2.7 CDATA Sections

CDATA sections may occur anywhere character data may occur; they are used to escape blocks of text containing characters which would otherwise be recognized as markup. CDATA sections begin with the string "`<![CDATA[`" and end with the string "`]]>`":

CDATA Sections

```
[18]  CDSect ::=  CDStart CData CDEnd
[19] CDStart ::=  '<![CDATA['
[20]   CData ::=  (Char* - (Char* ']]>' Char*))
[21]   CDEnd ::=  ']]>'
```

Within a CDATA section, only the `CDEnd` string is recognized as markup, so that left angle brackets and ampersands may occur in their literal form; they need not (and cannot) be escaped using "`<`" and "`&`". CDATA sections cannot nest.

An example of a CDATA section, in which "`<greeting>`" and "`</greeting>`" are recognized as character data, not markup:

```
<![CDATA[<greeting>Hello, world!</greeting>]]>
```

2.8 Prolog and Document Type Declaration

XML documents may, and should, begin with an **XML declaration** which specifies the version of XML being used. For example, the following is a complete XML document, well-formed but not valid:

```
<?xml version="1.0"?> <greeting>Hello, world!</greeting>
```

and so is this:

```
<greeting>Hello, world!</greeting>
```

The version number "`1.0`" should be used to indicate conformance to this version of this specification; it is an error for a document to use the value "`1.0`" if it does not conform to this version of this specification. It is the intent of the XML working group to give later versions of this specification numbers other than "`1.0`", but this intent does not indicate a commitment to produce any future versions of XML, nor if any are produced, to use any particular numbering scheme. Since future versions are not ruled out, this construct is provided as a means to allow the possibility of automatic version recognition, should it become necessary. Processors may signal an error if they receive documents labeled with versions they do not support.

The function of the markup in an XML document is to describe its storage and logical structure and to associate attribute-value pairs with its logical structures. XML provides a mechanism, the document type declaration, to define constraints on the logical structure and to support the use of predefined storage units. An XML document is valid if it has an associated document type declaration and if the document complies with the constraints expressed in it.

The document type declaration must appear before the first element in the document.

Prolog

```
[22]       prolog ::=  XMLDecl? Misc* (doctypedecl Misc*)?
[23]      XMLDecl ::=  '<?xml' VersionInfo EncodingDecl? SDDecl? S? '?>'
[24]  VersionInfo ::=  S 'version' Eq (' VersionNum ' | " VersionNum ")
[25]           Eq ::=  S? '=' S?
[26]   VersionNum ::=  ([a-zA-Z0-9_.:] | '-')+
[27]         Misc ::=  Comment | PI | S
```

The XML **document type declaration** contains or points to markup declarations that provide a grammar for a class of documents. This grammar is known as a document type definition, or DTD. The document type declaration can point to an external subset (a special kind of external entity) containing markup declarations, or can contain the markup declarations directly in an internal subset, or can do both. The DTD for a document consists of both subsets taken together.

A **markup declaration** is an element type declaration, an attribute-list declaration, an entity declaration, or a notation declaration. These declarations may be contained in whole or in part within parameter entities, as described in the well-formedness and validity constraints below. For fuller information, see "4. Physical Structures".

Document Type Definition

[28]	doctypedecl ::=	`'<!DOCTYPE' S Name (S ExternalID)? S? ('[' (markupdecl | PEReference | S)* ']' S?)? '>'`	[VC: Root Element Type]
[29]	markupdecl ::=	`elementdecl | AttlistDecl | EntityDecl | NotationDecl | PI | Comment`	[VC: Proper Declaration/ PE Nesting] [WFC: PEs in Internal Subset]

The markup declarations may be made up in whole or in part of the replacement text of parameter entities. The productions later in this specification for individual nonterminals (`elementdecl`, `AttlistDecl`, and so on) describe the declarations *after* all the parameter entities have been included.

Validity Constraint: Root Element Type

The `Name` in the document type declaration must match the element type of the root element.

Validity Constraint: Proper Declaration/PE Nesting

Parameter-entity replacement text must be properly nested with markup declarations. That is to say, if either the first character or the last character of a markup declaration (`markupdecl` above) is contained in the replacement text for a parameter-entity reference, both must be contained in the same replacement text.

Well-Formedness Constraint: PEs in Internal Subset

In the internal DTD subset, parameter-entity references can occur only where markup declarations can occur, not within markup declarations. (This does not apply to references that occur in external parameter entities or to the external subset.)

Like the internal subset, the external subset and any external parameter entities referred to in the DTD must consist of a series of complete markup declarations of the types allowed by the non-terminal symbol `markupdecl`, interspersed with white space or parameter-entity references. However, portions of the contents of the external subset or of external parameter entities may conditionally be ignored by using the conditional section construct; this is not allowed in the internal subset.

External Subset

```
[30]      extSubset ::=  TextDecl? extSubsetDecl
[31]  extSubsetDecl ::=  ( markupdecl | conditionalSect | PEReference | S )*
```

The external subset and external parameter entities also differ from the internal subset in that in them, parameter-entity references are permitted *within* markup declarations, not only *between* markup declarations.

An example of an XML document with a document type declaration:

```
<?xml version="1.0"?>
<!DOCTYPE greeting SYSTEM "hello.dtd">
<greeting>Hello, world!</greeting>
```

The system identifier "`hello.dtd`" gives the URI of a DTD for the document.

The declarations can also be given locally, as in this example:

```
<?xml version="1.0" encoding="UTF-8" ?>
 <!DOCTYPE greeting [ <!ELEMENT greeting (#PCDATA)>
]>
<greeting>Hello, world!</greeting>
```

If both the external and internal subsets are used, the internal subset is considered to occur before the external subset. This has the effect that entity and attribute-list declarations in the internal subset take precedence over those in the external subset.

2.9 Standalone Document Declaration

Markup declarations can affect the content of the document, as passed from an XML processor to an application; examples are attribute defaults and entity declarations. The standalone document declaration, which may appear as a component of the XML declaration, signals whether or not there are such declarations which appear external to the document entity.

Standalone Document Declaration

```
[32]  SDDecl ::=  S 'standalone' Eq (("'" ('yes'      [  VC: Standalone
                  | 'no') "'") | ('"' ('yes'              Document
                  | 'no') '"'))                           Declaration ]
```

In a standalone document declaration, the value "`yes`" indicates that there are no markup declarations external to the document entity (either in the DTD external subset, or in an external parameter entity referenced from the internal subset) which affect the information passed from the XML processor to the application. The value "`no`" indicates that there are or may be such external markup declarations. Note that the standalone document declaration only denotes the presence of external *declarations*; the presence, in a document, of references to external *entities*, when those entities are internally declared, does not change its standalone status.

If there are no external markup declarations, the standalone document declaration has no meaning. If there are external markup declarations but there is no standalone document declaration, the value "`no`" is assumed.

Any XML document for which `standalone="no"` holds can be converted algorithmically to a standalone document, which may be desirable for some network delivery applications.

Validity Constraint: Standalone Document Declaration

The standalone document declaration must have the value "`no`" if any external markup declarations contain declarations of:

- attributes with default values, if elements to which these attributes apply appear in the document without specifications of values for these attributes, or
- entities (other than `amp`, `lt`, `gt`, `apos`, `quot`), if references to those entities appear in the document, or
- attributes with values subject to normalization, where the attribute appears in the document with a value which will change as a result of normalization, or
- element types with element content, if white space occurs directly within any instance of those types.

An example XML declaration with a standalone document declaration:

```
<?xml version="1.0" standalone='yes'?>
```

2.10 White Space Handling

In editing XML documents, it is often convenient to use "white space" (spaces, tabs, and blank lines, denoted by the nonterminal `S` in this specification) to set apart the markup for greater readability. Such white space is typically not intended for inclusion in the delivered version of the document. On the other hand, "significant" white space that should be preserved in the delivered version is common, for example in poetry and source code.

An XML processor must always pass all characters in a document that are not markup through to the application. A validating XML processor must also inform the application which of these characters constitute white space appearing in element content.

A special attribute named `xml:space` may be attached to an element to signal an intention that in that element, white space should be preserved by applications. In valid documents, this attribute, like any other, must be declared if it is used. When declared, it must be given as an enumerated type whose only possible values are "`default`" and "`preserve`". For example:

```
<!ATTLIST poem xml:space (default|preserve) 'preserve'>
```

The value "`default`" signals that applications' default white-space processing modes are acceptable for this element; the value "`preserve`" indicates the intent that applications preserve all the white space. This declared intent is considered to apply to all elements within the content of the element where it is specified, unless overridden with another instance of the `xml:space` attribute.

The root element of any document is considered to have signaled no intentions as regards application space handling, unless it provides a value for this attribute or the attribute is declared with a default value.

2.11 End-of-Line Handling

XML parsed entities are often stored in computer files which, for editing convenience, are organized into lines. These lines are typically separated by some combination of the characters carriage-return (#xD) and line-feed (#xA).

To simplify the tasks of applications, wherever an external parsed entity or the literal entity value of an internal parsed entity contains either the literal two-character sequence "`#xD#xA`" or a standalone literal #xD, an XML processor must pass to the application the single character #xA. (This behavior can conveniently be produced by normalizing all line breaks to #xA on input, before parsing.)

2.12 Language Identification

In document processing, it is often useful to identify the natural or formal language in which the content is written. A special attribute named `xml:lang` may be inserted in documents to specify the language used in the contents and attribute values of any element in an XML document. In valid documents, this attribute, like any other, must be declared if it is used. The values of the attribute are language identifiers as defined by [IETF RFC 1766], "Tags for the Identification of Languages":

Language Identification

```
[33] LanguageID ::=  Langcode ('-' Subcode)*
[34]   Langcode ::=  ISO639Code | IanaCode | UserCode
[35] ISO639Code ::=  ([a-z] | [A-Z]) ([a-z] | [A-Z])
[36]   IanaCode ::=  ('i' | 'I') '-' ([a-z] | [A-Z])+
[37]   UserCode ::=  ('x' | 'X') '-' ([a-z] | [A-Z])+
[38]    Subcode ::=  ([a-z] | [A-Z])+
```

The `Langcode` may be any of the following:

- a two-letter language code as defined by [ISO 639], "Codes for the representation of names of languages"
- a language identifier registered with the Internet Assigned Numbers Authority [IANA]; these begin with the prefix "`i-`" (or "`I-`")
- a language identifier assigned by the user, or agreed on between parties in private use; these must begin with the prefix "`x-`" or "`X-`" in order to ensure that they do not conflict with names later standardized or registered with IANA

There may be any number of `Subcode` segments; if the first subcode segment exists and the Subcode consists of two letters, then it must be a country code from [ISO 3166], "Codes for the representation of names of countries." If the first subcode consists of more than two letters, it must be a subcode for the language in question registered with IANA, unless the `Langcode` begins with the prefix "`x-`" or "`X-`".

It is customary to give the language code in lower case, and the country code (if any) in upper case. Note that these values, unlike other names in XML documents, are case insensitive.

For example:

```
<p xml:lang="en">The quick brown fox jumps over the lazy dog.</p>
p xml:lang="en-GB">What colour is it?</p>
<p xml:lang="en-US">What color is it?</p>
<sp who="Faust" desc='leise' xml:lang="de">
 <l>Habe nun, ach! Philosophie,</l>
 <l>Juristerei, und Medizin</l>
 <l>und leider auch Theologie</l>
 <l>durchaus studiert mit heißem Bemüh'n.</l>
 </sp>
```

The intent declared with `xml:lang` is considered to apply to all attributes and content of the element where it is specified, unless overridden with an instance of `xml:lang` on another element within that content.

A simple declaration for `xml:lang` might take the form

```
xml:lang NMTOKEN #IMPLIED
```

but specific default values may also be given, if appropriate. In a collection of French poems for English students, with glosses and notes in English, the `xml:lang` attribute might be declared this way:

```
<!ATTLIST poem  xml:lang NMTOKEN 'fr'>
<!ATTLIST gloss xml:lang NMTOKEN 'en'>
<!ATTLIST note  xml:lang NMTOKEN 'en'>
```

3. Logical Structures

Each XML document contains one or more **elements**, the boundaries of which are either delimited by start-tags and end-tags, or, for empty elements, by an empty-element tag. Each element has a type, identified by name, sometimes called its "generic identifier" (GI), and may have a set of attribute specifications. Each attribute specification has a name and a value.

Element

```
[39]  element ::=  EmptyElemTag
                   | STag content ETag [  WFC: Element Type Match ]
                                       [  VC: Element Valid ]
```

This specification does not constrain the semantics, use, or (beyond syntax) names of the element types and attributes, except that names beginning with a match to `(('X'|'x')('M'|'m')('L'|'l'))` are reserved for standardization in this or future versions of this specification.

Well-Formedness Constraint: Element Type Match

The `Name` in an element's end-tag must match the element type in the start-tag.

Validity Constraint: Element Valid

An element is valid if there is a declaration matching `elementdecl` where the `Name` matches the element type, and one of the following holds:

1. The declaration matches `EMPTY` and the element has no content.
2. The declaration matches `children` and the sequence of child elements belongs to the language generated by the regular expression in the content model, with optional white space (characters matching the nonterminal `S`) between each pair of child elements.
3. The declaration matches `Mixed` and the content consists of character data and child elements whose types match names in the content model.
4. The declaration matches `ANY`, and the types of any child elements have been declared.

3.1 Start-Tags, End-Tags, and Empty-Element Tags

The beginning of every non-empty XML element is marked by a **start-tag**.

Start-tag

```
[40]       STag ::=  '<' Name (S Attribute)* S? '>' [  WFC: Unique Att Spec ]
[41]  Attribute ::=  Name Eq AttValue               [  VC: Attribute Value
                                                       Type ]
                                                    [  WFC: No External Entity
                                                       References ]
                                                    [  WFC: No < in Attribute
                                                       Values ]
```

The `Name` in the start- and end-tags gives the element's **type**. The `Name-AttValue` pairs are referred to as the **attribute specifications** of the element, with the `Name` in each pair referred to as the **attribute name** and the content of the `AttValue` (the text between the `'` or `"` delimiters) as the **attribute value**.

Well-Formedness Constraint: Unique Att Spec

No attribute name may appear more than once in the same start-tag or empty-element tag.

Validity Constraint: Attribute Value Type

The attribute must have been declared; the value must be of the type declared for it. (For attribute types, see "3.3 Attribute-List Declarations".)

Well-Formedness Constraint: No External Entity References

Attribute values cannot contain direct or indirect entity references to external entities.

Well-Formedness Constraint: No < in Attribute Values

The replacement text of any entity referred to directly or indirectly in an attribute value (other than "`<`") must not contain a <.

An example of a start-tag:

```
<termdef id="dt-dog" term="dog">
```

The end of every element that begins with a start-tag must be marked by an end-tag containing a name that echoes the element's type as given in the start-tag:

End-tag

```
[42]  ETag ::=  '</' Name S? '>'
```

An example of an end-tag:

```
</termdef>
```

The text between the start-tag and end-tag is called the element's **content**:

Content of Elements

```
[43]  content ::=  (element | CharData | Reference | CDSect | PI | Comment)*
```

If an element is **empty**, it must be represented either by a start-tag immediately followed by an end-tag or by an **empty-element tag**. An empty-element tag takes a special form:

Tags for Empty Elements

```
[44]  EmptyElemTag ::=  '<' Name (S Attribute)* S? '/>'   [  WFC: Unique
                                                              Att Spec ]
```

Empty-element tags may be used for any element which has no content, whether or not it is declared using the keyword EMPTY. For interoperability, the empty-element tag must be used, and can only be used, for elements which are declared EMPTY.

Examples of empty elements:

```
<IMG align="left"
 src="http://www.w3.org/Icons/WWW/w3c_home" />
<br></br>
<br/>
```

3.2 Element Type Declarations

The element structure of an XML document may, for validation purposes, be constrained using element type and attribute-list declarations. An element type declaration constrains the element's content.

Element type declarations often constrain which element types can appear as children of the element. At user option, an XML processor may issue a warning when a declaration mentions an element type for which no declaration is provided, but this is not an error.

An **element type declaration** takes the form:

Element Type Declaration

```
[45]  elementdecl ::=  '<!ELEMENT' S Name S contentspec S?  [ VC: Unique
                       '>'                                    Element Type
                                                              Declaration ]
[46]  contentspec ::=  'EMPTY' | 'ANY' | Mixed | children
```

where the `Name` gives the element type being declared.

Validity Constraint: Unique Element Type Declaration

No element type may be declared more than once.

Examples of element type declarations:

```
<!ELEMENT br EMPTY>
<!ELEMENT p (#PCDATA|emph)* >
<!ELEMENT %name.para; %content.para; >
<!ELEMENT container ANY>
```

3.2.1 Element Content

An element type has **element content** when elements of that type must contain only child elements (no character data), optionally separated by white space (characters matching the nonterminal `S`). In this case, the constraint includes a content model, a simple grammar governing the allowed types of the child elements and the order in which they are allowed to appear. The grammar is built on content particles (`cp`s), which consist of names, choice lists of content particles, or sequence lists of content particles:

Element-content Models

```
[47] children ::=  (choice | seq) ('?' | '*' | '+')?
[48]       cp ::=  (Name | choice | seq) ('?' | '*'
                   | '+')?
[49]   choice ::=  '(' S? cp ( S? '|' S? cp )* S? ')'   [ VC: Proper
                                                          Group/PE
                                                          Nesting ]
[50]      seq ::=  '(' S? cp ( S? ',' S? cp )* S? ')'   [ VC: Proper
                                                          Group/PE
                                                          Nesting ]
```

where each `Name` is the type of an element which may appear as a child. Any content particle in a choice list may appear in the element content at the location where the choice list appears in the grammar; content particles occurring in a sequence list must each appear in the element content in the order given in the list. The optional character following a name or list governs whether the element or the content particles in the list may occur one or more (+), zero or more (*), or zero or one times (?). The absence of such an operator means that the element or content particle must appear exactly once. This syntax and meaning are identical to those used in the productions in this specification.

The content of an element matches a content model if and only if it is possible to trace out a path through the content model, obeying the sequence, choice, and repetition operators and matching each element in the content against an element type in the content model. For compatibility, it is an error if an element in the document can match more than one occurrence of an element type in the content model. For more information, see "E. Deterministic Content Models".

Validity Constraint: Proper Group/PE Nesting

Parameter-entity replacement text must be properly nested with parenthetized groups. That is to say, if either of the opening or closing parentheses in a `choice`, `seq`, or `Mixed` construct is contained in the replacement text for a parameter entity, both must be contained in the same replacement text. For interoperability, if a parameter-entity reference appears in a `choice`, `seq`, or `Mixed` construct, its replacement text should not be empty, and neither the first nor last non-blank character of the replacement text should be a connector (| or ,).

Examples of element-content models:

```
<!ELEMENT spec (front, body, back?)>
<!ELEMENT div1 (head, (p | list | note)*, div2*)>
<!ELEMENT dictionary-body (%div.mix; | %dict.mix;)*>
```

3.2.2 Mixed Content

An element type has **mixed content** when elements of that type may contain character data, optionally interspersed with child elements. In this case, the types of the child elements may be constrained, but not their order or their number of occurrences:

Mixed-content Declaration

```
[51]  Mixed ::=  '(' S? '#PCDATA' (S? '|' S? Name)* S?
                 ')*' | '(' S? '#PCDATA' S? ')'       [ VC: Proper
                                                        Group/PE
                                                        Nesting ]
                                                      [ VC: No
                                                        Duplicate Types ]
```

where the `Names` give the types of elements that may appear as children.

Validity Constraint: No Duplicate Types

The same name must not appear more than once in a single mixed-content declaration.

Examples of mixed content declarations:

```
<!ELEMENT p (#PCDATA|a|ul|b|i|em)*>
<!ELEMENT p (#PCDATA | %font; | %phrase; | %special; | %form;)* >
<!ELEMENT b (#PCDATA)>
```

3.3 Attribute-List Declarations

Attributes are used to associate name-value pairs with elements. Attribute specifications may appear only within start-tags and empty-element tags; thus, the productions used to recognize them appear in "3.1 Start-Tags, End-Tags, and Empty-Element Tags". Attribute-list declarations may be used:

- To define the set of attributes pertaining to a given element type.
- To establish type constraints for these attributes.
- To provide default values for attributes.

Attribute-list declarations specify the name, data type, and default value (if any) of each attribute associated with a given element type:

Attribute-list Declaration

```
[52] AttlistDecl ::=  '<!ATTLIST' S Name AttDef* S? '>'
[53]      AttDef ::=  S Name S AttType S DefaultDecl
```

The `Name` in the `AttlistDecl` rule is the type of an element. At user option, an XML processor may issue a warning if attributes are declared for an element type not itself declared, but this is not an error. The `Name` in the `AttDef` rule is the name of the attribute.

When more than one `AttlistDecl` is provided for a given element type, the contents of all those provided are merged. When more than one definition is provided for the same attribute of a given element type, the first declaration is binding and later declarations are ignored. For interoperability, writers of DTDs may choose to provide at most one attribute-list declaration for a given element type, at most one attribute definition for a given attribute name, and at least one attribute definition in each attribute-list declaration. For interoperability, an XML processor may at user option issue a warning when more than one attribute-list declaration is provided for a given element type, or more than one attribute definition is provided for a given attribute, but this is not an error.

3.3.1 Attribute Types

XML attribute types are of three kinds: a string type, a set of tokenized types, and enumerated types. The string type may take any literal string as a value; the tokenized types have varying lexical and semantic constraints, as noted:

Attribute Types

```
[54]        AttType ::=  StringType | TokenizedType
                         | EnumeratedType
[55]     StringType ::=  'CDATA'
[56]  TokenizedType ::=  'ID'                    [ VC: ID ]
                                                 [ VC: One ID per
                                                   Element Type ]
                                                 [ VC: ID Attribute
                                                   Default ]
                         | 'IDREF'               [ VC: IDREF ]
                         | 'IDREFS'              [ VC: IDREF ]
                         | 'ENTITY'              [ VC: Entity Name ]
                         | 'ENTITIES'            [ VC: Entity Name ]
                         | 'NMTOKEN'             [ VC: Name Token ]
                         | 'NMTOKENS'            [ VC: Name Token ]
```

Validity Constraint: ID

Values of type `ID` must match the `Name` production. A name must not appear more than once in an XML document as a value of this type; i.e., ID values must uniquely identify the elements which bear them.

Validity Constraint: One ID per Element Type

No element type may have more than one ID attribute specified.

Validity Constraint: ID Attribute Default

An ID attribute must have a declared default of `#IMPLIED` or `#REQUIRED`.

Validity Constraint: IDREF

Values of type `IDREF` must match the `Name` production, and values of type `IDREFS` must match `Names`; each `Name` must match the value of an ID attribute on some element in the XML document; i.e. `IDREF` values must match the value of some ID attribute.

Validity Constraint: Entity Name

Values of type `ENTITY` must match the `Name` production, values of type `ENTITIES` must match `Names`; each `Name` must match the name of an unparsed entity declared in the DTD.

Validity Constraint: Name Token

Values of type `NMTOKEN` must match the `Nmtoken` production; values of type `NMTOKENS` must match Nmtokens.

Enumerated attributes can take one of a list of values provided in the declaration. There are two kinds of enumerated types:

Enumerated Attribute Types

```
[57] EnumeratedType ::=  NotationType | Enumeration
[58]   NotationType ::=  'NOTATION' S '(' S? Name        [ VC: Notation
                         (S? '|' S? Name)* S? ')'           Attributes ]
[59]    Enumeration ::=  '(' S? Nmtoken (S? '|'
                         S? Nmtoken)* S? ')'             [ VC: Enumeration ]
```

A `NOTATION` attribute identifies a notation, declared in the DTD with associated system and/or public identifiers, to be used in interpreting the element to which the attribute is attached.

Validity Constraint: Notation Attributes

Values of this type must match one of the notation names included in the declaration; all notation names in the declaration must be declared.

Validity Constraint: Enumeration

Values of this type must match one of the `Nmtoken` tokens in the declaration.

For interoperability, the same `Nmtoken` should not occur more than once in the enumerated attribute types of a single element type.

3.3.2 Attribute Defaults

An attribute declaration provides information on whether the attribute's presence is required, and if not, how an XML processor should react if a declared attribute is absent in a document.

Attribute Defaults

```
[60] DefaultDecl ::= '#REQUIRED' | '#IMPLIED'
                   | (('#FIXED' S)? AttValue) [ VC: Required Attribute ]
                                              [ VC: Attribute Default
                                                Legal ]
                                              [ WFC: No < in Attribute
                                                Values ]
                                              [ VC: Fixed Attribute
                                                Default ]
```

In an attribute declaration, `#REQUIRED` means that the attribute must always be provided, `#IMPLIED` that no default value is provided. If the declaration is neither `#REQUIRED` nor `#IMPLIED`, then the `AttValue` value contains the declared **default** value; the `#FIXED` keyword states that the attribute must always have the default value. If a default value is declared, when an XML processor encounters an omitted attribute, it is to behave as though the attribute were present with the declared default value.

Validity Constraint: Required Attribute

If the default declaration is the keyword `#REQUIRED`, then the attribute must be specified for all elements of the type in the attribute-list declaration.

Validity Constraint: Attribute Default Legal

The declared default value must meet the lexical constraints of the declared attribute type.

Validity Constraint: Fixed Attribute Default

If an attribute has a default value declared with the `#FIXED` keyword, instances of that attribute must match the default value.

Examples of attribute-list declarations:

```
<!ATTLIST termdef
          id      ID     #REQUIRED
          name    CDATA  #IMPLIED>
<!ATTLIST list
          type    (bullets|ordered|glossary)  "ordered">
<!ATTLIST form
           method  CDATA  #FIXED "POST">
```

3.3.3 Attribute-Value Normalization

Before the value of an attribute is passed to the application or checked for validity, the XML processor must normalize it as follows:

- a character reference is processed by appending the referenced character to the attribute value
- an entity reference is processed by recursively processing the replacement text of the entity
- a whitespace character (#x20, #xD, #xA, #x9) is processed by appending #x20 to the normalized value, except that only a single #x20 is appended for a "`#xD#xA`" sequence that is part of an external parsed entity or the literal entity value of an internal parsed entity
- other characters are processed by appending them to the normalized value

If the declared value is not CDATA, then the XML processor must further process the normalized attribute value by discarding any leading and trailing space (#x20) characters, and by replacing sequences of space (#x20) characters by a single space (#x20) character.

All attributes for which no declaration has been read should be treated by a non-validating parser as if declared `CDATA`.

3.4 Conditional Sections

Conditional sections are portions of the document type declaration external subset which are included in, or excluded from, the logical structure of the DTD based on the keyword which governs them.

Conditional Section

```
[61]     conditionalSect ::=  includeSect | ignoreSect
[62]         includeSect ::=  '<![' S? 'INCLUDE' S?
                              '[' extSubsetDecl ']]>'
[63]          ignoreSect ::=  '<![' S? 'IGNORE' S?
                              '[' ignoreSectContents* ']]>'
[64] ignoreSectContents ::=  Ignore ('<![' ignoreSectContents ']]>' Ignore)*
[65]              Ignore ::=  Char* - (Char* ('<![' | ']]>') Char*)
```

Like the internal and external DTD subsets, a conditional section may contain one or more complete declarations, comments, processing instructions, or nested conditional sections, intermingled with white space.

If the keyword of the conditional section is `INCLUDE`, then the contents of the conditional section are part of the DTD. If the keyword of the conditional section is `IGNORE`, then the contents of the conditional section are not logically part of the DTD. Note that for reliable parsing, the contents of even ignored conditional sections must be read in order to detect nested conditional sections and ensure that the end of the outermost (ignored) conditional section is properly detected. If a conditional section with a keyword of `INCLUDE` occurs within a larger conditional section with a keyword of `IGNORE`, both the outer and the inner conditional sections are ignored.

If the keyword of the conditional section is a parameter-entity reference, the parameter entity must be replaced by its content before the processor decides whether to include or ignore the conditional section.

An example:

```
<!ENTITY % draft 'INCLUDE' >
<!ENTITY % final 'IGNORE' >

<![%draft;[
<!ELEMENT book (comments*, title, body, supplements?)>
]]>
<![%final;[
<!ELEMENT book (title, body, supplements?)>
]]>
```

4. Physical Structures

An XML document may consist of one or many storage units. These are called **entities**; they all have **content** and are all (except for the document entity, see below, and the external DTD subset) identified by **name**. Each XML document has one entity called the document entity, which serves as the starting point for the XML processor and may contain the whole document.

Entities may be either parsed or unparsed. A **parsed entity's** contents are referred to as its replacement text; this text is considered an integral part of the document.

An **unparsed entity** is a resource whose contents may or may not be text, and if text, may not be XML. Each unparsed entity has an associated notation, identified by name. Beyond a requirement that an XML processor make the identifiers for the entity and notation available to the application, XML places no constraints on the contents of unparsed entities.

Parsed entities are invoked by name using entity references; unparsed entities by name, given in the value of `ENTITY` or `ENTITIES` attributes.

General entities are entities for use within the document content. In this specification, general entities are sometimes referred to with the unqualified term *entity* when this leads to no ambiguity. Parameter entities are parsed entities for use within the DTD. These two types of entities use different forms of reference and are recognized in different contexts. Furthermore, they occupy different namespaces; a parameter entity and a general entity with the same name are two distinct entities.

4.1 Character and Entity References

A **character reference** refers to a specific character in the ISO/IEC 10646 character set, for example one not directly accessible from available input devices.

Character Reference

```
[66]  CharRef ::=  '&#' [0-9]+ ';'
                   | '&#x' [0-9a-fA-F]+ ';' [  WFC: Legal Character ]
```

Well-Formedness Constraint: Legal Character

Characters referred to using character references must match the production for Char.

If the character reference begins with "`&#x`", the digits and letters up to the terminating ; provide a hexadecimal representation of the character's code point in ISO/IEC 10646. If it begins just with "`&#`", the digits up to the terminating ; provide a decimal representation of the character's code point.

An **entity reference** refers to the content of a named entity. References to parsed general entities use ampersand (`&`) and semicolon (;) as delimiters. **Parameter-entity references** use percent-sign (`%`) and semicolon (;) as delimiters.

Entity Reference

```
[67]    Reference ::=  EntityRef | CharRef
[68]    EntityRef ::=  '&' Name ';'        [ WFC: Entity Declared ]
                                           [ VC: Entity Declared ]
                                           [ WFC: Parsed Entity ]
                                           [ WFC: No Recursion ]
[69]  PEReference ::=  '%' Name ';'        [ VC: Entity Declared ]
                                           [ WFC: No Recursion ]
                                           [ WFC: In DTD ]
```

Well-Formedness Constraint: Entity Declared

In a document without any DTD, a document with only an internal DTD subset which contains no parameter entity references, or a document with "`standalone='yes'`", the `Name` given in the entity reference must match that in an entity declaration, except that well-formed documents need not declare any of the following entities: `amp`, `lt`, `gt`, `apos`, `quot`. The declaration of a parameter entity must precede any reference to it. Similarly, the declaration of a general entity must precede any reference to it which appears in a default value in an attribute-list declaration. Note that if entities are declared in the external subset or in external parameter entities, a non-validating processor is not obligated to read and process their declarations; for such documents, the rule that an entity must be declared is a well-formedness constraint only if `standalone='yes'`.

Validity Constraint: Entity Declared

In a document with an external subset or external parameter entities with "`standalone='no'`", the `Name` given in the entity reference must match that in an entity declaration. For interoperability, valid documents should declare the entities `amp`, `lt`, `gt`, `apos`, `quot`, in the form specified in "4.6 Predefined Entities". The declaration of a parameter entity must precede any reference to it. Similarly, the declaration of a general entity must precede any reference to it which appears in a default value in an attribute-list declaration.

Well-Formedness Constraint: Parsed Entity

An entity reference must not contain the name of an unparsed entity. Unparsed entities may be referred to only in attribute values declared to be of type `ENTITY` or `ENTITIES`.

Well-Formedness Constraint: No Recursion

A parsed entity must not contain a recursive reference to itself, either directly or indirectly.

Well-Formedness Constraint: In DTD

Parameter-entity references may only appear in the DTD.

Examples of character and entity references:

```
Type <key>less-than</key> (&#x3C;) to save options.
This document was prepared on &docdate; and
is classified &security-level;.
```

Example of a parameter-entity reference:

```
<!-- declare the parameter entity "ISOLat2"... -->
<!ENTITY % ISOLat2
        SYSTEM "http://www.xml.com/iso/isolat2-xml.entities" >
<!-- ... now reference it. -->
%ISOLat2;
```

4.2 Entity Declarations

Entities are declared thus:

Entity Declaration

```
[70]  EntityDecl ::=  GEDecl | PEDecl
[71]      GEDecl ::=  '<!ENTITY' S Name S EntityDef S? '>'
[72]      PEDecl ::=  '<!ENTITY' S '%' S Name S PEDef S? '>'
[73]   EntityDef ::=  EntityValue | (ExternalID NDataDecl?)
[74]       PEDef ::=  EntityValue | ExternalID
```

The `Name` identifies the entity in an entity reference or, in the case of an unparsed entity, in the value of an `ENTITY` or `ENTITIES` attribute. If the same entity is declared more than once, the first declaration encountered is binding; at user option, an XML processor may issue a warning if entities are declared multiple times.

4.2.1 Internal Entities

If the entity definition is an `EntityValue`, the defined entity is called an **internal entity**. There is no separate physical storage object, and the content of the entity is given in the declaration. Note that some processing of entity and character references in the literal entity value may be required to produce the correct replacement text: see "4.5 Construction of Internal Entity Replacement Text".

An internal entity is a parsed entity.

Example of an internal entity declaration:

```
<!ENTITY Pub-Status "This is a pre-release of the
specification.">
```

4.2.2 External Entities

If the entity is not internal, it is an **external entity**, declared as follows:

External Entity Declaration

```
[75] ExternalID ::=  'SYSTEM' S SystemLiteral
                   | 'PUBLIC' S PubidLiteral
                   S SystemLiteral
[76]  NDataDecl ::=  S 'NDATA' S Name           [  VC: Notation Declared ]
```

If the `NDataDecl` is present, this is a general unparsed entity; otherwise it is a parsed entity.

Validity Constraint: Notation Declared

The `Name` must match the declared name of a notation.

The `SystemLiteral` is called the entity's **system identifier**. It is a URI, which may be used to retrieve the entity. Note that the hash mark (#) and fragment identifier frequently used with URIs are not, formally, part of the URI itself; an XML processor may signal an error if a fragment identifier is given as part of a system identifier. Unless otherwise provided by information outside the scope of this specification (e.g. a special XML element type defined by a particular DTD, or a processing instruction defined by a particular application specification), relative URIs are relative to the location of the resource within which the entity declaration occurs. A URI might thus be relative to the document entity, to the entity containing the external DTD subset, or to some other external parameter entity.

An XML processor should handle a non-ASCII character in a URI by representing the character in UTF-8 as one or more bytes, and then escaping these bytes with the URI escaping mechanism (i.e., by converting each byte to %HH, where HH is the hexadecimal notation of the byte value).

In addition to a system identifier, an external identifier may include a **public identifier**. An XML processor attempting to retrieve the entity's content may use the public identifier to try to generate an alternative URI. If the processor is unable to do so, it must use the URI specified in the system literal. Before a match is attempted, all strings of white space in the public identifier must be normalized to single space characters (#x20), and leading and trailing white space must be removed.

Examples of external entity declarations:

```
<!ENTITY open-hatch
        SYSTEM "http://www.textuality.com/boilerplate/OpenHatch.xml">
<!ENTITY open-hatch
        PUBLIC "-//Textuality//TEXT Standard open-hatch boilerplate//EN"
        "http://www.textuality.com/boilerplate/OpenHatch.xml">
<!ENTITY hatch-pic
        SYSTEM "../grafix/OpenHatch.gif"
        NDATA gif >
```

4.3 Parsed Entities

4.3.1 The Text Declaration

External parsed entities may each begin with a **text declaration**.

Text Declaration

```
[77]  TextDecl ::=  '<?xml' VersionInfo? EncodingDecl S? '?>'
```

The text declaration must be provided literally, not by reference to a parsed entity. No text declaration may appear at any position other than the beginning of an external parsed entity.

4.3.2 Well-Formed Parsed Entities

The document entity is well-formed if it matches the production labeled `document`. An external general parsed entity is well-formed if it matches the production labeled `extParsedEnt`. An external parameter entity is well-formed if it matches the production labeled `extPE`.

Well-Formed External Parsed Entity

```
[78]  extParsedEnt ::=  TextDecl? content
[79]         extPE ::=  TextDecl? extSubsetDecl
```

An internal general parsed entity is well-formed if its replacement text matches the production labeled `content`. All internal parameter entities are well-formed by definition.

A consequence of well-formedness in entities is that the logical and physical structures in an XML document are properly nested; no start-tag, end-tag, empty-element tag, element, comment, processing instruction, character reference, or entity reference can begin in one entity and end in another.

4.3.3 Character Encoding in Entities

Each external parsed entity in an XML document may use a different encoding for its characters. All XML processors must be able to read entities in either UTF-8 or UTF-16.

Entities encoded in UTF-16 must begin with the Byte Order Mark described by ISO/IEC 10646 Annex E and Unicode Appendix B (the ZERO WIDTH NO-BREAK SPACE character, #xFEFF). This is an encoding signature, not part of either the markup or the character data of the XML document. XML processors must be able to use this character to differentiate between UTF-8 and UTF-16 encoded documents.

Although an XML processor is required to read only entities in the UTF-8 and UTF-16 encodings, it is recognized that other encodings are used around the world, and it may be desired for XML processors to read entities that use them. Parsed entities which are stored in an encoding other than UTF-8 or UTF-16 must begin with a text declaration containing an encoding declaration:

Encoding Declaration

```
[80] EncodingDecl ::= S 'encoding' Eq ('"'
                      EncName '"' | "'" EncName "'" )
[81]      EncName ::= [A-Za-z] ([A-Za-z0-9._]      /* Encoding
                      | '-')*                          name contains
                                                       only Latin
                                                       characters */
```

In the document entity, the encoding declaration is part of the XML declaration. The `EncName` is the name of the encoding used.

In an encoding declaration, the values "`UTF-8`", "`UTF-16`", "`ISO-10646-UCS-2`", and "`ISO-10646-UCS-4`" should be used for the various encodings and transformations of Unicode / ISO/IEC 10646, the values "`ISO-8859-1`", "`ISO-8859-2`", ... "`ISO-8859-9`" should be used for the parts of ISO 8859, and the values "`ISO-2022-JP`", "`Shift_JIS`", and "`EUC-JP`" should be used for the various encoded forms of JIS X-0208-1997. XML processors may recognize other encodings; it is recommended that character encodings registered (as *charsets*) with the Internet Assigned Numbers Authority [IANA], other than those just listed, should be referred to using their registered names. Note that these registered names are defined to be case-insensitive, so processors wishing to match against them should do so in a case-insensitive way.

In the absence of information provided by an external transport protocol (e.g. HTTP or MIME), it is an error for an entity including an encoding declaration to be presented to the XML processor in an encoding other than that named in the declaration, for an encoding declaration to occur other than at the beginning of an external entity, or for an entity which begins with neither a Byte Order Mark nor an encoding declaration to use an encoding other than UTF-8. Note that since ASCII is a subset of UTF-8, ordinary ASCII entities do not strictly need an encoding declaration.

It is a fatal error when an XML processor encounters an entity with an encoding that it is unable to process.

Examples of encoding declarations:

```
<?xml encoding='UTF-8'?>
<?xml encoding='EUC-JP'?>
```

4.4 XML Processor Treatment of Entities and References

The table below summarizes the contexts in which character references, entity references, and invocations of unparsed entities might appear and the required behavior of an XML processor in each case. The labels in the left-most column describe the recognition context:

Reference in Content

as a reference anywhere after the start-tag and before the end-tag of an element; corresponds to the nonterminal `content`.

Reference in Attribute Value

as a reference within either the value of an attribute in a start-tag, or a default value in an attribute declaration; corresponds to the nonterminal `AttValue`.

Occurs as Attribute Value

as a `Name`, not a reference, appearing either as the value of an attribute which has been declared as type `ENTITY`, or as one of the space-separated tokens in the value of an attribute which has been declared as type `ENTITIES`.

Reference in Entity Value

as a reference within a parameter or internal entity's literal entity value in the entity's declaration; corresponds to the nonterminal `EntityValue`.

Reference in DTD

as a reference within either the internal or external subsets of the DTD, but outside of an `EntityValue` or `AttValue`.

	Entity Type				
	Parameter	**Internal General**	**External Parsed General**	**Unparsed**	**Character**
Reference in Content	Not recognized	Included	Included if validating	Forbidden	Included
Reference in Attribute Value	Not recognized	Included in literal	Forbidden	Forbidden	Included
Occurs as Attribute Value	Not recognized	Forbidden	Forbidden	Notify	Not recognized
Reference in EntityValue	Included in literal	Bypassed	Bypassed	Forbidden	Included
Reference in DTD	Included as PE	Forbidden	Forbidden	Forbidden	Forbidden

4.4.1 Not Recognized

Outside the DTD, the `%` character has no special significance; thus, what would be parameter entity references in the DTD are not recognized as markup in `content`. Similarly, the names of unparsed entities are not recognized except when they appear in the value of an appropriately declared attribute.

4.4.2 Included

An entity is **included** when its replacement text is retrieved and processed, in place of the reference itself, as though it were part of the document at the location the reference was recognized. The replacement text may contain both character data and (except for parameter entities) markup, which must be recognized in the usual way, except that the replacement text of entities used to escape markup delimiters (the entities `amp`, `lt`, `gt`, `apos`, `quot`) is always treated as data. (The string "`AT&T;`" expands to "`AT&T;`" and the remaining ampersand is not recognized as an entity-reference delimiter.) A character reference is **included** when the indicated character is processed in place of the reference itself.

4.4.3 Included If Validating

When an XML processor recognizes a reference to a parsed entity, in order to validate the document, the processor must include its replacement text. If the entity is external, and the processor is not attempting to validate the XML document, the processor may, but need not, include the entity's replacement text. If a non-validating parser does not include the replacement text, it must inform the application that it recognized, but did not read, the entity.

This rule is based on the recognition that the automatic inclusion provided by the SGML and XML entity mechanism, primarily designed to support modularity in authoring, is not necessarily appropriate for other applications, in particular document browsing. Browsers, for example, when encountering an external parsed entity reference, might choose to provide a visual indication of the entity's presence and retrieve it for display only on demand.

4.4.4 Forbidden

The following are forbidden, and constitute fatal errors:

- the appearance of a reference to an unparsed entity.
- the appearance of any character or general-entity reference in the DTD except within an `EntityValue` or `AttValue`.
- a reference to an external entity in an attribute value.

4.4.5 Included in Literal

When an entity reference appears in an attribute value, or a parameter entity reference appears in a literal entity value, its replacement text is processed in place of the reference itself as though it were part of the document at the location the reference was recognized, except that a single or double quote character in the replacement text is always treated as a normal data character and will not terminate the literal. For example, this is well-formed:

```
<!ENTITY % YN '"Yes"' >
<!ENTITY WhatHeSaid "He said &YN;" >
```

while this is not:

```
<!ENTITY EndAttr "27'" >
<element attribute='a-&EndAttr;>
```

4.4.6 Notify

When the name of an unparsed entity appears as a token in the value of an attribute of declared type `ENTITY` or `ENTITIES`, a validating processor must inform the application of the system and public (if any) identifiers for both the entity and its associated notation.

4.4.7 Bypassed

When a general entity reference appears in the `EntityValue` in an entity declaration, it is bypassed and left as is.

4.4.8 Included as PE

Just as with external parsed entities, parameter entities need only be included if validating. When a parameter-entity reference is recognized in the DTD and included, its replacement text is enlarged by the attachment of one leading and one following space (#x20) character; the intent is to constrain the replacement text of parameter entities to contain an integral number of grammatical tokens in the DTD.

4.5 Construction of Internal Entity Replacement Text

In discussing the treatment of internal entities, it is useful to distinguish two forms of the entity's value. The **literal entity value** is the quoted string actually present in the entity declaration, corresponding to the non-terminal `EntityValue`. The **replacement text** is the content of the entity, after replacement of character references and parameter-entity references.

The literal entity value as given in an internal entity declaration (`EntityValue`) may contain character, parameter-entity, and general-entity references. Such references must be contained entirely within the literal entity value. The actual replacement text that is included as described above must contain the *replacement text* of any parameter entities referred to, and must contain the character referred to, in place of any character references in the literal entity value; however, general-entity references must be left as-is, unexpanded. For example, given the following declarations:

```
<!ENTITY % pub "&#xc9;ditions Gallimard" >
<!ENTITY rights "All rights reserved" >
<!ENTITY book "La Peste: Albert Camus,
&#xA9; 1947 %pub;. &rights;" >
```

then the replacement text for the entity "`book`" is:

```
La Peste: Albert Camus,
© 1947 Éditions Gallimard. &rights;
```

The general-entity reference "`&rights;`" would be expanded should the reference "`&book;`" appear in the document's content or an attribute value.

These simple rules may have complex interactions; for a detailed discussion of a difficult example, see "D. Expansion of Entity and Character References".

4.6 Predefined Entities

Entity and character references can both be used to **escape** the left angle bracket, ampersand, and other delimiters. A set of general entities (`amp`, `lt`, `gt`, `apos`, `quot`) is specified for this purpose. Numeric character references may also be used; they are expanded immediately when recognized and must be treated as character data, so the numeric character references "`<`" and "`&`" may be used to escape < and `&` when they occur in character data.

All XML processors must recognize these entities whether they are declared or not. For interoperability, valid XML documents should declare these entities, like any others, before using them. If the entities in question are declared, they must be declared as internal entities whose replacement text is the single character being escaped or a character reference to that character, as shown below.

```
<!ENTITY lt "&#38;#60;">
<!ENTITY gt "&#62;">
<!ENTITY amp "&#38;#38;">
<!ENTITY apos "&#39;">
<!ENTITY quot "&#34;">
```

Note that the < and `&` characters in the declarations of "`lt`" and "`amp`" are doubly escaped to meet the requirement that entity replacement be well-formed.

4.7 Notation Declarations

Notations identify by name the format of unparsed entities, the format of elements which bear a notation attribute, or the application to which a processing instruction is addressed.

Notation declarations provide a name for the notation, for use in entity and attribute-list declarations and in attribute specifications, and an external identifier for the notation which may allow an XML processor or its client application to locate a helper application capable of processing data in the given notation.

Notation Declarations

```
[82] NotationDecl ::=  '<!NOTATION' S Name S (ExternalID | PublicID) S? '>'
[83]     PublicID ::=  'PUBLIC' S PubidLiteral
```

XML processors must provide applications with the name and external identifier(s) of any notation declared and referred to in an attribute value, attribute definition, or entity declaration. They may additionally resolve the external identifier into the system identifier, file name, or other information needed to allow the application to call a processor for data in the notation described. (It is not an error, however, for XML documents to declare and refer to notations for which notation-specific applications are not available on the system where the XML processor or application is running.)

4.8 Document Entity

The **document entity** serves as the root of the entity tree and a starting-point for an XML processor. This specification does not specify how the document entity is to be located by an XML processor; unlike other entities, the document entity has no name and might well appear on a processor input stream without any identification at all.

5. Conformance

5.1 Validating and Non-Validating Processors

Conforming XML processors fall into two classes: validating and non-validating.

Validating and non-validating processors alike must report violations of this specification's well-formedness constraints in the content of the document entity and any other parsed entities that they read.

Validating processors must report violations of the constraints expressed by the declarations in the DTD, and failures to fulfill the validity constraints given in this specification. To accomplish this, validating XML processors must read and process the entire DTD and all external parsed entities referenced in the document.

Non-validating processors are required to check only the document entity, including the entire internal DTD subset, for well-formedness. While they are not required to check the document for validity, they are required to **process** all the declarations they read in the internal DTD subset and in any parameter entity that they read, up to the first reference to a parameter entity that they do *not* read; that is to say, they must use the information in those declarations to normalize attribute values, include the replacement text of internal entities, and supply default attribute values. They must not process entity declarations or attribute-list declarations encountered after a reference to a parameter entity that is not read, since the entity may have contained overriding declarations.

5.2 Using XML Processors

The behavior of a validating XML processor is highly predictable; it must read every piece of a document and report all well-formedness and validity violations. Less is required of a non-validating processor; it need not read any part of the document other than the document entity. This has two effects that may be important to users of XML processors:

Certain well-formedness errors, specifically those that require reading external entities, may not be detected by a non-validating processor. Examples include the constraints entitled Entity Declared, Parsed Entity, and No Recursion, as well as some of the cases described as forbidden in "4.4 XML Processor Treatment of Entities and References".

The information passed from the processor to the application may vary, depending on whether the processor reads parameter and external entities. For example, a non-validating processor may not normalize attribute values, include the replacement text of internal entities, or supply default attribute values, where doing so depends on having read declarations in external or parameter entities.

For maximum reliability in interoperating between different XML processors, applications which use non-validating processors should not rely on any behaviors not required of such processors. Applications which require facilities such as the use of default attributes or internal entities which are declared in external entities should use validating XML processors.

6. Notation

The formal grammar of XML is given in this specification using a simple Extended Backus-Naur Form (EBNF) notation. Each rule in the grammar defines one symbol, in the form

```
symbol ::= expression
```

Symbols are written with an initial capital letter if they are defined by a regular expression, or with an initial lower case letter otherwise. Literal strings are quoted.

Within the expression on the right-hand side of a rule, the following expressions are used to match strings of one or more characters:

`#xN`

where `N` is a hexadecimal integer, the expression matches the character in ISO/IEC 10646 whose canonical (UCS-4) code value, when interpreted as an unsigned binary number, has the value indicated. The number of leading zeros in the `#xN` form is insignificant; the number of leading zeros in the corresponding code value is governed by the character encoding in use and is not significant for XML.

`[a-zA-Z], [#xN-#xN]`

matches any character with a value in the range(s) indicated (inclusive).

`[^a-z], [^#xN-#xN]`

matches any character with a value *outside* the range indicated.

`[^abc], [^#xN#xN#xN]`

matches any character with a value not among the characters given.

`"string"`

matches a literal string matching that given inside the double quotes.

`'string'`

matches a literal string matching that given inside the single quotes.

These symbols may be combined to match more complex patterns as follows, where `A` and `B` represent simple expressions:

`(expression)`

`expression` is treated as a unit and may be combined as described in this list.

`A?`

matches `A` or nothing; optional `A`.

`A B`

matches `A` followed by `B`.

`A | B`

matches `A` or `B` but not both.

`A - B`

matches any string that matches `A` but does not match `B`.

`A+`

matches one or more occurrences of `A`.

`A*`

matches zero or more occurrences of `A`.

Other notations used in the productions are:

`/* ... */`

comment.

`[ wfc: ... ]`

well-formedness constraint; this identifies by name a constraint on well-formed documents associated with a production.

`[ vc: ... ]`

validity constraint; this identifies by name a constraint on valid documents associated with a production.

Appendices

A. References

A.1 Normative References

IANA

(Internet Assigned Numbers Authority) *Official Names for Character Sets*, ed. Keld Simonsen et al. See ftp://ftp.isi.edu/in-notes/iana/assignments/character-sets.

IETF RFC 1766

IETF (Internet Engineering Task Force). *RFC 1766: Tags for the Identification of Languages*, ed. H. Alvestrand. 1995.

ISO 639

(International Organization for Standardization). *ISO 639:1988 (E). Code for the representation of names of languages.* [Geneva]: International Organization for Standardization, 1988.

ISO 3166

(International Organization for Standardization). *ISO 3166-1:1997 (E). Codes for the representation of names of countries and their subdivisions — Part 1: Country codes* [Geneva]: International Organization for Standardization, 1997.

ISO/IEC 10646

ISO (International Organization for Standardization). *ISO/IEC 10646-1993 (E). Information technology — Universal Multiple-Octet Coded Character Set (UCS) — Part 1: Architecture and Basic Multilingual Plane.* [Geneva]: International Organization for Standardization, 1993 (plus amendments AM 1 through AM 7).

Unicode

The Unicode Consortium. *The Unicode Standard, Version 2.0.* Reading, Mass.: Addison-Wesley Developers Press, 1996.

A.2 Other References

Aho/Ullman

Aho, Alfred V., Ravi Sethi, and Jeffrey D. Ullman. *Compilers: Principles, Techniques, and Tools*. Reading: Addison-Wesley, 1986, rpt. corr. 1988.

Berners-Lee et al.

Berners-Lee, T., R. Fielding, and L. Masinter. *Uniform Resource Identifiers (URI): Generic Syntax and Semantics*. 1997. (Work in progress; see updates to RFC1738.)

Brüggemann-Klein

Brüggemann-Klein, Anne. *Regular Expressions into Finite Automata.* Extended abstract in I. Simon, Hrsg., LATIN 1992, S. 97-98. Springer-Verlag, Berlin 1992. Full Version in Theoretical Computer Science 120: 197-213, 1993.

Brüggemann-Klein and Wood

Brüggemann-Klein, Anne, and Derick Wood. *Deterministic Regular Languages*. Universitaüt Freiburg, Institut für Informatik, Bericht 38, Oktober 1991.

Clark

James Clark. Comparison of SGML and XML. See http://www.w3.org/TR/NOTE-sgml-xml-971215.

IETF RFC1738

IETF (Internet Engineering Task Force). *RFC 1738: Uniform Resource Locators (URL)*, ed. T. Berners-Lee, L. Masinter, M. McCahill. 1994.

IETF RFC1808

IETF (Internet Engineering Task Force). *RFC 1808: Relative Uniform Resource Locators*, ed. R. Fielding. 1995.

IETF RFC2141

IETF (Internet Engineering Task Force). *RFC 2141: URN Syntax*, ed. R. Moats. 1997.

ISO 8879

ISO (International Organization for Standardization). *ISO 8879:1986(E). Information processing — Text and Office Systems — Standard Generalized Markup Language (SGML)*. First edition — 1986-10-15. [Geneva]: International Organization for Standardization, 1986.

ISO/IEC 10744

ISO (International Organization for Standardization). *ISO/IEC 10744-1992 (E). Information technology — Hypermedia/Time-based Structuring Language (HyTime)*. [Geneva]: International Organization for Standardization, 1992. *Extended Facilities Annexe.* [Geneva]: International Organization for Standardization, 1996.

B. Character Classes

Following the characteristics defined in the Unicode standard, characters are classed as base characters (among others, these contain the alphabetic characters of the Latin alphabet, without diacritics), ideographic characters, and combining characters (among others, this class contains most diacritics); these classes combine to form the class of letters. Digits and extenders are also distinguished.

Characters

```
[84]      Letter ::=  BaseChar | Ideographic
[85]    BaseChar ::=  [#x0041-#x005A] | [#x0061-#x007A] | [#x00C0-#x00D6]
                      | [#x00D8-#x00F6]
                      | [#x00F8-#x00FF] | [#x0100-#x0131] | [#x0134-#x013E]
                      | [#x0141-#x0148] | [#x014A-#x017E] | [#x0180-#x01C3]
                      | [#x01CD-#x01F0] | [#x01F4-#x01F5] | [#x01FA-#x0217]
                      | [#x0250-#x02A8] | [#x02BB-#x02C1] | #x0386
                      | [#x0388-#x038A]
                      | #x038C | [#x038E-#x03A1] | [#x03A3-#x03CE]
                      | [#x03D0-#x03D6]
                      | #x03DA | #x03DC | #x03DE | #x03E0 | [#x03E2-#x03F3]
                      | [#x0401-#x040C] | [#x040E-#x044F] | [#x0451-#x045C]
                      | [#x045E-#x0481] | [#x0490-#x04C4] | [#x04C7-#x04C8]
                      | [#x04CB-#x04CC] | [#x04D0-#x04EB] | [#x04EE-#x04F5]
                      | [#x04F8-#x04F9] | [#x0531-#x0556] | #x0559
                      | [#x0561-#x0586]
                      | [#x05D0-#x05EA] | [#x05F0-#x05F2] | [#x0621-#x063A]
                      | [#x0641-#x064A] | [#x0671-#x06B7] | [#x06BA-#x06BE]
                      | [#x06C0-#x06CE] | [#x06D0-#x06D3] | #x06D5
                      | [#x06E5-#x06E6]
                      | [#x0905-#x0939] | #x093D | [#x0958-#x0961]
```

continues ▸

```
| [#x0985-#x098C]
| [#x098F-#x0990] | [#x0993-#x09A8] | [#x09AA-#x09B0]
| #x09B2
| [#x09B6-#x09B9] | [#x09DC-#x09DD] | [#x09DF-#x09E1]
| [#x09F0-#x09F1] | [#x0A05-#x0A0A] | [#x0A0F-#x0A10]
| [#x0A13-#x0A28] | [#x0A2A-#x0A30] | [#x0A32-#x0A33]
| [#x0A35-#x0A36] | [#x0A38-#x0A39] | [#x0A59-#x0A5C]
| #x0A5E
| [#x0A72-#x0A74] | [#x0A85-#x0A8B] | #x0A8D
| [#x0A8F-#x0A91]
| [#x0A93-#x0AA8] | [#x0AAA-#x0AB0] | [#x0AB2-#x0AB3]
| [#x0AB5-#x0AB9] | #x0ABD | #x0AE0 | [#x0B05-#x0B0C]
| [#x0B0F-#x0B10] | [#x0B13-#x0B28] | [#x0B2A-#x0B30]
| [#x0B32-#x0B33] | [#x0B36-#x0B39] | #x0B3D
| [#x0B5C-#x0B5D]
| [#x0B5F-#x0B61] | [#x0B85-#x0B8A] | [#x0B8E-#x0B90]
| [#x0B92-#x0B95] | [#x0B99-#x0B9A] | #x0B9C
| [#x0B9E-#x0B9F]
| [#x0BA3-#x0BA4] | [#x0BA8-#x0BAA] | [#x0BAE-#x0BB5]
| [#x0BB7-#x0BB9] | [#x0C05-#x0C0C] | [#x0C0E-#x0C10]
| [#x0C12-#x0C28] | [#x0C2A-#x0C33] | [#x0C35-#x0C39]
| [#x0C60-#x0C61] | [#x0C85-#x0C8C] | [#x0C8E-#x0C90]
| [#x0C92-#x0CA8] | [#x0CAA-#x0CB3] | [#x0CB5-#x0CB9]
| #x0CDE
| [#x0CE0-#x0CE1] | [#x0D05-#x0D0C] | [#x0D0E-#x0D10]
| [#x0D12-#x0D28] | [#x0D2A-#x0D39] | [#x0D60-#x0D61]
| [#x0E01-#x0E2E] | #x0E30 | [#x0E32-#x0E33]
| [#x0E40-#x0E45]
| [#x0E81-#x0E82] | #x0E84 | [#x0E87-#x0E88]
| #x0E8A | #x0E8D
| [#x0E94-#x0E97] | [#x0E99-#x0E9F] | [#x0EA1-#x0EA3]
| #x0EA5
| #x0EA7 | [#x0EAA-#x0EAB] | [#x0EAD-#x0EAE] | #x0EB0
| [#x0EB2-#x0EB3] | #x0EBD | [#x0EC0-#x0EC4]
| [#x0F40-#x0F47]
| [#x0F49-#x0F69] | [#x10A0-#x10C5] | [#x10D0-#x10F6]
| #x1100
| [#x1102-#x1103] | [#x1105-#x1107] | #x1109
| [#x110B-#x110C]
| [#x110E-#x1112] | #x113C | #x113E | #x1140 | #x114C
| #x114E
| #x1150 | [#x1154-#x1155] | #x1159 | [#x115F-#x1161]
| #x1163
| #x1165 | #x1167 | #x1169 | [#x116D-#x116E]
| [#x1172-#x1173]
| #x1175 | #x119E | #x11A8 | #x11AB | [#x11AE-#x11AF]
| [#x11B7-#x11B8] | #x11BA | [#x11BC-#x11C2] | #x11EB
| #x11F0
| #x11F9 | [#x1E00-#x1E9B] | [#x1EA0-#x1EF9]
| [#x1F00-#x1F15]
| [#x1F18-#x1F1D] | [#x1F20-#x1F45] | [#x1F48-#x1F4D]
| [#x1F50-#x1F57] | #x1F59 | #x1F5B | #x1F5D
```

```
                         | [#x1F5F-#x1F7D]
                         | [#x1F80-#x1FB4] | [#x1FB6-#x1FBC] | #x1FBE
                         | [#x1FC2-#x1FC4]
                         | [#x1FC6-#x1FCC] | [#x1FD0-#x1FD3] | [#x1FD6-#x1FDB]
                         | [#x1FE0-#x1FEC] | [#x1FF2-#x1FF4] | [#x1FF6-#x1FFC]
                         | #x2126
                         | [#x212A-#x212B] | #x212E | [#x2180-#x2182]
                         | [#x3041-#x3094]
                         | [#x30A1-#x30FA] | [#x3105-#x312C] | [#xAC00-#xD7A3]
[86]    Ideographic ::=  [#x4E00-#x9FA5] | #x3007 | [#x3021-#x3029]
[87]  CombiningChar ::=  [#x0300-#x0345] | [#x0360-#x0361] | [#x0483-#x0486]
                         | [#x0591-#x05A1]
                         | [#x05A3-#x05B9] | [#x05BB-#x05BD] | #x05BF
                         | [#x05C1-#x05C2]
                         | #x05C4 | [#x064B-#x0652] | #x0670 | [#x06D6-#x06DC]
                         | [#x06DD-#x06DF] | [#x06E0-#x06E4] | [#x06E7-#x06E8]
                         | [#x06EA-#x06ED] | [#x0901-#x0903] | #x093C
                         | [#x093E-#x094C]
                         | #x094D | [#x0951-#x0954] | [#x0962-#x0963]
                         | [#x0981-#x0983]
                         | #x09BC | #x09BE | #x09BF | [#x09C0-#x09C4]
                         | [#x09C7-#x09C8]
                         | [#x09CB-#x09CD] | #x09D7 | [#x09E2-#x09E3] | #x0A02
                         | #x0A3C
                         | #x0A3E | #x0A3F | [#x0A40-#x0A42] | [#x0A47-#x0A48]
                         | [#x0A4B-#x0A4D] | [#x0A70-#x0A71] | [#x0A81-#x0A83]
                         | #x0ABC
                         | [#x0ABE-#x0AC5] | [#x0AC7-#x0AC9] | [#x0ACB-#x0ACD]
                         | [#x0B01-#x0B03] | #x0B3C | [#x0B3E-#x0B43]
                         | [#x0B47-#x0B48]
                         | [#x0B4B-#x0B4D] | [#x0B56-#x0B57] | [#x0B82-#x0B83]
                         | [#x0BBE-#x0BC2] | [#x0BC6-#x0BC8] | [#x0BCA-#x0BCD]
                         | #x0BD7
                         | [#x0C01-#x0C03] | [#x0C3E-#x0C44] | [#x0C46-#x0C48]
                         | [#x0C4A-#x0C4D] | [#x0C55-#x0C56] | [#x0C82-#x0C83]
                         | [#x0CBE-#x0CC4] | [#x0CC6-#x0CC8] | [#x0CCA-#x0CCD]
                         | [#x0CD5-#x0CD6] | [#x0D02-#x0D03] | [#x0D3E-#x0D43]
                         | [#x0D46-#x0D48] | [#x0D4A-#x0D4D] | #x0D57 | #x0E31
                         | [#x0E34-#x0E3A] | [#x0E47-#x0E4E] | #x0EB1
                         | [#x0EB4-#x0EB9]
                         | [#x0EBB-#x0EBC] | [#x0EC8-#x0ECD] | [#x0F18-#x0F19]
                         | #x0F35
                         | #x0F37 | #x0F39 | #x0F3E | #x0F3F | [#x0F71-#x0F84]
                         | [#x0F86-#x0F8B] | [#x0F90-#x0F95] | #x0F97
                         | [#x0F99-#x0FAD]
                         | [#x0FB1-#x0FB7] | #x0FB9 | [#x20D0-#x20DC] | #x20E1
                         | [#x302A-#x302F] | #x3099 | #x309A
[88]          Digit ::=  [#x0030-#x0039] | [#x0660-#x0669] | [#x06F0-#x06F9]
                         | [#x0966-#x096F]
                         | [#x09E6-#x09EF] | [#x0A66-#x0A6F] | [#x0AE6-#x0AEF]
                         | [#x0B66-#x0B6F] | [#x0BE7-#x0BEF] | [#x0C66-#x0C6F]
                         | [#x0CE6-#x0CEF] | [#x0D66-#x0D6F] | [#x0E50-#x0E59]
```

continues ▸

```
                      | [#x0ED0-#x0ED9] | [#x0F20-#x0F29]
[89]   Extender ::=  #x00B7 | #x02D0 | #x02D1 | #x0387 | #x0640 | #x0E46
                      | #x0EC6 | #x3005
                      |[#x3031-#x3035] | [#x309D-#x309E] | [#x30FC-#x30FE]
```

The character classes defined here can be derived from the Unicode character database as follows:

- Name start characters must have one of the categories Ll, Lu, Lo, Lt, Nl.
- Name characters other than Name-start characters must have one of the categories Mc, Me, Mn, Lm, or Nd.
- Characters in the compatibility area (i.e. with character code greater than #xF900 and less than #xFFFE) are not allowed in XML names.
- Characters which have a font or compatibility decomposition (i.e. those with a "compatibility formatting tag" in field 5 of the database — marked by field 5 beginning with a "<") are not allowed.
- The following characters are treated as name-start characters rather than name characters, because the property file classifies them as Alphabetic: [#x02BB-#x02C1], #x0559, #x06E5, #x06E6.
- Characters #x20DD-#x20E0 are excluded (in accordance with Unicode, section 5.14).
- Character #x00B7 is classified as an extender, because the property list so identifies it.
- Character #x0387 is added as a name character, because #x00B7 is its canonical equivalent.
- Characters ':' and '_' are allowed as name-start characters.
- Characters '-' and '.' are allowed as name characters.

C. XML and SGML (Non-Normative)

XML is designed to be a subset of SGML, in that every valid XML document should also be a conformant SGML document. For a detailed comparison of the additional restrictions that XML places on documents beyond those of SGML, see [Clark].

D. Expansion of Entity and Character References (Non-Normative)

This appendix contains some examples illustrating the sequence of entity- and character-reference recognition and expansion, as specified in "4.4 XML Processor Treatment of Entities and References".

If the DTD contains the declaration

```
<!ENTITY example "<p>An ampersand (&#38;#38;) may be escaped
numerically (&#38;#38;#38;) or with a general entity
(&amp;amp;).</p>" >
```

then the XML processor will recognize the character references when it parses the entity declaration, and resolve them before storing the following string as the value of the entity "example":

```
<p>An ampersand (&#38;) may be escaped
numerically (&#38;#38;) or with a general entity
(&amp;amp;).</p>
```

A reference in the document to "&example;" will cause the text to be reparsed, at which time the start- and end-tags of the "p" element will be recognized and the three references will be recognized and expanded, resulting in a "p" element with the following content (all data, no delimiters or markup):

An ampersand (&) may be escaped numerically (&) or with a general entity (&).

A more complex example will illustrate the rules and their effects fully. In the following example, the line numbers are solely for reference.

```
1 <?xml version='1.0'?>
2 <!DOCTYPE test [
3 <!ELEMENT test (#PCDATA) >
4 <!ENTITY % xx '&#37;zz;'>
5 <!ENTITY % zz '&#60;!ENTITY tricky "error-prone" >' >
6 %xx;
7 ]>
8 <test>This sample shows a &tricky; method.</test>
```

This produces the following:

- in line 4, the reference to character 37 is expanded immediately, and the parameter entity "xx" is stored in the symbol table with the value "%zz;". Since the replacement text is not rescanned, the reference to parameter entity "zz" is not recognized. (And it would be an error if it were, since "zz" is not yet declared.)
- in line 5, the character reference "<" is expanded immediately and the parameter entity "zz" is stored with the replacement text "<!ENTITY tricky "error-prone" >", which is a well-formed entity declaration.
- in line 6, the reference to "xx" is recognized, and the replacement text of "xx" (namely "%zz;") is parsed. The reference to "zz" is recognized in its turn, and its replacement text ("<!ENTITY tricky "error-prone" >") is

parsed. The general entity "`tricky`" has now been declared, with the replacement text "`error-prone`".

- in line 8, the reference to the general entity "`tricky`" is recognized, and it is expanded, so the full content of the "`test`" element is the self-describing (and ungrammatical) string *This sample shows a error-prone method.*

E. Deterministic Content Models (Non-Normative)

For compatibility, it is required that content models in element type declarations be deterministic.

SGML requires deterministic content models (it calls them "unambiguous"); XML processors built using SGML systems may flag non-deterministic content models as errors.

For example, the content model `((b, c) | (b, d))` is non-deterministic, because given an initial `b` the parser cannot know which `b` in the model is being matched without looking ahead to see which element follows the `b`. In this case, the two references to `b` can be collapsed into a single reference, making the model read `(b, (c | d))`. An initial `b` now clearly matches only a single name in the content model. The parser doesn't need to look ahead to see what follows; either `c` or `d` would be accepted.

More formally: a finite state automaton may be constructed from the content model using the standard algorithms, e.g. algorithm 3.5 in section 3.9 of Aho, Sethi, and Ullman [Aho/Ullman]. In many such algorithms, a follow set is constructed for each position in the regular expression (i.e., each leaf node in the syntax tree for the regular expression); if any position has a follow set in which more than one following position is labeled with the same element type name, then the content model is in error and may be reported as an error.

Algorithms exist which allow many but not all non-deterministic content models to be reduced automatically to equivalent deterministic models; see Brüggemann-Klein 1991 [Brüggemann-Klein].

F. Autodetection of Character Encodings (Non-Normative)

The XML encoding declaration functions as an internal label on each entity, indicating which character encoding is in use. Before an XML processor can read the internal label, however, it apparently has to know what character encoding is in use—which is what the internal label is trying to indicate. In the general case, this is a hopeless situation. It is not entirely hopeless in XML, however, because XML limits the general case in two ways: each implementation is assumed to support only a finite set of character encodings, and the XML encoding declaration is restricted in position and content in order to make it feasible to autodetect the character encoding in use in each entity in normal cases. Also, in many cases other sources of information are available in addition to the XML data stream itself. Two cases may be distinguished, depending on whether the XML entity is presented to the processor without, or with, any accompanying (external) information. We consider the first case first.

Because each XML entity not in UTF-8 or UTF-16 format *must* begin with an XML encoding declaration, in which the first characters must be `'<?xml'`, any conforming processor can detect, after two to four octets of input, which of the following cases apply. In reading this list, it may help to know that in UCS-4, `'<'` is `"#x0000003C"` and `'?'` is `"#x0000003F"`, and the Byte Order Mark required of UTF-16 data streams is `"#xFEFF"`.

- `00 00 00 3C`: UCS-4, big-endian machine (1234 order)
- `3C 00 00 00`: UCS-4, little-endian machine (4321 order)
- `00 00 3C 00`: UCS-4, unusual octet order (2143)
- `00 3C 00 00`: UCS-4, unusual octet order (3412)
- `FE FF`: UTF-16, big-endian
- `FF FE`: UTF-16, little-endian
- `00 3C 00 3F`: UTF-16, big-endian, no Byte Order Mark (and thus, strictly speaking, in error)
- `3C 00 3F 00`: UTF-16, little-endian, no Byte Order Mark (and thus, strictly speaking, in error)
- `3C 3F 78 6D`: UTF-8, ISO 646, ASCII, some part of ISO 8859, Shift-JIS, EUC, or any other 7-bit, 8-bit, or mixed-width encoding which ensures that the characters of ASCII have their normal positions, width, and values; the actual encoding declaration must be read to detect which of these applies, but since all of these encodings use the same bit patterns for the ASCII characters, the encoding declaration itself may be read reliably
- `4C 6F A7 94`: EBCDIC (in some flavor; the full encoding declaration must be read to tell which code page is in use)
- other: UTF-8 without an encoding declaration, or else the data stream is corrupt, fragmentary, or enclosed in a wrapper of some kind

This level of autodetection is enough to read the XML encoding declaration and parse the character-encoding identifier, which is still necessary to distinguish the individual members of each family of encodings (e.g. to tell UTF-8 from 8859, and the parts of 8859 from each other, or to distinguish the specific EBCDIC code page in use, and so on).

Because the contents of the encoding declaration are restricted to ASCII characters, a processor can reliably read the entire encoding declaration as soon as it has detected which family of encodings is in use. Since in practice, all widely used character encodings fall into one of the categories above, the XML encoding declaration allows reasonably reliable in-band labeling of character encodings, even when external sources of information at the operating-system or transport-protocol level are unreliable.

Once the processor has detected the character encoding in use, it can act appropriately, whether by invoking a separate input routine for each case, or by calling the proper conversion function on each character of input.

Like any self-labeling system, the XML encoding declaration will not work if any software changes the entity's character set or encoding without updating the encoding declaration. Implementers of character-encoding routines should be careful to ensure the accuracy of the internal and external information used to label the entity.

The second possible case occurs when the XML entity is accompanied by encoding information, as in some file systems and some network protocols. When multiple sources of information are available, their relative priority and the preferred method of handling conflict should be specified as part of the higher-level protocol used to deliver XML. Rules for the relative priority of the internal label and the MIME-type label in an external header, for example, should be part of the RFC document defining the text/xml and application/xml MIME types. In the interests of interoperability, however, the following rules are recommended.

- If an XML entity is in a file, the Byte-Order Mark and encoding-declaration PI are used (if present) to determine the character encoding. All other heuristics and sources of information are solely for error recovery.
- If an XML entity is delivered with a MIME type of text/xml, then the `charset` parameter on the MIME type determines the character encoding method; all other heuristics and sources of information are solely for error recovery.

- If an XML entity is delivered with a MIME type of application/xml, then the Byte-Order Mark and encoding-declaration PI are used (if present) to determine the character encoding. All other heuristics and sources of information are solely for error recovery.

These rules apply only in the absence of protocol-level documentation; in particular, when the MIME types text/xml and application/xml are defined, the recommendations of the relevant RFC will supersede these rules.

G. W3C XML Working Group (Non-Normative)

This specification was prepared and approved for publication by the W3C XML Working Group (WG). WG approval of this specification does not necessarily imply that all WG members voted for its approval. The current and former members of the XML WG are:

Jon Bosak, Sun (Chair); James Clark (Technical Lead); Tim Bray, Textuality and Netscape (XML Co-editor); Jean Paoli, Microsoft (XML Co-editor); C. M. Sperberg-McQueen, U. of Ill. (XML Co-editor); Dan Connolly, W3C (W3C Liaison); Paula Angerstein, Texcel; Steve DeRose, INSO; Dave Hollander, HP; Eliot Kimber, ISOGEN; Eve Maler, ArborText; Tom Magliery, NCSA; Murray Maloney, Muzmo and Grif; Makoto Murata, Fuji Xerox Information Systems; Joel Nava, Adobe; Conleth O'Connell, Vignette; Peter Sharpe, SoftQuad; John Tigue, DataChannel

Index

Symbols

B

D

E

F

G

H

I

J

K-L

M

N

O

P

Q-R

S

T

W

X-Z

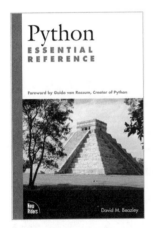

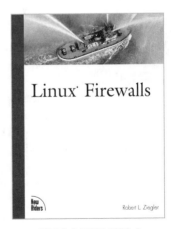

Advanced Information on Networking Technologies

New Riders Books Offer Advice and Experience

LANDMARK

Rethinking Computer Books

We know how important it is to have access to detailed, solution-oriented information on core technologies. *Landmark* books contain the essential information you need to solve technical problems. Written by experts and subjected to rigorous peer and technical reviews, our *Landmark* books are hard-core resources for practitioners like you.

ESSENTIAL REFERENCE

Smart, Like You

The *Essential Reference* series from New Riders provides answers when you know what you want to do but need to know how to do it. Each title skips extraneous material and assumes a strong base of knowledge. These are indispensable books for the practitioner who wants to find specific features of a technology quickly and efficiently. Avoiding fluff and basic material, these books present solutions in an innovative, clean format—and at a great value.

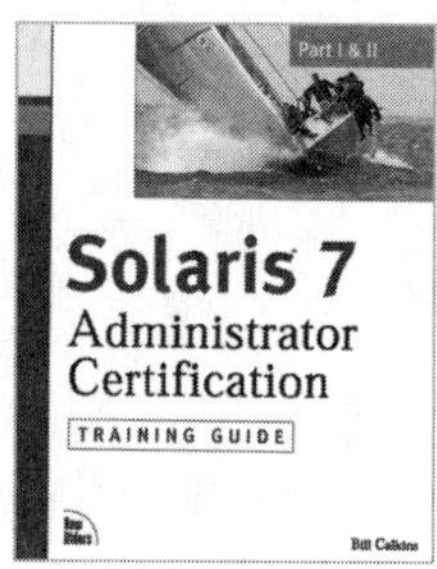

MCSE CERTIFICATION

Engineered for Test Success

New Riders offers a complete line of test preparation materials to help you achieve your certification. With books like the *MCSE Training Guide*, and software like the acclaimed *MCSE Complete* and the revolutionary *ExamGear*, New Riders offers comprehensive products built by experienced professionals who have passed the exams and instructed hundreds of candidates.

Selected Titles from New Riders

Microsoft Technologies

Inside Windows 2000 Server

By William Boswell
1st Edition
1515 pages, $49.99
ISBN: 1-56205-929-7

Taking the author-driven, no-nonsense approach we pioneered with our *Landmark* books, New Riders proudly offers something unique for Windows 2000 administrators—an interesting, discriminating book on Windows 2000 Server written by someone who can anticipate your situation and give you workarounds that won't leave a system unstable or sluggish.

Windows 2000 Active Directory

By Ed Brovick, Doug Hauger, and William Wade III
1st Edition
416 pages, $29.99
ISBN: 0-7357-0870-3

Written by three of Microsoft's key premium partners, with high-level access to people, information, and resources, this book offers a concise, focused, and informative *Landmark* format, filled with case studies and real-world experience for Windows 2000's most anticipated and most complex feature—the Active Directory.

Windows 2000 Essential Reference

By Steven Tate, et al.
1st Edition
670 pages, $35.00
ISBN: 0-7357-0869-X

Architected to be the most navigable, useful and value-packed reference for Windows 2000, this book uses a creative "telescoping" design that you can adapt to your style of learning. The authors give you answers based on their hands-on experience with Windows 2000 and apply their formidable credentials toward giving you the answers you won't find anywhere else.

Windows 2000 Routing and Remote Access Service

By Kackie Charles
1st Edition
400 pages, $34.99
ISBN: 0-7357-0951-3

Ideal for system administrators looking to create cost-effective and secure remote access across the network. Author Kackie Charles uses concrete examples to demonstrate how to smoothly integrate Windows 2000 routing with your existing routing infrastructure, and connect users to the network while maxmizing available bandwidth. Featured coverage includes new authentication models, routing protocols, configuration of the Windows 2000 router, design issues, security, and troubleshooting.

Windows 2000 Deployment & Desktop Management

By Jeffrey A. Ferris
1st Edition
408 pages, $34.99
ISBN: 0-7357-0975-0

More than a simple overview of new features and tools, this solutions-driven book is a thorough reference to deploying Windows 2000 Professional to corporate workstations. The expert real-world advice and detailed exercises make this a one-stop, easy-to-use resource for any system administrator, integrator, engineer, or other IT professional planning rollout of Windows 2000 clients.

Windows 2000 DNS

By Herman Knief, Jeffrey Graham, Andrew Daniels, and Roger Abell
2nd Edition
480 pages, $39.99
ISBN: 0-7357-0973-4

Focusing on such key topics as designing and securing DNS services, planning for interoperation, and installing and using DHCP and WINS services, *Windows 2000 DNS* is a comprehensive guide to the newest iteration of Microsoft's DNS. The authors provide you with real-world advice, best practices, and strategies you will need to design and administer DNS for optimal performance.

Windows 2000 User Management

By Lori Sanders
1st Edition
240 pages, $34.99
ISBN: 1-56205-886-X

With the dawn of Windows 2000, it has become even more difficult to draw a clear line between managing the user and managing the user's environment and desktop. This book, written by a noted trainer and consultant, provides a comprehensive, practical guide to managing users and their desktop environments with Windows 2000.

Windows 2000 Professional

By Jerry Honeycutt
1st Edition
330 pages, $34.99
ISBN: 0-7357-0950-5

Windows 2000 Professional explores the power available to the Windows workstation user on the corporate network and Internet. The book is aimed directly at the power user who values the security, stability, and networking capabilities of NT alongside the ease and familiarity of the Windows 9X user interface. This book covers both user and administration topics, with a dose of networking content added for connectivity.

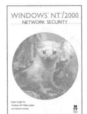

Windows 2000 TCP/IP

By Karanjit S. Siyan, Ph.D.
2nd Edition
920 pages, $39.99
ISBN 0-7357-0992-0

Focusing on ways to administer networks using Microsoft TCP/IP, this book is for professionals who want to read about best practices on using the technology. Without spending time on basics that readers already understand, *Windows 2000 TCP/IP* presents advanced solutions and is a must-have for any system administrator.

Windows NT Performance Monitoring, Benchmarking, and Tuning

By Mark Edmead and Paul Hinsberg
1st Edition
288 pages, $29.99
ISBN: 1-56205-942-4

Windows NT Performance Monitoring, Benchmarking, and Tuning provides a one-stop source for sound technical information on doing everything necessary to fine-tune your network. From benchmarking to analyzing performance numbers to isolating and solving resource bottlenecks, the authors provide a reliable blueprint for ensuring optimal Windows NT performance.

Windows NT Registry: A Settings Reference

By Sandra Osborne
1st Edition
576 pages, $29.99
ISBN:1-56205-941-6

More than a simple troubleshooting or optimization book, this solutions-driven guide shows you how to manage hardware, Windows NT Workstation and other clients, notebook computers, application software, and Internet settings using the Registry in the most efficient and cost-effective manner possible. If you're a network developer, system engineer, server administrator, or workstation technician, you'll come to rely on the expert advice contained in this comprehensive reference.

Windows NT Domain Architecture

By Gregg Branham
1st Edition
312 pages, $39.95
ISBN: 1-57870-112-0

As Windows NT continues to be deployed more and more in the enterprise, the domain architecture for the network becomes critical as the complexity increases. This book contains the in-depth expertise that is necessary to truly plan a complex enterprise domain.

Windows NT/2000 Native API Reference

By Gary Nebbett
1st Edition
528 pages, $50.00
ISBN:1-57870-199-6

This book is the first complete reference to the API functions native to Windows NT and covers the set of services that are offered by the Windows NT to both kernel- and user-mode programs. Coverage consists of documentation of the 210 routines included in the NT Native API, and the functions that will be added in Windows 2000. Routines that are either not directly accessible via the Win32 API or offer substantial additional functionality are described in especially great detail. Services offered by the NT kernel—mainly the support for debugging user mode applications—are also included.

Windows NT Device Driver Development

By Peter Viscarola and W. Anthony Mason
1st Edition
704 pages, $50.00
ISBN: 1-57870-058-2

This title begins with an introduction to the general Windows NT operating system concepts relevant to drivers, then progresses to more detailed information about the operating system, such as interrupt management, synchronization issues, the I/O Subsystem, standard kernel mode drivers, and more.

DCE/RPC over SMB: Samba and Windows NT Domain Internals

By Luke Leighton
1st Edition
312 pages, $45.00
ISBN: 1-57870-150-3

Security people, system and network administrators, and those writing tools for them all need to be familiar with the packets flowing across their networks. Authored by a key member of the Samba team, this book describes how Microsoft has taken DCE/RPC and implemented it over SMB and TCP/IP.

Delphi COM Programming

By Eric Harmon
1st Edition
500 pages, $45.00
ISBN: 1-57870-221-6

Delphi COM Programming is for all Delphi 3, 4, and 5 programmers. After providing readers with an understanding of the COM framework, it offers a practical exploration of COM to enable Delphi developers to program component-based applications. Typical real-world scenarios, such as Windows Shell programming, automating Microsoft Agent, and creating and using ActiveX controls, are explored. Discussions of each topic are illustrated with detailed examples.

Applying COM+

By Gregory Brill
1st Edition
450 pages, $49.99
ISBN: 0-7357-0978-5

By pulling a number of disparate services into one unified technology, COM+ holds the promise of greater efficiency and more diverse capabilities for developers who are creating applications—either enterprise or commercial software—to run on a Windows 2000 system. *Applying COM+* covers the features of the new tool, as well as how to implement them in a real case study. Features are demonstrated in all three of the major languages used in the Windows environment: C++, VB, and VJ++.

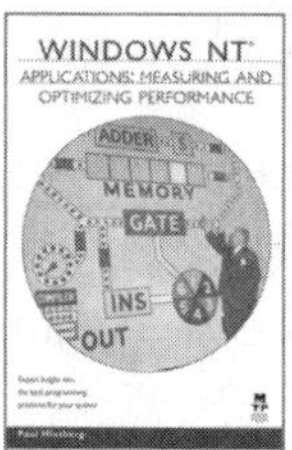

Windows NT Applications: Measuring and Optimizing Performance

By Paul Hinsberg
1st Edition
288 pages, $40.00
ISBN: 1-57870-176-7

This book offers developers crucial insight into the underlying structure of Windows NT, as well as the methodology and tools for measuring and ultimately optimizing code performance.

Exchange & Outlook: Constructing Collaborative Solutions

By Joel Semeniuk and Duncan Mackenzie
1st Edition
576 pages, $40.00
ISBN 1-57870-252-6

The authors of this book are responsible for building custom messaging applications for some of the biggest Fortune 100 companies in the world. They share their expertise to help administrators and designers use Microsoft technology to establish a base for their messaging system and to lay out the tools that can be used to help build those collaborative solutions. Actutal planning and design solutions are included along with typical workflow/collaborative solutions.

Windows Script Host

By Tim Hill
1st Edition
448 pages, $35.00
ISBN: 1-57870-139-2

Windows Script Host is one of the first books published about this powerful tool. The text focuses on system scripting and the VBScript language, using objects, server scriptlets, and ready-to-use script solutions.

Windows NT Shell Scripting

By Tim Hill
1st Edition
400 pages, $32.00
ISBN: 1-57870-047-7

A complete reference for Windows NT scripting, this book guides you through a high-level introduction to the Shell language itself and the Shell commands that are useful for controlling or managing different components of a network.

Win32 Perl Programming: The Standard Extensions

By Dave Roth
1st Edition
640 pages, $40.00
ISBN:1-57870-067-1

Discover numerous proven examples and practical uses of Perl in solving everyday Win32 problems. This is the only book available with comprehensive coverage of Win32 extensions, where most of the Perl functionality resides in Windows settings.

Windows NT/2000 ADSI Scripting for System Administration

By Thomas Eck
1st Edition
700 pages, $45.00
ISBN: 1-57870-219-4

Active Directory Scripting Interfaces (ADSI) allow administrators to automate administrative tasks across their Windows networks. This title fills a gap in the current ADSI documentation by including coverage of its interaction with LDAP and provides administrators with proven code samples that they can adopt to effectively configure and manage user accounts and other usually time-consuming tasks.

Windows NT Automated Deployment and Customization

By Richard Puckett
1st Editon
300 pages, $32.00
ISBN: 1-57870-045-0

This title offers time-saving advice that helps you install, update and configure software on each of your clients, without having to visit each client. Learn how to control all clients remotely for tasks, such as security and legal software use. Reference material on native NT tools, registry edits, and third-party tools is included.

SMS 2 Administration

By Darshan Doshi and Mike Lubanski
1st Edition
448 pages, $39.99
ISBN: 0-7357-0082-6

SMS 2 Administra-tion offers comprehensive coverage of how to design, deploy, and manage SMS 2.0 in an enterprise environment. This book follows the evolution of a software management system from the initial design through the implementation life cycle, to day-to-day management and usage of the system. Packed with case studies and examples pulled from the author's extensive experience, this book makes this complex product seem almost simple.

Internet Information Services Administration

By Kelli Adam
1st Edition
192 pages, $29.99
ISBN: 0-7357-0022-2

Administrators who know IIS from previous versions need this book to show them in concrete detail how to configure the new protocols, authenticate users with the new Certificate Server, and implement and manage the new e-commerce features that are part of IIS 5. This book gives you all of that: a quick read that provides real-world solutions, and doubles as a portable reference.

SQL Server System Administration

By Sean Baird and Chris Miller, et al.
1st Edition
352 pages, $29.99
ISBN: 1-56205-955-6

Assuming that the reader is familiar with the fundamentals of database administration and has worked with SQL Server in some capacity, this book focuses on the topics of interest to most administrators: keeping data consistently available to users. Unlike other SQL Server books that have little relevance to the serious SQL Server DBA, *SQL Server System Administra-tion* provides a hands-on approach that administrators won't find elsewhere.

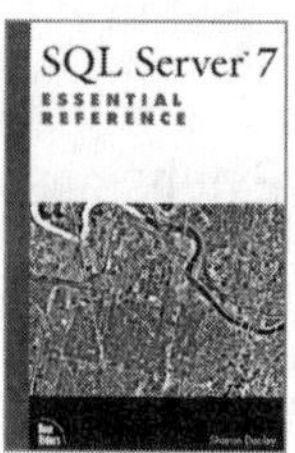

SQL Server 7 Essential Reference

By Sharon Dooley
1st Edition
400 pages, $35.00
ISBN: 0-7357-0864-9

SQL Server 7 Essential Reference is a comprehensive reference of advanced how-tos and techniques for developing with SQL Server. In particular, the book addresses advanced development techniques used in large application efforts with multiple users developing Web applications for intranets, extranets, or the Internet. Each section includes details on how each component is developed and then integrated into a real-life application.

Open Source

MySQL

By Paul DuBois
1st Edition
800 pages, $49.99
ISBN: 0-7357-0921-1

MySQL teaches readers how to use the tools provided by the MySQL distribution, covering installation, setup, daily use, security, optimization, maintenance, and troubleshooting. It also discusses important third-party tools, such as the Perl DBI and Apache/PHP interfaces that provide access to MySQL.

Linux/UNIX

Linux System Administration

By M. Carling, James T. Dennis, and Stephen Degler
1st Edition
368 pages, $29.99
ISBN: 1-56205-934-3

Today's overworked sysadmins are looking for ways to keep their networks running smoothly and achieve enhanced performance. Users are always looking for more storage, more services, and more Speed. *Linux System Administration* guides the reader in the many intricacies of maintaining a secure, stable system.

Linux Firewalls

By Robert Ziegler
1st Edition
496 pages, $39.99
ISBN: 0-7357-0900-9

This book details security steps thata small, non-enterprise business user might take to protect his system. These steps include packet-level firewall filtering, IP masquerading, proxies, tcp wrappers, system integrity checking, and system security monitoring with an overall emphasis on filtering and protection. The goal of *Linux Firewalls* is to help people get their Internet security measures in place quickly, without the need to become experts in security or firewalls.

Linux Essential Reference

By Ed Petron
1st Edition
368 pages, $24.95
ISBN: 0-7357-0852-5

This title is all about getting things done by providing structured organization to the plethora of available Linux information. Providing clear and concise instructions on how to perform important administration and management tasks, as well as how to use some of the more powerful commands and more advanced topics, the scope of *Linux Essential Reference* includes the best way to implement the most frequently used commands, manage shell scripting, administer your own system, and utilize effective security.

UnixWare 7 System Administration

By Gene Henriksen and Melissa Henriksen
1st Edition
560 pages, $39.99
ISBN: 1-57870-080-9

In great technical detail, this title presents the latest version of SCO UnixWare and is the definitive operating system resource for SCO engineers and administrators. SCO troubleshooting notes and tips are integrated throughout the text, as are tips specifically designed for those who are familiar with other UNIX variants.

Developing Linux Applications with GTK+ and GDK

By Eric Harlow
1st Edition
512 pages, $34.99
ISBN: 0-7357-0021-4

This handbook is for developers who are moving to the Linux platform, and those using the GTK+ library, including Glib and GDK using C. All the applications and code the author developed for this book have been released under the GPL.

GTK+/Gnome Application Development

By Havoc Pennington
1st Edition
528 pages, $39.99
ISBN: 0-7357-0078-8

More than one million Linux users are also application developers. *GTK+/Gnome Application Development* provides the experienced programmer with the knowledge to develop X Windows applications with the popular GTK+ toolkit. It contains reference information for more experienced users who are already familiar with usage, but require function prototypes and detailed descriptions.

KDE Application Development

By Uwe Thiem
1st Edition
190 pages, $39.99
ISBN: 1-57870-201-1

KDE Application Development offers a head start on KDE and Qt. The book covers the essential widgets available in KDE and Qt, and offers a strong start without the "first try" annoyances which sometimes make strong developers and programmers give up.

Grokking the GIMP

By Carey Bunks
1st Edition
342 pages, $45.00
ISBN: 0-7357-0924-6

Grokking the GIMP is a technical reference that covers the intricacies of the GIMP's functionality. The material gives the reader the ability to get up to speed quickly and start creating great graphics using the GIMP. Included as a bonus are step-by-step cookbook features used entirely for advanced effects.

GIMP Essential Reference

By Alex Harford
1st Edition
400 pages, $24.95
ISBN: 0-7357-0911-4

As the use of the Linux OS gains steam, so does the use of the GIMP. Many Photoshop users are starting to use the GIMP, recognized for its power and versatility. Taking this into consideration, GIMP Essential Reference has shortcuts exclusively for Photoshop users and puts the power of this program into the palm of the reader's hand.

Solaris Advanced System Administrator's Guide

By Janice Winsor
2nd Edition
587 pages, $39.99
ISBN: 1-57870-039-6

This officially authorized tutorial provides indispensable tips, advice, and quick-reference tables to help you add system components, improve service access, and automate routine tasks. this book also includes updated information on Solaris 2.6 topics.

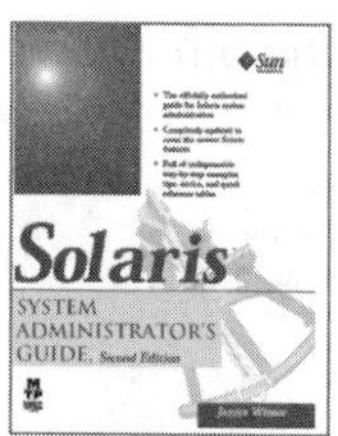

Solaris System Administrator's Guide

By Janice Winsor
2nd Edition
324 pages, $34.99
ISBN: 1-57870-040-X

Designed to work as both a practical tutorial and quick reference, this book provides UNIX administrators complete, detailed descriptions of the most frequently performed tasks for Solaris. Learn how to employ the features of Solaris to meet these needs of your users, and get tips on how to make administration easier.

Solaris Essential Reference

By John Mulligan
1st Edition
304 pages, $24.95
ISBN: 0-7357-0023-0

A great companion to the `solarisguide.com` website, *Solaris Essential Reference* assumes readers are well-versed in general UNIX skills and simply need some pointers on how to get the most out of Solaris. This book provides clear and concise instructions on how to perform important administration and management tasks.

Networking

Cisco Router Configuration &Troubleshooting

By Mark Tripod
2nd Edition
330 pages, $39.99
ISBN: 0-7357-0999-8

A reference for the network and system administrator who finds himself having to configure and maintain existing Cisco routers, as well as get new hardware up and running. By providing advice and preferred practices, instead of just rehashing Cisco documentation, this book gives networking professionals information they can start using today.

Understanding Directory Services

By Beth Sheresh and Doug Sheresh
1st Edition
390 pages, $39.99
ISBN: 0-7357-0910-6

Understanding Directory Services provides the reader with a thorough knowledge of the fundamentals of directory services: what Directory Services are, how they are designed, and what functionality they can provide to an IT infrastructure. This book provides a framework to the exploding market of directory services by placing the technology in context and helping people understand what directories can, and can't, do for their networks.

Understanding the Network: A Practical Guide to Internetworking

By Michael Martin
1st Edition
690 pages, $39.99
ISBN: 0-7357-0977-7

Understanding the Network addresses the audience in practical terminology, and describes the most essential information and tools required to build high-availability networks in a step-by-step implementation format. Each chapter could be read as a standalone, but the book builds progressively toward a summary of the essential concepts needed to put together a wide-area network.

Understanding Data Communications

By Gilbert Held
6th Edition
620 pages, $39.99
ISBN: 0-7357-0036-2

Gil Held's book is ideal for those who want to get up to speed on technological advances as well as those who want a primer on networking concepts. This book is intended to explain how data communications actually work. It contains updated coverage on hot topics like thin client technology, x2 and 56Kbps modems, voice digitization, and wireless data transmission. Whatever your needs, this title puts perspective and expertise in your hands.

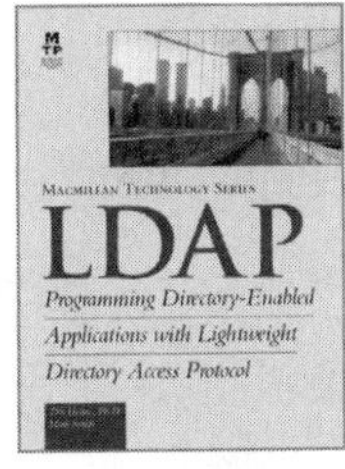

LDAP: Programming Directory Enabled Applications

By Tim Howes and Mark Smith
1st Edition
480 pages, $44.99
ISBN: 1-57870-000-0

This overview of the LDAP standard discusses its creation and history with the Internet Engineering Task Force, as well as the original RFC standard. LDAP also covers compliance trends, implementation, data packet handling in C++, client/server responsibilities and more.

Directory Enabled Networks

By John Strassner
1st Edition
752 pages, $50.00
ISBN: 1-57870-140-6

Directory Enabled Networks is a comprehensive resource on the design and use of DEN. This book provides practical examples side-by-side with a detailed introduction to the theory of building a new class of network-enabled applications that will solve networking problems. DEN is a critical tool for network architects, administrators, and application developers.

Gigabit Ethernet Networking

By David Cunningham and William Lane
1st Edition
560 pages, $50.00
ISBN: 1-57870-062-0

Gigabit Ethernet is the next step for speed on the majority of installed networks. Explore how this technology will allow high-bandwidth applications, such as the integration of telephone and data services, real-time applications, thin client applications, such as Windows NT Terminal Server, and corporate teleconferencing.

Supporting Service Level Agreements on IP Networks

By Dinesh Verma
1st Edition
270 pages, $50.00
ISBN: 1-57870-146-5

An essential resource for network engineers and architects, *Supporting Service Level Agreements on IP Networks* will help you build a core network capable of supporting a range of service. Learn how to create SLA solutions using off-the-shelf components in both best-effort and DiffServ/IntServ networks. Learn how to verify the performance of your SLA, as either a customer or network services provider, and use SLAs to support IPv6 networks.

Local Area High Speed Networks

By Dr. Sidnie Feit
1st Edition
655 pages, $50.00
ISBN: 1-57870-113-9

There is a great deal of change happening in the technology being used for local area networks. As Web intranets have driven bandwidth needs through the ceiling, inexpensive Ethernet NICs and switches have come into the market. As a result, many network professionals are interested in evaluating these new technologies for implementation. This book provides real-world implementation expertise for these technologies, including traces, so that users canrealistically compare and decide how to use them.

Wide Area High Speed Networks

By Dr. Sidnie Feit
1st Edition
624 pages, $50.00
ISBN: 1-57870-114-7

Networking is in a transitional phase between long-standing conventional wide area services and new technologies and services. This book presents current and emerging wide area technologies and services, makes them understandable, and puts them into perspective so that their merits and disadvantages are clear.

Differentiated Services for the Internet

By Kalevi Kilkki
1st Edition
400 pages, $50.00
ISBN: 1-57870-132-5

This book offers network architects, engineers, and managers of packet networks critical insight into the continuing development of Differentiated Services. It addresses the particular needs of a network environment as well as issues that must be considered in its implementation. Coverage allows networkers to implement DiffServ on a variety of networking technologies, including ATM, and to solve common problems related to TCP, UDP, and other networking protocols.

Quality of Service in IP Networks

By Grenville Armitage
1st Edition
310 pages, $50.00
ISBN: 1-57870-189-9

Quality of Service in IP Networks presents a clear understanding of the architectural issues surrounding delivering QoS in an IP network, and positions the emerging technologies within a framework of solutions. The motivation for QoS is explained with reference to emerging real-time applications, such as Voice/Video over IP, VPN services, and supporting Service Level Agreements.

Designing Addressing Architectures for Routing and Switching

By Howard Berkowitz
1st Edition
500 pages, $45.00
ISBN: 1-57870-059-0

One of the greatest challenges for a network design professional is making the users, servers, files, printers, and other resources visible on their network. This title equips the network engineer or architect with a systematic methodology for planning the wide area and local area network "streets" on which users and servers live.

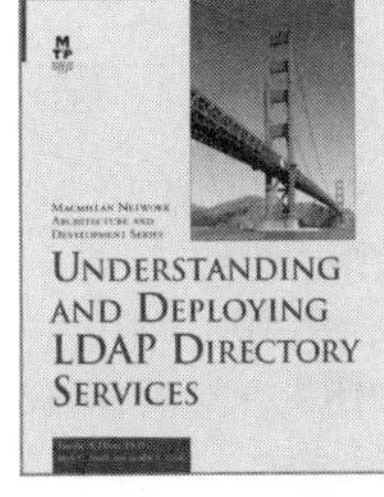

Understanding and Deploying LDAP Directory Services

By Tim Howes, Mark Smith, and Gordon Good
1st Edition
850 pages, $50.00
ISBN: 1-57870-070-1

This comprehensive tutorial provides the reader with a thorough treatment of LDAP directory services. Minimal knowledge of general networking and administration is assumed, making the material accessible to intermediate and advanced readers alike. The text is full of practical implementation advice and real-world deployment examples to help the reader choose the path that makes the most sense for his specific organization.

Switched, Fast, and Gigabit Ethernet

By Sean Riley and Robert Breyer

3rd Edition

615 pages, $50.00

ISBN: 1-57870-073-6

Switched, Fast, and Gigabit Ethernet, Third Edition is the one and only solution needed to understand and fully implement this entire range of Ethernet innovations. Acting both as an overview of current technologies and hardware requirements as well as a hands-on, comprehensive tutorial for deploying and managing switched, fast, and gigabit ethernet networks, this guide covers the most prominent present and future challenges network administrators face.

The DHCP Handbook

By Ralph Droms and Ted Lemon

1st Edition

535 pages, $55.00

ISBN: 1-57870-137-6

The DHCP Handbook is an authoritative overview and expert guide to the setup and management of a DHCP server. This title discusses how DHCP was developed and its interaction with other protocols. Learn how DHCP operates, its use in different environments, and the interaction between DHCP servers and clients. Network hardware, inter-server communication, security, SNMP, and IP mobility are also discussed. Also, included in the book are several appendices that provide a rich resource for networking professionals working with DHCP.

Wireless LANs: Implementing Interoperable Networks

By Jim Geier

1st Edition

432 pages, $40.00

ISBN: 1-57870-081-7

Wireless LANs covers how and why to migrate from proprietary solutions to the 802.11 standard, and explains how to realize significant cost savings through wireless LAN implementation for data collection systems.

Designing Routing and Switching Architectures for Enterprise Networks

By Howard Berkowitz

1st Edition

992 pages, $55.00

ISBN: 1-57870-060-4

This title provides a fundamental understanding of how switches and routers operate, enabling the reader to use them effectively to build networks. The book walks the network designer through all aspects of requirements, analysis, and deployment strategies, strengthens readers' professional abilities, and helps them develop skills necessary to advance in their profession.

Network Performance Baselining

By Daniel Nassar
1st Edition
736 pages, $50.00
ISBN: 1-57870-240-2

Network Performance Baselining focuses on the real-world implementation of network baselining principles and shows not only how to measure and rate a network's performance, but also how to improve the network performance. This book includes chapters that give a real "how-to" approach for standard baseline methodologies along with actual steps and processes to perform network baseline measurements. In addition, the proper way to document and build a baseline report will be provided.

The Economics of Electronic Commerce

By Soon-Yong Choi, Andrew Whinston, Dale Stahl
1st Edition
656 pages, $49.99
ISBN: 1-57870-014-0

This is the first electronic commerce title to focus on traditional topics of economics applied to the electronic commerce arena. While all other electronic commerce titles take a "how-to" approach, this focuses on what it means from an economic perspective.

Intrusion Detection

By Rebecca Gurley Bace
1st Edition
340 pages, $50.00
ISBN: 1-57870-185-6

Intrusion detection is a critical new area of technology within network security. This comprehensive guide to the field of intrusion detection covers the foundations of intrusion detection and system audit. *Intrusion Detection* provides a wealth of information, ranging from design considerations to how to evaluate and choose the optimal commercial intrusion detection products for a particular networking environment.

Understanding Public-Key Infrastructure

By Carlisle Adams and Steve Lloyd
1st Edition
300 pages, $50.00
ISBN: 1-57870-166-X

This book is a tutorial on, and a guide to the deployment of, Public-Key Infrastructures. It covers a broad range of material related to PKIs, including certification, operational considerations and standardization efforts, as well as deployment issues and considerations. Emphasis is placed on explaining the interrelated fields within the topic area, to assist those who will be responsible for making deployment decisions and architecting a PKI within an organization.

Network Intrusion Detection: An Analyst's Handbook

By Stephen Northcutt and Judy Novak
2nd Edition
480 pages, $45.00
ISBN: 0-7357-1008-2

Get answers and solutions from someone who has been in the trenches. Author Stephen Northcutt, original developer of the Shadow intrusion detection system and former Director of the United States Navy's Informa-tion System Security Office, gives his expertise to intrusion detection specialists, security analysts, and consultants responsible for setting up and maintaining an effective defense against network security attacks.

Domino System Administration

By Rob Kirkland
1st Edition
860 pages, $49.99
ISBN: 1-56205-948-3

Need a concise, practical explana-tion about the new features of Domino, and how to make some of the advanced stuff really work? *Domino System Administration* is the first book on Domino that attacks the technology at the professional level, with practical, hands-on assistance to get Domino 5 running in your organization.

Lotus Notes & Domino Essential Reference

By Dave Hatter and Tim Bankes
1st Edition
675 pages, $45.00
ISBN: 0-7357-0007-9

If you need something to facilitate your creative and technical abilities—something to perfect your Lotus Notes and Domino programming skills—this is the book for you. This title includes all of the objects, classes, functions, and methods found if you work with Lotus Notes and Domino. It shows the object hierarchy and the overlying relationship between each one, organized the way the language is designed.

Software Architecture and Engineering

Designing Flexible Object-Oriented Systems with UML

By Charles Richter
1st Edition
416 pages, $40.00
ISBN: 1-57870-098-1

Designing Flexible Object-Oriented Systems with UML details the UML, which is a notation system for designing object-oriented programs. The book follows the same sequence that a development project might employ, starting with requirements of the problem using UML case diagrams and activity diagrams. The reader is shown ways to improve the design as the author moves through the transformation of the initial diagrams into class diagrams and interaction diagrams.

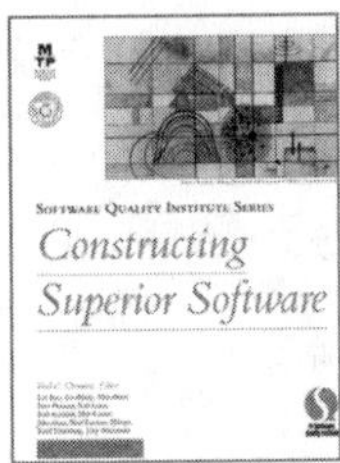

Constructing Superior Software

By Paul Clements, et al.

1st Edition

285 pages, $40.00

ISBN: 1-57870-147-3

Published in cooperation with the Software Quality Institute at the University of Texas, Austin, this title presents a set of fundamental engineering strategies for achieving a successful software solution, with practical advice to ensure that the development project is moving in the right direction. Software designers and development managers can improve the development speed and quality of their software, and improve the processes used in development.

A UML Pattern Language

By Paul Evitts

1st Edition

260 pages, $40.00

ISBN: 1-57870-118-X

While other books focus only on the UML notation system, this book integrates key UML modeling concepts and illustrates their use through patterns. It provides an integrated, practical, step-by-step discussion of UML and patterns, with real-world examples to illustrate proven software modeling techniques.

Other Books By New Riders

MICROSOFT TECHNOLOGIES

ADMINISTRATION

Inside Windows 2000 Server
1-56205-929-7 • $49.99 US / $74.95 CAN
Windows 2000 Essential Reference
0-7357-0869-X • $35.00 US / $52.95 CAN
Windows 2000 Active Directory
0-7357-0870-3 • $29.99 US / $44.95 CAN
Windows 2000 Routing and Remote Access Service
0-7357-0951-3 • $34.99 US / $52.95 CAN
Windows 2000 Deployment & Desktop Management
0-7357-0975-0 • $34.99 US / $52.95 CAN
Windows 2000 DNS
0-7357-0973-4 • $39.99 US / $59.95 CAN
Windows 2000 User Management
1-56205-886-X • $34.99 US / $52.95 CAN
Windows 2000 Professional
0-7357-0950-5 • $34.99 US / $52.95 CAN
Planning for Windows 2000
0-7357-0048-6 • $29.99 US / $44.95 CAN
Windows 2000 Server Professional Reference
0-7357-0952-1 • $75.00 US / $111.95 CAN
Windows 2000 Security
0-7357-0991-2 • $39.99 US / $59.95 CAN
Windows 2000 TCP/IP
0-7357-0992-0 • $39.99 US / $59.95 CAN
Windows NT/2000 Network Security
1-57870-253-4 • $45.00 US / $67.95 CAN
Windows NT/2000 Thin Client Solutions
1-57870-239-9 • $45.00 US / $67.95 CAN
Windows 2000 Virtual Private Networking
1-57870-246-1 • $45.00 US / $67.95 CAN • Available January 2001
Windows 2000 Active Directory Design & Development
1-57870-242-9 • $45.00 US / $67.95 CAN
Windows 2000 and Mainframe Integration
1-57870-200-3 • $40.00 US / $59.95 CAN
Windows 2000 Server: Planning and Migration
1-57870-023-X • $40.00 US / $59.95 CAN
Windows 2000 Quality of Service
1-57870-115-5 • $45.00 US / $67.95 CAN
Windows NT Power Toolkit
0-7357-0922-X • $49.99 US / $74.95 CAN
Windows NT Terminal Server and Citrix MetaFrame
1-56205-944-0 • $29.99 US / $44.95 CAN
Windows NT Performance: Monitoring, Benchmarking, and Tuning
1-56205-942-4 • $29.99 US / $44.95 CAN
Windows NT Registry: A Settings Reference
1-56205-941-6 • $29.99 US / $44.95 CAN
Windows NT Domain Architecture
1-57870-112-0 • $38.00 US / $56.95 CAN

SYSTEMS PROGRAMMING

Windows NDIS Miniport Development
1-57870-248-8 • $50.00 US / $74.95 CAN • Available March 2001
Windows NT/2000 Native API Reference
1-57870-199-6 • $50.00 US / $74.95 CAN
Windows NT Device Driver Development
1-57870-058-2 • $50.00 US / $74.95 CAN
DCE/RPC over SMB: Samba and Windows NT Domain Internals
1-57870-150-3 • $45.00 US / $67.95 CAN

WEB PROGRAMMING

Real World Web Code: Techniques for Structured ASP Programming
0-7357-1033-3 • $39.99 US / $59.95 CAN • Available March 2001
Exchange & Outlook: Constructing Collaborative Solutions
1-57870-252-6 • $40.00 US / $59.95 CAN

APPLICATION PROGRAMMING

Delphi COM Programming
1-57870-221-6 • $45.00 US / $67.95 CAN
Windows NT Applications: Measuring and Optimizing Performance
1-57870-176-7 • $40.00 US / $59.95 CAN
Applying COM+
0-7357-0978-5 • $49.99 US / $74.95 CAN

SCRIPTING

Windows Script Host
1-57870-139-2 • $35.00 US / $52.95 CAN
Windows NT Shell Scripting
1-57870-047-7 • $32.00 US / $45.95 CAN
Windows NT Win32 Perl Programming: The Standard Extensions
1-57870-067-1 • $40.00 US / $59.95 CAN
Windows NT/2000 ADSI Scripting for System Administration
1-57870-219-4 • $45.00 US / $67.95 CAN
Windows NT Automated Deployment and Customization
1-57870-045-0 • $32.00 US / $45.95 CAN
Win32 Perl Scripting: The Administrator's Handbook
1-57870-215-1 • $35.00 US / $52.95 CAN

BACK OFFICE

SMS 2 Administration
0-7357-0082-6 • $39.99 US / $59.95 CAN
Internet Information Services Administration
0-7357-0022-2 • $29.99 US / $44.95 CAN
SQL Server System Administration
1-56205-955-6 • $29.99 US / $44.95 CAN
SQL Server 7 Essential Reference
0-7357-0864-9 • $35.00 US / $52.95 CAN
Inside Exchange 2000 Server
0-7357-1027-9 • $49.99 US / $74.95 CAN • Available February 2001

WEB DESIGN & DEVELOPMENT

OPEN SOURCE

MySQL
0-7357-0921-1 • $49.99 US / $74.95 CAN
Web Application Development with PHP 4.0
0-7357-0997-1 • $39.99 US / $59.95 CAN
PHP Functions Essential Reference
0-7357-0970-X • $35.00 US / $52.95 CAN • Available February 2001
Python Essential Reference
0-7357-0901-7 • $34.95 US / $52.95 CAN
Qt: The Official Documentation
1-57870-209-7 • $50.00 US / $74.95 CAN
Berkeley DB
0-7357-1064-3 • $39.99 US / $59.95 CAN• Available February 2001
GNU Autoconf, Automake, and Libtool
1-57870-190-2 • $40.00 US / $59.95 CAN

CREATIVE MEDIA

Designing Web Usability
1-56205-810-X • $45.00 US / $67.95 CAN
Designing Web Graphics.3
1-56205-949-1 • $55.00 US / $81.95 CAN
Flash Web Design
0-7357-0896-7 • $45.00 US / $67.95 CAN
<creative.html design>
1-56205-704-9 • $39.99 US / $59.95 CAN
Creating Killer Web Sites, Second Edition
1-56830-433-1 • $49.99 US / $74.95 CAN
Secrets of Successful Web Sites
1-56830-382-3 • $49.99 US / $74.95 CAN

XML

Inside XML
0-7357-1020-1 • $49.99 US / $74.95 CAN
XHTML
0-7357-1034-1 • $39.99 US / $59.95 CAN• Available January 2001

LINUX/UNIX

ADMINISTRATION

Networking Linux: A Practical Guide to TCP/IP
0-7357-1031-7 • $39.99 US / $59.95 CAN • Available February 2001
Inside Linux
0-7357-0940-8 • $39.99 US / $59.95 CAN
Vi iMproved (VIM)
0-7357-1001-5 • $49.99 US / $74.95 CAN • Available January 2001
Linux System Administration
1-56205-934-3 • $29.99 US / $44.95 CAN
Linux Firewalls
0-7357-0900-9 • $39.99 US / $59.95 CAN
Linux Essential Reference
0-7357-0852-5 • $24.95 US / $37.95 CAN
UnixWare 7 System Administration
1-57870-080-9 • $40.00 US / $59.99 CAN

DEVELOPMENT

Developing Linux Applications with GTK+ and GDK
0-7357-0021-4 • $34.99 US / $52.95 CAN
GTK+/Gnome Application Development
0-7357-0078-8 • $39.99 US / $59.95 CAN
KDE Application Development
1-57870-201-1 • $39.99 US / $59.95 CAN

GIMP

Grokking the GIMP
0-7357-0924-6 • $39.99 US / $59.95 CAN
GIMP Essential Reference
0-7357-0911-4 • $24.95 US / $37.95 CAN

SOLARIS

Solaris Advanced System Administrator's Guide, Second Edition
1-57870-039-6 • $39.99 US / $59.95 CAN
Solaris System Administrator's Guide, Second Edition
1-57870-040-X • $34.99 US / $52.95 CAN
Solaris Essential Reference
0-7357-0023-0 • $24.95 US / $37.95 CAN
Solaris System Management
0-7357-1018-X • $39.99 US / $59.95 CAN • Available March 2001
Solaris 8 Essential Reference
0-7357-1007-4 • $34.99 US / $52.95 CAN • Available January 2001

NETWORKING

STANDARDS & PROTOCOLS

Cisco Router Configuration & Troubleshooting, Second Edition
0-7357-0999-8 • $34.99 US / $52.95 CAN
Understanding Directory Services
0-7357-0910-6 • $39.99 US / $59.95 CAN
Understanding the Network: A Practical Guide to Internetworking
0-7357-0977-7 • $39.99 US / $59.95 CAN
Understanding Data Communications, Sixth Edition
0-7357-0036-2 • $39.99 US / $59.95 CAN
LDAP: Programming Directory Enabled Applications
1-57870-000-0 • $44.99 US / $67.95 CAN
Gigabit Ethernet Networking
1-57870-062-0 • $50.00 US / $74.95 CAN
Supporting Service Level Agreements on IP Networks
1-57870-146-5 • $50.00 US / $74.95 CAN
Directory Enabled Networks
1-57870-140-6 • $50.00 US / $74.95 CAN
Differentiated Services for the Internet
1-57870-132-5 • $50.00 US / $74.95 CAN
Policy-Based Networking: Architecture and Algorithms
1-57870-226-7 • $50.00 US / $74.95 CAN
Networking Quality of Service and Windows Operating Systems
1-57870-206-2 • $50.00 US / $74.95 CAN
Policy-Based Management
1-57870-225-9 • $55.00 US / $81.95 CAN • Available March 2001
Quality of Service on IP Networks
1-57870-189-9 • $50.00 US / $74.95 CAN
Designing Addressing Architectures for Routing and Switching
1-57870-059-0 • $45.00 US / $69.95 CAN
Understanding & Deploying LDAP Directory Services
1-57870-070-1 • $50.00 US / $74.95 CAN
Switched, Fast and Gigabit Ethernet, Third Edition
1-57870-073-6 • $50.00 US / $74.95 CAN
Wireless LANs: Implementing Interoperable Networks
1-57870-081-7 • $40.00 US / $59.95 CAN
Wide Area High Speed Networks
1-57870-114-7 • $50.00 US / $74.95 CAN
The DHCP Handbook
1-57870-137-6 • $55.00 US / $81.95 CAN
Designing Routing and Switching Architectures for Enterprise Networks
1-57870-060-4 • $55.00 US / $81.95 CAN
Local Area High Speed Networks
1-57870-113-9 • $50.00 US / $74.95 CAN
Network Performance Baselining
1-57870-240-2 • $50.00 US / $74.95 CAN
Economics of Electronic Commerce
1-57870-014-0 • $49.99 US / $74.95 CAN

SECURITY

Intrusion Detection
1-57870-185-6 • $50.00 US / $74.95 CAN
Understanding Public-Key Infrastructure
1-57870-166-X • $50.00 US / $74.95 CAN
Network Intrusion Detection: An Analyst's Handbook, 2E
0-7357-1008-2 • $45.00 US / $67.95 CAN
Linux Firewalls
0-7357-0900-9 • $39.99 US / $59.95 CAN
Intrusion Signatures and Analysis
0-7357-1063-5 • $39.99 US / $59.95 CAN • Available February 2001
Hackers Beware
0-7357-1009-0 • $45.00 US / $67.95 CAN • Available March 2001

LOTUS NOTES/DOMINO

Domino System Administration
1-56205-948-3 • $49.99 US / $74.95 CAN
Lotus Notes & Domino Essential Reference
0-7357-0007-9 • $45.00 US / $67.95 CAN

PROFESSIONAL CERTIFICATION

TRAINING GUIDES

MCSE Training Guide: Networking Essentials, 2nd Ed.
1-56205-919-X • $49.99 US / $74.95 CAN
MCSE Training Guide: Windows NT Server 4, 2nd Ed.
1-56205-916-5 • $49.99 US / $74.95 CAN
MCSE Training Guide: Windows NT Workstation 4, 2nd Ed.
1-56205-918-1 • $49.99 US / $74.95 CAN
MCSE Training Guide: Windows NT Server 4 Enterprise, 2nd Ed.
1-56205-917-3 • $49.99 US / $74.95 CAN
MCSE Training Guide: Core Exams Bundle, 2nd Ed.
1-56205-926-2 • $149.99 US / $223.95 CAN
MCSE Training Guide: TCP/IP, 2nd Ed.
1-56205-920-3 • $49.99 US / $74.95 CAN
MCSE Training Guide: IIS 4, 2nd Ed.
0-7357-0865-7 • $49.99 US / $74.95 CAN
MCSE Training Guide: SQL Server 7 Administration
0-7357-0003-6 • $49.99 US / $74.95 CAN
MCSE Training Guide: SQL Server 7 Database Design
0-7357-0004-4 • $49.99 US / $74.95 CAN
MCSD Training Guide: Visual Basic 6 Exams
0-7357-0002-8 • $69.99 US / $104.95 CAN
MCSD Training Guide: Solution Architectures
0-7357-0026-5 • $49.99 US / $74.95 CAN
MCSD Training Guide: 4-in-1 Bundle
0-7357-0912-2 • $149.99 US / $223.95 CAN
A+ Certification Training Guide, Second Edition
0-7357-0907-6 • $49.99 US / $74.95 CAN
Network+ Certification Guide
0-7357-0077-X • $49.99 US / $74.95 CAN
Solaris 2.6 Administrator Certification Training Guide, Part I
1-57870-085-X • $40.00 US / $59.95 CAN
Solaris 2.6 Administrator Certification Training Guide, Part II
1-57870-086-8 • $40.00 US / $59.95 CAN
Solaris 7 Administrator Certification Training Guide, Part I and II
1-57870-249-6 • $49.99 US / $74.95 CAN
MCSE Training Guide: Windows 2000 Professional
0-7357-0965-3 • $49.99 US / $74.95 CAN
MCSE Training Guide: Windows 2000 Server
0-7357-0968-8 • $49.99 US / $74.95 CAN
MCSE Training Guide: Windows 2000 Network Infrastructure
0-7357-0966-1 • $49.99 US / $74.95 CAN
MCSE Training Guide: Windows 2000 Network Security Design
0-73570-984X • $49.99 US / $74.95 CAN
MCSE Training Guide: Windows 2000 Network Infrastructure Design
0-73570-982-3 • $49.99 US / $74.95 CAN
MCSE Training Guide: Windows 2000 Directory Svcs. Infrastructure
0-7357-0976-9 • $49.99 US / $74.95 CAN
MCSE Training Guide: Windows 2000 Directory Services Design
0-7357-0983-1 • $49.99 US / $74.95 CAN
MCSE Training Guide: Windows 2000 Accelerated Exam
0-7357-0979-3 • $69.99 US / $104.95 CAN
MCSE Training Guide: Windows 2000 Core Exams Bundle
0-7357-0988-2 • $149.99 US / $223.95 CAN

FAST TRACKS

CLP Fast Track: Lotus Notes/Domino 5 Application Development
0-73570-877-0 • $39.99 US / $59.95 CAN
CLP Fast Track: Lotus Notes/Domino 5 System Administration
0-7357-0878-9 • $39.99 US / $59.95 CAN
Network+ Fast Track
0-7357-0904-1 • $29.99 US / $44.95 CAN
A+ Fast Track
0-7357-0028-1 • $34.99 US / $52.95 CAN
MCSD Fast Track: Visual Basic 6, Exam #70-175
0-7357-0019-2 • $19.99 US / $29.95 CAN
MCSD FastTrack: Visual Basic 6, Exam #70-175
0-7357-0018-4 • $19.99 US / $29.95 CAN

SOFTWARE ARCHITECTURE & ENGINEERING

Designing for the User with OVID
1-57870-101-5 • $40.00 US / $59.95 CAN
Designing Flexible Object-Oriented Systems with UML
1-57870-098-1 • $40.00 US / $59.95 CAN
Constructing Superior Software
1-57870-147-3 • $40.00 US / $59.95 CAN
A UML Pattern Language
1-57870-118-X • $45.00 US / $67.95 CAN

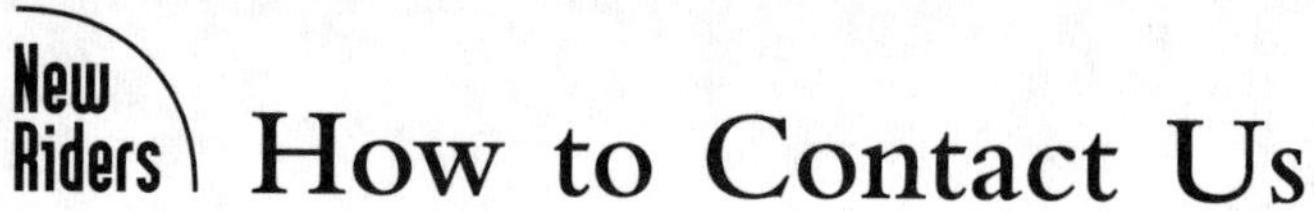

How to Contact Us

Visit Our Web Site

www.newriders.com

On our Web site you'll find information about our other books, authors, tables of contents, indexes, and book errata.

Email Us

Contact us at this address:

nrfeedback@newriders.com

- If you have comments or questions about this book
- To report errors that you have found in this book
- If you have a book proposal to submit or are interested in writing for New Riders
- If you would like to have an author kit sent to you
- If you are an expert in a computer topic or technology and are interested in being a technical editor who reviews manuscripts for technical accuracy
- To find an international distributor in your area

nrmedia@newriders.com

- For instructors from educational institutions who want to preview New Riders books for classroom use. Email should include your name, title, school, department, address, phone number, office days/hours, text in use, and enrollment, along with your request for desk/examination copies and/or additional information.
- For members of the media who are interested in reviewing copies of New Riders books. Send your name, mailing address, and email address, along with the name of the publication or Web site you work for.

Bulk Purchases/Corporate Sales

If you are interested in buying 10 or more copies of a title or want to set up an account for your company to purchase directly from the publisher at a substantial discount, contact us at 800-382-3419 or email your contact information to corpsales@pearsontechgroup.com. A sales representative will contact you with more information.

Write to Us

New Riders Publishing
201 W. 103rd St.
Indianapolis, IN 46290-1097

Call Us

Toll-free (800) 571-5840 + 9 + 7477
If outside U.S. (317) 581-3500. Ask for New Riders.

Fax Us

(317) 581-4663

New Riders

We Want to Know What You Think

To better serve you, we would like your opinion on the content and quality of this book. Please complete this card and mail it to us or fax it to 317-581-4663.

Name ___________________________________

Address ___________________________________

City_______________State_______________Zip ___________________

Phone ___________________________________

Email Address ___________________________________

Occupation ___________________________________

Operating System(s) that you use ___________________________________

What influenced your purchase of this book?

- ❑ Recommendation
- ❑ Cover Design
- ❑ Table of Contents
- ❑ Index
- ❑ Magazine Review
- ❑ Advertisement
- ❑ New Rider's Reputation
- ❑ Author Name

How would you rate the contents of this book?

- ❑ Excellent
- ❑ Very Good
- ❑ Good
- ❑ Fair
- ❑ Below Average
- ❑ Poor

How do you plan to use this book?

- ❑ Quick reference
- ❑ Self-training
- ❑ Classroom
- ❑ Other

What do you like most about this book? Check all that apply.

- ❑ Content
- ❑ Writing Style
- ❑ Accuracy
- ❑ Examples
- ❑ Listings
- ❑ Design
- ❑ Index
- ❑ Page Count
- ❑ Price
- ❑ Illustrations

What do you like least about this book? Check all that apply.

- ❑ Content
- ❑ Writing Style
- ❑ Accuracy
- ❑ Examples
- ❑ Listings
- ❑ Design
- ❑ Index
- ❑ Page Count
- ❑ Price
- ❑ Illustrations

What would be a useful follow-up book to this one for you?___________________________________

Where did you purchase this book? ___________________________________

____

Can you name a similar book that you like better than this one, or one that is as good? Why?

____

____

How many New Riders books do you own? ___________________________________

What are your favorite computer books?___________________________________

____

What other titles would you like to see us develop? ___________________________________

____

Any comments for us? ___________________________________

____

____

____

Inside XML, 0-7357-1020-1

Fold here and tape to mail

Place
Stamp
Here

New Riders Publishing
201 W. 103rd St.
Indianapolis, IN 46290